GENETICS:
ETHICS, LAW AND POLICY

Third Edition

■ ■ ■

By

Lori B. Andrews
Distinguished Professor of Law
Chicago–Kent College of Law
Illinois Institute of Technology

Maxwell J. Mehlman
Arthur E. Petersilge Professor of Law
Case Western Reserve University

Mark A. Rothstein
Herbert F. Boehl Chair of Law and Medicine
University of Louisville

AMERICAN CASEBOOK SERIES®

WEST®
A Thomson Reuters business

Mat #40902952

American Casebook Series is a trademark registered in the U.S. Patent and Trademark Office.

© West, a Thomson business, 2002, 2006
© 2010 Thomson Reuters
    610 Opperman Drive
    St. Paul, MN 55123
    1–800–313–9378
Printed in the United States of America

ISBN: 978–0–314–91186–5

For Christopher, Rory, Gabe, Julia, and Lisa

PREFACE

Every day thousands of people face individual choices about genetics. At the same time, hundreds of policy decisions are made about genetics—such as whether a particular test should be offered, what information should be provided in advance of a test, and who should have access to the results. Doctors determine whether to test patients for a newly-discovered genetic mutation. Health insurers analyze whether to reimburse for such a test. The Food and Drug Administration struggles with the question of whether university laboratories offering genetic tests should be regulated. State lawmakers debate whether an insurer should be able to deny an individual health insurance because his or her sibling or parent has a genetic disorder.

Developments in genetics touch us as individuals and as members of society. They raise important questions for health care providers, economists, public health officials, corporations, insurers, and employers. They also raise issues for lawyers, judges, and legislators that encompass all areas of law—from tort law to constitutional law, from intellectual property law to employment law, from family law to criminal law.

To introduce the legal, ethical, economic, and social implications of genetics, we have included a wide variety of materials in this book. It contains relevant judicial opinions drawn from the federal and state courts. The book also contains statutes, administrative regulations, medical professional guidelines, and international conventions. It includes informed consent forms and licensing agreements covering the actual practices governing genetics research, diagnosis, treatment, and product development. The book deals only with human genetics and does not cover genetically-modified plants or animals. It is designed for use by not only law students, but students of medicine, public health, and various other disciplines.

The casebook is divided into four major sections. The first section (chapters 1–3) provides an introduction to the context in which decisions about genetics have been made. It details the scientific basis for genetic technology and the historical use of genetic ideas.

The second section (chapters 4 and 5) covers genetic research, including issues related to federal and international regulations, intellectual property rights, and intriguing research initiatives such as the Human Genome Diversity Project and the Environmental Genome Project.

The third section (chapters 6 through 10) deals with medical applications of genetics, including prenatal testing, newborn screening, cancer testing, the testing of children, gene therapy, and the use of reproductive technologies. It includes information about federal, state and professional oversight of the quality of genetic services, as well as judicial opinions about liability in the provision of genetic services.

The fourth section (chapters 11 through 17) addresses the non-medical application of genetics, including paternity testing. The major focus of this section is on the use of genetic technologies by social institutions—such as law enforcement officials, courts, insurers, employers and schools.

We are grateful to our many talented colleagues from law, the social sciences, molecular biology, clinical genetics, philosophy, bioethics, economics, genetic counseling, and public health whose ideas and interactions with us have helped shape this book. We are also thankful to the colleagues who worked closely on the manuscript, including Tim Holbrook, Hal Krent, Laurie Rosenow, Nanette Elster, Julie Burger and Jake Meyer, as well as research assistants Atossa Alavi, Patrick Bickley, Sarah Blenner, Jason Braswell, Erin Chapman, Tracy Green, Dorislee Jackson, Nancy Pratt Kantor, Laura Kaper, Aaron Midler, Sherizaan Minwalla, Jordan Paradise, Kerry Rost, Cory Schmidt, Heather Stenmark, Laura Sluis, Keith Syverson and Sarah Zegar. And a special thanks goes to Robert Klein and Tim Welch for their administrative support.

LORI ANDREWS
MAXWELL MEHLMAN
MARK ROTHSTEIN

PREFACE TO THE THIRD EDITION

Genetics is entering all aspects of our lives. People use genetic genealogy to discover distant relatives. Hospitals apply cutting edge genetic technologies to diagnose and treat. Television shows feature the latest in forensic DNA, and courts use those techniques to convict or exonerate people. Lawmakers—or, in the case of the California stem cell initiative, voters themselves—seek to take advantage of new genetic technologies. Regulators like the Food and Drug Administration and U.S. Patent and Trademark Office struggle with how to regulate them. And certain genetic technologies raise profound moral questions of life and death—and of how to define "human."

The earlier editions of this casebook were used in a variety of settings—from law school courses and seminars to undergraduate bioethics courses to graduate health professional programs. In each of those settings, materials about genetics provoked fascinating discussions and novel policy proposals. In law schools, the casebook served an additional function. Courses using Genetics: Ethics, Law and Policy acted as a capstone to the law school education, providing a context for students to apply the knowledge they learned in tort, constitutional, medical, family, criminal, insurance, employment, and intellectual property law.

This subsequent edition expands upon the earlier editions, reflecting the evolving nature of the science and law in this area. Not only does the new edition include more cases, statutes, and commentaries dealing with scientific developments, such as pharmacogenomics and embryonic stem cell research, it also includes more readings to stimulate discussions of social and ethical issues, such as the marketing of race-based medications. The third edition has been updated to include everything from Octomom to President Obama's directive on stem cells. As new issues emerge in the field, the authors will continue to post relevant materials on the West website so that the course remains cutting edge.

ACKNOWLEDGMENTS

Allen, Anita L., Genetic Privacy: Emerging Concepts and Values, in Genetic Secrets: Protecting Privacy and Confidentiality in the Genetic Era, 31, 33–34 (Mark A. Rothstein, ed. 1997). Copyright © 1997 by Yale University. Reprinted by permission.

American Academy of Pediatrics, Newborn Screening: A Blueprint for the Future; A Call for a National Agenda on State Newborn Screening Programs, Report of the Task Force on Newborn Screening excerpted from Birth to the Medical Home; Pediatrics, volume 106: 2 (2000), used with permission of the American Academy of Pediatrics. Copyright © August 2000 American Academy of Pediatrics.

American College of Medical Genetics, Position Statement on Gene Patents and Accessibility of Gene Testing (August 2, 1999). Reprinted with permission of the American College of Medical Genetics.

American Medical Association, Code of Medical Ethics, Opinion 2.08: Commercial Use of Human Tissue (2000). Copyright © 2000 American Medical Association. Reprinted with permission from the American Medical Association.

American Medical Association, Code of Medical Ethics, Opinion 2.11 and Opinion 2.138: Gene Therapy (1995). Copyright © 1995 American Medical Association. Reprinted with permission from the American Medical Association.

American Society for Reproductive Medicine, Minimal Screening for Gamete Donors, Fertility and Sterility, 2008, volume 90, No. 5, Supplement, S44. Reprinted by permission from the American Society for Reproductive Medicine.

American Society of Gene Therapy, Policy of the American Society of Gene Therapy Financial Conflict of Interest in Clinical Research (adopted April 5, 2000). Reprinted with permission of the American Society of Gene Therapy, Copyright © 2000–2006. All rights reserved.

American Society of Human Genetics, Points to Consider: Ethical, Legal, and Psychosocial Implications of Genetic Testing in Children and Adolescents, in American Journal of Human Genetics, volume 57, 1233 (1995). Reprinted with permission of the University of Chicago Press excerpts from the American Society of Human Genetics and American College of Medical Genetics, Copyright © (1995) by the American Society of Human Genetics. All rights reserved.

American Society of Human Genetics, Social Issues Committee and American College of Medical Genetics, Social, Ethical, and Legal Issues Committee, Genetic Testing in Adoption, American Journal of Human Genetics, volume 66, 761–767 (2000). Copyright © 2000. Reprinted with permission of the American Society of Human Genetics.

American Society of Human Genetics, Statement on Informed Consent for Genetic Research, American Journal of Human Genetics 1996; volume 59, 471. Copyright © 1996, the American Society of Human Genetics. Reprinted with permission of the University of Chicago Press.

Andrews, Lori B. et al., Assessing Genetic Risks: Implications for Health and Social Policy, 118–121, 124–126, 128–29 (1994). Copyright © 1994. Reprinted with the permission of National Academy Press, Washington, D.C.

Andrews, Lori B., Future Perfect: Confronting Decisions About Genetics, 56–62, 140–141 (2001). Copyright © 2001, Lori B. Andrews. Columbia University Press. Reprinted with the permission of the publisher.

Andrews, Lori B., Is There a Right to Clone? Constitutional Challenges to Bans on Human Cloning, 11 Harv. J.L. & Tech. 643, 647–648, 661–667 (Summer, 1998). Copyright © 1998, the President & Fellows of Harvard College. Reprinted with the permission of the Harvard Journal of Law and Technology.

Andrews, Lori B., Predicting and Punishing Antisocial Acts: How the Criminal Justice System Might Use Behavioral Genetics, in Behavioral Genetics: The Clash of Culture and Biology, 120–122 (Ronald A. Carson and Mark A. Rothstein eds., 1999). Copyright © 1999 Johns Hopkins University Press. Reprinted by permission of the Johns Hopkins University Press.

Andrews, Lori B., Prenatal Screening and the Culture of Motherhood, 47 Hastings L.J. 967, 970–971, 994–1000 (April 1996). Copyright © 1996, the University of California, Hastings College of the Law. Reprinted from 47 Hastings Law Journal (1996), by permission.

Andrews, Lori B., The Clone Age: Adventures in The New World of Reproductive Technology. Copyright © 1999 by Lori B. Andrews. Reprinted by arrangement with Henry Holt & Company, LLC.

Andrews, Lori B., Torts and the Double Helix: Malpractice Liability for Failure to Warn of Genetic Risks, 29 Hous. L. Rev. 149, 152–57, 166–69 (1992). Copyright © 1992 by the Houston Law Review. Reprinted with the permission of Houston Law Review.

Andrews, Lori and Dorothy Nelkin, Body Bazaar: The Market For Human Tissue in the Biotechnology Age, 60–62, 102–103 (2001). Copyright © 2001, Random House Inc. Reprinted with permission of Random House.

Annas, George J., Genetic Privacy: There Ought to Be a Law, 4 Tex. Rev. L. & Politics 9, 9–13 (1999). Copyright © 1999 Texas Review of Law & Politics; George J. Annas. Reprinted by permission.

Annas, George J., Leonard H. Glantz and Patricia A. Roche, The Genetic Privacy Act and Commentary vii–ix (1995). Reprinted by permission of the authors.

Avise, John, The Genetic Gods: Evolution and Belief in Human Affairs, 50 (1998). Copyright © 1998 by the President and Fellows of Harvard College. Reprinted by permission of the publisher, Harvard University Press.

Baily, Mary Ann and Thomas H. Murray, Ethics, Evidence, and Cost in Newborn Screening, Hastings Center Report 23, 27–28 (May/June 2008). Used with permission.

Berg, P. et al., Letter: Potential Biohazards of Recombinant DNA Molecules, Science, volume 185, 303 (1974). Reprinted with permission.

Bloch, Maurice et al, Predictive Testing for HD in Canada: The Experience of Those Receiving an Increased Risk, American Journal of Medical Genetics, volume 42, 499–507 (1992). Reprinted with permission of Wiley–Liss, Inc. a subsidiary of John Wiley & Sons, Inc. Copyright © 1992.

Bok, Sissela, Secrets: On the Ethics of Concealment and Revelation, 20 (1983). Copyright © 1982 by Sissela Bok. Used by permission of Pantheon Books, a division of Random House, Inc.

Bork, Robert H., The Challenges of Biology for Law, 4 Tex. Rev. L. & Politics 1, 2–3 (1999). Copyright © 1999 Texas Review of Law & Politics; Robert H. Bork. Reprinted by permission.

Bowser, Rene, Race as a Proxy for Drug Response: the Dangers and Challenges of Ethnic Drugs, 53 DePaul Law Review 1111 (2004). Reprinted with permission.

Brock, Dan W., Allen Buchanan, Norman Daniels, and Dan Wikler (eds.), From Chance to Choice: Genetics and Justice, 27–28 (2000). Reprinted with the permission of Cambridge University Press. Copyright © 2000 Cambridge University Press.

Cavalli–Sforza, Luigi Luca, Remarks Upon Being Awarded the Balzan Prize for the Science of Human Origins (1999). Reprinted by permission.

Churchill, L.R. et al., Genetic Research as Therapy: Implication of 'Gene Therapy' for Informed Consent, 26 Journal of Law, Medicine, & Ethics, 38–47 (Spring 1998). Copyright © 1998, Reprinted with the permission of the American Society of Law, Medicine & Ethics. All rights reserved.

Chwalow, A. Judith, Ruth R. Faden, and Neil A. Holtzman, Parental Rights, Child Welfare, and Public Health: The Case of PKU Screening, American Journal of Public Health, volume 72, 1396 (1982). Reprinted with permission of the American Public Health Association. Copyright © 1982, the American Public Health Association.

College of American Pathologists, Advocacy on the Issues, Genes Patents Detrimental to Care, Training, Research (July 5, 2000). Reprinted with permission of College of American Pathologists.

Collins, Francis S., Shattuck Lecture—Medical and Societal Consequence of the Human Genome Project, New England Journal of Medicine, volume 341, 30–35 (1999). Copyright © 1999 Massachusetts Medical Society. Reprinted with permission. All rights reserved.

Collins, Francis S. and Victor A. McKusick, Implications of the Human Genome Project for Medical Science 285 JAMA, volume 285, 540 (2001). Reprinted with permission.

Dorozynski, Alexander, Privacy Rules Blindside French Glaucoma Effort, Science, volume 252, 369 (1991). Reprinted with permission.

Duster, Troy, Behavioral Genetics and Explanations of the Link Between Crime, Violence, and Race, In Wrestling with Behavioral Genetics: Science, Ethics, and Public Conversations (Erik Parens and Audrey R. Chapman, eds.). Copyright © 2006 Johns Hopkins University Press. Reprinted with permission of The Johns Hopkins Press.

Eichenwald, Kurt and Gina Kolata, Drug Trials Hide Conflicts for Doctors, The New York Times, May 16, 1999, 1. Copyright © 1999. Reprinted with the permission of the New York Times.

Epstein, Richard A., The Legal Regulation of Genetic Discrimination: Old Responses to New Technology 74 B.U. L. Rev. 1, 12–13 (1994). Copyright © 1994 by the Trustees of Boston University; Richard A. Epstein. Reprinted by permission.

Erramouspe, Matthew, Staking Patent Claims on the Human Blueprint: Rewards and Rent–Dissipating Races, 43 UCLA L. Rev. 961 (1996). Reprinted with the permission of the UCLA Law Review and the author. Originally published in 43 UCLA L. Rev. 961. Copyright © 1996, the Regents of the University of California. All Rights Reserved.

Fost, Norman, Genetic Diagnosis & Treatment Ethical Considerations, American Journal of Disease of Children, volume/edition 147 (11) (1993). Copyright © 1993 American Medical Association. Reproduced with permission of American Medical Association in the format Textbook via Copyright Clearance Center.

Foster, et al. Excerpts from Foster et al., A Model Agreement for Genetic Research in Socially Identifiable Populations, American Journal of Human Genetics, volume 63, 696–702 (1998). Copyright © 1998. Reprinted with the permission of the University of Chicago Press.

Ginsburg, Douglas H., Genetics and Privacy 4 Tex. Rev. L. & Politics 17, 22–23 (1999). Copyright © 1999 Texas Review of Law & Politics; Douglas H. Ginsburg. Reprinted by permission.

Glantz, Leonard H., Research with Children, 24 Am. J. L. and Med. 213 (1998). Reprinted with permission of the American Society of Law, Medicine & Ethics.

Goldstein, Norm, Owner of 'Genius' Sperm Bank Pleased by Results, The New York Times, December 11, 1984, A11. Reprinted with permission of the Associated Press. Copyright © 1984 the Associated Press.

Greely, Henry T., The Control of Genetic Research: Involving the "Groups Between," 33 Hous. L. Rev. 1397, 1400–1401 (1997). Copyright © 1997, Houston Law Review. Reprinted with permission of the University of Houston Law Review.

Hall, Mark A., Legal Rules and Industry Norms: The Impact of Laws Restricting Health Insurers' Use of Genetic Information 40 Jurimetrics 93, 94–99, 122 (1999). Copyright © 1999 American Bar Association; Mark A. Hall. Reprinted by permission.

Harsanyi, Zsolt and Richard Hutton, Genetic Prophecy: Beyond the Double Helix, 236–240 (1981). Copyright © 1981. Reprinted with permission of the authors.

Heller, Michael A. and Rebecca S. Eisenberg, Can Patents Deter Innovation? The Anticommons in Biomedical Research. Excerpted with permission from Science, volume 280, 698 (1998). Copyright © 1998 American Association for the Advancement of Science.

Hoffman, Sharona and Mark Rothstein, Genetic Tests, Genetic Medicine and Managed Care, Wake Forest Law Review, volume 34, 849, 875–76 (1999). Reprinted with permission of the Wake Forest Law Review.

Holtzman, Neil A., Putting the Search for Genes in Perspective, 31 Int'l J. Health Servs. 445, 457–458 (2001). Reprinted by permission.

HUGO Ethics Committee, Statement On Benefit–Sharing, April 9, 2000. Copyright © 2000. Reprinted with the permission of the HUGO Ethics Committee.

Hyman, Steven E., Using Genetics to Understand Human Behavior 113–166 (Erik Parens, Audrey R. Chapman, & Nancy Press eds. 2006) Copyright © Johns Hopkins University Press. Reprinted with permission of The Johns Hopkins Press.

Imwinkelried, Edward and D. H. Kaye, DNA Typing: Emerging or Neglected Issues, 76 Wash. L. Rev. 413 (2001). Copyright © 2001 Washington Law Review Association. Reprinted with permission of the authors.

Jensen, Kyle and Fiona Murray, Intellectual Property Landscape of the Human Genome, 310 Science 239 (October 14, 2005). Reprinted with permission.

Juengst, E. and E. Parens, Inadvertently Crossing the Germ Line, Science, volume 292, 397 (2001). Reprinted with permission of the American Association for the Advancement of Science. Copyright © 2001 American Association for the Advancement of Science.

Juengst, Eric T., The Perils of Genetic Genealogy, 10 CenterViews 253 (Winter 1996). Copyright © 1996. Reprinted with permission of the author.

Kaiser, Jocelyn, A More Rational Approach to Gauging Environmental Threats? Excerpted with permission from Science, volume 278, 570 (1997). Copyright © 1997 American Association for the Advancement of Science.

Kaiser, Jocelyn, A Plan to Capture Human Diversity in 1000 Genomes. Excerpted with permission from Science, volume 319, 395 (2008). Copyright © 2008 American Association for the Advancement of Science.

Kaiser, Jocelyn, Environment Institute Lays Plans for Gene Hunt. Excerpted with permission from Science, volume 278, 569 (1997). Copyright © 1997 American Association for the Advancement of Science.

Kass, Nancy E., The Implications of Genetic Testing for Health and Life Insurance, in Genetic Secrets: Protecting Privacy and Confidentiality in the Genetic Era, 299, 300–302 (Mark A. Rothstein, ed. 1997). Copyright © 1997 by Yale University. Reprinted by permission.

Kerouac, James D., The Regulation of Home Diagnostic Test for Genetic Disorders: Can the FDA Deny Premarket Application on the Basis of the Devices, 5 Journal of Biolaw & Business 34–43 (2002). Reprinted with permission.

Khan, Zeshan Q., Colonialism Revisited: Insights into the Human Genome Diversity Project, 3 J.L. & Soc. Challenges 89 (1999). Copyright © 1999. Reprinted with permission.

Khoury, Muin J., Wylie Burke, and Elizabeth Thomson, Genetics and Public Health: A Framework for the Integration of Human Genetics in Public Health Practice, Genetics and Public Health in the 21st Century. Copyright © 2000 Oxford University Press, Inc. Reprinted with permission.

Kitcher, Philip, The Lives to Come: The Genetic Revolution and Human Possibilities, 17–18 (1996). Copyright © 1996 by Andrew George Philip Kitcher. Reprinted by permission.

Krimsky, Sheldon, The Profit of Scientific Discovery and Its Normative Implications, 75 Chicago–Kent L. Rev. 15, 21–22, 28–37 (1999). Copyright © 1999, IIT Chicago–Kent College of Law. Reprinted with permission of Chicago–Kent Law Review.

Lacy, James V. et al., Technology Transfer Laws Governing Federally Funded Research and Development, 19 Pepp. L. Rev. 1, 9–11, 13–14 (1991). Copyright © 1991. Reprinted with the permission of the Pepperdine University School of Law, Law Review.

Lander, E.S. Scientific Commentary: The Scientific Foundations and Medical and Social Prospects of the Human Genome, volume 26, Journal of Law, Medicine & Ethics, 184–88 (Fall 1998). Copyright © 1998, Reprinted with the permission of the American Society of Law, Medicine & Ethics. All rights reserved.

Lander, Eric, DNA Fingerprinting: Science, Law, and the Ultimate Identifier, in The Code of Codes, (Daniel J. Kevles and Leroy Hood, eds., 1992). Reprinted by permission of the publisher from in The Code Of Codes: Scientific And Social Issues In The Human Genome Project, edited by Daniel J. Kevles and Leroy Hood, Cambridge, Mass.: Harvard University Press, Copyright © 1992 by Daniel J. Kevles and Leroy Hood.

Ledley, Fred, A Consumer Charter for Genomic Services, 20 Nature Biotechnology 767 (2002). Reprinted with permission.

Lewin, Tamar, Boom in Genetic Testing Raises Questions on Sharing Results, The New York Times, July 21, 2000, A1. Reprinted with permission from the New York Times Agency. Copyright © 2000, the New York Times Agency.

Lewis, C.S., The Abolition of Man, 57–58 (1947). Copyright © C.S. Lewis Pte. Ltd. 1943, 1946, 1978. Extract reprinted by permission.

Lombardo, Paul A., Three Generations, No Imbeciles: New Light on Buck v. Bell, in the New York University Law Review, volume 60, 49–62 (1985). Reprinted with permission from the New York University Law Review.

Lowden, J. Alexander, Genetic Risks and Mortality Rules, in Genetics and Life Insurance: Medical Underwriting and Social Policy, Mark A. Rothstein ed. Copyright © 2004, MIT Press. Reprinted with permission.

Malinowski, Michael J., Dealing with the Realities of Race and Ethnicity: A Bioethics–Centered Argument in Favor of Race–Based Genetics Research, 45 Hous. L. Rev. 1415, 1433–36 (2009). Reprinted by permission of the Houston Law Review.

Marchant, Gary E., Genetic Susceptibility and Biomarkers in Toxic Injury Litigation, 41 Jurimetrics 67, 87 (2000). Copyright © 2000 by American Bar Association, Gary E. Marchant. Reprinted by permission.

Marchant, Gary E., Toxicogenomics and Environmental Regulation, Genomics and Environmental Regulation: Science, Ethics, and Law. Copyright © Johns Hopkins University Press. Reprinted with permission of The Johns Hopkins Press.

Marshall, Eliot, Tapping Iceland's DNA. Excerpted with permission from Science, volume 278, 566 (1997). Copyright © 1997, American Association for the Advancement of Science.

Matthews, Anne L., Genetic Counseling, in the Encyclopedia of Ethical, Legal & Policy Issues in Biotechnology, volume 1, 349–50 (T.H. Murray and M.J. Mehlman, eds., 2000). Reprinted with permission of John Wiley & Sons, Inc. Copyright © 2000.

McEwen, Jean, Genetic Information, Ethics, and Information Relating to Biological Parenthood, in the Encyclopedia of Ethical, Legal & Policy Issues in Biotechnology, volume 1, 356, 359–62 (T.H. Murray and M.J. Mehlman, eds., 2000). Reprinted with permission of John Wiley & Sons, Inc. Copyright © 2000.

McGuire, Amy L., Rebecca Fisher, Paul Cuseman, Kathy Hudson, Mark A. Rothstein, Deven McGraw, Stephen Matterson, John Glasser, and Douglas Henley, Confidentiality, Privacy, and Security Considerations for the Storage of Genetic and Genomic Test Information in Electronic Health Records: Points to Consider. 10 Genetics in Med., 495, 495–499, (2009). Reprinted by permission.

Mehlman, Maxwell J., Access to the Genome and Federal Entitlement Programs, in The Human Genome Project and the Future of Health Care, 119–123. (T.H. Murray and M.J. Mehlman, R.F. Murray, Jr., eds., 1996). Reprinted with permission of Indiana University Press. Copyright © 1996 from Access to the Genome and Federal Entitlement Programs.

Mehlman, Maxwell J. Modern Eugenics and the Law, in A Century of Eugenics in America: From the "Indiana Experiment" to the Human Genome Era, Paul A. Lombardo, Ed. (Indiana University Press, Forthcoming 2010). Used with permission.

Mehlman, Maxwell J., Jessica W. Berg, Eric T. Juengst, and Eric Kodish, Ethical and Legal Issues in Enhancement Research on Human Subjects (forthcoming, Cambridge Q. J. of Ethics, 2009). Used with permission.

Murray, Thomas H., Genetic Exceptionalism and Future Diaries: Is Genetic Information Different from Other Medical Information?, in Genetic Secrets: Protecting Privacy and Confidentiality in the Genetic Era, 60, 71 (Mark A. Rothstein, ed. 1997). Copyright © 1997 by Yale University. Reprinted by permission.

National Research Council, Application of Toxicogenomic Technologies to Predictive Toxicology and Risk Assessment, 2007. Reprinted with permission by the National Academy of Sciences, Courtesy of the National Academies Press, Washington, DC.

National Research Council, The Evaluation of Forensic DNA Evidence, 171–73 (1996). Copyright © 1996, National Academy Press. Reprinted with permission of the National Academy of Sciences.

Obasogie, Osagie K., Playing the Gene Card? A Report on Race and Human Biotechnology (Center for Genetics and Society 2009). Used with permission.

Orentlicher, David, Genetic Privacy in the Patient–Physician Relationship, in Genetic Secrets: Protecting Privacy and Confidentiality in the Genetic Era, 77, 78–81 (Mark A. Rothstein, ed. 1997). Copyright © 1997 by Yale University. Reprinted by permission.

Parens, Erik, Authenticity and Ambivalence: Toward Understanding the Enhancement Debate, Hastings Center Report 34, 37–38 (2005). Reprinted with permission.

Pelias, Mary Z. and Margaret M. DeAngelis, The New Genetic Technologies: New Options, New Hope, and New Challenges, 45 Loy. L. Rev. 287, 289–91 (1999). Copyright © 1999. Reprinted with the permission of the Loyola Law Review.

Plomin, Robert et al., Behavioral Genetics, in Behavioral Genetics in the Post Genomic Era, 10–14 (Robert Plomin et al. eds., 2003). Copyright © 2003 by the American Psychological Association. Reprinted with permission.

Pollack, Andrew, Patient's DNA May Be Signal to Tailor Drugs, The New York Times, Dec. 30, 2008, at A1. Used with permission.

Portman, Robert M., Legislative Restriction On Medical And Surgical Procedure Patents Removes Impediment To Medical Progress, 4 U. Balt. Intell. Prop. L.J. 91, 91–92, 104–107 (Spring, 1996). Copyright © 1996, the University of Baltimore School of Law Intellectual Property Law Journal. Reprinted with the permission of the University of Baltimore Intellectual Property Law Journal.

Reilly, Philip R., Eugenics, Ethics, Sterilization Law, in the Encyclopedia of Ethical, Legal & Policy Issues in Biotechnology, 204–208, volume 1. (T.H. Murray and M.J. Mehlman, eds., 2000). Reprinted with permission of John Wiley & Sons, Inc. Copyright © 2000.

Ridley, Matt, Genome: The Autobiography of a Species in 23 Chapters 43–46 (1999). Copyright 1999 by Matt Ridley, reprinted by permission of HarperCollins Publishers, Inc.

Ridley, Matt, Nature Via Nurture: Genes, Experience, and What Makes Us Human 260–262 (2003). Copyright © 2003 by Matt Ridley, reprinted by permission of HarperCollins Publishers, Inc.

Roses, Allen D., Pharmacogenetics and the Practice of Medicine, Nature, volume 405, 857–865 (2000). Reprinted with permission from Pharmacogenetics and the Practice of Medicine, Nature, volume 405, 857–865 (2000). Copyright © 2000 Macmillan Magazines, Ltd.

Rothman, Barbara Katz, Genetic Maps and Human Imaginations: The Limits of Science in Understanding Who We Are, 18, 247–48 (1998). Copyright © 1998 by Barbara Katz Rothman. Used by permission of W.W. Norton & Company, Inc.

Rothstein, Laura F., Genetic Information in Schools, in Genetic Secrets: Protecting Privacy and Confidentiality in the Genetic Era, 317–320 (Mark A. Rothstein ed., 1997). Copyright © 1997 by Yale University. Reprinted by permission.

Rothstein, Mark A., Applications of Behavioural Genetics: Outpacing the Sciences, 6 Nature Reviews Genetics 793–798 (2005). Copyright © 2005 by the Nature Publishing Group. Reprinted by permission.

Rothstein, Mark A., Behavioral Genetic Determinism: Its Effects on Culture and Law, in Behavioral Genetics: The Clash of Culture and Biology, 89–96 (Ronald A. Carson and Mark A. Rothstein eds., 1999). Copyright © 1999 Johns Hopkins University Press. Reprinted by permission of the Johns Hopkins University Press.

Rothstein, Mark A., Expanding the Ethical Analysis of Biobanks, 33 J.L. Med. & Ethics 89 (Spring 2005). Reprinted with permission of the American Society of Law, Medicine & Ethics.

Rothstein, Mark A., Genetic Exceptionalism and Legislative Pragmatism, 35 Hastings Center Report No. 4, 27–33 (2005). Copyright © 2005. Reprinted with permission of the Hastings Center.

Rothstein, Mark A., Genetic Stalking and Voyeurism: A New Challenge to Privacy, 57 Kansas Law Review (2009) 539, 546–548. Reprinted by permission.

Rothstein, Mark A., Genetics and the Work Force of the Next Hundred Years, 2000 Colum. Bus. L. Rev. 371, 371–72 (2000). Copyright © 2000 Columbia Business Law Review; Mark A. Rothstein. Reprinted by permission.

Rothstein, Mark A., GINA's Beauty Is Only Skin Deep, 22 GeneWatch (2009) 9–12, Reprinted with the permission of GeneWatch, the magazine of the Council for Responsible Genetics. May not be reproduced for any political purpose, including use in candidate campaigns or for legislative lobbying.

Rothstein, Mark A., Legal Conceptions of Equality in the Genomic Age, 25 Journal of Law & Inequality: A Journal of Theory & Practice 429, 455–460, (2007). Reprinted with permission.

Rothstein, Mark A., Medical Privacy—An Oxymoron? Newsday, March 15, 1999, A25. Reprinted by permission of the author.

Rothstein, Mark A., Occupational Health and Discrimination Issues Raised by Toxicogenomics in the Workplace, Genomics and Environmental Regulation 184–188 (Richard R. Sharp, Gary E. Marchant, & Jamie Grodsky, eds., 2008). Copyright © Johns Hopkins University Press. Reprinted with permission of The Johns Hopkins Press.

Rothstein, Mark A., Policy Recommendations, in Genetics and Life Insurance: Medical Underwriting and Social Policy (Mark A. Rothstein, ed. 2004). Copyright © 2004, MIT Press. Reprinted by permission.

Rothstein, Mark A., Predictive Genetic Testing for Alzheimer's Disease in Long–Term Care Insurance, 35 Ga. L. Rev. 707, 714–731 (2001). Copyright © 2001 Georgia Law Review Association, Inc.; Mark A. Rothstein. Reprinted by permission.

Rothstein, Mark A., Preventing the Discovery of Plaintiff Genetic Profiles by Defendants Seeking to Limit Damages in Personal Injury Litigation, 71 Ind. L.J. 877 (1996). Copyright © 1996 by the Trustees of Indiana University; Mark A. Rothstein. Reprinted by permission.

Rothstein, Mark A., The ADA and Genetic Discrimination in Employment, 35 J.L. Med. & Ethics 837–839 (2008). Copyright © 2008. Reprinted with permission of the American Society of Law, Medicine & Ethics. May not be reproduced without express written consent.

Rothstein, Mark A. and Mary R. Anderlik, What is Genetic Discrimination and When and How Can it Be Prevented? 3 Genetics in Med. 354 (2001). Reprinted by permission.

Rothstein, Mark A., Yu Cai, and Gary E. Marchant, Ethical Implications of Epigenetic Research, 10 Nature Reviews Genetics 224 (2009). Copyright © 2009 Nature Publishing Group. Reprinted by permission.

Rothstein, Mark A. and Sandra Carnahan, Legal and Policy Issues in Expanding the Scope of Law Enforcement DNA Data Banks, 67 Brook. L. Rev. 127 (2001). Copyright © 2001. Reprinted with the permission of the Brooklyn Law Review.

Rothstein, Mark A. and Phyllis Griffin Epps, Ethical and Legal Implications of Pharmacogenomics, 2 Nature Reviews Genetics 228–230 (2001). Copyright © 2001, Macmillan Magazines, Ltd.

Rothstein, Mark A. and Yann Joly, Genetic Information and Insurance Underwriting: Contemporary Issues and Approaches in the Global Economy in Handbook of Genetics and Society (Paul Atkinson, Peter Glasner, & Margaret Lock, eds., 2009). Copyright © 2009. Reprinted with author permission.

Rothstein, Mark A. and Meghan K. Talbott, Compelled Disclosure of Health Information: Protecting Against the Greatest Potential Threat to Privacy, JAMA 295(24) 2882–2885 (2006). Copyright © 2006 American Medical Association All rights reserved. Reprinted with permission.

Sandel, Michael, The Case Against Perfection: What's Wrong with Designer Children, Bionic Athletes, and Genetic Engineering, Atlantic Monthly (April 2004). Reprinted with permission.

Stock, Gregory, Redesigning Humans: Our Inevitable Genetic Future (2002). Reprinted with permission.

Stolberg, S., The Biotech Death of Jesse Gelsinger, The New York Times Sunday Magazine, November 28, 1999, 137. Reprinted with permission, The New York Times Agency. Copyright © 1999, The New York Times Agency.

Sturges, Melissa L., Who Should Hold Property Rights to the Human Genome? An Application of the Common Heritage of Humankind, 13 Am. U. Int'l L. Rev. 219, 245–248 (1997). Copyright © 1997, American University Int'l L. Review. Reprinted with the permission of the American University International Law Review.

Taub, Sara, Karine Morin, Monique A. Spillman, Robert Sade, and Frank A. Riddick, for the Council on Ethical and Judicial Affairs of the American Medical Association, Managing Familial Risk in Genetic Testing, 8 Genetic Testing 356–359 (2004). Reprinted with permission.

Thompson, Nicholas, Gene Blues: Is the Patent Office Prepared to Deal with the Genomic Revolution? Washington Monthly, 9 (April 2001). Reprinted with permission of the Washington Monthly. Copyright © by Washington Monthly Publishing, LLC, 733 15th St. NW, Suite 1000, Washington, DC 20005. (202) 393–5155. Web site: www.washingtonmonthly.com.

Trefethen, Amanda, The Emerging Tort of Wrongful Adoption, 11 J. Contemp. Legal Issues 620 (2000). Copyright © 2000, Journal of Contemporary Legal Issues. Reprinted with the permission of the Journal of Contemporary Legal Issues.

Wertz, Dorothy, et al., Genetic Testing for Children and Adolescents: Who Decides?, Journal of the American Medical Association, volume/edition 272, 875 (1995). Copyright © 1995, American Medical Association. Reproduced with permission of the American Medical Association in the format Textbook via Copyright Clearance Center.

Willing, Richard, DNA and Daddy, USA Today, July 29, 1999, 1A. Copyright © 1999, USA Today. Reprinted with permission.

Winker, Margaret A., Race and Ethnicity in Medical Research: Requirements Meet Reality, 34 J. Law, Med., & Ethics 520, 520–522 (2006). Reprinted with permission of the Journal of Law, Medicine, and Ethics.

Wood, Alastair J.J., Racial Differences in the Response to Drugs—Pointers to Genetic Disorders, 344 New England Journal of Medicine 1393, 1395 (2001). Reprinted with permission.

Wright Clayton, Ellen, Screening and Treatment of Newborns, 29 Houston Law Review, 86 (1992). Reprinted with permission from the Houston Law Review, Copyright © 1992.

Zick, Cathleen D. et al., Genetic Testing, Adverse Selection, and the Demand for Life Insurance, 93 Am. J. Med. Genetics 29, 29–32, 35–38 (2000). Copyright © 2000 by Wiley–Liss, Inc. Reprinted by permission of Wiley–Liss, Inc., a subsidiary of John Wiley & Sons, Inc.

Zick, Cathleen D. et al., Genetic Testing for Alzheimer's Disease and Its Impact on Insurance Purchasing Behavior, 24 Health Affairs 483, 484–488

(2005). Copyright © 2005, by Project HOPE—The People-to-People Foundation, Inc. Reprinted by permission.

Zimmerman, B.K., Human Germ Line Therapy: The Case for its Development and Use, Journal of Medicine and Philosophy, volume 16, 593 (1991). Copyright © 1991 by Swets & Zeitlinger, Publishers. Reprinted with permission.

Summary of Contents

TABLE OF CONTENTS

―――――――

CHAPTER 5.   COMMERCIALIZATION OF GENETIC
RESEARCH: PROPERTY, PATENTS, AND CONFLICTS OF
INTEREST

CHAPTER 10. GENETIC ENHANCEMENT

CHAPTER 13.   MENTAL AND BEHAVIORAL GENETICS

CHAPTER 14. PRIVACY, CONFIDENTIALITY, AND DISCRIMINATION

CHAPTER 15. INSURANCE

CHAPTER 16.   EMPLOYMENT DISCRIMINATION

TABLE OF CASES

The principal cases are in bold type. Cases cited or discussed in the text are in roman type. References are to pages. Cases cited in principal cases and within other quoted materials are not included.

GENETICS:
ETHICS, LAW AND POLICY

Third Edition

CHAPTER 1

INTRODUCTION

■ ■ ■

For all of recorded human history—and undoubtedly long before—humans have been fascinated by parentage and familial relationships, as well as the inheritance of physical, mental, and behavioral traits. Until the last century, however, our knowledge of human inheritance was limited to observing the associations of expressed factors. Inherited afflictions were seemingly caused by the indecipherable and unpredictable hand of fate. We lacked the ability to predict or explain the inter-generational transmission of any of these characteristics.

It is only since the turn of the twentieth century that human genetics has emerged as a rigorous science. Building on the work of Charles Darwin and Gregor Mendel in the nineteenth century, Thomas Hunt Morgan, James Watson, Francis Crick, Sydney Brenner, Frederick Sanger and numerous other scientists began to unravel the mysteries inside the nucleus of the cell. By the start of the twenty-first century, a draft sequence of the entire 3 billion letters of human DNA had been completed.

Although the role of genes in human life is still vigorously debated in scientific, political, and theological circles, the impact of genetics goes well beyond understanding modes of inheritance and predisposition to illness. Genetics raises exciting possibilities for disease prevention, treatment, and cures. As we learn that virtually all health conditions are affected to some degree by genetic factors, genetics will become an increasingly essential part of primary care and all medical specialties. In the health care setting, genetics implicates important issues of privacy, confidentiality, informed consent, the physician-patient relationship, access to health care, public health, and myriad other issues. Beyond health care, genetics is becoming a more common issue in criminal and civil litigation, forensics, employment and insurance, family law, intellectual property, and other areas.

This chapter puts genetics in the broadest perspective, by viewing the past, future, and present of human life through the lens of genetics.

1

I.　GENES AND THE PAST

The study of genetics requires the widest possible perspective, beginning with evolution of life on earth, the emergence and migration of humans, and the nineteenth century discovery of natural selection and the basic principles of heredity.

JOHN AVISE, THE GENETIC GODS: EVOLUTION AND BELIEF IN HUMAN AFFAIRS
50 (1998).

Physicists and astronomers who subscribe to the big bang theory of the origin of the universe tell us that it took place roughly 15 billion years ago. If we compress these 15 billion years into one year, the big bang occurs on January 1. The earth comes into existence on approximately September 12, and the first known forms of life appear about October 7. Eukaryotic organisms begin to flourish by mid-November, and by December 17 diverse invertebrate life roams the planet. The first mammals appear on December 26, the first primates on December 29, and the first hominoids on December 30. It is not until late in the final day of our calendar year, December 31 at about 10:30 P.M., that the earliest human creatures amble onto the evolutionary stage. By 11:46 P.M., humans domesticate fire. Thirteen minutes later they are drawing extensive cave paintings, inventing agriculture, and beginning to cluster into the first large towns. Jesus is born four seconds before the present, at 11:59:56 P.M. Within the last second of the cosmic calendar, Europeans discovered the western hemisphere, many countries become mechanized and industrialized, and, perhaps most germane to the current discussion, the experimental method of science, which provides an objective and empirical illumination of the biotic geneses, emerged.

These scientific perspectives are sobering. No longer can we rationally see ourselves as the focal point of creation, either in space or time. We are dwarfed by the immensity of our surroundings, and by the vastness of time within which we participate for so brief an instant.

By measuring the degree of variation in DNA, scientists can determine the degree of relatedness of individual species of plants and animals. They also can estimate when any two lines of living things diverged to form separate branches of the evolutionary tree.

Humans are a young species and therefore have comparatively little intra-species genetic variation. Using new techniques, however, scientists can identify patterns of slight differences in human DNA. This information has been used to help write the history of our species, including migration patterns, the development of various language groups, and the genetic basis for differences in human appearance.

The following excerpt is from a speech given by Dr. Luigi Luca Cavalli–Sforza, a leading population geneticist, upon being awarded the Balzan Prize for his research.

LUIGI LUCA CAVALLI–SFORZA, REMARKS UPON BEING AWARDED THE BALZAN PRIZE FOR THE SCIENCE OF HUMAN ORIGINS

(1999).

The first approach I tried for reconstructing the history of human evolution was the use of evolutionary trees. Their application relies on the principle that the longer the separation of two populations, the greater is, in probability, the magnitude of the genetic difference between them. This requires [us] to measure a quantity we have called genetic distance. When one examines the genetic distance between species which have been separated for very long times, tens or hundreds of millions of years, one usually examines one individual per species, and finds species differ for many single genetic differences. The proportion of units of DNA which is different in two species is related in a simple way to their evolutionary time separation. But human populations have been separated for a comparatively very short time. Archeology shows that modern humans appeared only a little more than [one] hundred thousand years ago, in Africa, and spread first to Asia, between 100,000 and 50,000 years ago, and from S.E. Asia first to Oceania between 60,000 and 40,000 years ago. Europe was reached about 40,000 years ago from both West Asia and North Africa, and America from Siberia beginning 15,000 years ago.

Mutation first appears in one individual, and then it spreads to other individuals only in successive generations, when the individual carrying the mutated type has several progeny carrying the mutation, either because mutants are favored by selection and survive easily or have more children, or they are favored by chance. It usually takes a great number of generations before the mutation is found in many individuals, and even more for it to replace completely the original type. Thus between the first appearance of a mutation and the replacement of the original type there will usually elapse a very long time. During that period the mutant type is "polymorphic," i.e. there coexist in the population both the original (ancestral) type and the mutant one. It is extremely rare that a mutation has reached 100% in humans living in one part of the world and is absent in other parts. In fact, we find that any population, however small, has enormous genetic variation; on average, one finds 85% of the total human variation is within populations, and only 15% between.

* * *

I don't like the word "race" because it corresponds to old subdivisions that are inconsistent with genetic reality and unjustifiable by a rational classification. Moreover, there is no real use of such classifications and, what is worse, there is always an associated racist flavor. Darwin had already recognized the difficulty of a rational classification of races in what is almost a perfect continuum, and noted the futility of racial classifications, given the enormous variety of numbers and definitions of races which different taxonomists have traditionally offered, from two to more than one hundred. The current trend to increased admixture can only make races even less clear.

MATT RIDLEY, GENOME: THE AUTOBIOGRAPHY OF A SPECIES IN 23 CHAPTERS

43–46 (1999).

Darwin was not a little nervous on the subject. He had recently come under attack from a fierce Scottish professor of engineering, strangely named Fleeming Jenkin, who had pointed out the simple and unassailable fact that natural selection and blending inheritance did not mix. If heredity consisted of blended fluids, then Darwin's theory probably would not work, because each new and advantageous change would be lost in the general dilution of descent. Jenkin illustrated his point with the story of a white man attempting to convert an island of black people to whiteness merely by breeding with them. His white blood would soon be diluted to insignificance. In his heart Darwin knew Jenkin was right, and even the usually ferocious Thomas Henry Huxley was silenced by Jenkin's argument, but Darwin also knew that his own theory was right. He could not square the two. If only he had read Mendel.

Many things are obvious in retrospect, but still take a flash of genius to become plain. Mendel's achievement was to reveal that the only reason most inheritance *seems* to be a blend is because it involves more than one particle. In the early nineteenth century John Dalton had proved that water was actually made up of billions of hard, irreducible little things called atoms and had defeated the rival continuity theorists. So now Mendel had proved the atomic theory of biology. The atoms of biology might have been called all sorts of things: among the names used in the first years of this century were factor, gemmule, plastidule, pangene, biophor, id and idant. But it was 'gene' that stuck.

* * *

Yet even in his lifetime Mendel came tantalizingly close to full recognition. Charles Darwin, normally so diligent at gleaning ideas from the work of others, even recommended to a friend a book, by W.O. Focke, that contained fourteen different references to Mendel's paper. Yet he seems not to have noticed them himself. Mendel's fate was to be rediscovered, in 1900, long after his own and Darwin's deaths. It happened almost simultaneously in three different places. Each of his rediscoverers—Hugo de Vries, Carl Correns and Erich von Tschermak, all botanists—had laboriously duplicated Mendel's work on different species before he found Mendel's paper.

* * *

But the very fact that the dreaded [William] Bateson was Mendelism's champion led European evolutionists to be suspicious of it. In Britain, the bitter feud between Mendelians and 'biometricians' persisted for twenty years. As much as anything this passed the torch to the United States where the argument was less polarized. In 1903 an American geneticist called Walter Sutton noticed that chromosomes behave just like Mendelian factors: they come in pairs, one from each parent. Thomas Hunt Morgan, the father of American genetics, promptly became a late convert to Mendelism, so Bateson, who disliked Morgan, gave up being right and fought against the chromosomal theory. By such petty feuds is the history of science often decided. Bateson sank into obscurity while Morgan went on to great things as the founder of a productive school of genetics and the man who lent his name to the unit of genetic distance: the centimorgan. In Britain, it was not until the sharp, mathematical mind of Ronald Fisher was brought to bear upon the matter in 1918 that Darwinism and Mendelism were at last reconciled: far from contradicting Darwin, Mendel had brilliantly vindicated him. 'Mendelism', said Fisher, 'supplied the missing parts of the structure erected by Darwin.'

NOTES AND QUESTIONS

1. New discoveries in genetics are helping to write the history of our species and our relationship with other species. For example, we now know that humans and chimpanzees are 98%–99% alike genetically. The Human Genome Project has also confirmed the fundamental genetic homogeneity of our species. Any two individuals are 99.9% identical from a genetic standpoint. Genetics also helps to explain the relationships of groups of individuals, including ancient migration patterns and the development of language and culture. For example, population genetics demonstrates clearly that "race" is a social rather than a biological construct. Thus, new discoveries in genetics have had and will continue to have great importance in numerous fields of the natural and social sciences, as well as in the attitudes and ideals of ordinary citizens.

2. The astounding pace of genetic discovery needs to be put into perspective. Mendel's work was only rediscovered at the turn of the twentieth century; it has been only 50 years since the correct number of chromosomes in humans and the double helical structure of DNA were discovered; it was not until the 1990s that the loci of a substantial number of genes associated with debilitating diseases were determined; and it was not until the spring of 2001 that scientists were able to revise the approximation of the number of genes in humans from 80,000–100,000 to 32,000. By 2005, the estimate of the number of human genes was 20,0000–25,000—the same number as for the spotted green puffer fish.

3. In 2009, researchers announced that they had reconstructed the genome of Neanderthals, a human species that became extinct 30,000 years ago. When fully analyzed, the Neanderthal genome will help to trace the human lineage as it evolved over millions of years. Scientists also disclosed that there was no significant evidence of Neanderthal genes in modern

humans, dampening speculation that there could have been interbreeding. Dr. George Church, a Harvard researcher, said that a Neanderthal could be brought to life with present technology for about $30 million. He said he had no plans for such an experiment but, if someone eager to create a "Pleistocene Park" should supply the financing, "[w]e might go along with it." The New York Times, Feb. 13, 2009, at A13.

4.   There are numerous excellent and accessible books about evolution and genetics. Among the best are Steve Jones, The Language of Genes: Solving the Mysteries of Our Genetic Past, Present and Future (1993); Mark Ridley, The Cooperative Gene: How Mendel's Demon Explains the Evolution of Complex Beings (2001); Michael R. Rose, Darwin's Spectre: Evolutionary Biology in the Modern World (1998). For a further discussion of genes and human migration, see Luigi Luca Cavelli–Sforza, The History and Geography of Human Genes (1996).

II.   GENES AND THE FUTURE

Genetic engineering is destined to play a role in the future of humans, although the nature and extent of the effects are subject to extensive debate.

PHILIP KITCHER, THE LIVES TO COME: THE GENETIC REVOLUTION AND HUMAN POSSIBILITIES

17–18 (1996).

How should we assess the likely consequences of the genetic revolution? Should we recall the children whose lives are violated by their terrible inheritance and focus on the good of preventing more lives like theirs? Or should we think of the families whose lives will be disrupted by the disclosure to employers or insurance companies of information about their unlucky genes? Both, surely, and more besides.

For there are many other prospects. Imagine the medicine of the twenty-first century as it might be. Advances in molecular genetics have disclosed the causes of numerous diseases. Clever molecular techniques make it possible to detect and eliminate many types of cancer cells. Hereditary predispositions to cardiovascular disease can be discovered very early in life, and frequently future problems can be avoided. Understanding of the molecular mechanisms of viral replication is so far advanced that entire classes of infectious agents—including HIV, "the AIDS virus"—can be subdued. Some of our descendants live longer, all enjoy healthier, more vigorous lives.

But are they happier? There is yet another image, the darker side of the optimism about medical progress. Perhaps in probing the mechanics of our lives, we will disclose differences that would better have been left hidden. Will the society of our descendants embody a new class system, one that distinguishes people on the basis of their genes, genes that are supposed, rightly or wrongly, to affect traits that are most prized? Will they try to plan future generations, designing combinations of people with combinations of genes so as to form a harmonious society? Will human life be reduced to a product, something whose quality is carefully monitored and controlled, made by licensed manufacturers under expert medical supervision? Dimly, fearfully, thoughtful people glimpse enormous successors to Baron Frankenstein's laboratory, twenty-first-century hospitals equipped with the "decanting rooms" of *Brave New World*.

Alternately inspiring and appalling, kaleidoscopic images of possible futures whirl by. We sense that the molecular revolution will make large differences—how large, we do not know—in the lives our children will lead, we sense that we have the power now to channel the impact the new biology will have on society, but the kaleidoscope shifts too quickly. We do not know how to stop it, how to bring these images into focus, how to decide which of them represents something for which we should genuinely hope or of which we have reason to be afraid.

MARK A. ROTHSTEIN, GENETICS AND THE WORK FORCE OF THE NEXT HUNDRED YEARS

2000 Colum. Bus. L. Rev. 371, 371–72 (2000).

The December 5, 1999 issue of *The New York Times Magazine* is a special issue devoted to describing the efforts of *The New York Times* to create a time capsule to be opened in the year 3000. A panel of experts from various fields provided their opinions on, among other things, the location, architecture, contents, and style of the capsule. Besides these immediate issues, some of the experts observe that other likely events of the next thousand years would complicate any long-range planning for the year 3000, including the following: (1) the tectonic plates holding the American and European continents will drift apart by as much as sixty feet; (2) the sea level will rise by about eight feet; (3) the United States will cease to exist as a country by then; and (4) the language spoken by the inhabitants of New York City will be totally different from today's English—even today's English as spoken by the inhabitants of New York City.

Interestingly, the discussion of the New York City of the distant future failed to mention the biology of the inhabitants in the year 3000. When one thinks of the inhabitants of the Earth in one thousand years, one is easily drawn into a science fiction world of humans with unlimited lifespans, robots, cyborgs, chimeras, clones, and extraterrestrials. Even without such dramatic changes in the population of the planet, advances in our understanding of and ability to manipulate human biology are taking place at a rate much faster than the continental drift, and the consequences of at least some of the changes will be realized in our lifetimes.

C.S. LEWIS, THE ABOLITION OF MAN
70–71 (1947).

In reality, of course, if any one age really attains, by eugenics and scientific education, the power to make its descendants what it pleases, all men who live after it are the patients of that power. They are weaker, not stronger: for though we may have put wonderful machines in their hands we have pre-ordained how they are to use them. And if, as is almost certain, the age which had thus attained maximum power over posterity were also the age most emancipated from tradition, it would be engaged in reducing the power of its predecessors almost as drastically as that of its successors. And we must also remember that, quite apart from this, the later a generation comes—the nearer it lives to that date at which the species becomes extinct—the less power it will have in the forward direction, because its subjects will be so few. There is therefore no question of a power vested in the race as a whole steadily growing as long as the race survives. The last men, far from being the heirs of power, will be of all men most subject to the dead hand of the great planners and conditions and will themselves exercise least power upon the future. The real picture is that of one dominant age—let us suppose the hundredth century A.D.—which resists all previous ages most successfully and dominates all subsequent ages most irresistibly, and thus is the real master of the human species. But even within this master generation (itself an infinitesimal minority of the species) the power will be exercised by a minority smaller still. Man's conquest of Nature, if the dreams of some scientific planners are realized, means the rule of a few hundreds of men over billions upon billions of men. There neither is nor can be any simple increase of power on Man's side. Each new power won *by* man is a power *over* man as well. Each advance leaves him weaker as well as stronger. In every victory, besides being the general who triumphs, he is also the prisoner who follows the triumphal car.

NOTES AND QUESTIONS

1. Germ-line gene therapy, genetic enhancement, xenobiotics, and similar measures raise the issue of our genetic stewardship for future generations. A compelling argument could be made that scientists should not manipulate the gene pool until the consequences of such interventions are known with absolute certainty, and even then certain alterations of germ-lines should be impermissible. On the other hand, it also may be asserted that germ-line interventions in a small number of individuals are unlikely to affect the genetic heritage of a species with 6 billion people; countless other technological discoveries over thousands of years—from fire to agriculture to sanitation—have affected the gene pool to a much greater degree; and in an age of international scientific research there is very little that can be done to prevent scientists from performing virtually any research somewhere. For one view of the future, see Lee M. Silver, Remaking Eden: How Genetic Engineering and Cloning Will Transform the American Family (1998).

2. Is it possible to say no to science? Could we, as a society or world community, say that some measures have too much risk to be undertaken or that the consequences of some interventions undermine the fundamental characteristics of humans? Are there some activities that can truly be said to be "playing God"? See John H. Evans, Playing God? Genetic Engineering and the Rationalization of Public Bioethical Debate (2002).

3. Science works in progression, with each new discovery building on prior ones. As each new advance is made, the argument is raised that there is not much difference between the new measure and the last one. This reasoning has its critics. "Because we have to use numbers so much we tend to think of every process as if it must be like the numeral series, where every step to all eternity, is the same kind of step as the one before.... But you cannot go on 'explaining away' for ever; you will find that you have explained explanation itself away." C.S. Lewis, The Abolition of Man 90 (1947).

4. And who is to decide about possible alterations of the human germ-line?

> We recognize ourselves, measured against such goals and ideals, to be imperfect creatures. We wish to be more generous, more mathematically able, more musical, more athletic—less like brutes and more like gods, or demigods at least. Yet as noble as our aspirations for shedding our failings might be, our history also suggests that, being flawed as we are, we can never blindly trust our own aspirations to reshape ourselves.

Celeste M. Condit, The Meanings of the Gene: Public Debates About Human Heredity 245 (1999).

III. GENES AND THE PRESENT

Although it is enlightening and humbling to study the evolutionary past, and tantalizing and provocative to contemplate the distant future, we cannot ignore the present. In genetics, the present always includes the near future.

FRANCIS S. COLLINS & VICTOR A. MCKUSICK, IMPLICATIONS OF THE HUMAN GENOME PROJECT FOR MEDICAL SCIENCE

285 JAMA 540, 543–544 (2001).

The power of the molecular genetic approach for answering questions in the research laboratory will catalyze a similar transformation of clinical medicine, although this will come gradually over the course of the next 25 years.

By the year 2010, it is expected that predictive genetic tests will be available for as many as a dozen common conditions, allowing individuals who wish to know this information to learn their individual susceptibilities and to take steps to reduce those risks for which interventions are or will be available. Such interventions could take the form of medical surveillance, lifestyle modifications, diet, or drug therapy. Identification of persons at highest risk for colon cancer, for example, could lead to targeted efforts to provide colonoscopic screening to those individuals, with the likelihood of preventing many premature deaths.

Predictive genetic tests will become applicable first in situations where individuals have a strong family history of a particular condition; indeed, such testing is already available for several conditions, such as breast and colon cancers. But with increasing genetic information about common illnesses, this kind of risk assessment will become more generally available, and many primary care clinicians will become practitioners of genomic medicine, having to explain complex statistical risk information to healthy individuals who are seeking to enhance their chances of staying well. This will require substantial advances in the understanding of genetics by a wide range of clinicians. The National Coalition for Health Professional Education in Genetics, an umbrella group of physicians, nurses, and other clinicians, has organized to help prepare for this coming era.

* * *

By 2020, the impact of genetics on medicine will be even more widespread. The pharmacogenomics approach for predicting drug responsiveness will be standard practice for quite a number of disorders and drugs. New gene-based "designer drugs" will be introduced to the market for diabetes mellitus, hypertension, mental illness, and many other conditions. Improved diagnosis and treatment of cancer will likely be the most advanced of the clinical consequences of genetics, since a vast amount of molecular information already has been collected about the genetic basis of malignancy. By 2020, it is likely that every tumor will have a precise molecular fingerprint determined, cataloging the genes that have gone awry, and therapy will be individually targeted to that fingerprint.

* * *

In conclusion, this is a time of dramatic change in medicine. As we cross the threshold of the new millennium, we simultaneously cross a threshold into an era where the human genome sequence is largely known. We must commit ourselves to exploring the application of these powerful tools to the alleviation of human suffering, a mandate that undergirds all of medicine. At the same time, we must be mindful of the great potential for misunderstanding in this quickly developing field and make sure that the advancement of the social agenda of genetics is equally as vigorous as the medical agenda.

NEIL A. HOLTZMAN, PUTTING THE SEARCH FOR GENES IN PERSPECTIVE

31 Int'l J. Health Servs. 445, 457–458 (2001).

Only when disease-related genotypes are simultaneously present at many different loci, and when certain environmental exposures occur, do common diseases develop in the vast majority of individuals who will get the diseases. Moreover, no single constellation of genotypes will account for a large fraction of cases unless involving genotypes with frequencies of greater than 50 percent in the population. This is highly unlikely except for diseases that result from *new* environmental exposures or appear only after reproduction is complete, or for diseases in which the high-frequency genotypes are nonpenetrant by themselves but interact with other genotypes and environmental factors to increase the risk of disease. With these exceptions, finding all or most of the genes that contribute to any constellation will prove extremely difficult. The one or two genetic constituents of the constellation that researchers may discover will confer low relative risks for the disease. One consequence is that tests for these genotypes will have low positive predictive value; most people with positive test results will never develop the disease. Few healthy people will be interested in having tests when the positive predictive value is low. If there is no means of prevention or treatment that is uniquely effective in people with the detectable genotype, they are also unlikely to want testing even when the predictive value is higher. So far, interest in predictive genetic testing has been low.

* * *

I do not question the importance of basic genetic research with public funds, but I do question whether the National Institutes of Health and other tax-payer-supported agencies should continue to fund projects whose major aim is the quest for genes causing common diseases. In the past few years, not least because of genohype, the private sector has attracted huge amounts of capital for ventures of this sort. That is where research on common diseases should and will be done, at least until investors take the money and run, or lose it.

Although more attention to environmental risk factors for particular diseases will have greater yield than a genetic search, it will be difficult because of environmental-genetic and other interactions. The search for risk factors of particular diseases neglects the political and social milieu in which individuals swim or sink, and in which all diseases occur. Even in Mendelian disease the social milieu makes a difference. Patients with cystic fibrosis and low socio-economic status, for instance, have poorer pulmonary function (the strongest predictor of morbidity and morality) and are hospitalized more often and for longer duration than cystic fibrosis patients with higher socioeconomic status.

* * *

Political action to alter the social milieu by, for instance, improving air and water quality, reducing disparities between rich and poor, and strengthening primary care may do more to improve health than attacking ill health disease by disease. The improvements in everyone's health would result in a greater reduction in disease than focusing on the tail of the distribution. But the strategies entailed are a greater threat to the powers that be than is biomedical research, which seeks to find the seeds of disease in individuals, not in their social milieu.

BARBARA KATZ ROTHMAN, GENETIC MAPS AND HUMAN IMAGINATIONS: THE LIMITS OF SCIENCE IN UNDERSTANDING WHO WE ARE

18, 247–248 (1998).

Genetics isn't just a science; it is a way of thinking. Ruth Hubbard, professor emerita at Harvard and herself a biologist, points out that scientists are not detached observers of nature. They are constantly making decisions about what they will consider significant, and these choices are not merely individual or idiosyncratic, but reflect the society in which the scientists live and work. Genetic thinking, genetics as our society is developing it, genetics as we use it and think it and speak it, genetics as an ideology for our time, is about seeds. Genetics is the most obvious and direct scientific descendent of this traditional, father-based worldview, an attempt to understand the very meaning of life by understanding genes, bits of DNA, the updated version of seeds.

* * *

People map what they value, what they think is important. We are choosing to map the human genome. A map is a guide: it tells you what is there, but it also tells you how to get places. The genome map, as we have seen, may end up taking us places we don't want to go. What with slippery slopes, camels at the tent, and the way one thing leads to another, the world that we're creating with this map may not be a world in which we'd want to live. But how can anyone argue against mapping, against exploration? How can we stand here, of all places, in the "new world," and wring our hands and fret about exploration? Yet maybe exactly here, the land that native people lost to explorers, the land where the language blends the words of the British colonizers with the rhythms of the African slaves, maybe here in this unmeltable pot, we're best placed to think about maps, where they take us and where they lead.

Why are we spending our precious dollars on this map? What are we looking for? If our concern is with preventing disability and disease, with extending the life span, with lowering infant mortality, with making smarter people, there are better places to spend money. They want to find the genetic contribution to intelligence? Appreciate each baby with wonder and awe at its developing mind, nurture that intelligence in a rich and stimulating and safe environment, offer schools that inspire as well as instruct, and then get back to me on the question of individual—or racial—variation in intellectual potential. Don't start with schools that warehouse kids, televisions that stupefy them, and parents who are overburdened and overstressed, and then look for the genes for intelligence.

Cars, violence, lead and other poisons in the air and water, all kinds of things are destroying our children, their bodies and their minds, at higher rates than our genes. A mother's zip code is still the best predictor of infant mortality. Deal with poverty, and then get back to me on genetics research.

NOTES AND QUESTIONS

1.   The Collins and McKusick article has a quite different vision of the likely consequences of the genetic era of medicine from the Holtzman article. It is certainly understandable why there would be such optimism regarding each new medical technology developed, from gene therapy to stem cell research to "personalized medicine." Yet, the details of science are often more difficult and complicated to follow through on than the initial rushes of conceptual insight. The year 2010 has arrived, and few of the hopeful predictions of Collins and McKusick have been realized.

2.   The Rothman excerpt first raises the issue of whether science is really value neutral. According to the National Research Council:

> One myth about scientific research is that science is value neutral–that new scientific understandings await discovery, that these discoveries have no independent moral significance, and that they take on moral significance only when individuals and groups of individuals assign weight to scientific findings. One flaw in this argument is that there are seemingly limitless areas for scientific inquiry, yet there are finite numbers of scientists and limited resources to pursue research. Therefore, scientists and society must set priorities for research, and those priorities are a function of societal values. Even though scientists often make adventitious discoveries, they generally discover what they are looking for, and what they are looking for are the things that science and society value discovering.

Committee on Applications of Toxicogenomic Technologies to Predictive Toxicology, National Research Council, Applications of Toxicogenomic Technologies to Predictive Toxicology and Risk Assessment 173 (2007). Do you agree?

3.   Fundamental discoveries in science have the potential to effect drastic social change. What are the moral implications of these advances? Harold Shapiro, Former President of Princeton University and Chair of the National Bioethics Advisory Commission, stated: "We may or may not need new moral philosophies, but we are more likely to get to the moral high ground if scientists and others work together to help shape the uses of new knowledge. The fact that the moral context of scientific discoveries is defined by the objectives and applications of this new knowledge gives all of us additional responsibilities and inevitably new anxieties." Harold T. Shapiro, Reflections on the Interface of Bioethics, Public Policy, and Science, 9 Kennedy Inst. Ethics J. 209, 222 (1999).

4.   The effect on society of advances in science and technology is a familiar theme. Thoreau said: "We do not ride on the railroad; it rides upon us." Henry David Thoreau, Walden and Other Writings 83 (Random House ed. 1950). His concern, of course, was that we are not the masters, but the

servants of technology. The railroads opened up vast expanses of our country in the nineteenth century and greatly improved commerce and transportation. But the railroads literally carved a swath through cities, towns, and forests; belched smoke and sparks and noise; and forced people to live by its scheduled arrivals and departures.

To paraphrase Thoreau in the genetics context: We do not probe the gene; it probes us. New advances in genetics are forcing us to reassess the value systems and political assumptions on which our society is based. We now must probe what it means to be human, what it means to be normal, what we mean by equality and discrimination, what the social consequences are of individual and group genetic variability, what it means to be healthy, who should have access to health care, what property rights to biological discoveries should be recognized, what obligations exist among family members, what the contours are of the physician-patient relationship, what trade-offs exist between using DNA for identification and civil liberties, and how privacy and confidentiality can be protected without sacrificing other interests. These and numerous other foundational questions are sometimes framed as legal issues, but often they are combinations of ethics, law, policy, and other disciplines. That is why this book is called Genetics: Ethics, Law and Policy.

5. Beyond its obvious influence on health law, genetics will affect numerous other areas of the law, including criminal law, constitutional law, forensics, intellectual property, family law, civil rights law, insurance law, employment law, and tort law. This book deals with the legal issues raised by genetics, as well as the scientific, ethical, and social context in which they arise.

CHAPTER 2

SCIENTIFIC OVERVIEW

■ ■ ■

This chapter is designed for the reader who does not have a background in the science of human genetics. It provides an overview of the science pertaining to cells, chromosomes, genes, proteins, genetic differences among individuals, and patterns of inheritance, and a brief description of mapping and sequencing the human genome. It is intended to provide a scientific overview to assist in understanding the material in the remainder of the book. It also identifies some of the key legal and ethical issues that are raised by scientific developments.

I. HISTORY OF GENETIC SCIENCE

ERIC S. LANDER, SCIENTIFIC COMMENTARY: THE SCIENTIFIC FOUNDATIONS AND MEDICAL AND SOCIAL PROSPECTS OF THE HUMAN GENOME PROJECT

26 J. L., Med. & Ethics 184, 184–185 (1998).

* * *

Genetics is a remarkable discipline, because it offers a generic approach that enables scientists to pursue any disease-related question, from inflammatory bowel disease to schizophrenia. How is this possible? The foundations of this story, as almost everything in genetics, go back to the fundamental insight of Gregor Mendel in 1865.

Mendel noted that hereditary traits in the pea plant could be explained by the action of certain invisible but predictable "factors" (the word *gene* was coined only at the beginning of the twentieth century). Mendel noted that each individual inherited two copies of each factor—one from each parent. And, each individual passed on one copy to its offspring. For example, when a pure-breeding green plant is mated with a pure-breeding yellow plant, the offspring will inherit one color gene from the green parent and one from the yellow parent. Finally, when the resulting plant is crossed with itself, the genes reassort: offspring of different types reemerge in the next generation.

15

Mendel's extraordinarily important and simple concept—that discrete factors control inheritance—was not regarded as earthshaking in its time, probably because it was so abstract. Mendel did not know the identity of the factors. He simply inferred their existence to explain the results of his pea experiments. About thirty-five years passed before cell biologists studying the division of cells noticed strange structures that appear red when cells underwent division. When cells underwent meiosis to make gametes (sperm or eggs), the structures lined up in pairs, and one copy of each pair would be transmitted. When two gametes fused to give rise to an offspring, each parent thus contributed one copy of each such structure.

This strange choreography—pairs splitting, sending one to the offspring, and then rejoining—behaved just as Mendel's abstract factors had behaved. The cell biologists did not know what these objects were, but, because they stained them with certain dyes, they named them chromosomes—a Latinate term meaning *colored things*. These chromosomes seemed likely to hold the secret of inheritance.

Soon after this discovery, scientists set out to understand how chromosomes controlled inheritance. By about 1911, a student at Columbia University named Alfred Sturtevant made a key observation: by following the inheritance patterns of genes, it was possible to infer whether genes were nearby one another on a chromosome. Nearby genes would tend to be transmitted together, whereas distant genes would tend to be separated by recombination events (that is, exchanges of genetic material.) In other words, one could measure the location of genes on chromosomes by how frequently they were transmitted together. Sturtevant began building genetic maps, showing the locations of genes that controlled various traits in the fruit fly, such as body color and eye color. He was teasing apart the secrets of inheritance patterns that controlled traits, without knowing anything about the actual DNA that encoded them.

The idea that one could trace inheritance in this fashion was applied widely to flies, corn, and many other organisms. Moreover, it soon became clear that, in principle, the same basic ideas applied to the human being. However, one could not set up human matings to study inheritance, as in the fly or in corn. Also, one did not have simple, single-gene traits with which to trace inheritance patterns (with a few exceptions, such as a blood group). Thus, for most of this century, our understanding of human genetics was largely theoretical, not operational. Seventy years of scientific progress were required before human geneticists could do what Sturtevant was doing in 1911. The DNA revolution offered the key.

It took the seminal work of Francis Crick and James Watson in the 1950's to understand the structure of DNA and how its double-helical properties enabled it to encode information, to divide apart, and to pass the information on to daughter cells. Work conducted in the 1960's showed how DNA actually encodes information in the language of the genetic code, which specifies the instructions for making proteins. Finally, the tools of recombinant DNA, developed during the 1970's, allowed molecular biologists to copy (or clone) and read the sequence of individual pieces of DNA. After all of that work—from 1910 to 1980—it was finally possible to apply Sturtevant's techniques of genetic mapping to humans. To trace inheritance, one could not use curly wings and white eyes as with *Drosophila.* However, one could use simply the spelling differences in DNA.

II. STRUCTURE OF DNA

DNA (short for *deoxyribonucleic acid*) is a molecule consisting of a string of chemicals called *nucleotides*. Each nucleotide is composed of a sugar, a phosphate, and a base. To understand the structure of DNA, first think of a ladder cut in half down the middle of the rungs. The sugars and phosphates of the nucleotides are connected to one another to form a long strip like the side of the ladder. The half rungs of the ladder consist of the bases, sticking out from the side. The bases are the important part of the DNA molecule: their order, or *sequence*, forms the genetic code of the organism.

There are four nucleotide bases: adenine, guanine, cytosine, and thymine, known by their initials A, G, C and T. These bases attach or bond to one another according to a strict set of rules: A only bonds with T and vice versa, while G only bonds with C and vice versa.

In humans and other higher organisms, the DNA molecule actually is two strands of DNA, as if you reunited the two halves of the ladder. Each of the sides of the ladder is a strip of sugars and phosphates. The rungs are the bases that stick out and that are connected together in pairs according to the bonding rules: A with T, G with C. This double-stranded DNA molecule is twisted around the mid-point of the rungs to give it its famous "double-helix" appearance. See Figure 2–1.

Figure 2–1

DNA Molecule

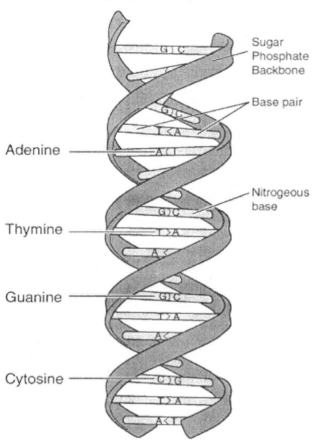

In human DNA, there are about 3 billion rungs of the ladder, or pairs of nucleotide bases. The DNA of the bacterium *E. coli* has about 4 million base pairs, and yeast has about 15 million.

Triggered by cellular enzymes, DNA duplicates or *replicates*. It does this first by unwinding from its twisted double-helix shape and breaking apart at the bonds between the base pairs, like unzipping a zipper. This produces two separate strands of DNA, like the two halves of our ladder. In the nucleus of the cell where replication takes place are many unattached nucleotides. When the double strand unzips, these free-standing bases bind to the exposed bases of the DNA strands according to the binding rules. This produces a complementary copy of the strand. Suppose, for example, that at one point on the original double helix DNA molecule, there was an A attached to a T, followed by a G attached to a C. After the molecule unzips into two separate strands, the exposed A on one of the single strands binds with a free-standing T, the exposed G binds with a free-standing C, and so on. The same thing happens with the other single strand: the T binds with a free-standing A, the C to a G, and so on. The result is two new double-helix-shaped, double-stranded DNA molecules each of which reproduces the sequence of base pairs in the original double-stranded molecule. See Figure 2–2.

Figure 2–2

DNA Replication

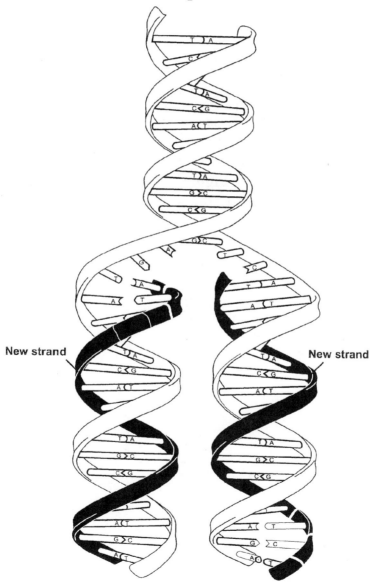

DNA replication occurs when cells divide, as described below.

III. CELLS AND CHROMOSOMES

Most human DNA is found in cell nuclei. Each cell nucleus contains chromosomes—physically-distinct, microscopic structures composed of double strands of DNA folded and twisted so they can fit into the confined space. (If the DNA in the chromosomes of a single cell nucleus were unwound and laid end-to-end, it would stretch more than five feet.) There are a total of 24 different chromosomes. Two of the chromosomes determine sex, and are called "X" and "Y." A normal female has two X chromosomes; a male has one X and one Y. The remaining 22 chromosomes, referred to by number, are called *autosomes*.

Most normal cell nuclei contain two sets of 23 chromosomes, or a total of 46. Each set is comprised of the 22 autosomes and a sex chromosome. One set of chromosomes derives from the person's mother and one set from the father. This fact helps explain why children have characteristics that cannot be found in either parent. See Figure 2–3 for a photograph image of a microscopic view of an individual's chromosomes, called a *karyotype*.

Figure 2–3

Karyotype of Human Chromosomes

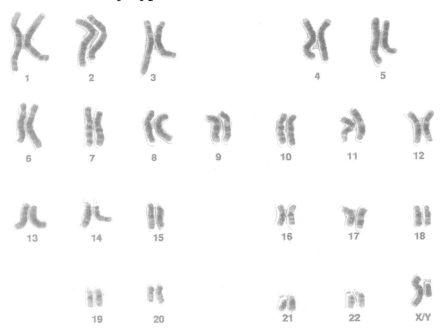

Some genetic diseases result from chromosomal abnormalities. For example, Down's syndrome occurs when an individual inherits an extra copy of chromosome 21. For this reason, it is also known as "Trisomy (meaning three copies) 21." Some males have an extra Y sex chromosome.

As described in Chapter 13, some people believed that this made them more aggressive and prone to engage in violent criminal behavior.

A small amount of human DNA is found outside the cell nucleus, in cell structures called *mitochondria*. As discussed in Chapter 4, this enables researchers to trace a population's pattern of genetic descent, and has implications for certain infertility treatments that involve inserting one person's nuclear DNA into another person's egg cell from which the nucleus has been removed.

IV.   GENES AND PROTEINS

Along certain stretches of DNA, the sequences of nucleotide bases contain instructions for making proteins. Proteins form the structural components of cells and tissue and the enzymes that control biochemical reactions, including the functioning of the genes themselves. The stretches of DNA containing protein instructions are called *genes,* and genes are said to *code for* specific proteins. Initially, the non-gene stretches of DNA were referred to as "junk DNA" on the assumption that they had no important function. It turns out that these non-protein coding regions of DNA are indeed important, for they contain instructions for turning genes on and off, and non-coding portions of human DNA have been associated with risks for prostate, breast, colon cancer, and heart attacks.

Proteins consist of long, complex chains of twenty different types of amino acids. Within the gene stretches of DNA, there are sequences of bases called *exons* that code for specific amino acids. Each of these sequences, called *codons* or *triplets*, is only three bases long. Other stretches of sequences within genes, called *introns*, do not code for amino acids. Thus, there appear to be large amounts of DNA, including both non-coding stretches between the genes and introns within the genes, that do not code for proteins.

The instructions for making proteins contained in genes are decoded via two processes called *transcription* and *translation*. In transcription, the portion of the double strand of DNA containing a gene first unwinds and breaks apart. But then, instead of making a copy of the DNA with free-standing nucleotides like during DNA replication, different enzymes–still following the binding rules—construct a different type of complimentary strand using three of the four DNA nucleotides (A, G, and C), a fourth nucleotide called uracil that binds with A the same as T, and a different type of sugar, ribose. Hence the name of this material: RNA (*ribonucleic acid*). This form of RNA contains not only the triplets, which code for amino acids, but also the introns, so enzymes strip out the intron sequences, producing a strand that only contains amino-acid coding sequences. This is called *messenger RNA (mRNA)*. It is the result or product of transcription.

So far this process has taken place inside the cell nucleus. But now the messenger RNA exits the cell nucleus and enters the cytoplasm, where it encounters a structure called a *ribosome*. In the process called translation, the ribosome reads the sequence in the messenger RNA and puts together a chain of amino acids which becomes a protein.

The number of DNA bases that are required to produce a protein varies from only 100 to a couple of million, depending on how complex a protein it codes for and how many of its bases are introns. The longest gene is 2.4 million bases long, and codes for the protein that malfunctions in muscular dystrophy.

Until recently, geneticists believed that a single human gene coded for a single protein. Since there are about 100,000 proteins, this meant that there should be about 100,000 human genes. It now appears that there are only around 20,000 to 25,000 human genes. This means the some genes can code for more than one protein, depending on how the amino acids are arranged and how the protein is shaped or folded. This has several implications. First, it shows that the greater complexity of a human, compared to other organisms such as the small flowering plant *Arabidopsis thaliana*, with about the same number of genes, is not due to the difference in the number of genes. Second, the more complex relationship between genes and proteins is likely to complicate the task of linking genes to specific diseases or traits and of finding effective treatments.

In 2003, the National Human Genome Research Institute at NIH established a research program called the Encyclopedia of DNA Elements (ENCODE) to identify all the functional elements of the human genome, not just the genes themselves. In 2007, researchers announced that a pilot project that had examined 1 percent of the genome had found that, while the protein-coding components of genes account for only about 2 percent of human DNA, 93 percent of the DNA is functionally active, in that it is transcribed into RNA. The non-protein-coding gene elements include genes that do not code for proteins, regulatory elements that control the transcription process, and elements that maintain the structure of chromosomes and mediate their replication. In addition, the ENCODE results showed that genes were not strings of nucleotides like beads along the DNA molecule, as had long been assumed, but instead, that many genes overlap one another and share stretches of DNA. In short, the ways in which DNA functions are far more complex than previously thought.

V. GENETIC DIFFERENCES AMONG INDIVIDUALS

The exact sequence of genes differs among people. For example, all humans have a gene that codes for the protein huntingtin. But the sequence of nucleotide bases of that gene can differ from one person to another. One stretch of the gene consists of a repeat of three bases, C, A, and G. Most people have 26 or fewer repeats. But some people have a lot more CAG repeats. The extra repeats interfere with the production of the huntingtin protein; as a result, these people will get Huntington disease, the fatal, neurological disorder that killed folksinger Woody Guthrie. We tend to say that these individuals "have the gene for Huntington disease." Since we all have the gene for the protein huntingtin, it is more accurate to say that affected individuals have a gene with the variation or *mutation*—an extra number of CAG repeats—that causes the disease.

Another example is cystic fibrosis. Everyone has a certain gene, called the CFTR gene, that affects the transport of chloride in the body. In the most common form of cystic fibrosis, there is a mutation on this gene: three bases, CTT, that code for the amino acid phenylalanine, are missing from a certain location, known as position 508.

Another term used to describe the different versions of the same gene among different individuals is *allele*: We say that people with 26 or fewer CAG repeats and people with a lot more repeats on the huntingtin gene, or people with and without the CTT sequence at position 508 of the CFTR gene, have different *alleles* of the same gene. These differences in alleles produce genetic disease. They also account for much of the variety in human observable characteristics—why some people have blue eyes and some brown, and so on. Put another way, these differences in genetic make-up, or *genotype*, produce differences in observable characteristics, or *phenotype*.

Most genetic sequences are the same from one person to the next; only about 0.1 percent differ. But these differences are the basis for genetic testing to diagnose and predict susceptibility to genetic diseases, discussed in Chapters 7 and 8; to inform reproductive decision-making, discussed in Chapter 6; to establish paternity, described in Chapter 11; and to distinguish individuals for identification purposes on the basis of samples of their DNA, which is covered in Chapter 12.

VI. THE HUMAN GENOME PROJECT

NATIONAL HUMAN GENOME RESEARCH INSTITUTE, NIH UNDERSTANDING OUR GENETIC INHERITANCE: THE U.S. HUMAN GENOME PROJECT THE FIRST FIVE YEARS: FISCAL YEARS

1991–1995 (1990).

The Human Genome Initiative is a worldwide research effort that has the goal of analyzing the structure of human DNA and determining the location of all human genes. In parallel with this effort, the DNA of a set of model organisms will be studied to provide the comparative information necessary for understanding the functioning of the human genome. The information generated by the human genome project is expected to be the source book for biomedical science in the 21st century. It will have a profound impact on and expedite progress in a variety of biological fields, including those such as developmental biology and neurobiology, where scientists are just beginning to understand the underlying molecular mechanisms. The analysis and interpretation of the information will occupy scientists for many years to come. Thus, the maximal benefit of the human genome project will only be achieved if it is surrounded by research efforts that are focused on understanding and taking advantage of the human genetic information.

* * *

III. SCIENTIFIC GOALS

A. Mapping and Sequencing the Human Genome

* * *

Although mapping of human genes began early in the twentieth century, it has been intensively pursued only for the past two decades. For most of this period the methods that were developed, though original and ingenious, have been inadequate for comprehensive mapping and have only allowed the construction of relatively crude maps with very little detail. Recently, much more effective technology has been introduced. * * *

A frequently asked question is: whose genome will be sequenced? The answer is: no one's. The first complete human genome to be sequenced will be a composite of sequences from many sources, most of these being cell lines that have existed in laboratories all over the world for some time. The sequence will thus be a generic sequence representative of humans in general and not of any particular individual. The complete sequence will provide a standard against which other partial sequences can be compared.

It has been suggested that, due to the great variability between individual human beings, a single sequence would not be very useful. While it is true that much valuable insight will come from comparing many different human sequences, the presumption is that functionally important DNA is conserved among humans as it is between humans and mice in those areas that have been studied. DNA regions of particular interest, such as genes involved in genetic disease, will be sequenced from many individuals in the course of research on those diseases. As more information about the extent of human polymorphism accumulates from these and other studies in the next few years, it will be evaluated to determine the impact on strategy for the human genome project.

1. Genetic Map

Genetic maps have many uses, including identification of the genes associated with genetic diseases and other biological properties. Genetic maps also form an essential backbone or scaffold that is needed to guide a physical mapping effort.

Genetic maps are constructed by determining how frequently two "markers," such as a physical trait, a particular medical syndrome, or a detectable DNA sequence, are inherited together. Genes which lie close together on a chromosome have a much higher chance of being inherited together than genes that lie farther apart. Genetic studies of families, to determine how frequently two traits are inherited together, lead to the production of "genetic maps" in which distance between genes is measured in centimorgans in honor of the American geneticist Thomas Hunt Morgan. Two markers are one centimorgan apart if they are separated during transmission from parents to children one percent of the time. A centimorgan corresponds to a highly variable physical distance, but the genome-wide average is believed to be roughly one million base pairs.

Among the technical advances that led to the Human Genome Initiative, the development of new genetic mapping tools is prominent. One of the most important innovations has been the introduction of DNA markers such as restriction fragment length polymorphisms, or RFLPs, to detect genetic variation among individuals. Such markers are relatively easy to find in large numbers and have been used to construct genetic maps. In the past two years, advances have continued to be made in this area. New types of DNA markers have been defined and techniques, such as denaturing gradient gel electrophoresis, have been adapted to detect subtle variation in DNA sequences. As a result, the number of useful markers has increased in the past two years. It is estimated that 3000 well-spaced and informative markers will be needed to achieve the goal of a completely linked map where markers are an average of one centimorgan apart, as recommended by the NRC. For the first five years, the genome program has set as its goal the creation of a 2–5 centimorgan map, which would require 600 to 1500 such markers.

* * *

2. *Physical Map*

The distance between sites on physical maps is measured in units of physical length, such as numbers of nucleotide pairs. Physical maps can be constructed in a variety of different ways. They are used as the basis for the characterization and isolation of individual genes or other DNA regions of interest, as well as to provide the starting material for DNA sequencing. The ability to construct physical maps derives from recombinant DNA techniques that allow the isolation and cloning of DNA fragments, the identification of specific sequence markers on DNA, and the determination of the order of and distance between such markers on a chromosome.

There are several kinds of physical maps, which can be conveniently categorized into two general types. One type describes the order and spacing of markers on a DNA molecule. The cytogenetic map is a map of this type. Based on microscopic analysis, cytogenetic maps record the location of genes or DNA markers relative to visible landmarks on the chromosomes. This is the oldest type of physical map and the resolution (precision in locating markers) is rather low, on the order of 10 million base pairs. Nevertheless, the cytogenetic map is still an extremely valuable tool and markers continue to be mapped in this way. At the recent 10th

Human Gene Mapping Workshop, the number of mapped markers was reported to be 4362, as opposed to 2057 only two years a go. Another example of this type of physical map is the long range restriction map, which records the order of and distance between specific sequences, known as restriction sites, on chromosomes. The resolution of long-range restriction maps is between 100,000 and 2 million base pairs.

The second type of physical map consists of a collection of cloned pieces of DNA that represent a complete chromosome or chromosomal segment, together with information about the order of the cloned pieces. There are a variety of techniques for cloning [which means producing an identical copy of] DNA and a number of methods for determining the order of the clones. The technology for constructing overlapping clone sets (known as "contigs") is continually improving. At present, a collection of ordered clones is typically the starting material for sequencing. However, novel approaches that do not require cloning, but still allow the investigator access to the DNA to be sequenced, are under development.

In the past two years, improvements in several techniques, such as pulsed field gel electrophoresis, yeast artificial chromosome cloning, the polymerase chain reaction (PCR), fluorescence in situ hybridization, and radiation hybrid analysis have made the initial stages in the construction of physical maps of large genomes significantly easier and more rapid than was predictable at the time of the NRC recommendations.

* * *

3. Sequencing

Three decades ago when Francis Crick and James Watson elucidated the double helix structure of DNA, there was no way of determining the sequence of even short molecules of DNA. Only years later, with the advent of recombinant DNA technology [combining DNA from one source with DNA from another] in the early 1970's, was it possible to think of isolating individual genes. That breakthrough, combined with the development of powerful DNA sequencing techniques, provided the technological basis for the Human Genome Initiative.

To date, the only organisms for which a complete DNA sequence has been determined are viruses. The largest published viral genome sequence is that of the Epstein–Barr virus (EBV), a sequence of 170,000 base pairs. Scientists are now attempting to sequence the DNA of certain bacteria, approximately 4,500,000 base pairs long. The size and complexity of human DNA, however, still makes the sequencing of the human genome awesome to contemplate. While many short stretches of human DNA have been sequenced, slightly more than 5 million base pairs in the aggregate, the human genome comprises about 3 billion base pairs of DNA and is nearly 1,000 times larger than that of a bacterial genome.

If such a large amount of DNA is to be sequenced, a substantial increase in the speed and reduction in the cost of sequencing technology will be required. The current cost of DNA sequencing, in laboratories that do it routinely, is estimated to be about $2 to $5 per base pair of finished sequence, that is, sequence whose accuracy has been adequately confirmed. In laboratories that sequence DNA only occasionally, the costs are much higher. The costs of DNA preparation, salaries and overhead are included in these figures. These costs must be reduced below $0.50 a base pair before large scale sequencing will be cost effective.

Sequencing technology has improved significantly in the last two years. Machines that automatically perform the basic steps of identifying the order of the base pairs in appropriately prepared DNA samples are now readily available. In the most advanced laboratories, using these machines, it is possible for one individual to generate about 2000 base pairs of finished DNA sequence per day per machine, starting with properly prepared cloned DNA. One approach to lowering the cost of DNA sequencing is further automation. The maximum reduction in cost of current sequencing technology will come from the creation of a fully automated assembly line for rapid DNA sequencing. Efforts are underway in both DOE and NIH-sponsored projects, as well as in private companies, to automate most of the preparatory steps in the sequencing process through the development of high speed robotic workstations for sample handling.

Notes

The first phase of the Human Genome Project (HGP) involved *mapping* the human genome. The goal was to locate all human genes on their chromosomes. There are basically two kinds of maps, referred to by the confusing names *genetic* or *genetic linkage*, and *physical*.

As the reading indicates, genetic or genetic linkage maps identify *genetic markers* on chromosomes. A genetic marker is a stretch of nucleotide bases that is physically located in the same region of DNA as a gene. The marker may actually include all or part of the gene, or it may consist of bases in the stretches between genes. To be useful, a marker must be close enough to a gene that the marker is likely to be inherited along with the gene. (As discussed more fully later, because DNA is somewhat chopped up during cell division, the physically farther away one stretch of DNA is from another, the less likely that the two stretches will be inherited together.) The bases that comprise the marker also must be known to be *polymorphic*, that is, to differ among individuals, or at least among the members of a family, depending, for example, on whether or not they have a genetic mutation.

Markers enable genetic information about individuals to be determined without knowing the exact location of genes or the sequences of their nucleotide bases. Suppose a person wants to know if he or she has inherited a certain genetic mutation, say one that causes disease. Geneticists test that person's DNA, as well as the DNA of members of that person's family. They are searching for a marker or set of markers that is present in the DNA of family members who have the mutation and that is not present in the family members who do not have the mutation. If the person has the marker, then it is likely that he or she also has inherited the mutation, and vice versa. The process of identifying markers by testing members of a family is called *linkage analysis*. Hence the term "genetic linkage map." In this manner, geneticists were able to test for a number of genetic diseases, including cystic fibrosis, sickle cell disease, and Tay–Sachs disease, before the actual genes for these diseases were identified or their sequences were decoded.

Gradually, researchers built up lists of markers that tended to be associated with various inherited diseases, called genetic or genetic linkage maps. By studying the frequency with which specific markers were associated with specific genetic mutations, moreover, they calculated the probability that the marker would be inherited along with the mutation. A genetic or genetic linkage map expresses the results in units called *centimorgans*. A marker and a gene are 1 centimorgan apart when there is a 1 percent chance that they will not be inherited together. Currently, over 2,200 disorders have been tied to specific genes.

Physical maps reflect actual physical distances between stretches of DNA, as opposed to the statistical calculations represented by the centimorgans on a genetic or genetic linkage map. Physical maps come with varying degrees of detail or resolution, ranging from the distance between regions on chromosomes observable by staining, to maps of fragments of DNA arranged in order along the chromosomes, to the ultimate physical map: the sequence of base pairs.

REMARKS BY THE PRESIDENT, PRIME MINISTER TONY BLAIR OF ENGLAND, DR. FRANCIS COLLINS, DIRECTOR OF THE NATIONAL HUMAN GENOME RESEARCH INSTITUTE, AND DR. CRAIG VENTER, PRESIDENT AND CHIEF OFFICER, CELERA GENOMICS CORPORATION, ON THE COMPLETION OF THE FIRST SURVEY OF THE ENTIRE HUMAN GENOME PROJECT

June 26, 2000.

THE EAST ROOM

THE PRESIDENT [WILLIAM CLINTON]: Good morning.

* * *

Nearly two centuries ago, in this room, on this floor, Thomas Jefferson and a trusted aide spread out a magnificent map—a map Jefferson had long prayed he would get to see in his lifetime. The aide was Meriwether Lewis and the map was the product of his courageous expedition across the American frontier, all the way to the Pacific. It was a map that defined the contours and forever expanded the frontiers of our continent and our imagination.

Today, the world is joining us here in the East Room to behold a map of even greater significance. We are here to celebrate the completion of the first survey of the entire human genome. Without a doubt, this is the most important, most wondrous map ever produced by humankind.

The moment we are here to witness was brought about through brilliant and painstaking work of scientists all over the world, including many men and women here today. It was not even 50 years ago that a young Englishman named Crick and a brash even younger American named Watson, first discovered the elegant structure of our genetic code. Dr. Watson, the way you announced your discovery in the journal "Nature," was one of the great understatements of all time. "This structure has novel features, which are of considerable biological interest."

How far we have come since that day. In the intervening years, we have pooled the combined wisdom of biology, chemistry, physics, engineering, mathematics and computer science; tapped the great strengths and insights of the public and private sectors. More than 1,000 researchers across six nations have revealed nearly all 3 billion letters of our miraculous genetic code. I congratulate all of you on this stunning and humbling achievement.

Today's announcement represents more than just an epic-making triumph of science and reason. After all, when Galileo discovered he could use the tools of mathematics and mechanics to understand the motion of celestial bodies, he felt, in the words of one eminent researcher, "that he had learned the language in which God created the universe."

Today, we are learning the language in which God created life. We are gaining ever more awe for the complexity, the beauty, the wonder of God's most divine and sacred gift. With this profound new knowledge, humankind is on the verge of gaining immense, new power to heal. Genome science will have a real impact on all our lives—and even more, on the lives of our children. It will revolutionize the diagnosis, prevention and treatment of most, if not all, human diseases.

In coming years, doctors increasingly will be able to cure diseases like Alzheimer's, Parkinson's, diabetes and cancer by attacking their genetic roots. Just to offer one example, patients with some forms of leukemia and breast cancer already are being treated in clinical trials with sophisticated new drugs that precisely target the faulty genes and cancer cells, with little or no risk to healthy cells. In fact, it is now conceivable that our children's children will know the term cancer only as a constellation of stars.

But today's historic achievement is only a starting point. There is much hard work yet to be done. That is why I'm so pleased to announce that from this moment forward, the robust and healthy competition that has led us to this day and that always is essential to the progress of science, will be coupled with enhanced public-private cooperation.

Public and private research teams are committed to publishing their genomic data simultaneously later this year, for the benefit of researchers in every corner of the globe. And after publication, both sets of teams will join together for an historic sequence analysis conference. Together, they will examine what scientific insights have been gleaned from both efforts, and how we can most judiciously proceed toward the next majestic horizons.

What are those next horizons? Well, first, we will complete a virtually error-free final draft of the human genome before the 50th anniversary of the discovery of the double helix, less than three years from now. Second, through sustained and vigorous support for public and private research, we must sort through this trove of genomic data to identify every human gene. We must discover the function of these genes and their protein products, and then we must rapidly convert that knowledge into treatments that can lengthen and enrich lives.

I want to emphasize that biotechnology companies are absolutely essential in this endeavor. For it is they who will bring to the market the life-enhancing applications of the information from the human genome. And for that reason, this administration is committed to helping them to make the kind of long-term investments that will change the face of medicine forever.

The third horizon that lies before us is one that science cannot approach alone. It is the horizon that represents the ethical, moral and spiritual dimension of the power we now possess. We must not shrink from exploring that far frontier of science. But as we consider how to use new discovery, we must also not retreat from our oldest and most cherished human values. We must ensure that new genome science and its benefits will be directed toward making life better for all citizens of the world, never just a privileged few.

As we unlock the secrets of the human genome, we must work simultaneously to ensure that new discoveries never pry open the doors of privacy. And we must guarantee that genetic information cannot be used to stigmatize or discriminate against any individual or group.

Increasing knowledge of the human genome must never change the basic belief on which our ethics, our government, our society are founded. All of us are created equal, entitled to equal treatment under the law. After all, I believe one of the great truths to emerge from this triumphant expedition inside the human genome is that in genetic terms, all human beings, regardless of race, are more than 99.9 percent the same.

What that means is that modern science has confirmed what we first learned from ancient fates. The most important fact of life on this Earth is our common humanity. My greatest wish on this day for the ages is that this incandescent truth will always guide our actions as we continue to march forth in this, the greatest age of discovery ever known.

NOTES AND QUESTIONS

1. The term "Human Genome Project" (HGP) technically refers to the publicly-sponsored effort to map and sequence the human genome. The HGP originally expected to complete its sequencing of the human genome by 2005, at a cost of approximately $3 billion. In the U.S., funding was provided by

Congress to the National Institute of Health (NIH) and, to a much smaller extent, the Department of Energy (which had an interest in genetics as a result of its concern about the effects of atomic radiation). The NIH in turn channeled the funds to a consortium of nine research establishments, with most of the funds going to Washington University at St. Louis, Baylor College of Medicine, and the Whitehead Institute in Cambridge, Massachusetts. At the NIH, the HGP initially was overseen by an "Office of Human Genome Research," created in 1988, and headed by James Watson. In 1990, the "office" was transformed into a free-standing "center," and in 1997, the center finally achieved the status of a full-fledged "institute." In the U.K., the Wellcome Trust sponsored research at the Sanger Center. Additional public efforts were made in other countries under a loose affiliation called HUGO (for "Human Genome Organization").

Compared to publicly-funded efforts, only a small amount of mapping and sequencing initially took place in the private sector. This changed in 1998 with the formation of a company called Celera Genomics. Celera grew out of the development of faster sequencing machines. With $200 million in funding from Perkin–Elmer Corporation, an old-line medical equipment manufacturer, and with a scientist named Craig Venter as its president, Celera set out from scratch to complete its own sequence map by 2001 by running 200 of the machines around the clock.

The sequencing technique Celera used, called a "shotgun" approach, differed from the HGP approach. The HGP identified specific regions of DNA and proceeded to sequence them. Celera sequenced chunks of DNA without knowing where they were located, and then relied on computers to identify overlapping sequences at the ends of the chunks to piece them together.

At first the two programs regarded each other with antagonism. This was due in part to the high historical and scientific stakes and to the impact of success and failure on personal reputations, but also to a fundamental difference in regard to the intended use of results. As a public-funded project, the HGP was committed to making its sequencing immediately available to the public for free, while Celera, a private, for-profit company, intended to extract commercial value from its research efforts. (For more discussion about the intellectual property aspects of the HGP, see Chapter 5.) Francis Collins, the director of the National Human Genome Research Institute (NHGRI) at NIH, responded to Celera's challenge by vowing to speed up the HGP and complete a "rough draft" of the human genome by 2000 and a final version by 2003, rather than by the original date of 2005. When Venter scoffed that the HGP would not meet this timetable, some HGP scientists raised concerns about whether Celera could reassemble its fragments into an accurate map of the entire genome. Both sides seemed vindicated when the HGP began cranking out large portions of sequences in keeping with its new schedule, and Celera published an accurate sequence of the genome of the fruit fly, *Drosophila*. The race heated up.

Ultimately, Ari Patrinos, the head of the human genome project at the Department of Energy, invited Collins and Venter to his home for pizza and beer and, after several more meetings, the two rivals agreed to cooperate in issuing a joint statement with President Clinton at the White House announcing the completion of their sequencing efforts, excerpts of which appear above. The HGP subsequently published its sequence map in the journal *Nature* while Celera published its map in *Science*.

Ironically, at the time of the June 26, 2000, announcement, neither sequencing effort was complete. The HGP had only finished a "working draft," with 97 percent of the human genome sequenced and only 85 percent placed in the proper order. Venter stated that Celera had sequenced 99 percent of the genome, but that its supercomputers (which comprised the largest private supercomputing capacity in the world) were still piecing the fragments together.

On April 14, 2003, the International Human Genome Sequencing Consortium announced that it had really finished the sequencing of the human genome. But even then, the sequencing was not quite complete. It was not until May 2006 that researchers announced that they had completed the sequencing of the last chromosome, chromosome 1.

2. Whose genome was sequenced? The NHGRI report said that the DNA came from a number of sources. But most of the DNA sequenced by the public consortium came from one man, although there were segments from eleven other people from different backgrounds. Celera sequenced DNA from three females and two males. The males were Caucasians; there was one African–American woman, one Hispanic woman, and one woman of Asian descent. Craig Venter has said that he was one of the two males. What are the scientific and policy consequences?

3. Having announced that they had finished sequencing the human genome, the scientists working on the Human Genome Project debated what they should do next. Some of them continued to work on sequencing the DNA of other organisms, successfully sequencing rice (2002), plague (2001), malaria (2002), and the mouse (2002). The genomes of a number of organisms are being sequenced by the large-scale sequencing capacity developed by the Human Genome Project. These include the dog, the rat, the chicken, the honey bee, two fruit flies, the sea urchin, two puffer fish, two sea squirts, two roundworms, several fungi, baker's yeast and many prokaryotes (bacteria and archaea) including *Escherichia coli*. Additional organisms already in the NHGRI sequencing pipeline are: the macaque, the orangutan, the kangaroo, the cow, the gray short-tailed opossum, the platypus, the red flour beetle, the domestic cat, the flatworm *Schimdtea mediterranea*, more species of fruit fly and several species of fungi.

4. The cost of DNA sequencing has continued to decline. The Human Genome Project originally estimated a cost of $1 per nucleotide base pair. (Given the estimated 3 billion base pairs in the entire human genome, this cost was the basis for the original estimate that the project would cost $3 billion.) By 2005, the cost had dropped to less than 1/10th of a cent.

Meanwhile, other researchers embarked on a new mega-project: creating a haplotype map of the human genome.

NATIONAL HUMAN GENOME RESEARCH INSTITUTE, INTERNATIONAL HAPMAP PROJECT OVERVIEW

September 2005.

The DNA sequence of any two people is 99.9 percent identical. The variations, however, may greatly affect an individual's disease risk. Sites in the DNA sequence where individuals differ at a single DNA base are called single nucleotide polymorphisms (SNPs). Sets of nearby SNPs on the same chromosome are inherited in blocks. This pattern of SNPs on a block is a haplotype. Blocks may contain a large number of SNPs, but a few SNPs are enough to uniquely identify the haplotypes in a block. The HapMap is a map of these haplotype blocks and the specific SNPs that identify the haplotypes are called tag SNPs.

The HapMap should be valuable by reducing the number of SNPs required to examine the entire genome for association with a phenotype from the 10 million SNPs that exist to roughly 500,000 tag SNPs. This will make genome scan approaches to finding regions with genes that affect diseases much more efficient and comprehensive, since effort will not be wasted typing more SNPs than necessary and all regions of the genome can be included.

In addition to its use in studying genetic associations with disease, the HapMap should be a powerful resource for studying the genetic factors contributing to variation in response to environmental factors, in susceptibility to infection, and in the effectiveness of and adverse responses to drugs and vaccines. All such studies will be based on the expectation that there will be higher frequencies of the contributing genetic components in a group of people with a disease or particular response to a drug, vaccine, pathogen, or environmental factor than in a group of similar people without the disease or response. Using just the tag SNPs, researchers should be able to find chromosome regions that have different haplotype distributions in the two groups of people, those with a disease or response and those without. Each region would then be studied in more detail to discover which variants in which genes in the region contribute to the disease or response, leading to more effective interventions. This should also allow the development of tests to predict which drugs or vaccines would be most effective in individuals with particular genotypes for genes affecting drug metabolism.

NOTES AND QUESTIONS

1. The haplotype mapping project, called the International HapMap Project, or simply, HapMap, began as a three-year program in 2002 with pledges of $100 million from six nations (Canada, China, Japan, Nigeria, the United Kingdom and the United States). By February 2005, the project had reached its initial goal of mapping one million SNPs. Currently over 10 million SNPs have been identified.

2. HapMap began analyzing blood samples from donors from 5 populations: Han Chinese in Beijing, Japanese in Tokyo, Yoruba in Ibadan, Niger-

ians, and Utah residents with ancestry from northern and western Europe. No medical or personal identifying information was obtained from the 270 donors. However, the samples are identified by the population from which they were collected. What ethical, legal, and social issues does this raise? For a more complete discussion, see Chapter 4.

3. In 2002, Craig Venter resigned as head of Celera and started a foundation called The J. Craig Venter Institute.

4. Studies that take advantage of new high-speed sequencing technologies (discussed in Chapter 4) have accelerated the search for SNPs associated with disease. These studies, referred to as whole genome or genome-wide association studies (GWAS), search for SNPs by comparing the entire genome of large numbers of individuals with particular diseases to the genomes of control groups without the diseases.

5. Another post-Human Genome Project research program is the 1000 Genomes Project, an international research consortium formed to sequence the genomes of approximately 1200 people from around the world to provide medically useful information on human genetic variation. The project was funded by the Wellcome Trust Sanger Institute in England, the Beijing Genomics Institute Shenzhen in China, and the National Human Genome Research Institute at the National Institutes of Health. The results of the project were made public in January 2009.

6. In 2007, the NIH initiated the Human Microbiome Project. The goal of this project is to use DNA sequencing to obtain a better understanding of the microbial communities that inhabit the human digestive system. These microorganisms are essential for human metabolism, and their cells outnumber human cells by a factor of ten to one.

VII. CELL DIVISION

There are two types of human cell division processes, *meiosis*, in which certain specialized cells form reproductive cells (eggs or sperm), and *mitosis*, which occurs when *somatic* or non-reproductive cells divide.

In mitosis, an enzyme in the cell nucleus first causes duplicates to be made of the chromosomes. This creates 92 chromosomes (2 sets of the original 46, itself composed of two sets of the 23 different chromosomes, one from each parent, with each chromosome consisting of a double-strand of DNA). The chromosomes arrange themselves in pairs joined near their centers and line up along the midline of the nucleus. The sets of pairs then split apart and are pulled toward the opposite sides of the nucleus. The cell itself pinches in two, creating two new cells, each with a full set of 46 chromosomes. These chromosomes are essentially identical to the original 46, except for alterations or mutations that occur by duplication error or that are introduced by environmental factors or through deliberate manipulation. (It is important to note that these alterations in somatic cell DNA will not be passed on to an individual's offspring. If the alterations occur early enough in human development, such as in an early-stage fetus, or if they affect enough of a person's somatic cells, they can have significant effects on the person's phenotype, including causing genetic disease. But the disease will not be inherited by the person's children.)

Meiosis is the process by which reproductive cells—eggs or sperm—are fashioned. It takes place either in the ovaries or the testes.

The first step in meiosis is the same as in mitosis: in a specialized cell, the 46 chromosomes (comprising two sets of 23, one of which was inherited from each parent) duplicate to form 92. The duplicated pairs of paternal and maternal chromosomes fuse together near their centers, and the pairs arrange themselves along the midline of the cell nucleus, with each paternal pair lining up across from its corresponding maternal pair (i.e., paternal chromosome 4 across from maternal chromosome 4, and so on). But the paternal and maternal pairs can line up on different sides of this midline independently of one another, so that the paternal pair of chromosome 4's may be lined up across from a maternal pair of 4's, but next to a maternal pair of 5's, which is across from a paternal pair of 5's, and so on. In addition, in an apparently random fashion, enzymes cut out pieces of the chromosomes and exchange them across the midline, so that one paternal chromosome 4 may now have a piece of maternal chromosome 4 and vice versa. This is called *crossing over* or *recombination*. See Figure 2–4.

Figure 2–4

Crossing Over or Recombination

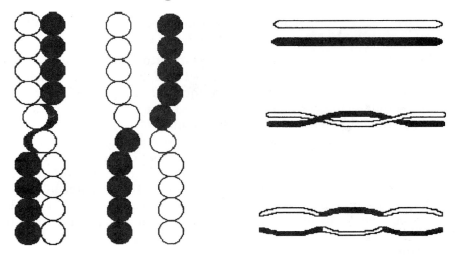

Now the cell begins to pull apart and eventually pinches off to form two new cells, each with 46 chromosomes. But note that these chromosomes are not duplicates of the original 46. Instead, they consist of a different mixture of maternal and paternal chromosomes, and each chromosome may contain DNA from the other parent. These cells then divide again, but without any duplicating of DNA, to yield 4 new cells, each with 23 chromosomes. Again, some of these chromosomes will be maternal and some paternal in origin, and their maternal and paternal DNA will be mixed up because of recombination.

In the case of eggs, 3 of the 4 new cells are discarded and the fourth becomes an egg. All of this takes place while the female fetus is in the womb: a woman is born with her full compliment of reproductive cells. In the case of sperm, each of the four cells becomes a sperm, and males continue to produce sperm through meiosis throughout their reproductive lifetimes. (This has an impact on, among other things, the techniques by which deliberate changes might be made in the DNA of reproductive cells, for example, to prevent offspring from inheriting a genetic disease.)

Genetic variation between parents and children results from three factors: the fact that the child inherits one set of chromosomes from each parent; the fact that the DNA gets mixed up in the process of meiosis; and the occurrence of spontaneous mutations, due either to errors that take place when cells divide, or to environmental factors such as x-rays. Someday, perhaps, variation may also result from intentional manipulation.

VIII. PATTERNS OF INHERITANCE

The simplest rules of inheritance apply to gender. Every egg that a woman produces will only have a copy of the X sex chromosome (since a person with a Y chromosome would be male). Since males have one X and one Y chromosome, a sperm has a 50/50 chance of containing either one. Therefore, when a sperm fertilizes an egg, if the sperm contains an X chromosome, the child will be female (since it will inherit an X from each parent). On the other hand, if the sperm contains a Y chromosome, the child will be male (since it will inherit an X chromosome from the mother and a Y from the father).

Characteristics other than gender can result from environmental factors, from genes, or from the interaction of environmental factors and genes. Genetic effects may result either from a single gene or from a number of genes interacting with one another, in which case it is called a *multigene* or *multifactorial* effect. Finally, genetic effects can either be *dominant* or *recessive*.

To understand the difference between dominant and recessive, remember that an individual inherits two sets of genes, one from the mother and one from the father. The sequences of the bases on those genes can be essentially identical (although there may be minor differences), in which case the individual is said to be *homozygous* for that gene, or the sequences of the bases of the two genes can be different in significant respects, in which case the individual is *heterozygous* for the gene. If the individual is homozygous for a gene that codes for a single-gene characteristic, for example, eye-color, then the phenotype will reflect the gene. Thus, a person who inherits two genes for blue eyes will have blue eyes, and a person who inherits two genes for brown eyes will be brown-eyed. But if the individual is heterozygous, the effect on the phenotype (here, eye color) will depend on which genetic characteristic is dominant and which is recessive. In terms of eye color, brown is a dominant characteristic, while blue is recessive. In a person who is heterozygous for eye color and who has one brown-eyed gene and one blue-eyed gene, the dominant brown-eyed gene will trump the recessive blue-eyed gene, and the person will have brown eyes. In order for the phenotype to exhibit a recessive genetic characteristic like blue eyes, the person must have two copies of the recessive gene, one from each parent.

Patterns of inheritance become especially complicated when we try to figure out whether children will display a particular phenotype based on their genetic inheritance from their parents. Parents who are both homozygous for the same eye color, for example, will have children all of whom have the same eye color as the parents. But suppose one parent has blue eyes and the other brown eyes. In order for the one parent's eyes to be blue, both copies of the eye-color gene have to be blue-eyed, since blue is recessive. The brown-eyed parent may be homozygous for brown eyes, or may be heterozygous; in either case, the parent's eyes will be brown because brown is dominant. If the brown-eyed parent is homozygous, then all the couple's children will have brown eyes, since each child will inherit one brown-eyed gene from the brown-eyed parent, and brown is dominant so it will override the blue-eyed gene from the other parent. If the brown-eyed parent is heterozygous, however, each child has a 50/50 chance of inheriting that parent's brown-eyed gene and a 50/50 chance of inheriting the parent's blue-eyed gene. So each child will have a 50/50 chance of having two blue-eyed genes (which will give them blue eyes) or one blue- and one brown-eyed gene, which, since brown is dominant, will give them brown eyes.

What if both parents have brown eyes, and both parents are heterozygous, each having a recessive blue-eyed and a dominant brown-eyed gene? Each child has a 50/50 chance of inheriting either one of either parent's eye-color genes, and this will average out to 1 in 4 children inheriting two blue-eyed genes and therefore being blue-eyed; 1 in 4 children inheriting two brown-eyed genes and therefore being brown-eyed; and 2 out of 4 children inheriting one of each gene, but still being brown-eyed because brown is dominant. Each child of these parents thus has a 25 percent chance of being blue-eyed and a 75 percent chance of being brown-eyed.

One final concept: The children in the foregoing example who inherit one dominant brown-eyed gene and one recessive blue-eyed gene will be brown-eyed, but they will be *carriers* for the blue-eyed trait. This means that they can pass the blue-eyed gene on to their children. This is why brown-eyed parents with brown-eyed children can have a blue-eyed grandchild. The grandchild can inherit two blue-eyed genes from brown-eyed parents who are carriers of the recessive blue-eyed trait.

So far we have been focusing on single-gene characteristics. These include Huntington disease, achondroplasia (a type of dwarfism), and the ability to roll your tongue into the shape of a "U." These three phenotypes happen to also be dominant: a person only needs to inherit one copy of the huntingtin gene with too many CAG repeats, for example, to get Huntington disease. (What is the chance that the child of a person with Huntington disease will also have the disease?) Other single-gene characteristics are recessive; a person must inherit copies of the gene from both parents to manifest the characteristic. Recessive single-gene characteristics include albinism, cystic fibrosis, sickle cell disease, and Tay–Sachs disease.

All of these phenotypes happen to be not only single-gene but *autosomal*. This means that the single gene that is associated with the characteristic is located on one of the 22 pairs of chromosomes that do not determine gender. As a result, a person can inherit the gene from either parent. There are other single-gene characteristics that are *sex-linked*, meaning that the gene is located on a sex chromosome, usually the X chromosome. A few of these *X-linked* characteristics are dominant; each child of a mother with a dominant X-linked characteristic has a 50/50 chance of inheriting the characteristic, and if the parent with the gene is the father, then only daughters can inherit the characteristic (since males must have inherited the father's Y chromosome, and a child who inherits the father's Y chromosome will not inherit a trait linked to the X chromosome). Most X-linked characteristics, such as color blindness, are recessive. (The children of a normal mother and a color-blind father will all be normal, but female children will be carriers; 1 in 4 of the children of a normal father and a mother who is a carrier will be a normal female, 1 in 4 will be a normal male, 1 in 4 will be a female carrier, and 1 in 4 will be a color-blind male.)

To add to the complexity, remember that so far we are only discussing single-gene characteristics. Many characteristics, however, result from the interaction of more than one gene. (Imagine the complexity of the patterns of inheritance for these multifactorial traits.)

Furthermore, genetic characteristics vary in terms of their *penetrance* and *expressivity*, and sometimes also in terms of their *age of onset*.

Penetrance refers to whether or not a gene will give rise to a phenotype. Some genes, like the gene for Huntington disease, are *completely penetrant*: if a person has too many CAG repeats, he or she invariably will exhibit symptoms of the disease at some point in their lives. Other genes, such as the gene for the disease retinoblastoma, are not completely penetrant; a person may have the gene and not get the disease.

Expressivity refers to the degree of the phenotypic effect—in the case of a genetic disease, the severity of the symptoms. Some genes are highly expressive: the gene will produce significant effects on the phenotype, and persons with a highly expressive genetic disease will have severe symptoms. Other genes have *variable expressivity*, meaning that there can be a range of symptoms. For example, the gene for a disease called neurofibromatosis produces multiple tumors and other serious conditions in some individuals, but others with the same gene merely have a few skin discolorations or a few tumors.

Some genes produce effects in people at different ages, depending on the sequence of bases. A person who has more than 40 CAG repeats on the huntingtin gene will definitely develop Huntington disease by the time he or she is 50 years old, but the greater the number of repeats beyond 40, the earlier the age of onset of symptoms, and people with as many as 60 repeats often develop symptoms in adolescence.

Finally, it is crucial to continue to bear in mind the influence of environmental factors. Consider the following statement by Ruth Hubbard and Richard Lewontin:

> * * * [E]ven in the case of so-called simple mendelian variations, the relation between the DNA sequence of a gene and the corresponding phenotype is far from simple. When we move from the relatively rare conditions whose patterns of inheritance follow Mendel's laws (such as cystic fibrosis, phenylketonuria, and Huntington's disease) to the more prevalent and usually late-onset conditions that sometimes have

familial components (such as diabetes, coronary heart disease, Alzheimer's disease, and certain cancers), the situation becomes even more complicated. In these diseases, the patterns of transmission are unpredictable and seem to depend on various other factors, be they social, economic, psychological, or biologic.

Ruth Hubbard & Richard Lewontin, Sounding Board: Pitfalls of Genetic Testing, 334 N. Eng. J. Med. 1192, 1193 (1996).

IX. GENES, RACE, AND ETHNICITY

The recent discovery that there are only about 25,000 human genes—far fewer than previously thought—underscores the fact that the genetic variation between individuals is extremely small. This is also true for genetic differences between specific populations, including minorities and ethnic groups. For the most part, members of minorities and ethnic groups will have the same distribution of genetic sequences as the majority. In some cases, however, members of minority and ethnic groups will have a different distribution of alleles. This raises questions about therapeutic testing for diseases that occur with varying frequencies in different populations. As Herbert Nickens points out:

> There is potential for discrimination and stigma in both circumstances. There is potential for differential treatment for minorities with "defective genes," even for those traits for which minorities have a similar distribution of variation as that for majority populations; and certainly there is potential for stigma for those negative traits or diseases which are strongly associated with minorities.

Herbert Nickens, The Genome Project and Health Services for Minority Populations 59, in The Human Genome Project and the Future of Health Care (Thomas H. Murray et al. eds. 1996). (As discussed in Chapter 6, problems also arise with genetic testing of minorities and ethnic groups for reproductive purposes.)

OSAGIE K. OBASOGIE, PLAYING THE GENE CARD? A REPORT ON RACE AND HUMAN BIOTECHNOLOGY

Center for Genetics and Society 2009.
www.thegenecard.org.

What does it mean to say that race is not biologically significant? Researchers in the social and life sciences have argued that race is not a meaningful biological category, that it is a "social construction" rather than a scientific fact.

But what does this mean? These phrases are typically used to convey the ideas that

- the importance placed on the outward physical distinctions that societies traditionally use to draw racial boundaries vary substantially over time and place,

- these physical distinctions do not reflect any inherent meanings, abilities, or disabilities, and

- racial differences in social and health outcomes do not correlate meaningfully with underlying biological or genetic mechanisms.

In short, as University of California, Berkeley Law Professor Ian Haney Lopez argues, the constructionist view "rejects the most widely accepted understanding of race ... [which holds that] there exist natural, physical, divisions among humans that are hereditary, reflected in morphology, and roughly captured by terms like Black, White, and Asian."

There are certainly biological components to race and health outcomes, though often only because of the way certain groups are treated in relation to how they are perceived. A key example of this phenomenon was demonstrated by John Hopkins epidemiologist Michael Klag, who found that rates of hypertension among Black Americans correspond to skin complexion; those with darker skin have higher rates. Klag showed that this is not simply a genetic or biological phenomenon, but rather a health outcome linked to skin tone discrimination and the higher degree of stress experienced by dark-skinned Blacks. While the effect was biological, the cause was largely social.

Of course, genes (along with other biological and environmental factors) shape human variation and outward physical appearance, and many of these characteristics are heritable. Evolutionary dynamics have conferred some different phenotypic traits and genetic signatures to geographically separated groups that may loosely resemble social categories of race. Thus, as Francis Collins notes, the ability to identify genetic variations that provide "reasonably accurate" yet "blurry" estimates of portions of an individual's ancestry suggest that "it is not strictly true that race or ethnicity has no biological connection."

But it is important to put even loose correlations between race and genes or genetic predispositions in an appropriate context. An early and enduring finding in human genetic studies is that there is typically more genetic variation within socially defined racial groups than between them. Another consistent finding is that for any observable "racial" trait, there are no corresponding genetic boundaries between population groups. They are discordant—that is, the collection of observable physical cues that society often uses to create the idea of discrete racial groups are not mirrored by corresponding genetic boundaries. Instead, biologists find graded variations in the percentages of groups with each characteristic.

In other words, the sharp delineations that society makes with regards to racial categories are not meaningfully reflected in our genes. That is why scientists such as Yale geneticist Kenneth Kidd conclude that "there's no such thing as race in *Homo sapiens*.... There's no place [in our genes] where you can draw a line and say there's a major difference on one side of the line from what's on the other side." To say that race is a social construction is to emphasize that in most cases, racial categories based upon phenotype (physical appearance) ultimately provide a poor way to proxy individual genotype, or genetic variations that may be exclusive to certain populations.

MICHAEL J. MALINOWSKI, DEALING WITH THE REALITIES OF RACE AND ETHNICITY: A BIOETHICS–CENTERED ARGUMENT IN FAVOR OF RACE–BASED GENETICS RESEARCH

45 Hous. L. Rev. 1415, 1433–1436 (2009).

Those in the scientific and medical communities opposed to research based on race and ethnicity emphasize that these groupings are inconsistent with the scientific reality of human genetics. They draw from the ample body of literature by Professors Cavalli–Sforza, Lewontin, and their contemporaries, and also reference recent findings that bolster the argument that race and ethnicity are more social constructs than genetic realities. Opponents assert that a preferred methodology for population genetics is research centered on diseases or at least specific and more reliable genetic particulars. They argue this approach will help avoid wasting resources, forcing outcomes, and chancing the affirmation of racial and ethnic groupings and social stereotypes. According to bioethicist and Ph.D scientist Mildred Cho, the race and ethnicity categories are unworkable: "Because social perceptions of the meaning of race and ethnicity are extremely fluid, basing research findings on these categories or applying scientific findings based on perceived race or ethnicity is fraught with problems. Thus, attempts to better define [the racial and ethnic] structure [of drug response] will be futile."

Sociologist Troy Duster and many other opponents raise concerns about biologic determinism, meaning that genetic protocols crafted around race and ethnicity will become self-fulfilling prophecies. They emphasize the genetic commonality in any group due to the youth of the human species and its overwhelming genetic sameness. Professor Duster also addresses the broader social implications of underscoring lines traditionally drawn around groups based upon race and ethnicity through genetics research protocols that suggest their validity. He warns that singling out these groups further affirms prejudices and increases their vulnerability to discrimination, exploitation, and health inequality. According to Professor Duster, the scientific community has shifted from "genetic sameness" as the mantra for mapping the human genome to a mantra of "genetic differentiation" through ongoing efforts to make medical sense out of the genome map, including population genetics, pharmacogenomics, and identification of SNPs.

A number of law academics have entered the debate and argued against the perpetuation of race in the biomedical context with cautions about the weighty social and legal implications involved. In fact, there is a discernible majority opinion among law academics that race-based genomics research is undesirable on multiple levels and perhaps even illegal. The literature includes articles by Professors Erik Lillquist and Charles Sullivan, Professor Sharona Hoffman, Professor Jonathon Kahn, and a University of Minnesota symposium chaired by Professor Wolf, which includes an article by Professor Dorothy Roberts.

Proposals have been made to distinguish basic, clinical, epidemiological, and other forms of research, and to introduce legal restraints on the use of race and ethnicity in a manner tailored to each research specialty. The general consensus among law opponents is that the use of race and ethnicity in biomedical research always warrants caution and legal restraints, but there is a continuum: use of race in clinical research is least acceptable; use in epidemiological research, such as research on the correlation between race and health disparities, is most acceptable; and other types of research place between the two. Also, the general consensus is that the use of race in research and medicine runs contrary to U.S. law and policy that broadly proscribes it. Lillquist & Sullivan conclude that the use of race in research and medicine should be severely circumscribed, if not prohibited almost entirely. Their proposed standard for using race in medical treatment is extremely restrictive. They would require a scientific basis to establish not simply that the use of race is helpful in diagnosis and treatment, but that it is the best known method at the time. Professor Hoffman declares that " 'race-based' medicine is an inappropriate and perilous approach" and proposes regulatory reforms to heavily restrain, if not entirely eliminate, both race-based research and medicine. She proposes "attributes-based" identification as a race-neutral alternative.

Collectively, legal academics generally approach race-based research from the standpoint of U.S. jurisprudence and public policy against discrimination and associated social and ethical concerns. Their analysis of potential legal constraints on race-centered research begins with restrictions on intentional disparate treatment based on race by government entities under the Equal Protection Clause of the Fourteenth Amendment and the Due Process Clause of the Fifth Amendment. They emphasize that government use of racial classifications triggers strict scrutiny, but recognize that government actions, including programs thoughtfully crafted to promote affirmative action, survive such scrutiny where there is a compelling government interest and the use of race is narrowly tailored to promote that interest. They generally concede that, under established jurisprudence, government sponsorship of responsible race-based genetics research is likely to survive such challenges, though the present Court recently questioned Seattle and Louisville school diversity policies and subjected them to further inquiry.

MARGARET A. WINKER, RACE AND ETHNICITY IN MEDICAL RESEARCH: REQUIREMENTS MEET REALITY

34 J. Law, Med. & Ethics 520, 520–522 (2006).

In medical research the assumption that race is an important factor is widespread. This may derive from the use of race as a patient descriptor throughout medical training. Medical students traditionally learned that patients' histories begin with "this is a [insert patient's age, presumed race, sex] who presents with a chief complaint of. . . ." In medical editing, peer reviewers sometimes ask that race be reported and analyzed even when originally omitted. However, medicine is hardly unique in its preoccupation with race. Reporting and analyzing medical studies by race may reflect the significant role, both real and perceived, that race plays in the broader society. * * *

Scientific research must be reported accurately to allow interpretation and replication. However, the terms used to describe race and ethnicity often have been inaccurate and inappropriate. The terms "Latino/Hispanic," "Asian," and "white" or "Caucasian" have all been criticized for inaccuracy and ambiguity. The problem is compounded when observers such as researchers or clinicians classify individuals by race based on skin color and appearances, but even self-classification raises issues. In some areas of the United States, fully one-quarter of individuals checked more than one box indicating race/ethnicity in the 2000 census. In addition, translating descriptions of race/ethnicity from the native language in which a survey was administered can lead to additional measurement error.

Despite the many difficulties posed by categorizing race, in some instances it can be important to assess race and ethnicity. First, reporting race can suggest whether the populations studied reflect the diversity of the population to whom the results might be applied. Clinicians, in particular, may need to know whether the characteristics of the study population are comparable to the population the clinician treats. For example, major cardiovascular risk factors were first defined in the middle-class white population of Framingham, Massachusetts, but it was unclear whether these risk factors were applicable to more diverse populations. In fact, the risk factors do predict cardiovascular disease in more diverse populations, but the relative importance of specific risk factors varies by the racial and ethnic background of the population. For similar reasons, the National Institutes of Health (NIH) requires that race and ethnicity be measured and reported in funded research, in part to ensure that traditionally understudied non-white populations are included.

Race also may be used as one of several parameters to determine whether randomization has been successful. This assessment may be useful to readers as one description of the population of research participants, but the existence of the variable tempts the researcher or reviewer to request results by race whether or not such analysis is appropriate. If such analyses are conducted without considering other contributing factors such as socioeconomic differences, the results may lead to incorrect interpretation and implications.

The third reason to assess race and ethnicity is that racial disparities in risk factors, treatment, and outcomes are common in the United States and race must be measured if reasons for the disparities are to be studied. Racial disparities often persist after controlling for socioeconomic measures such as income and education. However, the reasons underlying disparities are more complex than differential treatment or racism by clinicians. In a 2004 study, Elizabeth Bradley and colleagues found that when both admitting hospital and race were assessed, health care disparities varied primarily by hospital rather than by race; the association of disparities with race was a result of blacks being cared for in hospitals with worse process of care. Another 2004 study, by Peter Bach and colleagues, found that physicians treating black patients were less likely to be board-certified and had less access to high-quality specialists, diagnostic imaging, and ancillary services. These studies suggest that interventions to reduce health disparities will need to address more than socioeconomic differences. Eliminating disparities will require a nuanced understanding of patient care, quality of care, and behavior of clinicians and patients.

* * *

A fourth reason for assessing race is related to the tenuous connection between race and genetics. Genetic factors associated with drug metabolism can enhance or reduce a drug's effectiveness or adverse effects. In some cases, some of these genetic tendencies may be associated with a particular race. However, when race is used as a proxy for what presumably is a genetic marker for susceptibility to a given drug's effects, some members of the population who may benefit from the drug will be excluded from treatment and some members of the population targeted for the drug will not benefit. A statistical difference in drug response between different racial or ethnic groups should be the starting point for genetic studies, not the final conclusion resulting in different drug indications by race.

* * *

Given that some legitimate reasons to assess race exist in medical research, the measurement and reporting of race should be as accurate and transparent as possible.

NOTES AND QUESTIONS

1.   Given the lack of a genetic basis for racial categorizations, what is the proper role of the concept of race in genetic research, health care research, and policy more generally?

2.   What policy measures might be taken to reduce the risk of discrimination or stigma when members of minority and ethnic groups obtain therapeutic genetic testing?

3.   The Obasogie excerpt gives an example of how differences in hypertension based on skin complexion can lead to erroneous assumptions about racial determinants of health status. Another example was a finding that African–American steel workers have higher lung cancer rates compared with whites. It turned out that blacks were given the dirtiest, most dangerous jobs, such as standing on top of coke ovens, which exposed them to a higher risk of disease. See Elaine Draper, Risky Business: Genetic Testing and Exclusionary Practices in the Hazardous Workplace 65–96 (1991).

4. The relationship between genetics and race has also come up in connection with pharmacogenetics. See the discussion of the BiDil controversy in Chapter 9.

Chapter 3

Eugenics

■ ■ ■

I. INTRODUCTION

Current ethical, legal, and policy developments concerning human genetics cannot be understood without reference to the historical background. Part of this background, the history of the science of human genetics, was described in the preceding chapter and will be supplemented in later chapters in discussions of specific scientific applications, such as gene therapy. This chapter covers a different aspect of the historical setting—the eugenics movement that flourished during the first half of the twentieth century. It is safe to say that no phenomenon has done more to shape the ethical, legal, and policy attitudes toward human genetics than the philosophy of eugenics and the actions that it inspired.

This chapter begins with an explanation of the term "eugenics" and a historical description of the movement that bears its name. The chapter then explores the reaction of American law, and discusses the ways in which eugenic thinking continues to be reflected in public attitudes and policy. The chapter concludes with a description of the Ethical, Legal, and Social Implications (ELSI) Program at the National Human Genome Research Institute at the NIH and at the U.S. Department of Energy, one of the most tangible public policy responses to the shadow that eugenics has cast over the ongoing revolution in human genetics.

ALLEN BUCHANAN ET AL., FROM CHANCE TO CHOICE: GENETICS AND JUSTICE
27–28 (2000).

The current revolution in molecular biology is not the first but the second large-scale attempt to modify the pattern of human heredity for the better. The eugenics movement of 1870–1950 came first. These large-scale social movements, originating in England but ultimately involving public advocates and membership organizations from Brazil to Russia, located the source of social problems in the genes of individuals and sought to alter the pattern by which these genes would be transmitted to future generations. In the United States, the movement received substan-

47

tial funding from the great family fortunes, including Carnegie and the Rockefellers, and it was endorsed, with varying degrees of enthusiasm, by most scientists working in the field of human genetics. Indeed, eugenics was the motivation for much of the early scientific research in this field.

Nevertheless, the history of eugenics is not a proud one. It is largely remembered for its shoddy science, the blatant race and class biases of many of its leading advocates, and its cruel program of segregation and, later, sterilization of hundreds of thousands of vulnerable people who were judged to have substandard genes. Even worse, eugenics, in the form of "racial hygiene," formed part of the core of Nazi doctrine. Hitler endorses it in *Mein Kampf*, and once in power expanded both eugenic research and, borrowing from U.S. models, a program of sterilization that became the first step toward the murder of handicapped "Aryans" and ultimately millions of victims of the Holocaust.

II. EUGENICS PROGRAMS IN THE UNITED STATES

PHILIP R. REILLY, EUGENICS, ETHICS, STERILIZATION LAWS, IN 1 ENCYCLOPEDIA OF ETHICAL, LEGAL, AND POLICY ISSUES IN BIOTECHNOLOGY

204, 204–208 (Thomas H. Murray & Maxwell J. Mehlman eds. 2000).

ORIGINS AND RISE OF THE EUGENICS MOVEMENT

Although speculations about the perfectibility of humankind date at least as far back as the flowering of philosophy among the ancient Greek city states, the first serious social policy proposal to improve the gene pool of our species that was tied to scientific claims arose in England in the second half of the nineteenth century. Francis Galton, a Victorian polymath who was probably influenced by the revolutionary impact of *The Origin of Species* published in 1859 by his cousin, Charles Darwin, began investigating the inheritance of talent among eminent English families about 1864. He coined the term eugenics (from the Greek, fusing words for good and birth) in 1883 in *Inquiries into Human Faculty and its Development*. Public interest in the notion that success and failure in life might be closely tied to the germ plasm that one inherited grew rapidly, especially in England and the United States, and the new word enjoyed a certain vogue. In 1904, when he made a major financial gift to the Eugenics Record Office at the University of London, Galton drafted an official definition of "natural eugenics" as "the study of the agencies under social control that may improve or impair the racial qualities of future generations either physically or mentally."

In the United States eugenic policies, which flowered in the early twentieth century, germinated in the climate of progressive reform that took root in the last quarter of the nineteenth century. From 1850 to 1880, the states had built many prisons, hospitals, insane asylums, and colonies for the mentally retarded. Initial enthusiasm faded as funding problems arose and conditions declined. Richard Dugdale, a well-to-do Englishman who made New York City home, was an ardent social reformer and one of many who sought to improve such facilities. It was while inspecting prisons in upstate New York that he discovered a large family many of whose members seemed to be inhabiting one state facility or another. His book, *The Jukes,* based on an exhaustive study of the family, detailed the cost to taxpayers of their incarceration and support. He also championed two ideas that would become core beliefs among many Americans within a decade: that feeblemindedness, epilepsy, drunkenness, criminality, and insanity had strong hereditary influences, and that affected individuals tended to produce larger than average numbers of offspring.

Interest in eugenics was widespread in the United States just as biologists rediscovered the laws of inheritance that Gregor Mendel had postulated in 1865, but which had been reported in an obscure local scientific journal and been little noticed. Charles Davenport, a talented young biology professor, played an instrumental role in propagating "mendelism" in the United States. He was quick to apply the theory to problems of human heredity and about 1905 he secured a large gift from Mrs. E.H. Harriman (the wife of the railroad magnate) to develop and sustain a eugenics research facility at Cold Spring Harbor on Long Island, an entity which operated independently of the Station for Experimental Evolution that he had founded there a couple of years earlier. One of his most important decisions was to recruit a midwestern high school teacher named Harry Hamilton Laughlin to direct the Eugenics Record Office. In so doing, Davenport, a highly respected biologist who would become a member of the National Academy of Sciences, tied human genetics to eugenics and provided eugenics with a cloak of scientific legitimacy that it wore for more than three decades.

The indefatigable Laughlin became an ardent eugenicist who, from 1918 to 1939, played the premier role as a strategist for the eugenics movement in the United States. One of his early projects was to train cadres of young women as eugenic field-workers. Armed with knowledge on how to prepare detailed family pedigrees, many of these workers reviewed the records of thousands of institutionalized persons and interviewed their relatives, thereby gathering the raw material that became the basis for what might be considered the nation's first foray into sociobiology. Between 1910 and 1920 eugenicists working in association with the Eugenics Record Office and sometimes assisted by Laughlin's field-workers published a number of lengthy monographs with colorful names, such as *The Hill Folk: Report of a Rural Community of Hereditary Defectives.* These monographs reinforced the eugenic ideas propounded in *The Jukes* and the equally famous *The Kallikaks* (1912), written by Henry Herbert Goddard, a prominent psychologist who worked at the Vineland Training School in New Jersey and who imported IQ testing from France about 1905. These and similar works caught the attention of American journalists. About 1910 articles on eugenics constituted the second most popular topic in the print media according to the Index to Periodical Literature.

Laughlin played a critically important role in the effort to secure enactment of federal laws to limit the immigration of persons that he and many others believed were of inferior racial stock. He conducted and published surveys that purported to show that immigrants from southern Europe and Russia were much more likely than immigrants from north-western Europe to wind up in charity hospitals or need public assistance. In 1922 he served as the official expert on eugenics to the committee in the United States Congress charged with immigration matters. In that role he provided testimony that offered an apparent scientific basis to rationalize a legislative quota system that favored the immigration of some ethnic groups over others from 1924 to 1968.

During the 1920s Laughlin also spent an immense amount of time drafting and lobbying for the enactment of laws to permit state officials to sterilize institutionalized retarded persons without their consent. He helped propagate the second wave of such laws that swept through America in the 1920s, and he provided an important deposition in the lower court proceedings that led to *Buck v. Bell*, in which the United States Supreme Court ultimately upheld the constitutionality of a law he helped to craft. This opinion removed lingering doubts in many state legislatures and made possible the enactment of about a dozen new laws (discussed below) in the ensuing five years.

IMPACT OF VASECTOMY

Prior to 1910 in the United States proponents of eugenics tried a variety of methods to reduce child-bearing by persons thought to be unfit. In some states, notably California, the focus was on the insane; in others such as New York and New Jersey, there was special concern for "protecting" mentally retarded young women who, it was feared, were especially vulnerable to unscrupulous men. The typical proposals were to segregate the sexes in institutions and prohibit trysts. In society at large the problem was dealt with by the enactment of marriage restriction laws that forbade the insane, the retarded, the epileptic, public drunkards, those with tuberculosis, and even, in some states, the poor, from marrying. Unlike antimiscegenation laws which were vigorously prosecuted, marriage restriction laws were not much enforced. Those few that were legally challenged in the years before World War I did not survive constitutional scrutiny.

A clinical advance, the development of the vasectomy, about 1897 had an obvious, material impact on the rise of sterilization laws. A.J. Ochsner, chief surgeon at St. Mary's Hospital in Chicago, published his surgical experience with several cases in the *Journal of the American Medical Association* in 1899. The paper carried the remarkable title: "Surgical Treatment of Habitual Criminals." After describing the new surgical technique. Dr. Ochsner asserted: "if it were possible to eliminate all habitual criminals from the possibility of having children, there would soon be a very marked decrease in this class." Further, the same treatment "could reasonably be suggested for chronic inebriates, imbeciles, perverts and paupers." Although there was no comparable, safe operation for women, Ochsner opined that since most female criminals were also prostitutes and were highly likely to become infertile due to the impact of untreated gonorrhea, their class would produce relatively few children.

Ocshner's proposal received a large boost in 1902 when Dr. Harry C. Sharp, the surgeon for the Indiana Reformatory in Jeffersonville, reported on the follow-up of 42 prisoners who had agreed to undergo vasectomy, claiming that the patients "feel that they are stronger, sleep better, their memory improves, the will becomes stronger, and they do better in school." He urged his fellow physicians to lobby the leaders of state institutions of all kinds "to render every male sterile who passes its portals, whether it be almshouse, insane asylum, institute for the feeble-minded, reformatory or prison." Policy makers, who had viewed earlier, sporadic proposals to castrate criminals with distaste, greeted the suggestion to use the much less mutilating vasectomy with enthusiasm.

In the years 1902 to 1912, Sharp was an outspoken advocate for vasectomy as a social tool. He spoke on the subject frequently at regional and national medical meetings (often exaggerating the salubrious effects of sterilization), wrote political pamphlets on eugenics, and button-holed state legislators. It is no accident that in 1907 Indiana became the first state: (indeed, the first political jurisdiction in the world) to enact an involuntary sterilization law that had a demonstrably eugenic underpinning.

FIRST STERILIZATION LAWS

The nation's first sterilization bill was introduced in the Michigan legislature in 1897, but did not come to floor vote. In 1905 the Pennsylvania House of Representatives became the first legislative body to pass a bill proposing involuntary sterilization of certain institutionalized persons, but the governor vetoed it. On April 9, 1907, Indiana governor J. Frank Hanly, a month after a sizable majority of both houses had voted favorably, signed the nation's first eugenic sterilization law. The statute authorized the compulsory sterilization of "confirmed criminals, idiots, imbeciles and rapists" residing in a state institution if, after appropriate review, a panel of one physician and two surgeons concluded that it was "inadvisable" that the individual procreate and that there was "no probability of improvement." The new law was crafted to legitimize the program that Dr. Sharp was already vigorously pursuing in Jeffersonville, except it eliminated the pretense of obtaining consent.

In 1909 the legislatures in California, Connecticut, Oregon, and Washington passed similar laws. Despite overwhelming support in the legislature, the governor of Oregon vetoed the bill sent to him; the other three governors promptly signed their bills into law. In the ensuing four years (1910–1913), ten states (Iowa, New Jersey, Nevada, New York, North Dakota, Michigan, Kansas, Wisconsin, Vermont, and Nebraska) passed sterilization laws. In general, there was little opposition and most votes were lopsided. Only in the state where the vote was close (96–82 in the House), Vermont, did a governor cast a veto.

The California law, which launched the most active eugenical sterilization program in the United States until well into the 1920s, was slightly more sophisticated. Section 1 of the law covered institutionalized persons who had been diagnosed with "hereditary insanity," "incurable chronic mania," and "dementia," requiring that their discharge must be premised on "asexualization." Used in the early days as a synonym for vasectomy, this term was often confused with castration. Section 2 targeted recidivists in state prison. It identified three persons (the resident prison physician, the general superintendent of state hospitals, and the secretary of the state board of health) to review the cases of persons who had been convicted twice of rape or sexual assault or three times of having committed other crimes, and who while in prison continued to show evidence that they were moral or sexual degenerates. If two of the three reviewers concluded that there was no hope of "moral recovery," they could order that the prisoner be sterilized without his consent. The third section of the law directed the state to pay for the sterilization of institutionalized retarded children or adults so long as their parents or guardians consented. This relatively enlightened section may explain why the constitutionality of this law was not challenged.

By 1913 involuntary sterilization programs were active in 14 states. There were significant differences in their scope and pace, partly because in a number of the states opponents of eugenics attacked the constitutionality of the enabling laws. In every instance (Indiana, Iowa, Michigan, Nevada, New Jersey, New York, and Washington) in which the constitutionality was put at issue, the courts invalidated the laws, usually on the grounds that they violated the requirements of the Due Process Clause of the Fourteenth Amendment. Laws that targeted prisoners were held to violate the Eighth Amendment prohibiting cruel and unusual punishments. In Oregon the sterilization law, which also was challenged on constitutional grounds, was repealed by public referendum only months after the governor signed it.

From 1907 to 1922 activities in California account for the vast majority of reported involuntary sterilizations conducted pursuant to state law. Of a national total of 3,233 operations, 2,558 were performed there, most on institutionalized, mentally ill persons. During that era a substantial fraction of the men and women who were discharged from a California state hospital were sterilized. The women usually were subjected to oophorectomy (removal of the ovaries), in those days a risky operation that resulted in several deaths. Due to the vigorous commitment of its medical superintendent, Dr. John Reily, during this era the South California State hospital in Patton sterilized 1,009 of its residents. In March 1918, Dr. Reily reported that he had sterilized 43 persons.

* * *

During the years just before and during World War I, there was a hiatus in the enactment of sterilization laws. Almost certainly this was because of the failure of existing statutes to survive constitutional challenge. [The grounds for reversal were, in one state, that the law violated the prohibition against cruel and unusual punishment; and in other states, that these laws violated equal protection because they only applied to institutionalized persons, or that they violated due process by not providing adequate procedural safeguards.—Eds.] But the hiatus was probably also influenced by the sharp drop in immigration during that era. In the first two decades of the twentieth century American eugenicists were far more vexed by the massive influx of what they were convinced were racially inferior people than by the slowly growing number of retarded persons who were housed in state institutions. As the tide of immigration rapidly subsided during 1914 to 1919, the sense of urgency among eugenicists may have relaxed.

RESURGENCE OF STERILIZATION LAWS

Eugenic Thinking in the 1920s

During the 1920s the eugenics movement, which prior to the World War had begun to decline, grew and prospered. August institutions, such as Yale University, the Cold Spring Harbor Laboratory, and the New York Museum of Natural History numbered intellectual leaders of eugenics on their faculties. The Second International Congress of Eugenics met in New York City in 1921. By 1924 the New York based American Eugenics Society was lobbying in Albany against bills that its members thought were dysgenic (e.g., including those intended to provide financial assistance to poor women with school age children). Across the nation, local eugenic societies flowered. In 1926 the Human Betterment Foundation, the pet project of an eccentric California millionaire named Ezra S. Gosney, emerged as a major voice for eugenics on the West Coast. In Cleveland in 1928 Charles F. Brush, a successful inventor, launched the Brush Foundation for the Betterment of the Human Race with one stated goal being the propagation of eugenic goals. In Topeka, J.H. Pile, a self-made millionaire who had studied at Yale, founded the Eugenic Babies Foundation. Especially in the midwest, interest in positive eugenics (the search for methods to have genetically superior children) captured the imagination. County fairs sponsored "fitter family" contests in which people, not unlike the prize hogs or cattle they showed, competed for blue ribbons based on their pedigree, physical examinations, and their children's report cards.

At the Eugenics Record Office, Laughlin, stung by the constitutional defeats suffered by the involuntary sterilization laws between 1913 and 1918, produced a massive tome on the societal benefits of eugenic sterilization. He carefully analyzed the laws that the courts had found flawed, and then drafted and circulated a model sterilization law that he hoped would satisfy the constitutional concerns. In the early 1920s his work was widely used by legislators who wanted to sponsor such bills. His polemics on sterilization found their way to Nazi Germany where Laughlin was held in such high regard that he was awarded an honorary degree by the University of Heidelberg in 1934.

Beginning in 1923 there was a major resurgence of sterilization laws. After five years of legislative inactivity, new laws were enacted in Delaware, Michigan, Montana, and Oregon. Virginia adopted a law in 1924, and governors signed seven of the nine bills that were passed in 1925. By January 1926 eugenic sterilization laws were on the books of 17 states and small bands of pro-sterilization lobbyists were urging many others to follow suit. In some states directors of state institutions permitted involuntary eugenical sterilizations to occur despite the absence of enabling laws.

In mid–1925 the Michigan Supreme Court upheld the constitutionality of the new law which it held was "justified by the findings of Biological Science," and was a "proper and reasonable exercise of the police power of the state." This greatly encouraged other legislatures, but many still wondered how such laws would fare before the United States Supreme Court. In a bold move, pro-sterilization forces in Virginia decided to find out. The resulting decision, *Buck v. Bell*, was the single most important event in the history of the sterilization laws in the United States.

BUCK v. BELL
274 U.S. 200 (1927).

MR. JUSTICE HOLMES delivered the opinion of the Court.

This is a writ of error to review a judgment of the Supreme Court of Appeals of the state of Virginia, affirming a judgment of the Circuit Court of Amherst County, by which the defendant in error, the superintendent of the State Colony for Epileptics and Feeble Minded, was ordered to perform the operation of salpingectomy upon Carrie Buck, the plaintiff in error, for the purpose of making her sterile. The case comes here upon the contention that the statute authorizing the judgment is void under the Fourteenth Amendment as denying to the plaintiff in error due process of law and the equal protection of the laws.

Carrie Buck is a feeble minded white woman who was committed to the State Colony above mentioned in due form. She is the daughter of a feeble minded mother in the same institution, and the mother of an illegitimate feeble minded child. She was eighteen years old at the time of the trial of her case in the Circuit Court, in the latter part of 1924. An Act of Virginia, approved March 20, 1924, recites that the health of the patient and the welfare of society may be promoted in certain cases by the sterilization of mental defectives, under careful safeguard, etc.; that the sterilization may be effected in males by vasectomy and in females by salpingectomy, without serious pain or substantial danger to life; that the Commonwealth is supporting in various institutions many defective persons who if now discharged would become a menace but if incapable of procreating might be discharged with safety and become self-supporting with benefit to themselves and to society; and that experience has shown that heredity plays an important part in the transmission of insanity, imbecility, etc. The statute then enacts that whenever the superintendent of certain institutions including the above named State Colony shall be of opinion that it is for the best interests of the patients and of society that an inmate under his care should be sexually sterilized, he may have the operation performed upon any patient afflicted with hereditary forms of insanity, imbecility, etc., on complying with the very careful provisions by which the act protects the patients from possible abuse.

The superintendent first presents a petition to the special board of directors of his hospital or colony, stating the facts and the grounds for his opinion, verified by affidavit. Notice of the petition and of the time and place of the hearing in the institution is to be served upon the inmate, and also upon his guardian, and if there is no guardian the superintendent is to apply to the Circuit Court of the County to appoint one. If the inmate is a minor notice also is to be given to his parents if any with a copy of the petition. The board is to see to it that the inmate may attend the hearings if desired by him or his guardian. The evidence is all to be reduced to writing, and after the board has made its order for or against the operation, the superintendent, or the inmate, or his guardian, may appeal to the Circuit Court of the County. The Circuit Court may consider the record of the board and the evidence before it and such other admissible evidence as may be offered, and may affirm, revise, or reverse the order of the board and enter such order as it deems just. Finally any party may apply to the Supreme Court of Appeals, which, if it grants the appeal, is to hear the case upon the record of the trial in the Circuit Court and may enter such order as it thinks the Circuit Court should have entered. There can be no doubt that so far as procedure is concerned the rights of the patient are most carefully considered, and as every step in this case was taken in scrupulous compliance with the statute and after months of observation, there is no doubt that in that respect the plaintiff in error has had due process of law.

The attack is not upon the procedure but upon the substantive law. It seems to be contended that in no circumstances could such an order be justified. It certainly is contended that the order cannot be justified upon the existing grounds. The judgment finds the facts that have been recited and that Carrie Buck "is the probable potential parent of socially inadequate offspring, likewise afflicted, that she may be sexually sterilized without detriment to her general health and that her welfare and that of society will be promoted by her sterilization," and thereupon makes the order. In view of the general declarations of the legislature and the specific findings of the Court, obviously we cannot say as matter of law that the grounds do not exist, and if they exist they justify the result. We have seen more than once that the public welfare may call upon the best citizens for their lives. It would be strange if it could not call upon those who already sap the strength of the State for these lesser sacrifices, often not felt to be such by those concerned, in order to prevent our being swamped with incompetence. It is better for all the world, if instead of waiting to execute degenerate offspring for crime, or to let them starve for their imbecility, society can prevent those who are manifestly unfit from continuing their kind. The principle that sustains compulsory vaccination is broad enough to cover cutting the Fallopian tubes. Jacobson v. Massachusetts, 197 U.S. 11. Three generations of imbeciles are enough.

But, it is said, however it might be if this reasoning were applied generally, it fails when it is confined to the small number who are in the institutions named and is not applied to the multitudes outside. It is the usual last resort of constitutional arguments to point out shortcomings of this sort. But the answer is that the law does all that is needed when it does all that it can, indicates a policy, applies it to all within the lines, and seeks to bring within the lines all similarly situated so far and so fast as its means allow. Of course so far as the operations enable those who otherwise must be kept confined to be returned to the world, and thus open the asylum to others, the equality aimed at will be more nearly reached.

Judgment affirmed.

MR. JUSTICE BUTLER dissents.

PAUL A. LOMBARDO, THREE GENERATIONS, NO IMBECILES: NEW LIGHT ON BUCK v. BELL

60 N.Y.U.L. Rev. 30, 50–62 (1985).

The trial of Buck v. Bell took place November 18, 1924. Strode [counsel for the superintendent of the state institution] presented eight witnesses from the area near Carrie's home in an attempt to prove her "social inadequacy." Additionally, Strode introduced a lengthy deposition from a eugenical expert from New York and had another eugenicist testify at the trial, both of whom informed the court about Carrie's feeblemindedness in light of eugenical theory. He also put two Virginia physicians on the stand to bolster the case in favor of the sterilization law.

In contrast, Whitehead [counsel for Buck] called no witnesses to dispute the specific allegations against Carrie or to cast doubt on the "scientific" theories about which Strode's four "experts" had testified. Moreover, Whitehead's cross-examination of the witnesses for the State was so weak that it was often unclear which side he was representing. * * * A cursory review of the trial transcript readily supports this view; a more thorough analysis of the case Whitehead could have presented suggests a deliberate decision not to defend Carrie.

Among the allegations Whitehead chose not to dispute were several assertions about Carrie's background. For example, famed eugenicist Harry Laughlin never examined Carrie, but drew firm "scientific conclusions" from very sketchy information supplied by Priddy [id.], compelling one commentator to label Laughlin's analysis as "near-psychic." Laughlin's deposition relied on Priddy's "facts" as proof not only of Carrie's alleged feeblemindedness, but also of her generally undesirable character. She had, said Priddy, a "record during life of immorality, prostitution, and untruthfulness; [had] never been self-sustaining; [and] has had one illegitimate child * * * supposed to be mental defective." Her mother, Emma Buck, "was maritally unworthy; having been divorced from her husband on account of infidelity * * * [and] has had one illegitimate child and probably two others inclusive of Carrie Buck * * *." With regard to the Buck family generally, he concluded, "[t]hese people belong to the shiftless, ignorant, and worthless class of anti-social whites of the South * * * [about whom] it is impossible to get intelligent and satisfactory data * * *."

Most of these comments, left unchallenged by Whitehead, were not only of questionable relevance, but untrue. Had Whitehead chosen to investigate Carrie's background he easily could have collected evidence to refute most of Priddy's charges. For example, on the question of her illegitimacy, he could have found that her parents, Frank and Emma Buck, were married in 1896. The available records indicate that when Carrie was born in 1906, her parents were still married. A common law presumption effective in Virginia at that time would have established Carrie's legitimacy. Was Carrie feebleminded? This was the purported justification for her commitment to the Colony, yet the majority of witnesses called by Strode had no firsthand knowledge of Carrie. Seven of the eleven witnesses either had never met Carrie or refused to offer any conclusion about her mental condition. Several of Carrie's own teachers could have attested, with supporting documentation, that Carrie was not mentally deficient. School records indicate that Carrie was a normal child: In the five years that she attended school, she was promoted to the sixth grade. In fact, the year before she left school, her teacher entered the comment "very good—deportment and lessons" and recommended her for promotion. That teacher and her records would have contradicted the testimony of the single witness who claimed that Carrie was "anti-social" because she had written notes to boys in school.

Was Carrie immoral? Apart from how ridiculous this charge sounds today, broadly defined character traits such as immorality were at issue in the trial. Priddy linked Carrie's supposed predisposition to "anti-social" behavior to the same characteristics he had observed in her mother and the "generally accepted theory of the laws of heredity." Whitehead easily could have questioned the charge of "immorality" by calling witnesses of his own. Carrie had attended church and church school and had been a member of two church choirs in her hometown. Such testimony would have, at the least, posed doubts about the accuracy of the investigation into her character.

The eugenical basis of the Virginia sterilization law required that Carrie's inadequacies be hereditary—that she be the "probable potential parent of socially inadequate offspring." To show this hereditary link,

Strode elicited testimony that Carrie's mother, Emma, was a feebleminded patient at the Colony, that Carrie had exhibited "peculiarities" since childhood, that supposed members of Carrie's family were "peculiar," and that Carrie's child was slow. Strode's evidence was weak, yet Whitehead's cross-examination, when it took place at all, failed to attack the evidence.

Why, given the weakness of Strode's evidence, was Carrie chosen as the perfect candidate for sterilization? The answer to this question clarifies the unstated purpose of the sterilization policy: she had delivered a child, but was unmarried. Poor, and born of a disgraced mother herself, Carrie was likely to be the parent of more of the "shiftless, ignorant and worthless class of anti-social whites" from which she came. The single fact of her unwed motherhood was Priddy's proof of her deficiency.

However, strong evidence existed to mitigate Carrie's responsibility for her bastard child. The circumstances of her commitment and the contradictions in the testimony of her foster parents would have alerted any conscientious attorney to probe further. As Carrie's commitment papers show, the foster parents [the Dobbses] with whom she lived for fourteen years were very anxious to have her put away.

* * *

What the trial did not reveal was that, despite all the discussion of her immoral behavior, Carrie was pregnant because she had been raped.

Mrs. Dobbs was away "on account of some illness," in the summer of 1923. During her absence Carrie was raped by Mrs. Dobbs's nephew. Commitment to the Colony would hide Carrie's shame; more importantly for Mr. and Mrs. Dobbs, it would save the family reputation.

* * *

Whitehead neither called the Dobbses as witnesses nor challenged Priddy by introducing readily available data on Carrie's parents, her church attendance, or her school record—data Priddy (and presumably Whitehead) had considered "impossible to get." Whitehead failed as Carrie's attorney not because he was incompetent, underpaid, or merely ineffectual. He failed because he intended to fail.

Whitehead had long been associated with Strode and Priddy. He helped Strode with his election campaign and helped him obtain an Army commission. As a member of the Colony Board, Whitehead authorized Priddy's sterilization requests. A building named in Whitehead's honor was opened at the Colony just two months before Carrie's arrival. Strode, in turn, recommended Whitehead for a government position only six days before Carrie Buck's trial. Proof that Whitehead intended to lose Carrie Buck's case does not, however, rely primarily on the evidence of these close, personal associations. Whitehead's role and intent are amply documented in the minutes of the Colony Board.

* * *

In 1930 Doctor Bell reported that after her sterilization, Carrie Buck "was immediately returned to society and made good." That evaluation was only partially true. Although she was paroled as a domestic helper to a family in Bland, Virginia, she remained under the control of the Colony. Her discharge, like that of all sterilized Colony women, was conditioned on an annual visit to Doctor Bell for a physical examination. Had there been any complaints of ill behavior, she could have been returned to the Colony at once.

After Carrie left the Colony, she married and became a member of the Methodist Church in Bland where she sang in the choir as she had as a teenager in Charlottesville. After twenty-four years of marriage, her husband died and she traveled to Front Royal, Virginia, where she met and later married Charles Detamore. He took work in farms and orchards and Carrie assisted a local family in caring for an elderly relative.

In 1970, with Carrie suffering from ill health, the couple returned to Carrie's hometown. They moved into a single-room cinder block shed with no plumbing, which the owner allowed them to inhabit rent-free. They lived there ten years in abject poverty, until in 1980 Carrie was hospitalized for exposure and malnutrition. After she recovered partially, she and her husband were taken to a state-operated nursing home outside Waynesboro, Virginia. She died there on January 28, 1983, at the age of seventy-six. Her body was returned to Charlottesville, where she was buried only a few steps from the graves of her daughter, Vivian, and her foster parents, Mr. and Mrs. Dobbs.

Throughout Carrie's adult life she regularly displayed intelligence and kindness that belied the "feeblemindedness" and "immorality" that were used as an excuse to sterilize her. She was an avid reader, and even in her last weeks was able to converse lucidly, recalling events from her childhood. Branded by Holmes as a second generation imbecile, Carrie provided no support for his glib epithet throughout her life.

Carrie's daughter Vivian, like her mother, was wrongly accused. On the basis of a nurse's comment that she was "not quite normal," Vivian Buck was used to prove her mother's hereditary "defects." Although she lived barely eight years, she too disproved Holmes's epigram. In her two years of schooling, she performed quite well, at one point earning a spot on the school "Honor Roll."

Of the three generations, the least is known about Emma Buck. She died at the Colony, leaving few records of her life. She was, at worst, the "moron" that Priddy claimed; no one but Holmes charged her with imbecility. Her true shortcomings probably stemmed from poverty and perhaps promiscuity.

Notes and Questions

1. The decision in *Buck* was generally considered to be a progressive result. Brandeis, Stone, and Taft joined in Holmes' majority opinion. Only

Justice Butler, the Court's only Catholic, dissented (without opinion). (Many Catholics at the time were troubled by eugenics, which some people thought should authorize non-treatment of "defective" newborns.) The outcome in *Buck* was embraced by such progressives of the time as Clarence Darrow, Helen Keller, and Margaret Sanger, who founded Planned Parenthood.

2. Note the elaborate procedural protections provided for in the statute pursuant to which Carrie Buck was sterilized. Are there any additional protections that might have been provided? Given the scope of the existing protections, how can the outcome in her case be explained? Does this suggest anything about the usefulness of procedural protections to prevent abuses?

3. Is Justice Holmes correct in analogizing sterilization to "call[ing] upon the best citizens for their lives" to promote "the public welfare"? When is the government permitted to require someone to die for the public welfare? Could the state kill someone to prevent the spread of an infectious disease?

4. A recurrent theme in this course is the degree to which the government should be permitted to control human reproductive behavior. What does the *Buck* case suggest are the limits on the power of the state to restrict reproduction? Are there any circumstances in which the state would be justified in sterilizing people against their will? Does the answer turn on whether only certain types of individuals, such as those considered "defective," are being singled out? In the mid–1970s, one Indian state adopted a policy of sterilizing women after their third child. See Note, India's Compulsory Sterilization Laws: The Human Rights of Family Planning, 8 Cal. W. Int'l L. J. 342 (1978). Is population control a sufficiently important social purpose to justify forced sterilization?

5. Justice Holmes stated that "[t]he principle that sustains compulsory vaccination is broad enough to cover cutting the Fallopian tubes," and cited Jacobson v. Massachusetts, 197 U.S. 11 (1905). That case upheld a Massachusetts requirement of smallpox vaccinations against a challenge that they infringed personal liberty. In his opinion, Justice Harlan observed:

> According to settled principles the police power of a State must be held to embrace, at least, such reasonable regulations established directly by legislative enactment as will protect the public health and the public safety.

> * * *

> [I]n every well-ordered society charged with the duty of conserving the safety of its members the rights of the individual in respect of his liberty may at times, under the pressure of great dangers, be subjected to such restraint, to be enforced by reasonable regulations, as the safety of the general public may demand.

> * * *

> [T]he means prescribed by the State to that end [must have a] real and substantial relation to the protection of the public health and safety.

197 U.S. at 25, 29, 31. Does the statute at issue in *Buck* meet these standards?

6.   Beyond compulsory vaccination, "[g]overnment engages in a broad range of restrictions of the person to reduce the spread of infection—civil confinement (isolation, quarantine, and compulsory hospitalization), mandatory treatment, and criminal penalties for knowing or willful exposure to disease." Lawrence O. Gostin, Public Health Law: Power, Duty, Restraint 203 (2000). To what extent does a genetic disease resemble a communicable disease? Is a genetic disease sufficiently "communicable" that the government is entitled to invoke its public health authority to prevent the disease from being "spread"? If so, what public health measures would be appropriate? For example, could the government, under its power to protect the public health, require someone to undergo genetic testing to determine if a fetus was affected with a genetic abnormality or disorder? Would the answer depend on whether or not the condition was treatable? See the discussion of mandatory screening programs in Chapter 7.

7.   Following *Buck*, a total of 28 states had enacted compulsory sterilization laws by 1931. In California, the number of reported sterilizations rose from 322 in 1925 to 2,362 over the course of 1928 and 1929. Nationally, approximately 3,000 operations were reported annually prior to the Second World War. More occurred that were not reported. For more complete information, see Phillip R. Reilly, Eugenics, Ethics, Sterilization Laws, Encyclopedia of Ethical, Legal, and Policy Issues in Biotechnology 204 (Thomas H. Murray & Maxwell J. Mehlman, eds. 2000).

8.   Eugenics theories also were seized upon by the descendants of early, Northern European immigrants to preserve their political power in the face of later waves of immigration. As Celeste Condit writes in her book The Meanings of the Gene (1999), at 35:

> The turn of the century was an anxious era for the relatively well-to-do Americans whose ancestors had come from Europe and who had dominated the continent for 200 years. Massive migration from rural areas to cities was occurring. From 1800 to 1920 the population in the United States shifted from overwhelmingly rural (75 percent) to majority urban (51 percent). This migration was creating and amplifying what we now know to be the standard problems of urban poverty in industrializing areas. However, the scope and scale of these problems were probably both new and shocking to the members of the society. While absolute numbers of those involved in crime and poverty might not have increased, the proximity to crime, poverty, prostitution, and other social ills that accompanies life in a city environment was nonetheless capable of creating distress. The shock was exacerbated by the immigration of a variety of different ethnic groups with a vast array of languages, cultural values, and cultural practices different from those preferred by the people derived from Northern European ancestry and culture. As Diane Paul has noted, a third of the population in 1920 consisted of immigrants and their children, and the proportions were higher in cities. The descendants of the Northern Europeans who had gained dominance by displacing the native population 200 years earlier were now faced with losing that dominance in turn.

9. World War II marked a watershed in the eugenics movement because of the association between eugenics and the Nazis. As described by Buchanan et al.:

> Eugenics was central to the entire Nazi enterprise, joined with romantic nativist and racist myths of the purebred Nordic. The emphasis on "blood" called for a purifying of the nation's gene pool so that Germans could regain the nobility and greatness of their genetically pure forebears.
>
> As Robert Proctor and other historians have shown, the subsequent programs of sterilization, euthanasia of the unfit (a program that took the lives of tens of thousands of "Aryans," mostly young children), and eventually the Holocaust itself were part of the unfolding of this central idea. The sterilization and "euthanasia" programs, which did not initially target Jews and other minorities, were an exercise in negative eugenics designed to improve the native German stock from its degenerated condition. Legislation barring sexual relations between Jews and "Aryans," and ultimately the Holocaust were intended to prevent further adulteration of the "pure" German nation with inferior genes. Jews and others who contributed "evil" genes were the disease afflicting the German nation, which Hitler, the physician, would cure.

Allen Buchanan et al., From Chance to Choice: Genetics and Justice 37 (2000).

The Nazi sterilization program, although much larger in scope, employed many of the same legal mechanisms as the Americans:

> A comprehensive German eugenic sterilization law was enacted on July 14, 1933. Pursuant to it, the nation set up a network of Hereditary Health Courts empowered to sterilize persons about whom, in "the experience of medical science, it may be expected with great probability that their offspring may suffer severe physical damage." At first persons with any one of nine conditions were targeted: inborn feeblemindedness, schizophrenia, manicdepressive [sic] insanity, hereditary epilepsy, Huntington's chorea, hereditary blindness, hereditary deafness, severe hereditary physical deformity, and severe habitual drunkenness. Each special court had three members: a district judge, a local public health official, and a physician deemed to be expert in making the evaluations of the individuals thought to be at risk.
>
> The scale of the eugenic sterilization program in Nazi Germany dwarfed those in all other nations, including the United States. In 1934 more than 200 courts received 84,500 petitions to sterilize. These were sometimes filed by doctors or local public health officials, but often they were filed by one family member about another. In one of the more extreme examples of patriotism, substantial numbers of deaf persons volunteered to be sterilized as a show of support for the "fatherland." Of the 64,499 petitions that were heard, the courts decided for sterilization in 56,244 for a eugenic conviction rate of 87 percent. By 1935 more than 150,000 sterilizations had been approved, many based on judicial proceedings that must have taken under an hour.

Over the ensuing years the scope of the law was broadened. For example, in 1934 it was amended to apply to non-Germans living in Germany. During the 1940s people were often sterilized on the weakest of pretenses, such as being half-Jewish. In 1951, the Central Association of Sterilized People in West Germany estimated that the Nazi programs had sterilized 3,500,000 persons, although it is not possible to document the claim.

Philip R. Reilly, Eugenics, Ethics, Sterilization Laws, Encyclopedia of Ethical, Legal, and Policy Issues in Biotechnology 210 (Thomas H. Murray & Maxwell J. Mehlman, eds. 2000).

10.   The American eugenics movement was a major influence on the Nazis. Hitler was in jail and working on *Mein Kampf* in 1924 when he read about the Virginia sterilization statute, and a sterilization provision was the first law the Reichstag enacted after he gained power. Hitler's intent originally was to use sterilization to eliminate inferior populations, but once the war started and he needed hospital beds for wounded soldiers, he decided to empty the mental wards by killing the patients. This policy then grew to encompass the extermination of other undesirables, including Jews and Gypsies.

11.   The German sterilization law was based on a "prototypical Model Sterilization Law" drafted by Harry Laughlin, the director of the Eugenics Record Office at Cold Spring Harbor, Long Island. As noted in the Reilly excerpt, Laughlin was held in such high regard by the Nazis that he received an honorary degree from the University of Heidelberg in 1934.

12.   Although eugenics-based sterilization in the United States declined markedly after World War II, it did not disappear altogether. As Reilly reports (p. 211), between 1948 and 1955, approximately 186 women were sterilized in North Carolina. In 1958, Georgia, North Carolina and Virginia reported 574 sterilizations, 76 percent of the national total. At one South Carolina facility for the incurably mentally ill, 104 inmates, 102 of whom were black, were sterilized between 1949 and 1960. From 1970 to 1974, 23 sterilizations were performed in North Carolina state institutions, although most often at the request of relatives concerned that an inmate would become pregnant against her will.

13.   For more historical information about the eugenics movement in America, see Paul A. Lombardo, Three Generations, No Imbeciles: Eugenics, the Supreme Court, and Buck v. Bell (2008); Paul A. Lombardo, 'The American Breed': Nazi Eugenics and the Origins of the Pioneer Fund, 65 Albany L. Rev. 743–830 (2002), Paul A. Lombardo, Taking Eugenics Seriously: Three Generations of ??? are Enough?, 30 Fla. St. U. L. Rev. 191–218 (Winter 2003), and Michael J. Malinowski, Choosing the Genetic Makeup of Children: Our Eugenics Past–Present, and Future? 36 Conn. L. Rev. 125–224 (2003).

14.   On May 2, 2002, the Commonwealth of Virginia unveiled a highway marker to celebrate the 75th anniversary of Buck v. Bell. The text of the marker reads:

In 1924, Virginia, like a majority of states then, enacted eugenic sterilization laws. Virginia's law allowed state institutions to operate on individuals to prevent conception of what were believed to be "genetically inferior'' children. Charlottesville native Carrie Buck (1906–1983), involuntarily committed to a state facility near Lynchburg, was chosen as the first person to be sterilized under the new law. The U.S. Supreme Court, in *Buck v. Bell*, on May 2, 1927, affirmed the Virginia law. After Buck more than 8,000 other Virginians were sterilized before the most relevant parts of the act were repealed in 1974. Later evidence eventually showed that Buck and many others had no "hereditary defects." She is buried south of here.

At the ceremony, Governor Mark Warner apologized, stating: "The eugenics movement was a shameful effort in which state government never should have been involved." In 2002, Oregon Governor John Kitzhaber also apologized for the forced sterilization of more than 2,500 Oregonians between 1917 and 1983.

POE v. LYNCHBURG TRAINING SCHOOL & HOSPITAL
518 F.Supp. 789 (W.D.Va.1981).

TURK, J.

This case is filed as an individual and class action suit challenging the involuntary sterilization of a number of men and women by Virginia state officials acting pursuant to a statute enacted in 1924 by the Commonwealth of Virginia. The complaint also challenges the constitutionality of the purported refusal of appropriate Virginia state officials to notify all those persons who received such surgery as to their medical status and medical alternatives. In short, plaintiffs allege that many of those who were involuntarily sterilized are still unaware of the reason for their infertility as well as the medical ramifications of the procedure.

* * *

In 1924, the Commonwealth enacted legislation providing for the sexual sterilization of "mental defectives" in certain cases. 1924 Acts of Assembly, Chap. 394. As set forth in defendants' memorandum in support of the motion to dismiss, the statute specifically prescribed certain preliminary procedural steps including notification to the individual, or his or her parent, guardian, or committee as might be appropriate. Shortly after enactment of the statute, the constitutionality of the entire practice was tested in court, and the controversy eventually reached the United States Supreme Court. In Buck v. Bell (1927), the United States Supreme Court held that the statute was not violative of any constitutionally guaranteed rights. However, in 1974, the involuntary sterilization statute was repealed. 1974 Acts of Assembly, Chap. 296. The parties agree that the Commonwealth has no statutory procedures permitting involuntary sterilization at the current time.

Several of the individual plaintiffs in this case underwent involuntary sterilization pursuant to the statute. These plaintiffs also purport to sue on behalf of all persons who have been involuntarily sterilized at governmental institutions in Virginia under color of state law.

* * *

Plaintiffs' prayer for relief essentially tracks the contentions set forth in their complaint. Stated briefly, plaintiffs seek as follows:

1. Entry of a judgment declaring that:

(a) the forced surgical sterilization of the sterilized class by Virginia state officials and agencies violated the Fourteenth Amendment, 42 U.S.C. § 1983, and the common law of Virginia; and

(b) defendants' subsequent failure to notify and prevent further harm to members of the sterilized class violates the Fourteenth Amendment, 42 U.S.C. § 1983, the Developmentally Disabled Assistance and Bill of Rights Act, and the common law of Virginia.

2. Entry of an Order enjoining defendants from authorizing or conducting any surgical sterilization without prior informed consent; and

3. Entry of an Order requiring defendants to provide adequate notice to all members of the sterilized class of the facts and circumstances of their involuntary surgical sterilization, including the effects and possible reversibility of the operations, and to provide such medical, surgical, and psychological assistance as is necessary to prevent further harm to members of the sterilized class, including operations to reverse the sterilization where possible.

Plaintiffs also seek compensation for costs, attorneys' fees, and other relief as may prove appropriate.

Defendants' motion to dismiss for failure to state a claim is based on the assertions that the requested relief is barred by virtue of the Eleventh Amendment; that the complaint does not allege an actual case or controversy; and that the action is barred by virtue of the applicable statute of limitations.

* * *

The court has reached the conclusion that the motion must be granted in part and denied in part. Specifically, as to the different forms of relief sought by the complaint and as enumerated above, the court will enter an order granting the motion as to sections 1(a) and 2 of the prayer, and denying the motion as to sections 1(b) and 3.

* * *

Regardless of whatever philosophical and sociological valuation may be made regarding involuntary sterilizations in terms of current mores and social thought, the fact remains that the general practice and procedure under the old Virginia statute were upheld by the highest court in the land in Buck v. Bell, supra. It is no answer for the plaintiff to allude to changing patterns of social and constitutional thought as a ground for reopening the inquiry. Since 1974, well before the filing of the instant action, Virginia has had no involuntary sterilization statute. In short, this court has neither the authority nor the occasion to undertake an evaluation as to the constitutionality of the old Virginia statute permitting forced sterilizations. * * *[1]

Given the repeal of the involuntary sterilization statute, it is also apparent that plaintiffs are not entitled to an order, as sought in section 2 of the prayer, enjoining defendants from authorizing or conducting any surgical sterilization without prior informed consent. The complaint gives absolutely no indication that any of the defendants are likely to undertake such action in the future.

* * *

The court now directs its attention to those portions of plaintiffs' complaint and prayer dealing with defendants' alleged failure to notify plaintiffs of the fact of their sterilization and to otherwise provide information and assistance as might be appropriate. As suggested above, the old Virginia statute contained provisions which insured, at least in theory, that persons considered for involuntary sterilization, and their representatives, would be well advised prior to the surgery as to its purpose.

Plaintiffs have alleged facts which indicate that in at least some instances, such notification was not provided and that potential candidates were affirmatively misled as to the purpose of the surgery. Plaintiffs contend that many such persons who were inadequately or inaccurately informed have suffered and continue to suffer medical, emotional, and mental problems, arising in large part from unsuccessful and uninformed attempts to deal with their infertility. Plaintiffs contend that defendants continue to refuse to notify and inform all those affected persons despite the fact that defendants now have reason to believe that some involuntarily sterilized persons were not properly notified at the time of their hospitalization. In short, plaintiffs contend that, in actual practice, the notification provisions of the statute were often not honored and that state officials have continued to perpetrate the deprivation through their subsequent refusal to notify all involuntarily sterilized persons as to their status. To the extent that the complaint sets forth such allegations, and to the extent of sections 1(b) and 3 of the prayer for relief, the court must conclude that the complaint states a claim.

---

1. The court recognizes that in making these arguments, and in attempting to distinguish Buck v. Bell, supra, plaintiffs have relied primarily on what they perceive as a constitutional deficiency in the procedural aspects of the old Virginia statute. The court also recognizes that Buck dealt with an attack to the statute's substance rather than its procedure. Nevertheless, in delivering the court's opinion in Buck, Justice Holmes specifically noted that " ... there is no doubt that ... plaintiff in error has had due process of law." 274 U.S. at 207, 47 S. Ct. at 584. The court notes that plaintiffs have also alleged a deviation between the stated procedure and the actual procedure under the statute. While these allegations will be considered in more detail in the context of the contention of a "continuing deprivation" due to failure to notify, the court notes for purposes of this argument that, at the most, plaintiffs might establish that on some occasions, certain officials acted inconsistently with the procedural requirements of the statute. Such a circumstance certainly would not justify entry of a declaration holding all sterilizations under the statute to be illegal as per plaintiffs' prayer. Moreover, an allegation of such past deviations, standing alone, does not remotely suggest the existence of a present case and controversy, absent a viable demand for monetary damages and absent identification of any parties defendant who could now be held answerable for such damages.

NOTE

The *Poe* case was settled in 1983 when state officials agreed to attempt to locate all surviving victims and provide a small amount of compensation.

RELF v. WEINBERGER

372 F.Supp. 1196 (D.D.C. 1974), vacated as moot, 565 F.2d 722 (D.C. Cir. 1977).

GESELL, J.

These two related cases, which have been consolidated with the consent of all parties, challenge the statutory authorization and constitutionality of regulations of the Department of Health, Education and Welfare (HEW) governing human sterilizations under programs and projects funded by the Department's Public Health Service and its Social and Rehabilitation Service. 39 Fed. Reg. 4730–34 (1974). Plaintiffs are the National Welfare Rights Organization (NWRO), suing on behalf of its 125,000 members, and five individual women, proceeding by class action on behalf of all poor persons subject to involuntary sterilization under the challenged regulations. Defendants are the Secretary of HEW, under whose authority the regulations were issued, 42 U.S.C. § 216, and two high-level HEW officials charged with the administration of federal family planning funds.

The issues have been fully briefed and argued, and are now before the Court on separate motions for summary judgment by the respective plaintiffs and on the Secretary's motion for dismissal or summary judgment. Declaratory and injunctive relief is sought in both cases. The effective date of the regulations has been voluntarily deferred by the Secretary at the Court's request until March 18, 1974, to facilitate resolution of these issues.

Congress has authorized the funding of a full range of family planning services under two basic procedures. The Public Health Service administers federal grants to state health agencies and to public and private projects for the provision of family planning services to the poor, 42 U.S.C. §§ 300 et seq., 708(a), and the Social and Rehabilitation Service provides funds for such services under the Medicaid and Aid to Families of Dependent Children programs, 42 U.S.C. §§ 601 et seq., 1396 et seq.

Although there is no specific reference to sterilization in any of the family planning statutes nor in the legislative history surrounding their passage, the Secretary has considered sterilization to fall within the general statutory scheme and Congress has been made aware of this position. But until recently, there were no particular rules or regulations governing the circumstances under which sterilizations could be funded under these statutes.

Sterilization of females or males is irreversible. [This is not necessarily the case now.—Eds.] The total number of these sterilizations is clearly of national significance. Few realize that over 16 percent of the married couples in this country between the ages of 20 and 39 have had a sterilization operation. Over the last few years, an estimated 100,000 to 150,000 low-income persons have been sterilized annually under federally funded programs. Virtually all of these people have been adults: only about 2,000 to 3,000 per year have been under 21 years of age and fewer than 300 have been under 18. There are no statistics in the record indicating what percentage of these patients were mentally incompetent.

Although Congress has been insistent that all family planning programs function on a purely voluntary basis, there is uncontroverted evidence in the record that minors and other incompetents have been sterilized with federal funds and that an indefinite number of poor people have been improperly coerced into accepting a sterilization operation under the threat that various federally supported welfare benefits would be withdrawn unless they submitted to irreversible sterilization. Patients receiving Medicaid assistance at childbirth are evidently the most frequent targets of this pressure, as the experiences of plaintiffs Waters and Walker illustrate. Mrs. Waters was actually refused medical assistance by her attending physician unless she submitted to a tubal ligation after the birth. Other examples were documented.

When such deplorable incidents began to receive nationwide public attention due to the experience of the Relf sisters in Alabama, the Secretary took steps to restrict the circumstances under which recipients of federal family planning funds could conduct sterilization operations. On August 3, 1973, the Department published in the Federal Register a notice of Guidelines for Sterilization Procedures under HEW Supported Programs. 38 Fed. Reg. 20930 (1973). The notice directed that the policies set forth in the guidelines be implemented through regulations to be issued by the departmental agencies administering programs which provide federal financial assistance for family planning services. Notices of proposed rule making were duly published in the Federal Register on September 21, 1973. 38 Fed. Reg. 26459 (1973). Interested persons were given an opportunity to participate in the rule making by submitting comments on the proposed regulations. Approximately 300 comments, including those of plaintiff NWRO, were received and reviewed by the Department. The final regulations here under attack were issued on February 6, 1974.

These regulations provide that projects and programs receiving PHS or SRS funds, whether for family planning or purely medical services, shall neither perform nor arrange for the performance of a nontherapeutic sterilization unless certain procedures are carried out. These vary depending upon whether the patient is, under state law, a legally competent adult, a legally competent person under the age of 18, a legally incompetent minor, or a mental incompetent. Briefly, they are as follows:

(1) Legally competent adults must give their "informed consent" to sterilization. Such consent must be evidenced by a written and signed document indicating, inter alia, that the patient is aware of the benefits

and costs of sterilization and of the fact that he may withdraw from the operation without losing federal benefits. 42 CFR § 50.202(f); 45 CFR § 205.35(a)(2)(ii).

(2) Legally competent persons under the age of 18 must also give such written consent. In these situations, a special Review Committee of independent persons from the community must also have determined that the proposed sterilization is in the best interest of the patient, taking into consideration (a) the expected mental and physical impact of pregnancy and motherhood on the patient, if female, or the expected mental impact of fatherhood, if male, and (b) the expected immediate and long-term mental and physical impact of sterilization on the patient. 42 CFR § 50.206(a); 45 CFR § 205.35(a)(4)(i). The Review Committee must also (a) review appropriate medical, social and psychological information concerning the patient, including the age of the patient, alternative family planning methods, and the adequacy of consent, and (b) interview the patient, both parents of the patient (if available), and such other persons as in its judgment will contribute pertinent information. 42 CFR § 50.206(b)(1, 2); 45 CFR § 205.35(a)(4)(i)(A, B). However, parental consent is not required. 42 CFR § 50.203(c); 45 CFR § 205.35(a)(5)(ii).

(3) Legally incompetent minors must be afforded the above safeguards, and, in addition, a state court of competent jurisdiction must determine that the proposed sterilization is in the best interest of the patient. 42 CFR § 50.203(c); 45 CFR § 205.35(a)(1)(iv)(A, B).

(4) The sterilization of mental incompetents of all ages must also be sanctioned by a Review Committee and a court. However, personal consent is not required—it is enough that the patient's "representative" requests sterilization. 42 CFR § 50.203(a); 45 CFR § 205.35(a) (1). Although defendants interpret the term "representative" to mean a person empowered under state law to consent to the sterilization on behalf of the patient, no such definition appears in the regulations themselves.

Plaintiffs do not oppose the voluntary sterilization of poor persons under federally funded programs. However, they contend that these regulations are both illegal and arbitrary because they authorize involuntary sterilizations, without statutory or constitutional justification. They argue forcefully that sterilization of minors or mental incompetents is necessarily involuntary in the nature of things. Further, they claim that sterilization of competent adults under these regulations can be undertaken without insuring that the request for sterilization is in actuality voluntary. The Secretary defends the regulations and insists that only "voluntary" sterilization is permitted under their terms.

* * *

While plaintiffs invoke both statutory and constitutional principles, relying on the Fourth, Fifth, Sixth, Eighth and Ninth Amendments to the Constitution in support of their position, the issues tendered may be readily resolved simply by resort to the underlying statutes. Accordingly, no occasion exists to consider the related constitutional claims.

For the reasons developed below, the Court finds that the Secretary has no statutory authority under the family planning sections of the Social Security or Public Health Services Acts to fund the sterilization of any person incompetent under state law to consent to such an operation, whether because of minority or of mental deficiency. It also finds that the challenged regulations are arbitrary and unreasonable in that they fail to implement the congressional command that federal family planning funds not be used to coerce indigent patients into submitting to sterilization. In short, federally assisted family planning sterilizations are permissible only with the voluntary, knowing and uncoerced consent of individuals competent to give such consent. This result requires an injunction against substantial portions of the proposed regulations and their revision to insure that all sterilizations funded under the family planning sections are voluntary in the full sense of that term and that sterilization of incompetent minors and adults is prevented. The dispute with regard to minors and mental incompetents centers around two aspects of the statutory language. On the one hand, Congress included in every section mentioning family planning a requirement that such services be voluntarily requested. 42 U.S.C. §§ 300a–5, 602(a)(15), 708(a), 1396d(a)(4). On the other hand, these sections purport to offer family planning services to all poor people and two of them specifically include minors. 42 U.S.C. §§ 602(a)(15), 1396d(a)(4). The Secretary argues that this juxtaposition indicates that Congress intended that minors personally and incompetents through their representatives would be able to consent to sterilization under these sections. That conclusion is unwarranted.

Although the term "voluntary" is nowhere defined in the statutes under consideration, it is frequently encountered in the law. Even its dictionary definition assumes an exercise of free will and clearly precludes the existence of coercion or force. * * * And its use in the statutory and decisional law, at least when important human rights are at stake, entails a requirement that the individual have at his disposal the information necessary to make his decision and the mental competence to appreciate the significance of that information.

* * *

No person who is mentally incompetent can meet these standards, nor can the consent of a representative, however sufficient under state law, impute voluntariness to the individual actually undergoing irreversible sterilization. Minors would also appear to lack the knowledge, maturity and judgment to satisfy these standards with regard to such an important issue, whatever may be their competence to rely on devices or medication that temporarily frustrates procreation. This is the reasoning that provides the basis for the nearly universal common law and statutory rule

that minors and mental incompetents cannot consent to medical operations.

* * *

The statutory references to minors and mental incompetents do not
contradict this conclusion, for they appear only in the context of family
planning services in general. Minors, for example, are not legally incompetent for all purposes, and many girls of child-bearing age are undoubtedly
sufficiently aware of the relevant considerations to use temporary contraceptives that intrude far less on fundamental rights. However, the Secretary has not demonstrated and the Court cannot find that Congress
deemed such children capable of voluntarily consenting to an irreversible
operation involving the basic human right to procreate. Nor can the Court
find, in the face of repeated warnings concerning voluntariness, that
Congress authorized the imposition of such a serious deprivation upon
mental incompetents at the will of an unspecified "representative."

The regulations also fail to provide the procedural safeguards necessary to insure that even competent adults voluntarily request sterilization.
Plaintiffs would require an elaborate hearing process prior to the operation to remedy this problem. The Secretary, however, has determined that
the consent document procedure set forth in the existing regulations is
adequate in most instances to insure a knowledgeable decision, and the
Court finds that this determination is not unreasonable. In one respect,
however, the consent procedure must be improved. Even a fully informed
individual cannot make a "voluntary" decision concerning sterilization if
he has been subjected to coercion from doctors or project officers. Despite
specific statutory language forbidding the recipients of federal family
planning funds to threaten a cutoff of program benefits unless the
individual submits to sterilization and despite clear evidence that such
coercion is actually being applied, the challenged regulations contain no
clear safeguard against this abuse. Although the required consent document must state that the patient can withdraw his consent to sterilization
without losing other program benefits, there is nothing to prohibit the use
of such coercion to extract the initial consent. In order to prevent express
or implied threats, which would obviate the Secretary's entire framework
of procedural safeguards, and to insure compliance with the statutory
language, the Court concludes that the regulations must also be amended
to require that individuals seeking sterilization be orally informed at the
very outset that no federal benefits can be withdrawn because of a failure
to accept sterilization. This guarantee must also appear prominently at
the top of the consent document already required by the regulations. To
permit sterilization without this essential safeguard is an unreasonable
and arbitrary interpretation of the congressional mandate.

Since these conclusions are based on statutory rather than constitutional grounds, the Court need not reach the question of whether involuntary sterilization could be funded by Congress. It is sufficient to note that
there is no indication whatever that Congress intended to do so under the

existing legislation, and such an intent will not be lightly assumed in light of the fundamental interests at stake. The present statutes were passed to facilitate only voluntary family planning and thus to assist the individual in the exercise of his voluntary right to govern his own procreation. Involuntary sterilization is not only distinguishable from these services, but diametrically so. It invades rather than compliments the right to procreate.

This controversy has arisen during a period of rapid change in the field of birth control. In recent years, through the efforts of dedicated proponents of family planning, birth control information and services have become widely available. Aided by the growing acceptance of family planning, medical science has steadily improved and diversified the techniques of birth prevention and control. Advancements in artificial insemination and in the understanding of genetic attributes are also affecting the decision to bear children. There are even suggestions in the scientific literature that the sex of children may soon be subject to parental control. And over this entire area lies the specter of overpopulation, with its possible impact upon the food supply, interpersonal relations, privacy, and the enjoyment of our "inalienable rights."

Surely the Federal Government must move cautiously in this area, under well-defined policies determined by Congress after full consideration of constitutional and far-reaching social implications. The dividing line between family planning and eugenics is murky. And yet the Secretary, through the regulations at issue, seeks to sanction one of the most drastic methods of population control—the involuntary irreversible sterilization of men and women—without any legislative guidance. Whatever might be the merits of limiting irresponsible reproduction, which each year places increasing numbers of unwanted or mentally defective children into tax-supported institutions, it is for Congress and not individual social workers and physicians to determine the manner in which federal funds should be used to support such a program. We should not drift into a policy which has unfathomed implications and which permanently deprives unwilling or immature citizens of their ability to procreate without adequate legal safeguards and a legislative determination of the appropriate standards in light of the general welfare and of individual rights.

NOTES AND QUESTIONS

1. The *Relf* case ultimately was vacated after the Department of Health and Human Services adopted regulations conforming to the district court's order. Relf v. Weinberger, 565 F.2d 722 (D.C. Cir.1977).

2. How do the protections mandated by the court in *Relf* differ from those called for under the Virginia statute at issue in Buck? Are the protections in *Relf* sufficient? Are there any others that could be provided?

3. The minors sterilized with federal funds that Judge Gesell referred to in *Relf* included Mary Alice and Minnie Lee Relf, black children aged 12 and

14 respectively, who were sterilized without their knowledge or consent by authorities in Montgomery, Alabama. An older sister, Katie, 17, avoided surgery only by physically resisting. The children's mother, who was unable to read, had placed an "X" on the consent document without knowing what it said. She assumed, she explained later, that she was merely authorizing continued use of Depo–Provera injections, which the girls had been receiving as an experimental contraceptive. For more details on the Relfs and similar cases, see Donna Franklin, Beyond the Tuskegee Apology, Washington Post, May 29, 1997, at A23. How do the protections mandated by the court in *Relf* prevent this from happening again?

4.   As the administration of Depo–Provera to the Relf children suggests, compulsory contraception is a eugenic alternative to compulsory sterilization. After the FDA approved Norplant, a surgically-implanted, long-lasting contraceptive, legislators in a number of states proposed linking Norplant use to eligibility for welfare benefits. Although no such requirement has been adopted, Norplant has been covered under all state Medicaid programs.

5.   The United States and Germany are not the only countries to have engaged in eugenics-based sterilizations. Between 1935 and 1976, approximately 60,000 people, mostly women, were sterilized in Sweden. They were typically poor, had learning disabilities, or were non-Nordic, and were labeled as genetically or racially "inferior." One of the major justifications for this sterilization program was that it would reduce the cost of the Swedish welfare state by reducing the number of people who would have to be supported. One woman is reported to have been sterilized because she could not master her confirmation studies well enough to satisfy her priest. Another was judged to be mentally slow as a child because she could not read the blackboard; it later turned out that she merely needed glasses. For a fuller account of the Swedish program, see Dan Balz, Sweden Sterilized Thousands of "Useless" Citizens for Decades, Washington Post, August 29, 1997, at A1. In 1999, the Swedish government agreed to pay $20,780 to each surviving person who had been sterilized.

6.   In 1994, the Chinese national legislature passed a law entitled "Law of the People's Republic of China on Maternal and Infant Health Care." The statute requires every couple to undergo a premarital medical examination, and where this shows "genetic disease of a serious nature which is considered to be inappropriate for child bearing from a medical point of view, the two may be married only if both sides agree to take long term contraceptive precautions or to take ligation operation for sterility." Moreover, termination of pregnancy must be advised when a fetus has a "defect of a serious nature" or a "genetic disease of a serious nature." "Relevant mental diseases" include schizophrenia and manic depressive psychosis. The Chinese legislation is described in an editorial by Martin Bobrow, head of the genetics department at Cambridge University, Redrafted Chinese Law Remains Eugenic, 32 J. Med. Genetics 409 (1995).

A related use of compulsory sterilization is to punish the commission of a crime. The Supreme Court had occasion to consider the constitutionality of such an approach in the following case.

SKINNER v. OKLAHOMA
316 U.S. 535 (1942).

MR. JUSTICE DOUGLAS delivered the opinion of the Court.

This case touches a sensitive and important area of human rights. Oklahoma deprives certain individuals of a right which is basic to the perpetuation of a race—the right to have offspring. Oklahoma has decreed the enforcement of its law against petitioner, overruling his claim that it violated the Fourteenth Amendment. Because that decision raised grave and substantial constitutional questions, we granted the petition for certiorari.

The statute involved is Oklahoma's Habitual Criminal Sterilization Act. Okla. Stat. Ann. Tit. 57, §§ 171, et seq.; L. 1935, pp. 94 et seq. That Act defines an "habitual criminal" as a person who, having been convicted two or more times for crimes "amounting to felonies involving moral turpitude," either in an Oklahoma court or in a court of any other State, is thereafter convicted of such a felony in Oklahoma and is sentenced to a term of imprisonment in an Oklahoma penal institution. Machinery is provided for the institution by the Attorney General of a proceeding against such a person in the Oklahoma courts for a judgment that such person shall be rendered sexually sterile. §§ 176, 177. Notice, an opportunity to be heard, and the right to a jury trial are provided. §§ 177–181. The issues triable in such a proceeding are narrow and confined. If the court or jury finds that the defendant is an "habitual criminal" and that he "may be rendered sexually sterile without detriment to his or her general health," then the court "shall render judgment to the effect that said defendant be rendered sexually sterile" (§ 182) by the operation of vasectomy in case of a male, and of salpingectomy in case of a female. § 174. Only one other provision of the Act is material here, and that is § 195, which provides that "offenses arising out of the violation of the prohibitory laws, revenue acts, embezzlement, or political offenses, shall not come or be considered within the terms of this Act."

Petitioner was convicted in 1926 of the crime of stealing chickens, and was sentenced to the Oklahoma State Reformatory. In 1929 he was convicted of the crime of robbery with firearms, and was sentenced to the reformatory. In 1934 he was convicted again of robbery with firearms, and was sentenced to the penitentiary. He was confined there in 1935 when the Act was passed. In 1936 the Attorney General instituted proceedings against him. Petitioner in his answer challenged the Act as unconstitutional by reason of the Fourteenth Amendment. A jury trial was had. The court instructed the jury that the crimes of which petitioner had been convicted were felonies involving moral turpitude, and that the only question for the jury was whether the operation of vasectomy could be performed on petitioner without detriment to his general health. The jury found that it could be. A judgment directing that the operation of vasectomy be performed on petitioner was affirmed by the Supreme Court of Oklahoma by a five to four decision.

Several objections to the constitutionality of the Act have been pressed upon us. It is urged that the Act cannot be sustained as an exercise of the police power, in view of the state of scientific authorities respecting inheritability of criminal traits. It is argued that due process is lacking because, under this Act, unlike the Act upheld in Buck v. Bell, 274 U.S. 200, the defendant is given no opportunity to be heard on the issue as to whether he is the probable potential parent of socially undesirable offspring. It is also suggested that the Act is penal in character and that the sterilization provided for is cruel and unusual punishment and violative of the Fourteenth Amendment. We pass those points without intimating an opinion on them, for there is a feature of the Act which clearly condemns it. That is, its failure to meet the requirements of the equal protection clause of the Fourteenth Amendment. We do not stop to point out all of the inequalities in this Act. A few examples will suffice. In Oklahoma, grand larceny is a felony. Okla. Stats. Ann. Tit. 21, §§ 1705, 5. Larceny is grand larceny when the property taken exceeds $20 in value. Id. § 1704. Embezzlement is punishable "in the manner prescribed for feloniously stealing property of the value of that embezzled." Id. § 1462. Hence, he who embezzles property worth more than $20 is guilty of a felony. A clerk who appropriates over $20 from his employer's till (id. § 1456) and a stranger who steals the same amount are thus both guilty of felonies. If the latter repeats his act and is convicted three times, he may be sterilized. But the clerk is not subject to the pains and penalties of the Act no matter how large his embezzlements nor how frequent his convictions. A person who enters a chicken coop and steals chickens commits a felony (id. § 1719); and he may be sterilized if he is thrice convicted. If, however, he is a bailee of the property and fraudulently appropriates it, he is an embezzler. Id. § 1455. Hence, no matter how habitual his proclivities for embezzlement are and no matter how often his conviction, he may not be sterilized. Thus, the nature of the two crimes is intrinsically the same and they are punishable in the same manner. Furthermore, the line between them follows close distinctions—distinctions comparable to those highly technical ones which shaped the common law as to "trespass" or "taking." There may be larceny by fraud rather than embezzlement even where the owner of the personal property delivers it to the defendant, if the latter has at that time "a fraudulent intention to make use of the possession as a means of converting such property to his own use, and does so convert it." If the fraudulent intent occurs later and the defendant converts the property, he is guilty of embezzlement. Whether a particular act is larceny by fraud or embezzlement thus turns not on the intrinsic quality of the act but on when the felonious intent arose—a question for the jury under appropriate instructions.

It was stated in Buck v. Bell, that the claim that state legislation violates the equal protection clause of the Fourteenth Amendment is "the usual last resort of constitutional arguments." Under our constitutional system the States in determining the reach and scope of particular legislation need not provide "abstract symmetry." They may mark and set apart the classes and types of problems according to the needs and as dictated or suggested by experience. It was in that connection that Mr. Justice Holmes, speaking for the Court in Bain Peanut Co. v. Pinson, 282 U.S. 499, 501, stated, "We must remember that the machinery of government would not work if it were not allowed a little play in its joints." Only recently we reaffirmed the view that the equal protection clause does not prevent the legislature from recognizing "degrees of evil" by our ruling in Tigner v. Texas, 310 U.S. 141, 147, that "the Constitution does not require things which are different in fact or opinion to be treated in law as though they were the same." Thus, if we had here only a question as to a State's classification of crimes, such as embezzlement or larceny, no substantial federal question would be raised. For a State is not constrained in the exercise of its police power to ignore experience which marks a class of offenders or a family of offenses for special treatment. Nor is it prevented by the equal protection clause from confining "its restrictions to those classes of cases where the need is deemed to be clearest." As stated in Buck v. Bell, " . . . the law does all that is needed when it does all that it can, indicates a policy, applies it to all within the lines, and seeks to bring within the lines all similarly situated so far and so fast as its means allow."

But the instant legislation runs afoul of the equal protection clause, though we give Oklahoma that large deference which the rule of the foregoing cases requires. We are dealing here with legislation which involves one of the basic civil rights of man. Marriage and procreation are fundamental to the very existence and survival of the race. The power to sterilize, if exercised, may have subtle, far-reaching and devastating effects. In evil or reckless hands it can cause races or types which are inimical to the dominant group to wither and disappear. There is no redemption for the individual whom the law touches. Any experiment which the State conducts is to his irreparable injury. He is forever deprived of a basic liberty. We mention these matters not to reexamine the scope of the police power of the States. We advert to them merely in emphasis of our view that strict scrutiny of the classification which a State makes in a sterilization law is essential, lest unwittingly, or otherwise, invidious discriminations are made against groups or types of individuals in violation of the constitutional guaranty of just and equal laws. The guaranty of "equal protection of the laws is a pledge of the protection of equal laws." When the law lays an unequal hand on those who have committed intrinsically the same quality of offense and sterilizes one and not the other, it has made as invidious a discrimination as if it had selected a particular race or nationality for oppressive treatment. Sterilization of those who have thrice committed grand larceny, with immunity for those who are embezzlers, is a clear, pointed, unmistakable discrimination. Oklahoma makes no attempt to say that he who commits larceny by trespass or trick or fraud has biologically inheritable traits which he who commits embezzlement lacks. Oklahoma's line between larceny by fraud and embezzlement is determined, as we have noted, "with reference to the time when the fraudulent intent to convert the property to the taker's own use" arises. We have not the slightest basis for inferring that that line has any significance in eugenics, nor that the inheritability of criminal traits follows the neat legal distinctions which the law has marked between those two offenses. In terms of fines and imprisonment, the crimes of larceny and embezzlement rate the same under the Oklahoma code. Only when it comes to sterilization are the pains and penalties of the law different. The equal protection clause would indeed be a formula of empty words if such conspicuously artificial lines could be drawn. In Buck v. Bell, the Virginia statute was upheld though it applied only to feeble-minded persons in institutions of the State. But it was pointed out that "so far as the operations enable those who otherwise must be kept confined to be returned to the world, and thus open the asylum to others, the equality aimed at will be more nearly reached." Here there is no such saving feature. Embezzlers are forever free. Those who steal or take in other ways are not. If such a classification were permitted, the technical common law concept of a "trespass" based on distinctions which are "very largely dependent upon history for explanation" could readily become a rule of human genetics.

* * *

Reversed.

MR. CHIEF JUSTICE STONE, concurring:

I concur in the result, but I am not persuaded that we are aided in reaching it by recourse to the equal protection clause. If Oklahoma may resort generally to the sterilization of criminals on the assumption that their propensities are transmissible to future generations by inheritance, I seriously doubt that the equal protection clause requires it to apply the measure to all criminals in the first instance, or to none.

Moreover, if we must presume that the legislature knows—what science has been unable to ascertain—that the criminal tendencies of any class of habitual offenders are transmissible regardless of the varying mental characteristics of its individuals, I should suppose that we must likewise presume that the legislature, in its wisdom, knows that the criminal tendencies of some classes of offenders are more likely to be transmitted than those of others. And so I think the real question we have to consider is not one of equal protection, but whether the wholesale condemnation of a class to such an invasion of personal liberty, without opportunity to any individual to show that his is not the type of case which would justify resort to it, satisfies the demands of due process.

There are limits to the extent to which the presumption of constitutionality can be pressed, especially where the liberty of the person is concerned and there the presumption is resorted to only to dispense with a procedure which the ordinary dictates of prudence would seem to demand for the protection of the individual from arbitrary action. Although petitioner here was given a hearing to ascertain whether sterilization would be detrimental to his health, he was given none to discover whether his criminal tendencies are of an inheritable type. Undoubtedly a state may, after appropriate inquiry, constitutionally interfere with the personal liberty of the individual to prevent the transmission by inheritance of his socially injurious tendencies. Buck v. Bell, 274 U.S. 200. But until now we have not been called upon to say that it may do so without giving him a hearing and opportunity to challenge the existence as to him of the only facts which could justify so drastic a measure.

Science has found and the law has recognized that there are certain types of mental deficiency associated with delinquency which are inheritable. But the State does not contend—nor can there be any pretense—that either common knowledge or experience, or scientific investigation, has given assurance that the criminal tendencies of any class of habitual offenders are universally or even generally inheritable. In such circumstances, inquiry whether such is the fact in the case of any particular individual cannot rightly be dispensed with. Whether the procedure by which a statute carries its mandate into execution satisfies due process is a matter of judicial cognizance. A law which condemns, without hearing, all the individuals of a class to so harsh a measure as the present because some or even many merit condemnation, is lacking in the first principles of due process. And so, while the state may protect itself from the demonstrably inheritable tendencies of the individual which are injurious to society, the most elementary notions of due process would seem to require it to take appropriate steps to safeguard the liberty of the individual by affording him, before he is condemned to an irreparable injury in his person, some opportunity to show that he is without such inheritable tendencies. The state is called on to sacrifice no permissible end when it is required to reach its objective by a reasonable and just procedure adequate to safeguard rights of the individual which concededly the Constitution protects.

MR. JUSTICE JACKSON concurring:

I join the CHIEF JUSTICE in holding that the hearings provided are too limited in the context of the present Act to afford due process of law. I also agree with the opinion of MR. JUSTICE DOUGLAS that the scheme of classification set forth in the Act denies equal protection of the law. I disagree with the opinion of each in so far as it rejects or minimizes the grounds taken by the other.

Perhaps to employ a broad and loose scheme of classification would be permissible if accompanied by the individual hearings indicated by the CHIEF JUSTICE. On the other hand, narrow classification with reference to the end to be accomplished by the Act might justify limiting individual hearings to the issue whether the individual belonged to a class so defined. Since this Act does not present these questions, I reserve judgment on them.

I also think the present plan to sterilize the individual in pursuit of a eugenic plan to eliminate from the race characteristics that are only vaguely identified and which in our present state of knowledge are uncertain as to transmissibility presents other constitutional questions of gravity. This Court has sustained such an experiment with respect to an imbecile, a person with definite and observable characteristics, where the condition had persisted through three generations and afforded grounds for the belief that it was transmissible and would continue to manifest itself in generations to come. Buck v. Bell, 274 U.S. 200.

There are limits to the extent to which a legislatively represented majority may conduct biological experiments at the expense of the dignity and personality and natural powers of a minority—even those who have been guilty of what the majority define as crimes. But this Act falls down before reaching this problem, which I mention only to avoid the implication that such a question may not exist because not discussed. On it I would also reserve judgment.

NOTES AND QUESTIONS

1. Under *Skinner,* what sorts of sterilization laws, if any, would survive constitutional challenge? What other governmental interventions involving genetics and the regulation of human reproduction would the decision in *Skinner* support? What interventions would be prohibited?

2. Compare *Skinner* with Buck v. Bell. Does *Skinner* overrule *Buck*? What language in Skinner can you cite to support your position?

3. Was the Oklahoma statute at issue in *Skinner* drafted to use sterilization as a punishment and deterrent for crimes or a eugenic strategy for reducing crimes in future generations?

4. Which constitutional theory, equal protection or due process, do you think provides the most appropriate basis for striking down the statute?

5. Why do you think thieves but not embezzlers were covered by the statute?

6. Although *Skinner* is often cited as a great anti-eugenics decision, note how the Douglas and Stone opinions incorporate eugenic language and rationale.

7. Justice Jackson's concurrence, in which he questioned the legitimacy of "biological experiments" is ironic. After World War II, Justice Jackson was appointed chief prosecutor for the Nuremberg trials.

8. In contrast to *Skinner,* where state law authorized sterilization as a punishment for committing a crime, sterilization and other restrictions on reproduction may also be employed to deter the commission of future crimes. For example, in 1996 California enacted a law authorizing voluntary chemical

or surgical castration for the first offense of child molesting and mandating castration as a condition of parole for repeat offenders. Cal. Penal Code § 645. Georgia, Florida, and Montana have adopted similar statutes. Chemical castration involves the use of Depo–Provera, a synthetic progesterone that decreases testosterone, causing a reduction in sex drive and an improved ability to control sexual fantasizing. For more on chemical castration, see Avital Stadler, Comment, California Injects New Life Into an Old Idea: Taking a Shot at Recidivism, Chemical Castration, and the Constitution, 46 Emory L. J. 1285 (1997). One judge conditioned parole for a convicted child abuser on surgical implantation of the contraceptive Norplant. The defendant challenged the requirement, but the case was dismissed as moot after other parole violations occurred.

9.   Are there other current examples of eugenics programs in the United States? What about government maternal and prenatal health care programs? What about the use of the courts to collect wrongful birth damages from health care professionals whose negligent failure to provide appropriate genetic counseling or testing results in the birth of a child with genetic diseases or abnormalities?

TAYLOR v. KURAPATI

600 N.W.2d 670 (Mich. App. 1999).

WHITBECK, J.

Plaintiffs Brandy and Brian Taylor, individually, and Brandy Taylor as next friend and mother of Shelby Taylor, a minor, appeal as of right the trial court's order granting summary disposition in favor of defendants Surender Kurapati, M.D., and Annapolis Hospital with respect to their wrongful birth and negligent infliction of emotional distress claims.

* * *

The Taylors filed their complaint in August 1996. The Taylors alleged that Brandy Taylor had a doctor-patient relationship with Kurapati, a specialist in radiology, and Annapolis. On April 19, 1994, Brandy Taylor gave birth to the couple's daughter, Shelby Taylor. Throughout her pregnancy, Brandy Taylor had been treated by Dr. Leela Suruli. Suruli had ordered that a routine ultrasound be performed in Brandy Taylor's second trimester. The ultrasound was conducted on December 4, 1993, and interpreted by Kurapati, an agent of Annapolis. Kurapati concluded that the pregnancy was seventeen weeks along, plus or minus two weeks, and that there were no visible abnormalities with the fetus. A second ultrasound was conducted on March 16, 1994, and interpreted by another physician, Dr. M.B. Cash. Cash indicated that the baby's femurs could not be adequately identified and believed that a high resolution ultrasound could be helpful for further investigation. Suruli told Brandy Taylor that the baby had short femur bones and would merely be shorter than average. Brandy Taylor decided not to have another ultrasound. Shelby Taylor was born on April 19, 1994, with ''gross anatomical deformities including missing right shoulder, fusion of left elbow, missing digits on left hand, missing femur on left leg and short femur on right." A study at the University of Michigan Hospital suggested that Shelby Taylor had femur-fibula-ulna syndrome.

In their complaint, the Taylors alleged that the standard of care in performing the initial ultrasound had been breached by Kurapati when he failed to locate all four limbs at the time of the ultrasound. The Taylors alleged that the ultrasound should have shown Shelby Taylor's disabilities and that the failure to reveal the disabilities deprived the Taylors of their right to make a reproductive decision regarding the pregnancy. In addition to their claim of medical malpractice, the Taylors also alleged that, because of defendants' negligence, they suffered emotional distress at witnessing the birth of their child.

* * *

This review of the elements of tort liability points up the extraordinary nature of the trial court's holding that the plaintiffs were entitled to no recovery as a matter of law. We have here a negligent, wrongful act by the defendant, which act directly and proximately caused injury to the plaintiffs. What we must decide is whether there is justification here for a departure from generally applicable, well-established principles of law:

* * *

At its intellectual core, the wrongful birth tort this Court created in Eisbrenner relies on the benefits rule this Court adopted in Troppi. To say the very least, continued reliance on this rule has some far-reaching, and profoundly disturbing, consequences. This rule invites the jury in wrongful birth cases to weigh the costs to the parents of a disabled child of bearing and raising that child against the benefits to the parents of the life of that child. This rule thus asks the jury to quantify the unquantifiable with respect to the benefits side of the equation. Further, to posit a specific question: how does a jury measure the benefits to the parents of the whole life of the disabled child, when the potential of that child is unknown at the time of suit? How, for example, would a hypothetical Grecian jury, operating under Michigan jurisprudence, measure the benefits to the parents of the whole life of Homer, the blind singer of songs who created the Iliad and the Odyssey? Absent the ability to foretell the future and to quantify the value of the spoken and then the written word, how, exactly, would the jury do that?

Further, the use of the benefits rule in wrongful birth cases can slide ever so quickly into applied eugenics. The very phrase "wrongful birth" suggests that the birth of the disabled child was wrong and should have been prevented. If one accepts the premise that the birth of one "defective" child should have been prevented, then it is but a short step to accepting the premise that the births of classes of "defective" children should be similarly prevented, not just for the benefit of the parents but also for the benefit of society as a whole through the protection of the "public welfare." This is the operating principle of eugenics. James E.

Bowman provides a dark, single sentence description of eugenics: "Eugenics espouses the reproduction of the 'fit' over the 'unfit' (positive eugenics) and discourages the birth of the 'unfit' (negative eugenics)." Paul A. Lombardo more broadly, and more charitably, defines eugenics as the idea that the human race can be gradually improved and social ills simultaneously eliminated through a program of selective procreation and describes its most enthusiastic American advocates:

Francis Galton, Karl Pearson, and others who called themselves eugenicists believed in improving the human condition through the use of science. They understood their field as the marriage of the biological sciences, including medical genetics, with the then new discipline of biostatistics. The most passionate of American eugenicists, such as Charles Davenport and Harry Laughlin, wished to develop a taxonomy of human traits and to categorize individuals as "healthy" or "unhealthy," and "normal" or "abnormal," within their classification scheme. Working under the presumption that most, if not all, human traits are transmitted genetically, the eugenicists encouraged educated, resourceful, and self-sufficient citizens to mate and produce "wellborn" eugenic children. In contrast, the dysgenic were discouraged from reproducing. Harry Laughlin called dysgenic groups "socially inadequate" and defined them to include: the feebleminded, the insane, the criminalistic, the epileptic, the inebriated or the drug addicted, the diseased—regardless of etiology, the blind, the deaf, the deformed, and dependents (an extraordinarily expansive term that embraced orphans, "ne'er-do-wells," tramps, the homeless and paupers.)

To our eyes, this concept appears simultaneously cruel and laughable, but we should remember that the concept, and the values, of eugenics had a profound effect on American society. We should also recall that the courts were not above the use of this type of rhetoric. One of the most respected jurists in American history, Justice Oliver Wendell Holmes, wrote the decision in Buck v. Bell.

* * *

Finally, we should not forget the influence that the Third Reich's experiments with sterilization had on the American eugenics movement. As Lombardo notes, Dr. Joseph DeJarnette, who testified as an expert witness in the Buck trial, made the following comments about those experiments:

No person unable to support himself on account of his inherited mental condition has a right to be born. . . . In Germany the sterilization law embraces chronic alcoholics, certain hereditary physical diseases, the hereditarily blind and deaf, the criminally insane, feebleminded and epileptic. By December 31, 1934 Germany had sterilized 56,224 [persons].

Lombardo notes that Dr. DeJarnette continued to express his admiration for Hitler's campaign in the good doctor's last official comment regarding sterilization in 1938:

Germany in six years has sterilized about 80,000 of her unfit while the United States with approximately twice the population has sterilized about 27,869 to January 1, 1938, in the past 20 years. The death rates in Virginia from sterilization is [sic] negligible—not over one in a thousand.... The fact that there are 12,000,000 defectives in the United States should arouse our best endeavors to push this procedure to the maximum.

To our ears, at the close of the twentieth century, this talk of the "unfit" and of "defectives" has a decidedly jarring ring; we are, after all, above such lethal nonsense. But are we? We know now that we all have at least five recessive genes but, according to Bowman, when scientists map the human genome, they will unveil many more potentially harmful genes in each of us. Bowman states that "psychoses, hypertension, diabetes, early-and late-appearing cancers, degenerative disorders, susceptibility genes for communicable diseases, genes for various mental deficiencies, aging genes, and other variations and disorders will be ascertained." Will we then see the tort of wrongful birth extended to physicians who neglect or misinterpret genetic evidence and thereby fail to extend the option of a eugenic abortion to the unsuspecting parents of a genetically "unfit" and "defective" child? Our current acceptance of the wrongful birth tort would require the answer to this question in Michigan to be: yes. We further note that it is but another short half step from the concept of preventing the birth of an "unfit" or "defective" child to proposing, for the benefit of the child's overburdened parents and of the society as a whole, that the existence of the child should not be allowed to continue. Again, this sounds preposterous, but is it? As described by Bowman:

> Daniel Callahan, the former President and Founder of the Hastings Center, the preeminent center for bioethics in the United States, has proposed age-based rationing of health care for elderly persons to alleviate escalating health care costs. Pain relief would be in order, but not life-saving measures, including nutrition. In short, aged individuals past their late seventies or early eighties should go quietly into the night in order that the generation to follow would have access to health care—in their early years.

If the elderly have a duty to die—indeed, to be starved to death—then why not the disabled child? After all, if that child never should have been born, then that child has no real right to go on living, thereby imposing the costs of the child's continued existence on the parents and society. This, we conclude, is the logical end of the slippery slope inherent in the application of the benefits rule through the wrongful birth tort.

CONCLUSION

We conclude that this intermediate appellate court should not continue to recognize the wrongful birth tort without the slightest hint of approval from the Michigan Supreme Court or our Legislature.

Notes

See the discussion of wrongful birth actions in Chapter 6.

So far this chapter has been discussing primarily what is called "negative eugenics"—the use of state power to prevent the birth of "undesirable" offspring. Another form of eugenics is "positive eugenics," which encourages the birth of children with "desirable" traits.

The father of modern eugenics, Francis Galton, influenced by the views of Malthus, was appalled by his observation that "inferior" people were reproducing at great rates while the best and the brightest had small families. Positive eugenics captured the popular imagination during the 1920s, when state fairs hosted "Fitter Families Exhibits" and "Perfect Baby Competitions"; livestock was judged in one barn, human lineage in another. Students on field trips who obtained a good eugenics evaluation might win a "Goodly Heritage" medal. The American Eugenics Society also sponsored awards for church sermons extolling marriages of "the best" with "the best."

An extreme example of positive eugenics was the Nazi's "Lebensborn" program, where public health officials selected Aryan women to breed with SS soldiers and raised the resulting children in special foster families. At the same time, in a program promoted by the Army Air Corps in the United States, the Pioneer Fund, created by a group of wealthy conservatives, offered military pilots and crews who had three children $4,000 (about $45,000 today) to help educate a fourth. (For a description of what happened to the twelve children who were born under the program, see Douglas A. Blackmon, A Breed Apart: A Long–Ago Effort to Better the Species Yields Ordinary Folks, Wall St. J., Aug. 17, 1999, at A1.)

Are there any examples of positive eugenics programs in the United States today? Consider the following:

Associated Press, Owner of "Genius" Sperm Bank Pleased By Results

The New York Times, Dec. 11, 1984, at A17.

Robert Graham still gets some negative reaction to his sperm bank, but his list of genius donors is slowly growing and 15 children have been born to women chosen as recipients.

Mr. Graham vigorously denied that he was trying to create a super race through his Repository for Germinal Choice, popularly known as the Nobel Prize sperm bank, but he says he envisions a better society populated by smarter children born to parents who meet his standards for health and emotional stability.

"We are, I would think, selective," Mr. Graham said in a recent interview at his downtown office. "But we're not racist. We'll accept excellence in any race. What we're really trying to do is optimize the conditions for having children."

Most of the women who receive the semen, which is kept in a frozen state, are in their mid-to late 30's. Many have tried unsuccessfully for years to bear children with their husbands. Occasionally, the recipient's husband has a hereditary problem that he does not want to pass on.

* * *

Secrecy shrouds most of the names involved with the repository, started in 1979. Only William B. Shockley, who shared a Nobel Prize for the invention of the transistor and who says blacks as a group are intellectually inferior to whites for genetic reasons, has made his donations public.

Nine other men, all possessing an I.Q. of at least 140, are regular donors, Mr. Graham said.

Women who inquire about insemination through the repository are given a booklet showing the characteristics of the donors, who are not identified by name.

Sperm is given to the women free except for a $50 application fee, $10 a month for liquid nitrogen for storage and shipping costs. The women are required to be married and to prove it.

* * *

Mr. Graham, 78 years old, does not pay any fee to the repository's donors, but sends someone to pick up their donations.

"These are men who would never be on call to a doctor," Mr. Graham said. "And they don't do this because they need the money."

But running the nonprofit repository and paying its four employees costs Mr. Graham several hundred thousand dollars annually. He said money was no problem because he made a fortune by inventing shatterproof eyeglasses.

He Now Seeks Athletes

Since the repository's founding, Mr. Graham has been primarily interested in attracting men whose area of excellence is sciences or the arts. Since the 1984 Olympics in Los Angeles, he also has been looking for donors who are outstanding athletes and have high intelligence.

"We have an interview with a gold medal winner in a week or two," Mr. Graham said. "Our present donors are all geniuses. Now we're also emphasizing outstanding bodies."

* * *

MAXWELL J. MEHLMAN, MODERN EUGENICS AND THE LAW IN A CENTURY OF EUGENICS: FROM THE "INDIANA EXPERIMENT" TO THE HUMAN GENOME ERA

Paul A. Lombardo, ed. (Indiana University Press, Forthcoming 2010).

* * *

Commentators often distinguish between "state-sponsored" and "private" reproductive decisions, suggesting that only the former can be considered to be eugenics. [Troy] Duster states, for example: "[I]t is imperative to distinguish between state-sanctioned eugenics programs on the one hand, and private, individualized, *personal* decisions that are socially patterned on the other." But the exercise of state power, and the dividing line between state-sponsored and private decision-making, are less clear-cut than Duster implies. At one extreme, the state can prohibit a eugenic practice. In Skinner v. Oklahoma, for example, the Supreme Court held that it was unconstitutional for a state to require certain habitual criminals to be sterilized but not others. * * *

At the other extreme, the state may compel a eugenic practice, such as Indiana did when it enacted [the nation's first] involuntary sterilization law [in 1907]. Between these two extremes, however, there are a number of gradations. For example, the government can provide financial inducements for eugenic practices, such as tax breaks and welfare penalties for having desirable or undesirable children, or damages awarded by the judicial system to families whose physicians failed to prevent the birth of children with disabilities. Even when the government merely refrains from limiting or prohibiting eugenic practices, it might be said to be sanctioning them implicitly. Duster might regard reproductive decisions by parents as "personal," but the government arguably collaborates when it turns a blind eye.

In short, when the law influences reproductive decision-making in such a way as to encourage or discourage the birth of specifically types of desirable or undesirable individuals, this is at least suggestive of a eugenics objective. The more overt this objective, or the greater the impact of the law on individual reproductive decisions, the more frankly eugenic the law can be considered. This is not meant to imply that forced sterilization is on a par with government inaction in the face of private behavior. Yet ... society has employed indirect as well as direct means to control reproductive behavior in order to achieve eugenic goals. The memory of the victims of the Indiana law and its successors would be dishonored if we examined the current state of affairs using too narrow a view of this history.

A. LEGALLY-TOLERATED PRACTICES.

A number of practices typically are thought of as private because they result from private rather than public decision-making. But the fact that the law permits them to take place indicates a measure of public acquiescence, if not approval.

This category includes attempts to achieve what might be considered positive neoeugenic objectives. One example is selective breeding to produce a "better" genetic lineage. This has long taken place with animals, but it also takes place in humans. The most notorious recent case is the Chinese basketball player Yao Ming, whose parents were mated by the Chinese government because of their height and athletic prowess and who was forced to play basketball at an early age. Private forms of selective breeding are rampant in the United States, including mating within certain social circles, such as "coming out" at debutante balls, arranged marriages and semi-arranged marriages in which the couple is brought together by the parents, and most recently, computerized dating services in which participants select one another according to desirable traits. One such service, eHarmony.com, provides information about 29 personal characteristics, including appearance, intellect, industriousness, ambition, family background, education, and character. Those who avail themselves of these dating services can compress investigations that used to take a number of "dates" into the click of a button.

Some of the most glaring selective breeding practices are associated with gamete donation. The Genetics & IVF Institute, for example, provides the following information about egg donors: adult photos, childhood photos, audio interviews, blood type, ethnic background of donor's mother and father, height, weight, whether pregnancies have been achieved, body build, eye color, hair color and texture, years of education and major areas of study, occupation, Scholastic Aptitude Test (SAT) scores and grade point averages, special interests, family medical history, essays by donors, and personality typing based on the Keirsey test, which uses a Jungian approach to classify temperaments into 12 catagories, such as "rational and reserved" or "artisan and introspective." The California Cryobank, Inc. provides purchasers of donor sperm with a 26–page donor profile. A company called Fertility Alternatives pays a premium to "exceptional" egg donors. To qualify, the donor must have graduated from a major university, or be currently attending one, preferably Ivy League; have a GPA of 3.0 +; SAT scores of 1350 + or ACT scores of 30 +; and have a documented high IQ.

The degree to which the law accommodates these assisted reproductive practices is striking. Although health care is one of the most heavily regulated industries in the country, the only federal law specifically governing in vitro fertilization (IVF) services is the Fertility Clinic Success Rate and Certification Act of 1992, which merely requires infertility clinics to report success rates in a standardized fashion. State regulation is minimal. The criticisms leveled at the recent IVF-assisted birth of octuplets to an unmarried, unemployed woman illustrate this regulatory lacuna.

Conceivably, state law might encourage selective breeding by permitting parents to sue infertility clinics for negligence in failing properly to screen gamete donors. The leading case is Harnicher v. University of Utah Medical Center. [See Chapter 6]

* * *

While the parents in the *Harnicher* case used selective breeding in the hopes of achieving a positive neoeugenic goal, the law also countenances a number of practices that might be deemed negative neoeugenics. One obvious example is fetal testing followed by aborting the fetus for reasons that do not relate to the mother's health. Another is preimplantation genetic diagnosis (PGD) of fertilized embryos in the course of IVF, where only those embryos with the best genetic endowment are implanted in the uterus and allowed to gestate. The law leaves IVF services essentially unregulated. A third technique is community-based genetic testing for matchmaking purposes, such as screening programs for Tay–Sachs and other recessive genetic diseases prevalent in Jews of Ashkenazi descent. The pioneer program is Chevra Dor Yeshurim ("Association of the Upright Generation"), which screens Orthodox Jewish adolescents in New York and does not allow a matchmaker to arrange a marriage between two individuals who both carry a recessive mutation.

Finally, there are private family planning initiatives. One is Project Prevention (formerly "CRACK"). This was started in California in 1997 by a woman who wanted to punish the drug-addicted mother who had given birth to 4 children she had adopted. When she failed to persuade the state legislature to criminalize drug-addicted mothers, she created CRACK, which gives drug addicts $200 if they undergo sterilization or use long-term birth control. In 2003, the organization claimed to have 23 chapters nationwide and had paid 907 persons, including 361 who had tubal ligations. African–Americans and Hispanics accounted for 401 of the participants. At present, there is no state or federal law that would interfere with this project.

B. LEGALLY-FACILITATED PRACTICES.

In some instances, the law goes farther than turning a blind eye; it actually aids the practice of neoeugenics. One example is the ability of parents to bring so-called "wrongful birth" actions. [See Chapter 6]

* * *

Another method by which the government involves itself in what might be considered neoeugenics is providing public funding for family-planning programs aimed at preventing the birth of children to poor mothers. According to the Alan Guttmacher Institute, the government in 2001 spent $1.26 billion on reversible contraceptive services and $95 million on sterilization services. These funds are distributed through several programs: Medicaid, Title X, Title V (Maternal Child Block Grants), Social Services Block Grants, and TANF (Temporary Assistance for Needy Families). These programs would not be particularly neoeugenic if they provided family-planning assistance to all socio-economic groups, but virtually all of these funds are earmarked for the poor. * * *

Organizations that provide these federally-funded family planning services are typically non-profits, and therefore another way that the government facilitates their activities in by giving them a subsidy in the form of exempting them from federal and state taxes. . . .

Another government tax policy that might be considered neoeugenic is federal child tax credits. Until statutory limits are reached, the more children the taxpaying family has, the larger the number of credits that it can claim. The policy might be regarded as eugenic in that, since only families with enough income to pay taxes benefit from the credit, the policy creates an incentive for better-off families to have more children.

Contrast child tax credits with so-called family caps under state welfare programs. Unlike child tax credits that encourage taxpaying families to produce more offspring, family caps apply to families on welfare, discouraging them from becoming larger by halting increases in welfare benefits once there are more than a certain number of children. Currently 24 states have some version of this policy. Dorothy Roberts observes that "[l]ike birth control programs and reproductive punishments, contemporary welfare policies share features of eugenic thinking. * * * Of course, the current welfare family caps are not premised on notions of recipients' genetic inferiority. But, like eugenic programs of the past, they are seen as a way of ridding America of the burden poor people pose."

In Dandridge v. Williams, the Supreme Court upheld family caps in the face of constitutional challenge. The Court ruled that the state of Maryland did not violate the Equal Protection Clause of the Fourteenth Amendment because it had a reasonable basis for the policy, namely, "the state's legitimate interest in encouraging employment and in avoiding discrimination between welfare families and the families of the working poor." Interestingly, the state itself had articulated an additional goal— "providing incentives for family planning"—on which, without comment, the Court apparently declined to rely.

C.   LEGALLY-MANDATED PRACTICES.

So far we have considered government toleration or subsidization of practices that can be considered neoeugenic. Additionally, there are some practices that the government currently mandates by law. All of them are in aid of negative eugenics objectives in that they discourage reproduction by undesirable segments of the population. One example is sterilization and other restrictions on reproduction employed ostensibly to deter the commission of future crimes. For example, California in 1996 enacted a law authorizing voluntary chemical or surgical castration for the first offense of child molesting and mandating castration as a condition of parole for repeat offenders. * * * Although the intent of these laws arguably is to prevent child molestation, they are eugenic in that they decrease the likelihood that child molesters will reproduce.

The criminal justice system deters reproduction not only by sex offenders but by all incarcerated criminals. In a broader sense, then, the entire criminal system is a negative neoeugenic program. Only five states (California, Mississippi, New Mexico, New York, and Washington) permit prisoners to have conjugal visits with their spouses, despite some evidence that such visits reduce the incidence of prison rape.

In the early 20th century, eugenic goals fueled restrictive immigration laws. Similar objectives arguably are associated with current efforts to limit immigration, including the plan to construct a fence along the border with Mexico. * * *

* * *

The state-mandated initiative that most overtly raises eugenics concerns, however, is newborn-screening for nontreatable disorders. [See Chapter 7] * * *

The development of faster and cheaper technologies such as tandem mass spectrometry and microchip arrays enable programs to screen for far greater numbers of disorders, including many for which no readily effective treatments presently exist. Screening for these nontreatable disorders can be beneficial, in that it could spare families years of uncertainty once symptoms emerged; alert them to be on the watch for new discoveries that could provide their children with treatment; provide children with adjunctive if not curative interventions; and facilitate participation of the children in research on their disorders. Yet some public health advocates offer an additional rationale for screening for nontreatable disorders: that it can serve as a valuable tool in family planning. One recent article explains, for example: "Arguments for considering broader benefits from the early diagnosis that only newborn screening can provide include ... knowledge on which to base reproductive decision-making years before a disease would be diagnosed for the affected child ...."

Moreover, as noted above, newborn screening is mandatory. * * *

* * * Newborn screening for treatable disorders is laudable. Screening for nontreatable disorders, however, is another matter. The screening is mandated by the state, and is imposed on parents over their objection. Nontreatable disorders would be included in part in order to discourage parents from giving birth to additional children with those disorders. This will prevent these children from inheriting genes that will make them a burden on society. Viewed in this manner, the resemblance between this program and classic eugenic practices, especially on this, the centennial of the first eugenic law, is, at least, disconcerting.

NOTES AND QUESTIONS

1. To what extent should the programs and practices described by Mehlman count as eugenics?

2. In what ways do they rekindle or avoid the concerns raised by the efforts of the eugenics movement in the 20th century?

III. THE ELSI PROGRAM

The experience with eugenics in the twentieth century, as well as other controversial programs such as the sickle-cell screening effort in the early 1970s (see the discussion in Chapter 8), created concern about the potential abuses of the scientific advances made possible by the Human Genome Project. The response was to establish a special program within the Human Genome Project, called the Ethical, Legal and Social Implications or ELSI program, to focus on the project's ethical, legal, and social implications. The ELSI program was conceived by the first director of the

Human Genome Project at NIH, James Watson, who, along with Francis Crick, had discovered the structure of the DNA molecule.

Watson himself gives the following account of the origin of the ELSI program:

> In putting ethics so soon into the genome agenda, I was responding to my own personal fear that all too soon critics of the Genome Project would point out that I was a representative of the Cold Spring Harbor Laboratory that once housed the controversial Eugenics Record Office. My not forming a genome ethics program quickly might be falsely used as evidence that I was a closet eugenicist, having as my real long-term purpose the unambiguous identification of genes that lead to social and occupational stratification as well as genes justifying racial discrimination. So I saw the need to be proactive in making ELSI's major purpose clear from its start—to devise better ways to combat the social injustice that has at its roots bad draws of the genetic dice.

James Watson, A Passion for DNA: Genes, Genomes & Society 202 (2000).

Watson insisted that between 3 and 5 percent of the federal budget for the Human Genome Project be devoted to ELSI-sponsored studies by researchers outside of the government. Administration of the ELSI program was shared by the NIH, which created an ELSI Branch within what became the National Center for Human Genome Research, and the Department of Energy, which was interested in the Human Genome Project as a result of its effort to measure the biological effects of atomic radiation. (For a history of the Department of Energy's involvement in the inception of the Human Genome Project, see Robert M. Cook–Deegan, The Gene Wars: Science, Politics, and the Human Genome (1994)).

The ELSI program was unprecedented as an attempt to shape US science policy, and it has had its share of critics. As reported by Eric Juengst, the first chief of the ELSI Branch at NIH, one senior NIH official complained: "I still don't understand why you want to spend all this money subsidizing the vacuous pronouncements of self-styled 'ethicists'!" Watson replied that, for better or worse, "the cat was out of the bag." The official retorted: "But why inflate the cat? Why put the cat on TV?" Juengst adds:

> Pro-genomicists, like the NIH official quoted above, saw it as at best a waste of (increasingly scarce) NIH research dollars, and at worst an overblown hand-waving that could backfire badly on the scientific community if it actually succeeded in getting the public's attention. Anti-genomicists suspected that the program was, at best, a clever attempt to create a screen of ethical smoke behind which the [Human Genome Project's] juggernaut could build up speed, and, at worst, an attempt to buy off the very critics who might otherwise make trouble for the scientists.

Eric Juengst, Self–Critical Federal Science? The Ethics Experiment Within the U.S. Human Genome Project, 13 Social Philosophy & Policy 63, 66–67 (1996). Another criticism, voiced by George Annas and Sherman Elias, was that the one policy issue that received no attention from ELSI was whether the Human Genome Project should take place in the first place.

Since its inception in 1990, the ELSI program at NIH has sponsored more than 190 projects and the DOE program more than 95. By the end of fiscal year 1999, the combined programs had spent more than $76 million dollars. The DOE program focuses on privacy and the use of genetic information. The NIH program focuses on research and health care policy issues. See ELSI Research Planning and Evaluation Group, A Review and Analysis of the ELSI Research Programs at NIH and DOE (2000), http://www.genome.gov./10001727 for a description and evaluation of the twin programs.

In 2003, the NIH announced the establishment of the first "Centers of Excellence in ELSI Research." These are funded by large-scale grants and are research centers with the resources and expertise to design and implement multi-faceted and multi-disciplinary investigations of particularly complex, persistent or rapidly emerging ELSI issues. The creation of these centers is a sign that the ELSI program has attained the maturity and stature of the major clinical research enterprises at the NIH.

Chapter 4

Genetics Research

■ ■ ■

I. INTRODUCTION

Each year, more genetic mechanisms that underlie diseases are uncovered, new diagnostic tests to pinpoint genetic disorders are introduced into clinical practice, and experimental therapies to treat genetic diseases are developed. Since so many traits, conditions, diseases, and defects have a genetic basis, almost everyone is a potential subject of genetic research. Potential genetic research subjects range widely in age, including embryos, fetuses, newborns, children, and adults. They differ in condition—healthy, mentally disabled, physically ill. The experimental procedures and products range in the level of risk they pose to the subject. The methodology of the research varies widely as well, ranging from pedigree studies to complicated procedures involving identifying and manipulating genes for diagnostic and therapeutic purposes.

Experimentation with human subjects has existed since the beginning of the science of medicine. However, it was not until the early twentieth century that ethical and legal considerations regarding such research came to the fore. The atrocities committed by Nazi physicians in experiments (some done in the name of genetics or, more properly stated, eugenics) led to the development of certain principles and guidelines that affect research on humans today. In the trials of those physicians, the court set forth standards that should be complied with both before and during research. These standards, subsequently adopted by the United Nations General Assembly, are known as the Nuremberg Code. The tenets of the code significantly influenced later state laws and federal regulations in the United States dealing with research.

The Nuremberg Code provides guidance for assuring that participation in research is voluntary and that the risks of research are minimized. The Code requires that certain basic scientific research and animal research must be done before human research is undertaken, that the human research must be well-designed and undertaken only by scientifically qualified individuals, that the potential results justify the level of risk involved in the performance of the research, and that those results are not procurable by other means of study. The central tenet of the Nuremberg Code is that participation in research must be voluntary, informed, and uncoerced, and that the subject has the right to bring the experiment to an end. The Code also requires the minimization of research risks through the appropriate design and conduct of the research as well as through adequate preparation and facilities. Research is forbidden if there is an *a priori* reason to believe death or disabling injury will occur (although the Nuremberg Code does allow for a potential exception if the researchers also serve as subjects) and on-going research must be stopped if there is reason to believe that its continuation will lead to the injury, disability, or death of the subject.

Subsequent societal discussion of research in the decades since the adoption of the Nuremberg Code has highlighted some additional ethical concerns. One concern is that subjects for research must be selected equitably; for example, a particular class or race of subjects should not serve as subjects for research that primarily benefits people of another class or race. With respect to potential genetics research on fetuses, there is concern that a disproportionate share of the fetal research burden might fall upon people of color. Since African–American infants have a higher morbidity and mortality rate than do Caucasian infants, it might be argued that they stand to benefit more from fetal research. However, it can conversely be argued that research on infants from minority or poor families will more likely be used to benefit wealthier white mothers and infants who have better access to new medical technologies. There has also been a move toward requiring that research proposals be reviewed in advance by groups unrelated to the research project itself. This has led to the formation of Institutional Review Boards (IRBs), committees designed to approve, disapprove, review, and monitor biomedical research involving human subjects. The purpose of IRB review is to assure that proper steps are taken to protect the rights and welfare of human research subjects.

Federal regulations, adopted in 1975 to regulate federally-funded research, focus on avoiding unnecessary physical risks to the subject, assuring informed consent and confidentiality, and assessing the merits of the proposed research in advance. Genetics research, however, raises ethical and legal concerns not necessarily addressed by the federal regulations. Much genetics research is conducted with private funds (for example, by biotechnology companies) and thus is not covered by the federal regulations protecting human subjects, although if it will result in a marketable product it will be regulated by the Food and Drug Administration. Genetics research presents risks beyond physical risks—such as psychological risks and risks of discrimination. In addition, genetics research raises risks of stigmatization not only to the individual participating in the research, but to relatives or members of the ethnic group who share some of his or her genes. This has led to consideration about whether group consent, in addition to individual consent, should be required before certain types of genetic research are undertaken. Also of concern has been the question of how to operationalize consent and otherwise protect human subjects in the international setting as research-ers seek DNA from members of indigenous groups.

While the law has focused on protection of people from risks in their interactions with researchers, new concerns have been raised about genet-ic research undertaken on previously-collected tissue samples. All of us have DNA on file someplace. Since the late 1960s, virtually every newborn in the United States has undergone public health department testing for certain genetic diseases; many laboratories have saved those blood sam-ples. After blood tests or biopsies are undertaken in hospitals, the samples are saved and often made available, without the individual's knowledge or consent, for further research. A major policy question has arisen about whether the person whose blood or other tissue sample is used for genetic research should have the chance to either consent or refuse to participate in such research.

Another controversial area involves genetics research on embryos. In a society divided over the issue of abortion, there is no clear cut legal or moral consensus over the status of the embryo. Some experimental procedures are designed to diagnose or treat genetic disease in an embryo which may be destined to be implanted in a woman to create a child. Other experimental procedures—such as the development of embryonic stem cells—use the embryo as a means of providing treatment for some-one else's genetic disease.

II. REGULATION OF RESEARCH

A. TYPES OF GENETIC RESEARCH

Genetic sequencing research involves determining the chemical make-up of the genome, which consists of three billion base pairs of the nucleotides adenine, guanine, cytosine, and thymine. (See Chapter 2, Scientific Overview). In February of 2001, scientists announced the com-pletion of a rough draft of a model human genome sequence. Far from signaling the end of genomic research, scientists are now working with human subjects to make use of this information. Research is being undertaken to determine whether individuals with a certain genetic pro-file are also more likely to develop certain diseases than those with a different makeup. There are also studies underway to investigate the varying manifestations of each particular genetic profile, to understand the role of proteins created by genes, and to target drugs and therapies more precisely based on genetic information.

A related field is epigenetics, which focuses on chemical changes to DNA that modify gene activity without altering the genetic sequence itself. Epigenetic signals, such as methylation, may help guide stem cells as they develop into other types of cells. Researchers believe that the presence of a methyl group near the start of a gene marks the gene as turned off and blocks its activity. Epigenetic signals, which are established in the early embryo, can be influenced by environmental factors and random mutations throughout a person's life, and some signal patterns may be related to diseases such as cancer. Scientists suspect that differences in epigenetic signals due to environmental factors could account for why identical twins do not look exactly alike despite sharing the same genetic sequence. See Tina, Hesman Saey, Epigenetics: From Islands to the Shores, Science News, Feb. 14, 2009 at 5–6.

Once the connection between a particular genetic trait and an illness or characteristic is understood, clinical research can be undertaken, including DNA diagnostic studies (to develop techniques for determining the presence of specific DNA mutations) and gene therapy research (to develop treatments for genetic disease at the DNA level). See Chapter 9, Clinical Application of Genetics.

Genome Wide Association Studies

Currently, Genome Wide Association Studies (GWAS) are the most prevalent type of clinical genetics research conducted. Medical researchers are no longer limited to the study of a few diseases with simple genetic causes. The research field has expanded to cover diseases caused by the interactions between multiple genes as well as interactions between genes and the environment. Researchers employ GWAS to uncover these interactions.

GWAS depend upon variation in the human genome to uncover interactions. The most common variations are single nucleotide polymorphisms (SNPs). An SNP is a single change in the nucleotide sequence of a gene. For example, one person might have an AATGGCA genotype for a trait and another person might have an AATGTCA genotype. The human genome is estimated to contain 10 million SNPs.

GWAS analyze the distribution of SNPS in hundreds or thousands of individuals to determine which SNPs are associated with a particular disease. GWAS generally consist of two groups: a group of individuals known not to have a particular disease, and a group of individuals who are known to have a particular disease. The genetic information of these two groups is compared and the SNPs that occur in statistically significant amounts in the population known to carry the disease, which are also generally absent in the population known not to carry the disease, are said to be associated with the target disease. Once the GWAS identify the genes that are likely associated with increased risk of disease, further studies are free to focus on these genes and tease apart their interactions with each other and the environment. GWAS themselves do not directly lead to medical products that reach the public but rather pave the way for research that eventually will.

GWAS have proved to be an effective tool for studying linkages between genetic variation and disease. For example, in 2005, three independent research groups identified a link between age-related macular degeneration and a variation in a gene involved in creating a protein that regulates inflammation. Other studies have found links between genetic variation and increased or decreased risk for such diseases as Crohn's Disease, Parkinson's Disease, type 2 Diabetes, and others. See http://www.genome.gov/20019523 for more information.

However, GWAS also have limitations. The common genetic variations that they target equate to only a fraction of the total amount of variation in the genome. Additionally, many of these variations have low to moderate effects in explaining gene expression and protein function. It may be the case that an inordinately large number of such genetic variations is required to explain any sizeable percentage of variation in observable expression or function in relation to any given disease. Some believe that analyzing rarer genetic variations will lead to the discovery of more manageable genetic pathways that account for a larger portion of disease risk and have greater effect on gene expression and protein function. Currently, scientists are ill-equipped to detect these rare variations. See David B. Goldstein, Common Genetic Variation and Human Traits, 360 New Eng. J. Med. 1696 (April 23, 2009).

B. THE FEDERAL APPROACH

HENRY T. GREELY, THE CONTROL OF GENETIC RESEARCH: INVOLVING THE "GROUPS BETWEEN"

33 Hous. L. Rev. 1397, 1399–1402 (1997).

* * *

Existing regulation of biomedical research in the United States works at two levels. At one level, federal law in effect requires researchers to submit proposals for studies of human subjects to expert panels, which must judge those proposals based on their adherence to federal regulations for the protection of human subjects. Those regulations, bolstered by both international declarations and trends in United States domestic law, also enshrine the second level of control: the requirement that individual research subjects be fully informed about the nature, scope, and risks of the research and agree formally to participate in it.

Substantial federal regulation of biomedical research began in the aftermath of the disclosure of research that abused human subjects, notably the notorious Tuskegee syphilis study. This regulation is indirect but overpowering. First, any research funded by the federal government—and any research institution that receives federal funds—is required by regulation to take certain steps to protect human research subjects. These regulations may be promulgated separately by federal agencies that fund research, but they are largely identical. Substantively, the rules demand that the research risks to subjects be justified by the potential benefits of the research, that broad informed consent be provided, and that special protections be applied to particularly vulnerable populations. Procedurally, the regulations force all such research to be approved by IRBs [institutional review boards], which determine whether the research meets federal standards.

Second, any research to be used in supporting applications to the Food and Drug Administration (FDA) must also satisfy regulations for protecting subjects. The regulations are largely similar to those of the funding agencies, but they expand the reach of those provisions to research performed by institutions that do not receive federal grants: notably pharmaceutical and biotechnology companies. Importantly, these regulations apply not only to companies from the United States and those doing research in the United States, but to companies from any country doing biomedical research anywhere that plan to use the research in support of an application to the FDA. Those firms must also have their relevant research approved by IRBs.

Thus, the federal government effectively regulates biomedical research, not by asserting its direct governmental power to require that research follow certain rules, but by withholding federal benefits—research funding or regulatory approval—from institutions that have not met federal rules.

FEDERAL RESEARCH REGULATIONS
45 C.F.R. § 46.101 et seq.

PART 46—PROTECTION OF HUMAN SUBJECTS

SUBPART A—BASIC HHS POLICY FOR PROTECTION OF HUMAN RESEARCH SUBJECTS

§ 46.101   To what does this policy apply?

* * *

(b) Unless otherwise required by department or agency heads, research activities in which the only involvement of human subjects will be in one or more of the following categories are exempt from this policy:

* * *

(4) Research, involving the collection or study of existing data, documents, records, pathological specimens, or diagnostic specimens, if these sources are publicly available or if the information is recorded by the investigator in such a manner that subjects cannot be identified, directly or through identifiers linked to the subjects.

* * *

(e) Compliance with this policy requires compliance with pertinent federal laws or regulations which provide additional protections for human subjects.

(f) This policy does not affect any state or local laws or regulations which may otherwise be applicable and which provide additional protections for human subjects.

* * *

§ 46.102 Definitions.

* * *

(d) *Research* means a systematic investigation, including research development, testing and evaluation, designed to develop or contribute to generalizable knowledge. Activities which meet this definition constitute research for purposes of this policy, whether or not they are conducted or supported under a program which is considered research for other purposes. For example, some demonstration and service programs may include research activities.

* * *

(f) *Human subject* means a living individual about whom an investigator (whether professional or student) conducting research obtains

(1) Data through intervention or interaction with the individual, or

(2) Identifiable private information.

Intervention includes both physical procedures by which data are gathered (for example, venipuncture) and manipulations of the subject or the subject's environment that are performed for research purposes. Interaction includes communication or interpersonal contact between investigator and subject. *Private information* includes information about behavior that occurs in a context in which an individual can reasonably expect that no observation or recording is taking place, and information which has been provided for specific purposes by an individual and which the individual can reasonably expect will not be made public (for example, a medical record). Private information must be individually identifiable (i.e., the identity of the subject is or may readily be ascertained by the investigator or associated with the information) in order for obtaining the information to constitute research involving human subjects.

(g) *IRB* means an institutional review board established in accord with and for the purposes expressed in this policy.

(h) *IRB approval* means the determination of the IRB that the research has been reviewed and may be conducted at an institution within the constraints set forth by the IRB and by other institutional and federal requirements.

(i) *Minimal risk* means that the probability and magnitude of harm or discomfort anticipated in the research are not greater in and of themselves than those ordinarily encountered in daily life or during the performance of routine physical or psychological examinations or tests.

* * *

§ 46.107   IRB membership.

(a) Each IRB shall have at least five members, with varying backgrounds to promote complete and adequate review of research activities commonly conducted by the institution. The IRB shall be sufficiently qualified through the experience and expertise of its members, and the diversity of the members, including consideration of race, gender, and cultural backgrounds and sensitivity to such issues as community attitudes, to promote respect for its advice and counsel in safeguarding the rights and welfare of human subjects. In addition to possessing the professional competence necessary to review specific research activities, the IRB shall be able to ascertain the acceptability of proposed research in terms of institutional commitments and regulations, applicable law, and standards of professional conduct and practice. The IRB shall therefore include persons knowledgeable in these areas. If an IRB regularly reviews research that involves a vulnerable category of subjects, such as children, prisoners, pregnant women, or handicapped or mentally disabled persons, consideration shall be given to the inclusion of one or more individuals who are knowledgeable about and experienced in working with these subjects.

(b) Every nondiscriminatory effort will be made to ensure that no IRB consists entirely of men or entirely of women, including the institution's consideration of qualified persons of both sexes, so long as no selection is made to the IRB on the basis of gender. No IRB may consist entirely of members of one profession.

(c) Each IRB shall include at least one member whose primary concerns are in scientific areas and at least one member whose primary concerns are in nonscientific areas.

(d) Each IRB shall include at least one member who is not otherwise affiliated with the institution and who is not part of the immediate family of a person who is affiliated with the institution.

(e) No IRB may have a member participate in the IRB's initial or continuing review of any project in which the member has a conflicting interest, except to provide information requested by the IRB.

(f) An IRB may, in its discretion, invite individuals with competence in special areas to assist in the review of issues which require expertise beyond or in addition to that available on the IRB. These individuals may not vote with the IRB.

* * *

§ 46.111   Criteria for IRB approval of research.

(a) In order to approve research covered by this policy the IRB shall determine that all of the following requirements are satisfied:

(1) Risks to subjects are minimized: (i) By using procedures which are consistent with sound research design and which do not unnecessarily expose subjects to risk, and (ii) whenever appropriate, by using procedures already being performed on the subjects for diagnostic or treatment purposes.

(2) Risks to subjects are reasonable in relation to anticipated benefits, if any, to subjects, and the importance of the knowledge that may reasonably be expected to result. In evaluating risks and benefits, the IRB should consider only those risks and benefits that may result from the research (as distinguished from risks and benefits of therapies subjects would receive even if not participating in the research). The IRB should not consider possible long-range effects of applying knowledge gained in the research (for example, the possible effects of the research on public policy) as among those research risks that fall within the purview of its responsibility.

(3) Selection of subjects is equitable. In making this assessment the IRB should take into account the purposes of the research and the setting in which the research will be conducted and should be particularly cognizant of the special problems of research involving vulnerable populations, such as children, prisoners, pregnant women, mentally disabled persons, or economically or educationally disadvantaged persons.

(4) Informed consent will be sought from each prospective subject or the subject's legally authorized representative, in accordance with, and to the extent required by § 46.116.

(5) Informed consent will be appropriately documented, in accordance with, and to the extent required by § 46.117.

(6) When appropriate, the research plan makes adequate provision for monitoring the data collected to ensure the safety of subjects.

(7) When appropriate, there are adequate provisions to protect the privacy of subjects and to maintain the confidentiality of data.

(b) When some or all of the subjects are likely to be vulnerable to coercion or undue influence, such as children, prisoners, pregnant women, mentally disabled persons, or economically or educationally disadvantaged persons, additional safeguards have been included in the study to protect the rights and welfare of these subjects.

* * *

§ 46.116   General requirements for informed consent.

Except as provided elsewhere in this policy, no investigator may involve a human being as a subject in research covered by this policy unless the investigator has obtained the legally effective informed consent of the subject or the subject's legally authorized representative. An investigator shall seek such consent only under circumstances that provide the prospective subject or the representative sufficient opportunity to consider whether or not to participate and that minimize the possibility of coercion or undue influence. The information that is given to the subject or the representative shall be in language understandable to the subject or the representative. No informed consent, whether oral or written, may include any exculpatory language through which the subject or the representative is made to waive or appear to waive any of the subject's legal rights, or releases or appears to release the investigator, the sponsor, the institution or its agents from liability for negligence.

(a) Basic elements of informed consent. Except as provided in paragraph (c) or (d) of this section, in seeking informed consent the following information shall be provided to each subject:

(1) A statement that the study involves research, an explanation of the purposes of the research and the expected duration of the subject's participation, a description of the procedures to be followed, and identification of any procedures which are experimental;

(2) A description of any reasonably foreseeable risks or discomforts to the subject;

(3) A description of any benefits to the subject or to others which may reasonably be expected from the research;

(4) A disclosure of appropriate alternative procedures or courses of treatment, if any, that might be advantageous to the subject;

(5) A statement describing the extent, if any, to which confidentiality of records identifying the subject will be maintained;

(6) For research involving more than minimal risk, an explanation as to whether any compensation and an explanation as to whether any medical treatments are available if injury occurs and, if so, what they consist of, or where further information may be obtained;

(7) An explanation of whom to contact for answers to pertinent questions about the research and research subjects' rights, and whom to contact in the event of a research-related injury to the subject; and

(8) A statement that participation is voluntary, refusal to participate will involve no penalty or loss of benefits to which the subject is otherwise entitled, and the subject may discontinue participation at any time without penalty or loss of benefits to which the subject is otherwise entitled.

(b) Additional elements of informed consent. When appropriate, one or more of the following elements of information shall also be provided to each subject:

(1) A statement that the particular treatment or procedure may involve risks to the subject (or to the embryo or fetus, if the subject is or may become pregnant) which are currently unforeseeable;

(2) Anticipated circumstances under which the subject's participation may be terminated by the investigator without regard to the subject's consent;

(3) Any additional costs to the subject that may result from participation in the research;

(4) The consequences of a subject's decision to withdraw from the research and procedures for orderly termination of participation by the subject;

(5) A statement that significant new findings developed during the course of the research which may relate to the subject's willingness to continue participation will be provided to the subject; and

(6) The approximate number of subjects involved in the study.

(c) An IRB may approve a consent procedure which does not include, or which alters, some or all of the elements of informed consent set forth above, or waive the requirement to obtain informed consent provided the IRB finds and documents that:

(1) The research or demonstration project is to be conducted by or subject to the approval of state or local government officials and is designed to study, evaluate, or otherwise examine: (i) Public benefit of service programs; (ii) procedures for obtaining benefits or services under those programs; (iii) possible changes in or alternatives to those programs or procedures; or (iv) possible changes in methods or levels of payment for benefits or services under those programs; and

(2) The research could not practicably be carried out without the waiver or alteration.

(d) An IRB may approve a consent procedure which does not include, or which alters, some or all of the elements of informed consent set forth in this section, or waive the requirements to obtain informed consent provided the IRB finds and documents that:

(1) The research involves no more than minimal risk to the subjects;

(2) The waiver or alteration will not adversely affect the rights and welfare of the subjects;

(3) The research could not practicably be carried out without the waiver or alteration; and

(4) Whenever appropriate, the subjects will be provided with additional pertinent information after participation.

(e) The informed consent requirements in this policy are not intended to preempt any applicable federal, state, or local laws which require additional information to be disclosed in order for informed consent to be legally effective.

(f) Nothing in this policy is intended to limit the authority of a physician to provide emergency medical care, to the extent the physician is permitted to do so under applicable federal, state, or local law.

C. SPECIAL CONCERNS ABOUT GENETIC RESEARCH

U.S. DEPT. OF HEALTH AND HUMAN SERVICES, OFFICE OF PROTECTION FROM RESEARCH RISKS (OPRR) PROTECTING HUMAN RESEARCH SUBJECTS: INSTITUTIONAL REVIEW BOARD GUIDEBOOK

5–42 to 5–51 (1993), www.genome.gov/10001752.

HUMAN GENETIC RESEARCH

Human genetic research involves the study of inherited human traits. Much of this research is aimed at identifying DNA mutations that can help cause specific health problems. The identification of genetic mutations enables clinicians to predict the likelihood that persons will develop a given health problem in the future or pass on a health risk to their children. For many disorders, however, there will be a considerable time lag between the ability to determine the likelihood of disease and the ability to treat the disease.

Efforts to isolate DNA mutations involved in disease in order to understand the origins of the pathophysiological process are becoming increasingly common across the broad sweep of biomedical research, from cardiology to oncology to psychiatry. IRBs [Institutional Review Boards] should expect to see more of these kinds of studies in the future. * * *

* * *

Unlike the risks presented by many biomedical research protocols considered by IRBs, the primary risk involved in the first three types of genetic research [family linkage studies, identification of genes, and DNA diagnostic studies] are risks of social and psychological harm, rather than risks of physical injury. Genetic studies that generate information about subjects' personal health risks can provoke anxiety and confusion, damage familial relationships, and compromise the subjects' insurability and employment opportunities. [See Chapter 15 for a discussion of the legal issues raised by genetic discrimination.] For many genetic research protocols, these psychosocial risks can be significant enough to warrant careful IRB review and discussion. The fact that genetic studies are often limited to the collection of family history information and blood drawing should not, therefore, automatically classify them as "minimal risk" studies qualifying for expedited IRB review.

* * *

Subject Recruitment and Retention. The familial nature of the research cohorts involved in pedigree studies can pose challenges for ensuring that recruitment procedures are free of elements that unduly influence decisions to participate. The very nature of the research exerts pressure on family members to take part, because the more complete the pedigree, the more reliable the resulting information will be. For example, revealing who else in the family has agreed to participate may act as an undue influence on an individual's decision, as may recruiting individuals in the presence of other family members. (Both would also constitute a breach of confidentiality * * *.)

Recruitment plans, some of which are described here, can attempt to address these problems; each approach has its own strengths and weaknesses. One strategy is to use the proband as the point of contact for recruiting. [The proband is the person whose case serves as the stimulus for the study of other members of the family.] This approach insulates families from pressure by the investigator, but presents the risk that the proband may be personally interested in the research findings and exert undue pressure on relatives to enroll in the study. Furthermore, the proband may not want to act as a recruiter for fear that other family members will then know that he or she is affected by the disease. Another approach is direct recruitment by the investigator through letters or telephone calls to individuals whose identity is supplied by the proband. Direct recruitment by the investigator may, however, be seen as an invasion of privacy by family members * * *. A third approach is to recruit participants through support groups or lay organizations. Adopting this strategy requires investigator and IRB confidence that these organizations will be as scrupulous in their own efforts to protect subjects as the investigator would be. A fourth possibility is to contact individuals through their personal physicians. Prospective subjects contacted by their physician may, however, feel that their health care will be compromised if they do not agree to participate. In the end, the IRB must ensure that the recruitment plan minimizes the possibility of coercion or undue influence.

In contrast to inappropriate pressure placed on prospective participants to join the study is the possibility that a subject may agree to participate out of a misguided effort to obtain therapy. The purposes of the research and how subjects will or will not benefit by participation must be clearly explained.

* * *

Defining Risks and Benefits. Potential risks and benefits should be discussed thoroughly with prospective subjects. In genetic research, the primary risks, outside of gene therapy, are psychological and social (referred to generally as "psychosocial") rather than physical. IRBs should review genetic research with such risks in mind.

Psychological risk includes the risk of harm from learning genetic information about oneself (*e.g.*, that one is affected by a genetic disorder that has not yet manifested itself). Complicating the communication of genetic information is that often the information is limited to probabilities. Furthermore, the development of genetic data carries with it a margin of error; some information communicated to subjects will, in the end, prove to be wrong. In either event, participants are subjected to the stress of receiving such information. For example, researchers involved in developing presymptomatic tests for Huntington Disease (HD) have been concerned that the emotional impact of learning the results may lead some subjects to attempt suicide. They have therefore asked whether prospective participants should be screened for emotional stability prior to acceptance into a research protocol.

Note that these same disclosures of information can also be beneficial. One of the primary benefits of participation in genetic research is that the receipt of genetic information, however imperfect, can reduce uncertainty about whether participants will likely develop a disease that runs in their family (and possibly whether they have passed the gene along to their children). Where subjects learn that they will likely develop or pass along the disease, they might better plan for the future.

To minimize the psychological harms presented by pedigree research, IRBs should make sure that investigators will provide for adequate counseling to subjects on the meaning of the genetic information they receive. Genetic counseling is not a simple matter and must be done by persons qualified and experienced in communicating the meaning of genetic information to persons participating in genetic research or persons who seek genetic testing.

Debate about the social policy implications of genetic information is vitally important and is occurring on a national and international level, but is not literally a concern for IRBs. The IRB's concern is, first, to ensure that these risks will be disclosed to subjects, and, second, to protect subjects against unwarranted disclosures of information.

* * *

Privacy and Confidentiality Protections. Special privacy and confidentiality concerns arise in genetic family studies because of the special relationship between the participants. IRBs should keep in mind that within families, each person is an individual who deserves to have information about him-or herself kept confidential. Family members are not entitled to each other's diagnoses. Before revealing medical or personal information about individuals to other family members, investigators must obtain the consent of the individual.

Data must be stored in such a manner that does not directly identify individuals. In general, except where directly authorized by individual subjects, data may not be released to anyone other than the subject. An exception to requiring explicit authorization for the release of data may be secondary research use of the data, where the data are not especially sensitive and where confidentiality can be assured. IRBs should exercise their discretion in reviewing protocols that call for the secondary use of genetic data. Furthermore, when reviewing a consent document, IRBs should note agreements made by investigators not to release information without the express consent of subjects. Subsequent requests for access to the data are subject to agreements made in the consent process. For studies involving socially sensitive traits or conditions, investigators might also consider requesting a certificate of confidentiality.

* * *

Publication Practices. One final issue involving consent is the publication of research data. The publication of pedigrees can easily result in the identification of study participants. Where a risk of identification exists, participants must consent, in writing, to the release of personal information. Various authors have noted the problem of obtaining consent for the publication of identifying data, and have recommended that consent to the publication be obtained immediately prior to the publication, rather than as part of the consent to treatment or participation in research. It is worth noting, however, that to address this concern, IRBs must also resolve the following questions: Who determines the risk of identification, and on what grounds? Who are defined as participants (is it everyone listed in the pedigree, some of whom have been contacted by investigators, some of whom have had information about them provided by a family member)?

While IRBs must be careful to avoid inappropriate restrictions on investigators' research publications, some evaluation of publication plans is important as part of the IRB's overall interest in preserving the confidentiality of research subjects. One approach for investigators to use in evaluating their publication plans might be to work in a step-wise fashion: First, is publication of the pedigree essential? If publication of the pedigree or other identifying data (*e.g.*, case histories, photographs, or radiographs) is essential, can some identifying data be omitted without changing the scientific message? (The practice of altering data—such as changing the birth order and gender—is controversial, and no clear professional consensus yet exists as to whether this is an appropriate practice.) Finally, if the pedigree must be published, and if identifying data cannot be omitted in an appropriate manner without changing the scientific message, subjects must give their permission for publication of data that may reveal their identity.

ZSOLT HARSANYI & RICHARD HUTTON, GENETIC PROPHECY: BEYOND THE DOUBLE HELIX

187–188 (1981).

THE EXTRA Y: A CRIMINAL CHROMOSOME?

On July 13, 1966, a tall loner with "Born to Raise Hell" tattooed on his arm brutally murdered eight Chicago nurses in their residence. Soon after, Richard Speck was captured, tried, and imprisoned. Journalists covering the case had a field day. Several self-appointed genetic experts speculated loosely about his genes. They noted his height and his criminal record and suggested that he might belong to a class of criminals that had been discovered just the year before: a group of unusually tall men who carried an extra Y chromosome in addition to the normal male set of XY sex chromosomes.

High rates of XYY carriers in mental-penal institutions had been discovered in Edinburgh, Scotland. Subsequent studies confirmed the initial findings: The incidence of XYY chromosome carriers in the general population is about one in a thousand; but in institutions, it was found to be about two in a hundred. That difference was considered significant. Scientists and journalists alike theorized that the abnormality was a marker for criminal behavior; several lawyers tried to defend their XYY clients by pleading insanity based solely on the presence of the extra Y.

Richard Speck turned out to have the normal complement of chromosomes, and the furor surrounding the journalists' suspicions soon died out. But once questions about the criminal tendencies of those with XYY chromosomes had been raised, they had to be answered. In 1968, two Boston-based scientists, Stanley Walzer, a psychiatrist, and Park Gerald, a geneticist, decided to survey all male offspring born in Boston's Children's Medical Center, typing them for their sex chromosomes and following those who turned out to have more than the usual complement.

The project began quietly enough. But by 1973 it had aroused a storm of controversy around the Boston area. In an ideal world, the project might have been a fine bit of scientific investigation; but in a world that had managed to tag carriers of XYY as holders of the legacy of Richard Speck, it seemed dangerous.

Those who opposed the research raised serious questions both about its value and about its impact on its young subjects:

1. Had the devastating publicity given the XYY type crippled the Walzer study even before it began because of the "criminal" label that would be applied to anyone with the chromosomal abnormality?

2. Did the scientists' methodology, which involved informing the parents of the abnormality, render the study useless by changing parental behavior toward the offspring and affecting the critical issue of the environment?

3. Was the study endangering children who might otherwise grow up to be normal, leading to a kind of self-fulfilling prophecy?

NOTES AND QUESTIONS

1. If you were on an IRB evaluating the proposed XYY study, would you have voted for it to go forward? What alternative design might you use to determine if an XYY chromosomal complement was linked to a higher level of aggression? Ultimately, researchers in Denmark concluded that XYY men were less likely to be aggressive than their XY counterparts.

> The investigators examined the chromosomes of thousands of tall Danes (since those with the abnormality are, on the average, six inches taller than the general population) so that they could study a group of XYYs chosen from among ordinary citizens, rather than from among inmates of an institution. Then they took case histories to find out whether those in the sample had been convicted of crimes, evaluated the types of crimes, and examined their findings in the light of three possible explanations: that XYYs were, in fact, more aggressive and antisocial than the rest of the population; that the intellectual impairment known to be brought on by the extra Y chromosome made XYYs easier to catch; and that their added height made aggression easier and caused others to perceive them as more dangerous * * *.

> The Danish group found that about 42 percent of the XYYs they uncovered (five out of twelve) had criminal records, much more than the 9 percent who turned up among the controls. But except for one man who badly beat his wife while he was drunk, the crimes were neither aggressive nor violent. And some of the convictions were directly tied to crimes that someone with normal intelligence and impulses would never have been caught doing * * *.

Zsolt Harsanyi & Richard Hutton, Genetic Prophecy: Beyond the Double Helix 188–89 (1981). The issue of XYY karyotype is also discussed in Chapter 13, Mental and Behavioral Genetics.

2. Most Institutional Review Board assessments of research focus on the physical risks of participation in the research. If the research only involves a blood test, it might be viewed as a study presenting ''minimal risks.'' In what ways do the federal research regulations allow less scrutiny for a study with minimal risks? Why does the Office for Human Research Protections (formerly the Office for Protection from Research Risks (OPRR)) think genetic research presents more than minimal risks?

3. How, if at all, would the federal research regulations apply to the following research protocols:

a) A biotechnology company, using venture capital, institutes a project to identify genes associated with asthma.

b) Researchers propose to test Abraham Lincoln's blood from the cloak Mary Todd Lincoln wore on the night of the assassination to see if the president had a genetic predisposition to Marfan syndrome, a connective tissue disorder. See Robert Kurson, In Old Blood, Chicago Magazine,

March 2001, at 24. See also Philip R. Reilly, Abraham Lincoln's DNA and Other Adventures in Genetics (2000). For proposed guidelines regarding testing DNA from historic figures, see Lori Andrews et al., Constructing Ethical Guidelines for Biohistory, 304 Science 215–216 (2004).

c) A genetic researcher with a grant from the National Institutes of Health undertakes a study of the Huntington disease gene in a large family. The participants do not wish to know if they have inherited the mutated form of the gene. After he completes the study, he proposes to publish a family tree—without identifiers—to identify which family members have the mutation. By looking at the tree, a 19–year-old family member will realize he has the mutation. Would anything in the federal regulations prohibit the publication of the family tree? In The Ethics of Prediction: Genetic Risk and the Physician–Patient Relationship, 1 Genome Sci. & Tech. 21 (1995), Eric Juengst points to an actual study in which genetic information about misattributed paternity was revealed to participants in this manner. Should the researcher avoid a potential confidentiality breach by "disguising" the family tree by changing the number of siblings or the sex of certain family members? How would such a change affect the research utility of the family tree?

d) A state university with a federal grant appoints the following people from its faculty and administration as the only members of its Institutional Review Board: a female pathologist, a female geneticist, a female law professor, and the female head of the university tech transfer office. Is this IRB properly constituted? If not, why not?

4.   Should researchers inform participants of incidental findings that concern the participant's health, even if those findings are not the subject of the research project? For example, if a participant's genetic sample indicated that he was highly likely to develop Huntington's Disease in the future, is the researcher obligated to inform the participant? What if the study was meant to determine the genetic basis for baldness? What if the researcher who analyzed the sample was not a medical doctor?

5.   As GWAS become more powerful, researchers will likely be able to link increasing amounts of genetic variation with susceptibility to disease. What if certain racial or ethnic groups are found to be more vulnerable to certain diseases than others? Should that information be made public? Should we develop medications that are specifically approved for different races and ethnic groups?

D.   RESEARCH ON VULNERABLE POPULATIONS

FEDERAL REGULATIONS GOVERNING RESEARCH ON CHILDREN

45 C.F.R. 46.401 et seq.

§ 46.401   To what do these regulations apply?

(a) This subpart applies to all research involving children as subjects, conducted or supported by the Department of Health and Human Services.

* * *

§ 46.402   Definitions.

The definitions in § 46.102 of subpart A shall be applicable to this subpart as well. In addition, as used in this subpart:

(a) Children are persons who have not attained the legal age for consent to treatments or procedures involved in the research, under the applicable law of the jurisdiction in which the research will be conducted.

(b) Assent means a child's affirmative agreement to participate in research. Mere failure to object should not, absent affirmative agreement, be construed as assent.

(c) Permission means the agreement of parent(s) or guardian to the participation of their child or ward in research.

(d) Parent means a child's biological or adoptive parent.

(e) Guardian means an individual who is authorized under applicable State or local law to consent on behalf of a child to general medical care.

§ 46.403   IRB duties.

In addition to other responsibilities assigned to IRBs under this part, each IRB shall review research covered by this subpart and approve only research which satisfies the conditions of all applicable sections of this subpart.

§ 46.404   Research not involving greater than minimal risk.

HHS will conduct or fund research in which the IRB finds that no greater than minimal risk to children is presented, only if the IRB finds that adequate provisions are made for soliciting the assent of the children and the permission of their parents or guardians, as set forth in § 46.408.

§ 46.405   Research involving greater than minimal risk but presenting the prospect of direct benefit to the individual subjects.

HHS will conduct or fund research in which the IRB finds that more than minimal risk to children is presented by an intervention or procedure that holds out the prospect of direct benefit for the individual subject, or by a monitoring procedure that is likely to contribute to the subject's well-being, only if the IRB finds that:

(a) The risk is justified by the anticipated benefit to the subjects;

(b) The relation of the anticipated benefit to the risk is at least as favorable to the subjects as that presented by available alternative approaches; and

(c) Adequate provisions are made for soliciting the assent of the children and permission of their parents or guardians, as set forth in § 46.408.

§ 46.406   Research involving greater than minimal risk and no prospect of direct benefit to individual subjects, but likely to yield generalizable knowledge about the subject's disorder or condition.

HHS will conduct or fund research in which the IRB finds that more than minimal risk to children is presented by an intervention or procedure that does not hold out the prospect of direct benefit for the individual subject, or by a monitoring procedure which is not likely to contribute to the well-being of the subject, only if the IRB finds that:

(a) The risk represents a minor increase over minimal risk;

(b) The intervention or procedure presents experiences to subjects that are reasonably commensurate with those inherent in their actual or expected medical, dental, psychological, social, or educational situations;

(c) The intervention or procedure is likely to yield generalizable knowledge about the subjects' disorder or condition which is of vital importance for the understanding or amelioration of the subjects' disorder or condition; and

(d) Adequate provisions are made for soliciting assent of the children and permission of their parents or guardians, as set forth in § 46.408.

§ 46.407   Research not otherwise approvable which presents an opportunity to understand, prevent, or alleviate a serious problem affecting the health or welfare of children.

HHS will conduct or fund research that the IRB does not believe meets the requirements of § 46.404, § 46.405, or § 46.406 only if:

(a) the IRB finds that the research presents a reasonable opportunity to further the understanding, prevention, or alleviation of a serious problem affecting the health or welfare of children; and

(b) the Secretary, after consultation with a panel of experts in pertinent disciplines (for example: science, medicine, education, ethics, law) and following opportunity for public review and comment, has determined either:

> (1) that the research in fact satisfies the conditions of § 46.404, § 46.405, or § 46.406, as applicable, or (2) the following:
>
>> (i) the research presents a reasonable opportunity to further the understanding, prevention, or alleviation of a serious problem affecting the health or welfare of children;
>>
>> (ii) the research will be conducted in accordance with sound ethical principles;
>>
>> (iii) adequate provisions are made for soliciting the assent of children and the permission of their parents or guardians, as set forth in § 46.408.

* * *

§ 46.409   Wards.

(a) Children who are wards of the state or any other agency, institution, or entity can be included in research approved under § 46.406 or § 46.407 only if such research is:

(1) Related to their status as wards; or

(2) Conducted in schools, camps, hospitals, institutions, or similar settings in which the majority of children involved as subjects are not wards.

(b) If the research is approved under paragraph (a) of this section, the IRB shall require appointment of an advocate for each child who is a ward, in addition to any other individual acting on behalf of the child as guardian or in loco parentis. One individual may serve as advocate for more than one child. The advocate shall be an individual who has the background and experience to act in, and agrees to act in, the best interests of the child for the duration of the child's participation in the research and who is not associated in any way (except in the role as advocate or member of the IRB) with the research, the investigator(s), or the guardian organization.

LEONARD H. GLANTZ, RESEARCH WITH CHILDREN
24 Am. J. L. & Med. 213 (1998).

The first tests of immunization were performed on slaves and children. Edward Jenner vaccinated his one-year-old son with cowpox to see if it offered immunity to smallpox. His next subject was an eight-year-old child who was challenged with an inoculation of smallpox material in order to determine if the inoculation was effective. In 1802, Jenner's vaccine was tested on forty-eight children living in an almshouse. All the children were challenged with smallpox to see if they were effectively immunized.

Following the exploitation of children as laborers in the Industrial Revolution, the 1900s saw an increased interest in child welfare along with an increased desire to learn more about children's health problems. In the first decade of the 1900s, Alfred Hess, a respected pediatrician, became the medical director of the Hebrew Infant Asylum in New York. He noted that conducting research in an asylum was ideal because it approximated those "conditions which are insisted on in considering the course of experimental infection among laboratory animals, but which can rarely be controlled in a study of infection in man."

The germ theory was tested by intentionally infecting both adults and children with diseases. The health officer at a Hawaiian leprosarium injected six girls under his care with the syphilis virus. Dr. Henry Heiman reported that he was able to successfully produce gonorrhea in a four-year-old "idiot" with chronic epilepsy as well as in a sixteen-year-old male "idiot."

The invention of the x-ray prompted much research in children and adults. Physicians used x-rays to study the normal development of children and adults, including the fetus in utero.

In 1896, Dr. Arthur Wentworth published a paper describing spinal taps he performed on twenty-nine children at Children's Hospital in

Boston to determine if the procedure was harmful. He determined they were safe. However, John Roberts, a Philadelphia physician, noting that these procedures were with "no therapeutic indications for the operation" and for "purely and avowedly experimental" reasons, labeled Wentworth's use of these procedures "human vivisection."

In 1941, Francis Payton Rous, editor of the *Journal of Experimental Medicine*, rejected a manuscript from a physician and wrote to the author, "the inoculation of a twelve month old infant with herpes ... was an abuse of power, an infringement of the rights of an individual, and not excusable because the illness which followed had implications for science." The fact that "a child was 'offered as a volunteer'—whatever that may mean—does not palliate the action." This statement represents an important turning point in the discussion of research with children. It is one of the first statements to acknowledge that children themselves have rights as individuals and that the thought that one could be "offered as a volunteer" was a contradiction in terms.

In one of the initial research projects designed to determine if phenylalanine accumulations caused phenylketonuria (PKU), a metabolic disorder that causes mental retardation, the researchers first put a two-year-old girl with PKU on a diet low in phenylalinine. A gradual improvement resulted over a few months. Due to the importance of establishing the role of phenylalinine in this condition, the researchers decided to add phenylalinine to the child's special diet without telling the child's mother so that any change could be noted by her without bias. The mother reported a definite deterioration; within a few days, she reported that her daughter lost all the ground that had been gained in the past ten months. This was then repeated with the same child. From the 1950s through the 1970s, a research team at the Willowbrook State School systematically infected mentally retarded children with strains of hepatitis.

* * *

Concern about these past abuses have led to the adoption of federal regulations that are specifically designed to protect children when they are enrolled as research subjects. Indeed, a New York court which limited the use of children and mentally disabled individuals as research subjects began its opinion by stating:

> The mere mention of experimental medical research on incapacitated human beings—the mentally ill, the profoundly retarded, and minor children summons up visceral reactions with recollections of the brutal Nazi experimentation with helpless subjects of concentration camps, and elicits shudders of revulsion when parallels are suggested. Even without the planned brutality, we have had deplorable instances of over-reaching medical research in this country.

* * *

Children are particularly vulnerable as research subjects for numerous reasons. First, they may not be competent to volunteer to participate in a research project and so they will be participating either nonvoluntarily or involuntarily. Second, the person giving consent for the child's participation may have ulterior motives that go against the best interests of the child, especially considering the psychological effects an illness can have on a family. Furthermore, parents may be offered incentives for their child's participation that may influence their decisions to allow their child to participate. Third, the person proposing the research may have motives for conducting the research that are unrelated to, or even conflict with, the particular subject's welfare. Fourth, if the children are institutionalized or otherwise in state care, they are removed from the "ideal" protective parent. Fifth, the legal authority of parents or guardians to "volunteer" their children to participate as research subjects is unclear. Last, there may be subgroups of children, such as terminally ill children or children with rare conditions, that may place them at special risk.

* * *

A recently published study provides an example of the vagueness of the concept of minimal risk when applied to research on children. The study subjects were thirty-four impoverished African American and Hispanic boys, ranging from seven to eleven years of age, who were younger brothers of delinquents. Subjects underwent two psychiatric assessments in order to determine which children could be classified as being afflicted with oppositional defiant disorder, conduct disorder and attention-deficit hyperactivity disorder. The investigators then visited the children's homes to rate them on a number of variables. Finally, the investigators assessed the boys' serotonergic activity based on prior work that supposedly shows a relationship between serotonin levels and aggression. To accomplish this, all boys were free of medications for at least one month, all followed a low-monoamine diet for four days, and all fasted the night before the test (referred to as a "challenge"). On the day of the challenge, the boys received nothing by mouth and an intravenous catheter was inserted at 8:30 A.M. and remained in place for about five and a half hours. Researchers orally administered fenfluramine hydrochloride to the boys at 10:00 A.M. and took blood samples every hour from the catheter. By measuring certain biochemical responses to the fenfluramine challenge, the investigators would be able to make an assessment of the boys' central serotonergic activity. The investigators conducted this research in an attempt "to replicate results that have suggested that aggression in prepubertal children is positively correlated with central serotonergic activity" and to determine if "an association between adverse-rearing conditions and serotonin in children" existed.

Because this study presented no possible benefit to the minor subjects, the question is whether it should have be performed on this group of boys. Is this a minimal risk study or a greater than minimal risk study? The study involves conferring on the boys a psychiatric diagnosis related to aggressiveness that they apparently did not previously carry. Was this diagnosis passed on to the parents? If so, what is the effect on the children of such labeling? This negative diagnosis or labeling was created other than for the purpose of furthering research, not for developing a treatment or preventive program for the child. The children were placed on a special diet for four days, a catheter was inserted and remained in place for five and a half hours, and the children were administered a drug that has no pediatric indication solely for the purpose of producing a response to the drug. Is the probability and magnitude of harm not greater than those encountered in the "routine physical or psychological examinations or tests?" In "routine" physical and psychological tests, children are not exposed to substances that cannot possibly be of use in diagnosis and treatment of a condition from which they might suffer. Moreover, the administration of fenfluramine in adults had previously been documented to cause adverse reactions. * * * Further, the study raises the question of how one keeps children with "oppositional defiant disorder," "conduct disorder" and "attention-deficit hyperactivity disorder" from withdrawing from the study during the many long hours of study. If the study presents more than minimal risk to the child-subjects and is not "likely to yield generalizable knowledge about the subjects' condition which is of vital importance for the understanding or the amelioration of the subject's disorder or condition," then it would clearly be barred under the federal regulations. First, it is not clear that these children have a "disorder or condition," as those terms are used in the regulations. Indeed, it appears the only "diagnosis" these children had was the one conferred on them by the investigators. Second, nothing in this study was designed to be of "vital importance" to the amelioration of a condition or even the understanding of the condition. But the larger question is, Why should a parent have the authority to submit a child to such nonbeneficial procedures? Even if each individual procedure to which the children were subjected presented minimal risk, when a child is subjected to several minimal risk procedures, when does this amount to more than minimal risk?

GRIMES v. KENNEDY KRIEGER INST., INC.

782 A.2d 807 (Md. App. 2001).

CATHELL, J.

PROLOGUE

In these present cases, a prestigious research institute [KKI], associated with Johns Hopkins University, based on this record, created a nontherapeutic research program whereby it required certain classes of homes to have only partial lead paint abatement modifications performed, and in at least some instances, including at least one of the cases at bar, arranged for the landlords to receive public funding by way of grants or loans to aid in the modifications. The research institute then encouraged, and in at least one of the cases at bar, required the landlords to rent the premises to families with young children. In the event young children already resided in one of the study houses, it was contemplated that a child would remain in the premises, and the child was encouraged to remain, in order for his or her blood to be periodically analyzed. In other words, the continuing presence of the children that were the subjects of the study was required in order for the study to be complete. Apparently, the children and their parents involved in the cases *sub judice* were from lower economic strata and were, at least in one case, minorities.

The purpose of the research was to determine how effective varying degrees of lead paint abatement procedures were. Success was to be determined by periodically, over a two-year period of time, measuring the extent to which lead dust remained in, or returned to, the premises after the varying levels of abatement modifications, and, as most important to our decision, by measuring the extent to which the theretofore healthy children's blood became contaminated with lead, and comparing that contamination with levels of lead dust in the houses over the same periods of time.

* * *

Apparently, it was anticipated that the children, who were the human subjects in the program, would, or at least might, accumulate lead in their blood from the dust, thus helping the researchers to determine the extent to which the various partial abatement methods worked. There was no complete and clear explanation in the consent agreements signed by the parents of the children that the research to be conducted was designed, at least in significant part, to measure the success of the abatement procedures by measuring the extent to which the children's blood was being contaminated.

* * *

Nowhere in the consent form was it clearly disclosed to the mother that the researchers contemplated that, as a result of the experiment, the child might accumulate lead in her blood, and that in order for the experiment to succeed it was necessary that the child remain in the house as the lead in the child's blood increased or decreased, so that it could be measured. The Consent Form states in relevant part:

"PURPOSE OF STUDY:

As you may know, lead poisoning in children is a problem in Baltimore City and other communities across the country. Lead in paint, house dust and outside soil are major sources of lead exposure for children. Children can also be exposed to lead in drinking water and other sources. We understand that your house is going to have special repairs done in order to reduce exposure to lead in paint and dust. On a random basis, homes will receive one of two levels of repair. We are interested in finding out how well the two levels of repair work. The repairs are not intended, or expected, to completely remove exposure to lead.

* * *

BENEFITS

> To compensate you for your time answering questions and allowing us to sketch your home we will mail you a check in the amount of $5.00. In the future we would mail you a check in the amount of $15 each time the full questionnaire is completed. The dust, soil, water, and blood samples would be tested for lead at the Kennedy Krieger Institute at no charge to you. We would provide you with specific blood-lead results. *We would contact you to discuss a summary of house test results and steps that you could take to reduce any risks of exposure.*" [Emphasis added.]

Pursuant to the plans of the research study, KKI collected dust samples in the Monroe Street property on March 9, 1993, August 23, 1993, March 9, 1994, September 19, 1994, April 18, 1995, and November 13, 1995. The March 9, 1993 dust testing revealed what the researchers referred to as "hot spots" where the level of lead was "higher than might be found in a completely renovated [abated] house." This information about the "hot spots" was not furnished to Ms. Hughes until December 16, 1993, more than nine months after the samples had been collected and, as we discuss, *infra,* not until after Ericka Grimes's blood was found to contain elevated levels of lead.

* * *

On appeal, appellants seek review of the circuit courts' decisions granting KKI's respective summary judgment motions. They contend, contrary to the trial courts' findings, that KKI owed a duty to warn appellants of the presence of lead-based paint and dust because: (1) a "special relationship" existed between the parties; (2) of the contractual duty created by the consent agreement; (3) the danger was foreseeable; and (4) a Federal regulation exists, which created such a duty. Specifically, they contend that KKI had an affirmative duty to give appellants complete and accurate information concerning the risks and hazards of participating in the study—to include the XRF results and the Cyclone vacuum results.

* * *

Initially, we note that we know of no law, nor have we been directed to any applicable in Maryland courts, that provides that the parties to a scientific study, because it is a scientific, health-related study, cannot be held to have entered into special relationships with the subjects of the study that can create duties, including duties, the breach of which may give rise to negligence claims. We also are not aware of any general legal precept that immunizes nongovernmental "institutional volunteers" [the term one of the trial courts used to refer to the researchers] or scientific researchers from the responsibility for the breaches of duties arising in "special relationships." * * * We shall hold initially that the very nature of nontherapeutic scientific research on human subjects can, and normally will, create special relationships out of which duties arise. Since World

War II the specialness or nature of such relationships has been frequently of concern in and outside of the research community.

As a result of the atrocities performed in the name of science during the Holocaust, and other happenings in the World War II era, what is now known as The Nuremberg Code evolved. Of special interest to this Court, the Nuremberg Code, at least in significant part, was the result of legal thought and legal principles, as opposed to medical or scientific principles, and thus should be the preferred standard for assessing the legality of scientific research on human subjects. Under it, duties to research subjects arise.

* * *

The Sufficiency of the Consent Form

The consent form did not directly inform the parents of the fact that it was contemplated that some of the children might ingest lead dust particles, and that one of the reasons the blood of the children was to be tested was to evaluate how effective the various abatement measures were.

A reasonable parent would expect to be clearly informed that it was at least contemplated that her child would ingest lead dust particles, and that the degree to which lead dust contaminated the child's blood would be used as one of the ways in which the success of the experiment would be measured. The fact that if such information was furnished, it might be difficult to obtain human subjects for the research, does not affect the need to supply the information, or alter the ethics of failing to provide such information. A human subject is entitled to *all* material information. * * * Whether assessed by a subjective or an objective standard, the children, or their surrogates, should have been additionally informed that the researchers anticipated that, as a result of the experiment, it was possible that there might be some accumulation of lead in the blood of the children. The "informed" consent was not valid because full material information was not furnished to the subjects or their parents.

* * *

[The] federal regulations, especially the requirement for adherence to sound ethical principles [in 45 C.F.R. § 46.407], strike right at the heart of KKI's defense of the granting of the Motions for Summary Judgment. *Fully informed* consent is lacking in these cases. The research did not comply with the regulations. There clearly was more than a minimal risk involved. Under the regulations, children should not have been used for the purpose of measuring how much lead they would accumulate in their blood while living in partially abated houses to which they were recruited initially or encouraged to remain, because of the study.

* * *

Clearly, KKI, as a research institution, is required to obtain a human participant's fully informed consent, using sound ethical principles. It is clear from the wording of the applicable federal regulations that this requirement of informed consent continues during the duration of the research study and applies to new or changing risks. In this case, a special relationship out of which duties might arise might be created by reason of the federally imposed regulations. The question becomes whether this duty of informed consent created by federal regulation, as a matter of state law, translates into a duty of care arising out of the unique relationship that is researcher-subject, as opposed to doctor-patient. We answer that question in the affirmative. In this State, it may, depending on the facts, create such a duty.

Additionally, the Nuremberg Code, intended to be applied internationally, and never expressly rejected in this country, inherently and implicitly, speaks strongly to the existence of special relationships imposing ethical duties on researchers who conduct nontherapeutic experiments on human subjects. The Nuremberg Code specifically requires researchers to make known to human subjects of research "all inconveniences and hazards reasonably to be expected; and the effects upon his health or person which may *possibly* come from his participation in the experiment." (Emphasis added.) The breach of obligations imposed on researchers by the Nuremberg Code, might well support actions sounding in negligence in cases such as those at issue here.

* * *

It is, first and foremost, the responsibility of the researcher and the research entity to see to the harmlessness of such nontherapeutic research. Consent of parents can never relieve the researcher of this duty. We do not feel that it serves proper public policy concerns to permit children to be placed in situations of potential harm, during nontherapeutic procedures, even if parents, or other surrogates, consent. Under these types of circumstances, even where consent is given, *albeit* inappropriately, policy considerations suggest that there remains a special relationship between researchers and participants to the research study, which imposes a duty of care. This is entirely consistent with the principles found in the Nuremberg Code.

NOTES AND QUESTIONS

1. Why were children historically chosen as research participants? Do the federal regulations governing research on children provide sufficient protection?

2. How persuasive is Paul Ramsey's viewpoint that children should never be used as research subjects because they cannot give legally valid consent? Paul Ramsey, The Enforcement of Morals: Nontherapeutic Research on Children, 6 Hastings Center Report 21 (August 1976).

3. Since the 1980s, federally funded researchers have included foster children with HIV in experimental AIDS treatment trials. Despite being

required to provide an advocate by federal law, in many cases no advocates were appointed on behalf of the children to independently determine whether the child was being subjected to serious risks without receiving any personal health benefits. Some studies reported higher death rates among test subjects taking high doses of a drug, but the local agencies involved in bringing the children—mostly poor or minority children—into the study concluded that these deaths were not directly related to the drug trials. John Solomon, U.S. Tested AIDS Drugs on 200 Ill. Foster Children, Associated Press, May 5, 2005, http://www.usatoday.com/news/health/2005–05–04–drugs-foster%1-kids?dx. htm. Is this a situation where an advocate is needed for each child involved in the study? How should the agencies in charge of caring for these children balance the potential risk to them against the chance to gain access to cutting-edge medical care that the children might not otherwise get?

4. How should an IRB assess the level of risk permitted under § 46.406? If risks are allowed that are "reasonably commensurate with those inherent in their actual or expected medical, dental, psychological, social or educational situations," should it be permissible to expose children who are seriously ill or live in dangerous neighborhoods to a greater level of risk in the research than children who have a lesser baseline risk in their daily life?

5. Should it be considered to be more than minimal risk to undertake a blood test to determine if children are homozygous for a recessive disorder, such as cystic fibrosis or a sickle cell disorder?

6. Which provision—45 C.F.R. § 405, § 406 or § 407—should be applied to the serotonin research described in the Glantz article? Were the risks minimal? Did the subjects have a "disorder or condition"?

7. How should an IRB view a payment of $1000 to a parent to enroll a healthy child in gene therapy research? Would the federal regulations, or any other legal doctrine, prevent such a payment? On what grounds might an IRB refuse to authorize such a study?

8. What types of genetic research on children might be included by the *Grimes* decision? Were there any precautions KKI could have taken to minimize their liability in *Grimes*? Do you think the decision in *Grimes* would have been different if the research had been for therapeutic purposes?

E. STATE REGULATION OF RESEARCH

The federal research regulations specifically do not preempt state or local laws or regulations that provide additional protections for human subjects. Only a handful of states, such as Virginia, have adopted comprehensive laws governing human research. See Va. Code Ann. §§ 32.1–162.16–.20. Many states, however, have adopted laws governing research on certain vulnerable populations, such as children or people with mental disabilities. See Lori B. Andrews, Medical Genetics: A Legal Frontier 42–46 (1987). States have also adopted restrictive laws governing research on embryos and fetuses. The state laws on research are particularly important because, unlike the federal research regulations, they apply to research no matter what the source of funding.

Starting in the mid–1990s, a new trend in state laws emerged. Some states adopted laws forbidding genetic testing without an individual's written informed consent. Yet most of those laws created exceptions that allowed researchers to undertake certain types of genetic testing without informed consent. The Massachusetts law, Mass. Stat. Ann. 111 § 70G, for example, allows investigators undertaking pharmacological or clinical research to undertake genetic testing on a person's DNA without his or her consent if the research has been approved by an IRB. Other states exempt any researcher from having to comply with the informed consent provision, without even requiring IRB approval.

III. RESEARCH ON TISSUE SAMPLES

A. THE NATURE OF THE RESEARCH

NATIONAL BIOETHICS ADVISORY COMMISSION (NBAC), RESEARCH INVOLVING HUMAN BIOLOGICAL MATERIALS: ETHICAL ISSUES AND POLICY GUIDANCE

1–14 (1999).

Biomedical researchers have long studied human biological materials—such as cells collected in research projects, biopsy specimens obtained for diagnostic purposes, and organs and tissues removed during surgery—to increase knowledge about human diseases and to develop better means of preventing, diagnosing, and treating these diseases. Today, new technologies and advances in biology provide even more effective tools for using such resources to improve medicine's diagnostic and therapeutic potential. Yet, the very power of these new technologies raises a number of important ethical issues.

Is it appropriate to use stored biological materials in ways that originally were not contemplated either by the people from whom the materials came or by those who collected the materials? Does such use harm anyone's interest? Does it matter whether the material is identified, or identifiable, as to its source, or is linked, or linkable, to other medical or personal data regarding the source?

* * *

Although protection of human subjects in research is of primary concern in the U.S. biomedical research system, research that uses biological materials—materials that often are distanced in time and space from the persons from whom they were obtained—raises unique challenges regarding the appropriate protection of research subjects.

* * *

Policies and guidelines governing human subjects research should permit investigators—under certain circumstances and with the informed, voluntary consent of sample sources—to have access to identifying infor-

mation sufficient to enable them to gather necessary data regarding the
subjects. Provided that adequate protections exist (which usually, but not
always, include informed consent), such information gathering could include ongoing collection of medical records data and even requests for
individuals to undergo tests to provide additional research information. In
some cases, it even will be acceptable for investigators to convey information about research results to the persons whose samples have been
studied. Where identifying information exists, however, a well-developed
system of protections must be implemented to ensure that risks are
minimized and that the interests of sample sources are protected.

* * *

How well does the existing Federal Policy for the Protection of
Human Subjects (the so-called Common Rule, codified at 45 C.F.R. Part
46) meet these objectives? Specifically, does it provide clear direction to
research sponsors, investigators, IRBs, and others regarding the conduct
of research using human biological materials in an ethical manner? NBAC
finds that it does not adequately do so. In some cases, present regulatory
language provides ambiguous guidance for research using human biological materials. For example, confusion about the intended meaning of
terms such as "human subject," "publicly available," and "minimal risk"
has stymied investigators and IRB members. Beyond these ambiguities,
certain parts of current regulations are inadequate to ensure the ethical
use of human biological materials in research and require some modification.

B. MEDICAL ORGANIZATION GUIDANCE ABOUT RESEARCH ON TISSUE SAMPLES

AMERICAN SOCIETY OF HUMAN GENETICS, STATEMENT ON INFORMED CONSENT FOR GENETIC RESEARCH

59 Am. J. Human Genetics 471–474 (1996).

* * *

RESEARCH USING PROSPECTIVELY COLLECTED SAMPLES

In genetic studies that are designed to collect new biological samples
from individuals, the investigators generally have the opportunity to
communicate with potential subjects in advance and involve them in the
research by obtaining their informed consent. This should be encouraged,
except for the prospective studies in which samples are collected anonymously, or have been "anonymized."

Studies that maintain identified or identifiable specimens must maintain subjects' confidentiality * * *. To ensure maximum privacy, it is
strongly recommended that investigators apply to the Department of
Health and Human Services for a Certificate of Confidentiality. Investiga-

tors should indicate to the subject that they cannot guarantee absolute confidentiality.

Research results or samples should not be given to any of the subject's family members by the investigator without the explicit, written permission of the subject, except under extraordinary circumstances. Within the limits of the law, the results must not be shared with employers, insurance companies, or other parties without the written permission of the subject.

CONSENT DISCLOSURES

Subjects providing consent to prospective studies should be told about the types of information that could result from genetic research. Subjects must be given sufficient information to understand the implications and the limitations of research. Individuals should be told the purpose, limitations, possible outcomes, and means of communicating results and maintaining confidentiality. They should be informed of what information may reasonably be expected to result from the genetic study. Importantly, subjects should also understand that unexpected findings, including identification of medical risk, carrier status, or risk to offspring affected by genetic disease, may arise.

During the course of molecular genetic diagnosis, the results may indicate that the child is not the offspring of one or both the presumed parents. The investigator therefore should consider including in the consent form a statement that misidentified parentage will not be disclosed. Another example of unforeseen outcome is genetic heterogeneity in which disorders which were initially thought to be due to defects in a single allele or locus are associated with new ones.

Additional risks that should be disclosed to subjects of certain genetic research studies include the possibility of adverse psychological sequelae, disruption of family dynamics, and social stigmatization and discrimination. All genetic research studies involving identified or identifiable samples in which disclosure of results is planned should have medical geneticists and/or genetic counselors involved to ensure that the results are communicated to the subjects accurately and appropriately. The consent form should not promise significant breakthroughs in diagnosis, treatment or outcome to entice participation. Also, careful attention by all parties involved in genetic research should be given to avoiding actions that could be coercive to potential subjects.

DISPOSITION OF SAMPLES AND RESULTS

Depending on the study, subjects may be given the opportunity to determine if they want to be informed of the results of their testing. Subjects should be informed if the sample will be stored for later study, but they also need to be told that there is always the possibility of storage failure. Decisions related to disposition of results or samples after the subject's death should be specified by the subject.

In some studies researchers may wish to disclose results to subjects. If so, it is the obligation of the subjects to keep the investigator informed of how they may be contacted. Investigators should indicate to study subjects that certain results may not allow definite answers until an analysis of the entire study has been completed (and, sometimes, not even then). Under such circumstances, results cannot be communicated expeditiously.

Subjects involved in studies where the samples are identified or identifiable should indicate if their sample should be used exclusively in the study under consideration. If the sample is to be used more generally, subjects should be given options regarding the scope of the subsequent investigations, such as whether the sample can be used only for a specific disease under investigation, or for other unrelated conditions. It is inappropriate to ask a subject to grant blanket consent for all future unspecified genetic research projects on any disease or in any area if the samples are identifiable in those subsequent studies.

Subjects involved in studies in which the samples are identified or identifiable should indicate if unused portions of the samples may be shared with other researchers. If the subject is willing to have the sample shared with other researchers, it is the responsibility of the principal investigator to distribute the sample, so as to ensure that the agreement embodied in the informed consent is upheld. Finally, subjects should decide if subsequent researchers may receive their samples as anonymous or identifiable specimens.

Retrospective Studies of Existing Samples

We endorse the use of anonymous samples for genetic research. Importantly, in retrospective research proposing to use samples collected anonymously or anonymized, there is no possibility, or need, to obtain consent.

For many studies, there may be benefits to making identifiable samples anonymous, because this effectively protects subjects from some of the risks of genetic research. Importantly, making samples anonymous will eliminate the need for recontact to obtain informed consent. This will also reduce the chance of introducing bias due to inability to recontact some, or the possible refusal of others to participate. On the other hand, investigators should consider the appropriateness of anonymizing samples, especially when there is available medical intervention for the disorder being tested.

For research involving identifiable samples, the investigator should be required to recontact the subjects to obtain consent for new studies. However, an investigator may seek a waiver based on the following criteria of 45 CFR 46.116:

1. The research involves no more than minimal risk to the subjects;

2. The waiver or alteration will not adversely affect the rights and welfare of the subjects;

3. The research could not practically be carried out without the waiver or alteration; and

4. Whenever appropriate, the subjects will be provided with additional pertinent information after participation.

For research involving samples that retain identifiers, consent should be obtained. Waivers may be granted, although the waivers will be difficult to justify by the above criteria if identifiers are retained.

C. CASE STUDY OF RESEARCH ON EXISTING SAMPLES

The following is the text of a brochure distributed by the Centers for Disease Control and Prevention (CDC) for a study of Americans' health. In the course of the study CDC researchers conducted blood tests on tens of thousands of people, took their health histories, and undertook certain other procedures such as X-rays. After this was done, researchers wanted access to the blood samples to conduct genetic research. Officials at the CDC convened a panel of experts to determine whether there was anything in the federal regulations or the brochure itself that would preclude using the blood samples for genetic research without asking the people who provided the blood initially for consent for that new use.

CENTERS FOR DISEASE CONTROL AND PREVENTION, "NATIONAL HEALTH AND NUTRITION EXAMINATION SURVEY"

More than 70,000 persons have participated in the National Health and Nutrition Examination Surveys (NHANES).

It is the willingness of the people that makes this survey work. Since the early 1960's, NHANES has identified many health problems that affect all of us. Through continued research, health promotion and disease prevention, such health problems as heart disease have declined.

The third National Health and Nutrition Examination Survey (NHANES III) will be used to track the progress of combating disease in this country. Tracking our progress helps to prevent future disease. As a result, NHANES information that has been very valuable to our health in the recent past promises to be even more so in the future.

* * *

NHANES III Is Different From Other Surveys

NHANES III is different because it is the only national survey in which physical examinations are performed to measure a person's health. We are studying how current health habits and practices relate to future health. After several years, we will check back with you to note any changes in your health. A small sample of your blood will be kept in long-term storage for future testing. The examinations are conducted by a medical doctor and a highly trained medical staff in modern specially designed mobile units.

* * *

We Need Your Help

You were especially selected to be a part of NHANES III. You will represent hundreds of persons like yourself.

To show our appreciation for your participation, we provide:

Health Examinations

The data are collected through physical measurements, laboratory testing, and health interviews. There are no internal examinations given in this survey. Depending on your age you may be in the Examination Center for up to 3–1/2 hours. You will have the opportunity to learn about your health along with contributing to knowledge of the health needs of other Americans.

Your Examinations May Include:

Health Measurements

- Blood pressure
- Height, weight, and body fat
- Allergy test
- Lung capacity test
- Electrocardiogram
- Arthritis test (x rays of knees and hands)
- Bone density measurement (x rays of the hip)
- Ultrasound test for gallstones
- Dental check up

Laboratory Tests

Blood

- Cholesterol
- Anemia
- Kidney
- Liver
- Diabetes
- Lead
- Acquired immunodeficiency Syndrome (AIDS)
- Thyroid

Urine

- Drug use
- Kidney

Private Health Interviews

- Nutrition
- Reproductive health
- Sexual experience
- Physical activity
- Mental health
- Health habits

Q. What are the benefits for me?

A. • The opportunity to make an important contribution to the health of the nation

- Valuable health tests
- Cash payment for participating in the survey.

Q. Will I receive the results of my AIDS test?

A. No. The AIDS testing is being done in the NHANES III survey so we can determine how many people in the United States are infected with the AIDS virus. In order to make extra sure that the results are kept private, no information that would allow us to identify you will be attached to the blood specimens tested for AIDS virus. Therefore, your test results will be anonymous. If you would like to have an AIDS test and receive the results in a confidential manner, our staff can give you the name of a clinic in your area where you can go.

Q. How will I receive the results of my examination?

A. The results of your examination will be sent to you in about 12–16 weeks. Of course, if we should find something important to your health before that time, you will be notified.

* * *

Health information collected in the NHANES III is kept in strictest confidence. Without your approval our staff is not allowed to discuss your participation in this study with anyone under penalty of Federal law. Section 308(d) of the Public Health Service Act (42 USC 242m) and the Privacy Act of 1974 (5 USC 552A). However, in the case of children we will refer clear evidence of physical abuse to the responsible state agency for possible follow-up.

Notice—Information contained on this form which would permit identification of any individual or establishment has been collected with a guarantee that it will be held in strict confidence, will be used only for purposes stated for this study, and will not be disclosed or released to others without the consent of the individual or the establishment in accordance with section 308(d) of the Public Health Service Act (42 USC 242m).

NOTES AND QUESTIONS

1. How should an institutional review board assess a proposal to use the existing NHANES samples for new types of genetic research? Can such research go forward without consent? Would it fall within the exception of 45 C.F.R. § 46.101(b)(4)? Would it violate any provisions of the brochure, which participants signed as an informed consent form? Would the results of the new genetic tests have to be disclosed to people? Would identifiers have to be removed from the samples before they were analyzed?

For a discussion of how one interdisciplinary advisory workshop resolved these questions, see Ellen Wright Clayton et al., Informed Consent for Genetic Research on Stored Tissue Samples, 274 JAMA 1786 (1995). For alternative recommendations on research involving previously-collected tissue samples, see National Bioethics Advisory Commission, Research Involving Human Biological Materials: Ethical Issues and Policy Guidance (1999).

2. Clayton et al. suggest the following guidelines:

People should have the opportunity to decide whether their samples will be used for research. This option should be presented when samples are collected for whatever reason if it is likely that the samples will also be used for research. In addition, the possibility of future research should generally be discussed whenever tissue samples are collected for any research project.

If people agree to such use, they should then be offered the following options:

1. Whether they are willing to have their samples used in identifiable or linked research. To make this complex decision, potential subjects must be informed about (a) the risks and benefits of participation; (b) the extent to which confidentiality realistically will be maintained. Investigators are strongly encouraged to seek certificates of confidentiality; (c) under what circumstances, if any, they will be recontacted. If recontact may occur, subjects must be offered the opportunity to refuse to participate. Even if specific information will not be made available, researchers could offer to send a periodic newsletter to participants so that they can be aware of new findings and can seek them through their health care provider if they are interested. The circumstances under which the researcher will decline to provide preliminary results either in individual contacts or in the newsletters should also be defined; and (d) their ability to withdraw from the project in the future. In general, a decision to withdraw should allow the individual to stop any further personal involvement and to withdraw any samples or data that contain identifiers from use in research that occurs after the date of withdrawal.

Because of the complexity of the issues that individuals must consider in deciding whether to participate in such research, the workshop participants believe that it is not desirable to ask sources to sign statements in which they agree to the use of their identifiable samples for research without being informed about the scope and potential consequences of the projects.

2.   Whether they wish or are willing to have their samples stripped of identifiers for use in research. Individuals should be told that when their samples are used anonymously, they cannot be given specific information about findings related to their samples.

Whether people permit researchers to use identifiable or anonymous samples, they should be informed of the extent to which the researcher may be motivated by interests other than those of the source. People should be told whether they will share in the profits of any commercial products that might be developed based on findings from the research.

In addition, many at the workshop urged that people who provide tissue samples, particularly for use in identified or linkable research, should also be given the following choices:

1.   Whether they are willing to have their samples shared with other investigators either inside or outside the institution in which they are collected. Individuals may wish to permit their samples to be used only by investigators at academic institutions and not by those involved with commercial enterprises, although the distinctions between these two groups are increasingly difficult to define. In any event, samples should be shared with investigators who were not involved in the research project to which the subjects agreed only after identifiers have been removed.

2.   Whether they wish their samples to be used only to study certain disorders. Some individuals may wish to limit the use of their samples to specific diseases in which they are interested, such as breast cancer or cystic fibrosis. Others may wish to specify that their samples not be used to study certain classes of disorders, such as behavior-related diseases, disorders that are currently untreatable, diseases that are particularly stigmatizing to members of a group, or those for which prenatal diagnosis is the primary option.

Ellen Wright Clayton et al., Informed Consent for Genetic Research on Stored Tissue Samples, 274 JAMA 1786, 1791 (1995). What are the likely impacts of these suggestions on protecting human subjects? How will each of these suggestions affect the research effort itself?

3.   Do the ASHG's recommended guidelines for informed consent meet all the concerns raised in the Institutional Review Board Handbook?

4.   Since at least the time of adoption of the Nuremberg Code, research subjects have had the right to withdraw from a research project at any time. George Annas has suggested that, with respect to genetic research, this means that subjects should be able to order their DNA samples destroyed at any time. Annas also suggests that in order for the right of withdrawal to be meaningful, researchers should inform the people who provided DNA of their research agenda. George J. Annas, Rules for Research on Human Genetic Variation—Lessons from Iceland, 342 New Eng. J. Med. 1830, 1832 (2000).

How solid is the legal basis for such a right? What are the practical implications of such a right?

IV. BIOBANKS

A. OVERVIEW OF BIOBANKING

MARK A. ROTHSTEIN, EXPANDING THE ETHICAL ANALYSIS OF BIOBANKS

33 J.L. Med. & Ethics 89–91 (2005).

Biobanks are repositories of human biological materials collected for biomedical research. There are over 300 million stored specimens in the United States, and the number grows by 20 million per year. In the post-genome world of high throughput gene sequencing and computational biology, biobanks hold the promise of facilitating large-scale research studies. New organizational and operational models of research repositories also raise complex issues of big science, big business, and big ethical concerns.

Biobanks represent a new paradigm for biomedical research. Traditional research with biological specimens generally involves: (1) a single researcher or an established group of researchers; (2) obtaining and using the samples in defined ways to research in discrete areas; and (3) obtaining informed consent from each research subject to use his or her sample and, where appropriate, an authorization to obtain, use, and disclose the subject's health information. By contrast, with biobanks: (1) the individual or entity obtaining the sample may not be engaged in research, but may be only a broker or intermediary supplying specimens to other researchers; (2) the purpose of a biobank is to develop a repository that can be used for many research protocols, often in numerous scientific areas; (3) a biobank contemplates future research activities, including research by investigators who cannot be specified at the time of the sample collection; and (4) research using biobanks seeks to move beyond the one study/one informed consent model to a format of obtaining general (or blanket) consent to participate in the research activities of the biobank.

Some of the uncertainty surrounding the ethical and legal rules relating to biobanks can be traced to the fact that many developers and administrators of biobanks, researchers, regulators, and research subjects have viewed biobanks within the context of the traditional research paradigm.

* * *

It has been widely observed that the nature and degree of risk of biobank research depends on (1) the identifiability of the sample and any linked health information, and (2) whether the samples are extant or to be collected prospectively. Furthermore, just as the benefits of research go beyond the researchers and their affiliated institutions and entities to the public, the risks of research go beyond the individual human subjects to population groups with which the subject is associated as well as the general public. Therefore, societal interests appear on both the benefit and risk side of research.

The use of biobanks in research may be considered to raise the risks of both intrinsic harms and consequential harms, both of which may be manifested at the individual, group, or societal levels.

INTRINSIC HARMS

Research with identifiable samples raises the risk that there will be an invasion of the sample donor's privacy through disclosure of sensitive information. Research with unidentifiable samples raises the risk that the subject's sample will be used for research of which the sample donor does not approve (e.g., behavioral genetics) or otherwise violates the sample donor's strongly held beliefs (e.g., by failing to return bodily tissues in violation of religious precepts).

Even where direct personal identifiers have been removed, labels on biological samples and linked medical records may contain demographic data, such as gender, race, and ethnicity. Research findings indicating that members of certain subpopulations are more likely to have a genotype conferring an increased risk of disease or other traits could lead to stigma or discrimination against members of specific population groups. Thus, some forms of research may carry social risks beyond the donors of biological specimens. Another example of group intrinsic harm would be where a religious group opposed to abortion, such as Mormons in Utah, was concerned that its population database was being used in genetic research that might lead to more abortions (e.g., research on a gene linked to the likelihood of non-lethal birth defects).

CONSEQUENTIAL HARMS

Research with identifiable samples raises the risk of genetic discrimination by disclosure of individual research findings to third parties through clinical records or compelled disclosures.* * * Sometimes, harms may be considered both intrinsic and consequential. The ethical conduct of research exemplifies a society's respect for persons. Ethical lapses undermine public trust in the research enterprise and may result in widespread and long-lasting consequences, including reduced public funding for research, unwillingness of individuals or groups to participate in research, and distrust of the medical establishment that may extend to the clinical setting.

INFORMED CONSENT AND AUTHORIZATION

Informed consent has been variously defined as a legal doctrine, an ethical precept, and a system of shared decision making. Regardless of the specific meaning used, informed consent is a central tenet of biomedical research. The Nuremberg Code in 1947 established that the touchstone of ethical research is informed consent. The voluntary consent of the human subject is absolutely essential * * *. The primacy of informed consent is now codified in the federal Protection of Human Subjects Rule, also known as the Common Rule.

To some extent, the current research regulations are based on a narrow view of the research enterprise. The rules implicitly contemplate *individual* consent for particular research projects, *individual* risks and benefits, and largely *individual* consequences of the research. Under the current research rules, informed consent is an integral part of research, and it is obtained only after the specific elements of the research have been conceptualized and approved by an institutional review board (IRB). At present, IRBs attempting to protect group or societal interests in research are left without clear direction by the Common Rule.

Biobanks give rise to new relationships and ethical issues distinct from traditional concerns about the subjects of research. Biobanks frequently involve a separation of the sample collection process (and thus the informed consent process) from the actual research on the sample. The research may be undertaken years after the sample collection and may involve hypotheses and methods that could not have been contemplated at the time of the sample collection. With most sample collection, there are de minimis or no physical risks to the research subjects; the common risks are dignitary (e.g., use of specimens without consent in violation of religious or personal values). The social risks (e.g., stigmatization or discrimination) are often group-based (e.g., race/ethnicity) and implicate research subjects and non-subjects alike. The benefits of the research are often more diffuse and involve broader societal concerns about advancing scientific knowledge as well as the prevention, diagnosis, and treatment of disease. If informed consent is based on promoting autonomy and the rights of individuals, what ethical paradigm should govern the fundamentally social enterprise of biobank research?

There is considerable scholarly and professional debate on the necessity or nature of informed consent for biobank research. There are two main issues. First, informed consent is broadly required when samples will be collected, stored, or released in an individually identifiable form. Identifiability, however, is quite complicated. The literature is strewn with terms of indecipherable distinctions: anonymous, anonymized, linked, unlinked, coded, key-coded, double coded, masked, encrypted, identified, and deidentified. It is clear that a standard nomenclature is needed, but there are numerous proposed taxonomies that only seem to make matters more confusing.

Second, informed consent depends on whether the samples are extant or prospective. Nearly all proposals relax the rules on informed consent for archival samples, especially those that are not identifiable. The effect of applying contemporary informed consent criteria to samples collected many years ago would be to render these resources largely unavailable to researchers. For prospective samples, however, informed consent should be required, regardless of the identifiability or anonymity of the sample.

Simply stated, research ethics and respect for persons do not permit investigators to appropriate an individual's specimen without permission. Moreover, as discussed earlier, group-based harms do not require individually-identifiable specimens.

B. NOTE ON THE ICELAND BIOBANK

Harvard geneticist Kari Stefansson returned to his native Iceland last year to launch a remarkable enterprise: he aims to gather up and index the heredity of the entire nation—clinical records, DNA, family histories, and all. The result, he hopes, will be the world's finest collection of family data for studying the genetic causes of common diseases. He intends to make this resource available for a fee, and for pharmaceutical companies, part of the price will be free treatment for Icelanders if the research leads to a therapy * * *.

Iceland's 270,000 citizens offer a valuable resource, because they have been isolated from the outside world since the Vikings settled the island more than a millennium ago. In addition, Stefansson says, Icelanders passed through two bottlenecks that further increased their genetic homogeneity—an attack of bubonic plague in the 1400s that narrowed the population from 70,000 to 25,000 and the eruption of the volcano Hekla in the 1700s, which brought widespread famine. Because so many Icelanders share the same ancestors, and because family and medical records are so good (the national health service began in 1915), it should be easier to identify a genomic locus linked to disease among Icelanders than it would be in an outbred population.

Eliot Marshall, Tapping Iceland's DNA, 278 Science 566 (1997).

The Icelandic Parliament approved an arrangement where all health records of its citizens would be put in a central database. Stefansson's company, deCODE, was granted an exclusive 12–year license to operate the database and sell access to it to third parties. deCODE started collecting DNA from people to link to genealogical information and medical history. People's data is automatically entered unless they opt out, but their privacy is protected by encoding names, addresses, and birth dates in the data. Icelandic scientists, if approved by an access committee, can use the data for noncommercial research. And Icelanders will get free access to any drugs or diagnostics developed through use of the deCODE database for the period of the patent.

deCODE attracted venture capital, including $200 million from the pharmaceutical company Hoffmann–La Roche. The collaboration led to the identification of a gene that could be involved in triggering strokes and a gene linked to adult-onset diabetes.

deCODE Genetics has utilized the Icelandic population's acceptance of medical research, substantial private investments in software, and publicly accessible genealogy records spanning centuries in its isolation of 15 genes and drug targets. deCODE Genetics, *From Genes to Drugs*, 2005, http:// www.decode.com. In its first nine years, and with genotypic data from over 100,000 Icelanders, deCODE mapped predisposing genes for such diseases as peripheral artery disease, heart attack, asthma, hypertension, stroke, osteoporosis, and schizophrenia. Though there are concerns that the discoveries which may prove invaluable to the Icelandic population may not translate to foreign genetics, deCODE is hopeful that the diagnosis of particular proteins responsible for particular diseases will have international application. Corie Lok, Translating Iceland's Genes into Medicine, 107 Tech. Rev. 58 (2004).

The project has not been without critics, though. Some are of the opinion that Stefansson has appropriated Iceland's genetic heritage for his own gain. Matt Crenson, Iceland's Genetic Powerhouse, Chicago Tribune, April 2, 2001. The privacy protections are seen as inadequate. Iceland is small—with a population the size of Erie, Pennsylvania or Fayetteville, North Carolina. Even without names attached to the data, people's privacy could be invaded since just a few facts linked to the genetic information—a person's profession, family relations, and the five-year period in which he was born—could give away the individual's identity. Employers, for example, might use the information to discriminate. Martin Enserink, Physicians Wary of Scheme to Pool Icelanders' Genetic Data, 281 Science 890 (1998). The Icelandic Medical Association is concerned that the plan will damage the doctor-patient relationship. One-third of the country's physicians have declared they will not turn their patients' records over to deCODE. Within months of the law's passage, nearly 20,000 people had filed the forms necessary to opt out of the database. Colin Woodard, Putting a Price on Icelanders, San Francisco Chronicle, Oct. 23, 2000, at A6.

Ultimately, Iceland's genetic database did not materialize. Two years after receiving a license to operate the program, deCODE struggled with the data protection requirements established by the Icelandic Data Protection Commission. The company disclosed to its shareholders that the development of the database "may be more expensive and time consuming than deCODE anticipates, and may lead to litigation." deCODE Genetics, Form 10–K (fiscal year ending December 31, 2002), at 19, http://www. decode.com/files/file173160.pdf.

In addition to uncertainty regarding the profitability of the program, deCODE also faced legal challenges. In November 2003, the Icelandic Supreme Court held that a person could opt out of the program for their deceased relative. "Noting that Icelandic medical records were required by law to contain extensive information on people's health, their medical treatment, lifestyles, social circumstances, employment, and family, the court held that 'it is unequivocal that the . . . [Constitutional] provision that "everyone shall enjoy freedom from interference with privacy, home, and family life" appl[ies] to information of this kind and . . . guarantee protection of privacy in this respect.' " Moreover, "the 'vague limits' set by the provisions of the Health Sector Database Act inadequately provided for the protection of [Plaintiff's] constitutional right to privacy, and therefore her right to opt-out her deceased father's health information was affirmed." David E. Winickoff, Genome and Nation: Iceland's Health Sector Database and its Legacy, 1 Innovations 80–105, 95 (Spring 2006) (quoting Gudmundsdóttir v. the State of Iceland, No 151/2003 (Nov. 27, 2003) (Ice.)).

Shortly after the ruling, deCODE announced that it would no longer be pursuing the database because other business had become more profitable. In fact, without aid from the national database program, the company successfully collected medical information from over 90,000 volunteers via standard informed consent procedures to continue its genetic research. David E. Winickoff, Genome and Nation: Iceland's Health Sector Database and its Legacy, 1 Innovations 80–105, 95 (Spring 2006).

C. NOTE ON THE UK BIOBANK

The UK Biobank was founded in 2003 in Great Britain by the Medical Research Council, the Wellcome Trust and the Department of Health. The UK Biobank is a database of information and samples that will be used to undertake research on the effect environmental and genetic factors have on human health and disease. The 500,000 British citizens between the ages of 40–69 who volunteered to participate will provide blood and urine samples, complete questionnaires, have their physical measurements taken, and will give UK Biobank permission to access all of their health records for up to 30 years.

The Ethics and Governance Council is an independent committee consisting of ethicists, lawyers, scientists and experts on social and consumer issues created to act as an ethical watchdog over the UK Biobank. The Council will publicly report on the project's actions to ensure its accountability to the public, and has released a guideline of standards to make sure safeguards are enacted to ensure data and samples are only used for approved research. The information and medical histories are combined as a "(reversibly) anonymized national database." See The Ethics and Governance Framework, UK Biobank, http://www.ukbiobank.ac.uk/ethics/egf.php.

UK Biobank Limited will be the legal owner of the data and samples. Some have expressed concerns that UK Biobank would be able to sell or destroy the data or samples without the participants' consent. UK Biobank insists it will not sell the samples or the database. Law enforcement agencies will need a court order to access the data. The Data Protection Act provides a cause of action for breach of confidentiality if individually identifiable health information is transferred without the participant's consent.

NOTES AND QUESTIONS

1. How do the concerns over Iceland's deCODE project differ from the potential problems facing UK Biobank?

2. What legal issues stem from UK Biobank's ownership rights in the data and medical histories?

3. Should UK Biobank have an obligation to report medical findings to participants? See Johnston & Jane Kaye, Does the UK Biobank Have a Legal Obligation to Feedback Individual Findings to Participants? 12 Med. L. Rev. 239, Autumn 2004.

4. National biobanks have been started around the world including in Belgium, Canada, Estonia, Iceland, Japan, Latvia, Singapore, Sweden, and the United Kingdom. For a discussion of the lessons learned from the successes and failures of these biobank projects, see Helen Swede et al., National Population–Based Biobanks for Genetic Research, 9 Genetics in Medicine 141 (2007); New Challenges for Biobanks: Ethics, Law and Governance, Kris Dierickx and Pascal Barry, eds. (2009).

5. At the 2005 annual meeting of the American Society of Human Genetics, Francis Collins, head of the U.S. Human Genome Project, suggested that the United States should invest in its own population-based biobank of two or three million people. What controversies would such a move create? What legal protections might be necessary? For a discussion of the legal questions raised by biobanks, see the symposium issue "Regulation of Biobanks" (edited by Mark A. Rothstein and Bartha Maria Knoppers), 33 J. of L. Med. & Ethics 1–188 (2005).

6. Since the early 1980s, Dr. William Catalona, a prostate cancer surgeon, has asked his patients if they were willing to let him use the tissue removed during their surgery, blood, and other tissue for research. Over the years he amassed over 30,000 tissue samples and an enviable set of research results. Thanks to Dr. Catalona's research, men now routinely use a simple blood test to screen for prostate cancer. When Dr. Catalona decided to leave his job at Washington University to take a new position at Northwestern, he intended to take the tissue samples with him to continue his research. He sought permission from the research subjects to move the samples and over 6,000 people asked that their samples be transferred to Northwestern University.

Washington University sought to prevent the transfers by asking a federal court to declare that the university was the legal owner of the samples. Washington University v. Catalona, et al., Case No. 4:03cv–1065–SNL (E.D. Mo.2003). The patients were eventually added as necessary parties to the matter; they argued that they owned their samples and could thus transfer them. Washington University argued that the patients had no ownership rights to tissue that had been donated for research purposes. The patients and Dr. Catalona disputed that depiction, claiming that the tissue samples had not been donated or gifted to the University, but were instead provided to Dr. Catalona for a particular use—research on prostate cancer. The patients also claimed that, under the research informed consent forms, they had retained rights to control what happened to their tissue samples, including the right to withdraw samples from research and in some cases to have samples destroyed, and as such there could not have been a gift of their tissue samples to the University. In April 2006, the district court ruled that the informed consent form under which the patients retained rights was "inconsequential" and held that the samples were the property of Washington University. The court stated that the patients released their samples to Washington University as *inter vivos* gifts, finding all the elements of a gift were present on the facts: (1) present donative intent, (2) delivery of the gift, and (3) acceptance of the gift.

The Court of Appeals for the Eighth Circuit affirmed the judgment of the district court. In addressing the issue of whether the patients' limited rights to withdraw their tissue from research prevented them from making an *inter vivos* gift, the appellate court noted that under Missouri law, an individual can give a charitable donation as a valid gift, even if the donation is subject to a condition of revocation. In this case, the condition of revocation would be the patients' rights to withdraw from research. Thus, according to the court, the patients made valid *inter vivos* gifts to Washington University under Missouri law.

Additionally, the appellate court clarified what it meant if the patients withdrew from research. The district court had indicated that federal regulations permitted Washington University to use a patient's tissue for research if it removed all donor-identifying information, even if the patient expressed a desire to withdraw from the research process. In contrast, the Court of Appeals for the Eighth Circuit stated that patients have the right to withdraw from research by (1) prohibiting future research of any kind on their samples, (2) refusing to donate more samples, and (3) refusing to answer additional questions.

By deciding that tissue can be given as a gift and acknowledging that patients can retain rights to their tissue, the appellate court's decision implicitly recognizes that people have property interests in their tissue. See Washington University v. Catalona, 490 F.3d 667, 673–676 (8th Cir. 2007), cert. denied 128 S. Ct. 1122 (2008). Should the courts formally recognize a property interest in excised tissue? If so, how extensive should this interest be? Should individuals retain control of their samples even after donating them to research? Should relatives of donors be able to control the use of the donor's sample after the donor's death?

V. THE HUMAN GENOME DIVERSITY PROJECT AND ITS PROGENY

A. GENETIC RESEARCH ON ISOLATED POPULATIONS

HENRY T. GREELY, THE CONTROL OF GENETIC RESEARCH: INVOLVING THE "GROUPS BETWEEN"

33 Hous. L. Rev. 1397, 1414–1415 (1997).

The HGDP [Human Genome Diversity Project] intends to collect a representative sample of human genetic variation. It would like to collect DNA from members of about five hundred of the roughly five to ten thousand human populations in the world. This DNA would be stored in repositories and made available to researchers. The samples would all be subjected to analysis under a standard set of markers, and the results would be placed in a database, also generally available to researchers. The result would be a reference library of human genetic diversity, which the HGDP estimates could be completed in about five to seven years, for a cost of about twenty-five to thirty-five million dollars.

Improved information about human genetic diversity can be important for at least four different reasons. First, thus far the vast majority of detailed research into human genetics has been done with Europeans or North Americans of European descent, and thus omits the eighty percent of the world's population that is not of European ancestry. It is fundamentally unfair to the majority of humanity to describe the human genome without including a representative sample of all humans. Second, studying human genetic diversity will help us understand better the workings of evolution in humans, including the ways in which culture influences evolution. Third, greater knowledge of human genetic diversity will improve medicine, both because it will advance the study of those genetic diseases found largely in non-European populations, and because genetic variation is basic to better understanding a host of diseases found in all peoples. Finally, studying human diversity will help us uncover our shared human history. Genetic results, when interpreted along with evidence from anthropology, archaeology, history, linguistics, and other fields, will help map human migrations and expansions in prehistoric times.

ZESHAN Q. KHAN, COLONIALISM REVISITED: INSIGHTS INTO THE HUMAN GENOME DIVERSITY PROJECT

3 J.L. & Soc. Challenges 89, 89–115 (1999).

The HGDP, a Project created by Stanford geneticist Luigi Luca Cavalli–Sforza, intends to obtain DNA samples from between 400 to 722 indigenous groups throughout the world. By obtaining samples from peoples who have remained culturally, geographically and biologically isolated from the rest of the world, the Project hopes to obtain DNA samples from those whose blood has remained relatively consistent for centuries. Western scientists created this project for three primary reasons: (1) the location of genes among indigenous peoples that immunize them from genetic diseases (as well as the location of disease-causing genes); (2) the formation of a family tree that depicts the evolution and migratory patterns of existing humans; and (3) an increased sampling pool for the Human Genome Project.

* * *

Opponents of the HGDP have concerns on many levels. These include problems with the potential benefits depicted by the proponents of the Project, as well as fears that relate to histories of exploitation; the aboriginal people fear that once again, others will exploit them * * *. The primary argument against the Project * * * is that any medical advances associated with genes will not benefit indigenous peoples. Scientific advances may help those who can afford treatment or who live in a society where concerns such as mental disorders or genetic cancers supersede concerns about malaria. However, it is unlikely that such medical advances associated with genes will directly benefit those who provide the "raw materials" for the design of such knowledge. Moreover, if gene therapies were created, it is unlikely that indigenous peoples could afford them. Such a system, by its very nature, is colonialism in its purest form—the appropriation of resources from the colonized to benefit the colonizing people, without proper compensation, as determined by the subject indigenous people.

* * *

There are many examples of profiting from naturally occurring substances at the expense of indigenous peoples. One is the Indian neem tree. A U.S. chemicals company obtained a patent for a natural pesticide extracted by generations of Indian farmers from the seed of the neem tree. The traditional methods, however, were not protected by patent thus the chemical company only had to extract the pesticide and claim it as its own. Because a patent entitles one to control its use by others, Indian farmers must now pay a royalty to the chemical company to use the extract.

Another example of plant appropriation is quinine, the well-known cure for malaria. The drug comes from the bark of the cinchona tree of Peru. Indigenous Andean groups used quinine as a cure for fevers, learning to do so by supposedly watching feverish jaguars eat it. In addition, the rosy periwinkle plant of Madagascar has been found to possess certain cancer-fighting characteristics. Eli Lilly developed two drugs from the plant, resulting in $100 million in annual sales. Madagascar received none of the profits.

In 1990, scientist Sally Fox received a patent for colored cotton. This fabric is highly lucrative since it is environmentally friendly and some of the largest U.S. clothing manufacturers desire such material. The seed for

Sally Fox's cotton, however, came from a U.S. Department of Agriculture sample collected from Latin America. The seed is the result of centuries of cultivation and breeding by indigenous peoples. To date, 15,000 indigenous farmers grow the cotton, and over 50,000 indigenous women spin and weave it. These are just a few examples of the profiteering which has occurred over the past twenty-five years.

* * * One could argue that there is a clear difference between plants and human genetic material, however, members of indigenous peoples may not share this view of distinction. Many see themselves, as well as the plant-life around them, as parts of a natural gestaltic whole. The separation of plant-life from human genetic material is seen by some as a cultural imposition upon these people. Distinct ownership of living materials is not a part of their understanding. Notions of exclusive property rights over naturally occurring substances are a violation of the beliefs held by many of the indigenous people. Ownership is often a cultural construct of the colonizing world and its imposition upon indigenous peoples is commonly seen as a form of cultural imperialism.

* * *

[The indigenous groups have raised concerns about the patenting of their DNA.] Since patenting a U.S. citizen's DNA for profit is acceptable, it seems logical that the next target is DNA from other countries. In 1993, the U.S. government filed a patent claim for the cell line of a Guaymi woman from Panama. Although the government withdrew its claims, it has filed two other patent applications on human cell lines of indigenous peoples—one from the Solomon Islands, and the other from Papua New Guinea. Eventually, the government filed papers to forfeit its "rights" to the patent claims with the Patent and Trademark Office (PTO) * * *. The Guaymi tribal president stated that he, "never imagined people would patent plants and animals. It's fundamentally immoral, contrary to the Guaymi view of nature, and our place in it. To patent human material * * * to take human DNA and patent its products * * * that violates the integrity of life itself, and our deepest sense of morality."

* * *

[The indigenous groups are also concerned that genetic research will be used in an attempt to prove their "inferiority," like research on skull size was used in an earlier era in an attempt to prove the intellectual inferiority of Native Americans.] What many scientists seem to miss is that the scientific data, which to scientists are irreducible truths, are prone to the same socially arbitrary appropriation as already existing tools for racial subordination. Scientists themselves have claimed to discover the lack of a "novelty seeking gene" among Asians that may predispose them to an unchanging and settled lifestyle. Does this mean that "afflicted" Asians are incapable of innovation, and thus cultural evolution? Or have Asians hit an evolutionary plateau?

* * *

[There is also concern that indigenous peoples' samples are being used without their consent.] Janelle Noble [a scientist for a pharmaceutical company who collected tissue samples from people in South America], once questioned the purpose of obtaining informed consent from native peoples who had lived uncomplicated agrarian lifestyles for hundreds of years. According to Noble, "there is no point in telling them [indigenous people] we're going to do HLA typing on their genes since they would not understand what HLA typing is in the first place," and that the subjects of the HGDP "as much as they can understand, they are giving their informed consent." This comment implies that it is a waste of time to properly give these people information so that they can make a truly informed choice. Indeed, many proponents and opponents alike have questioned the ability of native peoples' ability to give truly informed consent. George Annas, bioethicist from Boston University's School of Public Health, claims that if many of these people knew the true purpose of the Project, they would not give their consent since the Project violates essential notions they hold of life. But Noble's condescension precludes the possibility of even remedial knowledge from being offered to these people. Many people have echoed the sentiment asserted by Annas. Upon awareness of the Project's basic agenda and methodology, a group of indigenous people in North and South America created the Declaration of Indigenous Peoples of the Western Hemisphere Regarding the Human Genome Diversity Project, which condemned the Project on many fronts. Seventeen organizations consisting of and representing indigenous people from British Columbia to Bolivia signed the document * * *.

JOCELYN KAISER, A PLAN TO CAPTURE HUMAN DIVERSITY IN 1000 GENOMES
319 Science 395 (2008).

It's sign of how fast horizons are changing in biology: Researchers who only a few years ago were being asked to justify the cost of sequencing a single human genome are now breezily offering to sequence 1000. And they say they can do it in a flash. Over the next 3 years, an international team plans to create a massive new genome catalog that will serve as "a gold-standard reference set for analysis of human variation," says Richard Durbin of the Sanger Institute in Hinxton, U.K., who proposed the project just last year.

The 1000 Genomes Project, as it's called, will delve much deeper than the sequencing of celebrity genomes, three of which were completed last year. It will help fill out the list of new genetic markers for common diseases that came out in 2007, says Francis Collins, director of the U.S. National Human Genome Research Institute (NHGRI) in Bethesda, Maryland. At the same time, new technologies will be put to the test, and researchers will work out how to handle a growing deluge of data. Such practical advances will be needed a few years from now when sequencing entire genomes will be routine, notes population geneticist Kenneth Weiss of Pennsylvania State University in State College, who is not part of the project. "This seems overall like a next logical step," he says.

The search for disease genes took off last year, building on the first human genome reference sequence in 2003 and the subsequent HapMap. The latter describes how blocks of DNA tagged by common variants, called single-nucleotide polymorphisms (SNPs), vary in different populations. These SNPs have turned up more than 100 new DNA markers associated with common illnesses such as diabetes and heart disease. But the HapMap includes only the most common markers, those present in at least 5% of the population.

To find rarer SNPs that occur at 1% frequency, genome leaders say, they need to sequence about 1000 genomes. According to a plan hammered out by about three dozen experts last year, the project will take advantage of new technologies that have slashed the cost of sequencing. The work will be done by the three U.S. sequencing centers funded by NHGRI, the Sanger Institute, and the Beijing Genomics Institute (BGI) in Shenzhen, China.

Because the technologies are so new, the consortium will start with three pilot projects. One will exhaustively sequence the entire genome of six individuals: two adults and both sets of their parents. DNA in these six genomes will be analyzed repeatedly up to 20 times to ensure almost complete coverage. A second project will sequence 180 individual genomes at light (2x) coverage, leaving gaps. The third project will be to fully sequence (20x coverage) the protein-coding regions of 1000 genes (5% of the total) in about 1000 genomes. The samples, all anonymous and with no clinical information, will mainly be drawn from those collected for the HapMap, which includes people of European, Asian, and African descent.

The pilots should take about a year and will put the new technologies to a "very vigorous test," Collins says. After that, the consortium will decide what coverage to use to sequence the entire set of 1000 genomes. Most of the project's $30 million to $50 million price tag will be paid from the existing sequencing budgets of institutes, organizers say.

The new catalog could help disease gene hunters in several ways. It may allow researchers simply to hunt through an index for a SNP in a particular location that alters a gene product rather than run a time-consuming sequencing project, Collins says. The project will also catalog genes that are sometimes lost or duplicated; such copy-number variants can cause disease. By compiling rarer variants, it should also help resolve a debate about the relative contribution of these mutations to disease risks. "There's no question it's going to be a tremendous resource," says Yale University's Judy Cho, who has used the HapMap to find a new gene for Crohn's disease.

China is also launching its own human genomes project. BGI Shenzhen this month announced that it is seeking 99 volunteers who will help pay to have their genomes sequenced as part of a study of diversity. The 3–year effort, called the Yanhuang Project after the Yan and Huang tribes that are believed to be ancestors of modern Chinese, will overlap with the 1000 Genomes Project. With proper consent, some volunteers' genomes will be sequenced for both efforts, says Wang Jun, director of BGI Hangzhou.

In a parallel effort, J. Craig Venter of the J. Craig Venter Institute in Rockville, Maryland, says his team will sequence up to 10 individuals this year and publish the data along with medical information. Venter—who dismisses the 1000 Genomes Project as "more survey work" because not all genomes will be sequenced to great depth—has even bolder plans. He says he aims for "complete diploid genome sequencing" of 10,000 human genomes in the next decade. Still, he says, "it's great that there's such an expansion of things."

NOTES AND QUESTIONS

1. By 2005, the Human Genome Diversity Project collected over 1,000 cell lines from more than 50 populations all over the world and sent those samples to over 50 research groups globally. Luigi Luca Cavalli–Sforza, The Human Genome Diversity Project: Past, Present, and Future, 6 Nature Genetics Reviews 333 (April 2005). However, the Human Genome Diversity Project appears not to have moved forward due to a lack of funding; in 2005 the National Institute of Health refused to fund the HGDP. See Henry T. Greely, Lessons From The HGDP?, 308 Science 1554 (2005).

2. The Genographic Project seeks to tell the genetic origin story of humanity, describing in detail the patterns of human migration over the past 150,000 years. It is a privately funded venture, sponsored by National Geographic and funded by the Waitt Family Foundation, as well as other private contributors. Although the general public is welcome to participate in the project by contributing DNA samples, the Genographic Project seeks to collect 100,000 samples from various indigenous and traditional peoples throughout the world to complete its goal. The Genographic Project relies on the genetic information of indigenous and traditional peoples it considers sufficiently isolated from the general population as reference points to determine paths of human migration throughout history. Ultimately, the Project hopes to produce its findings in a database that associates genetic variations in global populations with anthropological information about the cultures involved in the project—the creators of the project argue that such anthropological information is necessary to contextualizing and understanding the genetic data, particularly where globalization threatens to erase traditional cultures around the world. When the project ends in 2010, the Project hopes to release its database into the public domain. However, researchers involved in the project have already published several scientific papers utilizing the genetic data collected thus far. For more information, visit https://genographic. nationalgeographic.com/genographic/lan/en/faqs_about.html.

The Genographic Project hopes to quash speculation of "bioprospecting"—the appropriation of indigenous and traditional people's genetic material for the research and production of commercial products—by anonymizing genetic samples and requiring informed consent from both individuals and communities of indigenous or traditional descent. Additionally, The Geno-graphic Project does not create cell lines from collected samples and prohibits their use in medical research.

However, the Genographic Project's claim to tell the origin story of humanity is problematic. Some see the Genographic Project as diminishing the personhood of indigenous and traditional people by reinforcing a stereo-type that they are primal or primitive by characterizing their genetic heritage as isolated or unique. Additionally, the migration story told by the genetic data may conflict with indigenous peoples' understanding of their origins or could potentially be used against them in the resolution of legal issues such as land ownership conflicts. For a treatment of these issues see Kim TallBear, Narratives of Race and Indigeneity in The Genographic Project, 35 J.L. Med. & Ethics 412 (2007). Are there any situations, political, legal or otherwise, where genetic migration data might be useful or beneficial to indigenous and traditional peoples? For what reasons might indigenous people oppose such research?

3.   The International HapMap Project specifically aims to provide genetic information that medical researchers will later use to predict and treat disease. The Project is a publicly and privately funded venture, with financial support from several countries, including the United States. To accomplish its goal, the Project maps common genetic variations and shows where the variations occur in the genome. Additionally, it shows how these variations are distributed within different populations throughout the world. The Project also creates and maintains cell lines of its samples for medical researchers, first, to create the map of genetic variation (the HapMap), and second, for use in future medical research. The Project has collected genetic material from peoples of African, Asian, and European ancestry, including, but not limited to, indigenous peoples and continuously makes updates available on its website as new data is collected and analyzed. For more information, visit http://www.hapmap.org/thehapmap.html.en.

In an attempt to avoid ethical controversy, the International HapMap Project has instituted informed consent procedures for research participants. The Project's informed consent materials inform individual participants and their communities that their genetic material may later be used by medical researchers in studying disease. And to obtain informed consent at the communal and individual level, the project attempts to create relationships between researchers and participating communities through a number of devices, including Community Advisory Groups (CAG). CAGs act as interme-diaries between communities and researchers and facilitate discussion of the Project. As the Project continues, updates concerning the status and use of communal samples are sent through CAGs to communities for discussion and interpretation. The informed consent materials also provide that CAGs will help participating communities to understand how future research projects conducted with their samples might affect them. Additionally, all studies that use samples from the International HapMap Project need IRB approval.

However, the individuals and communities who provide samples do not have any direct influence over whether research will be conducted on those samples. Nor are communities able to prevent an organization from patenting future findings based on the study of their samples. What if the IRB approves a project that the study participants do not approve? Whose opinion should control the use of the samples in genetic research? See the discussion of the HapMap in Chapter 2.

4.   The Khan excerpt mentions concerns that the Guaymi tribe raised after cell lines derived from its people were patented. Other indigenous groups have also raised concerns about the benefits promised to them in exchange for donating blood samples. In 1996 a group of researchers visited the Karitiana tribe in Brazil promising medicine if the Karitiana would give blood for research. Eleven years later, the tribe never received medicine but discovered that their blood samples were on sale by a French blood and DNA repository for $85 a sample. The French repository, says it provides samples only to scientists who agree not to commercialize their findings or transfer the material to third parties. A major concern with retrieving blood samples from isolated tribes like the Karitiana is that often the tribes have had little to no contact with the outside world at the time of their agreements with researchers. Do you think it is possible for someone with "little to no understanding of the outside world, let alone the workings of Western medicine and modern capitalist economics" to be capable of giving informed consent? Members of other tribes have also raised religious objections. The Yanomami demanded their blood samples back because they believe a soul cannot rest until all of a person's tissue is cremated. See Larry Rohter, In the Amazon, Giving Blood but Getting Nothing, The New York Times, June 20, 2007 at A1.

B.   CONCERNS ABOUT "GROUP" HARMS

ERIC T. JUENGST, THE PERILS OF GENETIC GENEALOGY

10 CenterViews 1 (1996).

Origin stories are powerful. Think of the tenacity with which adoptees can pursue their birth parents' identities, or the pride that families often take in their geographical roots, or the controversies over teaching human evolution to school kids. No matter how new social conventions and technologies allow us to reinvent our identities, our sense of self nonetheless depends heavily on where we came from—that is, on our family tree and our family's travels * * *. Given this, it should have been anticipated that the Human Genome Diversity Project (HGDP) would attract attention.

* * *

First, it risks the appearance of granting biological legitimacy to social categories, inappropriately "naturalizing" the lines among groups and adding the authority of science to the attempt of those—both within and outside particular groups—to set those groups apart from the rest of society. The concept of "race" may be undermined, but in its place the thoroughly respectable concept of a "deme"—as a genetically differentiated subpopulation—can still serve as a scientific foundation for unjust attitudes and practices. If ethnic groups and minority communities are counted as human demes, the local tensions between them can take on the virulence of racism as new species of "demic discrimination."

Second, by identifying 500 populations as "particularly representative of ancestral populations," the project risks reifying these groups in the public's mind as representing the "original pure types" of humanity, reinforcing the idea that human groups can be graded, for better or worse, in terms of their distance from their stock. This could have stigmatizing consequences for either the target groups (if they are seen as "primitive") or for mixed groups (if they are seen as "polluted") depending on the local social context.

Third, even if we could prevent people from misinterpreting the HGDP's basic human taxonomy, what about the stories that would ultimately emerge? The stories that scientists will be able to tell after working with the HGDP's cell banks will be stories about lineage and land tenure: stories about who is most closely related to whom and who got where first. Here is where the power of our origin stories asserts itself. Even where ethnic tensions are not involved, stories about lineage and land tenure have always been humanity's two favorite excuses for claiming social privilege. Any new information that could add scientific credibility to the arguments of those disputing such claims could be easily abused. Would the HGDP archivists police the users and uses of their databank to discourage those seeking to settle political disputes?

Finally, looking for the genomic hallmarks of particular social groups could produce tools for carrying out a program of demic discrimination by making DNA identification tests possible. One can imagine two scenarios: one in which the privileged caste tests for their own definitive DNA hallmarks as inclusion criteria for social opportunities, and one in which a particular group's markers are used to identify them for oppression. At first, there seemed to be some comfort in scientific skepticism that any such unique markers could be found for any human groups larger than extended families. But consider this January 14, 1996 news flash:

> An extremely rare mutation on the Y chromosome may be a genetic marker that is unique to the people who first migrated to the Americas some 30,000 years ago researchers report * * * A group of Stanford University researchers have identified a mutation that in their sample (of 500 DNA samples from populations around the world) exists only in Indian populations in North and South America and in Eskimo groups * * * The Y chromosome mutation occurred in a stretch of DNA that is not related to a gene, but is part of the "junk" DNA that separates the genes.

Would it be fair for an American man to use a positive test for this mutation in supporting a claim to affirmative action benefits? What about native American women and men with maternal lines of descent, who could not show this proof of American Indian ancestry? Would it be right for a South American government to publish the results of this test for all political candidates? The capacity for both uses of this little tidbit from the human origin story is already with us in genotyping labs throughout the hemisphere.

MORRIS W. FOSTER ET AL., A MODEL AGREEMENT FOR GENETIC RESEARCH IN SOCIALLY IDENTIFIABLE POPULATIONS

63 Am J. Human Genetics 696, 696–702 (1998).

* * *

COMMUNAL DISCOURSE

We used a process of communal discourse to engage the participation of the Apache Tribe of Oklahoma. We began by conducting a health survey through 150 ethnographic interviews (20% of the adult population). The interviews included questions about who was consulted in making health-care decisions. We used the answers to those questions to identify public and private social units that Apaches were accustomed to consult about their well-being. These units were considered by community members to be the most appropriate entities to consult about the collective implications of genetic research. Our definition of "appropriate" is derived from the population's preexisting processes for reaching a communal consensus. Although such processes vary among populations, our procedure for identifying culturally appropriate decision-making units is generally applicable. Anthropology has well-defined methods for the study of collective decision making.

A related problem was the inclusion of a cross-section of appropriate social units sufficient to represent all segments of the Apache population. Here, we relied on a combination of information from the health-survey interviews and advice from Apache elders. Members of the Apache community were themselves very aware of the question of representativeness—a necessary element in reaching any communal consensus—and were able to guide us in including specific social units. In the Apache community, the major public unit is a five-person Apache Business Committee that is elected by tribal members. It is recognized as having public authority to make formal decisions about matters affecting the well-being of the community as a whole. Everyday private life, however, is ordered by five major extended families, which are the private units within which information about such matters as individual health status is confidential. The Apache Business Committee takes care to appoint members from each of the major families to any community panel.

We requested that the Apache Business Committee sponsor a series of public meetings, open to all tribal members, in which we explained our research goals. As a result of this initial dialogue, we modified our goals to take account of communal priorities * * *. [T]he Apache Business Committee * * * appointed a committee to evaluate the research proposal * * *. The Apache Business Committee designated this committee as a "tribal institutional review board" (IRB) but that designation may be somewhat misleading. What the Apaches called a "tribal IRB" functioned in a dual role that is not standard in bioethical practice; that is, it both evaluated the research project for its implications for the Apache community and then explained those implications to and negotiated them with researchers. Typically, an IRB undertakes only the first of these tasks, whereas inclusion of the second might be considered—according to Euro–American ethics—as creating a conflict of interest for the IRB. In the case of the Apache community, however, such a separation of responsibilities was seen by members as impractical. Those persons who were judged most knowledgeable in evaluating the cultural implications of the proposed research also were considered the most appropriate persons to negotiate community-specific concerns with researchers. The same qualities of personal and cultural authority were deemed necessary for both tasks. To avoid confusion with more typical IRBs, we will use the term "community review board," or "CRB," to refer to the Apache committee.

* * *

Apaches discussed implications for the community as issues separate from those for individuals. They recognized that risks of stigmatization and discrimination would apply to all tribal members, not just to those who might volunteer as study participants. They asserted a communal interest even for biological specimens that would be individually anonymous, because of the use of the collective name "Apache." This communal interest was no less for stored materials subject to studies in the future. Nevertheless, despite potential collective risks, Apaches were strongly motivated to participate in research on diabetes mellitus, which they perceived as a major health problem.

[Among the provisions that the Apaches negotiated were the following:]

PUBLICATIONS

All manuscripts that report project findings will be reviewed by the Apache CRB, which will have 60 days to raise objections to use of the tribal name. In that event, investigators either could revise the manuscript to satisfy Apaches' concerns or could publish the results without naming the Apache tribe. Although study populations traditionally have been named in scientific publications, keeping their identities confidential would not necessarily invalidate analyses of genetic factors for disease susceptibility and resistance.

INTELLECTUAL PROPERTY

According to long-established practice, as well as limited legal precedent, individuals who donate biological materials do not have legal claim on the intellectual property derived from them. In our agreement, the owner of any intellectual property is the university, the sponsoring institution. The subcontract, however, recognizes the unique contribution of the participating community in the creation of that intellectual property. The university will deduct 10% of royalties for legal and administrative costs. Of the remainder, the university will retain 30%, the tribe will receive 30%, and investigators will receive 30%. The unassigned 10% will be retained in a reserve fund for liability or litigation. The Apache CRB resolved that any royalties to the tribe be earmarked for the promotion of the health and education of tribal members.

ARCHIVAL STORAGE AND STUDY

At the conclusion of our project, we will negotiate with the tribal CRB the issue of long-term storage of biological specimens. If we are unable to reach an agreement, those materials will be disposed of in a culturally appropriate manner. However, if the tribal CRB permits storage of samples, explicit provisions will be negotiated to define how future research projects would receive community approval.

CULTURAL CONCERNS

We encountered some concerns that are culturally specific to the study population. Apaches have restrictions about physical contact that are specific to gender, family, and age. Thus, the tribal CRB decided that blood samples should be drawn by a non-Apache. Apaches also expressed an interest in what is done with biological materials that are not consumed by laboratory analyses. Those materials still are considered part of the body, so investigators and the tribal CRB will review procedures to ensure that the proper respect is accorded. More generally, each of the other provisions negotiated with the tribe was interpreted from a uniquely Apache cultural perspective. For instance, concerns about adverse affects from the publication of scientific findings focused on stigmatization of families with a history of diabetes within the community, rather than on discrimination from outside. Similarly, the primary concern about the use of archival specimens was in potential studies comparing the Apache genome with those of other Native peoples. Results from such comparative studies could contradict Apache origin narratives. Both these risks are based on how Apaches culturally construct their own sense of shared identity, not on how others view them.

LORI ANDREWS, HAVASUPAI TRIBE SUES GENETIC RESEARCHERS

4 Law and Bioethics Report 10–11 (2004), reprinted in 31 Privacy Journal, 5–6 (April, 2005).

The foundation of genetics research around the world was built on studies of Drosophila and lab rats. But with the advent of the Human Genome Project, genetics researchers turned increasingly to humans as research subjects. Now researchers are finding that the human subjects have a characteristic that other species do not: their concerns about informed consent, privacy, and fair dealing sometimes lead them to file lawsuits when researchers behave in a way that the subjects find unacceptable.

Litigation pending before Judge Fredrick J. Martone of the U.S. District Court for Arizona could help clarify the duties of genetics researchers toward their subjects. Members of the Havasupai Tribe allege that researchers of Arizona State University ("ASU") and the University of Arizona ("U of A") collected 400 blood samples from them for researching diabetes, but that additional unauthorized research was undertaken on those samples regarding schizophrenia, inbreeding, and population migration. They assert that the research on schizophrenia and inbreeding was stigmatizing to them and that they would not have authorized the migration research because it conflicts with their religious origin story.

The 650–member Havasupai Tribe are descendents of the Hohokam Indians, who migrated north from Mexico around 300 B.C. The Havasupai settled in an isolated and remote location in the Grand Canyon, which is still only assessible by horseback, foot, or helicopter. Such isolation is the reason that the Havasupai Tribe poses a restricted gene pool, in which certain genetic diseases are at higher incidence than in, say, a general urban population. In fact, the Havasupai have one of the highest incidences of type 2 diabetes anywhere in the world. In 1991, 55% of Havasupai women and 38% of the Havasupai men were diabetic.

In 1989, two tribe members approached an ASU faculty member, asking for help to stem the tribe's high incidence of diabetes. They allege that researcher Therese Markow and a colleague originally presented their project to the tribal counsel as consisting of three elements: (1) "diabetes education," (2) "collecting and testing blood samples from individual members to identify diabetics or persons susceptible to diabetes," and (3) "genetic testing to identify an association between certain gene variants and diabetes among Havasupai people." They allege that Markow did not inform them that she was in the process of, or had previously submitted, a grant application to study schizophrenia among the Havasupai. Nor were they subsequently told that Markow caused her medical assistant to surreptitiously examine their medical charts for schizophrenia after operating hours of the local health clinic. The complaint alleges that the defendants authored 15 publications dealing with schizophrenia, inbreeding, and theories about ancient human population migrations from Asia to North America—secondary uses of the samples to which the Havasupai say they would not have consented.

* * *

In defense of Markow, *Nature* reports that research into interbreeding and migration patterns is "an accepted procedure" for researching the extent to which the studied population is isolated. According to *Nature*, information on the extent to which a studied population is isolated is "important" for the genetic investigation of a disease. However, most research to identify human disease genes has proceeded without inbreeding studies and *Nature* fails to explain how schizophrenia is linked to diabetes research. Moreover, even if such studies were standard procedure, the Havasupai argue that they should have been told of these "accepted procedures" before they were asked whether they were willing to consent to the research.

TILOUSI v. ARIZONA STATE UNIVERSITY BOARD OF REGENTS

No. 04–CV–1290–PCT–FJM (D. Ariz. March 3, 2005).

MARTONE, J.

This action stems from a research project directed by Arizona State University professors John Martin and Therese Markow focusing on the Havasupai Indian Tribe. Defendants obtained blood samples and hand print samples from plaintiff tribe members ostensibly to be used to study diabetes within the tribe. However, plaintiffs claim the samples were also used for research on unrelated topics such as schizophrenia, inbreeding, and ancient human population migrations. Plaintiffs allege a number of injuries as a result of defendants' actions and these additional uses. Plaintiffs contend that had they known the purposes for which their blood samples would be used, they would not have consented to provide the samples.

We address each count of plaintiffs' second amended complaint separately.

COUNT I

Plaintiffs allege breach of fiduciary duty and lack of informed consent on the part of all defendants. Plaintiffs claim defendant Zuerlein represented to them that blood samples collected by Markow and Martin would be used solely to research and study diabetes among the Havasupai. Plaintiffs claim defendant Benyshek induced plaintiffs to provide blood samples by representing that they would be used solely to study diabetes. Plaintiffs allege that they would not have consented to provide their blood samples had they known they would be used in other studies.

Plaintiffs claim all defendants failed to obtain informed consent for drawing blood and failed to use the care and skill exercised by researchers of ordinary prudence. The Restatement requires informed consent to be "to the particular conduct, or substantially the same conduct" in order to be effective. Plaintiffs do not allege that the actual conduct towards plaintiffs, taking their blood samples, was not the result of proper consent. Instead, they claim plaintiffs did not consent to certain later uses of the blood samples. However, a comment to the Restatement notes that:

> The rule stated in § 892B, that a consent to a contact the particular character of which the other is fully aware, is not made ineffective by reason of the fraudulent misrepresentations which induce the other to give the consent, is of peculiar importance in determining the existence of liability for a merely offensive contact * * * [T]he consent,

though fraudulently procured, prevents the infliction of the contact from being itself a wrong and as such actionable. RESTATEMENT (SECOND) OF TORTS § 18 cmt f (1965).

Plaintiffs consented to having blood drawn and were fully aware of the character of the contact. Thus their consent is not made ineffective even if defendants did make fraudulent representations to induce that consent. Therefore, there is no cause of action for lack of informed consent and that component of Count I is dismissed.

Additionally, plaintiffs allege in Count I that all defendants violated 42 U.S.C. § 289, 45 C.F.R. § 46.116. However, this federal regulation regarding institutional review boards does not provide a private right of action nor does it evidence an intent to do so. A court must determine whether a statute "displays an intent to create not just a private right but also a private remedy." See Alexander v. Sandoval, 532 U.S. 275, 286 (2001). 42 U.S.C. § 289 instructs the Secretary of Health and Human services to engage in certain regulatory functions. The text and structure of the statute display no intent to establish a private right of action.

As to plaintiffs' claim that they had a fiduciary relationship with all defendants, plaintiffs allege no facts sufficient to establish such a relationship. As defendants point out, plaintiffs do not even allege that any of the defendants accepted the trust and confidence of plaintiffs, but instead plaintiffs' allegations focus on Martin and Benyshek's perception that the Havasupai trusted Martin. This does not establish that defendants accepted the trust of plaintiffs. See e.g. Greenberg v. Miami Children's Hospital, 264 F.Supp.2d. 1064 (S.D. Fla. 2003). For these reasons, plaintiffs' claims for breach of fiduciary duty are also dismissed. Therefore, Count I is dismissed in its entirety.

[The court dismissed the fraud and misrepresentation/fraudulent concealment counts since no specific statements were alleged.]

* * *

COUNT III

In Count III of their second amended complaint, plaintiffs allege negligent infliction of emotional distress against all defendants and intentional infliction of emotional distress against only defendants Martin, Markow, and Zuerlein.

In order to recover for the tort of negligent infliction of emotional distress, the shock or mental anguish of the plaintiff must be manifested as a physical injury. Plaintiffs claim they have suffered "severe mental and nervous emotional harm, suffering, fright, anguish, rage, shock, nervousness, anxiety, sleeplessness, unrest, depression, humiliation, loss of self esteem, and loss of dignity." The Restatement makes clear that "transitory, non-recurring physical phenomena, harmless in themselves, such as dizziness, vomiting, and the like, do not make the actor liable where such phenomena are in themselves inconsequential and do not amount to any substantial bodily harm." RESTATEMENT (SECOND) OF TORTS 436(A) cmt c (1965). Also, according to the Restatement,

> Long continued nausea or headaches may amount to physical illness, which is bodily harm; and even long continued mental disturbance, as for example in the case of repeated hysterical attacks, or mental aberration, may be classified by the courts as illness * * * Id.

Plaintiffs' complaint alleging continued mental and emotional harm may be adequate for a claim of bodily harm if plaintiffs can present evidence to establish long continued mental disturbance of the sort contemplated by the Restatement. Therefore, the motion to dismiss the negligent infliction of emotional distress claim in Count III is denied.

As to plaintiffs' claim for intentional infliction of emotional distress against defendants Martin, Markow, and Zuerlein, plaintiffs may recover only if defendants' conduct is extreme and outrageous, the defendant either intends to cause the emotional distress or recklessly disregards the near certainty that such distress will result, and severe emotional distress actually occurs.

Defendants' actions must be "so outrageous in character and so extreme in degree, as to go beyond all possible bounds of decency, and to be regarded as atrocious and utterly intolerable in a civilized community." We cannot say that defendants' alleged actions in collecting blood samples for different uses than those stated to plaintiffs do not meet this standard. Plaintiffs have alleged the elements of intent and severe emotional distress. Because plaintiffs have adequately alleged a claim for intentional infliction of emotional distress, defendants' motion to dismiss the intentional infliction of emotional distress claim in Count III is denied.

COUNT IV

Count IV of the second amended complaint alleges conversion against defendants Markow, Martin, and Zuerlein only, and not against defendant Benyshek or defendant Arizona Board of Regents et. al. (ABOR).

In order to state a claim for conversion, plaintiffs must allege a "right to immediate possession of the chattel at the time of the alleged conversion." Sears Consumer Fin. v. Thunderbird Products, 166 Ariz. 333, 335, 802 P.2d 1032, 1034 (Ct. App. 1990). Despite plaintiffs' voluntary donation of the blood samples, which suggests plaintiffs had no right to immediate possession of the blood, plaintiffs claim defendants committed conversion by intentionally "obtaining possession of a chattel from another by fraud or duress." RESTATEMENT (SECOND) OF TORTS § 221(b) (1965). However, Rule 9 of the Federal Rules of Civil Procedure applies to this claim grounded in fraud and requires plaintiffs to allege the who, what, when, where, and how of the alleged misconduct. Cooper v. Pickett, 137 F.3d 616, 627 (9th Cir. 1997). Plaintiffs fail to comply with the requirement of Rule 9 and therefore Count IV is dismissed in its entirety.

* * *

The remaining claims include: Count Three intentional infliction of emotional distress claims against Martin, Markow, and Zuerlein; Count Three negligent infliction of emotional distress claims against all defendants; Count V Violation of Civil Rights claims against Martin, Markow, and Benyshek, and Zuerlein; Count VI negligence and gross negligence claims against all defendants.

NOTES AND QUESTIONS

1.   What are some other examples of groups that might be harmed or stigmatized by genetic research? Which of those groups might benefit from the community consultation approach described in the Foster et al. study?

2.   Native American populations have elected tribal councils. But how should researchers determine the appropriate groups to consult if the population targeted by the study does not have such a structure? What groups might represent the affected community in a genetic study of women and math ability or African–Americans and kidney disease?

3.   The Tilousi case indicates that there is no private cause of action under the federal research regulations. What are the pros and cons of that approach?

4.   Tilousi v. Arizona State University Board of Regents was brought by members of the Havasupai Tribe for alleged misuse of their DNA samples by faculty of Arizona State University. As excerpted above, the federal district court dismissed several of the tribe members' claims, but not their negligent and intentional infliction of emotional distress, civil rights, and negligence claims. The federal district court then granted the plaintiffs' motion to remand the case to state court.

The Havasupai Tribe also filed suit on its own behalf in Havasupai Tribe v. Arizona Board of Regents. The defendants in the Havasupai case removed the case to federal court, where the district court subsequently dismissed several of the tribe's claims, but granted it leave to amend its complaint to allege breach of fiduciary duty, fraud, negligence, and trespass. The district court then remanded the case to state court.

Currently, the Arizona Supreme Court is reviewing some of the claims in both the Tilousi case and the Havasupai Tribe case based on an issue of Arizona civil procedure. However, several of the claims in both cases are moving ahead at the trial level. In the Tilousi case, the claims currently slated to go forward are those against Markow and the Arizona Board of Regents for negligent and intentional infliction of emotional distress, as well as negligence and gross negligence. And in the Havasupai Tribe case, the claims currently slated to go forward are those against Markow and the Arizona Board of Regents for breach of confidential or fiduciary duty, fraudulent nondisclosure, fraudulent concealment, negligence and gross negligence, and finally, trespass. As of May 2009, the state courts have not reached the substantive questions concerning the alleged misuse of DNA specimens in either the Havasupai Tribe or Tilousi case.

5. Various indigenous groups have taken formal stances against certain types of genetic research. In the "Declaration of Indigenous Peoples of the Western Hemisphere Regarding the Human Genome Diversity Project," www.ankn.uaf.edu/IKS/declaration.html for example, participating indigenous organizations stated "we particularly oppose the Human Genome Diversity Project which intends to collect, and make available our genetic materials which may be used for commercial, scientific and military purposes."

VI. THE ENVIRONMENTAL GENOME PROJECT

A. THE PURPOSE OF THE ENVIRONMENTAL GENOME PROJECT

JOCELYN KAISER, ENVIRONMENT INSTITUTE LAYS PLANS FOR GENE HUNT

278 Science 569, 569–570 (1997).

Twelve people died after members of the Aum Shinrikyo cult unleashed a potent nerve gas called sarin in the Tokyo subway 2 years ago. Some of these victims, scientists now know, may have been much more vulnerable than others. Circulating in the blood of 25% of Asians and 10% of Caucasians is a version of the enzyme paraoxonase that converts sarin to a less toxic chemical about 10 times more quickly than the enzyme found in most people.

The paraoxonase gene is one of dozens that toxicologists think make some individuals more susceptible to the effects of pollutants and other environmental chemicals, contributing to everything from cancer to birth defects and Parkinson's disease. Hoping to ferret out dozens more of these "environmental susceptibility" gene variants, National Institutes of Health (NIH) scientists are putting together a major effort to sequence DNA from perhaps 1000 people to try to demonstrate a link between certain genes and patterns of disease. "This is information that can really revolutionize public health policy" by making it possible to identify and protect people susceptible to hazards, says Ken Olden, director of the National Institute of Environmental Health Sciences (NIEHS), whose scientists conceived the so-called Environmental Genome Project.

* * *

The idea for the undertaking follows several decades of work on common variations of genes involved in activating or detoxifying drugs and chemicals that we breathe, drink, or eat. "Each person basically has his own unique fingerprint of drug-metabolizing enzymes and receptors, so we all handle drugs [and chemicals] differently," says Dan Nebert, director of the Center for Ecogenetics and Environmental Science at the University of Cincinnati.

Variations, or alleles, of the gene for paraoxonase—an enzyme that breaks down toxic organophosphate compounds, including many insecticides—is one example. Many other genes, such as those in the cytochrome P450 and NAT families—which metabolize carcinogens—can increase cancer risk, especially in smokers. For instance, a smoker with certain NAT variants may have up to a six-fold greater risk of bladder cancer than nonsmokers with other NAT variants * * *.

* * *

First, scientists would set up a DNA repository from 1000 individuals representative of the major U.S. ethnic groups. Next, teams would use some combination of DNA chips and sequencers to resequence alleles of roughly 200 "candidate" genes involved in everything from DNA repair to digestion * * *. Next, researchers would sort out which alleles are common enough to be classified as polymorphisms—versions shared by 1% or more of the population. The project would then sponsor molecular, animal, and, finally, population studies—of sick people who had been exposed to a suspect chemical, for example—to find out how important these polymorphisms are to disease.

NATIONAL INSTITUTE OF ENVIRONMENTAL HEALTH SCIENCES. ENVIRONMENTAL GENOME PROJECT

EGP Overview (2001).

Understanding genetic susceptibility to environmental agents will allow more precise identification of the environmental agents that cause disease and the true risks of exposures. This can lead to more effective disease prevention and improved public health * * *. The human health/disease condition is determined by the complex interplay between genetic susceptibility, environmental exposures and aging. The rapid advances in molecular genetic technology is providing us with new opportunities to understand the genetic basis for individual differences in susceptibility to environmental exposure. The NIEHS is expanding its research program on genetic susceptibility to environmentally-associated diseases through a new Environmental Genome Project. This project, which will makes use of technology developed by the Human Genome Project, is aimed at the identification of allelic variants (polymorphisms) of environmental disease susceptibility genes in the U.S. population, developing a central database of polymorphisms for these genes, and fostering population-based studies of gene-environment interaction in disease etiology. By identifying those genes and allelic variants that affect individual response to environmental agents, scientists can better predict health risks and assist regulatory agencies in the development of environmental protection policies.

* * *

Working with genetically susceptible (sub)populations will allow the more precise identification of environmental agents that cause disease and the true risks of exposure. However, it is of paramount importance to emphasize that identification of polymorphism(s) in an individual does not predict that individual's risk to exposure because of complex, multiple interactions. An individual's complete exposure risk can only be determined by consideration of additional exposure history, nutritional status, age and developmental changes, gender, and other factors. It is our intention that the Environmental Genome Project will generate data that will be utilized in epidemiological studies to enhance our understanding of environmental association with disease. As susceptible (sub)populations are identified, they must be distinguished from susceptible individuals within that population. Some individuals within the susceptible population will be at increased risk for specific exposures while some individuals in that population will have no increase in exposure risk.

* * *

Information gleaned from the Environmental Genome Project could refine current risk assessment capabilities to better protect sensitive subgroups such as children or people who are immunocompromised, and to potentially reduce regulatory costs. Although today's risk assessments and resulting chemical regulations do a pretty good job given the data that are available, "they make the assumption that there is an average individual and an average exposure," [National Institute of Environmental Health Sciences Director Kenneth] Olden says. "There may be an average exposure, but not an average individual." As it stands, he continues, "whether we're actually protecting the health of the American people is uncertain. We may be underregulating or overregulating," as the deviation from the norm can be enormous. Variances in the responsiveness to exposures caused by susceptibility genes may shed light, for example, on disease caused by exposure to the nerve gas "sarin" or other organophosphates used during the Persian Gulf War, Olden says. People with certain polymorphisms produce variants of the enzyme paraoxonase that have difficulty breaking down such nerve agents and related pesticides while people with other allelic variations are more resistant to disease. "The project has tremendous public health implications and will have a tremendous public health impact," Olden says. "If we can understand how these agents interact, we'll be in much better shape to prevent and not just treat end-stage diseases."

And knowing our genetic identity will help protect us all from environmental hazards, he says. The answers may begin trickling in within the next decade, say researchers orchestrating the Environmental Genome Project. The goal of the Environmental Genome Project is to identify variations in genes which, triggered by substances milling around in the environment and hidden in our food, predispose people to diseases and disorders.

* * *

Environmental agents often do not recognize boundaries; e.g., the same environmental toxin may cause cancer in one individual and induce birth defects in another. Examples of environmentally associated diseases/dysfunction are listed as follows:

- Cancer (lung, bladder, breast, prostate cancer)

- Pulmonary Diseases (asthma, cystic fibrosis)

- Neurodegenerative Disorders (Alzheimer's, Parkinson's, amyotrophic lateral sclerosis)

- Developmental Disorders (reduced intelligence, ADHD)

- Birth Defects (orofacial clefting)

- Reproductive Function (fertility, fibroids, endometriosis, precocious puberty)

- Autoimmune Disease (systemic lupus erythematosus, multiple sclerosis)

B. THE FUTURE LEGAL IMPLICATIONS OF THE ENVIRONMENTAL GENOME PROJECT

JOCELYN KAISER, A MORE RATIONAL APPROACH TO GAUGING ENVIRONMENTAL THREATS?

278 Science 570 (1997).

One of the biggest potential payoffs from an environmental genome project is that it could help policy-makers devise rules that better protect sensitive individuals. "To have intelligent environmental regulatory policy, one has to begin to unravel the role of genetics in determining the differences in susceptibility," says National Institute of Environmental Health Sciences (NIEHS) director Ken Olden.

Olden's words are music to the ears of members of Congress who have been clamoring for better science behind regulations. Risk assessors at the Environmental Protection Agency (EPA) and elsewhere now craft rules with a standard fudge factor to try to protect sensitive individuals: They set the permissible exposure level to a chemical, for instance, at a tenth of that deemed acceptable for the general population. Data on the prevalence of susceptibility genes could reduce the need for guesswork, says NIEHS's George Lucier, who's helping write the EPA's dioxin reassessment. "As we get more and more information on the variation of environmentally relevant genes across the population," he says, "we'll be able to more frequently * * * use real data."

In some cases real data might result in a less stringent standard and in others a tighter one. For example, some people may have a version of a detoxifying enzyme that makes them five times more sensitive than others to a pollutant. Risk assessors, then, might permit an exposure that's a fifth that of the acceptable level for the rest of the population—an exposure twice as high as they might set using the standard fudge factor.

"It could go either direction," Lucier says. "It could be a 100–fold factor or a twofold factor." But political factors and economics, in some cases, will inevitably pull rank on science—particularly if the sensitive population is tiny. "It would obviously become extremely expensive to protect a few individuals," says University of Washington, Seattle, toxicologist Dave Eaton.

Indeed, both scientist and regulators may struggle to "digest and understand the meaning and importance" of the initial data on environmental genes, says George Gray of the Harvard Center for Risk Analysis. For one thing, several genes may be involved in defining an individual's risk * * *.

Another bedeviling issue is how this information might be used to alter workplace exposure levels. One test case might be beryllium, an industrial metal that can cause an incurable lung disease. Four years ago, scientists found a genetic marker of susceptibility to beryllium disease carried by 30% of the population; 97% of a group of workers with the disease had the marker. Employers are now debating whether to screen workers for it. One worry is that a worker with a susceptibility gene could be denied a job.

NOTES AND QUESTIONS

1.   By 2009, the Environmental Genome Project (EGP) had sequenced 644 environmentally sensitive genes and discovered 92,377 potentially significant genetic variations called SNPs (single nucleotide polypmorphisms) across the 95 ethnically diverse individuals who provided DNA samples to the project. See http://egp.gs.washington.edu/summary_data.html for more information on the Environmental Genome Project's progress in genome sequencing.

2.   What role might the findings of the Environmental Genome Project play in revision of environmental protection laws?

3.   How might the Environmental Genome Project lead to improved public health?

4.   If a genetic test were available to indicate which people will not be harmed by an otherwise toxic gas, should the Armed Forces be able to use such a test to send only immune soldiers into combat?

5.   If employees can prove that their work environment is hazardous to them because of a gene they possess, should those employees be allowed to demand that the employer provide them with a safe working environment? At what expense? What if the hazard is fundamental to the employer's business? If only one employee possesses the predisposing gene, should the employer be required to abate the risk in order to eliminate the potential danger to the single employee? For a further discussion of employment issues, see Chapter 16.

6.   Plaintiffs in civil cases, particularly where so-called "toxic torts" are involved, are using evidence of genetic susceptibility to disease to clear the

hurdle of causation between exposure to an environmental contaminant and a medical injury. Should plaintiffs be able to introduce evidence of genetic predisposition to establish causation of injuries? Should they be required to undergo genetic testing to prove that they fit the genetic profile of susceptible populations to prove causation? (See Chapter 17, infra.)

7. What about defendants in criminal trials? Should evidence of genetic susceptibility to disease coupled with exposure to environmental factors serve to negate or mitigate a defendant's crime? How does this picture of mental disease fit into our criminal justice system's treatment of the criminal as a rational actor making the choice to commit crimes? See Erica Beecher–Monas, Circumventing Daubert in The Gene Pool, 43 Tulsa L. Rev. 241 (2007), for a treatment of both civil and criminal issues.

VII. RESEARCH ON HUMAN EMBRYOS

A. THE PURPOSE OF EMBRYO RESEARCH

In a society deeply divided over the moral and legal status of embryos, any scientific or medical project using tissue or cells from embryos is bound to raise serious philosophical and social concerns. Because varying viewpoints regarding the legal protection of embryos and fetuses have been enacted into law in different states, it is often difficult for researchers and physicians to determine which laws cover their work. Indeed, statutory and court precedents dealing with embryo and fetal research, abortion, organ transplant, and payment for body tissue all have ramifications for genetic research involving embryo stem cells. Yet no two states have identical laws covering these procedures. Federal law and regulations, too, limit the type of experimentation that may be undertaken with human embryos.

In the genetics realm, three types of embryo research are being pursued extensively. The first is research in which the embryo is intended to be used to create a child. This includes research to diagnose or treat genetic diseases in the embryo. Because of the link between some forms of embryo research and reproductive decisions, bans on embryo research of this type have been challenged as unconstitutional.

The second type of research involves embryos created in the process of in vitro fertilization but not implanted. These embryos are often frozen for a period of time and then destroyed. The third type of embryo research involves embryos created specifically for research purposes. The latter two types of research are intended to benefit other individuals, such as through the use of embryo stem cells to create potential therapeutic cell lines. Some state laws limit research on embryos. For example, Louisiana prohibits research on in vitro fertilized embryos. La. Rev. Stat. Ann. § 9:122. And because federal law bans research which destroys embryos, a controversial question has arisen about the circumstances under which federally-funded researchers can undertake embryo stem cell research.

B. CONSTITUTIONAL CONCERNS IN EMBRYO RESEARCH

LIFCHEZ v. HARTIGAN

735 F.Supp. 1361 (N.D. Ill. 1990).

Memorandum Opinion and Order

WILLIAMS, J.

Dr. Lifchez represents a class of plaintiff physicians who challenged an Illinois statute that banned research on fetuses and embryos in a way that appeared to prohibit certain novel reproductive technologies and experimental genetic testing.

* * *

VAGUENESS

Section 6(7) of the Illinois Abortion Law provides as follows:

(7) No person shall sell or experiment upon a fetus produced by the fertilization of a human ovum by a human sperm unless such experimentation is therapeutic to the fetus thereby produced. Intentional violation of this section is a Class A misdemeanor. Nothing in this subsection (7) is intended to prohibit the performance of in vitro fertilization.

Ill. Rev. Stat., Ch. 38 & 81–26, § 6(7) (1989). Dr. Lifchez claims that the Illinois legislature's failure to define the terms "experimentation" and "therapeutic" renders the statute vague, thus violating his due process rights under the Fourteenth Amendment. The court agrees.

Vague laws—especially criminal laws—violate due process in three ways. First, they fail to give adequate notice of precisely what conduct is being prohibited. Without such notice, it is impossible for people to regulate their conduct within legal bounds * * *. The second problem with vague statutes is that, by failing to explicitly define what conduct is unlawful, they invite arbitrary and discriminatory enforcement by the police, judges, and juries * * *.

Last, vague standards of unlawful conduct, coupled with the prospect of arbitrary enforcement, will inevitably cause people to "steer far wider of the unlawful zone * * * than if the boundaries of the forbidden areas were clearly marked." * * * This is an especially dangerous consequence of vague statutes that encroach upon constitutional rights * * *. It is a fundamental principle of due process that persons " 'of common intelligence' not be forced to guess at the meaning of the criminal law."

* * *

A. *Experiment or Routine Test?*

The Illinois legislature's failure to define "experimentation" and "therapeutic" in § 6(7) means that persons of common intelligence will be forced to guess at whether or not their conduct is unlawful. As Dr. Lifchez points out in his briefs, there is no single accepted definition of "experimentation" in the scientific and medical communities. Dr. Lifchez identifies four referents for the term. One meaning of experiment is pure research, where there is no direct benefit to the subject being experimented on, and the only goal of the research is to increase the researcher's knowledge * * *. This definition describes the defendants' "Orwellian nightmare" of laying out fetuses in a laboratory and exposing them to various harmful agents "just for the scientific thrill" of it * * *. A second meaning of experiment includes any procedure that has not yet been sufficiently tested so that the outcome is predictable, or a procedure that departs from present-day practice. This is the kind of definition adhered to by insurance companies, which often deny coverage for procedures whose effectiveness is not generally recognized * * *. Dr. Lifchez also cites to the definition of experiment by the American Fertility Society, which includes as "experimental" even standard techniques when those techniques are performed by a practitioner or clinic for the first time * * *. Finally, any medical therapy where the practitioner applies what he learns from one patient to another, could be described as an "experiment." * * * This definition of experiment is in line with that apparently contemplated by the federal regulations on protection of human research subjects: "Research means a systematic investigation designed to develop or contribute to generalizable knowledge." 45 C.F.R. § 46.102(e) (1989).

* * *

It is difficult to know where along this broad spectrum of possible meanings for "experiment" to fit the medical procedures performed by Dr. Lifchez and his colleagues. These procedures can be roughly divided into three kinds: diagnostic, in vitro fertilization and related technologies, and procedures performed exclusively for the benefit of the pregnant woman. The statute's vagueness affects all three kinds of procedures, but in different ways.

DIAGNOSTIC PROCEDURES

One of the more common procedures performed by reproductive endocrinologists is amniocentesis. Amniocentesis involves withdrawing a portion of the amniotic fluid in order to test it for genetic anomalies. It is performed on women considered to be at risk for bearing children with serious defects * * *. The purpose of the procedure is to provide information about the developing fetus; this information is often used by women in deciding whether or not to have an abortion. Although now routinely performed, amniocentesis could be considered experimental under at least two of Dr. Lifchez' definitions: it could be classified as pure research, since there is no benefit to the fetus, the subject being "experimented" on; it could also be experimental (as defined by the American Fertility Society) if the particular practitioner or clinic were doing it for the first time.

Amniocentesis illustrates well the problem of deciding at what point a procedure graduates from "experimental" to routine. Does this occur the fifth time a procedure is performed? the fiftieth? the five hundredth? the five thousandth?

* * *

B. *Therapeutic Intent*

The defendants claim that the scienter requirement in § 6(7), "Intentional violation of this section is a Class A misdemeanor," saves it from being unconstitutionally vague. It is true that a scienter requirement can do this for a statute * * *. However, a scienter requirement cannot save a statute such as § 6(7) that has no core of meaning to begin with.

* * *

[T]he legality of diagnostic or screening procedures such as amniocentesis and chorionic villi sampling will depend on whether they are "tests" or "experiments." If a practitioner is unable to tell whether a procedure he is about to perform is an experiment or a test, grafting on a requirement that he intend it to be one or the other does not mitigate the vagueness of what is being forbidden. In other words, while the physician may take comfort in the fact that he is administering a test in good faith, he still does not know which tests are tests and which are experiments. To the extent that amniocentesis and chorionic villi sampling (or attempts to improve them) may be experimental, they are almost certainly illegal under § 6(7). They are designed to give information about fetal development, and often aid women in making a decision about whether or not to have an abortion. Considering in addition the risk factor of spontaneous abortion from these procedures, they can hardly be called therapeutic to the fetus, no matter the practitioner's intent.

* * *

REPRODUCTIVE PRIVACY

Section 6(7) of the Illinois Abortion Law is also unconstitutional because it impermissibly restricts a woman's fundamental right of privacy, in particular, her right to make reproductive choices free of governmental interference with those choices * * *. Section 6(7) intrudes upon this "cluster of constitutionally protected choices." * * *

It takes no great leap of logic to see that within the cluster of constitutionally protected choices that includes the right to have access to contraceptives, there must be included within that cluster the right to submit to a medical procedure that may bring about, rather than prevent, pregnancy. Chorionic villi sampling is similarly protected. The cluster of constitutional choices that includes the right to abort a fetus within the first trimester must also include the right to submit to a procedure designed to give information about that fetus which can then lead to a decision to abort. Since there is no compelling state interest sufficient to prevent a woman from terminating her pregnancy during the first trimester, * * * there can be no such interest sufficient to intrude upon these other protected activities during the first trimester. By encroaching upon this protected zone of privacy, § 6(7) is unconstitutional.

Notes and Questions

1.   One of the reasons that the Illinois ban on embryo and fetal research was unconstitutional was that it was vague. Would the following, more specific laws be upheld as constitutional under the *Lifchez* logic?

a.   A law banning genetic testing for sex selection purposes.

b.   A law banning the use of human embryos to create stem cells to make heart cells for people who have had heart attacks.

c.   A law banning the creation of children through human cloning.

2.   For a further discussion of the constitutionality of human reproductive cloning, see Chapter 6.

C.   EMBRYO STEM CELL RESEARCH

1.   How Embryo Stem Cell Research is Performed

NATIONAL INSTITUTES OF HEALTH, PLURIPOTENT STEM CELLS: A PRIMER

(May 2000).

What Is a Stem Cell?

Stem cells have the ability to divide without limit and to give rise to specialized cells. They are best described in the context of normal human development. Human development begins when a sperm fertilizes an egg and creates a single cell that has the potential to form an entire human being—it is totipotent, meaning that its potential is total. In the first hours after fertilization, this cell divides into two identical totipotent cells. This means that either one of these cells, if placed into a woman's uterus, has the potential to develop into a human. In fact, identical twins develop when two totipotent cells separate and develop into two individual, identical human beings. After approximately four days, the totipotent cells enter the next stage of development that is characterized by specialization and the formation of a hollow sphere of cells, called a blastocyst. The blastocyst has an outer layer of cells and inside the hollow sphere, there are a cluster of cells called the inner cell mass.

The outer layer of cells will go on to form the placenta and other supporting tissues needed for fetal development in the uterus. The inner cell mass cells will go on to form all of the tissues of the human body. Although the inner cell mass cells can form virtually every type of cell found in the human body, they cannot form a human because they are unable to give rise to the placenta and supporting tissues necessary for development in the human uterus. These inner cell mass cells are pluripotent—they can give rise to many types of cells but not all types of cells. Because their potential is not total, they are not totipotent and they are not embryos. In fact, if an inner cell mass cell were placed into a woman's uterus, it would not develop into a human being.

The pluripotent stem cells undergo further specialization into stem cells that are committed to giving rise to cells with a particular function; for example, blood stem cells or skin stem cells. A blood stem cell will then give rise to the various types of blood cells—white blood cells, red blood cells and platelets. But once a pluripotent stem cell specializes into a blood stem cell, it does not change course and produce skin stem cells, liver cells or any cell other than a blood stem cell or a specific type of blood cell. In addition, pluripotent stem cells do not produce totipotent stem cells.

* * *

How are Pluripotent Cells Derived?

At present, human pluripotent cell lines have been developed from two sources with methods previously developed in work with animal models.

(1) In the work done by Dr. Thomson, pluripotent stem cells were isolated directly from the inner cell mass of human embryos at the blastocyst stage. Dr. Thomson received embryos from IVF (In Vitro Fertilization) clinics—these embryos were in excess of the clinical need and would otherwise have been discarded. The embryos were made for purposes of reproduction, not research. Informed consent was obtained from the donor couples. Dr. Thomson isolated the inner cell mass and cultured these cells producing a pluripotent stem cell line.

(2) In contrast, Dr. Gearhart isolated pluripotent stem cells from fetal tissue obtained from terminated pregnancies. Informed consent was obtained from the donors after they had independently made the decision to terminate their pregnancy. Dr. Gearhart took cells from the region of the fetus that was destined to develop into the testes or the ovaries. Although the cells developed in Dr. Gearhart's lab and Dr. Thomson's lab were derived from different sources, they appear to be very similar.

The use of somatic cell nuclear transfer (SCNT) [more commonly known as "cloning"] may be another way that pluripotent stem cells could be isolated. In studies with animals using SCNT, researchers take a normal animal egg cell and remove the nucleus (cell structure containing the chromosomes). The material left behind in the egg cell contains nutrients and other energy-producing materials that are essential for embryo development. Then, using carefully worked out laboratory conditions, a somatic cell—any cell other than an egg or a sperm cell—is placed next to the egg from which the nucleus had been removed, and the two are fused. The resulting fused cell, and its immediate descendants, are believed to have the full potential to develop into an entire animal, and hence are totipotent * * *. [T]hese totipotent cells will soon form a blastocyst. Cells from the inner cell mass of this blastocyst could, in theory, be used to develop pluripotent stem cell lines. Indeed, any method by which a human blastocyst is formed could potentially serve as a source of pluripotent stem cells.

POTENTIAL APPLICATIONS OF PLURIPOTENT STEM CELLS

There are several important reasons why the isolation of human pluripotent stem cells is important to science and to advances in health care. At the most fundamental level, pluripotent stem cells could help us to understand the complex events that occur during human development. A primary goal of this work would be the identification of the factors involved in the cellular decision-making process that results in cell specialization. We know that turning genes on and off is central to this process, but we do not know much about these "decision-making" genes or what turns them on or off. Some of our most serious medical conditions, such as cancer and birth defects, are due to abnormal cell differentiation and cell division. A better understanding of normal cell processes will allow us to further delineate the fundamental errors that cause these deadly illnesses.

Human pluripotent stem cell research could also dramatically change the way we develop drugs and test them for safety. For example, rather than evaluating the safety of a candidate drug in an animal model, these drugs could be tested against human cell lines. Cell lines are currently used in this way (for example cancer cells). Pluripotent stem cells would allow testing in more cell types. This would not replace testing in cell lines, whole animals, and testing in human beings, but it would streamline the process of drug development. Only the safest candidate would be likely to graduate to whole animal and then human testing.

Perhaps the most far-reaching potential application of human pluripotent stem cells is the generation of cells and tissue that could be used for so-called cell therapies. Many diseases and disorders result from disruption of cellular function or destruction of tissues of the body. Today, donated organs and tissues are often used to replace ailing or destroyed tissue. Unfortunately, the number of people suffering from these disorders far outstrips the number of organs available from transplantation. Pluripotent stem cells, stimulated to develop into specialized cells, offer the possibility of a renewable source of replacement cells and tissue to treat a myriad of diseases, conditions, and disabilities including Parkinson's and Alzheimer's diseases, spinal cord injury, stroke, burns, heart disease, diabetes, osteoarthritis and rheumatoid arthritis.

2. The Legal Implications of Embryo Stem Cell Research

REMOVING BARRIERS TO RESPONSIBLE SCIENTIFIC RESEARCH INVOLVING HUMAN STEM CELLS

EXECUTIVE ORDER OF PRESIDENT OBAMA

March 9, 2009.

http://www.whitehouse.gov/the_press_office/Removing–
Barriers-to-Responsible–Scientific–Research–
Involving–Human–Stem–Cells/.

By the authority vested in me as President by the Constitution and the laws of the United States of America, it is hereby ordered as follows:

Section 1. Policy. Research involving human embryonic stem cells and human non-embryonic stem cells has the potential to lead to better understanding and treatment of many disabling diseases and conditions. Advances over the past decade in this promising scientific field have been encouraging, leading to broad agreement in the scientific community that the research should be supported by Federal funds.

For the past 8 years, the authority of the Department of Health and Human Services, including the National Institutes of Health (NIH), to fund and conduct human embryonic stem cell research has been limited by Presidential actions. The purpose of this order is to remove these limitations on scientific inquiry, to expand NIH support for the exploration of human stem cell research, and in so doing to enhance the contribution of America's scientists to important new discoveries and new therapies for the benefit of humankind.

Sec. 2. Research. The Secretary of Health and Human Services (Secretary), through the Director of NIH, may support and conduct responsible, scientifically worthy human stem cell research, including human embryonic stem cell research, to the extent permitted by law.

Sec. 3. Guidance. Within 120 days from the date of this order, the Secretary, through the Director of NIH, shall review existing NIH guidance and other widely recognized guidelines on human stem cell research, including provisions establishing appropriate safeguards, and issue new NIH guidance on such research that is consistent with this order. The Secretary, through NIH, shall review and update such guidance periodically, as appropriate.

NATIONAL INSTITUTES OF HEALTH GUIDELINES FOR RESEARCH USING HUMAN STEM CELLS
Effective July 6, 2009,

http://stemcells.nih.gov/policy/2009guidelines.htm.

I.   Scope of Guidelines

These Guidelines apply to the expenditure of National Institutes of Health (NIH) funds for research using human embryonic stem cells (hESCs) and certain uses of induced pluripotent stem cells (See Section IV). The Guidelines implement Executive Order 13505.

* * *

These guidelines are based on the following principles:

1.   Responsible research with hESCs has the potential to improve our understanding of human health and illness and discover new ways to prevent and/or treat illness.

2.   Individuals donating embryos for research purposes should do so freely, with voluntary and informed consent.

* * *

II.   Eligibility of Human Embryonic Stem Cells for Research with NIH Funding

For the purpose of these Guidelines, "human embryonic stem cells (hESCs)" are cells that are derived from the inner cell mass of blastocyst stage human embryos, are capable of dividing without differentiating for a prolonged period in culture, and are known to develop into cells and tissues of the three primary germ layers. Although hESCs are derived from embryos, such stem cells are not themselves human embryos. All of the processes and procedures for review of the eligibility of hESCs will be centralized at the NIH as follows:

A.   Applicant institutions proposing research using hESCs derived from embryos donated in the U.S. on or after the effective date of these Guidelines may use hESCs that are posted on the new NIH Registry or they may establish eligibility for NIH funding by submitting an assurance of compliance with Section II (A) of the Guidelines, along with supporting information demonstrating compliance for administrative review by the NIH. For the purposes of this Section II (A), hESCs should have been derived from human embryos:

1.   that were created using in vitro fertilization for reproductive purposes and were no longer needed for this purpose;

2.   that were donated by individuals who sought reproductive treatment (hereafter referred to as "donor(s)") and who gave voluntary written consent for the human embryos to be used for research purposes; and

3.   for which all of the following can be assured and documentation provided, such as consent forms, written policies, or other documentation, provided:

a.   All options available in the health care facility where treatment was sought pertaining to the embryos no longer needed for reproductive purposes were explained to the individual(s) who sought reproductive treatment.

b. No payments, cash or in kind, were offered for the donated embryos.

c. Policies and/or procedures were in place at the health care facility where the embryos were donated that neither consenting nor refusing to donate embryos for research would affect the quality of care provided to potential donor(s).

d. There was a clear separation between the prospective donor(s)'s decision to create human embryos for reproductive purposes and the prospective donor(s)'s decision to donate human embryos for research purposes. Specifically:

    i. Decisions related to the creation of human embryos for reproductive purposes should have been made free from the influence of researchers proposing to derive or utilize hESCs in research. The attending physician responsible for reproductive clinical care and the researcher deriving and/or proposing to utilize hESCs should not have been the same person unless separation was not practicable.

    ii. At the time of donation, consent for that donation should have been obtained from the individual(s) who had sought reproductive treatment. That is, even if potential donor(s) had given prior indication of their intent to donate to research any embryos that remained after reproductive treatment, consent for the donation for research purposes should have been given at the time of the donation.

    iii. Donor(s) should have been informed that they retained the right to withdraw consent for the donation of the embryo until the embryos were actually used to derive embryonic stem cells or until information which could link the identity of the donor(s) with the embryo was no longer retained, if applicable.

e. During the consent process, the donor(s) were informed of the following:

    i. that the embryos would be used to derive hESCs for research;

    ii. what would happen to the embryos in the derivation of hESCs for research;

    iii. that hESCs derived from the embryos might be kept for many years;

    iv. that the donation was made without any restriction or direction regarding the individual(s) who may receive medical benefit from the use of the hESCs, such as who may be the recipients of cell transplants;

v. that the research was not intended to provide direct medical benefit to the donor(s);

vi. that the results of research using the hESCs may have commercial potential, and that the donor(s) would not receive financial or any other benefits from any such commercial development;

vii. whether information that could identify the donor(s) would be available to researchers.

* * *

V.   Other Research Not Eligible for NIH Funding

A.   NIH funding of the derivation of stem cells from human embryos is prohibited by the annual appropriations ban on funding of human embryo research (Section 509, Omnibus Appropriations Act, 2009, Pub. L. 111–8, 3/11/09), otherwise known as the Dickey Amendment.

B.   Research using hESCs derived from other sources, including somatic cell nuclear transfer, parthenogenesis, and/or IVF embryos created for research purposes, is not eligible for NIH funding.

NOTES AND QUESTIONS

1.   President Obama revoked President Bush's August 9, 2001 directive (which limited federal funding of research to 60 existing stem cell lines) and revoked President Bush's executive order 13435 of June 20, 2007, which allowed for the federal support of stem cell research, as long as the research was not based on the creation or destruction of a human embryo. Now, federal funds may be used for research involving privately created stem cell lines.

Nonetheless, federal funds may not be used to support research which directly results in the creation or destruction of a human embryo. Two days after President Obama issued his order regarding stem cell research, he signed into law the Omnibus Appropriations Act of 2009, which included the following provision:

SEC. 509:

(a) None of the funds made available in this Act may be used for—

(1) the creation of a human embryo or embryos for research purposes; or

(2) research in which a human embryo or embryos are destroyed, discarded, or knowingly subjected to risk of injury or death greater than that allowed for research on fetuses in utero under 45 CFR 46.204(b) and section 498(b) of the Public Health Service Act (42 U.S.C. 289g(b)).

The above provision, commonly referred to as a Dickey–Wicker amendment, has been included in annual appropriations bills since 1996. Should the federal government continue to implement Dickey–Wicker amendments or should it support research that directly involves the creation or destruction of a human embryo?

2.   Additionally, federal law limits the uses of human fetal tissue, which is one of the sources for human pluripotent stem cells. The Public Health Service Act prohibits the sale of human fetal tissue for valuable consideration as well as the directed donation of fetal tissue for transplantation. 42 U.S.C. 289g–2. The act also states that federal support for the "transplantation of fetal tissue for therapeutic purposes" may only be given where: (1) the woman donating the tissue has given informed consent, (2) the attending physician states that the consent was uncoerced and that no medical procedures were altered to acquire the fetal tissue, and (3) the researcher states that he or she is aware of the source of the tissue, communicates that information to the donee, and states that he or she had no part in terminating the pregnancy. 42 U.S.C. 289g–1. Moreover, federal regulation stipulates that any activities involving the biological tissues of a non-living fetus must conform to state and local law. 45 C.F.R. § 46.206.

3.   State law permitting stem cell research on fetal tissue varies widely. For example, New Jersey law permits research on non-living fetal tissue donated with informed consent, whereas South Dakota law prohibits any research on non-living fetal tissue that did not result from an abortion necessary to save the life of the mother. N.J. Stat. Ann. § 26:2Z–2(c); S.D. Codified Laws §§ 34–23A–17. Is this an issue better resolved by each individual state or by a policy set forth by the federal government?

4.   What were the advantages and disadvantages of President Bush's policy to allow embryo stem cell research only on existing cell lines? Did his position seem motivated by scientific concerns, policy concerns, or religious concerns?

5.   President Bush's former policy to limit federal funding to research on 60 existing stem cell lines. In an August 13, 2001 Newsday article, Embryo Decision Raises New Issues, Professor Lori Andrews articulated some of the ethical problems with President Bush's policy: (1) the stem cell lines may not be representative enough of human genetic diversity to create useful therapies for all racial and ethnic groups, (2) some of the existing stem cell lines were created without consent of the donors to use the fetal tissue for research purposes, and (3) due to licensing fees, the cost of research on existing stem cell lines may be prohibitive and may greatly increase the cost of both research and research products to the taxpayer. Does President Obama's policy address some of these concerns? Does it raise others?

6.   What concerns about informed consent should be raised when embryo stem cell research is undertaken? A 2007 study at nine infertility clinics found that donors preferred to donate to research rather than donate embryos to another couple or thaw embryos and discard them. Additionally, according to the study, the decision to donate was affected by the type of research proposed. For example, 62% of respondents stated that they would be somewhat or very likely to donate to stem cell research aimed at understanding and treating human disease or injury, whereas only 28% stated that they would be somewhat or very likely to donate embryos to improve cloning techniques. Anne Drapkin Lyerly, Ruth R. Faden, Willingness to Donate

Frozen Embryos for Stem Cell Research, 317 Science 46 (2007). Is the informed consent requirement under the federal rules met by asking the couple for consent to do research? Or must the couple be told the details of each specific study?

7.   A study reported in the *New England Journal of Medicine* showed that as often as 71% of the time couples change their minds about what they would like to do with excess embryos created during the in vitro fertilization process. See S.C. Klock, S. Sheinin, & R.R. Kazer, The Disposition of Frozen Embryos, 345 New Eng. J. Med. 69 (2001). How should researchers approach informed consent in light of this study? Should the couple be recontacted before specific research is undertaken?

8.   One controversial area involves determining whether research organizations should financially compensate women for their donation of eggs (oocytes) to research. Currently, most research organizations do not compensate egg donors, but donors are paid when they provide their eggs to infertility clinics.

There are two major arguments in favor of compensation. First, compensation of research subjects is common in the United States. Additionally, according to FDA guidelines on payment to research subjects, payment is often appropriate where the research subject receives no direct health benefit from participation. Generally, egg donors receive no direct health benefit from the research eventually conducted on their eggs. Second, as a practical matter, the National Research Council recognized in its 2005 Guidelines for Human Embryonic Stem Cell Research that compensation is a major motivator for egg donors. Researchers may argue that they need to compensate egg donors in some manner or else jeopardize their projects for lack of research materials.

The FDA guidelines are available at http://www.fda.gov/ScienceResearch/ SpecialTopics/RunningClinicalTrials/GuidancesInformationSheetsandNotices/ ucm116330.htm. The National Research Council's Guidelines for Human Embryonic Stem Cell Research are available at http://www.nap.edu/catalog. php?record_id=11278.

However, compensation could undermine the value of informed consent procedures. If a compulsive gambler needed to pay a gambling debt and donated eggs to research because the compensation was $5,000—exactly the amount she needed—would her informed consent be truly voluntary? Or did her predicament make her vulnerable and impel her to donate when ordinarily she would not?

In 2005, the California Senate Subcommittee on Stem Cell Research Oversight, the Senate Health Committee, and the Assembly Health Committee conducted a joint informational hearing to determine how to implement Proposition 71, which created the California Institute for Regenerative Medicine. Francine Coeytaux, a representative for the Pro-Choice Alliance for Responsible Research, spoke to the committee and expressed concern about the compensation of egg donors for research. Coeytaux argued that egg donors should not be compensated for donation to research due to the risk of coercing large numbers of poor women into donation. Many fertility clinics offer thousands of dollars in compensation to donors and presumably research organizations would need to offer similar amounts to induce potential donors.

Coeytaux also expressed concern about exposing large numbers of women to the risks of the egg donation process itself. According to Coeytaux, Luprin, a drug used in the in vitro fertilization process, has sometimes resulted in bone loss, liver disorders and severe muscle, joint, and bone pain in donors. Additionally, the drugs used to stimulate the ovary into producing several eggs at once can cause Ovarian Hyper–Stimulation Syndrome, a condition which can be life-threatening.

Currently, the regulations governing the California Institute for Regenerative Medicine (CIRM) do not permit researchers to compensate egg donors. The regulations also do not permit CIRM-funded researchers to use eggs acquired from fertility clinics, where the clinics have compensated egg donors in excess of the direct out-of-pocket expenses ("permissible expense") related to donation. Cal. Admin. Code tit. 17, § 100095; Guidance for CIRM Ethical and Medical Standards Regulations Governing Donation of Oocytes for CIRM–Funded Research, California Institute for Regenerative Medicine, Oct. 10, 2008.

Should we be concerned that fertility treatments are turning the process of procreation into a money-making venture? How should we proceed in light of the fact that a woman's eggs are now a valuable commodity? Does this recognition of market forces point toward compensating women for donating to research or not? Does the very existence of an active marketplace for egg donation undermine the concept of informed consent?

Is it paternalistic to think that special steps are needed to protect women from exploitation by the research community? Is it paternalistic to think that donating oocytes is any different from the donation of other tissue samples? Or is it simply a matter of accounting for the time commitment and discomfort related to the donation process?

9.   The California Initiative amended the California state constitution to guarantee a "right" to conduct embryonic stem cell research, apparently to protect the state from any subsequently enacted federal laws. How does this state constitutional right affect the level of scrutiny to be applied in judging any future state and federal legislative attempts to regulate stem cell research?

VIII.   CONFLICTS OF INTEREST IN RESEARCH

A.   PAYMENT TO PHYSICIANS

KURT EICHENWALD & GINA KOLATA, DRUG TRIALS HIDE CONFLICTS FOR DOCTORS

The New York Times, May 16, 1999, at 1.

Once clinical research was a staid enterprise primarily administered by academic researchers driven by a desire for knowledge, fame or career advancement. Now, it is a multibillion-dollar industry, with hundreds of testing and drug companies working with thousands of private doctors.

In this new industry, patients have become commodities, bought and traded by testing companies and doctors. Almost daily, the industry urges doctors to join the gold rush, bombarding them with faxes and letters blaring such come-ons as "Improve Your Cash Flow" and "Discover the Secret For Obtaining More Funded Studies." In an era of managed care, the pleas are seductive: the number of private doctors in research since 1990 has almost tripled, and top recruiters can earn as much as $500,000 to $1 million a year.

* * *

Testing companies often use doctors as clinical investigators regardless of their specialty, at times leaving patients in the care of doctors who know little about their condition. For example, psychiatrists have conducted Pap smears and asthma specialists have dispensed experimental psychiatric drugs.

A growing number of doctors conducting drug research have limited experience as clinical investigators, raising questions among some experts about the quality of their data.

* * *

A system that offers so much cash and so many benefits for quick recruitment assumes that doctors would never allow money to distort their judgment—in this case by causing them to put undue pressure on reluctant patients or to include patients who do not qualify. But the assumption that doctors can resist financial temptations has been proved wrong repeatedly in other situations.

For example, throughout much of the 1980's, doctors could refer patients to treatment centers—such as physical or radiation therapy sites—in which they had a stake. The practice was outlawed after studies found that doctors were overusing treatments and tests when they had financial interests in the centers that provided them. A 1992 study published in The New England Journal of Medicine found that doctors with investments in radiation sites prescribed such treatment as much as 60 percent more often than those without the financial conflict.

* * *

Dr. Shimm of Porter Adventist Hospital in Denver recalled that when he served on an ethics board at a university medical school, a good deal of time was spent discussing whether payments to patient volunteers were coercive. The concern was that patients might enter studies for the money rather than out of altruism, the ideal that is sought. But, immediately after such a discussion at one meeting, another proposal came up in which a doctor stood to receive thousands of dollars from the drug company for each patient recruited.

"I said, 'Wait a minute,' " Dr. Shimm said. "If it is coercive to pay a patient $500, why is it not coercive to pay the clinical investigator $5,000?"

But other members of the research board were not interested in the topic.

"I was told," Dr. Shimm said, "to sit down and shut up."

B. FEDERAL REGULATIONS AND GUIDELINES ON CONFLICTS OF INTERESTS

FEDERAL REGULATIONS ON THE RESPONSIBILITY OF APPLICANTS FOR PROMOTING OBJECTIVITY IN RESEARCH FOR WHICH PUBLIC HEALTH SERVICE FUNDING IS SOUGHT

42 C.F.R. § 50.604 et seq.

42 C.F.R. § 50.604 Institutional responsibility regarding conflicting interests of investigators.

Each Institution must:

(a) Maintain an appropriate written, enforced policy on conflict of interest that complies with this subpart and inform each Investigator of that policy, the Investigator's reporting responsibilities, and of these regulations. If the Institution carries out the PHS-funded research through subgrantees, contractors, or collaborators, the Institution must take reasonable steps to ensure that Investigators working for such entities comply with this subpart, either by requiring those Investigators to comply with the Institution's policy or by requiring the entities to provide assurances to the Institution that will enable the Institution to comply with this subpart.

(b) Designate an institutional official(s) to solicit and review financial disclosure statements from each Investigator who is planning to participate in PHS-funded research.

(c)(1) Require that by the time an application is submitted to PHS each Investigator who is planning to participate in the PHS-funded research has submitted to the designated official(s) a listing of his/her known Significant Financial Interests (and those of his/her spouse and dependent children):

(i) That would reasonably appear to be affected by the research for which PHS funding is sought; and

(ii) In entities whose financial interests would reasonably appear to be affected by the research.

(2) All financial disclosures must be updated during the period of the award, either on an annual basis or as new reportable Significant Financial Interests are obtained.

(d) Provide guidelines consistent with this subpart for the designated official(s) to identify conflicting interests and take such actions as necessary to ensure that such conflicting interests will be managed, reduced, or eliminated.

(e) Maintain records of all financial disclosures and all actions taken by the Institution with respect to each conflicting interest for at least three years from the date of submission of the final expenditures report or, where applicable, from other dates specified in 45 CFR 74.53(b) for different situations.

(f) Establish adequate enforcement mechanisms and provide for sanctions where appropriate.

* * *

45 C.F.R. § 50.605 Management of conflicting interests.

(a) The designated official(s) must: Review all financial disclosures; and determine whether a conflict of interest exists and, if so, determine what actions should be taken by the institution to manage, reduce or eliminate such conflict of interest. A conflict of interest exists when the designated official(s) reasonably determines that a Significant Financial Interest could directly and significantly affect the design, conduct, or reporting of the PHS-funded research. Examples of conditions or restrictions that might be imposed to manage conflicts of interest include, but are not limited to:

(1) Public disclosure of significant financial interests;

(2) Monitoring of research by independent reviewers;

(3) Modification of the research plan;

(4) Disqualification from participation in all or a portion of the research funded by the PHS;

(5) Divestiture of significant financial interests; or

(6) Severance of relationships that create actual or potential conflicts.

(b) In addition to the types of conflicting financial interests described in this paragraph that must be managed, reduced, or eliminated, an Institution may require the management of other conflicting financial interests, as the Institution deems appropriate.

PROPOSED TEXT OF S.301
THE PHYSICIAN PAYMENTS SUNSHINE ACT OF 2009

* * *

SEC. 1128G. TRANSPARENCY REPORTS AND REPORTING OF PHYSICIAN OWNERSHIP OR INVESTMENT INTERESTS.

(a) Transparency Reports-

(1) PAYMENTS OR OTHER TRANSFERS OF VALUE-

(A) IN GENERAL-Except as provided in subsection (e), on March 31, 2011, and on the 90th day of each calendar year beginning thereafter, any applicable manufacturer that provides a payment or other transfer of value to a covered recipient (or to an entity or individual at the request of or designated on behalf of a covered recipient), shall submit to the Secretary, in such electronic form as the Secretary shall require, the following information with respect to the preceding calendar year:

(i) The name of the covered recipient.

(ii) The business address of the covered recipient and, in the case of a covered recipient who is a physician, the specialty and Medicare billing number of the covered recipient.

(iii) The value of the payment or other transfer of value.

(iv) The dates on which the payment or other transfer of value was provided to the covered recipient.

(v) A description of the form of the payment or other transfer of value, indicated (as appropriate for all that apply) as—

(I) cash or a cash equivalent;

(II) in-kind items or services;

(III) stock, a stock option, or any other ownership interest, dividend, profit, or other return on investment; or

(IV) any other form of payment or other transfer of value (as defined by the Secretary).

(vi) A description of the nature of the payment or other transfer of value, indicated (as appropriate for all that apply) as—

(I) consulting fees;

(II) compensation for services other than consulting;

(III) honoraria;

(IV) gift;

(V) entertainment;

(VI) food;

(VII) travel;

(VIII) education;

(IX) research;

(X) charitable contribution;

(XI) royalty or license;

(XII) current or prospective ownership or investment interest;

(XIII) compensation for serving as faculty or as a speaker for a continuing medical education program;

(XIV) grant; or

(XV) any other nature of the payment or other transfer of value (as defined by the Secretary).

(vii) If the payment or other transfer of value is related to marketing, education, or research specific to a covered drug, device, biological, or medical supply, the name of that covered drug, device, biological, or medical supply.

(viii) Any other categories of information regarding the payment or other transfer of value the Secretary determines appropriate.

* * *

(10) PAYMENT OR OTHER TRANSFER OF VALUE-

(A) IN GENERAL—The term 'payment or other transfer of value' means a transfer of anything of value and includes, subject to subparagraph (B), without limitation, any compensation, gift, honorarium, speaking fee, consulting fee, travel, services, dividend, profit distribution, stock or stock option grant, or ownership or investment interest.

(B) EXCLUSIONS—An applicable manufacturer shall not be required to submit information under subsection (a) with respect to the following:

(i) Any payment or other transfer of value provided by an applicable manufacturer to a covered recipient where the aggregate amount transferred to, requested by, or designated on behalf of the covered recipient does not exceed $100 during the calendar year. Such aggregate amount shall be determined without taking into account any payment or other transfer of value described in clauses (ii) through (ix).

(ii) Product samples that are not intended to be sold and are intended for patient use.

(iii) Educational materials that directly benefit patients or are intended for patient use.

(iv) The loan of a covered device for a short-term trial period, not to exceed 90 days, to permit evaluation of the covered device by the covered recipient.

(v) Items or services provided under a contractual warranty, including the replacement of a covered device, where the terms of the warranty are set forth in the purchase or lease agreement for the covered device.

(vi) A transfer of anything of value to a covered recipient when the covered recipient is a patient and not acting in the professional capacity of a covered recipient.

(vii) Discounts (including rebates).

(viii) In-kind items used for the provision of charity care.

(ix) A dividend or other profit distribution from, or ownership or investment interest in, a publicly traded security and mutual fund (as described in section 1877(c)).

NOTES AND QUESTIONS

1. The Physician Payment Sunshine Act attempts to curtail the undue influence of private pharmaceutical and medical device companies over physicians by requiring companies to disclose any financial payments or valuable interests transferred to physicians in excess of $100. The act also provides that all the resulting information will be collected in a database and made available to the public. Keeping in mind that the cost of a single meal could easily exceed $100, should companies be required to report such small expenditures made on behalf of physicians?

2. Several states have also attempted to limit the undue influence of private companies over physicians by passing similar legislation. For example, Vermont, the District of Columbia, West Virginia, Maine, Massachusetts, Nevada, California and Minnesota have all passed laws requiring disclosure of marketing activities made by physicians on behalf of private companies. Vermont also recently passed a law that would require further disclosure of the kinds of financial payments and valuable interests covered by the Physician Payment Sunshine Act of 2009. Is this problem better handled by state legislatures than by the federal government?

3. A Congressional investigation spearheaded by Senator Grassley has highlighted several alleged undisclosed conflicts of interest incidents: psychiatrist Dr. Charles B. Nemeroff of Emory University reportedly failed to disclose $1.2 million in outside income from drug makers (including money from GlaxoSmithKline) while running a $3.9 million taxpayer-funded study to test GlaxoSmithKline drugs; Drs. Joseph Biederman and Timothy Wilens of Harvard each earned at least $1.6 million in consulting fees from drug makers but reportedly stated they earned only several hundred thousand dollars; Dr. Melissa DelBello of Univ. of Cincinnati allegedly reported around $100,000 from 8 drug companies over two years, while one alone had paid her $238,000.

Senator Grassley also asked the drug company Pfizer to provide information about any unreported payments made to *any* Harvard faculty members. Additionally, his letter asks for records, pictures, or files the drug company might have regarding medical students who held a demonstration protesting the relationship between their professors and drug and medical device companies. According to an article in *The New York Times*, a pharmacy representative was present at the demonstration and took pictures of the students with a cell phone. Duff Wilson, A Senator Asks Pfizer About Harvard Payments, The New York Times, March 4, 2009 at B3. Senator Grassley raised concerns that this could intimidate students and prevent them from freely expressing their opinions about their professors' ties with industry.

Should all ties between academic research entities and drug companies be cut? What would be the effect of such a move on the academic and the business sector? Why do drug companies approach academic institutions to conduct studies on their products in the first place?

C. MEDICAL ORGANIZATION GUIDELINES ON CONFLICTS OF INTEREST

POLICY OF THE AMERICAN SOCIETY OF GENE THERAPY, FINANCIAL CONFLICT OF INTEREST IN CLINICAL RESEARCH

Adopted April 5, 2000.

Potential conflicts of interest may arise in the course of all clinical research, including gene therapy. In principle, the ethical standards for clinical research in gene therapy should be the same as those demanded in all areas of medicine. Therapeutic agents used in clinical trials are often produced by for-profit companies, which can give rise to circumstances that present a financial conflict of interest to the investigators. An extreme case would be that a clinical reagent, be it a small molecule, a protein or a gene transfer vector, that is manufactured by a company wholly or partly owned by the Principal Investigator conducting the clinical trial. The guiding principle is clear: clinical investigators must be able to design and carry out clinical research studies in an objective and unbiased manner, free from conflicts caused by significant financial involvement with the commercial sponsors of the study.

Clinical trials are often sponsored by industry, where legitimate costs in conducting the research are covered. The Regulations on Objectivity in Research and the Investigator Financial Disclosure Policy adopted by the National Institutes of Health and the National Science Foundation on July 3, 1996 have established that: "Investigators are required to disclose to the institution a listing of Significant Financial Interests (and those of his/her spouse and dependent children) that would reasonably appear to be affected by the research proposed for funding by the PHS. The institution will review those disclosures and determine whether any of the reported financial interests could directly and significantly affect the design, conduct, or reporting of the research and if so, the institution must report the existence of such conflicting interests to the PHS Awarding Component and act to protect PHS-funded research from bias due to the conflict of interest". The same documents also established significant financial interests as equity ownership in companies exceeding 5%, and/or aggregate payments received from companies in excess of $10,000/year. Academic institutions have also established policies governing investigators' financial conflicts of interest that are consistent with these federal regulations.

The American Society of Gene Therapy is not a regulatory body and it should beware from becoming one. However, in order to pursue its mission to promote gene therapy research and development, the Ethics Committee recommends to the Board of Directors to adopt the following resolution:

"In Gene Therapy trials, as in all other clinical trials, the best interest of the patients must be always primary. International, national and institutional guidelines on standards of care must be rigorously followed, approved protocols strictly adhered to, serious adverse events promptly reported to all appropriate regulatory and review bodies. Relevant federally and institutionally established regulations and guidelines in financial conflicts must also be abided by. In addition, all investigators and team members directly responsible for patient selection, the informed consent process and/or clinical management in a trial must not have equity, stock options or comparable arrangements in companies sponsoring the trial. The American Society of Gene Therapy requests its members to abstain from or to discontinue any arrangement that is not consonant with this policy."

NOTES AND QUESTIONS

1.   Under a conflicts of interest policy, what types of financial interests should be forbidden entirely? What types should be disclosed?

2.   What are some examples of non-financial conflicts of interests? How should they be handled?

3.   The New York Times investigation revealed that physicians who recruit patients for research studies can profit handsomely. Is there anything in the federal regulations that would prohibit the arrangements described in the Eichenwald and Kolata article?

4.   At a cost of several million dollars, the National Institutes of Health collected tissue samples, including spinal fluid, from individuals afflicted with Alzheimer's Disease and also from healthy individuals, for use in future studies conducted by the National Institute for Mental Health (NIMH). When a researcher attempted to gain access to some of these samples for use in a new study, she was told by Dr. Pearson ("Trey") Sunderland III, the head of Geriatric Psychiatry at NIMH, that a freezer malfunction had destroyed 95% of the samples. However, Dr. Sunderland was unable to substantiate his claims and a Congressional investigation was launched to determine what happened to the samples.

The investigators discovered that Dr. Sunderland had provided over 3,000 tissue samples and associated clinical data to the pharmaceutical company Pfizer. The samples came from 538 patients over a 15 year period. Staff of H. Comm. on Energy and Commerce, 109th Cong., A Staff Report: For the Use of the Subcommittee on Oversight and Investigations In Preparation for Its Hearing, Human Tissue Samples: NIH Research Policies and Practices, June 13–14, 2006. The investigators also uncovered a previously undisclosed financial relationship between Dr. Sunderland and Pfizer. Pfizer paid Dr. Sunderland as a consultant at the same time that Pfizer was entering into official research partnerships with NIMH. As a result, Dr. Sunderland was often paid simultaneously by NIMH and Pfizer for the same work. Dr. Sunderland received hundreds of thousands of dollars from Pfizer for his consultations, but did not disclose this information or seek approval to act as a consultant for Pfizer as required by federal regulation.

Dr. Sunderland was ultimately charged with violations of a federal law which acts to prevent conflicts of interest—18 U.S.C. § 208(a)—which carried with it a potential 5–year prison sentence under 18 U.S.C. § 216(a)(2) if his actions were willful. 18 U.S.C. § 208(a) reads:

> (a) Except as permitted by subsection (b) hereof, whoever, being an officer or employee of the executive branch of the United States Government, or of any independent agency of the United States, a Federal Reserve bank director, officer, or employee, or an officer or employee of the District of Columbia, including a special Government employee, participates personally and substantially as a Government officer or employee, through decision, approval, disapproval, recommendation, the rendering of advice, investigation, or otherwise, in a judicial or other proceeding, application, request for a ruling or other determination, contract, claim, controversy, charge, accusation, arrest, or other particular matter in which, to his knowledge, he, his spouse, minor child, general partner, organization in which he is serving as officer, director, trustee, general partner or employee, or any person or organization with whom he is negotiating or has any arrangement concerning prospective employment, has a financial interest—Shall be subject to the penalties set forth in section 216 of this title.

Complaint at 8, United States v. Pearson Sunderland III, No. JFM–06–0537 (D. Md. Dec 4, 2006). Dr. Sunderland was allowed to plead guilty to a misdemeanor charge with two years of probation and 400 hours of community service at a geriatric psychology service. He also agreed to pay the government $300,000.

Paul W. Lewis, one of the research participants who provided tissue samples for the Alzheimer's studies, stated that he felt Dr. Sunderland received little more than "a slap on the wrist," and stated that he would attempt to retrieve his sample from the NIH. David Willman, NIH Researcher is Ordered to Forfeit Pfizer Payments, Los Angeles Times, Dec. 23, 2006, at A22. Did Dr. Sunderland do anything wrong? If so, do you think that he should have received a harsher punishment? What might be the legal basis for Paul Lewis to sue the NIH?

5. A 2008 study of 125 medical schools in the United States suggests that academic medical research institutions need to engage in more comprehensive oversight for institutional conflicts of interests. Of the 86 institutions that responded to the survey, by 2006 only 30 had adopted conflicts of interest policies applicable to the institution's financial interests. However, more than half of the responding institutions had policies in place that applied to senior officials, mid-level officials, governing board members, and IRB members.

The study also suggested that institutions need to provide their IRBs with more comprehensive information regarding potential conflicts of interest associated with research projects. Susan H. Eringhaus, et al., Responses of Medical Schools to Institutional Conflicts of Interest, 299 JAMA 665 (2008). How might comprehensive institutional conflicts of interest policies determine the kinds of research conducted at academic institutions? Would such policies hamper research or promote it?

6. A study of potential research participants found that most people wanted to be informed of the financial conflicts of interest of the researcher, but only a minority (2 percent to 32 percent, depending on how extensive the conflict of interest was) said they would refuse to participate in a clinical trial due to conflicts of interest. S.Y.H. Kim, R. W. Millard, P. Nisbet, C. Cox & E. D. Caine, Potential Research Participants' Views Regarding Researcher and Institutional Financial Conflicts of Interest, 30 J. Med. Ethics 73–79 (2004).

7. For an ethical argument that paying physicians to recruit patients is morally wrong, see Jammi N. Rao & L. J. Sant Cassia, Ethics of Undisclosed Payments to Doctors Recruiting Patients in Clinical Trials, 325 Brit. Med. J. 36–7 (2002). The authors also point out that the British Royal College of Physicians considers payment per patient for recruiting patients into studies to be unethical, but does allow reimbursement to cover the physician's time.

IX. OBLIGATIONS TO RESEARCH SUBJECTS

A. DUTIES WHEN RESEARCH ENDS

DAHL v. HEM PHARMACEUTICAL CORP.

7 F.3d 1399 (9th Cir. 1993).

KLEINFELD, J.

Dahl and seventeen others, afflicted with chronic fatigue syndrome, enrolled in an experimental program to test a new medication. HEM Pharmaceuticals makes the medication, called Ampligen. The patients received the medicine as part of the testing procedure used by the Food and Drug Administration to determine whether a medicine is safe and effective. When the test was over, HEM ceased providing the medication to the patients. They sued for injunctive and other relief, claiming that HEM promised to continue providing Ampligen to them after the study ended if statistical analysis showed efficacy compared to placebo. The district court granted a preliminary injunction, requiring HEM to continue providing Ampligen for twelve months. Because HEM initially failed to comply with the injunction, the district court held it in civil contempt. HEM appeals, claiming that it should not have been so enjoined. One of the patients cross-appeals, claiming that the preliminary injunction should not have been limited to twelve months. We affirm.

I. FACTS

New medicines go through several phases of clinical evaluation before general release onto the market. HEM conducted a clinical trial with 92 patients designed to evaluate the effectiveness, side effects, and risks of Ampligen, classified by the FDA as an "investigational new drug" not yet permitted to be sold freely as a prescription medication. The study was "double blind," which means that some patients got Ampligen, some got a placebo (saline solution), and neither the doctor nor the patient knew who was getting which. The Ampligen was administered as a liquid by slow injection into a vein. All the patients signed consent forms warning of the experimental status of Ampligen and possible side effects. Although the patients were free to withdraw at any time, if they remained in the study they were required to accept the risks of treatment, forgo other drugs, not become pregnant, and submit to uncomfortable testing.

The arrangement with the experimental subjects was that they would participate in the double-blind study for a year. This was to facilitate evaluation of the safety and effectiveness of Ampligen. After the double-blind phase of testing ended, they would be entitled to receive Ampligen for a full year at no charge. The consent forms included a conditional promise of additional Ampligen after the double-blind study was completed:

> If statistical analysis of the endpoints show that Ampligen R shows efficacy compared to placebo, then following completion of all termination procedures, you understand that if you received placebo on study, you will be offered Ampligen R and will re-enter and follow the same protocol as if you had been randomized to receive Ampligen on study. If you received Ampligen R on study, you understand that you will be offered continuation on Ampligen R and will re-enter and follow the same protocol.

After the double-blind study, HEM applied for permission to proceed with what the FDA calls a "treatment IND." IND is an FDA acronym for "investigational new drug application." 21 C.F.R. § 312.3(b). The application, had it been granted, would have allowed the use of Ampligen "in the treatment of patients not in the clinical trials." 21 C.F.R. § 312.34(a). This procedure can be used for an experimental new drug if the disease is serious and there is no satisfactory alternative treatment. 21 C.F.R. § 312.34(b). The FDA rejected the application for safety reasons, but allowed the next phase in clinical trials, an open label study, where the doctor and patient know that the patient is receiving Ampligen.

* * *

An "open label" study of Ampligen in patients with CFS will be allowed to continue. FDA Talk Paper T91–63 (Oct. 4, 1991). Thus, the FDA prohibited use of Ampligen on patients not in the clinical trials, but expressly allowed it for those who were.

* * *

III. HEM's Appeal

HEM makes two arguments: first, that the judicial process should have been suspended pending completion of the administrative process for reviewing the safety and efficacy of Ampligen by the FDA; second, that it had no contractual obligation to supply Ampligen at no charge for a year. The district judge was required to balance the probability of success on the merits with the possibility of irreparable injury. The grant or denial of a preliminary injunction will be reversed only where the district court abused its discretion or based its decision on an erroneous legal standard or on clearly erroneous findings of fact. Also, this injunction required affirmative conduct by Ampligen—it must provide Ampligen and inject it into the veins of the petitioners who want it. Such "mandatory preliminary relief" is subject to heightened scrutiny and should not be issued unless the facts and law clearly favor the moving party.

A. *Primary Jurisdiction*

HEM argues that the doctrine of primary jurisdiction, which seeks to reserve to administrative agencies those questions that are peculiarly within their domain, should have prevented the district court from issuing the injunction. * * *

HEM claims that the District Court was faced with questions that Congress has entrusted to the FDA: effectiveness and safety of Ampligen, and whether the clinical hold was violated by the district court's order. HEM correctly argues that the agreement for a year's treatment at no charge in the consent form was conditioned on statistical analysis showing "efficacy compared to placebo." But HEM does not show that the district court took this decision away from the FDA. The FDA has not made a finding one way or the other, so far as the record shows. HEM's application for approval of the drug must imply that HEM takes the position that Ampligen does more to relieve chronic fatigue syndrome than saline solution. See 21 C.F.R. § 312.34(b)(4); 21 U.S.C. § 355(b)(1)(A). HEM has offered no evidence against the proposition that "statistical evidence of the endpoints shows that Ampligen shows efficacy compared to placebo," the wording of its contractual condition.

HEM argues that 21 U.S.C. § 355(d) leaves the decision of effectiveness to the FDA, and so it does, on the basis of "substantial evidence." "Substantial evidence" is defined in that statutory section to include "clinical investigations," which would be augmented by the one year of Ampligen injections on petitioners. Supervised treatment of petitioners with Ampligen under "the same protocol," as the agreement provides, will not damage the open label phase of testing for safety and efficacy—it will be part of it. HEM has offered no argument or evidence to suggest that adding a few patients to the open label phase of its study would impair the value of the study or conflict with the study protocol as approved by the FDA. It would be difficult to make practical sense of the contract if it were interpreted to mean, as HEM's position implies, that patients should get Ampligen during the double blind test, then receive none of it until the FDA approves the drug for treatment, and then go back on Ampligen for another year. The FDA determination of efficacy did not have to precede the one year of Ampligen at no charge for patients who subjected themselves to the double-blind study.

HEM also argues that the preliminary injunction erroneously takes away the decision on safety from the FDA and gives it to the district court. * * *

Had the FDA decided that Ampligen should not be administered to human beings at all because of safety concerns, a court might well be in error if it ordered injection of Ampligen anyway because HEM had promised to do so. But that would be a distinguishable case. Here, the FDA has decided that Ampligen can be injected into humans in an open label study. This amounts to an implicit finding of sufficient safety for use in the open label study.

* * *

B. Contract obligation

HEM argues that as a matter of contract law, petitioners' probability of success on the merits was low, because its promise was not supported by consideration. This argument is without merit. The patients submitted themselves to months of periodic injections with an experimental drug, or unbeknownst to them, mere saline solution, combined with intrusive and necessarily uncomfortable testing to determine their condition as the tests proceeded. HEM sought to have them participate in its study so that it could obtain FDA approval for its new drug.

HEM argues that because petitioners participated voluntarily and were free to withdraw, they had no binding obligation and so gave no consideration. Somehow the category of unilateral contracts appears to have escaped HEM's notice. The deal was, "if you submit to our experiment, we will give you a year's supply of Ampligen at no charge." This form of agreement resembles that in the case taught in the first year of law school, Hamer v. Sidway, 124 N.Y. 538, 27 N.E. 256 (N.Y. 1891). There, an uncle promised his nephew that if he would refrain from drinking, using tobacco, or playing cards and billiards until age 21, he would receive $5000. The court held that consideration had been given because the nephew had refrained from the prohibited activities during the requisite period on the faith of his uncle's promise. He had accepted the offer by completing performance. See also Restatement (Second) of Contracts § 50(2)(acceptance by performance); Mohr Park Manor, Inc. v. Mohr, 83 Nev. 107, 424 P.2d 101, 104 (Nev. 1967)(recognizing unilateral contracts).

HEM did not bargain for or seek a promise by the patients to submit to the double-blind testing. It sought and obtained their actual performance. Mutuality of promises was unnecessary.

In this case, the petitioners performed by submitting to the double-blind tests. They incurred the detriment of being tested upon for HEM's studies in exchange for the promise of a year's treatment of Ampligen. Upon completion of the double-blind tests, there was a binding contract.

Dahl seeks sanctions against HEM under Fed. R. App. P. 38 on the ground that this appeal is frivolous. While the contract argument approaches frivolousness, the primary jurisdiction argument is serious. The FDA's role in the drug approval process and the FDA's concerns about the safety of Ampligen justified HEM in pursuing the appeal. HEM's arguments were not "wholly without merit," so no sanction will be imposed. McDougal v. County of Imperial, 942 F.2d 668, 680 (9th Cir. 1991).

* * *

AFFIRMED.

B. LIABILITY IN THE RESEARCH CONTEXT

ANDE v. ROCK

647 N.W.2d 265 (Wis. App. 2002).

BACKGROUND

ROGGENSACK, J.

C.E.A. was born to Linda and Charles Ande on July 13, 1993. There was then ongoing a cystic fibrosis research project which had begun in 1985. Philip Farrell and Norman Fost were the co-investigators. To test for the presence of factors indicative of cystic fibrosis, the study used excess blood that had been drawn from all newborns to conduct statutorily required tests for the presence of other congenital and metabolic disorders. The research protocol required that the parents of half of the newborns in the study were told if their child tested positive for cystic fibrosis. A nutritional plan was made available to them immediately, as it was the researchers' theory that treating the nutritional needs of children with cystic fibrosis before they became symptomatic would result in a less vigorous development of the disease with fewer impairments to overall health. The other half of the children who were tested were placed in the "blinded control" group. Their parents and their treating physicians were not told if they had tested positive for factors indicative of cystic fibrosis. C.E.A. was placed in the blinded group, and therefore, her parents and her primary physician, Dr. Amy Plumb, were not told that she had tested positive.

Prior to testing the blood of newborns for cystic fibrosis, a pamphlet was prepared that told about the different tests that were required to be completed on newborns' blood. It also told of the cystic fibrosis test that would be run as part of a research project. It described the dangers of cystic fibrosis and stated that cystic fibrosis was an inherited disorder. The pamphlet also arguably implied that positive test results would be reported to the infant's physician, and a phone number was listed for parents who wanted additional information about the test.[3] There is no assertion that the Andes were asked for or gave specific, written consent

---

3. The brochure was revised numerous times, with differing disclosures listed in each version. The edition that plaintiffs' attorneys aver was presented to the Andes states:

> One-half of the blood samples are tested for CF before the babies are one month old. The remaining blood samples are partially tested at this time. Testing on these blood samples is completed when the children are 4 years old. Positive test results are reported to your child's doctor.

> If the CF research test is done, you may contact your doctor, certified nurse-midwife, or the CF specialist at (608) 263–8555 for the result.

to have the cystic fibrosis test run on C.E.A. or to have the results of that test go unreported to them. Subsequent to birth, C.E.A. had difficulties thriving. On June 23, 1995, when C.E.A. was almost two years old, she was diagnosed with cystic fibrosis. At the time that the Andes learned that C.E.A. had cystic fibrosis, Linda Ande was pregnant with a second child. The Andes' second child, C.L.A., is also afflicted with cystic fibrosis.

In this lawsuit, the Andes' allegations may be summarized into the assertion that the defendants committed three wrongful acts that give rise to the Andes' various claims: (1) The cystic fibrosis test was run without their informed consent; (2) treatment was withheld from C.E.A. when the investigators had knowledge that nutritional treatment would reduce the severity of her cystic fibrosis; and (3) C.E.A.'s test results were withheld from them. They allege to have been harmed by these acts in two ways: (1) If they had been given the test results, they would have accepted treatment for C.E.A. to lessen the severity of the progression of her illness; and (2) if they had been given the test results, they would not have conceived C.L.A. They do not identify any harm they suffered from the alleged lack of informed consent to run the test in the first instance.

In response, the defendants assert that they did not test C.E.A.'s blood without the Andes' knowledge and consent. They also contend that although all the children in the blinded control group were tested as newborns, no one reviewed the test results for the control group, some of which were negative and some of which were positive for factors indicative of cystic fibrosis. Therefore, the defendants contend they did not withhold information from the Andes. The defendants also raised many affirmative defenses, including failure to state a claim and qualified immunity.

* * *

MEDICAL MALPRACTICE

* * *[E]ven if we were to assume arguendo that the researchers had a duty to obtain informed consent from the Andes, that the pamphlet that was provided was insufficient to do so, and that the researchers had a duty to share what information was available to them with the Andes, there is no allegation in the complaint of any relationships between the Andes and any of the researchers from which one could conclude that such duties arose from a physician-patient relationship, rather than from ordinary negligence principles.

FEDERAL CLAIMS

The Andes' federal claims invoke 42 U.S.C. § 1983 (1994).[8] They claim a due process violation because the defendants deprived them of

---

8. *42 U.S.C. § 1983* (1994) provides in relevant part:

Every person who, under color of any statute, ordinance, regulation, custom, or usage, of any State or Territory or the District of Columbia, subjects, or causes to be subjected, any citizen of the United States or other person within the jurisdiction thereof to the deprivation of any rights, privileges, or immunities secured by the Constitution and laws, shall be liable to the party injured in an action at law, suit in equity, or other proper proceeding for redress.

their liberty and property interests by arbitrarily placing C.E.A. in the blinded control group of the cystic fibrosis study and by withholding her test results from them for almost two years, during which time beneficial treatment was withheld from C.E.A. and the Andes conceived another child who also has cystic fibrosis. The respondents contend that the Andes' claims may not proceed because they are protected by qualified immunity.

1.   42 U.S.C. § 1983 overview

Section 1983, in and of itself, does not create substantive rights; rather, it provides a remedy for the deprivation of rights that are established elsewhere. In a § 1983 claim that alleges a violation of either procedural or substantive due process, a plaintiff must show a deprivation of an interest in life, liberty or property that is protected by the Constitution. Although the Andes allege the deprivation of substantive rights, based on what they characterize as the withholding of medical information about C.E.A., they are not clear about whether their due process claims implicate a property interest or a liberty interest. We will examine each interest in turn.

* * *

3.   Violation of a clearly established right

   a.   Property interest

* * *

* * * The Andes have cited no Wisconsin case to us which holds that they had a property interest in the test results of the cystic fibrosis study, nor have they cited any cases which are closely analogous. Additionally, our research has uncovered no such Wisconsin case that predates the disclosure of the information to the Andes in 1995. * * * Accordingly, the Andes have failed to establish the first step necessary to a due process claim based on the deprivation of a clearly established property right and therefore, their claim in this regard was properly dismissed.

   b.   Liberty interest

The Andes also allege a constitutional violation of a liberty interest based on the failure to obtain informed consent for the testing that was done, as well as on the alleged failure to disclose information. Liberty interests may arise under either state or federal law. For example, the Fourteenth Amendment of the United States Constitution protects an "individual interest in avoiding disclosure of personal matters." This personal liberty interest arises from a "guarantee" under federal law of certain zones of privacy. The Supreme Court has also recognized that there is a constitutionally protected liberty interest in bodily integrity and in the right to determine what medical treatment shall be accepted or refused, and that parents have a constitutionally protected right to obtain needed medical treatment for their child so long as the child's rights are protected by the process employed. While neither the Wisconsin Supreme

Court nor the United States Supreme Court has yet addressed whether there is a constitutionally protected liberty interest in receiving information from a research project relative to one's genetic predisposition to give birth to a child with a genetically transmitted disorder or in receiving information from a research project that would assist a parent in making informed health care choices for his or her child, we cannot say with certainty that the withholding of the results of C.E.A.'s test did not implicate a liberty interest in either the parents or C.E.A. Therefore, for purposes of our discussion we shall assume, without deciding, that a liberty interest could be established if this case were to go to trial.

Once a liberty interest has been established, it may not be denied without a constitutionally acceptable amount of procedural due process. In regard to the alleged failure to obtain informed consent before the cystic fibrosis test was run in the first instance, the Andes base none of their claimed injuries on an unauthorized disclosure of private information, as they might if the researchers had disclosed C.E.A.'s condition to third parties. And they identify no harm that they suffered by not giving consent to the test in the first instance. For example, they do not allege that they would not have permitted the test if they had known it was being conducted. Instead, all of their alleged injuries flow from not having the results of the test at or near the time it was conducted. Therefore, we will not address their claims in regard to an alleged lack of informed consent further.

We now turn to the alleged failure to timely disclose the results of C.E.A.'s cystic fibrosis test. The closest the Andes come in making an argument that the alleged failure to disclose was a clear violation of their rights is to contend that one of the defendants, Richard Aronson, as the Medical Director for the Wisconsin Newborn Screening Program conducted under the direction of the Wisconsin Department of Health and Family Services, had a statutory duty under Wis. Stat. § 253.13(5) to disclose the results of the testing for congenital disorders. Section 253.13(5) stated in relevant part:

> The department shall disseminate information to families whose children suffer from congenital disorders and to women of child-bearing age with a history of congenital disorders concerning the need for and availability of follow-up counseling and special dietary treatment and the necessity for testing infants. The department shall also refer families of children who suffer from congenital disorders to available health and family services programs and shall coordinate the provision of these programs. The department shall periodically consult appropriate experts in reviewing and evaluating the state's infant screening programs.

In 1993, the year C.E.A. was born, Wis. Admin. Code § HSS 115.04 (1993) set out the tests to be done and for which information was required to be provided under § 253.13. Cystic fibrosis was not then a required test under § HSS 115.04.

* * *

The Andes also allege a "general" violation of substantive due process, claiming that the actions of the defendants were arbitrary and capricious in the way in which they selected C.E.A for the control group and failed to disseminate the information they had about her. Substantive due process protects individuals from arbitrary, wrongful, governmental actions regardless of the process afforded prior to the deprivation. The Supreme Court has repeatedly explained that the touchstone of substantive due process is the protection of the individual against arbitrary action of government. Substantive due process against governmental actors who engage in conduct that "shocks the conscience" or conduct that interferes with rights "implicit in the concept of ordered liberty." However, even so generalized a claim of protection still requires the identification of a clearly protected interest that the actor's conduct violates. Due process claims are not a substitute for general tort claims. The Andes have failed to identify any Wisconsin or federal case law clearly establishing such an interest. Therefore, we conclude that qualified immunity bars all their federal claims.

CONCLUSION

Because we conclude that plaintiffs have made no showing of a physician-patient relationship with any remaining defendant, which relationship is necessary to support a medical malpractice claim, and that plaintiffs have made no showing of a clearly established state property right or a clearly established state or federal liberty interest that any named defendant's conduct violated, we affirm the judgment and order of the circuit court.

By the Court.—Judgment and order affirmed.

NOTES AND QUESTIONS

1. The *Dahl* case, like York v. Jones, 717 F.Supp. 421 (E.D. Va. 1989), holds that an informed consent to research is a contract under which certain duties are assumed. How is it that the *Ande* case finds no duties between a researcher and a subject?

2. In 2006, the Sixth Circuit suggested that under certain circumstances researchers owe an actionable duty to participants in therapeutic research. If informed consent materials provide that participants will have access to an experimental drug after clinical trials end, the researchers may be legally obligated to provide access, even if clinical trials have demonstrated mixed results and potential health hazards. Abney v. Amgen, 443 F.3d 540 (6th Cir. 2006). Should researchers be obligated to provide such drugs to participants based on a promise made before the results of clinical trials are known? How might researchers protect themselves from such an obligation?

3. The need for large numbers of research subjects has led to the proliferation of genomic biobanks from which researchers can draw samples. Do the researchers who use this data have an ethical duty to inform participants of their individual results? Consider different results that may be available to the participants: identification of a variant related to a treatable condition, identification of an environmental factor related to a treatable condition, identification of a variant that is related to an untreatable condition, or identification of a variant of unknown significance. What if the variant has unknown significance at the time of the study, but researchers later are able to determine some significance, should a continuing duty exist? Who should cover the costs of informing the individual? A study of 141 adults found a strong desire to be able to access individual results, as well as the ability to change their preferences over time. The study participants viewed access to results as a valuable incentive for participating in the biobank. Juli Murphy, et al., Public Expectations for Return of Results from Large–Cohort Genetic Research, 8 American Journal of Bioethics 36 (2008).

4. Drug companies are increasingly looking overseas to test new products because of an eager participant pool and less stringent bureaucratic requirements, but are far less likely to make the drugs available in the same test countries after the study is over because of a general inability to afford the drugs. Ethicists and biotech companies alike are struggling with what, if any, obligation is owed to poor study participants who are not able to afford drugs that can save lives or significantly improve quality of life. Given high overhead costs associated with establishing a market in a country, including hiring sales staff and purchasing office space, drug companies are unlikely to market to poor countries, and even more often cannot afford to provide the test participants with free drugs. "Compassionate use" of drug supplies requires a distribution system, training of physicians, and monitoring of patient reaction, making drug companies, particularly small ones, unable to financially justify the free distribution of life-improving drugs. Proponents of the view that drug companies should make post-study drugs available to study participants argue that these individuals faced considerable risks in enrolling in clinical trials, and should be reimbursed for their efforts. Gina Kolata, Companies Facing Ethical Issue As Drugs Are Tested Overseas, The New York Times, March 5, 2004, at A1.

Do drug companies owe a duty to clinical trial participants in poor countries to continue supplying the drug free of charge, or at least to market the drug in their country, even when this happens to conflict with the company's obligations to investors?

5. Many drug companies are able to pay doctors in poor countries more for conducting clinical trials than the doctors could possibly earn treating patients. Additionally, some companies provide doctors who perform clinical trials with technology and equipment that can enhance the doctor's private practice. Do you think these "perks" unethically persuade foreign doctors to recommend clinical trials to their poor patients?

CHAPTER 5

COMMERCIALIZATION OF GENETIC RESEARCH: PROPERTY, PATENTS, AND CONFLICTS OF INTEREST

■ ■ ■

I. INTRODUCTION

The framers of the U.S. Constitution realized that it was important to create incentives for technological innovation. The U.S. Constitution, Art. 1, § 8, cl. 8 provides that Congress shall have the power "To promote the Progress of Science and useful Arts, by securing for limited Times to Authors and Inventors the exclusive Right to their respective Writings and Discoveries."

Under the federal patent statute, inventors are rewarded with a 20 year period of exclusivity that allows them to forbid anyone else from making, using, selling or offering to sell their invention in order to make sure that novel, useful, and nonobvious technologies get developed that otherwise might not have been created.

Without the exclusive protection provided by a patent, individual inventors and institutions would not be willing to invest time and money in creating new products. Their research and development efforts could be too easily undermined if a competitor could use their work to introduce a duplicate product without the prior investment of resources. Since the development of a drug and its testing on research subjects generally involves hundreds of millions of dollars, patent protection is particularly important to the pharmaceutical industry.

A patent application spells out the process, composition of matter, or other invention being protected. It describes the invention and how to make it. In order to obtain a patent, the invention must be "novel." It cannot have been publicly described more than a year earlier in, for example, a scientific journal or at a professional meeting. It must be "nonobvious"—that is, people skilled in the field at issue must not think the invention is a trivial advance. (If there is a patent on a red ball, an inventor would not be able to obtain a patent on a yellow ball.) The patent

194

must be "useful." An inventor cannot patent a new chemical, for example, unless it has a specific and substantial utility.

The patent application must be adequately "enabling" as well. That is, it must describe the invention fully, in a way that would allow another person skilled in that field to make the invention. This requirement is particularly important since one of the purposes of the patent law is to assure that the public gets information back in exchange for the monopoly granted to the patent holder. When a patent is granted, the information in it becomes public. Other inventors can then use that information to further their own research, though they cannot make or use the patented invention or process itself without the permission of the patent holder.

Typically, a gene patent claims to cover one or more of the following: a purified and isolated gene, the protein for which the gene codes, the correlation between mutations of the gene and disease, cells or biological entities that have been engineered to express the gene, and the use of the gene or protein to detect or treat a disease or condition. In January 2001, the U.S. Patent and Trademark Office, which has the statutory authority to grant or deny patent applications, issued new guidelines clarifying the usefulness criteria in the context of patents involving DNA. The utility of the invention to be patented must be specific, substantial, and credible. "The Patent Office's new rules with more stringent requirements on real-world use for gene patents will help keep squatters from just putting their name on genes and hoping it will become valuable," Q. Todd Dickinson, the Patent Office's Director, told a Congressional hearing. "One simply cannot patent a gene itself without also clearly disclosing a use to which that gene can be put," he said. For example, raw DNA sequence data, such as that generated by the Human Genome Project, is not patentable.

When a company is issued a gene patent, it gains exclusive rights to commercialize the patented gene. Most companies' primary method of commercially exploiting patented genes is through agreements in which they license others to use their patents. An example of such an agreement would be a company charging a per test fee to doctors to use sequence information about the company's patented gene to identify whether a patient has a mutation in that gene. Licensing agreements can also be created that allow other researchers to conduct research involving patented genes. These licenses may take one of two forms. The license may charge a royalty for the use of the gene in research to create another product (such as a diagnostic test or a gene therapy). Or the license may include a reach-through agreement where the patent holder earns a percentage of the profits from the ultimate sales of other products that licensees created through research on the patented gene. For example, a company could enter an arrangement to receive a set percentage of gross sales from a gene therapy developed using its patented gene. A company is also free to prevent others from using its patented gene. The company can then develop commercial products utilizing its patented gene and enjoy the monopoly on those products that a gene patent provides.

There is much controversy regarding whether genes should be patentable under existing laws. The U.S. Patent and Trademark Office has determined that a genetic sequence can be patented if the patent applicant can describe that sequence and its function. But the U.S. Supreme Court has not ruled on the issue of whether genetic sequences and correlation between genetic mutations and diseases fall within the statutory definition of patentable subject matter. And Congress itself retains the power to eliminate gene patents if legislators were convinced that the patents were wrongly granted or excessively inhibit research or substantially interfere with patient care.

The patenting of genes has also led to legal questions about the type of informed consent that should be obtained from the person whose bodily tissue has been used to isolate a gene. Additional questions are raised about whether the person (or groups) whose genetic material has been patented should share in the proceeds. Vast sums of money are at stake. The patent related to the human erythropoietin gene (which codes for a protein needed by kidney disease patients) is worth more than $1.5 billion a year because a genetically engineered treatment can be made from it.

Concerns have been raised about the increasing focus on patenting and commercializing genetic discoveries within university and government molecular biology laboratories. Prior to the 1980s, government researchers and academic researchers funded by the government generally could not personally profit commercially from their research. Federal technology transfer laws changed that by allowing taxpayer-funded researchers to patent their inventions and form or contract with for-profit companies to exploit them.

Researchers with commercial interests—who are now the majority in the genetics field—sometimes protect their interests in ways that are fundamentally changing the nature of science. They keep information confidential that they once readily shared. There is also evidence that the sharing of research materials is decreasing. Scientists with access to biological materials from patients are now less likely to give samples of those materials to other researchers. This is true even with genes and cell lines, where replication techniques can create millions of copies of the genes or cells and thus sharing does not diminish the first scientist's ability to carry out research. Other researchers have reported difficulty in accessing research tools—such as gene segments—developed through taxpayer-funded research at the National Institutes of Health. There are questions about whether this approach will best serve society in the long run.

This chapter details the legal requirements for obtaining a patent, gives examples of licensing agreements, discusses concerns about gene patents, describes policy alternatives to the current approach to gene patents, and analyzes the rights of individuals whose bodies are the sources of patented genes.

II. THE PATENTING OF GENETIC MATERIALS

LILA FEISEE, ARE BIOTECHNOLOGY PATENTS IMPORTANT? YES!

PTO Today, Feb. 2000, at 9–12.
http://www.uspto.gov/web/offices/ac/ahrpa/opa/ptotoday/ptotoday02.pdf.

Biotechnology is one of the most research intensive and innovative industries in the global economy today. While the promise of new discovery is great, this does not come without cost. It takes hundreds of millions of dollars to bring a new pharmaceutical to the marketplace. Without patent protection for biotechnological research, there would be little incentive for investors to risk their capital and many of the potential benefits of biotechnology would not come to fruition. By rewarding inventors for their discoveries for a limited time, the patent system supports innovation while, at the same time, dedicating these discoveries to the public. Thus, both the private sector and the public benefit.

Patent protection in the area of biotechnology also serves the larger economy by providing a forum that encourages both innovation and investment. It also benefits society by providing the means to reduce disease and suffering for both humans and animals. Such results promote and enhance the dignity and quality of life * * *. Biotechnology patents allow for the dissemination of potentially valuable scientific information. The availability of the information disclosed in biotechnology patents enables others in the field of science to build on earlier discoveries. Not only can other researchers use the information in a patent, but by disclosing cutting edge scientific information, the patent system avoids expensive duplication of research efforts. It is only with the patenting of biotechnology that some companies, particularly small companies, can raise capital to bring beneficial products to the market place or fund further research.

In addition, this capital provides jobs that represent an immediate public benefit independent of the technological benefits. Continuing employment opportunities represent a national resource for the future because they encourage the youth of today to become the scientists and inventors of tomorrow. Thus, the patent system not only fosters benefits to our society today, but ensures our future ability to innovate and grow.

* * *

Gene discovery has been a prime area of research in biotechnology, especially as it relates to the determination of the underlying basis of human disease. One specific goal of the Human Genome Project has been to facilitate the discovery of genes that cause or contribute to human diseases. The granting of patents to genes allows inventors to obtain private sector funding for the development of methods of disease diagnosis and treatment. This additional capital obtained from private sources (such as venture capitalists) acts to supplement the increasingly limited funds available in the public sector (such as the National Institutes of Health and the National Cancer Institute). This synergism between private and public sector funding is evidenced by the nature and extent of subject matter that has been the object of patent protection.

For example, U.S. Patent 5,777,093, issued to Shiloh, Tagle, and Collins on July 7, 1998, is directed to nucleic acids encoding mutant forms of the gene that causes ataxia-telangiectasia (AT). AT is a genetic disease that affects the skin, nervous system, and immune system and is present in approximately 2 in 100,000 individuals. The cloning of this gene has allowed the development of diagnostic methods as well as screening procedures to facilitate discovery of drugs that might be valuable for the treatment of this disease.

U.S. Patent 5,888,722, issued to Costa De Beauregard et al., is directed to the gene that causes cystic fibrosis (CF). CF affects approximately 1 in 2000 live births in North America and about 1 in 20 persons are carriers of the disease. This patent is assigned to the Institut Curie of Paris, France and the Centre National de la Recherche Scientifique, Paris, France. The patented subject matter resulted from worldwide research efforts. This patent, while securing intellectual property rights to some mutant forms of the CF gene, did not affect the development of diagnostic methods for screening subjects for the presence of CF related genes. This patent also demonstrates the increasing support that the patent system plays in international commerce and discovery. The international economy and its underlying support in the intellectual property arena, is facilitating cooperation between inventors. This cooperation bridges national boundaries and serves to bring together innovators from around the world. By fostering this type of interaction, cooperation between the members of the brain trust of the world is occurring at an increasing rate, and the ultimate beneficiary is the public. Inventions that serve the public good are commercially successful and provide benefit to everyone.

III. CURRENT LEGAL REQUIREMENTS FOR GENE PATENTS

MATTHEW ERRAMOUSPE, STAKING PATENT CLAIMS ON THE HUMAN BLUEPRINT: REWARDS AND RENT–DISSIPATING RACES

43 UCLA L. Rev. 961, 964–968, 985–992 (1996).

Just as a gold rush exploits gold, the enormous race to patent genes will surely exploit the beneficial uses of genes sooner rather than later; but the value of the genes may also be substantially, if not entirely, dissipated by the overbidding of resources, as well as by wasteful, duplicative efforts among competitors to locate genes when only one contestant can ultimately win the patent.

* * *

The potential gold mine that gene-hunters ultimately seek is a patent. A patent, in essence, confers a twenty-year exclusive right over one's "invention," including the derivative right to exclude others—even innocent infringers who develop the same invention independently—from making, using, or selling the invention. In exchange for a patent, the inventor must publicly disclose details enabling others "skilled in the art" to make and use the invention. The patent system essentially amounts to an exchange of temporary monopoly rights for the significant advancement of public knowledge.

Patents come in three distinct varieties—utility, design, and plant. Utility patents—the most common and the type at issue with respect to genes—encompass machines, industrial processes, compositions of matter, and articles of manufacture. Utility patents basically consist of two kinds: process patents and product patents. A process patent prevents others from using the particular process without compensating the patent holder, but does not prevent other inventors from using or even patenting different processes yielding the same product. A product patent, on the other hand, prevents others from making or using the final product without compensating the patent holder, regardless of how the product is made. Thus, product patents, because they are broader, are often more valuable than process patents.

To qualify for a patent, an invention must satisfy certain statutory requirements. As a threshold requirement, the invention must constitute patentable subject matter. Beyond that, the invention must demonstrate sufficient nonobviousness, utility, and novelty.

A.   PATENTABLE SUBJECT MATTER

An invention is not patentable if it fails to constitute patentable subject matter. 35 U.S.C. § 101 defines the scope of patentable subject matter: "Whoever invents or discovers any new and useful process, machine, manufacture, or composition of matter, or any new and useful improvement thereof, may obtain a patent therefore, subject to the conditions and requirements of this title."

In interpreting § 101, courts have repeatedly stated that patentable subject matter does not include natural phenomena, that is, principles, powers, and products of nature. For instance, in O'Reilly v. Morse [56 U.S. (15 How.) 62 (1853)]—the leading case on patentable subject matter—the United States Supreme Court upheld all of Samuel Morse's claims covering the invention of the telegraph and ancillary telegraphic code, except his celebrated "eighth claim." In his eighth claim, Morse attempted to patent "electromagnetism, however developed for marking or printing intelligible characters, signs, or letters at any distances." Rejecting the claim, the Court found that Morse was trying to extend his monopoly rights over a force of nature he had not invented but rather had merely been the first to harness, and held that "a principle of nature" is not patentable subject matter.

* * *

Under the "natural phenomena" gloss, just as principles of nature are unpatentable, so too are products of nature. In Funk Bros. Seed Co. v. Kalo Inoculant Co. [333 U.S. 127 (1948)], the Supreme Court held that naturally existing products, even when combined in a new product, are not patentable.

STATUTORY AUTHORITY

35 U.S.C. §§ 101–103

§ 101. Inventions patentable

Whoever invents or discovers any new and useful process, machine, manufacture, or composition of matter, or any new and useful improvement thereof, may obtain a patent therefore, subject to the conditions and requirements of this title.

§ 102. Conditions for patentability; novelty * * *

§ 103. Conditions for patentability; non-obvious subject matter

(a) A patent may not be obtained though the invention is not identically disclosed or described as set forth in section 102 of this title, if the differences between the subject matter sought to be patented and the prior art are such that the subject matter as a whole would have been obvious at the time the invention was made to a person having ordinary skill in the art to which said subject matter pertains.

(b)(1) Notwithstanding subsection (a), and upon timely election by the applicant for patent to proceed under this subsection, a biotechnological process using or resulting in a composition of matter that is novel under section 102 and nonobvious under subsection (a) of this section shall be considered nonobvious if—

> (A) claims to the process and the composition of matter are contained in either the same application for patent or in separate applications having the same effective filing date; and

> (B) the composition of matter, and the process at the time it was invented, were owned by the same person or subject to an obligation of assignment to the same person.

(2) A patent issued on a process under paragraph (1)—

> (A) shall also contain the claims to the composition of matter used in or made by that process, or

> (B) shall, if such composition of matter is claimed in another patent, be set to expire on the same date as such other patent, notwithstanding section 154.

(3) For purposes of paragraph (1), the term "biotechnological process" means—

(A) a process of genetically altering or otherwise inducing a single-or multi-celled organism to—

(i) express an exogenous nucleotide sequence,

(ii) inhibit, eliminate, augment, or alter expression of an endogenous nucleotide sequence, or

(iii) express a specific physiological characteristic not naturally associated with said organism;

(B) cell fusion procedures yielding a cell line that expresses a specific protein, such as a monoclonal antibody; and

(C) a method of using a product produced by a process defined by subparagraph (A) or (B), or a combination of subparagraphs (A) and (B).

U.S. DEPARTMENT OF ENERGY OFFICE OF SCIENCE, OFFICE OF BIOLOGICAL AND ENVIRONMENTAL RESEARCH, HUMAN GENOME PROGRAM

http://www.ornl.gov/hgmis/elsi/patents.html.

GENETICS AND PATENTING

What are patents, and how do they work?

The patentability of inventions under U.S. law is determined by the Patent and Trademark Office (USPTO) in the Department of Commerce. A patent application is judged on four criteria. The invention must be "useful" in a practical sense (the inventor must identify some useful purpose for it), "novel" (i.e., not known or used before the filing), and "nonobvious" (i.e., not an improvement easily made by someone trained in the relevant area). The invention also must be described in sufficient detail to enable one skilled in the field to use it for the stated purpose (sometimes called the "enablement" criterion).

In general, raw products of nature are not patentable. DNA products usually become patentable when they have been isolated, purified, or modified to produce a unique form not found in nature.

The USPTO has 3 years to issue a patent. In Europe, the timeframe is 18 months. The USPTO is adopting a similar system. Patents are good for 20 years from filing date.

In the United States, patent priority is based on the "first to invent" principle: whoever made the invention first (and can prove it) is awarded property rights for the 20–year period. Inventors have a one-year grace period to file after they publish. All other countries except the Philippines, however, follow a "first inventor to file" rule in establishing priority when granting patents.

* * *

Currently over three million genome-related patent applications have been filed * * *. Those who use sequences from public databases today risk facing a future injunction if those sequences turn out to be patented by a private company on the basis of previously filed patent applications.

* * *

Genes and Gene Fragments

USPTO has issued a few patents for gene fragments. Full sequence and function often are not known for gene fragments. On pending applications, their utility has been identified by such vague definitions as providing scientific probes to help find a gene or another EST or to help map a chromosome. Questions have arisen over the issue of when, from discovery to development into useful products, exclusive right to genes could be claimed.

The 300– to 500–base gene fragments, called expressed sequence tags (ESTs), represent only 10 to 30% of the average cDNA, and the genomic genes are often 10 to 20 times larger than the cDNA. A cDNA molecule is a laboratory-made version of a gene that contains only its information-rich (exon) regions; these molecules provide a way for genome researchers to fast-forward through the genome to biologically important areas. The original chromosomal locations and biological functions of the full genes identified by ESTs are unknown in most cases.

Patent applications for such gene fragments have sparked controversy among scientists, many of whom have urged the USPTO not to grant broad patents in this early stage of human genome research to applicants who have neither characterized the genes nor determined their functions and uses.

In December 1999, the USPTO issued stiffer interim guidelines (made final in 2001) stating that more usefulness—specifically how the product functions in nature—must now be shown before gene fragments are considered patentable. The new rules call for "specific and substantial utility that is credible," but some still feel the rules are too lax.

The patenting of gene fragments is controversial. Some say that patenting such discoveries is inappropriate because the effort to find any given EST is small compared with the work of isolating and characterizing a gene and gene product, finding out what it does, and developing a commercial product. They feel that allowing holders of such "gatekeeper" patents to exercise undue control over the commercial fruits of genome research would be unfair. Similarly, allowing multiple patents on different parts of the same genome sequence—say on a gene fragment, the gene, and the protein—adds undue costs to the researcher who wants to examine the sequence. Not only does the researcher have to pay each patent holder via licensing for the opportunity to study the sequence, he also has to pay his own staff to research the different patents and determine which are applicable to the area of the genome he wants to study.

SNPs

Single nucleotide polymorphisms (SNPs) are DNA sequence variations that occur when a single nucleotide (A, T, C, or G) in the genome sequence is altered. For example a SNP might change the DNA sequence AAGGCTAA to ATGGCTAA. SNPs occur every 100 to 1000 bases along the 3–billion-base human genome. SNPs can occur in both coding (gene) and noncoding regions of the genome. Many SNPs have no effect on cell function, but scientists believe others could predispose people to disease or influence their response to a drug.

Variations in DNA sequence can have a major impact on how humans respond to disease; environmental insults such as bacteria, viruses, toxins, and chemicals; and drugs and other therapies. This makes SNPs of great value for biomedical research and for developing pharmaceutical products or medical diagnostics. Scientists believe SNP maps will help them identify the multiple genes associated with such complex diseases as cancer, diabetes, vascular disease, and some forms of mental illness. These associations are difficult to establish with conventional gene-hunting methods because a single altered gene may make only a small contribution to the disease.

In April 1999, ten large pharmaceutical companies and the U.K. Wellcome Trust philanthropy announced the establishment of a non-profit foundation to find and map 300,000 common SNPs (they found 1.8 million). Their goal was to generate a widely accepted, high-quality, extensive, publicly available map using SNPs as markers evenly distributed throughout the human genome. The consortium planned to patent all the SNPs found but to enforce the patents only to prevent others from patenting the same information. Information found by the consortium is freely available.

Gene Tests

As disease genes are found, complementary gene tests are developed to screen for the gene in humans who suspect they may be at risk for developing the disease. These tests are usually patented and licensed by the owners of the disease gene patent. Royalties are due the patent holder each time the tests are administered, and only licensed entities can conduct the tests.

Proteins

Proteins do the work of the cell. A complete set of genetic information is contained in each cell. This information provides a specific set of instructions to the body. The body carries out these instructions via proteins. Genes encode proteins.

All living organisms are composed largely of proteins, which have three main cellular functions: to provide cell structure and be involved in cell signaling and cell communication functions. Enzymes are proteins.

Proteins are important to researchers because they are the link between genes and pharmaceutical development. They indicate which genes are expressed or are being used. Important for understanding gene function, proteins also have unique shapes or structures. Understanding these structures and how potential pharmaceuticals will bind to them is a key element in drug design.

* * *

Why Patent?

Research scientists who work in public institutions often are troubled by the concept of intellectual property because their norms tell them that science will advance more rapidly if researchers enjoy free access to knowledge. By contrast, the law of intellectual property rests on an assumption that, without exclusive rights, no one will be willing to invest in research and development (R & D).

* * *

What are some of the potential arguments for gene patenting?

- Researchers are rewarded for their discoveries and can use monies gained from patenting to further their research.
- The investment of resources is encouraged by providing a monopoly to the inventor and prohibiting competitors from making, using, or selling the invention without a license.
- Wasteful duplication of effort is prevented.
- Research is forced into new, unexplored areas.
- Secrecy is reduced and all researchers are ensured access to the new invention.

What are some of the potential arguments against gene patenting?

- Patents of partial and uncharacterized cDNA sequences will reward those who make routine discoveries but penalize those who determine biological function or application (inappropriate reward given to easiest step in the process).
- Patents could impede the development of diagnostics and therapeutics by third parties because of the costs associated with using patented research data.
- Patent stacking (allowing a single genomic sequence to be patented in several ways such as an EST, a gene, and a SNP) may discourage product development because of high royalty costs owed to all patent owners of that sequence; these are costs that will likely be passed on to the consumer.
- Because patent applications remain secret until granted, companies may work on developing a product only to find that new patents have been granted along the way, with unexpected licensing costs and possible infringement penalties. [Beginning in 2001, patent

applications are published 18 months from their earliest filing date, unless the patent applicant requests non-publication and fulfills the requirements pursuant to 37 C.F.R. § 1.213.]

- Costs increase not only for paying for patent licensing but also for determining what patents apply and who has rights to downstream products.

- Patent holders are being allowed to patent a part of nature—a basic constituent of life; this allows one organism to own all or part of another organism.

- Private biotechs who own certain patents can monopolize certain gene test markets.

- Patent filings are replacing journal articles as places for public disclosure—reducing the body of knowledge in the literature.

A. PATENTABLE SUBJECT MATTER

DIAMOND v. CHAKRABARTY

447 U.S. 303 (1980).

BURGER, J.

We granted certiorari to determine whether a live, human-made micro-organism is patentable subject matter under 35 U.S.C. § 101.

I.

In 1972, respondent Chakrabarty, a microbiologist, filed a patent application, assigned to the General Electric Co. The application asserted 36 claims related to Chakrabarty's invention of "a bacterium from the genus *Pseudomonas* containing therein at least two stable energy-generating plasmids, each of said plasmids providing a separate hydrocarbon degradative pathway." This human-made, genetically engineered bacterium is capable of breaking down multiple components of crude oil. Because of this property, which is possessed by no naturally occurring bacteria, Chakrabarty's invention is believed to have significant value for the treatment of oil spills.

* * *

The patent examiner * * * rejected claims for the bacteria. His decision rested on two grounds: (1) that micro-organisms are "products of nature," and (2) that as living things they are not patentable subject matter under 35 U.S.C. § 101.

Chakrabarty appealed the rejection of these claims to the Patent Office Board of Appeals, and the Board affirmed the Examiner on the second ground. Relying on the legislative history of the 1930 Plant Patent Act, in which Congress extended patent protection to certain asexually reproduced plants, the Board concluded that § 101 was not intended to cover living things such as these laboratory created micro-organisms.

The Court of Customs and Patent Appeals, by a divided vote, reversed on the authority of its prior decision in In re Bergy, 563 F.2d 1031, 1038 (1977), which held that "the fact that microorganisms * * * are alive * * * [is] without legal significance" for purposes of the patent law.

* * *

II.

The Constitution grants Congress broad power to legislate to "promote the Progress of Science and useful Arts, by securing for limited Times to Authors and Inventors the exclusive Right to their respective Writings and Discoveries." Art. I, § 8, cl. 8. The patent laws promote this progress by offering inventors exclusive rights for a limited period as an incentive for their inventiveness and research efforts.

* * *

The question before us in this case is a narrow one of statutory interpretation requiring us to construe 35 U.S.C. § 101, which provides:

Whoever invents or discovers any new and useful process, machine, manufacture, or composition of matter, or any new and useful improvement thereof, may obtain a patent therefor, subject to the conditions and requirements of this title.

Specifically, we must determine whether respondent's micro-organism constitutes a "manufacture" or "composition of matter" within the meaning of the statute.

III.

* * *

"[C]omposition of matter" has been construed consistent with its common usage to include "all compositions of two or more substances and * * * all composite articles, whether they be the results of chemical union, or of mechanical mixture, or whether they be gases, fluids, powders or solids." * * *

The relevant legislative history also supports a broad construction. The Patent Act of 1793, authored by Thomas Jefferson, defined statutory subject matter as "any new and useful art, machine, manufacture, or composition of matter, or any new or useful improvement [thereof]." The Committee Reports accompanying the 1952 Act inform us that Congress intended statutory subject matter to "include anything under the sun that is made by man."

This is not to suggest that § 101 has no limits or that it embraces every discovery. The laws of nature, physical phenomena, and abstract ideas have been held not patentable. Thus, a new mineral discovered in the earth or a new plant found in the wild is not patentable subject matter. Likewise, Einstein could not patent his celebrated law that $E = mc^2$; nor could Newton have patented the law of gravity. Such discoveries are "manifestations of * * * nature, free to all men and reserved exclusively to none."

Judged in this light, respondent's micro-organism plainly qualifies as patentable subject matter. His claim is not to a hitherto unknown natural phenomenon, but to a nonnaturally occurring manufacture or composition of matter—a product of human ingenuity "having a distinctive name, character [and] use." The point is underscored dramatically by comparison of the invention here with that in Funk [Brothers Seed Co. v. Kalo Inoculant Co., 333 U.S. 127 (1948)]. There, the patentee had discovered that there existed in nature certain species of root-nodule bacteria which did not exert a mutually inhibitive effect on each other. He used that discovery to produce a mixed culture capable of inoculating the seeds of leguminous plants. Concluding that the patentee had discovered "only some of the handiwork of nature," the Court ruled the product nonpatentable.

* * *

Here, by contrast, the patentee has produced a new bacterium with markedly different characteristics from any found in nature and one having the potential for significant utility. His discovery is not nature's handiwork, but his own; accordingly it is patentable subject matter under § 101.

* * *

Congress is free to amend § 101 so as to exclude from patent protection organisms produced by genetic engineering. Cf. 42 U.S.C. § 2181(a), exempting from patent protection inventions "useful solely in the utilization of special nuclear material or atomic energy in an atomic weapon." Or it may chose to craft a statute specifically designed for such living things. But, until Congress takes such action, this Court must construe the language of § 101 as it is.

* * *

BRENNAN, J., WHITE, J., MARSHALL, J., and POWELL, J. join, dissenting.

* * *

The sweeping language of the Patent Act of 1793, as re-enacted in 1952, is not the last pronouncement Congress has made in this area. In 1930 Congress enacted the Plant Patent Act affording patent protection to developers of certain asexually reproduced plants. In 1970 Congress enacted the Plant Variety Protection Act to extend protection to certain new plant varieties capable of sexual reproduction. Thus, we are not dealing—as the Court would have it—with the routine problem of "unanticipated inventions." In these two Acts Congress has addressed the general problem of patenting animate inventions and has chosen carefully limited language granting protection to some kinds of discoveries, but specifically excluding others. These Acts strongly evidence a congressional limitation that excludes bacteria from patentability.

First, the Acts evidence Congress' understanding, at least since 1930, that § 101 does not include living organisms. If newly developed living organisms not naturally occurring had been patentable under § 101, the plants included in the scope of the 1930 and 1970 Acts could have been patented without new legislation. Those plants, like the bacteria involved in this case, were new varieties not naturally occurring.

* * *

Congress plainly has legislated in the belief that § 101 does not encompass living organisms. It is the role of Congress, not this Court, to broaden or narrow the reach of the patent laws. This is especially true where, as here, the composition sought to be patented uniquely implicates matters of public concern.

LABORATORY CORP. OF AMERICA HOLDINGS v. METABOLITE LABORATORIES, INC.

548 U.S. 124 (2006).

[In June 2006 the Supreme Court dismissed a writ of certiorari as improvidently granted because a challenge based on 35 U.S.C. § 101 on patentable subject matter had not been raised by the alleged infringers in the lower court. Three justices would have decided the issue and wrote a dissent discussing the reasons why it is important not to have patents on products of nature or on laws of nature.]

BREYER, J., with whom STEVENS, J. and SOUTER, J. join, dissenting.

This case involves a patent that claims a process for helping to diagnose deficiencies of two vitamins, folate and cobalamin. The process consists of using any test (whether patented or unpatented) to measure the level in a body fluid of an amino acid called homocysteine and then noticing whether its level is elevated above the norm; if so, a vitamin deficiency is likely.

The lower courts held that the patent claim is valid. They also found the petitioner, Laboratory Corporation of America Holdings (LabCorp), liable for inducing infringement of the claim when it encouraged doctors to order diagnostic tests for measuring homocysteine. The courts assessed damages. And they enjoined LabCorp from using any tests that would lead the doctors it serves to find a vitamin deficiency by taking account of elevated homocysteine levels.

We granted certiorari in this case to determine whether the patent claim is invalid on the ground that it improperly seeks to "claim a monopoly over a basic scientific relationship," Pet. for Cert. i, namely, the relationship between homocysteine and vitamin deficiency. The Court has dismissed the writ as improvidently granted. In my view, we should not dismiss the writ. The question presented is not unusually difficult. We have the authority to decide it. We said that we would do so. The parties and *amici* have fully briefed the question. And those who engage in medical research, who practice medicine, and who as patients depend upon proper health care, might well benefit from this Court's authoritative answer.

* * *

The relevant principle of law "[e]xclude[s] from . . . patent protection . . . laws of nature, natural phenomena, and abstract ideas." Diamond v. Diehr, 450 U.S. 175, 185, 101 S.Ct. 1048, 67 L.Ed.2d 155 (1981). This principle finds its roots in both English and American law. * * * The principle means that Einstein could not have "patent[ed] his celebrated law that $E=mc^2$; nor could Newton have patented the law of gravity." Diamond v. Chakrabarty, 447 U.S. 303 (1980). * * *

The justification for the principle does not lie in any claim that "laws of nature" are obvious, or that their discovery is easy, or that they are not useful. To the contrary, research into such matters may be costly and time-consuming; monetary incentives may matter; and the fruits of those incentives and that research may prove of great benefit to the human race. Rather, the reason for the exclusion is that sometimes *too much* patent protection can impede rather than "promote the Progress of Science and useful Arts," the constitutional objective of patent and copyright protection. U.S. Const., Art. I, § 8, cl. 8.

The problem arises from the fact that patents do not only encourage research by providing monetary incentives for invention. Sometimes their presence can discourage research by impeding the free exchange of information, for example by forcing researchers to avoid the use of potentially patented ideas, by leading them to conduct costly and time-consuming searches of existing or pending patents, by requiring complex licensing arrangements, and by raising the costs of using the patented information, sometimes prohibitively so.

Patent law seeks to avoid the dangers of overprotection just as surely as it seeks to avoid the diminished incentive to invent that underprotection can threaten. One way in which patent law seeks to sail between these opposing and risky shoals is through rules that bring certain types of invention and discovery within the scope of patentability while excluding others. And scholars have noted that "patent law['s] exclu[sion of] fundamental scientific (including mathematical) and technological principles," (like copyright's exclusion of "ideas") is a rule of the latter variety. * * *

Thus, the Court has recognized that "[p]henomena of nature, though just discovered, mental processes, and abstract intellectual concepts are . . . the basic tools of scientific and technological work." It has treated fundamental scientific principles as "part of the storehouse of knowledge" and manifestations of laws of nature as "free to all men and reserved exclusively to none." And its doing so reflects a basic judgment that protection in such cases, despite its potentially positive incentive effects, would too often severely interfere with, or discourage, development and the further spread of useful knowledge itself.

* * *

* * * [Claim 13 of the patent] seeks patent protection for:

"A method for detecting a deficiency of cobalamin or folate in warm-blooded animals comprising the steps of:

"assaying a body fluid for an elevated level of total homocysteine; and

"correlating an elevated level of total homocysteine in said body fluid with a deficiency of cobalamin or folate."

Claim 13, respondents argued, created a protected monopoly over the process of "correlating" test results and potential vitamin deficiencies. The parties agreed that the words "assaying a body fluid" refer to the use of any test at all, whether patented or not patented, that determines whether a body fluid has an "elevated level of total homocysteine." And at trial, the inventors testified that claim 13's "correlating" step consists simply of a physician's recognizing that a test that shows an elevated homocysteine level-by that very fact-shows the patient likely has a cobalamin or folate deficiency. They added that, because the natural relationship between homocysteine and vitamin deficiency was now well known, such "correlating" would occur automatically in the mind of any competent physician.

* * *

The jury found LabCorp liable on this theory. The District Court calculated damages based on unpaid royalties for some 350,000 homocysteine tests performed by LabCorp using the Abbott method. The court also enjoined LabCorp from performing "any homocysteine-only test, including, without limitation homocysteine-only tests via the Abbott method."

LabCorp appealed. It argued to the Federal Circuit that the trial court was wrong to construe claim 13 so broadly that infringement took place "every time a physician does nothing more than look at a patient's homocysteine level." Indeed, if so construed (rather than construed, say, to cover only *patented* tests), then claim 13 was "invalid for indefiniteness, lack of written description, non-enablement, anticipation, and obviousness." LabCorp told the Federal Circuit:

> If the Court were to uphold this vague claim, anyone could obtain a patent on any scientific correlation-that there is a link between fact A and fact B-merely by drafting a patent claiming no more than 'test for fact A and correlate with fact B'. . . . Claim 13 does no more than that. If it is upheld, [patentee] would improperly gain a monopoly over a basic scientific fact rather than any novel invention of its own. The law is settled that no such claim should be allowed. See, e.g., Diamond v. Diehr, 450 U.S. 175, 101 S.Ct. 1048, 67 L.Ed.2d 155 (1981) . . . ; Chisum on Patents § 1.03[6].

The Federal Circuit rejected LabCorp's arguments. * * *

* * * [T]he Circuit concluded, because any competent doctor reviewing test results would automatically correlate those results with the presence or absence of a vitamin deficiency, virtually every doctor who ordered and read the tests was a direct infringer. And because LabCorp "publishes ... Continuing Medical Education articles" and other pieces, which urge doctors to conduct the relevant tests and to reach a conclusion about whether a patient is suffering from a vitamin deficiency based upon the test results, LabCorp induces infringement.

LabCorp filed a petition for certiorari. Question Three of the petition asks "[w]hether a method patent ... directing a party simply to 'correlate' test results can validly claim a monopoly over a basic scientific relationship ... such that any doctor necessarily infringes the patent merely by thinking about the relationship after looking at a test result." Pet. for Cert. i. After calling for and receiving the views of the Solicitor General, we granted the petition, limited to Question Three.

* * *

I turn to the merits. The researchers who obtained the present patent found that an elevated level of homocysteine in a warm-blooded animal is correlated with folate and cobalamin deficiencies. As construed by the Federal Circuit, claim 13 provides those researchers with control over doctors' efforts to use that correlation to diagnose vitamin deficiencies in a patient. Does the law permit such protection or does claim 13, in the circumstances, amount to an invalid effort to patent a "phenomenon of nature"?

I concede that the category of non-patentable "phenomena of nature," like the categories of "mental processes," and "abstract intellectual concepts," is not easy to define. * * * Nor can one easily use such abstract categories directly to distinguish instances of likely beneficial, from likely harmful, forms of protection.

But this case is not at the boundary. It does not require us to consider the precise scope of the "natural phenomenon" doctrine or any other difficult issue. In my view, claim 13 is invalid no matter how narrowly one reasonably interprets that doctrine.

* * *

The respondents argue, however, that the correlation is nonetheless patentable because claim 13 packages it in the form of a "process" for detecting vitamin deficiency, with discrete testing and correlating steps. They point to this Court's statements that a "process is not unpatentable simply because it contains a law of nature," and that "an *application* of a law of nature ... to a known ... process may well be deserving of patent protection." They add that claim 13 is a patentable "application of a law of nature" because, considered as a whole, it (1) "entails a physical transformation of matter," namely, the alteration of a blood sample during whatever test is used, Brief for Respondents 33 (citing Cochrane v. Deener, 94 U.S. 780, 788, 24 L.Ed. 139 (1877); Gottschalk [v. Benson, 409 U.S.63], 70, 93 S.Ct. 253 [(1972)]), and because it (2) "produces a 'useful, concrete, and tangible result,' "namely, detection of a vitamin deficiency, Brief for Respondents 36 (citing State Street Bank & Trust Co. v. Signature Financial Group, Inc., 149 F.3d 1368, 1373 (C.A.Fed 1998)).

In my view, however, the cases to which respondents refer do not support their claim. Neither *Cochrane* nor *Gottschalk* can help them because the process described in claim 13 is *not* a process for transforming blood or any other matter. Claim 13's process instructs the user to (1) obtain test results and (2) think about them. Why should it matter if the test results themselves were obtained through an unpatented procedure that involved the transformation of blood? Claim 13 is indifferent to that fact, for it tells the user to use any test at all. Indeed, to use virtually any natural phenomenon for virtually any useful purpose could well involve the use of empirical information obtained through an unpatented means that might have involved transforming matter. Neither *Cochrane* nor *Gottschalk* suggests that that fact renders the phenomenon patentable. See Cochrane, supra, at 785 (upholding process for improving quality of flour by removing impurities with blasts of air); Gottschalk, supra, at 71–73, 93 S.Ct. 253 (rejecting process for converting numerals to binary form through mathematical formula).

Neither does the Federal Circuit's decision in *State Street Bank* help respondents. That case does say that a process is patentable if it produces a "useful, concrete, and tangible result." But this Court has never made such a statement and, if taken literally, the statement would cover instances where this Court has held the contrary. The Court, for example, has invalidated a claim to the use of electromagnetic current for transmitting messages over long distances even though it produces a result that seems "useful, concrete, and tangible." Morse, supra, at 116. Similarly the Court has invalidated a patent setting forth a system for triggering alarm limits in connection with catalytic conversion despite a similar utility, concreteness, and tangibility. [Parker v.] Flook, [437 U.S. 584 (1978)]. And the Court has invalidated a patent setting forth a process that transforms, for computer-programming purposes, decimal figures into binary figures-even though the result would seem useful, concrete, and at least arguably (within the computer's wiring system) tangible. Gottschalk, supra.

* * *

At most, respondents have simply described the natural law at issue in the abstract patent language of a "process." But they cannot avoid the fact that the process is no more than an instruction to read some numbers in light of medical knowledge. * * * One might, of course, reduce the "process" to a series of steps, *e.g.*, Step 1: gather data; Step 2: read a number; Step 3: compare the number with the norm; Step 4: act accordingly. But one can reduce *any* process to a series of steps. The question is what those steps embody. And here, aside from the unpatented test, they embody only the correlation between homocysteine and vitamin deficiency that the researchers uncovered. In my view, that correlation is an unpatentable "natural phenomenon," and I can find nothing in claim 13 that adds anything more of significance.

IV

If I am correct in my conclusion in Part III that the patent is invalid, then special public interest considerations reinforce my view that we should decide this case. To fail to do so threatens to leave the medical profession subject to the restrictions imposed by this individual patent and others of its kind. Those restrictions may inhibit doctors from using their best medical judgment; they may force doctors to spend unnecessary time and energy to enter into license agreements; they may divert resources from the medical task of health care to the legal task of searching patent files for similar simple correlations; they may raise the cost of healthcare while inhibiting its effective delivery.

PROMETHEUS LABORATORIES v. MAYO COLLABORATIVE SERVICES

581 F.3d 1336 (Fed. Cir. 2009).

LOURIE, J.

Prometheus Laboratories, Inc. ("Prometheus") appeals from the final judgment of the United States District Court for the Southern District of California granting summary judgment of invalidity of U.S. Patents 6,355,623 ("the '623 patent") and 6,680,302 ("the '302 patent") under 35 U.S.C. § 101. Because the district court erred as a matter of law in finding the asserted claims to be drawn to non-statutory subject matter, we reverse.

BACKGROUND

* * *

[Prometheus was the sole and exclusive licensee of the '623 and '302 patents, which claimed methods for calibrating the proper dosage of thiopurine drugs, used to treat gastrointestinal and non-gastrointestinal autoimmune diseases. These drugs include 6–mercaptopurine ("6–MP") and azathiopurine ("AZA"), which are broken down in the body into various metabolites including 6–methyl-mercaptopurine ("6–MMP") and 6–thioguanine ("6–TG"). The patents claimed methods of calibrating dosage of the drugs by measuring the level of these metabolites in the patient's blood. A metabolite level above a certain concentration indicated the dosage should be decreased to avoid toxic side effects. Conversely, a metabolite level below a certain concentration indicated the dosage should be increased to ensure efficacy. Mayo Collaborative Services and Mayo Clinic Rochester had formerly purchased and used Prometheus's test, but in 2004 announced they would begin using and selling their own version of the test. Mayo's test would measure the same metabolites as Prometheus's test but use different concentration levels.]

Claim 1 of the '623 patent is representative of the independent claims asserted by Prometheus in this case:

A method of optimizing therapeutic efficacy for treatment of an immune-mediated gastrointestinal disorder, comprising:

(a) administering a drug providing 6–thioguanine to a subject having said immune-mediated gastrointestinal disorder; and

(b) determining the level of 6–thioguanine in said subject having said immune-mediated gastrointestinal disorder,

wherein the level of 6–thioguanine less than about 230 pmol per 8×10^8 red blood cells indicates a need to increase the amount of said drug subsequently administered to said subject and

wherein the level of 6–thioguanine greater than about 400 pmol per 8×10^8 red blood cells indicates a need to decrease the amount of said drug subsequently administered to said subject.

* * *

DISCUSSION
* * *

B. *Section 101*

The issue before us is whether the claims meet the requirements of § 101, so we begin with the text of the statute. Section 101 provides that:

Whoever invents or discovers any new and useful process, machine, manufacture, or composition of matter, or any new and useful improvement thereof, may obtain a patent thereof, subject to the conditions and requirements of this title.

35 U.S.C. § 101. According to § 100(b), "[t]he term 'process' means process, art, or method, and includes a new use of a known process, machine, manufacture, composition of matter, or materials." But, as noted in *In re Bilski,* this definition of process is "unhelpful" because the definition itself uses the term "process." 545 F.3d 943, 951 n. 3 (Fed.Cir. 2008)(en banc), *cert. granted,* 129 S.Ct. 2735 (June 1, 2009). Thus, we turn to the case law to guide our understanding of what constitutes statutory subject matter under § 101.

[Although the Supreme Court has construed § 101 broadly,] the Court has held that a claim to a process is not patent-eligible if it claims "laws of nature, natural phenomena, and abstract ideas." Diamond v. Diehr, 450 U.S. 175, 185 (1981).

At the same time, it has also been established that "while a claim drawn to a fundamental principle"—*i.e.,* a law of nature, natural phenomenon, or abstract idea—"is unpatentable, 'an *application* of a law of nature or mathematical formula to a known structure or process may well be deserving of patent protection.' " *Bilski,* 545 F.3d at 953 (quoting *Diehr,* 450 U.S. at 187). The key issue for patentability, then, at least on the present facts, is whether a claim is drawn to a fundamental principle or an application of a fundamental principle. Although this inquiry is hardly straightforward, following the Supreme Court, we articulated in *Bilski* a "definitive test" for determining whether a process is patent-eligible under § 101: "A claimed process is surely patent-eligible under § 101 if: (1) it is tied to a particular machine or apparatus, or (2) it transforms a particular article into a different state or thing." *Id.* The machine-or-transformation test is a "two-branched inquiry," *i.e.,* the patentee "may show that a process claim satisfies § 101 either by showing that his claim is tied to a particular machine, or by showing that his claim transforms an article." *Id.* at 961.

The machine-or-transformation test has two further aspects: "the use of a specific machine or transformation of an article must impose mean-ingful limits on the claim's scope to impart patent-eligibility," and "the involvement of the machine or transformation in the claimed process must not merely be insignificant extra-solution activity." *Bilski,* 545 F.3d at 961–62. "This transformation must be central to the purpose of the claimed process." *Id.* at 962. Thus, in most cases, one cannot ground the transformative nature of a process in a step that is "insignificant extra-solution activity" or merely a "data-gathering step." In other words, if steps of a method are included for the purpose of data-gathering rather than being "central" to the purpose of the process, the patentee likely cannot rely on the data-gathering steps to prove that the claimed process is transformative and thus drawn to patentable subject matter.

* * *

C. Analysis

* * *

1. The administering and determining steps are transformative

* * *

We conclude that the methods of treatment claimed in the patents in suit squarely fall within the realm of patentable subject matter because they "transform an article into a different state or thing," and this transformation is "central to the purpose of the claimed process." *See Bilski,* 545 F.3d at 962. The transformation is of the human body following administration of a drug and the various chemical and physical changes of the drug's metabolites that enable their concentrations to be determined. Because the claimed methods meet the transformation prong under *Bilski,* we do not consider whether they also meet the machine prong.

Contrary to the district court, we do not view the disputed claims as merely claiming natural correlations and data-gathering steps.[3] The asserted claims are in effect claims to methods of treatment, which are always transformative when a defined group of drugs is administered to the body to ameliorate the effects of an undesired condition. More specifically, Prometheus here claimed methods for optimizing efficacy and reducing toxicity of treatment regimes for gastrointestinal and non-gastrointestinal autoimmune diseases that utilize drugs providing 6–TG by administering a drug to a subject. The invention's purpose to treat the human body is made clear in the specification and the preambles of the asserted claims.

When administering a drug such as AZA or 6–MP, the human body necessarily undergoes a transformation. The drugs do not pass through the body untouched without affecting it. In fact, the transformation that occurs, *viz.*, the effect on the body after metabolizing the artificially administered drugs, is the entire purpose of administering these drugs: the drugs are administered to provide 6–TG, which is thought to be the drugs' active metabolite in the treatment of disease, to a subject. The fact that the change of the administered drug into its metabolites relies on natural processes does not disqualify the administering step from the realm of patentability. As Prometheus points out, quite literally every transformation of physical matter can be described as occurring according to natural processes and natural law. Transformations operate by natural principles. The transformation here, however, is the result of the physical administration of a drug to a subject to transform—*i.e.*, treat—the subject, which is itself not a natural process. "It is virtually self-evident that a process for a chemical or physical transformation of *physical objects or substances* is patent-eligible subject matter." *See Bilski*, 545 F.3d at 962. The administering step, therefore, is not merely data-gathering but a significant transformative element of Prometheus's claimed methods of treatment that is "sufficiently definite to confine the patent monopoly within rather definite bounds." *Id.*

Mayo is correct that not all of the asserted claims contain the administering step. That omission, which occurs in claims 46 and 53 of the '623 patent, does not diminish the patentability of the claimed methods because the determining step, which is present in each of the asserted claims, is also transformative and central to the claimed methods. Determining the levels of 6–TG or 6–MMP in a subject necessarily involves a transformation, for those levels cannot be determined by mere inspection. Some form of manipulation, such as the high pressure liquid chromatography method specified in several of the asserted dependent claims or other modification of the substances to be measured, is necessary to extract the metabolites from a bodily sample and determine their concentration. As stated by Prometheus's expert, "at the end of the

---

3. In reaching its conclusion, the district court relied heavily on the opinion of three justices dissenting from the dismissal of the grant of certiorari in *Laboratory Corp. of America Holdings v. Metabolite Laboratories, Inc.*, 548 U.S. 124 (2006) (Breyer, J., dissenting). That dissent is not controlling law and also involved different claims from the ones at issue here.

process, the human blood sample is no longer human blood; human tissue is no longer human tissue." That is clearly a transformation. In fact, Mayo does not dispute that determining metabolite levels in the clinical samples taken from patients is transformative, but argues that this transformation is merely a necessary data-gathering step for use of the correlations. On the contrary, this transformation is central to the purpose of the claims, since the determining step is, like the administering step, a significant part of the claimed method of treatment. Measuring the levels of 6–TG and 6–MMP is what enables possible adjustments to thiopurine drug dosage to be detected for optimizing efficacy or reducing toxicity during a course of treatment. The determining step, by working a chemical and physical transformation on physical substances, likewise sufficiently confines the patent monopoly, as required by *Bilski*.

2. The administering and determining steps are not merely data-gathering

A further requirement for patent-eligibility is ensuring that the involvement of the transformation in Prometheus's claimed process is "not merely insignificant extra-solution activity." *Bilski*, 545 F.3d at 962. As made clear from the discussion above, the administering and determining steps are transformative and are central to the claims rather than merely insignificant extra-solution activity.

The crucial error the district court made in reaching the opposite conclusion was failing to recognize that the first two steps of the asserted claims are not merely data-gathering steps. While it is true that the administering and determining steps gather useful data, it is also clear that the presence of those two steps in the claimed processes is not "merely" for the purpose of gathering data. Instead, the administering and determining steps are part of a treatment protocol, and they are transformative. As explained above, the administering step provides thiopurine drugs for the purpose of treating disease, and the determining step measures the drugs' metabolite levels for the purpose of assessing the drugs' dosage during the course of treatment.

* * *

3. The presence of a mental step does not detract from patentability

We agree with the district court that the final "wherein" clauses are mental steps and thus not patent-eligible per se. However, although they alone are not patent-eligible, the claims are not simply to the mental steps. A subsequent mental step does not, by itself, negate the transformative nature of prior steps. Thus, when viewed in the proper context, the final step of providing a warning based on the results of the prior steps does not detract from the patentability of Prometheus's claimed methods as a whole. The data that the administering and determining steps provide for use in the mental steps is obtained by steps well within the realm of patentable subject matter. The addition of the mental steps to the claimed methods thus does not remove the prior two steps from that realm.

* * *

[The court then concluded that the claims did not wholly preempt the use of correlations between metabolite levels and efficacy or toxicity because the claims covered a particular application of a natural process to treat various diseases, and because the claims used the processes in a series of specific steps.] Regardless, because the claims meet the machine-or-transformation test, they do not preempt a fundamental principle. The inventive nature of the claimed methods stems not from preemption of all use of these natural processes, but from the application of a natural phenomenon in a series of transformative steps comprising particular methods of treatment. It is clear that these methods of treatment are § 101 patentable subject matter.

Thus, the claimed methods satisfy all of the requirements under *Bilski's* transformation prong for patent-eligible subject matter under § 101.

HARVARD COLLEGE v. CANADA (COMMISSIONER OF PATENTS)

[2002] 4 S.C.R. 45.

* * *

BASTARACHE, J.

I. INTRODUCTION

118   This appeal raises the issue of the patentability of higher life forms within the context of the *Patent Act*, R.S.C. 1985, c. P–4. The respondent, the President and Fellows of Harvard College, seeks to patent a mouse that has been genetically altered to increase its susceptibility to cancer, which makes it useful for cancer research. The patent claims also extend to all non-human mammals which have been similarly altered.

119   The Commissioner of Patents upheld the Patent Examiner's refusal to grant the patent. This decision was in turn upheld by the Federal Court, Trial Division, but was overturned by a majority of the Federal Court of Appeal. * * *

120   * * * [T]he sole question is whether Parliament intended the definition of "invention", and more particularly the words "manufacture" or "composition of matter", within the context of the *Patent Act*, to encompass higher life forms such as the oncomouse. In my opinion, Parliament did not intend higher life forms to be patentable. Had Parliament intended every conceivable subject matter to be patentable, it would not have chosen to adopt an exhaustive definition that limits invention to any "art, process, machine, manufacture or composition of matter". In addition, the phrases "manufacture" and "composition of matter" do not correspond to

common understandings of animal and plant life. Even accepting that the words of the definition can support a broad interpretation, they must be interpreted in light of the scheme of the Act and the relevant context. The Act in its current form fails to address many of the unique concerns that are raised by the patenting of higher life forms, a factor which indicates that Parliament never intended the definition of "invention" to extend to this type of subject matter. Given the unique concerns associated with the grant of a monopoly right over higher life forms, it is my view that Parliament would not likely choose the *Patent Act* as it currently exists as the appropriate vehicle to protect the rights of inventors of this type of subject matter.

II. FACTUAL BACKGROUND

121 On June 21, 1985, the respondent, the President and Fellows of Harvard College ("Harvard"), applied for a patent on an invention entitled "transgenic animals". The invention aims to produce animals with a susceptibility to cancer for purposes of animal carcinogenic studies. * * *

122 The technology by which a cancer-prone mouse ("oncomouse") is produced is described in the patent application disclosure. * * *

123 In its patent application, the respondent seeks to protect both the process by which the oncomice are produced and the end product of the process, i.e. the founder mice and the offspring whose cells are affected by the oncogene. The process and product claims also extend to all non-human mammals. In March 1993, by Final Action, a Patent Examiner rejected the product claims (claims 1 to 12) as being outside the scope of the definition of "invention" in s. 2 of the *Patent Act*, but allowed the process claims (claims 13 to 26). In August 1995, * * * the Commissioner confirmed the refusal to grant a patent for claims 1 to 12. The Federal Court, Trial Division dismissed the respondent's appeal from the decision of the Commissioner. The respondent's further appeal to the Federal Court of Appeal was allowed by a majority of the court, Isaac J.A. dissenting. The Commissioner of Patents appeals from that decision.

III. RELEVANT STATUTORY PROVISIONS

124 Patent Act, R.S.C. 1985, c. P–4

   2. In this Act, except as otherwise provided,

   "invention" means any new and useful art, process, machine, manufacture or composition of matter, or any new and useful improvement in any art, process, machine, manufacture or composition of matter;

* * *

V. ANALYSIS

* * *

B. *The Definition of "Invention": Whether a Higher Life Form Is a "Manufacture" or a "Composition of Matter"*

* * *

155   Having considered the relevant factors, I conclude that Parliament did not intend to include higher life forms within the definition of "invention" found in the *Patent Act*. In their grammatical and ordinary sense alone, the words "manufacture" and "composition of matter" are somewhat imprecise and ambiguous. However, it is my view that the best reading of the words of the Act supports the conclusion that higher life forms are not patentable. As I discuss below, I do not believe that a higher life form such as the oncomouse is easily understood as either a "manufacture" or a "composition of matter". For this reason, I am not satisfied that the definition of "invention" in the *Patent Act* is sufficiently broad to include higher life forms. This conclusion is supported by the fact that the patenting of higher life forms raises unique concerns which do not arise in respect of non-living inventions and which are not addressed by the scheme of the Act. Even if a higher life form could, scientifically, be regarded as a "composition of matter", the scheme of the Act indicates that the patentability of higher life forms was not contemplated by Parliament. Owing to the fact that the patenting of higher life forms is a highly contentious and complex matter that raises serious practical, ethical and environmental concerns that the Act does not contemplate, I conclude that the Commissioner was correct to reject the patent application. This is a policy issue that raises questions of great significance and importance and that would appear to require a dramatic expansion of the traditional patent regime. Absent explicit legislative direction, the Court should not order the Commissioner to grant a patent on a higher life form.

(1) The Words of the Act

156   The definition of "invention" in s. 2 of the *Patent Act* lists five categories of invention: art (*réalisation*), process (*procédé*), machine (*machine*), manufacture (*fabrication*) or composition of matter (*composition de matières*). The first three, "art", "process" and "machine", are clearly inapplicable when considering claims directed toward a genetically engineered non-human mammal. If a higher life form is to fit within the definition of "invention", it must therefore be considered to be either a "manufacture" or a "composition of matter".

* * *

158   I agree that the definition of "invention" in the *Patent Act* is broad. Because the Act was designed in part to promote innovation, it is only reasonable to expect the definition of "invention" to be broad enough to encompass unforeseen and unanticipated technology. I cannot however agree with the suggestion that the definition is unlimited in the sense that it includes "anything under the sun that is made by man". In drafting the *Patent Act*, Parliament chose to adopt an exhaustive definition that limits invention to any "art, process, machine, manufacture or composition of

matter". Parliament did not define "invention" as "anything new and useful made by man". By choosing to define invention in this way, Parliament signalled a clear intention to include certain subject matter as patentable and to exclude other subject matter as being outside the confines of the Act. This should be kept in mind when determining whether the words "manufacture" and "composition of matter" include higher life forms.

159   With respect to the meaning of the word "manufacture" (*fabrication*), * * * I am of the opinion that the word would commonly be understood to denote a non-living mechanistic product or process. For example, the Oxford English Dictionary (2nd ed. 1989), vol. IX, at p. 341, defines the noun "manufacture" as the following:

> The action or process of making by hand.... * * *

* * *

In [Diamond v.] Chakrabarty, [447 U.S. 303,] 308 [(1980)], "manufacture" was defined as

> the production of articles for use from raw or prepared materials by giving to these materials new forms, qualities, properties, or combinations, whether by hand-labor or by machinery.

These definitions use the terminology of "article", "material", and *"objet technique"*. Is a mouse an "article", "material", or an *"objet technique"*? In my view, while a mouse may be analogized to a "manufacture" when it is produced in an industrial setting, the word in its vernacular sense does not include a higher life form. * * * In my opinion, a complex life form such as a mouse or a chimpanzee cannot easily be characterized as "something made by the hands of man".

160   As regards the meaning of the words "composition of matter", I believe that they must be defined more narrowly than was the case in *Chakrabarty*, supra, at p. 308 namely "all compositions of two or more substances and ... all composite articles". If the words "composition of matter" are understood this broadly, then the other listed categories of invention, including "machine" and "manufacture", become redundant. This implies that "composition of matter" must be limited in some way. Although I do not express an opinion as to where the line should be drawn, I conclude that "composition of matter" does not include a higher life form such as the oncomouse.

* * *

164   Lastly, I wish also to address Rothstein J.A.'s assertion that "[t]he language of patent law is broad and general and is to be given wide scope because inventions are, necessarily, unanticipated and unforeseeable" (para. 116). In my view, it does not thereby follow that all proposed inventions are patentable. * * * Although Parliament would not have foreseen the genetically altered mouse and the process of genetic engineering used to produce it, Parliament was well aware of animal husbandry or

breeding. * * * Yet Parliament chose to define the categories of invention using language that does not, in common usage, refer to higher life forms. * * *

* * *

166   Patenting higher life forms would involve a radical departure from the traditional patent regime. Moreover, the patentability of such life forms is a highly contentious matter that raises a number of extremely complex issues. If higher life forms are to be patentable, it must be under the clear and unequivocal direction of Parliament. For the reasons discussed above, I conclude that the current Act does not clearly indicate that higher life forms are patentable. * * * [T]he Act supports the opposite conclusion—that higher life forms such as the oncomouse are not currently patentable in Canada.

* * *

205   * * * The respondent argues that it is apparent from this provision that plants and animals are considered patentable, unless specifically excluded from patentability. I see little merit to this argument since the *status quo* position in Canada is that higher life forms are not a patentable subject matter, regardless of the fact that there is no explicit exclusion in the *Patent Act.* * * *

206   As I remarked above, it is up to Parliament and not the courts to assess the validity of the distinction drawn by the Patent Office between higher life forms and lower life forms. Yet, even if this Court were to alter the *status quo* and find higher life forms patentable, it would be unable to avoid engaging in line-drawing. The majority of the Federal Court of Appeal, which found that the *Patent Act* did apply to higher life forms, was nonetheless compelled to draw a distinction between higher life forms and human beings. In doing so, it merely substituted one line, that between humans and animals, for the line preferred by the Patent Office, that between higher and lower life forms. In my opinion, the decision to move the line in this manner was ill-advised. As I stated earlier when considering the definition of "invention", the patenting of all plants and animals, and not just human beings, raises several concerns that are not appropriately dealt with in the *Patent Act.* In addition, a judicially crafted exception from patentability for human beings does not adequately address issues such as what defines a human being and whether parts of the human body as opposed to the entire person would be patentable.

VI.   CONCLUSION

207   For the reasons given above, the appeal is allowed. No order as to costs will be given in light of the Commissioner's oral submissions.

NOTES AND QUESTIONS

1.   Article 1, section 8, clause 8 of the United States Constitution provides that Congress shall have the power "To promote the Progress of

Science and useful Arts, by securing for limited Times to Authors and Inventors the exclusive Right to their respective Writings and Discoveries." Scholars have noted that the term "Discoveries," as utilized in Article I, Section 8, Clause 8, is synonymous with the modern term "inventions."

> An "invention," in the parlance of the Constitution and early patent laws, is a new creation consciously sought and successfully reduced to practice by the inventor. A "discovery," as used in the same parlance, was intended to denote a fortuitous creation of the inventor and not merely something found by him or her. Thus, an "invention" and a "discovery" share the requirement that the inventor create something original; the difference between the two is that an "invention" is consciously sought, while a "discovery" is created unexpectedly. A discovery in that era, as used in the intellectual property law, denoted something originating from the human intellect and not merely learned by that intellect.

Linda J. Demaine and Aaron Xavier Fellmeth, Reinventing the Double Helix: A Novel and Nonobvious Reconceptualization of the Biotechnology Patent, 55 Stan. L. Rev. 303, 370 (2002).

Writing in 1889, a patent law scholar noted that someone "may invent a machine, and may discover an island or law of nature. For doing the first of these things, the patent laws may reward him, because he is an inventor in doing it; but those laws cannot reward him for doing either of the others, because he is not an inventor in doing either." Albert A. Walker, Text–Book of the Patent Laws of the United States of America 2–3 (L. K. Strouse & Co., 2d ed. 1889). Does the sequence of a gene meet the Constitution's standard of a definition of a discovery?

Under the patent statute, 35 U.S.C. § 101, certain categories of inventions are deemed patentable: "[w]hoever invents or discovers any new and useful process, machine, manufacture, or composition of matter, or any new and useful improvement thereof, may obtain a patent therefore, subject to the conditions and requirements of this title * * *." The Supreme Court has limited the categories of patentable subject matter by excluding "products of nature" and "laws of nature" from patentability. "This Court has undoubtedly recognized limits to § 101 and every discovery is not embraced within the statutory terms. Excluded from such patent protection are laws of nature, natural phenomena, and abstract ideas." Diamond v. Diehr, 450 U.S. 175, 182 (1980). Is a gene sequence a "product of nature" or a "law of nature" or is it a patentable "invention"?

2. The Federal Circuit in In re Bilski, 545 F.3d 943 (Fed. Cir. 2008), attempted to construct a definitive test for § 101 patent-eligibility from Supreme Court precedents. "A claimed process is surely patent-eligible under § 101 if: (1) it is tied to a particular machine or apparatus, or (2) it transforms a particular article into a different state or thing." Id. at 954. The Supreme Court granted certiorari to hear the case in 2009. Bilski v. Doll, 129 S.Ct. 2735 (2009).

3. Many gene-related patents involve comparing a gene sequence from a patient to a normal gene sequence and correlating the existence of a mutation to a disease. Based on the dissent in Laboratory Corporation of America Holdings v. Metabolite Laboratories, Inc., 548 U.S. 124 (2006), should this be

patentable? Does a patent applicant in such cases actually invent the correlation or does an inventor merely discover a correlation? What arguments can be made under *Bilski* and *Prometheus* about whether the correlation between a mutation and a disease should be patentable subject matter under § 101?

4. In December 2001, the U.S. Supreme Court addressed one of the issues brought up by the dissenting justices in *Chakrabarty*: Does the enactment of the Plant Patent Act indicate that patents on living organisms were not appropriate under the patent act itself? J.E.M. Ag. Supply, Inc. v. Pioneer Hi–Bred Intern., Inc., 534 U.S. 124 (2001). The Supreme Court held that seeds were patentable under the general patent statute.

5. The United States and Canada have taken different positions on the patentability of the Harvard oncomouse. A patent on the oncomouse was granted by the USPTO (U.S. Patent No. 4,736,866) on April 12, 1988, and has not been subject to a challenge of its validity. How might the United States Supreme Court have ruled if the oncomouse patent was challenged under 35 U.S.C. § 101 for being a non-patentable subject matter?

B. UTILITY

IN RE FISHER

421 F.3d 1365 (Fed. Cir. 2005).

MICHEL, C.J.

The claimed invention relates to five purified nucleic acid sequences that encode proteins and protein fragments in maize plants. The claimed sequences are commonly referred to as "expressed sequence tags" or "ESTs." Before delving into the specifics of this case, it is important to understand more about the basic principles of molecular genetics and the role of ESTs.

Genes are located on chromosomes in the nucleus of a cell and are made of deoxyribonucleic acid ("DNA"). DNA is composed of two strands of nucleotides in double helix formation. The nucleotides contain one of four bases, adenine ("A"), guanine ("G"), cytosine ("C"), and thymine ("T"), that are linked by hydrogen bonds to form complementary base pairs (i.e., A–T and G–C).

When a gene is expressed in a cell, the relevant double-stranded DNA sequence is transcribed into a single strand of messenger ribonucleic acid ("mRNA"). Messenger RNA contains three of the same bases as DNA (A, G, and C), but contains uracil ("U") instead of thymine. mRNA is released from the nucleus of a cell and used by ribosomes found in the cytoplasm to produce proteins.

Complementary DNA ("cDNA") is produced synthetically by reverse transcribing mRNA. cDNA, like naturally occurring DNA, is composed of nucleotides containing the four nitrogenous bases, A, T, G, and C. Scientists routinely compile cDNA into libraries to study the kinds of genes expressed in a certain tissue at a particular point in time. One of the goals of this research is to learn what genes and downstream proteins are expressed in a cell so as to regulate gene expression and control protein synthesis.

An EST is a short nucleotide sequence that represents a fragment of a cDNA clone. It is typically generated by isolating a cDNA clone and sequencing a small number of nucleotides located at the end of one of the two cDNA strands. When an EST is introduced into a sample containing a mixture of DNA, the EST may hybridize with a portion of DNA. Such binding shows that the gene corresponding to the EST was being expressed at the time of mRNA extraction.

Claim 1 of the '643 application recites:

> A substantially purified nucleic acid molecule that encodes a maize protein or fragment thereof comprising a nucleic acid sequence selected from the group consisting of SEQ ID NO: 1 through SEQ ID NO: 5.

* * *

When Fisher filed the '643 application, he claimed ESTs corresponding to genes expressed from the maize pooled leaf tissue at the time of anthesis [the period during which a flower is fully open and functional]. Nevertheless, Fisher did not know the precise structure or function of either the genes or the proteins encoded for by those genes.

The '643 application generally discloses that the five claimed ESTs may be used in a variety of ways, including: (1) serving as a molecular marker for mapping the entire maize genome, which consists of ten chromosomes that collectively encompass roughly 50,000 genes; (2) measuring the level of mRNA in a tissue sample via microarray technology to provide information about gene expression; (3) providing a source for primers for use in the polymerase chain reaction ("PCR") process to enable rapid and inexpensive duplication of specific genes; (4) identifying the presence or absence of a polymorphism; (5) isolating promoters via chromosome walking; (6) controlling protein expression; and (7) locating genetic molecules of other plants and organisms.

* * *

Fisher contends that § 101 requires only that the claimed invention "not be frivolous, or injurious to the well-being, good policy, or good morals of society," essentially adopting Justice Story's view of a useful invention from Lowell v. Lewis, 15 F. Cas. 1018, 1019, F. Cas. No. 8568 (C.C. Mass. 1817). Under the correct application of the law, Fisher argues, the record shows that the claimed ESTs provide seven specific and substantial uses, regardless whether the functions of the genes corresponding to the claimed ESTs are known. * * * Fisher likewise argues that the general commercial success of ESTs in the marketplace confirms the utility of the claimed ESTs. Hence, Fisher avers that the Board's decision was not supported by substantial evidence and should be reversed.

The government agrees with Fisher that the utility threshold is not high, but disagrees with Fisher's allegation that the Board applied a heightened utility standard. The government contends that a patent applicant need disclose only a single specific and substantial utility pursuant to *Brenner* [v. Manson, 383 U.S. 519 (1965)], the very standard articulated in the PTO's "Utility Examination Guidelines" ("Utility Guidelines") and followed here when examining the '643 application. It argues that Fisher failed to meet that standard because Fisher's alleged uses are so general as to be meaningless. What is more, the government asserts that the same generic uses could apply not only to the five claimed ESTs but also to any EST derived from any organism. It thus argues that the seven utilities alleged by Fisher are merely starting points for further research, not the end point of any research effort. It further disputes the importance of the commercial success of ESTs in the marketplace, pointing out that Fisher's evidence involved only databases, clone sets, and microarrays, not the five claimed ESTs. Therefore, the government contends that we should affirm the Board's decision.

Several academic institutions and biotechnology and pharmaceutical companies write as amici curiae in support of the government. Like the government, they assert that Fisher's claimed uses are nothing more than a "laundry list" of research plans, each general and speculative, none providing a specific and substantial benefit in currently available form. The amici also advocate that the claimed ESTs are the objects of further research aimed at identifying what genes of unknown function are expressed during anthesis and what proteins of unknown function are encoded for by those genes. Until the corresponding genes and proteins have a known function, the amici argue, the claimed ESTs lack utility under § 101 and are not patentable.

We agree with both the government and the amici that none of Fisher's seven asserted uses meets the utility requirement of § 101. Section 101 provides: "Whoever invents ... any new and *useful* ... composition of matter ... may obtain a patent therefore...." (Emphasis added). In *Brenner*, the Supreme Court explained what is required to establish the usefulness of a new invention * * *:

> The basic *quid pro quo* contemplated by the Constitution and the Congress for granting a patent monopoly is the benefit derived by the public from an invention with *substantial utility*. Unless and until a process is refined and developed to this point–where *specific benefit exists in currently available form*–there is insufficient justification for permitting an applicant to engross what may prove to be a broad field.

Brenner, 383 U.S. at 534–35 (emphases added). Following *Brenner*, our predecessor court, the Court of Customs and Patent Appeals, and this court have required a claimed invention to have a specific and substantial utility to satisfy § 101.

* * *

[A]n application must show that an invention is useful to the public as disclosed in its current form, not that it may prove useful at some future date after further research. Simply put, to satisfy the "substantial" utility requirement, an asserted use must show that that claimed invention has a significant and presently available benefit to the public.

Turning to the "specific" utility requirement, an application must disclose a use which is not so vague as to be meaningless. Indeed, one of our predecessor courts has observed "that the nebulous expressions 'biological activity' or 'biological properties' appearing in the specification convey no more explicit indication of the usefulness of the compounds and how to use them than did the equally obscure expression 'useful for technical and pharmaceutical purposes' unsuccessfully relied upon by the appellant in In re Diedrich." In re Kirk, 376 F.2d 936, 941, 54 C.C.P.A. 1119 (C.C.P.A. 1967). Thus, in addition to providing a "substantial" utility, an asserted use must also show that that claimed invention can be used to provide a well-defined and particular benefit to the public.

In 2001, partially in response to questions about the patentability of ESTs, the PTO issued Utility Guidelines governing its internal practice for determining whether a claimed invention satisfies § 101. See Utility Examination Guidelines, 66 Fed. Reg. 1092 (Jan. 5, 2001). * * * According to the Utility Guidelines, a specific utility is particular to the subject matter claimed and would not be applicable to a broad class of invention. Manual of Patent Examining Procedure § 2107.01. The Utility Guidelines also explain that a substantial utility defines a "real world" use. In particular, "utilities that require or constitute carrying out further research to identify or reasonably confirm a 'real world' context of use are not substantial utilities." Id.

* * *

Fisher compares the claimed ESTs to certain other patentable research tools, such as a microscope. Although this comparison may, on first blush, be appealing in that both a microscope and one of the claimed ESTs can be used to generate scientific data about a sample having unknown properties, Fisher's analogy is flawed. As the government points out, a microscope has the specific benefit of optically magnifying an object to immediately reveal its structure. One of the claimed ESTs, by contrast, can only be used to detect the presence of genetic material having the same structure as the EST itself. It is unable to provide any information about the overall structure let alone the function of the underlying gene. Accordingly, while a microscope can offer an immediate, real world benefit in a variety of applications, the same cannot be said for the claimed ESTs. Fisher's proposed analogy is thus inapt. Hence, we conclude that Fisher's asserted uses are insufficient to meet the standard for a "substantial" utility under § 101.

* * *

Here, granting a patent to Fisher for its five claimed ESTs would amount to a hunting license because the claimed ESTs can be used only to gain further information about the underlying genes and the proteins encoded for by those genes. The claimed ESTs themselves are not an end of Fisher's research effort, but only tools to be used along the way in the search for a practical utility. Thus, while Fisher's claimed ESTs may add a noteworthy contribution to biotechnology research, our precedent dictates that the '643 application does not meet the utility requirement of § 101 because Fisher does not identify the function for the underlying protein-encoding genes. Absent such identification, we hold that the claimed ESTs have not been researched and understood to the point of providing an immediate, well-defined, real world benefit to the public meriting the grant of a patent.

NOTES AND QUESTIONS

1. In the dissent in *Fisher*, Judge Rader argues that ESTs are research tools with utility in a laboratory setting and, as such, satisfy the requirements of 35 U.S.C. § 101. Judge Rader notes that ESTs are similar to nucleotide sequencing techniques, screening assays, and gas chromatographs in that they are useful in analyzing compounds. If that is true, then why does the majority in *Fisher* find a lack of utility?

C. NOVELTY

AMGEN, INC. v. CHUGAI PHARMACEUTICAL CO., LTD.
927 F.2d 1200 (Fed. Cir. 1991).

LOURIE, J.

This appeal and cross appeal * * * involve issues of patent validity, infringement, and inequitable conduct with respect to * * * U.S. Patent 4,703,008 ('008), owned by Kirin–Amgen Inc. (Amgen) * * *.

Chugai Pharmaceutical Co., Ltd. (Chugai) and Genetics Institute, Inc. [GI] (collectively defendants) assert on appeal that the district court erred in holding that: 1) Amgen's '008 patent is not invalid under 35 U.S.C. §§ 102(g) and 103 * * *.

* * *

Erythropoietin (EPO) is a protein consisting of 165 amino acids which stimulates the production of red blood cells. It is therefore a useful therapeutic agent in the treatment of anemias or blood disorders characterized by low or defective bone marrow production of red blood cells.

The preparation of EPO products generally has been accomplished through the concentration and purification of urine from both healthy individuals and those exhibiting high EPO levels. A new technique for producing EPO is recombinant DNA technology in which EPO is produced from cell cultures into which genetically-engineered vectors containing the EPO gene have been introduced. The production of EPO by recombinant technology involves expressing an EPO gene through the same processes that occur in a natural cell.

* * *

U.S. Patent 4,703,008, entitled "DNA Sequences Encoding Erythropoietin" (the '008 patent), [was] issued on October 27, 1987, to Dr. Fu–Kuen Lin, an employee of Amgen. The claims of the '008 patent cover purified and isolated DNA sequences encoding erythropoietin and host cells transformed or transfected with a DNA sequence. [In 1983, Dr. Lin "obtained the amino acid sequence for EPO and designed two sets of probes to isolate the EPO gene from a 'genomic library,' a mixture containing most, if not all, of the human genes," making Amgen the first biotechnology company to clone the EPO gene. In July 1984, Dr. Edward Fritch, of GI, isolated the EPO gene using a very similar technique. "GI does not contest that Dr. Lin was the first actually to clone the gene, but, among other things, argues that Dr. Fritsch invented the methodology necessary to clone the gene in December, 1981 before Dr. Lin conceived of it and that by 1983 Dr. Lin's methodology was obvious." Amgen, Inc. v. Chugai Pharmaceutical Co., Ltd., 13 U.S.P.Q.2D (BNA) 1737 (D.Mass. 1989).]

* * *

The first issue we review is whether the district court erred in finding that the claims directed to a purified and isolated DNA sequence encoding human EPO were not invalidated by the work of GI's Dr. Fritsch. Section 102(g) provides in relevant part that:

A person is entitled to a patent unless—(g) before the applicant's invention thereof the invention was made * * * by another who had not abandoned, suppressed, or concealed it. In determining priority of invention there shall be considered not only the respective dates of conception and reduction to practice of the invention, but also the reasonable diligence of one who was first to conceive and last to reduce to practice, from a time prior to conception by the other.

* * *

The invention recited in claim 2 is a "purified and isolated DNA sequence" encoding human EPO. The structure of this DNA sequence was unknown until 1983, when the gene was cloned by Lin; Fritsch was unaware of it until 1984. As Dr. Sadler, an expert for GI, testified in his deposition: "You have to clone it first to get the sequence." In order to design a set of degenerate probes, one of which will hybridize with a particular gene, the amino acid sequence, or a portion thereof, of the protein of interest must be known. Prior to 1983, the amino acid sequence for EPO was uncertain, and in some positions the sequence envisioned was incorrect. Thus, until Fritsch had a complete mental conception of a purified and isolated DNA sequence encoding EPO and a method for its preparation, in which the precise identity of the sequence is envisioned, or in terms of other characteristics sufficient to distinguish it from other genes, all he had was an objective to make an invention which he could not then adequately describe or define.

A gene is a chemical compound, albeit a complex one, and it is well established in our law that conception of a chemical compound requires that the inventor be able to define it so as to distinguish it from other materials, and to describe how to obtain it. Conception does not occur unless one has a mental picture of the structure of the chemical, or is able to define it by its method of preparation, its physical or chemical properties, or whatever characteristics sufficiently distinguish it. It is not sufficient to define it solely by its principal biological property, *e.g.*, encoding human erythropoietin, because an alleged conception having no more specificity than that is simply a wish to know the identity of any material with that biological property. We hold that when an inventor is unable to envision the detailed constitution of a gene so as to distinguish it from other materials, as well as a method for obtaining it, conception has not been achieved until reduction to practice has occurred, *i.e.*, until after the gene has been isolated.

Fritsch had a goal of obtaining the isolated EPO gene, whatever its identity, and even had an idea of a possible method of obtaining it, but he did not conceive a purified and isolated DNA sequence encoding EPO and a viable method for obtaining it until after Lin. It is important to recognize that neither Fritsch nor Lin invented EPO or the EPO gene. The subject matter of claim 2 was the novel *purified and isolated* sequence which codes for EPO, and neither Fritsch nor Lin knew the structure or physical characteristics of it and had a viable method of obtaining that subject matter until it was actually obtained and characterized.

* * *

As expert testimony from both sides indicated, success in cloning the EPO gene was not assured until the gene was in fact isolated and its sequence known. Based on the uncertainties of the method and lack of information concerning the amino acid sequence of the EPO protein, the trial court was correct in concluding that neither party had an adequate conception of the DNA sequence until reduction to practice had been achieved; Lin was first to accomplish that goal.

* * *

CONCLUSION

We conclude that the district court did not err in its findings that claims 2, 4, and 6 of the '008 patent are valid and enforceable and have been infringed by GI * * *.

D. NON–OBVIOUSNESS

AMGEN, INC. v. CHUGAI PHARMACEUTICAL CO., LTD.

927 F.2d 1200 (Fed. Cir. 1991).

LOURIE, J.

[The facts of this case are recited in Section C of this chapter.]

* * *

I. AMGEN'S '008 PATENT (LIN)

* * *

B. Alleged obviousness of the inventions of claims 2, 4, and 6

Claim 2, as noted above, recites a purified and isolated DNA sequence, and claims 4 and 6 are directed to host cells transformed with such a DNA sequence. The district court determined that claims 2, 4, and 6 are not invalid under 35 U.S.C. § 103, concluding that the unique probing and screening method employed by Lin in isolating the EPO gene and the extensive effort required to employ that method made the invention nonobvious over the prior art.

Obviousness under Section 103 is a question of law. The district court stated that one must inquire whether the prior art would have suggested to one of ordinary skill in the art that Lin's probing and screening method should be carried out and would have a reasonable expectation of success, viewed in light of the prior art. "Both the suggestion and the expectation of success must be founded in the prior art, not in applicant's disclosure."

The district court specifically found that, as of 1983, none of the prior art references "suggest[s] that the probing strategy of using two fully-redundant [sic] sets of probes, of relatively high degeneracy [sic], to screen a human genomic library would be likely to succeed in pulling out the gene of interest." While it found that defendants had shown that these procedures were "obvious to try," the references did not show that there was a reasonable expectation of success.

Defendants challenge the district court's determination, arguing that, as of September 1983, one of ordinary skill in the art would have had a reasonable expectation of success in screening a gDNA library by Lin's method in order to obtain EPO. We agree with the district court's conclusion, which was supported by convincing testimony. One witness, Dr. Davies of Biogen, another biotechnology company that had worked on EPO, stated that he could not say whether Biogen scientists would have succeeded in isolating the EPO gene if Biogen had the EPO fragments that were available to Lin in 1983. Dr. Wall, a professor at UCLA, testified that it would have been "difficult" to find the gene in 1983, and that there would have been no more than a fifty percent chance of success. He said, "you couldn't be certain where in the genomic DNA your probe might fall." The court found that no one had successfully screened a genomic library using fully-degenerate probes of such high redundancy as the probes used by Lin. In the face of this and other evidence on both sides of the issue, it concluded that defendants had not shown by clear and convincing evidence that the procedures used by Lin would have been obvious in September 1983. We are not persuaded that the court erred in its decision.

Defendants assert that whether or not it would have been obvious to isolate the human EPO gene from a gDNA library with fully-degenerate probes is immaterial because it was obvious to use the already known monkey EPO gene as a probe. Defendants point out that, in the early 1980s, Biogen did significant work with an EPO cDNA obtained from a baboon, and that they used it as a probe to hybridize with the corresponding gene in a human gDNA library. However, this technique did not succeed until after Lin isolated the EPO gene with his fully-degenerate set of probes.

To support its obviousness assertion, defendants rely upon the testimony of their expert, Dr. Flavell, who testified that the overall homology of baboon DNA and human DNA was "roughly 90 percent". While this testimony indicates that it might have been feasible, perhaps obvious to try, to successfully probe a human gDNA library with a monkey cDNA probe, it does not indicate that the gene could have been identified and isolated with a reasonable likelihood of success. Neither the DNA nucleotide sequence of the human EPO gene nor its exact degree of homology with the monkey EPO gene was known at the time.

Indeed, the district court found that Lin was unsuccessful at probing a human gDNA library with monkey cDNA until after he had isolated the EPO gene by using the fully-degenerate probes. Based on the evidence in the record, the district court found there was no reasonable expectation of success in obtaining the EPO gene by the method that Lin eventually used. While the idea of using the monkey gene to probe for a homologous human gene may have been obvious to try, the realization of that idea would not have been obvious. There were many pitfalls. Hindsight is not a justifiable basis on which to find that ultimate achievement of a long sought and difficult scientific goal was obvious. The district court thoroughly examined the evidence and the testimony. We see no error in its result. Moreover, if the DNA sequence was not obvious, host cells containing such sequence, as claimed in claims 4 and 6, could not have been obvious. We conclude that the district court did not err in holding that the claims of the patent are not invalid under Section 103.

CONCLUSION

We conclude that the district court did not err in its findings that claims 2, 4, and 6 of the '008 Patent are valid and enforceable * * *.

AVENTIS PHARMA DEUTSCHLAND GmbH v. LUPIN, LTD.

499 F.3d 1293 (Fed. Cir. 2007).

LINN, C.J.

This is a patent infringement action concerning the pharmaceutical compound ramipril, which is marketed by King Pharmaceuticals, Inc. ("King") as a blood pressure medication under the name Altace®. Lupin Ltd. and Lupin Pharmaceuticals, Inc. (collectively, "Lupin") appeal from a final judgment of infringement entered by the United States District Court for the Eastern District of Virginia in favor of King and Aventis Pharma Deutschland GmbH ("Aventis"). The district court concluded at summary judgment that Lupin's filing of an Abbreviated New Drug Application (ANDA) for a generic version of ramipril infringed Aventis's U.S. Patent. No. 5,061,722 ("the '722 patent") under the doctrine of equivalents, and concluded after a bench trial that the asserted claims of the '722 patent were not invalid. Lupin appeals from these decisions. Aventis cross-appeals from the district court's decision to dismiss its claim of willful infringement. For the reasons that follow, we conclude that the subject matter of the asserted claims of the '722 patent would have been obvious. Accordingly, we reverse. The cross-appeal and the remaining issues raised by the parties are deemed moot and are not addressed.

I.   BACKGROUND

A.   The Claimed Technology

The patent at issue in this appeal is directed to the pharmaceutical compound ramipril in a formulation "substantially free of other isomers." Ramipril, like many complex organic molecules, is one of a family of stereoisomers. As the district court explained in greater detail in its opinion regarding validity, an isomer of a compound is a separate compound in which each molecule contains the same constituent atoms as the first compound, but with those atoms arranged differently. A stereoisomer is an isomer in which the same atoms are bonded to the same other atoms, but where the configuration of those atoms in three dimensions differs.
* * *

* * *

B.   The Development of Ramipril

Ramipril is one of a family of drugs known as "Angiotensin–Converting Enzyme inhibitors," or "ACE inhibitors." ACE inhibitors inhibit a biochemical pathway that constricts blood vessels and therefore are useful for treating high blood pressure. The earliest ACE inhibitors, dating back to the late 1960s, were based on the venom of the Brazilian Viper, which was known to reduce blood pressure. The active compound isolated from viper venom, known as BPP_{5a}, has six stereocenters, all of which are in the S configuration. Synthetic ACE inhibitors have been developed by making structural modifications to this venom and to successive generations of ACE inhibitors. * * *

Ramipril's immediate predecessor is an ACE inhibitor known as enalapril that was introduced by Merck in 1980. * * *

* * * Ramipril has the same overall structure as enalapril, with one distinction: where ramipril has two linked five-sided carbon rings (a "5, 5 fused ring system") * * *. The addition of the second ring gives rise to two more stereocenters than are present in enalapril; thus, ramipril has the same three stereocenters as enalapril, plus two new ones that span the fused ring system and are therefore known as "bridgehead" carbons, for a total of five as discussed above.

II. DISCUSSION

* * *

B. Obviousness of Claims 1 and 2

We turn to the question of obviousness. "Obviousness is a question of law, reviewed *de novo,* based upon underlying factual questions which are reviewed for clear error following a bench trial." The key question is whether the 5(S) stereoisomer of ramipril, in a form substantially free of other isomers, would have been obvious over the prior art listed above to one of ordinary skill in the art at the time of the '722 patent's priority date. See 35 U.S.C. § 103(a). * * *

The district court held that Lupin failed to meet its burden of proof by clear and convincing evidence that a person of ordinary skill in the art would have been motivated to purify 5(S) ramipril into a composition substantially free of other isomers. *Invalidity Opinion* at 74–75. The district court saw this as a close case based principally on the absence of a clear and convincing showing of motivation. Since the date of that decision, however, the Supreme Court decided KSR International Co. v. Teleflex Inc., [550 U.S. 398 (2007)], which counsels against applying the "teaching, suggestion, or motivation" ("TSM") test as a "rigid and mandatory formula[ ]." It remains necessary to show " 'some articulated reasoning with some rational underpinning to support the legal conclusion of obviousness,' "but such reasoning "need not seek out precise teachings directed to the specific subject matter of the challenged claim." Requiring an explicit teaching to purify the 5(S) stereoisomer from a mixture in which it is the active ingredient is precisely the sort of rigid application of the TSM test that was criticized in *KSR*.

* * *

The analysis is similar where, as here, a claimed composition is a purified form of a mixture that existed in the prior art. Such a purified compound is not always prima facie obvious over the mixture; for example, it may not be known that the purified compound is present in or an active ingredient of the mixture, or the state of the art may be such that discovering how to perform the purification is an invention of patentable weight in itself. However, if it is known that some desirable property of a mixture derives in whole or in part from a particular one of its components, or if the prior art would provide a person of ordinary skill in the art with reason to believe that this is so, the purified compound is prima facie obvious over the mixture even without an explicit teaching that the ingredient should be concentrated or purified. Ordinarily, one expects a concentrated or purified ingredient to retain the same properties it exhibited in a mixture, and for those properties to be amplified when the ingredient is concentrated or purified; isolation of interesting compounds is a mainstay of the chemist's art. If it is known how to perform such an isolation, doing so "is likely the product not of innovation but of ordinary skill and common sense." KSR [International Co. v. Teleflex Inc., 550 U.S. 398, 420 (2007)].

* * *

In sum, we hold that claims 1 and 2 of the '722 patent, which cover the 5(S) stereoisomer of ramipril in a composition substantially free of other isomers, are invalid under 35 U.S.C. § 103 over the SCH 31925 mixture, the '944 patent, and the enalapril references in the prior art.

* * *

III.   CONCLUSION

Having concluded that all asserted claims of the '722 patent are invalid as obvious, we need not reach Lupin's remaining arguments in favor of reversal. Likewise, Aventis's cross-appeal is moot. Because Lupin is entitled to entry of judgment in its favor, the judgment of the district court is

Reversed.

IN RE KUBIN

561 F.3d 1351 (Fed. Cir. 2009).

RADER, C.J.

Marek Kubin and Raymond Goodwin ("appellants") appeal from a decision of the Board of Patent Appeals and Interferences (the "Board") rejecting the claims of U.S. Patent Application Serial No. 09/667,859 ("'859 Application") as obvious under 35 U.S.C. § 103(a) and invalid under 35 U.S.C. § 112 ¶ 1 for lack of written description. Ex parte Kubin, No. 2007–0819, 83 U.S.P.Q.2d 1410 (B.P.A.I.2007) ("*Board Decision*"). Because the Board correctly determined that appellants' claims are unpatentably obvious, this court affirms.

I.

This case presents a claim to a classic biotechnology invention-the isolation and sequencing of a human gene that encodes a particular domain of a protein. * * * Specifically, appellants claim DNA molecules ("polynucleotides") encoding a protein ("polypeptide") known as the Natural Killer Cell Activation Inducing Ligand ("NAIL").

* * *

* * * Representative claim 73 of appellants' application claims the DNA that encodes the CD48–binding region of NAIL proteins:

> 73. An isolated nucleic acid molecule comprising a polynucleotide encoding a polypeptide at least 80% identical to amino acids 22–221 of SEQ ID NO: 2, wherein the polypeptide binds CD48.

In other words, appellants claim a genus of isolated polynucleotides encoding a protein that binds CD48 and is at least 80% identical to amino acids 22–221 of SEQ ID NO: 2—the disclosed amino acid sequence for the CD48–binding region of NAIL.

* * *

II.

The Board rejected appellants' claims as invalid under both § 103 and § 112. * * *

* * *

Regarding obviousness, the Board rejected appellants' claims over the combined teachings of U.S. Patent No. 5,688,690 ("Valiante") and Joseph Sambrook et al., Molecular Cloning: A Laboratory Manual 43–84 (2d ed.1989) ("Sambrook"). The Board also considered, but found to be cumulative to Valiante and Sambrook, Porunelloor Mathew et al., Cloning and Characterization of the 2B4 Gene Encoding a Molecule Associated with Non–MHC–Restricted Killing Mediated by Activated Natural Killer Cells and T Cells, 151 J. Immunology 5328–37 (1993) ("Mathew").

* * *

The Board found as a factual matter that appellants used conventional techniques "such as those outlined in Sambrook" to isolate and sequence the gene that codes for NAIL. The Board also found that appellants' claimed DNA sequence is "isolated from a cDNA library ... using the commercial monoclonal antibody C1.7 ... disclosed by Valiante." With regard to the amino acid sequence referred to as SEQ ID NO:2, the Board found that

> Valiante's disclosure of the polypeptide p38, and a detailed method of isolating its DNA, including disclosure of a specific probe to do so, i.e., mAb C1.7, established Valiante's possession of p38's amino acid sequence and provided a reasonable expectation of success in obtaining a polynucleotide encoding p38, a polynucleotide within the scope of Appellants' claim 73.

Because of NAIL's important role in the human immune response, the Board further found that "one of ordinary skill in the art would have recognized the value of isolating NAIL cDNA, and would have been motivated to apply conventional methodologies, such as those disclosed in Sambrook and utilized in Valiante, to do so.''

Based on these factual findings, the Board turned to the legal question of obviousness under § 103. Invoking the Supreme Court's decision in KSR International Co. v. Teleflex Inc., 550 U.S. 398 (2007), the Board concluded that appellants' claim was '' 'the product not of innovation but of ordinary skill and common sense,' leading us to conclude NAIL cDNA is not patentable as it would have been obvious to isolate it.''

* * *

III.

This court reviews the Board's factual findings for lack of substantial evidence, and its legal conclusions without deference.

Obviousness is a question of law based on underlying findings of fact. An analysis of obviousness must be based on several factual inquiries: (1) the scope and content of the prior art; (2) the differences between the prior art and the claims at issue; (3) the level of ordinary skill in the art at the time the invention was made; and (4) objective evidence of nonobviousness, if any. The teachings of a prior art reference are underlying factual questions in the obviousness inquiry.

A.

* * * Stated directly, the record shows repeatedly that Valiante's Example 12 produces for any person of ordinary skill in this art the claimed polynucleotide.

More to the point, however, any putative difference in Valiante's/Sambrook's and appellants' *processes* does not directly address the obviousness of representative claim 73, which claims a genus of *polynucleotides*. The difference between Valiante's and the application's techniques might be directly relevant to obviousness in this case if Kubin and Goodwin had claimed a method of DNA cloning or isolation. But they did not. Appellants claim a gene sequence. Accordingly, the obviousness inquiry requires this court to review the Board's decision that the claimed sequence, not appellants' unclaimed cloning technique, is obvious in light of the abundant prior art.

In any event, this court determines that the Board had substantial evidence to conclude that appellants used conventional techniques, as taught in Valiante and Sambrook, to isolate a gene sequence for NAIL.
* * *

* * *

* * * Because this court sustains, under substantial evidence review, the Board's finding that Valiante's p38 is the same protein as appellant's NAIL, Valiante's teaching to obtain cDNA encoding p38 also necessarily teaches one to obtain cDNA of NAIL that exhibits the CD48 binding property.

B.

The instant case also requires this court to consider the Board's application of this court's early assessment of obviousness in the context of classical biotechnological inventions, specifically In re Deuel, 51 F.3d 1552 (Fed. Cir. 1995). In *Deuel*, this court reversed the Board's conclusion that a prior art reference teaching a method of gene cloning, together with a reference disclosing a partial amino acid sequence of a protein, rendered DNA molecules encoding the protein obvious. In reversing the Board, this court in *Deuel* held that "knowledge of a protein does not give one a conception of a particular DNA encoding it." Id. Further, this court stated that "obvious to try" is an inappropriate test for obviousness.

* * * Thus, this court must examine *Deuel's* effect on the Board's conclusion that Valiante's teaching of the NAIL protein, combined with Valiante's/Sambrook's teaching of a method to isolate the gene sequence that codes for NAIL, renders claim 73 obvious.

With regard to *Deuel*, the Board addressed directly its application in this case. In particular, the Board observed that the Supreme Court in *KSR* cast doubts on this court's application of the "obvious to try" doctrine:

> To the extent *Deuel* is considered relevant to this case, we note the Supreme Court recently cast doubt on the viability of *Deuel* to the extent the Federal Circuit rejected an "obvious to try" test. See KSR Int'l Co. v. Teleflex Inc., [550 U.S. 398 (2007)] (citing Deuel, 51 F.3d at 1559). Under *KSR*, it's now apparent "obvious to try" may be an appropriate test in more situations than we previously contemplated.

Insofar as *Deuel* implies the obviousness inquiry cannot consider that the combination of the claim's constituent elements was "obvious to try," the Supreme Court in *KSR* unambiguously discredited that holding. In fact, the Supreme Court expressly invoked *Deuel* as a source of the discredited "obvious to try" doctrine.

The Supreme Court repudiated as "error" the *Deuel* restriction on the ability of a skilled artisan to combine elements within the scope of the prior art:

> The same constricted analysis led the Court of Appeals to conclude, in error, that a patent claim cannot be proved obvious merely by showing that the combination of elements was "obvious to try." When there is a design need or market pressure to solve a problem and there are a finite number of identified, predictable solutions, a person of ordinary skill has good reason to pursue the known options within his or her technical grasp. If this leads to the anticipated success, it is likely the product not of innovation but of ordinary skill and common sense. In that instance *the fact that a combination was obvious to try might show that it was obvious under § 103.*

The Supreme Court's admonition against a formalistic approach to obviousness in this context actually resurrects this court's own wisdom in In re O'Farrell [853 F.2d 894 (Fed. Cir. 1988)], which predates the *Deuel* decision by some seven years. * * *

To differentiate between proper and improper applications of "obvious to try," this court outlined two classes of situations where "obvious to try" is erroneously equated with obviousness under § 103. In the first class of cases,

> what would have been "obvious to try" would have been to vary all parameters or try each of numerous possible choices until one possibly arrived at a successful result, where the prior art gave either no indication of which parameters were critical or no direction as to which of many possible choices is likely to be successful.

Id. In such circumstances, where a defendant merely throws metaphorical darts at a board filled with combinatorial prior art possibilities, courts should not succumb to hindsight claims of obviousness. The inverse of this proposition is succinctly encapsulated by the Supreme Court's statement in *KSR* that where a skilled artisan merely pursues "known options" from a "finite number of identified, predictable solutions," obviousness under § 103 arises.

> The second class of *O'Farrell's* impermissible "obvious to try" situations occurs where what was "obvious to try" was to explore a new technology or general approach that seemed to be a promising field of experimentation, where the prior art gave only general guidance as to the particular form of the claimed invention or how to achieve it.

853 F.2d at 905. Again, *KSR* affirmed the logical inverse of this statement by stating that § 103 bars patentability unless "the improvement is more than the predictable use of prior art elements according to their established functions."

This court in *O'Farrell* * * * [r]esponding to concerns about uncertainty in the prior art influencing the purported success of the claimed combination, * * * stated: "[o]bviousness does not require absolute predictability of success ... *all that is required is a reasonable expectation of success.*" The Supreme Court in *KSR* reinvigorated this perceptive analysis.

* * *

This court also declines to cabin *KSR* to the "predictable arts" (as opposed to the "unpredictable art" of biotechnology). In fact, this record shows that one of skill in this advanced art would find these claimed "results" profoundly "predictable." The record shows the well-known and reliable nature of the cloning and sequencing techniques in the prior art, not to mention the readily knowable and obtainable structure of an identified protein. Therefore this court cannot deem irrelevant the ease and predictability of cloning the gene that codes for that protein. This court cannot, in the face of *KSR*, cling to formalistic rules for obviousness, customize its legal tests for specific scientific fields in ways that deem entire classes of prior art teachings irrelevant, or discount the significant abilities of artisans of ordinary skill in an advanced area of art. * * *

The record in this case shows that Valiante did not explicitly supply an amino acid sequence for NAIL or a polynucleotide sequence for the NAIL gene. In that sense, Kubin and Goodwin's disclosure represents some minor advance in the art. But "[g]ranting patent protection to advances that would occur in the ordinary course without real innovation retards progress." KSR, 550 U.S. at 419, "Were it otherwise patents might stifle, rather than promote, the progress of useful arts." * * *

IV.

For the reasons stated above, the Board did not err in finding appellants' claims obvious as a matter of law. Thus, this court need not address appellants' contention that the Board erred in finding its claims invalid under § 112 ¶ 1. Accordingly, this court affirms the decision of the Board.

Affirmed.

E. ENABLEMENT

AMGEN, INC. v. CHUGAI PHARMACEUTICAL CO., LTD.

927 F.2d 1200 (Fed.Cir.1991).

LOURIE, J.

[The facts of this case are recited in Section C of this chapter.]

* * *

D. *Enablement of claims 7, 8, 23–27, and 29*

Amgen argues that the district court's holding that GI "provided clear and convincing evidence that the patent specification is insufficient to enable one of ordinary skill in the art to make and use the invention claimed in claim 7 of the '008 patent without undue experimentation" constituted legal error. Amgen specifically argues that the district court erred because it "did not properly address the factors which this court has held must be considered in determining lack of enablement based on assertion of undue experimentation," citing this court's decision in In re Wands, 858 F.2d [731,] 737 [(Fed.Cir. 1988)].

Claim 7 is a generic claim, covering all possible DNA sequences that will encode any polypeptide having an amino acid sequence "sufficiently duplicative" of EPO to possess the property of increasing production of red blood cells. As claims 8, 23–27, and 29, dependent on claim 7, are not separately argued, and are of similar scope, they stand or fall with claim 7.

* * *

That some experimentation is necessary does not constitute a lack of enablement; the amount of experimentation, however, must not be unduly extensive. The essential question here is whether the scope of enablement of claim 7 is as broad as the scope of the claim.

* * *

Moreover, it is not necessary that a patent applicant test all the embodiments of his invention; what is necessary is that he provide a disclosure sufficient to enable one skilled in the art to carry out the invention commensurate with the scope of his claims. For DNA sequences, that means disclosing how to make and use enough sequences to justify grant of the claims sought. Amgen has not done that here * * *. What is relevant depends on the facts, and the facts here are that Amgen has not enabled preparation of DNA sequences sufficient to support its all-encompassing claims.

It is well established that a patent applicant is entitled to claim his invention generically, when he describes it sufficiently to meet the requirements of Section 112. Here, however, despite extensive statements in the specification concerning all the analogs of the EPO gene that can be made, there is little enabling disclosure of particular analogs and how to make them. Details for preparing only a few EPO analog genes are disclosed. Amgen argues that this is sufficient to support its claims; we disagree. This "disclosure" might well justify a generic claim encompassing these and similar analogs, but it represents inadequate support for Amgen's desire to claim all EPO gene analogs. There may be many other genetic sequences that code for EPO-type products. Amgen has told how to make and use only a few of them and is therefore not entitled to claim all of them.

In affirming the district court's invalidation of claims 7, 8, 23–27, and 29 under Section 112, we do not intend to imply that generic claims to genetic sequences cannot be valid where they are of a scope appropriate to the invention disclosed by an applicant. That is not the case here, where Amgen has claimed every possible analog of a gene containing about 4,000 nucleotides, with a disclosure only of how to make EPO and a very few analogs.

* * *

Considering the structural complexity of the EPO gene, the manifold possibilities for change in its structure, with attendant uncertainty as to what utility will be possessed by these analogs, we consider that more is needed concerning identifying the various analogs that are within the scope of the claim, methods for making them, and structural requirements for producing compounds with EPO-like activity. It is not sufficient, having made the gene and a handful of analogs whose activity has not been clearly ascertained, to claim all possible genetic sequences that have EPO-like activity. Under the circumstances, we find no error in the court's conclusion that the generic DNA sequence claims are invalid under Section 112.

CONCLUSION

We conclude that the district court did not err in its findings * * * that claims 7, 8, 23–27, and 29 of the '008 patent are invalid * * *.

NOTES AND QUESTIONS

1.   To obtain a patent, the inventor must show that the claimed invention is novel, nonobvious, and useful. Products of nature and formulas cannot be patented. Why have genetic sequences been found to be patentable?

2.   Does a claim to a gene sequence coding for a known protein (with or without a known sequence) satisfy the obviousness test after *KSR* and *Kubin*? See, for example, claim 1 of U.S. Patent No. 5,747,282:

1.   An isolated DNA coding for a BRCA1 polypeptide, said polypeptide having the amino acid sequence set forth in SEQ ID NO:2.

Would the claims to the gene sequences at issue in Amgen, Inc. v. Chugai Pharmaceutical Co., Ltd., Amgen v. Chugai, 927 F.2d 1200 (Fed. Cir. 1991) be allowed today by USPTO?

3.   Does *Aventis* call into question the logic that genes are patentable when they are "isolated and purified"? Under the U.S. Supreme Court's decision in *KSR* (discussed in *Aventis*), are gene sequences "obvious"?

4.   Can patent applicants credibly argue that they have "isolated and purified" the gene? In some instances, the patent applicant merely patents a gene mutation exactly as it occurs in nature. In others, the patent applicant only removes the non-coding region, but the remaining coding sequence still has the same effect and function as the naturally-occurring gene. Does isolating genes from their natural surroundings or purifying them from other cellular components sufficiently transform the genes from the original product of nature? Is "isolation" and "purification" enough, according to U.S. Supreme Court precedents?

5.   If a patent holder did not want the gene sequence at issue to be tested for prenatally due to opposition to abortion, how would this restriction be effectuated? Is it legal under patent law? If a woman wanted to challenge the decision because she planned to abort a fetus with a propensity to develop breast cancer, would she have any legal grounds to challenge the decision?

6.   A 2005 study that examined 1167 claims in 74 patents covering genetic materials found that 38% of claims failed to meet the requirements for patentability as set forth by the USPTO and the courts. Problems identified include written description, enablement and utility, definiteness, and novelty and nonobviousness. Jordan Paradise, Lori Andrews, and Timothy Holbrook, Patents on Human Genes: An Analysis of Scope and Claims, 307 Science 1566 (2005). What can be done to ensure that patent applications being granted in the USPTO are meeting the standards for patentability as set forth by that agency and the courts? Should patent examiners be required to have special-

ized training or degrees? Would some type of procedure allowing a third party to challenge a granted patent immediately after issuance be of any assistance?

IV. RESEARCH EXEMPTIONS

MADEY v. DUKE UNIVERSITY

307 F.3d 1351 (Fed. Cir. 2002).

GAJARSA, J.

Dr. John M.J. Madey ("Madey") appeals from a judgment of the United States District Court for the Middle District of North Carolina. Madey sued Duke University ("Duke"), bringing claims of patent infringement and various other federal and state law claims. Pursuant to a motion filed by Duke under Federal Rule of Civil Procedure ("FRCP") 12(b)(1), the district court dismissed-in-part certain patent infringement claims and dismissed certain other claims. Madey v. Duke Univ., 1999 U.S. Dist. LEXIS 21379, No. 1:97CV1170, slip op. at 12–14, 38–40 (M.D.N.C. Dec. 1, 1999) ("Dismissal Opinion"). After discovery, the district court granted summary judgment in favor of Duke on the remaining claims. For a first set of alleged infringing acts, it held that the experimental use defense applied to Duke's use of Madey's patented laser technology. For a second set of alleged infringing acts, it held that Duke was not the infringing party because a third-party owned and controlled the allegedly infringing laser equipment. Madey v. Duke Univ., No. 1:97CV1170, slip op. at 12–15, 18, 20 (M.D.N.C. June 15, 2001) ("Summary Judgment Opinion").

* * *

In the mid–1980s Madey was a tenured research professor at Stanford University. At Stanford, he had an innovative laser research program, which was highly regarded in the scientific community. An opportunity arose for Madey to consider leaving Stanford and take a tenured position at Duke. Duke recruited Madey, and in 1988 he left Stanford for a position in Duke's physics department. In 1989 Madey moved his free electron laser ("FEL") research lab from Stanford to Duke. The FEL lab contained substantial equipment, requiring Duke to build an addition to its physics building to house the lab. In addition, during his time at Stanford, Madey had obtained sole ownership of two patents practiced by some of the equipment in the FEL lab.

At Duke, Madey served for almost a decade as director of the FEL lab. During that time the lab continued to achieve success in both research funding and scientific breakthroughs. However, a dispute arose between Madey and Duke. Duke contends that, despite his scientific prowess, Madey ineffectively managed the lab. Madey contends that Duke sought to use the lab's equipment for research areas outside the allocated scope of certain government funding, and that when he objected, Duke sought to remove him as lab director. Duke eventually did remove Madey as director of the lab in 1997. The removal is not at issue in this appeal, however, it is the genesis of this unique patent infringement case. As a result of the removal, Madey resigned from Duke in 1998. Duke, however, continued to operate some of the equipment in the lab. Madey then sued Duke for patent infringement of his two patents, and brought a variety of other claims.

* * *

The district court acknowledged a common law "exception" for patent infringement liability for uses that, in the district court's words, are "solely for research, academic or experimental purposes." The district court recognized the debate over the scope of the experimental use defense, but cited this court's opinion in Embrex, Inc. v. Service Engineering Corp., 216 F.3d 1343, 1349, 55 U.S.P.Q.2D (BNA) 1161, 1163 (Fed. Cir. 2000) to hold that the defense was viable for experimental, non-profit purposes.

* * *

Before the district court, Madey argued that Duke's research in its FEL lab was commercial in character and intent. Id. Madey relied on Pitcairn v. United States, 212 Ct. Cl. 168, 547 F.2d 1106, 192 U.S.P.Q. (BNA) 612 (Ct. Cl. 1976), where the government used patented rotor structures and control systems for a helicopter to test the "lifting ability" and other attributes of the patented technology. The Pitcairn court held that the helicopters were not built solely for experimental purposes because they were also built to benefit the government in its legitimate business. Based on language in Duke's patent policy, Madey argues that Duke is in the business of "obtaining grants and developing possible commercial applications for the fruits of its 'academic research.' "

The district court rejected Madey's argument, relying on another statement in the preamble of the Duke patent policy which stated that Duke was "dedicated to teaching, research, and the expansion of knowledge ... [and] does not undertake research or development work principally for the purpose of developing patents and commercial applications." The district court reasoned that these statements from the patent policy refute any contention that Duke is "in the business" of developing technology for commercial applications. Id. According to the district court, Madey's "evidence" was mere speculation, and thus Madey did not meet his burden of proof to create a genuine issue of material fact. The court went on to state that "without more concrete evidence to rebut [Duke's] stated purpose with respect to its research in the FEL lab, Plaintiff has failed to meet its burden of establishing patent infringement by a preponderance of the evidence."

* * *

Madey argues, and we agree, that the district court had an overly broad conception of the very narrow and strictly limited experimental use defense. The district court stated that the experimental use defense inoculated uses that "were solely for research, academic, or experimental purposes," and that the defense covered use that "is made for experimental, non-profit purposes only." Id. at 9. Both formulations are too broad and stand in sharp contrast to our admonitions in Embrex and Roche that the experimental use defense is very narrow and strictly limited. In Embrex, we followed the teachings of Roche and Pitcairn to hold that the defense was very narrow and limited to actions performed "for amusement, to satisfy idle curiosity, or for strictly philosophical inquiry." Embrex, 216 F.3d at 1349, 55 U.S.P.Q.2D (BNA) at 1163. Further, use does not qualify for the experimental use defense when it is undertaken in the "guise of scientific inquiry" but has "definite, cognizable, and not insubstantial commercial purposes." Id. (quoting Roche, 733 F.2d at 863, 221 U.S.P.Q. (BNA) at 941). The concurring opinion in Embrex expresses a similar view: use is disqualified from the defense if it has the "slightest commercial implication." 216 F.3d at 1353, 55 U.S.P.Q.2D (BNA) at 1166. Moreover, use in keeping with the legitimate business of the alleged infringer does not qualify for the experimental use defense. See Pitcairn, 547 F.2d at 1125–26, 192 U.S.P.Q. (BNA) at 625. The district court supported its conclusion with a citation to Ruth v. Stearns–Roger Mfg. Co., 13 F. Supp. 697, 713 (D. Colo. 1935), a case that is not binding precedent for this court.

The Ruth case represents the conceptual dilemma that may have led the district court astray. Cases evaluating the experimental use defense are few, and those involving non-profit, educational alleged infringers are even fewer. In Ruth, the court concluded that a manufacturer of equipment covered by patents was not liable for contributory infringement because the end-user purchaser was the Colorado School of Mines, which used the equipment in furtherance of its educational purpose. Thus, the combination of apparent lack of commerciality, with the non-profit status of an educational institution, prompted the court in Ruth, without any detailed analysis of the character, nature and effect of the use, to hold that the experimental use defense applied. This is not consistent with the binding precedent of our case law postulated by *Embrex, Roche* and *Pitcairn*.

Our precedent clearly does not immunize use that is in any way commercial in nature. Similarly, our precedent does not immunize any conduct that is in keeping with the alleged infringer's legitimate business, regardless of commercial implications. For example, major research universities, such as Duke, often sanction and fund research projects with arguably no commercial application whatsoever. However, these projects unmistakably further the institution's legitimate business objectives, including educating and enlightening students and faculty participating in these projects. These projects also serve, for example, to increase the status of the institution and lure lucrative research grants, students and faculty.

In short, regardless of whether a particular institution or entity is engaged in an endeavor for commercial gain, so long as the act is in

furtherance of the alleged infringer's legitimate business and is not solely
for amusement, to satisfy idle curiosity, or for strictly philosophical
inquiry, the act does not qualify for the very narrow and strictly limited
experimental use defense. Moreover, the profit or non-profit status of the
user is not determinative.

In the present case, the district court attached too great a weight to
the non-profit, educational status of Duke, effectively suppressing the fact
that Duke's acts appear to be in accordance with any reasonable interpretation of Duke's legitimate business objectives.[7] On remand, the district
court will have to significantly narrow and limit its conception of the
experimental use defense. The correct focus should not be on the non-
profit status of Duke but on the legitimate business Duke is involved in
and whether or not the use was solely for amusement, to satisfy idle
curiosity, or for strictly philosophical inquiry.

NOTES AND QUESTIONS

1. Based on the description of the experimental use defense in *Madey*,
would a research project at an educational institution ever qualify? Aren't
educational institutions, by their very nature, always "educating and enlightening" students and faculty involved in research projects, even if such
projects are done solely for amusement? At what point does a research project
done for amusement become something more that no longer qualifies for the
experimental use defense?

2. What are the pros and cons of a general research exemption to patent
law? How does it compare to the "fair use" exemption in copyright law?

3. Many countries, including most European nations and Japan, China,
Canada, India, and Israel, have statutory research exemptions. The EU
members' exemptions are based on proposed Article 27 of the Community
Patent Convention (1989), which stated in part that "The rights conferred by
a Community patent shall not extend to * * * (b) acts done for experimental
purposes relating to the subject-matter of the patented invention." The
United States has a very limited research exemption in 35 U.S.C. § 271 (e)(1),
which exempts "uses reasonable related to the development and submission of
information under a Federal law which regulates the manufacture, use, or
sale of drugs or veterinary biological products." See also Jordan Paradise and
Christopher Janson, Decoding the Research Exemption, 7 Nature Reviews
148, 150 (2006). Considering the *Madey* case, does genetic research fall within
the statutory or common law research exemptions in the U.S.?

---

7. Duke's patent and licensing policy may support its primary function as an educational
institution. See Duke University Policy on Inventions, Patents, and Technology Transfer (1996),
available   at   [http://olv.duke.edu/Inventors/PoliciesAndProcedures/policy_on_inventions.pdf].
Duke, however, like other major research institutions of higher learning, is not shy in pursuing
an aggressive patent licensing program from which it derives a not insubstantial revenue stream.

V. LICENSING AGREEMENTS

[This is an excerpt from the agreement between the University of Wisconsin and the federal Department of Health and Human Services to allow federally-funded researchers to use patented embryonic cell lines.]

MEMORANDUM OF UNDERSTANDING BETWEEN WICELL RESEARCH INSTITUTE, INC. AND PUBLIC HEALTH SERVICE U.S. DEPARTMENT OF HEALTH AND HUMAN SERVICES

http://ott.od.nih.gov/pdfs/WiCellMOUnonhuman.pdf

* * *

WHEREAS certain technologies and materials concerning primate embryonic stem cells and their cultivation claimed in U.S. Patent 5,843,780, U.S. Patent 6,200,806, U.S. Patent Application 09/522,030 and corresponding U.S. or foreign patent rights and any patents granted on any divisional and continuation applications of any type but only to the extent it claims an invention claimed in a patent application listed herein ("Wisconsin Patent Rights") have usefulness in basic research conducted or funded by PHS as well as potential utility for commercial applications; and

WHEREAS specific human embryonic stem cell line materials, their unmodified and undifferentiated progeny or derivatives ("Wisconsin Materials") have been derived consistent with the Presidential Statement of August 9, 2001 from the research efforts of James A. Thomson of the University of Wisconsin–Madison working alone or with other investigators; and

WHEREAS PHS has a basic mission on behalf of the U.S. Government for the conduct and support of health research performed at its own facilities or through funding agreements to other institutions ("Recipient Institutions"); and

WHEREAS PHS funded primate research studies at the University of Wisconsin–Madison that led to certain discoveries claimed in Wisconsin Patent Rights and therefore the Government has certain use and other rights to the intellectual property comprising the Wisconsin Patent Rights granted by law and regulation; and

WHEREAS Wisconsin Materials were made using solely private funds and are the proprietary, tangible property of WiCell and, as such, their ownership is not subject to the rights and obligations granted the Government in the Wisconsin Patent Rights; and

WHEREAS the Wisconsin Alumni Research Foundation of the University of Wisconsin–Madison ("WARF") and WiCell have a mission to serve the public good and desire to serve the public interest by making the Wisconsin Materials and the Wisconsin Patent Rights widely available to PHS and other academic researchers; and

* * *

NOW, THEREFORE, the Parties hereby agree to the following terms and conditions regarding use of Wisconsin Materials or Wisconsin Patent

Rights for research conducted either by PHS or on behalf of PHS by its contractors:

* * *

(2) The Parties agree that Wisconsin Materials are to be made available by WiCell for use in PHS biomedical research programs, either by PHS or on behalf of PHS by its contractors. For purposes of transferring Wisconsin Materials to PHS or PHS contractors, WiCell agrees to utilize the Simple Letter Agreement For The Transfer of Materials including the following conditions:

(a) Wisconsin Materials are the property of WiCell and are being made available to investigators in the PHS research community as a service by WiCell. Ownership of Wisconsin Materials shall remain with WiCell.

(b) Wisconsin Materials are not to be used for diagnostic or therapeutic purposes.

(c) Wisconsin Materials may only be used in compliance with all applicable statutes, regulations and guidelines relating to their handling or use. Specifically, PHS agrees that its research program will exclude: (i) the mixing of Wisconsin Materials with an intact embryo, either human or non-human; (ii) implanting Wisconsin Materials or products of Materials in a uterus; and (iii) attempting to make whole embryos with Wisconsin Materials by any method.

* * *

(d) The use of Wisconsin Materials shall be for teaching or non-commercial research purposes only. As used herein, non-commercial research purposes specifically excludes sponsored research wherein the sponsor receives a right whether actual or contingent to the results of the sponsored research, other than a grant for non-commercial research purposes to the sponsor. The Wisconsin Materials may not be used for commercial purposes or the direct benefit of research sponsor, except as such research sponsor is permitted to use Wisconsin Materials under a separate written agreement with WiCell or WARF. Specifically, Wisconsin Materials shall not be used in a PHS research program where rights (either actual or contingent) have already been granted to a research sponsor who does not have a separate written agreement with WiCell permitting such commercial use of Wisconsin Materials.

(e) Wisconsin Materials may not be transferred by PHS or its contractors to third parties without the written consent of WiCell.

(f) PHS agrees to acknowledge the source of Wisconsin Materials in any publications or other disclosures reporting their use.

* * *

(h) The Parties recognize that Wisconsin Materials may be used in the PHS research program to make discoveries of different materials ("PHS Materials") which themselves may eventually be the basis of commercial products that benefit public health. Any grant of rights to Wisconsin Materials or Wisconsin Patent Rights that may be needed by a third party for commercialization of PHS Materials shall be done by a separate written agreement with WiCell permitting such use of Wisconsin Materials or Wisconsin Patent Rights under terms not less favorable than other similar commercial licenses to the extent such rights are available.

(i) Any Wisconsin Materials delivered pursuant to this Agreement are understood to be experimental in nature and may have hazardous properties. WiCell makes no representations and extends no warranties of any kind, either expressed or implied. There are no express or implied warranties of merchantability for fitness for a particular purpose, or that the use of the Wisconsin Materials will not infringe any patent, copyright, trademark or other proprietary rights. Unless prohibited by law, PHS assumes all liability for claims for damages which may arise from the use, storage, handling or disposal of Wisconsin Materials except that, to the extent permitted by law, WiCell shall be liable to PHS when the damage is caused by the gross negligence or willful misconduct of WiCell.

(j) A transmittal fee may be requested by WiCell to cover its preparation and distribution costs for samples of Wisconsin Materials requested by PHS. Such fees will be the responsibility of the requesting PHS laboratory and are not expected to exceed Five Thousand Dollars ($5,000) or as specified in the appropriate schedule of a U.S. Government procurement accompanying the PHS Simple Letter Agreement for the Transfer of Materials.

(3) Upon WiCell's written request, PHS agrees to provide without cost reasonable quantities of any PHS Materials that it makes in the course of its research program to WiCell for research purposes only after PHS has publicly disclosed or reasonably characterized such PHS Materials. For PHS Patent Rights, PHS also agrees to continue its current policy of retaining the right to grant research licenses to either non-profit or for-profit institutions.

* * *

(6) Nothing contained herein shall be considered to be the grant of a commercial license or right under the Wisconsin Patent Rights or to Wisconsin Materials. Furthermore, nothing contained herein shall be construed to be a waiver of WiCell's patent rights under the Wisconsin Patent Rights or WiCell's property rights in Wisconsin Materials.

NOTES AND QUESTIONS

1. In what way does the agreement limit the type of research a scientist can undertake with the embryo stem cells that are subject to the University of Wisconsin patent?

2. If a federally-funded researcher developed a therapeutic line of heart cells based on the embryo stem cells provided by the University of Wisconsin, could the researcher sell or patent the heart cells?

VI. CONCERNS ABOUT THE PATENTING OF GENES

MICHAEL A. HELLER & REBECCA S. EISENBERG, CAN PATENTS DETER INNOVATION? THE ANTICOMMONS IN BIOMEDICAL RESEARCH

280 Science 698, 698–701 (1998).

The "tragedy of the commons" metaphor helps explain why people overuse shared resources. However, the recent proliferation of intellectual property rights in biomedical research suggests a different tragedy, an "anticommons" in which people underuse scarce resources because too many owners can block each other.

* * *

Thirty years ago in Science, Garrett Hardin introduced the metaphor "tragedy of the commons" to help explain overpopulation, air pollution, and species extinction. People often overuse resources they own in common because they have no incentive to conserve. Today, Hardin's metaphor is central to debates in economics, law, and science and is a powerful justification for privatizing commons property. Although the metaphor highlights the cost of overuse when governments allow too many people to use a scarce resource, it overlooks the possibility of underuse when governments give too many people rights to exclude others. Privatization can solve one tragedy but cause another.

Since Hardin's article appeared, biomedical research has been moving from a commons model toward a privatization model. Under the commons model, the federal government sponsored premarket or "upstream" research and encouraged broad dissemination of results in the public domain. Unpatented biomedical discoveries were freely incorporated in "downstream" products for diagnosing and treating disease. In 1980, in an effort to promote commercial development of new technologies, Congress began encouraging universities and other institutions to patent discoveries arising from federally supported research and development and to transfer their technology to the private sector. Supporters applaud the resulting increase in patent filings and private investment, whereas critics fear deterioration in the culture of upstream research.

* * *

How a Biomedical Anticommons May Arise

Current examples in biomedical research demonstrate two mechanisms by which a government might inadvertently create an anticommons: either by creating too many concurrent fragments of intellectual property rights in potential future products or by permitting too many upstream patent owners to stack licenses on top of the future discoveries of downstream users.

* * *

A proliferation of patents on individual [gene] fragments held by different owners seems inevitably to require costly future transactions to bundle licenses together before a firm can have an effective right to develop these products.

* * *

Stacking licenses. The use of reach-through license agreements (RTLAs) on patented research tools illustrates another path by which an anticommons may emerge. As we use the term, an RTLA gives the owner of a patented invention, used in upstream stages of research, rights in subsequent downstream discoveries. Such rights may take the form of a royalty on sales that result from use of the upstream research tool, an exclusive or nonexclusive license on future discoveries, or an option to acquire such a license. In principle, RTLAs offer advantages to both patent holders and researchers. They permit researchers with limited funds to use patented research tools right away and defer payment until the research yields valuable results. Patent holders may also prefer a chance at larger payoffs from sales of downstream products rather than certain, but smaller, upfront fees. In practice, RTLAs may lead to an anticommons as upstream owners stack overlapping and inconsistent claims on potential downstream products. In effect, the use of RTLAs gives each upstream patent owner a continuing right to be present at the bargaining table as a research project moves downstream toward product development.

* * *

[T]here may be reasons to fear that a patent anticommons could prove more intractable in biomedical research than in other settings. Because patents matter more to the pharmaceutical and biotechnology industries than to other industries, firms in these industries may be less willing to participate in patent pools that undermine the gains from exclusivity. Moreover, the lack of substitutes for certain biomedical discoveries (such as patented genes or receptors) may increase the leverage of some patent holders, thereby aggravating holdout problems. Rivals may not be able to invent around patents in research aimed at understanding the genetic bases of diseases as they occur in nature.

More generally, three structural concerns caution against uncritical reliance on markets and norms to avoid a biomedical anticommons tragedy: the transaction costs of rearranging entitlements, heterogeneous interests of owners, and cognitive biases among researchers.

Transaction costs of bundling rights. High transaction costs may be an enduring impediment to efficient bundling of intellectual property rights in biomedical research. First, many upstream patent owners are public institutions with limited resources for absorbing transaction costs and limited competence in fast-paced, market-oriented bargaining. Second, the rights involved cover a diverse set of techniques, reagents, DNA sequences, and instruments. Difficulties in comparing the values of these patents will likely impede development of a standard distribution scheme. Third, the heterogeneity of interests and resources among public and private patent owners may complicate the emergence of standard license terms, requiring costly case-by-case negotiations. Fourth, licensing transaction costs are likely to arise early in the course of R & D when the outcome of a project is uncertain, the potential gains are speculative, and it is not yet clear that the value of downstream products justifies the trouble of overcoming the anticommons.

* * *

Heterogeneous interests of rights holders. Intellectual property rights in upstream biomedical research belong to a large, diverse group of owners in the public and private sectors with divergent institutional agendas * * *. For example, a politically accountable government agency such as NIH may further its public health mission by using its intellectual property rights to ensure widespread availability of new therapeutic products at reasonable prices * * *. By contrast, a private firm is more likely to use intellectual property to maintain a lucrative product monopoly that rewards shareholders and funds future product development. When owners have conflicting goals and each can deploy its rights to block the strategies of the others, they may not be able to reach an agreement that leaves enough private value for downstream developers to bring products to the market.

* * *

Cognitive biases. People consistently overestimate the likelihood that very low probability events of high salience will occur. For example, many travelers overestimate the danger of an airplane crash relative to the hazards of other modes of transportation. We suspect that a similar bias is likely to cause owners of upstream biomedical research patents to overvalue their discoveries. Imagine that one of a set of 50 upstream inventions will likely be the key to identifying an important new drug, the rest of the set will have no practical use, and a downstream product developer is willing to pay $10 million for the set. Given the assumption that no owner knows ex ante which invention will be the key, a rational owner should be willing to sell her patent for the probabilistic value of $200,000. However, if each owner overestimates the likelihood that her patent will be the key, then each will demand more than the probabilistic value, the upstream owners collectively will demand more than the aggregate market value of their inputs, the downstream user will decline the offers, and the new drug will not be developed.

* * *

Policy-makers should seek to ensure coherent boundaries of upstream patents and to minimize restrictive licensing practices that interfere with downstream product development. Otherwise, more upstream rights may lead paradoxically to fewer useful products for improving human health.

NICHOLAS THOMPSON, GENE BLUES: IS THE PATENT OFFICE PREPARED TO DEAL WITH THE GENOMIC REVOLUTION?

Washington Monthly, April 2001.

There are about 30,000 human genes in the genome; about 1,000 have already been claimed, and an estimated 10,000–20,000 applications are pending at the PTO. Facing this onslaught, the PTO's rules were tightened at the end of the Clinton administration: Patent applications must now show a "clear, substantial, and specific" utility for their applications. A company can no longer receive a patent simply for finding a gene that might help a virus enter cells. The company has to say which virus and which cells. That change has been universally welcomed. No company wants a new drug torpedoed because another company fortuitously patented the key gene years ago without really understanding it.

The patent office has not, however, tackled the more important issue of how companies use patents. Patenting a gene and releasing it into the public domain, as the National Institute of Health now usually does, harms no one. Some private companies, Incyte Genomics for example, have also earned reputations for allowing other companies to use their patents widely and cheaply, in no small part because money can often be made just as easily with lots of companies paying small fees to use a patent, instead of a few companies paying astronomical ones. But not everybody's sharing. Myriad Genetics, for example, used its patent over a gene that served as an indicator of breast cancer to stop research on it at the University of Pennsylvania. Two years ago, in another well-known case, the Miami Children's Hospital received a patent on a gene for the rare Canavan disease that it had identified in one of its patients, Jonathan Greenberg. Without informing Greenberg, the hospital set out to block free Canavan tests offered elsewhere.

Right now, the patent office is our only instrument for policing the gene industry, but the agency is unarmed and patrolling on foot.

* * *

From an industry standpoint, the problem with the current system is best understood if one thinks of upstream and downstream products. The downstream product is the actual drug sold at CVS or the genetic test conducted in a clinic. Upstream products are the test tubes, the original cell that's torn apart to look for the genes, and the genes themselves. Traditionally, the PTO has granted mainly patents to downstream products like actual drugs. By allowing patents on upstream products like genes the legal process has been turned upside down, with two major consequences. First, anyone who develops a drug or a clinical test has to look upstream to see whether anyone else had a claim on the genes used. Second, every company has an incentive to patent as many genes as possible. No one really knows how science will change, and having genes in the bank may be useful for your own research, so your competitor can't screw you, or so you can screw your competitor. Unsurprisingly, everyone's suing everybody else to grab rights to potentially lucrative genes. Elan is suing the Mayo Clinic; the University of Rochester is suing Pharmacia over a gene crucial to Celebrex, a painkiller, currently one of the best-selling drugs on the market; Amgen just won a case against Transkaryotic Therapies, a much-smaller company trying to make a competitor to Epogen, Amgen's anemia-fighting blockbuster.

From a public perspective, the problem isn't just that tests are being stopped, like Myriad Genetics' crackdown on breast-cancer screening, but that many tests aren't even getting started. Jon Merz and Mildred Cho, bioethicists at the University of Pennsylvania and Stanford, recently conducted a survey of laboratory physicians and found that one in four had abandoned a clinical test that they had developed because of patents, and almost half reported that they had not developed a test for fear that, the minute they cleaned their test tubes, a patent lawyer would come knocking. In a follow-up, Merz and Cho surveyed 100 laboratories to determine how they responded when GlaxoSmithKline was granted a patent over a gene critical to a screening test for hemochromotosis. Before Glaxo even decided to enforce the patent, 25 labs made a decision never to use it and five already using it chose to drop it. Even universities have been playing hardball, sending lawyers after companies and each other.

* * *

Even without the legal mess, there's a strong moral reason for government intervention. Gene patents are different from other patents. Biotech companies are not just putting fish genes in tomatoes to make them grow in cold weather; they're manipulating and owning parts of humans that have existed since well before the first hominoid speared his first antelope. Furthermore, all of the research, from the machines used to sequence genes to the actual structure of the genome, is based in large-part on a $15–billion investment by the public in the National Institute of Health's Human Genome Project.

* * *

Congress can and should give the PTO the authority and ability to issue conditional patents on human genes, deciding not just who should be granted patents, but how those patents should be used. The PTO under-stands the issues much better than Congress and can act quickly when needed; it just doesn't have the legal ability to do much right now.

The PTO should then take one specific step in the short run—non-commercial researchers should be given unlimited rights to use genes in their work and develop long-term standards that allow biotech companies to make reasonable profits while also protecting the public interest. The period of exclusive rights for genes should be shortened—it's odd to give 20–year protection to a company that has existed for three years—and companies that do not develop licensing agreements with their competi-tors should be penalized, perhaps by having previous patents moved into the public domain. This would reduce uncertainty because companies wouldn't have to look upstream constantly. It would also probably reduce lawsuits by moving patenting away from a winner-takes-all system where lawyers can make the difference between a billion-dollar patent and collapse.

* * *

The patent office took a large step in a positive direction at the end of the Clinton administration, publishing a paper suggesting that the biotech industry consider pooling patents, with companies entering cross-licensing agreements sharing patents with competitors. The office couldn't enforce the paper because Congress hasn't granted it that power yet. But the suggestion does point out a future path. Although important issues of anti-trust need to be considered so that big players don't use pools to squeeze out the small guys, such an approach has proved an effective way of sharing information in the electronics industry. The most recent example came when DVD manufacturers from Sony to Hitachi to Time Warner agreed to share their patents, ensuring each can comply with DVD–Video and DVD–ROM standard specifications.

Perhaps the most germane example, though, comes from 1917 when a committee chaired by Navy Assistant Secretary Franklin Roosevelt pushed the country's airplane manufacturers to pool their patents. Previously, two companies had been hoarding patents, as some gene companies are doing today, preventing the government from building the planes it needed to fight the war. Roosevelt twisted some arms and made the public aware of the problem. With the patents pooled, we built the planes needed to win the war.

The stakes now aren't that much different. Europe isn't being over-run, but science is spilling into uncharted technical and moral territory. The probable benefits are awesome, but the ethical, moral, and legal issues need clear government action-starting with the PTO. Calling balls and strikes just isn't enough anymore.

MELISSA L. STURGES, WHO SHOULD HOLD PROPERTY RIGHTS TO THE HUMAN GENOME? AN APPLICATION OF THE COMMON HERITAGE OF HUMANKIND

13 Am. U. Int'l L. Rev. 219, 245–248 (1997).

TRADITIONAL APPLICATIONS OF THE COMMON HERITAGE CONCEPT

The Common Heritage of Mankind principle is an international legal concept which conveys equal property interests to all people. Less developed countries have embraced the Common Heritage concept as the embodiment of the combination of customary international law with jus cogens status [a status which would not allow it to be overridden by a statute or treaty]. The Common Heritage doctrine includes four characteristics: 1) no country can appropriate for itself the territory in question; 2) all states share responsibility for managing the territory; 3) all states share in the benefits from exploitation of the territory or its resources; and 4) all countries must use the territory for exclusively peaceful purposes. In addition, legal bodies sometimes include a fifth characteristic, that all countries have a shared responsibility for preserving the unique or irreplaceable resources of the territory in question for future generations. The Common Heritage concept is unpopular with developed countries that do not agree with its goal of redistributing resources to less developed countries.

The United Nations has traditionally applied the Common Heritage doctrine to deep seabeds, Antarctica, the Moon and other celestial bodies, and certain worldwide historical sites. The United Nations tends to uniformly apply the Common Heritage concept to environmentally vulnerable sites because the environment transcends national borders and is not limited to domestic sovereignty. Thus, preservation of the environment can only occur through international cooperation.

Judging from the similarities between traditional applications of the Common Heritage concept and the human genome, and taking into account the grave ethical consequences of privatizing the genome, the Common Heritage of Mankind should apply to the human genome.

AMERICAN COLLEGE OF MEDICAL GENETICS POSITION STATEMENT ON GENE PATENTS AND ACCESSIBILITY OF GENE TESTING (AUGUST 2, 1999)

http://www.acmg.net/StaticContent/StaticPages/Gene_Patents.pdf.

The fruits of the human genome project are rapidly redefining the medical community's views of patient care and moving us from a focus on the treatment of disease to a broader perspective in which prevention and diagnosis play equally critical roles. The American College of Medical Genetics (ACMG) believes that gene testing * * * must remain widely accessible and affordable, and that the development and improvement of safe and effective genetic tests should not be hindered. The decision of the Patent and Trademark Office (PTO) to permit the patenting of naturally occurring genes and disease-causing mutations has produced numerous difficulties. While the ACMG disagrees with the PTO over this fundamental issue, we have further concerns over current patterns of enforcement of patents on genes that are important in the diagnosis, management and risk assessment of human disease.

This statement is directed at current practices related to such enforcement. Enforcement has been effected in one or more of these ways: monopolistic licensing that limits a given genetic test to a single laboratory, royalty-based licensing agreements with exorbitant up-front fees and per-test fees, and licensing agreements that seek proportions of reimbursement from testing services. These limit the accessibility of competitively priced genetic testing services and hinder test-specific development of national programs for quality assurance. They also limit the number of knowledgeable individuals who can assist physicians, laboratory geneticists and counselors in the diagnosis, management and care of at-risk patients.

Further, restricting the availability of gene testing has long-term implications beyond patient care. It affects the training of the next generation of medical and laboratory geneticists, physicians, and scientists in the area enveloped by the patent or license. It also retards the usually very rapid improvement of a test that occurs through the addition of new mutations or the use of new techniques by numerous laboratories that have accumulated samples from affected individuals over many years.

Therefore, it is the ACMG's position that:

● Genes and their mutations are naturally occurring substances that should not be patented.

● Patents on genes with clinical implications must be very broadly licensed.

● Licensing agreements should not limit access through excessive royalties and other unreasonable terms.

COLLEGE OF AMERICAN PATHOLOGISTS, STATEMENT TO THE SECRETARY'S ADVISORY COMMITTEE ON GENETICS, HEALTH AND SOCIETY (JUNE 26–27, 2006)

http://www.cap.org/apps/cap.portal?_nfpb=true&cntvwrPtlt
_actionOverride=/portlets/contentViewer/show&_windowLabel
=cntvwrPtlt&cntvwrPtlt{actionForm.contentReference}
=advocacy/testimony/sacghs.html&_state=maximized&_pageLabel=cntvwr.

* * *

We are in the midst of a scientific revolution in genetics that promises extraordinary advances in clinical medicine. As the medical specialists in the diagnosis of disease, College members recognize that genetic testing is an area of growth and change for pathology and medical practice in the decades to come. Pathologists therefore have a keen interest in ensuring that gene patents do not restrict the ability of physicians to provide quality diagnostic services to the patients they serve. Gene patents pose a serious threat to medical advancement, medical education, and patient care. When patents are granted, subsequent exclusive license agreements, excessive licensing fees, and other restrictive licensing conditions prevent physicians and laboratories from providing genetic based clinical testing services. As a consequence, patient access to care is limited, quality of patient care is jeopardized, clinical observations as the basis for new discoveries are compromised, and training of health care providers is restricted.

Throughout history, medical discoveries have progressed from the discovery of basic anatomy to histology and cytology, none of which are patented, to the more recent discovery of genes. The recent trend of using patents to monopolize gene-based testing services is a radical departure from historical precedent in clinical laboratories, and it works against the goal of making these procedures widely accessible and affordable for the public. Especially troubling is the fact that under patent protection, the increasing understanding of the utility of the test, as well as the underlying disease processes, also becomes proprietary, thereby imposing a profound change in how the profession and the public acquire knowledge about these rapidly evolving tests, the diseases diagnosed by the tests and their clinical utility.

Physicians and scientists can easily and rapidly translate the fundamental information derived from mapping the human genome into diagnostic genetic tests and use these tests for patient care. Because information about gene sequences is so fundamental to understanding specific diseases, patent holders can essentially gain ownership of diseases through patents. Exclusive or restrictive license agreements on gene-based tests have been used to prevent physicians and clinical laboratories from performing genetic tests as diagnostic medical procedures. Patients suffer because diagnostic test services are less readily and affordably accessible. Medical education and research related to laboratory testing also are threatened. In fact, College members have received "cease and desist" notification letters from patent holders or exclusive licensees indicating that continued patient testing would be patent infringement. Examples of diseases where testing has been halted due to patent enforcement include breast cancer, Alzheimer disease, Canavan disease, and Charcot–Marie–Tooth disease.

* * *

NOTES AND QUESTIONS

1. What problems might gene patenting cause for medical research and medical care?

2. A 2005 study found that nearly 20% of all human genes are explicitly claimed in United States patents. Kyle Jensen & Fiona Murray, Intellectual

Property Landscape of the Human Genome, 310 Science 239 (2005). Because there are only a finite number of human genes in existence, less than 30,000, what will happen when the vast majority of them are subject to patent protection? What types of subject matter related to the patented gene might still be available for patenting once the actual gene sequences themselves are protected?

3. How might a trade secret approach to genetic discoveries differ from that of a gene patenting approach? What is the likely impact of each on research? What is the likely impact of each on the development of gene therapies?

4. Why does the American College of Medical Genetics oppose gene patenting? What changes does the organization seem to want in the law?

5. A wide variety of other medical organizations signed a joint statement criticizing gene patents. In addition to advocating non-exclusive licenses at reasonable costs, the statement pointed out that the incentives of patent law are not necessary. "Most discoveries of pathogen or human disease genes can be effectively translated into genetic tests without recourse to the incentives provided by patents or exclusive license agreements." Association for Molecular Pathology, Clinical Practice Committee, AMP Position on Patenting of Genetic Tests (Nov. 22, 1999), http://www.amp.org/Gen/gen-tests.htm. The statement was developed by representatives from the following organizations: Academy of Clinical Laboratory Physicians and Scientists, College of American Pathologists, American College of Medical Genetics, American Society of Human Genetics, National Society of Genetic Counselors, American Medical Association, American College of Obstetricians and Gynecologists, American Society of Clinical Pathologists, Association of American Medical Colleges.

6. In 2009, a lawsuit was filed in the United States District Court for the Southern District of New York challenging the validity and constitutionality of patents on the BRCA1 and BRCA2 breast cancer genes owned by Myriad Genetics. Association for Molecular Pathology v. United States Patent and Trademark Office, 09 Civ. 4515. The plaintiffs in the lawsuit include: women who wish to have testing for the BRCA1 and BRCA2 genes; researchers who have the capabilities to offer testing for these genes but are unable to because of Myriad's patents on the BRCA1 and BRCA2 genes; medical organizations; and women's health organizations. The plaintiffs allege that Myriad's patents on the sequences of two genes related to breast cancer and correlations between mutations in those genes and breast cancer claim unpatentable subject matter under 35 U.S.C. § 101 and that the patents are unconstitutional under the First and Fourteenth Amendments of the United States Constitution. What arguments can be made that gene patents are not patentable subject matter? What arguments can be made that gene patents infringe on the right to free speech?

7. The World Medical Association considers genes to be part of "mankind's common heritage" and urges medical organizations around the globe to lobby against gene patenting. Matt Borsellino, World Med. Association Tackling Health Database Issue, 36 Med. Post 40 (2000).

8. About one-quarter of gene patent holders will not allow any other physician or laboratory to test for "their" patented gene. The company

holding the patent on a gene associated with Alzheimer's disease, for example, will not let any laboratory except its own perform the test. Doctors and labs across the country face a lawsuit if they try to determine whether one of their patients has the genetic form of Alzheimer's even though testing can easily be done by anyone who knows the gene sequence without using any product or device made by the patent holder.

This exclusivity can impede research to improve diagnosis. Various mutations in the same gene can cause a particular disease. But companies that do not let anyone else test for "their" gene make it more difficult to find mutations than if other labs were testing. In countries where the Alzheimer's gene and hemochromatosis gene were *not* patented, researchers found previously unknown mutations. These mutations can be used to diagnose people who would not otherwise be diagnosed.

9. Most drugs only work on a percentage of patients who use them. Genetic testing can help distinguish those patients for whom a drug will work from those for whom it will not. But such tests will also limit the market for drugs. For example, a pharmaceutical company has filed for a patent on a genetic test to determine the effectiveness of one of its asthma drugs. But the company says it will not develop the test—or let anyone else develop it. Geeta Anand, Big Drug Makers Try to Postpone Custom Regimens, Wall St. J., June 18, 2001 at B1. Should a company lose its patent in a case like this, where the company is not developing the invention? There is a concept in trademark law, under 15 U.S.C. § 1127, whereby the owner can lose a trademark he or she does not use for three consecutive years (since part of the requirement for trademark protection is use in commerce).

Would your opinion change if the patent owner had reasons other than financial ones for wanting to prevent the development of the patented invention? Some scientists have suggested creating a chimera, mixing human and chimp DNA to produce a subhuman species to do menial tasks. Biologist Stuart Newman filed a patent application on that technology. He planned to use the patent to prevent anyone from making such a creation for the 20–year period that he controlled the patent. His patent was denied on the grounds that the chimera "includes within its scope a human being" and people are not patentable. John Travis, Patently Unpatentable, 156 Science News 127 (1999).

VII. POLICY PROPOSALS TO CHANGE GENE PATENT LAW

There are various policy proposals to change the laws governing gene patents. One approach would be for a court to determine that genes are unpatentable products of nature. Another potential solution would be a patent pool that operated similarly to ASCAP (American Society of Composers, Authors and Producers), which handles the licensing of music under the copyright laws. A patent pool could potentially extend non-exclusive licenses for set fees. That way, a researcher who wanted to develop a treatment for breast cancer would not be prevented from doing so by the holder of a patent on all or a section of a gene related to breast cancer. Nor would the researcher have to negotiate with each holder of each patent for the various mutations related to breast cancer, thus saving transaction costs and preventing future litigation.

Since the U.S. Constitutional provision about promoting the useful arts is quite general, the actual provisions of patent law are enacted by Congress and can be modified by that body. For example, gene patents could be banned altogether. Another legislative approach would be Congressional action to create one or more exemptions. One exemption might allow researchers to use patented genes. Another could protect doctors and scientists from patent infringement suits when they undertake genetics tests based on information contained in a gene patent. An exemption for genetic diagnosis would be akin to the current exemption for physicians' use of patented medical procedures. Attention focused on the downside of patenting medical procedures when Dr. Samuel Pallin patented a method for performing cataract surgery and, in 1995, sued Dr. Jack Singer for using the technique without paying a royalty. As a result of Dr. Pallin's action, the American Medical Association amended its Code of Ethics to forbid doctors from patenting medical procedures because it found that these patents compromised patient care. The implications of such patents are troubling. Say a doctor patents the procedure for appendectomies. Not wanting to pay a high royalty fee to use that procedure, a doctor might use a less safe surgical procedure rather than risk infringing the patent. Responding to the concerns raised by patients and by the medical profession, Congress in 1996 created an exception in the patent law so that health care providers are not subject to patent infringement suits when they use a patented medical or surgical technique.

Yet another exception might be for an overriding public health purpose. In 2001, after terrorists began sending Anthrax to public officials, the Canadian government overrode Bayer's patent for the antibiotic Cipro and ordered a million tablets of a generic version of the drug. Amy Harmon & Robert Pear, Canada Overrides Patent for Cipro to Treat Anthrax, The New York Times, Oct. 29, 2001.

In South Africa, many people afflicted with AIDS could not afford the costly anti-retroviral drugs. Because the drugs were patented, and the international agreement on Trade–Related Aspects of International Property (TRIPS) requires countries to recognize other countries' patents, South African pharmaceutical companies could not make cheaper generic versions of the drugs. Activists in South Africa began to argue that the drug patents were giving rise to "genocide by intellectual property." The South African government passed a law allowing compulsory licensing and parallel importing.

Compulsory licensing allows a government to give a party other than the patent holder a license to use a patent, without consent of the patent owner. In the case of drugs, this practice tends to drive prices down when the drug is marketed under a generic name. Article 31 of the TRIPS Agreement requires that prior to requesting a compulsory license, the applicant must have attempted to obtain a voluntary license from the patent holder on reasonable commercial terms. An exception to this requirement is made for national emergencies and "other circumstances of extreme urgency" or "public non-commercial use" or anti-competitive practices. It also requires that where a compulsory license is granted, adequate royalties must be paid to the patent holder.

Parallel importing allows a country to import a product and then sell it to another country without the authorization of the patent holder. This tends to lower the price in situations where the reselling country is able to purchase the product at a lower price than the end-user country. The legal idea behind parallel importing is exhaustion: once a company sells its products, its patent rights attached thereto are exhausted and it no longer has any rights over what happens to that product.

ROBERT M. PORTMAN, LEGISLATIVE RESTRICTION ON MEDICAL AND SURGICAL PROCEDURE PATENTS REMOVES IMPEDIMENT TO MEDICAL PROGRESS

4 U. Balt. Intell. Prop. L.J. 91, 91–92, 104–107 (1996).

* * *

Strong public policy arguments led to Congress' decision to restrict the enforcement of medical procedure patents against physicians and other health care providers.

A.   MEDICAL PROCEDURE PATENTS HAVE A CHILLING EFFECT ON THE MEDICAL PROFESSION'S TRADITION OF OPEN EXCHANGE OF INFORMATION AND IDEAS

Assigning proprietary rights to medical and surgical procedures is contrary to the medical profession's history of free and open exchange of information on medical advances and discoveries: a tradition that has served the United States extremely well for more than two centuries. Typically, physicians who develop new and better treatments have promptly shared those advances with colleagues at scientific seminars, in textbooks and journal articles, and in teaching demonstrations.

This open sharing of information is not only firmly ingrained in the medical culture, it has long been an ethical duty. According to the American Medical Association's Code of Medical Ethics:

> Physicians have an obligation to share their knowledge and skills and to report the results of clinical and laboratory research. This tradition enhances patient care, leads to the early evaluation of new technologies, and permits the rapid dissemination of improved techniques . . . The intentional withholding of new medical knowledge, skills, and techniques from colleagues for reasons of personal gain is detrimental to the medical profession and to society and is to be condemned . . . Prompt presentation before scientific organizations and timely publi-

cation of clinical and laboratory research in scientific journals are essential elements in the foundation of good medical care.

* * *

[T]he enforcement of medical procedure patents against physicians for using, teaching or writing about medical discoveries would corrupt and commercialize the art and science of medicine, while limiting the widespread availability of new advances. The natural incentive for any potential patent applicant is to withhold information from others at least until the application has been filed, which, in some cases, may be a period of months or years. The mere threat of patent infringement litigation may deter a physician from using or teaching new medical advances, whether patented or not, because the physician has no readily available means of determining what is patented.

For these reasons, the American Medical Association has ruled that it is unethical for physicians to obtain or enforce medical procedure patents. Certainly, physicians who obtain patents for particular medical procedures and refuse to grant licenses or impose royalties on would-be licensees violate their ethical duty to share information and restrict the availability of the procedure to patients of other physicians.

But even if licenses are freely granted, such patents still inhibit the free flow of information and the availability of the procedure. First, the patenting process usually takes several years. A would-be patent holder has a strong incentive to withhold information from others until a patent application has been filed. Moreover, the pendency of a patent application could easily prevent the physician from reporting research results in an unbiased manner for fear of adversely affecting the future "marketability" of the procedure.

* * *

B. MEDICAL PROCEDURE PATENTS IMPEDE THE QUALITY OF HEALTH CARE

The possibility of infringing medical method patents also threatens to discourage the process of early evaluation and critical appraisal from within the medical profession and therefore impairs the quality of health care. First, an individual applying for a medical procedure patent has a natural incentive to withhold information from the peer review process to avoid exposing flaws in the procedure or the existence of prior discoveries that might undermine the application's issuance. Indeed, a public disclosure of a new medical procedure more than one year before filing is an absolute bar to obtaining a patent in the United States. This rule clearly discourages clinical testing of the technique.

Second, the possibility that a patent holder will retaliate against a critical peer reviewer by withholding permission to use a procedure tends to discourage open and frank evaluation of the safety and efficacy of a medical procedure. This obstruction of the peer review process is critical because, unlike drugs and medical devices, professional peer review is the only effective check on the safety and efficacy of medical procedures. The Food and Drug Administration (FDA), for instance, quite appropriately does not regulate medical procedures and techniques.

Medical procedure patents may also have the effect of substituting the judgment of patent examiners for highly trained medical experts in evaluating the efficacy of new procedures. To the lay public, a medical procedure patent may be misunderstood as a governmental seal of approval. As a result, patented medical procedures may gain more currency from their patent status than the peer review process would justify, especially if patent owners advertise that their techniques are "patented," which has occurred with some frequency in the United States.

C. MEDICAL PROCEDURE PATENTS WILL UNNECESSARILY DRIVE UP THE COST OF HEALTH CARE

The problem of rising health care costs needs little exposition here. In an era where health care expenditures engulf fourteen percent of the gross domestic product (GDP) and are rising at several times the rate of inflation, any policies that contribute to these escalating costs should be subject to the most exacting scrutiny.

Medical method patents fit squarely in this suspect class. As their popularity increases, the cost of licensing fees alone could be substantial. By their nature, patents afford the holder the right to charge monopoly prices. Men's Health of Overland Park, the owner of the patent for treating male impotence, demanded an annual license fee of $350 per physician. Dr. Pallin had requested as much as $10,000 per year per physician for use of his patented incision method [for eye surgery].

35 U.S.C. § 287

§ 287. Limitation on damages and other remedies; marking and notice

* * *

(c)(1) With respect to a medical practitioner's performance of a medical activity that constitutes an infringement under section 271(a) or (b) of this title, the provisions of sections 281, 283, 284, and 285 of this title shall not apply against the medical practitioner or against a related health care entity with respect to such medical activity.

(2) For the purposes of this subsection:

(A) the term "medical activity" means the performance of a medical or surgical procedure on a body, but shall not include (i) the use of a patented machine, manufacture, or composition of matter in violation of such patent, (ii) the practice of a patented use of a composition of matter in violation of such patent, or (iii) the practice of a process in violation of a biotechnology patent.

(B) the term "medical practitioner" means any natural person who is licensed by a State to provide the medical activity described in subsection (c)(1) or who is acting under the direction of such person in the performance of the medical activity.

* * *

(E) the term "body" shall mean a human body, organ or cadaver, or a nonhuman animal used in medical research or instruction directly relating to the treatment of humans.

* * *

(3) This subsection does not apply to the activities of any person, or employee or agent of such person (regardless of whether such person is a tax exempt organization under section 501(c) of the Internal Revenue Code), who is engaged in the commercial development, manufacture, sale, importation, or distribution of a machine, manufacture, or composition of matter or the provision of pharmacy or clinical laboratory services (other than clinical laboratory services provided in a physician's office), where such activities are:

(A) directly related to the commercial development, manufacture, sale, importation, or distribution of a machine, manufacture, or composition of matter or the provision of pharmacy or clinical laboratory services (other than clinical laboratory services provided in a physician's office), and

(B) regulated under the Federal Food, Drug, and Cosmetic Act, the Public Health Service Act, or the Clinical Laboratories Improvement Act.

(4) This subsection shall not apply to any patent issued based on an application the earliest effective filing date of which is prior to September 30, 1996.

JEANNE CLARK, ET AL., PATENT POOLS: A SOLUTION TO THE PROBLEM OF ACCESS IN BIOTECHNOLOGY PATENTS?

U.S. Patent and Trademark Office,
http://www.uspto.gov/web/offices/pac/dapp/opla/patentpool.pdf.

One of the biggest public concerns voiced against the granting of patents by the United States Patent Office (USPTO) to inventions in biotechnology, specifically inventions based on genetic information, is the potential lack of reasonable access to that technology for the research and development of commercial products and for further basic biological research. One possible solution lies in the formation of patent pools.

* * *

Of present concern to the public is the removal of valuable research resources from the public domain. The characterization of nucleic acid sequence information is only the first step in the utilization of genetic information. Significant and intensive research efforts, however, are required to glean the information from the nucleic acid sequences for use in, inter alia, the development of pharmaceutical agents for disease treatment, and in elucidating basic biological processes. Many feel that by allowing genetic information to be patented, researchers will no longer have free access to the information and materials necessary to perform biological research. This issue of access to research tools relates to the ability of a patent holder to exclude others from using the material. Further, if a single patent holder has a proprietary position on a large number of nucleic acids, they may be in a position to "hold hostage" future research and development efforts.

* * *

A "patent pool" is an agreement between two or more patent owners to license one or more of their patents to one another or third parties * * *. Over the last one hundred and fifty years, patent pools have played an important role in shaping both the industry and the law in the United States. In 1856, the Sewing Machine Combination formed one of the first patent pools consisting of sewing machine patents. In 1917, as a result of a recommendation of a committee formed by the Assistant Secretary of the Navy (The Honorable Franklin D. Roosevelt), an aircraft patent pool was privately formed encompassing almost all aircraft manufacturers in the United States. The creation of the Manufacturer's Aircraft Association was crucial to the U.S. government because the two major patent holders, the Wright Company and the Curtiss Company, had effectively blocked the building of any new airplanes, which were desperately needed as the United States was entering World War I * * *. In 1998, Sony, Philips and Pioneer formed a patent pool for inventions that are essential to comply with certain DVD–Video and DVD–ROM standard specifications.

* * *

A first benefit associated with the pooling of patents is the elimination of problems caused by "blocking" patents or "stacking" licenses. In biotechnology, the granting of patents to nucleic acids may create blocking patents or lead to stacking licenses. As demonstrated in the emerging airplane technology in the early 1900's, corporations that hold patents on an industry's basic building blocks can prevent each other, as well as others, from bringing commercial products to the market. By creating a patent pool of these basic patents, businesses can easily obtain all the necessary licenses required to practice that particular technology concurrently from a single entity. This, in turn, can facilitate rapid development of new technology since it opens the playing field to all members and licensees of the patent pool. For example, the recent patent pool encompassing MPEG–2 technology led to the rapid formation of a standardized protocol to protect copyrighted works on the Internet. Similarly, patent pools can eliminate the problems associated with blocking patents or stacking licenses in the field of biotechnology, while at the same time encouraging the cooperative efforts needed to realize the true economic and social benefits of genomic inventions. In addition, since each party in a patent pool would benefit from the work of others, the members may focus on their core competencies, thus spurring innovation at a faster rate.

A second benefit is that patent pools have the potential to significantly reduce several aspects of licensing transaction costs. First, patent pools can reduce or eliminate the need for litigation over patent rights because such disputes can be easily settled, or avoided, through the creation of a patent pool. A reduction in patent litigation would save businesses time and money, and also avoid the uncertainty of patent rights caused by litigation. In addition, small businesses, which cannot usually endure the costs of litigation, are more likely to survive and prosper if they are free from legal suits over patent rights in the future. Second, a patent pool creates an efficient mechanism for obtaining rights to a patented technology. Parties interested in a certain technology covered by a patent pool can, in one stop, license all the patents essential to a core technology. Without a patent pool, a company would have to obtain licenses separately from each holder of the essential patents. Not only does the process of individual licensing require more time, money and resources, but it also establishes a motivation for some patent owners to hold out on licensing their patent. For example, if a company knows that they own the last patent a consumer needs to practice a particular technology, they can demand a substantially higher royalty because they realize that the value of all the other licenses that the consumer already purchased depends on obtaining this last license. Patent pools address this anticompetitive "hold out" problem by providing a means in which most, if not all, necessary licenses are obtained at one time. In addition, patent pools often require a grantback license of any improvement patents on the core technology of the patent pool to reduce the risk of future lawsuits. A reduction in transaction costs is particularly important to biotechnology firms, where a significant portion of their research and development funds are being diverted to cover transaction costs, thus slowing down further innovation.

A third major benefit from patent pooling is the distribution of risks. Like an insurance policy, a patent pool can provide incentive for further innovation by enabling its members to share the risks associated with research and development. The pooling of patents can increase the likelihood that a company will recover some, if not all, of its costs of research and development efforts. Depending on the structure of the pool, all members may receive a set income based upon a percentage of the pool's royalty regardless of the "economic" value of their individual patent. For example, under the MPEG LA patent pool, all essential patents are equal in value no matter the cost of the research and development required for their actualization. This arrangement evenly distributes the wealth of the pool to all its members. In addition, all members of a patent pool have equal access to the technology in the pool, which may enhance the commercial potential of the patented invention of an individual member. A mechanism that distributes risks and provides greater access to related technology should be extremely attractive to biotechnology businesses that have to fund the high research and development costs inherent in this area of innovation.

* * *

Critics have stated that patent pools have several anticompetitive effects. The first criticism is that patent pools inflate the costs of competitively priced goods. This argument is based on the assumption that while certain patents may be considered to be legally blocking, such patents actually cover competitive alternatives to a certain technology, and that the pooling of these patents will expand monopoly pricing.

* * *

A second reason why critics feel patent pools should not be encouraged is that pools shield invalid patents. Companies who fear that their patents will be invalidated in court are eager to settle by creating a patent pool. This, in turn, will force the public to pay royalties on technology that would have become part of the public domain if the patents were actually litigated in court. While certainly a valid concern, patent pools can avoid this situation if the patents for the pool are selected and monitored by an independent expert to evaluate the patents. In addition, oversight of patent pools by the Department of Justice and the FTC provide further assurance that the pools are not shielding invalid patents. For example, recently, a FTC complaint against Summit and VISX charged the companies with unlawful price fixing involving their patent pool. In addition, the FTC challenged the patent pool because it was protecting an invalid patent. Thus, the formation of a patent pool does necessarily prevent the technology in an invalid patent from being returned to the public domain.

A final criticism of patent pools is that such pools eliminate competition by encouraging collusion and price fixing. Careful evaluation of patent pools under the IP Guidelines [Antitrust Guidelines for the Licensing of Intellectual Property, prepared by the Justice Department and Federal Trade Commission] should alleviate this important concern. One of the many factors that the IP Guidelines evaluate is the patents' relationship to the industry and to each other. If the patent pool harms competition and reduces further innovation, then the members of that pool may face antitrust violations, which should discourage the formation of anticompetitive patent pools.

NOTES AND QUESTIONS

1. What policy arguments do you think convinced Congress to allow health care providers to use patented medical and surgical procedures without being liable for infringing the patents? What is the value of patents on such procedures now that 35 U.S.C. § 287 (c) has been enacted?

2. If a physician undertook a genetic test on a patient without paying a royalty to the patent holder, would he or she be protected under 35 U.S.C. § 287 (c)(1) of the patent law? If not, what changes in the statute might be necessary to achieve that protection?

3. What are the pros and cons of patent pools?

VIII. INTERNATIONAL ASPECTS OF GENE PATENTING

DIRECTIVE 98/44/EC OF THE EUROPEAN PARLIAMENT AND OF THE COUNCIL OF 6 JULY 1998 ON THE LEGAL PROTECTION OF BIOTECHNOLOGICAL INVENTIONS

Official Journal of the European Communities L 213, 30/07/1998 P.0013–0021.

Chapter I. Patentability

Article 1

1. Member States shall protect biotechnological inventions under national patent law. They shall, if necessary, adjust their national patent law to take account of the provisions of this Directive.

* * *

Article 2

1. For the purposes of this Directive,

(a) "biological material" means any material containing genetic information and capable of reproducing itself or being reproduced in a biological system;

(b) "microbiological process" means any process involving or performed upon or resulting in microbiological material.

* * *

Article 3

1. For the purposes of this Directive, inventions which are new, which involve an inventive step and which are susceptible of industrial application shall be patentable even if they concern a product consisting of or containing biological material or a process by means of which biological material is produced, processed or used.

2. Biological material which is isolated from its natural environment or produced by means of a technical process may be the subject of an invention even if it previously occurred in nature.

Article 4

1. The following shall not be patentable:

(a) plant and animal varieties;

(b) essentially biological processes for the production of plants or animals.

2. Inventions which concern plants or animals shall be patentable if the technical feasibility of the invention is not confined to a particular plant or animal variety.

3. Paragraph 1(b) shall be without prejudice to the patentability of inventions which concern a microbiological or other technical process or a product obtained by means of such a process.

Article 5

1. The human body, at the various stages of its formation and development, and the simple discovery of one of its elements, including the sequence or partial sequence of a gene, cannot constitute patentable inventions.

2. An element isolated from the human body or otherwise produced by means of a technical process, including the sequence or partial sequence of a gene, may constitute a patentable invention, even if the structure of that element is identical to that of a natural element.

3. The industrial application of a sequence or a partial sequence of a gene must be disclosed in the patent application.

Article 6

1. Inventions shall be considered unpatentable where their commercial exploitation would be contrary to ordre public or morality; however, exploitation shall not be deemed to be so contrary merely because it is prohibited by law or regulation.

2. On the basis of paragraph 1, the following, in particular, shall be considered unpatentable:

   (a) processes for cloning human beings;

   (b) processes for modifying the germ line genetic identity of human beings;

   (c) uses of human embryos for industrial or commercial purposes;

   (d) processes for modifying the genetic identity of animals which are likely to cause them suffering without any substantial medical benefit to man or animal, and also animals resulting from such processes.

AGREEMENT ON TRADE–RELATED ASPECTS OF INTELLECTUAL PROPERTY RIGHTS (TRIPS)

http://www.wto.org/english/docs_e/legal_e/27–trips.pdf

Section 5: Patents

Article 27 Patentable Subject Matter

1. Subject to the provisions of paragraphs 2 and 3 below, patents shall be available for any inventions, whether products or processes, in all fields of technology, provided that they are new, involve an inventive step

and are capable of industrial application * * *. [P]atents shall be available and patent rights enjoyable without discrimination as to the place of invention, the field of technology and whether products are imported or locally produced.

2.   Members may exclude from patentability inventions, the prevention within their territory of the commercial exploitation of which is necessary to protect *ordre public* or morality, including to protect human, animal or plant life or health or to avoid serious prejudice to the environment, provided that such exclusion is not made merely because the exploitation is prohibited by domestic law.

3.   Members may also exclude from patentability:

(a) diagnostic, therapeutic and surgical methods for the treatment of humans or animals;

(b) plants and animals other than microorganisms, and essentially biological processes for the production of plants or animals other than non-biological and microbiological processes. However, Members shall provide for the protection of plant varieties either by patents or by an effective *sui generis* system or by any combination thereof. The provisions of this subparagraph shall be reviewed four years after the date of entry into force of the WTO [World Trade Organization] Agreement.

EUROPEAN PATENT OFFICE ENLARGED
BOARD OF APPEAL

G 0002/06, 25 November 2008.

* * *

II.   The appeal pending before the referring Board 3.3.08 is against the decision of 13 July 2004 of the Examining Division, refusing European patent application No. 96 903 521.1 This decision related to a set of claims 1 to 10 of which Claim 1 reads:

1.   A cell culture comprising primate embryonic stem cells [including human embryonic stem cells] which (i) are capable of proliferation in vitro [sic] culture for over one year, (ii) maintain a karyotype in which all chromosomes normally characteristic of the primate species are present and are not noticeably altered through culture for over one year, (iii) maintain the potential to differentiate to derivatives of endoderm, mesoderm, and ectoderm tissues throughout the culture, and (iv) are prevented from differentiating when cultured on a fibroblast feeder layer.

* * *

VI.   The main points submitted by the Appellant [Wisconsin Alumni Research Foundation] in written submissions of 31 October 2006 and 22 May 2008, and at the oral proceedings on 24 June 2008 can be summarized as follows:

Introductory comment:

> In 1998 the named inventor using the methods suggested in the application was, the first to successfully isolate and culture human embryonic stem, cells that can grow *in vitro*. The provision of these is a major scientific breakthrough and pioneering invention opening up a new and very exciting field of research having great potential for promising medical therapies and other applications, and worthy of patent protection.

* * *

*Q2. * * * [D]oes Rule 23d(c) [now 28(c)] EPC forbid the patenting, of claims directed to products (here: human embryonic stem cell cultures) which—as described in the application—at the filing date could be prepared exclusively by a method which necessarily involved the destruction of the human embryos from which the said products are derived if the said method is not part of the claims?*

15.   The present invention concerns *inter alia* human embryonic stem cell cultures which at the filing date could be prepared exclusively by a method which, necessarily involved the destruction of the human embryos from which they are derived, said method not being part of the claims. Rule 28 (formerly 23d) EPC provides, *inter alia:* "Under Article 53(a), European patents shall not be granted in respect of biotechnological inventions which, in particular, concern ... (c) uses of human embryos for industrial or commercial purposes". The question thus is whether the present invention falls under the prohibition of this provision.

* * *

18.   On its face, the provision of Article 6(2) (c) of the Directive and thus also of Rule 28(c) EPC is straightforward and prohibits the patenting if a human embryo is used for industrial or commercial purposes. Such a reading is also in line with the concern of the legislator to prevent a misuse in the sense of a commodification of human embryos (see the decision of the German Bundespatentgericht (BPatG) of 5 December. 2006, 3 Ni 42/04, point IV 2.2 i.f.) and with one of the essential objectives of the whole Directive to protect human dignity. This concern is also evidenced by the selective policy of the Community in funding stem cell research. The Appellant argues that the very fact that the Community funds such research shows that the legislator did not want to exclude activities such as those underlying the present invention and which include the use (and destruction) of human embryos. However, Council press release 11554/06 (Presse 215) of 24 July 2006, states on page 7 that as regards Community Research "... the Commission confirmed that it will continue the current practice and will not submit to the Regulatory Committee proposals for projects which include research activities which destroy human embryos, including for the procurement of

stem cells. The exclusion of funding for this step of research will not prevent the Community funding of subsequent steps involving human embryonic stem cells." This selective funding in no way supports the Appellant's position.

19. Against a reading of Rule 28(c) EPC being applicable to the invention in this case, the Appellant has put forward several arguments. Firstly it argues for a very specific meaning of embryo, as being embryos of 14 days or older, in accordance with usage in the medical field.

20. Neither the EU legislator nor the EPC legislator have chosen to define the term "embryo", as used in the Directive or now in Rule 28 EPC. This contrasts with the German law (Gesetz zum Schutz von Embryonen of 13 December 1990, § 8) where embryo is defined as including a fertilized egg, or the, UK law (Human Fertilisation and Embryology Act 199.0, Section 1(1)) where embryo includes the two cell zygote and an egg in the process of fertilisation. The EU and the EPC legislators must presumably have been aware of the definitions used in national laws on regulating embryos, and yet chose to leave the term undefined. Given the purpose to protect human dignity and prevent the commercialization of embryos, the Enlarged Board can only presume that "embryo" was not to be given any restrictive meaning in Rule 28 EPC, as to do so would undermine the intention of the legislator, and that what is an embryo is a question of fact in the context of any particular patent application.

21. Secondly the Appellant contends that, in order to fall under the prohibition of Rule 28(c) EPC, the use of human embryos must be claimed.

22. However, this Rule (as well as the corresponding provision of the Directive) does not mention claims, but refers to "invention" in the context of its exploitation. What needs to be looked at is not just the explicit wording of the claims but the technical teaching of the application as a whole as to how the invention is to be performed. Before human embryonic stem cell cultures can be used they have to be made. Since in the case referred to the Enlarged Board the only teaching of how to perform the invention to make human embryonic stem cell cultures is the use (involving their destruction) of human embryos, this invention falls under the prohibition of Rule 28(c) EPC (compare also the decision of the BPatG of 5 December 2006, loc.cit., points IV 2.1 to 2.3). To restrict the application of Rule 28(c) EPC to what an applicant chooses explicitly to put in his claim would have the undesirable consequence of making avoidance of the patenting prohibition merely a matter of clever and skilful drafting of such claim.

23. In a case like the present one, where the teaching to obtain the embryonic human stem cells claimed is confined to the use (involving their destruction) of human embryos, the argument raised by the Appellant, namely that the exclusion from patentability would go

much too far if one would consider all the steps preceding an invention for the purposes of Rule 28(c) EPC, is not relevant.

24. The Appellant further argues that the use of human embryos to make the claimed human embryonic stem cell cultures is not a use "for industrial or commercial purposes", as required by Rule 28(c) EPC, but some other form of use not prohibited by this Rule.

25. A claimed new and inventive product must first be made before it can be used. Such making is the ordinary way commercially to exploit the claimed invention and falls within the monopoly granted, as someone having a patent application with a claim directed to this product has on the grant of the patent the right to exclude others from making or using such product. Making the claimed product remains commercial or industrial exploitation of the invention even where there is an intention to use that product for further research. On the facts which this Board must assume in answering the referred question 2, making the claimed product involves the destruction of human embryos. This use involving destruction is thus an integral and essential part of the industrial or commercial exploitation of the claimed invention, and thus violates the prohibition of Rule 28(c) EPC.

26. In the context of the terms "for industrial or commercial purposes" used in Rule 28 EPC and Article 6(2)(c) of the Directive, the Appellant has also pointed to the legislative history of the Directive and argued that the replacement of the terms "methods in which human embryos are used" by "uses of human embryos for industrial or commercial purposes" meant a narrowing of the provision, excluding inventions such as the present one from its scope.

27. However, this Board cannot detect such a narrowing. The reason given in Point 37 of the Common Position for this amendment is that a distinction was wanted between the uses of human embryos for industrial or commercial purposes, which were excluded from patentability, and inventions for therapeutic or diagnostic purposes applied to the human embryo and useful to it, the latter not being excluded from patentability. To clarify this exception from the exception, a new Recital 42 was introduced into the Directive. Thus, if anything, these reasons point in the direction of the opinion of this Board that in the present case human embryos are used for industrial or commercial purposes, since patentability was only considered if the invention was to the benefit of the embryo itself (compare also decision of the BPatG of 5 December 2006, loc. cit., point IV 3). That this is not the case here is evident, since the embryos used to perform the invention are destroyed.

* * *

29. * * * In this context, it is important to point out that it is not the fact of the patenting itself that is considered to be against *ordre*

public or morality, but it is the performing of the invention, which includes a step (the use involving its destruction of a human embryo) that has to be considered to contravene those concepts.

* * *

35.   In view of the questions referred, this decision is not concerned with the patentability in general of inventions relating to human stem cells or human stem cell cultures. It holds unpatentable inventions concerning products (here human stem cell cultures) which can only be obtained by the use involving their destruction of human embryos.

NOTES AND QUESTIONS

1.   How does the European patent system differ from that of the United States?

2.   Can a scientist patent a gene in Europe? Under the European directive, can a scientist patent the process of analyzing a particular gene sequence in patients and preclude anyone else from testing patients for that gene sequence?

3.   If the patenting of genetic tests were shown to interfere with health care or scientific research, could there be recourse to eliminate such patents in Europe? What about in the United States?

4.   In *eBay v. MercExchange*, the Supreme Court held that lower courts must consider the interest of the public before granting an injunction in patent cases. eBay Inc. v. MercExchange, L.L.C., 547 U.S. 388 (2006). The interest of the public could include public health. Julie Burger and Justin Brunner, A Court's Dilemma: When Patents Conflict with Public Health, 12 Virginia Journal of Law & Technology 7 (Fall 2007). How similar is the decision in *eBay* to Article 27 of TRIPS?

5.   Under the European patent law, can a company patent embryonic stem cells or the process to remove stem cells from an embryo? What about a human embryo that has been genetically enhanced? Would such an embryo be patentable in the United States?

6.   In 2001, Myriad Genetics obtained three patents related to the BRCA1 gene from the European Patent Office (EPO): EP 699754 (methods used to detect mutations in the BRCA1 gene that predispose a person to cancer); EP 705902 (an isolated gene comprising the BRCA1 gene sequence); and EP 705903 (method for diagnosing a predisposition to cancer by detecting alterations in the BRCA1 gene). Myriad Genetics also obtained a patent on the BRCA2 gene from the EPO in 2003: EP 785216 (an isolated gene comprising the BRCA1 gene sequence). After obtaining the patents, Myriad told doctors and researchers in France that they could no longer diagnose breast cancer by comparing patients' samples with the genetic sequence for the gene patented by Myriad. Instead, the company required that all samples be sent to its lab in Salt Lake City, Utah for testing. French physicians protested on various grounds, including a concern that Myriad's test only identified 10 to 20 percent of the mutations in the gene. In fact, a French physician had found a mutation in an American family (which consisted of a

deletion of a large section of the gene–12,000 base pairs) that the Myriad test had missed.

The Institut Curie, the Social Democratic Party of Switzerland, Greenpeace Germany, Assistance publique—Hôpitaux de Paris, the Institut Gustave Roussy, the Belgian Society of Human Genetics, the Netherlands Ministry of Health, the Austrian Federal Ministry of Social Security, the Institut Gustave Roussy, and the Associazione Angela Serra per la Ricerca sul Cancro challenged Myriad's BRCA1 and BRCA2 patents through the EPO's opposition procedure. The Opposition Division of the European Patent Office revoked EP 699754 and allowed amended narrower versions of the other two patents to be maintained. On appeal, the Technical Board of Appeals overturned the decision to revoke EP 699754 and ultimately found that all three of BRCA1 patents could be maintained in amended forms, but denied Myriad's claim on the sequences. In their amended forms, EP 699754 covers a method for diagnosing a predisposition to cancer by detecting certain mutations in the BRCA1 gene; EP 705902 covers nucleic acid probes; and EP 705903 covers a method for diagnosing a predisposition to cancer by detecting a specific mutation (185delAG) in the BRCA1 gene that has a high frequency of occurrence in Ashkenazi Jews but also occurs throughout the general population. Technical Board of Appeal Decisions: T 1213/05; T 0080/05; and T 0666/05. Technical Board of Appeals Maintains Two "Myriad/Breast Cancer" Patents in Limited Form, Nov. 19, 2008, http://www.epo.org/topics/news/2008/20081119.html.

The Opposition Division of the European Patent Office decided that Myriad's BRCA2 patent, EP 785216, could be maintained in a narrower amended form. EP 785216 was amended to cover the use of a BRCA2 gene with a specific mutation (6174delT) for the diagnosis of a predisposition to breast cancer in Ashkenazi–Jewish women. The rationale for granting this amended patent was that the specific mutation occurs at a higher frequency in Ashkenazi women than in the general population. Commentators have suggested that this use of race by the EPO carries the risk of characterizing the Ashkenazi as a distinct genetic group. The danger is that the EPO's position lends legitimacy to the view that Ashkenazi Jews are genetically different. This is troubling since Jews have been historically persecuted on the premise of being genetically different. At the time of the Myriad controversy, Gert Matthijs, of the Catholic University of Leuven (KUL) in Belgium and a member of the European Society of Human Genetics said "we believe there is something fundamentally wrong if one ethnic group can be singled out by patenting. . . . It means that someone is exploring the limits of what is acceptable legally and ethically." Patents Single Out Ashkenazi Jewish Women, New Scientist, July 9, 2005, http://www.newscientist.com/article/mg18725073.300.

Canadian health care providers have also criticized Myriad's patents on the BRCA1 and BRCA2 genes. The government-funded health plan pays $800 for each genetic test for breast cancer done at Canadian laboratories. Myriad wanted the tests sent to its own lab at a charge of $3,850 each. This high cost caused the province of British Columbia to eliminate the genetic test for breast cancer from its health plan. Premier Mike Harris of Ontario, however, kept the test in his province's plan, but called on political leaders to address the patent issue, since the increasing number of gene patents could bankrupt the health care system entirely. "The benefits of a worldwide effort such as the Human Genome Project should not be the property of a handful of people or companies," said Harris. Ontario Won't Halt Gene Test for Cancer, London Free Press, Sept. 20, 2001, at A10. In 2002, Ontario, Health Canada, and the Patent Policy Directorate at Industry Canada met to resolve the Myriad patent problem. Ontario and Health Canada were concerned that broad patents on genes would put health research and Canadian health services at risk. After over seven years of policy debate, Ontario has continued a policy of ignoring Myriad's patents and providing BRCA1 and BRCA2 testing. Thus far Myriad has not sued. E. Richard Gold & Julia Carbone, Myriad Genetics: In the Eye of the Storm, International Expert Group on Biotechnology, Innovation, and Intellectual Property, 1–59, 29 (2008), http://ssrn.com/abstract= 120098.

IX. TECHNOLOGY TRANSFER LAWS AND COMMERCIALIZATION

JAMES V. LACY, ET AL., TECHNOLOGY TRANSFER LAWS GOVERNING FEDERALLY FUNDED RESEARCH AND DEVELOPMENT

19 Pepp. L. Rev. 1, 9–11, 13–14 (1991).

Economists have long realized that innovation affects demand and is thus one of the key forces that drives capitalism. A robust economy requires investment in research and development, as technological change most often results in production shifts, which can form the cornerstone of economic development and expansion. Technological innovation, however, can only be economically meaningful when it impacts the market. Therefore, a good idea which is never commercialized simply remains only a good idea.

The absence of a federal technology transfer policy prior to 1980 resulted in an enormous investment of money in R & D, which yielded a great deal of government-owned, but unlicensed, patents. Technological, bureaucratic, legal and communications problems, as well as a lack of basic incentives, prevented the transfer of this technology to American industry.

* * *

The commercialization of federal technology is a complicated problem. Historically, there were no incentives for institutions or individuals who performed government research to produce commercially viable technology. A major stumbling block was the lack of a statutory basis for royalty sharing. Without such explicit authority, it was unlikely that inventors in the public sector would be motivated by salary alone.

* * *

An economic parable states: "Lease a man a garden and in time he will leave you a patch of sand. Make a man a full owner of a patch of sand and he will grow there a garden on the sand." This parable highlights one of the basic problems with federal patent policy and technology transfer prior to 1980. There was no incentive for government inventors or institutions to create commercially viable technology because there was no legal basis to gain a piece of the resulting monetary rewards. As a result, commercially viable technology was not being created, and the wealth of federal inventions that were available for licensing were not being transferred for use in the private sector.

* * *

As a result of this concern, Congress enacted a series of bipartisan initiatives in the 1980s. These initiatives were aimed at revising government patent policy, reducing legal and bureaucratic barriers, and creating incentives to improve federal technology transfer to the private sector.

* * *

In short, recipients of government contracts, grants and cooperative agreements for the performance of experimental, developmental or research work funded in whole or in part by the federal government may now elect to retain title to any subject invention made in the course of that work.

* * *

[T]he government by statute must retain certain residual rights to the invention, including a government-use license to practice the invention, the right to limit exclusive licenses into which the funding recipient may wish to enter, and so-called "march-in" rights.

The government-use license that the Bayh–Dole Act imposes on contractors and grantees must provide the federal government with, at a minimum, "a nonexclusive, nontransferable, irrevocable, paid-up license to practice or have practiced for or on behalf of the United States any subject invention throughout the world." The statute also provides that the license may provide for such additional rights in favor of the government as are determined to be necessary by the government agency entering into grant, contract or cooperative agreement.

* * *

Finally, the government retains so-called "march-in" rights to inventions made with full or partial government funding. The government is provided the right to "march-in" and retake title to inventions in those cases where: (1) "action is necessary because the contractor or assignee has not taken, or is not expected to take within a reasonable time, effective steps to achieve practical application of the subject invention;" or (2) "action is necessary to alleviate health or safety needs which are not reasonably satisfied" by the contractor or grantee; or (3) "action is necessary to meet requirements for public use specified by Federal regulations and such requirements are not reasonably satisfied" by the contractor or grantee; or (4) the contractor or grantee has granted an exclusive license in violation of the "Preference for United States Industry."

SHELDON KRIMSKY, THE PROFIT OF SCIENTIFIC DISCOVERY AND ITS NORMATIVE IMPLICATIONS

75 Chi.–Kent L. Rev. 15, 21–22, 28–37 (1999).

[S]everal pieces of legislation were enacted in 1980 to create more cooperation between industries and universities. The Stevenson–Wydler Technology Transfer Act of 1980 encouraged interaction and cooperation among government laboratories, universities, big industries and small businesses. In the same year, Congress passed the Bayh–Dole Patent and Trademark Laws Amendment, which gave intellectual property rights to research findings to institutions that had received federal grants. Discoveries and inventions from public funds could be patented and licensed, initially to small businesses, with exclusive rights of royalties given to the grantee * * *. In 1983, by executive order, President Reagan extended the Bayh–Dole Act to all industry. To close the circle of research partnerships among industry, universities and government, Congress passed the Federal Technology Transfer Act of 1986, which expanded science-industry collaboration to laboratories run by the federal government. Governmental standards for keeping an arm's length from industry were being turned on their head. Through this act, a government scientist could form a "Cooperative Research and Development Agreement" ("CRADA") with a company as a route to commercializing discoveries made in a federal laboratory. Government scientists could accept royalty income up to a given amount [$150,000], fifteen percent of the National Institutes of Health (the "NIH") share, to supplement their salaries. At the time this policy was enacted, there was virtually no public discussion about the blatant conflicts of interest that this would introduce. The CRADA required government scientists to keep company data confidential and impeded the sharing of information in government laboratories.

* * *

By the mid–1980s, genetic technology had spawned hundreds of new companies, many with academic scientists as officers, board members or consultants. Small venture capital companies colonized the faculty of prestigious universities for building their intellectual capital. Major corporations that had sector interests in drugs, therapeutics, and agriculture invested large sums into multi-year contracts with universities.

* * *

A number of studies published in the early 1990s began to shed some light on the extent to which the burgeoning field of biotechnology had begun to impact universities.

* * *

* * * [T]hese new arrangements * * * impeded the "free, rapid, and unbiased dissemination of research results." Biotechnology faculty with industry support were four times as likely as other biotechnology faculty to report that trade secrets had resulted from their research. The vast majority of the faculty without industry support viewed the commercial relationships as undermining intellectual exchange and cooperation within departments. The surveys also revealed that faculty believed the new relationships were responsible for skewing the research agenda in biology toward applied research.

* * *

[T]wo concerns flowing from the intense commercialization of science that could not be resolved by ethical standards established within universities were conflicts of interest and scientific bias * * *. Of the 789 articles and 1105 Massachusetts authors reviewed in * * * [a] study, thirty-four percent of the papers met one or more of the criteria for possessing a financial interest. Furthermore, none of the articles revealed the authors' financial interests.

* * *

[A] study which appeared in the Journal of General Internal Medicine reported that clinical trials sponsored by pharmaceutical companies were much more likely to favor new drugs (an outcome beneficial to the sponsoring companies in this case) than studies not supported by the companies.

A recent study [found] that * * * those authors who were supportive of the obesity drugs were significantly more likely than the authors who were neutral or critical of the drugs to have a financial agreement with a manufacturer of a calcium channel blocker (ninety-six percent, sixty percent and thirty-seven percent respectively).

* * *

Because every biomedical discovery has potential monetary value, the new culture of science will seek to protect that discovery from becoming part of the "knowledge commons." * * * Scientists, instead of sharing their discoveries in a timely fashion, are protecting them as trade secrets. This has resulted in wasteful duplication of research, not for the sake of verifying results, but rather for establishing the unpublished data needed to secure intellectual property rights over the discovery. Writing in Science, Eliot Marshall noted, "[w]hile some duplication is normal in research, experts say it is getting out of hand in microbe sequencing. Tuberculosis, like *Staph aureus* and *H. pylori* will be sequenced many times over in part because sequencers aren't sharing data, whether for business reasons or because of interlab rivalries."

* * *

Companies have taken out patents on disease causing bacteria and viruses, sometimes keeping confidential parts of the sequenced genome.

This may inhibit two companies competing in the search for a cure or treatment for a disease. Why should anyone own the natural sequence of a natural microorganism? Pharmaceutical companies can now exercise property ownership over both the drug to treat a disease and the microorganism that causes it. The intense privatization of biomedical knowledge that has evolved since the 1980s threatens the entire edifice of public health medicine.

LORI ANDREWS AND DOROTHY NELKIN, BODY BAZAAR: THE MARKET FOR HUMAN TISSUE IN THE BIOTECHNOLOGY AGE

60–62 (2001).

Nowhere are these fundamental changes in scientific research more evident than at the National Institutes of Health, where scientists who are paid with taxpayer dollars can patent their research and pad their salaries with royalties. Allowing publicly-funded researchers to gain commercially, however, means that government-funded laboratories are experiencing some of the same problems with secrecy and conflicts of interest as industry-funded academic laboratories.

When government scientists enter joint ventures with business, their lips must be sealed concerning their data. Cooperative research and development agreements (CRADAs) restrict free access of information in NIH labs because of the requirement that company data be kept confidential. Anthony S. Fauci, the director of the National Institute of Allergy and Infectious Diseases, is worried about the effect of "CRADA fever." For the first time in his several decades at NIH, he says, scientists are reluctant to share information.

Leslie Roberts, writing in Science, points out, "The obvious concern is that some investigators might use the resources developed with public funds for their own proprietary interest. Yet another question is how will the genome project receive impartial advice when nearly everyone has a financial stake in it?"

People increasingly feel they are paying twice for research—once to the government to fund the research, and then again to the biotech companies who sell them products developed from taxpayer-funded research. In the pharmaceutical field, patents are generally thought to be necessary in order to encourage the discovery of drugs, and to fund the testing of these drugs on animals and humans. But genetic discoveries are very different from drug development. The public pays for the research that yields discoveries of genetic associations with disease. Genetic testing can be applied to humans as soon as the gene is accurately identified, without costly clinical trials. Financial compensation is thus less warranted.

The high costs of genetic tests and treatments seems ludicrous, given that taxpayers have provided much of the funding for their discovery. The

NIH paid $4.6 million toward discovery of a gene predisposing women to breast cancer.

This situation—in which private companies [such as Myriad, which holds the patent on the BRCA1 gene and the BRCA2 gene predisposing to cancer] get a boost from taxpayer-funded research—occurs daily. Sixty-three percent of gene patents are based on research funded with federal money. The same thing occurs with funding for drug research. A Boston Globe investigative report revealed "a billion-dollar taxpayers' subsidy for pharmaceutical companies already awash in profits." Of the 50 top-selling drugs, 48 benefited from federal research money in their development or testing phases. A kidney cancer drug, Proleukin, benefited from $46 million in research funds. Patients nevertheless pay up to $20,000 per treatment. Taxcol, a breast and ovarian cancer treatment, received a $27 million federal subsidy; the treatment cost—$5,500.

Federal subsidies could have a much different impact on drug prices. The federal research handout could come with a requirement that the drug company lower prices to the consumer. When the federal Department of Health and Human Services patented the genetic sequence used for diagnosing Tay–Sachs in 1995, it made a deliberate attempt to hold down the price of tests. The genetic test for Tay–Sachs costs a mere $100, in contrast to the $2,580 for Myriad's breast cancer test.

Protests against federal subsidies of pharmaceutical companies erupted in the 1980s around the drug AZT, which was developed through taxpayer-funded research at the National Cancer Institute. Studies in 1986 determined that AZT could be used to treat AIDS, and the FDA rapidly approved the drug. Burroughs–Wellcome received the exclusive right to market the drug and charged $10,000 to $12,000 for a year's supply. AIDS activists questioned the high price, given that the drug's development had been subsidized by the federal government. In response, Burroughs–Wellcome lowered the price to $2,500 and in 1989 the NIH responded by imposing a "reasonable pricing clause" in its subsequent contracts with companies. The reasonable pricing clause required companies to which the NIH licensed its products to prove that there was "a reasonable relationship between the pricing of license product, the public investment in the product, and health and safety needs of the public." This approach made good sense, but in April 1995 NIH Director Harold Varmus unilaterally decided to eliminate the reasonable pricing clause. A federal bill to reinstate it has been introduced in Congress, but at this writing it is languishing in committee. U.S. Representative Bernard Sanders of Vermont suggests a more direct approach: cutting the prices of drugs that are developed with public funds.

NOTES AND QUESTIONS

1. What was the purpose of the technology transfer laws?

2. Should products such as genetic tests or gene therapies that are developed with substantial amounts of public funds be priced or marketed differently than privately developed tests and therapies?

3. When a researcher has a financial interest in the gene or drug that he or she studies, should that fact be disclosed in publications? Since the publication of the Krimsky article, the journal Nature has changed its policy and now requires disclosures of conflicts of interest.

4. If you wanted to design a study to determine if the technology transfer laws have been effective, how would you do it? How would you define and measure "success"? The number of patents obtained by government employees and federally-funded researchers has increased since the laws' passage. Is that a sufficient indicator of success?

X. PATIENTS: THE SOURCES OF GENES AND CELL LINES

MOORE v. REGENTS OF THE UNIVERSITY OF CALIFORNIA

793 P.2d 479 (Cal. 1990).

PANELLI, J.

We granted review in this case to determine whether plaintiff has stated a cause of action against his physician and other defendants for using his cells in potentially lucrative medical research without his permission. Plaintiff alleges that his physician failed to disclose preexisting research and economic interests in the cells before obtaining consent to the medical procedures by which they were extracted.

* * *

The plaintiff is John Moore (Moore), who underwent treatment for hairy-cell leukemia at the Medical Center of the University of California at Los Angeles (UCLA Medical Center). The five defendants are: (1) Dr. David W. Golde (Golde), a physician who attended Moore at UCLA Medical Center; (2) the Regents of the University of California (Regents), who own and operate the university; (3) Shirley G. Quan, a researcher employed by the Regents; (4) Genetics Institute, Inc. (Genetics Institute); and (5) Sandoz Pharmaceuticals Corporation and related entities (collectively Sandoz).

Moore first visited UCLA Medical Center on October 5, 1976, shortly after he learned that he had hairy-cell leukemia. After hospitalizing Moore and "withdr[awing] extensive amounts of blood, bone marrow aspirate, and other bodily substances," Golde confirmed that diagnosis. At this time all defendants, including Golde, were aware that "certain blood products and blood components were of great value in a number of commercial and scientific efforts" and that access to a patient whose blood contained these substances would provide "competitive, commercial, and scientific advantages."

On October 8, 1976, Golde recommended that Moore's spleen be removed. Golde informed Moore "that he had reason to fear for his life, and that the proposed splenectomy operation ... was necessary to slow down the progress of his disease." Based upon Golde's representations, Moore signed a written consent form authorizing the splenectomy.

Before the operation, Golde and Quan "formed the intent and made arrangements to obtain portions of [Moore's] spleen following its removal" and to take them to a separate research unit. Golde gave written instructions to this effect on October 18 and 19, 1976. These research activities "were not intended to have ... any relation to [Moore's] medical ... care." However, neither Golde nor Quan informed Moore of their plans to conduct this research or requested his permission. Surgeons at UCLA Medical Center, whom the complaint does not name as defendants, removed Moore's spleen on October 20, 1976.

Moore returned to the UCLA Medical Center several times between November 1976 and September 1983. He did so at Golde's direction and based upon representations "that such visits were necessary and required for his health and well-being, and based upon the trust inherent in and by virtue of the physician-patient relationship...." On each of these visits Golde withdrew additional samples of "blood, blood serum, skin, bone marrow aspirate, and sperm." On each occasion Moore travelled to the UCLA Medical Center from his home in Seattle because he had been told that the procedures were to be performed only there and only under Golde's direction.

"In fact, [however,] throughout the period of time that [Moore] was under [Golde's] care and treatment, ... the defendants were actively involved in a number of activities which they concealed from [Moore]...." Specifically, defendants were conducting research on Moore's cells and planned to "benefit financially and competitively ... [by exploiting the cells] and [their] exclusive access to [the cells] by virtue of [Golde's] ongoing physician-patient relationship...."

Sometime before August 1979, Golde established a cell line from Moore's T-lymphocytes.[2] On January 30, 1981, the Regents applied for a

---

2. A T-lymphocyte is a type of white blood cell. T-lymphocytes produce lymphokines, or proteins that regulate the immune system. Some lymphokines have potential therapeutic value. If the genetic material responsible for producing a particular lymphokine can be identified, it can sometimes be used to manufacture large quantities of the lymphokine through the techniques of recombinant DNA. (See generally U.S. Congress, Office of Technology Assessment, *New Developments in Biotechnology: Ownership of Human Tissues and Cells* (1987) at pp. 31–46 (hereafter OTA Report)) * * *.

While the genetic code for lymphokines does not vary from individual to individual, it can nevertheless be quite difficult to locate the gene responsible for a particular lymphokine. Because T-lymphocytes produce many different lymphokines, the relevant gene is often like a needle in a haystack. (OTA Rep., supra, p. 42.) Moore's T-lymphocytes were interesting to the defendants because they overproduced certain lymphokines, thus making the corresponding genetic material easier to identify. (In published research papers, defendants and other researchers have shown that the overproduction was caused by a virus, and that normal T-lymphocytes infected by the virus will also overproduce * * *.)

Cells taken directly from the body (primary cells) are not very useful for these purposes. Primary cells typically reproduce a few times and then die. One can, however, sometimes continue to use cells for an extended period of time by developing them into a "cell line," a culture capable of reproducing indefinitely. This is not, however, always an easy task. "Long-term growth of human cells and tissues is difficult, often an art," and the probability of succeeding with any given cell sample is low, except for a few types of cells not involved in this case.

patent on the cell line, listing Golde and Quan as inventors. "[B]y virtue of an established policy ..., [the] Regents, Golde, and Quan would share in any royalties or profits ... arising out of [the] patent." The patent issued on March 20, 1984, naming Golde and Quan as the inventors of the cell line and the Regents as the assignee of the patent. (U.S. Patent No. 4,438,032 (Mar. 20, 1984).)

The Regent's patent also covers various methods for using the cell line to produce lymphokines. Moore admits in his complaint that "the true clinical potential of each of the lymphokines ... [is] difficult to predict, [but] ... competing commercial firms in these relevant fields have published reports in biotechnology industry periodicals predicting a potential market of approximately $3.01 Billion Dollars by the year 1990 for a whole range of [such lymphokines]...."

* * *

Based upon these allegations, Moore attempted to state 13 causes of action. [These were: (1) "Conversion"; (2) "lack of informed consent"; (3) "breach of fiduciary duty"; (4) "fraud and deceit"; (5) "unjust enrichment"; (6) "quasi-contract"; (7) "bad faith breach of the implied covenant of good faith and fair dealing"; (8) "intentional infliction of emotional distress"; (9) "negligent misrepresentation"; (10) "intentional interference with prospective advantageous economic relationships"; (11) "slander of title"; (12) "accounting"; and (13) "declaratory relief."] Each defendant demurred to each purported cause of action. The superior court, however, expressly considered the validity of only the first cause of action, conversion [and rejected it] * * *.

[T]he Court of Appeal reversed, holding that the complaint did state a cause of action for conversion * * *.

A. BREACH OF FIDUCIARY DUTY AND LACK OF INFORMED CONSENT

Moore repeatedly alleges that Golde failed to disclose the extent of his research and economic interests in Moore's cells before obtaining consent to the medical procedures by which the cells were extracted. These allegations, in our view, state a cause of action against Golde for invading a legally protected interest of his patient. This cause of action can properly be characterized either as the breach of a fiduciary duty to disclose facts material to the patient's consent or, alternatively, as the performance of medical procedures without first having obtained the patient's informed consent.

Our analysis begins with three well-established principles. First, "a person of adult years and in sound mind has the right, in the exercise of control over his own body, to determine whether or not to submit to lawful medical treatment." Second, "the patient's consent to treatment, to be effective, must be an informed consent." Third, in soliciting the patient's consent, a physician has a fiduciary duty to disclose all information material to the patient's decision.

These principles lead to the following conclusions: (1) a physician must disclose personal interests unrelated to the patient's health, whether research or economic, that may affect the physician's professional judgment; and (2) a physician's failure to disclose such interests may give rise to a cause of action for performing medical procedures without informed consent or breach of fiduciary duty.

* * *

Indeed, the law already recognizes that a reasonable patient would want to know whether a physician has an economic interest that might affect the physician's professional judgment. As the Court of Appeal has said, "[c]ertainly a sick patient deserves to be free of any reasonable suspicion that his doctor's judgment is influenced by a profit motive." The desire to protect patients from possible conflicts of interest has also motivated legislative enactments. Among these is Business and Professions Code section 654.2. Under that section, a physician may not charge a patient on behalf of, or refer a patient to, any organization in which the physician has a "significant beneficial interest, unless [the physician] first discloses in writing to the patient, that there is such an interest and advises the patient that the patient may choose any organization for the purposes of obtaining the services ordered or requested by [the physician]." Similarly, under Health and Safety Code section 24173, a physician who plans to conduct a medical experiment on a patient must, among other things, inform the patient of "[t]he name of the sponsor or funding source, if any, . . . and the organization, if any, under whose general aegis the experiment is being conducted."

* * *

Yet a physician who treats a patient in whom he also has a research interest has potentially conflicting loyalties. This is because medical treatment decisions are made on the basis of proportionality—weighing the benefits *to the patient* against the risks *to the patient*. * * * A physician who adds his own research interests to this balance may be tempted to order a scientifically useful procedure or test that offers marginal, or no, benefits to the patient. The possibility that an interest extraneous to the patient's health has affected the physician's judgment is something that a reasonable patient would want to know in deciding whether to consent to a proposed course of treatment. It is material to the patient's decision and, thus, a prerequisite to informed consent.

* * *

B. CONVERSION

Moore also attempts to characterize the invasion of his rights as a conversion—a tort that protects against interference with possessory and ownership interests in personal property. He theorizes that he continued to own his cells following their removal from his body, at least for the purpose of directing their use, and that he never consented to their use in potentially lucrative medical research. Thus, to complete Moore's argument, defendants' unauthorized use of his cells constitutes a conversion. As a result of the alleged conversion, Moore claims a proprietary interest in each of the products that any of the defendants might ever create from his cells or the patented cell line.

* * *

Since Moore clearly did not expect to retain possession of his cells following their removal, to sue for their conversion he must have retained an ownership interest in them. But there are several reasons to doubt that he did retain any such interest. First, no reported judicial decision supports Moore's claim, either directly or by close analogy. Second, California statutory law drastically limits any continuing interest of a patient in excised cells. Third, the subject matters of the Regents' patent—the patented cell line and the products derived from it—cannot be Moore's property.

Neither the Court of Appeal's opinion, the parties' briefs, nor our research discloses a case holding that a person retains a sufficient interest in excised cells to support a cause of action for conversion. We do not find this surprising, since the laws governing such things as human tissues, transplantable organs, blood, fetuses, pituitary glands, corneal tissue, and dead bodies deal with human biological materials as objects sui generis, regulating their disposition to achieve policy goals rather than abandoning them to the general law of personal property. It is these specialized statutes, not the law of conversion, to which courts ordinarily should and do look for guidance on the disposition of human biological materials.

* * *

Moore, adopting the analogy originally advanced by the Court of Appeal, argues that "[i]f the courts have found a sufficient proprietary interest in one's persona, how could one not have a right in one's own genetic material, something far more profoundly the essence of one's human uniqueness than a name or a face?" However, as the defendants' patent makes clear—and the complaint, too, if read with an understanding of the scientific terms which it has borrowed from the patent—the goal and result of defendants' efforts has been to manufacture lymphokines. Lymphokines, unlike a name or a face, have the same molecular structure in every human being and the same, important functions in every human being's immune system. Moreover, the particular genetic material which is responsible for the natural production of lymphokines, and which defendants use to manufacture lymphokines in the laboratory, is also the same in every person; it is no more unique to Moore than the number of vertebrae in the spine or the chemical formula of hemoglobin.

Another privacy case offered by analogy to support Moore's claim establishes only that patients have a right to refuse medical treatment * * *. Yet one may earnestly wish to protect privacy and dignity without accepting the extremely problematic conclusion that interference with those interests amounts to a conversion of personal property. Nor is it necessary to force the round pegs of "privacy" and "dignity" into the square hole of "property" in order to protect the patient, since the fiduciary-duty and informed-consent theories protect these interests directly by requiring full disclosure.

* * *

The extension of conversion law into this area will hinder research by restricting access to the necessary raw materials. Thousands of human cell lines already exist in tissue repositories, such as the American Type Culture Collection and those operated by the National Institutes of Health and the American Cancer Society. These repositories respond to tens of thousands of requests for samples annually. Since the patent office requires the holders of patents on cell lines to make samples available to anyone, many patent holders place their cell lines in repositories to avoid the administrative burden of responding to requests. At present, human cell lines are routinely copied and distributed to other researchers for experimental purposes, usually free of charge. This exchange of scientific materials, which still is relatively free and efficient, will surely be compromised if each cell sample becomes the potential subject matter of a lawsuit.

* * *

For these reasons, we hold that the allegations of Moore's third amended complaint state a cause of action for breach of fiduciary duty or lack of informed consent, but not conversion.

* * *

BROUSSARD, J., concurring and dissenting.

* * *

With respect to the conversion cause of action, I dissent from the majority's conclusion that the facts alleged in this case do not state a cause of action for conversion * * *. [T]he pertinent inquiry is not whether a patient generally retains an ownership interest in a body part after its removal from his body, but rather whether a patient has a right to determine, before a body part is removed, the use to which the part will be put after removal. Although the majority opinion suggests that there are "reasons to doubt" that a patient retains "any" ownership interest in his organs or cells after removal, the opinion fails to identify any statutory provision or common law authority that indicates that a patient does not generally have the right, before a body part is removed, to choose among the permissible uses to which the part may be put after removal. On the contrary, the most closely related statutory scheme—the Uniform Anatomical Gift Act—is quite clear that a patient does have this right.

* * *

Although the majority opinion does not acknowledge that plaintiff's conversion action is supported by existing common law principles, its reasoning suggests that the majority would, in any event, conclude that considerations of public policy support a judicially crafted limitation on a patient's right to sue anyone involved in medical research activities for conversion of a patient's excised organs or cells * * *.

One of the majority's principal policy concerns is that "[t]he extension of conversion law into this area will hinder research by restricting access to the necessary raw materials"—the thousands of cell lines and tissues already in cell and tissue repositories. The majority suggests that the "exchange of scientific materials, which still is relatively free and efficient, will surely be compromised if each cell sample becomes the potential subject matter of a lawsuit."

This policy argument is flawed in a number of respects * * *. For example, if a patient donated his removed cells to a medical center, reserving the right to approve or disapprove the research projects for which the cells would be used, and if another medical center or a drug manufacturer stole the cells after removal and used them in an unauthorized manner for its own economic gain, no breach-of-fiduciary-duty cause of action would be available and a conversion action would be necessary to vindicate the patient's rights. Under the majority's holding, however, the patient would have no right to bring a conversion action, even against such a thief. As this hypothetical illustrates, even if there were compelling policy reasons to limit the potential liability of innocent researchers who use cells obtained from an existing cell bank, those policy considerations would not justify the majority's broad abrogation of *all* conversion liability for the unauthorized use of body parts.

* * *

Because potential liability under a conversion theory will exist in only the exceedingly rare instance in which a doctor knowingly concealed from the patient the value of his body part or the patient's specific directive with regard to the use of the body part was disregarded, there is no reason to think that application of settled conversion law will have any negative effect on the primary conduct of medical researchers who use tissue and cell banks.

* * *

Under established conversion law, a "subsequent innocent converter" does not forfeit the proceeds of his own creative efforts, but rather "is entitled to the benefit of any work or labor that he has expended on the [property]."

* * *

Finally, the majority's analysis of the relevant policy considerations tellingly omits a most pertinent consideration. In identifying the interests of the patient that are implicated by the decision whether to recognize a conversion cause of action, the opinion speaks only of the "patient's right to make autonomous medical decisions" * * * and fails even to mention the patient's interest in obtaining the economic value, if any, that may adhere in the subsequent use of his own body parts. Although such economic value may constitute a fortuitous "windfall" to the patient * * *, the fortuitous nature of the economic value does not justify the creation of a novel exception from conversion liability which sanctions the intentional misappropriation of that value from the patient.

* * *

It is certainly arguable that, as a matter of policy or morality, it would be wiser to prohibit any private individual or entity from profiting from the fortuitous value that adheres in a part of a human body, and instead to require all valuable excised body parts to be deposited in a public repository which would make such materials freely available to all scientists for the betterment of society as a whole * * *. But the majority's rejection of plaintiff's conversion cause of action does not mean that body parts may not be bought or sold for research or commercial purposes or that no private individual or entity may benefit economically from the fortuitous value of plaintiff's diseased cells. Far from elevating these biological materials above the marketplace, the majority's holding simply bars *plaintiff*, the source of the cells, from obtaining the benefit of the cells' value, but permits *defendants*, who allegedly obtained the cells from plaintiff by improper means, to retain and exploit the full economic value of their ill-gotten gains free of their ordinary common law liability for conversion.

* * *

Mosk, J., dissenting

* * *

[T]he majority conclude that the patent somehow cut off all Moore's rights—past, present, and future—to share in the proceeds of defendants' commercial exploitation of the cell line derived from his own body tissue. The majority cite no authority for this unfair result, and I cannot believe it is compelled by the general law of patents: a patent is not a license to defraud. Perhaps the answer lies in an analogy to the concept of "joint inventor." I am aware that "patients and research subjects who contribute cells to research will not be considered inventors." Nor is such a person strictly speaking a "joint inventor" within the meaning of the term in federal law. (35 U.S.C. § 116.) But he does fall within the spirit of that law: "The joint invention provision guarantees that all who contribute in a substantial way to a product's development benefit from the reward that the product brings. Thus, the protection of joint inventors encourages scientists to cooperate with each other and ensures that each contributor is rewarded fairly."

* * *

The majority begin their analysis by stressing the obvious facts that research on human cells plays an increasingly important role in the progress of medicine, and that the manipulation of those cells by the methods of biotechnology has resulted in numerous beneficial products and treatments. Yet it does not necessarily follow that, as the majority claim, application of the law of conversion to this area "will hinder research by restricting access to the necessary raw materials," i.e., to cells, cell cultures, and cell lines.

* * *

To begin with, if the relevant exchange of scientific materials was ever "free and efficient," it is much less so today. Since biological products of genetic engineering became patentable in 1980 (Diamond v. Chakrabarty, 447 U.S. 303 (1980)), human cell lines have been amenable to patent protection and, as the Court of Appeal observed in its opinion below, "The rush to patent for exclusive use has been rampant." * * * Thus defendants herein recited in their patent specification, "At no time has the Mo cell line been available to other than the investigators involved with its initial discovery and only the conditioned medium from the cell line has been made available to a limited number of investigators for collaborative work with the original discoverers of the Mo cell line."

* * *

"Record keeping would not be overly burdensome because researchers generally keep accurate records of tissue sources for other reasons: to trace anomalies to the medical history of the patient, to maintain title for other researchers and for themselves, and to insure reproducibility of the experiment."

* * *

In any event, in my view whatever merit the majority's single policy consideration may have is outweighed by two contrary considerations, i.e., policies that are promoted by recognizing that every individual has a legally protectible property interest in his own body and its products. First, our society acknowledges a profound ethical imperative to respect the human body as the physical and temporal expression of the unique human persona. One manifestation of that respect is our prohibition against direct abuse of the body by torture or other forms of cruel or unusual punishment. Another is our prohibition against indirect abuse of the body by its economic exploitation for the sole benefit of another person. The most abhorrent form of such exploitation, of course, was the institution of slavery. Lesser forms, such as indentured servitude or even debtor's prison, have also disappeared. Yet their specter haunts the laboratories and boardrooms of today's biotechnological research-industrial complex. It arises wherever scientists or industrialists claim, as defendants claim here, the right to appropriate and exploit a patient's tissue for their sole economic benefit—the right, in other words, to freely mine or harvest valuable physical properties of the patient's body.

* * *

The majority's final reason for refusing to recognize a conversion cause of action on these facts is that "there is no pressing need" to do so because the complaint also states another cause of action that is assertedly adequate to the task; that cause of action is "the breach of a fiduciary duty to disclose facts material to the patient's consent or, alternatively, . . . the performance of medical procedures without first having obtained the patient's informed consent".

* * *

The remedy is largely illusory * * *. Few if any judges or juries are likely to believe that disclosure of such a possibility of research or development would dissuade a reasonably prudent person from consenting to the treatment. For example, in the case at bar no trier of fact is likely to believe that if defendants had disclosed their plans for using Moore's cells, no reasonably prudent person in Moore's position—i.e., a leukemia patient suffering from a grossly enlarged spleen—would have consented to the routine operation that saved or at least prolonged his life.

* * *

The second reason why the nondisclosure cause of action is inadequate for the task that the majority assign to it is that it fails to solve half the problem before us: it gives the patient only the right to *refuse* consent, i.e., the right to prohibit the commercialization of his tissue; it does not give him the right to *grant* consent to that commercialization on the condition that he share in its proceeds.

* * *

In sum, the nondisclosure cause of action (1) is unlikely to be successful in most cases, (2) fails to protect patients' rights to share in the proceeds of the commercial exploitation of their tissue, and (3) may allow the true exploiters to escape liability. It is thus not an adequate substitute, in my view, for the conversion cause of action.

GREENBERG v. MIAMI CHILDREN'S HOSPITAL RESEARCH INSTITUTE, INC.

264 F.Supp.2d 1064 (S.D. Fla. 2003).

MORENO, J.

Plaintiffs Daniel Greenberg ("Greenberg"), Fern Kupfer ("Kupfer"), Frieda Eisen ("Eisen"), David Green ("Green"), Canavan Foundation, Dor Yeshorim, and National Tay–Sachs and Allied Diseases Association, Inc. (collectively "Plaintiffs") brought this diversity action for damages and equitable and injunctive relief to redress Defendants' alleged breach of informed consent, breach of fiduciary duty, unjust enrichment, fraudulent concealment, conversion, and misappropriation of trade secrets. The individual plaintiffs Greenberg, Kupfer, Eisen, and Green are parents of children who were afflicted with Canavan disease. The other Plaintiffs are non-profit organizations that provided funding and information to Defendants to research and discover the Canavan disease gene. Defendants are the physician-researcher, Dr. Reuben Matalon ("Matalon"), Variety Children's Hospital d/b/a Miami Children's Hospital ("MCH"), and the hospital's research affiliate, Miami Children's Hospital Research Institute ("MCHRI").

The Complaint alleges a tale of a successful research collaboration gone sour. In 1987, Canavan disease still remained a mystery—there was no way to identify who was a carrier of the disease, nor was there a way to identify a fetus with Canavan disease. Plaintiff Greenberg approached Dr. Matalon, a research physician * * * [and] requested Matalon's involvement in discovering the genes that were ostensibly responsible for this fatal disease, so that tests could be administered to determine carriers and allow for prenatal testing for the disease.

Greenberg and the Chicago Chapter of the National Tay–Sachs and Allied Disease Association, Inc. ("NTSAD") located other Canavan families and convinced them to provide tissue (such as blood, urine, and autopsy samples), financial support, and aid in identifying the location of Canavan families internationally.

* * *

The individual Plaintiffs allege that they provided Matalon with these samples and confidential information "with the understanding and expectations that such samples and information would be used for the specific purpose of researching Canavan disease and identifying mutations in the Canavan disease which could lead to carrier detection within their families and benefit the population at large." Plaintiffs further allege that it was their "understanding that any carrier and prenatal testing developed in connection with the research for which they were providing essential support would be provided on an affordable and accessible basis, and that Matalon's research would remain in the public domain to promote the discovery of more effective prevention techniques and treatments and, eventually, to effectuate a cure for Canavan disease." This understanding stemmed from their "experience in community testing for Tay–Sachs disease, another deadly genetic disease that occurs most frequently in families of Ashkenazi Jewish descent."

Using Plaintiffs' blood and tissue samples, familial pedigree information, contacts, and financial support, Matalon and his research team successfully isolated the gene responsible for Canavan disease. * * * [U]nbeknownst to Plaintiffs, a patent application was submitted for the genetic sequence that Defendants had identified. This application was granted in October 1997. * * * Through patenting, Defendants acquired the ability to restrict any activity related to the Canavan disease gene, including without limitation: carrier and prenatal testing, gene therapy and other treatments for Canavan disease and research involving the gene and its mutations.

Plaintiffs allege that they did not learn of [the patent] until November 1998, when MCH revealed their intention to limit Canavan disease testing through a campaign of restrictive licensing of the Patent.

* * *

Based on these facts, Plaintiffs filed a six-count complaint on October 30, 2000, against Defendants asserting the following causes of action: (1) lack of informed consent; (2) breach of fiduciary duty; (3) unjust enrichment; (4) fraudulent concealment; (5) conversion; and (6) misappropriation of trade secrets. Plaintiffs generally seek a permanent injunction restraining Defendants from enforcing their patent rights, damages in the form of all royalties Defendants have received on the Patent as well as all financial contributions Plaintiffs made to benefit Defendants' research. Plaintiffs allege that Defendants have earned significant royalties from Canavan disease testing in excess of $75,000 through enforcement of their gene patent, and that Dr. Matalon has personally profited by receiving a recent substantial federal grant to undertake further research on the gene patent.

* * *

A. LACK OF INFORMED CONSENT

Plaintiffs * * * claim that Defendants breached this duty [of informed consent] * * * when they did not disclose the intent to patent and enforce for their own economic benefit the Canavan disease gene. The duty was also breached by the misrepresentation of the research purpose that Matalon had included on the written consent forms. Finally, the Plaintiffs allege that if they had known that the Defendants would "commercialize" the results of their contributions, they would not have made the contributions.

* * *

The question of informed consent in the context of medical research, however, is a relatively novel one in Florida. Medical consent law does not apply to medical researchers. Florida Statute § 760.40 does require, however, that a person's informed consent must be obtained when any genetic analysis is undertaken on his or her tissue.

* * *

Since the law regarding a duty of informed consent for research subjects is unsettled and fact-specific and further, Defendants conceded at oral argument that a duty does attach at some point in the relationship, the Court finds that in certain circumstances a medical researcher does have a duty of informed consent. Nevertheless, without clear guidance from Florida jurisprudence, the Court must consider whether this duty of informed consent in medical research can be extended to disclosure of a researcher's economic interests.

* * *

Defendants assert that extending a possible informed consent duty to disclosing economic interests has no support in established law, and more ominously, this requirement would have pernicious effects over medical research, as it would give each donor complete control over how medical research is used and who benefits from that research. The Court agrees and declines to extend the duty of informed consent to cover a researcher's economic interests in this case.

* * *

In declining to extend the duty of informed consent to cover economic interests, the Court takes note of the practical implications of retroactively imposing a duty of this nature. First, imposing a duty of the character that Plaintiffs seek would be unworkable and would chill medical research as it would mandate that researchers constantly evaluate whether a discloseable event has occurred. Second, this extra duty would give rise to a type of dead-hand control that research subjects could hold because they would be able to dictate how medical research progresses. Finally, the Plaintiffs are more accurately portrayed as donors rather than objects of human experimentation, and thus the voluntary nature of their submissions warrants different treatment. Accordingly, the Court finds that Plaintiffs have failed to state a claim upon which relief may be granted, and this count is DISMISSED.

B.   BREACH OF FIDUCIARY DUTY

The individual Plaintiffs allege in Count II of the Complaint that all the Defendants were in a fiduciary relationship with them, and as such, they should have disclosed all material information relating to the Canavan disease research they were conducting, including any economic interests of the Defendants relating to that research.

* * *

Defendants assert that the Complaint does not allege any facts that show that the trust was recognized and accepted. Plaintiffs allege, however, that Defendants accepted the trust by undertaking research that they represented as being for the benefit of the Plaintiffs. * * * Taking all the facts alleged as true, the Court finds that Plaintiffs have not sufficiently alleged the second element of acceptance of trust by Defendants and therefore have failed to state a claim. There is no automatic fiduciary relationship that attaches when a researcher accepts medical donations and the acceptance of trust, the second constitutive element of finding a fiduciary duty, cannot be assumed once a donation is given. Accordingly, this claim is DISMISSED.

C.   UNJUST ENRICHMENT

In Count III of the Complaint, Plaintiffs allege that MCH is being unjustly enriched by collecting license fees under the Patent. * * * The Court finds that Plaintiffs have sufficiently alleged the elements of a claim for unjust enrichment to survive Defendants' motion to dismiss.

* * *

[T]he facts paint a picture of a continuing research collaboration that involved Plaintiffs also investing time and significant resources in the race to isolate the Canavan gene. Therefore, given the facts as alleged, the Court finds that Plaintiffs have sufficiently pled the requisite elements of an unjust enrichment claim and the motion to dismiss for failure to state a claim is DENIED as to this count.

D.   FRAUDULENT CONCEALMENT

Count IV of the Complaint alleges that MCH fraudulently concealed from the Plaintiffs that (1) the Hospital would economically benefit from Canavan research; (2) it would patent the Canavan gene mutation; and (3) it would license the testing under the Patent.

* * *

[T]here was no duty of disclosure to the Plaintiffs. Allegations of fraudulent concealment by silence must be accompanied by allegations of a special relationship that gives rise to a duty to speak. * * * [T]he facts asserted as fraudulently concealed were accessible to the Plaintiffs. A patent becomes public knowledge when issued and Plaintiffs could have undertaken due diligence to uncover the facts surrounding the patent application. Plaintiffs' allegations that they were prevented from making reasonable inquiries because they had no reason to believe that patenting would occur is unavailing because if they were so concerned about a possible intent to patent then a simple phone inquiry to the Defendants would have uncovered this fact.

* * *

Plaintiffs contend that, but for the fraudulent non-disclosure, they would have acted differently. Nevertheless, fraud must be specially pled, and the Complaint does not adequately allege a claim based on a special relationship or of injury nor does it allege more specifics about efforts at concealment or about any representations made by Matalon as to what he would do with the test results. Therefore, the Court finds that the Complaint lacks the specificity required by Fed.R.Civ.P. 9(b). Accordingly, the fraudulent concealment claim is DISMISSED.

E.   CONVERSION

The Plaintiffs allege in Count V of their Complaint that they had a property interest in their body tissue and genetic information, and that they owned the Canavan registry in Illinois which contained contact information, pedigree information and family information for Canavan families worldwide. They claim that MCH and Matalon converted the names on the register and the genetic information by utilizing them for the hospitals' "exclusive economic benefit." The Court disagrees and declines to find a property interest for the body tissue and genetic information voluntarily given to Defendants. These were donations to research without any contemporaneous expectations of return of the body tissue and genetic samples, and thus conversion does not lie as a cause of action.

In Florida, the tort of "conversion is an unauthorized act which deprives another of his property permanently or for an indefinite time." Using property given for one purpose for another purpose constitutes conversion.

First, Plaintiffs have no cognizable property interest in body tissue and genetic matter donated for research under a theory of conversion. This case is similar to Moore v. Regents of the University of California, where the Court declined to extend liability under a theory of conversion to misuse of a person's excised biological materials. 51 Cal.3d 120 (Cal. 1990). The plaintiff in Moore alleged that he had retained a property right in excised bodily material used in research, and therefore retained some control over the results of that research. The California Supreme Court, however, disagreed and held that the use of the results of medical research inconsistent with the wishes of the donor was not conversion, because the donor had no property interest at stake after the donation was made. The Court also recognized that the patented result of research is "both factually and legally distinct" from excised material used in the research.

Second, limits to the property rights that attach to body tissue have been recognized in Florida state courts * * * Similarly, the property right in blood and tissue samples also evaporates once the sample is voluntarily given to a third party.

Plaintiffs rely on Pioneer Hi–Bred v. Holden Foundation, 1987 WL 341211 (S.D.Iowa, Oct.30, 1987), aff'd, 35 F.3d 1226 (8th Cir.1994), for their assertion that genetic information itself can constitute property for the purposes of the tort of conversion. In that case, the Court held that a corn seed's property interest in the genetic message contained in a corn seed variety is property protected by the laws of conversion. Plaintiffs argue that giving permission for one purpose (gene discovery) does not mean they agreed to other uses (gene patenting and commercialization). Yet, the Pioneer court recognized that, "where information is gathered and arranged at some cost and sold as a commodity on the market, it is properly protected as property." This seemingly provides more support for property rights inherent in Defendants' research rather than the donations of Plaintiffs' DNA. * * *

Plaintiffs have not cited any case that interprets the statute as applying to an analogous factual situation, and this Court's investigation did not find any relevant case either. Moreover, even assuming, arguendo, that the statute does create a property right in genetic material donated for medical research purposes, it is unclear whether this confers a property right for conversion, a common law cause of action.

Finally, although the Complaint sets out that Plaintiff Greenberg owned the Canavan Registry, the facts alleged do not sufficiently allege the elements of a prima facie case of conversion, as the Plaintiffs have not alleged how the Defendants' use of the Registry in their research was an expressly unauthorized act. The Complaint only alleges that the Defendants "utilized the information and contacts for their exclusive economic benefit." There is no further allegation of the circumstances or conditions that were attached to the Defendants' use of the Canavan Registry. Nor are there any allegations about any of the Plaintiffs' entitlement to possess the Registry.

The Court finds that Florida statutory and common law do not provide a remedy for Plaintiffs' donations of body tissue and blood samples under a theory of conversion liability. Indeed, the Complaint does not allege that the Defendants used the genetic material for any purpose but medical research. Plaintiffs claim that the fruits of the research, namely the patented material, was commercialized. This is an important distinction and another step in the chain of attenuation that renders conversion liability inapplicable to the facts as alleged. If adopted, the expansive theory championed by Plaintiffs would cripple medical research as it would bestow a continuing right for donors to possess the results of any research conducted by the hospital. At the core, these were donations to research without any contemporaneous expectations of return. Consequently, the Plaintiffs have failed to state a claim upon which relief may be granted on this issue. Accordingly, this claim is DISMISSED.

F. MISAPPROPRIATION OF TRADE SECRETS

The Canavan Registry was not misappropriated by MCH because there is no allegation that MCH knew or should have known that the Canavan Registry was a confidential trade secret guarded by Plaintiffs, and furthermore, that Matalon had acquired through improper means. Plaintiffs cannot donate information that they prepared for fighting a disease and then retroactively claim that it was a protected secret. * * * This claim is therefore DISMISSED.

AMERICAN MEDICAL ASSOCIATION, COUNCIL ON ETHICAL AND JUDICIAL AFFAIRS, CODE OF MEDICAL ETHICS: CURRENT OPINIONS WITH ANNOTATIONS
(2000).

2.08   Commercial Use of Human Tissue

The rapid growth of the biotechnology industry has resulted in the commercial availability of numerous therapeutic and other products developed from human tissue. Physicians contemplating the commercial use of human tissue should abide by the following guidelines:

(1) Informed consent must be obtained from patients for the use of organs or tissues in clinical research.

(2) Potential commercial applications must be disclosed to the patient before a profit is realized on products developed from biological materials.

(3) Human tissue and its products may not be used for commercial purposes without the informed consent of the patient who provided the original cellular material.

(4) Profits from the commercial use of human tissue and its products may be shared with patients, in accordance with lawful contractual agreements.

(5) The diagnostic and therapeutic alternatives offered to patients by their physicians should conform to standards of good medical practice and should not be influenced in any way by the commercial potential of the patient's tissue.

Issued June 1994 based on the report Who Should Profit from the Economic Value of Human Tissue? An Ethical Analysis, adopted June 1990.

HUGO ETHICS COMMITTEE STATEMENT ON BENEFIT–SHARING

http://www.eubios.info/BENSHARE.htm.

April 9, 2000.

A. INTRODUCTION

[The Human Genome Organization (HUGO) is the international organisation of scientists involved in the Human Genome Project (HGP), the global initiative to map and sequence the human genome. HUGO was established in 1989 by a group of the world's leading genome scientists to promote international collaboration within the project.]

The HUGO Ethics Committee subscribes to the following four principles presented in the HUGO Statement on the Principled Conduct of Genetic Research (1996):

- Recognition that the human genome is part of the common heritage of humanity:

- Adherence to international norms of human rights:

- Respect for the values, traditions, culture, and integrity of participants: and

- Acceptance and upholding of human dignity and freedom.

The above Statement further provided:

"That undue inducement through compensation for individual participants, families and populations should be prohibited. This prohibition does not include agreements with individuals, families, groups, communities or populations that foresee technology transfer, local training, joint ventures, provision of health care or of information, infrastructures, reimbursement of costs, or the possible use of a percentage of any royalties for humanitarian purposes."

* * *

G.   BENEFIT–SHARING

A benefit is a good that contributes to the well-being of an individual and/or a given community (e.g. by region, tribe, disease-group * * *). Benefits transcend avoidance of harm (non-maleficence) in so far as they promote the welfare of an individual and/or of a community. Thus, a benefit is not identical with profit in the monetary or economic sense. Determining a benefit depends on needs, values, priorities and cultural expectations.

In genetic research in general, benefit-sharing has also been established as a principle of international law in the area of biodiversity and genetic resources in food and agriculture.

People with common multifactorial diseases, may have few shared beliefs about benefit. Indeed, benefit will often be that of eventual prevention or treatment and affordable medical services.

Prior consultation with individuals and communities and their involvement and participation in the research design is a preliminary basis for the future distribution of benefit and may be considered a benefit in itself. Such prior discussion should include consideration of affordability and accessibility of eventual therapy, and preventive and diagnostic products of research.

The actual or future benefits discussed should not serve as an inducement to participation. Nor should there be any financial gain from participation in genetic research. This does not exclude, however, the possibility of reimbursement for an individual's time, inconvenience and expenses (if any), even if there is a general distribution of benefits to the community. Participants should be told of such general distribution at the outset.

In the very rare case where the extended family or a small group/tribe harbours an unusual gene, yet the research eventually benefits those with another disorder, justice may require that the original group deserve recognition. In this situation, benefits could be provided to all members of the group regardless of their participation in the research. Limiting the returns to only those who participated could create divisiveness within a group and is inconsistent with solidarity.

Even if there are no results or profits, at a minimum, individuals, families and groups participating in research should be thanked (e.g. letter, or a small token or gift where the culture expects this). They should also receive information about the general outcome(s) of research in understandable language. The ethical advisability of provision of information to individuals about their results should be determined separately for each specific project. Moreover, immediate benefits such as medical care, technology transfer, or contribution to the local community infrastructure (e.g., schools, libraries, sports, clean water * * *) could be provided.

In the case of profit-making endeavours, the general distribution of benefits should be the donation of a percentage of the net profits (after taxes) to the health care infrastructure or for vaccines, tests, drugs, and treatments, or, to local, national and international humanitarian efforts.

RECOMMENDATIONS

Whereas:

- we all share a common genetic heritage, and
- there are different definitions of community, and
- communities may have different beliefs about what constitutes a benefit, and
- genetic research should foster health for all human beings,

The HUGO Ethics Committee recommends:

1) that all humanity share in, and have access to, the benefits of genetic research.

2) that benefits not be limited to those individuals who participated in such research.

3) that there be prior discussion with groups or communities on the issue of benefit-sharing.

4) that even in the absence of profits, immediate health benefits as determined by community needs could be provided.

5) that at a minimum, all research participants should receive information about general research outcomes and an indication of appreciation.

6) that profit-making entities dedicate a percentage (e.g. 1%–3%) of their annual net profit to healthcare infrastructure and/or to humanitarian efforts.

NOTES AND QUESTIONS

1. On what legal grounds does the patient have a right to be informed of a physician's research interests and commercial interests?

2. Why does Justice Mosk believe that the nondisclosure causes of action are inadequate?

3. Is it likely that granting Moore a property interest in his tissue would have hampered research? How?

4. Are there situations in which an individual should have a property interest in his or her tissue or genes?

5. Would allowing a person to have a property right in his or her genes "commodify" individuals? If selling genes is permitted, what about other

parts of people like organs? What about selling people as a whole—i.e., slavery?

It is important to note that just because something is legally considered to be property does not preclude limiting its sale or use. Justice Mosk in his *Moore* dissent points out, "For a variety of policy reasons, the law limits or even forbids the exercise of certain rights over certain forms of property. For example, both law and contract may limit the right of an owner of real property to use his parcel as he sees fit. Owners of various forms of personal property may likewise be subject to restrictions on the time, place, and manner of their use. Limitations on the disposition of real property, while less common, may also be imposed. Finally, some types of personal property may be sold but not given away, while others may be given away but not sold, and still others may neither be given away nor sold." What restrictions, if any, are appropriate for genes?

6. Justice Broussard suggests an alternative to patenting: making cell lines and genes available to all scientists through a public repository. What are the pros and cons of this more communitarian alternative instead of allowing either the patients or the scientists to have a property right in cells or genes?

7. The majority in *Moore* makes much of the fact that California statutes (such as public health laws on the disposal of human tissue) limit patients' control over their cells. Justice Mosk, in dissent, notes that the statutory law also "does not authorize the principal use that defendants claim the right to make of Moore's tissue, i.e., its commercial exploitation." Do the existing statutes shed light on the question of whether patients should have a property right in their tissue or genes?

8. The court in *Greenberg* notes in its discussion of conversion that Florida law limits the property rights a person has in body tissue. What if such a law did not exist? Would the court have come to the same conclusion with only the decision in *Moore* to rely on?

The court also states that any property rights that might exist in body tissues evaporate once the body tissues are voluntarily given to a third party. What would happen, however, if some property rights were retained? If the person providing the body tissues to the third party retained the right to have the tissues removed from the research being undertaken, or retained the right to have the tissues destroyed, would the outcome be the same?

9. Assume that couples have submitted to blood tests to determine if they are carriers of a particular genetic disease. Unbeknownst to them, their doctor uses their blood sample to find the gene for another disease and patents it and receives royalties. Has the doctor violated the AMA Code of Ethics?

What if the doctor removed patient names from a large number of patients' blood samples and gave them to a scientist at a for-profit biotechnology company who then found a new gene, patented it, and received royalties? Would the doctor have violated his fiduciary duty or duty of informed consent? Would the scientist for the for-profit company have violated the AMA Code of Ethics or the federal research regulations (discussed in Chapter

4)? If the scientist were at the National Institutes of Health, would he or she have violated the AMA Code or federal regulations? Could the government scientist personally profit if the research were funded with taxpayer money?

10. A company, DNA Copyright Institute of San Francisco, offers to copyright celebrities' DNA for $1,500 by filing their DNA code with the U.S. copyright office. The company's founder says copyrighting DNA will protect against unauthorized cloning of celebrities. Although codes in general are protectible by copyright, some copyright experts argue that such a procedure is inappropriate for the genetic code, since individuals are not the "author" of their DNA. Philip Cohen, Born to Make You Happy, New Scientist, April 25, 2001, at 12.

11. Although much attention has been paid to the John Moore case, he is not the first person whose cell lines were made commercially available. In 1951, a 31–year-old African–American woman, Henrietta Lacks, was dying of ovarian cancer. Dr. George Otto Grey, a cell biologist at Johns Hopkins University at the time, used her cancerous tissue to create the first immortalized human cell line, the HeLa cell line, which could grow continuously in vitro. The HeLa cells have been used by generations of scientists for research. In a recent interview, her husband said, "As far as them selling my wife's cells without my knowledge and making a profit—I don't like it at all. They are exploiting us both." Harriet A. Washington, Henrietta Lacks—An Unsung Hero, Emerge, Oct. 1994, at 29.

12. Patients' tissue samples are now a commercial resource for hospitals. Duke University Medical Center entered into a commercial agreement with Ardais, granting the start-up genomics company access to Duke's patients' tissue. Harvard Beth Israel Deaconess Medical Center entered into a similar arrangement. Should patients whose tissue is part of these deals be informed of the arrangements? Should they receive compensation? For information about the agreements, see Deborah Josefsen, Human Tissue for Sale: What Are the Costs?, 173 Western J. Med. 302 (2000).

13. A person on whose land oil was discovered would receive a percent of the profits generated when the oil is extracted, refined, and sold. Should people whose genes are patented similarly receive compensation? The HUGO recommendations reject such compensation and argue in favor of "benefit sharing." What is the rationale for a system that benefits the community rather than the individual who is the source of the genes?

14. In the *Moore* case, Justice Mosk suggested that patients or research subjects who were the source of genes or cell lines could be listed as co-inventors on the patent. A decade later, in 2000, the patient group PXE International followed that approach. The patients suffered from pseudoxanthoma elasticum, a genetic disorder that causes connective tissue in the skin, eyes, and arteries to calcify. Because PXE had been an under-researched disease, PXE International took the initiative to set up a tissue bank of families afflicted with the disease. Before researchers gained access to the tissue bank, they had to sign a contract saying that they would share with PXE International the ownership and profits from research using those samples. When University of Hawaii pathobiologist Charles Boyd found the PXW gene in 2000, he filed a patent application listing Sharon Terry, the

founder of PXE International and the mother of two children with the disorder, as a co-inventor on the patent. PXE International will split royalties gained from the patent equally with the university, and will have control over licensing arrangements for the gene patent. Matt Fleisher, Seeking Rights to Crucial Genes, National Law Journal, June 25, 2001 at C 1.

If you were representing a patient group, what provisions might you want to put into an agreement with researchers?

15.   When arrangements to be a co-inventor or co-owner of a patent are not made in advance, the people whose DNA was used to find a particular gene may not be able to assert a claim to be recognized on the patent. Eric Fuchs realized he had been repeatedly exposed to HIV infection without becoming symptomatic. He suggested to researchers that they search his blood for the unique factor that appeared to make him immune. When researchers at the Aaron Diamond AIDS Research Center found it, they patented it. Fuchs believes that his role in the research should be recognized via co-ownership of the patent.

In an analogous case, a non-scientist who conceived of a particular type of research was not granted any rights to share in the proceeds of the resulting patent. Marlo Brown, a veterinary hospital manager who maintained a shelter for sick, stray, and abandoned cats, brought detailed observations and records of her cats' illnesses to a well-known animal virologist at U.C. Davis School of Veterinary Medicine. Brown provided the cats' histories and blood samples, as well as her belief that the cats were infected with a virus similar to the human AIDS virus. After extensive lab work, the virologist and a colleague received a patent based on their isolation and substantial purification of the virus. Though the doctors widely and publicly credited Brown for her role in the discovery of the new virus, "FIV," the court ruled that she was not a joint inventor under patent law. The court reasoned, "she at most played a substantial role in the discovery of FIV * * * regardless of the value of her research leads, she cannot be deemed to have contributed to the conception of the inventions covered by the patents." Brown v. Regents of Univ. of California, 866 F.Supp. 439 (N.D.Cal.1994).

CHAPTER 6

GENETIC TESTING AND REPRODUCTION

■ ■ ■

I. GENETIC TESTING TECHNOLOGY

Information about an individual's genetic endowment can come from a variety of sources, such as family history, physical appearance, and physical examination (including laboratory tests for levels of cholesterol, blood glucose, and other chemicals that may vary, to some degree, as a result of genes). This chapter focuses on one specific type of laboratory testing: DNA testing.

Until fairly recently, knowledge about an individual's genetic inheritance was based on indirect information, such as observations of the symptoms of genetic disease, detection of gene products (e.g., elevated chloride levels in the sweat of persons with cystic fibrosis), or descriptions of symptoms in other family members. In addition, cell nuclei can be collected and cultured and a visual image obtained of the chromosomes. This permits the detection of chromosomal abnormalities such as Down syndrome, caused by an extra copy of chromosome 21. Typically the cellular material is obtained prenatally through amniocentesis or chorionic villus sampling, and facilitates reproductive decision-making such as whether or not to have an abortion. Originally, the chromosomes were visually inspected under a microscope. More recently, a technique called FISH (for "Fluorescence In Situ Hybridization") employs fluorescence to "paint" the chromosomes.

A more direct type of information about genes can be obtained by linkage analysis. This technique is used when the exact location and sequence of the disease gene (or genes) is not yet known. Linkage analysis relies on the identification of "markers," discussed in Chapter 2 (these markers, it will be recalled, are stretches of DNA believed to be near to or containing disease genes)—and on an analysis of DNA from family members. (The analysis of DNA from family members is necessary because markers differ among families.)

Until recently, it was difficult to detect a gene correlated with disease in a person's DNA because of the large number of genes in a human cell. The first breakthrough came when a Scottish scientist, Edward Southern, developed a powerful method to pinpoint a specific genetic sequence containing, or near, the "target" gene.

This simple technique named Southern blotting after its creator begins with a sample of DNA from a patient's blood or saliva. The DNA is chopped up by a chemical, called a restriction enzyme, which cuts the DNA into fragments at specific places. Then the fragments are separated by size by being sifted through a porous jelly-like substance through which an electric current is passed. This process is called gel electrophoresis. Since smaller fragments move faster through the gel than larger ones, the different-sized fragments end up at different positions. A chemical is used to "denature" or unzip the two strands of DNA into single strands. The single-stranded fragments are blotted out of the gel onto a special paper without changing their relative positions, and the paper copy of the gel is bathed in a solution containing "probes." Probes are radioactively labeled short lengths of single-stranded DNA that match a specific DNA sequence in the gene of interest. Where the probe recognizes its "complementary" sequence, it will attach to the paper and its location can be detected by placing an x-ray film on top of the paper. The radioactivity discolors the x-ray film, resulting in a pattern of "bands" which can be compared to the band patterns of DNA from unaffected individuals that do not have the target mutation.

Southern blotting or hybridization was the first technique that allowed detection and isolation of abnormal genes in a number of diseases, including sickle cell anemia and Huntington disease, before the precise sequence of the entire gene was known.

This technique used to be expensive and time consuming but with the advent of PCR, it has become easy, fast and inexpensive. In the mid 1980s a young scientist, Kary Mullis, developed a method called polymerase chain reaction or PCR. This technique is used to copy, or amplify, small fragments of DNA within a test tube. For DNA testing, a sample of DNA is mixed with three types of chemicals: a primer, which attaches to the DNA and begins the duplication process; an enzyme that makes copies of the DNA; and the nucleotides that are necessary to form the duplicates. This mixture is put in a machine that increases and reduces the temperature every few minutes, doubling the "target" sequence with each cycle. This results in hundreds of millions of copies in a matter of hours. When the final mixture is run through an electrophoretic gel, the amplified stretch of DNA can be seen visually as a band at a known position on the gel. This technique can be used to copy a specific stretch of the DNA that contains the target mutation. If the target mutation is present, it will be amplified and appear on the gel.

PCR is fast and inexpensive. However, it has some limitations, such as the fact that it does not provide information about the entire sequence of the gene, so that if certain mutations are not known or are not tested for, they can be missed.

The third and most sophisticated technique is called DNA sequencing. In the most common type of sequencing, developed by Fred Sanger, a stretch of DNA is amplified and single strands of it are produced. Again, a primer chemical and enzymes are added which make copies of the DNA, but this time the mixture contains special nucleotides that stop the copying at specific points depending on where they are incorporated into the copied sequence. This produces fragments of different lengths. The reaction is repeated four times, for each of the four nucleotides, and the result is run though an electrophoretic gel which reveals the location of the different nucleotides on the original stretch of DNA. The resulting sequence of bases is then analyzed to reveal mutations.

This technique yields the most detailed information compared to the others, but is more expensive and time consuming and requires large quantities of DNA.

Currently, most sequencing is automated. PCR is used to produce the desired amounts of DNA, and automated sequencers, which use a computer and laser to read the banding pattern produced on a gel, translate the pattern into the sequence of nucleotides in a matter of seconds.

Most recently, DNA microarrays (''chips'') have been developed that speed the analysis by several orders of magnitude. These consist of a small glass plate encased in plastic which is manufactured using a process similar to the one used to make computer microchips. The surface of the glass plate, or chip, contains a number of synthetic, single-stranded DNA sequences corresponding to stretches of bases in a ''normal'' gene. A sample of the individual's DNA, together with a sample of ''normal'' DNA, are separated into single strands, cut into more manageable sizes, and labeled with different fluorescent dyes—for example, green for the individual's and red for the normal sample. Both samples are then inserted into the chip. There, they bind with any sequences on the chip that have a complementary set of bases. Both a normal sequence from the individual and the corresponding sequence from the normal sample will bind to the complementary sequence on the chip, creating a position on the chip that is red and green. If the individual's sample has a mutation in that sequence, however, only the normal sample will bind to the chip, leaving a position that is red. The result is then analyzed to reveal which mutations, if any, are present in the patient's DNA.

The advantage of chips over conventional methods is that they require smaller DNA samples, and can run tests in parallel to detect large numbers of mutations.

Another new technique being developed uses a very fine carbon rod (about half a diameter of a DNA double helix) like a phonograph needle to ''feel'' what the DNA molecule looks like. The result is translated into a computer image. In the near future, this technology may be able to read the sequence directly from the DNA molecule.

For more detailed descriptions of these techniques and case studies, see Chapters 4 and 5 of Andrew Read and Dian Donnai, New Clinical Genetics (2007).

This chapter focuses on genetic testing for clinical purposes, that is, to facilitate the diagnosis, treatment, or prevention of genetic disease. It addresses a number of the ethical, legal, and social issues raised by this form of genetic testing. Specifically, it covers the regulation of genetic testing products and laboratory services, the liability of health care professionals for failing to provide access to genetic testing for therapeutic purposes, and several specific problem areas: unanticipated misattributed paternity and maternity (which occurs when a genetic test performed for therapeutic purposes unintentionally reveals that a parent is not biologically related to a child); access to genetic testing; and genetic testing for minorities and ethnic groups. The chapter also discusses the medical and nonmedical uses of genetic testing in the context of reproduction and assisted reproductive technologies.

One type of therapeutic function for genetic testing is to facilitate a diagnosis or prognosis for a person exhibiting disease symptoms. For example, a person experiencing muscle stiffness may have a genetic disease called myotonic dystrophy, which can be pinpointed by genetic testing.

Genetic testing also can be used to predict the risk of future disease, sometimes enabling steps to be taken to prevent or mitigate the disease. One common genetic disorder which can be detected pre-symptomatically is hereditary hemochromatosis (HH), which occurs in 1 in 200 whites, and which is readily treated with phlebotomy (similar to the discredited technique of "bleeding"). Genetic testing also can reveal HIV infection much earlier than traditional antibody-based tests like the ELISA test.

One of the major issues with genetic testing is its predictive accuracy. This is especially important when the test results might lead to drastic actions, such as radical preventive measures. A good example is genetic testing to detect the risk for breast cancer. In the mid–1990s, researchers identified mutations in two genes, BRCA1 and BRCA2, that were associated with an elevated risk of breast and ovarian cancer in women who have the mutations. A commercial test for the mutations was quickly developed. Some women with a positive test result have undergone prophylactic radical mastectomies—the removal of their breasts in an attempt to eliminate the tissue at risk for cancer. The problem is that the predictive value of the genetic tests is limited. In the first place, most forms of breast cancer do not appear to be inherited: only about 5 to 10 percent of the 200,000 women annually diagnosed with breast cancer have an inherited form of the disease. Second, these mutations are incompletely penetrant—that is, some women with the mutations will not develop breast cancer as a result. Even in families with a high risk of breast cancer, based on identified cases in the biologic line, between 10 and 15 percent of women with the BRCA1 mutation will not develop breast cancer. One in one hundred Ashkenazic Jewish people carry the 185delAG mutation. Approximately 20% of Ashkenazic Jewish people diagnosed with breast cancer before 42 years of age carry the 185delAG mutation. The predictive value of the genetic tests increases substantially with knowledge about other factors, such as whether there is a family history of both breast and ovarian cancer, and the woman's ethnic group, since much of the initial information came from research on Ashkenazic Jews.

Another problem raised by therapeutic genetic testing is the danger of misinterpreting a negative test result. The concern is that persons with negative test results will conclude that they will not get the disease. This could lead them to reduce their vigilance or refrain from taking preventive measures. A woman with a negative genetic test for breast cancer, for example, might reduce her frequency of mammograms. But a negative result does not mean that the person will not get the disease. As noted, most cases of breast cancer do not appear to be inherited. Even when a test for a mutation known to occur in the individual's family is negative, this only means that the individual did not inherit that particular mutation; she may have other genetic mutations for the disease that the test does not detect. Finally, the person may have had the mutation but the laboratory performing the test may have made an error in interpretation or accidentally switched samples, resulting in a "false negative" test result.

For a more complete discussion of the issues raised by genetic tests for breast cancer, see the symposium at 7 Health Matrix 1 (1997). For a good overview of genetic testing, see Wylie Burke, Genetic Testing, 347 New Eng. J. Med. 1867–1875 (2002).

A distinction is usually made between "genetic testing" and "genetic screening" for therapeutic purposes. The actual tests are often the same (although the techniques used to interpret the results may differ). The difference between them lies mainly in the degree of suspicion that the person being tested is at risk for the disease in question. The term "genetic testing" is usually reserved for genetic tests on persons with symptoms of the disease or a known family history. "Genetic screening" is conducted on populations of non-symptomatic individuals regardless of whether or not the individual has a family history of the disease. This chapter addresses genetic testing; the chapter that follows, Chapter 7, discusses genetic screening.

Some genetic testing is conducted for non-therapeutic purposes. Some testing is conducted purely for research purposes, which was discussed earlier in Chapter 4. Another principal non-therapeutic use of genetic testing is for forensic purposes, mainly identification, which is discussed later in Chapter 12.

Note that the line between therapeutic and reproductive genetic testing is not always a bright one. Reproductive testing may lead to a decision to prevent a pregnancy or live birth. If this decision is based on a desire to avoid the birth of a person who may suffer from a genetic disease, for some geneticists the decision is preventive.

II. REGULATION OF GENETIC TESTING PRODUCTS AND SERVICES

Genetic testing is a complex industry involving a number of technologies. Clinicians or researchers obtain test samples—usually blood samples—from patients. The test samples are processed by a laboratory. This may be a free-standing commercial laboratory to which the clinician sends the sample, or a laboratory operated by the health care or research facility with which the clinician or researcher is affiliated. The laboratory processes the sample. This involves the use of certain machinery such as DNA sequencers, PCR machines, microscopes, plastic and glassware, as well as the use of certain chemicals, called reagents, to interact with the test sample. The laboratory may develop and use its own reagents in its own testing process (which is called an "in-house" test or "home brew"); purchase the reagents for use in its own testing process; or it may purchase a "test kit" from a commercial manufacturer containing reagents, instructions, and usually some equipment. In addition, some companies have patented the genetic mutation that the laboratory is testing for. In some cases, they operate commercial laboratory services that process the patient samples. But they also may seek royalty payments from independent laboratories that use the patented information about the location and sequence of the gene. For example, Myriad Genetics, the company that owns the patents on the BRCA1 and BRCA2 gene mutations for breast cancer, and which previously had performed genetic tests for these mutations exclusively in its own laboratories, has agreed to license NIH researchers to perform the tests themselves if they pay a royalty.

These different technologies are regulated differently. A broad distinction is made between products and laboratory services. The former are regulated by the FDA, while the latter are regulated by the FDA, the Centers for Disease Control and Prevention, and the Centers for Medicare and Medicaid Services (formerly called the Health Care Financing Administration), all units of the U.S. Department of Health and Human Services, and in a few cases, by state governmental entities. Professional and industry organizations impose additional requirements. The result is a web of controls that is often criticized for its complexity and for its gaps.

A. REGULATION OF TEST PRODUCTS

The FDA regulates testing machinery, reagents and kits as medical devices under the Federal Food, Drug, and Cosmetic Act.

LORI ANDREWS ET AL., ASSESSING GENETIC RISKS: IMPLICATIONS FOR HEALTH AND SOCIAL POLICY

128–29 (1994).

ENSURING THE SAFETY AND EFFECTIVENESS OF NEW GENETIC TESTS

FDA regulates medical devices under the Medical Devices Act of 1976 and the Safe Medical Device Amendments of 1990. This legislation gives FDA the authority to regulate an "in vitro reagent, or any other similar or related article, including any component, part or accessory, which is: intended for use in the diagnosis of disease or other conditions in man" (21 CFR 201(h)). Through classification of such "devices," FDA implements the legislation's intent to provide a "level of regulation necessary to afford reasonable assurance of safety and effectiveness of the device." Safety cannot be considered entirely separately from effectiveness. If a test cannot properly distinguish those at high risk of genetic disease from those at low risk, individuals who are mislabeled will suffer harm. False negatives will not be treated, while false positives may suffer from both unnecessary intervention and anxiety.

Only a small proportion of genetic tests in widespread use have been reviewed by FDA; these include tests for hypothyroidism, phenylketonuria (PKU), and MSAFP tests. The technologies used for the detection of most disease-related genotypes have not been submitted to FDA; these include biochemical reagents and DNA probes used in tests for CF, Huntington disease, muscular dystrophy, fragile X syndrome, and other disorders.

Premarket Approval of Medical Devices

Before a medical device can be legally marketed for in vitro diagnostic use, its sponsor (manufacturer, university, or individual scientist) must obtain premarket approval (PMA) or clearance. On receiving premarket notification from a sponsor, FDA will determine whether the device is "substantially equivalent" to a legally marketed "predicate" device. "Substantial equivalence means the new device must have the same intended use as the predicate device, the same technological characteristics (or, if different,) strong comparability of intended use and performance characteristics, and [not raise] new questions of safety and effectiveness." For the FDA to make a determination of substantial equivalence, the manufacturer has to demonstrate equivalent performance characteristics (as good as other legally marketed devices). If so, FDA will give the device either Class I or II designation, depending on the class of the predicate device. The safety and efficacy of Class I devices can be reasonably ensured if the manufacturer adheres to general controls that include good manufacturing practices in their production. Class II devices must meet not only general controls, but also special controls, in order to reasonably ensure safety and efficacy.

If FDA fails to find the device substantially equivalent, it will require full premarket approval, designating it a Class III device. This requires the manufacturer to present evidence of the device's safety and effectiveness. Genetic tests and devices placed in Class III include MSAFP [maternal serum alpha-fetoprotein] kits (MSAFP is not approved by the FDA for use as a screening test for Down syndrome, although it is widely used for that purpose) and kits for the Philadelphia chromosome, tumor markers, and gene rearrangements. Class II tests include the sweat chloride test for CF, creatine kinase test for Duchenne muscular dystrophy, phenylalanine test for PKU, tests for coagulation defects (including detection of carriers of coagulation defects), and tests for sickle cell trait or disease. The copper test for Wilson disease is Class I.

* * *

Although the [FDA's current definition of "substantial equivalence"] is reassuringly comprehensive, the FDA could interpret substantial equivalence too broadly, permitting a manufacturer to avoid the premarket approval process by claiming, for instance, that a DNA test marketed to detect sickle cell carriers was substantially equivalent to electrophoretic tests already on the market. Once marketed to detect carriers, the DNA test, unlike the electrophoretic test, could also be used for prenatal diagnosis. This would constitute an unapproved or "off-label" use of the device. Similarly, a DNA-based test for some CF mutations might be approved for the diagnosis of CF on the basis of substantial equivalence to the sweat chloride test, although only the DNA test could be used for carrier detection or prenatal diagnosis.

NOTES AND QUESTIONS

1.   For an overview and history of FDA regulation generally, see Richard A. Merrill, The Architecture of Government Regulation of Medical Products, 82 Va. L. Rev. 1753 (1996).

2.   An example of a genetic test that was approved on the basis of a full-scale Class III premarket approval application is PATHWAY™ Her 2 (Clone CB11), which helps determine which breast cancer patients will benefit from a certain treatment that reduces levels of the Her2 protein.

3.   Many devices relating to genetic testing have been marketed in reliance on 21 U.S.C. § 360(k) "substantial equivalence" provisions, which essentially allow a manufacturer to market a product without going through the full approval process for a new device. For example, the FDA approved a § 360(k) for a test that counts the chromosomes of bone marrow transplant donors and recipients of different genders.

4.   In 1998, the FDA announced that it regarded reagents used in genetic testing as Class I devices, and that it will not even require adherence to good manufacturing practices, thus placing reagents in the device category with the least regulatory oversight. Furthermore, the agency has taken the position that it will not exert any oversight over reagents developed and used within a laboratory, as opposed to reagents sold to other laboratories.

B. REGULATION OF LABORATORY SERVICES

LORI ANDREWS ET AL., ASSESSING GENETIC RISKS: IMPLICATIONS FOR HEALTH AND SOCIAL POLICY

124–26 (1994).

HISTORY

The Clinical Laboratory Improvement Act of 1967 (CLIA67) established federal control of laboratories providing more than 100 tests per year in interstate commerce for a profit. Only about 12,000 laboratories reimbursed by Medicare and Medicaid were covered. CLIA67 was originally administered by CDC, but authority was transferred to the Health Care Finance Administration in 1978. For laboratories under its purview, CLIA67 required the establishment of standards for laboratory directors and other laboratory personnel. The College of American Pathologists was recognized to set laboratory and personnel standards, and to develop a laboratory inspection system nationwide.

The Clinical Laboratory Improvement Amendments of 1988 (CLIA88) were enacted in response to rising concern over media reports of serious errors and variability in laboratory results, and inadequate training and supervision of personnel performing clinical laboratory tests. In particular, so-called Pap mills were found to have serious deficiencies in their cytology analysis of Papanicolaou tests, intended to detect cervical cancer. Public concern had also intensified about the quality of the increasing amount of unregulated laboratory services provided in physicians' office laboratories and other laboratories reimbursed by Medicare and Medicaid.

LABORATORIES COVERED BY CLIA88

With few exceptions, laboratories performing an "examination of materials derived from the human body for the purpose of providing information for the diagnosis, prevention, or treatment of any disease or impairment of, or the assessment of the health of, human beings" must obtain certification from HCFA under CLIA88. The exceptions are laboratories performing tests only for forensic purposes, research laboratories that do not report patient-specific results for the purposes defined above, and laboratories of federal agencies to the extent excepted by the Secretary of Health and Human Services. How a laboratory derives its revenues, or even whether it charges for tests, is no longer a determinant of coverage under CLIA88. Thus, any laboratory that provided a genetic test result on which a clinical decision was based is subject to regulation.

More than 200,000 laboratories are estimated to be covered by CLIA88, over 100,000 of them in physicians' offices. Compliance with CLIA88, including CLIA certification is required for Medicare reimbursement of laboratory services, and many other third-party payers use Medicare certification as one criterion for reimbursement. However,

HCFA may not know about laboratories that do not obtain certificates unless there is a complaint.

CLIA88 REGULATIONS

In implementing CLIA88 the government sets standards for laboratories according to whether the tests they perform are of "moderate" or "high" complexity. The distinction between moderate and high complexity depends on a number of factors including knowledge needed to perform the test, characteristics of operational steps, judgment required, and interpretation of results. Thus far, CDC has classified 10,000 tests, approximately 25 percent as high complexity and 75 percent as moderate complexity.

Laboratories performing tests of moderate or high complexity must conform to general quality control standards as well as those of the "specialty" under which the tests they perform are classified. (Some specialties are microbiology, chemistry, pathology, and hematology.) Laboratories must participate in proficiency testing programs for each specialty in which they perform tests and for which proficiency programs have been established. By 1995, a laboratory that fails a proficiency test two consecutive times or two out of three times will be subject to sanctions and may not continue to perform that test under its CLIA certificate. Nor will it be eligible for Medicare reimbursement for that test. HCFA had approved 12 of the 19 proficiency testing programs that had applied as of December 1992. None of these is in genetics * * *.

The absence of a complexity rating for a test does not exempt a laboratory performing only unrated tests from quality control. A laboratory test whose complexity has not been categorized "is considered to be a test of high complexity until PHS (Public Health Service), upon request, reviews the matter and notifies the applicant of its decision." In the meantime, "the laboratory must have a system for verifying the accuracy and reliability of its test results at least twice a year." Moreover, all laboratories filing a certificate of registration with HCFA will be inspected every two years, and the laboratory's quality control and internal proficiency test system will be assessed. HCFA has a training program for laboratory inspectors—many of whom are sent by states—provided by the Department of Laboratory Medicine of the Johns Hopkins University School of Medicine. HCFA may soon deem other organizations (CAP, Joint Committee on Accreditation of Health Organizations, specific states) as capable of conducting its surveys and accrediting laboratories. State accreditation can supplant HCFA accreditation when a state's program is deemed equivalent or more stringent than the federal program.

Quality control under CLIA88 is funded by fees charged to laboratories. Compliance fees vary substantially from hundreds to thousands of dollars depending on how many different types of tests the laboratory performs, their complexity, and the volume of testing.

GENETIC TESTS UNDER CLIA88

Very few genetic tests are on the list of tests whose complexity has been defined under CLIA88. Those that are listed have been classified as of moderate complexity including sweat chloride for CF, creative kinase, and alpha-fetoprotein (AFP) for tumor marker. A test subspecialty called "clinical cytogenetics" has been established, but there is no other genetic test subspecialty under CLIA88. Moreover, no proficiency testing for cytogenetic laboratories is required, although well-established programs (e.g. New York State and CAP) have been operating for years. Proficiency tests are not required for any other genetic tests, either.

Few laboratories performing genetic tests as their sole or principal activity are yet complying with the CLIA88 regulations. Based on the committee's workshops and other information, it appears that few genetics laboratories have applied for certification from HCFA even though they provide genetic test information for clinical use. Committee staff also surveyed the directors of 12 genetics laboratories in academic centers to ask if their laboratory had applied for certification, and only 1 laboratory indicated that it had.

RESEARCH LABORATORIES AND TESTS FOR RARE DISORDERS

Research laboratories are covered under CLIA88 if they also provide tests on which clinical decisions are based. Some of these laboratories provide genetic tests as clinical services that are not directly related to the research they perform, and they may have limited expertise in performing or interpreting such tests. In many large academic hospitals, the central laboratory is not even aware of all the laboratories that provide services.

NOTES AND QUESTIONS

The regulation of laboratory services under CLIA is divided among three federal agencies. The Centers for Medicare and Medicaid Services (CMS) oversees the inspection and certification of laboratories. (Why would an agency whose main function is running the federal Medicare and Medicaid programs be given this responsibility?) The Centers for Disease Control and Prevention (CDC) assures the accuracy and reliability of testing services provided by non-commercial laboratories. The FDA is responsible for regulating the accuracy and reliability of commercial tests, including approving the test products themselves as described in Section A, and, since 2000, assigning complexity ratings.

In August 2007, CMS denied a petition by the Genetics and Public Policy Center, Public Citizen, and the Genetic Alliance to create a genetic testing specialty under CLIA88 and to establish standards for proficiency testing for genetic tests. The agency cited "technological and financial issues" as the reason for the lack of proficiency testing, rather than the absence of federal regulatory requirements.

LORI ANDREWS ET AL., ASSESSING GENETIC RISKS: IMPLICATIONS FOR HEALTH AND SOCIAL POLICY

118–21 (1994).

STATE ASSESSMENTS OF LABORATORIES PROVIDING GENETIC TESTS

New York State began mandatory regulation of genetic testing when it established the first program assessment for cytogenetics laboratories in the United States in 1972, with cytogenetics proficiency testing beginning in 1974. Since 1990, New York has been the only state that has specific mandatory standards and permits for DNA genetics laboratories performing tests on its citizens. It has a list of DNA tests approved for testing, including tests for sickle cell anemia, cystic fibrosis (CF), Duchenne and Becker muscular dystrophy, Tay–Sachs, and the thalassemias. * * * To be approved to perform DNA tests from this list, the laboratories must demonstrate that they successfully perform the accepted test methodologies. New York developed a special training program for all inspectors who survey laboratories that perform genetic testing. New York has also developed standards for proficiency testing for DNA tests, but these standards have not yet been implemented. The reach of the New York State program extends beyond the geographic borders of the state, since any laboratory wishing to perform a genetic test on a citizen of New York must be certified just as if it were located in New York; thus, most large commercial genetic testing laboratories who accept specimens from around the United States are licensed to meet New York DNA laboratory standards. Currently, no other state has developed as rigorous a program for the quality control of genetic testing as New York.

The California Department of Health Services contracts with private laboratories to provide newborn screening and maternal serum alpha-fetoprotein (MSAFP) testing. As part of the process it assesses the quality of the laboratories with whom it contracts. Since 1980, California has limited newborn screening to eight state-monitored laboratories, with centralized computer data collection, quality control, blind proficiency testing, and case follow-up. Fees for newborn screening are collected from the birth hospital or birth attendant. California also has centralized laboratory testing, quality control, and blind proficiency testing for its MSAFP screening program, which must be offered to every pregnant woman in California. California has developed draft regulations on DNA, cytogenetics, and microbiological testing, and for prenatal diagnosis centers and clinical centers; these draft regulations are awaiting public comment and public hearing.

Maryland has regulations requiring genetic testing and screening laboratories to demonstrate "continuing satisfactory performance" in external proficiency testing programs where they exist. The only approved laboratory for newborn screening in Maryland is the state laboratory, which participates in the U.S. Centers for Disease Control proficiency testing program for newborn screening. Fourteen laboratories (including the state laboratory) are approved for MSAFP screening. Maryland regulations require laboratories doing Tay–Sachs testing to participate successfully in the proficiency testing program of the International Tay–Sachs Disease Quality Control Reference Standards and Data Collection Center.

New Jersey requires its laboratories to comply with the New York system for genetic tests. and it now also recognizes College of American Pathology (CAP) proficiency testing for cytogenetics. Florida licenses cytogenetics laboratories using CAP guidelines and proficiency testing, but its legislation is now expiring. Iowa requires that MSAFP testing be done centrally in the state laboratory at the University of Iowa.

In addition, states in the Pacific Northwest Region (PacNoRGG) of the Council of Regional Networks for Genetic Services (CORN), including Washington, Oregon, Idaho, and Alaska, have adopted PacNoRGG proficiency testing standards as a condition for state laboratory license as a cytogenetics laboratory. The PacNoRGG cytogenetics proficiency test involves the provision of blind samples and requires the interpretation of clinical information on individuals and families. Each round of proficiency testing gets more difficult as the proficiency of the participating laboratories improves.

NOTES

1.   The Council of Regional Networks for Genetic Services (CORN) was abolished in 1999.

2.   A laboratory seeking to perform tests it developed in-house, including genetic tests, on specimens originating in New York may apply for approval to perform such tests, but must demonstrate that the test is "of proven reliability and generally accepted by leading authorities in the specialties of laboratory medicine and/or approved by the department." N.Y.Comp.Codes R. & Regs. Tit. 10, § 58–1.10. To win approval to perform any molecular genetic test a laboratory must submit its standard operating procedure manual and test validation data.

New York issues permits for laboratories to perform tests it categorizes as cytogenetics (the analysis of the numerical and structural chromosome complement of human cells) and genetic testing (diagnosis of a genetic disease or its carrier state or risk assessment for drug metabolism, disease susceptibility and/or hemostasis). Laboratories performing cytogenetic tests must achieve a proficiency score of at least 80 percent. While proficiency testing is not offered for laboratories performing genetic testing, each laboratories must create an internal system for verifying the reliability and accuracy of its results and must utilize this system twice a year.

3.   For a spirited defense of a highly-regulated state approach to genetic testing services, see George C. Cunningham, A Public Health Perspective on the Control of Predictive Screening for Breast Cancer, 7 Health Matrix 31 (1997).

LORI ANDREWS ET AL., ASSESSING GENETIC RISKS: IMPLICATIONS FOR HEALTH AND SOCIAL POLICY

121 (1994).

VOLUNTARY QUALITY ASSURANCE AND PROFICIENCY TESTING IN GENETICS

The Council of Regional Networks of Genetic Services, the College of American Pathologists, the Centers for Disease Control and Prevention, and several other organizations have developed specific genetic tests or tests for specific disorders. These include maternal serum alpha-fetoprotein, Tay–Sachs disease, and Huntington disease, for which the organizations have established voluntary proficiency tests. Other organizations interested in the quality of genetic tests include the Organization for Clinical Laboratory Genetics, the American Society for Histocompatibility and Immunogenetics, the American Association of Blood Banks, the Technical Working Group on DNA Analysis Methods (TWGDAM), the National Reference System for the Clinical Laboratory, the National Committee for Clinical Laboratory Standards (NCCLS), and the new American College of Medical Genetics (ACMG). Many of the voluntary quality assurance programs grew from the efforts of the American Society of Human Genetics (ASHG).

CORN was established in 1985 as a coordinating body for state genetic services programs organized in 10 regions. CORN is funded by the Genetic Services Program of the Maternal and Child Health Program, Health Resources and Services Administration (HRSA), U.S. Department of Health and Human Services (DHHS). Laboratory quality assurance quickly became and remains a high priority for CORN. CORN has a Quality Assurance Committee (for laboratory services), as well as other committees on quality assurance and proficiency testing, and education. CORN's national proficiency testing programs include alpha-fetoprotein, biochemical genetics, hemoglobinopathies and newborn screening, and most recently, DNA-based tests.

The College of American Pathologists developed guidelines, criteria, and methods for quality control and standards for clinical laboratories. CAP played a key role in the implementation of the Clinical Laboratory Improvement Act of 1967 when its quality assurance and proficiency testing standards and activities were recognized ("deemed") by the Secretary of Health and Human Services to fulfill the requirements of the law. Since 1967, CAP has worked to maintain itself and M.D.-pathologists as the appropriate professional group to judge the quality of clinical laboratories. CAP has voluntary proficiency testing programs for cytogenetics and MSAFP screening that are recognized by some states. With input from ASHG, CAP has spent two years developing guidelines for what it calls "molecular pathology." The ASHG role in setting standards for laboratory genetics will be assumed by the ACMG in 1993. ACMG laboratory standards for genetics are now under final revision and will be very important in quality assurance in genetic testing.

NOTES AND QUESTIONS

1. The American College of Medical Genetics (ACMG) issued standards in 1993 and revised the standards in 2005. See http://www.acmg.net/Pages/ACMG_Activities/ stds–2002/stdsmenu-n.htm. For a discussion of FDA regulation of genetic testing, see Gail H. Javitt, In Search of a Coherent Framework: Options for FDA Oversight of Genetic Tests, 62 Food Drug L. J. 617 (2007). Javitt states that "for most genetic tests there is no independent external review of analytic or clinical validity before tests are offered to the public. As a result, there is no external assessment of whether the laboratory can reliably identify the presence or absence of a mutation or whether the presence of the mutation actually is correlated with disease or risk of disease in an individual." Id. at 639.

2. What are the relative merits of federal, state, and voluntary industry regulation? Which approach makes the most sense for regulating genetic testing?

3. Does the regulatory distinction between genetic testing products and laboratory services make sense? Should genetic testing be regulated by a single entity? If so, which one?

4. Some commentators argue that the FDA should regulate both test products and widely marketed tests offered as a service. See, e.g., Anny Huang, Genetic Information, Legal, FDA Regulation of Genetic Testing, Encyclopedia of Ethical, Legal, and Policy Issues in Biotechnology 441 (Murray and Mehlman, eds. 2000). The latter would include commercial testing services that analyze samples sent to them by clinicians, and that have patented the genetic mutation in question so that independent laboratories seeking to offer a similar service would have to pay royalties. Myriad Genetics, for example, has patented the BRCA1 and BRCA2 mutations for breast cancer and sells them as testing services. Its laboratory is certified by CMS under CLIA, but it has not submitted its tests to the government for a complexity rating (by default, they would be regarded as "high complexity"), and since they are not sold as kits or reagents, neither the FDA nor any other federal agency has evaluated the accuracy and reliability of the tests themselves.

One problem with giving the FDA regulatory authority over laboratory services is that the agency traditionally has been deemed to lack the authority to regulate the practice of medicine. Is a laboratory service the practice of medicine? What if it is provided by a non-physician, for example, a Ph.D.?

5. In 1998 the Secretary of Health and Human Services created the Secretary's Advisory Committee on Genetic Testing (SACGT). The SACGT issued a set of recommendations at the end of 2000, which included the following:

- "Additional oversight is warranted for all genetic tests."
- "FDA should be the federal agency responsible for the review, approval, and labeling of all new genetic tests that have moved beyond the basic research phase."
- "Development of data formats for post-market information gathering to update the utility of genetic tests should be the responsibility of CDC in collaboration with FDA, other federal agencies, and private sector organizations, as appropriate."
- "The CLIA regulations should be augmented to provide more specific provisions for ensuring the quality of laboratories conducting genetic tests."
- "Using principles employed for the review of new genetic tests, a multidisciplinary group, given deemed status[1] for this purpose, should review genetic tests that are already on the market for evaluation of clinical efficacy and development of guidelines about their appropriate use."

The SACGT also stated:

In the future, tests may be developed that raise major social and ethical concerns. Because FDA's review will focus on assuring the analytical and clinical validity of a test, the agency's capacity to assess the ethical and social implications of a test may not be sufficient. The Secretary should consider the development of a mechanism to ensure the identification and appropriate review of tests that raise major social and ethical concerns.

What does this suggest regarding the FDA's ability to regulate genetic tests, and genetic technologies in general?

In a January 19, 2001, letter responding to the committee's recommendations, Secretary of HHS Shalala went on to stipulate that "HCFA would begin immediately to identify and register all clinical laboratories that are providing genetic tests results to patients or their care providers but are not already CLIA certified." She also stated that "oversight of genetic tests will cover clinical genetic testing services (so-called 'home brews') as well as genetic test kits."

How helpful are these recommendations?

The SACGT also initially recommended that FDA differentiate between two "levels" of genetic tests in conducting its reviews, but later abandoned this approach in favor of an FDA proposal that would review all genetic tests according to a standardized "template."

III. PRENATAL SCREENING

A. INTRODUCTION

For centuries, parents followed folk myths in attempts to control the characteristics of their children. In earlier generations, people believed

---

1. "Deemed status" means that, for purposes of fulfilling federal legal requirements, the findings of the multidisciplinary group would be accepted as if they were government findings.

that conceiving under certain circumstances (a full moon or with a particular item under the bed) would influence the traits of their off-spring. As physicians gained greater knowledge about inheritance, couples began to incorporate into their reproductive decisions facts about the risks, based on family history, of passing on a particular genetic disease to their children. Some people choose not to conceive children in order to avoid passing on a serious untreatable genetic disorder such as Huntington disease.

In recent decades, genetic testing has entered the obstetric realm to provide more precise predictions about the risks of passing on a particular genetic disease. Couples planning to conceive can be screened to see if they are carriers of genetic diseases. During pregnancy, tests can be undertaken on the embryo or fetus itself. A large proportion of pregnant women in the United States now undergo some form of prenatal screening, such as ultrasound, amniocentesis, chorionic villi sampling, or other tests. New technologies are available such as simple blood tests of the mother to analyze the health status or genetic makeup of the fetus. By testing the woman's blood for a particular gene product from the fetus (known as maternal serum alpha-fetoprotein), a physician can assess whether the child will have a neural tube defect such as spina bifida or anencephaly. An even more cutting edge blood test analyzes fetal cells circulating in the mother's blood to determine whether there are any genetic mutations which would indicate the child will experience Down syndrome, Tay–Sachs, or another genetic disease.

In the wake of the Human Genome Project, the range of genes that can be tested prenatally has grown exponentially. Ethical questions arise about whether fetuses should be tested for diseases that will not manifest until later in life, such as breast cancer, or for traits that do not represent diseases, such as by using the controversial genetic test that purports to indicate homosexuality. Legal questions also abound about which genetic tests health care professionals should offer and the circumstances under which they may be found liable for negligence in testing.

B. PRENATAL SCREENING TECHNIQUES

LORI B. ANDREWS, FUTURE PERFECT: CONFRONTING DECISIONS ABOUT GENETICS

56–62 (2001).

Family history has long been used to predict a couple's general chance of giving birth to a child with a particular disorder. Starting thirty years ago with the advent of prenatal diagnosis through amniocentesis, specific genetic information about a particular fetus became available to parents. Today, genetic information related to reproduction is obtainable in numerous ways. One partner may have a mutation associated with Huntington disease or breast cancer, for example, and face a decision about whether the fetus should be tested for that mutation. In other instances, the parents may not know their genetic make-up, but each (or maybe both) may be tested in advance of reproduction (or even during pregnancy) for mutations that are common in their ethnic group—such as cystic fibrosis for Caucasians, sickle cell anemia for African Americans, or Tay–Sachs for Ashkenazi Jews. Or the fetus itself may be tested, which can reveal previously unknown genetic information about the mother, the father, or both. Parents-to-be may learn that both are carriers of a recessive disorder, that one has a mutation associated with a dominant disorder, or that the woman has passed on a mutation associated with an X-linked disorder.

The range of conditions that can be screened for prenatally is growing exponentially each year. More than 500 different conditions can be diagnosed through chorionic villi sampling or amniocentesis. The availability of these tests affects even those people who decide not to have them done. Some women say that friends and relatives have made them feel irresponsible for not having genetic testing; others have felt guilty and responsible if they had a child with a genetic disorder (either after refusing testing or after deciding to carry through the pregnancy of an affected child). Yet, as more and more prenatal genetic tests become available, parents are increasingly feeling that they are put into the position of playing God. Should they have prenatal screening for a disorder that won't affect their child until much later in life—or should they bank on a cure being developed in the child's lifetime? Should they abort a fetus whose disorder is treatable, albeit at some expense? As testing becomes available to tell whether a fetus is at a higher likelihood of suffering from breast cancer, colon cancer, heart disease, diabetes, and Alzheimer's disease, should such tests be utilized? What about for alcoholism, violence, and other behavioral traits? In studies with varying degrees of scientific repute, genes have been implicated in shyness, bedwetting, attempted rape, homosexuality, manic-depressive disorder, arson, tendency to tease, traditionalism, tendency to giggle or to use hurtful words, and zest for life. Should testing for such traits be done prenatally? If so, what should be done with the resulting information?

* * *

Many couples who use genetic services in conjunction with reproduction feel that it has offered them an overall benefit by allowing them to make an informed choice about their pregnancies. In fact, couples have sued when they felt deprived of prenatal genetic information. At least one federal court [Lifchez v. Hartigan, 735 F.Supp. 1361, 1377 (N.D. Ill.1990), cert. denied, 498 U.S. 1069 (1991)] has recognized the importance of this choice by indicating that the constitutional protections of the abortion decision logically "must also include the right to submit to a procedure designed to give information about that fetus which can then lead to a decision to abort."

* * *

THE PHYSICAL RISK OF PRENATAL SCREENING

Some forms of prenatal testing present physical risks to the fetus, but others are relatively unintrusive. Sampling blood from the fetus while it is in utero through fetoscopy, one of the first means of prenatal tests developed for fetuses, is associated with a 3 to 6 percent risk of fetal death. Amniocentesis, in which fluid from the amniotic sac is withdrawn and analyzed, causes spontaneous abortions in approximately two to three in every 1,000 pregnancies. [This is 0.3% higher than for pregnant women who do not have amniocentesis.] Chorionic villi sampling (CVS), in which a tissue surrounding the fetus is sampled and analyzed between eight and twelve weeks gestation, is associated with a spontaneous abortion rate of about 3.6 percent. [Because many miscarriages occur naturally in the first semester, the additional risk from CVS is approximately 0.8%.] In addition, CVS in early pregnancy presents a risk of limb deformities in approximately one in 3,000 cases. These procedures entail physical risks to pregnant women as well, particularly risks of infection. Some women have chosen to undergo prenatal screening despite the risks because they intend to terminate a pregnancy if the fetus is diagnosed as having a serious disorder.

The prenatal diagnostic techniques of fetoscopy, amniocentesis, and chorionic villi sampling have generally been limited to women whose fetuses are at greater-than-average risk of having a genetic or chromosomal disorder, such as women over age thirty-five (who are at a greater-than-average risk of giving birth to a child with Down syndrome) or women with family histories of or ethnic-group familiarity with genetic disorders. In many instances, the women being offered such prenatal testing have had some experience with the disorders for which the fetus is being tested. Most women are familiar with Down syndrome. Those who have a family history of a disorder such as cystic fibrosis or sickle cell anemia have an affected relative and thus are likely to have some knowledge about the disorder. And in ethnic groups that have a higher-than-average risk of certain genetic diseases, there is often widespread knowledge among members of the community about the particular disorder.

Now, however, prenatal testing is being developed that is less physically risky to the fetus and to the pregnant woman. Some testing can be performed with a sample of the pregnant woman's blood. Genetic mutations affecting the fetus can be identified through maternal/fetal cell sorting, a technique that can analyze fetal cells circulating in the woman's blood. Since the physical risk has been reduced, women who might not otherwise have sought prenatal testing are being asked to do so. One result is that women who have no personal knowledge or experience with a disease or disorder are faced with having to decide whether they are willing to raise a child with these conditions. This stands in contrast to those in situations in which such disorders are generally understood within the woman's community. The more accessible prenatal testing becomes, the more important it is to adequately inform and educate potential parents about their fetus's condition as well as about the long-term consequences of whatever decisions they make.... A survey found that 39 percent of people felt that every pregnant woman should have prenatal testing and 22 percent felt that a woman should be required to abort if the baby has a serious genetic defect.

NOTES AND QUESTIONS

While still not widely used in practice, advances in technology have improved upon the technique of maternal/fetal cell sorting. H. Christina Fan et al., Noninvasive Diagnosis of Fetal Aneuploidy by Shotgun Sequencing DNA from Maternal Blood, PNAS (Oct. 6, 2008). What are some of the ethical and legal implications if such technology becomes widely available, or even standard?

C. LIABILITY FOR MALPRACTICE IN PRENATAL SCREENING

LORI B. ANDREWS, TORTS AND THE DOUBLE HELIX: MALPRACTICE LIABILITY FOR FAILURE TO WARN OF GENETIC RISKS

29 Hous. L. Rev. 149, 152–57, 166–69 (1992).

The legal issues surrounding the dissemination of genetic information first reached the courts in the wrongful birth and wrongful life cases. Various courts have held that physicians and geneticists have a duty to disclose information to prospective parents concerning both the genetic risks to their potential offspring and the diagnostic procedures available to ascertain those risks so that they might choose whether to refrain from conceiving or to abort a fetus with a serious disorder.

Courts initially resisted recognizing a cause of action for wrongful birth. The early cases befuddled the courts because, unlike traditional malpractice cases, nothing that the health care provider could have done would have prevented the harm to the child. The logic behind these early suits was that if the parents of the affected child had received proper counseling or diagnosis, they could have decided not to conceive or to seek an abortion. Early case law dealing with wrongful birth actions rejected the notion that the failure to warn the parents of a fetus' risk of serious defect was actionable because the physician was not the proximate cause of the defect. However, liability for a missed diagnosis in other areas of medicine was, and still is, common even though, in such cases, the physician did not cause the illness.

Another reason that courts were reluctant to recognize the wrongful birth cause of action was that the post-conception remedy available—abortion—was illegal. This reasoning is no longer valid after Roe v. Wade [410 U.S. 113 (1973)], which upheld a woman's constitutional right to undergo an abortion during the first two trimesters of pregnancy. As one court noted, "the value of genetic testing programs ... is based on the opportunity of parents to abort afflicted fetuses, within appropriate time limitations.''

Wrongful birth cases are now widely recognized. A cause of action exists when physicians fail to warn prospective parents that they are at risk of conceiving or giving birth to a child with a serious genetic disorder. This potential liability includes instances in which a reasonable physician should have known of the risk because the couple's previous child had a genetic disorder or because of the woman's advanced age. Liability can also arise if the health care provider fails to advise prospective parents of known risks due to one or both parents belonging to a particular ethnic or racial group. Finally, courts find physicians liable for failing to discuss the availability of genetic services when specific risk assessment services are available. Thus, physicians may be liable for failing to inform a couple about the availability of carrier status testing (to determine whether the parents' genes harbor a defect which, if passed to the child, could cause a genetic disorder) or prenatal diagnosis (to determine if the fetus is currently affected or will develop the genetic disorder).

In addition to the wrongful birth suits that parents can bring when a physician does not accurately advise them of the possibilities of genetic defects in their children, parents can also bring wrongful life suits on behalf of the children. In a wrongful life action,

> [t]he child does not allege that the physician's negligence caused the child's deformity. Rather, the claim is that the physician's negligence—his failure to adequately inform the parents of the risk—has caused the birth of the deformed child. The child argues that but for the inadequate advice, it would not have been born to experience the pain and suffering attributable to the deformity.

The controversy surrounding this cause of action stems from the nature of the claim: the allegation that one would be better off in a state of non-existence than in a state of impaired existence. While certain jurisdictions have recognized the validity of wrongful life actions, others have refused to grapple with the philosophical and ethical implications of such an allegation.

Wrongful life and wrongful birth causes of action present similar fact situations in jurisdictions that recognize wrongful life as a cause of action. For example, courts have recognized a wrongful life cause of action when doctors failed to advise prospective parents of genetic risks or provided erroneous information. Courts have also recognized this cause of action in non-genetic circumstances in which parents were not advised of other fetal risks.

In both wrongful birth and wrongful life cases, the current trend with respect to damages is to allow the recovery of only the additional costs of treatment and special resources for the child, not the entire cost of rearing the child. In fact, Maine has codified that approach: ''Damages for the birth of an unhealthy child born as the result of professional negligence shall be limited to damages associated with the disease, defect or handicap suffered by the child.''

KEEL v. BANACH

624 So.2d 1022 (Ala. 1993).

SHORES, J.

The plaintiffs are Karen and Danny Keel, parents of Justin Keel, who was born on January 18, 1985, with severe multiple congenital abnormalities. Justin died in February 1991, at the age of six. The defendants are Warren Banach, M.D., who was Karen's doctor and who performed the sonographic examinations of the fetus, and his professional corporation. The Keels charged the defendants with medical malpractice in failing to discover several severe, life-threatening fetal abnormalities that, the Keels say, had they been known to them, would have caused them to terminate the pregnancy. Actions such as that filed by the Keels have come to be called actions for "wrongful birth."

* * *

The sole issue on appeal is whether this State recognizes a cause of action for wrongful birth. At the outset, we must emphasize the posture in which this case is now before this Court: The question presented for review is not whether the plaintiffs should ultimately prevail in this litigation, but whether their complaint states a claim upon which relief can be granted.

On October 22, 1984, Karen Keel had her first prenatal visit with Dr. Banach, an obstetrician practicing in Ozark, Alabama. There is conflicting testimony as to the content of the conversations between the physician and his patient pertaining to the couple's medical history. The Keels say that they relayed their concerns regarding this pregnancy because Danny had earlier fathered a stillborn infant with anencephaly, the congenital absence of brain and spinal cord, which is the most severe of spinal cord abnormalities. Spinal cord defects are known to be hereditary, and the Keels contend that they told Dr. Banach that they did not want their child to suffer such a fate.

Dr. Banach did a sonogram on October 26, 1984. He derived a biparietal diameter consistent with 19 weeks' gestation, and a femur length consistent with 22 weeks' gestation. Under "obvious anomalies" he wrote: "none seen." The Keels say that, to alleviate their fears, Dr. Banach moved the transducer around to show them what appeared to be a healthy fetus's head, body, arms, and legs. The sonogram machine produced several photographs of the sonographic images. Two were given to Karen.

Another sonogram was performed on January 4, 1985. Again Dr. Banach marked under "obvious anomalies" "none seen." During this sonogram, Dr. Banach determined that the fetus was a male. As during the first sonogram, the machine produced photographs, and all were retained in the medical records.

Justin was born on January 18, 1985, with severe multiple congenital abnormalities. He had only a two-vessel umbilical cord (as opposed to the normal three-vessel cord), a short cord, ventriculomegaly, absent right leg, imperforate anus, one testicle, one kidney, a vertebrae anomaly in the lumbar sacral region, hydrocephaly, a large fluid-filled sac extending off the right aspect of the sacrum consistent with meningocele (spina bifida). Justin underwent numerous surgeries during his life. A shunt from his brain to his heart channeled fluids, which, for the most part, prevented any brain damage due to the hydrocephaly. Blood clots from the heart, impregnating the lungs, a known but unpreventable risk of the shunt, were the direct cause of Justin's death.

According to Dr. Banach, the fact that Danny had fathered a stillborn with anencephaly was not revealed to him until after Justin was born.

The Keels sued Dr. Banach, alleging that he had failed to meet the standard of prenatal care and that, had he done so, he would have further investigated questionable sonogram findings. The plaintiffs contend that there were discrepancies in the fetus measurements that should have prompted further investigation. They contend that there were images on the sonogram that showed an oblong head with open frontal bones visible (known as a "lemon sign," frequently noted in spina bifida). They contend that the sonogram findings should have prompted an amniocentesis, which, had it been performed, would in all likelihood have diagnosed this fetus's neurotube defect.

As described by the considerable literature and litigation in this area, a "wrongful birth action" refers to a claim for relief by parents who allege they would have avoided conception or would have terminated the pregnancy but for the negligence of those charged with prenatal testing, genetic prognosticating, or counseling parents as to the likelihood of giving birth to a physically or mentally impaired child. The underlying premise is that prudent medical care would have detected the risk of a congenital or hereditary genetic disorder either before conception or during pregnancy. In such an action, the parents allege that as a proximate result of this negligently performed or omitted genetic counseling or prenatal testing they were foreclosed from making an informed decision whether to conceive a potentially handicapped child or, in the event of a pregnancy, to terminate it.

* * *

This case involves an alleged failure by Dr. Banach to properly perform prenatal tests that would have revealed severe multiple congenital abnormalities in the fetus, which, if known to the parents, would have weighed in their decision whether to exercise their constitutional right to terminate the pregnancy.

The defendants make compelling policy arguments for rejecting the plaintiffs' cause of action. These include:

"(1) [T]he tort will be particularly subject to fraudulent claims. The cause of action is dependent entirely upon the retrospective and subjective testimony of the mother that had she known of the defects during the pregnancy, she would have aborted the child.

"(2) [T]he wrongful birth action would place a heavy burden on obstetricians/gynecologists. Appellee claims that with respect to obstetrics and gynecology the wrongful birth action will:

"a. Increase abortions;

"b. Increase abortions of healthy fetuses as a risk management action;

"c. Increase the cost of prenatal care as the result of more prenatal testing and the burden on OB/GYNs to obtain detailed informed consent; and

"d. Lead to the reduction of OB/GYNs practicing in the state.

"(3) Another concern is ... the negative impact the cause of action may have on the child by creating an 'emotional bastard.'

"(4) Since the wrongful birth views nonexistence as being greater than life with a disability, the cause of action would have a negative impact on the disabled. The cause of action cries out that children with disabilities constitute injury to parents. This will lead to a stigmatism and high toll on the self-esteem of persons with disabilities at a time when our state and country are moving forward at great lengths to recognize the rights and privileges of the disabled as ordinary citizens."

* * *

Although the arguments of the defendants set out above are compelling, the great weight of authority to the contrary forces us to agree with the majority of the courts and the legal commentators and to hold that an action for the wrongful birth of a genetically or congenitally defective child may be maintained by the parents of such a child.

The nature of the tort of wrongful birth has nothing to do with whether a defendant caused the injury or harm to the child, but, rather, with whether the defendant's negligence was the proximate cause of the parents' being deprived of the option of avoiding a conception or, in the case of pregnancy, making an informed and meaningful decision either to terminate the pregnancy or to give birth to a potentially defective child. Like most of the other courts that have considered this cause of action, we hold that the parents of a genetically or congenitally defective child may maintain an action for its wrongful birth if the birth was the result of the negligent failure of the attending prenatal physician to discover and inform them of the existence of fetal defects.

* * *

The basic rule of tort compensation is that the plaintiff should be put in the position that he would have been in absent the defendant's negligence * * *. "It is a fundamental tenet of tort law that a negligent tortfeasor is liable for all damages that are the proximate result of his negligence."

We follow the holding of other courts that have considered this issue. "[T]he current trend with respect to damages is to allow the recovery of only the additional costs of treatment and special resources for the child, not the entire cost of rearing the child." * * * The primary element of damages that may be recovered in an action for wrongful birth is the pecuniary loss to the plaintiffs, the child's parents, resulting from the care and treatment of the child. The plaintiffs are entitled to recover for the extraordinary expenses they incur because of the child's unhealthy condition, including: (1) hospital and medical costs, (2) costs of medication, and (3) costs of education and therapy for the child.

It is generally recognized that, in a wrongful birth action, parents may recover the extraordinary costs necessary to treat the birth defect and any additional medical or educational costs attributable to the birth defect during the child's minority.

Emotional distress suffered by the parents of an unhealthy child is compensable in a wrongful birth action. A jury could conclude that the defendants, in failing to inform Mrs. Keel of the possibility of giving birth to a child with severe multiple congenital abnormalities, directly deprived her and, derivatively, her husband, of the option to accept or reject a parental relationship with the child and thus caused them to experience mental and emotional anguish upon their realization that they had given birth to a child afflicted with severe multiple congenital abnormalities.

We conclude that the following items are compensable, if proven: (1) any medical and hospital expenses incurred as a result of a physician's negligence; (2) the physical pain suffered by the wife; (3) loss of consortium; and (4) mental and emotional anguish the parents have suffered.

NOTES AND QUESTIONS

1. What are the policy reasons for and against the recognition of wrongful birth cases?

2. In Azzolino v. Dingfelder, 337 S.E.2d 528 (N.C. 1985), the court refused to recognize a wrongful birth cause of action. The court was concerned, in part, about its eugenic implications. The court said:

[S]ince the parents will decide which "defects" would have led them to abort the fetus, other questions will rapidly arise in jurisdictions recognizing wrongful birth claims when determining whether such claims will be permitted in particular cases. When will parents in those jurisdictions be allowed to decide that their child is so "defective" that given a chance they would have aborted it while still a fetus and, as a result, then be allowed to hold their physician civilly liable? When a fetus is only the carrier of a deleterious gene and not itself impaired? When the fetus is of one sex rather than the other? Should such issues be left exclusively to the parents with doctors being found liable for breaching their duty to inform parents of any fetal conditions to which they know or should know the parents may object?

* * *

Inevitably this will place increased pressure upon physicians to take the "safe" course by recommending abortion. This is perhaps best illustrated by a story drawn from a real life situation.

A clinical instructor asks his students to advise an expectant mother on the fate of a fetus whose father has chronic syphilis. Early siblings were born with a collection of defects such as deafness, blindness, and retardation. The usual response of the students is: "Abort!" The teacher then calmly replies: "Congratulations, you have just aborted Beethoven."

3. In traditional tort cases, the plaintiffs have a duty to mitigate damages. Should parents in wrongful birth cases be required to mitigate damages by putting their child up for adoption?

4. What types of evidence can be used to establish the standard of care in wrongful birth suits?

5. What should be the scope of damages in wrongful birth cases? The Illinois Appellate court allowed a couple to plead damages that encompassed the care of their child born with Angelman Syndrome after physicians failed to diagnose the disease in his older brother. Clark v. The Children's Memorial Hospital, 329 Ill.Dec. 730, 907 N.E.2d 49 (Ill. App. 1st Dist. April 9, 2009). In Basten v. United States, 848 F.Supp. 962 (M.D. Ala. 1994), liability was found for wrongful birth when physicians failed to inform a couple of the availability of prenatal testing that would help diagnose spina bifida. In addition to allowing the parents to recover millions of dollars in damages, the court allowed the healthy sister of the affected child to recover $25,000 for "loss of parental services"—the loss of care, counsel, training and education she would have received were it not for her parents' necessity to devote attention to her seriously ill sibling. The court in a footnote said it was awarding those damages "reluctantly" and was doing so because the parties jointly stipulated that the sister of the affected child should recover damages for loss of parental services. What are the arguments for and against such damages? If the "healthy" child can recover such damages because a child born with a genetic impairment takes an excessive amount of parental time, could a first-born child sue his or her parents for having several additional children, thus reducing the attention the first-born will receive?

6. If parents can recover for wrongful birth, why not grandparents? A New Jersey appellate court held that a grandfather cannot bring a wrongful birth suit on his behalf to recover emotional distress damages arising from the birth of his grandson. The grandfather alleged that a grandparent is a

"filament of family life" and that the birth of a child with Tay–Sachs disease affected the entire family. Thus, he argued, he should also be entitled to recover damages for the emotional distress he had when the defendants failed to inform the mother of his grandson of fetal abnormalities. The appellate court held that only the parents of the child may recover for pain and suffering resulting from the birth of the child. Michelman v. Erlich, 709 A.2d 281 (N.J. Super. A.D. 1998).

7.   Should wrongful birth actions only be permitted where the disorder at issue is serious? Some courts have considered the severity of the disorder as a factor in assessing the health care professional's liability for failing to provide information about genetic risks. For example, in Turpin v. Sortini, 643 P.2d 954 (Cal. 1982), a wrongful birth case, the California Supreme Court asserted, "[i]n this case, in which the plaintiff's only affliction is deafness, it seems quite unlikely that a jury would ever conclude that life with such a condition is worse than not being born at all." Using the reasoning presented in *Turpin*, a slight disadvantage such as short stature would probably not be sufficient to find liability. In Zepeda v. Zepeda, 190 N.E.2d 849, 859 (Ill. App. 1963), the court refused to allow an illegitimate son to sue his father for wrongful life. The court refused to recognize a cause of action because it felt it was the legislature's job to redress such a far-reaching tort. The court noted:

> Encouragement would extend to all others born into the world under conditions they might regard as adverse. One might seek damages for being born of a certain color, another because of race; one for being born with a hereditary disease, another for inheriting unfortunate family characteristics; one for being born into a large and destitute family, another because a parent has an unsavory reputation.

8.   Currently, at least six states, Idaho, Michigan, Minnesota, Missouri, Pennsylvania, and South Dakota have laws that prohibit parents from bringing wrongful birth suits against health care providers. Could such statutes be challenged as a violation of the couple's reproductive liberty by eliminating an incentive for physicians to give parents-to-be information necessary to make procreative decisions? In a Utah case, a couple challenged the constitutionality of a Utah statute which prohibited any cause of action "based on [a] claim that but for the act or omission of another, a person would not have been permitted to have been born alive but would have been aborted." Several genetic tests had been conducted, but the parents alleged that they were never accurately informed about the results of the tests or the risks of the fetus having Downs Syndrome. The Utah Supreme Court rejected a due process challenge to Utah's prohibition on wrongful birth lawsuits because the court found the law did not place an undue burden on a woman's ability to abort a fetus with a genetic anomaly. It also rejected an equal protection challenge to the law because it held that the class of people who choose to abort a fetus with a genetic anomaly is not a recognized class under the equal protection clause. Wood v. University of Utah Medical Center 67 P.3d 436 (Utah 2002). Utah subsequently repealed its wrongful birth statute in 2008.

9.   The North Carolina Supreme Court allowed the parents of a child born with sickle cell disease to bring a medical malpractice suit against a physician, even though North Carolina statutorily bars wrongful birth and

wrongful life actions where the claim is the parents would have aborted. The parents alleged that the physician negligently failed to advise them of their own genetic test results showing they were carriers of sickle cell anemia and thus would have a 25% risk of having a child with sickle cell disease. See McAllister v. Ha, 496 S.E.2d 577, 584 (N.C. 1998). In this case, the couple could have chosen not to procreate (rather than abort). However, the court refused to allow the parents to recover damages for any costs associated with child-rearing (including the extraordinary costs of caring for the child due to illness), but would allow the recovery of costs associated with the pregnancy and severe emotional distress.

10. Most cases alleging negligence in prenatal screening deal with false negatives—situations in which parents are erroneously told that their fetus is not afflicted with a serious genetic disorder. What about false positives, though? A couple might erroneously be told their fetus has a serious genetic disease. Such a case is not a wrongful birth case because the fetus is not brought to term, but may be looked at as a wrongful abortion case. In Martinez v. Long Island Jewish Hillside Medical Center, 512 N.E.2d 538 (N.Y. 1987), defendants negligently advised Carmen Martinez that her baby would be born with the congenital birth defect of microcephaly (small brain) or anencephaly (no brain). Based on the extraordinary circumstances, she submitted to an abortion believing that it would be justified. Because of her religious beliefs, she felt abortion was a sin except under justifiable circumstances such as these.

When it was shown that the diagnosis was erroneous and that Ms. Martinez had aborted a healthy fetus, she was allowed to maintain a cause of action for emotional distress.

11. The existence of prenatal screening may alter physician's ideas of responsible parental behavior. When pregnant women do not undergo available prenatal testing, health care professionals blame them for the resulting genetic condition of their child. Theresa M. Marteau & Harriet Drake, Attributions for Disability: The Influence of Genetic Screening, 40 Soc. Sci. Med. 1127–1132 (1995).

12. Currently, in the Orthodox Jewish community of New York, where arranged marriages are still common, genetic information is increasingly being taken into consideration at the matchmaking stage. People who are of Ashkenazi Jewish descent have a one-in–25 chance of having a Tay–Sachs genetic mutation; if two such carriers marry, each child has a one-in-four chance of having the devastating disease. A child with Tay–Sachs appears normal at birth, but later loses motor functions, suffers massive neurological deterioration and seizures, and generally dies by age three. A program in New York known as Chevra Dor Yeshorim (Association of an Upright Generation) offers Tay–Sachs carrier screening to Orthodox Jewish adolescents. Before a marriage is arranged, the matchmaker calls the program with the identification numbers of the two individuals. If they both carry the gene for Tay–Sachs, they are not matched for marriage. To preserve medical confidentiality, they are not informed why they are not a good match. The program has generated controversy because it has added screening for other disorders, such as cystic fibrosis, which are not necessarily fatal in childhood.

In the Chevra Dor Yeshorim program, if both individuals are carriers, they are found to be "genetically incompatible," but the program does not disclose information of individual genetic risks. In contrast, the Thalassaemia Screening Program (TSP) in Cyprus does disclose carrier status of individual genetic risks. Another difference between the programs is that Chevra Dor tests for diseases such as Tay–Sachs, which is fatal at a very early age; thalassaemia is treatable but at a high cost. Does premarital genetic testing raise any ethical questions? Do you think there is any danger in labeling a couple "genetically incompatible"? See Barbara Prainsack and Gil Siegal, The Rise of Genetic Couplehood? A Comparative View of Premarital Genetic Testing, 1 BioSocieties 17 (2006).

What if a couple undergoing testing in the Chevra Dor Yeshorim program are told that they both carry the Tay–Sachs mutation—and do not marry as a result. If the information is later found to be erroneous, could they sue? What potential damages would there be for the loss of a chance to marry, particularly if each member of the couple marries someone else?

MUNRO v. REGENTS OF THE UNIVERSITY OF CALIFORNIA

263 Cal.Rptr. 878 (Cal. App. 1989).

LILLIE, J.

Plaintiffs Pamela and Allen Munro are a married couple. In September 1984 Mrs. Munro saw Dr. William Growdon, an obstetrician-gynecologist. Dr. Growdon confirmed that Mrs. Munro, then 37 years old, was pregnant with her second child. Because of the increased risk of Down Syndrome in children born to women over the age of 35, Dr. Growdon referred Mrs. Munro to defendant Barbara Crandall, a physician, for genetic counseling.

In October 1984 Mrs. Munro met with Dr. Crandall at the UCLA Neuropsychiatric Institute. At this meeting Dr. Crandall took a family history of Mr. and Mrs. Munro. Mrs. Munro told Dr. Crandall her father's background was "primarily German" and her mother's background was English and Canadian. She said that her husband's father's father was Scottish and his father's mother was either Scottish or Irish. Mrs. Munro also told Dr. Crandall that Mr. Munro's mother's father was Norwegian and his "mother's father's [sic] family was some peculiar type of French." The information Dr. Crandall obtained from Mrs. Munro indicated that neither she nor Mr. Munro is of Jewish heritage. Because of the extremely low incidence of non-Jewish carriers of Tay–Sachs disease, Dr. Crandall does not recommend genetic testing for Tay–Sachs disease unless one or both parents indicate they are of Ashkenazic (eastern European) Jewish background. Accordingly, when Mrs. Munro underwent genetic testing at UCLA Medical Center in November 1984, no test was given to determine whether she or her husband had the genetic makeup for transmission of Tay–Sachs disease to their unborn child. About three weeks later an employee of the UCLA Medical Center telephoned Mrs. Munro and told her she was carrying a healthy baby boy.

On May 11, 1985, Pamela Munro gave birth to plaintiff Alexander Munro. In March 1986 Alexander was diagnosed as suffering from Tay–Sachs disease. When Mrs. Munro came to her for genetic counseling in 1984, Dr. Crandall knew that in addition to Ashkenazic Jews, there is a small inbred community in French Canada which is said to have a slightly higher prevalence of Tay–Sachs disease than the general population. Not until after the counseling session did the Munros learn that Mr. Munro's maternal grandfather's parents were French Canadian.

Plaintiffs sued defendants for medical malpractice and intentional and negligent infliction of emotional distress. The complaint's first cause of action ("negligence"), on behalf of all plaintiffs, alleged that plaintiff Alexander Munro, by his guardians ad litem plaintiffs Pamela and Allen Munro, engaged the services of defendants to care for and treat "a problem pertaining to the health and well-being" of Alexander Munro and Pamela Munro. Defendants undertook to provide genetic counseling for Pamela Munro, and consequently for Alexander Munro. In providing such counseling defendants negligently failed to possess and exercise the degree of knowledge and skill ordinarily possessed and exercised by other physicians and hospitals in the same locality as defendants. As a direct result of said negligence plaintiffs Pamela Munro and Allen Munro suffered severe, serious and permanent physical and emotional injuries. Plaintiff Alexander Munro, by and through his guardians ad litem, incurred hospital and medical expenses and will continue to incur such expenses for an indefinite period of time in the future.

The second cause of action (intentional infliction of emotional distress), on behalf of plaintiffs Pamela and Allen Munro, incorporated the allegations of the first cause of action and further alleged: When she received genetic counseling from defendants, Pamela Munro was pregnant with Alexander and sought the services of defendants for the purpose of diagnosis and treatment of any genetic fetal abnormality. Defendants held themselves out to the general public, including plaintiffs, as experts in the field of genetic counseling and diagnosis; plaintiffs had no education or training in that field and relied upon defendants to undertake all necessary and proper testing so as to render a professional opinion regarding potential genetic disorders in Alexander. Defendants represented to plaintiffs that all such testing would be done. Plaintiffs believed that tests to rule out Tay–Sachs disease were performed by defendants and that said tests were negative. In fact, defendants intentionally and maliciously either omitted said tests or if said tests were performed, recklessly disregarded their results and failed to inform plaintiffs Pamela and Allen Munro that Alexander, in utero, was afflicted with Tay–Sachs disease. As a result of defendants' conduct plaintiffs suffered severe emotional distress.

Defendants moved for summary judgment on the ground defendant Barbara Crandall acted within the operative standard of care in her genetic counseling of plaintiffs. In support of the motion defendants presented excerpts from the depositions of Dr. Crandall and plaintiffs Pamela and Allen Munro. Defendants also presented the declaration of Dr. Michael Kaback, a physician certified by the American Board of Pediatrics and the American Board of Medical Genetics. Dr. Kaback is the director of the State of California Tay–Sachs Disease Prevention Program and the director of the International Tay–Sachs Disease Testing, Quality Control and Data Collection Center. Based on his medical knowledge and expertise and his knowledge of the facts of this case, Dr. Kaback expressed the opinion that plaintiffs did not meet the profile characteristics necessary to warrant performing a Tay–Sachs screening test and therefore it was within the standard of care for defendants not to perform such testing on plaintiffs.

Plaintiffs opposed the motion for summary judgment, submitting the declaration of plaintiff Pamela Munro wherein she stated inter alia: If the basis of defendants' exclusion of Tay–Sachs testing was the fact that she and her husband are not Jewish, this should have been made known to plaintiffs; regardless of the rarity of the carrier status of Tay–Sachs disease in non-Jews, plaintiffs would have availed themselves of the Tay–Sachs test if the easy availability of that test had been made known to them. Plaintiffs presented no expert medical evidence.

The motion was granted as to the entire complaint. Summary judgment was entered in favor of defendants and against plaintiffs. This appeal followed.

* * *

[The summary judgment in favor of defendants on the medical malpractice claim was upheld because the plaintiffs did not present an expert on the standard of care. Then the court turned to the wrongful birth claim.]

Plaintiffs contend that defendants had a duty to disclose material information to enable plaintiffs to make an informed decision whether to take the Tay–Sachs test. Plaintiffs further argue that because such duty of disclosure is not governed by the standard practice of the physicians' community, but is instead a duty imposed by law, expert evidence is not required to establish the existence of the duty and a triable issue of fact was presented as to whether defendants complied with that duty.

Defendants reply that inasmuch as plaintiffs did not allege breach of the duty of disclosure, they may not advance that theory on appeal. "Generally, the rules relating to the scope of appellate review apply to appellate review of summary judgments. An argument or theory will generally not be considered if it is raised for the first time on appeal. Specifically, in reviewing a summary judgment, the appellate court must consider only those facts before the trial court, disregarding any new allegations on appeal. Thus, possible theories that were not fully developed or factually presented to the trial court cannot create a 'triable issue' on appeal."

Plaintiffs' second cause of action, while labeled "intentional infliction of emotional distress," appears to allege fraud on the part of defendants by falsely representing to plaintiffs that testing for all "potential genetic disorders" would be done. In her declaration in opposition to the motion for summary judgment plaintiff Pamela Munro stated: During genetic counseling by defendants, plaintiff was not told why she was asked questions about her family history and that of her husband. If defendants' exclusion of Tay–Sachs testing was based on the fact that plaintiffs are not Jewish, defendants should have so informed plaintiff. They also should have told her of the easy availability of Tay–Sachs screening. If plaintiffs had known this, they would have availed themselves of such screening regardless of the rarity of the Tay–Sachs trait in non-Jewish people.

In Willard v. Hagemeister, 175 Cal.Rptr. 365 [(Cal. App. 2d 1981)], a dental malpractice case in which summary judgment was entered in favor of defendants, plaintiff alleged that she consented to certain dental treatment on the basis of false representations that such treatment would save a tooth. The court concluded that in addition to fraud, plaintiff attempted to charge defendants with a failure to disclose material facts necessary for an informed consent to their proposed treatment. The court noted that the requisite causal relationship between defendants' failure to inform and plaintiff's injury was supplied by plaintiff's counterdeclaration that if the inherent risks had been revealed, she would not have consented to the treatment given. Summary judgment for defendants on the cause of action for fraud was reversed with directions that plaintiff be permitted to amend her complaint and to litigate the issue of informed consent.

We decline to follow a similar course because, under the circumstances of the present case, as a matter of law plaintiffs cannot prevail on the theory of lack of informed consent.

In Cobbs v. Grant, 502 P.2d 1 [(Cal.1972)], the Supreme Court held that "as an integral part of the physician's overall obligation to the patient there is a duty of reasonable disclosure of the available choices with respect to proposed therapy and of the dangers inherently and potentially involved in each." In Truman v. Thomas, 611 P.2d 902 [(Cal. 1980)], it was held the duty of disclosure applies whether the proposed procedure involves treatment or a diagnostic test. Further, a patient must be informed of the risks of refusing to undergo a proposed treatment or test as well as the risks of consenting to proposed treatment or testing.

In Scalere v. Stenson, 260 Cal.Rptr. 152 [(Cal. App. 2d 1989)], we recently held that under *Cobbs* and *Truman* a physician has no duty to disclose where no diagnostic testing or treatment is recommended. There, plaintiff underwent a diagnostic surgical procedure (angiogram) performed on the brachial artery of her right arm. After surgery plaintiff complained of pain in her right arm. Defendant, a cardiologist, examined and tested the arm and concluded it was progressing satisfactorily. He therefore neither told plaintiff about nor recommended any further diagnostic tests or therapy. A year later plaintiff underwent a saphenous vein bypass of her right brachial artery with resultant damage. While plaintiff alleged only ordinary negligence (" 'negligently examined, diagnosed, prognosed, cared for, treated, and performed surgical procedures upon the body and person of plaintiff' ") at trial she relied on the theory that defendant improperly failed to disclose material facts necessary for plaintiff to evaluate her condition and seek post-operative care. In affirming judgment in favor of defendant we rejected that theory, noting that in *Cobbs* the predicate for the duty to disclose was proposed therapy (duodenal ulcer surgery) while in Truman the predicate for the duty was a proposed diagnostic procedure (pap smear). We concluded that inasmuch as defendant, following the surgery, recommended neither further therapy nor further diagnostic testing, no duty of disclosure arose.

In rejecting the contrary view expressed by the dissent, we stated: "The dissent would draw a new duty-to-disclose line. Though a doctor proposes neither surgery nor medical procedure, though he recommends no therapy and is unaware of any other school of doctors who would recommend therapy, the dissent would require such a doctor to disclose 'the risks and benefits of non-treatment.' Such a line, like one drawn with a finger in the air, is without precision and predictability. It would impose significant new burdens on already harried doctors without awarding demonstrable benefits to their patients. 'It seems obviously prohibitive and unrealistic to expect physicians to discuss with their patients every risk of proposed treatment [[l]et alone non treatment]—no matter how small or remote—and generally unnecessary from the patient's viewpoint as well.' "

The passage quoted in *Scalere* is a complete answer to plaintiffs' argument that even though defendants did not recommend plaintiffs undergo a Tay–Sachs screening test, defendants were under a duty to inform plaintiffs of the incidence of Tay–Sachs disease in the general population, the higher incidence of the disease among French Canadians, and that the Tay–Sachs test is simply a blood test which, together with the amniocentetic culture test therefor, costs $500. As is natural in view of their son's tragic affliction, plaintiffs focus on defendants' failure to give them any information which would have enabled them to decide whether or not to undergo testing for Tay–Sachs disease. However, when Pamela Munro received genetic counseling she provided defendants with no facts which should have alerted them to the possibility that one or both of the plaintiffs might be carriers of Tay–Sachs disease, which is but one of approximately 70 genetic disorders that can be detected by testing. This is truly a case in which it can be said that the information plaintiffs now claim defendants were under a duty to divulge related to a " 'small or remote' " risk [the incidence of non-Jewish carriers of Tay–Sachs is between 1 in 200 and 1 in 300] and was " 'generally unnecessary from the patient's viewpoint' '' in light of what plaintiffs knew of their respective ethnic backgrounds at the time of genetic counseling.

Plaintiffs would have us impose on defendants a duty to give plaintiffs information regarding a genetic test defendants did not recommend because it was not indicated by any facts which plaintiffs told to defendants, or even any facts of which plaintiffs were aware. Reason, as well as precedent, compels our refusal to impose such a duty.

* * *

The judgment is affirmed.

WOODS, J., concurs.

JOHNSON, J.

I concur in the result the majority reaches but not in its reasoning.

For the reasons I explained at length in my dissent in *Scalere* a doctor's duty of disclosure includes the duty of explaining the risks and benefits of non-treatment. This duty arises from the same principle that imposes a duty to explain the risks and benefits of treatment: "so that patients might meaningfully exercise their right to make decisions about their own bodies...."

Whether the physician's recommendation is to treat or not to treat, or, as here, to test or not to test, there are risks and benefits to either course which must be explained to the patient.

The principle that a doctor's duty of disclosure includes the duty of explaining the risks of not performing tests has been recognized in other jurisdictions. * * *

In contrast to *Scalere*, *Goldberg* [v. *Ruskin*, 471 N.E.2d 530, 537 (Ill. 1984) aff'd on appeal from a separate issue, 499 N.E.2d 406, 407 (1986)] and *Phillips* [v. United States 566 F.Supp. 1 (D.C.S.C. 1981)], nothing Dr. Crandall knew about the Munros triggered a duty to disclose the risks and benefits of not testing for Tay–Sachs. Neither of the Munros were of Jewish heritage. Mr. Munro had some distant relatives of French heritage but Dr. Crandall had no reason to know or even suspect any of these relatives came from a small inbred community of French Canadians which is said to have a slightly higher incidence of Tay–Sachs disease than the general population.

In the present case, summary judgment against the Munros should be affirmed because the undisputed facts show Dr. Crandall was not aware of any facts that would trigger a duty to disclose to the Munros the risk of not performing a test for Tay–Sachs. Thus, the majority reaches the correct result in this case. What concerns me is the majority would have reached the same result in the case of the Goldbergs and the Phillips.

NOTES AND QUESTIONS

1.   Carrier frequency of Tay–Sachs in non-Jews is 1 in 200 to 1 in 300, with 1 in 160,000 to 1 in 360,000 affected. When would the incidence be high enough to make genetic testing part of the standard of care?

2.   Was there a duty to tell the parents in *Munro* about the existence of other tests that were not being recommended? In 1984, there were tests for about 70 disorders; in 2002, there are tests for over 600 disorders.

3.   To what extent do you think the standard of care (and thus the result in *Munro*) was based on the risks and benefits of the testing based on 1984 technology? Might the result be different with the advent of multi-plex or chip-based tests performed after a maternal blood test?

4.   Women generally visit their obstetricians numerous times during pregnancy. Should obstetricians have a duty to at least provide written material that would inform patients what type of background family information is necessary to determine if the patients are in a high risk group for passing on a genetic disease?

CURLENDER v. BIO–SCIENCE LABORATORIES

165 Cal.Rptr. 477 (Cal. App. 1980).

JEFFERSON, J.

The appeal presents an issue of first impression in California: What remedy, if any, is available in this state to a severely impaired child genetically defective born as the result of defendants' negligence in conducting certain genetic tests of the child's parents tests which, if properly done, would have disclosed the high probability that the actual, catastrophic result would occur?

* * *

In the first cause of action against the named defendants, plaintiff Shauna alleged that on January 15, 1977, her parents, Phillis and Hyam Curlender, retained defendant laboratories to administer certain tests designed to reveal whether either of the parents were carriers of genes which would result in the conception and birth of a child with Tay–Sachs disease, medically defined as "amaurotic familial idiocy." The tests on plaintiff's parents were performed on January 21, 1977, and, it was alleged, due to defendants' negligence, "incorrect and inaccurate" information was disseminated to plaintiff's parents concerning their status as carriers.

The complaint did not allege the date of plaintiff's birth, so we do not know whether the parents relied upon the test results in conceiving plaintiff, or, as parents-to-be when the tests were made, relied upon the results in failing to avail themselves of amniocentesis and an abortion. In any event, on May 10, 1978, plaintiff's parents were informed that plaintiff had Tay–Sachs disease.

As the result of the disease, plaintiff Shauna suffers from "mental retardation, susceptibility to other diseases, convulsions, sluggishness, apathy, failure to fix objects with her eyes, inability to take an interest in her surroundings, loss of motor reactions, inability to sit up or hold her head up, loss of weight, muscle atrophy, blindness, pseudobulper palsy, inability to feed orally, decerebrate rigidity and gross physical deformity." It was alleged that Shauna's life expectancy is estimated to be four years. The complaint also contained allegations that plaintiff suffers "pain, physical and emotional distress, fear, anxiety, despair, loss of enjoyment of life, and frustration ....."

The complaint sought costs of plaintiff's care as damages and also damages for emotional distress and the deprivation of "72.6 years of her life." In addition, punitive damages of three million dollars were sought, on the ground that "[a]t the time that Defendants ... [tested the parents], Defendants, and each of them, had been expressly informed by the nation's leading authority on Tay–Sachs disease that said test procedures were substantially inaccurate and would likely result is disasterous [sic] and catastrophic consequences to the patients, and Defendants knew that said procedures were improper, inadequate and with insufficient controls and that the results of such testing were likely to be inaccurate and that a false negative result would have disasterous [sic] and catastrophic consequences to the Plaintiff, all in conscious disregard of the health, safety and well-being of Plaintiff ...."

* * *

The term "wrongful life" has to date served as an umbrella for causes of action based upon any distinguishable factual situations; this has led to some confusion in its use. For purposes of our discussion, the term "wrongful life" will be confined to those causes of action *brought by the infant* alleging that, due to the negligence of the defendant, birth occurred; * * *.

* * *

The high court in Pennsylvania issued an exhaustive opinion in 1979 concerning the various aspects of the "wrongful-life" problem. The case was Speck v. Finegold, 408 A.2d 496 (Pa. 1979), a malpractice suit by parents and child occasioned by the birth of the child with neurofibromatosis, a seriously crippling condition already evidenced in the child's siblings. Overruling the trial court, *Speck* recognized the parents' cause of action but not that of the infant plaintiff.

We quote at length from the *Speck* court's opinion: "In the instant case, we deny Francine's [infant plaintiff's] claim to be made whole. When we examine Francine's claim, we find regardless of whether her claim is based on 'wrongful life' or otherwise, there is a failure to state a legally cognizable cause of action even though, admittedly, the defendants' actions of negligence were the proximate cause of her defective birth. Her claims to be whole have two fatal weaknesses. First, there is no precedent in appellate judicial pronouncements that holds a child has a fundamental right to be born as a whole, functional human being. Whether it is better to have never been born at all rather than to have been born with serious mental defects is a mystery more properly left to the philosophers and theologians, a mystery which would lead us into the field of metaphysics, beyond the realm of our understanding or ability to solve . . . . [This] cause of action . . . demands a calculation of damages dependent on a comparison between Hobson's choice of life in an impaired state and nonexistence. This the law is incapable of doing . . . unfortunately, . . . this is not an action cognizable in law. Thus, the recognized principle, not peculiar to traditional tort law alone, that it would be a denial of justice to deny all relief where a wrong is of such a nature as to preclude certain ascertained damages, is inapposite and inapplicable here.''

* * *

The circumstance that the birth and injury have come hand in hand has caused other courts to deal with the problem by barring recovery. The reality of the ''wrongful-life'' concept is that such a plaintiff both *exists* and *suffers*, due to the negligence of others. It is neither necessary nor just to retreat into meditation on the mysteries of life. We need not be concerned with the fact that had defendants not been negligent, the plaintiff might not have come into existence at all. The certainty of genetic impairment is no longer a mystery. In addition, a reverent appreciation of life compels recognition that plaintiff, however impaired she may be, has come into existence as a living person with certain rights.

One of the fears expressed in the decisional law is that, once it is determined that such infants have rights cognizable at law, nothing would prevent such a plaintiff from bringing suit against its own parents for allowing plaintiff to be born. In our view, the fear is groundless. The ''wrongful-life'' cause of action with which we are concerned is based upon negligently caused failure by someone under a duty to do so to inform the prospective parents of facts needed by them to make a conscious choice *not* to become parents. If a case arose where, despite due care by the medical profession in transmitting the necessary warnings, parents made a conscious choice to proceed with a pregnancy, with full knowledge that a seriously impaired infant would be born, that conscious choice would provide an intervening act of proximate cause to preclude liability insofar as defendants other than the parents were concerned. Under such circumstances, we see no sound public policy which should protect those parents from being answerable for the pain, suffering and misery which they have wrought upon their offspring.

* * *

The extent of recovery, however, is subject to certain limitations due to the nature of the tort involved. While ordinarily a defendant is liable for all consequences flowing from the injury, it is appropriate in the case before us to tailor the elements of recovery, taking into account particular circumstances involved.

The complaint seeks damages based upon an actuarial life expectancy of plaintiff of more than 70 years—the life expectancy if plaintiff had been born without the Tay–Sachs disease. The complaint sets forth that plaintiff's actual life expectancy, because of the disease, is only four years. We reject as untenable the claim that plaintiff is entitled to damages as if plaintiff had been born without defects and would have had a normal life expectancy. Plaintiff's right to damages must be considered on the basis of plaintiff's mental and physical condition at birth and her expected condition during the short life span (four years according to the complaint) anticipated for one with her impaired condition. In similar fashion, we reject the notion that a "wrongful-life" cause of action involves any attempted evaluation of a claimed right *not* to be born. In essence, we construe the "wrongful-life" cause of action by the defective child as the right of such child to recover damages for the pain and suffering to be endured during the limited life span available to such a child and any special pecuniary loss resulting from the impaired condition.

In California, infants are presumed to experience pain and suffering when injury has been established, even if the infant is unable to testify and describe such pain and suffering * * *.

The complaint sought costs of care as an element of special damages, an appropriate item of recovery in cases where, for one reason or another, there is no suit brought by the parents seeking recovery for this pecuniary loss. We are informed, however, that such a suit is pending by the parents of the plaintiff before us. Upon remand, consideration should be given to consolidating plaintiff's cause of action with those of the parents in the interest of efficient use of trial time and the prevention of duplication of effort, as well as the prevention of possible double recovery. Costs of plaintiff's care may only be awarded once.

Finally, we considered the matter of punitive damages. The complaint makes such a request. Our Civil Code section 3294 allows such damages "where the defendant has been guilty of oppression, fraud, or malice, express or implied"; they are given "for the sake of example and by way of punishing the defendant." We need not speculate on the means by which plaintiff plans to establish facts showing oppression, fraud or malice—as related to either the third cause of action stated in the complaint or the entitlement of plaintiff to punitive damages. Such will be the concern of judge and jury when this matter is tried. For our purposes, we find that plaintiff has adequately pleaded a cause of action for punitive damages. We see no reason in public policy or legal analysis for exempting from liability for punitive damages a defendant who is sued for committing a "wrongful-life" tort.

DOOLAN v. IVF AMERICA (MA) INC.

2000 WL 33170944 (Mass. Super. 2000).

CRATSLEY, J.

Pursuant to the summary judgment record, the undisputed material facts are as follows:

In 1993, plaintiff Laureen Doolan gave birth to her first child, Samantha, who was born afflicted with cystic fibrosis. Laureen and her husband, plaintiff John Doolan, subsequently learned that they were both carriers of a cystic fibrosis gene mutation known as Delta F–508. Mr. and Mrs. Doolan wished to have another child, but they wanted some assurance that their second child would not have cystic fibrosis.

In 1996 Mr. and Mrs. Doolan agreed to participate in a series of procedures conducted jointly by the co-defendants that were designed to provide the Doolans with a degree of certainty that their second child would not be afflicted with cystic fibrosis. In November 1996 defendant Ronald Carson, Ph.D. ("Dr. Carson"), the Scientific and Laboratory Director at defendant MPD, harvested a series of Mrs. Doolan's eggs, fertilized the eggs with Mr. Doolan's sperm in vitro, and prepared the resulting embryos for genetic testing. A cell from each of the resulting ten embryos was then retrieved by MPD, whereupon the cells were sent to defendant Genzyme Corporation ("Genzyme").

In December 1996 Genzyme tested the ten cells to ascertain which embryos were (1) afflicted with, (2) carriers of, or (3) free of the cystic fibrosis gene mutation, Delta F–508. In a letter dated December 23, 1996, defendant Katherine Klinger, Ph.D. ("Dr. Klinger"), the Vice President of Science at Genzyme, advised MPD that Embryo No. 7 was free of the cystic fibrosis gene mutation and suitable for implantation. As a result of this finding, Mr. and Mrs. Doolan decided to have MPD implant Embryo No. 7 into Mrs. Doolan on March 10, 1997.

On November 21, 1997, Mrs. Doolan gave birth to her son, minor plaintiff Thomas Doolan. Shortly after Thomas' birth, it was discovered that he did, in fact, suffer from cystic fibrosis and that his condition was due to the Delta F–508 genetic mutation. All three plaintiffs assert claims arising out of (1) MPD's and Dr. Carson's alleged negligence in implanting an embryo that contained the cystic fibrosis gene mutation, and (2) Genzyme's and Dr. Klinger's alleged negligence in advising MPD that Embryo No. 7 was free of the Delta F–508 gene mutation and therefore was suitable for implantation.

* * *

MINOR PLAINTIFF THOMAS DOOLAN'S NEGLIGENCE CLAIM

The almost universal rule in this country is that a physician is not liable to a child who was born because of the physician's negligence.

Courts have generally referred to claims alleging that the physician negligently failed to inform the child's parents of the possibility of their bearing a severely defective child, thereby preventing a parental choice to avoid the child's birth, as "wrongful life" cases. The Massachusetts Supreme Judicial Court (SJC) has reasoned that granting the minor plaintiff a cause of action in wrongful life cases would require a comparison of the relative monetary values of existence and nonexistence, a task that is beyond the competence of the judicial system.

* * *

Perhaps sensing the tenuous nature of his "wrongful life" claim, * * * minor plaintiff Thomas Doolan asserts that his negligence claim against the defendants is not a "wrongful life" claim, but rather it is a pre-conception tort, and as such it is not foreclosed under Massachusetts law. Unlike "wrongful life" claims, * * * the SJC has yet to address the viability of pre-conception tort claims * * *. [But] the essence of Thomas Doolan's claim is not that the alleged negligence of the defendants caused him to be born with cystic fibrosis, but rather that the alleged negligence of the defendants denied his parents the opportunity to choose not to conceive and give birth to him. This is precisely the "fundamental problem of logic" that the SJC sought to avoid when it denied the minor plaintiff a cause of action for "wrongful life" * * *.

JOHN AND LAUREEN DOOLAN'S CLAIMS FOR LOSS OF CONSORTIUM

Plaintiffs John and Laureen Doolan advance two arguments in support of their claims for loss of consortium. The plaintiffs first argue that M.G.L. c. 231, § 85X creates a cause of action for parents seeking to recover for the loss of consortium of a dependent child. Section 85X provides:

> The parents of a minor child or an adult child who is dependent on his parents for support shall have a cause of action for loss of consortium of the child who has been seriously injured against any person who is legally responsible for causing such injury.

The plain language of the preceding section indicates that the plaintiffs may only recover for the loss of consortium of Thomas Doolan against any person who is legally responsible for causing such injury. Plaintiffs have failed to put forth any evidence suggesting that the defendants are legally responsible for causing Thomas Doolan to be born afflicted with cystic fibrosis. This analysis is similar to that found * * * regarding Thomas Doolan's own negligence claims. Therefore, this Court holds as a matter of law that M.G.L. c. 231, § 85X does not confer a cause of action for loss of consortium on the plaintiffs, John and Laureen Doolan.

The second argument made by the plaintiffs in support of their loss of consortium claims asks this Court to undertake an analysis in the realm of the hypothetical. Mr. and Mrs. Doolan assert that were it not for the alleged negligence of the defendants, they would currently be raising a boy named Thomas, and that this child would not be afflicted with cystic fibrosis. Since this hypothetical "healthy" Thomas Doolan would be more likely to be able to offer society and companionship to his parents for the duration of their lifetimes than would the actual Thomas Doolan, plaintiffs reason that they have a cause of action for loss of consortium.

Plaintiffs' argument fails for two reasons. First, the extent of any loss of consortium damages for a child that was never born would be far too speculative to uphold plaintiffs' cause of action. For example, the jury would have to consider the quality of the relationship plaintiffs might have had with their hypothetical son in assessing Mr. and Mrs. Doolan's loss of consortium damages. Furthermore, plaintiffs' assertion that this hypothetical Thomas Doolan would have been "healthy" discounts the possibility that he might have been afflicted with another type of birth defect or long term illness.

Notes and Questions

1. What are the policy arguments for and against wrongful life actions? How do the policy arguments regarding wrongful life cases compare to those involving wrongful birth cases?

2. Should a child be able to bring a wrongful life cause of action against his or her parents in addition to, or instead of, the negligent health care provider? In *dicta*, the *Curlender* court said:

> If a case arose where, despite due care by the medical profession in transmitting the necessary warnings, parents made a conscious choice to proceed with a pregnancy, with a full knowledge that a seriously impaired infant would be born.... Under such circumstances, we see no sound policy which should protect those parents from being answerable for the pain, suffering and misery which they have wrought upon their offspring.

Subsequently, the California legislature passed the following statute:

Cal. Civ. Code § 43.6 (2001)

§ 43.6. Wrongful life action

(a) No cause of action arises against a parent of a child based upon the claim that the child should not have been conceived or, if conceived, should not have been allowed to have been born alive.

(b) The failure or refusal of a parent to prevent the live birth of his or her child shall not be a defense in any action against a third party, nor shall the failure or refusal be considered in awarding damages in any such action.

3. Examples of genetic diseases commonly tested for by preimplantation genetic diagnosis include Down syndrome, cystic fibrosis, thalassemia, sickle cell anemia, Gaucher disease, and hemophilia. Other heritable traits that have been screened in the clinical setting include a gene that predisposes carriers to deafness and a gene that causes early onset Alzheimer's disease. Recently, studies have indicated that embryos have been screened and selected to not have genes correlating with an increased risk of developing colon cancer or breast cancer. A child was born in January 2009 in the United Kingdom who

had been screened to be free of BRCA genetic mutations linked to breast cancer. Sarah–Kate Templeton, Gene Parents Plan More Babies, The Sunday Times (London), January 11, 2009, at 3. Note that in Great Britain only 5% of the cases of breast cancer are caused by the BRCA gene mutation.

D. MANDATORY PRENATAL SCREENING

LORI B. ANDREWS, PRENATAL SCREENING AND THE CULTURE OF MOTHERHOOD

47 Hastings L.J. 967, 970–971, 994–1000 (1996).

The range of tests offered is growing continually, due in large measure to concerted efforts by the Human Genome Project, a $3 billion federally funded endeavor to map and sequence the complete set of genes in the human body. Prenatal testing is now possible not just for serious, life-threatening disorders but also for disorders that are treatable after birth, for disorders that do not manifest until later in life, such as breast cancer, and even for conditions not thought to be medical problems, such as homosexuality.

At the same time, a developing technology offers more women the option of prenatal testing. This technology, fetal cell sorting, provides fetal information without creating a physical risk to the fetus or the pregnant woman. A "simple" blood test is performed on the woman. In the laboratory, technicians use complex procedures to capture minute quantities of fetal blood cells circulating in the woman's blood. Prenatal diagnosis is undertaken on those cells, to determine, for example, whether the fetus has Down syndrome, cystic fibrosis, Tay–Sachs disease, or other disorders.

Researchers developing fetal cell sorting have pointed out that it could be used to screen large populations of women. One group of researchers has noted that,

> because the * * * procedure requires sampling of maternal blood rather than amniotic fluid, it could make widespread screening in younger women feasible * * *. Widespread screening is desirable because the relatively large number of pregnancies in women below 35 years old means that they bear the majority of children with chromosomal abnormalities despite the relatively low risk of such abnormalities in pregnancies in this age group.

* * *

[The article then documents how some types of genetic testing have been undertaken on pregnant women without their knowledge or consent. It then discusses the policy issues that would be raised by a public health mandate requiring that pregnant women undergo fetal cell sorting.]

* * *

Various blue ribbon panels of government, ethics organizations, and entities like the Institute of Medicine have already concluded that, due to the various psychological and social risks of genetic testing, genetics services should be voluntary. With respect to prenatal testing, the National Institutes of Health Workshop on Reproductive Genetic Testing: Impact Upon Women has recommended that "[r]eproductive genetic services should be meticulously voluntary." Similarly, the Committee on Assessing Genetic Risks of the Institute of Medicine has recommended that "voluntariness should be the cornerstone of any genetic testing program. The committee [finds] no justification for a state-sponsored mandatory public health program involving genetic testing of adults, or for unconsented-to genetic testing of patients in the clinical setting."

Overriding autonomy by mandating fetal cell sorting clearly has the most impact on women. Women are the people subject to genetic testing on their fetuses' behalf, and the action that the state subtly may be trying to encourage is one that the women would have to take—abortion. Additionally, diagnosis of the fetus more often provides information about the mother than about the father. In the case of a recessive disease, an X-linked disease, and some instances of dominant diseases, the fetus' genetic status will provide information to the mother about her genetic status, thus influencing her self-image, her personal relationships, and her relationships with third-party institutions.

Moreover, the intrusion on autonomy may be especially egregious to women, who, more than men, feel that doctors should keep out of reproductive decisions. A Swedish study assessing the attitudes of women and men towards prenatal diagnosis found that autonomy in the decision-making process was more important to women than to men. In response to the question: "[W]ho should decide about prenatal diagnosis, the couple itself or somebody else?," 82% of women indicated the couple should make the decision, compared to 20% of the male partners.

* * *

Currently, the constitutional protections supporting a woman's right to refuse medical interventions during pregnancy are four-fold: privacy protection of certain personal information; protection against unreasonable searches and seizures; protection of bodily integrity; and protection of reproductive decision-making and decisions regarding child-rearing.

* * *

1. INFORMATIONAL PRIVACY

Medical information is protected as private, in part because of the psychological, social and financial risks associated with its disclosure. Common law privacy protections exist for certain types of medical information, as do federal constitutional protections. Just as "the sensitive nature of medical information about AIDS makes a compelling argument for keeping this information confidential," so too does the sensitive nature of genetic information. Since mandatory genetic testing would provide medical information about the woman or fetus to third parties (the laboratory personnel, the woman's physician), this could arguably be a breach of privacy. Such testing would violate one's privacy right not to know medical information about oneself and one's right to refuse medical information that is part of the right of informed consent in the health care setting.

2. FOURTH AMENDMENT PROTECTIONS

A pregnant woman could assert a Fourth Amendment right to refuse the fetal cell sorting test. Mandatory blood testing is considered a search and seizure that must comply with Fourth Amendment standards that balance the nature and quality of the intrusion against the strength of a given state interest. Under such an analysis, for example, mandatory testing of an incarcerated individual for HIV infection absent a warrant has been found unconstitutional under the Fourth Amendment. Similarly, mandatory HIV testing of state employees working with developmentally disabled clients was enjoined as an unreasonable search and seizure under the Fourth Amendment, since the employees' privacy interests outweighed the state's interest in preventing the low risk of clients' contracting AIDS from employees. Such precedents would likewise apply to blood tests to obtain genetic information.

3. PROTECTION OF BODILY INTEGRITY, REPRODUCTIVE AUTONOMY AND PARENTING DECISIONS

Women could also argue that they have a right to refuse fetal cell sorting based on the common law (and, in some cases, constitutional) protections of an individual's bodily integrity, as well as on constitutional protections of reproductive autonomy. Recent cases have begun to recognize a woman's right to refuse invasive interventions, such as Cesarean sections, during pregnancy. In In re A.C. [573 A.2d 1235 (D.C.1990)], the D.C. Court of Appeals held that the decision about whether a pregnant woman should undergo a Cesarean section should be controlled by the woman's wishes, articulated either through her informed consent or, if she is incompetent, through substituted judgment. A similar result was reached in an Illinois case, In re Baby Boy Doe [632 N.E.2d 326 (Ill.Ct. App.1994)]. In that case, a woman refused a Cesarean section on religious grounds, and the state attorney brought suit to force her to undergo the operation. The court upheld the woman's right to refuse, recognizing her right to privacy and bodily integrity. The court held that a woman has no duty to guarantee the physical and mental health of her child and that a woman may refuse forced interventions even if the refusal would be harmful to the fetus.

Parents also have a liberty interest in the type of children that they conceive and raise. In U.S. Supreme Court cases involving child-rearing decisions, the Court has held that the determination of a child's social traits is a matter for the parents to decide (even if state control arguably could produce a better child). A strong argument similarly could be made that a child's genetic traits should be determined by the parents rather than the state. Similar reasoning was used in dicta in Planned Parenthood v. Casey [505 U.S. 833 (1992)], in which the U.S. Supreme Court said,

> If indeed the woman's interest in deciding whether to bear and beget a child had not been recognized as in Roe [v. Wade, 410 U.S. 113 (1973)], the State might as readily restrict a woman's right to choose to carry a pregnancy to term as to terminate it, to further asserted state interests in population control, or eugenics, for example. Yet *Roe* has been sensibly relied upon to counter any such suggestions.

NOTES AND QUESTIONS

1. Some physicians undertake genetic testing on pregnant women without informed consent—and tell them the results of the testing only if it indicates a problem. When questioned about this practice, physicians state that other types of unconsented-to testing (such as for gestational diabetes) is routinely done on pregnant women without their consent. Are genetic tests distinguishable? Standard, nongenetic tests are often done in order to be able to treat the fetus. Genetic testing often reveals that the fetus is untreatable, so the "benefit" is the possibility of abortion. There is a much wider range of moral and personal opinion about the advisability of abortion than about treatment of fetuses or newborns. Some women understandably may not want information about their genetic status or the fetus's genetic status because they do not intend to abort or because they do not want to risk genetic discrimination against themselves or their future child. Standard tests are also generally for transitional, pregnancy-related conditions, whereas the genetic information revealed about a woman or her fetus is permanent and immutable in character.

2. What effect does mandatory genetic testing have on social expectations for women?

IV. REPRODUCTIVE TECHNOLOGY AND GENETICS

A. PROCEDURES

MARY Z. PELIAS & MARGARET M. DEANGELIS, THE NEW GENETIC TECHNOLOGIES: NEW OPTIONS, NEW HOPE, AND NEW CHALLENGES

45 Loyola L. Rev. 287, 289–91 (1999).

The new reproductive technologies are used both for medical treatment of infertility and for helping people circumvent the threat of conceiving and bearing a child with a genetic problem. Most of these technologies are founded in the technique of in vitro fertilization. This method involves the retrieval of mature egg cells and subsequent fertilization of these egg cells in a glass dish in the laboratory. Once fertilization takes place, the resulting conceptus can be carefully monitored in the laboratory for evidence of healthy cell division and growth. Further, its genetic material can be examined to determine the presence or absence of a grave genetic risk should the conceptus ever become part of a pregnancy that is carried to term birth. In vitro embryos are subsequently transferred into the uterus of the woman who expects to become pregnant and bear a child.

One approach to avoiding the possibility of genetic difficulties in offspring is *gamete donation*, or the use of gametes, either egg cells or sperm cells, that have been harvested from donor individuals. Egg cells may be harvested from the woman who expects to become the mother or from a woman who agrees to donate some of her own eggs to other women who either cannot furnish their own eggs or who do not wish to risk transmitting their own genes to their offspring. Fertilization is accomplished with semen collected either from the prospective father or from an anonymous sperm donor, depending on the needs of the individual couple. While retrieval of egg cells is of necessity more difficult than collecting sperm samples, both types of gametes can now be stored at ultra-low temperatures for use in the future by persons not yet identified. In the event that a clinic or laboratory stores gametes for donations to third persons, the careful assembly of genetic histories of donors is critical to ensuring, within the limits of available tests and technologies, that donors are themselves free of genes that could cause problems in the children of gamete recipients.

Another approach to assuring the birth of healthy children is *preimplantation genetic diagnosis* (PGD) to examine the genetic status of an in vitro embryo before the embryo is transferred to the woman who expects to become pregnant. PGD includes *blastomere analysis before implantation* (BABI) which is the technical union between in vitro fertilization and the molecular examination of the DNA of a very early in vitro embryo. This technique depends on sufficient knowledge of the molecular structure of a gene to allow identification of an embryo that has a significant deleterious genetic risk. Parents who know that they are both carriers of a deleterious recessive gene, for example, may opt for in vitro fertilization, using their own gametes, so that the genotypes of the resulting embryos can be examined before the embryos are transferred to the mother. Embryos that are determined to have a deleterious gene from both parents can be discarded before the embryo transfer procedure so that only embryos which are free from deleterious genes will have a chance to develop into a healthy infant.

An alternative to in vitro fertilization is the relatively simple procedure of *gamete intrafallopian transfer* (GIFT). This technique permits healthy gametes, either sperm or both eggs and sperm, to be introduced into the mother's reproductive tract before fertilization, so that fertilization can take place in its natural locus. Any resulting conceptuses may then reach a receptive uterus and implant to establish a pregnancy. Depending on the reasons for the procedure, gametes may be those of the couple, or they may be gametes donated by healthy, usually unidentified third persons. In any event, fertilization and implantation proceed according to natural biological pathways with less dependency on laboratory technologies and skills.

B. GENETIC SCREENING IN THE CONTEXT OF ASSISTED REPRODUCTION

MINIMUM GENETIC SCREENING FOR GAMETE DONORS, APPROVED BY THE BOARD OF DIRECTORS OF THE AMERICAN SOCIETY FOR REPRODUCTIVE MEDICINE

90 Fertility and Sterility S44 (2008).

The Donor

A. Should not have any major mendelian disorder. Mendelian disorders fall into the following categories:

1. Autosomal dominant or X-linked disorders in which age of onset extends beyond the age of the donor, such as Huntington disease.

2. Autosomal recessive inheritance (homozygous). Donors who are heterozygous need not necessarily be excluded if recipients are not carriers.

B. Should not have (or have had) any major malformation of complex cause (multifactorial/polygenic), such as spina bifida or heart malformation. A major malformation is defined as one that carries serious functional or cosmetic handicap. However, the definition of "major" is a matter of judgment.

C. Should not have any significant familial disease with a major genetic component, particularly in their first-degree relatives (parents, siblings, and offspring).

D. Should not carry a known karyotypic abnormality that may result in chromosomally unbalanced gametes. Among healthy young adults, the chance of having a chromosomal rearrangement that could be transmitted in unbalanced form to offspring is small. For this reason, routine karyotyping of all donors is optional.

E. A member of a high-risk group should be tested to determine carrier status for those disorders they are at higher risk of carrying. The list of tests may change as new tests for other disorders are developed. Heterozygosity need not necessarily exclude a donor, but certain donors may be inappropriate in a given case.

F. Screening guidelines for cystic fibrosis in the general population have been developed recently by the American College of Obstetricians and Gynecologists and other organizations and apply to gamete donors. All gamete donors should be evaluated by the current tests recommended at the time of the donation.

G.   Oocyte donors may be tested for fragile X carrier status at the discretion of the individual program.

H.   Donors should be generally healthy and young. Males 40 years and older are at increased risk for new mutations. Women 35 years and older are at increased risk for producing offspring with aneuploidy.

The donor's first-degree relatives (parents, siblings, and offspring) should be free of:

A.   Mendelian disorders as described in Section I.A.

B.   Major malformations as described in Section I.B.

C.   A chromosomal abnormality, unless the donor has a normal karyotype.

If family history reveals a disorder for which definitive testing is available, and it is important to consider that candidate further as a donor, then it is appropriate to test for that specific disorder. Results will determine appropriateness of that donor.

C.   LIABILITY IN REPRODUCTIVE TECHNOLOGY

JOHNSON v. SUPERIOR COURT OF LOS ANGELES COUNTY

95 Cal.Rptr.2d 864 (Cal. App. 2000).

MALLANO, J.

Petitioners Diane L. Johnson and Ronald G. Johnson, along with their minor daughter Brittany L. Johnson, filed an action against real parties in interest, California Cryobank, Inc., Cappy M. Rothman, M.D., and Charles A. Sims, M.D., claiming that real parties failed to disclose that the sperm they sold came from a donor with a family history of kidney disease called Autosomal Dominant Polycystic Kidney Disease (ADPKD). That sperm was used to conceive Brittany who has been diagnosed with this serious kidney disease.

* * *

The novel issue presented here is whether parents and their child, conceived by the sperm of an anonymous sperm donor, may compel the donor's deposition and production of documents in order to discover information relevant to their action against the sperm bank for selling sperm that they alleged transmitted ADPKD to the child.

* * *

Petitioners sued Cryobank, as well as its employees, officers, and directors, Doctors Sims and Rothman, for professional negligence, fraud, and breach of contract. In their second amended complaint, petitioners allege as follows. Diane and Ronald Johnson decided to conceive a child through the use of a sperm donor upon the recommendation of their infertility doctors. The Johnsons contacted Cryobank's sperm bank facility in Los Angeles. Ultimately, Cryobank sold the Johnsons frozen sperm specimens donated by donor No. 276. At or near the time of sale, the Johnsons signed Cryobank's form agreement that provided, in relevant part, that "Cryobank shall destroy all information and records which they may have as to the identity of said donor, it being the intention of all parties that the identity of said donor shall be and forever remain anonymous."

At the time of their purchase, Cryobank assured the Johnsons that the anonymous sperm donor had been fully tested and genetically screened. The Johnsons' doctors then implanted the purchased sperm in one of Diane Johnson's fallopian tubes. The procedure was successful and Brittany was born on April 18, 1989. In May 1995, the Johnsons were informed that Brittany was positively diagnosed with ADPKD.

As neither Ronald nor Diane Johnson has ADPKD or a family history of the disease, it was donor No. 276 who genetically transmitted ADPKD to Brittany. At the time donor No. 276 sold his sperm to Cryobank in December 1986, Doctors Sims and Rothman at Cryobank interviewed him and learned that the donor's mother and his mother's sister both suffered from kidney disease and hypertension, and the donor's mother suffered a 30 percent hearing loss before the age of 60. The presence of multiple instances of kidney disease coupled with hypertension and neurological disorders, such as deafness, are red flag indicators of the presence of ADPKD in donor No. 276's family, and thus, Cryobank and Doctors Sims and Rothman knew that donor No. 276's sperm could be at risk of genetically transferring kidney disease.

* * *

During the course of the action, petitioners propounded discovery to Cryobank seeking information regarding donor No. 276, including his name, address, and medical history. Cryobank objected to providing any information regarding donor No. 276, claiming the donor's right to privacy and his physician-patient privilege. Cryobank did, however, produce two donor consent agreements that were in use at the time donor No. 276 sold his sperm. Both of these agreements state that the donor will be compensated for each sperm specimen, that he will not attempt to discover the identity of the persons to whom he is donating his sperm, and that his identity "will be kept in the strictest confidence unless a court orders disclosure for good cause...." Cryobank also produced a document showing that on September 6, 1991, Cryobank informed Diane Johnson that donor No. 276 had been withdrawn from the donor program because "new information on his family members ... indicates that he is at risk for kidney disease" and that a "few small cysts were found" after performing a "renal ultrasound." Cryobank's responses to interrogatories indicated that donor No. 276 had sold 320 deposits of his semen to Cryobank. Donor No. 276's agreement with Cryobank indicated that he received approximately $35 per semen specimen. Donor No. 276 thus received a total of $11,200 for his sperm.

* * *

THE SCOPE OF DISCOVERY

Code of Civil Procedure section 2017 provides the framework for discovery in civil cases. Unless otherwise limited by court order, "any party may obtain discovery regarding any matter, not privileged, that is relevant to the subject matter involved in the pending action . . . if the matter either is itself admissible in evidence or appears reasonably calculated to lead to the discovery of admissible evidence." This same section further provides that "[d]iscovery may be obtained of the identity and location of persons having knowledge of any discoverable matter, as well as of the existence, description, nature, custody, condition, and location of any document. . . ."

* * *

THE PHYSICIAN–PATIENT PRIVILEGE

In order for a party to invoke the physician-patient privilege under Evidence Code section 994, there must be a patient. A "patient" is defined under section 991 as "a person who consults a physician or submits to an examination by a physician for the purpose of securing a diagnosis or preventative, palliative, or curative treatment of his physical or mental or emotional condition." Therefore, if a person does not consult a physician for diagnosis or treatment of a physical or mental ailment, the privilege does not exist. (Kizer v. Sulnick, [248 Cal. Rptr. 712 (Cal.App.1988)] [persons were not patients when they consulted with a physician as part of a study to determine whether residents shared similar medical complaints to determine further whether the presence of a waste facility was the cause of these symptoms because the purpose was not to obtain a diagnosis]).

Real parties in interest have failed to demonstrate that the physician-patient privilege is applicable in this case. The evidence presented to the trial court revealed that donor No. 276 visited Cryobank for the sole purpose of selling his sperm. That he consulted with Cryobank's physicians and medical personnel as part of the process of donating his sperm does not change the dominant purpose for his visit. There was no evidence presented to the trial court that donor No. 276 visited Cryobank "for the purpose of securing a diagnosis or preventative, palliative, or curative treatment of his physical or mental or emotional condition." Thus, we conclude that the physician-patient privilege has no application here.

JOHN DOE'S STATUS AS THIRD PARTY BENEFICIARY

John Doe next claims that petitioners are not entitled to discover his identity because their contract with Cryobank prohibits it. John Doe argues that petitioners' agreement with Cryobank providing that the sperm donor's identity would never be disclosed was made for his benefit and thus, as a third party beneficiary, he is entitled to keep his identity confidential as the agreement requires. While we agree that John Doe is a third party beneficiary, we disagree that the agreement precludes disclosure of his identity or related information under any circumstance.

* * *

The express terms of Family Code section 7613, subdivision (a) provide that a husband's written consent to the insemination must be retained by the physician "as part of the medical record." "All papers and records pertaining to the insemination" wherever located—which we construe as being broader than, and including, the "medical record" previously mentioned—are subject to being inspected "upon an order of the court for good cause." Such "papers and records pertaining to the insemination" would be expected in most cases to include the name and address and related information of the sperm donor whose sperm is used in the insemination, as is apparently the case here.

* * *

And enforcement under all circumstances of a confidentiality provision such as the one in Cryobank's contract with the Johnsons conflicts with California's compelling interest in the health and welfare of children, including those conceived by artificial insemination. There may be instances under which a child conceived by artificial insemination may need his or her family's genetic and medical history for important medical decisions. For example, such genetic and medical history can lead to an early detection of certain diseases and an increased chance of curing them. In some situations, a person's ability to locate his or her biological relative may be important in considering lifesaving transplant procedures. While in most situations the donor's genetic and medical information may be furnished without the need of disclosing the donor's identity, there may be other situations that require disclosure of the donor's identity in order to obtain the needed information. In either event, a contract that completely forecloses the opportunity of a child conceived by artificial insemination to discover the relevant and needed medical history of his or her genetic father is inconsistent with the best interests of the child.

We conclude that Cryobank's agreement with the Johnsons precluding disclosure of the donor's identity and other information pertaining to the donor under all circumstances is contrary to public policy and therefore unenforceable.

* * *

THE CONSTITUTIONAL RIGHT OF PRIVACY

Finally, real parties in interest contend that petitioners are precluded from deposing John Doe because to do so would violate his constitutional right of privacy under the federal and California Constitutions. We agree with real parties that donor No. 276 has a right of privacy in his medical history and his identity. We disagree, however, that such a right precludes his deposition and the production of the records requested in the deposition subpoena.

The California Constitution expressly provides that all people have the inalienable right to privacy.

* * *

"Legally recognized privacy interests are generally of two classes: (1) interests in precluding the dissemination or misuse of sensitive and confidential information ('informational privacy'); and (2) interests in making intimate personal decisions or conducting personal activities without observation, intrusion, or interference ('autonomy privacy')."

* * *

A person's medical history undoubtedly falls within the recognized zones of privacy.

* * *

We conclude that although donor No. 276 does indeed have a limited privacy interest in his identity as a sperm donor and in his medical history, under the circumstances of this case, it would be unreasonable for donor No. 276 to expect that his genetic and medical history, and possibly even his identity, would never be disclosed.

* * *

Petitioners seek to take John Doe's deposition in order to learn of all relevant facts he disclosed to Cryobank regarding his medical history of kidney disease. Petitioners also seek all of John Doe's records pertaining to "his family's affliction with [ADPKD], ... secondary health problems diagnosed as being caused or related to ADPKD," and "the history of deponent's medical health as it relates to symptomology of ADPKD...." As a result, what is at stake here is not only the disclosure of John Doe's identity and medical history, but of his family's as well. We conclude that such disclosure would involve an invasion of privacy unless reasonably curtailed.

* * *

Because discovery orders involve state-compelled disclosure, such disclosure is treated as a product of state action. Consequently, whenever the compelled disclosure treads upon the constitutional right of privacy, there must be a compelling state interest.

We conclude that there are compelling state interests in this case. First, the state has a compelling interest in making certain that parties comply with properly served subpoenas and discovery orders in order to disclose relevant information to the fullest extent allowable. Second, the state has an interest in seeking the truth in court proceedings. "The state has enough of an interest in discovering the truth in legal proceedings, that it may compel disclosure of confidential material." This includes medical records. Third, the state has a compelling interest in ensuring that those injured by the actionable conduct of others receive full redress of those injuries. Petitioners have demonstrated a compelling need to depose the only independent percipient witness that apparently can reveal the extent of information donor No. 276 disclosed to Cryobank. Such information is not only directly relevant to petitioners' claims, but is also relevant to Cryobank's affirmative defense of comparative fault. Thus, where, as here, the information sought "is essential to the fair resolution of the lawsuit, a trial court may properly compel such disclosure."

* * *

While donor No. 276 has an interest in maintaining the confidentiality of his identity and medical history, we hold that in the context of the particular facts of this case the state's interests, as well as those of petitioners, outweigh donor No. 276's interests. Accordingly, John Doe must appear at his deposition and answer all questions and produce documents that are relevant to the issues raised in the litigation. But this does not mean that John Doe's identity must automatically be disclosed if he indeed is donor No. 276.

* * *

For example, an order could be fashioned which would allow John Doe's deposition to proceed and documents produced on matters relevant to the issues in the litigation but in a manner which maintains the confidentiality of John Doe's identity and that of his family. Attendance at the deposition could be limited to the parties' counsel and the deposition transcript might refer simply to "John Doe" as the deponent. But we leave it to the trial court to craft the appropriate order.

* * *

We conclude that the trial court abused its discretion in denying petitioners' motion to compel John Doe's deposition and production of documents and in granting real parties' motion to quash. The trial court failed to consider the state and petitioners' countervailing interests that favor disclosure and failed to consider an order with "partial limitations rather than [an] outright denial of discovery." Petitioners are entitled to take John Doe's deposition and inquire whether he is donor No. 276, and if he is, delve into his and his family's health and medical history, and his communications with Cryobank, but only as to those issues which are relevant to the pending litigation. Similarly, we conclude that petitioners are entitled to the production of documents identified in their renotice of John Doe's deposition which are relevant and in the possession, custody, or control of John Doe. But John Doe's identity is to be protected to the fullest extent possible and the identities of his family members are not to be disclosed.

HARNICHER v. UNIVERSITY OF UTAH MEDICAL CENTER

962 P.2d 67 (Utah 1998).

Howe, J.

Plaintiffs David and Stephanie Harnicher, parents of triplets born after in vitro fertilization using donor sperm, brought this action for medical malpractice alleging negligent infliction of emotional distress against defendant University of Utah Medical Center for using sperm from a donor other than the one that the couple had allegedly selected. The trial court found no evidence of physical injury or illness to support an action for negligent infliction of emotional distress and granted summary judgment in favor of the Medical Center. The Harnichers appeal.

David and Stephanie Harnicher sought treatment for infertility at the University of Utah Medical Center Fertility Clinic. Artificial insemination using David's sperm yielded no results. The Harnichers then contacted Dr. Ronald L. Urry of the Fertility Clinic regarding the possibility of in vitro fertilization. Dr. Urry suggested a procedure known as "micromanipulation" wherein holes are drilled in the mother's harvested ova [eggs] to facilitate fertilization. The ova are then placed in a petri dish with harvested sperm and the fertilized ova are subsequently implanted in the uterine wall, enabling the mother to bear her own child. Dr. Urry recommended using a mixture of the husband's sperm and donor sperm.

The Harnichers agreed. The micromanipulation method increased the chances that Stephanie would bear David's biological child. Additionally, the "mixed sperm" procedure potentially allowed the couple to believe and represent that any child born would be David's because if the donor closely matched David in physical characteristics and blood type, the parents would never be sure which sperm actually fertilized the ovum. Therefore the Harnichers evaluated the donor information provided by the Medical Center on that basis. The Medical Center maintains that the couple narrowed the selection to four donors and signed consent forms acknowledging that their doctor would make the final selection. The Harnichers assert, however, that they specifically and exclusively selected donor #183. Stephanie testified that when clinic employee Doug Carroll informed her that only frozen sperm, which has a lower success rate than fresh, was available from donor #183 and asked her if she still wanted to do the donor backup, she replied, "Only if you can get 183. . . . I'll take my lower chances. Let's just go with 183."

The procedure was performed, and Stephanie gave birth to triplets, two girls and one boy. Shortly after their birth, one of the babies became ill, requiring blood tests. Two of the children's blood type revealed that they could not possibly have been the children of either David or donor #183. A DNA test on one of the children established that the father was actually donor #83, another donor on the Harnichers' list.

Donor #183, like David, had curly dark hair and brown eyes. Donor #83 had straight auburn hair and green eyes. One of the triplets has red hair. The Harnichers maintain that the Medical Center's mistaken use of the wrong donor thwarted their intention of believing and representing that David is the children's biological father. They brought this action against the Medical Center alleging that they have "suffered severe anxiety, depression, grief, and other mental and emotional suffering and distress which has adversely affected their relationship with the children and with each other." However, both David and Stephanie testified in their depositions that they had not experienced any bodily harm as a result of the mistake.

* * *

The Harnichers contend that their disappointment in their children has caused them severe emotional distress to the point of mental illness. They ask us to hold that "diagnosed mental illness," standing alone, is sufficient to support a claim for negligent infliction of emotional distress.

* * *

As a result of their fertility treatment, the Harnichers became the parents of three normal, healthy children whom the couple suggest do not look as much like David as different children might have and whose blood type could not be descended from his. This result thwarted the couple's intention to believe and represent that the triplets are David's biological children. Exposure to the truth about one's own situation cannot be considered an injury and has never been a tort. Therefore, destruction of a fiction cannot be grounds for either malpractice or negligent infliction of emotional distress.

The Harnichers' assertion that David did not want children unless they were biologically his own is belied by the couple's knowing consent to the use of donor sperm. Stephanie testified that she could say "with probability," without ever having seen either donor, that the children of donor #183 would have been better looking than her triplets and that in her mind, she was damaged by that fact.

* * *

Realistically, however, it is impossible to know whether the children of donor #183 would have been superior in any way to the triplets or, indeed, whether the same number of babies or none at all would have resulted from the use of the less effective frozen sperm. The supposition that the road not taken would have led to a better result is a common human fallacy; it cannot support an action for negligent infliction of emotional distress. The Harnichers do not allege that the triplets are unhealthy, deformed, or deficient in any way. Nor do they claim any racial or ethnic mismatch between the triplets and their parents. In fact, the couple has presented no evidence at all that the physiological characteristics of three normal healthy children, which could not have been reliably predicted in any event, present circumstances with which " 'a reasonable [person,] normally constituted, would be unable to adequately cope.' "

* * *

DURHAM, J., dissenting.

* * *

The majority appears to be reluctant to view the Harnichers' response to their asserted loss as a damaging one, in view of the fact that they do indeed have three healthy and loved children despite the University's negligence in performing this procedure. The alleged facts, however, clearly meet the traditional standard for negligence: 1) the existence of a duty on the part of the University to use the donor sperm selected by the Harnichers that would have permitted them to believe the children to be their full biological children; 2) a breach of that duty through the University's mistake in using sperm from the wrong donor; 3) injury consisting of the Harnichers' loss of the opportunity to believe their children to be their full biological offspring; and 4) damages in the form of mental illness requiring treatment, accompanied by physical symptoms....

* * *

In conclusion, I believe that a compensable loss and eligible damages have been asserted by plaintiffs and that they are entitled to have their cause of action tried by a jury. I would reverse.

NOTES AND QUESTIONS

1. What type of genetic screening of gamete donors is appropriate? Should donors be liable if they knew (or should have known) that they risked passing on a certain genetic disease to the resulting children? Should a donor's confidentiality be protected? Should a blood sample of each donor be kept for later genetic testing? Should a donor be required to update the clinic on subsequently-discovered genetic diseases in his or her family so that the children can be warned?

2. The Utah Supreme Court justices decided three to two that the Harnichers could not collect damages when artificial insemination helped them produce three children who were healthy, but did not resemble the husband. Was the case rightly decided? Does this case seem consistent with, or at odds with, the wrongful birth cases?

The dissenting justices in *Harnicher* suggest that if a couple requests sperm from a certain donor, and are given sperm from another donor, that mistake is actionable. Would such an analysis apply if the couple chose sperm or eggs from a donor whom they chose for certain genetic characteristics (e.g., intelligence or perfect pitch), but instead were given gametes from a donor who was not so gifted?

3. Would artificial insemination by donor to avoid passing on the husband's genetic disease be covered under the following insurance mandate:

215 Ill. Comp. Stat. 5/356m (2001)

Infertility Coverage

(a) No group policy of accident and health insurance providing coverage for more than 25 employees that provides pregnancy related benefits may be issued, amended, delivered, or renewed in this State ... unless the policy contains coverage for the diagnosis and treatment of infertility including, but not limited to, in vitro fertilization, uterine embryo lavage, embryo transfer, artificial insemination, gamete intrafallopian tube transfer, zygote intrafallopian tube transfer, and low tubal ovum transfer.

(b) The coverage required under subsection (a) is subject to the following conditions:

(1) Coverage for procedures for in vitro fertilization, gamete intrafallopian tube transfer, or zygote intrafallopian tube transfer shall be required only if:

(A) the covered individual has been unable to attain or sustain a successful pregnancy through reasonable, less costly medically appropriate infertility treatments for which coverage is available under the policy, plan, or contract;

(B) the covered individual has not undergone 4 completed oocyte retrievals, except that if a live birth follows a completed oocyte retrieval, then 2 more completed oocyte retrievals shall be covered; and

(C) the procedures are performed at medical facilities that conform to the American College of Obstetric and Gynecology guidelines for in vitro fertilization clinics or to the American Fertility Society minimal standards for programs of in vitro fertilization.

(2) The procedures required to be covered under this Section are not required to be contained in any policy or plan issued to or by a religious institution or organization or to or by an entity sponsored by a religious institution or organization that finds the procedures required to be covered under this Section to violate its religious and moral teachings and beliefs.

(c) For purpose of this Section, "infertility" means the inability to conceive after one year of unprotected sexual intercourse or the inability to sustain a successful pregnancy.

4.   Should sperm and egg donors be compensated for their genetic material? Such payment is banned in many European countries, but generally not in the United States. Should higher payments be allowed to donors thought to have "better" genes? An ad ran in the Ivy League college newspapers offering $50,000 to an egg donor who was tall, athletic and had scored at least 1400 out of a perfect 1600 SAT score. Kenneth Weiss, The Egg Brokers, L. A. Times, May 27, 2001 at A1. Is such an approach reminiscent of eugenics?

5.   Sperm donors are often unmarried medical students who do not yet have children of their own. On occasion, donor insemination produces a child with a rare recessive genetic disorder when the donor did not realize he was a

carrier. Should he be told that fact so that he can take it into consideration when making his own reproductive plans? What if, as is often the case, the infertility clinic has told him in advance that they will not let him know if his sperm results in a pregnancy (so that he will not track down any resulting child)? In a study of sperm banks faced with the issue of contacting donors, half tracked down the donor to warn of the genetic risk and half did not.

6.   An article in the *Journal of the American Medical Association* describes the case of a 23–year-old man in good health who donated sperm to a U.S. sperm bank almost a hundred times over a two year period. Barry J. Maron et al., Implications of Hypertrophic Cardiomyopathy Transmitted by Sperm Donation, 302 JAMA 1681–1684 (2009). The sperm bank followed protocols standard in the industry at the time of the donation: doctors gave the donor a comprehensive medical evaluation including a complete personal and family medical history in addition to laboratory testing for communicable diseases. Several years later, a woman inseminated with the donor's sperm gave birth to a child diagnosed with Hypertrophic Cardiomyopathy (HCM)—a heart disease characterized by the thickening of the heart muscle.

What are the pros and cons of undertaking chromosomal analysis on all sperm and egg donors? Would the cost make these procedures less accessible?

Should other women who conceived children with the donor's sperm be told of the birth of the affected child? Most sperm banks do not have records of which recipients conceived. In the case reported in JAMA, however, the sperm bank notified the donor and all other recipients of his sperm that their children were at risk for HCM. Twenty-two children were born using the donor's sperm in addition to two children born to the donor's wife. Five children showed evidence of HCM including one two and a half year old child who died waiting for a heart transplant.

7.   The Sixth Circuit Court of Appeals has held that surrogate brokers, lawyers, doctors and psychologists in infertility settings have a heightened responsibility which "gives rise to affirmative duties to act on the part of the surrogacy broker and program participants in order to reduce the risk of harm to the child and to the surrogate mother and the contracting father." These duties include designing and administering a program that provides appropriate testing for sexually transmitted diseases, in that case, cytomegalovirus. Stiver v. Parker, 975 F.2d 261 (6th Cir. 1992). Could these duties also extend to testing for genetic conditions?

8.   For cases and notes about who the legal parents are when an egg or sperm donor is used, see Chapter 11, Parentage and Family Law.

V. THE GENETIC FRONTIER: HUMAN CLONING

LORI B. ANDREWS, IS THERE A RIGHT TO CLONE? CONSTITUTIONAL CHALLENGES TO BANS ON HUMAN CLONING

11 Harv. J.L. & Tech. 643, 647–648, 661–667 (1998).

Mammalian "cloning" is the manipulation of a cell from an animal or human in such a way that it grows into a virtual copy of that animal or human with identical nucleic DNA. One way to think about it is that cloning is a way to create later-born twins of an individual who is living or has already lived. Unlike naturally occurring twins, however, the clone will not be one hundred percent genetically identical because it will have mitochondrial DNA from the donor of the enucleated egg. In the case of Dolly the sheep, an adult mammary cell containing a copy of every gene needed to make the lamb was extracted, then starved of its nutrients, forcing the cell into a quiescent state. This cell was then fused with an enucleated egg cell—one in which the nucleus has been extracted—and an electric current was run through the fused cell, activating it and causing it to begin to divide. These active cells were then implanted into a surrogate mother and carried to term.

Cloning may be an attractive means of creating a child to people in a variety of situations. If one or both members of a couple are infertile, cloning presents one viable reproductive option. If one member of the couple has a genetic disorder that the couple does not wish to pass on to a child, they could clone the unaffected member of the couple. If both husband and wife are carriers of a recessive genetic disease and are unwilling to run the twenty-five percent risk of bearing a child with the disorder, they may seek to clone one or the other of them. This may be the only way in which the couple will be willing to have a child that will carry on their genetic line.

* * *

WOULD A BAN ON CLONING INFRINGE UPON A CONSTITUTIONAL RIGHT OF SCIENTIFIC INQUIRY?

If Congress (or a state) were to adopt a ban on human cloning, one possible constitutional challenge would be that the law unduly interferes with a right of scientific inquiry * * *. The strongest claims have been made for a First Amendment right of scientific inquiry * * *. If the First Amendment protects a marketplace of ideas, it seems likely that it would protect the generation of information that will be included in the marketplace. Indeed, the [Supreme] Court's jurisprudence has protected activity under this theory in a variety of settings, such as the financing of speech and the gathering of news * * *. A federal district court similarly suggested that scholars have a right "to do research and advance the state of man's knowledge."

But what does that "right" consist of? Scientists have a right of access to existing information. For example, that federal court suggested in dicta that obscenity laws could not be applied to prohibit the Kinsey Institute from studying obscene materials. However, courts have held there is no fundamental right of scientific inquiry to undertake experiments—in particular, to conduct research on fetuses.

Cloning is sufficiently analogous to embryo research that restrictions on it should not be considered protected by a right of scientific inquiry. In holding that the right to conduct medical research is not fundamental under the Constitution, a federal court held that a state could regulate experimentation involving the unborn so long as the regulation was rational. The court explained, in words that are particularly applicable to cloning, "[g]iven the dangers of abuse inherent in any rapidly developing field, it is rational for a State to act to protect the health and safety of its citizens."

Even if cloning research on humans were protected by the Constitution, certain restrictions would be permissible. The freedom to pursue knowledge is distinguishable from the right to choose the method for achieving that knowledge, which may permissibly be regulated to some extent. Although the government may not prohibit research in an attempt to prevent the development of new knowledge, it may restrict or prohibit the means used by researchers that threaten interests in which the state has a legitimate concern. Research may be restricted, for example, to protect the subject's right to autonomy and welfare by requiring informed, free and competent consent.

* * *

WOULD A BAN ON CLONING INFRINGE UPON THE RIGHT TO MAKE REPRODUCTIVE DECISIONS?

A variety of personal desires may motivate people to utilize cloning. The NBAC [National Bioethics Advisory Commission] report suggests it would be "understandable, or even, as some have argued desirable," to create a child from one adult if both members of the couple have a lethal recessive gene; from a dying infant if his father is dead and the mother wants an offspring from her late husband; or from a terminally ill child to create a bone marrow donor.

* * *

The right to make decisions about whether or not to bear children is constitutionally protected under the constitutional right to privacy and the constitutional right to liberty. The Supreme Court in 1992 reaffirmed the "recognized protection accorded to liberty relating to intimate relationships, the family, and decisions about whether or not to beget or bear a child." Early decisions protected a married couple's right to privacy to make procreative decisions, but later decisions focused on individuals' rights as well: "If the right of privacy means anything, it is the right of the individual, married or single, to be free from unwarranted governmental intrusion into matters so fundamentally affecting a person as the decision whether to bear or beget a child."

A federal district court has indicated that the right to make procreative decisions encompasses the right of an infertile couple to undergo medically-assisted reproduction, including in vitro fertilization and the use of a donated embryo. Lifchez v. Hartigan [735 F.Supp. 1361 (N.D. Ill. 1990)] held that a ban on research on fetuses was unconstitutional not only because it was impermissibly vague, but also because it impermissibly infringed upon a woman's fundamental right to privacy. Although the Illinois statute banning embryo and fetal research at issue in the case permitted in vitro fertilization, it did not allow embryo donation, embryo freezing, or experimental prenatal diagnostic procedures. The court stated: "It takes no great leap of logic to see that within the cluster of constitutionally protected choices that includes the right to have access to contraceptives, there must be included within that cluster the right to submit to a medical procedure that may bring about, rather than prevent, pregnancy."

* * *

However, cloning is too qualitatively different from normal reproduction and from the types of assisted reproduction protected by the *Lifchez* case to simply assume the same Constitutional protections apply. As George Annas suggests, "[t]his change in kind in the fundamental way in which humans can 'reproduce' represents such a challenge to human dignity and the potential devaluation of human life (even comparing the 'original' to the 'copy' in terms of which is to be more valued) that even the search for an analogy has come up empty handed."

Cloning is not a process of genetic mix, but of genetic duplication. In even the most high-tech reproductive technologies available, a mix of genes occurs to create an individual with a genotype that has never before existed on earth. Even in the case of twins, their futures are unknown and the distinction between the offspring and their parents is acknowledged. In the case of cloning, however, the genotype in question has already existed. Even though it is clear that a clone will develop into a person with different traits because of different social, environmental, and generational influences, there is strong speculation that the fact that he or she has a genotype that already existed will affect how the resulting clone is treated by himself, his family, and social institutions.

Just as in the scientific inquiry context, even if a fundamental constitutional right to clone were recognized, any legislation that would infringe unduly upon this right would be permissible if it were narrowly tailored to further a compelling state interest.

111th CONGRESS, 1st Session
H.R. 1050

To amend title 18, United States Code, to prohibit human cloning.

IN THE HOUSE OF REPRESENTATIVES

February 12, 2009

Mr. STUPAK (for himself and Mr. WAMP) introduced the following bill; which was referred to the Committee on the Judiciary

A BILL

To amend title 18, United States Code, to prohibit human cloning.

Be it enacted by the Senate and House of Representatives of the United States of America in Congress assembled,

SECTION 1. SHORT TITLE.

This Act may be cited as the 'Human Cloning Prohibition Act of 2009'.

SEC. 2. FINDINGS.

Congress finds that—

(1) some individuals have announced that they will attempt to clone human beings using the technique known as somatic cell nuclear transfer already used with limited success in sheep and other animals;

(2) nearly all scientists agree that such attempts pose a massive risk of producing children who are stillborn, unhealthy, or severely disabled, and considered opinion is virtually unanimous that such attempts are therefore grossly irresponsible and unethical;

(3) efforts to create human beings by cloning mark a new and decisive step toward turning human reproduction into a manufacturing process in which children are made in laboratories to preordained specifications and, potentially, in multiple copies;

(4) because it is an asexual form of reproduction, cloning confounds the meaning of 'father' and 'mother' and confuses the identity and kinship relations of any cloned child, and thus threatens to weaken existing notions regarding who bears which parental duties and responsibilities for children;

(5) because cloning requires no personal involvement by the person whose genetic material is used, cloning could easily be used to reproduce living or deceased persons without their consent;

(6) creating cloned live-born human children (sometimes called 'reproductive cloning') necessarily begins by creating cloned human embryos, a process which some also propose as a way to create embryos for research or as sources of cells and tissues for possible treatment of other humans;

(7) the prospect of creating new human life solely to be exploited and destroyed in this way has been condemned on moral grounds by many, including supporters of a right to abortion, as displaying a profound disrespect for life, and recent scientific advances with adult stem cells indicate that there are fruitful and morally unproblematic alternatives to this approach;

(8) in order to be effective, a ban on human cloning must stop the cloning process at the beginning because—

(A) cloning would take place within the privacy of a doctor-patient relationship;

(B) the transfer of embryos to begin a pregnancy is a simple procedure; and

(C) any government effort to prevent the transfer of an existing embryo, or to prevent birth once the transfer has occurred, would raise substantial moral, legal, and practical issues, so that it will be nearly impossible to prevent attempts at 'reproductive cloning' once cloned human embryos are available in the laboratory;

(9) the scientifically and medically useful practices of cloning of DNA fragments, known as molecular cloning, the duplication of somatic cells (or stem cells) in tissue culture, known as cell cloning, and whole-organism or embryo cloning of nonhuman animals are appropriate uses of medical technology;

(10) in the preamble to the 1998 Additional Protocol on the Prohibition of Cloning Human Beings the Council of Europe agreed that 'the instrumentalisation of human beings through the deliberate creation of genetically identical human beings is contrary to human dignity and thus constitutes a misuse of biology and medicine';

(11) collaborative efforts to perform human cloning are conducted in ways that affect interstate and even international commerce, and the legal status of cloning will have a great impact on how biotechnology companies direct their resources for research and development;

(12) at least 23 countries have banned all human cloning, including Canada, France, and Germany;

(13) the United Nations has passed a declaration calling for all human cloning to be banned by member nations; and

(14) attempts to create cloned human embryos for development of embryonic stem cell lines have been unsuccessful, most recently involving the exploitation of over a hundred women in South Korea to provide over 2,000 human eggs without the production of a single stem cell line.

SEC. 3. PROHIBITION ON HUMAN CLONING

(a) In General—Title 18, United States Code, is amended by inserting after chapter 15, the following:

CHAPTER 16—HUMAN CLONING

Sec. 301. Definitions

In this chapter:

(1) HUMAN CLONING—The term 'human cloning' means human asexual reproduction, accomplished by introducing the nuclear material of a human somatic cell into a fertilized or unfertilized oocyte whose nucleus has been removed or inactivated to produce a living organism (at any stage of development) with a human or predominantly human genetic constitution.

(2) SOMATIC CELL—The term 'somatic cell' means a diploid cell (having a complete set of chromosomes) obtained or derived from a living or deceased human body at any stage of development.

Sec. 302. Prohibition on human cloning

(a) In General—It shall be unlawful for any person or entity, public or private, in or affecting interstate commerce—

(1) to perform or attempt to perform human cloning;

(2) to participate in an attempt to perform human cloning; or

(3) to ship or receive the product of human cloning for any purpose.

(b) Importation—It shall be unlawful for any person or entity, public or private, to import the product of human cloning for any purpose.

(c) Penalties—

(1) IN GENERAL—Any person or entity that is convicted of violating any provision of this section shall be fined under this section or imprisoned not more than 10 years, or both.

(2) CIVIL PENALTY—Any person or entity that is convicted of violating any provision of this section shall be subject to, in the case of a violation that involves the derivation of a pecuniary gain, a civil penalty of not less than $1,000,000 and not more than an amount equal to the amount of the gross gain multiplied by 2, if that amount is greater than $1,000,000.

(d) Scientific Research—Nothing in this section shall restrict areas of scientific research not specifically prohibited by this section, including research in the use of nuclear transfer or other cloning techniques to produce molecules, DNA, cells other than human embryos, tissues, organs, plants, or animals other than humans.

NOTES AND QUESTIONS

1. What types of compelling interests would be sufficient to uphold a ban on human cloning? What level of physical risks to the child might be enough to justify a ban? In animals, cloning only results in a successful

pregnancy 3 to 5 percent of the time. Even in those rare instances, many of the resulting offspring suffer. One-third die shortly before or right after birth. Other cloned animals seem perfectly healthy at first and then suffer heart and blood vessel problems, underdeveloped lungs, diabetes, immune system deficiencies, severe growth abnormalities or premature aging.

2.   If research on cloning in animals found ways to make the procedure less physically risky, would it be constitutional to ban the procedure because of psychological risks to the child? Andrews asserts that

> The unique origins of a clone might create unreasonable expectations about [the clone] * * *. Whether or not genetics actually play such a large role in human development, parents may raise a clone as if they do. After all, regardless of their belief in genetic determinism, the only reason people want to clone (as opposed to adopting or using an egg or sperm donor in the case of infertility) is to assure that a child has a certain genetic make-up. It seems absurd to think that they would forget about that genetic make-up once the clone was born. We already limit parents' genetic foreknowledge of their children because we believe it will improperly influence their rearing practices. Medical genetics groups often caution parents against having their children tested for late-onset genetic disorders, because a child who tested positive could "grow up in a world of limited horizons and may be psychologically harmed even if treatment is subsequently found for the disorder."

> Cloning could undermine human dignity by threatening the replicant's sense of self and autonomy. A vast body of developmental psychology research has demonstrated children's need to have a sense of an independent self. This might be difficult for the clone of a parent or of a previous child who died. Even if the clone did not believe in genetic determinism, the original's life "would always haunt the later twin, standing as an undue influence on the latter's life, and shaping it in ways to which others lives are not vulnerable."

Andrews, Is There A Right To Clone?, at 653.

3.   Why does the federal bill, H.R. 1050, ban the importation of cloned human embryos? Some researchers want to create cloned human embryos to create embryo stem cells for treatment. What justification does H.R. 1050 give for banning all cloning of human embryos?

4.   In 2009, researchers at the Max Planck Institute for Evolutionary Anthropology in Liepzig Germany announced they had sequenced the Neanderthal genome and learned that Neanderthals were 99.9% similar to humans. The Institute, in conjunction with 454 Life Sciences Corporation in Bradford Connecticut, isolated and sequenced nuclear DNA retrieved from three shards of female Neandrathal limb bone found in the Vindija Cave in Croatia. The bone shards are estimated to be at least 38,000 years old.

Based on their genetic profile, researchers think that Neanderthals resembled modern humans in many ways. Physically they are described as having "a stocky muscular body with short forearms and legs; a large head with bony brow ridges; a jutting face with a very big nose; and perhaps reddish hair and fair skin." The University of Barcelona's Lalueza–Fox found a unique Neanderthal variant of a pigmentation gene, *mc1r*, which can result in pale skin and red hair. Neanderthals had big brains 1200–1600 cubic centimeters, which is slightly larger than modern humans. Their genetic profile indicates that they were capable of speech. A 2007 analysis of a 43,000 year old Neanderthal bone showed the same FOXP2 gene variant that is related to speech in modern humans, rather than the variant that is found in chimps.

Neanderthals are the closest relatives of humans and lived until about 30,000 years ago. They lived in Europe, where fossils have been discovered from Spain to Southern Siberia. Neanderthals survived for about 15,000 years after modern humans appeared. There is no evidence of warfare between Neanderthals and homo sapiens, and competing theories for Neanderthals' extinction are that homo sapiens outcompeted against Neanderthals for resources, or that Neanderthals did not survive the last ice age. See Elizabeth Pennisi, Tales of a Prehistoric Human Genome, 323 Science 866–871, 866 (2009): Max Planck Society, Neanderthal Genome Completed, February 12, 2009, http://www.eva.mpg.de/english/presskit-neandertal/pdf/MaxPlanck Society_release_English.pdf; and Michael Balter, A Neandertal Primer, 323 Science 870, 13 February 2009.

Professor Svante Pääbo of the Institute has organized a consortium of researchers to analyze the genome and publish results later in 2009. The researchers are looking at: genes involved in speech and language in modern humans, such as FOXP2 and genes involved in brain development in modern humans, such as microcelaphin–1. They are also trying to determine if there was some interbreeding between Neanderthals and humans.

Some anthropologists have suggested cloning a Neanderthal. Would that activity run afoul of laws banning human cloning? If a Neanderthal was born (a tool-making, speaking, redhead), would the U.S. Constitution protect that individual? On what philosophical or legal grounds would you decide whether to consider a Neanderthal a "human"?

VI. USE OF GENETICS AND REPRODUCTIVE TECHNOLOGIES FOR NON–MEDICAL PURPOSES

A. SEX SELECTION

LORI B. ANDREWS, THE CLONE AGE: ADVENTURES IN THE NEW WORLD OF REPRODUCTIVE TECHNOLOGY
142–144 (2001).

In many parts of the world, technology is making the admission standards for birth tougher and tougher. In India, China, Taiwan, and Bangladesh, technicians with portable ultrasound machines go from village to village scanning pregnant women who are desperate to learn whether they are carrying a boy. Many abort when they fail to see a penis on the tiny out-of-focus screen. In Bombay alone, 258 clinics offered amniocentesis for sex selection. In one study of 8,000 abortions in India, 7,999 were female fetuses, leading human rights activists to protest this clear evidence of "gyne"cide. In China, when the one-child policy was strictly enforced, families so preferred males that the sex ratio changed to 153 males for each 100 females.

At Dr. John Stephens's clinics in California, Washington and New York, Western couples too can have prenatal testing for sex selection. One Australian client actually terminated a pregnancy because she couldn't get to Stephens's clinic in time to learn the sex of the fetus. She carried the next pregnancy to term when Stephens vetted it as a boy. Although most couples want a boy, an Israeli couple went to great lengths to have a girl out of fear of losing a son in a military engagement. They aborted a fetus when they learned it was a boy. In the next pregnancy, the wife was carrying twins, a boy an a girl. She used selective reduction to abort only the boy.

Thirty-four percent of U.S. geneticists said they would perform prenatal diagnosis for a family who want a son, and another 28 percent said they would refer the couple to another doctor who would perform such testing. Dorothy Wertz, the social scientist at the Shriver Center for Mental Retardation in Waltham, Massachusetts, who conducted the study, said the percentage of practitioners willing to respond to sex selection request had increased 10 percent from 1985 to 1995. "Autonomy just runs rampant over any other ethical principle in this country," Wertz says. "And it's only going to increase."

* * *

What if a sexual imbalance occurred in the United States, as is now happening in China and India? Sociologist Amitai Etzoni speculated that since women consume more culture and men commit more crimes, sex selection would create a more frontierlike society—with less art and more violence. Since men are more likely to vote Republican, politically there would be a shift to the right.

The overwhelming tilt toward boys is not as pronounced yet in the United States as it is in other countries, but social psychologist Roberta Steinbacher of Cleveland State University worries about the effect on society if couples were able to predetermine their baby's sex. Twenty-five percent of people say they would use a sex selection technique, with 81 percent of the women and 94 percent of the men desiring to ensure their first-born would be a boy. Since other research reveals firstborns are more successful in their education, income, and achievements than latterborns, Steinbacher worries that "second class citizenship of women would be institutionalized by determining that the firstborn would be a boy."

THE AMERICAN SOCIETY FOR REPRODUCTIVE MEDICINE'S POSITION ON GENDER SELECTION

In 1999, the ASRM Ethics Committee in a report endorsed by the ASRM Board of Directors concluded, "The initiation of IVF with PGD [preimplantation genetic diagnosis] solely for sex selection holds even greater risk of unwarranted gender bias, social harm and the diversion of medical resources from genuine medical need. It therefore should be discouraged."

Sex selection through PGD involves the screening of embryos for gender prior to implantation and may result in the discarding of embryos of the undesired gender. In contrast, preconception gender selection methods attempt to separate sperm cells by whether they have an X or Y chromosome, allowing insemination with sperm cells that will produce offspring of the desired sex. Although ethical concerns such as reinforcing gender discrimination, reinforcing gender stereotypes, and causing societal sex-ratio imbalances exist with preconception gender selection, preconception gender selection does not result in the destruction of embryos and the ASRM has taken a more permissive stance on the use of preconception gender selection than with sex selection through PGD.

In May of 2001 the Ethics Committee, again with the support of the ASRM Board, issued a report on preconception methods of gender selection. This report concluded, "If flow cytometry or other methods of preconception gender selection are found to be safe and effective, physicians should be free to offer preconception gender selection in clinical settings to couples who are seeking gender variety in their offspring if the couples [1] are fully informed of the risks of failure, [2] affirm that they will fully accept children of the opposite sex if the preconception gender selection fails, [3] are counseled about having unrealistic expectations about the behavior of children of the preferred gender, and [4] are offered the opportunity to participate in research to track and access the safety, efficacy and demographics of preconception gender selection. Practitioners offering assisted reproductive services are under no legal or ethical obligation to provide nonmedically indicated preconception methods of gender selection."

The full text of both reports are available (on the ASRM web site, http://www.asrm.org/Media/Ethics/ethicsmain.html or in Fertility and Sterility—Volume 72, No. 4, October 1999 and Volume 75 No. 5, May 2001). The reports were reviewed by the Ethics Committee in 2006 and left unchanged.

Notes and Questions

1.   Should prenatal sex selection be permitted? Would it be an unconstitutional infringement on the couple's reproductive liberty to ban it? If a couple seek to have a boy and the geneticist negligently tells them they are carrying a male fetus, would they be able to sue for wrongful birth if the child turned out to be a girl? What damages could they recover? (For example, could they recover the lifetime difference in salary, since women make 21% less than men in the same jobs?)

2.   Should there be a legal or ethical difference between sex selection using sperm sorting prior to conception versus preimplantation screening versus amniocentesis? Does it matter if the testing is used to select against male embryos when there is the risk of an X-linked disorder? Does it matter if it is used to select in favor of female embryos when a family already has three boys?

3.   What are the appropriate limits of prenatal testing? In one instance, a woman had two children with celiac disease which made them unable to digest carbohydrates. She wanted help from a physician to conceive a third child with the disease. Because the diet for her two children was so complicated, she did not want a child who required an alternative "normal" diet.

A couple who both had inherited the autosomal-dominant condition achondroplasia (dwarfism) had a 50% chance of having a child with this condition. They called the researcher who had cloned the gene and asked for aid in screening and aborting a fetus who would not have achondroplasia.

Ronald M. Green discusses these cases in Prenatal Autonomy and the Obligation Not to Harm One's Child Genetically, 25 J.L., Med. & Ethics, 5, 13 (1997). He advocates the following standard:

> Parents are best suited to understand and shape the lives of their offspring. Their freedom of decision in this area should have presumptive priority in our moral and legal thinking. Only in extreme cases are we warranted as a society in denying them access to the professional services they need to realize their choices or in preventing them from exercising those choices. These extreme cases are characterized by the following two features: (1) the likelihood that, relative to others in the birth cohort, the child will experience significant pain, disability or limitations in life options as a result of avoidable genetic factors; and (2) the parents' reasons for bringing the child into the world in this condition do not constitute reasonable or compelling grounds for respecting their choice.

4.   Atlas Sports Genetics offers parents a $149 test which identifies variations in their child's ACTN3 gene it claims is a measure of natural-born athletic ability. Using the test, the company claims it can determine whether a child will be a better football player, sprinter, or distance runner. While the science behind the test is questionable, the availability of the test raises the question of whether parents should be allowed to use preimplantation genetic diagnosis to select for these traits. Juliet Macur, Born to Run? Little Ones Get Test for Sports Gene, The New York Times, November 30, 2008, at A1.

Genetic imprinting disorders are a rare type of birth defect where only a copy of a gene from the mother or the father is expressed, while the copy from the other parent is suppressed or not present. Three types of imprinting disorders (Beckwith–Wiedemann syndrome, Angelman syndrome and hypomethylation syndrome) have been associated with in vitro fertilization, which is the first step in preimplantation diagnosis. What effect does the possibility of an increase in birth defects have in your analysis? For more information on ACTN3, see Chapter 10.

5.   An article in the *Journal of the American Medical Association* surveyed some of the ethical considerations involved in PGD. According to the authors, "[f]ocus group surveys and interviews have found that the US public, as well as users of PGD, emphasized the importance of individual decision making regarding the use of reproductive technologies. Individuals stressed ethical as well as personal considerations, including the nature of the trait being avoided." Moreover, "[t]he emotional burden on mutation carriers, who have to cope with their high risk for cancer and make decisions regarding prevention options, is heightened by the knowledge that they might pass the mutation to their children."

To address some of the concerns associated with PGD, the study authors suggest a framework for deciding whether the procedure should be performed to test for cancer susceptibility. The clinician ordering the test should take into account four considerations. First, does the disease develop at an early age of onset? Second, if a person inherits the genetic mutation, how likely is it that he or she will develop the disease? Third, how severe are the disease's symptoms? Four, what options are available for treating the disease or for risk-reducing surgery?

Do you think this framework provides an effective means for evaluating the concerns raised by PGD? What are some of the issues raised by PGD that this framework misses? The authors suggest that PGD also creates the possibility of "genetic selection according to economic means" because PGD is usually only covered by insurance companies in the United States when there is coexisting infertility. However, if the couple "desires PGD solely for the purpose of avoiding the risk of transmitting a cancer causing mutation to their children," insurance companies generally will not cover it. Kenneth Offit, et al., Preimplantation Genetic Diagnosis for Cancer Syndromes: A New Challenge for Preventative Medicine, 296 JAMA 2727 (2006).

B.   CONCEIVING A SIBLING TO BE A DONOR

When Anissa Ayala was diagnosed with chronic myelogenous leukemia, a disease usually fatal within five years, her best chance of survival was a bone marrow donation from a relative. However, neither her parents nor her brother was a close enough match. A nationwide search was unable to locate a compatible donor.

Anissa's parents decided to conceive another child to serve as a donor. Her father underwent surgery to reverse a vasectomy. Her mother was 42 when she conceived. Genetic testing when the fetus was six months old revealed the new daughter would be an appropriate match. When she was 14 months old, she was anesthetized and doctors inserted long needles into her hip bone to withdraw marrow to donate to her ill older sister. Gina Kolata, More Babies Born to Be Donors of Tissue, The New York Times, June 4, 1991 at A1.

In the years since the Ayala case, over one hundred children have been conceived as prospective donors. Couples get pregnant, have the fetus tested prenatally to see if it is a match, and then abort and try again if the new child cannot serve as a donor. There are no figures on how many fetuses have been aborted under these circumstances. One couple who chose not to abort created three additional children yet none was a suitable match. In another family, a baby was created to be a donor—but the infant turned out to have the same rare metabolic disease as the existing child.

In 2000, a Colorado couple, Lisa and Jack Nash, used in vitro fertilization followed by preimplantation genetic testing to conceive a child to be a tissue donor for his older sister who had a rare genetic disease, Fanconi anemia. Of 15 embryos created, only one was a genetic match. When the sibling was born, cells from his cast-off umbilical cord were transfused into his sister. Peter Gorner, A Child is Born and So Is a Genetic Dilemma, Chicago Tribune, October 8, 2000 at 1C. In another case, when a remarried woman learned that a child from her first marriage needed a bone marrow transplant, she used artificial insemination with sperm from her first husband to conceive a child.

FERRELL v. ROSENBAUM

691 A.2d 641 (D.C. App. 1997).

RUIZ, J.

Susan Ferrell and her daughter, Alexis Ferrell, brought a medical malpractice action against Kenneth N. Rosenbaum, M.D., and Children's National Medical Center ("CNMC") based upon their allegedly negligent failure to diagnose Alexis Ferrell as suffering from Fanconi anemia, a potentially fatal genetic blood disorder. The trial court awarded summary judgment to Dr. Rosenbaum and CNMC and denied the Ferrells' motion for reconsideration.

Alexis Ferrell is a young girl who suffers from Fanconi anemia, a progressive aplastic anemia that prevents the production of red and white blood cells and platelets. The physical signs of Fanconi anemia include thumb and kidney abnormalities, small stature and microcephaly. Without a bone marrow transplant, the odds of survival into adulthood are minimal.

Alexis was born on March 27, 1985, at the George Washington University Medical Center in Washington D.C. ("GWUMC"). Shortly after delivery, Alexis was noted to have hypoplastic thumbs and no external auditory canals. Consequently, Susan Ferrell and her husband, Barron

Fento Ferrell, were referred to Dr. Rosenbaum, who was Director of Clinical Genetics at CNMC. The morning after Alexis was born, Dr. Rosenbaum examined Alexis at GWUMC and found that in addition to the hypoplastic thumbs and lack of external auditory canals, she also had a slightly anteriorly placed anus and small ears. A renal sonogram also indicated that Alexis was missing a kidney. At this time, Dr. Rosenbaum indicated to Mrs. Ferrell that he would have various diagnostic tests, including a chromosome test, performed on Alexis.

Two days later, on March 30, 1985, an analysis of Alexis's blood performed at GWUMC showed that Alexis had abnormally elevated mean corpuscular volume ("MCV") and mean corpuscular hemoglobin ("MCH") levels and an abnormally low red blood cell ("RBC") count. However, Dr. Rosenbaum did not review these results. After several follow-up visits, Dr. Rosenbaum misdiagnosed Alexis with having a malformation syndrome referred to as the VATER association. Alexis first went to CNMC approximately two weeks after birth, at which time her deformed left thumb was surgically removed. Thereafter, Alexis was continuously seen by Dr. Rosenbaum at CNMC. When Alexis was approximately thirteen months old, Dr. Rosenbaum noted that Alexis was having trouble gaining weight, that her head was abnormally small, and that he "did not think that these problems could be attributed solely to her malformation syndrome."

Hematological data taken from the tests done at GWUMC three days after Alexis's birth on March 30, 1985, and from further tests conducted at CNMC on October 27, 1985, and April 26, 1986, consistently showed that Alexis had abnormally high MCV and MCH levels and an abnormally low RBC. These abnormal results, which were all indicative of Fanconi anemia, were marked on the laboratory reports with asterisks to alert the physicians of their abnormality. However, neither Dr. Rosenbaum, nor anyone else at CNMC, reviewed the results of the blood tests. Further, Dr. Rosenbaum did not pursue his belief that Alexis's problems could not be attributed solely to the malformation syndrome he believed to be affecting her. Instead, when Dr. Rosenbaum last saw Alexis on April 28, 1987, he noted that Alexis's malformation syndrome was following the expected course, and his only recommendation was to see her in one year for a follow-up visit.

Susan Ferrell and her husband separated in June 1987. Mr. Ferrell moved to California two years later and subsequently has contacted Mrs. Ferrell only twice, by telephone, in October 1989 and in Spring 1991. His whereabouts are currently unknown. During their last conversation, Mr. Ferrell told Mrs. Ferrell he was homeless.

Alexis was admitted to Arlington Hospital in April of 1990 with pneumonia. When she was released, Alexis was referred to a hematologist, Dr. Joseph E. Gootenberg, who informed Mrs. Ferrell that because of her physical deformities and blood count, he strongly suspected that Alexis suffered from Fanconi anemia and that he would need to send blood and bone marrow samples to New York for testing in order to confirm his diagnosis. On October 30, 1990, Dr. Gootenberg informed Mrs. Ferrell that his suspicion was correct: Alexis had tested positive for Fanconi anemia.

The basis for Mrs. Ferrell's claim of injury is that had Alexis been diagnosed properly while under Dr. Rosenbaum's care, the Ferrells would have been informed that a matched bone marrow transplant from a sibling donor was the best treatment for their daughter's condition. Because they were then living together and loved Alexis, they would have taken the opportunity to have another child who could have donated a matched bone marrow for transplantation. However, due to Dr. Rosenbaum's and CNMC's negligence, Alexis was misdiagnosed until October 1990 and, consequently, the Ferrells were not informed of the necessary treatment during the time that Mr. Ferrell was part of the family. Since Mr. Ferrell cannot now be found, Alexis's only chance for a matched sibling donor has been foreclosed. Consequently, as a result of Dr. Rosenbaum's and CNMC's negligence, Alexis's chance to obtain the matched bone marrow transplant donor she needs for survival has been significantly reduced.

* * *

Appellees filed a motion for summary judgment stating that there was no genuine issue as to any material fact and that they were entitled to judgment as a matter of law. Mrs. Ferrell responded by filing a motion for partial summary judgment and opposing appellees' motion for summary judgment. Mrs. Ferrell's motion for partial summary judgment was based on appellees' violation of their specific duty to at least review Alexis's blood data. In support of her opposition, Mrs. Ferrell argued that the record contained "ample evidence to support a finding by a jury that [appellees] violated the applicable standard of care and that the negligence effectively deprived Alexis of her only chance of survival."

The Superior Court denied Mrs. Ferrell's motion for partial summary judgment and granted summary judgment to Dr. Rosenbaum and CNMC. First, the trial court found that there were no disputed issues of material fact. Second, the trial court considered that Mrs. Ferrell had not demonstrated that Dr. Rosenbaum and CNMC departed from the applicable standard of care, and that even if she could so demonstrate, "the undisputed evidence does not suggest that an earlier diagnosis would have provided [Alexis] with a sufficiently substantial chance of survival."

* * *

Applying the summary judgment standard to the record before us, we conclude that there was a genuine dispute over material facts. Further, the record contains sufficient evidence from which a jury could find that Dr. Rosenbaum and CNMC violated the standard of care and that this negligence deprived Alexis of a substantial chance for survival. Therefore, appellees are not entitled to judgment as a matter of law. We reverse and remand the case to the trial court.

* * *

Mrs. Ferrell's last contention is that the trial court's conclusion that "there is no prima facie showing of proximate cause" was erroneously based on a misapprehension of Alexis's alleged injury to be that the missed diagnosis of Fanconi anemia delayed a bone marrow transplant. Instead, the claimed injury is the loss of Alexis's best opportunity to have a transplant by a potential sibling donor.

* * *

In her filings in the trial court, as in this court, Mrs. Ferrell has consistently argued that appellees' misdiagnosis harmed Alexis by depriving her parents from being informed, prior to their separation and estrangement, that a sibling could serve as the best bone marrow donor for Alexis, thereby precluding Alexis from any chance of ever obtaining a matched sibling bone marrow donor. Although Dr. Alter's testimony tends to show that the transplant was not appropriate at the time Alexis was diagnosed as suffering from Fanconi anemia, it does not defeat Mrs. Ferrell's showing of proximate cause * * *. [T]he *possibility* remained that, had the Ferrells known about the Fanconi anemia and its optimum treatment with a matched donor transplant, they would have taken steps to conceive a sibling or siblings who could have provided a compatible bone marrow donor whenever the transplant was appropriate. Because the Ferrells did not know of Alexis's anemia and its best treatment, however, they did not take any of these steps at the time. That lost opportunity has meant that the possibility of a matched donor was permanently foreclosed due to Mr. Ferrell's subsequent estrangement from his family. Therefore, appellees' negligence caused Alexis's loss of the opportunity for the best treatment, a transplant from a compatible sibling donor.

* * *

Proximate cause is divided into cause in fact and policy considerations that limit the liability of persons who have, in fact, caused the injury " 'where the chain of events appears highly extraordinary in retrospect.' " Appellees argue that the alleged negligence was not the cause in fact of Alexis's injury because Mrs. Ferrell was unable to demonstrate that she would have certainly conceived a compatible donor sibling.

In determining whether there has been cause in fact, the plaintiff is not required to prove causation to a certainty. The bare possibility that the Ferrells could have had another child, or children, that could have been a suitable bone marrow donor for Alexis, however, is not sufficient to defeat a motion for summary judgment for failure to show proximate causation. Something more is needed. The proper test is whether the plaintiff can prove, by a preponderance of the evidence, that the asserted negligence was a "substantial factor" in causing the injury.

In Daniels [v. Hadley Mem'l Hosp., 566 F.2d 749 (D.C. 1977)], the court applied the substantial factor test in a medical malpractice case where the plaintiff sought damages for a "lost chance of survival." The substantial factor test "is the appropriate test for causation in cases, such at [sic] this, where the harm appears to have been brought about by two or more concurrent causes." The court, applying District of Columbia law, rejected the claim that a plaintiff must conclusively show that the harm would not still have occurred absent the malpractice.

As the court noted:

[I]t does not lie in the defendant's mouth to raise conjectures as to the measure of the chances that he has put beyond the possibility of realization. *If there was any substantial possibility of survival and the defendant has destroyed it, he is answerable.* Rarely is it possible to demonstrate to an absolute certainty what would have happened in circumstances that the wrongdoer did not allow to come to pass.

In determining whether the negligence was a substantial factor in causing the harm, the *Daniels* court focused on two questions: a) what chance the plaintiff had to survive if properly diagnosed and treated and b) the extent to which the defendants' negligence reduced this chance.

We conclude that *Daniels'* two-pronged analysis correctly applies District of Columbia law on proximate causation in a case such as this involving negligent treatment of a potentially fatal condition. Applying the analysis to this case, we determine that Mrs. Ferrell made a showing, sufficient for summary judgment purposes, that Dr. Rosenbaum's and CNMC's negligence was a substantial factor in causing Alexis's injury. The first prong of the analysis involves Alexis's chances to survive had she been properly diagnosed and treated. Proper treatment in this case, meant a bone marrow transplant from a suitable matched donor. The record clearly supports a finding that had Dr. Rosenbaum or any other qualified person at CNMC reviewed the blood data, a diagnosis of Fanconi anemia would have resulted in 1985, and the Ferrells would have at least been given the opportunity to conceive a child or children who would be compatible donors for Alexis. Mrs. Ferrell testified that she would have done anything possible to help Alexis, including having another child or children; the record supports an inference that Mr. Ferrell would have been supportive of such efforts.[2] According to the expert testimony, the

---

2. Appellees contend that the record does not support a finding that Mr. Ferrell would have agreed to attempt to conceive another child even if the Ferrells had known that Alexis had Fanconi anemia when Mr. Ferrell was still part of the family. This argument was not made below; therefore it is not before us for consideration. Even were it properly before us, it is without merit. Alexis was born in March 1985. Mrs. Ferrell testified that Mr. Ferrell was very attentive to Alexis and that Mr. Ferrell would spend a lot of time with his daughter. The Ferrells were separated sometime in 1987, and Mr. Ferrell left for California in September 1989. Therefore, Mr. Ferrell was available for four years after Alexis was born. Mrs. Ferrell testified that during that time Mr. Ferrell wanted a reconciliation, but that she did not.

In her response to appellees' Interrogatory No. 14, Mrs. Ferrell stated that had she known that Alexis had Fanconi anemia she would have immediately taken all appropriate steps necessary to assure, to the maximum extent possible, the availability of a bone marrow transplant (BMT) for

chances were significant that the Ferrells, had they conceived a child, would have yielded a suitable donor for Alexis. Thus, the evidence showed that had Alexis been properly diagnosed when Mr. Ferrell was in her life, and had Alexis received a transplant from a compatible sibling donor Alexis would have had "an appreciable chance of saving [her] life." Id. at 566 F.2d at 758 (concluding that there was an "appreciable chance" that patient's life would have been saved, after bench trial including testimony that 75–85% of patients survived if given proper treatment).

The second prong, whether the defendants interfered with the plaintiff's chance to avoid the harm is easily met in this case. It is plain from the record that Dr. Rosenbaum's and CNMC's alleged negligence directly interfered with the possibility of Alexis having a transplant from a matched sibling donor. Whatever may be said about the speculative nature of the Ferrells having had a child who could donate bone marrow to Alexis, it is beyond doubt that the alleged negligence eliminated *any* chance that the Ferrells would even consider and implement that course of action. Mrs. Ferrell therefore sufficiently demonstrated that the claimed negligence was a substantial factor in the loss of Alexis's best chance for survival. The trial court's conclusion that Mrs. Ferrell did not make a prima facie showing of proximate cause was erroneous.

NOTES AND QUESTIONS

1. In some cases, an existing family member is a match for an ill child but does not want to go through the painful procedure of bone marrow extraction. Does it seem fair to create a child and force him or her to do something that an existing sibling, cousin or parent will not do? And where should we draw the line? Should parents conceive a second child to be a kidney donor for the first?

2. There are also questions about access to the technologies for prenatal and preimplantation screening for tissue matching. When a child is diagnosed with a disease that would benefit from matched tissue, should the physician have a duty to tell the parents that they could conceive a sibling for donation? Should insurers reimburse for the procedure? The cost to the Nashes of in vitro fertilization and preimplantation screening was $50,000.

Alexis when needed, including efforts to become pregnant immediately and have as many children as necessary and possible, in light of her maternal age, to obtain a matching sibling donor.

While appellees could argue to a jury that Mr. Ferrell was unlikely to have agreed to conceive another child or children, the record at this point would support a jury finding that Mr. Ferrell would have helped to save his daughter's life.

Our dissenting colleague states that the fact that "Mr. Ferrell might have been willing to reconcile with his estranged wife prior to June 1987 would not reasonably permit a trier of fact to infer that he might have been interested in doing so after October 1990." This conclusion misses the point of Mrs. Ferrell's argument because it assumes the alleged negligence. Had Dr. Rosenbaum adhered to the standard of care, Alexis would have been properly diagnosed in 1985, not in 1990, two years before her parents separated and four years before Mr. Ferrell left for California. The dissent's conclusion is also flawed because it assumes that a reconciliation would have been required to avert the injury suffered by Alexis as a result of the negligence. In fact, only Mr. Ferrell's willingness to *sire* another child or children is at issue. This would require a donation of sperm, and not necessarily reconciliation with the mother.

CHAPTER 7

GENETIC TESTING AND SCREENING FOR NEWBORNS, CHILDREN, AND ADOLESCENTS

■ ■ ■

I. NEWBORN SCREENING PROGRAMS

AMERICAN ACADEMY OF PEDIATRICS, REPORT OF THE TASK FORCE ON NEWBORN SCREENING, PUBLISHED AS A CALL FOR A NATIONAL AGENDA ON STATE NEWBORN SCREENING PROGRAMS

106 Pediatrics 389 (Supp.) (2000).

Newborn screening in the United States is a public health program aimed at the early identification of conditions for which early and timely interventions can lead to the elimination or reduction of associated mortality, morbidity, and disabilities. This screening takes place within the context of a newborn screening system, and involves the following components: screening, short-term follow-up, diagnosis, treatment/management, and evaluation. Inherent to each of these components is an education process.

* * *

THE HISTORY OF NEWBORN SCREENING

Newborn screening programs began in the early 1960s with the original work of Dr Robert Guthrie, who developed a screening test for phenylketonuria (PKU) and a system for collection and transportation of blood samples on filter paper. By 1962, Massachusetts launched a voluntary newborn PKU screening program that demonstrated the feasibility of mass genetic screening.

Initially, newborn screening for PKU was not a health department role or a legislated activity. Health professionals were slow to adopt the practice of screening for PKU, and the responsibility for screening was not defined (e.g., should it be the responsibility of the hospital in which the infant was born, the mother's obstetrician, or the infant's pediatrician or

381

primary care health professional). The American Academy of Pediatrics (AAP), acting as the professional association that develops policy for the care of children, raised concerns about the sensitivity and specificity of PKU screening tests, as well as the efficacy of early intervention for PKU. Out of these concerns, the need for further research about this testing was recognized, and the federal Children's Bureau (now the federal Maternal and Child Health Bureau [MCHB]) funded a collaborative study to address questions and concerns about the effectiveness of the PKU screening test.

At the same time, advocates for children remained concerned that children with undetected PKU were at high risk for mental retardation. The National Association for Retarded Citizens (now the ARC) proposed model legislation for creation of public programs to address low detection rates, and also conducted an extensive grass-roots lobbying effort to support passage of mandatory PKU screening legislation. Many state health departments supported the adoption of such legislation. The Kennedy Administration, with the guidance of the Presidential Advisory Commission on Mental Retardation, was also supportive. The Commission hired the Advertising Council, which mounted a public campaign for mandatory PKU screening. Other advocacy groups, such as the March of Dimes Birth Defects Foundation, mobilized volunteers to lobby for passage of legislation at the state level. As a result of this multidimensional advocacy campaign, most states passed laws in the early 1960s that mandated newborn screening for PKU. Forty-three states had formal statutes by 1973. State health departments, particularly their maternal and child health (MCH) programs (funded by Title V of the Social Security Act of 1935), assumed the central role in implementation of these new laws.

As a response to this mandate, some states set up screening laboratories or added phenylalanine analysis to their state laboratory's repertoire of tests. In other states, private laboratories played a major role. Quality control was difficult because of the number of and the variability among testing sites; and became even more difficult as states added other genetic tests to their newborn screening batteries. Early in the 1970s, the need to improve quality assurance through systematic proficiency testing was recognized. In an early proficiency-testing study, the Centers for Disease Control and Prevention (CDC) found marked variability among health department laboratories. As a result, the Newborn Screening Quality Assurance Program was begun at the CDC, with additional funding from the Health Resources and Services Administration (HRSA).

In 1976, federal legislation to support screening for genetic diseases was adopted, and in fiscal years 1979 and 1980, 34 state genetic service programs received federal funding. This support was welcomed by the states, as the cost of screening tests and the health departments' coordination of screening activities had not been completely covered by many state budgets.

As a result of the laws mandating PKU testing, and the establishment of health department newborn screening units that occurred in the 1960s and 1970s:

- Every newborn had an opportunity to be screened for PKU when laws were properly implemented; consequently, most were screened.

- Financial barriers to screening and diagnosis were removed, but families often had to pay for the special formula, special foods, and other related treatments.

- State newborn screening programs evolved, with the goal of providing safe screening tests and appropriate follow-up to every newborn.

During the 1980s, further systems development took place at the state and regional level. Newborn screening systems were set up by public health agencies to ensure coordination between the hospitals from which most specimens were received, the public health laboratory, the infant's pediatrician or primary care health professional to whom positive results were reported, and pediatric subspecialists to whom infants were referred for diagnosis and treatment. Together these entities comprised the backbone of newborn screening systems. Some state newborn screening systems also played a role coordinating follow-up; depending on their public health structure, medical care structure, and available resources. In many states, the Title V Children With Special Health Care Needs (CSHCN) programs performed this role.

In 1985, the Council of Regional Networks for Genetic Services (CORN) was developed in response to the need for an organization to facilitate state genetic program efforts through coordination and special initiatives. The CORN published newborn screening system guidelines that defined a 5–part system of screening, follow-up, diagnosis, treatment/management, and evaluation. These guidelines were not treatment guidelines or standards of care, but provided public health agencies with a detailed framework for a systems approach to newborn screening.

By 1985, 12 states had laws allowing charges or fees for screening tests. Today, a majority of the states have established newborn screening fees to be collected from the health care professional, birthing facility, third-party payer, or the parent of the newborn. Although newborn screening fees are collected in most states, financing the treatment of children identified with genetic conditions through newborn screening remains problematic. Eligible families in many states are ensured access to therapy (e.g., low phenylalanine diet for PKU), particularly when the special formula is deemed a prescription drug. Families deemed ineligible financially may be burdened by the cost of necessary treatments. However, when special PKU formula is classified as a food, many health insurers refuse to cover it at all; creating a problem for both eligible and ineligible families.

Now, after 30 years of experience with PKU, it is clear that knowledge regarding PKU and the approach to newborn screening were rudimentary when the programs were first launched. Studies to validate the screening test, and to assess the safety and effectiveness of a special diet to prevent mental retardation, were completed after laws were implemented. However, the history of these efforts has set the context for the role of public health in newborn screening and genetics.

UNITED STATES GENERAL ACCOUNTING OFFICE, NEWBORN SCREENING: CHARACTERISTICS OF STATE PROGRAMS

GAO–03–449 (2003).

Most state newborn screening programs screen for 8 disorders or fewer. The number of disorders included in state programs ranges from 4 to 36.

* * *

Programs are implemented through state statutes and/or regulations, which often require screening for certain disorders. According to the Resource Center, all states require screening for PKU and congenital hypothyroidism, and 50 states require screening for galactosemia. Table 1 lists the disorders most commonly included in state newborn screening programs. * * * Some states provide screening for certain disorders to selected populations, through pilot programs, or by request. For example, in addition to the 44 states that require screening for sickle cell diseases for all newborns, 6 states provide screening for sickle cell diseases to selected populations or through pilot programs. Some states are taking steps that could expand the number of disorders included in their programs.

The criteria that state newborn screening programs reported they consider in selecting disorders to include in their programs are generally consistent across states. For example, they generally include how often the disorder occurs in the population, whether an effective screening test exists to identify the disorder, and whether the disorder is treatable. These criteria are also consistent with recommendations of the American Academy of Pediatrics (AAP) newborn screening task force. Neither the criteria states use nor AAP's recommendations include benchmarks, such as the lowest incidence or prevalence rate that would be acceptable for population-based newborn screening or measurements of treatment effectiveness or screening reliability.

ELLEN WRIGHT CLAYTON, SCREENING AND TREATMENT OF NEWBORNS

29 Hous. L. Rev. 85, 103–134 (1992).

Even assuming that the identified disorder causes substantial morbidity and that effective treatment is available and accessible, accurately labelling a child as deviant may nonetheless be harmful in other ways. In American society, a substantial number of children are born to single women or into marriages that are under stress. A number of commentators have expressed concern that labelling a baby as "ill," particularly in the newborn period, may cause the dissolution of the family or cause the father to flee a relationship in which he otherwise would have remained. These authors are particularly fearful that the fathers fleeing will occur when further testing reveals nonpaternity.

Another set of problems arises because newborn screening, like any medical test, is not completely accurate. Even under the most ideal testing conditions, some children who actually have disease will be missed, and some healthy children will inappropriately be labelled as "ill." From one perspective, "false negative" tests that fail to detect affected children should not seem particularly troubling. After all, the argument goes, the disease surely would have gone undetected had there been no program at all, so children are not harmed when the program fails to work.

Things, however, are not that simple. To begin with, the existence of newborn screening programs can create a false sense of reassurance in physicians, possibly causing them to fail to make a diagnosis as quickly as they would have were there no screening in place once symptoms begin to appear.

The most common reason that affected children are missed, however, is not because of the inherent inaccuracy of testing but because the tests were not properly administered, if at all. Screening programs have encountered many problems, ranging from difficulties in getting adequate samples, to lab errors, to problems in recording and reporting results. For a significant number of children, blood samples simply do not reach the state departments of health at all. Although the move toward centralization of testing and emphasis on proficiency testing and quality assurance has improved procedures, some states still do not keep statistics on lapses in screening. Given all these problems with newborn screening programs, it is hardly surprising that litigation often results when a child's PKU or congenital hypothyroidism are not detected by screening tests.

Not only are some affected children missed, but some unaffected children are mislabelled as ill. Sometimes the screening test is diagnostic: the child with an abnormal result, in fact, has the disease being tested. In most instances, however, screening programs are set up as multistep processes in which, is order to capture all the true positives, the first step also yields abnormal results for some unaffected children who will later be distinguished by more sophisticated testing. Hence, mislabelling is inherent in the early stages of the screening process. The number of unaffected children, the "false positives," who are identified as potentially ill in the initial screening depends on the nature of the illness and the test. The presence of false negatives is troubling because labelling any child as ill in the newborn period, even if only for a few weeks or months, can disrupt the developing parent-child relationship, sometimes with long-term adverse consequences for the child.

Inadequate medical knowledge also causes mislabelling. For example, when screening for PKU began, it was not known that some children with high levels of phenylalanine did not in fact have PKU, but rather had hyperphenylalaninemia, which does not cause significant mental retardation. Until this fact was understood, children with this latter, benign condition were inappropriately thought to be ill and subjected to the restrictions and expense of treatment. Ironically, the treatment actually harmed some of these children, causing the very mental retardation that screening was supposed to avoid. The increased understanding of human variation that has emerged from this experience is desirable in itself, but this example and the problems described earlier demonstrate that screening is not an entirely benign procedure for children. Those who engage in traditional legal analysis or who advocate widespread testing often seem to forget, or at least give inadequate weight to, these very real harms.

Legal implications of screening for children. The effects of newborn screening on children have a wide range of legal consequences as well. Some are relatively straightforward. For those affected children whose diagnoses were missed as "false negatives," the question is usually whether some institution involved in the screening process failed to exercise due care. Traditional rules of negligence govern this issue but reflect the continuing erosion of charitable and governmental immunity. Even when an affected child who was missed can show negligence, he still must shoulder the burden of proving that he would have received adequate, effective therapy had the diagnosis been made in a timely fashion. For the "false positives," those healthy children who are inappropriately diagnosed as ill, the existence of a private legal remedy is more doubtful and raises such questions as whether a child can receive damages for interference with her relationship with her parents.

A larger problem is how the law can be used to limit the social consequences of labelling. For many years, this country has been engaged in a struggle involving how to deal with perceived or real differences between individuals—differences based upon race, gender, and disability. Federal legislation, such as Title VII of the Civil Rights Act of 1964, the Education for All Handicapped Children Act of 1975, and the Americans with Disabilities Act of 1990, embodies efforts to alleviate the problem of discrimination. State legislatures have enacted similar statutes. Despite this legislation, the ongoing debate about such strategies as affirmative action and accommodation demonstrates that there is no consensus about what to do.

In addition, these laws are only partial responses to the problem of discrimination. As a result, some children identified as different by newborn screening will not be covered by these laws. Some children, to be sure, will be protected because they will develop a dysfunction that allows them to qualify as disabled and will suffer at the hands of entities that are covered by the acts. Others, however, will not be officially disabled either because the manifestations of their diseases are effectively controlled by treatment or because their "disorders" have no clinical manifestations. One could hope that medical norms of confidentiality would protect such children; if no one knows that they have a particular condition, they cannot be the victims of discrimination on the basis of being affected. Such information, however, is hard to keep completely private. One need only remember the way that schoolmates are aware of and tease peers who take medicine or eat a special diet. Even when a condition requires no intervention, mere entry of the diagnosis into medical records makes it available to a wide array of people and institutions. Other children will be symptomatic but will be discriminated against by institutions or individuals not governed by these laws. These children who fall between the legislative cracks may nonetheless suffer real injury by virtue of being identified as different.

* * *

It is necessary to decide whether the labelling of children as genetically ill, either accurately or inaccurately, will adversely affect those children by subjecting them to differential treatment in school or in sports, or the parents of those children by making it more difficult to change jobs or obtain insurance because of their child's expensive treatment. It is also possible that these hurdles facing such parents will, in turn, impair their ability to care for their children. The challenge then is to decide which differences ought not to make a difference—which should not be the basis for distinguishing one person from another—and to extend to children the protection of the law, which often is already at least partially available to adults. The first step in this inquiry is to recognize the potential power of present and future newborn screening techniques to demonstrate ways in which children vary from one another as well as the fact that the results obtained are not always accurate.

* * *

Legal implications of newborn screening for parents. Newborn screening affects parents' relationships with their children as well as parents' own decision making about future childbearing in a variety of ways. Regardless of whether the effects of such screening appear to the outside observer to be beneficial or harmful, these consequences have legal implications because they represent intrusions into matters that society has generally concluded the family, and not the state, is to decide. Newborn screening can alter what parents know and do about their children's health care. While most families may well value this knowledge, some will not, especially when they understand the broader implications of being informed.

* * *

The state has been the primary provider of newborn screening since shortly after such tests were developed. In some ways, having the state in this role should confer advantages. At the most mundane level, the existence of a state-run program usually means that the testing is paid for, thus avoiding the inequities inherent in the piecemeal health insurance that exists in this country. The involvement of the state should also mean that all children are tested, especially in states where screening is mandatory. In reality, the states vary widely in the percentage of children who are tested. Finally, given the fact that families move and change health care providers frequently, the state has more tools at its disposal with which to find children who are diagnosed with serious conditions at birth and to ensure that they receive continuity of care. Here as well, the success of states in the context of finding and tracking children varies widely.

Limits upon state action in the name of health. * * * The state has two sources of power with which to protect the public health, each applying in different circumstances and having different limits. The more commonly invoked and broader power is the police power-the state's authority to prevent one person from harming another. * * * The second and narrower power is that of the state as *parens patriae,* the authority to intervene to prevent a person at risk from the self-infliction of serious harm.

* * *

[I]f the affected child is the target, the state cannot justify screening as an exercise of the police power. Because genetic disorders are not "catching," the child does not pose a health risk to others. One might argue that the parents could "harm" future children by passing on the genetic disorder and that the state can appropriately intervene to prevent this injury. The problem with this argument is that the only way to protect the child from getting the genetic disorder is to prevent the child from being born. Even if one concedes that some conditions may make a child's life not worth living, the disorders for which newborn screening is currently performed do not qualify. Nor is it likely that the diseases sought in newborn screening will ever be the basis for wrongful life claims because newborn screening is most appropriate when effective treatment is available.

The state, then, is far more likely to invoke its role as *parens patriae* as the source of its authority to conduct newborn screening. At first, the analogy between the state as parent and parents as parents seems compelling, but further analysis reveals two problems with viewing the state as "parent." First, these children have "real" parents, whether by biological or other social connections, who have far-reaching authority to make important decisions regarding their children. The state is not completely free to override the parents' choices.

Second, concern for children does not seem to be the state's primary motivation for participation in newborn screening. The fact that the state bases its decisions about which diseases to seek on cost-benefit analyses makes clear that avoiding burdens on the public fisc is a major reason for screening. Further, the cost-benefit analyses that have been done are fundamentally flawed because they are based on the invalid premise that affected children receive care. This assumption is invalid because many states neither provide treatment nor require insurers to pay for it and many families have trouble meeting the demands of dietary and other therapeutic regimens necessary to provide care for affected children.

To be fair, the state must engage in a balancing process in deciding how to spend its money because money spent for one program is then not available for others. Even so, it is one thing to decide whether a particular expenditure is an effective way to help people and another to establish a program in order to avoid future burdens. One simply cannot assume that the state will have the child's interest primarily at heart.

How newborn screening became a function of the state. The political process that led to the adoption of newborn screening laws reveals another reason to scrutinize the state's motives. As Katherine Acuff and Ruth Faden recently pointed out, there is real reason to question why the issue of newborn screening ever entered into the public health and legislative/regulatory arenas at all. The process by which PKU screening came to be required by law is illustrative.

Some suggest that states enacted PKU screening laws to overcome the reluctance of individual physicians to test newborns. Although many practitioners were already incorporating these tests into their routine neonatal care, institutions such as the American Academy of Pediatrics initially opposed legislatively mandated screening. Yet the perception of medical foot-dragging regarding newborn screening does not suffice to explain the state's virtually complete occupation of this field. After all, legislators usually do not intervene merely because they believe that changes in medical practice are coming too slowly.

To say that states enacted newborn screening laws because of lobbying by individual practitioners and political interest groups is closer to the truth. For example, early PKU laws were put into place largely in response to the pressure exerted by Dr. Robert Guthrie, the developer of the test for PKU, and the National Association for Retarded Children (NARC). Although the legislative process typically moves in response to the voices of individual and institutional advocates, this response still does not resolve the question of whether the state may justifiably involve itself in newborn screening.

* * *

Moreover, while the states' approaches to screening vary widely, most of the approaches taken present some serious problems. In some states, the legislature defines which diseases are to be sought. In New York, for example, the legislature directs the state department of health to test for PKU, sickle cell anemia, congenital hypothyroidism, branched chain keto-nuria (maple syrup urine disease), galactosemia, and homocystinuria. While one may applaud this "laundry-list" as permitting more accountability, such an approach presents some difficulties. If, for example, the state were to mandate testing for a disorder such as histidinemia that was later determined to be a benign condition, it is hard to imagine who would push for amendment of the statute to stop testing for the condition. Certainly, the families of the few children with the particular inborn error of metabolism are unlikely to have the political clout to do so. Furthermore, the companies that make the test and the laboratories that perform it might lobby against change.

Other state legislatures delegate authority to agencies to establish programs and to decide what to treat for. One might expect this approach to lead to better choices because it not only permits greater flexibility but also ensures that individuals who have greater expertise than legislators will make the decisions. The requirement in many states of public hearings prior to administrative action makes it even more likely that there is some public input into the process. Yet administrative agencies have less direct accountability to the public than do legislators. The possibility that regulators will be subject to less restraint is of some importance because they may not be even-handed in their actions, if for no other reason than their need to respond to the pressures of the bottom line and the implications of cost-benefit analyses. Moreover, evidence suggests that eugenic or other concerns that are publicly unacceptable motivate some administrators consciously or subconsciously. Consequently, there is reason to question whether the state will necessarily make better decisions about screening than the medical profession.

Thus, the state's role in newborn screening is complex and problematic. One can ask whether the states exceed their constitutional authority in establishing such programs. Certainly, the powers that generally justify state intervention into matters of health do not fit comfortably here, and the state's interest, no matter how well conceived, is hardly compelling. Even assuming that the states are acting within the limits of their power, it is not obvious that these programs should be in the public domain at all, particularly since similar screening efforts are undertaken as a matter of course in the context of routine medical care. No reasons suggest that the state is a particularly dispassionate or wise decision-maker in this area, for the state is subject to cost constraints that can oppose the interests of the children being screened and their families. In addition, history reveals that political advocacy by individual practitioners and special interest groups greatly influenced the development of newborn screening programs. Finally, although one can argue that the involvement of the state can lead to more uniform access, this potential has only been partially met.

NOTES AND QUESTIONS

1. For a table of the disorders included in mandatory newborn screening policies by states, see the website of the National Newborn Screening and Genetics Resource Center at http://genes-r-us.uthscsa.edu/nbsdisorders.pdf.

This center was established by the Health Resources and Services Administration (HRSA) in the Department of Health and Human Services as a joint project of HRSA's Maternal and Child Health Bureau and the University of Texas Health Sciences Center at the San Antonio Department of Pediatrics. (As an indication of the center's enthusiasm for genetic testing, its website is GeNeS–R–US). The center appears to serve primarily as a clearinghouse for information about newborn screening and genetic testing programs, rather than as a source of testing standards or guidelines.

2. What genetic conditions should be the subject of newborn screening tests and how should they be selected? Over the years, several groups of experts have addressed these questions. In 1975, the National Academy of Sciences issued a report setting forth a number of criteria for newborn screening tests:

1. acceptance by healthcare professionals;

2. previous feasibility studies;

3. satisfactory test methodology;

4. appropriate laboratory facilities and quality control;

5. adequate resources for counseling, treatment, and follow-up;

6. acceptable costs;

7. effective education;

8. informed consent; and

9. adequate means of evaluation.

Another NAS report in 1994 focused on three criteria:

1. clear indication of benefit to the newborn;

2. a system in place to confirm the diagnosis; and

3. available treatment and follow-up.

The Task Force on Newborn Screening of the American Academy of Pediatrics emphasized:

1. screening should be of primary benefit to the infant;

2. the test should have analytical and clinical validity and utility; and

3. interventions to improve outcomes for the infant should be safe and effective.

What are the differences between these approaches? What values do they share?

A 2005 report by the American College of Medical Genetics (ACMG) commissioned by the U.S. Department of Health and Human Services identified the following 29 conditions as a "core panel" that should be included in every state newborn screening program: isovaleric isodemia, glutaric acidemia type I, 3–hydroxy 3–methyl glutaric aciduria, multiple carboxylase deficiency, mutase deficiency, 3–Methylcrotonyl-CoA carboxylase deficiency, methylmalonic acidemia, proprionic acidemia, beta-Ketothiolase deficiency, medium-chain acyl-CoA dehydrogenase deficiency, very long-chain acyl-CoA dehydrogenase deficiency, long-chain L–3–OH acyl-CoA dehydrogenase deficiency, trifunctional protein deficiency, carnitine uptake deficiency, PKU, maple syrup disease, homocystinuria, citrullinemia, argininosuccinic acidemia, tyrosinemia type I, sickle cell anemia, beta-thalassemia,Hb S/C disease, congenital hypothyroidism, biotinase deficiency, congenital adrenal hyperplasia, galactosemia, hearing loss, and cystic fibrosis. The ACMG selected the core panel of tests based on the availability of specific and sensitive test methods, a well-understood history of the condition, and the existence of available and efficacious treatments.

The March of Dimes, an organization focused on preventing birth defects and infant mortality, criticized the Task Force report for not calling for screening for an unlimited number of diseases: "We believe that a test (even for a rare disease)—as long as its early discovery makes a difference to the child—must be conducted for every newborn." Mike Mitka, Neonatal Screening Varies by State of Birth, 284 JAMA 2044 (2000). What kinds of "differences to the child" should count?

The National Academy of Sciences recommends that newborns not be screened for disorders for which no beneficial treatment is available. What if there is beneficial treatment, but it is equally effective if it is delayed until symptoms occur, rather than initiated as the result of newborn screening? Some studies suggest that this is the case with newborn screening for galactosemia, one of the standard newborn screening tests. There is also controversy over whether detecting cystic fibrosis in newborns improves patient health. The GAO expects controversy over testing for non-treatable disorders to increase with the spread of new tandem mass spectrometry (MS/MS) screening technology, which can screen for multiple disorders in a single analysis, including disorders for which treatment is not currently available.

Is treatment the only benefit that might derive from screening? What about research needs? What about information to aid the child and its family in planning for the future? At least one state has screened infants for Duchenne muscular dystrophy in order to provide reproductive information for the parents. (See also the discussion in Chapter 3 of newborn screening in the context of eugenics.)

What reasons might there be for not including as many tests as possible in a newborn screening program—even tests for extremely rare disorders as the March of Dimes suggests? The National Academy of Sciences (NAS) 1994 report includes the following observations:

> Newborn screening is not a trivial intervention and may raise important health and social issues. For example, detection of an affected child can disrupt the relationship between the parents and the newborn. Parents often experience guilt at having passed on a genetic disorder to their child. In addition, there may be social stigma, and such stigma may be increased if a reliable carrier screening test was available *before* pregnancy or birth.

Lori Andrews et al., Assessing Genetic Risks: Implications for Health and Social Policy 162 (1994).

3. The 1994 NAS report recommends that screening be done only for conditions for which there is "available treatment and follow-up." What is meant by "available"? Suppose there is a treatment for the condition, but it is not readily available? Consider the following from the 2000 report of the Task Force on Newborn Screening:

> Funding for comprehensive medical care and treatment is challenging, and treatment of some conditions identified through newborn screening is costly. Not all children have health coverage or the means to purchase needed treatment. Managed care plans and other third-party payers often do not cover items such as special formulas, special foods, neurodevelopmental assessments, and therapies. Important psychosocial services and other support services for families are also less likely to be funded through health plans. Many managed care plans restrict access to specialized services or require that in-network health professionals who lack appropriate expertise deliver care. For children with complex conditions, treatment may best be delivered by a multidisciplinary team with specialized expertise; however, development and support of such teams requires financing beyond that provided through any form of insurance. Thus, many children with the disorders identified by neonatal screening do not receive optimal care because they have inadequate insurance coverage and/or lack access to qualified health professionals. For many, the situation is exacerbated when they reach adulthood and no longer qualify for public programs such as Medicaid.

4. In 2003, a jury awarded a brain-damaged boy more than $70 million in damages in a suit claiming that the Stanford Hospital and the Palo Alto Medical Clinic where he was treated had failed to diagnose the boy's phenylketonuria (PKU) disease. The hospitals were held liable in part because the boy had been given newborn screening for PKU too soon after he was born, resulting in a false negative result.

According to the GAO, states reported that they spent over $120 million on newborn screening in state fiscal year 2001, with individual states' expenditures ranging from $87,000 to about $27 million. Seventy-four percent of these expenditures supported laboratory activities. The primary funding source for most states' newborn screening expenditures was newborn screening fees. The fees are generally paid by health care providers submitting specimens; they in turn may receive payments from Medicaid and other third-party payers, including private insurers. Other funding sources that states identified included the Maternal and Child Health Services Block Grant, direct payments from Medicaid, and other state and federal funds. Approximately 4 million babies are screened each year for genetic conditions. Approximately 3000 cases of severe genetic disease are detected. In the late 1980s, the congressional Office of Technology Assessment calculated that, for every 100,000 babies screened for PKU and congenital hypothyroidism, the nation saved $3.2 million (in

1986 dollars), and that the net savings per detected and treated case was $93,000.

MARY ANN BAILY AND THOMAS H. MURRAY, ETHICS, EVIDENCE, AND COST IN NEWBORN SCREENING

Hastings Center Report 23, 27–28 (May/June 2008).

Could greater benefits or a fairer distribution of benefits be achieved by reallocating newborn screening resources to another use? In answering this question, all costs should be considered, and costs are often understated in newborn screening policy debates. A common error is to consider only the cost of the individual test. Advocates may say: "If Baby A had only had a fifty-dollar screening test for MCADD [medium chain acyl-coenzyme A dehydrogenase deficiency], his life could have been saved. Surely a child's life is worth fifty dollars!" That would indeed be a small price to pay to save an infant's life. But newborn screening programs must test many newborns in order to identify the few with MCADD, Thus, even if only the cost of testing itself is counted—ignoring for a moment many other activities that must accompany the testing—saving one life costs much more than the price of a single test.

Cost is also understated when advocates claim that the cost of testing all newborns for an additional condition is low because the blood sample is already being collected and the infrastructure is in place. For example, if tandem mass spectrometry is already used for PKU and MCADD, then adding one more metabolic disorder seems to add only a little to the cost. The real cost is more than the cost of testing, however. After we factor in the full costs of parental education, follow-up of all positives to a definitive diagnosis, treatment of affected children, and ongoing data collection and evaluation, adding a new disorder to an existing panel can be very expensive. Moreover, if the natural history of the condition is poorly understood and plainly effective treatments are lacking, children may receive no benefit, or may even be harmed by unnecessary interventions.

Another way to understate the cost of newborn screening is to count only the net cost of state budget appropriations earmarked for the program. In fact, adding a test to a mandatory newborn screening panel automatically imposes costs on private insurance (which is expected to pay for the screening test, follow-up, and treatment for insured infants) and on both the state and the federal government (which through the Medicaid program cover about a third of births in the United States). Other costs fall directly on families. These include the cost in time and money that families of children who test positive must bear to obtain a definitive diagnosis, and the unnecessary worry and anxiety experienced by families whose children turn out either not to have the disorder or to have a clinically insignificant form of it.

Finally, the full cost of newborn screening includes the cost of program-related research and quality improvement. The ACMG report concludes that the development and evaluation of evidence before and after introducing a test is an essential part of a national screening system, and it makes recommendations for incorporating ongoing research and quality improvement activities into newborn screening programs. It does not attempt to estimate the cost of all this work, however, and thus inevitably underestimates the total cost of newborn screening.

Once the full costs of newborn screening are understood, the benefits must be assessed and compared to the benefits that could be achieved from other ways of using the resources. The framework for equitable allocation of health care resources we used in our project starts from the premise that society has a moral obligation to ensure that every child has access to adequate health care and to distribute the cost of achieving this outcome fairly. The adequate level of care should be determined by considering the relative merits of different health services in the light of the reasons for the special importance of health care. This means that the resources devoted to newborn screening and treatment for genetic disorders should be established in the context of determining the entire adequate level of health care and the importance of health care relative to other important social goods. Unfortunately, the policy process is biased against doing this. The American health care system is not really a system. It has no institutional structure to take responsibility for stewardship of collective resources and force consideration of opportunity costs of decisions about public health programs or additions to standard clinical care. In newborn screening, this system-level problem has been made worse because each state makes its own decisions on newborn screening; furthermore, program financing is plagued by a lack of transparency. Advocacy by health professional groups, makers of screening technologies, and consumer groups such as the March of Dimes and associations supporting parents of children with genetic conditions also affects policy development. These advocates provide important perspectives, but often no one steps up to advocate for the programs that will not be undertaken and the people who will not be helped because health care resources have been directed elsewhere. Think again of Mississippi: a state expands newborn screening at the same time that it cuts support for prenatal care for poor women. The advocates for those women, and the children they were carrying, were either silent or ineffective.

RUTH R. FADEN ET AL., PARENTAL RIGHTS, CHILD WELFARE, AND PUBLIC HEALTH: THE CASE OF PKU SCREENING

72 Am. J. Pub. Health 1396, 1397–98 (1982).

THE FUNCTION OF PARENTAL CONSENT

Until recently, there has been little analysis of the function of a parental consent requirement when several competing interests are involved. Although case law links parental consent with the protection of parental self-interest and prerogatives, parental consent is generally not viewed as a mechanism for protecting the *autonomy* of parents or of parents' rights in medicine and biomedical research. Rather, parental consent is defended as a mechanism for protecting the welfare of children, on the theory that parents are their children's most conscientious advocates and have their children's best interest most accurately in focus. This analysis of the primary function of a parental consent requirement presupposes, but does not argue for, a well entrenched view in the literature of biomedical ethics, viz, that third-party consent is grounded in the principle of beneficence rather than the principle of autonomy. Even such starkly different positions as those defended by Paul Ramsey and the National Commission for the Protection of Human Subjects of Biomedical and Behavioral Research converge on this point.

Even if we consider general theories of proxy consent that allegedly are rooted in the principle of autonomy, such as the theory of substituted judgment, the focus of the obligation is not to respect the autonomy of the proxy but rather to honor the proxy's ability to infer, based on prior knowledge of the compromised person's values and preferences, what the individual would choose, if he or she had been competent. It is very doubtful, however, whether substituted judgment can be made an adequate theory for justifying policies of parental consent, particularly in the case of newborns.

If the primary function of a parental consent requirement is to protect the welfare of children, how does this apply to the case of PKU screening? In this form of screening, the intervention poses minimal risk of harm to normal infants and holds promise of the remote but important benefit of preventing mental retardation, which threatens not only the general well-being of infants, but also their future abilities to develop as autonomous agents. Thus, there appears to be no reasonable question or issue of judgment as to what is in the best interest of infants.

Under these conditions, is a public policy that grants parents the right to consign their children to a state of irreversible mental retardation morally acceptable? We think not, and it is for this reason that we question the moral justification for requiring parental consent for PKU screening. To require parental consent entails an obligation to respect parental refusal, and it is the validity of such refusals that we question. If the principle consideration is the welfare of children, their welfare is best served in this case by a program of compulsory and exceptionless screening.

CHILD WELFARE AND THE HARM PRINCIPLE

By making child welfare the overriding consideration in policy determinations about participation in child health programs, we are taking the position that in this context, any right of parents independent of their role as advocates for their children's welfare is subservient. The general outlines of this position in contemporary ethical theory can be traced historically to John Stuart Mill's *On Liberty,* where he discusses what is now popularly referred to as the harm principle. This principle states that a person's liberty may justifiably be restricted if the person's (e.g., a parent's) action or negligence poses significant risk of harm to another (e.g., the parent's child). The point of this appeal for our purposes is that parental refusal of PKU screening unjustifiably poses a risk of harm to the child.

Central to this argument for compulsory newborn screening for PKU is the absence of any reasonable question as to the welfare of children. To the extent that potential benefits to *individual* children may be present, a justification for a parental consent requirement is enhanced. Thus, from the perspective of a general policy on parental consent in public health programs, a central issue is whether risk/benefit judgments for individual children may sometimes differ from judgments about risks and benefits for children in general. If some children would be better off without the program, then parental consent may be required as a safeguard to protect the interests of those children. However, only if there is a reasonable possibility that some children would be better off should a policy permitting parental refusal be adopted.

It is important to clarify our position, which is based on the position that there is no *reasonable* question or issue of judgment as to the net beneficial character of the policy we propose. We do not mean that there can be no doubt in any parent's mind about the net benefit of the intervention. In the case of PKU, one could imagine parents opposing screening based on bizarre views about child welfare. For example, parents might believe that the screening test condemns children to eternal damnation. We would not interpret such metaphysical beliefs about damnation as providing a *reasonable* judgment as to the best interests of infants.

NORMAN FOST, GENETIC DIAGNOSIS AND TREATMENT: ETHICAL CONSIDERATIONS

147 Am. J. Diseases of Children 1190 (1993).

An important breach in the rule of informed consent occurred when newborn screening for phenylketonuria (PKU) was mandated by law in most states beginning in the 1960s. The origin of this mandate was the strong belief by advocates that the test was accurate, sensitive, and specific and that safe and effective treatment was available. Furthermore, given the rarity of the disease, there was concern that physicians left to their own devices would fail to perform the test on many infants, resulting in preventable harm. Finally, some believed that the benefits of testing and treatment were so clear and the risks of nontesting were so high that parents should not be allowed to refuse testing anyway, because to do so would constitute a form of medical neglect.

These presumptions all were later shown to be flawed. The Guthrie screening test turned out to be a remarkably nonspecific test, with a false-positive rate of between 15 and 20 to 1. As a result, many infants who, in fact, had benign forms of hyperphenylalaninemia were falsely labeled as having PKU. Confidence in the safety of the diet was also premature, resulting in brain damage and death in some infants who suffered from excessive restriction of an essential amino acid. The combination of these errors resulted in serious harm to an uncertain number of normal children.

Apart from disagreements about the practicality of informed consent in the setting of routine clinical care, there is stronger consensus, and clearer laws stating, that experimental treatments require stricter attention to explicit standards of informed consent. As an added precaution, approval by an institutional review board is required for experimental interventions. These strict standards for experimentation have been commonly ignored in genetic testing. The original PKU trials were begun before contemporary standards for institutional review were established, and consent from parents, to this day, is rarely obtained. Those who do not study history are doomed to repeat it, and the errors of the PKU program are repeated on a regular basis. Once the difficulties with PKU testing and treatment were resolved, it became common to add tests to the program, typically without institutional review or informed consent. In some cases, such as screening for hypothyroidism, there was a clearly positive outcome. In others, such as urine testing for iminoglycinuria or blood testing for CF [cystic fibrosis], the benefits were absent, as in the former case, or controversial, as in the latter. A positive outcome, of course, is not sufficient to justify bypassing the rules of experimentation; ends do not justify means.

The success of the PKU program also led to the widespread feeling that parental consent was now irrelevant because it would be unethical and possibly illegal for a parent to refuse permission for testing and treatment. It was also argued that it was inefficient to obtain consent for a simple test obtained from every newborn. These assumptions have also been shown to be flawed. Many states do allow parents to refuse testing for PKU, but they are seldom given the opportunity to do so. The notion that parents commit neglect when they expose a child to a 1:10,000 risk of serious harm is inconsistent with our general tolerance for refusal of circumcision, which is associated with comparable risks, and with decisions to allow a child to ride a bicycle or compete in gymnastics, activities with a higher risk than that of refusal of PKU testing. Finally, the claim that high standards for consent are impractical and inefficient are inconsistent with a study by Faden et al. showing that high standards for consent can result in higher compliance rates than those in states that mandate testing without consent.

These are the simple questions. The success of the PKU program is now clear if measured by the benefits and risks of preventing retardation in affected individuals. But treatments can have late effects that complicate assessment of benefits, risks, and costs. A pregnant woman who was successfully treated for PKU in childhood exposes her fetus to the most potent human teratogen, high maternal serum phenylalanine. Over 90% of such fetuses will be seriously damaged. Prevention of such damage requires strict adherence to a difficult diet throughout pregnancy, possibly from the moment of conception. It is not yet known how many children will be injured from such exposure. Because such women generally would not have borne children in the prescreening era, the net costs and benefits of screening cannot be assessed accurately. This high risk to exposed fetuses has also raised complex questions of law and ethics regarding forced treatment of women who cannot or do not consent to treatment.

Notes and Questions

1. What are the arguments in favor of and against obtaining parental consent for newborn screening tests? Which arguments do you find most persuasive?

In addition to the points made in the excerpt by Faden et al. in support of mandatory testing without parental consent, consider the following:

> Those who oppose the informed consent model contend that the logistical constraints of newborn-screening protocols make meaningful informed consent an unrealistic goal. The perceived limitations on time available to discuss complex screening issues prior to discharge, the logistical realities of varied birth settings, and the massive numbers of neonates to be screened can present genuine challenges to the implementation of the informed consent model. * * * In addition, some fear that it would be disruptive to established programs and might have a negative impact on both efficacy and cost-effectiveness. * * *

Elaine H. Hiller et al., Public Participation in Medical Policy–Making and the Status of Consumer Autonomy: The Example of Newborn–Screening Programs in the United States, 87 Am. J. Pub. Health 1280, 1286 (1997).

2. Only two states, Maryland and Wyoming, currently seek parental consent for newborn screening. (Massachusetts recently has begun doing so in a pilot program.) In Maryland, the consent is for the total screening package; parents are not asked to consent to each test. Thirty-three states provide an exemption from screening if contrary to parents' religious beliefs, but except in Maryland and Wyoming, it is up to the parents to assert the objection without being asked.

DOUGLAS COUNTY v. ANAYA

694 N.W.2d 601 (Neb. 2005).

WRIGHT, J.

Nature of Case

The Douglas County District Court ordered Josue Anaya and Mary Anaya to submit their daughter to testing for metabolic diseases as required by Neb.Rev.Stat. § 71–519 (Cum.Supp.2002). The Anayas appeal, asserting that § 71–519 violates their rights guaranteed under the 1st and 14th Amendments to the U.S. Constitution and that the issue is moot.

* * *

FACTS

Rosa Ariel Anaya was born in the Anayas' home, without a physician present, on July 11, 2003. The birth was reported to the Department of Health and Human Services (DHHS) on July 17.

In August 2003, a DHHS employee received Rosa Anaya's birth certificate, checked DHHS' database, and determined that the testing for metabolic diseases required by § 71–519 had not been performed. A certified letter was sent to the Anayas explaining the statute's requirements. Enclosed with the letter was a brochure detailing the screening process, which included drawing a small amount of blood from the heel of the infant to be tested. The Anayas declined to submit Rosa Anaya for the screening, stating that it was in direct conflict with their sincerely held religious beliefs that life is taken from the body if blood is removed from it and that a person's lifespan may be shortened if blood is drawn.

Douglas County brought an action seeking to compel the Anayas to comply with § 71–519. At a hearing on September 26, 2003, Mary Anaya testified as to the Anayas' religious beliefs.

The Anayas subsequently filed a motion for judicial exemption from prosecution and dismissal of the petition. They alleged that it was impossible for them to comply with § 71–519 because 70 days had passed since the birth was registered and DHHS regulations required that the testing be completed within 48 hours of the registration of the birth if the birth was not attended by a physician. They also claimed the statute violated the 14th Amendment to the U.S. Constitution.

The district court found that the State has a compelling state interest in the screening of infants for metabolic diseases and that the Anayas' religious beliefs did not outweigh the State's compelling interest that "these children can grow and develop to be free of a metabolic disease particularly in light of the minimal invasion of the blood test administration which is merely a pinprick to the child's heel." The court rejected the Anayas' claim that the issue was moot due to Rosa Anaya's age. Although testing procedures are most effective when administered shortly after birth, the court found that it was not too late to administer the test even if Rosa Anaya was 6 months of age or older. The court ordered the Anayas to comply with § 71–519 by submitting Rosa Anaya for metabolic screening forthwith.

* * *

The Anayas argue that § 71–519 infringes upon their First Amendment right to freely exercise their religion and that the district court erred in concluding that the State had shown a compelling interest which justifies the infringement.

"The free exercise of religion means, first and foremost, the right to believe and profess whatever religious doctrine one desires." Employment Div., Ore. Dept. of Human Res. v. Smith, 494 U.S. 872, 877, 110 S.Ct. 1595, 108 L.Ed.2d 876 (1990). The " 'exercise of religion' " involves "not only belief and profession but the performance of (or abstention from) physical acts * * *." Smith, 494 U.S. at 877, 110 S.Ct. 1595. The statute which the Anayas challenged provides:

> (1) All infants born in the State of Nebraska shall be screened for phenylketonuria, primary hypothyroidism, biotinidase deficiency, galactosemia, hemoglobinopathies, medium-chain acyl co-a dehydrogenase (MCAD) deficiency, and such other metabolic diseases as [DHHS] may from time to time specify * * *.

> (2) * * * If a birth is not attended by a physician and the infant does not have a physician, the person registering the birth shall cause such tests to be performed within the period and in the manner prescribed by [DHHS].

§ 71–519. When Rosa Anaya was born, regulations prescribed by DHHS provided that if a birth was not attended by a physician and "the tests have not been performed within 48 hours of birth as otherwise required by these regulations, the person registering the birth must cause newborn screening tests for metabolic diseases to be performed within 48 hours of registration of the birth." 181 Neb. Admin. Code, ch. 2, § 008 (2002).

The Anayas argue that because they have raised a free exercise of religion claim along with a parental substantive due process claim, they have a hybrid constitutional rights claim, which requires strict scrutiny review. Under a strict scrutiny review, the law must be justified by a compelling governmental interest and must be narrowly tailored to advance that interest. See Church of Lukumi Babalu Aye, Inc. v. Hialeah, 508 U.S. 520, 113 S.Ct. 2217, 124 L.Ed.2d 472 (1993). The Anayas claim *Smith* held that strict scrutiny is required in cases in which a free exercise claim has been raised along with a claim of violation of another constitutional right.

In *Smith*, the claimants ingested peyote during a religious ceremony and were subsequently dismissed from their employment because Oregon law prohibited use of the drug. The question was whether the state's prohibition was permissible under the Free Exercise Clause. In upholding the Oregon law, the Court stated that it had never held that an individual's religious beliefs excused him from compliance with an otherwise valid law prohibiting conduct that a state is free to regulate. "[T]he right of free exercise does not relieve an individual of the obligation to comply with a 'valid and neutral law of general applicability on the ground that the law proscribes * * * conduct that his religion prescribes * * *.' " Smith, 494 U.S. at 879, 110 S.Ct. 1595 citing United States v. Lee, 455 U.S. 252, 102 S.Ct. 1051, 71 L.Ed.2d 127 (1982) (Stevens, J., concurring in judgment).

We do not read *Smith* as supporting the Anayas' claim concerning strict scrutiny. Although *Smith* discussed prior decisions that involved not only the Free Exercise Clause but other constitutional provisions, the Court did not hold that a strict scrutiny review is required simply because more than one constitutional right might be implicated.

In *Hialeah,* the Court again held that to be found constitutional, a neutral law of general applicability does not require demonstration of a compelling governmental interest. "In addressing the constitutional protection for free exercise of religion, our cases establish the general proposition that a law that is neutral and of general applicability need not be justified by a compelling governmental interest even if the law has the incidental effect of burdening a particular religious practice." Hialeah, 508 U.S. at 531, 113 S.Ct. 2217.

Federal courts have also discussed hybrid rights claims. In Swanson By and Through Swanson v. Guthrie ISD I–L, 135 F.3d 694 (10th Cir.1998), the federal court addressed an argument that a school policy violated a home-schooled student's free exercise rights and the parents' right to direct her education. The court stated: "[W]e believe that simply raising such a claim is not a talisman that automatically leads to the application of the compelling-interest test." Id. at 699. "[I]t cannot be true that a plaintiff can simply invoke the parental rights doctrine, combine it with a claimed free-exercise right, and thereby force the government to demonstrate the presence of a compelling state interest." Id. at 700.

In Miller v. Reed, 176 F.3d 1202, 1207 (9th Cir.1999), the court stated, "[W]e recently held that, to assert a hybrid-rights claim, 'a free exercise plaintiff must make out a "colorable claim" that a companion right has been violated—that is, a "fair probability" or a "likelihood," but not a certitude, of success on the merits.' " The court further stated that "a plaintiff does not allege a hybrid-rights claim entitled to strict scrutiny analysis merely by combining a free exercise claim with an utterly meritless claim of the violation of another alleged fundamental right or a claim of an alleged violation of a non-fundamental or non-existent right." Id. at 1208. See, also, Boone v. Boozman, 217 F.Supp.2d 938 (E.D.Ark. 2002) (court found that case did not present hybrid rights theory).

In rejecting the idea of strict scrutiny analysis for hybrid rights claims, the U.S. Court of Appeals for the Sixth Circuit has stated:

> Such an outcome is completely illogical; therefore, at least until the Supreme Court holds that legal standards under the Free Exercise Clause vary depending on whether other constitutional rights are implicated, we will not use a stricter legal standard than that used in *Smith* to evaluate generally applicable, exceptionless state regulations under the Free Exercise Clause.

Kissinger v. Board of Trustees, 5 F.3d 177, 180 (6th Cir.1993).

We conclude that the Anayas' assertion of a hybrid rights claim does not implicate a strict scrutiny review of § 71–519. A party may not force the government to meet the strict scrutiny standard by merely asserting claims of violations of more than one constitutional right.

The second constitutional rights violation asserted by the Anayas seems to suggest that § 71–519 violates their rights as parents to make decisions concerning the upbringing of their children. They rely upon Pierce v. Society of Sisters, 268 U.S. 510, 45 S.Ct. 571, 69 L.Ed. 1070 (1925), and Wisconsin v. Yoder, 406 U.S. 205, 92 S.Ct. 1526, 32 L.Ed.2d 15 (1972).

In *Pierce,* the Court held that a compulsory education law deprived parents of the right to select a school for their children. It held that the Oregon compulsory education statute "unreasonably interfere[d] with the liberty of parents and guardians to direct the upbringing and education of children under their control." Pierce, 268 U.S. at 534–35, 45 S.Ct. 571. The Court concluded that the challenged law served no state interest and therefore had no reasonable relation to any state purpose.

In *Yoder,* the Court held that a state could not compel Amish parents to require their children to attend formal high school and that the compulsory education law violated the 1st and 14th Amendments. The Court noted that no harm to the physical or mental health of the child was inferred but that when the health and safety of a child was involved, different considerations applied.

> To be sure, the power of the parent, even when linked to a free exercise claim, may be subject to limitation under Prince [v. Massachusetts, 321 U.S. 158, 64 S.Ct. 438, 88 L.Ed. 645 (1944),] if it appears that parental decisions will jeopardize the health or safety of the child, or have a potential for significant social burdens.

Yoder, 406 U.S. at 233–34, 92 S.Ct. 1526. The Court did not conclude that strict scrutiny was required.

It is true that "the custody, care and nurture of the child reside first in the parents." Prince v. Massachusetts, 321 U.S. 158, 166, 64 S.Ct. 438, 88 L.Ed. 645 (1944). However, the Court has never held that parental rights to childrearing as guaranteed under the Due Process Clause of the 14th Amendment must be subjected to a strict scrutiny analysis. See Troxel v. Granville, 530 U.S. 57, 120 S.Ct. 2054, 147 L.Ed.2d 49 (2000). "[T]he Supreme Court has yet to decide whether the right to direct the upbringing and education of one's children is among those fundamental rights whose infringement merits heightened scrutiny." Brown v. Hot, Sexy and Safer Productions, Inc., 68 F.3d 525, 533 (1st Cir.1995). *Pierce* and *Yoder* do not support an inference that parental decisionmaking requires a strict scrutiny analysis.

The question is not whether the Anayas have set forth a hybrid rights claim but whether the law they have challenged is neutral and has general application.

This case is analogous to cases in which courts have upheld the State's right to require immunization of children. In Boone v. Boozman, 217 F.Supp.2d 938 (E.D.Ark.2002), the court upheld the constitutionality of an immunization statute, finding that the free exercise claim challenged a neutral law of general applicability. The law applied to all school children except those whose health would be endangered by immunization. Because the law was neutral, heightened scrutiny was not required even though compulsory immunization might burden a plaintiff's right to free exercise.

The court stated, "It is well established that the State may enact reasonable regulations to protect the public health and the public safety, and it cannot be questioned that compulsory immunization is a permissible exercise of the State's police power." Id. at 954. Society's interest in protecting against the spread of disease takes precedence over parental rights and the right to free exercise of religion. *Id.*

In Prince, 321 U.S. at 166–67, 64 S.Ct. 438 the Court held that neither rights of religion nor rights of parenthood are beyond limitation. Acting to guard the general interest in youth's well being, the state as *parens patriae* may restrict the parent's control by requiring school attendance, regulating or prohibiting the child's labor and in many other ways. Its authority is not nullified merely because the parent grounds his claim to control the child's course of conduct on religion or conscience. Thus, he cannot claim freedom from compulsory vaccination for the child more than for himself on religious grounds. The right to practice religion freely does not include liberty to expose the community or the child to communicable disease or the latter to ill health or death * * *. [T]he state has a wide range of power for limiting parental freedom and authority in things affecting the child's welfare; and * * * this includes, to some extent, matters of conscience and religious conviction.

A law is neutral and of general applicability "if it does not aim to 'infringe upon or restrict practices because of their religious motivation,' and if it does not 'in a selective manner impose burdens only on conduct motivated by religious belief[.]' "San Jose Christian College v. Morgan Hill, 360 F.3d 1024, 1031 (9th Cir.2004), quoting Church of Lukumi Babalu Aye, Inc. v. Hialeah, 508 U.S. 520, 113 S.Ct. 2217, 124 L.Ed.2d 472 (1993). Section 71–519 is a neutral law of general applicability. It is generally applicable to all babies born in the state and does not discriminate as to which babies must be tested. Its purpose is not directed at religious practices or beliefs. Pursuant to Employment Div., Dept. of Human Res. v. Smith, 494 U.S. 872, 110 S.Ct. 1595, 108 L.Ed.2d 876 (1990), and its progeny, a neutral law of general applicability need not be supported by a compelling governmental interest even though it may have an incidental effect of burdening religion.

Section 71–519 does not contain a system of particularized exemptions that allow some children to be excused from testing. See Kissinger v. Board of Trustees, 5 F.3d 177 (6th Cir.1993). The statute does not unlawfully burden the Anayas' right to freely exercise their religion, nor does it unlawfully burden their parental rights. Section 71–519 cannot be construed as directly regulating religious-based conduct. See Cornerstone Bible Church v. City of Hastings, 948 F.2d 464 (8th Cir.1991). There is no evidence that the State had an anti-religious purpose in enforcing the law. See *id.*

Whether a statute is constitutional is a question of law; accordingly, the Nebraska Supreme Court is obligated to reach a conclusion independent of the decision reached by the court below. Slansky v. Nebraska State Patrol, 268 Neb. 360, 685 N.W.2d 335 (2004). A statute is presumed to be constitutional, and all reasonable doubts will be resolved in favor of its constitutionality. *Id.*

We conclude that the effect of § 71–519 upon the constitutional claims the Anayas have asserted is properly analyzed under a rational basis review. Evidence was presented concerning the effects of the diseases that are tested for under the statute. Early diagnosis allows for prevention of death and disability in children. The State has determined that it is appropriate to test for these diseases soon after a child is born in order to address treatment options. The health and safety of the child are of particular concern, as are the potential social burdens created by children who are not identified and treated.

The State has an interest in the health and welfare of all children born in Nebraska, and the purpose of § 71–519 is to protect such health and welfare. This is a rational basis for the law, and it is constitutional.

[The discussion of mootness is omitted.]

NOTES AND QUESTIONS

1. A 1982 study in Maryland reported that only 27 out of approximately 50,000 mothers (0.05 percent) refused to consent to newborn screening when given the opportunity.

2. The report of the Task Force on Newborn Screening, American Academy of Pediatrics, recommends that "parents should always * * * have the opportunity to refuse testing." The 1994 report of the National Academy of Sciences recommended that screening be voluntary, but added that mandatory screening would be justified if there was "evidence that—without mandatory screening—newborns will not be screened for treatable illnesses in time to institute effective treatments (e.g., in PKU or congenital hypothyroidism)." The NAS went on to observe: "There is no evidence that a serious harm will result if autonomy is recognized, just as there is no evidence that mandating newborn screening is necessary to ensure that the vast majority of newborns are screened." Lori Andrews et al., Assessing Genetic Risks: Implications for Health and Social Policy 276 (1994). If parental consent is only permitted so long as parents give their consent, is the consent requirement meaningful?

What should a health professional do if parents refuse to consent to screening, especially for a disease that can be treated or prevented if it is detected early enough? Consider the following definition of child abuse and neglect under the federal Child Abuse Prevention and Treatment Act (CAP-TA), under which states must require health professionals to report to child protective services agencies in order to receive federal grants: "Any recent act or failure to act on the part of a parent or caretaker, which results in death, serious physical or emotional harm, sexual abuse, or exploitation, or an act or failure to act which presents an imminent risk of serious harm." 42 U.S.C. § 5106g(2). Would a parental refusal to permit newborn screening fall under these provisions?

3. Is newborn screening analogous to vaccination, as the court suggests? Vaccination is seen as a proper exercise of the police power because it protects third parties with whom the child might come into contact. Newborn screening will only affect that child and, with a 1 in 15,000 incidence of PKU, the child is unlikely to be "harmed" by the parents' refusal to test. (In fact, parents consent all the time to more risky activities of their children, such as participating in football.) Since the court views parents' refusal to consent to screening as creating a risk to the child, would the outcome be different for screening for one of the many other disorders that some states screen for in which there either is no treatment or the screening is just done for carrier status, to aid in the parents' future reproductive choices?

AMERICAN ACADEMY OF PEDIATRICS, REPORT OF THE TASK FORCE ON NEWBORN SCREENING (PUBLISHED AS A CALL FOR A NATIONAL AGENDA ON STATE NEWBORN SCREENING PROGRAMS)

106 Pediatrics 389, 389–415 (Supp.) (2000).

Almost all infants screened have residual blood samples retained by the state programs. Enough blood is obtained when performing heelstick newborn screening to permit programs to repeat tests when necessary. However, because repeat tests are not always necessary, and a repeat test may not use up the blood sample, the vast majority of infants screened (in excess of 95%) will have residual blood samples retained by the state programs. Currently, state programs hold these samples for variable lengths of time: 10 programs save samples for 21 years or more; 6 programs for 5 to 7 years; 2 programs for 1 to 3 years; 6 programs for 6 to 12 months; 21 programs for 1 to 6 months; and 5 programs for 1 to 4 weeks. Only 1 program is known to save the samples under optimal conditions for later use in biochemical analyses. Optimal storage conditions are much less critical for genetic analyses, and samples stored in many states are adequate for genetic analyses. The lack of uniformity between programs reflects uncertainty and debate over whether residual blood samples should be retained and, if so, for how long and under what conditions.

* * *

Residual blood samples may be used for several purposes including:

- Research related to new or existing newborn screening modalities. As technology advances for newborn screening programs, new testing modalities will be developed for conditions included in current programs, and new tests will be added for other health conditions. Residual heelstick blood samples can be used to ascertain the validity of new testing modalities for existing conditions and of tests for new conditions. Identifiers are sometimes retained to enable follow-up contact with an infant's family if an effective intervention is available for children diagnosed with the condition.

● Epidemiologic research relevant to clinical medicine and public health. Public health officials need population-based data to determine the appropriate allocation of resources to care for children with specific conditions. A thorough understanding of many health conditions requires epidemiologic data on the prevalence of specific genetic or biochemical attributes in the general population. Residual newborn screening samples constitute a specimen bank of a large cohort of the population of states. As genetic technology advances, such a comprehensive bank, linked to basic demographic information, may be useful for certain types of research. The potential utility of such a resource will need to be carefully evaluated because residual blood samples in this context will not be linked to clinical data on the children.

● Clinical or forensic testing. For children who have moved and cannot be located, the heelstick blood sample may represent the only source of a biological specimen from a given child. The sample may be useful for forensic purposes. Testing of residual blood samples may be essential in the postmortem identification of a genetic condition that may have contributed to a child's death. At least 1 state has decided to store newborn blood spots indefinitely to permit identification of children who have been kidnapped.

ETHICAL CONCERNS RELATED TO USE OF RESIDUAL BLOOD SAMPLES

Storage and use of residual newborn screening blood samples raise a number of practical and ethical challenges. Ethical challenges include the development of guidance regarding the use of residual blood spots for purposes other than those for which they were originally obtained. The protection of privacy and confidentiality among children and families is a serious concern. In the case of newborn screening, when blood samples are collected from infants as a matter of law, there is additional reason to ensure appropriate storage and use.

At the same time, residual newborn screening samples have been used to address important public health issues. The prevalence of in utero exposure to drugs and environmental agents; the allele frequency of genes associated with significant morbidity, mortality, or disability in infancy or childhood; and the prevalence of serious maternal or intrauterine infections have been determined in various populations by anonymous use of residual blood spots. Samples linked to outcome have been used to assess the feasibility of screening for various diseases of the newborn and infant, and to determine risk factors for birth defects and developmental disabilities. To date, there have been no published reports of misuse of residual newborn screening samples in research projects; however, the potential for use and misuse is expanding.

NOTES AND QUESTIONS

1. How does the storage and retention of these newborn blood samples compare with other DNA or tissue banks discussed in Chapter 4?

2. What policies should govern the storage and retention of these blood samples? The Task Force on Newborn Screening of the American Academy of Pediatrics states that "[c]urrent national standards stipulate that epidemiological research may be conducted without consent, so long as identifiers are removed." In regard to identifiable samples, the report states:

> The Task Force concluded that parental permission should be sought for the use of identifiable samples in research to validate tests for additional diseases, or for epidemiologic research. Identifiable samples from newborns should be used for research only if: 1) IRB approval is obtained for the proposed research, 2) consent is obtained from the child's parent(s) or guardian for the proposed research, 3) newborn samples represent the optimal source of available tissue for the research, 4) unlinked samples will not suffice, and 5) acceptable samples from consenting adults are not available.

Are these recommendations appropriate?

II. GENETIC TESTING OF CHILDREN AND ADOLESCENTS

Genetic testing of minors creates special problems. For example, when, if ever, is it appropriate to test children and adolescents? Is it ever appropriate to test them without their knowledge and consent? Without the assent of their parents? What if the minor and parents disagree? Who should have access to the test results?

AMERICAN SOCIETY OF HUMAN GENETICS AND AMERICAN COLLEGE OF MEDICAL GENETICS, POINTS TO CONSIDER: ETHICAL, LEGAL, AND PSYCHOSOCIAL IMPLICATIONS OF GENETIC TESTING IN CHILDREN AND ADOLESCENTS

57 Am. J. Human Gen. 1233 (1995).

Rapid developments in genetic knowledge and technologies increase the ability to test asymptomatic children for late-onset diseases, disease susceptibilities, and carrier status. These developments raise ethical and legal issues that focus on the interests of children and their parents. Although parents are presumed to promote the well-being of their children, a request for a genetic test may have negative implications for children, and the health-care provider must be prepared to acknowledge and discuss such issues with families.

This report is grounded in several social concepts: First, the primary goal of genetic testing should be to promote the well-being of the child. Second, the recognition that children are part of a network of family relationships supports an approach to potential conflicts that is not adversarial but, rather, emphasizes a deliberative process that seeks to promote the child's well-being within this context. Third, as children grow through successive stages of cognitive and moral development, parents and professionals should be attentive to the child's increasing interest and ability to participate in decisions about his or her own welfare.

Counseling and communication with the child and family about genetic testing should include the following components: (1) assessment of the significance of the potential benefits and harms of the test, (2) determination of the decision-making capacity of the child, and (3) advocacy on behalf of the interests of the child. The following points should be considered:

I.   POINTS TO CONSIDER

A.   *The Impact of Potential Benefits and Harms on Decisions about Testing*

1.   *Timely medical benefit to the child should be the primary justification for genetic testing in children and adolescents.* Under this condition, genetic testing is similar to other medical diagnostic evaluations. Medical benefits include preventive measures and therapies, as well as diagnostic information about symptomatic children. If the medical benefits are uncertain or will be deferred to a later time, this justification for testing is less compelling.

2.   *Substantial psychosocial benefits to the competent adolescent also may be a justification for genetic testing.* The benefits and harms of many genetic tests are psychosocial rather than physical. Relevant issues include anxiety, self-image, uncertainty, and the impact on decisions relating to reproduction, education, career, insurance, and lifestyle.

3.   *If the medical or psychosocial benefits of a genetic test will not accrue until adulthood, as in the case of carrier status or adult-onset diseases, genetic testing generally should be deferred.* Exceptions to this principle might occur when the adolescent meets conditions of competence, voluntariness, and adequate understanding of information. Further consultation with other genetic services providers, pediatricians, psychologists, and ethics committees may be appropriate to evaluate these conditions.

4.   *If the balance of benefits and harms is uncertain, the provider should respect the decision of competent adolescents and their families.* These decisions should be based on the unique circumstances of each family. The provider should enter into a thorough discussion about the potential benefits and harms and should assess the family's understanding of these issues.

5.   *Testing should be discouraged when the provider determines that potential harms of genetic testing in children and adolescents outweigh the potential benefits.* A health-care provider has no obli-

gation to provide a medical service for a child or adolescent that is not in the best interest of the child or adolescent.

B.   The Family's Involvement in Decision Making

1.   *Education and counseling for parents and the child, commensurate on maturity, should precede genetic testing.* Follow-up genetic counseling and psychological counseling also should be readily available. Providers of genetic testing should be prepared to educate, counsel, and refer, as appropriate.

2.   *The provider should obtain the permission of the parents and, as appropriate, the assent of the child or consent of the adolescent.* Decisions about competence should not depend arbitrarily on the child's age but should be based on an evaluation of the child's cognitive and moral development. The provider should also attempt to establish that the child's decision is voluntary.

3.   *The provider is obligated to advocate on behalf of the child when he or she considers a genetic test to be—or not to be—in the best interest of the child.* Continued discussion about the potential benefits and harms—and about the interests of the child—may be helpful in reaching a consensus.

4.   *A request by a competent adolescent for the results of a genetic test should be given priority over parents' requests to conceal information.* When possible, these issues should be explored prior to testing. When a younger child is tested and the parents request that the provider not reveal results, the provider should engage the parents in an ongoing discussion about the benefits and harms of the nondisclosure, the child's interest in the information, and when and in what manner the results should be disclosed.

* * *

II.   DISCUSSION

Benefits and Harms of Genetic Testing in Children

Parents sometimes request that their children be tested for adult-onset problems, so that they can address psychosocial issues. Such non-medical uses by parents are one of the most controversial issues in testing children. While some providers argue that parents should be able to obtain such information, other providers suggest that access to such information should be restricted or prohibited if the children will realize little or no immediate medical benefit. Some geneticists already limit testing for adult-onset diseases to individuals who are > 18 years of age, e.g., in some protocols for Huntington disease and breast cancer. One justification has been that, since such testing requires informed consent, and since children are not competent to give consent, therefore children should not be tested. However, this argument is so broad that it would preclude all pediatric care.

As with any other medical intervention, when children do not have the capacity to provide voluntary, informed consent, the decisive consideration in genetic testing in children should be the welfare of the child. Decisions about genetic testing in children should be based on an assessment of the possible benefits and harms that may be associated with the tests. The putative benefits and harms include medical, psychosocial, and reproductive issues that have implications for the child, the immediate family, and more distant relatives.

Medical issues

Medical issues include the possibilities of treatment and prevention, decisions about surveillance, and the resolution of questions about prognosis and diagnosis.

1. *Treatment and prevention.* Tests that offer children the potential for therapeutic benefit are most likely to be supported by the public and by medical professionals. For example, testing for familial hypertrophic cardiomyopathy, a disease associated with increased risk for sudden death, allows drug therapy to prevent arrhythmias. Individuals identified as having genetic diseases or disease susceptibility may also benefit from preventive advice about lifestyle changes. For example, children with familial hyperlipidemia may benefit from dietary restrictions.

Although some medical benefits from diagnosis in childhood are established, others remain unconfirmed-and may even be associated with the possibility of harm. One possible harm to a child determined to have a deleterious gene is increased medical tests and treatment regimens that may not have proved benefits. For example, presymptomatic diagnosis of cystic fibrosis has not yet demonstrated any medical benefit and may be associated with increased costs, unnecessary treatments, and familial distress. Thus, the potential for benefit of unestablished treatment and/or prevention regimens is a questionable justification for testing. Empirical verification of the benefits and harms of prevention and treatment should precede recommendations for routine testing.

2. *Surveillance.* Genetic testing can identify patients with an increased susceptibility to disease. The identification of genes associated with cancer might prompt surveillance to detect presymptomatic cancer. * * *

3. *Reduction of surveillance.* When genetic testing excludes a child from risk for a disease, the child may benefit from discontinued medical surveillance. * * *

4. *Refinement of prognosis.* Genetic testing can be helpful in refining prognosis, either when it leads to a precise diagnosis or when the genotype is well correlated with phenotype. * * *

5. *Clarification of diagnosis.* Genetic testing may provide clarification of an uncertain diagnosis if diagnostic data from other sources

are inconclusive, or if interpretations of diagnostic data are limited by the sensitivity of other evaluations.

Testing children may also benefit other family members when it is necessary to improve the reliability of linkage analysis and mutation analysis desired by other family members. However, participants in such studies should understand that unexpected information about paternity or adoption could be revealed.

Psychosocial issues

Psychosocial issues associated with medical problems or preexisting issues may be either exacerbated or alleviated by testing. The provider should discuss these issues with children and parents. The presence of severe anxiety or other psychopathology should be an indication for further psychological intervention-and not necessarily an indication for genetic testing.

1. Reduction of uncertainty.

* * *

Both parents and children may be anxious about their uncertain future. Genetic testing, even if confirming the presence of disease, may remove the uncertainty and allow parents the opportunity to confront the issues directly. When test results are favorable, psychological benefits may accrue to both parents and children.

2. Alteration of self-image. Children with genetic diseases may suffer a loss of self-esteem during a critical period when children's self-identity is developing. Children's understanding of illness and disease is often limited and may foster self-blame for their disease. If a child's genetic information is disclosed outside the family, the ensuing loss of privacy may exacerbate poor self-esteem. Alternatively, in some instances, an affected child may view the disease state as being normal and may even develop positive attitudes of identification with the affected family member.

Those individuals whose tests reveal that they are not at genetic risk may develop "survivor guilt," based on the knowledge that one or more of their siblings will develop-and perhaps die from-a serious genetic disease. For a child who is at risk of carrying recessive genes, the status of "not knowing" may allow the child to assume that he or she is a carrier and to share some of the burden. For some children, whose assumption of carrier status provides an important source of self-identity, the knowledge of being a noncarrier could generate a shift in such identity. * * *

3. Impact on family relationships. * * * A child known to have a deleterious gene may be overindulged, rejected, or treated as a scapegoat. * * * Unaffected siblings may also experience altered relationships with their parents, particularly in the case of children who feel disenfranchised if they see that an affected sibling is receiving a disproportionate amount of care and attention.

Testing a child for an adult-onset disease may inadvertently provide predictive information to other family members, who may not be interested in this information. However, identifying a child with a genetic disease or a gene predisposing to disease could benefit relatives who may wish to consider testing for themselves. Although the provider might presume an obligation to inform other family members at risk, some patients may prefer not to inform other family members. Current recommendations and practices suggest that the patient's wishes for confidentiality should be respected as long as the failure to disclose genetic information is not likely to result in immediate serious physical harm to the relative.

4. *Impact on life planning.* * * * The possibility of serious disease or early death may influence an individual's educational goals, occupational choices, and specific career plans. This information also may influence choice of domicile, perhaps to live closer to family, to other support systems, or to adequate medical facilities. Genetic test results may have financial implications for retirement planning and for obtaining life, disability, and health insurance.

Individuals at risk for developing a disease or for transmitting a deleterious gene to their children may be stigmatized and subject to inappropriate discrimination. * * *

Reproductive issues

* * *

Reproductive benefits may be of minimal value to children—and even to sexually active adolescents who are not likely to make family-planning decisions primarily on the basis of their genetic status. Additionally, children may not receive genetic information in an understandable or usable form-or at the appropriate time for the benefit to accrue. However, the knowledge of presymptomatic disease in a young child could have some impact on the reproductive decisions of parents, who may use this information for prenatal diagnosis in future pregnancies or to make decisions about the number or spacing of future children.

Promoting the Interests of Children and Their Families

Parents generally have the authority to make medical decisions for their children. This authority may be limited if a decision is likely to cause a child serious harm without the prospect of compensating benefit. What further complicates these issues in genetic testing is the uncertainty about the putative benefits and harms. Additionally, as children grow, their ability to participate in decisions increases, and, at times, their choices may be at odds with the wishes of their parents. These issues emphasize the provider's obligations to explore both the interests of children and the interests of their parents.

Presumption of parental authority

1.   Presumption of parental authority is a fundamental principle for families and professionals who are discussing genetic testing for children.

* * *

The most compelling justification for parental authority focuses on the well-being of the child and acknowledges that parents are usually in the best position to make such a determination and have the greatest interest in making decisions to promote the well-being of the child. A second justification for parental authority rests on the interests of parents in their own self-determination, including the authority to make decisions on behalf of their children. * * *

2.   *Limits of parental authority.* In spite of the presumption of parental prerogative, parental authority can be limited if there are objective reasons to believe that a decision or action has significant potential for an adverse impact on the health or well-being of the child. Such limitations are best exemplified by child-abuse and-neglect laws, which prohibit parents from acts of omission or commission that could or do result in serious harm to the child.

The law also requires parents to provide certain medical benefits for their children, even if those benefits are contrary to the beliefs of the parents. * * *

* * *

In the clinical setting, providers may refuse to provide requested diagnostic or therapeutic interventions that offer no or few benefits but that incur more than minimal risk or cost. * * * The provider does, however, have a responsibility to explain why he or she will not provide the requested intervention and, if feasible, to identify other providers who may be willing to provide the requested services.

3.   *Legal trend to recognize the authority of minors.* Although the law protects the autonomy of adults, on the presumption that adults are competent to make their own decisions, the law presumes that minors are not competent in this respect. Many states, however, permit adolescents to consent to medical treatment in the absence of parental consent. These states recognize a "mature minor rule," which views some adolescents as capable of understanding the consequences of some medical decisions. Mature-minor rules are circumstance specific and generally address situations in which the state has an interest in the adolescent's seeking medical attention that might not be sought if the problem were disclosed to the parents. These circumstances typically include reproductive issues, such as contraception, as well as sexually transmitted diseases. Other sensitive areas, such as treatment for drug and alcohol abuse and psychotherapy, are protected as well. The "emancipated minor" status also acknowledges

an adolescent as competent to make decisions, by virtue of adult status under the law. For example, adolescents who are living on their own or who are married, pregnant, or have children are generally permitted to make medical and other decisions usually reserved for adults.

The decision-making capacity of the child

Although 18 years of age is the general legal standard for decision making, the concepts of the mature minor and the emancipated minor derive, in part, from empirical observations about the gradual development of a child's cognitive skills and moral reasoning.

* * *

By the age of 7 years, children can usually begin to participate in decisions, since they have sufficient cognitive and language skills to understand some information. Thus, in the United States, a 7–year-old is generally entitled to give "assent" to participation in research involving human subjects (45 CFR 46.408, 1994).

During adolescence, children begin to develop concepts of mortality, cause and effect, and right and wrong, as well as a sense of connection to the future. As adolescents' decision-making capacity increases, additional consideration should be given to their wishes, even when these wishes differ from those of their parents or when these wishes are not clearly in the child's best interest. Adolescents may have a genuine interest in information about career and child-bearing choices, although they may still be vulnerable to coercion by family or peers, to stigmatization, or to altered self-image. By the age of 12 or 14 years, some children, though, will have sufficient decision-making capacity to evaluate the specific risks and benefits of tests or treatments.

The provider as a fiduciary for the child

The provider, as fiduciary for the child, must be conscientious about considering requests for testing, as well as requests for nondisclosure.

   1. *Assessing requests for tests.* * * * Although providers generally should respect parents' wishes, the provider ultimately must balance the responsibilities to the health and well-being of the child and to the wishes of the parents.

   Until more information is available regarding the risks and benefits of genetic testing, the provider's guiding principle continues to be primum non nocere—first do no harm. Thus, when faced with uncertainty, the provider may be obligated to avoid the possibility of harm, rather than to provide unclear benefits. There may be a rebuttable presumption to defer testing unless the risk/benefit ratio is favorable. On the other hand, in specific cases where the benefits and harms of genetic testing are more uncertain, more weight should be given to the wishes of the competent adolescent and the parents. These issues are not always straightforward, and, at the very least, the provider has a responsibility to engage in detailed conversations with the family. Parents may overestimate the power of genetic testing or be unaware of potential risks. It also may be advisable to obtain consultation from other genetic-service providers, pediatricians, psychologists, and ethics committee, to evaluate benefits/harms, decision-making capacity, and voluntariness. Sometimes a dialogue with parents about the nature of testing will lead to a consensus about its value to the child and the family. If a consensus is not attainable, the provider may decline to conduct the test or might suggest other providers, who may be willing to provide the testing.

The practice of medical genetics provides some examples of tests that may not be in the best interest of the child. For example, parents may request a determination of their young daughter's Tay–Sachs carrier status, for the purpose of encouraging her to be sexually responsible when she is older. The possibility of stigmatization without any clear immediate benefit is a serious concern. On the other hand, different issues may arise when, to help the parents make their own family-planning and socioeconomic decisions, parents request that young children be tested for adult-onset diseases. For example, the parents' choice about future children might be dependent on the genetic status of the child, or parents may wish to know about adult-onset diseases prior to deciding how much to save for a college education. In such cases, the balance swings between benefit to the family and benefit to the child. The unique potential of presymptomatic genetic testing to predict a child's future should be approached with great caution.

Adolescents who request tests prompt additional considerations. For example, if an adolescent requests testing for Huntington disease, it may be important to ascertain whether the request originates from the adolescent or from the parent. In the face of uncertain benefits and harms, an adolescent's request for a test necessitates an individual assessment of competence and voluntariness.

2. *Assessing requests for nondisclosure.* Parents occasionally may request that a test result not be disclosed to the child. This may pose a conflict between the interest of the parents in making decisions that they believe are for the well-being of the child and the interest of the child in self-determination. As the child matures, justifying such a request may become more difficult, even if the provider agrees that disclosure might not promote the well-being of the child. * * *

If genetic testing occurs prior to the request for nondisclosure to the child, the provider may wish to defer a decision about disclosure until after the issues have been explored fully. * * * It is recommended that, on reaching adulthood, the individual should be informed of the existence of the test results and should be given the option to know the results.

DOROTHY C. WERTZ ET AL., GENETIC TESTING FOR CHILDREN AND ADOLESCENTS: WHO DECIDES?

272 JAMA 875 (1994).

* * *

Genetic testing of minors poses questions of privacy and disclosure. It seems appropriate that the person(s) who requested the information should receive it and should also have some control over its dissemination to others. If the minor requested the test, ideally he or she should receive the results and should be able to keep these confidential, even from his or her parents. In the reality of family living, this will often be impossible. Genetic information, especially if it determines one's future, is uniquely private. If the information will benefit other family members, the "mature" minor has a moral obligation to opt for disclosure. If the minor refuses to disclose and there is a high risk of serious harm to identifiable individuals, the physician may override confidentiality, provided that the conditions set by the President's Commission are met. The situation occurs rarely, however, because testing of minors is ordinarily conducted only in families already at known risk. Minors who request testing should be informed, before testing, that third parties such as employers, insurers, and schools may be able to coerce their consent for access to test results by employment, insurance, or school admission.

If the parents requested testing, with the minor's assent, they should receive the results. The minor should also receive the results (in understandable form) if she or he is old enough to assent to testing. In cases where small children are tested specifically on behalf of other family members, there should be a way of ensuring that the information reaches them if, when they reach adulthood, they indicate a desire to know. It should not be assumed that parents will convey full and accurate information years after a test is performed. Although there is as yet no relevant case law, a few legal experts believe that professionals may have a duty to make sure that results eventually reach the minor.

It may be desirable to tell children about their genetic risks early on. Studies of children with cancer and other serious illnesses suggest that children cope better with their conditions if informed as early as possible. Adoption studies also support early disclosure. The possible benefits of early disclosure, however, do not necessarily support actual testing. There are varying degrees of disclosure. If an inherited disorder is present in the family, the healthiest approach may be to disclose its presence to a child at potential risk early on, so that the child can develop coping mechanisms. As the child grows in understanding and awareness, the child can then work toward a decision, over a period of several years or more, about whether to be tested. Early disclosure of a disorder's existence offers greater psychological benefits than concealment. Those who find out only in adulthood that a serious disorder such as HD exists in the family fare more poorly than those who know earlier. Parents often seek to protect their children by concealing a condition or the seriousness of a condition. For example, in some studies the mean age at which persons at risk for HD learned that the disorder existed in the family was 25 years. Many siblings of children with cystic fibrosis do not know that the disorder may cause early death. But if the ill sibling dies, the surviving siblings may lose trust in the parents who failed to warn them.

COMMENT

In view of the increasing respect for minors' autonomy in the overall context of medical care, and mindful that maturity is an extended developmental process, we propose the following guidelines for presymptomatic genetic testing.

1.   *The test may detect conditions for which treatment or preventive measures are available.* For disorders for which proven methods of treatment or prevention exist, testing of minors should proceed according to consent guidelines established for other necessary medical treatments. Testing should be offered at the earliest age when health benefits accrue, but need not be offered before this time. If parents refuse testing that would benefit the child, the problem could be handled under current child abuse statutes. For many adult-onset genetic disorders, early testing does not lead to clearly beneficial treatment or effective prevention. It may be difficult to establish efficacy until sufficient numbers of children reach the age of majority. Tests should fall into the "ordinary" or "necessary medical care" category only if treatment or prevention has an acknowledged and proven efficacy. In all other cases, the treatment associated with a test should be presented to the family as experimental, and the consent or assent procedure requirements for testing should follow a research protocol.

2.   *The test has no health benefits for the minor, but may be useful to the minor in making reproductive decisions now or in the near future.* This is one of the more common reasons for requests for testing. In such cases, it may be useful to a minor of reproductive age to know his or her genetic status. In such cases, the minor should be the primary decision maker. Professionals should probe to discern whether the minor is acting on her or his own behalf (perhaps in agreement with parental suggestion) or is merely carrying out parental wishes without actually desiring to be tested. Minors should have the "negative right" of not knowing at all if they so desire. Autonomy includes both the right to know and the right not to know one's genetic status.

Testing done to inform reproductive decision-making should be limited to situations where the potential risk to a minor's offspring is high (e.g., for dominant disorders). Ordinarily, carrier testing for autosomal recessive disorders will not be warranted unless both the minor and the minor's partner have a family history of the disorder.

3.   *There are no medical benefits and no current reproductive benefits from testing, but parents or the minor requests it.* Testing in the absence of

medical benefit or current reproductive benefit is the most ethically problematic category of testing. There are no real parallels: it is not necessary medical care and does not relate to reproductive rights. Perhaps the closest parallels are elective procedures such as cosmetic surgery.

The age at which the emotional maturity required for consent appears is highly variable and also depends on the seriousness of the genetic disorder. Often it may be advisable to defer testing until adulthood. If no clear benefits exist, parents should restrain their desire to know. The professional should ensure that both minor and parents are aware of potential harms. A physician who perceives testing to pose harm to the child should evaluate for cognitive and emotional maturity, using referrals if necessary. Ordinarily competence should not be assumed before the age of 16 years. Testing before this age in cases without medical or reproductive benefits requires careful evaluation.

Some minors may benefit from testing carried out to make plans for the future, provided that they themselves initiate the request. Thorough counseling of both the minor and family (including siblings) should precede testing, to assess the inner strength of all concerned. New measures are needed to enable professionals to evaluate a minor's competence, probably through sets of open-ended questions about the future or responses to vignettes describing future life problems, followed by careful interviewing. In some cases it may be possible to increase reasoning ability or to help develop a consistent set of values through an educational process, as has been done with the concept of rights.

Professionals should find out precisely how each child or adolescent views the cause of a genetic disorder and should take the child's conceptions seriously. They should remember that well-informed, articulate children or adolescents are not necessarily coping well with the prospect of illness. Sometimes basic decision making about parenthood precedes actual reproductive activity by several years. Girls' play activities frequently revolve around motherhood; they begin to think of themselves as mothers (or as not becoming mothers) well before menarche. A negative test result would undoubtedly relieve anxiety at this age, especially if a member of the immediate family were symptomatic. The benefits and harms of a positive test result, however, are more difficult to weigh. There is no research or evidence about the optimum timing or the benefit of testing. For some, it may be less traumatic to find out about genetic risks to offspring early on, before a self-image as a parent is developed, than to find out later. For others, it may be better to wait, and others might benefit most from not knowing until adulthood. It may be difficult for professionals to evaluate the minor's locus of control, given the tendency of many teenagers to base their actions on the wishes of parents or other outside authorities The minor should have reached the age at which she or he is beginning to make life plans and can understand the implications of genetic knowledge for the future. There is ordinarily no ethical justification for testing before the age of 11 or 12 years in the absence of proven medical benefits.

Individuals become capable of understanding the future implications of testing and of making an informed decision at widely different ages, partly based on cultural background. Psychological research, in setting general stages of cognitive development, has not explored all dimensions of cultural and social differences. The basic theories were developed in studies of middle-class, white boys and girls. Therefore, no fixed age can be set. Cultural beliefs or practices that may cause harm to others or that are oppressive, however, need not be respected, nor is it ethnocentric to oppose them.

Sometimes the physician must reject a request, whether from a parent or a minor, if in the physician's judgment it serves no useful purpose and may lead to harm For example, a parental request to test a 7–year-old for predisposition to familial Alzheimer's disease provides no medical benefit to the child and may lead to stigmatization. Decisions that challenge parental autonomy may be necessary to prevent harm and to preserve a minor's future autonomy, which should be the paramount considerations.

4. *Testing is carried out solely for the benefit of another family member.* Such testing may have a clear medical benefit, but not to the individual tested. One analogy is organ donation, which is ordinarily permitted if a minor provides the closest tissue match for a family member and if both parents and minor give consent (or assent, depending on age). No person can be forced to assent to organ donation, even to save the life of a family member. Similar rules would seemingly apply to providing tissue for DNA linkage analysis. In all cases, the test should have a clear usefulness for others, and the rationale for the test, including the name and description of the disorder (but not the name of the person on whose behalf the minor is to be tested, except with that person's permission), should be explained insofar as possible.

Parent–Child Conflict

When parent(s) and child disagree about testing, professional advocacy should be based on the four situations described above. (1) If testing offers medical benefits, the professional should advocate testing, unless it becomes apparent that harms could outweigh possible benefits. (2) If testing offers no benefits to the minor but would be useful in the minor's reproductive decision-making, the minor should have the final say, provided that he or she has reached reproductive age. (3) If there are no medical or reproductive benefits, it is usually best to postpone testing. If the parents wish the test but the minor does not, the professional should act as an advocate for the minor. If the minor wishes the test but the parents do not, testing should be postponed until majority, on the grounds that the parents may be aware that the minor is not sufficiently mature. (4) If testing is conducted solely for someone else's benefit, children over the age of 7 years should be able to refuse, as with organ donation. An objective hearing by a standing review committee, established by the clinic for this purpose, would help to clarify whose wishes should prevail in situations 2 through 4 above.

COUNCIL ON ETHICAL AND JUDICIAL AFFAIRS, AMERICAN MEDICAL ASSOCIATION, CODE OF MEDICAL ETHICS: CURRENT OPINION 2.138

(1995).

Genetic testing of children implicates important concerns about individual autonomy and the interest of the patients. Before testing of children can be performed, there must be some potential benefit from the testing that can reasonably be viewed as outweighing the disadvantages of testing, particularly the harm from abrogating the children's future choice in knowing their genetic status. When there is such a potential benefit, parents should decide whether their children will undergo testing. If parents unreasonably request or refuse testing of their child, physician should take steps to change or, if necessary, use legal means to override the parents' choice. Applying these principles to specific circumstances yields the following conclusions:

(1) When a child is at risk for a genetic condition for which preventive or other therapeutic measures are available, genetic testing should be offered or, in some cases, required.

(2) When a child is at risk for a genetic condition with pediatric onset for which preventive or other therapeutic measures are not available, parents generally should have discretion to decide about genetic testing.

(3) When a child is at risk for a genetic condition with adult onset for which preventive or other therapeutic measures are not available, genetic testing of children generally should not be undertaken. Families should still be informed of the existence of tests and given the opportunity to discuss the reasons why the tests are generally not offered for children.

(4) Genetic testing for carrier status should be deferred until either the child reaches maturity, the child needs to make reproductive decisions or, in the case of children too immature to make their own reproductive decisions, reproductive decisions need to be made for the child.

(5) Genetic testing of children for the benefit of a family member should not be performed unless the testing is necessary to prevent substantial harm to the family member.

When a child's genetic status is determined incidentally, the information should be retained by the physician and entered into the patient record. Discussion of the existence of this finding should then be taken up when the child reaches maturity or needs to make reproductive decisions, so that the individual can decide whether to request disclosure of the information. It is important that physicians be consistent in disclosing both positive and negative results in the same way since if physicians raise the existence of the testing results only when the results are positive, individuals will know what the results must be. This information should not be disclosed to third parties. Genetic information should be maintained in a separate portion of the medical record to prevent mistaken disclosure.

When a child is being considered for adoption, the guidelines for genetic testing should be the same as for other children.

NOTES AND QUESTIONS

1.   Minors of the same age differ in terms of their maturity. Do all of the foregoing sets of recommendations take this into consideration? How should maturity and mental competence be measured? For an overview, see Leonard H. Glantz, Research with Children, 24 Am. J. L. & Med. 213 (1998).

Typically, age restrictions under the law, such as minimum ages for driving or voting, are irrebuttable presumptions; minors are not permitted to argue that they should qualify for the privilege despite being under-age. Which of the foregoing recommendations advocate irrebuttable presumptions with regard to genetic testing of minors? Rebuttable presumptions? Should the approach for rules regarding genetic testing be different than for rules for, say, driving or voting? Why?

In some cases, the recommendations state that the rules for genetic testing of children and adolescents should be the same as the general rules for medical treatment or for medical research using children and adolescents as subjects. What are those rules? Are they different for treatment and research? For example, are children given the power to veto medical treatment? What about vetoing their participation in research? If the rules differ for the research and treatment contexts, which rules should apply to genetic testing?

2.   What benefits might accrue from genetic testing of minors and adolescents? Which of these benefits do the foregoing recommendations recognize? Which harms? How do the recommendations balance benefit and harm? Do you agree with the result?

One issue is the impact of genetic test information on the child or adolescent. A number of studies suggest that disclosing test results to children is preferable to postponing the disclosure until they are adults. Do the recommendations agree?

3.   How do the recommendations differ regarding the decision-making role of parents? Of health care professionals?

4.   How do the recommendations differ with regard to adult-onset and pediatric-onset conditions? How valid is this distinction?

5.   Are there any instances, according to these recommendations, in which health care professionals should act contrary to the views of both parents and minors? What do the recommendations suggest that professionals should do in these situations? Do you agree?

6. The Huntington Disease Society of America recommends against testing asymptomatic minors for Huntington disease, a nontreatable, adult-onset disease. Nevertheless, 53 percent of health professionals stated that they would perform the testing at the request of parents. In a survey of genetic testing laboratories, 22 percent reported that they performed tests for Huntington disease in children under the age of 12. Is it desirable that there be a single, uniform national policy on genetic testing of children and adolescents? Who should administer such a policy?

7. The Committee on Bioethics of the American Academy of Pediatrics issued a policy statement in 2001 entitled "Ethical Issues with Genetic Testing in Pediatrics" (107 Pediatrics 1451–1455) in which it recommended against routine carrier screening for newborns, children or adolescents, with the exception of adolescents who are pregnant or considering becoming pregnant. The committee also recommended against predictive testing for late-onset disorders "unless there is anticipated benefit to the child."

8. The federal National Childhood Vaccine Injury Act, 42 U.S.C. §§ 300aa–1 to 300aa–34, allows for compensation when the administration of a vaccine has resulted in an injury. The families of children with who were healthy until vaccinated but then developed autism have tried to seek compensation under the fund, but have had difficulty proving a link between vaccines and their child's autism.

In 2007, however, the Department of Health and Human Services, Division of Vaccine Injury Compensation, recommended that compensation be awarded to ten-year-old Hannah Poling, concluding that the child's vaccinations from July, 2000 "significantly aggravated an underlying mitochondrial disorder, which predisposed her to deficits in cellular energy metabolism, and manifested as a regressive encephalopathy with features of autism spectrum disorder." Respondent's Rule 4(c) Report, Child v. Secretary of Health and Human Services, (Ct. Fed. Cl. Office of Special Masters Nov. 9, 2007).

The import of that decision is that certain children with genetic mutations in their mitochondrial DNA could conceivably be harmed by vaccines and thus could be compensated from the federal fund. If you were a parent, would you want to have a genetic test on your child before submitting her to a vaccine? Should the federal government require such testing?

CHAPTER 8

GENETIC COUNSELING, ACCESS TO
GENETIC SERVICES, AND
LIABILITY ISSUES

∎ ∎ ∎

I. DUTIES OF HEALTH CARE PROFESSIONALS

A. GENETIC COUNSELING

Individuals and families concerned about genetic disorders may obtain information and advice from a variety of health care professionals, including primary care physicians, physicians specializing in clinical genetics, and nurses. In addition, masters degrees are offered in genetic counseling. Masters-level genetic counselors are not licensed in an overwhelming number of states (California being a notable exception), but they may be certified by the American Board of Genetic Counseling. The National Society of Genetic Counselors (NSGC) had 2648 members as of 2008. Roles may overlap, but a basic distinction is that, while any of these professionals may provide information and counseling, only physicians can make diagnoses and order genetic testing.

A major issue for health care professionals in general, and for those providing genetic counseling services in particular, is whether their interactions with patients and families should be directive or non-directive.

ANNE L. MATTHEWS, GENETIC COUNSELING, IN ENCYCLOPEDIA OF ETHICAL, LEGAL, AND POLICY ISSUES IN BIOTECHNOLOGY

349–50 (Thomas H. Murray & Maxwell J. Mehlman, eds. 2000).

* * *

From Sheldon Reed's first publication defining genetic counseling as a "a kind of social work done for the benefit of the whole family entirely without eugenic connotations," genetic counseling has been equated with the concept of nondirectiveness. Nondirectiveness appealed to the genetics

424

community as a way to distance itself from the eugenics movement associated with Nazi Germany. Genetic counseling embraced Carl Rogers's client-centered counseling approach. Rogers felt that counselors need to provide a warm, accepting environment free from pressure or coercion for clients to reach a successful self-acceptance and self-understanding. Nondirectiveness is understood to mean nonprescriptive. Fine defines nondirectiveness as a genetic counseling strategy that supports autonomous decision making by clients. NSGC Code of Ethics states, "Therefore, genetic counselors strive to: * * * Enable their clients to make informed independent decisions, free of coercion, by providing or illuminating the necessary facts and clarifying the alternatives and anticipated consequences." Genetic counselors therefore are facilitators and advocates of informed decision making, with the goal of having the counselee make a decision based solely on his or her own values and beliefs.

However, consensus regarding the terms directiveness and nondirectiveness is difficult to find among genetics professionals and in the literature. Kessler notes that depending on how one defines the term nondirective will determine whether or not it can be achieved. White notes that nondirectiveness is often equated with value neutrality, which may "either imply that the counseling approach as a whole does not represent any values or moral positions, or it may refer to value-free communication, representing an ideal in which concepts and facts are expressed in impartial terms." A number of authors have argued that counseling is never value-neutral. The types of information provided or not provided, the tone of voice, body language, all convey counselor values. Singer elaborates on this theme by noting that many of the decisions that patients make take place in an atmosphere of crisis and that the issues are often highly emotional. Counselors relay information that is often highly technical, while most counselees are likely to have limited knowledge of the biological and statistical issues that arise; they are a vulnerable population. Thus a counselor, who has a duty to provide all the information that clients need in order to make informed decisions, must decide what information the counselee needs and how to present the information. In this sense the genetic counselor utilizes her expertise to decide what and how much information the counselee needs to make the best possible decision for her. Brunger and Lippman would agree. They conclude that genetic counseling is not a "one-size-fits-all" endeavor; rather, it is information that is tailored to specific counselees in specific situations. For some, this would be considered a directive approach. However, authors such as Kessler or Singer would suggest that the counselor is facilitating the goal of genetic counseling by providing information upon which counselees can make autonomous, independent, and informed decisions.

One of the often quoted mechanisms for deciding whether or not a counselor is being directive is to ask whether or not counselors answer questions such as "What would you do in my situation?"

* * *

While the literature regarding nondirective counseling remains unsettled, research suggests that nondirectiveness is not the only guiding principle employed by genetic counselors. In their efforts to provide and facilitate autonomous, independent, and informed decision making by counselees, genetic counselors strive to maintain a delicate balance between a nondirective stance and enhanced counselee understanding.

NOTES AND QUESTIONS

1.   One approach Matthews describes for identifying whether counseling is directive or non-directive is whether the counselor answers the question "What would you do in my situation?" One reason people may consult health care professionals is to obtain the professional's expert opinion on what to do. How appropriate is it for professionals to refuse to provide this advice? Is there a way to provide advice in a non-directive manner? If not, is the goal of non-directiveness misguided?

2.   Although, in theory, genetic counseling is non-directive, the reality is somewhat different. See Barbara A. Bernhardt, Empirical Evidence That Genetic Counseling Is Directive: Where Do We Go From Here?, 60 Am. J. Human Genetics 17 (1997). It is also clear from consumer surveys that clients do not want complete non-directiveness.

3.   For a discussion of privacy issues in genetic counseling, see Barbara Bowles Biesecker, Privacy in Genetic Counseling, in Genetic Secrets: Protecting Privacy and Confidentiality in the Genetic Era 108–25 (Mark A. Rothstein ed. 1997). For a discussion of the role of genetic counselors in prenatal screening, see Sonia Suter, The Routinization of Prenatal Testing, 28 Am. J. L. & Med. 233 (2002).

MAURICE BLOCH ET AL., PREDICTIVE TESTING FOR HUNTINGTON DISEASE IN CANADA: THE EXPERIENCE OF THOSE RECEIVING AN INCREASED RISK

42 Am. J. Med. Genetics 499, 499–507 (1992).

Candidates who have received increased risk results are considered to be at high risk for emotional difficulties. Our clinical experience with these individuals in interviews and support groups suggest that all of them undergo a difficult immediate period of adjustment, while some experience a prolonged period of significant emotional distress. During the early follow-up period, a few candidates have expressed regret at taking the test. However, most have reiterated their commitment to the process and stated that it has been helpful and that given the choice they would do it again. It should be appreciated that this program has been carried out in the context of the availability of continued support.

* * *

The stringent protocol of precounselling and assessment used in our program has made it possible to assess the psychosocial status of each candidate, to develop rapport with the candidate and to identify those candidates who require further assessment and possibly treatment before proceeding in the predictive testing program. The development of good rapport is important to allow the candidate to fully engage in the precounselling process of exploring motivation for taking the test and actively preparing to take the test so that individuals who are uncertain do not prematurely participate in predictive testing. Furthermore, with the establishment of open communication the candidate is more likely to seek professional support, if needed, in the follow-up phase.

Our protocol requires that candidates who are either incapable of an informed decision or considered a current suicidal risk should have the delivery of results postponed until these concerns have been resolved. Four candidates have been referred for further assessment based on psychosocial concerns. Of those only one has had testing postponed and this was due to active suicidal risk. The decision to postpone testing can never be taken lightly. The stress of *undergoing testing,* receiving a result, and *adjusting to* the new risk status must be weighed against the stress and uncertainty of living at risk for HD, the blow to the candidate's self-respect by being denied testing, and the possible sense of humiliation and helplessness by having one's autonomy undermined. For example, the first candidate was able to cope with both divorce and job change in the follow-up period. The third candidate had mild depressive symptoms but strongly resisted any suggestion of postponement of testing. The candidate in the fourth case report went through divorce and entered a new relationship. *No candidate who has received an increased risk result in our program has yet made a suicide attempt or required psychiatric hospitalization.* The candidate who had the process postponed due to suicidal risk later resolved some of her personal issues and decided that she did not wish to proceed with predictive testing at that time. At the present time, based on our experience, only a small number of candidates will have testing postponed for psychosocial reasons.

In the second case report we described some of the ramifications of testing for other relatives. The decision to take the test or not must ultimately be made by the person at risk. However, the effects of this decision are not isolated but have a ripple effect throughout the family. The nontested spouse receives information about his/her partner as well as a change in the risk of his/her children and possibly grandchildren. It is this spouse who may later be the primary caregiver for this at risk individual and this person's hopes for the future may also be drastically affected by the test result. Similarly the children of the candidate are simultaneously receiving an alteration in their risk status. Counseling should also be available for relatives as part of any predictive testing program to alleviate some of these potential adverse events.

* * *

In general, open communication is encouraged for candidates in the predictive testing program as it tends to facilitate intimacy, support, and understanding. However, the risks of open communication need also be discussed. It might leave the candidate more vulnerable to rejection, to discriminating policies by employers who may, for example, deny a high risk candidate a deserved promotion. In addition, the candidate may have to deal with the emotional distress of others.

Candidates vary considerably in the defensive postures they adopt in order to live with HD and to prepare and deal with the predictive test results. Although, during precounselling and preparation for results we have strategies to assist candidates to prepare for the impact of the results, their attitudes are usually related to entrenched personality characteristics and are often not fully recognized and dealt with during that phase of the program. The third candidate had convinced herself that she would get an increased risk result and she felt prepared to receive this and thought that she could cope. Nevertheless she experienced considerable distress and prolonged difficulty coping with results. It became apparent in discussion that she had held a deep, powerful, and inadmissible belief that she would receive a decreased risk result. Exploration in the precounselling phase of the candidates beliefs about HD and the expected outcome of predictive testing may allow counseling strategies to deal with this before test results are given.

The fourth candidate, on the other hand, convinced himself that he would get a low risk result. The juvenile onset in one sibling and an early onset in another supported this bias. Neither of these candidates was able to project themselves effectively into both the low-risk and high-risk positions and, therefore, may have failed to effectively acknowledge their *full* range of hopes and fears which may be crucial in the process of psychologically preparing for results. This inability to prepare for both possible outcomes has been an impediment to successful assimilation of decreased risk results as well. The third and fourth case reports illustrate the possible distress that arises in part from not fully preparing for an adverse test result. The precounselling, using discussion, visual imagery, rehearsal, and other techniques has proven helpful for candidates to prepare more *fully* for the eventuality of any outcome.

* * *

Two issues emerged from our experience with the second candidate and his sibling participating concurrently in the program. He indicated at the results session that he did not intend to tell his brother his results at that time. His right to confidential treatment of this information has been clearly established. However, it did impose a challenge upon the counseling team not to let any of his information be disclosed to his brother, as he had told his brother that delivery had been postponed due to laboratory problems. However, some weeks later the candidate did disclose his results to his brother. This reinforced our belief that the candidate is, in most instances, best able to pace him or herself with respect to crucial decisions such as whether and when to take the test, to disclose information about HD or the test, and to join the support group. This experience also reinforced the importance of addressing the needs of each candidate individually even if more than one family member has requested testing concurrently.

Thus far there have been no catastrophic responses to increased risk results in the Canadian program. The candidates, in general, appear to be coping fairly well, although all have experienced some difficult episodes. Symptoms of depression and anxiety are most common and occur most frequently shortly after receiving results, which is clearly a period when persons are more vulnerable. However, in the longer term, candidates generally become more present-centered in their awareness with a heightened perception of the here and now, but have increased difficulty in planning for the future.

Longitudinal evaluation over the ensuing years will provide much needed information about the long term impact of living at increased risk for Huntington's disease, particularly as the candidates get close to the expected age of manifestation. These evaluations will have relevance for similar testing programs which may be developed for other late onset genetic disorders.

NOTES AND QUESTIONS

1. Under the protocol employed by the Canadian Huntington disease testing program, counselors evaluated candidates to determine whether they were suitable for testing. In one case, for example, the candidate was found to be experiencing significant emotional distress and to be moderately depressed. However, "[a]s she did not appear to be a suicidal risk, had a stable marriage and sound social supports, was motivated to seek additional individual psychotherapy outside the program, and was able to make an informed decision, we proceeded with predictive testing." Block et al. at 504. Is it appropriate to withhold testing because of these concerns? Is the Canadian protocol consistent with general principles governing informed consent to health care? To what extent, for example, is it appropriate to withhold testing because of fears that the results may emotionally upset the patient? See generally Jessica Berg et al., Informed Consent: Legal Theory and Clinical Practice 79–85 (2001).

2. The Canadian study also found that approximately 10 percent of those persons receiving a negative result from the test for Huntington's disease experienced psychological difficulties, including "survivor guilt," stress from having made irreversible personal and financial decisions based on an expectation that they were affected, and depression once the realization sets in that many problems in their lives remain unchanged. See Marlene Huggins et al., Predictive Testing for Huntington Disease in Canada: Adverse Effects and Unexpected Results in Those Receiving a Decreased Risk, 42 Am. J. Med. Genetics 508 (1992).

3. Other researchers have studied the impact of genetic testing for breast cancer and Alzheimer's disease. One study, for example, found that both women who were found to be carrying the BRCA1 mutation and those whose test results were negative increased their frequency of mammograms

after testing, and that 30 percent of the women who had the mutation had their ovaries removed to prevent the risk of ovarian cancer, while none of the women with positive test results obtained prophylactic mastectomies. Jeffrey R. Botkin et al., Genetic Testing for a BRCA1 Mutation: Prophylactic Surgery and Screening Behavior in Women 2 Years Post Testing, 118A Am. J. Med. Genetics 201–209 (2003).

4. In 1993, researchers announced that they had discovered a gene, APOE, that is associated with Alzheimer disease. In 1995, a working group of the American College of Medical Genetics and the American Society of Human Genetics issued a consensus statement that clinicians should not offer predictive testing, even to members of high-risk families. See Statement on the Use of Apolipoprotein E Testing for Alzheimer Disease, 274 JAMA 1627 (1995). The group noted uncertainties about the predictive value of test results (including that 35 to 50 percent of patients with Alzheimer's disease do not have the mutation), and took the position that predictive testing "may be valuable only if prevention can be affected by lifestyle changes or early drug intervention," which was not the case with Alzheimer's disease. Is this an appropriate stance? Should the decision be left up to the individuals seeking testing? What standards should be used to determine if a genetic test is predictive enough to be suitable for clinical use? Who should establish these standards? In a 2004 article, researchers studying attitudes toward genetic testing for an inherited form of amyotrophic lateral sclerosis (Lou Gehrig's disease) recommended that individuals considering being tested be informed that the purpose of the testing is for research rather than disclosure of individual results. See Joanna H. Fanos, Deborah F. Gelinas, and Robert G. Miller, "You Have Shown Me My End": Attitudes Toward Presymtomatic Testing for Familial Amyotrophic Lateral Sclerosis, 129A Am. J. Med. Genetics 248–253 (2004). Another group of commentators recommended that community input be obtained before establishing policies on offering genetic testing and screening for clinical and public health purposes. See Sarah E. Gollust, Kira Apse, Barbara P. Fuller, Paul Steven Miller, and Barbara B. Biesecker, Community Involvement in Developing Policies for Genetic Testing: Assessing the Interests and Experiences of Individuals Affected by Genetic Conditions, 95 Am. J. Public Health 35–41 (2005).

5. A 2005 study of the children of Alzheimer's patients who underwent genetic testing for a genetic mutation, ApoE4, associated with a higher risk of developing Alzheimer's disease, found that persons whose test results were positive had no increase in anxiety or depression compared with those whose test results were negative. The study was part of a large-scale series of investigations known as REVEAL (Risk Evaluation and Education for Alzheimer's Disease). See http://www.alz.org/preventionconference/pc2005/062005genesTesting.asp.

TAMAR LEWIN, BOOM IN GENETIC TESTING RAISES QUESTIONS ON SHARING RESULTS

The New York Times, July 21, 2000, at A1.

As genetic testing becomes increasingly common, those who choose to learn their genetic risks, and the health professionals who treat them, are facing difficult decisions about how—and whether—to share the results with family members who share their genes.

And the new genetic information is creating new kinds of rifts, when one family member finds out what another family member does not want to know, or when family members react differently to the same knowledge.

"One woman who'd had ovarian cancer was tested for the breast cancer gene mutations mostly for the sake of her two adult daughters," said Katherine Schneider, senior genetics counselor at the Dana Farber Cancer Institute in Boston. "But when she told them she had it, they were so devastated that they didn't talk with her for two years. They didn't want to know."

"I tell that story a lot. There's nothing easy about any of this. But before testing, it's important to talk not only about what the information will mean for you, but what it might mean to your sisters, your children, your cousins."

Genetic tests are now commonplace, what with prenatal tests diagnosing hundreds of syndromes, midlife tests for mutations linked to breast and ovarian cancer, and—with the human genome newly mapped—more and more familial disorders.

The scientific advances have created debate about public policy on genetic discrimination. But the private effects on family dynamics are just as complex, as patients and health professionals adjust to thinking about family not just as flesh and blood, but flesh and blood and genes.

Usually, patients are happy to share health information with family members for whom it may be important, often asking the doctor or genetic counselor for a written explanation to pass along.

But when patients want to keep the information to themselves, health professionals may encounter situations that mix social problem and soap opera, and be ethically and legally pulled into uncharted waters.

A young man in Washington State called his genetics counselor to confess a guilty conscience: Several months earlier, he told her, he had made a sperm donation. And while he knew his test results had shown that he had an inheritable syndrome that causes heart trouble and, often, early death, he did not mention it to the sperm bank. Troubled, the counselor called the sperm bank and found that there had, indeed, been successful pregnancies with the man's sperm. She offered to counsel those families but does not know whether the sperm bank even passed on the information.

In a New York family with three adult daughters, the two married daughters know that their mother, who had breast cancer as a young woman, has been tested and found to carry a gene mutation associated with a high risk of breast and ovarian cancer. The mother has forbidden them to tell their unmarried sister, who has always felt herself to be the least attractive, for fear that it might make her less marriageable. They have obeyed, but want the family doctor to make sure she has frequent mammograms and screenings.

Two sisters who know their mother had genetic testing before she died of ovarian cancer want to find out her test results. But the Pennsylvania medical center that did the testing will not release the results to the young women without the consent of their stepfather, who has a dismal relationship with them. The sisters could, of course, have had their own genetic tests, but they had hoped by learning more about their family's history to avoid the process. The center's ethics committee is now revising its consent forms to require all patients tested to specify which family members should have access to the results after their death.

* * *

Often, the decision to pass on information is a delicate one, depending not only on such factors as the relatives' closeness, ages and emotional health, but also the nature of the disease and the severity of the risk. Where there is no treatment, or the risk is small, the case for sharing painful knowledge becomes less compelling. And the need to share information may be temporary, experts say, as the era approaches when complete genetic profiles become a routine part of individual health records. Meanwhile, the cost of testing even a single gene can run from several hundred to several thousand dollars.

Still, Josephine Wagner Costalas, a genetic counselor at Fox Chase Cancer Center in Philadelphia, has an unspoken worry whenever she counsels a patient who has tested positive for the breast cancer gene mutations.

"My worst nightmare is the scenario where I might have a patient who tests positive and doesn't tell her relatives," Ms. Costalas said, "and a few years later her sister will discover she has metastatic cancer, with a bad prognosis, and she'll find out that there was this information showing she was at risk. And maybe she'll sue me, saying I should have picked up the phone and told her, 'Your sister's positive, you should get tested.' This is all so new, and there are no clear guidelines, so I worry."

Still, Ms. Costalas does not pressure her patients to share their results. "If people aren't sure about sharing the information, I ask them to think about what it would be like if the situation were reversed," she said. "Would they want to know? But I do believe patients need to decide for themselves what they want to do."

And when several family members come in together, there are other issues. "What if they have different results?" Ms. Costalas said. "Who do you tell first? What if they have different reactions?"

* * *

Two years ago, the American Society of Human Genetics adopted a position recognizing the conflict between the health professions' duty to maintain confidentiality and the duty to warn about serious health risks.

Health professionals should tell patients about potential genetic risks to their relatives, the statement said, and in some cases, they may be allowed to breach confidentiality to warn relatives at risk if the harm is "serious, imminent and likely" and prevention or treatment is available.

But there is little consensus on where to draw those lines. Generally, genetic counselors are more concerned about confidentiality and not pressuring patients, while physicians specializing in genetics are more concerned about the duty to warn, according to research by Dorothy C. Wertz, senior scientist at the Shriver Center in Waltham, Mass. As a practical matter, though, most health professionals cannot warn relatives.

"In the end it's up to the patient, because in real life, we don't have relatives' names and phone numbers," said Helen Hixon, a genetic counselor in cardiology at Cedars Sinai hospital in Los Angeles. "We do tell people pretty strongly that they should warn their relatives, that they may have a legal duty to do so."

SARA TAUB, KARINE MORIN, MONIQUE A. SPILLMAN, ROBERT M. SADE, AND FRANK A. RIDDICK, FOR THE COUNCIL ON ETHICAL AND JUDICIAL AFFAIRS OF THE AMERICAN MEDICAL ASSOCIATION, MANAGING FAMILIAL RISK IN GENETIC TESTING

8 Genetic Testing 356–359 (2004).

INTRODUCTION

In the past, genetic information has been sought primarily in the context of reproductive counseling. It is now being sought by individuals who wish to learn whether they have a predisposition to an adult onset genetic condition. At the same time, increased exposure to health information in general, through the media and especially through the Internet, has heightened public attention to medical disorders, including genetic conditions. Consequently, more people are obtaining individual genetic information that, unlike other medical information, directly concerns not only the tested individuals (proband), but their biological relatives (kindred) as well. This familial aspect poses new ethical quandaries for physicians by challenging the limits of medical confidentiality.

According to many commentators. the role of genetic testing in medicine has not fundamentally changed the responsibility of physicians to respect patient autonomy and act in their patients' best interests. However, according to others, it has raised new questions regarding physicians' responsibilities when an individual patient's genetic information reveals serious information that could be directly relevant to kindred's health.

In this report, we examine the informed consent process in the specific context of genetic testing; other aspects of medical genetics such as gene therapy fall outside the scope of this report. We consider whether there are circumstances in which the familial quality of genetic information justifies the compromise of physicians' duty of confidentiality, which is central to the patient physician relationship. We also address how physicians should handle patients' genetic information when it could be relevant to their biological relatives.

GENETIC INFORMATION AND CONFIDENTIALITY

In general, American Medical Association (AMA) ethics policy includes and is derived from principles that recognize physicians' duty to safeguard the confidences of their patients (Principle IV) to whom their responsibilities are paramount (Principle VIII). Physicians have a general duty to treat information acquired from the patient in the context of the patient physician relationship as confidential. As stated in Opinion 5.05, "Confidentiality," "the physician should not reveal confidential communications or information without the express consent of the patient, unless required to do so by the law".

In the medical ethics literature, there is a spectrum of opinions about the stringency of confidentiality regarding genetic information. At one end of the spectrum, commentators focus on the sensitivity of genetic information and call for more stringent confidentiality measures to protect it. Genetic testing has the potential to reveal medical risks to an individual. Such risks usually are highly uncertain because of uneven scientific validity and reliability of genetic testing findings, variable penetrance of genes, and absence of recognized interventions for some identified predispositions. Regardless of whether genetic information signals risks that are likely to materialize into an illness or disability, such information may warrant special protection for fear of discrimination and stigmatization.

Commentators at the opposite end of the confidentiality spectrum focus on the nonindividualistic or biological cohort ownership of genetic information and question the practice of asking physicians to withhold this information from potentially affected kindred. Some of these commentators would argue that the familial quality of genetic information requires extending the obligation of physicians beyond the patient, to the wider circle of immediate biological relatives. The rationale behind this position is that when a physician's knowledge of information pertains as much to the family as to the patient, a professional obligation is created that extends to other affected parties, especially when the physician already has a professional relationship with the patient's biological relatives. Under this view, confidentiality's basis in the claim of individual privacy is significantly compromised in the family context, where the information is at once individual and familial (Safer v. Estate of Pack, 1996). Beyond the circle of affected relatives, however, the physician's obligation toward the confidentiality of patient information is considered to remain unchanged.

Finally, an intermediate perspective exists among those who reject genetic exceptionalism. The limits of confidentiality are no more and no less stringent than those that already exist for other kinds of medical information. As such, confidentiality is near absolute: Physicians have a duty to maintain the confidentiality of genetic information about a patient, save "certain exceptions which are ethically and legally justified because of overriding social considerations".

Informed consent

Genetic information poses some special challenges, due to its inherited, and therefore shared, nature. Challenges can arise when the need to maintain an individual patient's confidentiality and autonomy conflicts with an obligation to inform kindred of information that may be directly relevant to their health. The pretesting period offers health care professionals the opportunity to educate and counsel their patients in an effort to prepare for test results, including findings that could have significant implications for biological relatives.

Before they can arrive at a voluntary, informed decision about whether to undergo genetic testing, individuals need to receive information regarding the overall risks and benefits associated with the procedure, including potential implications of test results for them and immediate biological relatives. Patients need to understand why relatives may have a substantial interest in this information, as it may influence relatives' decisions to seek treatment, reproductive decisions, or lifestyle choices. Patients also need to understand that some relatives may prefer not to know whether they are affected by a genetic condition, for reasons such as fear of social stigmatization, loss of insurance, or work related discrimination.

Once individuals understand the consequences for themselves and for others of obtaining genetic test results, they can address another important step of the pretesting phase. Guided by a professional with special genetic expertise, they can begin to contemplate, before any information is uncovered, whether to invite biological family members to participate in the testing process directly by undergoing testing, or indirectly by sharing in the findings.

For individuals who are comfortable with notifying immediate biological relatives that they intend to undergo genetic testing, the pretesting period is an opportune time to communicate their intention to family members. Genetic specialists can help patients inform their relatives by providing them with educational materials aimed at lay audiences and by offering themselves or another appropriate person as a resource to discuss opportunities for counseling and testing.

Just as families can benefit from discussing advance care planning or other health care matters before there is reason for concern, so they can benefit from exploring considerations that surround genetic testing to clarify an individual's preferences prior to obtaining test results. Relatives' early involvement provides ample time to offer family members genetic counseling to help them make informed decisions about whether they would like to share in the findings once they become available.

Knowing their preferences at this stage will shield physicians and patients from the awkward situation of trying to determine whether to involve family members after important information has been uncovered. It will also help prevent the unfortunate circumstance in which results for which kindred are unprepared are accidentally communicated to them by the proband before the relatives can receive counseling or arrive at an informed decision about the willingness to share in the results. Physicians cannot predict how individuals will react to genetic information, but they have the ability and the responsibility to encourage people to seek appropriate counseling to prepare them to receive results from testing.

Some individuals will opt not to tell their immediate biological relatives that they are contemplating testing. Even when this is clear from the start, there are still benefits to discussing the possibility of discovering familial genetic risk before the testing is done. Physicians can help their patients reach a decision about what they will do with information that could be important to immediate biological relatives, and, if they should decide to share genetic information with affected relatives, to encourage family members to seek genetic counseling before receiving the information. Whether genetic information is reassuring, neutral, or alarming, relatives may not want to know it, but if they do, they deserve to be prepared.

Finally, addressing the implications to biological relatives of genetic information gives professionals an opportunity to identify circumstances under which they would expect patients to notify biological relatives of the availability of information related to risk of disease. The use of what one bioethics scholar coined the "genetic Miranda warning" gives the patient the opportunity to decline testing from a physician whose conditions seem unacceptable.

An adequate informed consent is likely to avert most situations that could conflict the physician between the competing obligations to respect the patient's confidentiality and to warn third parties of potential harm. When patients and physicians discuss the patient's intended uses of genetic information during the pretesting phase, they will almost certainly identify any fundamental disagreements regarding the circumstances in which the physician would expect the patient to notify kindred that information related to risk for disease was available. Referral of the patient to another health professional might be indicated if such differences weaken the patient physician relationship.

Disclosure of familial risk

After testing has occurred, there may be instances in which, despite a satisfactory informed consent process, patient and physician find themselves at odds regarding who should share in the information revealed by test results. Physicians should make themselves available to assist patients in communicating with relatives to discuss opportunities for counseling and testing. In breaching patient confidentiality against the patient's will, the physician would be giving more weight to the health interests of a third party than to the patient's interest, thus compromising a core constituent of the patient physician relationship. The American Society of Human Genetics (ASHG), in Professional Disclosure of' Familial Genetic Information, warns that social, psychological, and financial harms as well as discrimination and stigmatization can accompany genetic findings. Failure to disclose to a patient's affected family members the availability of genetic testing results can also lead to harm, particularly when knowledge could result in avoidance, treatment, or prevention of a genetic condition or in significant changes to reproductive choices or lifestyle.

ASHG guidelines for familial disclosure are related to the magnitude of harm that may be incurred. Accordingly:

> Disclosure should be permissible where: attempts to encourage disclosure on the part of the patient have failed; the harm is highly likely to occur and is serious, imminent, and foreseeable; the at risk relative(s) is identifiable; and the disease is preventable, treatable, or medically accepted standards indicate that early monitoring will reduce the genetic risk. * * * The harm from failing to disclose should outweigh the harm from disclosure (American Society of Human Genetics, 1998).

The standard these guidelines establish with their requirement that harm be likely to occur, serious, imminent, and foreseeable is so stringent that it may only exist as a theoretical requirement that is unlikely to be met in practice. Indeed, in light of what is known of human genetics, no genetic test currently can result in the diagnosis of a condition with a high likelihood of causing imminent harm. For practical purposes, then, the ASHG's guidelines would not allow a physician to breach patient confidentiality by notifying immediate biological relatives of genetic information that might impact their health. On balance, the guidelines suggest that the harm potentially caused by the disclosure of information to relatives exceeds the harm potentially caused by withholding such information.

The President's Commission for the Study of Ethical Problems in Medicine and Biomedical and Behavioral Research (1983) arrived at similar, but more measured, conclusions when it stated that disclosure without the patient's consent is only justified if:

> 1. Reasonable efforts to elicit voluntary consent to disclosure have failed;

> 2. there is a high probability both that harm will occur if the information is withheld and that the disclosed information will actually be used to avert harm;

> 3. the harm the identifiable individuals would suffer would be serious; and

> 4. appropriate precautions are taken to ensure that only the genetic information needed for diagnosis and/or treatment of the disease in question is disclosed.

The Commission's conclusions were less stringent than the ASHG's in that they did not require the harm from withholding information to be imminent. Still, the requirements they established, especially those included in item 2, would justify breach of confidentiality only in very rare circumstances.

QUESTIONS

What legitimate interests do family members have in the results of an individual's genetic testing? What is the proper way to satisfy these interests? What is the obligation of clinicians—primary care physicians, geneticists, genetic counselors, and so on—toward family members?

B. UNANTICIPATED MISATTRIBUTED PATERNITY

Genetic testing can be used intentionally to establish whether a man is the biological father of a child. This is discussed more fully in Chapter 10. However, genetic tests for therapeutic purposes sometimes reveal that the presumed father of a child is not the biological father. Since the purpose of the test was to aid in the diagnosis or treatment of the child, rather than to establish biological parenthood, this finding is termed "unanticipated non-paternity" or misattributed paternity. Health care professionals providing the testing face difficult questions about what to do with this information.

JEAN MCEWEN, GENETIC INFORMATION, ETHICS, AND INFORMATION RELATING TO BIOLOGICAL PARENTHOOD

1 Encyclopedia of Ethical, Legal, and Policy Issues in Biotechnology 356, 359–62 (Thomas H. Murray & Maxwell J. Mehlman eds. 2000).

GENETIC DETERMINATION OF PARENTAGE AS A CONSEQUENCE OF GENETIC TESTING FOR NONIDENTIFICATION PURPOSES: FINDINGS OF MISATTRIBUTED PATERNITY

While genetic testing in the forensics context is the common way in which information regarding biological parentage or other familial relationships is brought to light, such information can also be uncovered inadvertently in the course of genetic testing undertaken for completely unrelated purposes, such as in clinical medicine. The common incidental finding that occurs in the context of nonforensic genetic testing is the finding of misattributed paternity (or sometimes grand-paternity). The true incidence of misattributed paternity is unknown, and undoubtedly varies widely depending on geographical region, age group, and cultural or ethnic group, among other factors. However, 10 percent is the figure most commonly cited, and estimates as high as 30 percent have been proposed. While more recent studies suggest that both of these figures may be substantial exaggerations, the accumulated experience of large-scale genetic screening programs (e.g., newborn screening programs) shows that the aggregate number of children born each year whose paternity is misattributed is by no means insignificant.

The incidental finding that the presumed father of a child is not the biological father can arise in a number of situations, such as when several family members are being tested to locate a suitable donor for a bone marrow or organ transplant, to take part in genetic linkage testing, or to participate in other types of genetic risk assessment that require samples from multiple family members. In cases where testing for bone marrow or donor organ compatibility yields evidence of misattributed paternity, it is often possible to communicate the fact that the individual tested and the intended recipient (e.g., two half-siblings) would not be a good match without mentioning anything about misconceptions regarding the degree of their biological relatedness. This is because it is easy to explain the *fact* of a mismatch without going into the apparent *reason* for the mismatch; there may be many reasons other than misattributed paternity why two people might not be suitably matched for transplantation purposes. The nondisclosure approach in the transplantation situation can also probably be justified ethically and legally because at least in most cases the nondisclosure is unlikely to have any direct, potentially adverse, effect on the parties' future personal medical or reproductive decision making.

On the other hand, when a finding of misattributed paternity surfaces in the context of genetic risk assessment, the stakes are higher because genetic risk estimates are based on the assumption that the biological relationships assumed to exist within a family are correct. A person's misunderstanding about his or her biological relationship to other family members can confound the clinical determination of whether he or she is at increased risk for an inherited disorder or for passing on an inherited disorder-with crucial ramifications for health and reproductive planning.

A common situation regarding misattributed paternity occurs when genetic testing is sought to determine recurrence risk following the birth of a child affected with an autosomal recessive genetic disorder, for which both parents must be obligate carriers. In some cases the woman may already suspect that another man fathered her child, and may thus seek out counseling on her own without involving her husband or partner. However, where the woman does not realize (or is in denial of the possibility that) the child has a different father, the entire family may become involved. If carrier testing in such a case reveals the presumed father not to be a carrier, this means that he cannot be the biological father. The genetic counselor or other provider then faces a dilemma: how to convey to the couple the reason *why* they are not at increased genetic risk for bearing another affected child without simultaneously disclosing the fact that the child they already have must have been fathered by someone other than the husband (or other presumed father).

Reconciling the competing interests in cases like these can be very difficult, and no one strategy for resolving the issue is likely to be entirely satisfactory. In fact international surveys of genetic service providers performed as recently as the 1990s revealed a marked lack of consensus regarding the appropriate resolution of this dilemma, even though it is one that genetics professionals have been wrestling with for years.

ALTERNATIVE APPROACHES TO HANDLING FINDINGS OF MISATTRIBUTED PATERNITY

Full Disclosure. One approach to the problem of misattributed paternity—the approach recommended in 1983 by the President's Commission for the Study of Ethical Problems in Medicine and Medical and Behavioral Research—is for the genetic counselor or other provider frankly to disclose the finding, including the conclusion that the recurrence risk in any future pregnancy of the couple is virtually zero because the existing affected child is not biologically the husband's. This approach accords maximal weight to the principles of autonomy and beneficence. It also reflects the practical consideration that deception regarding a child's paternity is likely eventually to be discovered in any event, and that in the long run, greater disruption to the family may result from this than from the frank revelation of misattributed paternity made when the information first surfaces in the clinical setting.

However, this approach has been criticized (at least in many cases) as placing form over substance, giving insufficient allegiance to the integrity of the family unit, and naive in its failure to recognize that many women—especially those who are in abusive relationships or who are economically disempowered—may suffer tangible detriment, in the form of physical, psychological, social, or economic harm, from the disclosure to their husbands or partners of misattributed paternity. In fact, in some cultures, the social environment may be such that an almost certain consequence of such a revelation would be clear harm to both the woman and the child. Indeed, it was this concern that led the Hereditary Diseases Programme of the World Health Organization to conclude that there is probably never a justification for a provider to reveal such a finding to a husband. Thus, at the very least, in cases where a decision is made to reveal information regarding misattributed paternity to both partners simultaneously, the provider should be prepared to offer appropriate psychological and other support.

Nondisclosure, Partial Disclosure, or Disclosure Only to the Woman. Another possible approach to dealing with findings of misattributed paternity is either to misrepresent the finding (or the basis for the finding) or skirt the issue in some other way, either through some form of partial disclosure or by telling the woman alone. The justification for this approach is that the genetic counselor owes greater loyalty to the integrity of the family unit than to any one family member, and that for the reasons mentioned above, revealing the complete truth simultaneously to both the husband and wife could do more harm than good.

An approach that misrepresents the facts, however, is also problematic, both from an ethical and a legal standpoint. First, to the extent that overt deception is involved (e.g., explaining away the child's disorder, and thus the reason for the lack of recurrence risk, as merely a spontaneous mutation or some other anomaly, or explaining away the test results as having been confounded by a mix-up in the testing laboratory), it risks jeopardizing the provider's professional integrity and lowers the standards of practice. Moreover, if the explanations given are viewed by the couple as implausible, the approach is likely to engender suspicion and mistrust. In fact, should the deception eventually be discovered, the provider could conceivably be liable for medical malpractice.

A particularly risky practice from the standpoint of legal liability is for the provider to lie outright if asked by the husband whether he is in fact the biological father. Nevertheless, surveys indicate that many providers follow this approach, sometimes justifying it on the basis that because the genetic testing is not being done for the purpose of discovering paternity, they have no obligation to reveal the finding, even when asked. In fact two-thirds of all United States geneticists in one survey stated that they would not tell a man that he is not the father of a child, even if he asked. On the one hand, in cases where a genuine and serious risk of harm to the woman or to the family appears likely if the information were to be disclosed, this approach may have considerable justification. On the other hand, as earlier discussed, it can be argued that making a genetic counselor complicit in the woman's intentional deception is always unethical, that secrets of this type are in any event unlikely to remain buried forever, and that when the truth does come out, the well-being of the woman and the family may be even more seriously jeopardized than if the deception had never been perpetuated in the first place.

A form of partial disclosure that may be less risky legally but that still raises significant ethical concerns is simply to avoid any discussion of the specifics regarding actual recurrence risk (e.g., by characterizing the results as inconclusive), thus obviating the need to discuss the husband's noncarrier status. This approach, however, may lead the couple to make inappropriate future reproductive decisions based on the erroneous belief that they are both in fact carriers (and thus have a 25 percent chance of having another affected child), when the actual risk is close to zero. Based on this inaccurate assumption, the couple may later resort unnecessarily to artificial insemination by donor, forgo future pregnancies altogether, or even divorce and seek new noncarrier mates. If they do decide to conceive another child together based on the misapprehension that such a child is at increased genetic risk, they may suffer needless anxiety and incur needless risk and expense associated with amniocentesis or other prenatal testing that is not in fact medically indicated.

Another approach is to convey to the couple the actual risk (close to zero, in the example discussed) while withholding the information about genetic transmission that would explain the reason for the risk and raise suspicions regarding non-paternity (the fact that in order for a child to be born with an autosomal recessive disorder, both parents must carry the gene). This approach, however, may leave the couple feeling anxious and confused and lead them to suspect that something important is being withheld.

Yet another approach is to relate the finding only to the woman (who is likely in many cases to suspect anyway that another man fathered her child) and leave with her the choice as to whether or how to tell her husband or partner. This approach—the approach recommended by the Institute of Medicine's Committee on Assessing Genetic Risks in its 1994 report—avoids the above described difficulties that may arise when such a finding is revealed by an outsider, and at the same time, requires no overt misrepresentation or skirting of the issues in the provider's conversations with the couple. However, the approach seems difficult to reconcile with the notion that the ethical and legal obligations of genetic counselors run equally to both partners. Thus, if this approach is followed, the potential psychological benefits of disclosure, including relief from the burden of keeping a secret and greater honesty in family relationships, should be stressed with the woman. However, the potential for adverse consequences should also be raised, and once again, the provider should stand ready to provide other necessary support.

Informed Consent Approach. An emerging approach to dealing with unexpected findings of misattributed paternity is to try to avoid many of the above-described problems by addressing the issue before the testing takes place, as part of the informed consent process. Under this approach the woman (or in some cases, both partners) are informed, prior to taking the test, of the possibility that misattributed paternity will be discovered. The woman (or the couple) can then (at least in theory) agree *in advance* on the way such information, if discovered, will be handled. This approach has the advantage of making the persons most likely to be affected active participants in any decision about disclosure. However, it too has limitations, due the practical realities of the context in which genetic testing typically occurs. The very inclusion of the subject of paternity among the subjects treated in an informed consent document may provoke anxiety, and where the woman is aware that misattributed paternity may be an issue, she may well "panic" in the situation, having never seriously thought before about the ramifications of that possibility. Even if the pre-test counseling is done separately, the woman may feel confused about how to now "get out" of a test she had previously seemed to agree to (before the possibility was called to her attention). In the end this approach could discourage some women who would like to obtain genetic information from participating in genetic testing-perhaps, in some cases, to the future detriment of themselves and their families.

Some genetic testing centers include in their standard informed consent form a reference to the possibility of an incidental finding of misattributed paternity, but simply state what the center's policy is regarding the communication of such findings without giving the woman (or the couple) an opportunity to communicate her (or their) preference in this regard. This approach is problematic for many of the same reasons. In addition it is based on the (typically erroneous) assumption that a couple who is uncomfortable with a center's policy can simply "go elsewhere" for testing. Testing for some genetic disorders (particularly those that are relatively rare) may, as a practical matter, only be available at a single location. Insurance and other practical constraints may also limit a couple's ability to "shop around" for a center with a more favorable disclosure policy.

QUESTIONS

1. Which of the approaches described by McEwen is the best and why?

2. Can intentional nondisclosure or misrepresentation of paternity ever be justified?

II. ACCESS TO GENETIC SERVICES

A. ECONOMIC ISSUES

Genetic testing for therapeutic purposes can provide valuable information to aid in the diagnosis and treatment of genetic disease. As with any new medical technology, however, it may not be readily accessible to the public. A number of factors may limit access. The person may not know he or she is ill or at risk, and not seek professional services. Alternatively, the individual's primary care physician may not be familiar with the genetic basis of the condition in question; as noted earlier in this chapter in the excerpt from the 1997 Report of the Task Force on Genetic Testing, many physicians are not adequately informed about genetics or genetic testing. As a result, the primary care physician may not suggest testing to the patient, or refer the patient to a clinical geneticist or genetic counselor for additional information. Even if the patient is aware of the possibility of testing, health care professionals for ethical reasons may decline to provide testing. As discussed in Chapter 7, for example, many health care professionals reject parental requests for certain types of predictive testing for children.

As discussed in Chapters 15 and 16, even if health care professionals recommend testing, individuals may decline because of fears of discrimination.

Finally, genetic testing may not be covered by the person's health insurance, and depending on how expensive it is, the person may not be able to afford to pay for it out-of-pocket. Some genetic tests can be obtained for little more than $100 (for hereditary hemochromatosis at some laboratories, with free genetic counseling). But other tests, together with counseling, cost several thousand dollars.

MAXWELL J. MEHLMAN, ACCESS TO THE GENOME AND FEDERAL ENTITLEMENT PROGRAMS, IN THE HUMAN GENOME PROJECT AND THE FUTURE OF HEALTH CARE

119–123 (Thomas H. Murray et al. eds. 1997).

TRENDS IN ACCESS

To predict how FEPs [federal entitlement programs] are likely to cope with the demand for genetic services that will result from the HGP [Human Genome Project], we can examine how these programs are reacting to pressures to increase access, on the one hand, and to reduce health care spending on the other.

One way or another, limits on access due to the inability to meet eligibility criteria are bound to disappear. Whether the approach that eventually is taken will be to expand eligibility under the FEPs themselves, or to create new governmental entitlement programs, or to mandate that individuals be covered under private insurance, is unclear. * * *

At the same time that it faces pressures to expand eligibility, however, the government also is being called upon to reduce national health care expenditures. The movement to expand third-party payment programs removes a common method of reducing spending: limiting access by restricting eligibility. To stem budget increases, for example, state Medicaid programs traditionally have lowered income thresholds in order to exclude persons who would otherwise be eligible. Prior to the increase in eligibility to cover all persons with incomes below the federal poverty level, or FPL, for example, the Oregon Medicaid program only provided benefits to persons who qualified for AFDC [Aid to Families with Dependent Children] if their incomes fell below 58 percent of the FPL.

Even if the federal government mandates universal health insurance, it might impose eligibility restrictions under future FEPs. For example, if Medicare and Medicaid were retained and government-subsidized private health insurance were provided for those who were not covered by FEPs or insured by their employers, a means test might be added to the eligibility criteria for Medicare, with those persons over 65 who had incomes or assets above the means threshold relegated to purchasing private insurance with their own funds. So long as the nation remained committed to providing universal access to health care, however, this would merely shift costs from government to private programs rather than lowering overall spending. Therefore, the government will need to pursue other methods in order to curtail health care costs.

Undoubtedly; the federal government will attempt to reduce prices for health care, and it will be aided in doing so by the increased leverage it will have as a result of the expansion of eligibility under government programs. However, price controls alone are unlikely to be able to curtail spending in the face of increased demand for services, particularly for genetic services stemming from the HGP. The government will continue to feel strong pressure to restrict access to health care generally, and to new, expensive genetic services in particular. Having lost the ability to restrict access by limiting eligibility, the government will be left instead with the options of co-payment, and restrictions on coverage and/or availability.

Maintaining or increasing the amounts that individuals pay for health care under government programs might be one way of limiting access to the genetic services that will emerge from the HGP. Those persons who could not afford the co-payments would not receive services, even though they were technically "eligible" for benefits. Medicare in particular has increased co-payments as a means to help control program costs. * * * Furthermore, the most recent effort to *reduce* co-payments under Medicare—the Medicare Catastrophic Coverage Act—failed miserably when Congress repealed the law under pressure from those elderly persons who would have footed the bill.

Co-payments represent fairly obvious limitations on access, however. In a nation committed to universal access, they are likely to be increasingly unacceptable as a cost-containment approach.

The same is true of overt restrictions on availability, or supply, particularly those that affect specific geographic areas or minority populations. For example, the government is likely to be under political pressure to increase the number of physicians and facilities for rural and inner-city residents. Yet shortages are likely to be an inevitable result of efforts to control costs, particularly if prices for health care are forced down substantially. Hospitals may be unwilling to purchase new technologies if their revenues are reduced, and health care professionals may refuse to treat patients who cannot supplement third-party reimbursement from their own resources. The government might try to force unwilling providers to treat patients, but it is unclear if it could do so successfully; or what the effect would be, for example, on the number of physicians entering or remaining in the market.

Furthermore, the government may be tempted to foster shortages deliberately as a method to contain costs, particularly if it can rationalize its behavior as something other than overt rationing. For example, the government might assert that it was merely encouraging "regionalization" or volume-based "centers of excellence" for certain high-technology services. This technique appears to be employed by national health systems such as Canada's, for example, where widespread queuing, at least for elective services, is reported. Whether deliberate or not, therefore, limitations on access as a result of the unavailability of services are likely to persist.

The final approach to limiting access is to restrict coverage. Faced with budget shortfalls, the government might well insist that it is unable to provide access under FEPs to specific services, particularly to the new, cost-increasing technologies emerging from the HGP.

While Medicare law precludes coverage for certain categories of services such as dental, eye, and nursing home care, as noted earlier, the Medicare program historically has defined the scope of covered services very broadly: The law itself stipulates that, with the exception of the categorical exclusions, beneficiaries are entitled to all items and services that are "reasonable and necessary for the diagnosis or treatment of illness or injury or to improve the functioning of a malformed body part." This has been interpreted to preclude the government from refusing to pay for care on the ground that it is too expensive. In 1989 the Health Care Financing Administration (HCFA) proposed to allow Medicare to refuse to cover a technology if it was not "cost effective"—that is, if it yielded no greater net benefit than a cheaper alternative. This proposal has triggered intense opposition, and was never finalized. In any-event, such a regulation would have little impact on new, cost-increasing technologies for which there were no alternatives, which is likely to be characteristic of many genetic services emerging from the HGP.

As a result of the scope of coverage embodied in the statutory language, it has been difficult for the government to limit coverage of specific technologies under Medicare in order to achieve cost savings. The government has had some success in controlling cost by limiting the amount of time patients can remain in the hospital. * * * Restrictions on length of stay alone do not discourage access to specific technologies, however, and would be of little use in restricting access to new genetic services.

The primary method by which the government has limited access to new technologies under Medicare has been to deem them "experimental." For many years, for example, Medicare refused to pay for heart transplants on the ground that their safety and efficacy had not been adequately demonstrated, and that therefore they had not been shown to be "reasonable and necessary." Medicare finally agreed to cover the transplants in 1979, but only if they were performed at the Stanford Medical Center. This policy lasted only nine months, at which time the HCFA revoked Stanford's authorization on the basis that the government lacked adequate data on the success and long-term implications of transplant technology. It was not until 1990 that Medicare once again agreed to reimburse for heart transplants, but then only under strict criteria limiting both the hospitals that could perform the procedure and the patients who could be selected.

The technologies emerging from the HGP initially will be experimental, and it will be some time before Medicare can be expected to reimburse providers for them. How much time it will take will depend on the significance of the expected benefit from the technology; the ratio of benefits to risks, and the degree of demand from both patients and health care professionals. Recent experience with AIDS drugs suggests that the government can be forced to accelerate the transition from experimental to therapeutic (and reimbursable) status given enough public clamor. This is likely to be the pattern for genetic services that promise to prevent or ameliorate serious genetic disorders.

Even after the safety and efficacy of a technology has been demonstrated, the government may delay paying for it on the basis that it remains experimental when the real reason is to hold down costs. For example, it is widely believed that the government has continued to maintain that heart transplants and certain other new technologies are experimental in large part in order to contain program costs. The government might be expected to resist paying for expensive, new genetic services under Medicare for the same reason.

Coverage restrictions under Medicare that limited access to genetic services on the basis of cost are not likely to survive for long, however. The elder lobby is too powerful, and its political power is growing as the population continues to age. Coincidentally, the post-World War II baby boom generation will become eligible for Medicare at approximately the same time that the HGP is expected to be completed. Even if younger voters somehow acquired the ability to thwart the interests of the elderly, they may be unwilling to restrict access to services that they may someday need themselves.

In contrast to Medicare, the Medicaid program is much more likely to restrict coverage of expensive, new technologies. A trend in this direction already is apparent. Until 1988 federal law required state Medicaid programs to provide liver transplants in order to receive federal matching funds. Coverage for these procedures became optional in 1988, and many states have since refused to reimburse for them. The Oregon demonstration project is even more far-ranging. * * * It has created a list of health services ranked on the basis of importance, and denies coverage for all services below an arbitrary cutoff chosen by the state legislature on the basis of budgetary constraints.

* * *

Several factors explain why the trend for Medicaid is so different from Medicare. First, the law underlying the Medicaid program is less clear-cut than the Medicare statute in terms of what services must be provided. There is no statutory language for Medicaid comparable to the "reasonable and necessary" standard under Medicare. Although courts generally have engrafted the Medicare standard onto Medicaid, they have shown some willingness to allow states to deny coverage for services because of their cost.

A second reason that Medicaid is likely to restrict overage is the growth of the program as a proportion of state budgets. * * * State budgetary woes have convinced the middle class that the only alternative to increasing taxes is to decrease the scope of benefits provided under Medicaid and other programs for the poor.

In contrast to the growing political dominance of elder Americans, the political power of the poor is weak. While everyone eventually hopes to be eligible for Medicare, most middle-and upper-class taxpayers never expect to be eligible for Medicaid, and therefore have no incentive to retain a generous coverage policy many consider to be contrary to their own self-interest.

Finally, coverage restrictions under Medicaid have been rationalized on the basis that they forestall cuts in eligibility. As noted earlier, the customary method for trimming Medicaid budgets has been to disqualify individuals from being entitled to any benefits, such as by lowering income thresholds. Limited coverage would seem preferable to none at all. Going a step farther, the Oregon project has justified its coverage limits on the basis that they allow the state to *expand* Medicaid eligibility, and to provide benefits, albeit incomplete, to all persons whose incomes are below the federal poverty level.

In summary, if current trends continue eligibility under FEPs is likely to increase, with more individuals entitled to receive benefits. To hold down costs, the government may try to increase the proportion that individuals must pay for their own care, and to promote "health planning" measures that limit the availability of services in certain geographic areas, but these efforts will be constrained by political pressures aimed at assuring access to some level of health care for all citizens. The most promising approach for limiting health care spending at the same time that eligibility restrictions are relaxed is to deny coverage under FEPs for certain technologies, particularly those that are new and expensive, and particularly for politically weak patient populations such as the poor.

MARK A. ROTHSTEIN & SHARONA HOFFMAN, GENETIC TESTING, GENETIC MEDICINE, AND MANAGED CARE

34 Wake Forest L. Rev. 849, 875–876 (1999).

Managed care organizations vary widely in their coverage and provision of genetic tests. According to a 1997 survey, of 197 responding HMOs, 45% covered predictive tests for breast cancer. In addition, 42% covered tests for colon cancer for some of their subscribers.

Managed care organizations first must decide whether a particular genetic test should be offered at all to their patient population and then whether it is appropriate for any particular individual. On June 29, 1998, the Secretary's Advisory Committee on Genetic Testing was established. The committee, with an initial term of two years, will advise the Secretary of Health and Human Services regarding all aspects of incorporating genetic testing into the health care system and surely will address questions relating to managed care. In addition, the Task Force on Genetic Information and Insurance issued a report in 1993, and several other groups continue to develop position statements and policy recommendations regarding genetic testing and insurance coverage issues. Ultimately, a clear standard of care regarding the provision of genetic tests should be developed to guide managed care organizations and other medical providers.

A few general principles can be articulated. Managed care entities should not adopt a per se rule of refusing predictive testing in the absence of an effective intervention, because, at times, knowledge itself provides tremendous psychological comfort or invaluable opportunities for life planning in light of a known future. Individuals at-risk should neither be coerced into testing nor discouraged from undergoing appropriate genetic testing. Furthermore, genetic testing must be accompanied by suitable genetic counseling both before and after the testing. Currently, genetic counseling is often not covered by insurance and genetic counselors cannot bill separately for their services. Counseling, however, should be covered by the insurer to ensure its availability to all patients, regardless of their financial resources.

NOTES AND QUESTIONS

1. You are the medical director of a large health plan. What process should the plan use to decide whether to provide coverage of genetic testing? What criteria should it employ?

2. No federal or state laws currently mandate that health plans cover genetic testing. State legislatures have enacted so-called "state mandates" that require health plans to cover certain specific technologies, such as breast reconstruction after mastectomies, but none have been adopted so far for genetic testing technologies. In any event, due to the effect of the Employee Retirement Income Security Act (ERISA), these state laws do not affect employer self-insured health plans. Would it be appropriate for Congress to give states the power to impose state mandates for genetic testing? Would it be appropriate for Congress to enact a requirement that all health plans cover genetic testing?

3. In 1993, President Clinton proposed a comprehensive program of national health insurance. While his plan contained a number of provisions governing what services would be covered, there were few specific details of the extent of coverage for genetic testing. See generally, Maxwell J. Mehlman et al., Coverage of Genetic Technologies Under National Health Reform, 55 Am. J. Hum. Genet. 1054 (1994). President Obama is facing similar issues with the latest effort to reform health insurance.

4. In April 2005, the Secretary's Advisory Committee on Genetics, Health, and Society issued a draft report entitled "Coverage and Reimbursement of Genetic Tests and Services." Among its "potential" recommendations was that the Secretary of Health and Human Services should "task an appropriate group or body to develop a set of principles to guide coverage decision making for genetic tests."

5. For a further discussion of health insurance coverage, see Chapter 15.

6. In 2004, the National Human Genome Research Institute at NIH began funding an effort to reduce the cost of sequencing a mammalian genome from $5 or $10 million to $1,000. This became known as the "$1,000

genome project." In 2009, the institute reiterated its goal of achieving the 4–fold cost reduction by 2014. What would be the pros and cons of a state mandating or a health plan offering genome sequencing?

III. LIABILITY ISSUES

PATE v. THRELKEL

661 So.2d 278 (Fla.1995).

WELLS, J.

We have for review the following question certified to be of great public importance:

DOES A PHYSICIAN OWE A DUTY OF CARE TO THE CHILDREN OF A PATIENT TO WARN THE PATIENT OF THE GENETICALLY TRANSFERABLE NATURE OF THE CONDITION FOR WHICH THE PHYSICIAN IS TREATING THE PATIENT?

We have jurisdiction. Art. V, § 3(b)(4), Fla. Const. We answer the question in the affirmative provided the children of the patient first establish that pursuant to the prevailing standard of care set forth in section 766.102, Florida Statutes (1989), a reasonably prudent physician would give such warning to his or her patient in light of all relevant circumstances.

In March 1987, Marianne New received treatment for medullary thyroid carcinoma, a genetically transferable disease. In 1990, Heidi Pate, New's adult daughter, learned that she also had medullary thyroid carcinoma. Consequently, Pate and her husband filed a complaint against the physicians who initially treated New for the disease as well as the physicians' respective employers. Pate and her husband alleged that the physicians knew or should have known of the likelihood that New's children would have inherited the condition genetically; that the physicians were under a duty to warn New that her children should be tested for the disease; that had New been warned in 1987, she would have had her children tested at that time; and if Pate had been tested in 1987, she would have taken preventative action, and her condition, more likely than not, would have been curable. Pate claimed that as a direct and proximate cause of the physicians' negligence, she suffers from advanced medullary thyroid carcinoma and its various damaging effects.

The respondent health care providers moved to dismiss the complaint for failure to state a cause of action. Specifically, the respondents alleged that Pate did not demonstrate the existence of a professional relationship between her and respondents and thus failed to establish that respondents owed her a duty of care. The trial court granted the motion and dismissed the Pates' complaint with prejudice, finding that the plaintiffs were not patients of the respondents and that they did not fit within any exception to the requirement that there be a physician-patient relationship between the parties as a condition precedent to bringing a medical malpractice action.

The district court affirmed the trial court's dismissal. The court rejected the Pates' argument that it should, based upon past decisions recognizing a doctor's duty to inform others of a patient's contagious disease, extend a physician's duty to cover the child of a patient who suffers from an inheritable disease. The court also rejected the Pates' reliance on Schroeder v. Perkel, 432 A.2d 834 (N.J.1981), in which the parents of a four-year-old child brought suit against the child's pediatricians for failing to diagnose the child with cystic fibrosis early enough to prevent the parents from having a second diseased child. The New Jersey court in Schroeder recognized that due to the special nature of the family relationship, a physician's duty may extend beyond a patient to members of the patient's immediate family.

* * *

We conclude that to answer the certified question we must consider two questions related to duty. First, we must determine whether New's physicians had a duty to warn New of the genetically transferable nature of her disease. We find that to make this determination we must apply section 766.102, Florida Statutes (1989), which defines the legal duty owed by a health care provider in a medical malpractice case. That section provides in part:

> (1) In any action for recovery of damages based on the death or personal injury of any person in which it is alleged that such death or injury resulted from the negligence of a health care provider as defined in s. 768.50(2)(b), the claimant shall have the burden of proving by the greater weight of evidence that the alleged actions of the health care provider represented a breach of the prevailing professional standard of care for that health care provider. The prevailing professional standard of care for a given health care provider shall be that level of care, skill, and treatment which, in light of all relevant surrounding circumstances, is recognized as acceptable and appropriate by reasonably prudent similar health care providers.

§ 766.102, Fla. Stat. (1989). In applying this statute to the instant case, we conclude that a duty exists if the statutory standard of care requires a reasonably prudent health care provider to warn a patient of the genetically transferable nature of the condition for which the physician was treating the patient.

In medical malpractice cases, the standard of care is determined by a consideration of expert testimony. Because this case comes to us on appeal from an order granting the physicians' motion to dismiss, the record has yet to be developed in respect to such testimony. However, the court's dismissal requires us to assume that the factual allegations in the complaint are true. * * * Accordingly, we must accept as true the Pates' allegations that pursuant to the prevailing standard of care, the health care providers were under a duty to warn New of the importance of testing her children for medullary thyroid carcinoma. Whether these allegations are supported by the statutorily required expert medical authority will have to be determined as the action progresses. We do note, however, that the plaintiffs have pled good-faith compliance with section 766.104, Florida Statutes (1989).

The second question we must address in answering the certified question is to whom does the alleged duty to warn New of the nature of her disease run? The duty obviously runs to the patient who is in privity with the physician. * * * In other professional relationships, however, we have recognized the rights of identified third party beneficiaries to recover from a professional because that party was the intended beneficiary of the prevailing standard of care. In such cases, we have determined that an absence of privity does not necessarily foreclose liability.

* * *

Here, the alleged prevailing standard of care was obviously developed for the benefit of the patient's children as well as the patient. We conclude that when the prevailing standard of care creates a duty that is obviously for the benefit of certain identified third parties and the physician knows of the existence of those third parties, then the physician's duty runs to those third parties. Therefore, in accord with our decision in Baskerville–Donovan Engineers, we hold that privity does not bar Heidi Pate's pursuit of a medical malpractice action. Our holding is likewise in accord with McCain because under the duty alleged in this case, a patient's children fall within the zone of foreseeable risk.

Though not encompassed by the certified question, there is another issue which should be addressed in light of our holding. If there is a duty to warn, to whom must the physician convey the warning? Our holding should not be read to require the physician to warn the patient's children of the disease. In most instances the physician is prohibited from disclosing the patient's medical condition to others except with the patient's permission. See § 255.241(2), Fla. Stat. (1989). Moreover, the patient ordinarily can be expected to pass on the warning. To require the physician to seek out and warn various members of the patient's family would often be difficult or impractical and would place too heavy a burden upon the physician. Thus, we emphasize that in any circumstances in which the physician has a duty to warn of a genetically transferable disease, that duty will be satisfied by warning the patient.

Accordingly, we conclude that the trial court erred by dismissing the complaint with prejudice. Whether the Pates can recover for medical malpractice depends upon the prevailing standard of care pursuant to section 766.102. The pleadings were prematurely terminated based upon the trial court's conclusion that a lack of privity prevented the Pates from stating a cause of action. We therefore quash the decision of the district court affirming the dismissal of the complaint with prejudice and remand for further proceedings in accord with this opinion.

It is so ordered.

SAFER v. PACK

677 A.2d 1188 (N.J. Super. Ct. App. Div. 1996).

KESTIN, J.

Plaintiffs appeal from the trial court's order dismissing their complaint and denying their cross-motion for partial summary judgment as to liability only. We reverse that portion of the order dismissing the complaint and affirm the denial of plaintiffs' motion.

Donna Safer's claim arises from the patient-physician relationship in the 1950s and 1960s between her father, Robert Batkin, a resident of New Jersey, and Dr. George T. Pack, also a resident of New Jersey, who practiced medicine and surgery in New York City and treated Mr. Batkin there. It is alleged that Dr. Pack specialized in the treatment and removal of cancerous tumors and growths.

In November 1956, Mr. Batkin was admitted to the hospital with a pre-operative diagnosis of retroperitoneal cancer. A week later, Dr. Pack performed a total colectomy and an ileosigmoidectomy for multiple polyposis of the colon with malignant degeneration in one area. The discharge summary noted the finding in a pathology report of the existence of adenocarcinoma developing in an intestinal polyp, and diffuse intestinal polyposis "from one end of the colon to the other." Dr. Pack continued to treat Mr. Batkin postoperatively.

In October 1961, Mr. Batkin was again hospitalized. Dr. Pack performed an ileoabdominal perineal resection with an ileostomy. The discharge summary reported pathology findings of "ulcerative adenocarcinoma of colon Grade II with metastases to Levels II and III" and "adenomatous polyps." Dr. Pack again continued to treat Mr. Batkin postoperatively. He also developed a physician-patient relationship with Mrs. Batkin relative to the diagnosis and treatment of a vaginal ulcer.

In December 1963, Mr. Batkin was hospitalized once again at Dr. Pack's direction. The carcinoma of the colon had metastasized to the liver with secondary jaundice and probable retroperitoneal disease causing pressure on the sciatic nerve plexus. After some treatment, Mr. Batkin died on January 3, 1964, at forty-five years of age. Donna was ten years old at the time of her father's death. Her sister was seventeen.

In February 1990, Donna Safer, then thirty-six years of age and newly married, residing in Connecticut, began to experience lower abdominal pain. Examinations and tests revealed a cancerous blockage of the colon and multiple polyposis. In March, Ms. Safer underwent a total abdominal colectomy with ileorectal anastamosis. A primary carcinoma in the sigmoid colon was found to extend through the serosa of the bowel and multiple polyps were seen throughout the entire bowel. Because of the detection of additional metastatic adenocarcinoma and carcinoma, plaintiff's left ovary was also removed. Between April 1990 and mid–1991, Ms. Safer underwent chemotherapy treatment.

In September 1991, plaintiffs obtained Robert Batkin's medical records, from which they learned that he had suffered from polyposis. Their complaint was filed in March 1992, alleging a violation of duty (professional negligence) on the part of Dr. Pack in his failure to warn of the risk to Donna Safer's health.

Plaintiffs contend that multiple polyposis is a hereditary condition that, if undiscovered and untreated, invariably leads to metastatic colorectal cancer. They contend, further, that the hereditary nature of the disease was known at the time Dr. Pack was treating Mr. Batkin and that the physician was required, by medical standards then prevailing, to warn those at risk so that they might have the benefits of early examination, monitoring, detection and treatment, that would provide opportunity to avoid the most baneful consequences of the condition.

* * *

In dismissing, the trial court held that a physician had no "legal duty to warn a child of a patient of a genetic risk[.]" In the absence of any evidence whether Dr. Pack had warned Mr. Batkin to provide information concerning his disease for the benefit of his children, the motion judge "assumed that Dr. Pack did not tell Robert Batkin of the genetic disease."

The motion judge's reasoning proceeded from the following legal premise: "in order for a doctor to have a duty to warn, there must be a patient/physician relationship or circumstances requiring the protection of the public health or the community [at] large." Finding no physician-patient relationship between Dr. Pack and his patient's daughter Donna, the court then held genetically transmissible diseases to differ from contagious or infectious diseases or threats of harm in respect of the duty to warn, because "the harm is already present within the non-patient child, as opposed to being introduced, by a patient who was not warned to stay away. The patient is taking no action in which to cause the child harm."

The motion judge relied on Pate v. Threlkel, 640 So. 2d 183 (Fla.Dist. Ct.App.1994), as the only "on point" authority respecting genetically transmissible disease.

* * *

Because the issue before us arose on a motion for summary judgment, we, too, are obliged to accept plaintiffs' proffer through their medical expert that the prevailing standard of care at the time Dr. Pack treated Mr. Batkin required the physician to warn of the known genetic threat.

* * *

We see no impediment, legal or otherwise, to recognizing a physician's duty to warn those known to be at risk of avoidable harm from a genetically transmissible condition. In terms of foreseeability especially, there is no essential difference between the type of genetic threat at issue here and the menace of infection, contagion or a threat of physical harm. See generally, e.g., McIntosh v. Milano, 168 N.J. Super. 466, 483–85, 403 A.2d 500 (Law Div.1979); Tarasoff v. Regents of Univ. of Cal., 17 Cal. 3d 425, 551 P.2d 334, 344, 131 Cal. Rptr. 14 (Cal. 1976); Restatement (Second) of Torts §§ 314, 314A (1965); T.A. Bateman, Annotation, Liability of Doctor or Other Health Practitioner to Third Party Contracting Contagious Disease from Doctor's Patient, 3 A.L.R. 5th 370 (1992). The individual or group at risk is easily identified, and substantial future harm may be averted or minimized by a timely and effective warning.

The motion judge's view of this case as one involving an unavoidable genetic condition gave too little significance to the proffered expert view that early monitoring of those at risk can effectively avert some of the more serious consequences a person with multiple polyposis might otherwise experience. We cannot conclude either, as the trial court did, that Dr. Pack breached no duty because avoidable harm to Donna was not foreseeable, i.e., "that Dr. Pack's conduct did not create a 'foreseeable zone of risk.' "Such a determination would ignore the presumed state of medical knowledge at the time.

* * *

Although an overly broad and general application of the physician's duty to warn might lead to confusion, conflict or unfairness in many types of circumstances, we are confident that the duty to warn of avertable risk from genetic causes, by definition a matter of familial concern, is sufficiently narrow to serve the interests of justice. Further, it is appropriate, for reasons already expressed by our Supreme Court, that the duty be seen as owed not only to the patient himself but that it also "extends beyond the interests of a patient to members of the immediate family of the patient who may be adversely affected by a breach of that duty."

* * *

We need not decide, in the present posture of this case, how, precisely, that duty is to be discharged, especially with respect to young children who may be at risk, except to require that reasonable steps be taken to assure that the information reaches those likely to be affected or is made available for their benefit. We are aware of no direct evidence that has been developed concerning the nature of the communications between physician and patient regarding Mr. Batkin's disease: what Dr. Pack did or did not disclose; the advice he gave to Mr. Batkin, if any, concerning genetic factors and what ought to have been done in respect of those at risk; and the conduct or expressed preferences of Mr. Batkin in response thereto. There may be enough from Mrs. Batkin's testimony and other evidence for inferences to be drawn, however.

We decline to hold as the Florida Supreme Court did in Pate v. Thelkel, supra, that, in all circumstances, the duty to warn will be satisfied by informing the patient. It may be necessary, at some stage, to resolve a conflict between the physician's broader duty to warn and his fidelity to an expressed preference of the patient that nothing be said to family members about the details of the disease. We cannot know presently, however, whether there is any likelihood that such a conflict may be shown to have existed in this matter or, if it did, what its qualities might have been. As the matter is currently constituted, it is as likely as not that no such conflict will be shown to have existed and that the only evidence on the issue will be Mrs. Batkin's testimony, including that she received no information, despite specific inquiry, that her children were at risk. We note, in addition, the possible existence of some offsetting evidence that Donna was rectally examined as a young child, suggesting that the risk to her had been disclosed.

This case implicates serious and conflicting medical, social and legal policies, many aptly identified in Sonia M. Suter, Whose Genes Are These Anyway? Familial Conflicts Over Access to Genetic Information, 91 Mich. L. Rev. 1854 (1993) and in other sources, including some referred to by the motion judge. Some such policy considerations may need to be addressed in ultimately resolving this case. For example, if evidence is produced that will permit the jury to find that Dr. Pack received instructions from his patient not to disclose details of the illness or the fact of genetic risk, the court will be required to determine whether, as a matter of law, there are or ought to be any limits on physician-patient confidentiality, especially after the patient's death where a risk of harm survives the patient, as in the case of genetic consequences. See generally Janet A. Kobrin, Confidentiality of Genetic Information, 30 UCLA L. Rev. 1283 (1983).

Issues of fact remain to be resolved, as well. What was the extent of Donna's risk, for instance? We are led to understand from the experts' reports that the risk of multiple polyposis was significant and that, upon detection, an early full colectomy, i.e., an excision of her entire colon, may well have been the treatment of choice to avoid resultant cancer—including metastasis, the loss of other organs and the rigors of chemotherapy. Full factual development may, however, cast a different light on these issues of fact and others.

Difficult damage issues portend also. Not the least of these will involve distinguishing between the costs of the medical surveillance that would have followed a timely and effective warning, and the costs of medical care attributable to any breach of duty that may be found to have occurred.

Because of the necessarily limited scope of our consideration, we have highlighted only a few of the potentially troublesome issues presented by this case. Such questions are best conceived and considered in the light of a fully developed record rather than in the abstract.

* * *

The order of the trial court dismissing the complaint is reversed. For similar reasons, the trial court's order denying plaintiffs' motion for summary judgment on liability is affirmed. The matter is remanded to the trial court for further proceedings.

NEIL A. HOLTZMAN & MICHAEL S. WATSON, PROMOTING SAFE AND EFFECTIVE GENETIC TESTING IN THE UNITED STATES

Final Report of the Task Force on Genetic Testing 67 (1997).

Despite the advantages of non-genetic providers being the gateway to genetic testing, there are drawbacks. One is the limited knowledge of genetics and genetic tests of some non-geneticist providers. In a 1991 survey of physicians selected at random from ten states, non-genetic, non-academic physicians in five specialties (family practice, internal medicine, obstetrics-gynecology, pediatrics, and psychiatry) were able to correctly answer an average of 73.1% of questions deemed important by a panel of non-genetic providers who helped develop the questionnaire. Physicians who graduated from medical school between 1971 and 1985 scored significantly higher than those who graduated between 1950 and 1970. Having a genetics course in medical school was significantly associated with higher scores but was not as important a predictor as the year of graduation. Physicians in specialties that had been exposed to genetic problems in their practices (family physicians who delivered babies, pediatricians, and obstetrician-gynecologists) had significantly higher scores than physicians in the other specialties. Over one-third of family physicians who did not deliver babies, internists, and psychiatrists had scores of 65% correct or lower.

In a 1996 survey on testing for genetic susceptibility to cancer, Burke and Press found that of the first 124 primary care physicians to respond, over 20% had not heard of a test for a genetic predisposition to breast cancer.

NOTES AND QUESTIONS

1. Both of the conditions that the physicians in *Pate* and *Safer* allegedly failed to warn the plaintiffs about, medullary thyroid carcinoma and familial adenomatous polyposis, are autosomal dominant disorders with nearly complete penetrance. Each child of an affected parent has a 50 percent chance of inheriting the mutation, and unless treated, has an extremely high probability of becoming ill. Does the physician's duty depend on the probability of inheriting the disorder? On its severity?

2. What harms might be caused by disclosing genetic test results to family members at risk?

3. If the genetic disorder is not treatable, does the health care professional still have a duty to warn third parties at risk? What benefits, if any, would disclosure provide? See Carol McCrehan Parker, Camping Trips and

Family Trees: Must Tennessee Physicians Warn Their Patients' Relatives of Genetic Risks?, 65 Tenn. L. Rev. 585, 601–02 (1998).

4.   The classic case addressing the duty of a health care professional to warn third parties of a risk of harm created by a patient is Tarasoff vs. Regents of the University of California, 551 P.2d 334 (Cal. 1976). In that case, the Supreme Court of California held that a psychotherapist had a duty to take reasonable care to warn a foreseeable victim of a threat of a serious danger of violence created by a patient. (The patient allegedly told the psychotherapist that he planned to kill a female acquaintance, and later did so.) In what ways do the facts alleged in *Pate* and *Safer* resemble the facts alleged in *Tarasoff*? Should the physician's duty to warn only extend to cases where the patient actively creates the harm? See Michelle R. King, Physician Duty to Warn a Patient's Offspring of Hereditary Genetic Defects: Balancing the Patient's Right to Confidentiality Against the Family Member's Right to Know—Can Or Should *Tarasoff* Apply?, 4 Quinnipiac Health L. J. 1 (2000).

The physician's duty to warn third parties has been extended to contagious and even non-contagious diseases. On the latter, see Bradshaw v. Daniel, 854 S.W.2d 865 (Tenn. 1993) (duty to warn husband that wife had Rocky Mountain Spotted Fever). Are genetic disorders "contagious"?

5.   Under the rule adopted by the court in *Safer*, what if the patient instructs the physician not to disclose the information to anyone? New Jersey has a statute that reads as follows:

N.J. STAT. ANN. § 10:5–47 (2001)

Conditions for disclosure of genetic information

a.   Regardless of the manner of receipt or the source of genetic information, including information received from an individual, a person may not disclose or be compelled, by subpoena or any other means, to disclose the identity of an individual upon whom a genetic test has been performed or to disclose genetic information about the individual in a manner that permits identification of the individual, unless:

(1)   Disclosure is necessary for the purposes of a criminal or death investigation or a criminal or juvenile proceeding;

(2)   Disclosure is necessary to determine paternity in accordance with the provisions of section 11 of P.L.1983, c.17 (C.9:17–48);

(3)   Disclosure is authorized by order of a court of competent jurisdiction;

(4)   Disclosure is made pursuant to the provisions of the "DNA Database and Databank Act of 1994," P.L.1994, c.136 (C.53:1–20.17 et seq.);

(5)   Disclosure is authorized by the tested individual or the tested individual's representative by signing a consent which complies with the requirements of the Department of Health and Senior Services;

(6) Disclosure is for the purpose of furnishing genetic information relating to a decedent for medical diagnosis of blood relatives of the decedent;

(7) Disclosure is for the purpose of identifying bodies;

(8) Disclosure is pursuant to newborn screening requirements established by State or federal law;

(9) Disclosure is authorized by federal law for the identification of persons; or

(10) Disclosure is by an insurer pursuant to the requirements of P.L.1985, c.179 (C.17:23A–1 et seq.).

b. The provisions of this section apply to any subsequent disclosure by any person after another person has disclosed genetic information or the identity of an individual upon whom a genetic test has been performed.

Under this statute, may a physician disclose genetic information to a family member over the patient's objection? If not, how can the physician fulfill the duty to warn recognized in *Pate* and *Safer*? See Natalie Anne Stepanuk, Comment, Genetic Information and Third Party Access to Information: New Jersey's Pioneering Legislation as a Model for Federal Privacy Protection of Genetic Information, 47 Cath. U. L. Rev. 1105, 1128 (1998). In some states, the law immunizes health care professionals from civil or criminal liability in certain circumstances. Title 410, section 513/30 of the Illinois Compiled Statutes, part of that state's Genetic Information Privacy Act, states: "No civil or criminal sanction under this Act shall be imposed for any disclosure or nondisclosure of a test result to a spouse by a physician acting in good faith under this paragraph." Would this protect a physician who disclosed test results to a spouse without the consent of the person who was tested? Would the protection of the statute extend to disclosure to children?

6. The Health Insurance Portability and Accountability Act (HIPAA) Privacy Rule prohibits the disclosure of individually identifiable health information without the authorization of the individual. 45 C.F.R. Parts 160, 164. One of the exceptions permits disclosures "required by law," and this includes common law as well as statutes. 45 C.F.R. § 164.512(a). Another exception permits disclosures "to prevent or lessen a serious and imminent threat to the health or safety of a person or the public." 45 C.F.R. § 164.512(j) Therefore, the Privacy Rule would not be a bar to *Tarasoff*-required disclosures. In theory, the Privacy Rule would not prohibit a state without a genetic privacy statute from judicially recognizing a duty to warn as suggested by *Safer*. On the other hand, the combination of widespread legislative action to protect genetic privacy and the spirit—if not the letter—of the Privacy Rule, would likely deter a court from imposing such a requirement.

7. In *Safer*, the patient's wife asked the physician if his condition could affect their children and was "told not to worry." Does the patient or the patient's family have a duty to inquire? If they fail to inquire, should that discharge the physician's duty to warn? If the patient fails to ask the right

questions, should she be deemed contributorily negligent? In Brown v. Dibbell, 595 N.W.2d 358 (Wis. 1999), the court stated:

> A patient's duty to exercise ordinary care in an informed consent action generally does not impose on the patient an affirmative duty to ascertain the truth or completeness of the information presented by the doctor; to ask questions of the doctor; or to independently seek information when a reasonable person would want such information. * * * We do not conclude, however, that a patient may never be contributorily negligent for failing to take such steps. We merely conclude that it would require a very extraordinary fact situation * * *.

Can you think of such a fact situation in regard to information about an inherited disorder?

8. The court in *Pate* states: "Thus, we emphasize that in any circumstances in which the physician has a duty to warn of a genetically transferable disease, that duty will be satisfied by warning the patient." Do you agree? Can you think of a situation in which warning the patient would not be sufficient to discharge the physician's duty? (See Molloy v. Meier, *infra*, for one example.) What if the patient said that she did not intend to disclose the information to members of her family who might be affected?

9. The decision in *Safer* requires the physician to take "reasonable steps" to see that warning information reaches the person to whom the physician owes a duty to warn. What steps might be "unreasonable"? The plaintiff was a child when her father was diagnosed. Dr. Pack died before she reached maturity. What effect should this have on the duty to warn?

10. A 2003 literature review identified 12 studies that found a lack of knowledge about genetics on the part of physicians. See Sandy Suther and Patricia Goodson, Barriers to the Provision of Genetic Services By Primary Care Physicians: A Systematic Review of the Literature, 5 Genetics in Med. 70–76 (2003). One survey found that only 13 percent of internists, 21 percent of OB/GYNs, and 40 percent of oncologists correctly answered questions about the genetic aspects of breast cancer and breast cancer testing. See Teresa Doksum, Barbara A. Bernhardt, & Neil A. Holtzman, Does Knowledge About the Genetics of Breast Cancer Differ Between Nongeneticist Physicians Who Do or Do Not Discuss or Order BRCA1 Testing?, 5 Genetics in Med. 99–105 (2003). Harold Varmus, former director of NIH, commented in 2002 that the pace of the transformation to gene-based medicine "will be limited not only by the pace of discovery, but also by the need to educate practicing physicians, their coworkers, and their patients about the uses and shortcomings of genetic information." Harold Varmus, Getting Ready for Gene–Based Medicine, 347 New Eng. J. Med. 1526 (2002). Varmus noted that most medical schools had not anticipated the impact of molecular genetics, and that, as a result, "many physicians struggle with the new biology." Id.

MOLLOY v. MEIER

679 N.W.2d 711 (Minn. 2004).

MEYER, JUSTICE.

Kimberly Molloy (Molloy) and her husband, Glenn Molloy, brought a medical malpractice action against appellants Dr. Diane Meier, Dr. Reno

Backus, and Dr. Kathryn Green, claiming they were negligent in failing to diagnose a genetic disorder in Molloy's daughter and their negligence caused Molloy to conceive another child with the same genetic disorder. The district court denied the appellants' motion for summary judgment and concluded that a physician who performs genetic tests on a child owes a duty to the biological parents of that child; that the action did not accrue until the time of conception and, therefore, was not time-barred; and that the action was not barred by Minn.Stat. § 145.424 (2002), which prohibits causes of action for wrongful birth and wrongful life. The court of appeals answered three certified questions and upheld the denial of summary judgment. We granted review and now affirm the court of appeals.

This case arises out of the medical treatment of S.F., the daughter of Kimberly Molloy and her ex-husband, Robert Flomer. As a young girl, S.F. was treated by appellant Dr. Diane M. Meier at Partners in Pediatrics (formerly Oakdale Pediatrics). When S.F. was three years old, Dr. Meier noted during a check-up that S.F. was developmentally delayed. Dr. Meier ordered a number of tests, but the results did not reveal the source of S.F.'s difficulties. On May 18, 1992, Dr. Meier met with Molloy, Robert Flomer, and S.F. to discuss the possible causes for S.F.'s developmental delays, including the possibility of a genetic cause. Molloy told Dr. Meier about Molloy's mentally retarded half-brother and asked Dr. Meier to conduct genetic tests on S.F. to determine whether S.F. had inherited any abnormalities from Molloy.

In her notes from the May 18 visit, Dr. Meier wrote "? chromosomes + fragile X," which meant she intended to order chromosomal testing and testing for Fragile X syndrome. In May of 1992, a Fragile X chromosomal test capable of diagnosing the disorder with 70 to 80 percent accuracy was in widespread use. A parent who is a carrier of Fragile X has up to a 50 percent chance of giving birth to a child with the condition. Although physicians can treat the symptoms of Fragile X, the condition itself is incurable. Dr. Meier conceded that "it was appropriate to test [S.F.] for [F]ragile X in keeping with accepted standards of pediatric practice on May 18, 1992." According to Molloy, Dr. Meier told her that if S.F. tested positive for a genetic disorder, Molloy should be tested herself.

On June 17, 1992, the chromosome testing ordered by Dr. Meier was performed at North Memorial Medical Center. On July 18, 1992, North Memorial's laboratory reported normal chromosome testing for S.F. Dr. Meier received the test results, telephoned the Flomers and informed them that the test results were negative; i.e., normal. However, Dr. Meier failed to mention that Fragile X testing had not been performed. The Flomers then informed Molloy that the test results were "normal." Based on the fact that Dr. Meier had mentioned Fragile X in her discussion of chromosomal testing, Molloy assumed that the negative test results included a negative result for Fragile X.

Meanwhile, on June 23, 1992, S.F. was referred by Dr. Meier to the Minneapolis Clinic of Neurology where she was seen by Dr. Reno Backus.

Dr. Backus testified in his deposition that his role was to evaluate S.F. and report back to Dr. Meier, the referring physician. Dr. Backus met with S.F., Molloy, and the Flomers, and diagnosed S.F. with a pervasive developmental delay of unknown origin. Molloy inquired about her chances of conceiving another child with S.F.'s defect. According to Molloy, Dr. Backus responded that S.F.'s problems were not genetic in origin and the risk that Molloy might give birth to another child like S.F. was extremely remote, especially with a father other than Robert Flomer. Dr. Backus was aware that chromosomal testing had been done but he made his assessment before the test results were known.

Several years later S.F. was referred to Dr. Kathryn Green, who was an employee of the Minneapolis Clinic of Neurology. When Dr. Green saw S.F. on April 30, 1996, she had the office chart of Minneapolis Clinic, including Dr. Backus's 1992 report. There were no Fragile X testing results in the chart because the testing had never been done. Dr. Green knew of Molloy's mentally retarded half-brother who had exhibited problems similar to S.F.'s. Despite having this information, Dr. Green did not order or recommend Fragile X testing. Dr. Green testified that she recognized the importance of Fragile X testing in general, but she assumed such tests had already been performed on S.F. and had come back negative, as S.F. had already seen three physicians.

In the meantime, Molloy remarried and gave birth to M.M. on June 30, 1998. M.M. showed signs of the same developmental difficulties as S.F., so his pediatrician, Dr. David Tilstra, ordered Fragile X testing for him. The Fragile X test results were positive; i.e., M.M. carried the Fragile X genetic disorder. When Dr. Tilstra received the positive results, he counseled Kimberly and Glenn Molloy about Fragile X syndrome and recommended that they and other potentially affected family members receive testing. Based on Dr. Tilstra's recommendation, S.F. and Kimberly Molloy were tested for Fragile X, and it was discovered that they both carried the genetic disorder.

Molloy commenced this lawsuit on August 23, 2001, alleging that Drs. Meier, Backus, and Green and their employers were negligent in the care and treatment rendered to S.F., Kimberly Molloy, and Glenn Molloy by failing to order Fragile X testing on S.F., failing to properly read those lab tests that were performed, mistakenly reporting that S.F. had been tested for Fragile X, and failing to provide counseling to Kimberly and Glenn Molloy regarding the risk of passing an inheritable genetic abnormality to future children. Molloy claimed she would not have conceived M.M. if Drs. Meier, Backus, and Green had correctly diagnosed S.F. with Fragile X and informed Molloy of the diagnosis.

Drs. Meier, Backus, and Green and their employers moved for summary judgment, arguing that they did not owe a duty to the family of a patient and that, in any event, Molloy's action was barred by the four-year statute of limitations for medical malpractice claims. In opposition, Molloy presented expert testimony of a pediatrician and a pediatric neurologist who described the prevailing standard of care in the medical community with respect to testing and counseling for genetic disorders. The experts indicated that a patient who exhibits the symptoms of this disorder with a family history of mental retardation should be tested for Fragile X. Further, a physician who identifies the possibility of Fragile X has a responsibility to follow up to confirm that the tests are performed. Finally, the physician of a child with Fragile X has an obligation to provide genetic counseling to the child's family.

In deposition testimony, the appellants each somewhat confirmed the standard of care described by Molloy's expert witnesses. Dr. Meier admitted that her practice is to communicate the results of Fragile X testing to the child's "primary" parents and inform them that the condition may be inherited. Dr. Backus acknowledged that Fragile X testing would have been appropriate for a child such as S.F. and that diagnoses of diseases such as Fragile X have implications for the entire family. Dr. Green conceded that a physician should share the genetic implications of positive genetic test results with the parents of a child diagnosed with an inheritable disorder.

The district court denied summary judgment, concluding that the defendants owed a duty to the biological parents of the child, the cause of action was not barred by the four-year statute of limitations, and a claim for wrongful conception was permitted under Minn.Stat. § 145.424. Subsequently, the district court certified the following questions to the court of appeals as "important and doubtful" under Minn. R. Civ.App. P. 103.03(i).

(a) Does a physician who allegedly fails to test for and diagnose a genetic disorder in an existing child leading to the birth of a subsequent child with that disorder owe a legal duty to the child's parents?

(b) When does the statute of limitations begin to run pursuant to Minn.Stat. § 541.076 (2002) in a parents' medical negligence claim alleging failure to test for and diagnose a genetic disorder in an existing child leading to the birth of a subsequent child with that disorder?

(c) Does Minn.Stat. § 145.424 prohibit parents from bringing an action alleging that they would not have conceived the subsequent child described in question (b)?

The court of appeals answered the first certified question in the affirmative: the appellants owed a legal duty to Molloy because appellants "should have foreseen that negligently rendering care to S.F. or erroneously reporting genetic test results to S.F.'s biological parents could result in the birth of another child with fragile X." *Molloy,* 660 N.W.2d at 452. The court of appeals answered the second certified question by concluding that the statute of limitations began to run at the time of M.M.'s conception, the point at which Molloy could establish damages and a viable cause of action in tort. *Id.* at 455. In answering the third certified question, the court concluded that Molloy's action was not barred by

Minn.Stat. § 145.424 because she did not claim that, but for the negligence of the appellants, M.M. would have been aborted.

I.

We begin by addressing the first certified question, whether the appellants owed a duty to Molloy regarding the genetic testing and diagnosis of S.F. for Fragile X syndrome. When we review certified questions arising from the denial of summary judgment, we must decide "whether there are any genuine issues of material fact and whether the lower courts erred in their application of the law." *Employers Mut. Cas. Co. v. A.C.C.T., Inc.,* 580 N.W.2d 490, 493 (Minn.1998) (quoting *Art Goebel, Inc. v. North Suburban Agencies, Inc.,* 567 N.W.2d 511, 515 (Minn.1997)). The existence of a duty in a negligence case is a question of law. *Funchess v. Cecil Newman Corp.,* 632 N.W.2d 666, 672 (Minn.2001). We consider the evidence in the light most favorable to the nonmoving party. *Gradjelick v. Hance,* 646 N.W.2d 225, 231 (Minn.2002).

Molloy advances two legal theories. She first argues that a physician-patient relationship existed between her and the appellants that gave rise to a legal duty to warn her about the risks of becoming pregnant as a carrier of Fragile X. Additionally, citing *Skillings v. Allen,* 143 Minn. 323, 173 N.W. 663 (1919), Molloy urges this court to hold that even if a physician-patient relationship cannot be established, a physician's duty to warn others of a patient's genetic disorder arises from the foreseeability of injury.

The appellants argue that their duty is owed only to S.F., the person with whom they had a physician-patient relationship. The appellants claim that they met with S.F. solely for S.F.'s own benefit and not for the benefit of her family. If any duty extended beyond the minor patient, the appellants argue that it should reach only those parties who have a contractual relationship with the physician, in this case the Flomers, S.F.'s custodial parents.

The question of whether a physician owes a duty to inform a child's family about the genetic implications of a child's genetic disorder is one of first impression in Minnesota. A medical malpractice action is based on principles of tort liability for negligence; the existence of a duty running to the plaintiff is a prerequisite to a finding of negligence. *See Plutshack v. Univ. of Minn. Hosps.,* 316 N.W.2d 1, 8 (Minn.1982).

We begin our analysis by observing that a duty to a third party who is not a patient of the physician has been recognized in only a few Minnesota cases. *See Lundgren v. Fultz,* 354 N.W.2d 25, 28–29 (Minn.1984) (psychiatrist owed duty to third party where patient threatens foreseeable harm to that party and psychiatrist has the ability to control the risk of harm); *Cairl v. State,* 323 N.W.2d 20, 25 n. 7, 26 (Minn.1982) (treatment facility may owe duty to warn identifiable third parties of violent propensities of a mentally disabled youth whom it released if that youth poses a specific threat to those parties). We also recognized a physician's duty to third parties in *Skillings v. Allen,* 143 Minn. 323, 325–26, 173 N.W. 663, 664 (1919). In that case, a minor child was hospitalized with scarlet fever. *Id.* at 324, 173 N.W. at 663. When the parents asked the child's physician about the nature of the disease and the danger of infection, the physician negligently informed them that they could safely visit their daughter in the hospital and take her home, even though the disease was in its most contagious stage. *Id.* We held that the doctor owed a duty to the parents, reasoning that "one is responsible for the direct consequences of his negligent acts whenever he is placed in such a position with regard to another that it is obvious that if he does not use due care in his own conduct he will cause injury to that person." *Id.* at 325, 173 N.W. at 663–64. We declined to label the duty contractual or noncontractual, noting that under either construct, liability extends to the parents because the physician had an obligation to use due care in a situation where it was likely known that the parents would rely on the advice. *See id.* at 326, 173 N.W. at 664.

Similarly, we noted in an attorney malpractice case, *Togstad v. Vesely, Otto, Miller & Keefe,* that an attorney-client relationship existed "under circumstances which made it reasonably foreseeable to [the defendant] that [the plaintiff] would be injured if the advice were negligently given." 291 N.W.2d 686, 693 (Minn.1980). Our decision in *Togstad* derived from the professional relationship. The plaintiff in that case consulted with the attorney defendant to discuss the medical treatment of her husband, whom she believed suffered permanent brain damage as a result of a hospital's negligence. *Id.* at 689–90. After taking notes and asking questions of the plaintiff, the defendant told her that she did not have a case for medical malpractice. *Id.* at 690. In reliance on these statements, the plaintiff did not pursue her case further until the statute of limitations for medical malpractice had run. *See id.* The plaintiff obtained expert testimony that a competent attorney would, at a minimum, obtain medical records and consult with an expert in the field before informing a client that she did not have a case. *Id.* at 691–92. We held that there was sufficient evidence to support an attorney-client relationship because it was reasonably foreseeable that negligent advice would injure the plaintiff. *Id.* at 693. We declined to adopt either tort or contract theory in resolving the case because under either legal theory the evidence established that the plaintiff "sought and received legal advice * * * under circumstances which made it reasonably foreseeable to [the attorney] that [the plaintiff] would be injured if the advice were negligently given." *Id.*

Only a few other jurisdictions have addressed the question of whether a physician owes a legal duty to the family of a patient who received negligent care in the field of genetics. In a case most analogous to the instant one, the New Jersey Supreme Court held that a physician owes a duty to members of the patient's immediate family who might be injured by the physician's breach of duty to the patient. *Schroeder v. Perkel,* 87 N.J. 53, 432 A.2d 834, 839 (1981). The court held that liability could extend to the patient's family where a doctor's failure to diagnose a first-born child with cystic fibrosis led to the birth of a second child with that disorder and it was foreseeable that the parents would rely on the diagnosis. *Id.* at 839–40; *cf. Lininger v. Eisenbaum,* 764 P.2d 1202, 1205 (Colo.1988) (holding that a physician's failure to diagnose the hereditary nature of a child's blindness that led his parents to conceive a second blind child stated a cause of action).

The Supreme Court of Florida has also held that a duty exists where "the prevailing standard of care creates a duty that is obviously for the benefit of certain identified third parties and the physician knows of the existence of those third parties." *Pate v. Threlkel,* 661 So.2d 278, 282 (Fla.1995). In *Pate,* the defendant physician diagnosed the plaintiff's mother with medullary thyroid carcinoma, a genetically inheritable disease. *Id.* at 279. When the plaintiff learned that she also carried the disease, she sued, alleging that the defendant should have known of the inheritable nature of the disease and owed a duty to inform her mother that the plaintiff may have carried it as well. *Id.* The plaintiff presented expert testimony that the prevailing standard of care required physicians to inform patients of the genetically transferable nature of their conditions. *Id.* at 281. The Florida Supreme Court noted that the standard of care was developed for the benefit of third parties and therefore held that a physician owes a duty to those third parties of whom the physician has knowledge. *Id.* at 282.

Other courts have drawn upon the prevailing standard of care to define the duties physicians owe in the context of genetic counseling. For example, the California Court of Appeals found no duty to parents to disclose the possibility of having a child with Tay–Sachs disease when the physicians did not have any reason to suspect that the parents were in a high-risk group for the disease. *Munro v. Regents of Univ. of Cal.,* 215 Cal.App.3d 977, 263 Cal.Rptr. 878, 882 (1989). That court recognized that it was impossible to test all patients and relied on expert testimony that the prevailing standard of care required testing only when parents had specific ethnic backgrounds. *Id.* Similarly, the New Jersey Court of Appeals relied upon "the presumed medical knowledge at the time [of treatment]" to find a duty to warn the patient's immediate family of a patient's genetically transferable condition. *Safer v. Estate of Pack,* 291 N.J.Super. 619, 677 A.2d 1188, 1192 (App.Div.1996).

Cases such as *Safer; Munro,* and *Pate* recognize that the field of genetic counseling is rapidly evolving as new methods of testing become more practical and reliable, and the legal duty of physicians will be driven, at least in part, by the standard of care in the medical profession. As this occurs, it is unlikely that the medical community will adopt a standard of care that is either unduly burdensome or unbeneficial to patients.

Our decision today is informed by the practical reality of the field of genetic testing and counseling; genetic testing and diagnosis does not affect only the patient. Both the patient and her family can benefit from accurate testing and diagnosis. And conversely, both the patient and her family can be harmed by negligent testing and diagnosis. Molloy's experts indicate that a physician would have a duty to inform the parents of a child diagnosed with Fragile X disorder. The appellants admit that their practice is to inform parents in such a case. The standard of care thus acknowledges that families rely on physicians to communicate a diagnosis of the genetic disorder to the patient's family. It is foreseeable that a negligent diagnosis of Fragile X will cause harm not only to the patient, but to the family of the patient as well. This is particularly true regarding parents who have consulted the physicians concerning the patient's condition and have been advised of the need for genetic testing.

We therefore hold that a physician's duty regarding genetic testing and diagnosis extends beyond the patient to biological parents who foreseeably may be harmed by a breach of that duty. In this case, the patient suffered from a serious disorder that had a high probability of being genetically transmitted and for which a reliable and accepted test was widely available. The appellants should have foreseen that parents of childbearing years might conceive another child in the absence of knowledge of the genetic disorder. The appellants owed a duty of care regarding genetic testing and diagnosis, and the resulting medical advice, not only to S.F. but also to her parents. In recognizing this duty, we apply the principles of negligence law set forth in *Skillings* and *Togstad* and conclude that the duty arises where it is reasonably foreseeable that the parents would be injured if the advice is negligently given. " '[T]he risk reasonably to be perceived defines the duty to be obeyed, and risk imports relation; it is risk to another or to others within the range of apprehension.' " *Connolly v. Nicollet Hotel*, 254 Minn. 373, 381, 95 N.W.2d 657, 664 (1959) (quoting *Palsgraf v. Long Island R. Co.*, 248 N.Y. 339, 162 N.E. 99, 100 (1928)).

Under our standard of review for summary judgment, there is sufficient evidence in the record to indicate that each of the appellants was on notice that S.F. displayed symptoms of Fragile X but that the testing was never carried out. Drs. Meier and Backus met face-to-face with Molloy and were aware of her specific need for accurate genetic information. Dr. Green did not meet face-to-face with Molloy but that does not relieve her of her duty of reasonable care to the patient and the patient's biological parents to provide accurate genetic testing results. We find sufficient evidence in the record to submit the negligence of each physician to a jury for a determination on whether one or more of the physicians breached the standard of care.

Appellants suggest that recognizing a duty to Molloy would extend a physician's duty to an unreasonable extent, requiring the physician to seek out and inform distant relatives. The court of appeals held that the "physician must notify a biological parent" to discharge his or her duty. *Molloy*, 660 N.W.2d at 453. Molloy concedes that the appellants could have discharged their duty by informing an appropriate contact person, who in this case would be Robert Flomer or Randine Flomer, the custodial parents, or Molloy, the noncustodial biological parent. In light of this concession, the facts of this case, and the limitation of the certified question to whether a duty extends to a minor patient's parents, we need not, and do not, address whether the duty recognized here extends beyond biological parents who foreseeably will rely on genetic testing and diagnosis and therefore foreseeably may be injured by negligence in discharging the duty of care.

* * *

The final certified question concerns whether Minn.Stat. § 145.424 prohibits Molloy's cause of action. The statute provides in pertinent part:

Subdivision 1. Wrongful life action prohibited. No person shall maintain a cause of action or receive an award of damages on behalf of that person based on the claim that but for the negligent conduct of another, the person would have been aborted.

Subd. 2. Wrongful birth action prohibited. No person shall maintain a cause of action or receive an award of damages on the claim that but for the negligent conduct of another, a child would have been aborted.

Subd. 3. Failure or refusal to prevent a live birth. Nothing in this section shall be construed to preclude a cause of action * * * [claiming that] but for the negligent conduct of another, tests or treatment would have been provided * * * which would have made possible the prevention, cure, or amelioration of any disease, defect, deficiency, or handicap.

The appellants argue that Molloy's action is essentially a "wrongful birth" action, and therefore prohibited by section 145.424, subdivision 2 (2002). Molloy contends that the statute prohibits only claims that but for the negligent conduct, an abortion would have been sought. Because Molloy claims that she would have sought a tubal ligation, not an abortion, if the appellants had fulfilled their duty to her, she argues that her claim is not prohibited. The district court held that Molloy's wrongful-conception cause was not prohibited by the statute and the court of appeals agreed, concluding that the plain language of Minn.Stat. § 145.424 did not bar the action.

When we interpret statutes, we first determine whether the language of the statute, on its face, is clear or ambiguous. *Gomon v. Northland Family Physicians, Ltd.*, 645 N.W.2d 413, 416 (Minn.2002). A statute is ambiguous if it is susceptible to more than one reasonable interpretation. *Wynkoop v. Carpenter*, 574 N.W.2d 422, 425 (Minn.1998). "Words and phrases are construed * * * according to their common and approved usage." Minn.Stat. § 645.08(1) (2002). However, "[i]f the words of the statute are 'clear and free from all ambiguity,' further construction is neither necessary nor permitted." *Owens v. Water Gremlin Co.*, 605 N.W.2d 733, 736 (Minn.2000).

The plain language of section 145.424 does not support the appellants' contention that Molloy's claim is barred by statute. The statute bars claims that but for the negligence, the pregnancy would have been aborted. Molloy makes no claim that she would have aborted M.M. if she had more accurate information about S.F.'s genetic condition. Rather, Molloy's complaint alleges that "[h]ad [she and her husband] known that [S.F.] had Fragile X, they would not have conceived [M.M.]." This states an action not for wrongful life or birth, but rather for wrongful conception—an action that has been recognized in this state for over a quarter century. *Sherlock*, 260 N.W.2d at 174 (holding that parents may sue physician for damages proximately caused by a negligently performed sterilization procedure). Because Molloy's action is properly characterized as one for wrongful conception rather than wrongful birth, it is not barred by Minn.Stat. § 145.424. We answer this certified question in the negative, and affirm the court of appeals.

NOTE

Fragile X syndrome affects approximately 1 in 3,600 males and 1 in 4,000 females, although females tend to be less severely affected. It is a trinucleotide repeat disorder like Huntington disease, but it has a much more complicated pattern of inheritance, as explained in the following.

NATIONAL INSTITUTE OF CHILD HEALTH AND HUMAN DEVELOPMENT, HOW IS FRAGILE X SYNDROME INHERITED?

http://www.nichd.nih.gov/publications/pubs/fragile
X/sub5.cfm (last modified Aug. 18, 2006).

The gene for Fragile X is carried on the X chromosome. Because both males (XY) and females (XX) have at least one X chromosome, both can pass on the mutated gene to their children.

A father with the altered gene for Fragile X on his X chromosome will only pass that gene on to his daughters. He passes a Y chromosome on to his sons, which doesn't transmit the condition. Therefore, if the father has the altered gene on his X chromosome, but the mother's X chromosomes are normal, all of the couple's daughters would have the altered gene for Fragile X, while none of their sons would have the mutated gene.

Current research indicates that a father can pass on the premutation form of the FMR1 gene only to his daughters. In other words, if a daughter inherits the mutated FMR1 gene from her father, she will get only the premutation from him, not the full mutation. Even if the father himself has a full mutation, it appears that sperm can carry only the premutation. Scientists don't understand how or why fathers can only pass on the milder form of Fragile X to their daughters. This remains an area of focused research.

Because mothers pass on only X chromosomes to their children, if the mother has the altered gene for Fragile X, she can pass that gene to either her sons or her daughters. If the mother has the mutated gene on one X chromosome and has one normal X chromosome, and the father has no genetic mutations, all the children have a 50–50 chance of inheriting the mutated gene.

The odds noted here apply to each child the parents have. Having one child who receives an X chromosome with the FMR1 mutation does not increase or decrease the chances of having another child with the mutated FMR1 gene. Nor do these odds influence the severity of the symptoms. Having one child with mild symptoms does not mean that the other children will have severe symptoms, and having a child with severe symptoms does not mean that other children will have mild symptoms.

A premutation gene is less stable than a full mutation. In some cases, the mutated gene may expand from the premutation to the full mutation as it is passed on from mother to child. The chances of expansion depend on the number of repeats in the promoter of the premutation gene; the higher the number of repeats, the more likely it is that the gene will expand. These chances also increase with each generation. Children of a mother who has the premutation, then, may have no genetic mutation, the premutation, or the full mutation.

Further, because an altered FMR1 gene can be passed on without symptoms, many people are unaware that they have it. As a result, a premutation form of the FMR1 gene can be silently passed through a family for generations, with no one ever showing any symptoms. However, with each generation, it becomes more likely that the premutation gene will expand its number of repeats to become a full mutation gene, which would also increase the number of and seriousness of symptoms.

NOTES AND QUESTIONS

1.   Is it correct, as the court in *Molloy* did, to describe both mother and daughter as ''carriers'' of the Fragile X mutation?

2.   The fact that the child in *Molloy* had the Fragile X mutation could be important for other family members. According to the court, does the physician have a duty to inform other family members? Is it sufficient if the physician informs the child's parents? See Mark Hallberg and Teresa Fariss McClain, Note: Recent Developments in Health Care Law: Molloy v. Meier Extends Genetic Counseling Duty of Care to Biological Parents and Establishes That Legal Damages Must Occur Before a Wrongful Conception Action Accrues for Statute of Limitations Purposes, 31 Wm. Mitchell L. Rev. 939, 954 (2005).

IV. DIRECT–TO–CONSUMER GENETIC TESTING

MAXWELL J. MEHLMAN, DIRECT-TO-CONSUMER GENETIC TESTING

Cyberounds® (2009).

More than a dozen companies now sell direct-to-consumer (DTC) or, as it is sometimes called, "home" genetic testing, purporting to reveal information relevant to health and lifestyle. Other companies offer only ancestry or paternity testing (e.g., www.familytreedna.com, http://www.dnaancestryproject.com, http://www.oxfordancestors.com, https://genographic.nationalgeographic.com/genographic/index.html, http://www.dna-worldwide.com). One company, Identigene (http://www.dnatesting.com), sells its paternity testing both by mail and as kits that can be purchased in drugstores. Still other companies provide nutritional guidance purportedly based on the results of genetic tests (e.g., http://www.mycellf.com).

POTENTIAL BENEFITS FROM DTC GENETIC TESTING

Like patent medicines in the 19th century and modern over-the-counter drugs, DTC genetic testing offers certain advantages to consumers. It is generally cheaper than genetic testing obtained through a physician, in part because DTC testing dispenses for the most part with the services of physicians and genetic counselors. Mail-order genetic testing may be more accessible for people in rural or medically-underserved communities and those with mobility constraints. DTC testing also may provide a greater sense of privacy. Unlike genetic testing by one's physician, the fact that someone has sought or obtained DTC genetic testing, as well as the test results themselves, do not become part of the patient's medical record unless the patient shares them with his or her physician. For persons concerned about the risk of social stigma and genetic discrimination in insurance and employment, DTC genetic testing thus offers many of the same advantages as anonymous testing, which colleagues and I described as follows in 1996 in an article in the *American Journal of Human Genetics*:

> It would encourage individuals to acquire important personal information at the same time that it safeguarded the information against disclosure. Anonymous testing would promote patient autonomy by making the proband the only person who could reveal identifiable test results to third parties. It would effectively eliminate concerns over unauthorized disclosure by the test provider. By avoiding automatic or unauthorized disclosure to insurers and employers, anonymous testing would reduce the potential for discrimination. It would be up to the proband to decide whether to reveal the fact that he or she had been counseled and tested, and the test results, to insurers, employers, physicians, and family members.

Arguably, concerns about discrimination have been lessened as a result of the enactment of the federal Genetic Information Nondiscrimination Act. [See the discussion in Chapters 15 and 16]. But people still may be concerned about the confidentiality of information from genetic tests performed by their physicians and placed in their medical records. Under the Health Insurance Portability and Accountability Act (HIPAA), medical records may be shared among an individual's clinicians and given to health insurers for claims administration purposes. Indeed, a major impetus for shifting the health care system to electronic medical records is the ease with which individual health care information in electronic form can be accessed by care givers. Individuals may blanch at the possibility that genetic information that becomes part of their medical record may be available to virtually anyone who works in a health care system where they obtain care, and they may turn to DTC companies in an effort to maintain greater control over the information.

How confidential is information from DTC genetic tests? The testing companies have privacy policies in which they state their intention not to let anyone outside the company see test information linked to a specific individual without the individual's permission, and although DTC genetic testing companies do not appear to be covered by the privacy protections of HIPAA, such as they are, some companies claim to be "HIPAA-compliant." It is unclear how easy is it for an outsider to discover the identity of the person who was tested, and how well the security systems employed by the companies work.

Ironically, despite all of the concern over genetic privacy, some DTC genetic testing companies are touting the ability of their customers to share their genetic information with others. 23andMe, for example, states: "Seeing your own genetics is just the beginning of the 23andMe experience. Our features also give you the ability to share and compare yourself to family, friends and people around the world." The company website goes on to urge people to "add some excitement at your family reunion" by "track[ing] the inheritance of specific genes in your family," having siblings "see which parts of their parents' DNA they share, and which they don't," and letting grandchildren "find out which genes they inherited from each grandparent." As a publicity stunt, 23andMe even hosted a "spit party" in Manhattan attended by such celebrities as Rupert Murdoch, film executive Harvey Weinstein, and fashion designer Diane von Furstenberg. As reported by the *New York Times*, participants spit into sample collection bottles and looked forward to using their genomes "as a basis for social networking."

CONCERNS ABOUT DTC GENETIC TESTING

Despite the possible benefits from DTC genetic testing, the practice has come in for substantial criticism. Aside from concerns about the confidentiality of identifiable information, critics complain about the validity of the tests and the difficulties of interpreting the results. 23andMe, for example, offers tests for 107 conditions and traits. (See https://www.23

andme.com/health/all/ for a complete list.) The company calls 28 of the tests "clinical reports," which refers to "conditions and traits for which there are genetic associations supported by multiple, large, peer-reviewed studies," and that also have "a substantial influence on a person's chances of developing the disease or having the trait." These tests include BRCA cancer mutations, Crohn's disease, cystic fibrosis, hemochromatosis, prostate cancer, Parkinson's disease, and type 1 and 2 diabetes. The company calls the remaining 79 tests "research reports," and describes them as "information from research that has not yet gained enough scientific consensus to be included in our Clinical Reports. This research is generally based on high-quality but limited scientific evidence." The company also classifies as research reports "scientifically accepted, established research that does not have a dramatic influence on a person's risk for a disease." The conditions covered by these tests include such non-disease traits as "avoidance of errors," "breastfeeding and IQ," "measures of intelligence," and "memory," as well as diseases such as asthma, brain aneurysm, lung cancer, ands ulcerative colitis. Some companies, such as Navigenics, only test for conditions which, they claim, bear directly on health.

Clearly there are different views on the validity and utility of various genetic tests. One would think that the government would play some role in assuring that only appropriate genetic tests were sold to consumers. The Food and Drug Administration (FDA) does require manufacturers of some home tests to obtain agency approval before the tests can be marketed, but this only applies to what are called "home test kits," which enable the user to obtain test results without sending a biological sample to a laboratory. (Examples of FDA-approved home test kits are tests for cholesterol, illicit drugs, fecal occult blood, glucose, hepatitis, HIV, menopause, ovulation, pregnancy, prothrombin time, and vaginal pH.) When the test sample must be sent to a laboratory for analysis, however, there may be no requirement of FDA approval for the test itself. The FDA has reviewed and approved only a handful of genetic tests, and purchasers of DTC tests are not likely to know which ones. [See the discussion in Chapter 7].

The Federal Trade Commission (FTC) is another government agency that is supposed to protect consumers from businesses that make false or misleading claims. In 2006, the FTC issued a warning to consumers about DTC genetic tests. In addition to explaining the limited ability of genetic testing in general to determine an individual's susceptibility to disease, the FTC advised consumers to be especially wary of claims about at-home testing. According to the commission, the FDA and the Centers for Disease Control and Prevention (CDC), which also plays a role in regulating medical tests, are not aware "of any valid studies that prove these tests give accurate results," and these agencies advise that, "because of the complexities involved in both the testing and the interpretation of the results, genetic tests should be performed in a specialized laboratory, and the results should be interpreted by a doctor or trained counselor who understands the value of genetic testing for a particular situation.''

Some states also attempt to regulate DTC genetic testing. A 2007 survey by the Genetics and Public Policy Center at Johns Hopkins University reported that only 25 states and the District of Columbia allowed the marketing of DTC genetic testing; 13 states prohibit it explicitly; and the remaining 12 may prohibit it indirectly. In April 2008, the New York State Department of Health sent cease-and-desist letters to Navigenics, 23andMe, and 21 other DTC testing companies, ordering them to stop selling their tests in New York unless they obtained a permit from the state. In June 2008, the California Department of Public Health followed suit, issuing cease-and-desist orders to 13 companies. In addition to requiring the companies to obtain a state license to furnish clinical laboratory services, the state regulators warned that state law required residents to obtain genetic tests through a physician. At least one DTC genetic testing company, DNA Direct, was notified by the California Department of Public Health that it was in compliance with state law.

One of the main concerns about DTC genetic testing is the difficulty consumers may have in interpreting the test results. The companies issue results on-line, in the form of charts and tables purporting to explain whether, compared with the general population, the individual is at increased or decreased risk for the conditions and traits for which they have been tested. Making sense of a large number of these comparisons is challenging, to say the least. The problem may be exacerbated if the results do not include information about the prevalence of the condition in the wider population. It is one thing to learn that, due to your genes, you have a 25% higher risk of suffering from a certain disease than others; it is another matter if the disease only affects only 1 out of a million people, rather than 1 out of 100. Moreover, the tests invariably reveal increased and decreased risks for different disorders. Assuming there is something individuals can do to reduce their risk, which risks should they focus on? All of them? And what preventive steps are warranted? Should someone who is told that they have a 10 percent greater risk of breast cancer obtain a prophylactic mastectomy? On the other hand, should someone told that they have a reduced risk of lung cancer start smoking?

Consumers of DTC genetic testing might have it somewhat easier if they received expert guidance in interpreting their test results. But none of the on-line testing companies requires the test results to be delivered by a physician, geneticist, or genetic counselor, although at least one company (DNA Direct), requires customers to speak with a counselor before ordering tests and gives them access to an on-line genetic specialist at no extra cost after they receive their test results. Another company, LabSafe, permits its customers to consult a staff physician by telephone at a cost of $75 for 15 minutes. Commentators also worry that company counselors who discuss testing with consumers before the tests are ordered may steer them towards making especially expensive purchases.

How do the testing companies justify the risk of confusing and misleading consumers? The answer is that they all disclaim that they are giving health advice. 23andMe, for example, states in its online consent document that "accessing your genetic information through 23andMe does not translate into a personal prediction"; that the information "should not be used to estimate your overall risk of future disease"; that its services are "not a test or kit designed to diagnose disease or medical conditions," "nor are they intended to be medical advice"; and that "you should not change your health behaviors on the basis of this information." But if customers took all these disclaimers seriously, what would be the point of spending between $300 and $1200 to obtain DTC genetic testing?

In 2006, the U.S. Government Accountability Office (GAO) issued a report on DTC sites that provided "nutragenetic" testing, that is, genetic tests that supposedly yield recommendations about nutrition and lifestyle. Like 23andMe, the four websites that were investigated all stressed that they do not provide information intended to diagnose or treat any disease or disorder. Yet all of the test results obtained by the investigators contained "predictions that a consumer may interpret as a diagnosis," including that the consumers were at risk for osteoporosis, high blood pressure, type 2 diabetes, heart disease, a reduced ability to clear toxins, brain aging, and cancer. Furthermore, the nutrition and lifestyle recommendations that supposedly were based on the results of the genetic tests were in fact based on the results of fictitious information provided by the investigators on questionnaires that were submitted as part of the testing process. To add insult to injury, two of the four sites recommended that the consumer buy expensive, "personalized" dietary supplements from them, at a cost of $1200 a year in one case and $1880 a year in the other. The investigators purchased and analyzed some of the supplements, and found that their ingredients essentially were multivitamins that could be purchased in a supermarket for about $35 a year. Far from being "personalized," moreover, each of the three fictitious consumers that the investigators created for each of the websites were told to purchase the same product, despite that the fact that the DNA samples that were sent to the companies came from two different donors, and each had a different lifestyle profile described in their questionnaires.

Some DTC genetic testing companies require consumers to agree to allow them to use test results for research purposes. As noted earlier, although the companies promise that, unless the consumer agrees otherwise, researchers will be given access only to de-identified information, consumers must take the company's word that their coding and security systems would withstand an attempt to link test results to specific individuals. In addition, consumers may be told that the company is entitled to use the research to develop commercial products and services, and that they should not expect to receive any financial benefit.

Professional Acceptance of DTC Genetic Testing

All of these criticisms of DTC genetic testing have led some professional medical groups to declare their opposition to the practice. In 2004, the American College of Medical Genetics issued a policy statement describing DTC genetic testing as "potentially harmful" and declaring that "genetic testing should be provided to the public only through the services of an appropriately qualified health care professional." In June 2008, the House of Delegates of the American Medical Association adopted a similar policy statement that also called for the Federal Trade Commission to increase its oversight of DTC genetic testing companies.

The position of the American Society for Human Genetics, however, is more nuanced, and considers the benefits as well as the risks of DTC genetic testing:

> Potential benefits of DTC testing include increased consumer awareness of and access to testing. In the current environment, consumers are at risk of harm from DTC testing if testing is performed by laboratories that are not of high quality, if tests lack adequate analytic or clinical validity, if claims made about tests are false or misleading, and if inadequate information and counseling are provided to permit the consumer to make an informed decision about whether testing is appropriate and about what actions to take on the basis of test results.

In the same way that historic objections to patent medicines might be seen, at least in part, as an effort by physicians to avoid competition from unlicensed salespersons and commercial drug manufacturers, so too condemnations of DTC genetic testing by physicians, geneticists, and genetic counselors may strike some as self-serving attempts by medical professionals to protect their turf. This view is reinforced by studies showing that primary care physicians are not well-informed about genetics and genetic testing. If this holds true, it is unclear how much better off patients would be if they obtained genetic testing through their primary care physicians, unless the physician had specialized training in genetics.

JAMES D. KEROUAC, THE REGULATION OF HOME DIAGNOSTIC TESTS FOR GENETIC DISORDERS: CAN THE FDA DENY PREMARKET APPLICATION ON THE BASIS OF THE DEVICE'S SOCIAL IMPACTS?

5 J. Biolaw & Business 34–43 (2002).

* * *

Psychological Effects

The availability of over-the-counter (OTC) diagnostics for genetic disorders may lead to serious psychological difficulties for the users of these devices and their family and friends. Genetic information revealed through OTC diagnostics may provide the test subject with devastating information about his or her prospects of fixture health or disease. The psychological effects may be particularly acute for subjects using OTC tests for late-onset genetic disorders that are presently untreatable.

For example, Huntington's Disease is a late-onset degenerative neurological disorder. Huntington's Disease causes degenerative effects on the patient's ability to walk, talk, and reason, eventually causing complete dependence on others for daily needs. The ultimate result is death due to complications from the disease, such as "choking, infection or heart failure." The current genetic test for this disorder, not available over-the-counter, provides a conclusive determination of the subject's status. Thus, if the test subject receives a positive test result, they are effectively receiving a death sentence, condemning the subject to a long, slow death. "For those whose results are positive, the suicide rate is approximately thirty-five percent higher than among the general population." It is also noted that even those who receive a negative test result for this disorder may likewise suffer psychological effects.

Genetic tests are currently available for the BRCA breast cancer genes; which are related to other late-onset genetic disorders. These genes pose a more complex situation than that of the Huntington's Disease gene. In this case, the [BRCA] genes may confer a lifetime risk of eighty percent for developing breast cancer and fifty percent for developing ovarian cancer. This situation is further complicated by speculation that women with no family history of breast cancer who possess this gene sequence may have only a forty percent or less chance of developing the disease. Clearly, women who test positive for genetic mutations in the BRCA genes are faced with an uncertain fate and may feel psychologically pressed to make a radical decision to prevent the potential, but not certain, onset of breast or ovarian cancer. Given the uncertainty of the correlation between the detection of BRCA mutations and the eventual onset of breast and ovarian cancer and the dearth of available treatments for these diseases, women who test positive for these mutations are faced with a psychologically disturbing choice to have preventive surgery or to do nothing and be faced with the constant uncertainty that they may eventually contract the disease. Both choices are likely to result in psychological trauma.

A third type of late-onset disorder may not pose such a psychological risk: late-onset genetic disorders for which adequate treatment or non-intrusive preventive measures can be taken to avoid the disease exist. [sic] For example, a genetic test for the genetic mutations relating to adult onset diabetes would not pose significant risk of psychological trauma to the test subject.

While this discussion clearly is not a comprehensive analysis of all the potential psychological effects resulting from genetic test results, it illustrates a few important points relevant to the overall position advocated by this paper. (1) The results of genetic tests for some disorders, particularly those for which adequate treatment does not exist and those for which there is not a one-to-one correlation between the mutation and the disease, may have almost certain devastating psychological effects on the test subjects. (2) The balance between the psychological and social impacts of home diagnostic genetic tests and the benefits of those tests is delicate and is intimately entwined with the current technology available to treat the disease relating to that mutation. (3) The psychological effects of genetic test results are not uniform in the context of different genetic mutations, and thus the regulation of tests for these disorders should not reflect a per se reluctance to approve genetic tests for home use. A case-by-case approach is supported by the different impacts expected in the different contexts. (4) The availability of adequate counseling may counterbalance these psychological impacts in certain cases.

* * *

Overtreatment & Misdiagnosis Causing Unnecessary, Risky or Painful Treatment

Home use genetic testing devices could potentially lead to overtreatment or to the application of unnecessary treatments if the patient receives a false positive test result. The term "overtreatment" refers to the tendency to provide treatment for a disease when there is a less than one-to-one correlation between the genotype of the test subject and the expression of that genotype. For example, [mutations in] the BRCA genes are believed to confer an 85% to 90% lifetime risk of breast cancer. If all women who tested positive had preventive surgery then there would be a 10% to 15% rate of overtreatment due to the genetic test results.

Similarly, if a particular OTC genetic test leads to many false positive results, the test subjects may be forced to undergo unnecessary and risky treatments. For example, one commentator cites such risky and unnecessary treatment of children who falsely tested positive for phenylketonuria (PKU) in mass screening for the genetic disorder.

These potential harms may easily fit into the PMA [Pre Market Application] calculus as probable risks of injury under the safety analysis. However, they do also constitute social harms because of their potentially detrimental effects on public health.

Selective Abortion

The potential availability of prenatal OTC genetic tests for certain conditions may raise serious social risks about selective abortion and eugenics. * * * Specifically, the selective termination of a fetus because the fetus tests positive for ALS may be socially unwarranted because a person afflicted with ALS does not suffer from the disease until relatively late in life and perhaps later in that potential individual's life science would find a cure for the disease. Selective termination also raises concerns about false positive test results.

The possibility of temptation to selectively abort due to uninformed decisions made by parents based on home use genetic tests supports a high level of FDA wariness about approving such devices. These devices would require, at the very least, professional consultation to aid parents in understanding the implications of the tests as well as the implications of their choices based on the tests. Also, the risk of selective termination illustrates that the FDA must use caution to examine the context in which OTC genetic tests will be used. The social risks of using prenatal diagnostics in the home are relatively graver than those of testing for some treatable late onset disease by the test subject herself.

THE FDA'S PAST EXPERIENCE IN REGULATING HOME USE DIAGNOSTIC TESTS

This section will discuss how the FDA dealt with home use diagnostic tests for HIV and drugs of abuse in the recent past. While neither case actually resulted in the denial of a PMA on the basis of social impacts, they do illustrate that the FDA takes social impacts very seriously as risks of home use devices. * * * For example, in the case of HIV, there is a strong public policy in favor of early detection to avoid further transmission of the disease, while in the case of Huntington's Disease early detection will result in primarily negative social impacts and there are no treatment options available—the positive result is merely a death sentence. In the latter case, therefore, the social impacts will outweigh the benefits to health.

The Saga of Regulating Home Use Diagnostics for HIV

The approval of home tests for diagnosis of HIV is illustrative of FDA's use of social risk information in the PMA process and in determining what restrictions are appropriate for devices raising significant social risks to assure that the devices are safe. As in the case of genetic home tests, many commentators believed OTC HIV tests raised serious social risks. Prior to the FDA's approval of HIV home test kits, many commentators cited psychological risks as one of the risks associated with the use of home HIV diagnostics. The standard argument that home testing for HIV posed psychological risks for patients receiving a positive test result is as follows: (1) A positive HIV test result amounts to a death sentence due to the lack of effective treatments for the disease. (2) Studies indicate that persons testing positive for HIV are more likely to commit suicide. This increased risk of suicide and the desperation accompanying a positive test result is clearly a psychological risk of HIV testing. (3) The only way to mitigate this risk is face-to-face counseling about the condition. The arguments about psychological risks of HIV home test kits clearly tracks those made above in the OTC genetic test kit context.

Similarly, the arguments against home HIV testing also track those against OTC genetic test kits regarding the social risks of insurance and employment discrimination. Some argued prior to the approval of home HIV test kits that marketing home HIV test kits would allow employers to screen potential employees "quickly, easily, secretly, and *without resort to any necessary intervention* of *health care professionals*. This faculty would enhance an employer's ability to fire or refuse to hire persons who are HIV-positive, with *reduced risk of liability for illegal discrimination*."

Concerns about the removal of health care professionals from the HIV testing process also gave rise to similar fears of insurance discrimination.

* * *

The Lessons of the HIV Home Testing Saga

The FDA's history of institutional reluctance to grant PMA applications for home use HIV diagnostics, coupled with the counseling restrictions the agency placed on such test systems is instructive for the purposes of this paper for a number of reasons. First, the FDA's HIV home diagnostic PA/1A history indicates that the agency believes social risks are cognizable in the PMA approval process for home use diagnostic tests for certain conditions. Second, the agency's cost-benefit analysis in the PMA process for home use diagnostic systems includes such factors as the availability of therapies for the condition for which the home use diagnostic test is indicated. Third, when the public health benefits of a home use diagnostic test (e.g., the increased screening of high risk minorities due to the widespread availability of home use diagnostics) outweigh the risks (e.g., social risks such as the risk of suicide due to the serious nature of the diagnosis), the agency will approve the PMA application. This lesson would appear especially true when the test subject will be empowered to take precautions to prevent the further spread of a serious public health threat like HIV Finally, the FDA is likely to engage in some brand of social engineering to avoid certain social risks when those risks are serious, though they do not outweigh the potential benefits of the home use diagnostic system.

These lessons can and should be applied to any future PMA applications for OTC genetic tests.

REGULATION OF HOME USE DIAGNOSTICS FOR DRUGS OF ABUSE

The Social Risks of Home Testing for Drugs of Abuse

As in the context of genetic home diagnostics and HIV home diagnostics, home testing for drugs of abuse raises certain social risks that may or may not be cognizable in the PMA process. These risks, however, it is urged, do not rise to the same level as those in those contrasting contexts. The FDA's approach to regulating home tests for drugs of abuse should therefore reflect the lower level of social risks.

One social impact that was widely noted in relation to OTC tests for drugs of abuse was the potential for "family discord" resulting from parents' ability to handle drugs tests they administer themselves to their children. This social risk is clearly of a lower magnitude than those cited above in relation to genetic testing and HIV antibody testing. The congressional committee charged with oversight of the FDA reacted to claims regarding the threat of familial discord caused by drugs of abuse home test kits with little enthusiasm. Another possible risk of home use drugs of abuse testing systems is the risk of a consumer receiving a false positive being labeled a social pariah. Similarly, the receipt of a false negative result of a test for drugs of abuse would "cause the individual requesting the testing to miss the opportunity to obtain treatment for the problem."

* * *

The Lessons of the FDA's Drugs of Abuse Home Test Regulations

The FDA's regulatory history of test systems for drugs of abuse provides a number of lessons that are instructive in the context of home use genetic diagnostic test regulation. First, political pressure from Congress and the President can affect the FDA's reading of its statutory authority to recognize social risks in the regulatory calculus. Second, the agency can engage in significant social engineering to avoid certain social risks through device restrictions, even when the FDA has not classed the diagnostic device in Class III. These restrictions on the marketing of diagnostic devices are powerful tools to avoid certain social risks, even though the agency never explicitly expresses that it is attempting to address those social risks. The social risks in the context of home testing for drugs of abuse are incomparable to those in the HIV and genetic testing settings and do not warrant stringent regulation. This final lesson should be considered when the agency is poised to consider a PMA for a home diagnostic test for a genetic condition and the agency should thus avoid drawing analogies to the drugs of abuse situation in regulating home use genetic tests.

The FDA Has Authority to Consider Social Impacts in the PMA Process

The FDA's history regulating home use HIV test systems and drugs of abuse test collection systems indicates that social risks of medical devices may play a role in the regulatory calculus. This role may be explicit or it may subtly underlie the restrictions placed on the device. The consideration of social risks of a new home use diagnostic system is warranted by the unique context of each particular device, including the treatment options available for the disorder tested for and the ability to reduce the spread of disease.

Thus, when the agency considers social risks as part of its regulatory calculus in the PMA process for new home use genetic diagnostic systems, the agency should consider the availability of therapies for the condition and the reliability of the testing technology available. For example, in the case of a home use diagnostic test for Huntington's disease or Alzheimer's disease, the agency should, consider the high risk of social harms, such as psychological risk to the patient and the risk of insurance and employment discrimination. If there are no available treatment options, then it is likely that the social costs of the device will outweigh the benefits to health and safety of such devices. However, where there are adequate options for treatment or disease prevention, the benefits to health and safety of home use genetic diagnostic kits will likely outweigh the social risks. Thus, for conditions like adult onset diabetes approving home use diagnostic kits may likely create incentives for at risk individuals to undergo testing and, if they receive a positive test result, alter their habits that contribute to the onset of the disease.

In Less Severe Cases FDA May Impose Restrictions on Devices Based on Social Impacts

In cases where the benefits associated with the availability of home use genetic diagnostics outweigh the risks of such technology, the agency will still need to engineer some protections into its device regulations to ensure safety and effectiveness of the devices. Given the power of genetic information to result in discrimination and cause significant psychological angst, the FDA will likely engage in some form of social engineering when it approves PMA applications for OTC genetic testing devices. The restrictions placed on such devices will likely be of the same nature as those placed on home use HIV diagnostics and drugs of abuse home collection systems, including requiring counseling with the provision of a positive test result.

CONCLUSION

The FDA appears to have authority to consider social impacts of OTC genetic testing technology in the PMA process. This is clearly indicated by the historical analysis of the FDA's regulation of home use HIV diagnostics and home use collection systems for drugs of abuse test kits. The consideration of social impacts, however, should be dictated by the particular technology available to screen and treat the condition tested for. Social impacts, at the extreme, may justify the denial of a PMA application when there is no available treatment for the disorder. However, the normal situation will likely be that the social impacts can be mitigated through the use of restrictions of the marketing of the devices. Such restrictions can include the provision of counseling services with the product and are well within the purview of the FDA's medical device regulatory authority.

FRED LEDLEY, A CONSUMER CHARTER FOR GENOMIC SERVICES

20 Nature Biotechnology 767 (2002).

Direct access to testing. Every individual has a fundamental right to obtain genetic information about himself or herself in a confidential manner by having genetic tests performed privately and receiving the test results directly from a testing laboratory. The consumer-focused model empowers consumers with direct and private access to genetic tests and services. To ensure quality, direct consumer services should be coupled to a valid informed consent process and sources of counseling, follow-up, and referrals to specialty healthcare providers.

NOTES AND QUESTIONS

1. Home testing is available for both HIV and drug abuse. Is genetic testing different? If so, how, and what do these differences mean in terms of how home genetic testing should be regulated?

2.   For a discussion of the reasons for limiting home genetic testing, see Gail H. Javitt, Erica Stanley, and Kathy Hudson, Direct-to-Consumer Genetic Tests, Government Oversight, and the First Amendment: What the Government Can (and Can't) Do to Protect the Public's Health, 57 Okla. L. Rev. 251, 264–267 (2004).

3.   One option is for the government to ban home genetic testing. Another is to permit testing as long as it meets certain requirements. What should these requirements be?

4.   One type of direct-to-consumer testing that has spawned litigation is testing that purports to tell pregnant women the sex of their child. According to Lori Andrews,

> the pregnant woman pricks her finger, then collects three drops of blood on a test card and sends it to the company for testing. For $275, Acu–Gen Biolab, Inc. offers pregnant women such a test which analyzes fetal cells circulating in maternal blood to make the assessment. The company claims that their Baby Gender Mentor Test is "highly accurate." However, the lawyer for a group of women suing Acu–Gen Biolab alleges that the company officials admit that 10 to 20 percent of customers have asked for refunds because of incorrect results. In addition to a class action for fraud filed in 2007, mothers in New York filed suit last month charging negligence and fraud against Acu-gen. One of the plaintiffs underwent testing because she wanted a boy and Acu-gen allegedly told her she would have a boy. She didn't, and she blames the company for her marriage breaking up. * * * Some of the women who have used on-line genetic testing for fetal sex and had the sex misdiagnosed allege that they were told by the company not that the test was inaccurate but that their fetus was abnormal. The distraught mothers then sought costly chromosomal testing through the medical system to find the source of this "abnormality."

Lori Andrews, Lawsuits in Pink and Blue: Sex Selection Cases Hit the Courts, http://blogs.kentlaw.edu/islat/2009/07/lawsuits-in-pink-and-blue-sex-selection-cases-hit-the-courts.html.

CHAPTER 9

CLINICAL APPLICATIONS OF GENETICS

■ ■ ■

Earlier chapters describe some of the therapeutic advances made possible by the decoding of the human genome, including genetic testing to diagnose and predict genetic illnesses. As more knowledge is gained about genes and how they function, new therapeutic approaches are becoming possible, such as pharmacogenetics, or the use of genetic information to fashion better drug therapies, and gene therapy, which involves altering defective genes or inserting corrected genes into the patient's body. If genetic alterations affect a person's reproductive cells and therefore are passed on to offspring, the result is what is termed germ line gene therapy.

This chapter examines the ethical, legal, and social implications of the use of genetic science in medical treatment. It begins with a history of gene therapy, and then provides a brief description of the underlying science. The chapter then introduces the main regulatory mechanisms—professional self-regulation, the Recombinant DNA Advisory Committee at the National Institutes of Health (NIH), and the Food and Drug Administration (FDA). It proceeds to a discussion of germ line gene therapy, pharmacogenetics, and personalized genomic medicine. It concludes with a discussion of the public health uses of genetic science.

There is considerable debate over the effects that new discoveries in human genetics will have on the practice of medicine. In an address to the Massachusetts Medical Society in May of 1999, Francis S. Collins, the director of the National Human Genome Research Institute at NIH, described how the isolation of disease genes will provide "the best hope for understanding human disease at its most fundamental level." Francis S. Collins, Shattuck Lecture—Medical and Societal Consequences of the Human Genome Project, 341 New Eng. J. Med. 28, 30 (1999). "Even before a gene's role in disease is fully understood," he went on, "diagnostic applications can be useful in preventing or minimizing the development of health consequences." He noted that "successes in reducing disease through treatment have been achieved for the hereditary disorders hemochromatosis, phenylketonuria, and familial hypercholesterolemia, among others. Risk reduction through early detection and lifestyle changes may be possible in the case of disorders associated with predisposing mutations, such as some cancers. As therapies build on knowledge gained about the molecular basis of disease, increasing numbers of illnesses that are now refractory to treatment may yield to molecular medicine in the future.''

Collins also described the manner in which genetic knowledge will facilitate what is called "personalized genomic medicine":

> Identifying human genetic variations will eventually allow clinicians to subclassify diseases and adapt therapies to the individual patient. There may be large differences in the effectiveness of medicines from one person to the next. Toxic reactions can also occur and in many instances are likely to be a consequence of genetically encoded host factors. That basic observation has spawned the burgeoning new field of pharmacogenomics, which attempts to use information about genetic variation to predict responses to drug therapies.

* * *

> Not only will genetic tests predict responsiveness to drugs on the market today, but also genetic approaches to disease prevention and treatment will include an expanding array of gene products for use in developing tomorrow's drug therapies. Since the Food and Drug Administration's approval of recombinant human insulin in 1982, over 50 additional gene-based drugs have become available for clinical use. These include drugs for the treatment of cancer, heart attack, stroke, and diabetes, as well as many vaccines.[1]

> Not all therapeutic advances for gene discovery will be genes or gene products. In other instances, molecular insights into a disorder, derived from gene discovery, will suggest a new treatment.

Id. at 33.

Collins then used a hypothetical case to describe how "gene-based medicine" will affect the delivery of primary care in 2010:

> John, a 23–year-old college graduate, is referred to his physician because a serum cholesterol level of 255 mg per deciliter was detected in the course of a medical examination required for employment. He is in good health but has smoked one pack of cigarettes per day for six years. Aided by an interactive computer program that takes John's family history, his physician notes that there is a strong paternal history of myocardial infarction and that John's father died at the age of 48 years. To obtain more precise information about his risks of contracting coronary artery disease and other illnesses in the future, John agrees to consider a battery of genetic tests that are available in 2010. After working through an interactive computer program that explains the benefits and risks of such tests, John agrees (and signs informed consent) to undergo 15 genetic tests that provide risk

---

1. New medicines in development: biotechnology. 1998. Washington, D.C.: Pharmaceutical Research and Manufacturers of America, 1998:35.

information for illnesses for which preventive strategies are available. He decides against an additional 10 tests involving disorders for which no clinically validated preventive interventions are yet available.

A cheek-swab DNA specimen is sent off for testing, and the results are returned in one week [table omitted]. John's subsequent counseling session with the physician and a genetic nurse specialist focuses on the conditions for which his risk differs substantially (by a factor of more than two) from that of the general population. Like most patients, John is interested in both his relative risk and his absolute risk.

John is pleased to learn that genetic testing does not always give bad news—his risks of contracting prostate cancer and Alzheimer's disease are reduced, because he carries low-risk variants of the several genes known in 2010 to contribute to these illnesses. But John is artery disease, colon cancer, and lung cancer. Confronted with the reality of his own genetic data, he arrives at that crucial "teachable 2010, the field of pharmacogenomics has blossomed, and a prophylactic drug regimen based on the knowledge of John's personal genetic data can be precisely prescribed to reduce his cholesterol level and the risk of coronary artery disease to normal levels. His risk of colon cancer can be addressed by beginning a program of annual colonoscopy at the age of 45, which in his situation is a very cost-effective way to avoid colon cancer. His substantial risk of contracting lung cancer provides the key motivation for him to join a support group of persons at genetically high risk for serious complications of smoking, and he successfully kicks the habit.

Id. at 34–35.

Francis Collins was just as optimistic 6 years later, when, in an article he wrote with Alan F. Guttmacher, he stressed the continued reduction in the cost of genetic sequencing as hastening the introduction of genomic medicine into clinical practice. Again, he used the example of colon cancer: "In a relatively few years, when the role of specific genetic factors in disease is more fully understood and a human genome can be sequenced for less than the cost of a colonoscopy (for example), an individual's sequence will likely become part of the standard medical record, especially since, unlike the colon, an individual's genome sequence is relatively static. Thus, unlike colonoscopy, sequencing will not require frequent repetition. Similarly, it will become the standard of care to sequence cancer patients' tumors and to use that information to refine prognosis and guide therapy." Alan E. Guttmacher and Francis S. Collins, Realizing the Potential of Genomics in Biomedical Research, 294 JAMA 1399, 1400 (2005).

Not everyone agrees with these optimistic predictions about the imminence or significance of new genetic insights for the practice of medicine. In an essay entitled "Will Genetics Revolutionize Medicine?" for example, Neil Holtzman and Theresa Marteau assert that the development of treatments will lag behind the identification of genes that cause inherited disorders, and that only a small proportion of the population suffers from such disorders. Holtzman and Marteau caution against concentrating on genetics rather than the contributions that changes in social structure, lifestyle, and environment can make in improving the public health. For their views, see 343 New Eng. J. Med. 141 (2000). Angus Clarke is especially skeptical of the utility of genetic information in connection with common diseases that are believed to result from a number of genetic and non-genetic factors: "The fact that so many genes and nongenetic factors are involved in the etiology of these common diseases means that the identification of inherited predisposition is of little use at the individual level; it will never be possible to predict those who will be affected nor to know when an individual will develop a disease if he does so at all." Angus J. Clarke, The Genetic Dissection of Multifactorial Disease: The Implications of Susceptibility Screening, in Genetics, Society, and Clinical Practice (Peter S. Harper and Angus J. Clarke eds. 1997).

I. GENE THERAPY

A. HISTORY OF GENE THERAPY

The first attempt at human gene therapy is said to have occurred in 1970, when Stanfield Rogers, a biochemist and physician, attempted to insert into three German girls a virus carrying a gene to combat an inherited liver disease. None of the girls improved.

In 1980, Martin Cline, a UCLA researcher and Chief of Hematology/Oncology at the UCLA Medical Center, attempted to insert DNA into the bone marrow of two patients, one in Italy and the other in Israel, suffering from beta thalassemia, a hereditary blood disorder. Cline submitted a protocol to the UCLA Institutional Review Board (IRB), but went ahead with the experiment before receiving IRB approval. The IRB later rejected Cline's protocol because of insufficient studies in animals. Cline's experiments were uncovered by a newspaper reporter for the L.A. Times. As a result, Cline lost his department chair and his funding from the National Institutes of Health (NIH). The Cline incident raises issues of research ethics, such as the following: What is the reach of a research protocol? Should a protocol from a U.S. university extend to a professor's work abroad?

Ten years later, on September 14, 1990, the third attempt at gene therapy occurred at the NIH in Bethesda, Maryland. The patient, Ashanti DeSilva, was a four year-old suffering from SCID (severe combined immune deficiency). As a result of a genetic error inherited from both parents, patients with this disease do not manufacture the enzyme adenosine deaminase, required for proper functioning of the immune system. DeSilva led a cloistered, endangered existence, being vulnerable to severe infections. A team of physicians removed some of her white blood cells, inserted normal copies of the gene into the cells, and returned the cells into her bloodstream. After four infusions over four months, she improved. She continues to receive infusions every few months, however, because the cells with the normal gene do not continue to work indefinitely. Moreover, she continues to receive traditional drug therapy (PEGADA, a form of the missing enzyme) to supplement the effect of the gene therapy. Nevertheless, many regard DeSilva's experiment to be the first partially successful use of gene therapy.

Ten years after that, in April 2000, French scientists announced that they had used gene therapy to successfully treat several infants suffering from a form of SCID (SCID–X1). Unlike in the case of DeSilva, the French researchers claimed to have inserted correctly-functioning genes in the babies' bone marrow, where they can continue to proliferate, thereby avoiding the need for repeat infusions. Moreover, the babies' immune systems have become normal, and they do not receive traditional drug therapy.

Three years later, however, the French scientists announced that, although 9 of the 10 babies developed normal immune systems, 2 of them developed T-cell leukemia, a form of cancer. The FDA placed a hold on 3 U.S. gene therapy trials that used the same retroviral vector, as did France and Germany. Subsequently, researchers determined that the leukemia resulted from the coincidental insertion of the retrovirus near a cancer gene that it activated. It was hoped that improved vectors could alleviate the problem. But in 2004, one of the two babies died, and in 2005, a third child in the French experiment developed leukemia.

The events in France followed years of unsuccessful efforts to use gene therapy to treat diseases such as cystic fibrosis, familial hypercholesterolemia, Gaucher's disease, and cancer. They also followed the death in October 1999, of Jesse Gelsinger.

Gelsinger, eighteen years old, enrolled in an experiment at the University of Pennsylvania to develop a gene therapy for OTC (ornithine transcarbamylase) deficiency, an x-linked, dominant, single-gene liver disorder whose sufferers, numbering about one out of every 40,000 births, are unable to metabolize ammonia, which is a by-product of the breakdown of protein in the body. The disease is especially severe in newborns. Affected babies slip into a coma within 72 hours of birth and suffer severe brain damage. Half die within one month, and half of the survivors die before they reach six months of age.

Interestingly, Gelsinger himself did not inherit the disease. Instead, it resulted from a genetic mutation. Furthermore, Gelsinger had what is called mosaicism—the genetic makeup of his cells were not all the same and some of his liver cells were producing the missing enzyme, enough so that he did not become comatose after birth and was able to control the illness with a combination of a non-protein diet and enzyme pills. However, by the time he reached eighteen, he was taking 35 pills a day, and was likely to have had to increase the dosage as time went on. He was eager to help find a cure—both for himself and for the more severely-affected infants.

The study Gelsinger enrolled in was not intended to treat OTC. Instead, it was what is called a "Phase I" trial. The plan was to use an adenovirus as a vector; the DNA in the nucleus of the virus would be altered by recombinant DNA techniques to carry the correct gene, and an infusion of the adenovirus vector would be inserted into the subjects' livers. The purpose of the Phase I trial was to determine if, once inserted, the corrected genes would proceed to produce the missing enzyme, and to determine the "maximum tolerated dose" of the infusion—that is, the highest dose that would produce the desired effect without serious side effects.

At first, the Penn researchers proposed to conduct the experiment on a group of severely affected newborns, since their form of the disease was the ultimate target of the therapy. But Arthur Caplan, a leading bioethicist at Penn, objected that the parents of these infants could not give valid informed consent, since parents of dying babies were subject to too much "emotional coercion." Sheryl Gay Stolberg, The Biotech Death of Jesse Gelsinger, The New York Times Sunday Magazine, Nov. 28, 1999, at 137. Consequently, the Penn researchers decided to do the Phase I study on adults, both female carriers and persons like Gelsinger with only partial enzyme deficiencies.

The Penn research was funded by the NIH. Therefore, the researchers submitted their protocol, or plan for the design of the study, to NIH for review. (The review was conducted by the Recombinant DNA Advisory Committee, known as the "RAC," discussed later in this chapter.) The NIH reviewers were concerned about imposing the risks of the experiment on asymptomatic volunteers like Gelsinger, but Caplan's position prevailed and the NIH gave Penn the go-ahead. The researchers also submitted their protocol to the FDA, as required by federal law, and the agency approved it. Finally, the protocol was reviewed and approved by Penn's own Institutional Review Board (IRB), a group made up primarily of Penn researchers.

There were 18 subjects in all, divided into three groups, with each group getting a higher dose. Gelsinger was in the highest dosage group. Everything seemed to be going fine. A story in The New York Times tells what happened next:

> The treatment began on Monday, Sept. 13. Jesse would receive the highest dose. Seventeen patients had already been treated, including one woman who had been given the same dose that Jesse would get, albeit from a different lot, and had done "quite well," Raper [the surgeon who administered the infusion] says. That morning, Jesse was taken to the interventional-radiology suite, where he was sedated and strapped to a table while a team of radiologists threaded two catheters into his groin. At 10:30 a.m., Raper drew 30 milliliters of the vector and injected it slowly. At half past noon, he was done.

> That night, Jesse was sick to his stomach and spiked a fever, 104.5 degrees. Raper was not particularly surprised: other patients had experienced the same reaction. Paul Gelsinger [the patient's father] called; he and Jesse talked briefly, exchanging I love yous. Those were the last words they ever spoke.

> Early Tuesday morning a nurse called Raper at home; Jesse seemed disoriented. When Raper got to the hospital, about 6:15 a.m., he noticed that the whites of Jesse's eyes were yellow. That meant jaundice, not a good sign. "It was not something we had seen before," Raper says. A test confirmed that Jesse's bilirubin, a breakdown product of red blood cells, was four times the normal level. Raper called Gelsinger, and Batshaw [a physician who proposed the experiment] in Washington, who said he would get on a train and be there in two hours.

Both doctors knew that the high bilirubin meant one of two things: either Jesse's liver was failing or he was suffering a clotting disorder in which his red blood cells were breaking down faster than the liver could metabolize them. This was the same disorder the scientists had seen in the monkeys that had been given the stronger vector. The condition is life-threatening for anyone, but particularly dangerous for someone with Jesse's disease, because red blood cells liberate protein when they break down.

By midafternoon Tuesday, a little more than 24 hours after the injection, the clotting disorder had pushed Jesse into a coma. By 11:30 p.m., his ammonia level was 393 micromoles per liter of blood. Normal is 35. The doctors began dialysis.

Paul Gelsinger had booked a red-eye flight. When he arrived in the surgical intensive care unit at 8 Wednesday morning, Raper and Batshaw told him that dialysis had brought Jesse's ammonia level down to 72 but that other complications were developing. He was hyperventilating, which would increase the level of ammonia in his brain. They wanted to paralyze his muscles and induce a deeper coma, so that a ventilator could breathe for him. Gelsinger gave consent. Then he put on scrubs, gloves and a mask and went in to see his son.

By Wednesday afternoon, Jesse seemed to be stabilizing. Batshaw went back to Washington. Paul felt comfortable enough to meet his brother for dinner. But later that night Jesse worsened again. His lungs grew stiff; the doctors were giving him 100 percent oxygen, but not enough of it was getting to his bloodstream. They consulted a liver-transplant team and learned that Jesse was not a good candidate. Raper was beside himself. He consulted with Batshaw and Wilson, and they decided to take an extraordinary step, a procedure known as ECMO, for extracorporeal membrane oxygenation, essentially an external lung that filters the blood, removing carbon dioxide and adding oxygen. It had been tried on only 1,000 people before, Raper says. Only half had survived.

"If we could just buy his lungs a day or two," Raper said later, they thought "maybe he would go ahead and heal up."

The next day, Thursday, Sept. 16, Hurricane Floyd slammed into the East Coast. Mickie Gelsinger [the patient's stepmother] flew in from Tucson just before the airport closed. (Pattie Gelsinger, Jesse's mother, was being treated in a psychiatric facility and was unable to leave.) Batshaw spent the day trapped outside Baltimore on an Amtrak train. He ran down his cell phone calling Raper; when it went dead, he persuaded another passenger to lend him his. The ECMO, Raper reported, appeared to be working. But then another problem cropped up: Jesse's kidneys stopped making urine. "He was sliding into multiple-organ-system failure," Raper says.

That night, at his hotel, Paul Gelsinger couldn't sleep. He left his wife a note and walked the half mile to the Penn medical center to see

Jesse. The boy was bloated beyond recognition; even his ears were swollen shut. Gelsinger noticed blood in Jesse's urine, an indication, he knew, that the kidneys were shutting down. How can anybody, he thought, survive this?

On the morning of Friday the 17th, a test showed that Jesse was brain dead. Paul Gelsinger didn't need to be told: "I knew it already." He called for a chaplain to hold a bedside service, with prayers for the removal of life support.

The room was crowded with equipment and people: 7 of Paul's 15 siblings came in, plus an array of doctors and nurses. Raper and Batshaw, shellshocked and exhausted, stood in the back. The chaplain anointed Jesse's forehead with oil, then read the Lord's Prayer. The doctors fought back tears. When the intensive-care specialist flipped two toggle switches, one to turn off the ventilator and the other to turn off the ECMO machine, Raper stepped forward. He checked the heart-rate monitor, watched the line go flat and noted the time: 2:30 p.m. He put his stethoscope to Jesse's chest, more out of habit than necessity, and pronounced the death official. "Goodbye, Jesse," he said. "We'll figure this out."

Sheryl Gay Stolberg, The Biotech Death of Jesse Gelsinger, The New York Times Sunday Magazine, Nov. 28, 1999, at 137.

Gelsinger was believed to be the first patient to die in the course of a gene therapy experiment. But after his death, reports surfaced of other adverse events, including several deaths, that had not been disclosed to reviewers, experimental subjects, or the public. In some cases, researchers had reported the events to the FDA, but FDA rules call for the reports to be kept confidential as "trade secrets." Adverse events for studies funded by the NIH also were supposed to be reported to the NIH, which made them public. An investigation revealed, however, that of 691 serious side effects disclosed to NIH following Gelsinger's death, only 39 had been reported when they occurred, as the NIH rules required. The FDA revealed that it received an average of 1,000 adverse event reports a year relating to gene therapy experiments, which it protected as trade secrets.

Two months after Gelsinger's death, the FDA inspected the research operation at Penn and, after finding a number of deficiencies, suspended all gene therapy experiments. The deficiencies included problems with the informed consent process in the OTC trial. The FDA also determined that Gelsinger was not a proper subject for enrollment into the study, since his liver was not functioning well-enough at the time he received the adenovirus infusion.

In February 2005, the Justice Department settled a lawsuit against the Gelsinger researchers that had accused them of making false statements to the FDA, including misrepresentations that would have resulted in the FDA shutting down the experiment. Under the terms of the settlement, the University of Pennsylvania agreed to pay $517,000 in fines and the Children's National Medical Center (where Batshaw worked)

$514,622. This was twice the amount of NIH funding for the experiment. The agreement also barred Wilson until 2010 from conducting clinical research under FDA jurisdiction, and imposed a 3–year ban on clinical research by Raper and Batshaw.

After several months during which he defended the researchers at Penn, Gelsinger's father filed a lawsuit for wrongful death. Arthur Caplan was initially named as a defendant, in what is regarded as the first suit against a biomedical ethicist for advice in connection with the design of a clinical trial. Caplan was subsequently dismissed as a defendant, however, and the suit eventually settled for an undisclosed amount.

The government reacted to Gelsinger's death and the revelations that followed it with several proposed new policies, discussed later in this chapter.

The question will be whether efforts to develop successful gene therapies will continue to move forward expeditiously, spurred on by successes such as those claimed by the French scientists, or whether concerns over safety and other ethical matters, raised dramatically by Gelsinger's death, will slow research by creating additional greater regulatory hurdles.

B. SCIENCE OF GENE THERAPY

The concept of gene therapy is broad and encompasses a number of different techniques that share a common approach: the administration of DNA to combat disease. This can occur in several ways, including replacing flawed genetic material in chromosomes; adding cells with properly-functioning DNA to an organism; altering the function of existing defective genes (such as by blocking messenger RNA, which in turn produces proteins); interrupting the aberrant functioning of mutant proteins (for example, by creating other proteins that block or destroy them); or creating "gene factories" that manufacture therapeutic substances in the body. In the experiment in which Jesse Gelsinger died, for example, the second technique was being used: infusing his liver with virus cells containing genes that would produce a missing enzyme. Moreover, gene therapy can be "somatic," meaning that it does not affect reproductive cells and therefore the altered DNA is not passed on to the patient's offspring, or it can be germ line therapy, in which the altered DNA intentionally or unintentionally changes the genetic endowment of future generations. Finally, the same techniques of genetic modification might be aimed at altering normal, non-disease traits, in which case they would not be considered gene therapy but "genetic enhancement." For a fuller description of gene therapy techniques, see Stuart H. Orkin & Arno G. Motulsky, Report and Recommendations of the Panel to Assess the NIH Investment in Research on Gene Therapy, December 7, 1995; Theodore Friedmann, Overcoming the Obstacles to Gene Therapy, Scientific American, June 1997, 96–101. Genetic enhancement is discussed later in chapter 10.

Gene therapy faces a number of technical hurdles. First, the DNA has to get into the patient. There are a variety of ways this might be accomplished, including the use of artificial chromosomes and "naked DNA." The most common technique in gene therapy experiments is to insert the desired DNA into an organism, such as a virus, and then insert the organism either into the patient directly, or into cells in the laboratory that are then inserted into the patient. In the Gelsinger experiment, for example, DNA that produces the enzyme that metabolizes ammonia was inserted into an adenovirus—the type of virus associated with the common cold—and infused into the study subjects. An organism such as a virus that delivers DNA into a patient or into a cell is called a "vector." The two most common vectors are viruses, such as the adenovirus used in the Gelsinger experiment, and retroviruses, which contain RNA rather than DNA. It is important that the pathological or disease-causing elements of the viral vector be deleted as much as possible before the vector is used.

Once a suitable vector is chosen to deliver the DNA (or RNA), the next problem is making sure that the genetic material gets to the correct site. The site in the Gelsinger experiment was the liver, so the vector was inserted into the hepatic artery. Some vectors may not need to be so site-specific. A treatment for hemophilia (a clotting disorder) might only need to be introduced into the circulatory system. But other treatments, such as those for cancer, might fail, or be accompanied by unacceptably serious side effects, if they cannot be delivered directly to tumors.

Even if therapeutic genes reach the appropriate site, it is necessary that they function, or are expressed, rather than remain dormant. Every cell nucleus contains essentially a complete set of a person's DNA, but only some of the genes are "turned on"; otherwise, the genes in the nuclei of liver cells, for example, would produce not only liver enzymes but biochemicals that were supposed to be manufactured in the pancreas or the gall bladder, and so on. The therapeutic genetic material must not only function, but function correctly. It must produce the correct amount of an enzyme, for example, and not cause problems such as cell death, sterility, or uncontrolled cell division (cancer).

Finally, the gene therapy must continue to function for the amount of time necessary to achieve the desired therapeutic effect. The body discards cells after a certain amount of time; even the oldest tissues in our bodies, our bones, are completely regenerated within approximately three years. Yet the target condition may persist throughout the patient's lifetime, or for longer than the corrected genes would remain functional. One approach is to replace the therapeutic genes as they wear out or are discarded. DeSilva continues to receive infusions of corrected genes every few months. An alternative is to insert the genetic material in such a way that it is replicated as cells divide. This is one advantage of using retroviruses, which integrate the therapeutic genetic material into the host genome, over viruses, like the adenovirus used in the experiment in which Gelsinger died, which only have short-term effects. In the Gelsinger experiment, the researchers believed that a short-acting viral vector would be sufficient; their aim was to ward off the comas that produce devastating neurological effects in newborns with OTC within 72 hours of their birth.

Another gene therapy approach that is attracting significant interest is RNA interference (RNAi). Recall from Chapter 2 that during the process of transcription, the DNA double helix breaks apart and each strand combines with adenine, guanine, cytosine, and, instead of thymine, a nucleotide called uracil, to create messenger RNA. If the messenger RNA exits the cell nucleus and encounters a structure in the cytoplasm called a ribosome, the ribosome reads the information in the messenger RNA and constructs proteins, the process known as translation.

While messenger RNA usually consists of single strands, some forms of RNA come in double strands. This is often the case with RNA from viruses. When the cell detects double-stranded RNA, it regards it as an invader and destroys it. It turns out that cells use the same basic method to deactivate portions of DNA so that there is no translation—that is, the protein that the DNA codes for is not produced. This method of preventing translation is called RNA interference. In the context of gene therapy, the idea is to use RNAi to silence disease genes—that is, to deactivate stretches of DNA that, if active, would produce proteins that caused illness. The FDA has approved clinical trials of RNAi to prevent macular degeneration and respiratory syncytial virus, a disease that can cause pneumonia and other respiratory problems in infants and the elderly.

The great advantage of RNAi therapy is that it does not alter the DNA itself. One problem is that RNA degrades relatively quickly in the bloodstream, so that methods must be found to deliver the RNAi to the target cells quickly and accurately. For a discussion of regulatory issues raised by RNAi, see Reese McKinght, RNA Interference: A Critical Analysis of the Regulatory and Ethical Issues Encountered in the Development of a Novel Therapy, 15 Albany L. J. of Science & Technology 73–108 (2004).

C. REGULATION OF GENE THERAPY

1. The Recombinant DNA Advisory Committee (RAC)

PAUL BERG ET AL., LETTER
185 Science 303 (1974).

POTENTIAL BIOHAZARDS OF RECOMBINANT DNA MOLECULES

Recent advances in techniques for the isolation and rejoining of segments of DNA now permit construction of biologically active recombinant DNA molecules in vitro. For example, DNA restriction endonucleases, which generate DNA fragments containing cohesive ends especially suitable for rejoining, have been used to create new types of biologically functional bacterial plasmids carrying antibiotic resistance markers and to link *Xenopus laevis* ribosomal DNA to DNA from a bacterial plasmid. This latter recombinant plasmid has been shown to replicate stably in *Escherichia coli* where it synthesizes RNA that is complementary to X. laevis ribsomal DNA. Similarly, segments of *Drosophila* chromosomal DNA have been incorporated into both plasmid and bacteriaphage DNA's to yield hybrid molecules that can infect and replicate in *E. coli.*

Several groups of scientists are now planning to use this technology to create recombinant DNAs from a variety of other viral, animal, and bacterial sources. Although such experiments are likely to facilitate the solution of important theoretical and practical biological problems, they would also result in the creation of novel types of infectious DNA elements whose biological properties cannot be completely predicted in advance.

There is serious concern that some of these artificial recombinant DNA molecules could prove biologically hazardous. One potential hazard in current experiments derives from the need to use a bacterium like *E. coli* to clone the recombinant DNA molecules and to amplify their number. Strains of *E. coli* commonly reside in the human intestinal tract, and they are capable of exchanging genetic information with other types of bacteria, some of which are pathogenic to man. Thus, new DNA elements introduced into *E. coli.* might possibly become widely disseminated among human, bacterial, plant, or animal populations with unpredictable effects.

Concern for these emerging capabilities was raised by scientists attending the 1973 Gordon Research Conference on Nucleic Acids, who requested that the National Academy of Sciences give consideration to these matters. The undersigned members of a committee, acting on behalf of and with the endorsement of the Assembly of Life Sciences of the National Research Council on this matter, propose the following recommendations.

First, and most important, that until the potential hazards of such recombinant DNA molecules have been better evaluated or until adequate methods are developed for preventing their spread, scientists throughout the world join with the members of this committee in voluntarily deferring the following types of experiments.

Type I: Construction of new, autonomously replicating bacterial plasmids that might result in the introduction of genetic determinants for antibiotic resistance or bacterial toxin formation into bacterial strains that do not at present carry such determinants; or construction of new bacterial plasmids containing combinations of resistance to clinically useful antibiotics unless plasmids containing such combinations of antibiotic resistance determinants already exist in nature.

Type II: Linkage of all or segments of the DNA's from oncogenic or other animal viruses to autonomously replicating DNA elements such as bacterial plasmids or other viral DNA's. Such recombinant DNA molecules might be more easily disseminated to bacterial populations in humans and other species, and thus possibly increase the incidence of cancer or other diseases.

Second, plans to link fragments of animal DNA's to bacterial plasmid DNA or bacteriophage DNA should be carefully weighed in light of the fact that many types of animal cell DNA's contain sequences common to RNA tumor viruses. Since joining of any foreign DNA to a DNA replication system creates new recombinant DNA molecules whose biological properties cannot be predicted with certainty, such experiments should not be undertaken lightly.

Third, the director of the National Institutes of Health is requested to give immediate consideration to establishing an advisory committee charged with (i) overseeing an experimental program to evaluate the potential biological and ecological hazards of the above types of recombinant DNA molecules; (ii) developing procedures which will minimize the spread of such molecules within human and other populations; and (iii) devising guidelines to be followed by investigators working with potentially hazardous recombinant DNA molecules.

Fourth, an international meeting of involved scientists from all over the world should be convened early in the coming year to review scientific progress in this area and to further discuss appropriate ways to deal with the potential biohazards of recombinant DNA molecules.

The above recommendations are made with the realization (i) that our concern is based on judgments of potential rather than demonstrated risk since there are few available experimental data on the hazards of such DNA molecules and (ii) that adherence to our major recommendations will entail postponement or possibly abandonment of certain types of scientifically worthwhile experiments. Moreover, we are aware of many theoretical and practical difficulties involved in evaluating the human hazards of such recombinant DNA molecules. Nonetheless, our concern for the possible unfortunate consequences of indiscriminate application of these techniques motivates us to urge all scientists working in this area to join us in agreeing not to initiate experiments of types I and II above until attempts have been made to evaluate the hazards and some resolution of the outstanding questions has been achieved.

Paul Berg, *Chairman,* David Baltimore, Herbert W. Boyer, Stanley N. Cohen, Ronald W. Davis, David S. Hogness, Daniel Nathans, Richard Roblin, James D. Watson, Sherman Weissman, Norton D. Zinder, Committee on Recombinant DNA Molecules, Assembly of Life Sciences, National Research Council, National Academy of Sciences

NOTES AND QUESTIONS

The Berg letter called on scientists to adopt a voluntary, world-wide moratorium on rDNA experiments until further deliberations could determine whether rDNA could be performed safely. A voluntary moratorium is a form of self-regulation, an alternative to external restraints, such as legal prohibitions. Is voluntary action a viable method of regulating gene therapy? What are its strengths and weaknesses as a regulatory approach? For an early discussion of these issues, see Barry Furrow, Governing Science: Public Risks and Private Remedies, 131 U. Pa. L. Rev. 1403 (1983).

Professional self-regulation may take the form of individual choices about behavior, such as when a physician refuses to perform procedures that violate the physician's moral or religious beliefs. It also may be embodied in the views of professional organizations, such as the ethical codes of physician groups or official positions adopted by scientific bodies.

AMERICAN MEDICAL ASSOCIATION COUNCIL ON ETHICAL AND JUDICIAL AFFAIRS

Current Opinion E–2.11.
Gene Therapy (Updated 1994).

Gene therapy involves the replacement or modification of a genetic variant to restore or enhance cellular function or to improve the reaction of non-genetic therapies.

Two types of gene therapy have been identified: (1) somatic cell therapy, in which human cells other than germ cells are genetically altered, and (2) germ line therapy, in which a replacement gene is integrated into the genome of human gametes or their precursors, resulting in expression of the new gene in the patient's offspring and subsequent generations. The fundamental difference between germ line therapy and somatic cell therapy is that germ line therapy affects the welfare of subsequent generations and may be associated with increased risk and the potential for unpredictable and irreversible results. Because of the far-reaching implications of germ line therapy, it is appropriate to limit genetic intervention to somatic cells at this time.

The goal of both somatic cell and germ line therapy is to alleviate human suffering and disease by remedying disorders for which available therapies are not satisfactory. This goal should be pursued only within the ethical tradition of medicine, which gives primacy to the welfare of the patient whose safety and well-being must be vigorously protected. To the extent possible, experience with animal studies must be sufficient to assure the effectiveness and safety of the techniques used, and the predictability of the results.

* * *

As gene therapy becomes feasible for a variety of human disorders, there are several practical factors to consider to ensure safe application of this technology in society. First, any gene therapy research should meet the Council's guidelines on clinical investigation (Opinion 2.07) and investigators must adhere to the standards of medical practice and professional responsibility. The proposed procedure must be fully discussed with the patient and the written informed consent of the patient or the patient's legal representative must be voluntary.

Investigators must be thorough in their attempts to eliminate any unwanted viral agents from the viral vector containing the corrective gene. The potential for adverse effects of the viral delivery system must be disclosed to the patient. The effectiveness of gene therapy must be evaluated fully, including the determination of the natural history of the disease and follow-up examination of subsequent generations. Gene therapy should be pursued only after the availability or effectiveness of other possible therapies is found to be insufficient. These considerations should be reviewed, as appropriate, as procedures and scientific information develop.

NOTES AND QUESTIONS

Is the AMA's approach, which relies on investigators adhering to the organization's ethical standards, a suitable one for regulating gene therapy? What are the consequences if a physician-researcher violates these provisions? See generally David Orentlicher, The Influence of a Professional Organization on Physician Behavior, 57 Alb. L. Rev. 583 (1994). Do these provisions apply to non-physicians?

———————

Following publication of the Berg letter, another conference was held at the Asilomar Conference Center in California. The meeting was attended by 150 scientists, 4 lawyers, and 16 journalists. The focus was on how rDNA experiments could be conducted safely. As one attendee observed:

> The recombinant DNA issue was defined as a technical problem to be solved by technical means. Larger ethical issues regarding the purposes and the long-term goals of the research were excluded, despite the rich discussion that had occurred among geneticists and other biologists in the 1960s about where to draw the line when it became possible to do genetic engineering. * * * Instead of these longer-term issues, the focus at Asilomar in 1975 was on safety of newly-developed technical tools for genetic engineering, on the means not the ends.

Charles Weiner, Recombinant DNA Policy: Asilomar Conference, in 2 Encyclopedia of Ethical, Legal and Policy Issues in Biotechnology 909, 910–911 (Thomas H. Murray & Maxwell J. Mehlman, eds. 2000). For a description of the conference by one of the lawyers who attended, see Roger B. Dworkin, Science, Society, and the Expert Town Meeting: Some Comments on Asilomar, 51 S. Cal. L. Rev. 1471 (1978).

Shortly before the Asilomar Conference, the director of NIH established an advisory committee called the Recombinant DNA Advisory Committee, the "RAC." The RAC originally had 12 members, all scientists. It met for the first time immediately after the conference, and began to draft safety guidelines for recombinant DNA research based on the conference proceedings. The guidelines, published at 41 Fed. Reg. 27902 (1976), required all large-scale NIH-funded rDNA experiments to be approved by the RAC.

In 1978, the RAC was expanded to 25 members, one-third of whom were "public" members, including lawyers and bioethicists, and the RAC issued revised guidelines (42 Fed. Reg. 49596) which, recognizing that rDNA experiments were less risky than originally had been thought, relaxed some of the restrictions on rDNA research. For a history of the early RAC, see Sheldon Krimsky, Genetic Alchemy: The Social History of the Recombinant DNA Controversy (1982).

In 1982, a report entitled *Splicing Life* was issued by the President's Commission for the Study of Ethical Problems in Medicine and Biomedical and Behavioral Research. The President's Commission, best known for the 1979 *Belmont Report*, which laid out the ethical ground rules for human subjects research, called for expanded consideration of the ethical and social implications of gene therapy. However, the report was broadly supportive of the technology.

In response to the President's Commission report and to congressional hearings (Human Genetic Engineering, Hearing Before the Subcommittee on Investigations and Oversight, House Committee on Science and Technology, 97th Cong. 2nd Sess., November 16–18, 1982), the RAC and NIH began to consider whether the RAC, which hitherto had focused on laboratory and animal experiments using rDNA techniques, should review proposals for human gene therapy experiments. In 1984, it established a Human Gene Therapy Working Group (later called the Human Gene Therapy Subcommittee). The Working Group, chaired by a bioethicist, LeRoy Walters, and comprising three laboratory scientists, three clinicians, three lawyers, three ethicists, two public policy specialists and a representative of the public, issued a 4000–word document called "Points to Consider" to guide researchers seeking RAC approval for federally-funded human gene therapy trials:

DEPARTMENT OF HEALTH AND HUMAN SERVICES, RECOMBINANT DNA RESEARCH; REQUEST FOR PUBLIC COMMENT ON "POINTS TO CONSIDER IN THE DESIGN AND SUBMISSION OF HUMAN SOMATIC–CELL GENE THERAPY PROTOCOLS"

National Institutes of Health 50 Fed. Reg. 2940 (1985).

Experiments in which recombinant DNA * * * is introduced into cells of a human subject with the intent of stably modifying the subject's genome are covered by Section III–A–4 of the National Institutes of Health (NIH) Guidelines for Research Involving Recombinant DNA Molecules (49 FR 46266). Section III–A–4 requires such experiments to be reviewed by the NIH Recombinant DNA Advisory Committee (RAC) and approved by the NIH. RAC consideration of each proposal will follow publication of a precis of the proposal in the Federal Register, an opportunity for public comment, and review of the proposal by a working group of the RAC. RAC recommendations on each proposal will be forwarded to the NIH Director for a decision, which will then be published in the Federal Register. In accordance with Section IV–C–1–B of the NIH Guidelines, the NIH Director may approve proposals only if he finds that they present "no significant risk to health or the environment."

In general, it is expected that somatic-cell gene therapy protocols will not present a risk to the environment as the recombinant DNA is expected to be confined to the human subject. Nevertheless, item I–B–4–b of the "Points to Consider" document asks the researchers to address specifically this point.

This document is intended to provide guidance in preparing proposals for NIH consideration under Section III–A–4. Not every point mentioned in the document will necessarily require attention in every proposal. It is expected that the document will be considered for revision at least annually as experience in evaluating proposals accumulates.

A proposal will be considered by the RAC only after the protocol has been approved by the local Institutional Biosafety Committee (IBC) and by the local Institutional Review Board (IRB) in accordance with Department of Health and Human Service regulations for the protection of human subjects (45 CFR, Part 46). If a proposal involves children, special attention should be paid to Subpart D of these regulations. The IRB and IBC may, at their discretion, condition their approval on further specific deliberation by the RAC and its working group. Consideration of gene therapy proposals by the RAC may proceed simultaneously with review by any other involved federal agencies (e.g., the Food and Drug Administration) provided that the RAC is notified of the simultaneous review. The committee expects that the first proposals submitted for RAC review will contain no proprietary information on trade secrets; therefore, the review will be open to the public. The public review of these protocols will serve to educate the public not only on the technical aspects of the proposals but also on the meaning and significance of the research.

The clinical application of recombinant DNA techniques to human gene therapy raises two general kinds of questions. Part I of this document deals with the short-term risks and benefits of the proposed research to the patient and to other people as well as with issues of equity in the selection of subjects, informed consent, and privacy and confidentiality. In Part II, investigators are requested to address broader ethical and social issues pertaining to the research and its longer-term implications. These broader questions go beyond the usual purview of IRBs and reflect the kinds of public concerns discussed by a recent presidential commission in its report entitled Splicing Life: The Social and Ethical Issues of Genetic Engineering with Human Beings. Responses to the questions raised in these "Points to Consider" should be in the form of either written answers or references to specific sections of the protocol or other documentation which accompanies the proposal. In addition, Part III of the

"Points to Consider" summarizes other documentation that will assist the RAC and its working group in their review of gene therapy proposals.

I. DESCRIPTION OF PROPOSAL

A. Objectives and rationale of the proposed research. State concisely the overall objectives and rationale of the proposed study. Please provide information on the following specific points:

1. Why is the disease selected for treatment by means of gene therapy a good candidate for such treatment?

2. Describe the natural history and range of expression of the disease selected for treatment. In your view, are the usual effects of the disease predictable enough to allow for meaningful assessment of the results of gene therapy?

3. Is the protocol designed to prevent all manifestations of the disease, to halt the progression of the disease after symptoms have begun to appear, or to reverse manifestations of the disease in seriously ill victims?

4. What alternative therapies exist? In what groups of patients are these therapies effective? What are their relative advantages and disadvantages as compared with the proposed gene therapy?

B. Research design, anticipated risks and benefits.

* * *

3. Clinical procedures, including patient monitoring. Describe the treatment that will be administered to patients and the diagnostic methods that will be used to monitor the success or failure of the treatment.

a. Will cells (e.g., bone marrow cells) be removed from patients and treated in vitro in preparation for gene therapy? If so, what kinds of cells will be removed from the patients, how many, how often, and at what intervals?

b. Will patients be treated to eliminate or reduce the number of cells containing malfunctioning genes (e.g., through radiation or chemotherapy) prior to gene therapy?

c. What treated cells (or vector/DNA combination) will be given to patients in the attempt to administer gene therapy? How will the treated cells be administered? What volume of cells will be used? Will there be single or multiple treatments? If so, over what period of time?

d. What are the clinical endpoints of the study? How will patients be monitored to assess specific effects of the treatment on the disease? What is the sensitivity of the analyses? How frequently will follow-up studies be done? How long will patient follow-up continue?

e. What are the major potential beneficial and adverse effects of treatment that you anticipate? What measures will be taken in an attempt to control or reverse these adverse effects if they occur? Compare the probability and magnitude of potential adverse effects on patients with the probability and magnitude of deleterious consequences from the disease if gene therapy is not performed.

f.   Serious adverse effects of treatment should be reported immediately to both your local IRB and the NIH Office for Protection from Research Risks (phone: 301–496–7005).

g.   Reports regarding the general progress of patients should be filed at six-month intervals with both your local IRB and the NIH Office of Recombinant DNA Activities (phone: 301–496–6051). These twice-yearly reports should continue for a sufficient period of time to allow observation of all major effects (at least three to five years).

h.   If a treated patient dies, will an autopsy be requested? If so, please indicate what special studies, if any, will be performed.

4.   Public health considerations. Describe the potential benefits and hazards of the proposed therapy to persons other than the patients being treated.

a.   What potential benefits or hazards are postulated?

b.   Is there any expectation that the recombinant DNA will spread from the patient to others or to the environment?

c.   What precautions will be taken, if any, to protect others (e.g., patients sharing a room, health-care workers, or family members) from such potential hazards?

5.   Qualifications of investigators, adequacy of laboratory and clinical facilities. Indicate the relevant training and experience of the personnel who will be involved in the preclinical studies and clinical administration of gene therapy. In addition, please describe the laboratory and clinical facilities where the proposed study will be performed.

a.   What professional personnel (medical and nonmedical) will be involved in the proposed study? What are their specific qualifications and experience with respect to the disease to be treated and with respect to the techniques employed in molecular biology? Please provide curricula vitae.

b.   At what hospital or clinic will the treatment be given? Which facilities of the hospital or clinic will be especially important for the proposed study? Will patients occupy regular hospital beds or clinical research center beds?

C.   Selection of subjects. Estimate the number of patients to be involved in the proposed study of gene therapy. Describe recruitment procedures and patient eligibility requirements. Indicate how equity consideration in the selection of subjects will be handled.

2.   How many eligible patients do you anticipate being able to identify each year?

3.   What recruitment procedures do you plan to use?

4. What selection criteria do you plan to employ? What are the exclusion and inclusion criteria for the study?

5. What equity issues, if any, are likely to arise in the selection of patients? How will these issues be addressed?

D. Informed consent. Indicate how patients will be informed about the proposed study and how their consent will be solicited. If the study involves pediatric or mentally handicapped patients, describe procedures for seeking the permission of parents or guardians and, where applicable, the assent of each patient. Areas of special concern include potential adverse effects, financial costs, privacy, and the right to withdraw from further participation in the study.

1. Will the major points covered in IA–IC of this document be disclosed to potential participants in this study and/or parents or guardians in language that is understandable to them? (Include a copy of the patient contest form as part of the documentation requested in Part II below).

2. Will the innovative character and the theoretically-possible adverse effects of gene therapy be discussed with patients and/or parents or guardians? Will the potential adverse effects be compared with the consequences of the disease? What will be said to convey that some of these adverse effects, if they occur, could be irreversible?

3. Will the financial costs of gene therapy and any available alternative therapies be explained to patients and/or parents or guardians?

4. Will patients and/or parents or guardians be informed that the innovative character of gene therapy may lead to great interest by the media in the research and in treated patients? What special procedures, if any, will be followed to protect the privacy of patients and their families?

5. Will patients and/or their parents or guardians be informed of their right to withdraw at any time from the proposed study and of the consequences of withdrawal at the various stages of the experiment? State the extent to which subjects will be specifically advised of the reversibility or irreversibility of procedures that are performed during the course of the experiment.

E. Privacy and confidentiality. Indicate what measures will be taken to protect the privacy of gene therapy patients and their families as well as to maintain the confidentiality of research data.

1. What provisions will be made to honor the wishes of individual patients (and the parents or guardians of pediatric or mentally handicapped patients) as to whether, when, or how the identity of patients is publicly disclosed?

2. What provision will be made to maintain the confidentiality of research data, at least in cases where data could be linked to individual patients?

II. SOCIAL ISSUES

The following issues are beyond the normal purview of local IRBs. However, since these issues have arisen in public debates about human gene therapy and the potential future applications of genetic techniques, the RAC and its working group request that investigators respond to questions A and B below and discuss, at their discretion, the general issues enumerated in point C.

A. What steps will be taken to ensure that accurate information is made available to the public with respect to such public concerns as may arise from the proposed study?

B. Do you or your funding sources intend to protect under patent or trade secret laws either the products or the procedures developed in the proposed study? If so, what steps will be taken to permit as full communication as possible among investigators and clinicians concerning research methods and results?

C. The following issues will also be considered by the RAC and its working group in reviewing each gene therapy proposal:

1. How strong is the evidence that the proposed somatic-cell gene therapy will not affect the reproductive cells of patients?

2. Is the proposed somatic-cell gene therapy an extension of existing methods of health care, or does it represent a distinct departure from present treatments of disease?

3. Is it likely that somatic-cell therapy for human genetic disease will lead to: (a) germ-line gene therapy, (b) the enhancement of human capabilities through genetic means, or (c) eugenic programs encouraged or even mandated by governments?

NOTES AND QUESTIONS

1. Do the "Points to Consider" adequately address the ethical, legal, and social issues that might be raised by gene therapy experiments? Which issues does it mention, and which, if any, does it neglect? For a critique, see Eric Juengst, The NIH "Points to Consider" and the Limits of Human Gene Therapy, 1 Human Gene Therapy 425 (1990).

2. The institution where the research is conducted is required to have an Institutional Review Board (IRB) and an Institutional Biosafety Committee (IBC) to approve and oversee the research. IBCs were required by the NIH's first guidelines for rDNA research, 41 Fed. Reg. 27,902 (1976). According to the guidelines, institutional biohazards committees, as they were then called, are required to (1) advise the institution on policies regarding containment of rDNA organisms; (2) create a reference resource; (3) develop a procedures manual; and (4) certify to NIH that they have reviewed and approved the safety of rDNA experiments.

3. The first protocol for a human experiment was received by the RAC in 1988. It was not an actual treatment experiment but a "gene marking"

study in which the researcher, Steven Rosenberg, proposed to use cells (specifically, tumor-infiltrating lymphocytes) "marked" with an inserted bacterial gene to track the path of the tumor-fighting cells in cancer patients. The RAC approved the experiment, and after a lawsuit filed by the Foundation on Economic Trends, a group headed by Jeremy Rifkin, complaining of procedural irregularities in the RAC review process, was settled, the experiment took place. For a description of the suit and its aftermath, see Joseph M. Rainsbury, Biotechnology on the RAC: FDA/NIH Regulation of Human Gene Therapy, 55 Food & Drug L. J. 575, 584 (2000); Kennedy Institute of Ethics, National Reference Center for Bioethics Literature, Scope Note 24 (February 2000), at www.georgetown.edu/research/ncrbl/publications/scopenotes/sn24. htm; Foundation on Economic Trends, Petition to Amend the National Institutes of Health Guidelines for Research Involving Recombinant DNA Molecules to Establish a Public Policy Advisory Committee, 2 Human Gene Therapy 131 (1991).

4. Rosenberg's experiment was followed by W. French Anderson's trial involving Ashanti DeSilva, described earlier.

5. In 1993, the director of NIH, Bernadine Healey, approved an exception to the normal RAC review process for "compassionate use"—in this case, for a patient suffering from Stage IV glioblastoma, a highly aggressive form of brain cancer. "Compassionate use" is an approach used by physicians to obtain supplies of experimental drugs for specific patients before the drugs are approved by the FDA. See 21 U.S.C. § 360bbb. The approval, which followed a letter to Healy from Senator Tom Harkin, sparked considerable debate within the RAC, and led to the adoption of the following amendment to the Points to Consider providing for "expedited review":

Recombinant DNA Research: Actions Under the Guidelines

IV. Procedures to be Followed for Expedited Review

1. An investigator submitting a request to the NIH for expedited review of a gene transfer protocol must provide detailed information regarding the necessity of expedited review.

2. No protocol shall be considered without Institutional Biosafety Committee (IBC) and Institutional Review Board (IRB) approval.

3. At this time, all gene transfer protocols must be considered experimental.

4. Regardless of the method of review, the Points to Consider must be the standard of review for all gene transfer protocols.

5. Review of such protocols may include intramural NIH experts but must include extramural experts.

6. Among other factors to be considered by the reviewer, is the similarity of the new protocol to previously approved protocols.

7. The NIH will report to the RAC following expedited review and will include all of the materials on which the decision was based. The RAC will formally review the protocol at its next scheduled meeting. Patient privacy will be maintained.

8. Protocols that are deferred or not approved by the RAC in its normal review process are not eligible for expedited review. No protocol shall have more than one patient approved under expedited review.

9. As requested in the context of non-expedited review, none of the costs of the experimental protocol should be borne by the patient or the patient's family.

10. Data on all patients undergoing gene transfer shall be provided to the RAC within six months of the procedure.

58 Fed. Reg. 21,737 (1993). The idea behind the compassionate use exemption in general is to make experimental products available to patients who are not enrolled in clinical trials. When, if ever, is it appropriate to make an exception to established procedures designed to protect human subjects? Is this appropriate for gene therapy? Do these provisions provide adequate protection? How do these provisions compare to the Points to Consider? Which regime is stricter?

6. In 1985, the RAC issued a revised version of its "Points to Consider." 50 Fed. Reg. 33,462. The revision contained the following new language:

The acceptability of human somatic-cell gene therapy has been addressed in several recent documents as well as in numerous academic studies.

* * *

Civic, religious, scientific, and medical groups have all accepted, in principle, the appropriateness of gene therapy of somatic cells in humans for specific genetic diseases. Somatic cell gene therapy is seen as an extension of present methods of therapy that might be preferable to other technologies.

Concurring with this judgment, the RAC and its working group are prepared to consider for approval somatic-cell therapy protocols, provided that the design of such experiments offers adequate assurance that their consequences will not go beyond their purpose, which is the same as the traditional purpose of all clinical investigations, namely, to benefit the health and well-being of the individual being treated while at the same time gathering generalizable knowledge.

The two possible undesirable consequences of somatic-cell therapy would be unintentional (1) vertical transmission of genetic changes from an individual to his or her offspring or (2) horizontal transmission of viral infection to other persons with whom the individual comes in contact. Accordingly, this document requests information that will enable the RAC and its working group to assess the likelihood that the proposed somatic-cell gene therapy will inadvertently affect reproductive cells or lead to infection of other people (e.g., treatment personnel or relatives).

In recognition of the social concern that surrounds the general discussion of human gene therapy, the working group will continue to consider the possible long-range effects of applying knowledge gained from these and related experiments. While research in molecular biology could lead to the development of techniques for germ line intervention or for the use of genetic means to enhance human capabilities rather than to correct defects in patients, the working group does not believe that these effects will follow immediately or inevitably from experiments with somatic-cell gene therapy. The working group will cooperate with other groups in assessing the possible long-term consequences of somatic-cell gene therapy and related laboratory and animal experiments in order to define appropriate human applications of this emerging technology.

Note that the RAC for the first time declared its willingness to consider protocols for human gene therapy experiments.

2.   Food and Drug Administration

The Food and Drug Administration within the federal Department of Health and Human Services regulates drugs, medical devices, and a class of products called "biologics." Three weeks before the RAC issued its "Points to Consider" in 1985, the FDA issued a policy statement declaring its intention to assert regulatory authority over biotechnology products, including gene therapies, and describing the sources of its regulatory authority.

FOOD AND DRUG ADMINISTRATION, STATEMENT OF POLICY FOR REGULATING BIOTECHNOLOGY PRODUCTS

49 Fed. Reg. 50,878 (1984).

INTRODUCTION

A small but important and expanding fraction of the products the Food and Drug Administration (FDA) regulates represents the fruits of new technological achievements. These achievements are in areas as diverse as polymer chemistry, molecular biology, and micro-miniaturization. It is also noteworthy that technological advancement in a given area may give rise to very diverse product classes, some or all of which may be under FDA's regulatory jurisdiction. For example, new developments in recombinant DNA research can yield products as divergent as food additives, drugs, biologics, and medical devices.

Although there are no statutory provisions or regulations that address biotechnology directly, the laws and regulations under which the Agency operates place the burden of proof of safety as well as effectiveness of products on the manufacturer, except for traditional foods and cosmetics. The administrative review of products using biotechnology is based on the intended use of each product on a case-by-case basis.

This notice describes the regulatory policy of the FDA applicable to biotechnology in general. The manner in which regulations for biotechnology are implemented in the United States could have a direct impact on the competitiveness of U.S. producers in both domestic and world markets. Inconsistent or duplicative domestic regulation will put U.S. producers at a competitive disadvantage. In addition, certification systems which favor domestic products, if adopted by our trading partners, could create substantial nontariff barriers to trade and block market access. Therefore during the development of the U.S. regulatory procedures for biotechnology products, attention is being paid to the need for achieving consistency in national regulation and international harmonization. With respect to international harmonization the U.S. is seeking to promote scientific cooperation, mutual understanding of regulatory approaches, international agreement on a range of common technical problems such as the development of consistent test guidelines, laboratory practices and principles for assessing potential risks. In achieving national consistency and international harmonization, regulatory decisions can be made in a socially responsible manner, protecting human health and the environment, while allowing U.S. producers to remain competitive.

The Agency possesses extensive experience with the administrative and regulatory regimens described as applied to the products of biotechnological processes, new and old, and proposes no new procedures or requirements for regulated industry or individuals. Public comment is requested on scientific and regulatory policy issues raised by this notice.

The marketing of new drugs and biologics for human use, and new animal drugs, requires prior approval of an appropriate new drug application (NDA), license, or new animal drug application (NADA). For new medical devices, including diagnostic devices for human use either a premarket approval application or reclassification petition is required. If the device is determined to be equivalent to an already marketed device, a premarket notification under section 510(k) of the Federal Food, Drug, and Cosmetic Act (the act) is required. For food products, section 409 of the act requires FDA preclearance of food additives including those prepared using biotechnology. Section 706 of the act requires preclearance of color additives. The implementing regulations for food and color additive petitions and for affirming generally recognized as safe (GRAS) food substances are sufficiently comprehensive to apply to those involving new biotechnology.

Genetic manipulations of plants or animals may enter FDA's jurisdiction in other ways; for example, the introduction into a plant of a gene coding for a pesticide or growth factor may constitute adulteration of the foodstuff derived from the plant, or the use of a new microorganism found in a food such as yogurt could be considered a food additive. Such situations will be evaluated case-by-case, and with cooperation with the U.S. Department of Agriculture (USDA), where appropriate.

THE REGULATORY PROCESS

Congress has provided FDA authority under the act and the Public Health Service (PHS) Act to regulate products regardless of how they are manufactured.

GENERAL REQUIREMENTS FOR HUMAN DRUGS AND BIOLOGICS

A new drug is, in general terms, a drug not generally recognized by qualified scientific experts as safe and effective for the proposed use. New drugs may not be marketed unless they have been approved as safe and effective, and clinical investigations on human subjects by qualified experts are a prerequisite for determination of safety and effectiveness. Sponsors of investigations of new drugs or new drug uses of approved drugs file an Investigational New Drug Application (IND) to conduct clinical investigations on human subjects. The IND must contain information needed to demonstrate the safety of proceeding to test the drug in human subjects, including, for example, drug composition, manufacturing and controls data, results of animal testing, training and experience of investigators, and a plan for clinical investigation. In addition, assurance of informed consent and protection of the rights and safety of human subjects is required. FDA evaluates IND submissions and reviews ongoing clinical investigations. Significant changes in the conditions of the study, including changes in study design, drug manufacture or formulation, or proposals for additional studies, must be submitted to FDA as amendment to the IND.

FDA approval of a New Drug Application (NDA) or an abbreviated New Drug Application (ANDA) is required before the new drug can be marketed. The NDA must contain:

— Full reports of investigations, including the results of clinical investigations, that show whether or not the drug is safe and effective;

— A list of components of the drug and a statement of the drug's quantitative composition;

— A description of the methods used in, and the facilities and controls used for, the manufacturing, processing, and packaging of the drug;

— Samples of the drug and drug components as may be required; and

— Specimens of the proposed labeling.

NDA holders who intend to market an approved drug under conditions other than those approved in the NDA must submit a supplemental NDA containing clinical evidence of the drug's safety and effectiveness for the added indications. Extensive changes such as a changed formula, manufacturing process, or method of testing differing from the conditions of approval outlined in the NDA may also require additional clinical testing.

Section 351 of the PHS Act defines a "biological product" as "any virus, therapeutic serum, toxin, antitoxin, vaccine, blood, blood component or derivative, allergenic product, or analogous product * * * applicable to the prevention, treatment, or cure of diseases or injuries of man * * *." Biologics are regulated similarly to new drugs during the IND phase; approval for marketing is granted by license, which is only issued upon demonstration that both the manufacturing establishment and the product meet standards designed to ensure safety, purity, potency, and efficacy. All biologics are subject to general provisions in the regulations that assure potency, general safety, sterility, and purity. In addition, specific tests and standards are established for particular products. To obtain a license, the manufacturer must submit information demonstrating that the manufacturing facility and the product meet FDA standards, and the facility must pass a prelicensing inspection. Licensed products are subject to specific requirements for lot release by FDA.

Manufacturers of new drugs and biologics must operate in conformance with current good manufacturing practice (CGMP) regulations, which address: adequately equipped manufacturing facilities; adequately trained personnel; stringent control over the manufacturing process; and appropriate finished product examination. CGMP's are designed to protect the integrity and purity of the product. Approval of the product application is also approval of the sponsor's process techniques.

* * *

GENERAL REQUIREMENTS FOR MEDICAL DEVICES

Medical devices for human use are regulated by requirements of the act as amended by the Medical Device Amendments of 1976. In general terms, a device is defined in the act as any health care product that does not achieve any of its principal intended purposes by chemical action in or on the body or by being metabolized. Devices include diagnostic aids such as reagents, antibiotic sensitivity discs, and test kits for in vitro diagnosis of disease. Veterinary medical devices are subject to the act but are not subject to preclearance requirements.

Regulations promulgated under the Medical Device Amendments control introduction of medical devices into commerce. In May 1976 when these device amendments were enacted, expert advisory committees recommended classifications for all medical devices of the types marketed at that time. The law segregates medical devices into three classes:

Class I devices are subject to the minimum level of control; general controls include the CGMP's.

Class II devices have been declared to require performance standards to assure their safety and/or effectiveness. They must also meet the controls of class I.

Class III devices require formal FDA approval of a Premarket Approval Application (PMAA) for each make and model of the device to assure its safety and effectiveness. The controls of class I are also required.

Before a manufacturer may introduce into commerce any medical device not previously marketed, the manufacturer must formally declare that intent to FDA and proceed along one of two legal avenues. The manufacturer can file a premarket notification to FDA seeking a determination that the device is substantially equivalent to a preamendment device and proceed to market the device subject to whatever controls apply to the older versions of the device depending on its classification. This is the so-called "510(k)" process, which takes its name from a paragraph in the act.

A new device—that is, one not substantially equivalent to a preenactment device—is automatically a class III device requiring FDA approval of a PMAA unless FDA reclassifies it into class I or class II. In the premarket approval process, the manufacturer must establish that the device is safe and effective. This is typically accomplished by scientific analysis by the Agency of product performance and data from clinical trials, submitted by the manufacturer in the PMAA.

For a "significant risk device," as defined in FDA's regulations, the sponsor must submit an application to FDA for approval to conduct the investigation. This application is known as the Investigational Device Exemption (IDE). When the manufacturer believes there are sufficient data to establish the safety and effectiveness of its device, the manufacturer may file a premarket approval application, or PMAA. The law requires that FDA act on such an application within 180 days.

REGULATION OF SPECIFIC PRODUCTS

Within the framework of FDA's statutes and regulations, strategies have been developed for the evaluation of various kinds of "biotechnological" or "genetically engineered" products, as well as for other products. These strategies are product-specific rather than technology-specific. For example, review of the production of human viral vaccines routinely involves a number of considerations including the purity of the media and the serum used to grow the cell substrate, the nature of the cell substrate, and the characterization of the virus. In the case of a live viral vaccine, the final product is biologically active and is intended to replicate in the recipient. Therefore, the composition, concentration, subtype, immunogenicity, reactivity, and nonpathogenicity of the vaccine preparation are all considerations in the final review, whatever the techniques employed in "engineering" the virus.

Scientific considerations may dictate areas of generic concerns or the use of certain tests for specific situations. For example, a hepatitis B vaccine produced in yeast (via recombinant DNA techniques) would be monitored for yeast cell contaminants, while distinctly different contaminants would be of concern in a similar vaccine produced from the plasma of infected patients.

In order to provide guidance to current or prospective manufacturers of drugs and biological products, the FDA has developed a series of documents describing points that manufacturers might wish to consider in the production of interferon, monoclonal antibodies, and products of recombinant DNA technology, as well as in the use of new cell substrates. These documents, called "Points to Consider . . . ", are available from the Agency upon request.

Administrative jurisdiction within FDA's various organizational units are the same for a given product, whatever the processes employed in its production.

Nucleic acids used for human gene therapy trials will be subject to the same requirements as other biological drugs. It is possible that there will be some redundancy between the scientific reviews of these products performed by the National Institutes of Health and FDA.

* * *

Scientific Issues Surrounding Specific Products

There are some scientific issues raised by specific products manufactured with recombinant DNA technology. First, the molecular structure of some products is different from that of the active molecule in nature. For example, the "human growth hormone" from recombinant microorganisms has an extra amino acid, an amino-terminal methionine; hence, it is an analogue of the native hormone. Such differences may affect the drug's activity or immunogenicity and these considerations, among others, may affect the amount of clinical testing required. However, FDA possesses extensive experience with evaluation of analogues of native human polypeptides, a number of which have been approved for marketing.

Second, approval of the product application for pharmaceuticals is also approval of the sponsor's processing techniques, and FDA must determine whether the quality assurance within the manufacturing process is adequate to detect deviations that might occur, such as the occurrence of mutations in the coding sequence of the cloned gene during fermentation. Such mutations could, in theory, give rise to a subpopulation of molecules with an anomalous primary structure and altered activity. This is a potential problem inherent in the production of polypeptides in any fermentation process. One way FDA has dealt with these situations in existing IND's is to require batch-by-batch testing with appropriate techniques to ensure that the active drug substance is homogenous and has the correct identity.

Summary

FDA's administrative review of products, including those that employ specialized biotechnological techniques such as recombinant DNA in their manufacture, is based on the intended use of product on a case-by-case basis. Although scientific considerations may dictate areas of generic concerns for certain techniques, e.g., the possibility of contamination with adventitious agents or oncogenes when cultured mammalian cells are the source of a drug, the use of a given biotechnological technique does not require a different administrative process. Regulation by FDA must be based on the rational and scientific evaluation of products, and not on a priori assumptions about certain processes.

NOTES AND QUESTIONS

1. In its policy statement, the FDA states: "The Agency possesses extensive experience with the administrative and regulatory regimens described as applied to the products of biotechnological processes, new and old, and proposes no new procedures or requirements for regulated industry or individuals. * * * Nucleic acids used for human gene therapy trials will be subject to the same requirements as other biological drugs." This represents the core of the FDA's approach to biotechnology: Biotechnology products and processes, including gene therapy, are subject to the same regulatory requirements as any other product or process, no more and no less. This position is noteworthy because it heralded the agency's long-standing approach to the whole range of biotechnology products, including genetically-engineered foods, that they would not be subject to any special review for safety. This approach has only recently begun to unravel. In January 2001, for example, the agency's Center for Food Safety and Nutrition announced its intent to require manufacturers to notify the FDA 120 days prior to marketing a genetically engineered food and provide special evidence of safety. (see http://www.cfsan. fda.gov/~lrd/stbioeng.html.) Following Jesse Gelsinger's death, the FDA also announced its intent to impose special regulatory requirements on human gene therapy experiments, discussed below.

The FDA's position in the 1984 policy statement that the agency will apply its existing regulatory requirements to gene therapy is also noteworthy because it indicates the agency's willingness to regulate practices that might be regarded as the practice of medicine rather than the marketing of a product. Historically, the FDA has been deemed to lack the authority to regulate the practice of medicine. See, e.g., Chaney v. Heckler, 718 F.2d 1174, 1179 (D.C. Cir. 1983) (noting that legislative history of the Federal Food, Drug, and Cosmetic Act reflects congressional intent to prohibit FDA from regulating the practice of medicine), rev'd on other grounds, 470 U.S. 821 (1985); David A. Kessler, The Regulation of Investigational Drugs, 320 New Eng. J. Med. 281, 285 (1989). The agency itself has traditionally accepted this view. See 37 Fed. Reg. 16,503, 16,504 (1972) (concluding that "it is clear that Congress did not intend the [FDA] to regulate or interfere with the practice of medicine"); Online Pharmacies FAQs (Jan. 28, 2000) (www.fda.gov/oc/ buyonline/faqs.html) (FDA will "continue to defer to states to regulate the practice of medicine and pharmacy"). The agency's lack of authority over the practice of medicine is what allows physicians to prescribe drugs for uses which the agency has not approved—a practice known as "off-label use"— without violating federal law. The FDA's lack of authority to regulate off-label use is discussed infra in the section on the regulation of genetic enhancement. (The agency's lack of authority is cited by some commentators as a reason why it does not have jurisdiction to regulate human cloning, despite its claims to the contrary. See Elizabeth C. Price, Does the FDA Have Authority to Regulate Human Cloning?, 11 Harv. J. L. & Tech. 619 (1998).)

2. The FDA policy statement observes: "It is possible that there will be some redundancy between the scientific reviews of these products performed by the National Institutes of Health and FDA." How do the procedures set

forth in the FDA policy statement compare with the procedures established in the RAC's "Points to Consider"? Is the FDA's regulatory scheme truly "redundant"? Does the RAC consider issues that the FDA does not? For a history of the early interaction between the FDA and the RAC, see Richard A. Merrill & Gail H. Javitt, Gene Therapy: Law and FDA Role in Regulation, in 1 Encyclopedia of Ethical, Legal and Policy Issues in Biotechnology 321, 323–324 (Thomas H. Murray & Maxwell J. Mehlman, eds. 2000).

3. In 1985, the RAC issued a revised version of its "Points to Consider." 50 Fed. Reg. 33,462. The revision contained the following new language:

> "Applicability: These 'Points to Consider' apply only to research conducted at or sponsored by an institution that receives any support for recombinant DNA research from the National Institutes of Health (NIH). This includes research performed by NIH directly."

The revision also contained a footnote stating: "The Food and Drug Administration (FDA) has jurisdiction over drug products intended for use in clinical trials of human somatic-cell gene therapy." Yet in 1987, the RAC issued a statement reiterating that gene therapy trials had to be reviewed and approved by the RAC even if they were approved by another agency.

4. Following the gene therapy trial with Ashanti DeSilva in 1990, the FDA intensified its efforts to regulate human gene therapy experimentation. In 1991, it issued its own "Points to Consider" document: Center for Biologics Evaluation and Research, Food and Drug Administration, Points to Consider in Human Somatic Cell Therapy and Gene Therapy (1991). In 1992, the FDA clarified that regulation of human gene therapy experiments would be coordinated by a new Division of Cellular and Gene Therapies in a new Office of Therapeutics Research and Review, housed in the agency's Center for Biologics Evaluation and Research (CBER). The new division was headed by Phillip Noguchi.

5. Toward the middle of the 1990s, gene therapy researchers and the biotechnology industry became increasingly frustrated at what many of them viewed as a duplication of regulatory oversight by the RAC and the FDA. Efforts were made to streamline the review process and eliminate the need to submit protocols using two different formats, one for FDA and the other for the RAC. In 1995, a committee headed by Inder Verma recommended to the director of the NIH, Harold Varmus, that the FDA take over the responsibility for reviewing most gene therapy protocols; the RAC would only review proposals that raised novel questions. Varmus decided to go even further. In 1996, he announced his intention to cede all regulatory authority to the FDA. His position was described in a publication in the Federal Register in July 1996 (61 Fed. Reg. 35,774) and formally set forth in a Federal Register publication in 1997 (62 Fed. Reg. 59,032, October 31, 1997). The size of the RAC was reduced to 15 members, and its functions reduced to three: (1) identifying "novel human gene transfer experiments deserving of public discussion" by the committee and transmitting its comments to the investigators, the sponsor, and the FDA; (2) identifying "novel scientific, safety, social, and ethical issues" and recommending revisions to the NIH's Points to Consider; and (3) recommending topics for "Gene Therapy Policy Conferences"—public discussions on "broad overarching policy and scientific issues

related to gene therapy research." 62 Fed. Reg. 59,032. (The first Gene Therapy Policy Conference was held on September 11, 1997. The topic was the regulation of genetic enhancement.)

An article in the New York Times stated that part of Varmus' motivation was his concern over the quality of the research proposals the RAC was being asked to review, and his disapproval of the way that biotechnology companies touted a favorable RAC review for business purposes. See Sheryl Gay Stolberg, The Biotech Death of Jesse Gelsinger, The New York Times Sunday Magazine, Nov. 28, 1999, at 137. Varmus' concern over the quality of research was no doubt influenced by the 1995 Report and Recommendations of the Panel to Assess the NIH Investment in Research on Gene Therapy, headed by Stuart Orkin and Arno Motulsky. (www.nih.gov/news/panelrep.html.) The report concluded that "significant problems remain in all basic aspects of gene therapy. Major difficulties at the basic level include shortcomings in all current gene transfer vectors and inadequate understanding of the biological interaction of these vectors with the host." The panel made a number of recommendations for changes in the direction of NIH-sponsored gene therapy research.

As noted in Chapter 6, the Secretary's Advisory Committee on Genetic Testing concluded that the FDA may not possess the capacity to assess the ethical and social implications of a genetic test, and that the Secretary therefore "should consider the development of a mechanism to ensure the identification and appropriate review of tests that raise major social and ethical concerns." What does this suggest regarding the FDA's ability to regulate gene therapy and genetic technologies in general?

6. As noted in its 1984 Statement of Policy, the FDA has basic regulatory authority over drugs, medical devices, and biologics (as well as foods and cosmetics). The FDA regulates drugs, devices and biologics somewhat differently, but all three regulatory schemes share common features. The manufacturer of the product, called the "sponsor," must demonstrate that the product is safe and efficacious[1] in order to be permitted to ship the product across state lines.

Under the Commerce Clause of the Constitution, federal regulatory authority is limited to interstate commerce. As in other areas, however, the courts have interpreted the scope of the FDA's authority over "interstate commerce" broadly. See, e.g., Baker v. United States, 932 F.2d 813 (9th Cir. 1991) (ingredients shipped in interstate commerce). In terms of gene therapies, the FDA states:

---

1. "Efficacious" is a term of art that relates to the performance of a product in human experiments. The term "effectiveness" is reserved for the performance of a product in actual use. For a variety of reasons, a product may be efficacious, meaning that it performs satisfactorily in clinical trials, but turn out to be ineffective when marketed for widespread use. For example, the types of patients enrolled in clinical trials are usually carefully controlled to produce the maximum effects, effects that may not be seen when physicians use the product in broader patient populations. In addition, the physicians who treat the experimental subjects may be more expert at using the product than the physicians who provide the product after it is approved. The efficacy-effectiveness distinction was dramatically illustrated by the drug chymopapain, which was efficacious in clinical trials when injected into patient's spines to treat slipped lumbar discs without surgery but which proved lethal when used by less well-trained physicians following FDA approval. See Drug for Slipped Disks is Linked to 5 Deaths, 28 Serious Disorders, Wall St. J., June 7, 1984, at 7.

The interstate commerce nexus needed to require premarket approval under the statutory provisions governing biologics and drugs may be created in various ways in addition to shipment of the finished product by the manufacturer. For example, even if a biological drug product is manufactured entirely with materials that have not crossed State lines, transport of the product into another State by an individual patient creates the interstate commerce nexus. If a component used in the manufacture of the product moves interstate, the interstate commerce prerequisite for the prohibition against drug misbranding is also satisfied even when the finished product stays within the State.

Food and Drug Administration, Application of Current Statutory Authorities to Human Somatic Cell Therapy Products and Gene Therapy Products, 58 Fed. Reg. 53,248, 53,249 (1993).

FDA approval to ship across state lines is required for experimental products as well as for products that have received marketing approval. Before an experimental gene therapy can be given to human subjects in a clinical investigation, the sponsor must have submitted an application to the FDA describing the experiment, and the FDA must have given its approval. The process differs slightly for drugs, devices, and biologics. As described in the 1984 statement, sponsors of drug trials must submit an Investigational New Drug application, called an "IND." The agency then has 30 days in which to object to the study going forward, or the application is deemed approved. See 21 C.F.R. § 312.42. The same application is used for biologics. See 21 C.F.R. § 312.2. In the case of a medical device, the application is called an Investigational Device Exemption application, or "IDE." See 21 C.F.R. § 812 1(a). Once clinical trials are satisfactorily completed, the sponsor must file an application for marketing approval. For drugs, this is a New Drug Application or "NDA," described in 21 C.F.R. Part 314. Following passage of the FDA Modernization Act of 1997, 21 U.S.C. §§ 355–397, biologics manufacturers are required to obtain an approved Biologics License Application or "BLA." (Previously they had to obtain separate product and establishment licenses.)

The system for medical devices is more complicated. As described in the 1984 Statement of Policy, medical devices are divided into three classes; only Class III devices must have the equivalent of an approved NDA or BLA, called, in the case of medical devices, an approved Premarket Approval Application or "PMA." Most gene therapies that would be regarded as medical devices would be considered Class III or "significant risk devices," requiring an approved PMA.

Given the different regulatory processes for drugs, devices, and biologics, it is important for sponsors of gene therapy products to know which route to follow, that is, whether their gene therapy is a drug, device, or biologic. A device, by definition, does not achieve its effect by chemical or metabolic action in the body. See 21 U.S.C. § 321(h). Genetic test kits and the reagents used by testing laboratories therefore were medical devices, but not most gene therapies. The distinction between a drug and a biologic was more troublesome. The 1984 Statement of Policy provided little guidance. A subsequent policy statement, Center for Biologics Evaluation and Research, Points to

Consider in Human Somatic Cell Therapy and Gene Therapy (1991), defined the term "gene therapy" ("a medical intervention based on modification of the genetic material of living cells"), but did not clarify whether a gene therapy was a drug or biologic. Finally, in 1993, the FDA issued a document entitled Application of Current Statutory Authorities to Human Somatic Cell Therapy Products and Gene Therapy Products (58 Fed. Reg. 53248), in which the agency explained that "synthetic products" (including "a synthetic polynucleotide sequence intended to alter a specific genetic sequence in human somatic cells after systemic administration") were drugs and required INDs and NDAs, while viral and retroviral vectors inserting natural DNA were biologics. 58 Fed. Reg. at 53251. Consequently, the experiments on Ashanti DeSilva and Jesse Gelsinger, as well as virtually all of the other gene therapy trials to date, fall into the regulatory category of biologics.

3. Protecting Human Subjects

LARRY R. CHURCHILL ET AL., GENETIC RESEARCH AS THERAPY: IMPLICATIONS OF "GENE THERAPY" FOR INFORMED CONSENT

26 J. L., Med. & Ethics 38 (1998).

In March 1996, the General Accounting Office (GAO) issued the report Scientific Research: Continued Vigilance Critical to Protecting Human Subjects. It stated that "an inherent conflict of interest exists when physician-researchers include their patients in research protocols. If the physicians do not clearly distinguish between research and treatment in their attempt to inform subjects, the possible benefits of a study can be overemphasized and the risks minimized." The report also acknowledged that "the line between research and treatment is not always clear to clinicians. Controversy exists regarding whether certain medical procedures should be categorized as research."

This problem currently plagues gene transfer research. A few months prior to the GAO report, an ad hoc committee appointed by National Institutes of Health (NIH) Director Harold Varmus expressed similar concerns in its assessment of NIH investment in research on gene therapy. The committee's report stated:

> Expectations of current gene therapy have been oversold. Overzealous representation of clinical gene therapy has obscured the exploratory nature of the initial studies, colored the manner in which findings are portrayed to the scientific press and public, and led to the widely held, but mistaken, perception that clinical gene therapy is already highly successful.

In mid 1996, the Recombinant DNA Advisory Committee's (RAC) five-year status report of gene therapy described the situation this way:

> It is clearly too early ... to assess the therapeutic efficacy of gene therapy or even to predict its promise. Numerous studies have reported the ability to express recombinant DNA in vivo, but few have

reported clinical efficacy.... The few "dramatic" successes claimed are not dissimilar to those that were reported with a variety of other therapeutic techniques for which enthusiasm ultimately dampened over time.

Yet despite this cautionary report, and despite the fact that no therapeutic benefit has been clearly demonstrated for the more than 2,100 subjects enrolled in gene transfer research worldwide, enthusiasm for gene therapy persists unabated.

* * *

At present, gene transfer research amplifies the already existing confusions between research and therapy and intensifies extant problems of informed consent.

* * *

Consider, for instance, the following excerpt from the minutes of 1991 meetings of RAC and its Human Gene Therapy Subcommittee. In the subcommittee's 1991 review of a protocol for gene therapy for familial hypercholesterolemia, not only is the research described by some discussants as treatment, but some subcommittee members also considered it "discriminatory" to "treat" adults before children were entered in the protocol. This is not an isolated example of the conflation of research and therapy. Indeed, the basis of this ambiguity is built into the ethical guidelines that RAC uses to review protocols for gene transfer research. The most recent version of RAC's "Points to Consider" document refers to research participants as "patients" in some places and "subjects" in others, and sometimes refers to clinical studies as "treatments." This oscillation in language cannot be helpful for the process of informed consent.

* * *

Yet although gene therapy is conceived as revolutionary, its administration is viewed as routine. For example, many advocates describe gene therapy as merely "a novel form of drug delivery," where this description does not refer to the practice of manufacturing traditional drugs with recombinant DNA techniques, but to gene transfer. Almost everyone agrees that germ-line intervention—affecting future generations and involving a host of unknowable consequences—presents major new ethical issues, but the accepted wisdom is that somatic cell gene transfer is simply a part of the therapeutic continuum, presenting no novel ethical dilemmas.

* * *

The revolutionary rhetoric about addressing the essence of disease in scientific research is fueled, of course, by the agendas of those with major social and economic investments in the gene therapy enterprise. Physicians and researchers working on gene transfer techniques have substantial interests in promoting this nascent field of medical science. Biotechnology companies, moreover, have an interest in turning out numerous products related to the so-called genetic revolution—for example, diagnostic tests and DNA-based medicines. The cluster of scientific, economic, and cultural hopes swirling around our genes seems to intensify and sustain the future promise of gene therapy at the same time that it frames this revolutionary concept in traditional garb—as merely the next wave of therapeutic options. The failure to discuss these factors candidly leads regulators, professionals, and the public to perpetuate confusion, misrepresentation, and disappointment in the sometimes appropriate, and occasionally misguided, pursuit of medical advancement.

* * *

CONCLUSION

Informed consent is fundamentally about language, about how doctors and patients, researchers, and subjects communicate. As a practice, informed consent is intended to foster genuinely collaborative decision making in both the research and patient care settings. But in the current milieu of therapeutic enthusiasm for research, informed consent has become a way of not talking, or more precisely, a way of not talking with sufficient candor. By failing to dispel confusion about the therapeutic intentions of gene transfer research, the consent process often perpetuates a false promise to subjects. To promote conversation, researchers must earn the trust of their subjects through communication that avoids the false appeal of a beneficence warranted only by compassionate intent and devoid of evidence of benefit. In promoting an ethically sound genetic research enterprise involving human subjects, policy-makers should craft institutional opportunities for meaningful informed consent discussions in which the nuances can be sorted out.

To achieve these goals, the minimum requirement is conceptual clarity. We argue that rectifying the language of the regulatory bodies is essential for restoring informed consent for research to its original role as a collaboration-oriented process that promotes appropriate access and yet fully informs and protects subjects from inflated promises of benefit.

Specifically, with regard to gene therapy, we suggest the following.

First, RAC, FDA, and the Office for Protection from Research Risks should delete the terms gene therapy and gene therapy research and any language that would imply that a gene therapy already exists from the informed consent process and committee deliberation. This conceptual clarity is essential in those oversight institutions that set the tone for researcher-subject discussions. The term gene transfer research more accurately conveys the experimental practice that is currently at issue.

Second, RAC should rewrite its "Points to Consider" to differentiate clearly patients from subjects and research from treatment where those references are misleading. In this regard, the recent diminution of RAC's oversight role is troubling. Over the past few years, RAC has received an abundance of criticism, including charges that it has exceeded its authority, delayed approval of protocols, and functioned in a "purely cosmetic" way. Members of RAC have seen their role differently, recognizing that they are charged with reviewing a "new form of medical experimentation." In many cases, RAC has changed the language of consent forms to delete terms like therapy and often challenged what it has perceived as overestimates of potential benefit from participation in gene transfer protocols, similar to the concerns we have discussed here. If the confusions about gene therapy are to be dispelled, we believe a more robust role for RAC is required, rather than a diminished one.

Third, all institutions [and investigators] charged with responsibility for protecting human subjects and ensuring their informed participation in research should critically rethink the ethical norms that currently shape the language of informed consent in areas like human gene transfer re search. The meaning of the principle of beneficence as direct benefit to the patient-subject should be clearly distinguished from beneficence as a possible benefit to future patients. The use of beneficence to refer to motivations of compassionate intent or desperate use in research contexts is misleading, especially to patient-subjects, and should be eliminated. The appropriate place for beneficence in genetic research is almost always as a long-range, aggregate good stemming from research results, and not as an immediate benefit resulting directly from research participation. The goal of genetic research is generalizable knowledge to benefit future patients, not current subjects. This is especially relevant to the Phase I and II protocols for gene transfer now extant. Subjects are treated ethically only when a robust exercise of consent is combined with a commitment to eliminate or reduce harms. Beneficence is too often translated into false promises of therapy for subjects, and this compromises the consent process.

Fourth, consent forms should state clearly and explicitly that there is no expected benefit to the individual patient who becomes a subject in current gene transfer research. Moreover, researchers should work to minimize the unwarranted therapeutic assumptions that inevitably result when research is conducted in the physical environment and moral context of ongoing patient care. One way to achieve this would be for each protocol and informed consent document to provide a separate section entitled "Evidence of Benefit," thereby calling attention to whatever evidence for individual benefit exists and laying it open to critical scrutiny by federal oversight bodies, IRBs, investigators, and subjects.

Finally, the NIH training program in research ethics should make a significant investment in educating investigators to view informed consent as conversation, in the service of subject autonomy and professional self-scrutiny, and aimed ultimately at an improved, collaborative decision-making process in research.

1. What are the differences between research and therapy? Are there differences between research subjects and patients undergoing treatment in terms of protections to prevent harm? Review the earlier discussion of the ethics of genetic research. Is the informed consent process the same in the cases of research and therapy? If not, how do they differ? Under federal law and the terms of NIH grants, all proposals for human subjects research involving the administration of a drug, device, or biologic must be reviewed by institutional review boards (IRBs), groups of individuals at the institution conducting the study. Is there an equivalent entity or function in the case of therapy?

2. Especially troublesome problems arise when a patient's physician is also a researcher. As George Annas states: "When physician and researcher are merged into one person, it is unlikely that patients can ever draw the distinction between these two conflicting roles because most patients simply do not believe that their physician would knowingly harm them or would knowingly use them as a means for their own ends." George J. Annas, Questing for Grails: Duplicity, Betrayal and Self–Deception in Postmodern Medical Research, 12 J. Contemp. Health L. & Pol'y 297, 311–312 (1996). Do the recommendations suggested by Churchill et al. respond to this concern?

3. Is the conflation of research and therapy a particular problem in gene therapy experimentation, or a general problem with medical research? Does the article by Churchill make a persuasive argument that gene therapy research is special?

4. Will the recommendations in the article solve the problem? If not, what other approaches can you think of?

5. Recently a great deal of attention has been given to the problems created by researchers' financial stake in the outcome of their experiments. See Catherine D. DeAngelis, Conflict of Interest and the Public Trust, 284 JAMA 2237 (2000); David Korn, Commentary: Conflicts of Interest in Biomedical Research, 284 JAMA 2234 (2000); Bernard Lo et al., Conflict-of-Interest Policies for Investigators in Clinical Trials, 343 New Eng. J. Med. 1616 (2000); S. Van McCrary et al., A National Survey of Policies on Disclosure of Conflicts of Interest in Biomedical Research, 343 New Eng. J. Med. 1621 (2000).

The experiment in which Jesse Gelsinger died was part of a large-scale gene therapy research program at the University of Pennsylvania's Institute of Gene Therapy, headed by James M. Wilson. At the time, the institute had 250 employees and an annual budget of $25 million, and was considered the largest academic gene therapy research program in the country. Wilson was also the founder and a stockholder, along with the university, in a company called Genovo. Genovo did not fund the Gelsinger study, but it did provide twenty percent of the institute's budget, and had the exclusive right to commercialize any institute discoveries. According to the university's general counsel, the relationship between Wilson, Genovo, and Penn was so complicated that the university set up two committees to oversee it. When Genova was sold in 2000 to a company called Targeted Genetics Corp., Wilson was due to receive stock worth $13.5 million.

In May 2000, the FDA criticized researchers at the St. Elizabeth's Medical Center in Boston for failing to report a death in an experiment designed to determine if patients with blocked blood vessels of the heart could be improved by injecting them with genes that produce a substance that promotes revascularization. It turned out that the patient was not appropriate for the study because he had a lung tumor and was a heavy smoker, raising the concern that the inserted genes would promote tumor growth. The chief researcher was a founder of and major stockholder in the company sponsoring the experiment.

6. In the aftermath of Gelsinger's death, it was discovered that there had been a number of adverse events associated with gene therapy experiments that had never been made public. Many of them had been reported to the FDA, as required by FDA regulations. See 21 C.F.R. § 312.32 (requiring IND safety reports within 15 days of any serious or unexpected adverse events, and immediate notification of fatal or life-threatening adverse events). In accordance with long-standing FDA policy, however, these reports were considered trade secrets and not disclosed to the public. Even the fact that a sponsor had filed an IND (or IDE) was kept secret.

NIH also required that it be notified of serious adverse events occurring in gene therapy studies that it funded or that were conducted at an institution that received NIH funding. See Appendix M–VII–C, Points to Consider in the Design and Submission of Protocols for the Transfer of Recombinant DNA Molecules into One or More Human Subjects (http://www4.od.nih.gov/oba/rac/guidelines_02/Appendix_M.htm). In contrast to the FDA, however, the NIH made these reports public. Sponsors therefore were reluctant to make the reports. After Gelsinger's death, the NIH received reports of 691 serious adverse events; only 39 had been reported when they occurred, as required by the NIH rules.

The lack of public awareness of safety problems with gene therapy trials not only impaired the ability of researchers to inform subjects of potential risks in obtaining informed consent; it hampered the researcher's ability to design and conduct safe studies. In reviewing gene therapy research INDs, the FDA was not always able to consider the full implications of the adverse event reports it received for other investigations, and researchers would only hear about these events if their occurrence was "leaked" by their colleagues, for example, at science conferences or in private conversations.

Gelsinger's death and the resulting disclosures of the lack of awareness of adverse events prompted several government reactions. In March 2000, the Department of Health and Human Services announced a new Gene Therapy Trial Monitoring Plan whereby the FDA would more closely review the procedures employed by a sponsor to monitor gene therapy trials, and established a program of Gene Transfer Safety Symposia which would bring researchers together 4 times a year to review safety results from gene therapy experiments. See Food and Drug Administration, New Initiatives to Protect Participants in Gene Therapy Trials, March 7, 2000 (www.fda.gov/bbs/topics/NEWS/NEW00717.html). The Secretary of Health and Human Services proposed to ask Congress for new authority to levy $250,000 fines against investigators who violated human subjects protection rules, and $1 million fines against their institutions.

Finally, the FDA published proposed regulations which would provide for the public disclosure of IND safety reports for two types of experiments: gene therapy and xenotransplantation (the transplantation into humans of non-human organs or tissue). The proposal can be found at 66 Fed. Reg. 4688 (2001). This marked the first time that the FDA proposed to adopt formal regulations specifically dealing with gene therapy; all previous FDA pronouncements had been in the form of policy statements.

If adopted, the regulations would mark a significant change in the agency's attitude toward gene therapy and biotechnology more generally. As noted earlier, until now, the FDA has taken the position that biotechnology products should be subject to the same regulatory requirements as any other products. The proposed regulations, by pertaining only to gene therapy and xenotransplantation would signal that the agency had abandoned this viewpoint. This might lead to a broader shift in the government's regulatory policy toward biotechnology, with repercussions for areas such as genetically engineered foods and plants.

In March 2004, the NIH and FDA announced the creation of a new web data base, the Genetic Modification Clinical Research Information System (GeMCRIS). Information reported to the NIH about adverse events that occur in gene therapy trials will be posted on the data base and be available to researchers and to the public.

D. GERM LINE THERAPY

The foregoing discussion of gene therapy focused on "somatic cell therapy," that is, therapeutic interventions that do not affect reproductive cells. The infusions of genes that Ashanti DeSilva received, for example, did not alter her oocytes, or eggs. Another approach, however, is "germ line therapy"—therapeutic genetic interventions that, intentionally or not, affect the genetic material of reproductive cells. As a result, the modifications directly alter the genetic endowment of the person's offspring, and their progeny in turn.

The distinction between somatic cell and germ line therapy is not always clear. Somatic cell treatments that enabled people to have children, whether by repairing their reproductive systems or simply by saving their lives while they were still capable of reproducing, would affect the genes of offspring by making the lives of the offspring possible. Similarly, abortions performed because of fetal health problems or health-based decisions about which embryos to implant following IVF might be considered germ line therapy because they affect the genes of a person's children, precluding the aborted fetuses or discarded embryos from passing on their genes via reproduction. But these interventions all involve naturally inherited genes; therapeutic abortions and embryo selection for implantation merely select among offspring on the basis of their natural genetic endowment.

Most commentators reserve the term "germ line therapy" for interventions that actually change the genes of surviving offspring.

Some commentators also distinguish somatic and germ line therapy in terms of the target of the intervention. The goal of somatic cell therapy, they say, is to treat the person who is the subject of the procedure, while the goal of germ line therapy is to treat that person's children. This distinction is blurred as well, however. As discussed below, one therapeutic approach might be to insert genes into an early stage embryo or fetus with the intent of correcting an abnormality or preventing a disease. If the insertion is made at an early-enough stage of development, the altered genes will be incorporated not only into the somatic cells of a surviving individual but into that person's reproductive cells.

Germ-line therapy refers to genetic manipulation of germ cells or "gametes": the egg and the sperm. In practice, it also refers to genetic alteration of the fertilized egg and genetic alteration of the cells of an early embryo (or embryonic stem (ES) cells), because these alterations will be incorporated in all the cells of the resultant child, including his or her germ cells. Therefore, the altered gene will pass down the generations. Currently, the following techniques show the most potential:

1.   Gene addition or "non-homologous recombination."

This technique is similar to the one currently used in somatic gene therapy, where cells are injected that contain copies of the normal gene. But in germ-line therapy, the genes are introduced into a fertilized egg where they get incorporated into the genome of the offspring and result in the correction or prevention of genetic disease in the progeny of the treated individual.

There has been success using this method in mice, where it produces the so-called "transgenic" animals. Diseases that have been successfully prevented include pituitary dwarfism and Lesch–Nyhan disease. However, there are several problems with this technique that make it particularly unsuitable for human germ-line therapy. First, it is inefficient. Only a minority of cells seem to take up the gene, and even when they do, the gene often is expressed at sub-optimal levels. Animals that demonstrate inadequate distribution or incorrect expression of the added gene, or that are damaged by the procedure, are destroyed, but this is problematic for humans. Furthermore, this technique may have unpredictable side effects. This is because chromosomes have two types of genetic elements along their DNA: genes themselves, each of which codes for a functional protein that contributes in some way to the functioning of the organism, and regulatory sequences, which control when and where particular genes are expressed. For an "added" gene to be effective, it must be expressed in the right place in the body, at the right time, and in the right amount. If only a gene sequence is added to the cell DNA, without its accompanying regulatory sequences, its expression will be unknown; it may become over-expressed, under-expressed, or not expressed at all. Another problem with this type of manipulation is that the added gene may become incorporated in the wrong location. This will result, at best, in perturbation of the added gene's activity, or in no gene activity at all. But at worst, it can have an effect on other genes in the cell, altering their expression and leading to cell death or other serious problems such as cancer.

2. Gene replacement or "targeting" or "homologous recombination."

In this procedure, the defective gene is replaced with a corrected gene. This technique overcomes a number of problems associated with "gene addition," since it ensures that the replaced gene will be in its normal chromosomal location, and since its sequences and genes will not be changed. As a result, it will function in the right cells, at the right time, and at the right level.

Gene replacement appears to be the preferred technique for germline therapy. In particular, the advent of cloning or nuclear transfer has made this technique feasible in the near future. A possible scenario is as follows: IVF would be used to generate an embryo from the sperm and eggs donated by each parent. The embryos would be permitted to progress to a four-cell stage. Then three of these embryonic stem (ES) cells would be frozen for future use and the fourth cell grown in culture. After about twenty cell divisions, a million cells would be generated. The cells would then be genetically manipulated and those cells that have taken up the genes would be isolated and carefully examined to ensure that the genetic modification was accurate. At this point, the nucleus of one of the mother's eggs, or one of the three frozen ES cells, would be removed and replaced with the nucleus from a cell containing the prescribed genetic modification. The cell would then be allowed to divide in culture once or twice, and the resultant embryo would be implanted into the mother's womb. A child reproduced in this way will be a clone of the original embryo, with a single gene difference, and the genetic modifications would be incorporated in all of his or her cells, including the germ cells. Many of these techniques are being done now in animals. However, cloning humans presents a number of technical and moral problems that would have to be addressed before gene replacement could be used safely and ethically in humans. Another drawback is that, in animals, this technique is usually used for only one genetic modification at a time, while combating genetic diseases may require simultaneous manipulation of multiple genes. However, progress in solving this problem has been made recently by the addition of large numbers of genes through "artificial chromosomes," described below.

3. Artificial chromosomes.

A new technique has been developed where an artificial chromosome, consisting of large numbers of modified genes together with their appropriate regulatory sequences, is introduced into a human cell. This procedure not only ensures proper gene expression, but also allows the introduction of large numbers of genes in order to alter characteristics that result from complex genetic combinations. So far, it has been shown that such a chromosome is stable and can persist through repeated divisions of the cell. However, potential problems with this technique may occur in the second generation. The side-effects of having an additional chromosome are not known. For example, the additional chromosome may cause sterility.

Although the ethical issues associated with human germline gene therapy are more complex than those of somatic gene therapy, some of the technical hurdles are actually less complex. Three major obstacles encountered in somatic gene therapy do not pose a problem in germline therapy, namely, gene delivery, gene expression, and immunological reactions. The delivery problem is solved since the gene will be automatically delivered to all cells in the body. The gene will be incorporated in the correct location to ensure proper expression. Finally, since the gene is expressed during fetal development, the altered gene product will be recognized as "self" and will not elicit an immune response.

In its Revised Points to Consider, the FDA stated that it would not approve any protocols for germ line therapy:

> A distinction should be drawn between making genetic changes in somatic cells and in germ line cells. The purpose of somatic cell gene therapy is to treat an individual patient, e.g., by inserting a properly functioning gene into a patient's bone marrow cells in vitro and then reintroducing the cells into the patient's body. In germ line alterations, a specific attempt is made to introduce genetic changes into the germ (reproductive) cells of an individual, with the aim of changing the set of genes passed on to the individual's offspring. The RAC and its working group will not at present entertain proposals for germ line alterations but will consider for approval protocols involving somatic-cell gene therapy.

50 Fed Reg. 33,462, 33,464 (1985).

So far as is known, there have been no attempts yet to deliberately alter genes in a person's reproductive cells. However, there has been at least one successful inadvertent germ line intervention. This involves a technique called "ooplasmic transfer" to treat a type of female infertility in which embryos do not properly grow and develop in the womb because of deficiencies, often related to age, in the portion of the egg, called the cytoplasm, that surrounds the nucleus. To correct the deficiencies, doctors remove the nucleus and insert it into an egg from another woman that has had its nucleus removed, leaving only the other woman's healthier cytoplasm. Using standard IVF techniques, the egg then is fertilized in the laboratory and implanted. Researchers using this approach reported the first successful birth in 1997.

Although most of a person's genetic material is found in the cell nucleus, a very small amount is contained in organelles or structures in the cytoplasm called mitochondria, which produce energy. Therefore, when an infertile woman's nucleus is implanted in the cytoplasm from another woman's donor egg, the resulting egg contains not only the mother's nuclear genetic material, but the donor's mitochondrial DNA, and as the fertilized egg divides, this mitochondrial DNA will be incorporated in the cells of the resulting child, including its reproductive cells, and passed on to its children. In short, a germ line modification has been introduced, as confirmed by researchers in New Jersey who examined the resulting mitochondrial DNA in two children born as the result of ooplasmic transfer.

Given the RAC's de facto ban on germ line alterations as reflected in its 1985 revised Points to Consider, how could any of these ooplasmic transfers have been lawfully conducted in the United States? In an editorial in Science, Eric Juengst and Erik Parens give the following answer:

> First, their intervention did not use recombinant DNA (rDNA). When RAC's guidelines, which apply only to interventions using rDNA, were articulated in the late 1980's, no one was thinking about transplanting ooplasm to treat a form of infertility. Insofar as the ooplasmic transfer technique does not involve rDNA, it falls outside of RAC's purview. However, as a recent American Association for the Advancement of Science (AAAS) report suggested, RAC's purview is unduly restricted to a consideration of techniques that now are more than two decades old. The AAAS working group (of which we were a part) argued that if new techniques raise the same ethical concerns as those raised by "traditional" germline gene transfer techniques, then either RAC's purview should be expanded to encompass them, or a new, RAC-like body should be created to oversee them. The working group argued that even though some inheritable genetic modifications (IGMs) might not involve rDNA, might not alter single genes, and might not alter nuclear DNA (nDNA), they should be subject to the same public scrutiny if they raise the same ethical questions as the traditional germline interventions. Examples of IGMs in the report included the introduction of artificial chromosomes, the use of oligonucleotides to repair genes in situ—and the transfer of mtDNA [mitochondrial DNA].

> Second, federal funds did not support this ooplasmic transfer experiment. RAC guidelines are binding only on those who receive federal funds. If, however, their protocol had aimed at achieving traditional germline interventions, they probably would have felt compelled to approach RAC, as do other privately funded researchers whose work raises novel issues. Given their recognition that they were engaged in "germline modification," it is unfortunate—though perfectly legitimate—that they did not bring their protocol before RAC.

> Third, gene transfer was an inadvertent effect of their intervention. Since the creation of the RAC guidelines, however, researchers have had to demonstrate that the chances of inadvertent germline gene transfer are miniscule. When an in utero gene transfer pre-protocol was recently put before RAC, the idea was rejected largely because the

chances of inadvertent germline effects were too great. If the ooplasmic transplantation protocol had been within RAC's official purview, it probably would not have received RAC's blessing. We will never know.

Erik Parens & Eric Juengst, Inadvertently Crossing the Germ Line, 292 Science 397 (2001). Note that at least some attempts at ooplasmic transfer were being made before the RAC's authority to review gene transfer protocols was ceded to the FDA.

In June 2001, the FDA sent a letter to 6 fertility clinics warning them that ooplasmic transfer was a clinical experiment for which an approved Investigational New Drug application was required.

In 1998, W. French Anderson and Emil Zanjani proposed a study in which corrected genes would be inserted by viral vectors into fetuses affected with the same immune deficiency disorder as Ashanti DeSilva, as well as fetuses with alpha thalassemia, a severe form of anemia. The idea was that by intervening at such an early stage of development, the corrected genes would become incorporated into virtually all of the child's cells and be perpetuated along with the child's natural DNA by means of normal cell division. The researchers were aware, however, that since the experiment would be performed before all of the fetal cells had differentiated, some of the inserted DNA might become incorporated into the child's reproductive cells. The corrected DNA then would be passed on to the child's offspring, creating another instance of germ line alteration.

Mindful of the RAC's position on germ line therapy, Anderson and Zinjani took the unusual step of submitting a preliminary plan for their experiments to the RAC for discussion. (See Minutes of the RAC Meeting, September 24–25, 1998, http://www4.od.nih.gov/oba/rac/minutes/9–98rac. htm). This generated considerable discussion in the media (see, e.g., Robert Cooke, Pushing a Human Limit, Gene Therapy That Could Affect Future Generations, Too, Newsday, Aug. 30, 1998, at A6; Rick Weiss, Scientists Seek Panel's Advice on In–Womb Genetic Tests, Wash. Post, Sept. 25, 1998, at A2; Rick Weiss, Science on the Ethical Frontier: Engineering the Unborn, Wash. Post, Mar. 22, 1998, at A1) and in the scholarly literature (see, e.g., see Emily Marden & Dorothy Nelkin, Displaced Agendas: Current Regulatory Strategies for Germline Gene Therapy, 45 McGill L. J. 461 (2000)).

In September 2000, the American Association for the Advancement of Science issued a report, Human Inheritable Genetic Modifications, which recommended that, in light of the potential for genetic harms, "any somatic genetic therapy applications where there is a reasonably foreseeable possibility of [germ line modifications] should not proceed at this time." The AAAS stated that before any germ line modifications are attempted, there should be evidence that they can be accomplished safely and effectively, including, when new genetic material is added, data from multiple generations. For a more permissive view, see John A. Robertson, Oocyte Cytoplasm Transfers and the Ethics of Germ–Line Intervention, 26 J. L., Med. & Ethics 211 (1998).

The FDA has not issued any guidance on whether it will entertain INDs for germ line therapy, nor what criteria it will apply in its review. Are there any impediments to that agency's ability to review research plans involving deliberate or inadvertent germ line alterations? One potential issue is whether the FDA has authority to regulate germ line therapy insofar as it consists of the practice of medicine. Is ooplasmic transfer performed by a physician treating infertility subject to FDA regulation?

NOTES AND QUESTIONS

1. Should intentional germ line therapy be regulated differently than somatic cell therapy? Should it be banned? Does it raise special health or ethical concerns? If so which ones?

2. Under what circumstances, if any, would it be appropriate to initiate an experiment deliberately intended to alter the human germ line? What safety information from laboratory and animal experiments should be required first? What kinds of conditions should the researchers target? Should the experiment be tried in subjects who are so severely ill that they will die unless the experiment succeeds? Or should it be tried in subjects who are less ill and therefore better able to withstand the physical rigors of the experiment? What special issues might be raised if the subjects are children, or fetuses, or embryos?

In view of the safety concerns voiced in the AAAS Report, would it ever be ethical to initiate a deliberate germ line therapy experiment? In this regard, the report states:

> For the reasons outlined above, many members of the working group, including several of the scientists, question whether we will ever have enough confidence in the safety of IGM to proceed to clinical use. This assessment led some to conclude that it would never be scientifically and ethically appropriate to begin human applications until we can surmount this problem.

AAAS Report at 26.

3. All biomedical interventions are accompanied by some degree of risk. The question is whether the risks are outweighed by the benefits. What are the potential benefits from germ line therapy? The AAAS Report did not regard the potential benefits as significant, stating (at p. 13):

> The working group could identify few instances where IGM would be needed. There are currently several alternative approaches available that will help parents avoid passing on defective genes to their offspring. These include genetic screening and counseling, prenatal diagnosis, and abortion, pre-implantation diagnosis and embryo selection, gamete donation, and adoption. In the future, *in utero* somatic gene therapy and gene therapy on patients after birth are likely to offer effective means for correcting defects.

Is the AAAS Report correct? If there were no significant benefits from germ line therapy, why would researchers want to try doing it?

———————

Although they too are mindful of the need to proceed with caution, other commentators are more supportive of germ line therapy in view of its potential benefits.

BURKE K. ZIMMERMAN, HUMAN GERM–LINE THERAPY: THE CASE FOR ITS DEVELOPMENT AND USE

16 J. Med. & Philosophy 593 (1991).

So-called genetic diseases afflict approximately two percent of all live births. Some of these are so severe that the victim faces only a few short years of painful existence. Others, such as cystic fibrosis or sickle-cell disease, can be managed with treatment which often becomes more heroic with increasing age. Although at present the afflicted face almost certain premature death, the outlook that such treatments may soon include somatic-cell gene therapy is quite promising. The first human experiments involving the implantation of a genetic marker in tumor-infiltrating lymphocytes have been carried out at the U.S. National Institutes of Health and clinical trials to treat patients with severely debilitating afflictions, such as ADA deficiency, have begun. Such trials have been approved in the United States by the Subcommittee on Human Gene Therapy of NIH's Recombinant DNA Advisory Committee.

While these trials represent milestone achievements in the development of molecular genetics as an important tool in human medicine, somatic-cell gene therapy is a treatment of existing pathology. But somatic-cell gene therapy cannot prevent genetic disease. In fact, should it become widely successful, it will increase the number of homozygous disease gene carriers, who will face the certainty of passing problem genes to their children. Moreover, somatic cell therapy is a strategy that is only appropriate for the treatment of a subset of the wide scope of clinical disorders that have a clearly established genetic component. Disorders involving developmental abnormalities may not be adequately reversible, even if diagnosed during early pregnancy. Those problems involving organ or tissue structure and function may not be correctable at all, if intervention is not made early in development. The bone marrow stem cells are easily accessible and may be replaced by new populations, making them ideal targets for somatic cell therapy. But disorders involving solid tissues or a function intimately dependent on structure (e.g., the brain) may be forever inaccessible to somatic cell therapy.

Clearly, if technically feasible, a strategy that can correct genetic anomalies before or during conception, or at the zygote stage, is one that would achieve true prevention. Even if such a strategy is complex and costly initially, the suffering and the costs in treating (even by somatic cell therapy) and caring for a severely handicapped individual is many times greater.

* * *

THE CASE FOR THE DEVELOPMENT AND USE OF METHODS FOR DIRECT GENETIC MODIFICATION OF PRE–IMPLANTATION EMBRYOS

The case for the development and eventual use of germ-line gene therapy (GLGT) rests on the following arguments.

A. *It is the moral obligation of the medical profession to use the best available methods and technology to prevent genetic pathology.* It has long been the acknowledged responsibility of the medical profession and public health practitioners in Western society to treat and, if possible, prevent infectious diseases and non-infectious diseases (such as cancer and athero-sclerosis), using techniques proven to be efficacious and safe. Conversely, it is considered to be unethical to withhold medical intervention that is known to be effective in the treatment or prevention of pathology. Should not a similar responsibility apply to genetic disease? In fact, the borderline between the major non-infectious diseases and the overtly genetic disorders is not a clearly defined one. We know, for example, that severe hyperlipidemia, leading to heart attacks at an early age, is in large part due to genetic factors. Recently, genetic defects leading to a high incidence of breast and other specific types of cancer have been reported. Moreover, susceptibility to many infectious diseases, and the severity of possible sequelae such as the auto-immune destruction of vital tissue, have a very strong genetic bias.

The application of the principle that the medical profession must act primarily in the interests of the patient clearly extends to the welfare of prospective parents carrying a genetic disability who seek restoration of reproductive health. A direct corollary of this responsibility is a broadening of the definition of 'patient' to include the genetic health of their baby, and the ensuing future generations. The criterion that must govern any strategies to be used is that the procedure must promise to help the patient more than it may harm him. In this case, that criterion must apply to the entire genetic legacy that may result from intervention in the germ-line, which imposes rather stringent requirements on the degree of uncertainty acceptable in any such procedure.

B. *Direct intervention in the germ-line is medically necessary to prevent certain classes of disorders or situations where screening and selection procedures will not work.* While the most often discussed targets of genetic counseling and somatic cell therapy are the severe homozygous recessive disorders, the number of medical problems that are known to be genetically determined or predisposed continue to increase. Those involving complex genetics, cases with more than one genetic locus, will not be readily able to screening and selection. Parents, who may have been treated by somatic cell therapy and are homozygous for the trait in question, can, at best, have a child who will at least carry the trait. GLGT will allow genetically normal children to result in all such cases.

C. The principle of parental autonomy should permit parents to choose to use GLGT to ensure a normal child. At least in Western societies, parents are generally considered to have the right to have their own child, and to choose to use whatever means, consistent with established norms of medical ethics, that will ensure a normal pregnancy and a healthy baby. While the concept of state paternalism has in some instances prevailed over maternal autonomy with respect to the right to terminate a pregnancy, or in preventing a parental choice to withhold necessary medical care, the right of parental autonomy to nurture a pregnancy has been upheld overwhelmingly; any public policies that would deny parental autonomy in such cases would be grossly inconsistent with prevailing practices. Just as parents with reproductive disabilities are free to choose *in vitro* fertilization procedures, they should also be accorded the right to subject their viable embryos to screening and selection, or to direct genetic intervention, in order to guarantee the genetic health of their children.

D. Germ-line therapy is more efficient than the repeated use of somatic cell therapy in successive generations. Although many genetic disorders are not amenable to treatment through somatic cell therapy, an increasing number are, enabling the afflicted to reach reproductive age themselves. By comparison, the somatic cell treatments now contemplated are heroic in dimension and accompanied by substantial risk. Why subject each generation to having to undergo major, invasive intervention, when elimination of the culprit genes from the germ-line is possible? It is far more efficient, in terms of suffering and discomfort, risk, and cost, and technically, to correct such disorders at the beginning of life.

E. The prevailing ethic of science and medicine is that knowledge has intrinsic value, and that its pursuit should not be impeded except under extraordinary circumstances. Knowledge, the result of basic research into the nature of things, is the foundation upon which any technology must be built. The process from principle to practice, however, first requires an intermediate stage, in which new techniques and methods are developed. Moreover, since the results of basic research are often unforeseen, the opportunities for application will expand in unpredictable directions, as long as the enterprise of research remains healthy. But the development of the needed methodology and, hence, the useful applications, will generally not come about before the underlying phenomena are understood. Thus, major programs to direct research toward specific goals before the basic knowledge was in place have generally not succeeded (e.g., the 'War on Cancer'), just so attempts to suppress the freedom of inquiry have failed. Yet the question of whether or not the concept of "forbidden knowledge" should be considered with respect to human germ-line therapy has received recent discussion.

1. One concern that is sometimes voiced against germ line therapy is that it could adversely affect the human gene pool, perhaps by eliminating genes that might have enabled future generations to respond to new environmental challenges. The AAAS Report disagreed, stating (at p. 34):

> It is also doubtful that IGM would have a serious impact on the gene pool. The number of carriers of recessive alleles related to monogenic impairments is far greater than the number of homozygotes with the diseases. Therefore, if we treat the latter with IGM, we would eliminate only a miniscule percentage of the carriers and would not have a major effect on the gene pool.

2. Another objection to germ line therapy is that it is "playing God." For a discussion of religious views, see AAAS Report at 27–32.

3. For European views on regulating germ line interventions, see Emily Marden & Dorothy Nelkin, Displaced Agendas: Current Regulatory Strategies for Germline Gene Therapy, 45 McGill L. J. 461, 479–480 (2000). For a bibliography on gene therapy, see Kennedy Institute of Ethics, National Reference Center for Bioethics Literature, Scope Note 24 (February 2000), at www.georgetown.edu/research/ncrbl/publications/scopenotes/sn24.htm.

4. In 2009, Japanese researchers reported that they had produced marmoset babies that glowed green under ultraviolet light, just like their genetically engineered parents, who had had fluorescent jellyfish genes inserted into their DNA when they were embryos. This was the first successful germ line gene transfer in primates. See Marmoset Model Takes Centre Stage, 459 Nature 515–516 (2009).

II. PHARMACOGENETICS

ALLEN D. ROSES, PHARMACOGENETICS AND THE PRACTICE OF MEDICINE

405 Nature 857 (2000).

Every individual is a product of the interaction of their genes and the environment. Pharmacogenetics is the study of how genetic differences influence the variability in patients' responses to drugs. Through the use of pharmacogenetics, we will soon be able to profile variations between individuals' DNA to predict responses to a particular medicine. The medical significance and economic value of a simple, predictive medicine response profile, which will provide information on the likelihood of efficacy and safety of a drug for an individual patient, will change the practice and economics of medicine. The ability to rapidly profile patients who are likely to benefit from a particular medicine will also streamline drug development and provide opportunities to develop discrete medicines concurrently for different patients with similar disease phenotypes. Other than relatively rare and highly penetrant diseases related to mutations of a single gene inherited in families, science has never before had the tools to characterize the nuances of inherited metabolic variations that interact over time and lead to common diseases. Powerful pharmacogenetic research tools are now becoming available to classify the heterogeneity of disease as well as individual responses to medicines.

* * *

TARGET SELECTION

Target validation that will predict a well-tolerated and effective medicine for a clinical indication in humans is a widely perceived problem; but the real challenge is target selection. A limited number of molecular target families have been identified, including receptors and enzymes, for which high-throughput screening is currently possible. A good target is one against which many compounds can be screened rapidly to identify active molecules (hits). These hits can be developed into optimized molecules (leads), which have the properties of well-tolerated and effective medicines. Selection of targets that can be validated for a disease or clinical symptom is a major problem faced by the pharmaceutical industry. The best-validated targets are those that have already produced well-tolerated and effective medicines in humans (precedented targets). Many targets are chosen on the basis of scientific hypotheses and do not lead to effective medicines because the initial hypotheses are often subsequently disproved.

Two broad strategies are being used to identify genes and express their protein products for use as high-throughput targets. These approaches of genomics and genetics share technologies but represent distinct scientific tactics and investments. Discovery genetics uses human disease populations to identify disease-related susceptibility genes. Discovery genomics uses the increasing number of databases of DNA sequence information to identify genes and families of genes for tractable or screenable targets that are not known to be genetically related to disease.

The advantage of information on disease-susceptibility genes derived from patients is that, by definition, these genes are relevant to the patients' genetic contributions to the disease. However, most susceptibility genes will not be tractable targets or amenable to high-throughput screening methods to identify active compounds. The differential metabolism related to the relevant gene variants can be studied using focused functional genomic and proteomic technologies to discover mechanisms of disease development or progression. Critical enzymes or receptors associated with the altered metabolism can then be used as targets. Gene-to-function-to-target strategies that focus on the role of the specific susceptibility gene variants on appropriate cellular metabolism become important.

* * *

The difference between the genomic approach and the genetic approach is that the former creates a need to functionally validate the tissue distribution and other aspects of each identified gene and find a relevant disease or clinical indication. In contrast, once the disease-related variants of susceptibility disease genes are identified, a single susceptibility gene is automatically validated in human disease. The major distinction between the genomic and genetic approaches is target selection, with genetically defined genes and variant-specific targets already known to be involved in the disease process. The current vogue of discovery genomics for nonspecific, wholesale gene identification, with each gene in search of a relationship to a disease, creates great opportunities for development of medicines. However, there are also enormous economical costs associated with searching huge lists of genes for 'the right disease for the available gene'. It is correct to state that target validation is a major challenge to the pharmaceutical industry, but it is also critical to realize that the core problem for drug development is poor target selection. The screening use of unproven technologies to imply disease-related validation, and the huge investment necessary to progress each selected gene to proof of concept in humans, is based on an unproven and cavalier use of the word 'validation'. Each failure is very expensive in lost time and money.

* * *

PHARMACOGENETICS AND MEDICAL PRACTICE

Diagnosis

When we go to see our doctor, our symptoms and physical signs are evaluated, and appropriate tests (for example, blood, urine, X-ray and magnetic resonance imaging) are undertaken. To the non-physician, this process of disease diagnosis seems straightforward. However, for a patient to have all the classical symptoms and signs of a particular disease is the exception rather than the rule. How these diagnoses relate to the underlying mechanism of disease is often unknown. For example, patients with mutations in different genes may present as clinically identical. Mutations of APP, presenilin 1 and presenilin 2 lead to clinically indistinguishable forms of Alzheimer's disease. It is also important to note that mutations at different sites along the *APP* gene can lead to two distinct diseases, early-onset Alzheimer's disease and recurrent intracerebral hemorrhages. For many common diseases, the situation may be assumed to be even more complicated, with many contributing molecular variants of several interacting susceptibility genes leading to multiple clinical effects over varying time frames. Thus many of the diseases that we classify clinically may be syndromes with several distinct contributing pathogenic mechanisms. With all this clinical and genetic heterogeneity we should not lose sight of the fact that the major objective is to treat, cure or prevent disease. It is significant that a medicine works; does it matter whether it is effective in patients who may have different diagnoses? The goal of medicine is to relieve pain and suffering. Similar mechanisms may exist for quite diverse clinical diseases. As the targets and mechanisms are validated in humans, additional clinical indications may become more obvious because of shared mechanisms rather than similar clinical presentations.

How does your doctor know when making the diagnosis that medicines that are effective for you have not been precluded? Pharmacogenetics will enable individuals to be classified according to their likely response to a medicine. This is not a new concept as clinical subtypes are often classified by drug responsiveness (for example, steroid-sensitive and steroid-resistant asthma). Application of pharmacogenetics will expand the population to those who can be helped but might have otherwise been missed because their clinical syndrome did not fit neatly into a traditional disease category. Alosetron is a recently approved medicine in the United States for the treatment of female patients with diarrhoea-predominant irritable bowel syndrome (IBS). Most physicians will acknowledge that the diagnosis of IBS can be imprecise—in fact, the 'disease' is truly a syndrome. The value of a diagnostic test to sub-classify IBS into different types may be limited, but a simple medicine response profile to determine whether the patient's symptoms will be alleviated by alosetron could have considerable value. Pharmacogenetic approaches will no doubt confirm what clinicians already know—disease diagnosis is not easy nor necessarily homogeneous and accurate.

Apparently distinct diseases may have similar underlying mechanisms. A medicine developed for a specific indication could have value in treating other related or non-related conditions. This is also not a new concept. There are many medicines that were initially registered with a single indication, which have then been expanded as more clinical research is conducted. For example, carbamazepine was initially registered as a treatment for trigeminal neuralgia, a syndrome with intermittent severe lightning-like bursts of facial pain, but was later extended to treat various forms of epilepsy. By understanding the genetic basis of patient responses to medicines, and perhaps also by having a better understanding of how the medicine works, we will be able to identify additional clinical indications more quickly.

Treatment

How does a physician know if the medicine and the dose prescribed will be effective and whether or not the patient will experience adverse effects? Information is available from clinical trials in the medicine's data sheet/label in which similar patients were included and the physician may use experience of treating previous patients. On many occasions, the prescribed medicine will be effective and not cause serious side effects. Other patients may not respond or suffer adverse reactions. By applying the results of pharmacogenetic research to clinical practice, physicians will be able to use information from patients' DNA to determine how patients are likely to respond to a particular medicine. The clinical fact that the drug dose for some patients must be individualized has been accepted for years. Polymorphisms in genes encoding P450 enzymes, *N*-acetyltransferase and other key enzymes in drug metabolism account for the concentration variation of certain drugs in patients' blood. It is also well established that some patients can be slow in activating drugs and respond inadequately to some prodrugs, or exhibit reduced clearance and increased effects from some pharmacologically active agents. Enzyme tests that measure those variants have, in some cases, already been replaced with genetic variants on chips. In the future, metabolic screens of genetic variants will be standardized so that automated read-outs of each person's predicted response to each medicine could be generated. These DNA-based screens will not provide disease-specific diagnosis, but useful information to aid in individual dosing of medications or avoidance of side effects.

* * *

PHARMACOGENETICS AND DRUG DEVELOPMENT

More efficient clinical trials and enhanced drug surveillance

Application of SNP mapping technologies will enable effective medicines to be developed and made available for clinical use more rapidly. Using abbreviated SNP linkage disequilibrium mapping, medicine response profiles could be identified during phase II clinical trials. These could be used in the selection of patient groups enriched for efficacy in phase III studies. This is likely to make these trials smaller, faster and more efficient.

Regulatory agencies would correctly be concerned that there were not enough patients in these streamlined phase III trials to evaluate adverse events, although larger clinical trials that do not select "efficacy" patients are also unlikely to detect rare adverse events (less than 1 in 1,000). Regulatory authorities would also be apprehensive that, when the drug is marketed, patients who did not meet the pharmacogenetic criteria for prescription may be prescribed the drug without study of their potential benefits or adverse events. However, the risk-benefit ratio for patients with poor efficacy predictions may exclude them from phase III studies on ethical grounds as they would now knowingly be included solely to experience potential adverse events. Furthermore, in clinical practice, access to the medicine could be determined by prescriptions based on pharmacogenetic profiles.

In fact, pharmacogenetic technology may enable a significantly enhanced post-approval surveillance system to be established for approved medicines. Regulatory agencies, pharmaceutical companies and the public recognize the need to improve strategies for drug surveillance. In this proposed concept of regulated surveillance, hundreds of thousands of patients who receive the medicine would have blood spots taken and stored on filter papers in an approved location using the original blood sample screened for the initial medicine response profile for efficacy. As rare, serious adverse events are documented and characterized, DNA from patients who experienced the adverse event could be extracted and compared with DNA from control patients who received the drug but did not experience the adverse event. This would enable abbreviated SNP profiles for patients susceptible to the adverse event to be determined. These adverse event profiles would be combined with efficacy profiles to produce a comprehensive medicine response profile. This would allow selection of patients for both efficacy and lower complications of therapy.

A predictive pharmacogenetic adverse event profile derived from hundreds of thousands of patients taking the drug would be a major advance on the present system of documenting reported serious adverse events during the use of the medicine in clinical practice, as this current system often obtains little or no predictive information to help subsequent patients, other than broad warnings.

Over the next few years, as we approach the ability to differentiate patients by their therapeutic responses, regulatory agencies and pharmaceutical companies will need to work together to pilot and examine methods to evaluate fewer total patients in faster, more efficient clinical trials while enhancing drug surveillance systems. Initial studies using medicine response profiles would no doubt use nested populations of patients within trials designed to meet current guidelines and regulations in order to demonstrate proof of concept.

Medicines for all

The application of pharmacogenetics will not diminish the population in whom a drug is effective, but simply allow prediction of patient response rather than prolonged and expensive prescribing by trial and error. Just as it will be possible to identify patients with drug efficacy, it will also be possible to identify those patients who do not respond early in the process of drug development. The ability to target heterogeneous groups of patients for parallel drug development early, rather than waiting years for non-responsive populations to emerge after extensive clinical use of the medicine, will be a significant benefit. For example, SNP profiling of different medicine-responsive association groups during phase II trials will enable identification of the location of genes contributing to heterogeneous forms of the disease, leading to the discovery of new medicines and additional susceptibility targets.

By focusing clinical trials on patients who are most likely to respond, drug development resources could be targeted to those patients with continued unmet medical need. In particular, molecules that show less than a 30% response rate in a large population, but have clear efficacy in an identifiable smaller population of patients, would become viable as they could be readily identified for development and clinical practice.

As a result of disease heterogeneity, there may be large, definable subgroups of patients suffering with a common phenotype, for example Alzheimer's disease, which represent only 10–15% of patients with that diagnosis. Focusing drug development on sub-groups of patients selected by either a disease-specific diagnostic or a medicine response profile will provide opportunities to develop more medicines for a larger proportion of patients with heterogeneous diseases. Similarly, patient groups who have vaguely defined phenotypes that are more difficult to categorize by objective criteria, such as depression, could be studied more efficiently using medicine response profiles as selection variables.

VALUE OF PHARMACOGENETICS TO HEALTH-CARE DELIVERY

The cost-effectiveness of new medicines (which are the product of considerable investment in research and development) is a significant concern to patients, funding bodies and governments. The application of pharmacogenetics to the delivery of medicines will maximize the value of each medicine. Medicines would be prescribed to only those patients where a high probability of efficacy without significant adverse events is expected. This is a much-preferred scenario than the problems facing funding agencies and governments at the present time. Medicines that might be prescribed to 100 patients to achieve an effect in 20 are becoming more difficult for sponsors of medical care to consider. However, selection of predicted responders offers a more efficient and economical solution to a growing problem that is leading governments and health-care providers to deny effective medicines to the few, because a proportion of patients do not respond to the treatment. The economy of predictable efficacy, limited adverse events, lower complications owing to targeted delivery, and increased cost-effectiveness of medicines will improve health-care delivery and eliminate the need for rationing. Effective and well-tolerated medicines with predictive medicine response profiles will obviate the need for formulary restrictions on prescribing and new policies to mandate cost-effectiveness to be proved in a broad population of patients.

Pharmacogenetics will impact medical care at multiple levels. As well-tolerated and effective medicines that treat, cure or prevent common diseases become a greater proportion of the medical care bill, the costs of chronic debilitating illnesses will be significantly reduced. As treatment and prevention of chronic and common diseases improves, a significant proportion of money saved by reducing hospitalization and long-term care costs could be transferred to well-tolerated and effective medicines.

FOOD AND DRUG ADMINISTRATION, GUIDANCE FOR INDUSTRY: PHARMACOGENOMIC DATA SUBMISSIONS

March 2005.

Background

The promise of pharmacogenomics lies in its potential to help identify sources of inter-individual variability in drug response (both effectiveness and toxicity); this information will make it possible to individualize therapy with the intent of maximizing effectiveness and minimizing risk. However, the field of pharmacogenomics is currently in early developmental stages, and such promise has not yet been realized. The Agency has heard that pharmaceutical sponsors have been reluctant to embark on programs of pharmacogenomic testing during FDA-regulated phases of drug development because of uncertainties in how the data will be used by

FDA in the drug application review process. This guidance is intended to help clarify FDA policy in this area.

Sponsors submitting or holding INDs, NDAs, or BLAs are subject to FDA requirements for submitting to the Agency data relevant to drug safety and effectiveness (including 21 CFR 312.22, 312.23, 312.31, 312.33, 314.50, 314.81, 601.2, and 601.12). Because these regulations were developed before the advent of widespread animal or human genetic or gene expression testing, they do not specifically address when such data must be submitted. The FDA has received numerous inquiries about what these regulations require of sponsors who are conducting such testing.

From a public policy perspective, a number of factors should be considered when interpreting how these regulations apply to the developing field of pharmacogenomics. Because the field of pharmacogenomics is rapidly evolving, in many circumstances, the experimental results may not be well enough established scientifically to be suitable for regulatory decision making. For example:

- Laboratory techniques and test procedures may not be well validated. In addition, test systems may vary so that results may not be consistent or generalizable across different platforms. A move to standardize assays is underway, and much more information should be available within the next several years.

- The scientific framework for interpreting the physiologic, toxicologic, pharmacologic, or clinical significance of certain experimental results may not yet be well understood.

- The findings from a specific study often cannot be extrapolated across species or to different study populations (e.g., various human subpopulations with different genetic backgrounds).

- The standards for transmission, processing, and storage of the large amounts of highly dimensional data generated from microarray technology have neither been well defined nor widely tested.

Despite these concerns, some pharmacogenetic tests—primarily those related to drug metabolism—have well-accepted mechanistic and clinical significance and are currently being integrated into drug development decision making and clinical practice.

It is important for FDA to have a role in the evaluation of pharmacogenomic tests, both to ensure that evolving FDA policies are based on the best science and to provide public confidence in the field. The FDA developed this guidance to facilitate the use of pharmacogenomic tests during drug development and encourage open and public sharing of data and information on pharmacogenomic test results.

To this end, the Agency has undertaken a process for obtaining input from the scientific community and the public. On May 16 and 17, 2002, the Agency held a workshop, cosponsored by pharmaceutical industry groups, to identify key issues associated with the application of pharmacogenetics and pharmacogenomics to drug development. Subsequently, on

April 8, 2003, a public presentation was made to the FDA Science Board. This presentation contained a proposal for developing guidance on the submission of information on pharmacogenomic tests and a potential algorithm for deciding whether submission of such data is voluntary or required. The Science Board endorsed moving forward with both of these proposals. In November 2003, FDA published a draft version of this guidance and received public comment on the draft guidance. The Agency also has developed internal policy related to pharmacogenomics and voluntary submissions.

The policies and processes outlined in this final guidance are intended to take the above factors into account and to assist in advancing the field in a manner that will benefit both drug development programs and the public health.

SUBMISSION POLICY

General Principles

The FDA recognizes that its pharmacogenomic data submission policies must be consistent with the relevant codified regulatory submission requirements for investigational and marketing application submitters and holders. At present, many pharmacogenomic results are not well enough established scientifically to be appropriate for regulatory decision making. This guidance interprets FDA's regulations for investigational and marketing submissions, with the goal of clarifying FDA's current thinking about when the regulations require pharmacogenomic data to be submitted and when the submission of such data would be welcome on a voluntary basis. In some cases, complete reports of pharmacogenomic studies suffice, while in others, an abbreviated report or synopsis should or must be submitted.

Because FDA regulations establish different requirements for investigational applications, unapproved marketing applications, and approved marketing applications, this guidance sets out different submission algorithms for each of these categories. The guidance also clarifies how the Agency currently intends to use such data in regulatory decision making—that is, when the data will be considered sufficiently reliable to serve as the basis for regulatory decision making; when it will be considered only supportive to a decision; and when the data will not be used in regulatory decision making.

This guidance also makes a distinction between pharmacogenomic tests that may be considered either probable or known *valid biomarkers,* which may be appropriate for regulatory decision making, and other less well-developed tests that are either observational or exploratory biomarkers that, alone, are insufficient for making regulatory decisions. Although, currently, most pharmacogenomic measurements are not considered valid biomarkers, certain markers (e.g., for drug metabolism) are well established biomarkers with clear clinical significance. Undoubtedly, the distinction between what tests are appropriate for regulatory decision making and those that are not will change over time as the science evolves. Throughout the development of these tests, as appropriate, FDA will continue to seek public comment as we evaluate whether a biomarker is a *valid biomarker* (e.g., via discussions at Advisory Committee meetings).

For the purposes of this guidance, a pharmacogenomic test result may be considered a *valid biomarker* if (1) it is measured in an analytical test system with well-established performance characteristics and (2) there is an established scientific framework or body of evidence that elucidates the physiologic, pharmacologic, toxicologic, or clinical significance of the test results. For example, the consequences for drug metabolism of genetic variation in the human enzymes CYP2D6 and thiopurine methyltransferase are well understood in the scientific community and are reflected in certain approved drug labels. The results of genetic tests that distinguish allelic variants of these enzymes are considered to be well established and, therefore, valid biomarkers.

This guidance makes an additional distinction between known valid biomarkers that have been accepted in the broad scientific community and probable valid biomarkers that appear to have predictive value for clinical outcomes, but may not yet be widely accepted or independently verified by other investigators or institutions. When a sponsor generates, or possesses, data sufficient to establish a significant association between a pharmacogenomic test result and clinical outcomes, the test result represents a probable valid biomarker. It would be expected that this biomarker would meet criteria (1) and (2) above, and its association with a meaningful outcome would have been demonstrated in more than one experiment.

The algorithms described below for investigational and marketing application holders describe when to submit to FDA data on known valid biomarkers. Data on probable valid biomarkers need not be submitted to the IND unless they are used by a sponsor to make decisions regarding specific animal safety studies or clinical trials (e.g., using biomarker data as inclusion or exclusion criteria, assessment of treatment-related prognosis, or stratifying patients by dose) or are a probable valid biomarker in human safety studies. However, we recommend that sponsors or applicants submit reports on all probable valid biomarkers to new (i.e., unapproved) NDAs or BLAs according to the algorithm in section IV.B.

Many pharmacogenomic testing programs implemented by pharmaceutical sponsors or by scientific organizations are intended to develop the knowledge base necessary to establish the validity of new genomic biomarkers. During such a period of scientific exploration, test results are not useful in making regulatory judgments pertaining to the safety or effectiveness of a drug and are not considered known or probable valid biomarkers. However, scientific development of this sort is highly desirable for advancing the understanding of relationships between genotype or gene expression and responses to drugs and, therefore, should be encouraged and facilitated. For these reasons, although submission of exploratory pharmacogenomic data is not required under the regulations, FDA is encouraging *voluntary submission* of such data, as described below.

Specific Uses of Pharmacogenomic Data in Drug Development and Labeling

As the field of pharmacogenomics advances, it is likely (and desirable) that sponsors will begin to use pharmacogenomic tests to support drug development and/or to guide therapy. Sponsors may choose to submit pharmacogenomic data that have not achieved the status of a valid biomarker to an investigational or marketing application to support scientific contentions related to dosing and dosing schedule, safety, or effectiveness. For example, a sponsor may wish to provide supportive data demonstrating that changes in drug-induced gene expression differ between species that have different toxicologic responses to a drug, thus correlating changes in certain gene expression patterns with a specific toxicity. Or, a pharmacogenomic test result might also be used to stratify patients in a clinical trial or to identify patients at higher risk for an adverse event to correlate test results with clinical outcome.

If a pharmacogenomic test shows promise for enhancing the dose selection, safety, or effectiveness of a drug, a sponsor may wish to fully integrate pharmacogenomic data into the drug development program. This integration could occur in two ways:

1.   The pharmacogenomic data may be intended to be included in the drug labeling in an informational manner. For example, such data might be used to describe the potential for dose adjustment by drug metabolism genotype (e.g., CYP2D6*5) or to mention the possibility of a side effect of greater severity or frequency in individuals of a certain genotype or gene expression profile. In such cases, the pharmacogenomic test result would be considered a known valid biomarker. However, an FDA-approved pharmacogenomic test may not be available or required to be available, or a commercial pharmacogenomic test may not be widely available. Given this level of complexity, at the current time, sponsors should consult the relevant FDA review division for advice on how to proceed in a specific case. However, whenever a sponsor intends to include pharmacogenomic data in the drug label, complete information on the test and results must be submitted to the Agency as described under §§ 314.50 and 601.2.

2.   The pharmacogenomic data and resulting test or tests may be intended to be included in the drug labeling to choose a dose and dose schedule, to identify patients at risk, or to identify patient responders. Inclusion of a pharmacogenomic test in the labeling would be contingent upon its performance characteristics. For example:

   • Patients will be tested for drug metabolism genotype and dosed according to the test results.

   • Patients will be selected as potential responders for an efficacy trial (or deselected because of a high risk) based on genotype (e.g., of either the patient or the patient's tumor) or gene expression profile.

- Patients will be excluded from a clinical trial based on genotype or gene expression profile (e.g., biomarker for risk of an adverse event).

In all of these cases, FDA recommends co-development of the drug and the pharmacogenomic tests, if they are not currently available, and submission of complete information on the test/drug combination to the Agency. The FDA plans to issue further guidance on co-development of pharmacogenomic tests and drugs.

The Office of In Vitro Diagnostics in CDRH, appropriate review divisions in CBER, and the Clinical and Clinical Pharmacology Review divisions in CBER or CDER are willing to meet jointly with sponsors to discuss both scientific and regulatory issues with regard to new pharmacogenomic tests. The CDRH has both formal (IDE) and informal (pre-IDE) processes to evaluate protocols for pharmacogenomic test development.

NOTES AND QUESTIONS

1. The terms "pharmacogenetics" and "pharmacogenomics" are often used inaccurately and interchangeably. As Roses explains, the difference lies in the starting point. With pharmacogenetics, the starting point is a human population with a genetic disease, and the task is to identify the genes that are associated with the disease. With pharmacogenomics, the starting point is the genome, the sequence of human DNA, and the task is to identify the diseases that are associated with differences in the genome, or polymorphisms. Pharmacogenetics is the older technique; pharmacogenomics was not feasible until stretches of the human genome were sequenced and the technology was available to rapidly identify single nucleotide polymorphisms, or "SNPs."

In both cases, the goals are the same: to improve the diagnosis of genetic disease; to develop drugs to fight genetic disease; to make clinical testing of drugs more efficient by identifying populations in which the drugs are likely to be especially efficacious (and presumably for whom they would be indicated on the labeling); and, using genetic information about patients, to maximize therapeutic benefit and minimize harmful side effects by prescribing drugs to targeted patient populations.

A related field is "proteomics," which focuses on the proteins that genes code for and the association of the proteins with disease.

2. The fields of pharmacogenetics, pharmacogenomics, and proteomics are still in their early stages. However, some findings are beginning to be commercialized and to find their way into clinical use. For example, a Cytochrome P4502D6 gene test, which will help determine how patients metabolize a number of drugs, is expected to be available soon. Other applications include the use of a test for a gene known as TPMT that makes some patients highly sensitive to the chemotherapy agent used to treat acute lymphoblastic leukemia, the most common form of childhood cancer. The test

reportedly can tell if a patient should get only 5% of the standard dosage to avoid serious side effects without significant loss of effectiveness. Another test can reveal if congestive heart failure will be responsive to drug therapy, or if a heart transplant will be necessary.

Warfarin is the most widely-used oral anticoagulant, which is used in patients with cardiovascular disease to prevent the formation of blood clots that can cause strokes. The dosage of the drug must be carefully calibrated for each patient to produce avoid catastrophic side-effects. Traditionally this was done on a risky trial-and-error basis, but pharmacogenomic research demonstrated that people with a variant of the genes CYP2C9 or VKORC1 break down the drug more slowly, which means that it stays in the body longer and causes bleeding. In 2007, the FDA announced that a new label is being prepared for Warfarin, which states under "precautions": "Certain variations in two key genes may increase the need for more frequent monitoring and the use of lower doses." Genetic tests for the two key genes cost $300–$500 and the turnaround time for test results means that initial dosing and titration of Warfarin levels must begin before the results are available. On May 4, 2009, the Centers for Medicare and Medicaid Services announced it will not pay for the genetic tests because of a lack of clinical utility.

3.   Not everyone is optimistic that positive developments will occur rapidly. See, e.g., Leslie Roberts, SNP Mappers Confront Reality and Find It Daunting, 287 Science 1898 (2000). In an article in the New Eng. J. Med., two respected genetics experts stated:

> [T]he new genetics will not revolutionize the way in which common diseases are identified or prevented. Mapping and sequencing the human genome will lead to the identification of more genes causing mendelian disorders and to the development of diagnostic and predictive tests for them. The development of safe and effective treatments, however, will usually lag behind, although occasionally a treatment does precede the discovery of the disease-causing allele, as was the case for hemochromatosis. Furthermore, only a small proportion of the population has mendelian disorders, and this will limit the ultimate impact of the Human Genome Project.

> Our doubts stem from the incomplete penetrance of genotypes for common diseases, the limited ability to tailor treatment to genotypes, and the low magnitude of risks conferred by various genotypes for the population at large.

Neil A. Holtzman & Theresa M. Marteau, Will Genetics Revolutionize Medicine?, 343 New Eng. J. Med. 141 (2000).

Andrew Pollack in an article in *The New York Times* describes some of the problems encountered in using pharmacogenetic testing to refine the prescribing of the drugs Herceptin and tamoxifen:

> * * * The hurdles include drug makers, which can be reluctant to develop or encourage tests that may limit the use of their drugs. Insurers may not pay for tests, which can cost up to a few thousand dollars. For makers of the tests, which hope their business becomes one of health care's next big growth industries, a major obstacle is proving that their

products are accurate and useful. While drugs must prove themselves in clinical trials before they can be sold, there is no generally recognized process for evaluating genetic tests, many of which can be marketed by laboratories without F.D.A. approval.

Genentech, a developer of cancer drugs, petitioned the F.D.A. this month to regulate such tests. It warned of "safety risks for patients, as more treatment decisions are based in whole or in part on the claims made by such test makers."

A cautionary case is Herceptin, a Genentech breast cancer drug that is considered the archetype of personalized medicine because it works only for women whose tumors have a particular genetic characteristic. But now, 10 years after Herceptin reached the market, scientists are finding that the various tests—some approved by the F.D.A., some not—can be inaccurate.

Moreover, doctors do not always conduct the tests or follow the results. The big insurer UnitedHealthcare found in 2005 that 8 percent of the women getting the drug had tested negative for the required genetic characteristic. An additional 4 percent had not been tested at all, or their test results could not be found.

Tamoxifen, * * * illustrates the promise and current limitations of genetic testing. In 2003, more than 25 years after tamoxifen was introduced, researchers led by Dr. David A. Flockhart at Indiana University School of Medicine figured out that the body coverts tamoxifen into another substance called endoxifen. It is endoxifen that actually exerts the cancer-fighting effect. The conversion is done by an enzyme in the body called CYP2D6, or 2D6 for short.

But variations in people's 2D6 genes mean the enzymes have different levels of activity. Up to 7 percent of people, depending on their ethnic group, have an inactive enzyme, Dr. Flockhart said, while another 20 to 40 percent have an only modestly active enzyme.

The implications were "scary," Dr. Flockhart said. Many women were apparently not being protected against cancer's return because they could not convert tamoxifen to endoxifen.

The economic implications could be just as scary to big pharmaceutical companies.

Tamoxifen, now a generic drug, costs as little as $500 for the typical five-year treatment. But most patients in the United States are currently treated with a newer, much more expensive class of drugs, called aromatase inhibitors, that cost about $18,000 over five years. Those drugs—made by AstraZeneca, Novartis and Pfizer—performed better than tamoxifen in clinical trials before the role of 2D6 was generally understood.

If only women with active 2D6 had been assessed, tamoxifen might have worked as well or better than the newer drugs, according to researchers at the Dana–Farber Cancer Institute in Boston.

But proving these suppositions and having them incorporated into medical practice have not been easy.

The F.D.A., in its meeting this month, said clinical trials were the ideal way to validate a test. But many test developers argue that trials would be too costly and time-consuming, so many tests are validated by reanalyzing patient data from old trials.

In the case of tamoxifen, Dr. Matthew P. Goetz of the Mayo Clinic and colleagues went back to an old trial and used stored tumor samples to test the 2D6 genes of each patient. The researchers reported in 2005 that 32 percent of the women with inactive 2D6 enzyme had relapsed or died within two years, in contrast to only 2 percent of the other women.

But while some subsequent studies have backed those conclusions, two had contradictory results. That leaves many experts hesitant to use the test, which costs about $300.

There are other complications. Dozens of variants of the 2D6 gene exist, and laboratories can differ in their interpretation of test results. And it is not always clear how to act upon the information the test provides.

* * *

Such complexities are not confined to tamoxifen testing. The labels of about 200 drugs now contain some information relating genes to drug response, said Lawrence J. Lesko, the F.D.A.'s head of clinical pharmacology. But in many cases, he said, doctors are not told specifically enough what to do with the test results, such as how much to change the dose.

Andrew Pollack, Patient's DNA May Be Signal to Tailor Drugs, The New York Times, Dec. 30, 2008, at A1.

4. Nutrigenomics is the study of the way dietary nutrients interact with individual genetic makeup to affect health outcomes. Scientifically, nutrigenomics is still in its infancy, and experts believe it will take years, if not decades, before research will support its widespread application to human diet. Nevertheless, marketers are already touting genetic testing for nutrition-related genetic factors and selling customized vitamin supplements and food based on personalized genetic factors. The assessments and products run from $249.95 to $595.00. See Rhonda L. Rundle, Can Genetic Tests Aid in Nutrition? Wall St. J. March 1, 2005, at D6. How, if at all, should the law regulate these practices?

MARK A. ROTHSTEIN & PHYLLIS GRIFFIN EPPS, ETHICAL AND LEGAL IMPLICATIONS OF PHARMACOGENOMICS
2 Nature Reviews Genetics 228 (2001).

Pharmacogenomics is changing the way that drugs are developed, approved, marketed and prescribed. The objective of pharmacogenomics is to define the pharmacological significance of genetic variation among individuals and to use this information in drug discovery, thereby decreasing the number of adverse drug responses that injure and kill thousands each year. By determining which genetic variations are likely to affect a person's ability to metabolize a drug, drug manufacturers intend to develop more predictable and effective therapeutic agents. Towards this end, pharmaceutical companies are investing huge amounts of capital in the technologies that will revolutionize both how researchers identify drug targets and the amount of time needed to move a drug through development and approval. Pharmacogenomics promises to streamline the clinical trial phase of drug development. Researchers hope to use knowledge gained from high-throughput screening and other technologies to construct clinical trial groups that are composed of people most likely to benefit from a particular drug. The ability to streamline clinical trials by genotyping will enable researchers to "rescue" drugs that could not be approved under conventional models of research trials. In other words, drugs that were previously rejected after giving unacceptable rates of adverse responses in traditionally constructed trials will yield lower adverse-response rates after testing under the new model, thereby becoming acceptable candidates for approval. Pharmacogenomics will not only produce better drugs but also yield greater efficiency in the allocation of resources in drug development.

Other changes attributable to pharmacogenomics will be less welcome. Notwithstanding the increasingly efficient research and development process, pharmacogenomic-based drugs will be expensive, because of, for example, the need to recoup the cost of investment in new technologies. The ability to develop specialized drugs that are ultimately approved for smaller populations rather than for general use will fragment the market for pharmaceuticals. Will a pharmaceutical manufacturer react to this economic reality in a way that better suits profit margins than health, and is that socially acceptable? The use of groups in clinical trials that are increasingly similar genotypically raises several important ethical issues regarding social inclusion and the adequacy of current regulatory frameworks. Because polymorphisms of pharmacological interest might vary in frequency among different population subgroups, important social issues arise in multi-ethnic countries, such as the United States. Finally, pharmacogenomics will change the standard of care for pharmaceutical companies and health professionals, including physicians and pharmacists.

This article provides an overview of some ethical and social concerns that arise with the integration of pharmacogenomics into the discovery of drugs and the practice of preventive and therapeutic medicine. Specifically, the article addresses issues associated with the design of clinical trials, the relatively higher cost of pharmaceuticals developed using pharmacogenomics, and the allocation of ethical and legal responsibility. The objective is to highlight a few of the questions and challenges that will require further attention in the near future.

A NEW MODEL OF CLINICAL TRIALS

Pharmacogenomics promises to reduce the time and money required to develop a drug. The ability to predict drug efficacy by genotyping participants during the early stages of clinical trials for a drug would enable researchers to recruit for later trials only those patients who, according to their genotype, are likely to benefit from the drug. As a result, clinical trials could become smaller, cheaper and faster to run.

The prospect of clinical trials that are composed of smaller groups with the same polymorphisms at one or more loci of interest poses some risks, however. A group that reflects the diversity of the population yields information on how a drug will behave in a greater number of people. If the clinical trial group is smaller, or is less genotypically diverse, there is a greater risk that some side effects will go undetected. So, the trials will yield a greater quantity and quality of information, but on a smaller segment of the population. Whereas the conventional model yielded information about harmful side effects in a greater proportion of the population, the concentration of individuals pre-selected for a favourable response under the newer model might not produce the same information. Compared with traditionally designed human clinical trials, genotype-specific human clinical studies might be subject to equal or greater limitations in that the relatively short duration of the study, combined with the narrower subject population and smaller size, would hinder the ability of the studies to identify rare or delayed adverse reactions or drug interactions. A drug could reach the market with less information about the side effects or risk of harm from its non-prescribed uses. An unresolved issue is whether the ethical principles of beneficence and non-maleficence (that is, not causing harm to others) would preclude the deliberate inclusion of anyone who is not likely to respond favourably to treatment. With the advent of genotype-specific clinical trials, manufacturers and regulators must be ready to carefully evaluate post-market data by strengthening the existing guidelines for phase IV, or post-approval, clinical trials.

As in other areas of genetic research that involve human subjects, the likely effect of pharmacogenomics on clinical trials raises important questions regarding informed consent, which might include considerations of privacy and confidentiality. Current ideas regarding patient autonomy and informed consent require that patients agree to enter into research on the basis of adequate information regarding the risks and consequences of participation. Genotyping that is appropriate to pharmacogenomic research might not produce information regarding susceptibility to disease or early death, but it might reveal evidence of genetic variation that could lead to individuals being classified as "difficult to treat," "less profitable to treat," or "more expensive to treat." The fear of being so classified could act as a barrier to the recruitment of research participants.

Fear of stigmatization might prove to be a significant barrier to participation in clinical trials among members of population subgroups. Genetic variations of pharmacological significance are known to occur in varying frequency in groups categorized by their ethnicity. For example, different variants of glucose–6–phosphate dehydrogenase (G6PD—an enzyme critical for NADPH (nicotinamide-adenine dinucleotide phosphate reduced) generation in mature red blood cells) are found at a high frequency in African, Mediterranean and Asiatic populations, some of which disrupt the function of the enzyme. A deficiency of G6PD can predispose individuals from these populations to haemolytic anaemia, both in individuals with loss-of-function G6PD mutations and in response to some drugs, such as the malarial drug primaquine. Isoniazid is an anti-tuberculosis drug that is inactivated by acetylation; its impaired metabolism by slow acetylation causes it to accumulate to toxic levels. Variation in the *N*-acetyl transferase 2 (*NAT2*) gene accounts for whether individuals are rapid or slow acetylators of isoniazid, as well as of other therapeutic and carcinogenic compounds. About 50% of individuals in many Caucasian populations are genotypically slow acetylators of isoniazid, but more than 80% of individuals in certain Middle Eastern populations and fewer than 20% in the Japanese population have the slow acetylator phenotype.

The significance of data that imply a role for ethnicity in research has been a source of considerable debate among the research ethics community. One issue is how to advise potential research participants about the possibility of social harms from group-based findings even where the research is conducted without using the names of participants. Another matter of considerable debate in the literature is whether it is necessary or feasible to engage in community consultation when genetic research focuses on socially or politically distinct population subgroups.

COST AS A BARRIER TO ACCESS

Pharmacogenomic drugs will be expensive, cheaper clinical trials notwithstanding. Collectively, the pharmaceutical industry is investing huge amounts of time and money in the development of new technologies that will yield drugs that are more effective than those already available. Without the opportunity to recoup their investment, drug companies will not continue their efforts. At the same time, insurance systems and consumers are struggling to absorb the rising costs of pharmaceutical products.

Pharmacogenomics is based on the idea that pharmaceutical consumers will be better served by drug therapy once they have been subdivided by genotype and matched with the most suitable drug. From the industry perspective, the subdivision of a market into smaller markets is hardly ideal. Incentives for pharmaceutical companies to invest time, effort and resources into the development of drugs to treat limited populations are few compared with the development of drugs to treat more prevalent genotypes in the context of pharmacogenomics. Most drug companies might be expected to direct their resources towards the development of drugs to treat the more prevalent genotypes.

Those groups characterized by less-profitable genotypes are at risk of becoming therapeutic "orphans". At present, pharmaceuticals for rare diseases are termed "orphan drugs." The United States and Japan have enacted legislation to stimulate research and the development of orphan drugs through market mechanisms, such as tax-based cost incentives and time-limited monopolies, with varying degrees of governmental intervention. Canada, Sweden, France, the United Kingdom and other countries rely on broader national drug policies based on more substantial governmental intervention. The European Union has entertained initiatives to stimulate legislative action on orphan drugs, and the European Agency for the Evaluation of Medicinal Products has a provision that exempts drug companies from having to pay application fees to develop a drug if it is an orphan drug. Despite allegations of overpricing of orphan drugs under the American model, nearly all efforts have been followed by a measurable increase in the number of drugs that have been developed and approved for the treatment of rare diseases. As clinical trials increasingly consist of genetically non-diverse groups, policy makers will need to consider whether to expand the concepts underlying orphan drug policies to stimulate research into and the development of drugs for populations who, by virtue of their genetic make-up, face inequities in drug development efforts.

Cost might act as a barrier to access to pharmacogenomics in that the cost of participating in clinical trials or of the resulting drug therapy might be excluded from insurance coverage. Particularly in the United States, where managed care systems attempt to contain costs by rationing medical services, public and private third-party payers have refused or been reluctant to pay for treatments that they deem "experimental" or not "medically necessary." Increasingly, these terms have more political than legal or medical significance. There is some evidence that the insurers' disinclination to cover expenses that are associated with new drug therapies can be countered by high physician or consumer demand for the new drug. If consumers must absorb rising pharmaceutical costs, pharmacogenomics will not introduce new questions so much as it will intensify existing ones about equitable access to medical care.

PROFESSIONAL STANDARDS OF CARE

As pharmacogenomic-based drugs enter into the marketplace, physicians will encounter alternatives to conventional drug therapy and prescription practices. Although the evaluation of genetic variation among patients to determine proper medication and dosage during the course of treatment is not the standard of care at present, ethical concerns, economic considerations and the threat of malpractice liability are likely to encourage physicians to begin testing for and prescribing medications designed for use by specific, smaller groups of individuals. Moral and ethical proscriptions against causing harm might require a physician to integrate pharmacogenetics into clinical practice where necessary to minimize risk to a patient. By contrast, budgetary constraints imposed by insurers could slow the acceptance of drugs developed through pharmacogenomics by limiting their use by physicians and their availability to patients. The issues raised are not unique to pharmacogenomics but do require new applications of ethical principles and legal doctrine.

In countries where the legal systems are based on common law (that is, the English tradition of law-making based on the court decisions of judges), physicians and pharmacists are subject to liability under theories of negligence, which involve the violation of a duty based on a "reasonableness" standard or a standard of reasonable care. The standard of care is defined by how a similarly qualified practitioner would act in treating a patient under the same or similar circumstances. The literature, which includes professional scholarship and guidelines published by professional societies, and clinical experience establish the standard of care. In cases based on negligence in the form of medical malpractice, the standard of care is defined through the testimony of witnesses regarding what constitutes conventional practice within the medical community.

As pharmacogenomic-based drugs increase in prevalence over the next several years, the use of genotyping or genetic testing as a diagnostic tool and the prescription of medications based on genotypic information will become the standard of care for physicians. Physicians and pharmacists might be subject to liability if they lack sufficient knowledge of genetics to adequately interpret diagnostic tests, prescribe appropriate pharmacogenomic-based drug therapy in proper dosages, consider pharmacogenomic-based drug interactions, or properly dispense pharmacogenomic-based prescriptions. With greater knowledge comes greater responsibility. Pharmacogenomics might provide greater information about the likelihood of a drug being effective or causing adverse reactions in persons possessing a particular genetic characteristic, and will certainly yield drugs that are more likely to be suitable for smaller, specific groups of individuals. By increasing the information available for consideration in drug therapy and the importance of matching the right drug to the right person, pharmacogenomics will raise the standard of care applicable to all involved in the safe prescription and distribution of pharmaceuticals.

Pharmacists are primarily charged with the dispensation of prescriptions as administered by physicians, but the scope of their responsibilities has expanded over time to include ensuring that prescriptions and patient directions are correct and appropriate. Pharmacists also have a duty to warn their customers of the potential adverse effects or other problems associated with a prescribed drug therapy. Even if a pharmacist has dispensed a prescription according to a physician's instructions, some jurisdictions have imposed liability on pharmacists for the harm that resulted from a drug that was properly dispensed in accordance with an improper or harmful prescription. As information regarding the genotype of an individual becomes increasingly important to safe prescription and dosage, pharmacists might be charged with greater knowledge of their customers' genetic information than they now require. The increased amount of genetic information in pharmacies raises privacy and confidentiality concerns, especially where pharmacists belong to large pharmacy chains or corporations with widely accessible, centralized records. For physicians and pharmacists, the issue of continuing professional education and record maintenance will become more important, not only for improving competence but also for preventing liability.

Pharmacogenomics is likely to increase the burden shared by the pharmaceutical industry to provide adequate warnings of the limitations and dangers of their products. In the United States, for example, pharmaceutical manufacturers have a duty to warn physicians about any known or knowable risks, or dangers, of the use of a manufactured drug. Many states in the US will impose strict liability on a drug company for harm caused by the failure to adequately warn against the dangerous propensities of a drug that it has manufactured. Unlike negligence theory, the rules of strict liability are not concerned with the standard of care nor the reasonableness of the manufacturer's conduct; and an aggrieved party need only prove that the manufacturer did not adequately warn of a particular risk that was knowable in the light of generally recognized and prevailing best scientific and medical knowledge available at the time of manufacture and distribution. Pharmaceutical companies must consider the potential for liability if patients are harmed because they were excluded from the subgroup for which a pharmacogenomic-based drug is deemed safe and efficacious, particularly if the exclusion leads to a failure to yield information on possible side effects or alternative therapies. Not all adverse side effects are predictable, owing to the number of genes relevant to drug responsiveness, as well as environmental factors. The question is how to allocate responsibility for taking the greatest advantage of drugs specialized to suit relatively smaller segments of the population.

In June 2000, four individuals filed a class action lawsuit against SmithKline Beecham, alleging that the manufacturer of a vaccine for Lyme disease knew that some individuals would be susceptible to arthritis on exposure to the vaccine because of their genotype, but failed to warn about this by labeling. The case is still pending. Similar cases involve malpractice actions by the patient against the prescribing physician, who in turn seeks to recover against the manufacturer for failure to provide adequate information. Put simply, pharmacogenomics will raise the legal stakes for all involved whenever a patient suffers adverse reactions from the use of a drug that might have been contraindicated based on his or her genotype.

CONCLUSION

By lessening the uncertainty associated with the selection of drug targets and the design of human clinical studies in the development of new drugs, pharmacogenomics will result in the production of safer, more effective drugs for use in therapeutic medicine. The integration of pharmacogenomic technology into the drug development process and the practice of medicine will require consideration of ethical, social and legal questions. Answers to these questions might well determine the level of social acceptance and realization of the benefits of pharmacogenomic technology.

NOTES AND QUESTIONS

1. Both pharmacogenetics and pharmacogenomics raise questions of the privacy and confidentiality of individually-identifiable genetic information and

the potential for discrimination. Pharmacogenetics, which involves genetic testing of individuals and families, could cause individuals and lineages to be classified as expensive or "hard to treat," making it difficult for them to get health care or health insurance, as Rothstein and Epps point out. In theory, pharmacogenetic testing is restricted to narrow tests for pharmacologic responsiveness:

> "Genetic testing" needs to be defined carefully. The magnitude of the ethical, legal and social implications of genetic testing is dependent on the information derived from the test. Genetic tests for mutations in single genes that are causally related to rare diseases and are inherited in a simple mendelian fashion can have profound implications for the individual and family members. Genetic tests for disease-susceptibility gene polymorphisms—which are risk factors for the disease—have the added complication of uncertainty. In both cases the lack of effective intervention drives many of the issues. Pharmacogenetic profiles, on the other hand, will predict if an individual patient is likely to benefit from a medicine and be free of serious side effects. These profiles will not be designed to provide any other information, as the profile data are derived from the patients who respond with efficacy or adverse event when taking the drug, compared with patients who did not respond. It does not differentiate disease. Should a polymorphism that is found to be related to disease association be included in a profile, it can be removed and replaced by another SNP that is in linkage disequilibrium, thus avoiding any disease-specific association, even if inadvertent. This would be similar to replacing the *ApoE4* SNP by one or more of the others in linkage disequilibrium with *ApoE4* but not specifically associated with Alzheimer's disease. The ethical, legal and social implications of pharmacogenetic profiles are therefore of a lower magnitude of societal concern compared with specific genetic tests for disease.

Allen D. Roses, Pharmacogenetics and the Practice of Medicine, 405 Nature 857 (legend for Fig. 5) (2000). To what extent do Roses' expectations depend on the care with which genetic testing is performed? Should the law require potentially revealing information in a genetic profile to be replaced with less sensitive information, as Roses suggests? Who would impose such a legal requirement and on whom?

Pharmacogenomics, on the other hand, involves the analysis of DNA from random persons. The DNA can be stored and analyzed anonymously, as Dr. Roses assures is the case with the data bank maintained by his employer, GlaxoSmithKline. See Gina Kolata, Tailor–Made Medicine, The New York Times, Dec. 20, 1999, at A1.

2.   The prospect of drug variants for small patient populations whose genetic profile makes the variant especially safe and effective raises questions about how safety and efficacy would be determined. To meet FDA requirements, sponsors typically must conduct clinical trials in large numbers of subjects. (The studies mentioned in the previous note exploring racial differences in drug response employed 1996 and 1087 subjects respectively.) It may be difficult to enroll enough subjects in studies of drug variants for small populations. Should the FDA relax its safety and efficacy requirements to

facilitate pharmacogenetic testing? Should it proceed on a case-by-case basis for specific drugs? What factors should the agency consider in deciding what requirements to impose? Does the new FDA guidance document adequately answer these questions?

3. As indicated by the class action suit against SmithKline Beecham mentioned in the article by Rothstein and Epps, Cassidy v. SmithKline Beecham, 1999 WL 33645128 (Pa. Com. Pl. 1999), drug manufacturers face products liability actions for failing to warn patients about small group susceptibilities to adverse drug reactions. The suit charged that 30 percent of the general population has the gene HLA–DR4+, which produces an autoimmune arthritic reaction triggered by an outer surface protein, Osp A, contained in the manufacturer's LYMErix vaccine. The suit charged that the manufacturer was aware of the connection because of its documentation in the literature, but did not advise physicians to recommend genetic testing for HLA–DR4+ prior to prescribing the vaccine. The suit was settled in 2003.

4. The "Learned Intermediary Doctrine" makes health professionals such as physicians and pharmacists rather than the manufacturer responsible for providing safety warnings to patients, but the manufacturer can still be liable if in product labeling it does not make health professionals aware of safety information of which the manufacturer is aware (see, e.g., Schenebeck v. Sterling Drug, Inc., 423 F.2d 919, 923 (8th Cir. 1970)) or if it directs advertising to patients and omits warnings about serious side effects (see Perez v. Wyeth Laboratories, Inc., 734 A.2d 1245 (N.J. 1999)).

Would manufacturers be liable for marketing a drug with a design defect if the drug harmed a subgroup of patients but was safe for others? See Margaret Gilhooley, When Drugs Are Safe for Some But Not Others: The FDA Experience and Alternatives for Products Liability, 36 Hous. L. Rev. 927 (1999). As Gilhooley notes, the newly-adopted Restatement (Third) of Torts provides that a prescription drug is defective only if it is unsafe "for any class of patients." Restatement (Third) of Torts: Products Liability § 6 (c) (1998), and a comment by the authors of the Restatement explains that "a prescription drug * * * that has usefulness to any class of patients is not defective in design even if it is harmful to other patients." (Comment b).

5. Note that, as Rothstein and Epps point out, not only manufacturers but physicians, pharmacists, and other health professionals also may be liable if they fail to meet the applicable standard of care in regard to the use of pharmacogenetic information in treating their patients.

6. The FDA has begun approving pharmacogenetic tests as medical devices. In April 2002, the FDA approved an HIV genotyping test. The test helps determine if a patient is infected with strains of the HIV virus that are resistant to certain antiretroviral drugs so that a different drug combination can be prescribed. In December 2004, the agency approved a P450 genotyping test, the first DNA test to use a microarray chip to help determine whether a patient is more or less likely to suffer side effects from several commonly-prescribed drugs. Recall from Chapter 6 that a microarray chip permits a large number of polymorphisms to be tested simultaneously. The P450 test analyzes one of the genes from a family of genes called cytochrome P450, which affect the ability of the liver to metabolize certain drugs and other

compounds, including those found in certain antidepressants, anti-psychotics, beta-blockers, and some chemotherapy drugs. In August 2005, the FDA approved a test to detect a gene called UGT1A1, which affects the ability of the liver to metabolize drugs used in treating colorectal cancer.

FOOD AND DRUG ADMINISTRATION, FDA APPROVES BIDIL HEART FAILURE DRUG FOR BLACK PATIENTS

June 23, 2005.
http://www.fda.gov/bbs/topics/NEWS/2005/NEW01190.html.

The Food and Drug Administration (FDA) approved BiDil (bye-DILL), a drug for the treatment of heart failure in self-identified black patients, representing a step toward the promise of personalized medicine.

Heart failure is a condition in which the heart is weakened and does not pump enough blood. It can be caused by a variety of damage to the heart, including heart attacks, high blood pressure, and infections.

The approval of BiDil was based in part on the results of the African–American Heart Failure Trial (A–HeFT). The study, which involved 1,050 self-identified black patients with severe heart failure who had already been treated with the best available therapy, was conducted because two previous trials in the general population of severe heart failure patients found no benefit, but suggested a benefit of BiDil in black patients. Patients on BiDil experienced a 43% reduction in death and a 39% decrease in hospitalization for heart failure compared to placebo, and a decrease of their symptoms of heart failure.

"Today's approval of a drug to treat severe heart failure in self-identified black population is a striking example of how a treatment can benefit some patients even if it does not help all patients," said Dr. Robert Temple, FDA Associate Director of Medical Policy. "The information presented to the FDA clearly showed that blacks suffering from heart failure will now have an additional safe and effective option for treating their condition. In the future, we hope to discover characteristics that identify people of any race who might be helped by Bidil."

BiDil is a combination of two older drugs, neither approved for heart failure—hydralazine and isosorbide dinitrate.

As an anti-hypertensive agent, hydralazine relaxes the arteries, and decreases the work of the heart. The anti-anginal agent, isosorbide dinitrate, relaxes the veins as well as the arteries. Isosorbide seems to work by releasing nitric oxide at the blood vessel wall, but its effect usually wears off after half a day. Hydralazine may prevent this loss of effect. But how the two drugs work together is not fully known.

Some common side effects with the use of BiDil are headache and dizziness.

BiDil is marketed by NitroMed, Inc. of Lexington, MA.

ALASTAIR J.J. WOOD, RACIAL DIFFERENCES IN THE RESPONSE TO DRUGS—POINTERS TO GENETIC DIFFERENCES

344 New Eng. J. Med. 1393, 1395 (2001).

* * *

Why do patients have different responses to a given drug, and more specifically, why do patients of different racial and ethnic groups have different responses? In the past, our understanding was relatively simplistic and included the recognition that such differences were fundamentally determined by variability in the concentrations of a drug (pharmacokinetic variability) or by variability in the responses to a drug at a given concentration (pharmacodynamic variability). Racial and ethnic differences in drug responses have now been well described for a range of drugs and reflect genetic differences, environmental differences (including shared cultural and dietary habits), and fundamental differences in the pathogenesis of diseases.

Genetic differences among racial and ethnic groups usually reflect differences in the distribution of polymorphic traits, which occur at different frequencies in different populations, rather than a trait unique to a particular racial or ethnic group. The underlying genetic determinants of the response to a drug and, specifically, racial and ethnic differences in that response are beginning to be unraveled and do indeed appear to be based on the varying distributions of polymorphisms in drug receptors or drug-metabolizing enzymes among different racial and ethnic groups. Persons whose genes encode drug-metabolizing enzymes that lack normal activity have impaired metabolism of the drug substrates of the affected enzyme. Polymorphisms of the enzymes responsible for drug metabolism are distributed differently among different racial and ethnic groups, so the proportion of people with impaired metabolism differs among these groups.

Thus, CYP2D6, the cytochrome P–450 enzyme responsible for the metabolism of drugs such as beta-blockers (including carvedilol) and tricyclic antidepressants, and for the metabolism of codeine to morphine, is functionally absent in 8 percent of whites but fewer than 1 percent of Asians, resulting in different drug concentrations and responses in these racial groups. Black Americans and Africans have a high frequency of a CYP2D6 allele that encodes an enzyme with impaired activity. This allele is virtually absent from white and Asian populations. It is particularly relevant to the study by Yancy et al., because CYP2D6 is responsible for the metabolism of one of the isomers of carvedilol, and stereoselective metabolism would be expected to contribute to differences in the toxicity and efficacy of carvedilol. Patients with the CYP2D6 phenotype of poor metabolism and black patients homozygous for the other CYP2D6 allele encoding impaired metabolism would be at particular risk of excess alpha-adrenergic blockade, perhaps even during the initial period of open-label therapy before randomization. It would therefore be of great interest to extend the study of Yancy et al. to determine whether the CYP2D6 genotype determined either therapeutic responses to carvedilol or its toxic effects.

Recent studies have addressed the role of differing rates of drug metabolism in patients' responses in clinical practice and clinical trials. CYP2C9 is the cytochrome P–450 enzyme responsible for the metabolism of the isomer of warfarin that is principally responsible for the anticoagulant effect of the drug. Two CYP2C9 alleles that produce a phenotype of poor metabolism occur in 11 percent and 8 percent of whites but only 3 percent and 0.8 percent of blacks. Such persons have impaired metabolism of warfarin and thus increased plasma concentrations of the drug. Of more importance to clinical practice, persons with the genotype of impaired metabolism require lower doses of warfarin to achieve an anticoagulant effect similar to that in patients with the normal genotype and are more likely to have an excessive anticoagulant response after the initial dose. In addition, bleeding episodes tend to be more common in persons with the genotype of impaired metabolism.

The proton-pump inhibitor omeprazole is metabolized by CYP2C19, another drug-metabolizing enzyme that exhibits polymorphism with phenotypes of varying distributions among different racial groups. For CYP2C19, in contrast to CYP2D6, the phenotype of poor metabolism is relatively rare in whites (occurring in < 2 percent) but is frequent in Asians (occurring in 18 to 20 percent). Omeprazole is frequently used as part of a combination regimen to eliminate *Helicobacter pylori* in patients with peptic ulcer disease, and the rate of response is dependent on the CYP2C19 genotype, ranging from 28 percent in patients who are homozygous for the extensive-metabolism allele to 100 percent in those with poor metabolism. Thus, the frequency of genetic polymorphisms of the enzymes responsible for drug metabolism varies among racial groups and contributes to variability in drug response among these groups.

Another genetically determined variable that is responsible for differences in drug response among racial and ethnic groups involves the drug receptors themselves, which also exhibit functionally important genetic polymorphisms. Our understanding of the role of receptor polymorphisms is less advanced than that of drug-metabolism polymorphisms. Polymorphisms of receptors relevant to therapy for heart failure, including β and ¥ adrenergic receptors, endothelial nitric oxide synthase receptors, and angiotensin II type 1 receptors, have all been described and in some cases have been linked to function or therapeutic response in patients with heart failure. The distribution of receptor polymorphisms differs among populations of different racial backgrounds. Such racial differences in receptor polymorphisms may contribute to previously recognized racial differences in the vascular response to adrenergic agonists, a potentially important pathophysiological mechanism in heart failure. There are marked differences among whites, blacks, and Asians in the frequency of polymorphisms of adrenergic receptors, including the β_1-, β_2-, and ¥_1 adrenergic receptors.

Thus, racial differences in the response to drugs not only have practical importance for the choice and dose of drugs but should also alert physicians to the important underlying genetic determinants of drug response. The logical extension of the studies reported in this issue of the *Journal* will be the identification of the genetic determinants of the reported racial differences, rather than attention to the external phenotypic manifestations of race. The identification of such genetic determinants will make possible better definition of the targets of current and future therapies and will lead to therapies that are more specific. However, an increased specificity of therapies is likely to increase the differences in response among persons of different genetic backgrounds.

RENE BOWSER, RACE AS A PROXY FOR DRUG RESPONSE: THE DANGERS AND CHALLENGES OF ETHNIC DRUGS

53 DePaul L. Rev. 1111 (2004).

* * *

IV.   RACIAL REPACKAGING—THE STORY OF BiDIL

Even though race has not been shown to be a strong proxy for drug metabolism, a drug called BiDil is poised to become the first drug ever approved by the FDA to treat heart failure in African Americans, and only in African Americans. BiDil is a combination of two vasodilators, hydralazine and isosorbide dinitratre (H/I). Vasodilators dilate blood vessels and ease the strain put on the heart in pumping blood. BiDil is thought to have an added benefit of improving levels of nitric oxide in the blood, which is also thought to be of great benefit to individuals suffering from heart failure.

BiDil is an underused drug that has been around for decades; it certainly did not begin as an ethnic drug. This brief review of BiDil's origins demonstrates the centrality of commerce and the exploitation of racial categories in the repackaging of BiDil as a wonder drug for African Americans.

It all begins with the first Vasodilator Heart Failure Trial (V–HeFT I). In this medical trial, which lasted from 1980 to 1985, cardiologists found that the H/I (BiDil) combination appeared to have a beneficial impact in reducing mortality from heart disease. The V–Heft I trial was soon followed by another trial, V–HeFT II, which lasted from 1986 to 1991. This trial compared the efficacy of the H/I (BiDil drugs) against the drug enalapril, an angiotensin-converting enzyme (ACE) inhibitor. The second trial found that enalapril had a more beneficial effect on mortality than the H/I combination. The results of the second trial established ACE inhibitors as the front-line therapy for heart failure. ACE inhibitors have not totally replaced H/I, however, because between 20% and 30% of congestive heart failure patients do not respond well to them. That is roughly 1.5 million patients annually (including members of all racial groups), and current guidelines still recommend the H/I combination for these patients.

The V–HeFT investigators presented the H/I (BiDil drugs) as generally efficacious in the population at large, without regard to race. In 1987, Dr. Jay Cohn, one of the principal investigators in the V–HeFT studies applied for and received a patent on the H/I drugs. In the patent description, Cohn made no mention of race, asserting that H/I substantially and significantly reduces the incidence of mortality in congestive heart patients. Clearly, he believed the BiDil drugs would be used to treat all people suffering from heart failure.

The H/I drugs are generic drugs. Cohn and others combined them into a single pill for easy administration. By 1994, tests were conducted to make sure that the pill form was just as effective as the administration of the drugs separately. They were. Cohn and Medco, which had acquired the intellectual property rights from Cohn, were now ready to approach the FDA for the approval of BiDil for use in the general population.

In 1996, Medco submitted a new drug application (NDA) to the FDA. Jay Cohn optimistically asserted at the time that the BiDil formulation represented a very convenient dosage that, once approved by the FDA, would lead to an increased usage of this therapy in the general population. An industry report estimated a potential market of up to sixty million dollars in annual sales for BiDil.

In an unanticipated move, however, the FDA voted nine to three against approving BiDil, even though extensive findings in peer reviewed journals supported Cohn's claim that the H/I combination substantially and significantly reduced the incidence of mortality in congestive heart failure patients. The agency concluded that while the drug had clinical significance, it failed to meet the biostatistical criteria of probability and efficacy sufficient for the FDA to grant a NDA. In particular, the FDA noted that data from the V–Heft studies contained too many variables specified as endpoints for them to interpret the data with biostatical certainty. The next day, Medco's stock dropped by 25%.

To salvage the drug, the BiDil promoters repackaged it along racial lines. Jay Cohn went back one more time to the V–HeFT data, this time to analyze the differential effects of BiDil and enalapril by race. In 1999, Cohn and others published a paper asserting that the H/I combinations worked better in blacks than ACE inhibitors. Specially, they concluded:

> The H–I combination appears to be particularly effective in prolonging survival in black patients and is as effective as enalapril in this subgroup. In contrast, enalapril shows its more favorable effect in the white population . . . the consistency of observations of a racial difference in response in V–HeFT I and V–HeFT II . . . lend credence to the suggestion that therapy for heart failure might appropriately be racially tailored.

That same year Daniel Dries coauthored a study in the prestigious New England Journal of Medicine suggesting that racial differences exist in the natural progression of congestive heart failure. The implicit conclusion is that heart disease is a different disease in blacks and whites and, therefore, it must be treated with different therapies. This theory of biological difference is consistent with Jay Cohn's claim that the black/white disparity in death rates from heart failure is partly attributable to "a pathophysiology found in black patients that may involve Nitric Oxide (NO) insufficiency arising from either reduced NO production, enhanced NO inactivation or both."

In 1999, NitroMed Inc., a Boston area biotech firm specializing in the development and commercialization of nitric oxide enhanced medicines, acquired the intellectual property rights to BiDil. NitroMed announced its plans to amend the NDA to seek approval for the use of BiDil to treat and prevent mortality associated with heart failure in African–American patients. After a meeting in Washington, the FDA approved the use of BiDil as a drug to treat heart failure in African Americans, pending the successful results of a confirmatory trial. That trial, A–HeFT, the African American Heart Failure Trial, is currently underway.

The FDA's tentative approval represents a significant expansion of the potential BiDil market. NitroMed currently estimates that approximately 750,000 African Americans suffer from heart disease. The implication is that all African Americans suffering from heart disease should be taking BiDil (because it is a different disease), not just those who cannot tolerate or do not respond well to ACE inhibitors. Without doubt, the huge commercial implications of the first ethnic niche market allowed NitroMed to raise over $31.4 million from several private venture capital firms to support the confirmatory trials. Recently, pharmaceutical giant Merck & Co., Inc. formed a multi-year research collaboration with NitroMed, even though BiDil is the company's most advanced product to date.

V. A NEW THERAPY OR A NEW MARKET FOR AN UNDERUSED DRUG?

BiDil started as a drug for use in the general population but has emerged as a drug for use only in African Americans. A fundamental question is whether significant scientific evidence demonstrates that all African Americans with heart problems should take this drug, or are NitroMed's claims merely a scheme to expand and exploit a potentially lucrative market. As discussed below, substantial evidence raises serious questions about the underpinnings of NitroMed's claims.

First, the study authored by Peter Carson along with Jay Cohn, claiming that blacks respond better to H/I than to ACE inhibitors, retrospectively analyzed data from V–HeFT I and II. It was not prospectively designed to study racial differences in response to treatment, rather, an existing and rather old data set was reanalyzed. There are well documented statistical problems involving randomization and stratification by race in such retrospective studies.

Second, black participants had higher levels of comordid factors such as diabetes and hypertension. Essentially, the white and black populations were not the same. Few doctors would use monotherapy (a single drug) for cardiovascular disease in patients with concomitant diabetes and hypertension. Therefore, this study may simply confirm what we already know: use of a single ACE inhibitor at a standard dose is not effective for patients who also have diabetes and hypertension, but is effective for patients without these conditions.

Third, the study purports to consider relevant nongenetic environmental influences on the development and progression of heart failure, and includes two such factors—education and "financial distress (yes vs. no) during the past twelve months." While education and experience of financial distress are relevant factors to consider in examining nongenetic environmental influences, the implicit understanding is that they are exhaustive of all such relevant factors.

Vast medical and public health literature shows that a host of deleterious conditions accompany black status in the United States, including differential exposures to environmental toxins, discrimination, residential segregation, and differential political power, both in terms of individual level of control and the allocation of resources. Indeed, a Harvard study shows that the stress of experiencing racism raises blood pressure. It is now well established that physiological processes respond to psychosocial stress. Therefore, the unmeasured variation in environmental exposures could account for the differential response in hospitalization and survival, not differences in drug metabolism.

Fourth, as fortune would have it, one of the strongest critiques has come from one of the coauthors of the original study, Dr. Daniel Dries. In 2002, Dries took issue with the earlier New England Journal of Medicine piece arguing that the ACE inhibitor, enalapril, worked equally well in blacks and whites:

> Despite recent concerns that angiotensin-converting enzyme (ACE) inhibitors may be less efficacious in black patients with [heart failure], the present study demonstrates that enalapril significantly reduced the risk of development of [heart failure] in both blacks and whites * * *. The consistency of results in black and white subjects strengthens the argument that ACE inhibitor-therapy should continue to be used in black patients with [heart failure].

These findings are consistent with the recent African American Study of Kidney Disease and Hypertension that demonstrated a benefit of ACE inhibitor therapy in patients with renal disease.

Finally, NitroMed has relied heavily on the claim that African Americans have twice the risk of dying from heart failure than whites. If this is true, then it is highly plausible that the difference is due to genetic rather than environmental factors. This two-to-one disparity has been floating around uncontested in the scientific literature for decades. Dr. Jonathan Kahn of the University of Minnesota has demonstrated conclusively that the NitroMed claim about the scope of black and white differences is simply untrue. Dr. Kahn traced the citation sources back nearly two decades, and found that the difference between blacks and whites is actually 1.2 to 1. While there is a difference, it is far less than the two-to-one ratio that would warrant special trials for blacks. Thus, "substantial scaffolding of the BiDil clinical trials is based upon incorrect statistical data on racial disparities."

NOTES AND QUESTIONS

1.   Recall the discussion about genetics and race in Chapter 2. Does the BiDil case illustrate the problem? Consider the following:

> The Association of Black Cardiologists, Inc. (ABC), co-sponsor of the landmark African American Heart Failure Trial (A–HeFT), is pleased that the U.S. Food and Drug Administration (FDA) approved BiDil® (isosorbide dinitrate/hydralazine hydrochloride) for the treatment of heart failure in black patients on [sic] yesterday. A–HeFT was the first clinical trial conducted in an all black heart failure population. BiDil is an orally-administered medicine shown in A–HeFT to improve survival, reduce the rate of first hospitalization for heart failure and improve patient-reported functional status, as an adjunct to current standard heart failure therapy in self-identified black patients.

> "The approval of BiDil is a major step toward eliminating existing cardiovascular-related health disparities affecting African Americans, a population that is disproportionately burdened by heart failure," said B. Waine Kong, Ph.D., J.D., chief executive officer of the Association of Black Cardiologists, Inc. "The ABC is proud to have played an integral role in the African American Heart Failure Trial and we look forward to continued progress in cardiovascular health for African Americans."

Press Release, Association of Black Cardiologists, FDA Approval of BiDil® Brings New Hope to Black Heart Failure Patients (June 24, 2005).

In an article in the Cambridge Quarterly of Healthcare Ethics, Joon–Ho Yu, Sara Goering and Stephanie Fullerton provide an interesting explanation for the support for BiDil among many leaders in the African–American community:

> BiDil's approval has been widely critiqued in academic circles on numerous grounds. Nevertheless, many advocates for African American health concerns have argued that BiDil is an important step toward reducing disparities in healthcare by creating medical therapies that are responsive to African American needs. Many of these advocates also publicly rejected the notion that BiDil is a race-specific drug, arguing that social race is a poor surrogate for the biological differences that underlie BiDil's efficacy. Thus, competing commitments to reducing health disparities while rejecting a biologically deterministic view of race have placed African American community leaders and health advocates in a state of conflict, both among themselves and with academic scholars of race, with respect to the desirability of BiDil.

In this paper, we offer a sympathetic reading of this response to BiDil by some African American community leaders and aim to show how many of the academic critiques have failed to adequately account for the competing commitments of community stakeholders. We argue that justice involves not only the fair distribution of benefits but also an element of recognition, such that socially marginalized groups have the opportunity to be heard and to participate in decisionmaking. In the case of BiDil, we believe that African American community leaders capitalized on an opportunity to bring attention to African American health issues, even as they risked complicity with an inaccurate portrayal of race as biological. Using Nancy Fraser's bivalent theory of justice (involving both recognition and redistribution),14 we argue that community leaders can be viewed as strategically affirming the use of race in hopes of ultimately transforming the process of drug development and garnering more careful attention to the problem of health disparities. Given the context of health disparities and statements made by community advocates that explicitly link BiDil to remedying such disparities, we believe this strategy is best understood not simply as a calculated risk assumed for the sake of some consequentialist benefit but rather as a means of asserting a demand for justice.

Joon–Ho Yu, Sara Goering, and Stephanie M. Fullerton, Race–Based Medicine and Justice as Recognition: Exploring the Phenomenon of BiDil, 18 Cambridge Q. of Healthcare Ethics 57, 57–58 (2009).

III. PUBLIC HEALTH GENETICS

MUIN J. KHOURY, WYLIE BURKE, & ELIZABETH THOMSON, GENETICS AND PUBLIC HEALTH: A FRAMEWORK FOR THE INTEGRATION OF HUMAN GENETICS INTO PUBLIC HEALTH PRACTICE IN GENETICS AND PUBLIC HEALTH IN THE TWENTY–FIRST CENTURY: USING GENETIC INFORMATION TO IMPROVE HEALTH AND PREVENT DISEASE

5–6, (Muin J. Khoury, Wylie Burke, & Elizabeth Thomson eds. 2000).

In recent years, a new hybrid subspecialty of genetics and public health has emerged. Public health genetics (a term mostly used in the United States) has been defined as the application of advances in genetics and molecular biotechnology to improve public health and prevent disease. Community genetics (a term mostly used in Europe) has been defined as "a branch of genetics that has service and science components." The service component seeks to integrate genetic services into community interventions. The science component encompasses the research needed to develop and evaluate services. Public health genetics and community genetics could be viewed as one and the same. Nevertheless, as we think about the broader mission of public health, namely "to fulfill society's interest in assuring conditions in which people can be healthy," there will be unavoidable integration of new genetic information into all public health programs and across all diseases, whether or not the diseases are labeled "genetic diseases" or the services are termed "genetic services." All public health professionals, therefore, will need an increasing appreciation for integrating genetic research, policy, and program development into their daily work. This is not different from the expected integration of genetics into health care in general and across the various medical subspecialties. Although recognizing the need for a cadre of public health researchers and practitioners fully trained in genetics, we also believe that all public health professionals will be using advances in human genetics in research and practice. We do not particularly endorse the creation of a new public health subspecialty in genetics; rather, we encourage and emphasize the smooth integration of genetics into public health practice.

* * *

One might wonder, What is the meaning of prevention in the context of genetics and public health? Juengst used the terms "genotypic prevention"—the interruption of genetic trait transmission from one generation to the next through reproductive counseling, carrier testing, prenatal diagnosis, and pregnancy termination—and "phenotypic prevention"—the prevention of disease and death among people with specific genotypes. In its strategic plan the CDC clearly endorses the concept of phenotypic prevention as the strategy for public health-driven programs. Phenotypic prevention can be achieved by interrupting harmful interaction of environmental cofactors with human genetic variation or by using gene therapy to correct deficiencies in gene products.

MARK A. ROTHSTEIN, PRIVACY ISSUES IN PUBLIC HEALTH GENOMICS, IN GENOMICS AND PUBLIC HEALTH: LEGAL AND SOCIO–ETHICAL PERSPECTIVES

152–154, 161 (Bartha Maria Knoppers ed. 2007).

Another area of confusion is the relationship between public health and individual clinical interventions, a misunderstanding caused, at least in part, by the mistaken belief that government programmes that provide health care to indigent populations is "public health." To eliminate this confusion, it is helpful to note the three criteria that distinguish public health from individual clinical care, including clinical care provided by a public entity. First, public health acts when the health of the population is threatened. Although the prototypical public health activity is infectious disease control, the threat to the public need not be based on horizontal, person-to-person transmission, such as with environmental health hazards. Second, public health relies on the unique powers and expertise of the government. For example, disease reporting and surveillance are responsibilities of government action through the public health system. Third, public health action by the government is more efficient or more likely to produce an effective intervention. Newborn screening would be an example where public health action is justified in providing the framework for supporting an important aspect of individual health care.

Based on these definitions and considerations, public health genomics is the use of genome wide analytical tools (or data derived from the application of those tools) by public officials, who are acting pursuant to specific legal authority to protect the health of the public.

It is important to note that the integration of genomics (and genetics) into public health interventions must be done carefully and with discretion because the values underlying public health are quite different from those underlying genomics and genetics The exercise of public health authority not only involves governmental action, but it also means the possible use of coercive powers to enforce governmental objectives. Public health action is based on utilitarian and communitarian ethics, under which societal interests take precedence over individual interests. An example is the imposition of quarantine to fight the spread of an epidemic. By contrast, the dominant social values of genomics and genetics are autonomy, privacy, and reproductive freedom. Politically, it is more libertarian than communitarian. An example is the traditional client-centered, nondirective approach that has become a hallmark of genetic counselling. The role of the genetic counselor or medical geneticist is to educate the individual and to provide options, but the ultimate decision rests with the individual.

The inherent conflict between the values underlying public health and those underlying genetics and genomics strongly suggests that any undertaking in the field of public health genomics should be approached with great care. This need for caution is underscored by the history of eugenics, which represented a failed and discredited attempt at reproductive, public health genetics. Today, members of the public overwhelmingly are concerned about the applications to individuals of genetic technologies (especially with regard to reproduction) to achieve social goals. Eugenics continues to be a dark cloud over public health genomics, and we ignore this fact at our peril.

How do these values, interests, and concerns play out in practice? A good example is screening for hereditary hemochromatosis. Hemochromatosis is an autosomal recessive disorder characterized by excess iron absorption and deposition in tissue. If left untreated, it can result in liver disease, diabetes, cardiomyopathy, and other serious disorders. Before the advent of genetic testing, a definitive diagnosis of hemochromatosis required a liver biopsy or other invasive testing, and there was no way to identify individuals who were presymptomatic. Furthermore, the recessive inheritance pattern of the disorder often did not make at-risk individuals or their physicians aware of their condition before the internal organ damage caused by excessive iron accumulation.

At first glance, hemochromatosis seems like an ideal candidate for public health intervention. The condition is relatively common, with as many as one million affected persons in the United States, prompt detection can prevent harm; there is a cheap, easy and effective therapy (periodic phlebotomy); there is a cheap simple test; and the most affected group is not medically or socially vulnerable (hemochromatosis disproportionately affects white males). Nevertheless, most experts and consensus panels to consider the issue have concluded that it is premature to offer population screening because of inadequate data on prevalence and penetrance of the most common mutations, lack of laboratory standardization, lack of agreement on optimal care for asymptomatic mutation carriers, and the fear that individuals testing positive will be subject to stigmatization and discrimination.

In the extensive literature on hemochromatosis, there has been some inconsistency about whether efforts to promote population screening should be considered "public health" or "population health." This determination will affect the role of government agencies vis à vis individual clinicians, medical societies, medical speciality groups, and payers in implementing testing. Applying the three factors mentioned above (threat to population health, unique governmental powers and expertise, and government intervention as more efficient and effective), it is clear that population screening for hemochromatosis is not a proper public health activity. It is an open question whether, in the future, a compelling case can be made for routine hemochromatosis testing in clinical settings. If such data could be marshaled, however, then hemochromatosis testing should be implemented in a manner more akin to cholesterol and PSA testing (i.e., under individual or population health principles) than to newborn screening or immunizations (i.e., proper domains of a government-directed public health programme).

* * *

Because the purpose of public health is to advance the well-being of the population, sometimes at the expense of individual interests, public health may conflict with the ethical tradition of autonomy that has become ingrained in genetics. Only by carefully limiting the scope of public health activities in genetics can the public be assured that the government is not unreasonably encroaching into some of the most sensitive and private realms of individual health.

New genomic and bioinformatics technologies also will substantially increase the amount of genetic and genomic information contained in health records. Stringently enforced confidentiality and security safeguards must apply to the protection of this information. At the same time, public officials should be required to present a compelling justification before individual genetic or genomic information is mandated to be disclosed for public health purposes, including for use in biosurveillance. Even then, such disclosures should be the minimum necessary to achieve the purpose of the disclosure and in the least identifiable form. As with other types of sensitive health information, vigilance in protecting the privacy of genetic and genomic information is especially warranted where, as is the case with public health genomics, the ostensible purpose for the disclosure is benign.

NOTES AND QUESTIONS

1.   Think back to Chapter 3 on Eugenics. Do you agree with the following statement in the Rothstein excerpt: "Eugenics continues to be a dark cloud over public health genomics, and we ignore this fact at our peril."

2.   Why is it important whether a medical intervention is considered a part of clinical practice or public health?

3.   Other aspects of public health genetics are discussed elsewhere in this book, including newborn screening, pharmacogenomics, and toxicogenomics. See also Grace Wang & Carolyn Watts, The Role of Genetics in the Provision of Essential Public Health Services, 97 Am. J. Pub. Health 620 (2007).

4.   The literature of public health genetics has been expanding. See, e.g., Melissa A. Austin, Patricia A. Peyser, & Muin J. Khoury, The Interface of Genetics and Public Health: Research and Educational Challenges, 21 Ann. Rev. Pub. Health 81 (2000); Ellen Wright Clayton & Mark A. Rothstein, Integrating Genetics Into Public Health Policy and Practice, Law in Public Health Practice, 2d ed., Richard A. Goodman et al. eds. 2007; Muin J. Khoury, Linda L. McCabe, & Edward R.B. McCabe, Population Screening in the Age of Genomic Medicine, 348 New Eng. J. Med. 50 (2003); Gilbert S. Omenn, Public Health Genetics: An Emerging Interdisciplinary Field for the Post–Genomic Era, 21 Ann. Rev. Pub. Health 1 (2000); George Davey Smith et al., Genetic Epidemiology and Public Health: Hope, Hype, and Future Prospects, 366 Lancet 1484 (2005).

CHAPTER 10

GENETIC ENHANCEMENT

■ ■ ■

As the human genome is more completely deciphered and the techniques of genetic testing, gene therapy, and pharmacogenetics and pharmacogenomics are perfected, the possibility arises that these technologies might be targeted at non-therapeutic or "enhancement" objectives. As the American Association for the Advancement of Science (AAAS) Report notes, "[t]he technology for therapy and enhancement procedures is basically the same." AAAS Report, Human Inheritable Genetic Modifications at 43 (2000).

Distinguishing between "therapy" and "enhancement" is not easy. If "enhancement" is defined in terms of making improvements beyond what is "natural," does it include preventive measures like vaccines which confer an immunity beyond what people naturally would enjoy? The NIH has approved the use of gene transfer technology to boost the functioning of low density lipoprotein receptors above the normal range in persons suffering from hypercholesterolemia (an inherited inability to clear cholesterol from the blood). According to one expert, the result was to give these patients a "super-cleansing ability." Yet both of these interventions are aimed at preventing, or reducing the severity of, disease, and therefore seem therapeutic rather than enhancing in their objective.

Another approach might be that therapy is aimed at preserving or restoring "normal" function, while the goal of enhancement is to make a person more than "normal." This conceptualization is endorsed by Norman Daniels, who conceives of the "normal" in terms of the typical functioning of the species. (See Norman Daniels, Just Health Care (1986); Allen Buchanan, et al., From Chance to Choice: Genetics and Justice (2000).) But it has been strongly criticized by Eric Juengst, who points out that it rests on questionable assumptions about what is "normal." See Eric Juengst, What Does Enhancement Mean? in Enhancing Human Traits 29 (Erik Parens, ed. 1998).

Perhaps the clearest distinction is between having a therapeutic or non-therapeutic goal. After all, this is the distinction that health insurance companies must make when presented with a claim for surgery that may be "cosmetic," and therefore not covered by the policy. But even this distinction is problematic on the ground that it depends on how we define "disease" or "disability," or on what we regard as "normal" appearance and functionality.

Depending on how "genetic enhancement" is defined, it could be achieved by a number of different types of techniques. For example, it could include drugs that affected non-disease traits and that were made with recombinant DNA manufacturing methods or using knowledge gained from decoding the genome. One example is human growth hormone (HGH), which is used by athletes to enhance performance, and by the general public to retard aging. Another hormone made using recombinant DNA engineering that is attractive to athletes is erythropoietin (EPO). This is a naturally-occurring hormone that influences how many of a person's blood cells are red, since the more red blood cells, the more oxygen is carried to the tissues. Recombinant DNA technology clones the human EPO gene and implants it into hamster ovary cells, which then act as genetically-programmed factories to make the protein. A third hormone with potential value to athletes and that is synthesized using recombinant DNA is Insulin-like Growth Factor–1 (IGF–1).

Not only can genetic factories produce synthetic versions of naturally-occurring substances, but the factories themselves can be inserted into organisms and programmed to turn on and off. A company called Oxford bioMedica has created a product called Repoxygen®. This is an EPO gene under the control of a gene which, when inserted into muscle cells, acts as a switch to turn the gene on to produce EPO in the presence of low amounts of oxygen. The company developed the product for the treatment of anemia, but it holds obvious interest for athletes, since they can obtain the benefit of EPO only when they need it, and more importantly, they may be able to avoid detection by anti-doping testing when the gene is turned off.

As genetic tests become available for non-disease traits, people can test themselves and prospective mates and use the results to decide whether or not to go ahead and have children. Or they could test a set of fertilized embryos in vitro to decide which ones to implant, or even use the results of prenatal testing to decide whether to abort a fetus. The use of genetic testing to make reproductive decisions based on non-disease traits might be termed "passive genetic enhancement," since it merely selects from naturally occurring genetic endowments. But genetic enhancement also might take the form of somatic or germ-line gene transfer, using the basic techniques of gene therapy to produce enhancement rather than therapeutic effects.

NIH funding is not available for research on genetic enhancement in human subjects. But in May 2007, NIH scientists announced that they had identified a genetic mutation in racing dogs that helps explain why some dogs run faster than others. The mutation is in the gene that codes for a muscle protein called myostatin. The researchers found that whippets with one mutated copy of the gene were the fastest racers, while dogs with two mutated copies had oversized muscles that slowed them down. Although the research was in dogs, Elaine A. Ostrander, the leader of the research team, acknowledged that it "could have implications for competitive sports in dogs, horses and possibly even humans." Medical researchers are seeking ways to turn off or counteract the production of myostatin in order to treat muscle-wasting diseases such as muscular dystrophy. They have developed an antibody that blocks myostatin in adult mice. The same techniques could enable healthy individuals to grow bigger muscles.

Another field of genetic research being watched closely by athletes involves genes that code for fast- and slow-twitch muscles. Fast-twitch muscles are associated with sports that require short bursts of energy, such as sprinting and weightlifting. People with more slow-twitch muscles are better at endurance sports, such as long-distance running. The discovery of genetic variations associated with the two different types of muscles already is impacting the sports world. Researchers have identified one variant of the ACTN3 gene in humans that codes for a protein called α-actinin–3, which helps to produce slow-twitch muscles. People who do not have this variant, called R577X, have more fast-twitch muscles. An Australian company is selling a genetic test that detects the variant for $93. The ACTN3 test is likely to be followed by many more performance-associated genetic indicators. For a critique of the science behind the test, see Lori Andrews, Testing Children for Sports Genes, http://blogs.kentlaw. edu/islat/2009/01/testing-children-for-sports-genes.html. In 2006, one group of researchers published a human gene map for "performance and health-related fitness phenotypes," or traits. It contained over 100 entries.

Pharmacogenetics, discussed in Chapter 9, also has important implications for athletes. The same knowledge that explains why certain people respond better than others to specific drugs can be applied to the use of performance-enhancing substances by athletes. Because of their genes, some athletes are likely to respond better to certain of these substances than to others. Not only might this increase the impact of the substance on performance, but athletes may be able to avoid many if not most of the side effects.

Genetic enhancement research is targeting traits besides athletic ability. Parents are reported to seek human growth hormone, which is now made using rDNA manufacturing techniques, to increase the height of children of normal or even greater-than-normal height. Scientists at McGill University in Montreal have discovered a gene that codes for a memory-blocking protein, eIF2α. Mice with a mutation that blocks production of the protein performed better than normal mice at remembering how to swim to a hidden platform, and did better on a "fear-conditioning" test that measures their recall of a stimulus that precedes a mild foot shock. One researcher observed that "[i]f a person were reading a page of a textbook, it might take several times to memorize it. A human equivalent of these mice would get the information right away." The NIH itself sponsored a study to determine if a drug for Parkinson's disease called tolcapone improved memory in schizophrenics. The subjects included a number of normal individuals acting as controls who were grouped based on differences in a particular gene, catecholamine-*O*-methyltransferase (COMT). The investigators reported that the drug significantly improved executive function and verbal episodic memory in subjects with one variant of the gene, while it impaired these abilities in subjects with another variant.

Genetic enhancement by actually inserting or deleting DNA remains a more distant prospect, since it faces the same hurdles described at the beginning of the chapter that beset gene therapy. Yet in 2004, a team of US and South Korean researchers, led by Ronald Evans at the Salk Institute, announced the creation of a "marathon mouse" that can run twice as far as a normal mouse. The researchers were able to increase the activity of a "master regulator" called the PPARdelta gene, which decreased the production of fast-twitch muscles in favor of slow-twitch muscles. One key question was whether the genetic manipulation would disrupt the animals' reproductive capacity, but the mice remained fertile and the mutation was inherited by offspring. Researchers at the University of Pennsylvania also claim to have genetically engineered a strain of "smart" mice by boosting their production of a protein called NR2B that controls the brain's ability to associate one event with another, and Boston University scientists report that the mice maintain their superior learning and memory function into old age.

No type of biomedical enhancement generates more concern than human germ line genetic enhancement, whereby changes in an individual's DNA would be passed on to their offspring. So far as is known, the direct manipulation of DNA to produce germ line enhancement has not yet occurred in humans, although as illustrated by the preceding discussion of the marathon mouse, it has been accomplished in animals. As discussed in Chapter 9, however, human germ line genetic manipulation for medical purposes occasionally does occur inadvertently.

JON W. GORDON, GENETIC ENHANCEMENT IN HUMANS

283 Science 2023 (1999).

Dramatic advances in gene transfer technology since the early 1980s have prompted consideration of its use in humans to enhance phenotypic traits. The notion that genetic modification could confer special advantages on an individual has generated excitement. Controversial issues surround this prospect, however. A practical concern is determining how to ensure equal access to such advanced medical technologies. There has also been speculation that genetic enhancement might affect human evolution, and philosophical objections have been raised, based on the belief that to intervene in such fundamental biological processes is to "play God." Although such philosophical questions cannot be resolved through data analysis, we nevertheless have the tools in hand to objectively assess our state of progress. We can also assess the impact that promulgation of such technology might have on human evolution and formulate sensible guidelines for developing policies governing human genetic enhancements.

DEFINING GENETIC ENHANCEMENT

Some experts have argued that "enhancement" can have different meanings depending on the circumstances. For example, when a disease is common, the risk for developing the disorder may be considered the norm, and genetic alleviation of that risk might be regarded as a form of enhancement. This kind of semantic gamesmanship is misleading. The obvious public concern does not relate to improvement of traits for alleviation of deficiencies or reduction of disease risk, but to augmentation of functions that without intervention would be considered entirely normal. To raise the athletic capabilities of a schoolyard basketball player to those of a professional or to confer the talents of Chopin on a typical college music professor is the sort of genetic enhancement that many find troublesome. The experts in the gene transfer field should acknowledge the distinction in order to avoid causing public distrust and undermining the deliberative process.

Another important distinction is that between genetic changes that are heritable and those that cannot be genetically transmitted. At the present time, gene transfer approaches that involve the early embryo are far more effective than somatic cell gene therapy methodologies. Embryo gene transfer affords the opportunity to transform most or all cells of the organism and thus overcomes the inefficient transformation that plagues somatic cell gene transfer protocols. Moreover, the commonly used approaches to embryo gene insertion—pronuclear microinjection and transfection of embryonic stem cells—are associated with stable, high expression of donor DNA. Typically, however, genetic changes introduced into the embryo extend to the gametes and are heritable.

Scenarios can be constructed wherein introduced genes could be deleted from germ cells or early embryos derived from the treated individual. For example, transferred genes could reside on artificial chromosomes that could be deleted by activating a recombinase that induced recombination of the chromosome ends. Such approaches, however, are currently only speculative. Germline gene transfer has already succeeded in several animal species. Because of this and the general belief that voluntary abstention from germline modification in humans is unlikely, a candid discussion of genetic enhancement must include the possibility that changes introduced will be transmitted to offspring.

THE STATE OF THE ART

Animal experiments thus far have attempted to improve what are intuitively regarded as "simple" traits such as growth rate or muscle mass. Efforts to genetically improve the growth of swine have involved insertion of transgenes encoding growth hormone. Nevertheless, despite the fact that growth hormone transgenes are expressed well in swine, increased growth does not occur. Although the transgenic animals fortuitously have less body fat, these unexpected benefits cannot be extrapolated to human clinical protocols. Before a human embryo is treated with recombinant DNA, we must know exactly what we are doing.

Another spectacular failed attempt at enhancement resulted from efforts to increase muscle mass in cattle. When expressed in mice, the avian c-*ski* gene, the cellular counterpart of the retroviral v-*ski* oncogene, induced massive muscle hypertrophy. This prompted efforts to produce cattle expressing a c-*ski* transgene. When gene transfer was accomplished, the transgenic calf initially exhibited muscle hypertrophy, but muscle degeneration and wasting soon followed. Unable to stand, the debilitated animal was killed.

Why did these enhancement experiments fail? For clues, it is useful to compare modern-day gene transfer technology with the more traditional approach to genetic engineering: selective breeding. Selective breeding maximizes the reproductive efficiency of individuals that exhibit desired characteristics. The selection strategy is oblivious to the number of genes responsible for generating the phenotype. Swine selected for rapid growth may consume more food, produce more growth hormone, respond more briskly to endogenous growth hormone, divert proteins toward somatic growth, and possess skeletal anatomy that allows the animal to tolerate increased weight. Dozens or perhaps hundreds of genes may influence these traits, but in selective breeding, favorable alleles at all loci can simultaneously be selected. In contrast, gene transfer selects one relevant locus and attempts to improve it in isolation. It is little wonder that this approach, albeit potentially powerful and efficient, is more chancy, and has, despite more than 10 years of effort, failed to yield even one unequivocal success. Greater success has been achieved in genetic enhancement of plants, which are more easily manipulated genetically and reproductively.

Given the inherent limitations of the gene transfer approach to enhancement, discussion of extending such procedures to humans is scientifically unjustified. We clearly do not yet understand how to accomplish controlled genetic modification of even simple phenotypes. Where more complex traits such as intelligence are concerned, we have no idea what to do, and in fact we may never be able to use gene transfer for enhancement of such phenotypes. A useful way to appreciate the daunting task of manipulating intelligence through gene transfer is by considering the fact that a single cerebellar Purkinje cell may possess more synapses than the total number of genes in the human genome. There are tens of millions of Purkinje cells in the cerebellum, and these cells are involved in only one aspect of brain function: motor coordination. The genome only provides a blueprint for formation of the brain; the finer details of assembly and intellectual development are beyond direct genetic control and must perforce be subject to innumerable stochastic and environmental influences.

GENETIC ENGINEERING AND HUMAN EVOLUTION

Some have suggested that genetic enhancement and related reproductive technologies now give us the power to control human evolution. This solemn pronouncement is totally without scientific foundation. The evolution of the human species may be understood as a nonrandom change in allelic frequencies resulting from selective pressure. The change progresses over generations because individuals with specific patterns of alleles are favored reproductively. If new alleles were introduced by gene transfer, the impact on the species would be negligible. Every month worldwide approximately 11 million babies are born. The addition of one genetically modified individual could not significantly affect gene frequencies. Moreover, if the "enhanced" individual had his or her first child at the age of 20, then 2,640,000,000 unengineered children would be born during the interval between the birth and procreation of the gene recipient. Even if 1000 successful gene transfers were performed per year, a number not likely to be achieved in the foreseeable future, those newborns would constitute only 1/132,000 of all live births. Thus, any effort to enhance the human species experimentally would be swamped by the random attempts of Mother Nature.

Finally, there is no certainty that genetically enhanced individuals would have greater biological fitness, as measured by reproductive success. A genius or great athlete who has no children has no biological fitness as defined in evolutionary theory. For these reasons, neither gene transfer nor any of the other emerging reproductive technologies will ever have a significant impact on human evolution.

DEVELOPING POLICY

If we accept the notion that genetic enhancement is not practicable in the near future, what policies should we develop concerning the use of such technology? The decision to undertake any form of invasive medical intervention immediately renders the treatment subject a patient who has a right to informed consent as well as to protection from unjustifiably dangerous medical manipulation. Our inability to predict the consequences of an attempt at genetic enhancement makes informed consent impossible, and current knowledge from animal experiments tells us that embryo gene transfer is unsafe: The common approach of pronuclear microinjection is characterized by random integration of donor DNA, a lack of control of the number of gene copies inserted, significant rearrangements of host genetic material, and a 5 to 10% frequency of insertional mutagenesis. Homologous recombination in embryonic stem cells overcomes many of these shortcomings, but human embryonic stem cell transfection would necessarily be followed by nuclear transfer into enucleated oocytes. Because nuclear transfer in at least two animal models is associated with a low birth rate and a very high rate of late pregnancy loss or newborn death, this procedure is also unsafe. The risks are so high and the documented efficacy is so low for gene transfer that it could not compare favorably to straightforward prenatal diagnosis even when a compelling need for therapy exists, as in cases of genetic disease. The use of gene transfer for elective purposes such as enhancement would stray far beyond the limits of acceptable medical intervention.

To attempt genetic enhancement with extant methods would clearly be medically unacceptable, but attempts to ban gene transfer legally could be a cumbersome approach to limiting its clinical use. Verification of compliance would be difficult. The diverse resources required for gene transfer necessitate that the procedure be carried out in facilities equipped for in vitro fertilization. Direct inspection would be required to uncover gene transfer procedures in such facilities. This would impose on the privacy of patients undergoing accepted assisted reproduction procedures such as sperm injection. Moreover, gene transfer can be easily concealed; in the case of pronuclear microinjection, only a few seconds are needed to complete the process. Legal restrictions can also be easily avoided by performing the procedure outside the area of jurisdiction.

Finally, and perhaps most important, broad legal restrictions incur the risk of limiting invaluable research. Exemplifying this problem is the current overly broad ban on federal funding for experiments with human embryos. The recent derivation of human embryonic stem cells from preimplantation embryos has created important new research opportunities, accompanied by pressure to provide federal funds for the work. This pressure has led to the odd situation in which federal funds will likely be allowed for research with embryonic stem cells but not for manipulating human embryos to produce embryonic stem cell lines. If, as a society, we feel compelled to make a statement against genetic enhancement, we need not enact anticipatory legislation. Instead we can evaluate such manipulations as we would any other invasive clinical procedure. If we require that gene transfer be accompanied by informed consent, that it have a reasonable possibility of succeeding, that its cost not be excessive, that it have acceptable side effects and toxicities, that it not be accompanied by a burdensome requirement for long-term follow-up evaluation, and that it compare favorably with other treatment options, we will currently reject the procedure on all counts as medically unethical. Were entities such as the National Bioethics Advisory Commission or Congress to make such statements formally, no responsible physician would attempt genetic enhancement. Irresponsible use of technology can never be stopped, even by legislation.

Fear of genetic manipulation may encourage proposals to limit basic investigations that might ultimately lead to effective human gene transfer. History has shown that effort is far better spent in preparing society to cope with scientific advances than in attempting to restrict basic research. Gene transfer studies may never lead to successful genetic enhancement, but they are certain to provide new treatment and prevention strategies for a variety of devastating diseases. No less significant is the potential for this research to improve our understanding of the most complex and compelling phenomenon ever observed—the life process. We cannot be expected to deny ourselves this knowledge.

NOTES AND QUESTIONS

1. Is Gordon correct that "genetic enhancement is not practicable in the near future"? It may depend on how genetic enhancement is defined. If it includes drugs made with genetic knowledge or rDNA techniques, then as shown earlier, examples already exist.

On September 11, 1997, the National Institutes of Health convened the first of its "Gene Therapy Policy Conferences." The meeting was prompted by a request to NIH to approve a protocol for conducting a gene therapy experiment in healthy volunteers, rather than in patients. Although the experiment was part of an effort to develop treatments for cystic fibrosis, the proposed use of healthy subjects raised for the first time the question of whether and in what circumstances it was appropriate to use gene insertion technology in "normal" individuals. Officials at NIH realized that it was but a short step from preliminary testing in healthy subjects of a genetic treatment for disease to experiments the goal of which was to genetically enhance a normal person's physical or mental characteristics. As the President's Council on Bioethics observed in its report, Beyond Therapy: Biotechnology and the Pursuit of Happiness: "We have every reason to expect exponential increases in biotechnologies and, therefore, in their potential uses in all aspects of human life." President's Council on Bioethics, Beyond Therapy: Biotechnology and the Pursuit of Happiness 303 (2003).

As discussed in Chapter 6, some parents already base reproductive decisions on non-disease characteristics detected with genetic (and other) testing—namely, tests that reveal gender. See Dorothy C. Wertz & John C. Fletcher, Fatal Knowledge? Prenatal Diagnosis and Sex Selection, 19 Hastings Center Rep. 21 (1989)(discussing the common use of prenatal diagnosis for sex screening); Lynne Marie Kohm, Sex Selection Abortion and the Boomerang Effect of a Woman's Right to Choose: A Paradox of the Skeptics, 4 William & Mary J. Women & L. 91, 92 (1997) (discussing how sex selection results in an unbalanced sex ratio). For an expansive view of genetic selection of offspring characteristics, including gender, see John A. Robertson, Genetic Selection of Offspring Characteristics, 76 B.U.L. Rev. 421, 479 (1996) (arguing that "commitment to procreative liberty necessarily leaves parents wide prebirth discretion to select or not the characteristics of their offspring").

Gene transfer for enhancement purposes may indeed be very far down the road, as Gordon suggests. But the potential demand may be so great that private companies may soon begin making a substantial commitment toward enhancement research and development.

Why is Gordon so skeptical (and he is not alone)? What difference does it make to him if some people want to speculate about genetic enhancement? The answer is found in the policy discussion of his article. Does this suggest that he may be distorting the scientific prospects in order to protect what he regards as more worthwhile forms of genetic research? If so, is this appropriate?

MAXWELL J. MEHLMAN, JESSICA W. BERG, ERIC T. JUENGST, AND ERIC KODISH, ETHICAL AND LEGAL ISSUES IN ENHANCEMENT RESEARCH ON HUMAN SUBJECTS

(forthcoming, Cambridge Q. J. of Ethics, 2009).

* * *

The United States, along with other nations and international organizations, has developed an elaborate system of ethical norms and legal rules to govern biomedical research using human subjects. These policies govern research which might provide direct health benefits to participants, and research in which there is no prospect for participant health benefits. There has been little discussion, however, about how well these rules would apply to research designed to improve participants' capabilities or characteristics beyond the goal of good health. When mentioned at all in the literature, this so-called "enhancement research," as opposed to research aimed at diagnosing, preventing, curing, or treating illnesses or medical conditions, is usually dismissed without explanation.

* * *

One concern raised by enhancement research is how to decide if the risks from an experiment would be outweighed by the potential benefits. The degree of potential benefit depends on the nature of the benefit as well as its amount: The more important or valuable the potential benefit, the greater the risks that researchers ethically can impose on subjects.

It might be wondered, therefore, whether the benefit from an enhancement was inherently of so much less value than health-oriented research that it would be unethical to conduct an enhancement study unless it offered a much better ratio of benefits to risks. Suppose there was a drug used to increase muscle mass in people with muscle-wasting diseases, and that was known to cause liver damage in a small number of patients. Should an IRB [Institutional Review Board] approve a study to see if the drug increased muscle mass in normal individuals? Should an IRB approve a study to measure patient satisfaction with a new surgical technique for facelifts, given that any surgical procedure carries with it a certain risk of scarring? Would a risk of scarring that was acceptable in a study of plastic surgery to correct a facial deformity be acceptable in a study of cosmetic use? The answer is that the value of a benefit clearly depends on the nature of the benefit. It is reasonable to expect that some health-oriented benefits would be regarded as more valuable than some enhancement benefits. On the other hand, some enhancement benefits may be perceived to be more valuable than medical benefits. An enhancement that potentially increased cognitive function substantially, for example, might be deemed more valuable than a substance to treat a minor skin irritation. . . .

A second question is how much to defer to the subjects in assessing potential enhancement benefits. The Common Rule [For the Protection of

Human Subjects] takes a highly paternalistic approach, allowing investigators to approach potential subjects to seek their informed consent to participate only after experts, in the form of institutional review boards, government sponsors, government regulators, and the investigators themselves, are satisfied that the potential benefits outweigh the risks. This may be justified in the case of health-oriented research on the ground that physicians and other medical experts are best suited to gauge medical benefits and risks. But it is not clear that these experts possess any particular advantage when it comes to assessing enhancement benefits. It will be difficult to measure many enhancement benefits against an objectively agreed upon standard since there is no baseline "normal" point of reference. And even in cases where there is some agreed upon standard of comparison, the perception of actual benefit may be highly subjective. This suggests that subjects in enhancement studies should be given more leeway than subjects in health-oriented research in accepting risks in return for potential benefits.

But it is important to recognize that experts continue to play a crucial role in protecting subjects even in enhancement experiments. Experts may be necessary to evaluate and explain medical risks of enhancement interventions. Moreover, only experts are likely to possess the ability to determine if a proposed study was properly designed, so that the risks to subjects can be justified in light of valid and reproducible results; or if the investigators had misrepresented the potential benefits, deemphasized risks, failed to disclose information necessary for informed consent, devalued subjects' welfare, or possessed an unacceptable conflict of interest. Experts also can prevent subjects from falling prey to the enhancement equivalent of the therapeutic misconception—what we might call the "melioristic misconception"—in which subjects mistakenly assume that they will derive some direct enhancement benefit from participating in a study, without realizing that they may be randomly assigned to a group of subjects that receives a placebo instead of the experimental enhancement, or that the experimental intervention may turn out to provide no enhancement benefits to the subjects who actually receive it.

IRB review also plays an important role in ensuring public support for the general research enterprise by limiting the types of research in which human subjects may be enrolled. In part this determination is made based on an analysis of the risk-benefit ratio. But another question is whether the mechanisms relied upon by the Common Rule to prevent unethical experimentation are adequate to protect against the potential adverse *social* impacts of biomedical enhancements? One common concern, for example is that widespread use of enhancement interventions would exacerbate the divide between the "haves" and "have nots" by allowing those that could afford the interventions to gain biological advantages over those that could not, creating separate social classes of genetic haves and have-nots. It is not clear, however, that IRBs have the authority to consider this and similar social concerns, whether in enhancement or health-oriented research. On the one hand, the Common Rule says that an

IRB may approve a study only if it concludes that the risks are reasonable in relation to the anticipated benefits, including benefits to subjects and the importance of the knowledge to be gained. Hence, the knowledge to be gained from a study of an enhancement that would increase inequality might not be deemed important enough to justify imposing any substantial risks on the subjects. But another section of the federal regulations specifically prohibits IRBs from considering these risks at all, saying:

> The IRB should not consider possible long-range effects of applying knowledge gained in the research (for example, the possible effects of the research on public policy) as among those research risks that fall within the purview of its responsibility. (45 C.F.R. § 46.111)

This category of risk was interpreted explicitly by the architects of this prohibition—the members of the National Commission for the Protection for Human Subjects in Biomedical and Behavioral Research—as including just the sort of speculative group harms raised by enhancement research. If social inequality is deemed to be a public policy concern, the rules may preclude IRBs from taking it into account in evaluating proposed human experiments. Additional guidance on this issue of long-term risks may be important both in the context of enhancement research and for more traditional health-oriented research.

Nᴏᴛᴇs ᴀɴᴅ Qᴜᴇsᴛɪᴏɴs

1.   Are special rules needed to govern enhancement research in humans? If so, what should the rules be?

2.   A special set of concerns arises in connection with research on so-called vulnerable populations. The federal research regulations establish special protections for pregnant women, fetuses and newborns, prisoners, and children, and adds that other populations may be "vulnerable to coercion or undue influence, such as * * * mentally disabled persons, or economically or educationally disadvantaged persons." (45 C.F.R. § 46.111(b)) These same populations may be vulnerable in the context of enhancement research, raising the question of whether the current protections, which were aimed at health-oriented research, provide adequate protections when the goal of the research is enhancement. A second question is whether the nature of enhancements, particularly their ability to confer a competitive advantage, requires that other distinct groups receive special protection.

In connection with enhancement research in children, consider the following:

> Children have already served as subjects in some biomedical enhancement research. For example, there have been at least seven studies on the effects of caffeine in normal children. Some ethicists might think that it is unethical for parents to enroll their children in any enhancement trials, on the ground that biomedical enhancement is contrary to a child's best interest. Parents might be deemed to be sacrificing the children's welfare in order to further the parents' own ambitions or social status, or to be valuing the children too much in terms of their capabilities, that is,

"commodifying" them. But there is little objection to parents placing their children in experimental educational settings in order to try to make them better learners. Why should parents be prohibited from enrolling their children in a study simply because it involves a biomedical rather than an educational enhancement?

The regulatory protections relating to children focus on risk-benefit assessments. Few if any experiments in which children were given biomedical enhancements would be likely to qualify as minimal risk under section 404 [45 CFR § 404]. It is less clear whether enhancement studies could fall under section 406 of the regulations, which pertains to research that presents only a "minor increase over minimal risk." Although this term is not defined in the regulations, most biomedical enhancements probably would be deemed to create a greater risk than this, and besides, section 406 requires the study to yield "generalizeable knowledge about the subjects' disorder or condition which is of vital importance for the understanding or amelioration of the subjects' disorder or condition," and an enhancement by definition does not address a disorder or condition. However, an NIH panel that reviewed a study in which normal-but-short children were to be given HGH concluded that the study could proceed under section 406. The implications of this decision for enhancement research troubled bioethicist Carol Tauer, who worried that:

> Such an application of 46.406 creates a precedent for approving greater than minimal risk research with healthy children in order to study any condition researchers or clinicians would like to be able to modify.

An "enhancement" modification is designed to alter a condition that is considered undesirable, either absolutely or relatively. Given the precedent in the NIH committee report, section 46.406 could be used to approve greater-than-minimal-risk enhancement research on children

Section 405 of the regulations allows an IRB to approve research with children that entails greater than minimal risk as long at there is a prospect of direct benefit to the individual subjects from the intervention in question, and the IRB determines that the risks are balanced by the potential benefits to the subjects, and that the ratio of risks to benefits is at least as favorable as that which would be provided by alternative treatments. The question is whether a direct enhancement benefit would count as a "direct benefit." The regulations fail to define the term, and a survey of the heads of IRBs showed that they were unclear about what it means. The regulation does not speak in terms of a "direct *medical* benefit," but the focus of the Common Rule is on health-oriented research, and the regulation does require the potential benefit to be compared to the benefit from alternative "treatments." Still, since the regulation on its face does not rule out enhancement research, it might allow enhancement research presenting more than minimal risk to be conducted on children if an IRB were convinced that the risks were outweighed by the potential benefits.

The final section of the regulations, 407, is a catch-all that applies to research on children that does not fall under one of the other three sections. It allows children to participate as subjects if a special review panel appointed by the NIH's Office of Human Research Protections finds that "the research presents a reasonable opportunity to further the understanding, prevention, or alleviation of a serious problem affecting the health or welfare of children." (45 C.F.R. § 46.407) If an enhancement study would be deemed to address "a serious problem affecting the health or welfare of children," a 407 panel might be willing to approve even relatively risky enhancement research on children.

While no 407 panels have been convened to review enhancement research, one study that did receive approval through the 407 process, although it was never carried out, involved administering to normal children methylphenidate and dextroamphetamine, which are controlled substances approved for treating ADHD but which are also used off-label to enhance cognition. The purpose of the study was to see whether magnetic resonance imaging could be useful as a means of diagnosing children with ADHD. To find this out, the researchers needed to determine if children with ADHD who were taking the drugs exhibited different brain images than siblings who did not have ADHD but who were given the drugs.

Similar to the regulations for children, federal regulations currently permit research to take place on fetuses if the research holds out the prospect of "direct benefit" to subjects. (45 C.F.R. § 46.204(b)) Since the regulations do not define the term "direct benefit," there is no obvious reason why research that presented the prospect of a direct enhancement rather than a health benefit would be prohibited. Examples of enhancement research with fetuses may include manipulation of embryonic and fetal DNA to produce enhancement effects, and the administration of enhancement drugs in utero. The regulations permit research on fetuses that does not offer the prospect of direct benefit only if the risk is minimal and the purpose of the research is to develop important medical knowledge that cannot be otherwise obtained. (45 C.F.R. § 46.204(b)) But since it is unlikely that a study of a biomedical enhancement effect on fetuses would be regarded as presenting no more than minimal risk, enhancement research involving fetuses would have to entail a direct benefit either to the fetus or to the pregnant woman to be permissible under the current guidelines.

One concern is that, in their eagerness to give their offspring every advantage (and societal pressures to do so), parents may agree to participate in experiments that expose children (or fetuses) to undue risk. The parents also may fall prey to the melioristic misconception—mistakenly thinking that the trial will provide actual enhancement benefits to all subjects. This suggests that IRBs and other external sources need to protect children and fetuses from research risks even when the parents would give their consent. On the other hand, parents traditionally are accorded considerable discretion in exposing their children to risks; the law only steps in when parental actions amount to "abuse or neglect." Assuming that the parents are not operating under a type of melioristic misconception, this would seem to call for deferring to parental decisions about participating in enhancement research. Under such an approach, oversight bodies such as IRBs would be entitled to limit parental decision making only when the oversight body was convinced that reasonable parents, having paramount regard for the welfare of the child or fetus, would not subject the child or fetus to such risks.

Note that this is not necessarily the same as the standard that the federal regulations establish for IRB review in general: that the IRB must determine, among other things, that the risks to subjects are reasonable in relation to the anticipated benefits. (45 C.F.R. § 46.111(a)(2)) The general standard would seem to allow an IRB to refuse to approve a study when the IRB members felt that, from their perspective, the risks would be unreasonable. The standard suggested above would require the IRB to assess a research protocol from the viewpoint of a parent, rather than from the members' own perspectives.

Maxwell J. Mehlman, Jessica W. Berg, Eric T. Juengst, and Eric Kodish, Ethical and Legal Issues in Enhancement Research on Human Subjects (forthcoming, Cambridge Q. J. of Ethics, 2009).

Other study populations that are especially vulnerable in the context of enhancement research are workers, students, athletes, and members of the military. What special protections are provided for these groups in the current regulations? Are they adequate? See Maxwell J. Mehlman, Jessica W. Berg, Eric T. Juengst, and Eric Kodish, Ethical and Legal Issues in Enhancement Research on Human Subjects (forthcoming, Cambridge Q. J. of Ethics, 2009).

3. Valid and reliable efficacy data for genetic enhancement technologies are likely to be extremely scarce not only because of ethical questions about how to conduct enhancement research on humans, but because of gaps in the current legal system for regulating drugs. Depending on how genetic enhancement is achieved, providers and suppliers may not be required to submit safety and efficacy data to the government and obtain government approval before marketing enhancement technologies. To the extent that genetic enhancement is deemed a surgical or medical procedure, as opposed to the administration of a drug, biological, or medical device, it will not require prior approval by the FDA, with the attendant requirement that this approval be based on adequate and well-controlled clinical investigations. Without being required to submit these data, it is unlikely that anyone would go to the enormous expense of creating them. Furthermore, even if regulators regard genetic enhancements as drugs, biologicals, or medical devices, these technologies are likely to emerge first as unapproved or "off-label" uses of therapeutic technologies—that is, uses for which the manufacturers are not labeling or promoting the technologies—and manufacturers are not required to conduct clinical investigations to support these uses. The experience with HGH, mentioned earlier, is a good example. The drug was approved by the FDA for use in individuals who were deficient in growth hormone. But pediatric endocrynologists began prescribing it for other individuals with short stature, and as noted earlier, there are reports that parents are seeking the drug—and no doubt obtaining it—for use in children who are of normal height and even for use in some who are tall. Efficacy data exist for the approved use of HGH,

but there are likely to be only unconfirmed reports from uncontrolled case studies for the off-label uses.

MICHAEL SANDEL, THE CASE AGAINST PERFECTION: WHAT'S WRONG WITH DESIGNER CHILDREN, BIONIC ATHLETES, AND GENETIC ENGINEERING

Atlantic Monthly, April 2004.

Breakthroughs in genetics present us with a promise and a predicament. The promise is that we may soon be able to treat and prevent a host of debilitating diseases. The predicament is that our newfound genetic knowledge may also enable us to manipulate our own nature—to enhance our muscles, memories, and moods; to choose the sex, height, and other genetic traits of our children; to make ourselves "better than well." When science moves faster than moral understanding, as it does today, men and women struggle to articulate their unease. In liberal societies they reach first for the language of autonomy, fairness, and individual rights. But this part of our moral vocabulary is ill equipped to address the hardest questions posed by genetic engineering. The genomic revolution has induced a kind of moral vertigo.

* * *

Though some maintain that genetic enhancement erodes human agency by overriding effort, the real problem is the explosion, not the erosion, of responsibility. As humility gives way, responsibility expands to daunting proportions. We attribute less to chance and more to choice. Parents become responsible for choosing, or failing to choose, the right traits for their children. Athletes become responsible for acquiring, or failing to acquire, the talents that will help their teams win.

One of the blessings of seeing ourselves as creatures of nature, God, or fortune is that we are not wholly responsible for the way we are. The more we become masters of our genetic endowments, the greater the burden we bear for the talents we have and the way we perform. Today when a basketball player misses a rebound, his coach can blame him for being out of position. Tomorrow the coach may blame him for being too short. Even now the use of performance-enhancing drugs in professional sports is subtly transforming the expectations players have for one another; on some teams players who take the field free from amphetamines or other stimulants are criticized for "playing naked."

The more alive we are to the chanced nature of our lot, the more reason we have to share our fate with others. Consider insurance. Since people do not know whether or when various ills will befall them, they pool their risk by buying health insurance and life insurance. As life plays itself out, the healthy wind up subsidizing the unhealthy, and those who live to a ripe old age wind up subsidizing the families of those who die before their time. Even without a sense of mutual obligation, people pool their risks and resources and share one another's fate.

But insurance markets mimic solidarity only insofar as people do not know or control their own risk factors. Suppose genetic testing advanced to the point where it could reliably predict each person's medical future and life expectancy. Those confident of good health and long life would opt out of the pool, causing other people's premiums to skyrocket. The solidarity of insurance would disappear as those with good genes fled the actuarial company of those with bad ones.

The fear that insurance companies would use genetic data to assess risks and set premiums recently led the Senate to vote to prohibit genetic discrimination in health insurance. But the bigger danger, admittedly more speculative, is that genetic enhancement, if routinely practiced, would make it harder to foster the moral sentiments that social solidarity requires.

Why, after all, do the successful owe anything to the least-advantaged members of society? The best answer to this question leans heavily on the notion of giftedness. The natural talents that enable the successful to flourish are not their own doing but, rather, their good fortune—a result of the genetic lottery. If our genetic endowments are gifts, rather than achievements for which we can claim credit, it is a mistake and a conceit to assume that we are entitled to the full measure of the bounty they reap in a market economy. We therefore have an obligation to share this bounty with those who, through no fault of their own, lack comparable gifts.

A lively sense of the contingency of our gifts—a consciousness that none of us is wholly responsible for his or her success—saves a meritocratic society from sliding into the smug assumption that the rich are rich because they are more deserving than the poor. Without this, the successful would become even more likely than they are now to view themselves as self-made and self-sufficient, and hence wholly responsible for their success. Those at the bottom of society would be viewed not as disadvantaged, and thus worthy of a measure of compensation, but as simply unfit, and thus worthy of eugenic repair. The meritocracy, less chastened by chance, would become harder, less forgiving. As perfect genetic knowledge would end the simulacrum of solidarity in insurance markets, so perfect genetic control would erode the actual solidarity that arises when men and women reflect on the contingency of their talents and fortunes.

Thirty-five years ago Robert L. Sinsheimer, a molecular biologist at the California Institute of Technology, glimpsed the shape of things to come. In an article titled "The Prospect of Designed Genetic Change" he argued that freedom of choice would vindicate the new genetics, and set it apart from the discredited eugenics of old.

> To implement the older eugenics ... would have required a massive social programme carried out over many generations. Such a programme could not have been initiated without the consent and co-operation of major fraction of the population, and would have been continuously subject to social control. In contrast, the new eugenics

could, at least in principle, be implemented on a quite individual basis, in one generation, and subject to no existing restrictions.

According to Sinsheimer, the new eugenics would be voluntary rather than coerced, and also more humane. Rather than segregating and eliminating the unfit, it would improve them. "The old eugenics would have required a continual selection for breeding of the fit, and a culling of the unfit," he wrote. "The new eugenics would permit in principle the conversion of all the unfit to the highest genetic level."

Sinsheimer's paean to genetic engineering caught the heady, Promethean self-image of the age. He wrote hopefully of rescuing "the losers in that chromosomal lottery that so firmly channels our human destinies," including not only those born with genetic defects but also "the 50,000,-000 'normal' Americans with an IQ of less than 90." But he also saw that something bigger than improving on nature's "mindless, age-old throw of dice" was at stake. Implicit in technologies of genetic intervention was a more exalted place for human beings in the cosmos. "As we enlarge man's freedom, we diminish his constraints and that which he must accept as given," he wrote. Copernicus and Darwin had "demoted man from his bright glory at the focal point of the universe," but the new biology would restore his central role. In the mirror of our genetic knowledge we would see ourselves as more than a link in the chain of evolution: "We can be the agent of transition to a whole new pitch of evolution. This is a cosmic event."

There is something appealing, even intoxicating, about a vision of human freedom unfettered by the given. It may even be the case that the allure of that vision played a part in summoning the genomic age into being. It is often assumed that the powers of enhancement we now possess arose as an inadvertent by-product of biomedical progress—the genetic revolution came, so to speak, to cure disease, and stayed to tempt us with the prospect of enhancing our performance, designing our children, and perfecting our nature. That may have the story backwards. It is more plausible to view genetic engineering as the ultimate expression of our resolve to see ourselves astride the world, the masters of our nature. But that promise of mastery is flawed. It threatens to banish our appreciation of life as a gift, and to leave us with nothing to affirm or behold outside our own.

GREGORY STOCK, REDESIGNING HUMANS: OUR INEVITABLE GENETIC FUTURE

1–5 (2002).

* * *

We know that *Homo sapiens* is not the final word in primate evolution, but few have yet grasped that we are on the cusp of profound biological change, poised to transcend our current form and character on a journey to destinations of new imagination.

At first glance, the very notion that we might become more than "human" seems preposterous. After all, we are still biologically identical in virtually every respect to our cave-dwelling ancestors. But this lack of change is deceptive. Never before have we had the power to manipulate human genetics to alter our biology in meaningful, predictable ways.

Bioethicists and scientists alike worry about the consequences of coming genetic technologies, but few have thought through the larger implications of the wave of new developments arriving in reproductive biology. Today in vitro fertilization is responsible for fewer than 1 percent of births in the United States; embryo selection numbers only in the hundreds of cases; cloning and human genetic modification still lie ahead. But give these emerging technologies a decade and they will be the cutting edge of human biological change.

These developments will write a new page in the history of life, allowing us to seize control of our evolutionary future. Our coming ability to choose our children's genes will have immense social impact and raise difficult ethical dilemmas. Biological enhancement will lead us into unexplored realms, eventually challenging our basic ideas about what it means to be human.

Some imagine we will see the perils, come to our senses, and turn away from such possibilities. But when we imagine Prometheus stealing fire from the gods, we are not incredulous or shocked by his act. It is too characteristically human. To forgo the powerful technologies that genomics and molecular biology are bringing would be as out of character for humanity as it would be to use them without concern for the dangers they pose. We will do neither. The question is no longer whether we will manipulate embryos, but when, where, and how.

We have already felt the impact of previous advances in reproductive technology. Without the broad access to birth control that we take so for granted, the populations of Italy, Japan, and Germany would not be shrinking; birth rates in the developing world would not be falling. These are major shifts, yet unlike the public response to today's high-tech developments, no impassioned voices protest birth control as an immense and dangerous experiment with our genetic future. Those opposing family planning seem more worried about the immorality of recreational sex than about human evolution.

* * *

The emerging reproductive technologies for selecting and altering human embryos * * * culminating in germline engineering—the manipulation of the genetics of egg or sperm (our "germinal" cells) to modify future generations—will have large consequences. Already, procedures that influence the germline are routine in labs working on fruit flies and mice, and researchers have done early procedures on nonhuman primates. Direct human germline manipulations may still be a decade or two away, but methods of choosing specific genes in an embryo are in use today to prevent disease, and sophisticated methods for making broader choices are arriving every year, bringing with them a taste of the ethical and social questions that will accompany comprehensive germline engineering.

The arrival of safe, reliable germline technology will signal the beginning of human self-design. We do not know where this development will ultimately take us, but it will transform the evolutionary process by drawing reproduction into a highly selective social process that is far more rapid and effective at spreading successful genes than traditional sexual competition and mate selection.

Considering the barrage of press reports about the project, we naturally wonder how much is hype. Extravagant metaphor has not been lacking. We are deciphering the "code of codes," "reading the book of life," "looking at the holy grail of human biology." It is reminiscent of the enthusiasm that attended Neil Armstrong's 1969 walk on the moon. Humanity seemed poised to march toward the stars, but 2001 has come and gone, and there has been no sentient computer like HAL, no odyssey to the moons of Jupiter. Thirty years from now, however, I do not think we will look back at the Human Genome Project with a similar wistful disappointment. Unlike outer space, genetics is at our core, and as we learn to manipulate it, we are learning to manipulate ourselves.

Well before this new millennium's close, we will almost certainly change ourselves enough to become much more than simply human.

* * *

Many bioethicists do not share my perspective on where we are heading. They imagine that our technology might become potent enough to alter us, but that we will turn away from it and reject human enhancement. But the reshaping of human genetics and biology does not hinge on some cadre of demonic researchers hidden away in a lab in Argentina trying to pick up where Hitler left off. The coming possibilities will be the inadvertent spinoff of mainstream research that virtually everyone supports. Infertility, for example, is a source of deep pain for millions of couples. Researchers and clinicians working on in vitro fertilization (IVF) don't think much about future human evolution, but nonetheless are building a foundation of expertise in conceiving, handling, testing, and implanting human embryos, and this will one day be the basis for the manipulation of the human species. Already, we are seeing attempts to apply this knowledge in highly controversial ways: as premature as today's efforts to clone humans may be, they would be the flimsiest of fantasies if they could not draw on decades of work on human IVF.

Similarly, in early 2001 more than five hundred gene-therapy trials were under way or in review throughout the world. The researchers are trying to cure real people suffering from real diseases and are no more interested in the future of human evolution than the IVF researchers. But their progress toward inserting genes into adult cells will be one more piece of the foundation for manipulating human embryos.

Not everything that can be done should or will be done, of course, but once a relatively inexpensive technology becomes feasible in thousands of laboratories around the world and a sizable fraction of the population sees it as beneficial, it will be used.

ERIK PARENS, AUTHENTICITY AND AMBIVALENCE: TOWARD UNDERSTANDING THE ENHANCEMENT DEBATE

35 Hastings Center Report 34, 37–38 (May/June 2005).

Although there are important disagreements among both critics and proponents, I want briefly to describe what I take to be an important difference between critics and proponents.

I have come to think that these different understandings of authenticity grow out of what I will call two different ethical frameworks. By "frameworks," I mean a constellation of commitments that support and shape our responses to questions about, among many other things, new enhancement technologies. When I refer to those different frameworks as "ethical," I use that term in its broadest possible sense, as designating habits of thought and being. Were it a more felicitous neologism, I would refer to "psycho-ethical frameworks," to emphasize that these frameworks have an important psychological (and perhaps aesthetic) dimension. Instead, I will say simply that I believe these different conceptions of authenticity grow, at least in part, out of different prerational experiences and understandings of our selves and of our proper relationships to the world.

These frameworks are built of answers to questions that do not have only one good answer. In another place I have described some of those questions at length, but for now I will merely mention some: Can we meaningfully distinguish between "natural" and "artificial" human interventions into nature? Should we conceive of technology as morally neutral or morally loaded? What do we mean when we claim that we are free, and to what extent are we free? And so forth.

To emphasize that these two frameworks are intimately related even as they are importantly different, I will dare to remind you of a single figure in an oft-cited book. In the book of Genesis, Jacob's wife Rachel, who was unable to bear children, begs him: "Give me children, or I shall die." Jacob famously responded to Rachel's injunction with a question, "Am I in the place of God?" With this question, Jacob expresses one of the book's central and best-known ideas: that we human beings are not the creators of life; we are creatures, whose job is to remember that life is a gift. It is our responsibility to express our gratitude for the mysterious whole, which we have not made.

This sort of attitude does not require a commitment to any particular religious tradition, indeed to any religion at all. Many a pagan environmentalist (like Bill McKibben, author of The End of Nature and Enough:

Genetic Engineering and the End of Human Nature) adopts such an attitude. Many a left-leaning critic of corporatization (like Rich Hayes, who directs the Center for Genetics and Society) adopts it. Michael Sandel invokes the secular version of this idea when he writes, "If bioengineering made the myth of the 'selfmade man' come true, it would be difficult to view our talents as gifts for which we are indebted, rather than as achievements for which we are responsible. This would transform three key features of our moral landscape: humility, responsibility, and solidarity." Leaving aside whether Sandel's predictions are accurate, we can discern in his words the sort of view symbolized by Jacob's question: if we forget that life is a gift—albeit from an unknown giver—we will make a mistake about the sort of creatures we really are and the way the world really is.

But this very same Jacob, who exhibits a kind of gratitude that many today associate with "religion," also exhibits a radically different stance, which Genesis also celebrates. After all, as has been noted more than once, Jacob, the very one whose name would become Israel, was "the first genetic engineer"; he was the one with the creativity to fashion a device ("rods of poplar and almond, into which he peeled white streaks" [Gen. 30:38]) with which he induced his uncle's goats to produce only the valuable "speckled and spotted" (Gen. 30:39) young. According to Genesis, and it seems to me much of Judaism, our responsibility is not merely to be grateful and remember that we are not the creators of the whole. It is also our responsibility to use our creativity to mend and transform ourselves and the world. As far as I can tell, Genesis and Judaism do not exhort us to choose between gratitude and creativity. Rather, or so it seems to this pagan, it is our job to figure out how to maintain that fertile tension, making sure that neither stance gets more than its share.

When we observe scholars and others debate about "enhancement technologies," I believe that we often see people who have at least for the moment adopted either the gratitude or creativity framework, as I am calling them. As one side emphasizes our obligation to remember that life is a gift and that we need to learn to let things be, the other emphasizes our obligation to transform that gift and to exhibit our creativity. As one framework emphasizes the danger of allowing ourselves to become, in Heidegger's famous formulation, "standing reserve," the other emphasizes the danger of failing to summon the courage to, as Nietzsche put it, "create" ourselves, to "become who we are."

Indeed, sometimes the same scholar moves between frameworks in the same talk. I believe I saw my friend Eric Juengst, a philosopher who has thought deeply about human enhancement, do just that during a lecture at Hiram College in the summer of 2004; he operated out of the creativity framework when he criticized those who would oppose all efforts at extending life, and he operated out of the gratitude framework when he criticized efforts that would bring normal aging under the control of medical science. Again, most of us can be comfortable in both frameworks, even if most of us are considerably more comfortable in one framework than in the other. I should hurry to add: moving between frameworks, being ambivalent, seems to me to be a sign of openness and thoughtfulness, not confusion.

It's not only because I love that we find both attitudes in one figure that I invoke Jacob. Yes, it is essential to remember that none of us who is thoughtful inhabits only one of those frameworks. But it is also useful to remember that the figure of Jacob appears in a book that is "religious." In fact, one might tell a creation story about bioethics that has the field grow out of a battle between two titans, both of whom were theologians: Paul Ramsey, the Ur-critic of biotechnology, and Joseph Fletcher, the Ur-proponent. If one looked to the history of presidential commissions that broached the enhancement question, one would notice that each of them has brought out theologians from both the gratitude and creativity frameworks: one side reminds us of the importance of letting things be, eschewing arrogance, and so on, while the other reminds us with equal passion of our obligation to find the courage to become creative in our efforts to ameliorate human suffering.

Suggesting that we find religious soil at the roots of the critical and the enthusiastic stances toward enhancement helps me bring to the fore concerns I have about both sides of the enhancement debate. Beginning with the side I feel most comfortable on: the critics. Sometimes, when we critics speak, we sound as if we have forgotten or don't even fully appreciate that, in principle, the creativity framework is as worthy as the gratitude framework. When we try to make the case "against perfection" or when we raise problems with the "ethic of willfulness," we risk forgetting that at the core of that ethic is the noble impulse to be creative, to mend and transform ourselves and the world. Were we to speak, instead, of "the ethic of creativity," we might be more prone to give the other side its due.

By calling attention to the religious element of the commitments on both sides, I am trying to emphasize what I take to be an obvious but under-appreciated fact: the proponent is not as neutral as she sometimes seems to believe. She has no more than anyone else escaped the maw of extra-rational commitments.

Having identified these two ethical frameworks, I need to emphasize several caveats. First, I've tried to make abundantly clear that I don't think the difference between critics and proponents is the same as the difference between people who are religious and those who are secular. You find both kinds in both camps. Second, the distinction between the gratitude and creativity frameworks is not the same as that between political conservatism and liberalism; conservatives and liberals operate out of each.

Finally, I do not for a moment forget that distinguishing between the gratitude framework of the critics and the creativity framework of the proponents is a very crude heuristic. The outlines of the gratitude and creativity frameworks are neat only in speech. Nonetheless, I think that when we engage in debates about enhancement technologies, it can help to recognize that people on both sides are speaking out of the framework in which they feel most comfortable. And I think it is crucial to recognize that none of us, if we are reflective, feels comfortable only in one of these frameworks. Even if we settle in one for the sake of debating each other, in our day-to-day lives we shuttle between them. One might say that in our day-to-day lives we are often more prone to allow ourselves such thoughtfulness—and ambivalence—than when we sit down to engage in scholarship.

NOTES AND QUESTIONS

The debate over the ethical, legal and social implications of genetic enhancement is part of a larger conversation about the use of biomedical enhancement in general. Within the world of sports, for example, a war against the use of performance-enhancing drugs has been waged since the late 1960's. Beginning in the late 1980's, however, the use of drugs in sports, generally referred to as "doping," began to attract the attention of the government. After a series of hearings in 1988, 1989, and 1990, Congress placed anabolic steroids on the list of controlled substances, making it a felony to distribute them for non-medical purposes, and amended the Federal Food, Drug, and Cosmetic Act to make it a felony to distribute, or possess with the intent to distribute, human growth hormone other than to treat disease. When the dietary supplement manufacturer Balco was accused of concocting and distributing steroid analogues, known as "designer steroids," that could not be detected by existing tests and that technically were not covered by the Controlled Substances Act, Congress amended the act in 2004 to close this loophole. In the winter of 2005, the U.S. Senate investigated the use of steroids in baseball, firing off subpoenas at players and executives. Senator John McCain threatened to revoke baseball's exemption from federal antitrust laws if it did not clean up its players. Later hearings targeted professional basketball and football. And in his first State of the Union message since the invasion of Iraq, President Bush declared:

> To help children make right choices, they need good examples. Athletics play such an important role in our society, but, unfortunately, some in professional sports are not setting much of an example. The use of performance-enhancing drugs like steroids in baseball, football, and other sports is dangerous, and it sends the wrong message—that there are shortcuts to accomplishment, and that performance is more important than character. So tonight I call on team owners, union representatives, coaches, and players to take the lead, to send the right signal, to get tough, and to get rid of steroids now.

States have not directly addressed doping in competitive athletics. However, most states have updated their controlled substance acts to reflect the federal stance against anabolic steroids. They have also made additional efforts to regulate steroids in schools and to disseminate information about the dangers of anabolic steroids.

1. What accounts for this intrusion of government into the private world of sports? By what authority does it act? And most importantly, what does this bode for the legal status of biomedical enhancement use outside of sports?

2. What are the distinctions between the use of biomedical enhancements for performance enhancement in sports and other uses? Are there significant differences between genetic enhancement and biomedical enhancement in general?

3. The readings by Sandel and Parens deal with the use of enhancements for purposes of self-fulfillment. Whose argument seems more persuasive? Another important purpose for using genetic enhancements is to obtain a competitive advantage. Depending on the nature of the enhancement, this could be an advantage in a sports competition (e.g., a performance enhancing intervention), or in school or at work (e.g., a cognition enhancing intervention). If third-party payers, such as health insurers, treat genetic enhancements like cosmetic surgery, they will not pay for them, and only persons who can afford them out-of-pocket will obtain them. Depending on how expensive they are, only relatively well-off individuals and families may gain access, since the cost may make government subsidies too expensive. If genetic enhancements are highly effective at conferring advantages, this may erode the belief in equality of opportunity that is a fundamental tenet of western liberal democracies.

4. An article in the September 2009 issues of The Chronicle of Higher Education notes the use of cognition-enhancing drugs by college students and quotes an Australian researcher predicting that they may soon face doping tests at exam time. Would this be appropriate? Paul Bisken, At Exam Time, Students May Face a Separate Test–for "Smart Drugs," The Chronicle of Higher Education (Sept. 30, 2009).

MAXWELL J. MEHLMAN, THE LAW OF ABOVE AVERAGES: LEVELING THE NEW GENETIC ENHANCEMENT PLAYING FIELD

85 Iowa L. Rev. 517, 541–544 (2000).

* * *

Is it fair for some people to have greater genetic advantages than others? This is an age-old question, forming the crux of the problem of "natural inequality" that has plagued philosophers and social theorists for centuries. If it is unfair, then presumably society should do what it can to mitigate the consequences. Yet, what forms of intervention should society take, and how feasible would they be?

* * *

Maintaining a liberal democratic form of government is an important social goal. This goal is directly threatened by wealth-based genetic enhancement: The inequality of social opportunity that results may be so great that a liberal democratic form of government becomes unsustainable, and our political system instead becomes autocratic or oligarchic. This follows from the assumption that a minimum degree of equality is necessary for the existence of a modern liberal democracy. If social inequality becomes too pronounced, liberal democratic political systems, and the capitalist economic system upon which they rest, become unstable. As one sociologist states:

> Inequality in the distribution of rewards is always a potential source of political and social instability. Because upper, relatively advantaged strata are generally fewer in number than disadvantaged lower strata, the former are faced with crucial problems of social control over the latter. One way of approaching this issue is to ask not why the disprivileged often rebel against the privileged but why they do not rebel more often than they do.

The characteristics of genetic enhancement that threaten to destabilize liberal democratic government are the features that distinguish genetic enhancement from other forms of self-improvement: its high cost, which may place it beyond the reach of all but the very wealthy; the broad and fundamental nature of the traits that it could enhance; the magnitude of its effects; their multiplicity; the resulting ability to gain advantages in multiple spheres of social activity; and the possibility—created by germ line enhancement—that these advantages would be passed on to successive generations.

These characteristics not only give rise to social inequality; more insidiously, they undermine the belief in equality of opportunity. A widespread belief in equality of opportunity is the method by which liberal democracies accommodate the reality of capitalist inequality—that everyone is not equally endowed with equally beneficial natural assets or blessed with the same luck. Sociologists point out that "whereas most Americans are willing to tolerate sizeable inequalities in the distribution of resources, they typically insist that individuals from all backgrounds should have an equal opportunity to secure these resources." John Schaar notes that the belief in equal opportunity is instrumental in maintaining the prevailing social order, stating that "no policy formula is better designed to fortify the dominant institutions, values, and ends of the American social order than the formula of equality of opportunity, for it offers *everyone* a fair and equal chance to find a place within that order."

Assuming, as discussed earlier, that the price of genetic enhancements prohibits people of ordinary means from acquiring them, genetic enhancement would create profound differences in ability that would endow the wealthy with opportunities utterly and irrevocably beyond the reach of the majority of the citizens. World history is filled with examples of societies similar to those that would result from wealth-based genetic enhancement. In medieval Europe, for example, individuals were born with a social status, and barring the infrequent case in which peasants were able to obtain education in religious institutions or became apprenticed and eventually esquired to knights, individuals remained members of the class into which they were born. Similarly, in slave-owning societies, people were born into bondage and could be freed only by escape (self-exile) or at the pleasure of their masters. The most obvious surviving example of such a society is the caste system in India. The caste system remains a constant threat to that nation's democratic institutions.

Genetic social stratification thus would undermine our current social system, but it is not certain how seriously. Perhaps society will adapt to the social artifacts of the genetic revolution and the result, while markedly different from present arrangements, will be relatively stable. The genetic underclass might cede power to their genetic superiors in return for enjoying the material benefits made possible by genetic advances. In this scenario, the underclass would accept the division between social strata, and be content with being upwardly mobile only within the confines of their own class. The genobility, in turn, would rule according to enlight-ened principles of noblesse oblige, taking care to permit sufficient benefits to trickle down to maintain political and social equilibrium. A democracy of sorts might even persist, with the underclass electing representatives who either belonged to the upper class or who were committed to preserving its privileges. In essence, such a system might not look very different from our own, given the extent to which we increasingly elect representatives who are considerably more privileged than their constitu-ents.

This system, however, seems highly unstable. For one thing, the members of the genetic upper class would require great self-control to avoid over-reaching. At minimum, they would need to maintain effective means of monitoring and regulating the behavior of their peers to prevent antisocial excesses of greed. The system also would be vulnerable to demagogues who achieved power by promising to redistribute genetic endowments more evenly. Assuming that the principle of one-person/one-vote persisted, a numerically inferior genetic upper class could be out-voted by the underclass and Congress could become dominated by elected officials pledged to employ the full force of government to rectify genetic imbalances.

The genobility might respond with reprisals in an effort to preserve its privileged status. At one extreme these could range from threats to withhold the fruits of genetic medicine from non-privileged segments of society, to overt interference with the democratic process. At the other, the genetic upper class is liable to amass sufficient wealth and influence to enable it to control the media, which would in turn permit it to affect the outcome of elections in a manner quite out of proportion to its numbers. Efforts by the underclass to preserve its hegemony might prove no more successful than current efforts to reform campaign finance laws in order to dilute the power of special interests.

In the end, we might embark on an era of social chaos as the system swung in ever-widening arcs between rule by underclass demagogues and by the genetic aristocracy. Eventually, this could degenerate into mob rule and, then, anarchy. To rid itself of its status as the class of the genetically disadvantaged, the mob might even destroy the scientific foundations of the genetic revolution, perhaps by physically dismantling research centers and erasing mapping and sequencing data.

Alternatively, post-genorevolutionary society could devolve into totalitarian rule by a genetic autocracy. The genetic upper class would employ whatever repressive techniques were necessary in order to obtain power and to keep the underclass in check. Advances in genetic science might even enable the genobility to genetically manipulate the underclass in ways that make it more docile.

While it is impossible to predict with certainty what effect wealth-based genetic enhancement will have on society, what is clear is that it creates not only a moral challenge but a political threat. From a moral standpoint, those who obtain enhancement may not have done anything to deserve it. Adults may have obtained the means necessary to purchase enhancement in objectionable or morally irrelevant ways—through exploitation or the brute luck of inheritance. Moreover, it is difficult to argue that children earned their new-found advantages. Yet genetic enhancement poses more than an ethical quandary. Even if the resources necessary to purchase genetic enhancement are earned in a moral sense, wealth-based enhancement is likely to have a severe societal impact. Somatic enhancement alone could dramatically widen the gap between the haves and have-nots, and crippling class warfare would ensue. Germ line enhancement could create, quite literally, a master race. A future as bleak as this is not perhaps inevitable, but it is unquestionably within the realm of possibility. The question then becomes whether there is any practical way to prevent this.

NOTES AND QUESTIONS

1. Is there a solution to the equality problem? See Mehlman, id. at 570–574 (suggesting licensing the use of genetic enhancements for public benefit and a national lottery in which everyone was enrolled). The high cost of enhancements also would create unfairness problems when the enhanced competed with the unenhanced for scarce societal resources, whether Olympic gold medals or admission to Harvard Law School. For possible ways of leveling the playing field, see Mehlman, id. at 576–592.

2. A particular concern is the prospect of germ line genetic enhancement. A September 2000 report by the American Association for the Advancement of Science entitled "Human Inheritable Genetic Modifications" stated:

In theory, genetic enhancement could be accomplished through either somatic or germ line intervention. Whether or not the latter will start us down a slippery slope toward enhancements, the desire to undertake enhancements will most likely favor IGM over somatic technology. Genetic enhancements are likely to require altering several genes that work in concert with each other. Such genetic interventions are likely to be more effective when conducted early in the development of the embryo or on the fetus *in utero,* although this remains to be demonstrated. In many, perhaps most instances, such early intervention would result in alteration of the germ line whether or not it was intended. The very considerable expense involved might incline parents to try to get the most for their investment, again favoring the IGM option.

AAAS Report, Human Inheritable Genetic Modifications at 43 (2000).

3.   As with any germ line modification, there may be latent risks that do not materialize for several generations. Moreover, if only the well-off can afford genetic enhancement, then highly effective germ-line modifications threaten to create a genetic aristocracy or "genobility" that passes genetic advantages on to their offspring. See Maxwell J. Mehlman & Jeffrey Botkin, Access to the Genome: The Challenge to Equality, 98–109 (1998). Should this risk prevent the development of therapeutic germ line interventions? LeRoy Walters, former chair of the RAC, states: "Think about confronting a person in the future with a genetic disease that you could have prevented and telling them that even though you knew how to fix it, you stopped because you thought society might abuse this thing." Rick Weiss, Scientists Seek Panel's Advice on In–Womb Genetic Tests, Wash. Post, March 22, 1998, at A2. At what point, if any, would the risks from germ line genetic enhancement outweigh this benefit? Which risks should count?

4.   To the extent that genetic enhancement products seek to alter the structure or function of the human body, the FDA has regulatory authority over them as drugs or devices. (A "biologic" comprises only products "applicable to the prevention or cure of diseases or injuries of man." 42 USC § 262(a)). Is the FDA well-suited to regulate enhancement products, however? See Maxwell J. Mehlman, How Will We Regulate Genetic Enhancement?, 34 Wake Forest L. Rev. 671, 701–703 (1999).

5.   Given concerns about the adverse impact of genetic enhancement in general or germ line genetic enhancement in particular, one alternative might be to attempt to prohibit it by law. In that case, the agency with regulatory authority might not be the FDA, but the Drug Enforcement Administration, acting pursuant to its authority under the Controlled Substances Act. See Maxwell J. Mehlman, How Will We Regulate Genetic Enhancement?, 34 Wake Forest L. Rev. 671, 704–705 (1999). This may seem far-fetched, but anabolic steroids are now classified as controlled substances in an effort to restrict their use by athletes, and the Federal Food, Drug, and Cosmetic Act contains a little known provision, added by Congress in 1991, that makes it a federal felony to distribute or possess human growth hormone "for any use in humans other than the treatment of disease or other recognized medical condition." 21 U.S.C. § 333(e)(1). How successful would a ban be? Would a black market arise similar to the current black market in illegal substances? Could the government stop citizens from traveling abroad to obtain enhancements that were illegal in the US? See Maxwell J. Mehlman and Kristen Rabe, Any DNA to Declare? Regulating Offshore Access to Genetic Enhancement, 28 American Journal Law & Medicine 179 (2002) (with Kristen Rabe).

6.   Since some forms of genetic enhancement, including in particular methods that altered the germ line, would be likely to require the expertise of health professionals, one regulatory approach would be professional self-regulation. The American Medical Association's Council on Ethical and Judi-

cial Affairs, for example, has issued an ethics opinion stating that "[e]fforts to enhance 'desirable' characteristics through the insertion of a modified or additional gene, or efforts to 'improve' complex human traits—the eugenic development of offspring—are contrary not only to the ethical tradition of medicine but also to the egalitarian values of our society." The statement goes on to assert that "genetic interventions to enhance traits should be considered permissible only in severely restricted situations: (1) clear and meaningful benefits to the fetus or child; (2) no trade-off with other characteristics or traits; and (3) equal access * * * irrespective of income or other socioeconomic characteristics." AMA Council on Ethical and Judicial Affairs, Report on Ethical Issues Related to Prenatal Genetic Tests, 3 Archives Fam. Med. 633, 637–39 (1994). Presumably, a physician who failed to comply with these conditions would be violating the physician's code of professional ethics.

Do these conditions make sense? How is a single physician supposed to ensure "equal access"? Why should a parent be prohibited from deciding that an enhancement is worth a certain price in terms of a trade-off of other characteristics or traits?

For a more thorough discussion of these and other issues relating to biomedical enhancement, see Maxwell J. Mehlman, The Price of Perfection: Individualism and Society in the Era of Biomedical Enhancement (Baltimore: Johns Hopkins University Press 2009).

CHAPTER 11

PARENTAGE AND FAMILY LAW

■ ■ ■

I. INTRODUCTION

Throughout human history, the delicate relations among family members have engendered complex legal disputes. In particular, courts have faced questions about how to characterize the relationship between children and parents. What is the legal status of children? How should parentage be determined, and what rights and responsibilities does it entail? What happens when parents separate or divorce?

Beginning in medieval times and even until the start of the twentieth century, children were viewed as the property of their parents. Under English common law, fathers had primary decision-making authority over children if parents separated. It was not until the last half of the nineteenth century that courts developed the "tender years" doctrine, creating a presumption that young children were better off being reared by their mothers. The "tender years" doctrine was completely abolished by the 1970s when ideas of equality influenced courts to give equal weight to each parent's interests, with the goal being to determine the "best interests of the child."

The legal assignment of parental rights and responsibilities over children has combined both biological and social criteria. For countless generations, maternal rights over children were easy to assign. The woman who gave birth to the child was the legal mother. This concept still prevails in the language of the paternity laws of many states. For example, California has a statutory provision which states that a parent and child relationship may be established "between a child and the natural mother * * * by proof of her having given birth to the child."

Yet, new reproductive technologies are challenging the traditional determination of maternity. It is now possible for an infertile woman to contract with an egg donor and a surrogate mother to bear a child for her. Which of these three mothers—the genetic one, the gestational one, or the social one, should be considered the legal mother? In such cases, assignment of legal maternity relies less on biology and more on social constructs, looking at the intent of the parties prior to conception to deter-

600

mine in whom rights and responsibilities with respect to the child should vest.

With respect to fathers, determination of paternity has been more complicated. In large measure, paternity has been based on social, rather than biological, factors. Paternity statutes generally provide that, if a woman is married, her husband is the father of her child, unless the husband proves he was sterile or had no access to the wife at the time of conception (for example, he was away at sea for months). Now, though, DNA paternity tests can demonstrate to a high degree of certainty (99 + %) who the biological father is, thereby generating questions about whether a biological assignment of fatherhood should replace the social one within marriage. Should the husband be able to authorize DNA testing on the child without the mother's consent in order to determine if he is the biological father? Should such DNA testing only be done by court order? If the couple divorces, should the ex-husband be able to sever ties with a child he reared for years, simply on the grounds that he was not the sperm provider? What about the ex-husband who wants custody of a child with whom he has a loving bond, but who is told by the ex-wife that he should have no rights because he is not actually the child's biological father? Does the social approach to parenthood serve important goals, such as protecting marriages and assuring support for children?

And what about the lover of a married woman, who wants to use DNA testing to gain rights to the child? Should a man be able to gain visitation rights to visit a five year-old with whom he has had no social relationship just because a DNA test says he is the father? Generally, when an unmarried biological father is trying to gain rights to a child, he must show that he has some social relation with that child. In Lehr v. Robertson, 463 U.S. 248 (1983), for example, an unmarried father petitioned to vacate the order of adoption of his two-year-old child by the mother's husband. The biological father, however, had never supported the child nor entered his name into a putative father registry. The Court held that the biological father's due process and equal protection rights were not violated when he was not given notice and an opportunity to be heard before his child was adopted, since the father had never had any significant custodial, personal, or financial relationship with the child.

The matter is entirely different if the issue is not rights, but responsibilities. If a mother is not married, a biological paternity determination is used to establish that a man owes child support to the child. Over the years, paternity testing has evolved to be more accurate. In many early cases, the baby was held in the air in the courtroom and the jury had to assess whether the baby resembled the putative father. Obviously, DNA testing is a more precise way to determine paternity.

DNA testing can play other roles in establishing family relationships. In some countries, it is used to provide evidence of family bonds in the context of immigration. Genetic testing could be used in the adoption setting to determine the fitness of parents—or the potential future health of the children available for adoption. In any of these settings, as with more traditional legal decisions about maternity and paternity, social values will be as important as biological predictions in determining the appropriate legal policies.

II. REASSESSING TRADITIONAL PRESUMPTIONS OF PATERNITY IN THE DNA ERA

MICHAEL H. v. GERALD D.

491 U.S. 110 (1989).

SCALIA, J.

* * *

Under California law, a child born to a married woman living with her husband is presumed to be a child of the marriage. Cal. Evid. Code Ann. § 621 (West Supp. 1989). The presumption of legitimacy may be rebutted only by the husband or wife, and then only in limited circumstances. The instant appeal presents the claim that this presumption infringes upon the due process rights of a man who wishes to establish his paternity of a child born to the wife of another man, and the claim that it infringes upon the constitutional right of the child to maintain a relationship with her natural father.

I.

The facts of this case are, we must hope, extraordinary. On May 9, 1976, in Las Vegas, Nevada, Carole D., an international model, and Gerald D., a top executive in a French oil company, were married. The couple established a home in Playa del Rey, California, in which they resided as husband and wife when one or the other was not out of the country on business. In the summer of 1978, Carole became involved in an adulterous affair with a neighbor, Michael H. In September 1980, she conceived a child, Victoria D., who was born on May 11, 1981. Gerald was listed as father on the birth certificate and has always held Victoria out to the world as his daughter. Soon after delivery of the child, however, Carole informed Michael that she believed he might be the father.

In the first three years of her life, Victoria remained always with Carole, but found herself within a variety of quasifamily units. In October 1981, Gerald moved to New York City to pursue his business interests, but Carole chose to remain in California. At the end of that month, Carole and Michael had blood tests of themselves and Victoria, which showed a 98.07% probability that Michael was Victoria's father. In January 1982, Carole visited Michael in St. Thomas, where his primary business interests were based. There Michael held Victoria out as his child. In March, however, Carole left Michael and returned to California, where she took up residence with yet another man, Scott K. Later that spring, and again in the summer, Carole and Victoria spent time with Gerald in New York City, as well as on vacation in Europe. In the fall, they returned to Scott in California.

In November 1982, rebuffed in his attempts to visit Victoria, Michael filed a filiation action in California Superior Court to establish his paternity and right to visitation.

* * *

On October 19, 1984, Gerald, who had intervened in the action, moved for summary judgment on the ground that under Cal. Evid. Code § 621 there were no triable issues of fact as to Victoria's paternity. This law provides that "the issue of a wife cohabiting with her husband, who is not impotent or sterile, is conclusively presumed to be a child of the marriage." The presumption may be rebutted by blood tests, but only if a motion for such tests is made, within two years from the date of the child's birth, either by the husband or, if the natural father has filed an affidavit acknowledging paternity, by the wife.

On January 28, 1985, having found that affidavits submitted by Carole and Gerald sufficed to demonstrate that the two were cohabiting at conception and birth and that Gerald was neither sterile nor impotent, the Superior Court granted Gerald's motion for summary judgment, rejecting Michael's and Victoria's challenges to the constitutionality of § 621. The court also denied their motions for continued visitation pending the appeal under Cal. Civ. Code § 4601, which provides that a court may, in its discretion, grant "reasonable visitation rights ... to any ... person having an interest in the welfare of the child." It found that allowing such visitation would "violat[e] the intention of the Legislature by impugning the integrity of the family unit."

On appeal, Michael asserted, inter alia, that the Superior Court's application of § 621 had violated his procedural and substantive due process rights. Victoria also raised a due process challenge to the statute, seeking to preserve her de facto relationship with Michael as well as with Gerald. She contended, in addition, that as § 621 allows the husband and, at least to a limited extent, the mother, but not the child, to rebut the presumption of legitimacy, it violates the child's right to equal protection. Finally, she asserted a right to continued visitation with Michael under § 4601. After submission of briefs and a hearing, the California Court of Appeal affirmed the judgment of the Superior Court and upheld the constitutionality of the statute.

* * *

III.

* * *

Michael raises two related challenges to the constitutionality of § 621. First, he asserts that requirements of procedural due process prevent the

State from terminating his liberty interest in his relationship with his child without affording him an opportunity to demonstrate his paternity in an evidentiary hearing. We believe this claim derives from a fundamental misconception of the nature of the California statute. While § 621 is phrased in terms of a presumption, that rule of evidence is the implementation of a substantive rule of law. California declares it to be, except in limited circumstances, *irrelevant* for paternity purposes whether a child conceived during, and born into, an existing marriage was begotten by someone other than the husband and had a prior relationship with him. As the Court of Appeal phrased it:

> " 'The conclusive presumption is actually a substantive rule of law based upon a determination by the Legislature as a matter of overriding social policy, that given a certain relationship between the husband and wife, the husband is to be held responsible for the child, and that the integrity of the family unit should not be impugned.' "

Of course the conclusive presumption not only expresses the State's substantive policy but also furthers it, excluding inquiries into the child's paternity that would be destructive of family integrity and privacy.

* * *

Michael contends as a matter of substantive due process that, because he has established a parental relationship with Victoria, protection of Gerald's and Carole's marital union is an insufficient state interest to support termination of that relationship. This argument is, of course, predicated on the assertion that Michael has a constitutionally protected liberty interest in his relationship with Victoria.

It is an established part of our constitutional jurisprudence that the term "liberty" in the Due Process Clause extends beyond freedom from physical restraint * * *. Without that core textual meaning as a limitation, defining the scope of the Due Process Clause "has at times been a treacherous field for this Court," giving "reason for concern lest the only limits to ... judicial intervention become the predilections of those who happen at the time to be Members of this Court." * * *

In an attempt to limit and guide interpretation of the Clause, we have insisted not merely that the interest denominated as a "liberty" be "fundamental" (a concept that, in isolation, is hard to objectify), but also that it be an interest traditionally protected by our society. As we have put it, the Due Process Clause affords only those protections "so rooted in the traditions and conscience of our people as to be ranked as fundamental." * * * Our cases reflect "continual insistence upon respect for the teachings of history [and] solid recognition of the basic values that underlie our society...."

* * *

It is a question of legislative policy and not constitutional law whether California will allow the presumed parenthood of a couple desiring to retain a child conceived within and born into their marriage to be rebutted.

We do not accept Justice Brennan's criticism [in his dissenting opinion in this case] that this result "squashes" the liberty that consists of "the freedom not to conform." It seems to us that reflects the erroneous view that there is only one side to this controversy—that one disposition can expand a "liberty" of sorts without contracting an equivalent "liberty" on the other side. Such a happy choice is rarely available. Here, to *provide* protection to an adulterous natural father is to *deny* protection to a marital father, and vice versa. If Michael has a "freedom not to conform" (whatever that means), Gerald must equivalently have a "freedom to conform." One of them will pay a price for asserting that "freedom"—Michael by being unable to act as father of the child he has adulterously begotten, or Gerald by being unable to preserve the integrity of the traditional family unit he and Victoria have established. Our disposition does not choose between these two "freedoms," but leaves that to the people of California. Justice Brennan's approach chooses one of them as the constitutional imperative, on no apparent basis except that the unconventional is to be preferred.

IV.

We have never had occasion to decide whether a child has a liberty interest, symmetrical with that of her parent, in maintaining her filial relationship. We need not do so here because, even assuming that such a right exists, Victoria's claim must fail. Victoria's due process challenge is, if anything, weaker than Michael's. Her basic claim is not that California has erred in preventing her from establishing that Michael, not Gerald, should stand as her legal father. Rather, she claims a due process right to maintain filial relationships with both Michael and Gerald. This assertion merits little discussion, for, whatever the merits of the guardian ad litem's belief that such an arrangement can be of great psychological benefit to a child, the claim that a State must recognize multiple fatherhood has no support in the history or traditions of this country. Moreover, even if we were to construe Victoria's argument as forwarding the lesser proposition that, whatever her status vis-à-vis Gerald, she has a liberty interest in maintaining a filial relationship with her natural father, Michael, we find that, at best, her claim is the obverse of Michael's and fails for the same reasons.

Victoria claims in addition that her equal protection rights have been violated because, unlike her mother and presumed father, she had no opportunity to rebut the presumption of her legitimacy. We find this argument wholly without merit. We reject, at the outset, Victoria's suggestion that her equal protection challenge must be assessed under a standard of strict scrutiny because, in denying her the right to maintain a filial relationship with Michael, the State is discriminating against her on the basis of her illegitimacy. Illegitimacy is a legal construct, not a natural trait. Under California law, Victoria is not illegitimate, and she is treated in the same manner as all other legitimate children: she is entitled to maintain a filial relationship with her legal parents.

We apply, therefore, the ordinary "rational relationship" test to Victoria's equal protection challenge. The primary rationale underlying § 621's limitation on those who may rebut the presumption of legitimacy is a concern that allowing persons other than the husband or wife to do so may undermine the integrity of the marital union. When the husband or wife contests the legitimacy of their child, the stability of the marriage has already been shaken. In contrast, allowing a claim of illegitimacy to be pressed by the child—or, more accurately, by a court-appointed guardian ad litem—may well disrupt an otherwise peaceful union. Since it pursues a legitimate end by rational means, California's decision to treat Victoria differently from her parents is not a denial of equal protection.

The judgment of the California Court of Appeal is

Affirmed.

RICHARD WILLING, DNA AND DADDY

USA Today (July 29, 1999), at 1A.

From a billboard above a Baltimore expressway, a very pregnant version of Leonardo da Vinci's Mona Lisa soon will aim her enigmatic smile at motorists.

"Who's The Daddy?" the billboard asks. The ad supplies the phone number of a Baltimore laboratory that uses DNA tests to determine paternity.

These days, not everyone is smiling about using DNA for paternity testing. For men such as Gerald Miscovich, who discovered through a DNA-based paternity test that he had not fathered the boy born during his marriage, the tests are serious business.

"I've spent the last seven years of my life trying to get this sorted out fairly," says Miscovich, 36, a computer programmer who lives near Philadelphia. "The test is just a beginning. You've got to be able to deal with what comes with it."

DNA-based paternity testing is booming, thanks to expanding technology and to laws that require women to name their child's father when applying for public assistance. Aggressive marketing, such as the Mona Lisa campaign that Baltimore's BRT Laboratories has used before and will mount again in October, helps drive the trend.

The tests, which are based on the same DNA technology that police use to catch criminals, are faster, cheaper and more accurate than the old-fashioned blood typing that was state-of-the-art until the late 1980s. DNA-based paternity testing has more than tripled during the past 10 years, to an estimated 247,000 cases in 1998. The new technology is clearing up inheritance controversies, fueling a $100 million annual business and even resolving age-old historical disputes like whether Thomas

Jefferson fathered a child with the slave Sally Hemings. The DNA says he probably did.

"When you think of where we are and where we were just a short time ago, it's nothing short of a revolution," says Howard Coleman, founder of the GeneLex Corp., a Seattle test laboratory. "You want to catch your breath and say, 'What's next?'"

But experts in psychology and in family law are discovering that the phenomenon has a down side.

They say divorces have become more contentious and family ties strained as parents seek to avoid child support payments by testing children. Increasingly, laboratory technicians say, they must offer comfort and counsel to customers who are emotionally devastated by the test results.

Perhaps most significantly, the time-honored legal concept of parenthood, put in place centuries ago to protect children, is being re-evaluated in courtrooms across the country in light of the new testing.

'SIMPLE' TEST HAS SERIOUS REPERCUSSIONS

The old doctrine states that children born to a married woman are deemed to have been fathered by her husband. It makes no allowances for modern tests such as DNA.

"People say that we have a simple test and we ought to let technology decide for us, but there's a real human cost we haven't focused on," says Joan Entmacher, who directs the Family Economic Security Project at the National Women's Law Center in Washington, D.C., a nonprofit organization that represents women in cases involving child support and other issues.

"The technology is a tool, and we should use it when it's useful but take care to see that it's appropriate."

Paternity testing is possible because when a child is conceived, he or she receives two pieces of genetic material, one from the mother and one from the father. If a gene is present that cannot be traced to the mother, it must be the father's. For years, scientists used red blood cells and blood antigens to exclude potential fathers and to identify the correct gene donor.

But blood typing was expensive—about $800 to $1,200 for a family— as well as slow and limited. It required blood to be drawn from mother, child and potential father, and the blood needed to be used quickly. And the accuracy was open to challenge.

The development of DNA analysis in the 1980s moved the science forward in a quantum jump. DNA, the cellular acid that contains an individual's genetic code, could now be examined directly, and fatherhood could be determined with a better than 99% probability. The tests, which cost $450 to $600 a family, can be completed within days and can use samples collected by mouth swabs as well as blood samples.

* * *

AN EXPLOSION IN DNA SUCCESS STORIES

Business has taken off. In 1988, the nation's labs performed 75,716 paternity tests, according to the American Association of Blood Banks, the national accrediting group. Most of those tests were blood tests. Last year's estimated 247,000 tests almost exclusively relied on DNA.

The success stories came quickly: The number of fathers acknowledging paternity tripled, from 512,000 in 1992 to 1.5 million last year, according to the U.S. Department of Health and Human Services. It is not known exactly how many of those cases were resolved through paternity testing, though the labs say the number rises every year.

"Men want to do the right thing, but they don't want to be fooled," says Neal Hurowitz of Philadelphia, who specializes in marital law. "Nowadays, you can get tested, know where you stand and make arrangements for the child, all without the adversarial situation of being pulled into court. And men are doing just that."

DNA testing has helped resolve inheritance disputes and clear up family mix-ups, including some celebrated cases:

> Last year, DNA testing helped a Virginia couple show that the University of Virginia Medical Center had sent them home with another family's baby. The mother who had the DNA test, Paula Johnson, is now suing for custody of both children.

> The children of four Filipino, Vietnamese and Micronesian bar girls have begun to share in the $500 million estate of air freight mogul Larry Hillblom, who died without marrying any of the mothers.

> Using a variation of the standard paternity test, descendants of a slave owned by George Washington's half-brother are attempting to verify an old family tale: that the Father of Our Country was their literal ancestor, too.

* * *

But not all the stories are happy ones. In about a third of the welfare cases and 10% of other cases, lab directors say that the father named by the mother turns out not to be the biological parent.

Caskey, of Houston's Identigene lab, prepares test candidates by warning them of the possibility that the results could be disturbing, particularly because the science of DNA is considered so accurate. "I want to make sure they want to go through with it," she says.

At Baltimore's BRT Laboratories, which sponsors the Mona Lisa billboard, molecular biologist Frank Chiafari recently found himself counseling a civil servant who learned that his teen-age son had been fathered by another man.

"He broke down and cried; it was pretty awful," Chiafari recalls.

"His wife, like people do sometimes, had dropped a reference to it in anger, so he decided to check it out. (Before DNA–based testing,) he probably would have let it go."

* * *

'DOUBLE BLOW' FOR A DIVORCED FATHER

Gerald Miscovich's experience with DNA testing is especially compelling. During a visit with Gerald Jr. in 1992, two years after his marriage ended, Miscovich noted that the boy, then 4, had brown eyes. Both Miscovich and his former wife had blue eyes, making a brown-eyed child nearly impossible. A DNA–based paternity test confirmed that another man was Gerald Jr.'s father.

"It was a double blow," Miscovich says. "That my wife had stepped outside the marriage, and that my son wasn't my son."

To Miscovich's surprise, a Pennsylvania court nevertheless ordered him to pay his ex-wife $537 a month in child support. The court relied on a 500–year-old English common-law doctrine that presumes a child born in a marriage is the offspring of the spouses, unless the husband is impotent or can show he was abroad at the time of conception.

"The law is designed for the economic protection of children," says Jane Mattes, a New York psychotherapist and specialist in single mothers. In medieval England, "a child shown to be illegitimate would have virtually no rights."

Miscovich fought an unsuccessful seven-year battle to have the court order revoked. He gave up in May when the U.S. Supreme Court declined to hear his appeal.

"Certainly protect the child, but do it by requiring the man who produced him to pay," Miscovich says.

STATES BEGINNING TO CHANGE THEIR LAWS

Miscovich's ex-wife has remarried, and he has had no contact with Gerald Jr. for the past seven years. He says he would have liked to have played "some part" in the boy's life but was advised that to do so would have undercut his case. Telephone calls to a lawyer for Miscovich's former wife were not returned.

"This was good law for centuries, but that was before DNA and trans–Atlantic travel and other things that can make mockery out of the idea that a woman can only be pregnant by her husband," says Miscovich's lawyer, Neal Hurowitz. "The law has got to catch up."

THAT PROCESS IS UNDER WAY

In about two-thirds of the states, judges now allow DNA–based paternity testing to be admitted as evidence in child custody cases, though they are not bound to let deceived husbands off the hook for payments. Massachusetts permits husbands to file affidavits stating that a child was fathered by another man. And an Oregon judge recently granted a rare order excusing an ex-husband from child support payments after DNA tests excluded him as the father of his former wife's young son.

NOT EVERYONE LIKES THE TREND

"Are we saying that if you cared for a child for 15 years, (a test) is then going to make you walk away?" Entmacher says. "It does force you to think what it means to be a parent."

LACH v. WELCH

1997 WL 536330 (Conn. Super. Ct. 1997).

Memorandum of Decision Re: Motion to Cite in Party Defendant and Motion for Genetic Testing

DRANGINIS, J.

On October 21, 1993, the plaintiff, Shannon Lach, commenced this paternity action against the defendant, Richard J. Welch, as administrator of the estate of Michael R. Welch. Pursuant to General Statutes 46b–160, the plaintiff seeks an adjudication of paternity of Kaitlyn Ruddy, her minor child. Kaitlyn was born out of wedlock on November 12, 1990. In her petition, the plaintiff alleges that Kaitlyn was fathered by Michael Welch, who lived with the plaintiff from January 1990, through and including April 1990. On June 1, 1991, prior to the commencement of any paternity proceedings, Michael Welch died as the result of an automobile accident.

Presently before the court are two motions. The first is a motion to cite in Patricia Welch, Michael's mother, claiming that she is a necessary party to a determination of paternity and estate distribution. The second motion seeks genetic testing of Patricia Welch, Richard Welch, the plaintiff and the minor child to determine whether Michael is Kaitlyn's father. The plaintiff filed memoranda of law in support of both motions.

The attorney for the minor child filed a brief in support of both motions requesting that the court grant both motions and consider adding the defendant, Richard J. Welch, in his individual capacity. In the alternative, or in addition to DNA testing of the putative grandparents, counsel for the minor child seeks an order of exhumation of the body of the deceased putative father for purposes of genetic testing.

The defendant filed objections to both the motion to cite in Patricia Welch and the motion for genetic testing along with supporting memoranda. The defendant, however, did not object to the request for exhumation of the body of the deceased putative father for purposes of genetic testing beyond claiming that the court lacks subject matter jurisdiction to determine paternity after the death of the putative father.

I. MOTION TO CITE IN PARTY DEFENDANT

* * *

The defendant argues that Patricia Welch has no interest in the present case in controversy whereas the plaintiff argues that Patricia Welch, as an heir to her deceased son's estate, does have an interest in the paternity determination because any disposition of the intestate estate will be affected if Kaitlyn is Michael's child.

This court finds that Patricia Welch is an indispensable party to this paternity action * * *. Although the question of the decedent's estate is not at issue in the present case, Patricia Welch's interest in the paternity action is that her share in the intestate succession of her deceased son's estate will be affected if Kaitlyn is found to be the daughter of Michael Welch.

* * *

The defendant also argues that General Statutes 46b–160 allows for commencement of paternity proceedings by "service on the putative father of a verified petition. . . ." Accordingly, the defendant argues, the statute is devoid of any provision for service on any party defendant other than the putative father and nothing else in chapter 825y provides vehicle for bringing a paternity action against anyone but the putative father. Thus, the defendant argues, the motion to add Patricia Welch as a party defendant should be denied.

* * *

In essence, the defendant is arguing that Patricia Welch cannot be added as a party because there is only one individual that is subject to a paternity action and that is the putative father. The court finds this argument unpersuasive especially in light of its previous holdings regarding posthumous paternity determinations.

Additionally, the defendant argues that Patricia Welch has no legal duty nor suffers any penalty in her capacity as the putative grandmother, and is thus immune from liability. Under General Statutes 52–102, "no person who is immune from liability shall be made a defendant in the controversy." Aside from setting forth the language of the statute and a definition of immunity as taken from Black's Law Dictionary, the defendant offers no authority to support the immunity argument. This court was not able to uncover any authority one way or the other on the issue of possible immunity under the circumstances of this case.

Lastly, the defendant argues that her presence is not necessary for a complete determination of any question involved in this action because DNA testing is not the only method possible to resolve plaintiff's claims equitably. Thus, Patricia Welch is not necessary within the meaning of

General Statutes 52–102. As stated above, this court finds Patricia Welch to be, not only necessary, but indispensable to this paternity action. Although this court recognizes that exhumation of the deceased putative father provides an alternate to DNA testing on Richard and Patricia Welch, it also recognizes the inherent proof problems of posthumous DNA testing and in fairness to all parties grants the motion to cite in Patricia Welch as a party defendant and adds Richard J. Welch in his individual capacity as requested by counsel for the minor child.

II. MOTION FOR GENETIC TESTING

The plaintiff has moved for genetic testing of the plaintiff, the minor child, Patricia and Richard Welch. Counsel for the minor child has joined in this motion and requests, as an alternative, exhumation of the body of the deceased putative father for purposes of DNA testing. The defendant objected to the request for DNA testing of Michael and Patricia Welch.

Modern scientific tests can determine, with nearly perfect accuracy, who is the true biological father of a child.

* * *

When both parents of the child are tested, the possibility of paternity, as expressed in a percentage, will either approach one hundred percent or zero percent.

When one parent is unavailable, as in the present case, DNA fingerprinting may also be utilized to effectively establish a "probability" of paternity by testing relatives of the unavailable parent. The DNA "print" of a father, mother, or other relative of the deceased putative father can be compared to the DNA prints of the child and the available mother to determine whether the parties are related. Although the process can not be deemed conclusive, it has been recognized by the scientific community as quite valuable.

* * *

Furthermore, other courts, including one state Supreme Court has recognized the reliability of testing relatives for purposes of establishing paternity. In Sudwischer v. Estate of Hoffpauir, 589 So. 2d 474 (La.1991), cert. denied sub nom., Estate of Hoffpauir v. Sudwisher, 504 U.S. 909 (1992), the Supreme Court of Louisiana affirmed an order that the legitimate daughter of a deceased father provide a blood test to determine the paternity of an illegitimate daughter. The court reasoned that the DNA fingerprinting of the legitimate daughter would produce relevant evidence which could establish the probability of a relationship between the deceased legitimate daughter and the illegitimate daughter. The DNA expert testified that the probability of the relationship could be as low as one in five or as high as one in a hundred thousand.

* * *

In consideration of the scientific techniques available to determine paternity, this court will not deny Kaitlyn the right to prove her paternity so that she may equitably share in her father's estate. The plaintiff's motion for genetic testing is granted. The plaintiff, minor child, Patricia and Richard Welch are hereby ordered to submit to DNA testing. In addition, the court orders exhumation of the body of Michael Welch for purposes of conducting DNA testing.

NOTES AND QUESTIONS

1. What was the social policy behind a statute providing that the husband of a woman is presumed to be the father of her child? Is assignment of paternity based on DNA testing a preferable approach?

2. Courts are currently struggling with the question of whether a genetic test indicating a high probability of paternity should trump other means of establishing legal fatherhood. Previously, social factors were considered in determining fatherhood. Courts considered it to be in the best interests of the child for the husband of the woman who gave birth to be declared the legal father. If the woman was not married and either she or the state wanted to assert that a man was the legal father, legal fatherhood was assigned based on the man's biological connection to the child. However, in situations in which the child had passed infancy, and the unwed mother wanted to give the child to a stranger for adoption or have the child adopted by her subsequent spouse and the biological father objected, a mere biological bond was insufficient for the man to establish paternity. He needed to show that he had a relationship with the child. Now questions have arisen whether genetic paternity testing with its high level of accuracy should change that scheme.

The various means of assigning legal fatherhood came into conflict in the case of N.A.H. and A.H. v. S.L.S., 9 P.3d 354 (Colo. 2000). A married woman conceived a child in an affair with a co-worker. Her husband believed he was the biological father and began raising the child. However, his wife left the child for 10 hours a week with the biological father and let him take the child on a week-long trip to meet his relatives. When the child was one-and-a-half years old, the mother abruptly terminated the biological father's visitation and he sued for a determination of his parent-child relationship with the child. Thus, the husband became aware that he was not the biological father.

The Colorado Supreme Court noted that both DNA testing and marriage to the woman created rebuttable presumptions of paternity. The court said DNA testing is the most accurate way to determine paternity "unless this presumption is outweighed by consideration of public policy." The court reversed the magistrate's order to declare the biological father to be the legal father (which had included an order to change the child's name and work with a psychologist to integrate the biological father into the child's life). Instead, the court held parenthood should be determined by the "best interests of the child." The married couple was unsuccessful in arguing that the best interest standards should be applied earlier—before a decision to order paternity testing is made by the court in the first place. The dissenting justices in the case urged that DNA paternity testing in and of itself should determine legal parenthood.

3.   In Evelyn H. v. David H., 729 N.Y.S.2d 570 (N.Y.Sup.2000), a divorce proceeding, a mother and her children were ordered by the court to submit to DNA testing to establish paternity even though the court recognized that the testing was not in the best interests of the children. Should a court order be necessary for such testing? Should a presumed father be able to get DNA testing without the mother's knowledge or consent? Would this invade the mother's privacy? In Identigene, Inc. v. Goff, 774 So.2d 48 (Fla. App. 2000), a mother sued a DNA testing company for various intentional torts for taking a saliva sample from her minor son without her consent. The case was dismissed for lack of personal jurisdiction over the company.

4.   What if a woman's husband wants custody of the children despite learning through DNA testing that he is not the biological father? In Moss v. Moss, 2000 WL 1349242 (Ark. App. 2000), an ex-husband won custody in such a situation under a best interests analysis. In In re Marriage of Slayton, 685 N.E.2d 1038 (Ill. App. 1997) an ex-husband was granted visitation rights for a child he had previously believed to be his son based on the best interests of the child. In Karen P. v. Christopher J.B., 878 A.2d 646 (Md. Ct. Spec. App. 2005), a man was awarded custody of his biological son and non-biological daughter even though he had not been married to the children's mother. The mother took both children from school and moved from Maryland to New Jersey upon filing for divorce, and the man did not learn that he might not be the daughter's father until the divorce proceedings. The court determined that granting the father custody, with visitation from the mother, was in the best interests of the children. But, in Killingbeck v. Killingbeck, 711 N.W.2d 759 (Mich. Ct. App. 2005), the court did not award parental rights to the father. In that case, a man married a woman with whom he thought he had fathered a child. After their divorce, DNA paternity testing revealed that he was not the biological father of the child. The court refused to apply an equitable parent doctrine to grant rights to the man because he had not been married to the child's mother at the time of the child's conception.

5.   Should paternity be relitigated each time an improved test is available? See S.C.G. v. J.G.Y., 794 So.2d 399 (Ala. Civ. App. 2000). The biological mother of the child filed a paternity action against two men she thought could be the father of her child. Human leukocyte antigen (H.L.A.) testing [a 95% accurate test which examines proteins found on the surface of white blood cells] indicated that both men were excluded from being the father of the child. Seven years later, one of the men who had the H.L.A. testing submitted to DNA testing, and it was found 99.9% sure that he was the father of the child. When the mother requested the paternity case be reopened based on scientific evidence, the court was not willing to do so. The court held that reopening the paternity action would not be in the best interests of the child.

6.   A man who thinks he is the father of a child may learn through genetic disease testing that he is not. In one case, a seven-year-old boy was diagnosed with cystic fibrosis. Since he was not a carrier of the cystic fibrosis gene, the boy's "father" realized that his "son" was not his biological child. However, the court did not let him reopen his earlier divorce case because

even though he knew his wife had been unfaithful, he had not sought paternity testing at the time of the divorce. Wise v. Fryar, 49 S.W.3d 450 (Tex. App. 2001).

7. French actor Yves Montand died in 1991. In 1994, a court declared that he was the father of a teenager, based on evidence that he'd had an affair with the girl's mother, and based on the resemblance between the girl and him (she smiled the same sardonic way he did and looked through half-closed eyes). When Montand's heirs appealed the ruling, the higher court ordered his body exhumed for DNA testing. The testing found that the girl was not his child. The decision to exhume the corpse offended the French secretary of state for health and has led to calls to ban posthumous paternity testing.

8. Was it appropriate to undertake DNA testing to determine the likelihood that Thomas Jefferson fathered a child with his slave Sally Hemings? See Eugene A. Foster, et al., Jefferson Fathered Slave's Last Child, 396 Nature 27 (1998). What are the potential issues with conducting such studies? The authors of the study published in *Nature* quickly came under criticism for failing to fully consider the possible paternity of other male relatives of Thomas Jefferson who lived in the area and could have had a relationship with Sally Hemings. See Eugene A. Foster, et al., Reply: The Thomas Jefferson Paternity Case, 397 Nature 32 (1999). Was such criticism justified?

9. Should genetic analysis be done on deceased individuals' tissue to determine if they fathered existing children? In Anne R. v. Estate of Francis C., 634 N.Y.S.2d 339 (N.Y. Fam. Ct. 1995), the court ordered DNA testing on a deceased individual's frozen blood sample. In Malone ex rel. Randolph v. Burnhart, 2004 WL 1794912 (N.D. Ill. 2004), an administrative law judge in the Social Security Administration did not admit a DNA test using a one-year-old sample from the decedent's autopsied organs to establish paternity because of concerns about scientific validity, but a federal magistrate reversed the decision.

10. Should genetic testing be done only if a sample of the putative father's DNA is available short of disinterment of his corpse (for example, through analysis of a hair follicle from a comb or a blood sample at a hospital)? Should disinterment be allowed only if the child is still alive and needs financial support? Consider the case of In re Estate of Nasert, 748 N.Y.S.2d 654 (N.Y. Sur. Ct. 2002), in which DNA testing was performed on the decedent's willing identical twin to establish whether the decedent had fathered a child.

11. Should a lawyer advise the executor of a client's estate to destroy DNA samples to avoid posthumous paternity tests? After the death of millionaire Larry Hillblom, his mistress purportedly buried his hairbrush, toothbrush, and clothes on the advice of his business consultants in order to prevent posthumous paternity testing. AP, Dead Millionaire's Belongings Found Buried, Chicago Tribune, Aug. 23, 1998 at 6.

12. What are the arguments for and against a court ordering DNA testing on a deceased putative father's parents or legitimate children in order to assess paternity? Should the answer depend on the accuracy of the test? Should testing only be allowed if the parents or legitimate child will inherit

from the estate and therefore might be reluctant to volunteer for such testing due to a financial conflict of interest?

13. Some states set time bars on paternity actions by children. In Rushford v. Caines, 2001 WL 310006 (Ohio App.10 Dist. 2001), a woman in her 40's learned through an anonymous note that a man who died testate might be her biological father. She brought an action in probate court to release the decedent's DNA for testing, but the court applied a provision of the Ohio paternity statute that bars an action brought by a child more than five years after the child reaches age 18. The court was unpersuaded by her argument that the statute of limitations should have been tolled during the period she did not know that the decedent might be her biological father.

14. DNA testing for parentage was put to a new use recently by Major League Baseball. After several scandals in which foreign athletes playing for U.S. teams claimed to be younger than they were, the MLB established an investigative team to subject potential players and their family members to bone scans and DNA testing. The MLB's vice president of investigation, Dan Mullin, dispatches investigators to the Dominican Republic to verify birth certificates, school records, and hospital records. However, according to Mullin, these documents are neither certified nor notarized. Players have been known to assume the identity of younger siblings or of a younger child of a neighboring family, just to appear two or three years younger. Because of this uncertainty, MLB investigators ordered bone scans of the player and his siblings in conjunction with DNA tests of the family to confirm a familial relationship and the age of the player. Michael S. Schmidt & Alan Schwarz, Baseball's Use of DNA Raises Questions, The New York Times at A1, July 22, 2009, http://www.nytimes.com/2009/07/22/sports/baseball/22dna.html?_r=1

Even if the investigators only test the DNA sample for parentage, the results could be inconclusive and cause negative psychological impacts. This kind of DNA test will only show if a child's parents are who he claims them to be; it cannot rule out the possibility that an athlete is assuming the role of a younger sibling. As The New York Times article points out, there is possibility that the child could learn that his parents are not who he thought they were. In addition to the psychological trauma of learning that the person the player thought was his father is not actually his dad, the player would probably not be signed because he would "fail" the DNA test.

15. For information on the ethical, legal, and social implications of DNA-based paternity testing, see Mark A. Rothstein et al., Genetic Ties and the Family (2005).

III. GENETICS AND SWITCHED BABIES
MAYS v. TWIGG
543 So.2d 241 (Fla. Dist. Ct. App. 1989).

PATTERSON, J.

Robert and Kimberly Mays petition this court for a writ of certiorari to review a non-final order of the circuit court entered in the course of an ongoing suit for declaratory relief. We grant the petition.

The facts surrounding this case are exceptionally delicate and unique. The respondents, Ernest and Regina Twigg, have alleged that some ten years ago staff personnel at Hardee Memorial Hospital, Wauchula, switched their healthy newborn daughter with one born on approximately the same date to Robert Mays' late wife, Barbara, and that both couples went on to raise children not actually their own natural offspring. The child raised by the Twiggs, Arlena Beatrice, later died from a congenital heart condition. Shortly before Arlena's death the Twiggs learned, based on the child's blood type, that neither of them could have been her biological parent. Kimberly Mays was the only other white female in occupancy at Hardee Memorial Hospital at the time of Arlena's birth.

Respondents began the underlying litigation by filing a "Petition for Order Compelling Blood Test to Confirm Paternity of Female Child," later substituting a complaint for declaratory relief. The amended complaint demands a declaration that Kimberly Mays is the Twiggs' natural biological child.

We hold that in cases such as this, before a putative father may obtain discovery relating to the paternity of the child, he must first prove the requisite standing to go forward with the suit * * *. Admittedly, natural parents have certain presumptive rights of custody as to their offspring. Those rights, however, are not absolute. Children are not property, but individuals whose needs and physical and mental well-being find protection in the law. The cases dealing with custody contests between a natural parent and a third party are replete with declarations that the privilege of custody of the natural parent must yield if such custody will be detrimental to the welfare of the child.

The facts of this case demand the application of the bifurcated procedure of *Van Nostrand* [v. Olivieri, 427 So. 2d 374 (Fla. 2d Dist. Ct. App. 1983)]. The same rights of privacy and freedom from unjustified humiliation and psychological damage are present. Before permitting further discovery on the issue of the paternity of Kimberly Mays, the trial court must first determine the standing of the Twiggs to go forward; in effect, a determination of probability that the Twiggs will prevail. If the trial court finds that the ultimate relief sought should not be granted because of probable detrimental effects upon the child, no additional discovery on the issue of paternity should be allowed.

This conclusion requires us to go further and consider the propriety of the trial court's denial of the Mays' motion to dismiss. The problem simply stated is that the Amended Complaint does not set forth the ultimate relief sought, and, therefore, the court below cannot determine whether or not it would have such a detrimental effect on the child that it should be denied. The Amended Complaint prays that the trial court declare Kimberly Mays to be the "natural biological child" of the Twiggs. The interests of the child, which we consider paramount in this case, require that the trial judge be without doubt as to why the declaration is demanded. In this respect the pleading is fatally defective.

Section 86.011(2) Florida Statutes (1987) provides that the circuit courts of this state have jurisdiction to render declaratory judgments on the existence or nonexistence of "any fact upon which the existence or nonexistence of [any] immunity, power, privilege or right, does or may depend." The complaint must define the immunity, power, privilege or right to which the declaration is pertinent and should allege an actual need for the declaration. The relief sought cannot be merely to satisfy the curiosity of the plaintiff. A complaint which states, or as in this case, implies that a dispute between the parties as to specific rights may occur in the future, does not state a cause of action for declaratory relief. In considering a motion to dismiss, the trial court must confine itself to the allegations within the four corners of the complaint. The allegations of the original complaint seeking a determination of paternity cannot be used to bolster the amended complaint which does not seek such relief. We are mindful that review of the denial of a motion to dismiss by certiorari is not favored; however, we find it necessary here due to the unusual nature of the action.

Accordingly, we quash the lower court's order of December 19, 1988, in its entirety. The amended complaint stands dismissed with leave to amend. Upon the resumption of the action, we direct the circuit court to permit no further discovery except as in accord with this opinion.

PERRY–ROGERS v. FASANO

276 A.D.2d 67 (N.Y. App. Div. 2000).

SAXE, J.

This appeal concerns a tragic mix-up at a fertility clinic through which a woman became a "gestational mother" to another couple's embryo, when the embryo was mistakenly implanted into the wrong woman's uterus. Since a determination of the issues presented may have far-ranging consequences, we attempt here to ensure that our holding is appropriately limited.

FACTS

In April 1998, plaintiffs Deborah Perry–Rogers and Robert Rogers began an in vitro fertilization and embryo transfer program with the In Vitro Fertility Center of New York. However, in the process, embryos consisting entirely of the Rogerses' genetic material were mistakenly implanted into the uterus of defendant Donna Fasano, along with embryos from Ms. Fasano's and her husband's genetic material. It is undisputed that on May 28, 1998 both couples were notified of the mistake and of the need for DNA and amniocentesis tests. The Rogerses further allege, and the Fasanos do not deny, that the Fasanos were unresponsive to the Rogerses' efforts to contact them.

On December 29, 1998, Donna Fasano gave birth to two male infants, of two different races. One, a white child, is concededly the Fasanos' biological child, named Vincent Fasano. The other, initially named Joseph

Fasano, is a black child, who subsequent tests confirmed to be the Rogerses' biological son, now known as Akeil Richard Rogers.

The Fasanos took no action regarding the clinic's apparent error until the Rogerses, upon discovering that Ms. Fasano had given birth to a child who could be theirs, located and commenced an action against them.

PROCEDURAL HISTORY OF THE LITIGATION

On March 12, 1999, the Rogerses commenced a Supreme Court action against the Fasanos as well as the fertility clinic and its doctors. As against the medical defendants, the complaint alleged medical malpractice and breach of contract; as against the Fasanos, it sought a declaratory judgment declaring the rights, obligations and relationships of the parties concerning Akeil.

On April 1 and April 2, 1999, DNA testing was conducted. The results of the test, issued on April 13, 1999, established that the Rogerses were the genetic parents of Akeil. However, according to Ms. Perry–Rogers, the Fasanos agreed to relinquish custody of Akeil to the Rogerses only upon the execution of a written agreement, which entitled the Fasanos to future visitation with Akeil. Ms. Perry–Rogers states that during the period between Akeil's birth on December 29, 1998 and May 10, 1999, the Fasanos only permitted her two brief visits with Akeil, and that she felt compelled to sign the agreement in order to gain custody of her son. The agreement, executed April 29, 1999, contains a visitation schedule providing for visits one full weekend per month, one weekend day each month, one week each summer, and alternating holidays. The agreement also contained a liquidated damages clause, providing that a violation of the Fasanos' visitation rights under the agreement would entitle them to $200,000.

On May 5, 1999 the Fasanos signed affidavits acknowledging that the Rogerses were the genetic parents of the infant, and consenting to the entry of a final order of custody of the child in favor of the Rogerses and to an amendment of the birth certificate naming the Rogerses as the biological and legal parents of the infant. On May 10, 1999, the Fasanos turned over custody of Akeil to the Rogerses, and the following day, May 11, 1999, counsel for the parties signed a stipulation discontinuing with prejudice the plenary action as against the Fasanos.

Despite the discontinuance, by order to show cause dated May 25, 1999, using the same index number of the plenary action, the Rogerses served a petition seeking a declaratory judgment against the Fasanos, naming the Rogerses as Akeil's legal and biological parents, granting them sole and exclusive custody, and permitting them to amend the birth certificate to reflect Akeil's biological heritage. Their application made no mention of the April 29, 1999 visitation agreement. The Fasanos submitted no opposition to the application, and the court granted the application without opposition in a decision dated June 7, 1999, directing settlement of an order.

The Fasanos then sought vacatur of the June 7, 1999 decision on the grounds that the Rogerses had failed to inform the court of the April 29, 1999 agreement, which they contended was a condition precedent to the signing of an order. The Fasanos proposed, in the alternative, a counterorder which specifically acknowledged the visitation agreement.

Although on July 16, 1999, the motion court signed the Rogerses' proposed order, which made no mention of the April 29, 1999 visitation agreement, at the same time the motion court "So Ordered" those paragraphs in the April 29, 1999 agreement which provided for visitation by the Fasanos.

The Rogerses assert that over the next few months, the IAS [International Adoption Services] Court issued oral "visitation orders" in apparent reliance upon the visitation agreement, and directed that a full forensic psychological evaluation of the parties and their infants be conducted by two sets of mental health experts. On January 14, 2000, the IAS Court granted the Fasanos visitation with the child every other weekend.

The Rogerses now challenge the court's January 14, 2000 visitation order. For their part, the Fasanos appeal from the order of July 16, 1999 giving the Rogerses custody of the child, contending that in view of the discontinuance and the failure to thereafter properly commence a new custody proceeding, the court lacked jurisdiction as well as statutory authority to award custody.

* * *

SUBJECT MATTER JURISDICTION AND STANDING

The Rogerses suggest that the Supreme Court lacks subject matter jurisdiction over this dispute because the Fasanos are "genetic strangers" to Akeil. We decline to dispose of the Fasanos' claim on this basis alone. The Supreme Court of the State of New York has subject matter jurisdiction over petitions for custody and visitation pursuant to both the Domestic Relations Law and the Family Court Act.

This is not to say that the Fasanos necessarily have standing to seek visitation with Akeil. However, on this issue we will not simply adopt the Rogerses' suggestion that no gestational mother may ever claim visitation with the infant she carried, in view of her status as a "genetic stranger" to the infant. In recognition of current reproductive technology, the term "genetic stranger" alone can no longer be enough to end a discussion of this issue. Additional considerations may be relevant for an initial threshold analysis of who is, or may be, a "parent."

In referring to the rights and responsibilities of parents, the laws of this State, as well as the commentaries and case law, often use the term "natural parents," as distinguished from adoptive parents, stepparents, and foster parents. Until recently, there was no question as to who was a child's "natural" mother. It was the woman in whose uterus the child was conceived and borne.

It was only with the recent advent of in vitro fertilization technology that it became possible to divide between two women the functions that traditionally defined a mother, at least prenatally. With this technology, a troublesome legal dilemma has arisen: when one woman's fertilized eggs are implanted in another, which woman is the child's "natural" mother?

Although the technology is still fairly new, several cases have been decided that focus on competing claims to child custody arising out of the use of in vitro fertilization technology. These cases are not dispositive here, since visitation rights rather than custody is at issue. However, they contain analysis that provides important background for the issues raised on this appeal.

In Johnson v. Calvert (851 P.2d 776 (Cal.1993), cert. denied 510 U.S. 874 (1993)), a surrogate mother, unrelated genetically to the child she had carried, declined to give the child to its genetic parents upon its birth, as had been agreed in a surrogacy contract. While "recogniz[ing] both genetic consanguinity and giving birth as means of establishing a mother and child relationship," the California Supreme Court concluded that "when the two means do not coincide in one woman, she who intended to procreate the child—that is, she who intended to bring about the birth of a child that she intended to raise as her own—is the natural mother under California law." It therefore affirmed an award of custody to the genetic parents.

The Second Department applied this "intent" analysis to the converse situation, to recognize the parental rights of a gestational mother who had carried a fetus created from the egg of an anonymous donor which was fertilized with her husband's sperm (see, McDonald v. McDonald, 196 A.D.2d 7 (N.Y.App.Div.1994)). The Court rejected the father's position, in the context of a divorce proceeding, that as "the 'only genetic and natural parent available,'" his claim to custody was superior to that of his wife, and held that the gestational mother was legally the mother of the child to whom she had given birth.

While the foregoing cases are not directly on point, since they deal with a gestational, nongenetic mother's asserted right to be regarded as the infant's sole natural mother, a claim for visitation by a gestational mother and her family also requires examination and clarification of their legal relationship to the child.

It is apparent from the foregoing cases that a "gestational mother" may possess enforceable rights under the law, despite her being a "genetic stranger" to the child. Given the complex possibilities in these kinds of circumstances, it is simply inappropriate to render any determination solely as a consequence of genetics.

Parenthetically, it is worth noting that even if the Fasanos had claimed the right to custody of the child, application of the "intent" analysis suggested in Professor Hill's article, and employed in Johnson v. Calvert and McDonald v. McDonald would—in our view—require that custody be awarded to the Rogerses. It was they who purposefully arranged for their genetic material to be taken and used in order to attempt to create their own child, whom they intended to rear.

Standing to Seek Visitation

To establish their claim that the Fasanos lack standing, the Rogerses focus upon the strict limits of New York statutory and case law regarding who may seek visitation. Under New York statutory law, the only people who have the right to seek visitation are parents, grandparents and siblings related by whole or half-blood. The Rogerses rely on the proposition that because the statutes must be strictly construed, they must be interpreted to preclude the Fasanos from within their framework. Specifically, they suggest that by their act of ceding Akeil to the Rogerses, the child's genetic parents, the Fasanos have surrendered any conceivable right to the parental status necessary to claim visitation rights.

We agree that under the circumstances presented, the Fasanos lack standing under Domestic Relations Law § 70 to seek visitation as the child's parents. However, this is not because we necessarily accept the broad premise that in *any* situation where a parent, possessed of that status by virtue of having borne and given birth to the child, acknowledges another couple's entitlement to the status of parent by virtue of their having provided the genetic materials that created the child, the birth parent automatically gives up all parental rights.

Rather, we recognize that in these rather unique circumstances, where the Rogerses' embryo was implanted in Donna Fasano by mistake, and where the Fasanos knew of the error not long after it occurred, the happenstance of the Fasanos' nominal parenthood over Akeil should have been treated as a mistake to be corrected as soon as possible, *before the development of a parental relationship*. It bears more similarity to a mix-up at the time of a hospital's discharge of two newborn infants, which should simply be corrected at once, than to one where a gestational mother has arguably the same rights to claim parentage as the genetic mother. Under such circumstances, the Fasanos will not be heard to claim the status of parents, entitled to seek an award of visitation.

Additionally, the Fasanos' child, Vincent, is not a sibling "by half or whole blood" with the right to proceed under Domestic Relations Law § 71, since the statute makes no reference to "gestational siblings."

In addition to the absence of statutory support for the Fasanos' visitation application, the policy underlying two important visitation cases in this State militates against their position as well. Even though, as we have noted, it is inaccurate to refer to a child's gestational mother as a "biological stranger," the strong policy considerations behind these cases, in which the Court considered visitation claims by "biological strangers," apply here. Where a child is properly in the custody of parents, it has been repeatedly held, those parents are accorded extremely broad rights to exclude any visitation, *even by a person who has raised and nurtured the child as his or her own*.

APPLICABILITY OF A "BEST INTERESTS" APPROACH

* * *

In the present case, any bonding on the part of Akeil to his gestational mother and her family was the direct result of the Fasanos' failure to take timely action upon being informed of the clinic's admitted error. Defendants cannot be permitted to purposefully act in such as way as to create a bond, and then rely upon it for their assertion of rights to which they would not otherwise be entitled.

Nor may the parties' visitation agreement form the basis for a court order of visitation. "[A] voluntary agreement ... will not of itself confer standing upon a person not related by blood to assert a legal claim to visitation or custody".

Finally, the circumstances presented, tragic as they are, do not form the basis for application of the doctrine of equitable estoppel to prevent the Rogerses from challenging the Fasanos' standing to seek visitation.

NOTES AND QUESTIONS

1. What factors should be taken into consideration when determining whether biological parents should have a right to custody, visitation, or information about their biological child who was mistakenly given as an embryo to another couple? Should these factors differ if the child was mistakenly switched after birth?

2. In 2009, Carolyn Savage and her husband Sean learned that a fertility clinic had mistakenly implanted the wrong embryo in her. The Savages say that their doctor told them that if they did not abort, the law would require her to give the child over to the other couple. Since the couple's moral beliefs precluded abortion, they turned over the child to the genetic parents. For information on the case, see Janet Romaker and Tom Troy, Sylvania Township Mom who Received Wrong Embryo Gives Birth to a Boy, Toledo Blade, (September 26, 2009). Can you think of any legal arguments that would have allowed Carolyn Savage to assert parental rights over the child? Would the *Michael H* case discussed earlier in this chapter provide support for such an argument?

What legal arguments could be made that the Savages should have visitation rights to the child or even joint custody with the genetic parents? Full joint parenting was the legal solution in a California case. Susan Buchweitz, a single woman, sought in vitro using a donated egg and donated sperm. Instead, she was implanted with the embryo of a married couple (created with sperm from a woman's husband and an egg from the same donor used by Buchweitz) who were also undergoing in vitro fertilization. Allegedly, the doctor knew within minutes of the procedure that there had been a mistake but Buchweitz was not informed until the child was ten months old. She was sued by the genetic father for full custody of the child. A California court declared Buchweitz the legal mother of the boy and the married man the legal father. She must send the child to the genetic father's house several days a week. Joan Ryan, Biology, Technology in Conflict, San Francisco Chronicle, (April 14, 2005) at B–1.

Bushweitz and other women have brought malpractice cases against the infertility clinics that have mixed up their sperm, eggs, or embryos. Bushweitz received one million dollars in damages after giving birth to the married couple's embryo. Chris Ayres, Mother Wins $1 M for IVF Mix-up But May Lose Son, The Times (London), August 5, 2004, at 3. When a Long Island, New York woman thought she was being inseminated with her dead husband's sperm, she instead received a stranger's sperm and gave birth to a child of another race. She won a $400,000 settlement with the doctor and sperm bank. True Parents?, San Jose Mercury News, August 2, 2002.

A recent scandal at another clinic indicated the problem of embryo mix-ups may be more common than previously thought. In most instances, a mix-up is discovered when a child of a different race than the parents is born. Perhaps many more mix-ups have occurred, but were not noticed because the baby was the same race as the parents. On September 25, 2009, a New Orleans hospital suspended operations at its in vitro fertilization center because so many embryos had been mislabeled. Michelle Hunter, Ochsner Shuts Down In Vitro Fertilization Center after Mix-up in Labeling Embryos, The Times–Picayune, (September 25, 2009).

Can money damages adequately compensate the people who suffer through these infertility mishaps or should greater oversight be considered as well? As a result of an embryo mix-up in Great Britain, the Government's Chief Medical Officer commissioned an examination of Britain's 90 IVF units, which resulted in the issuance of a 180–page report. The report, entitled "Assisted Reproduction: a Safe, Sound Future," is available at Britain's Medical Research Council website, http://www.mrc.ac.uk/prn/pdf-assisted_ reproduction.pdf. Does the U.S. need a similar close scrutiny of the protocols at in vitro fertilization clinics?

3. Under what circumstances should hospitals be considered negligent when babies are switched shortly after birth? In 1995, two baby girls were switched at the University of Virginia Medical Center. Photographs and medical records of the girls showed their ID bands were loose at times and absent at others. Subsequently, the hospital began to use identification tags clamped on newborns' umbilical cords rather than identification bracelets. When sued, the hospital offered a $2 million settlement to each family. See Michael D. Shear, Mother of Switched Baby Sues for $31M, Washington Post, May 25, 1999, at B1.

IV. PATERNITY AND ASSISTED REPRODUCTION

PEOPLE v. SORENSEN

437 P.2d 495 (Cal. 1968).

McCOMB, J.

Defendant appeals from a judgment convicting him of violating section 270 of the Penal Code (willful failure to provide for his minor child), a misdemeanor.

The settled statement of facts recites that seven years after defendant's marriage it was medically determined that he was sterile. His wife desired a child, either by artificial insemination or by adoption, and at first defendant refused to consent. About 15 years after the marriage defendant agreed to the artificial insemination of his wife. Husband and wife, then residents of San Joaquin County, consulted a physician in San Francisco. They signed an agreement, which is on the letterhead of the physician, requesting the physician to inseminate the wife with the sperm of a white male. The semen was to be selected by the physician, and under no circumstances were the parties to demand the name of the donor. The agreement contains a recitation that the physician does not represent that pregnancy will occur. The physician treated Mrs. Sorensen, and she became pregnant. Defendant knew at the time he signed the consent that when his wife took the treatments she could become pregnant and that if a child was born it was to be treated as their child.

A male child was born to defendant's wife in San Joaquin County on October 14, 1960. The information for the birth certificate was given by the mother, who named defendant as the father. Defendant testified that he had not provided the information on the birth certificate and did not recall seeing it before the trial.

For about four years the family had a normal family relationship, defendant having represented to friends that he was the child's father and treated the boy as his son. In 1964, Mrs. Sorensen separated from defendant and moved to Sonoma County with the boy. At separation, Mrs. Sorensen told defendant that she wanted no support for the boy, and she consented that a divorce be granted to defendant. Defendant obtained a decree of divorce, which recites that the court retained "jurisdiction regarding the possible support obligation of plaintiff in regard to a minor child born to defendant."

In the summer of 1966 when Mrs. Sorensen became ill and could not work, she applied for public assistance under the Aid to Needy Children program. The County of Sonoma supplied this aid until Mrs. Sorensen was able to resume work. Defendant paid no support for the child since the separation in 1964, although demand therefore was made by the district attorney. The municipal court found defendant guilty of violating section 270 of the Penal Code and granted him probation for three years on condition that he make payments of $50 per month for support through the district attorney's office.

From the record before us, this case could be disposed of on the ground that defendant has failed to overcome the presumption that "A child of a woman who is or has been married, born during the marriage or within 300 days after the dissolution thereof, is presumed to be a legitimate child of that marriage. This presumption may be disputed only by the people of the State of California in a criminal action brought under Section 270 of the Penal Code or by the husband or wife, or the descendant of one or both of them. In a civil action, this presumption may be rebutted only by clear and convincing proof."

* * *

Under the facts of this case, the term "father" as used in section 270 cannot be limited to the biologic or natural father as those terms are generally understood. The determinative factor is whether the legal relationship of father and child exists. A child conceived through heterologous artificial insemination[1] does not have a "natural father," as that term is commonly used. The anonymous donor of the sperm cannot be considered the "natural father," as he is no more responsible for the use made of his sperm than is the donor of blood or a kidney. Moreover, he could not dispute the presumption that the child is the legitimate issue of Mr. and Mrs. Sorensen, as that presumption "may be disputed only by the people of the State of California or by the husband or wife, or the descendant of one or both of them." With the use of frozen semen, the donor may even be dead at the time the semen is used. Since there is no "natural father," we can only look for a lawful father.

It is doubtful that with the enactment of section 270 of the Penal Code and its amendments the Legislature considered the plight of a child conceived through artificial insemination. However, the intent of the Legislature obviously was to include every child, legitimate or illegitimate, born or unborn, and enforce the obligation of support against the person who could be determined to be the lawful parent.

* * *

[A] reasonable man who, because of his inability to procreate, actively participates and consents to his wife's artificial insemination in the hope that a child will be produced whom they will treat as their own, knows that such behavior carries with it the legal responsibilities of fatherhood and criminal responsibility for nonsupport. One who consents to the production of a child cannot create a temporary relation to be assumed and disclaimed at will, but the arrangement must be of such character as to impose an obligation of supporting those for whose existence he is directly responsible. As noted by the trial court, it is safe to assume that without defendant's active participation and consent the child would not have been procreated.

* * *

In the absence of legislation prohibiting artificial insemination, the offspring of defendant's valid marriage to the child's mother was lawfully begotten and was not the product of an illicit or adulterous relationship. Adultery is defined as "the voluntary sexual intercourse of a married person with a person other than the offender's husband or wife." It has

---

1. There are two types of artificial insemination in common use: (1) artificial insemination with the husband's semen, homologous insemination, commonly termed A.I.H. and (2) artificial insemination with semen of third-party donor, heterologous insemination, commonly termed A.I.D. Only the latter raises legal problems of fatherhood and legitimacy.

been suggested that the doctor and the wife commit adultery by the process of artificial insemination. Since the doctor may be a woman, or the husband himself may administer the insemination by a syringe, this is patently absurd; to consider it an act of adultery with the donor, who at the time of insemination may be a thousand miles away or may even be dead, is equally absurd. Nor are we persuaded that the concept of legitimacy demands that the child be the actual offspring of the husband of the mother and if semen of some other male is utilized the resulting child is illegitimate.

In California, legitimacy is a legal status that may exist despite the fact that the husband is not the natural father of the child. The Legislature has provided for legitimation of a child born before wedlock by the subsequent marriage of its parents, for legitimation by acknowledgment by the father, and for inheritance rights of illegitimates, and since the subject of legitimation as well as that of succession of property is properly one for legislative action, we are not required in this case to do more than decide that, within the meaning of section 270 of the Penal Code, defendant is the lawful father of the child conceived through heterologous artificial insemination and born during his marriage to the child's mother.

The judgment is affirmed.

JHORDAN C. v. MARY K.

224 Cal.Rptr. 530 (Cal. App. 1986).

KING, J.

I. HOLDING

By statute in California a "donor of semen provided to a licensed physician for use in artificial insemination of a woman other than the donor's wife is treated in law as if he were not the natural father of a child thereby conceived." (Civ. Code, § 7005, subd. (b).) In this case we hold that where impregnation takes place by artificial insemination, and the parties have failed to take advantage of this statutory basis for preclusion of paternity, the donor of semen can be determined to be the father of the child in a paternity action.

Mary K. and Victoria T. appeal from a judgment declaring Jhordan C. to be the legal father of Mary's child, Devin. The child was conceived by artificial insemination with semen donated personally to Mary by Jhordan. We affirm the judgment.

II. FACTS AND PROCEDURAL HISTORY

In late 1978, Mary decided to bear a child by artificial insemination and to raise the child jointly with Victoria, a close friend who lived in a nearby town.[1] Mary sought a semen donor by talking to friends and

---

1. As many as 20,000 women each year are artificially inseminated in the United States. By one estimate some 1,500 of these women are unmarried.

acquaintances. This led to three or four potential donors with whom Mary spoke directly. She and Victoria ultimately chose Jhordan after he had one personal interview with Mary and one dinner at Mary's home.

The parties' testimony was in conflict as to what agreement they had concerning the role, if any, Jhordan would play in the child's life. According to Mary, she told Jhordan she did not want a donor who desired ongoing involvement with the child, but she did agree to let him see the child to satisfy his curiosity as to how the child would look. Jhordan, in contrast, asserts they agreed he and Mary would have an ongoing friendship, he would have ongoing contact with the child, and he would care for the child as much as two or three times per week.

None of the parties sought legal advice until long after the child's birth. They were completely unaware of the existence of Civil Code section 7005. They did not attempt to draft a written agreement concerning Jhordan's status.

Jhordan provided semen to Mary on a number of occasions during a six-month period commencing in late January 1979. On each occasion he came to her home, spoke briefly with her, produced the semen, and then left. The record is unclear, but Mary, who is a nurse, apparently performed the insemination by herself or with Victoria.

Contact between Mary and Jhordan continued after she became pregnant. Mary attended a Christmas party at Jhordan's home. Jhordan visited Mary several times at the health center where she worked. He took photographs of her. When he informed Mary by telephone that he had collected a crib, playpen, and high chair for the child, she told him to keep those items at his home. At one point Jhordan told Mary he had started a trust fund for the child and wanted legal guardianship in case she died; Mary vetoed the guardianship idea but did not disapprove the trust fund.

Victoria maintained a close involvement with Mary during the pregnancy. She took Mary to medical appointments, attended birthing classes, and shared information with Mary regarding pregnancy, delivery, and child rearing.

Mary gave birth to Devin on March 30, 1980. Victoria assisted in the delivery. Jhordan was listed as the father on Devin's birth certificate. Mary's roommate telephoned Jhordan that day to inform him of the birth. Jhordan visited Mary and Devin the next day and took photographs of the baby.

Five days later Jhordan telephoned Mary and said he wanted to visit Devin again. Mary initially resisted, but then allowed Jhordan to visit, although she told him she was angry. During the visit Jhordan claimed a right to see Devin, and Mary agreed to monthly visits.

Through August 1980 Jhordan visited Devin approximately five times. Mary then terminated the monthly visits. Jhordan said he would consult an attorney if Mary did not let him see Devin. Mary asked Jhordan to sign a contract indicating he would not seek to be Devin's father, but Jhordan refused.

In December 1980, Jhordan filed an action against Mary to establish paternity and visitation rights. In June 1982, by stipulated judgment in a separate action by the County of Sonoma, he was ordered to reimburse the county for public assistance paid for Devin's support. The judgment ordered him to commence payment, through the district attorney's office, of $900 in arrearages as well as future child support of $50 per month. In November 1982, the court granted Jhordan weekly visitation with Devin at Victoria's home.

Victoria had been closely involved with Devin since his birth. Devin spent at least two days each week in her home. On days when they did not see each other they spoke on the telephone. Victoria and Mary discussed Devin daily either in person or by telephone. They made joint decisions regarding his daily care and development. The three took vacations together. Devin and Victoria regarded each other as parent and child. Devin developed a brother-sister relationship with Victoria's 14–year-old daughter, and came to regard Victoria's parents as his grandparents. Victoria made the necessary arrangements for Devin's visits with Jhordan.

In August 1983, Victoria moved successfully for an order joining her as a party to this litigation. Supported by Mary, she sought joint legal custody (with Mary) and requested specified visitation rights, asserting she was a de facto parent of Devin. Jhordan subsequently requested an award of joint custody to him and Mary.

After trial the court rendered judgment declaring Jhordan to be Devin's legal father. However, the court awarded sole legal and physical custody to Mary, and denied Jhordan any input into decisions regarding Devin's schooling, medical and dental care, and day-to-day maintenance. Jhordan received substantial visitation rights as recommended by a court-appointed psychologist. The court held Victoria was not a de facto parent, but awarded her visitation rights (not to impinge upon Jhordan's visitation schedule), which were also recommended by the psychologist.

Mary and Victoria filed a timely notice of appeal, specifying the portions of the judgment declaring Jhordan to be Devin's legal father and denying Victoria the status of de facto parent.

III. DISCUSSION

We begin with a discussion of Civil Code section 7005, which provides in pertinent part: "(a) If, under the supervision of a licensed physician and with the consent of her husband, a wife is inseminated artificially with semen donated by a man not her husband, the husband is treated in law as if he were the natural father of a child thereby conceived * * *. (b) The donor of semen provided to a licensed physician for use in artificial insemination of a woman other than the donor's wife is treated in law as if he were not the natural father of a child thereby conceived."

Civil Code section 7005 is part of the Uniform Parentage Act (UPA), which was approved in 1973 by the National Conference of Commissioners on Uniform State Laws. The UPA was adopted in California in 1975. Section 7005 is derived almost verbatim from the UPA as originally drafted, with one crucial exception. The original UPA restricts application of the nonpaternity provision of subdivision (b) to a "married woman other than the donor's wife." The word "married" is excluded from subdivision (b) of section 7005, so that in California, subdivision (b) applies to all women, married or not.

Thus, the California Legislature has afforded unmarried as well as married women a statutory vehicle for obtaining semen for artificial insemination without fear that the donor may claim paternity, and has likewise provided men with a statutory vehicle for donating semen to married and unmarried women alike without fear of liability for child support. Subdivision (b) states only one limitation on its application: the semen must be "provided to a licensed physician." Otherwise, whether impregnation occurs through artificial insemination or sexual intercourse, there can be a determination of paternity with the rights, duties and obligations such a determination entails.

A. *Interpretation of the Statutory Nonpaternity Provision.*

Mary and Victoria first contend that despite the requirement of physician involvement stated in Civil Code section 7005, subdivision (b), the Legislature did not intend to withhold application of the donor nonpaternity provision where semen used in artificial insemination was not provided to a licensed physician. They suggest that the element of physician involvement appears in the statute merely because the Legislature assumed (erroneously) that all artificial insemination would occur under the supervision of a physician. Alternatively, they argue the requirement of physician involvement is merely directive rather than mandatory.

We cannot presume, however, that the Legislature simply assumed or wanted to recommend physician involvement, for two reasons.

First, the history of the UPA (the source of § 7005) indicates conscious adoption of the physician requirement. The initial "discussion draft" submitted to the drafters of the UPA in 1971 did not mention the involvement of a physician in artificial insemination; the draft stated no requirement as to how semen was to be obtained or how the insemination procedure was to be performed. The eventual inclusion of the physician requirement in the final version of the UPA suggests a conscious decision to require physician involvement.

Second, there are at least two sound justifications upon which the statutory requirement of physician involvement might have been based. One relates to health: a physician can obtain a complete medical history of the donor (which may be of crucial importance to the child during his or her lifetime) and screen the donor for any hereditary or communicable diseases. Indeed, the commissioners' comment to the section of the UPA on artificial insemination cites as a "useful reference" a law review article which argues that health considerations should require the involvement of a physician in statutorily authorized artificial insemination. This suggests that health considerations underlie the decision by the drafters of the UPA to include the physician requirement in the artificial insemination statute.

* * *

It is true that nothing inherent in artificial insemination requires the involvement of a physician. Artificial insemination is, as demonstrated here, a simple procedure easily performed by a woman in her own home. Also, despite the reasons outlined above in favor of physician involvement, there are countervailing considerations against requiring it. A requirement of physician involvement, as Mary argues, might offend a woman's sense of privacy and reproductive autonomy, might result in burdensome costs to some women, and might interfere with a woman's desire to conduct the procedure in a comfortable environment such as her own home or to choose the donor herself.

However, because of the way section 7005 is phrased, a woman (married or unmarried) can perform home artificial insemination or choose her donor and still obtain the benefits of the statute. Subdivision (b) does not require that a physician independently obtain the semen and perform the insemination, but requires only that the semen be "provided" to a physician. Thus, a woman who prefers home artificial insemination or who wishes to choose her donor can still obtain statutory protection from a donor's paternity claim through the relatively simple expedient of obtaining the semen, whether for home insemination or from a chosen donor (or both), through a licensed physician.

Regardless of the various countervailing considerations for and against physician involvement, our Legislature has embraced the apparently conscious decision by the drafters of the UPA to limit application of the donor nonpaternity provision to instances in which semen is provided to a licensed physician. The existence of sound justifications for physician involvement further supports a determination the Legislature intended to require it. Accordingly, section 7005, subdivision (b), by its terms does not apply to the present case. The Legislature's apparent decision to require physician involvement in order to invoke the statute cannot be subject to judicial second-guessing and cannot be disturbed, absent constitutional infirmity.

B. Constitutional Considerations.

Mary and Victoria next contend that even if section 7005, subdivision (b), by its terms does not apply where semen for artificial insemination has not been provided to a licensed physician, application of the statute to the present case is required by constitutional principles of equal protection and privacy (encompassing rights to family autonomy and procreative choice).

1. Equal protection.

Mary and Victoria argue the failure to apply section 7005, subdivision (b), to unmarried women who conceive artificially with semen not provided to a licensed physician denies equal protection because the operation of other paternity statutes precludes a donor's assertion of paternity where a *married* woman undergoes artificial insemination with semen not provided to a physician.

This characterization of the effect of the paternity statutes as applied to married women is correct. In the case of the married woman her husband is the presumed father (Civ. Code, § 7004, subd. (a)(1)), and any outsider—including a semen donor, regardless of physician involvement—is precluded from maintaining a paternity action unless the mother "relinquishes for, consents to, or proposes to relinquish for or consent to, the adoption of the child." (Civ. Code, § 7006, subd. (d).) An action to establish paternity by blood test can be brought only by the husband or mother.

But the statutory provision at issue here—Civil Code section 7005, subdivision (b)—treats married and unmarried women equally. Both are denied application of the statute where semen has not been provided to a licensed physician.

The true question presented is whether a completely different set of paternity statutes—affording protection to husband and wife from any claim of paternity by an outsider (Civ. Code, §§ 7004, 7006; Evid. Code, § 621)—denies equal protection by failing to provide similar protection to an unmarried woman. The simple answer is that, within the context of this question, a married woman and an unmarried woman are not similarly situated for purposes of equal protection analysis. In the case of a married woman, the marital relationship invokes a long-recognized social policy of preserving the integrity of the marriage. No such concerns arise where there is no marriage at all. Equal protection is not violated by providing that certain benefits or legal rights arise only out of the marital relationship. For example, spousal support may be awarded pursuant to Civil Code section 4801 upon the breakup of a marital relationship, but not upon the breakup of a nonmarital relationship.

2. Family autonomy.

Mary and Victoria contend that they and Devin compose a family unit and that the trial court's ruling constitutes an infringement upon a right they have to family autonomy, encompassed by the constitutional right to privacy. But this argument begs the question of which persons comprise the family in this case for purposes of judicial intervention. Characterization of the family unit must precede consideration of whether family autonomy has been infringed.

The semen donor here was permitted to develop a social relationship with Mary and Devin as the child's father. During Mary's pregnancy Jhordan maintained contact with her. They visited each other several times, and Mary did not object to Jhordan's collection of baby equipment or the creation of a trust fund for the child. Mary permitted Jhordan to visit Devin on the day after the child's birth and allowed monthly visits thereafter. The record demonstrates no clear understanding that Jhordan's role would be limited to provision of semen and that he would have no parental relationship with Devin; indeed, the parties' conduct indicates otherwise.

We do not purport to hold that an oral or written nonpaternity agreement between the parties would have been legally binding; that difficult question is not before us (and indeed is more appropriately addressed by the Legislature). We simply emphasize that for purposes of the family autonomy argument raised by Mary, Jhordan was not excluded as a member of Devin's family, either by anonymity, by agreement, or by the parties' conduct.

In short, the court's ruling did not infringe upon any right of Mary and Victoria to family autonomy, because under the peculiar facts of this case Jhordan was not excluded as a member of Devin's family for purposes of resolving this custody dispute.

3. Procreative choice.

Mary and Victoria argue that the physician requirement in Civil Code section 7005, subdivision (b), infringes a fundamental right to procreative choice, also encompassed by the constitutional right of privacy.

But the statute imposes no restriction on the right to bear a child. Unlike statutes in other jurisdictions proscribing artificial insemination other than by a physician, subdivision (b) of section 7005 does not forbid self-insemination; nor does the statute preclude personal selection of a donor or in any other way prevent women from artificially conceiving children under circumstances of their own choice. The statute simply addresses the perplexing question of the legal status of the semen donor, and provides a method of avoiding the legal consequences that might otherwise be dictated by traditional notions of paternity.

C. *Victoria's Status as a De Facto Parent.*

Finally, Mary and Victoria contend that even if the paternity judgment is affirmed Victoria should be declared a de facto parent, based on her day-to-day attention to Devin's needs, in order to guarantee her present visitation rights and ensure her parental status in any future custody or visitation proceedings. Present resolution of the de facto parenthood issue for these purposes would be premature and merely advisory. Victoria's visitation rights have been legally recognized and preserved by court order. If no further custody or visitation proceedings occur, the issue of Victoria's de facto parent status and its legal effect will never arise.

IV. CONCLUSION

We wish to stress that our opinion in this case is not intended to express any judicial preference toward traditional notions of family structure or toward providing a father where a single woman has chosen to bear a child. Public policy in these areas is best determined by the legislative branch of government, not the judicial. Our Legislature has already spoken and has afforded to unmarried women a statutory right to bear children by artificial insemination (as well as a right of men to donate semen) without fear of a paternity claim, through provision of the semen to a licensed physician. We simply hold that because Mary omitted to invoke Civil Code section 7005, subdivision (b), by obtaining Jhordan's semen through a licensed physician, and because the parties by all other conduct preserved Jhordan's status as a member of Devin's family, the trial court properly declared Jhordan to be Devin's legal father.

SOOS v. SUPERIOR COURT IN AND FOR COUNTY OF MARICOPA

897 P.2d 1356 (Ariz. App. 1994).

CLABORNE, J.

This is a Petition for Special Action from the trial court's order declaring the surrogate parentage contracts statute unconstitutional and ordering an evidentiary hearing to determine which person would be the better "mother" for the triplets. Petitioner Ronald A. Soos ("the Father") contends that the trial court erred as a matter of law in holding the statute unconstitutional and that she exceeded her jurisdiction and legal authority. We disagree and find that the statute violates the Equal Protection Clause of the United States and Arizona Constitutions. We previously accepted jurisdiction and denied relief with an Opinion to follow. This is that Opinion.

FACTS AND PROCEDURAL HISTORY

The Father and his then wife, Pamela J. Soos ("the Mother"), entered into a surrogate parentage contract with Debra Ballas ("the Surrogate") because the Mother was unable to have children because of a partial hysterectomy. Eggs were removed from the Mother and fertilized in vitro (in a test tube) by sperm obtained from the Father. Pursuant to a "Host Uterus Program" at the Arizona Institute of Reproductive Medicine, the fertilized eggs were implanted in the Surrogate. The Surrogate became pregnant with triplets.

During the pregnancy of the Surrogate, the Mother filed a petition for dissolution of marriage requesting shared custody of the unborn triplets. The Father responded to the petition, alleging that he was the biological father of the unborn triplets, and that pursuant to A.R.S. [Arizona Revised Statutes] section 25–218 (1991), the Surrogate was the legal mother of the triplets. The Father further alleged that since the Surrogate was the legal mother of the triplets, the Mother had no standing to request custody.

In September of 1993, the Surrogate gave birth to triplets. The Father and the Surrogate filed a request for order of paternity with the Maricopa County Superior Court. An order was entered naming the Father as the natural father of the triplets, and the Father took custody of the triplets.

The Mother responded by filing a motion for appointment of counsel for the triplets, a motion for temporary emergency visitation, and a motion to consolidate the dissolution proceeding with the paternity action. In her motions, the Mother attacked the constitutionality of A.R.S. section 25–218(B) declaring the Surrogate to be the legal mother. The trial court in its minute entry said:

> THE COURT FINDS that there is not a compelling state interest that justifies terminating the substantive due process rights of the genetic mother in such a summary fashion.

> The current law could leave a child without any mother, as a gestational mother may have no desire to do more than she was hired to do, which is to carry and give birth to a child. The current law also ignores the important role that generations of genetics may play in the determination of who a child is and becomes. The current law does not consider what is in the best interest of each individual child.

> THE COURT FINDS A.R.S. § 25–218(B) to be unconstitutional.

An evidentiary hearing was set to determine which mother could better assume the social and legal responsibilities of motherhood. The trial court also ordered that the Mother have visitation rights with the triplets, and that the triplets would remain in the temporary custody of the Father. Following the denial of a motion for reconsideration, the Father filed this Petition for Special Action.

* * *

DISCUSSION

* * *

A.R.S. section 25–218 provides in relevant part:

> A.   No person may enter into, induce, arrange, procure or otherwise assist in the formation of a surrogate parentage contract.

> B.   A surrogate is the legal mother of a child born as a result of a surrogate parentage contract and is entitled to custody of that child.

> C.   If the mother of a child born as a result of a surrogate contract is married, her husband is presumed to be the legal father of the child. *This presumption is rebuttable.* (Emphasis added.)

This statute was fashioned after the Michigan statute and enacted for the purpose of prohibiting surrogate parentage contracts. The minutes of the House Committee on Human Resources & Aging meeting of February

16, 1989, and the minutes of the House Committee on Judiciary of April 4, 1989, reflect the governmental interests in prohibiting surrogate contracts. The statute was designed to stop "baby brokers" and to stop the trafficking of human beings.

The question before us is whether the State's reasons for enacting the surrogate parentage contracts statute are sufficient to withstand constitutional scrutiny under the due process, equal protection, and privacy rights guaranteed by the United States and Arizona Constitutions. We must keep in mind that we are dealing with a custody issue between the biological mother and biological father and the constitutional issues surrounding their competing interests. This is not a case of the surrogate mother versus the biological mother. We are not dealing with the constitutional questions that arise when the surrogate mother wishes to keep the child she bore. Thus, we limit ourselves to the question of whether the statute withstands constitutional scrutiny when it affords a biological father an opportunity to prove paternity and gain custody, but does not afford a biological mother the same opportunity.

EQUAL PROTECTION

We first address the equal protection argument. The Mother argues that A.R.S. section 25–218 unconstitutionally denies her the right to equal protection of the laws. The Equal Protection Clause of the Fourteenth Amendment of the United States Constitution denies "to states the power to legislate that different treatment be accorded to persons placed by a statute into different classes on the basis of criteria wholly unrelated to the objective of that statute."

In reviewing the statute, we must determine which of three standards applies. The first standard is a strict scrutiny test. It is applied to statutes that involve a suspect class or impinge on a fundamental right. The second standard of review, the means-end scrutiny, has been limited to classifications involving gender and illegitimacy of birth. The final standard, the rational basis test, is used when the legislation does not involve a suspect classification or a fundamental right.

We are dealing with a statute that affects one of the basic civil rights. The due process clauses of the state and federal constitutions, together with the rights emanating from the guarantees of the Bill of Rights, protect "individual decisions in matters of childbearing from unjustified intrusion by the State." "Marriage and procreation are fundamental to the very existence and survival of the race." A parent's right to the custody and control of one's child is a fundamental interest guaranteed by the United States and Arizona Constitutions. Therefore, although a gender-based distinction is at issue, the statute must be tested against a strict scrutiny analysis. That is, the government can only "justify the abridgment of such a fundamental right by demonstrating that a countervailing compelling state interest is thereby promoted and that the means are closely tailored to the end sought to be achieved."

A.R.S. section 25–218(C) allows a man to rebut the presumption of legal paternity by proving "fatherhood" but does not provide the same opportunity for a woman.[1] A woman who may be genetically related to a child has no opportunity to prove her maternity and is thereby denied the opportunity to develop the parent-child relationship. She is afforded no procedural process by which to prove her maternity under the statute. The Mother has parental interests not less deserving of protection than those of the Father. "By providing dissimilar treatment for men and women who are thus similarly situated," the statute violates the Equal Protection Clause.

The Father responds to this problem by arguing that mere biology alone is not enough to create the parental rights guaranteed by our constitutions. We find this argument inapplicable. Lehr v. Robertson [463 U.S. 248 (1983)] holds that mere existence of a biological link is not enough to give rise to constitutional protections. Before a parent can claim a fundamental right, *a developed parent-child relationship must exist*. However, this rule cannot hold true in the surrogacy context. The biological mother can prove maternity only through her genetic or biological link. Further, since the surrogate statute does not recognize the biological mother as the "legal mother," she has no opportunity to develop a parent-child relationship. She must rely on her biology to protect her fundamental liberties.

The usual understanding of 'family' implies biological relationships, and most decisions treating the relation between parent and child have stressed this element * * *. The 'biological connection' is itself a relationship that creates a protected interest. Thus the 'nature' of the interest is the parent-child relationship; how well developed that relationship has become goes to its 'weight,' not its 'nature.'

By affording the Father a procedure for proving paternity, but not affording the Mother any means by which to prove maternity, the State has denied her equal protection of the laws. "A classification must be reasonable, not arbitrary, and must rest upon some ground of difference having a fair and substantial relation to the object of the legislation, so that all persons similarly circumstanced shall be treated alike." The surrogate statute violates this principle. We hold that the State has not shown any compelling interest to justify the dissimilar treatment of men and women similarly situated (the biological mother and father). The statute is unconstitutional on equal protection grounds.

CONCLUSION

We find that the surrogate statute affects a fundamental liberty interest. The surrogate statute as it exists violates the equal protection guarantees of the United States and Arizona Constitutions. Because of our

---

1. A.R.S. section 25–218(C) provides that '[i]f the mother of a child born as a result of a surrogate contract is married, her husband is presumed to be the legal father of the child. *This presumption is rebuttable.*'

resolution, we decline to address the remaining issues raised by the Father and the Mother.

IN RE MARRIAGE OF BUZZANCA

72 Cal.Rptr.2d 280 (Cal. App. 1998).

SILLS, J.

INTRODUCTION

Jaycee was born because Luanne and John Buzzanca agreed to have an embryo genetically unrelated to either of them implanted in a woman—a surrogate—who would carry and give birth to the child for them. After the fertilization, implantation and pregnancy, Luanne and John split up, and the question of who are Jaycee's lawful parents came before the trial court.

Luanne claimed that she and her erstwhile husband were the lawful parents, but John disclaimed any responsibility, financial or otherwise. The woman who gave birth also appeared in the case to make it clear that she made no claim to the child.

The trial court then reached an extraordinary conclusion: Jaycee had no lawful parents. First, the woman who gave birth to Jaycee was not the mother; the court had—astonishingly—already accepted a stipulation that neither she nor her husband were the "biological" parents. Second, Luanne was not the mother. According to the trial court, she could not be the mother because she had neither contributed the egg nor given birth. And John could not be the father, because, not having contributed the sperm, he had no biological relationship with the child.

* * *

Perhaps recognizing the inherent lack of appeal for any result which makes Jaycee a legal orphan, John now contends that the surrogate is Jaycee's legal mother; and further, by virtue of that fact, the surrogate's husband is the legal father. His reasoning goes like this: Under the Uniform Parentage Act (the Act), and particularly as set forth in section 7610 of California's Family Code, there are only two ways by which a woman can establish legal motherhood, i.e., giving birth or contributing genetically. Because the genetic contributors are not known to the court, the only candidate left is the surrogate who must therefore be deemed the lawful mother. And, as John's counsel commented at oral argument, if the surrogate and her husband cannot support Jaycee, the burden should fall on the taxpayers.

The law doesn't say what John says it says. It doesn't say: "The legal relationship between mother and child shall be established only by either proof of her giving birth or by genetics." The statute says "may," not "shall," and "under this part," not "by genetics." Here is the complete text of section 7610: "The parent and child relationship may be established as follows: (a) Between a child and the natural mother, it may be established by proof of her having given birth to the child, or under this part. (b) Between a child and the natural father, it may be established under this part. (c) Between a child and an adoptive parent, it may be established by proof of adoption."

* * *

In addition to blood tests there are several other ways the Act allows paternity to be established. Those ways are not necessarily related at all to any biological tie. Thus, under the Act, paternity may be established by:

— marrying, remaining married to, or attempting to marry the child's mother when she gives birth;

— marrying the child's mother after the child's birth and either consenting to being named as the father on the birth certificate (§ 7611, subd. (c)(1)) or making a written promise to support the child.

A man may also be deemed a father under the Act in the case of artificial insemination of his wife * * *.

* * *

Sorensen [People v. Sorensen, 437 P.2d 495 (Cal. 1968)] expresses a rule universally in tune with other jurisdictions. "Almost exclusively, courts which have addressed this issue have assigned parental responsibility to the husband based on conduct evidencing his consent to the artificial insemination."

* * *

One New York family court even went so far as to hold the lesbian partner of a woman who was artificially inseminated responsible for the support of two children where the partner had dressed as a man and the couple had obtained a marriage license and a wedding ceremony had been performed prior to the inseminations. Echoing the themes of causation and estoppel which underlie the cases, the court noted that the lesbian partner had "by her course of conduct in this case . . . brought into the world two innocent children" and should not "be allowed to benefit" from her acts to the detriment of the children and public generally.

Indeed, in the one case we are aware of where the court did not hold that the husband had a support obligation, the reason was not the absence of a biological relationship as such, but because of actual lack of consent to the insemination procedure.

It must also be noted that in applying the artificial insemination statute to a case where a party has caused a child to be brought into the world, the statutory policy is really echoing a more fundamental idea—a sort of grundnorm to borrow Hans Kelsen's famous jurisprudential word—already established in the case law. That idea is often summed up in the legal term "estoppel." Estoppel is an ungainly word from the Middle French (from the word meaning "bung" or "stopper") expressing the law's distaste for inconsistent actions and positions—like consenting to an act which brings a child into existence and then turning around and disclaiming any responsibility.

* * *

Luanne is the Lawful Mother of Jaycee, Not the Surrogate, and Not the Unknown Donor of the Egg

In the present case Luanne is situated like a husband in an artificial insemination case whose consent triggers a medical procedure which results in a pregnancy and eventual birth of a child. Her motherhood may therefore be established "under this part," by virtue of that consent. In light of our conclusion, John's argument that the surrogate should be declared the lawful mother disintegrates.

* * *

The legal paradigm adopted by the trial court, and now urged upon us by John, is one where all forms of artificial reproduction in which intended parents have no biological relationship with the child result in legal parentlessness. It means that, absent adoption, such children will be dependents of the state. One might describe this paradigm as the "adoption default" model: The idea is that by not specifically addressing some permutation of artificial reproduction, the Legislature has, in effect, set the default switch on adoption. The underlying theory seems to be that when intended parents resort to artificial reproduction without biological tie the Legislature wanted them to be screened first through the adoption system. (Thus John, in his brief, argues that a surrogacy contract must be "subject to state oversight.")

The "adoption default" model is, however, inconsistent with both statutory law and the Supreme Court's *Johnson* decision [Johnson v. Calvert, 19 Cal.Rptr.2d 494 (Cal. 1993)]. As to the statutory law, the Legislature has already made it perfectly clear that public policy (and, we might add, common sense) favors, whenever possible, the establishment of legal parenthood with the concomitant responsibility. Family Code section 7570, subdivision (a) states that "There is a compelling state interest in establishing paternity for all children."

* * *

John now argues that the Supreme Court's statement should be applied only in situations, such as that in the *Johnson* case, where the intended parents have a genetic tie to the child. The context of the *Johnson* language, however, reveals a broader purpose, namely, to emphasize the intelligence and utility of a rule that looks to intentions.

* * *

John is the Lawful Father of Jaycee Even If Luanne Did Promise to Assume All Responsibility for Jaycee's Care

The same reasons which impel us to conclude that Luanne is Jaycee's lawful mother also require that John be declared Jaycee's lawful father.

Even if the written surrogacy contract had not yet been signed at the time of conception and implantation, those occurrences were nonetheless the direct result of actions taken pursuant to an oral agreement which envisioned that the fertilization, implantation and ensuing pregnancy would go forward. Thus, it is still accurate to say, as we did the first time this case came before us, that for all practical purposes John caused Jaycee's conception every bit as much as if things had been done the old fashioned way.

When pressed at oral argument to make an offer of proof as to the "best facts" which John might be able to show if this case were tried, John's attorney raised the point that Luanne had (allegedly, we must add) promised to assume all responsibility for the child and would not hold him responsible for the child's upbringing. However, even if this case were returned for a trial on this point (we assume that Luanne would dispute the allegation) it could make no difference as to John's lawful paternity. It is well established that parents cannot, by agreement, limit or abrogate a child's right to support.

* * *

CONCLUSION

Even though neither Luanne nor John are biologically related to Jaycee, they are still her lawful parents given their initiating role as the intended parents in her conception and birth. And, while the absence of a biological connection is what makes this case extraordinary, this court is hardly without statutory basis and legal precedent in so deciding. Indeed, in both the most famous child custody case of all time,[19] and in our Supreme Court's Johnson v. Calvert decision, the court looked to intent to parent as the ultimate basis of its decision.[20] Fortunately, as the *Johnson* court also noted, intent to parent " 'correlate[s] significantly' " with a child's best interests. That is far more than can be said for a model of the law that renders a child a legal orphan.

Again we must call on the Legislature to sort out the parental rights and responsibilities of those involved in artificial reproduction. No matter what one thinks of artificial insemination, traditional and gestational surrogacy (in all its permutations), and—as now appears in the not-too-distant future, cloning and even gene splicing—courts are still going to be faced with the problem of determining lawful parentage. A child cannot be ignored. Even if all means of artificial reproduction were outlawed with draconian criminal penalties visited on the doctors and parties involved, courts will still be called upon to decide who the lawful parents really are

---

19. See I Kings 3:25–26 (dispute over identity of live child by two single women, each of whom had recently delivered a child but one child had died, resolved by novel evidentiary device designed to ferret out intent to parent).

20. While in each case intent to parent was used as a tie-breaker as between two claimants who either had or claimed a biological connection, it is still undeniable that, when push came to shove, the court employed a legal idea that was unrelated to any necessary biological connection.

and who—other than the taxpayers—is obligated to provide maintenance and support for the child. These cases will not go away.

Courts can continue to make decisions on an ad hoc basis without necessarily imposing some grand scheme, looking to the imperfectly designed Uniform Parentage Act and a growing body of case law for guidance in the light of applicable family law principles. Or the Legislature can act to impose a broader order which, even though it might not be perfect on a case-by-case basis, would bring some predictability to those who seek to make use of artificial reproductive techniques. As jurists, we recognize the traditional role of the common (i.e., judge-formulated) law in applying old legal principles to new technology * * *. However, we still believe it is the Legislature, with its ability to formulate general rules based on input from all its constituencies, which is the more desirable forum for lawmaking.

K.M. v. E.G.

117 P.3d 673 (Cal. 2005).

MORENO, J.

In the present case, we must decide whether a woman who provided ova to her lesbian partner so that the partner could bear children by means of in vitro fertilization is a parent of those children. For the reasons that follow, we conclude that Family Code section 7613, subdivision (b), which provides that a man is not a father if he provides semen to a physician to inseminate a woman who is not his wife, does not apply when a woman provides her ova to impregnate her partner in a lesbian relationship in order to produce children who will be raised in their joint home. Accordingly, when partners in a lesbian relationship decide to produce children in this manner, both the woman who provides her ova and her partner who bears the children are the children's parents.

* * *

On March 6, 2001, petitioner K.M. filed a petition to establish a parental relationship with twin five-year-old girls born to respondent E.G., her former lesbian partner. K.M. alleged that she "is the biological parent of the minor children" because "[s]he donated her egg to respondent, the gestational mother of the children." E.G. moved to dismiss the petition on the grounds that, although K.M. and E.G. "were lesbian partners who lived together until this action was filed," K.M. "explicitly donated her ovum under a clear written agreement by which she relinquished any claim to offspring born of her donation."

On April 18, 2001, K.M. filed a motion for custody of and visitation with the twins.

A hearing was held at which E.G. testified that she first considered raising a child before she met K.M., at a time when she did not have a partner. She met K.M. in October, 1992 and they became romantically involved in June 1993. E.G. told K.M. that she planned to adopt a baby as a single mother. E.G. applied for adoption in November, 1993. K.M. and E.G. began living together in March, 1994 and registered as domestic partners in San Francisco.

E.G. visited several fertility clinics in March, 1993 to inquire about artificial insemination and she attempted artificial insemination, without success, on 13 occasions from July, 1993 through November, 1994. K.M. accompanied her to most of these appointments. K.M. testified that she and E.G. planned to raise the child together, while E.G. insisted that, although K.M. was very supportive, E.G. made it clear that her intention was to become "a single parent."

In December, 1994, E.G. consulted with Dr. Mary Martin at the fertility practice of the University of California at San Francisco Medical Center (UCSF). E.G.'s first attempts at in vitro fertilization failed because she was unable to produce sufficient ova. In January, 1995, Dr. Martin suggested using K.M.'s ova. E.G. then asked K.M. to donate her ova, explaining that she would accept the ova only if K.M. "would really be a donor" and E.G. would "be the mother of any child," adding that she would not even consider permitting K.M. to adopt the child "for at least five years until [she] felt the relationship was stable and would endure." E.G. told K.M. that she "had seen too many lesbian relationships end quickly, and [she] did not want to be in a custody battle." E.G. and K.M. agreed they would not tell anyone that K.M. was the ova donor.

K.M. acknowledged that she agreed not to disclose to anyone that she was the ova donor, but insisted that she only agreed to provide her ova because she and E.G. had agreed to raise the child together. K.M. and E.G. selected the sperm donor together. K.M. denied that E.G. had said she wanted to be a single parent and insisted that she would not have donated her ova had she known E.G. intended to be the sole parent.

On March 8, 1995, K.M. signed a four-page form on UCSF letterhead entitled "Consent Form for Ovum Donor (Known)." The form states that K.M. agrees "to have eggs taken from my ovaries, in order that they may be donated to another woman." After explaining the medical procedures involved, the form states on the third page: "It is understood that I waive any right and relinquish any claim to the donated eggs or any pregnancy or offspring that might result from them. I agree that the recipient may regard the donated eggs and any offspring resulting therefrom as her own children." The following appears on page 4 of the form, above K.M.'s signature and the signature of a witness: "I specifically disclaim and waive any right in or any child that may be conceived as a result of the use of any ovum or egg of mine, and I agree not to attempt to discover the identity of the recipient thereof." E.G. signed a form entitled "Consent Form for Ovum Recipient" that stated, in part: "I acknowledge that the child or children produced by the IVF procedure is and shall be my own legitimate child or children and the heir or heirs of my body with all rights and privileges accompanying such status."

E.G. testified she received these two forms in a letter from UCSF dated February 2, 1995, and discussed the consent forms with K.M. during February and March. E.G. stated she would not have accepted K.M.'s ova if K.M. had not signed the consent form, because E.G. wanted to have a child on her own and believed the consent form "protected" her in this regard.

K.M. testified to the contrary that she first saw the ovum donation consent form 10 minutes before she signed it on March 8, 1995. K.M. admitted reading the form, but thought parts of the form were "odd" and did not pertain to her, such as the part stating that the donor promised not to discover the identity of the recipient. She did not intend to relinquish her rights and only signed the form so that "we could have children." Despite having signed the form, K.M. "thought [she] was going to be a parent."

Ova were withdrawn from K.M. on April 11, 1995, and embryos were implanted in E.G. on April 13, 1995. K.M. and E.G. told K.M's father about the resulting pregnancy by announcing that he was going to be a grandfather. The twins were born on December 7, 1995. The twins' birth certificates listed E.G. as their mother and did not reflect a father's name. As they had agreed, neither E.G. nor K.M. told anyone K.M. had donated the ova, including their friends, family and the twins' pediatrician. Soon after the twins were born, E.G. asked K.M. to marry her, and on Christmas Day, the couple exchanged rings.

* * *

K.M. asserts that she is a parent of the twins because she supplied the ova that were fertilized in vitro and implanted in her lesbian partner, resulting in the birth of the twins * * *. The Court of Appeal in the present case concluded, however, that K.M. was not a parent of the twins, despite her genetic relationship to them, because she had the same status as a sperm donor. Section 7613(b) states: "The donor of semen provided to a licensed physician and surgeon for use in artificial insemination of a woman other than the donor's wife is treated in law as if he were not the natural father of a child thereby conceived." In Johnson, we considered the predecessor statute to section 7613(b), former Civil Code section 7005. (Johnson v. Calvert, supra, 5 Cal.4th 84, 100, fn. 14(1993.)) We did not discuss whether this statute applied to a woman who provides ova used to impregnate another woman, but we observed that "in a true 'egg donation' situation, where a woman gestates and gives birth to a child formed from the egg of another woman with the intent to raise the child as her own, the birth mother is the natural mother under California law." We held that the statute did not apply under the circumstances in Johnson, because the husband and wife in Johnson did not intend to "donate" their sperm and ova to the surrogate mother, but rather "intended to procreate a child genetically related to them by the only available means."

The circumstances of the present case are not identical to those in Johnson, but they are similar in a crucial respect; both the couple in

Johnson and the couple in the present case intended to produce a child that would be raised in their own home. In Johnson, it was clear that the married couple did not intend to "donate" their semen and ova to the surrogate mother, but rather permitted their semen and ova to be used to impregnate the surrogate mother in order to produce a child to be raised by them. In the present case, K.M. contends that she did not intend to donate her ova, but rather provided her ova so that E.G. could give birth to a child to be raised jointly by K.M. and E.G. E.G. hotly contests this, asserting that K.M. donated her ova to E.G., agreeing that E.G. would be the sole parent. It is undisputed, however, that the couple lived together and that they both intended to bring the child into their joint home. Thus, even accepting as true E.G.'s version of the facts (which the superior court did), the present case, like Johnson, does not present a "true 'egg donation' " situation. K.M. did not intend to simply donate her ova to E.G., but rather provided her ova to her lesbian partner with whom she was living so that E.G. could give birth to a child that would be raised in their joint home.

* * *

The superior court in the present case found that K.M. signed a waiver form, thereby "relinquishing and waiving all rights to claim legal parentage of any children who might result." But such a waiver does not affect our determination of parentage. Section 7632 provides: "Regardless of its terms, an agreement between an alleged or presumed father and the mother or child does not bar an action under this chapter." (See In re Marriage of Buzzanca, supra, 61 Cal.App.4th 1410, 1426 (1998) ["It is well established that parents cannot, by agreement, limit or abrogate a child's right to support."].) A woman who supplies ova to be used to impregnate her lesbian partner, with the understanding that the resulting child will be raised in their joint home, cannot waive her responsibility to support that child. Nor can such a purported waiver effectively cause that woman to relinquish her parental rights.

NOTES AND QUESTIONS

1.   What are the advantages and disadvantages of a pre-conception intent approach to determining legal parenthood? In the adoption context, pre-birth agreements cannot be enforced if the biological mother changes her mind within a certain period after the birth. Why should it be any different for surrogate motherhood? What if the surrogate mother's own egg is used to create the child? See In the Matter of Baby M, 537 A.2d 1227 (N.J. 1988).

2.   Should the adoption model be used when neither member of the couple has a genetic or gestational tie to the child? In what ways, if any, does the production of a child through the use of a sperm donor, egg donor, or surrogate differ from the adoption of a child? Would home study and court oversight for adoption be appropriate with a Buzzanca-style situation?

3.   In Jhordan C., the court held that, because the artificial insemination had not been undertaken by a physician, the sperm donor's parental rights

were not extinguished. Is it likely that the legislature actually intended the determination of paternity to hinge on whether a doctor was involved in the process? If an unmarried woman uses artificial insemination, should it be permissible for her to choose that the baby has no legal father? If the woman has a female partner (or if two gay men arrange for a surrogate mother to bear a child for them), should the child be legally determined to have two parents of the same sex?

4. The court in *Soos* refers to the genetic mother as the "biological" mother. Could it be argued, though, that the surrogate mother who gestated the child is a biological mother as well? What might be the implication of her biological connection for purposes of defining legal parenthood?

5. While many states have laws severing sperm donors' legal relationship with the child, only ten states have statutes providing that an egg donor is not the legal parent of the child created with her egg. What would happen if an Ivy League undergrad in a state without a statute were paid $100,000 for an egg—but the procedure of egg removal was negligent and left her infertile? Should she be able to sue for parental rights to the child born to the egg recipient? If the donor doesn't realize she is infertile until years later, should she later be able to win visitation rights to the child?

6. In the past, most lesbians with children had their children in the context of a marriage before they became involved in lesbian relationships. See Nancy D. Polikoff, This Child Does Have Two Mothers: Redefining Parenthood to Meet the Needs of Children in Lesbian–Mother and Other Non–Traditional Families, 78 Geo. L.J. 459, 464–65 (1990). More recently, many lesbians have chosen assisted reproductive technology (ART) to create families. IVF and AID are the most widely used techniques. However, because the current state of the law accords more weight to biology than intent, the legal assignment of parental status may contradict and can frustrate the intentions of the participants. Anne Reichman Schiff, Frustrated Intentions and Binding Biology: Seeking AID In The Law, 44 Duke L.J. 524, 538 (1994). Known sperm donors may elect to assert paternal rights. In some jurisdictions, when a known sperm donor is used, even where there is an agreement to relinquish all parental rights, the donor may change his mind after the birth and institute a paternity suit. There is more legal protection when a sperm donor is anonymous. Now, some female couples are arranging for one to provide an egg and the other to gestate the fetus, but even that arrangement can lead to legal conflicts, despite the fact that both women have a biological link to their child.

7. Some hospital officials are crossing out the word "father" on birth certificates and writing the phrase "second parent" for children born to same-sex couples in Massachusetts. However, it is unclear whether these birth certificates with strikeouts on them are valid documents. There is concern that these "corrected" birth certificates could be challenged by government officials, foreign governments, and passport agents. Michael Levenson, Birth Certificate Policy Draws Fire: Change Affects Same–Sex Couples, Boston Globe, July 22, 2005 at B1.

8. In January 2009, 33–year-old Nadya Suleman gave birth via Cesarean section to octuplets—the first surviving set of octuplets in the world. The

public did not react favorably when it was revealed that Suleman (quickly dubbed "Octomom") was divorced, unemployed, and already the mother of six children. She had apparently found a physician willing to implant six embryos she had created using donor sperm and two of the embryos had split, forming twins.

There is no law in the United States that would prevent Suleman's use of assisted reproductive technology (ART). While patients sometimes ask for more embryos to be transferred, research demonstrates that implanting more than two embryos does not increase pregnancy success rates and that both the mother and the child fare better when no more than two embryos are transferred. In the U.K. and several other northern European countries, clinics are restricted on the number of embryos that can transferred based on the woman's age, health of the embryos, and number of IVF attempts. Under British law, no more than two embryos can be transferred to a woman under 40. In Germany, doctors can be jailed for up to three years if they put more than three embryos in a woman. Given U.S. constitutional considerations, who should regulate the use of ART and what kinds of regulation would you recommend?

States regularly set standards for persons wishing to adopt children or be foster parents. Should similar standards be developed for persons wishing to have their own children? Should clinics be required to consider the ability of the prospective parent to care for any resulting children? Compare the rationale behind requiring minimal parental competence with state requirements for those who wish to practice law, pharmacy, or psychiatry, or even drive a car. See Hugh LaFollete, Licensing Parents, 9 Phil. & Pub. Aff. 182 (1980). Should a clinic even be able to voluntarily consider the well-being of future children in deciding whom to treat? What standards should be considered?

9.   Should a child born through assisted reproduction have a right to know the identity of his or her biological parents? In January 2009, the Missouri legislature considered, but did not pass, a bill which would allow a child born using ART to obtain identifying information regarding the "biological parent," the sperm or egg donor, which the bill would require to be listed on a birth certificate. H.B. 355, 95th Gen. Assem., First Reg. Sess. (Mo. 2009). Do you find the use of the term "biological parent" to identify the donor troubling?

10.   How will the growth of public and private DNA databases affect the anonymity promises made by sperm banks to their donors? In 2005, the British journal *New Scientist* reported that a 15–year-old boy conceived using donor sperm had succeeded in tracking down his biological father using only a $289 DNA test offered by an on-line genealogy service, genealogical records, and some internet searches. Alison Motluk, Anonymous Sperm Donor Traced on Internet, New Scientist, November 3, 2005. The boy's biological father had never supplied DNA to the genealogy service, but two men from the same paternal line were on file. Because the sperm bank had told his mother the donor's place and date of birth, the boy was able to purchase through another online service the names of everyone that had been born in that place on that

day. One man's surname matched the surname of the men from the DNA site, and the boy made contact with the donor.

11. Should a legal right *not* to be a parent be recognized? Consider situations in which a married couple undergoing in vitro fertilization divorce, but several pre-embryos exist that were not implanted. Should the husband be allowed to prohibit the wife from obtaining and implanting the embryos? Would your answer change depending on whether the husband would be considered the legal parent of the resulting child and be responsible for the child's support? I. Glenn Cohen, The Right Not to Be a Genetic Parent?, 81 S. Cal. L. Rev. 1115 (2008). Professor Cohen has identified at least three severable negative rights: the right not to be a gestational parent, the right not to be a legal parent, and the right not to be a genetic parent. In Kass v. Kass, 696 N.E.2d 174 (N.Y. 1998) the Court of Appeals of New York enforced an agreement in which the parties had indicated their desire that the embryos be used for research by the IVF clinic if the parties were unable to agree on their disposition. But the Supreme Court of Iowa, in In re Marriage of Witten, 672 N.W.2d 768 (Iowa 2003), refused to enforce a prior agreement, instead holding that neither party could use or dispose of embryos without the other party's consent. What if no contract exists concerning disposition? The Supreme Court of Tennessee in Davis v. Davis, 842 S.W.2d 588 (Tenn. 1992), refused to give either the ex-husband or the ex-wife an automatic veto, but weighed the interests of both parties, and indicated that in most cases the party wishing to avoid procreation would prevail. The court, however, indicated that the court would enforce the donor preferences had they been given in an agreement at the time of fertilization or mutually altered later.

V.   GENETICS AND IMMIGRATION

Great Britain uses DNA paternity testing in the country of origin on immigration applicants attempting to prove they are related to their sponsors in Great Britain; Canada has a similar system. Although the applicants have a right to refuse such testing, most are afraid to do so for fear that officials will become suspicious. Immigrant organizations, though, claim that such testing is expensive and is required only of certain ethnic groups and thus is designed to discourage immigration of people from certain "undesirable" countries. For further discussion see Lori Andrews & Dorothy Nelkin, Body Bazaar: The Market For Human Tissue in the Biotechnology Age 115–116 (2001).

Under United States law, a child born abroad out of wedlock to a U.S. citizen mother and non-citizen father is automatically granted U.S. citizenship. If the father is a citizen and the mother is not, though, the child can only become a citizen if, before the child reaches 18, the child is legitimated under the law of the father's domicile; the father acknowledges paternity in a writing under oath; or paternity is established by a court. 8 U.S.C. § 1409. In 2001, the U.S. Supreme Court addressed the question of whether, in light of the existence of DNA paternity testing which establishes paternity to a high degree, this statutory scheme violates the equal protection guarantee embedded in the Fifth Amendment's

Due Process Clause. Tuan Anh Nguyen v. Immigration & Naturalization Service, 533 U.S. 53 (2001).

In that case, a child born out of wedlock in Vietnam to a Vietnamese mother and an American father was taken to the U.S. when he was six years old and raised by the father as a permanent U.S. resident. However, when the child was 22 years old, he pled guilty to two counts of sexual assault on a child whereupon the INS began deportation proceedings. His father then took a paternity test to establish his parenthood in order to keep his son in the country by establishing citizenship. The U.S. Supreme Court, in a 5–4 decision, ruled that because the father did not meet the statutory requirements of 8 U.S.C. § 1409 while his son was under the age of 18, the son was ineligible for citizenship.

The Court upheld the differential classification between children born abroad to U.S. mothers and those born to U.S. fathers on the grounds that "fathers and mothers are not similarly situated with respect to proof of biological parenthood." The majority opined that the woman demonstrates her biological connection by giving birth. The court assumed that birth ensures a mother-child relationship. For fathers, the justices required proof not only of a biological tie but a father-child bond. "That interest's importance is too profound to be satisfied by a DNA test because scientific proof of biological paternity does not, by itself, ensure father-child contact during a child's minority."

The majority totally ignored the fact that the father had, by the time the case reached the U.S. Supreme Court, spent 32 years caring for his son. Rather than acknowledge this very real bond, the majority expressed fear about opening the floodgates to a vast number of children claiming U.S. citizenship based on DNA tests. The court provided figures about how many American military personnel were stationed abroad in 1969, the year Nguyen was born (1,041,094) and in 1999 (252,763). The court stated that modern travel (with 25 million trips abroad in 1999) provided "even more substantial grounds to justify the statutory distinction." The court expressed concerns: "The fact of paternity can be established even without the father's knowledge, not to say his presence. Paternity can be established by taking DNA samples even from a few strands of hair, even after birth. Yet scientific proof of biological paternity does nothing by itself, to ensure contact between father and child during the child's minority."

Four dissenting justices (Justices O'Connor, Souter, Ginsburg and Breyer) opined that the statute violated equal protection, noting, "Sex-based statutes, even when accurately reflecting the way most men or women behave, deny individuals opportunity." The dissenters stated that the differential clarification failed to relate substantially to the achievement of important governmental objectives.

NOTES AND QUESTIONS

1. What are the implications of determining family ties in the immigration context based on DNA testing?

2. Isaac Owusu emigrated from Ghana to the United States with the hope that he would one day be reunited with his sons. Fourteen years after immigrating, he became an American citizen and had the opportunity to bring his sons to the United States, provided that paternity could be proved through genetic testing. But when DNA results came back, only one of the four sons was biologically related—calling into question the relationship that he had had with his deceased wife. While Isaac Owusu was able to bring the one biologically related son to the United States, the other three sons that he has cared for and loved cannot leave Ghana. Is this just? How should paternity or fatherhood be defined in the immigration context? While Isaac Owusu will not be able to bring the other three boys to the United States based on paternity, he may be able to challenge the decision, claiming status as a stepfather. See Rachel L. Swarns, DNA Tests Offer Immigrants Hope or Despair, New York Times, April 10, 2007.

3. Section 212 (a)(4) of the United States Immigration and Nationality Act of 1952 provided:

(a) Except as otherwise provided in this Act, the following classes of aliens shall be ineligible to receive visas and shall be excluded from admission into the United States:

* * *

(4) Aliens afflicted with psychopathic personality, epilepsy, or a mental defect * * *.

Several cases used this statute as a basis to deport homosexuals. See, e.g., Boutilier v. Immigration & Naturalization Service, 387 U.S. 118 (1967); see also Quiroz v. Neelly, 291 F.2d 906 (5th Cir. 1961) (adhering to the Congressional rather than the psychiatric interpretation of ''psychopathic personality'' in including homosexuals within the meaning of the term).

The current version of this statute, 8 U.S.C.S. § 1182 (a)(1), provides:

(a) * * * Except as otherwise provided in this Act, aliens who are inadmissible under the following paragraphs are ineligible to receive visas and ineligible to be admitted to the United States:

(1) Health-related grounds.

(A) In general. Any alien—

(i) who is determined (in accordance with regulations prescribed by the Secretary of Health and Human Services) to have a communicable disease of public health significance, which shall include infection with the etiologic agent for acquired immune deficiency syndrome,

* * *

(iii) who is determined (in accordance with regulations prescribed by the Secretary of Health and Human Services in consultation with the Attorney General)—

(I) to have a physical or mental disorder and behavior associated with the disorder that may pose, or has posed, a threat to the property, safety, or welfare of the alien or others, or

(II) to have had a physical or mental disorder and a history of behavior associated with the disorder, which behavior has posed a threat to the property, safety, or welfare of the alien or others and which behavior is likely to recur or to lead to other harmful behavior, or

(iv) who is determined (in accordance with regulations prescribed by the Secretary of Health and Human Services) to be a drug abuser or addict,

is inadmissible.

Could this statute be used to exclude individuals with a genetic propensity for violent behavior or to exclude people with costly-to-treat genetic diseases?

VI.   GENETICS, ADOPTION, AND DISABILITY

Genetic testing has been used in family law to assign legal rights and responsibilities. Such testing looks for genetic similarities between a putative parent and child. However, other types of genetic testing may enter the family law realm. In adoption, genetic testing could be undertaken to identify a predisposition to a genetic disease—to screen children genetically prior to adoption or to screen parents to determine current or future fitness to adopt. In order to assess whether such uses would be legal or ethical, it is useful to review how courts have dealt with genetic disability and other types of disability in the adoption realm.

CESNIK v. EDGEWOOD BAPTIST CHURCH

88 F.3d 902 (11th Cir. 1996).

TJOFLAT, J.

This case arises out of the adoptions of two newborn babies. The adopting parents contend that the adoption agency deliberately misrepresented that the infants were healthy when, in fact, they were severely mentally and physically disabled. The adopting parents brought this suit against the church that operates the adoption agency and against three individuals involved directly or indirectly in the adoptions. The parents' complaint presented multiple common-law and statutory (both state and federal) tort claims and a claim for breach of contract. On motion for summary judgment, the district court dismissed all of the parents' claims. This appeal followed.

* * *

I.

Blane and Kristi Cesnik, who live in St. Cloud, Minnesota, are the parents of four severely mentally and physically disabled children, all of whom they have adopted. They adopted their two youngest children, Caleb and Eli, through the New Beginnings Adoption and Counseling Agency, an unincorporated entity operated by the Edgewood Baptist Church, a corporation organized under Georgia law with its place of business in Columbus.

In November of 1989, Kristi Cesnik called Phoebe Dawson, the director of New Beginnings, and told Dawson that she and her husband were seeking to adopt a healthy, non-disabled child of any sex and any race. On November 20, 1989, a baby boy, whom the Cesniks would name Caleb, was born at a hospital in Columbus. Dawson contacted the Cesniks by telephone and told them that she had obtained and reviewed the medical records of Caleb's delivery, including the results of tests that the Cesniks had asked to be performed. Dawson told them that all of the medical records and other information she had obtained indicated that the boy was perfectly healthy. Dawson also told the Cesniks that Caleb's birth mother had received prenatal care since the sixth week of pregnancy and that she had not used drugs during the pregnancy.

Dawson delivered Caleb to the Cesniks on December 10, 1989, at an airport in Minnesota. The Cesniks soon noticed that Caleb had health problems. Four to six months after the placement, the Cesniks received Caleb's medical records. The records showed that the birth mother had, in fact, received no prenatal care, that she had tested positive for opiates and barbiturates at the time of delivery, that the delivery had been complicated, and that Caleb had been born prematurely. The Cesniks' doctors soon diagnosed Caleb with cerebral palsy, asthma, developmental disorders, and severe behavioral problems. The doctors suspect that most or all of these conditions were caused by exposure to drugs and alcohol during the pregnancy and by a lack of prenatal care.

When the Cesniks asked Dawson about the discrepancy between the medical records and what she had told them, Dawson explained that she had not actually reviewed Caleb's medical records before he was placed with the Cesniks because the records had been switched at the New Beginnings agency with those of another mother with the same name. Dawson also claimed that Caleb's birth mother had lied about her condition and her use of drugs. The Cesniks accepted Dawson's explanations. The adoption of Caleb became final on July 10, 1990.

In December of 1990, the Cesniks contacted New Beginnings again, seeking to adopt a healthy, non-disabled, black or mixed-race child. On February 12, 1991, a baby boy, whom the Cesniks would name Eli, was born at a hospital in Columbus. Dawson contacted the Cesniks by telephone and told them that she had obtained and reviewed the medical records of Eli's delivery, including the results of tests that the Cesniks had asked to be performed. Dawson told them that all of the medical records and other information she had obtained indicated that the boy was perfectly healthy. Dawson also told the Cesniks that Eli's birth mother had received prenatal care since the early stages of her pregnancy, and that Dawson knew the birth mother's personal history, including the fact that the birth mother had not used drugs during the pregnancy.

Dawson delivered Eli to the Cesniks on April 6, 1991, at an airport in Minnesota. The Cesniks soon noticed that Eli had health problems, and they contacted Dawson by telephone and requested his medical records. The agency sent the medical records a week or two later. The records showed that Eli's birth mother had, in fact, received no prenatal care and that she had experienced severe preeclampsia and toxemia. Furthermore, no drug test had been performed on Eli at the time of birth, as had been requested by the Cesniks. A drug test performed on April 1 indicated the presence of codeine and morphine, although that may have been the result of medication that Eli was taking at the time. The records also showed that Eli had intrauterine growth retardation and low Apgar scores. The Cesniks' doctors soon diagnosed Eli with cerebral palsy, pseudobulbar palsy, asthma, stomach problems, fetal alcohol syndrome, facial deformities, colitis, a sleeping disorder, and behavior problems associated with autism. The doctors suspect, as they do with Caleb, that most or all of these conditions were caused by exposure to drugs and alcohol during the pregnancy and by a lack of prenatal care.

When the Cesniks asked Dawson about the discrepancy between the medical records and what she had told them, Dawson explained, as she did after Caleb's placement, that she had not actually reviewed Eli's medical records before he was placed with the Cesniks because the records had been switched at the New Beginnings agency with those of another mother with a similar name. Dawson also claimed that Eli's birth mother had lied about her condition and her use of drugs. This time, the Cesniks did not accept Dawson's explanations.

* * *

II.

On December 9, 1993, the Cesniks filed a complaint in the United States District Court for the Middle District of Georgia against the Edgewood Baptist Church, Andy Merritt (the associate pastor of Edgewood Baptist Church who had supervisory authority over New Beginnings), Phoebe Dawson (the executive director of New Beginnings), and Mary Ellen Slaughter Winton (the social case worker hired by New Beginnings to work with Eli's birth mother during her pregnancy). The complaint consists of three counts, which are preceded by ninety-nine numbered paragraphs of factual recitations that are incorporated by reference into each of the three counts. In addition, count two incorporates all of the allegations—including the causes of action—of count one, and count three, in turn, incorporates all of the allegations—including the causes of action—of counts one and two.

* * *

The district court concluded that the Cesniks' common-law tort claims were barred by the applicable two-year statute of limitations. It concluded that the Cesniks' contract claim was foreclosed because they "could have avoided" the injury they allegedly sustained by the use of reasonable effort after they learned of the mental and physical conditions of the children because under the terms of the placement agreement the Plaintiffs could simply have ended the adoption proceedings and could have returned the children to the Agency.

Finally, the court found no merit in the Cesniks' federal and state RICO claims because the record contained no evidence of a conspiracy to defraud the Cesniks or the predicate acts of mail or wire fraud. The court said nothing regarding the Cesniks' failure to describe the enterprise allegedly involved in the appellees' conspiracy; nor did it indicate which substantive provision of 18 U.S.C. § 1962 the appellees were supposed to have conspired to violate.

III.

* * *

The situation is analogous to a seller misrepresenting the quality of goods being sold to a buyer. Ordinarily, a buyer of goods that are not of the quality represented has two options. He can rescind the transaction by returning the goods to the seller and demanding a return of the purchase price, or he can stand on the transaction and sue for damages—measured by the difference in value between the goods as represented and the goods as received. Here, the Cesniks kept the children and seek to recover the expenses they will incur in excess of those they would have incurred had the children not been disabled.

The district court held, in effect, that the Cesniks did not have the option of standing on the contract and suing for damages. Rather, according to the court, the Cesniks had but one remedy: rescission. The court cited no authority for its holding and the appellees have likewise cited none; nor can we find any. Under the circumstances, we cannot sustain the court's summary rejection of the Cesniks' claim for breach of contract against the Edgewood Baptist Church. Because there is nothing in the record, however, that indicates that appellees Dawson, Merritt, and Winton were parties to the Cesniks' contract with the church, we affirm the district court's disposition of the breach of contract claim brought against them individually.

MERACLE v. CHILDREN'S SERVICE SOCIETY OF WISCONSIN

437 N.W.2d 532 (Wis. 1989).

Callow, J.

* * *

We address two issues in this case. First, is the cause of action of Quentin and Nancy Meracle (the Meracles) barred by the statute of limitations? Second, is the Meracles' cause of action barred by public policy? We conclude that the Meracles' claim for future, extraordinary medical expenses is not barred by either the statute of limitations or by public policy. We also hold, however, that the Meracles' claim for emotional distress must be dismissed because the alleged emotional distress was not manifested by physical injury.

In 1977, the Meracles contacted Children's Service Society of Wisconsin (CSS), an adoption agency, about adopting a child. They told CSS they wanted a "normal, healthy child," which they defined as a child without a "disabilitating" or terminal disease, who is not deformed and who is of average or above average intelligence.

On October 10, 1979, the Meracles met with Josephine Braden (Braden), a social worker at CSS, to discuss the foster placement and adoption of Erin, a twenty-three month-old child. According to the Meracles' deposition testimony, Braden told them the following at the meeting: that Erin's paternal grandmother had died of Huntington's Disease; that Huntington's was a degenerative brain disease which is genetically transmitted between generations; that if one generation was free of the disease, the next generation would be free of it; that each child of a Huntington's Disease victim had a fifty-fifty chance of developing the disease; and that the disease was always fatal. According to the Meracles, Braden also told them that Erin's father had tested negative for the disease and that, therefore, Erin had no more chance of developing the disease than did any other child.

In her deposition, Braden recalled discussing Huntington's Disease with the Meracles at this meeting. However, she did not recall telling the Meracles there was no chance of Erin developing the disease, and could not believe she had done so.

On October 18, 1979, CSS placed Erin with the Meracles, and on November 12, 1980, the adoption was completed.

On February 8, 1981, Nancy Meracle saw a segment of the television program 60 Minutes which dealt with Huntington's Disease. The show stated that a child of a Huntington's Disease victim has a fifty percent chance of developing the disease. It also stated that there was no reliable test for someone at risk to determine whether he or she had inherited the disease.

"Alarmed" and "frightened," Nancy told her husband about the program. The Meracles obtained a pamphlet about Huntington's Disease from a library the next day which confirmed there was no test for the disease. They took no further action at this time.

On September 27, 1984, a neurologist diagnosed Erin as having Huntington's Disease. On September 25, 1985, the Meracles filed a complaint against CSS in the Milwaukee County Circuit Court. They subsequently amended the complaint twice to include two insurance companies as co-defendants: American Home Assurance Company (American Home) and St. Paul Fire & Marine Insurance Company.

* * *

[The trial court granted summary judgment for the defendants and the Meracles appealed.]

We first turn to CSS's contention that the Meracles' claim is barred by the three-year statute of limitations for negligence. CSS notes that Borello v. U.S. Oil Co., 388 N.W.2d 140 (Wis.1986), set forth the following rule for when a cause of action accrues:

> [U]nder Wisconsin law, a cause of action will not accrue until the plaintiff discovers, or in the exercise of reasonable diligence should have discovered, not only the fact of injury but also that the injury was probably caused by the defendant's conduct or product.

It insists that the Meracles' cause of action accrued in 1981 when the Meracles first learned of the negligent misrepresentation.

We find that in 1981, while the Meracles had learned of CSS's negligence, they had suffered no injury which would support a cause of action * * *. CSS contends that the Meracles could have stated a claim for the $1000 adoption fee and for the cost of raising Erin between the time of her adoption and the discovery of the disease in 1981. This is incorrect. These are costs which would have been incurred in any case during the adoption of a child. The Meracles wanted to adopt a child. These were ordinary expenses pursuant to that end. It is only the extraordinary expenses, the unexpected expenses resulting from Erin's special needs, which are actionable.

CSS also contends that the Meracles could have stated a claim for Erin's future medical expenses in 1981. This also is incorrect. In order to sue for future medical expenses in 1981, while Erin had not yet contracted the disease, the Meracles would have had to base their claim on the mere possibility that Erin would develop the disease. To recover for future expenses due to an injury, a plaintiff must demonstrate that the anticipated expenses are reasonably certain to occur. "[R]ecovery may be had for *reasonably certain* injurious consequences of the tortfeasor's negligent conduct, not for merely possible injurious consequences."

* * *

There was no reasonable medical certainty in 1981 that the Meracles would incur any future medical expenses because Erin had not developed Huntington's Disease. At the time, the Meracles only knew that Erin's paternal grandmother had developed the disease. They did not know whether her father would develop it. While Erin's father was not known to have developed the disease, there is a fifty percent chance that a Huntington's victim will genetically transmit the disease to his or her off-spring. The Meracles only knew that Erin's grandmother had the disease and her father had a fifty percent chance of developing Huntington's, and therefore Erin had only a twenty-five percent chance of developing the disease.

Further, Erin's chances of developing the disease within her first eighteen years, when the Meracles would have been responsible for medical payments, was even smaller. Deposition testimony revealed that only four to five percent of the people who develop Huntington's Disease do so while they are juveniles. In sum, even assuming that Erin would develop the disease at some point in her life, in 1981 there was only a four to five percent chance that the Meracles would incur future medical expenses for Erin. This risk constitutes a "mere possibility" and it was not an injury for which the Meracles could have recovered in 1981. They could not have shown with a reasonable medical certainty in 1981 that they would incur any future medical expenses. Thus, they did not suffer a pecuniary injury which would support a cause of action.

The Meracles likewise did not have a compensable claim for emotional distress in 1981. The general rule in Wisconsin is that, to recover for the negligent infliction of emotional distress, the "plaintiff's emotional distress must be manifested by physical injury." In Garrett [v. City of New Berlin, 362 N.W.2d 137 (Wis.1985)], we held that hysteria is a physical injury which can form the basis of a claim for negligent infliction of emotional distress. This rule exists because of the "fear of flooding the courts with fraudulent claims and exposing defendants to potentially unlimited liability for every type of mental disturbance." The existence of physical injury makes the genuineness of the claim much more likely.

CSS correctly points out that an exception to this rule exists. In La Fleur [v. Mosher, 325 N.W.2d 314 (Wis.1982)], we allowed a fourteen-year-old girl to recover damages for emotional distress when she was negligently confined in a police department cell for thirteen hours with no food, water or blankets. We stated that, "under the unique facts presented in this case," the nature of the confinement itself guaranteed the genuineness of the claim. We emphasized the fact that the tort involved "a substantial and unwarranted deprivation of liberty," which itself was "a sufficient guarantee that the claim is not frivolous."

CSS contends that the Meracles' claim in 1981 was such that we should make another exception to the requirement that a claim for the negligent infliction of emotional distress be accompanied by physical injury. We disagree. *La Fleur* involved unique facts and the decision emphasized the narrowness of its holding. The Meracles were not deprived of liberty or any other constitutional right in 1981 nor does the nature of their claim present a similar guarantee of the genuineness and severity of the injury.

We find, therefore, that the Meracles suffered no injury, pecuniary or emotional, which would support a compensable claim in 1981.

The Meracles did suffer an injury which could form the basis for a cause of action in 1984 when they learned that Erin had developed Huntington's Disease. The Meracles had a cause of action for pecuniary damages at this time. They could then demonstrate with reasonable medical certainty that Erin would need extensive future medical care. They were now certain to incur future expenses because of the adoption which they allege was induced by the affirmative misrepresentation that Erin's father had tested negative for the disease and therefore that Erin would not contract it. In 1984, the Meracles had "a claim capable of present enforcement."

As in 1981, however, the Meracles could not maintain a claim for emotional distress in 1984. They still did not demonstrate the existence of any physical injury accompanying their claim. The distress that is usually experienced by close relatives when illness strikes a family member is normal and is not compensable. The rule that a claim for the negligent infliction of emotional distress must be accompanied by physical injury is important and strikes "the appropriate balance between the rights of injured parties to obtain a remedy for a wrong, and the rights of defendants to be free from potentially unlimited liability and the meritless claims." The claim for emotional distress must be dismissed.

Under the discovery rule of *Borello*, the Meracles' cause of action for medical expenses accrued on September 27, 1984, when Erin was diagnosed with the disease. They filed their first complaint on September 25, 1985, well within the three-year limitations period. Therefore, their claim for future medical expenses is not time-barred and should be remanded for trial.

CSS also contends that, even if the Meracles' suit is not barred by the statute of limitations, it should be barred because it violates public policy. CSS, citing Rieck [v. Medical Protective Co., 219 N.W.2d 242 (Wis.1974)], notes that:

> Even where the chain of causation is complete and direct, recovery may sometimes be denied on grounds of public policy because: (1) The injury is too remote from the negligence; or (2) the injury is too wholly out of proportion to the culpability of the negligent tort-feasor; or (3) in retrospect it appears too highly extraordinary that the negligence should have brought about the harm; or (4) because allowance of recovery would place too unreasonable a burden (in the case before us, upon physicians and obstetricians); or (5) because allowance of recovery would be too likely to open the way for fraudulent claims; or (6) allowance of recovery would enter a field that has no sensible or just stopping point.

In support of its position CSS cites two California decisions which discuss the policy implications of wrongful adoption actions. In Richard P. v. Vista Del Mar Child Care Service, 165 Cal.Rptr. 370 (Cal.App.1980), the California Court of Appeals held that it would violate public policy to allow the adoptive parents of a child to sue an adoption agency which stated that the child, who later developed severe neurological damage, was healthy. The court feared that allowing such a suit to proceed would make adoption agencies the guarantors of the health of the children they place.

In Michael J. v. Los Angeles County Department of Adoptions, 247 Cal.Rptr. 504 (Cal.App.1988), the California Court of Appeals held that public policy did not bar a suit based on intentional misrepresentation by an adoption agency. However, the court reaffirmed its decision in *Richard P.* that adoption agencies were not liable for negligence in placing adoptive children. CSS likewise contends that allowing this suit to proceed would place an unreasonable burden on adoption agencies, exposing them to potentially unlimited liability and making them guarantors of the health of the children they place.

Before determining whether we should bar this cause of action on public policy grounds, we feel it necessary to emphasize the uniqueness of this case. This is not a case in which an adoption agency placed a child without discovering and informing the prospective parents about the child's health problems. Therefore we need not and do not address the question of whether adoption agencies have a duty to discover and disclose health information about children they place for adoption. In this case, accepting the alleged facts as true for purposes of this summary judgment motion, CSS affirmatively misrepresented Erin's risk of developing Huntington's Disease. The agency assumed the duty of informing the Meracles about Huntington's Disease and about Erin's chances of developing the disease. Having voluntarily assumed this duty, the complaint alleges, CSS negligently breached it.

Given these unique circumstances, we hold that the Meracles' claim is not barred by public policy. Such a conclusion does not expose adoption agencies to potentially unlimited liability nor does it make such agencies guarantors of the health of adopted children. To avoid liability, agencies simply must refrain from making affirmative misrepresentations about a child's health. We do not hold that agencies have any duty to disclose health information. Further, our decision will not inhibit adoption. Indeed, it will give potential parents more confidence in the adoption process and in the accuracy of the information they receive. Such confidence would be eroded if we were to immunize agencies from liability for false statements made during the adoption process.

We also emphasize that we do not create liability which is remote from or out of proportion to the negligence because, as we discussed above, we only allow recovery for the *extraordinary* medical expenses which will be incurred by the Meracles as a result of the negligent misrepresentation. This case is very different from *Rieck*, in which we determined based upon public policy that parents could not maintain a wrongful birth action to recover ordinary expenses of raising a normal child against a doctor who failed to diagnosis a pregnancy. Finally, this decision does not open the way for fraudulent claims to be brought. There is no greater chance of fraud in a case like this than in any case in which the dispute centers over what words were spoken during a particular conversation. Based upon the unique factors in this case we conclude this suit is not barred by public policy.

AMANDA TREFETHEN, THE EMERGING TORT OF WRONGFUL ADOPTION

11 J. Contemp. Legal Issues 620, 620–624 (2000).

Betty and Russell Burr were elated when the county social worker called to say that a "nice big, healthy, baby boy" had recently become available for adoption. According to the social worker, the mother was a healthy unwed 18–year-old who was financially unable to care for him. The Russells decided to adopt the 17–month-old, named him Patrick, and devoted their lives to caring and providing for him.

Soon the Burrs discovered that Patrick was mildly mentally retarded. A little while later he began to suffer from twitching, speech impediments, and poor motor skills; and later on, hallucinations. When he turned 20, Patrick was diagnosed with Huntington's disease, a genetically inherited, fatal disorder that destroys the nervous system.

The Burrs then obtained a court order to unseal the records concerning Patrick's history prior to adoption, and discovered that his mother was not an unwed teenager. Instead, she was a 31–year-old institutionalized mental patient with a history of psychotic reactions; and Patrick's unknown father was presumably also a mental patient at the same hospital. The Burrs also learned that Patrick had been in foster homes since birth; and that the county knew he was learning impaired and his medical background, which put him at risk for Huntington's disease, at the time of the adoption.

The Burrs filed a civil action against the adoption agency alleging false misrepresentation and fraudulent concealment of material information with the intent to deceive. In affirming the trial court's award of $125,000 in their favor, the Ohio Supreme Court [in Burr v. Bd. of County Com'rs, 491 N.E.2d 1101 (Ohio 1986)] concluded that the Burrs had established every element of fraud, and held:

> It would be a travesty of justice and a distortion of the truth to conclude that deceitful placement of this infant, known by appellants to be at risk, was not actionable when the tragic but hidden realities of the child's infirmities finally came to light.

The Burr decision ushered an erratic stream of cases premised on an emerging tort that came to be known as "Wrongful Adoption." Commentators as well as courts recognize that each of these cases requires a delicate balancing of the interests of prospective parents to whom pertinent family-history information is critical in making an informed decision and the interests of the adoption agency, concerned that disclosure requirements will require it to become the guarantor of children put up for adoption.

Inevitably difficult issues arise. Are adoptive parents entitled to a greater guarantee of health and well-being in their children than natural parents have in theirs? Does an adoption agency act in the child's best interests when it discloses, or instead intentionally withholds, pertinent negative medical history and background information in the hopes of finding the child a home? Can an adoption agency ever state that a child is "healthy" without inviting liability? Must adoptive parents prove, in order to establish their claim, that if they had known the risks involved they would not have adopted the child?

Responses to these questions have varied from state to state. Every state has adoption disclosure statutes that either require or permit access by adoptive parents to the medical records and relevant history of the adoptee. Nevertheless, adoptive parents are seeking remedies for an assortment of "wrongful adoption" tort claims ranging from intentional misrepresentation and fraud, to negligent misrepresentation, and on to intentional and negligent infliction of emotional distress. Courts diverge in the treatment of these tort claims arising from misinformation or failure to disclose in the adoption process.

The most successful of the potential wrongful adoption actions have been like *Burr*; they allege deliberate acts of misconduct such as fraud and intentional misinformation. The common law fraud claim requires that adoptive parents allege and prove (1) a material misrepresentation or omission was made to them in the course of the adoption, (2) made either with the intent of misleading them or with reckless disregard for the truth, (3) upon which they justifiably relied, and (4) in relying they were injured. Courts following *Burr* have upheld complaints or judgments that compensate adoptive parents for reasonable damages sustained as a result of the fraud perpetrated by the adoption agency. These decisions represent nothing more than the natural extension into the adoption arena of longstanding common law principles, the application of which has very little to do with adoption procedures per se.

But what of the duties of adoption agencies to disclose all known information? Increasingly the torts of negligent misrepresentation, negligent nondisclosure, and failure to investigate are finding application in the adoption context. A growing number of courts have held adoption agencies liable for negligently failing to disclose information or negligently misrepresenting the mental and physical background of the child. In holding an agency has a duty to disclose all known information about prospective adoptees, the Massachusetts Supreme Court reasoned that the duty is demanded by the notion of good faith and fair dealing. The court found that the burden on adoption agencies to disclose was substantially outweighed by the adoptive parents' need to for full disclosure. Other courts have shown reluctance to extend liability in negligence beyond this point. For example, no court as yet has held that an adoption agency has a duty to investigate, and several have specifically rejected such a claim.

Most wrongful adoption cases include claims for intentional or negligent infliction of emotional distress. Few courts have recognized the claim in the adoption context; and those that have set a difficult standard to meet, requiring that the adoptive parents show the defendant's reckless conduct was "outrageous and extreme." Other courts hold that unless the adoptive parent manifests symptoms of physical injury, he or she must show the defendant's conduct was "willful, wanton, or malicious."

Adopting a child is a permanent choice, much like the choice of those who have their own children. Natural parents have the information in front of them—their own medical histories and family backgrounds—and thus have the opportunity to weigh the risks and to make informed choices. Should not adoptive parents be permitted these same liberties? Absent a specific duty to investigate and disclose, adoption agencies will continue to choose silence and, in doing so, avoid any potential liability. But gone are the days in which quiet discretion and secrecy surrounded adoption. Advances in medical technology and the social sciences make knowledge, awareness, and early detection too critical to permit medial and historical information to be swept carelessly under an adoption agency's carpet. The interests of adopted children and their parents are best served when full disclosure is forthcoming.

AMERICAN SOCIETY OF HUMAN GENETICS SOCIAL ISSUES COMMITTEE AND AMERICAN COLLEGE OF MEDICAL GENETICS SOCIAL, ETHICAL, AND LEGAL ISSUES COMMITTEE, GENETIC TESTING IN ADOPTION

66 Am. J. Human Genetics 761–767 (2000).

Reports from geneticists have stated that prospective adoptive parents and adoption agencies are requesting a wider range of genetic tests before, during, or immediately after the adoption process. It is possible that certain children who are determined to have various harmful or undesirable genetic predispositions or characteristics will have a difficult time being adopted or, if adopted, will be treated differently by adoptive parents. Although these reports must be considered anecdotal or preliminary at the present time, it is clear that the pressure for genetic testing in adoption will increase as the range of available genetic tests increases.

The American Society of Human Genetics (ASHG) and the American College of Medical Genetics (ACMG) recommend the following:

1. All genetic testing of newborns and children in the adoption process should be consistent with the tests performed on all children of a similar age for the purposes of diagnosis or of identifying appropriate prevention strategies.

2. Because the primary justification for genetic testing of any child is a timely medical benefit to the child, genetic testing of newborns and children in the adoption process should be limited to testing for conditions that manifest themselves during childhood or for which preventive measures or therapies may be undertaken during childhood.

3. In the adoption process, newborns and children should not be tested for the purpose of detecting genetic variations of or predisposi-

tions to physical, mental, or behavioral traits within the normal range.

* * *

The welfare of children affected by genetic conditions should be the first concern in the practice of medical genetics. In assessing which genetic tests are appropriate for all children, including adopted children, the nature of the tests is an important consideration. Among the types of tests currently available are (1) tests for diseases that can be prevented or the health consequences of which can be reduced through early treatment; (2) tests for serious childhood diseases; (3) tests for conditions that do not manifest themselves until adulthood and for which no treatment or preventive action is available in childhood; (4) tests indicating a predisposition to a common adult-onset disorder for which some general preventive measures may be taken in childhood; (5) tests for behavioral traits; (6) tests for carrier state and other conditions that may impact the child's future reproductive decisions; (7) tests that parents request without any direct relation to treatment or reproductive options for the child; and (8) tests performed solely for the benefit of another family member. Additional classifications or smaller subsets of available tests are possible and some of the categories may overlap when the same test is performed for more than one reason, but the eight types of tests described provide a good starting point for discussion of the appropriateness of genetic testing.

Of the eight categories of tests, only the first two categories should be viewed with unqualified approval. The immediate availability of medical benefits for a child who has or may soon develop a genetic condition provides the strongest reason for genetic testing. An often-cited example of the first type of test is newborn screening for phenylketonuria (PKU). Such tests serve the interests of the child directly, are medically indicated, and comply with the standards set forth in the 1995 ASHG/ACMG report and the statements of other medical groups and organizations. The test for PKU is used to screen newborns for a genetic condition that, left untreated, will result in severe mental and motor retardation. Where the condition is identified through testing, effective dietary therapy is available. Such screening is also frequently required by law. All states either mandate or offer testing for PKU.

The second type of test, which screens for serious childhood conditions, should also be supported when there is some health-related indication of the need to test. Such indications include symptoms and family history. An example would be a child with a birth sibling who was already diagnosed with cystic fibrosis (CF). Interests of other parties, including the right of the adoptive parents to choose not to adopt a child with a catastrophic disease, are discussed in the sections that follow.

Although only these first two categories of tests are clearly justified, the remaining categories must also be addressed, because "the entry of such tests into the marketplace is raising the specter of their widespread use." In this regard, technology has increased the number of genetic conditions identifiable through testing, and entities with commercial interests in genetic tests are exerting pressure to expand state screening programs and increase the number of genetic tests available to the public. In addition, some suggest that genetic testing of children in situations in which no immediate medical benefit is expected should not be summarily dismissed as inappropriate, because testing may be otherwise beneficial to the child depending on the purpose of the test, the use to which the test results will be put, the level of maturity of the child, and other individually determined factors. Such testing requires greater consideration and caution, however, even if allowed under some circumstances.

The third type of test, which screens for conditions that do not manifest until adulthood and for which no treatment or preventive action is available in childhood, includes tests for Huntington disease (HD) and Alzheimer disease. Presymptomatic tests for such serious, untreatable, late-onset disorders are personal in nature and should only be conducted on a voluntary basis. Moreover, where no treatment exists for the condition even if revealed, the test is unnecessary, at least from a medical standpoint. Currently, diagnosis for genetic diseases far outstrips treatment technology. As a result, the decision about whether to test for most late-onset or untreatable genetic conditions is better left to the individual at a time when he or she is mature enough to consider all the ramifications of testing. Importantly, many adults with family histories of genetic predispositions for certain diseases choose not to be tested. For example, only 15% of those having a parent affected with HD choose to learn their own risk for the disease. Thus, tests that fall within the third category generally do not comport with the best interest of the child.

The fourth type of test involves screening for predisposition to common adult-onset disorders for which some general preventive measures may be taken in childhood. The benefits of such tests, however, may not outweigh the costs sufficiently to warrant their support. Tests that screen for an increased risk of skin cancer or heart disease fall within the fourth type of test. Some of the primary criticisms of these types of tests are that they may label children prematurely and they may result in the implementation of a course of medication that could last 50 years and cause side effects and have no guarantee of a change in life expectancy. Because of the potential for stigmatization where individualized testing is conducted, a more population-oriented approach should be taken. Numerous studies show that a majority of the population would benefit from a more healthful lifestyle, including reducing fat, increasing exercise, and limiting sun exposure. To the extent that selective screening is necessary, family histories can be used. Because such testing for genetic predispositions in newborns and children often lacks predictive value and is rarely justified, no special exception should be made for children in the adoption process.

The fifth type of test attempts to screen for behavioral traits, such as learning disabilities and personality traits. One of the major problems with this type of test is that biological or genetic markers have not been identified for most childhood behavioral disorders. Other problems include the unpredictable variability in the timing or severity of the disorder or how it will affect the child's functioning. Even where a genetic marker is identified, the stigmatization of the child and the potential for uncritical reliance on pharmacological solutions are possible. Tests for genetic mutations that cause severe mental retardation, such as fragile X syndrome, would not be included in this category and would be considered as a test of the second category.

The sixth type of test is directed at a child's future reproductive decisions and includes carrier tests for autosomal recessive or X-linked disorders, such as CF and Duchenne muscular dystrophy, and presymptomatic tests for adult-onset disorders, such as HD. Tests that may affect a child's reproductive choices later in life are unnecessary at the newborn stage or in the adoption process and serve no immediate medical need of the child. These tests should be postponed until the child is mature enough to decide whether to be tested.

The seventh type of test offers no present medical benefit or future reproductive benefit but is conducted solely at the request of the adopting parents. Carrier tests for autosomal recessive or X-linked disorders and presymptomatic tests for adult-onset disorders can also fall within this category of tests when the child is nowhere near reproductive age. As in the case of the sixth category of tests, tests that fall within the seventh category do not serve an immediate interest of the child, are not medically indicated, and do not comply with the stated positions of ASHG, ACMG, and other medical groups and organizations that have examined and addressed the wisdom of genetic testing of newborns and children.

The eighth type of test analyzes the DNA of several members of a biologically related family to determine the likelihood of a single individual within that family having a certain gene mutation. In the context of adoption, this category of test lacks justification. DNA linkage analysis is relevant only to biologically related individuals. Consequently, such tests serve no benefit to the child or the adoptive family because they are not biologically related.

* * *

The issue of testing is further complicated by the ambiguity associated with predictive testing. Genetic tests usually do not predict when or to what degree a genetic disease or condition will manifest itself. More importantly, the mere presence of a gene coding for a genetic disease or condition does not mean that a child will invariably develop the disease or condition. Such test results supply only "probabilities, not certainties." At best, predictive genetic tests can only provide a range of risk. To subject a child to the potential for stigmatization, discrimination, and poor self-image based on ambiguous information is especially problematic. When the disadvantages of testing are weighed against the advantages of testing, the balance favors not testing, except in cases where genetic conditions manifest themselves during childhood or where effective, preventive measures may be undertaken during childhood.

IN RE VALERIE W. v. GREG W.

75 Cal.Rptr.3d 86 (Cal. App. 2008).

NARES, J.

Greg W. and S.W. appeal judgments terminating parental rights to their minor children, Valerie W. and Gregory W. (together the children), under Welfare and Institutions Code section 366.26.[1]

* * *

FACTUAL AND PROCEDURAL BACKGROUND

[Two-year-old Valerie and nine-month-old Gregory were removed from parental custody in June 2006. The children's father, Greg, was a relapsed heroin addict, and the children's mother, S.W. had an extensive criminal and substance abuse history. The children were placed in the home of a non-relative, Vera. Vera's adult daughter, Juana, who did not live with her, and Juana's partner, Andrea, helped to care for the children, including providing daycare. After an initial six-month review period during which Greg did not maintain his sobriety and S.W. did not contact the social worker or visit the children, the court terminated reunification services and set a hearing regarding termination of parental rights under 366.26.

In its reports for the hearing, the San Diego Health and Human Services Agency (the Agency) reported that Valerie, now four, was healthy and doing well in school, but had behavior problems for which she was receiving treatment. The Agency reported that three-year-old Gregory was healthy, but was small for his age and had fallen below pediatric growth charts. Gregory suffered from asthma, had had a seizure the previous year, and had some delay in speech development, which may have been caused by a very small lower jaw and overbite. Because of these issues, a public health nurse recommended that Gregory undergo genetic testing.

In its reports, the Agency indicated Gregory had undergone an electroencephalogram (EEG), had a pediatric examination scheduled the following month to monitor his growth, and was scheduled to "undergo a thorough genetics test as well." However, in subsequent addendum reports, the Agency did not provide any information concerning the results of Gregory's pediatric examination, EEG results, or any genetic tests.

Greg and S.W. each filed a petition to leave the children in foster care to give them more time to demonstrate their suitability as parents. Greg also argued that the children might not be adoptable because of their unresolved medical and emotional problems and because no assessment was made whether other homes would be available to Valerie and Gregory if Vera was not approved for adoption.

---

1. All further statutory references are to the Welfare and Institutions Code, unless otherwise specified.

The court denied both parents' petitions, finding that the children were likely to be adopted by Vera if parental rights were terminated. The court noted that Vera had already taken steps to adopt both Valerie and Gregory. The court terminated parental rights and designated Vera as the children's prospective adoptive parent.]

* * *

DISCUSSION

* * *

II.   ADOPTABILITY

A.   *Introduction*

Greg contends insufficient evidence supports the court's finding that the children were likely to be adopted within a reasonable time. S.W. joins in Greg's argument. Greg asserts the evidence shows Valerie was emotionally fragile and her behaviors were deteriorating, and Gregory had unresolved neurological and genetic issues that required further testing. He further asserts the Agency's assessment report does not constitute substantial evidence of the children's adoptability because it contained only limited information concerning the prospective adoptive parents, who did not live together, and the Agency did not report on the nature of each caregiver's relationship to the children, the children's living arrangements, and whether other families were interested in adopting the children.

In supplemental briefing, S.W. contends the Agency did not specifically identify Vera and Juana as the children's prospective adoptive parents, and the record does not clearly reflect who was seeking to adopt the children. She asserts the children are not generally adoptable; thus, the Agency must identify the prospective adoptive parents to allow the court to assess the suitability of the prospective adoptive home.

* * *

Minors' counsel * * * asserts Gregory had and continues to have significant medical issues for which medical professionals recommended genetic and neurological testing, and the Agency did not provide any test results in its assessment report as required by section 366.21, subdivision (i)(3) [which requires the Agency to address, among other things, the child's medical, developmental, and emotional status]. Minors' counsel asserts the children's best interests will be served by remanding the matter to the trial court for a new hearing on the issue of the children's adoptability.

The Agency now admits Vera and Juana applied to adopt the children jointly. * * * With respect to Gregory's test results, the Agency argues that Gregory's caregivers were involved in his medical treatment and were aware of the concerns about his condition. It contends the totality of the evidence provided to the court constitutes a sufficient basis for a finding that Gregory did not suffer from severe problems that impacted his adoptability.

B. *Statutory Framework*

* * *

The assessment report is "a cornerstone of the evidentiary structure" upon which the court, the parents and the child are entitled to rely. The Agency is required to address seven specific subjects in the assessment report, including the child's medical, developmental, scholastic, mental, and emotional status. (§ 366.21, subd. (i).) In addition, the assessment report must include an analysis of the likelihood that the child will be adopted if parental rights are terminated. * * *

* * *

A finding of adoptability requires "clear and convincing evidence of the likelihood that adoption will be realized within a reasonable time." The question of adoptability usually focuses on whether the child's age, physical condition and emotional health make it difficult to find a person willing to adopt that child. If the child is considered generally adoptable, we do not examine the suitability of the prospective adoptive home. When the child is deemed adoptable based solely on a particular family's willingness to adopt the child, the trial court must determine whether there is a legal impediment to adoption.

* * *

C. *The Assessment Report Did Not Substantially Comply with Section 366.21, Subdivision (i)*

* * *

The Agency is also required to assess the capability of any identified prospective adoptive parent to meet the child's needs. This requirement presupposes the Agency has identified the child's needs. Where, as here, the record suggests the child has been or will be tested for a serious genetic or neurological disorder, a lack of evidence concerning the child's condition, prognosis and treatment needs, if any, undermines the basis for the determination that a prospective adoptive parent is capable of meeting that child's needs.

* * *

D. *The Inadequate Assessment Report Undermines the Court's Decision to Select Adoption As The Children's Permanent Plan*

1. *The Finding of Adoptability Is Not Supported by Substantial Evidence*

* * *

Further, the incomplete assessment of Gregory's condition under-mines the court's determination that Gregory is adoptable. We are not persuaded by the Agency's argument that the "totality" of the evidence supports a finding that Vera and/or Juana were able to meet Gregory's needs. Gregory's needs are not identified and documented in the required reports. The court and the parties were not informed of Gregory's diagnosis or possible diagnoses, prognosis or any needs for treatment or special care. Without this crucial information, the court was foreclosed from assessing whether each prospective adoptive parent had "the capability to meet [Gregory's] needs, and the understanding of the legal and financial rights and responsibilities of adoption."(§ 366.21, subd. (i)(4).)

The deficiencies in the assessment report were significantly egregious to undermine the basis of the court's decision. We conclude the court's finding of adoptability is not supported by substantial evidence.

  2. *The Inadequate Assessment Report Did Not Allow the Court to Consider Whether There Was a Legal Impediment to Adoption*

When a child is deemed adoptable based solely on a particular family's willingness to adopt the child, the trial court must determine whether there is a legal impediment to adoption. No such determination was made here.

The court made a specific finding of adoptability when it determined the children were likely to be adopted *by Vera*. However, neither the Agency nor Vera and Juana intended to proceed with Vera as the children's sole adoptive parent. We cannot determine from the record whether the court was aware of the Agency's plan to allow Vera and Juana to jointly adopt the children.

* * *

Because substantial evidence does not support a finding of adoptability, we remand the case to the trial court to determine whether the minors are adoptable based on an assessment report prepared in full compliance with section 366.21, subdivision (i) and other evidence that the parties may present, and after determining whether there is a legal impediment to adoption in view of the statutory framework for the adoption of a dependent child.

IN RE MARRIAGE OF CARNEY

598 P.2d 36 (Cal. 1979).

MOSK, J.

Appellant father (William) appeals from that portion of an interlocutory decree of dissolution which transfers custody of the two minor children of the marriage from himself to respondent mother (Ellen).

In this case of first impression we are called upon to resolve an apparent conflict between two strong public policies: the requirement that a custody award serve the best interests of the child, and the moral and legal obligation of society to respect the civil rights of its physically handicapped members, including their right not to be deprived of their children because of their disability. As will appear, we hold that upon a realistic appraisal of the present-day capabilities of the physically handicapped, these policies can both be accommodated. The trial court herein failed to make such an appraisal, and instead premised its ruling on outdated stereotypes of both the parental role and the ability of the handicapped to fill that role. Such stereotypes have no place in our law. Accordingly, the order changing custody on this ground must be set aside as an abuse of discretion.

* * *

In August 1976, while serving in the military reserve, William was injured in a jeep accident. The accident left him a quadriplegic, i.e., with paralyzed legs and impaired use of his arms and hands. He spent the next year recuperating in a veterans' hospital; his children visited him several times each week, and he came home nearly every weekend. He also bought a van, and it was being fitted with a wheelchair lift and hand controls to permit him to drive.

In May 1977 William filed the present action for dissolution of his marriage. Ellen moved for an order awarding her immediate custody of both boys. It was undisputed that from the date of separation (Nov. 1972) until a few days before the hearing (Aug. 1977) Ellen did not once visit her young sons or make any contribution to their support. Throughout this period of almost five years her sole contact with the boys consisted of some telephone calls and a few letters and packages. Nevertheless the court ordered that the boys be taken from the custody of their father, and that Ellen be allowed to remove them forthwith to New York State. Pursuant to stipulation of the parties, an interlocutory judgment of dissolution was entered at the same time. William appeals from that portion of the decree transferring custody of the children to Ellen.

William contends the trial court abused its discretion in making the award of custody. Several principles are here applicable. First, since it was amended in 1972 the code no longer requires or permits the trial courts to favor the mother in determining proper custody of a child "of tender years". Civil Code section 4600 now declares that custody should be awarded "To either parent according to the best interests of the child." Regardless of the age of the minor, therefore, fathers now have equal custody rights with mothers; the sole concern, as it should be, is "the best interests of the child."

* * *

Ellen first raised the issue in her declaration accompanying her request for a change of custody, asserting that because of William's handicap "it is almost impossible for [him] to actually care for the minor children," and "since [he] is confined to a hospital bed, he is never with the minor children and thus can no longer effectively care for the minor children or see to their physical and emotional needs." When asked at the hearing why she believed she should be given custody, she replied inter alia, "Bill's physical condition." Thereafter she testified that according to her observations William is not capable of feeding himself or helping the boys prepare meals or get dressed; and she summed up by agreeing that he is not able to do "anything" for himself.

The trial judge echoed this line of reasoning throughout the proceedings. Virtually the only questions he asked of any witness revolved around William's handicap and its physical consequences, real or imagined. Thus although William testified at length about his present family life and his future plans, the judge inquired only where he sat when he got out of his wheelchair, whether he had lost the use of his arms, and what his medical prognosis was.

* * *

The final witness was Dr. Jack Share, a licensed clinical psychologist specializing in child development, who had visited William's home and studied his family. Dr. Share testified that William had an IQ of 127, was a man of superior intelligence, excellent judgment and ability to plan, and had adapted well to his handicap. He observed good interaction between William and his boys, and described the latter as self-disciplined, sociable, and outgoing. On the basis of his tests and observations, Dr. Share gave as his professional opinion that neither of the children appeared threatened by William's physical condition; the condition did not in any way hinder William's ability to be a father to them, and would not be a detriment to them if they remained in his home; the present family situation in his home was a healthy environment for the children * * *.

Ellen made no effort on cross-examination to dispute any of the foregoing observations or conclusions, and offered no expert testimony to the contrary. The judge then took up the questioning, however, and focused on what appears to have been one of his main concerns in the case—i.e., that because of the handicap William would not be able to participate with his sons in sports and other physical activities. Thus the court asked Dr. Share, "It's very unfortunate that he's in this condition, but when these boys get another two, three years older, would it be better, in your opinion, if they had a parent that was able to actively go places with them, take them places, play Little League baseball, go fishing? Wouldn't that be advantageous to two young boys?" Dr. Share replied that "the commitment, the long-range planning, the dedication" of William to his sons were more important, and stated that from his observations William was "the more consistent, stable part of this family regardless of his physical condition at this point." The judge nevertheless persisted in stressing that William "is limited in what he can do for the boys," and demanded an answer to his question as to "the other activities that two growing boys should have with a natural parent." Dr. Share acknowledged William's obvious physical limitations, but once more asserted that "On the side dealing with what I have called the stability of the youngsters, which I put personally higher value on, I would say the father is very strong in this area." Finally, when asked on redirect examination what effect William's ability to drive will have, Dr. Share explained, "this opens up more vistas, greater alternatives when he's more mobile such as having his own van to take them places. . . . "

* * *

More importantly, the judge conceded that Dr. Share "saw a nice, loving relationship, and that's absolutely true. There's a great relationship between [William] and the boys. . . . " Yet despite this relationship the judge concluded "I think it would be detrimental to the boys to grow up until age 18 in the custody of their father. *It wouldn't be a normal relationship between father and boys.*" And what he meant by "normal" was quickly revealed: "It's unfortunate [William] has to have help bathing and dressing and undressing. *He can't do anything for the boys himself except maybe talk to them and teach them, be a tutor, which is good, but it's not enough.* I feel that it's in the best interests of the two boys to be with the mother even though she hasn't had them for five years." (Italics added.)

Such a record approaches perilously close to the showing in Adoption of Richardson, 251 Cal.App.2d 222 (1967). There the trial court denied a petition to adopt an infant boy because of the physical handicap of the proposed adoptive parents, who were deaf-mutes. As here, professional opinions were introduced—and remained uncontradicted—stating that the petitioners had adjusted well to their handicap and had a good relationship with the child, and that their disability would have no adverse effects on his physical or emotional development. Nevertheless, in language strangely similar to that of the judge herein, the trial court reasoned: " 'Is this a normally happy home? There is no question about it, it is a happy home, but is it a normal home? I don't think the Court could make a finding that it is a normal home when these poor unfortunate people, they are handicapped, and what can they do in the way of bringing this child up to be the type of citizen we all want him to be.' " The Court of Appeal there concluded from this and other evidence that the trial judge was prejudiced by a belief that no deaf-mute could ever be a good parent to a "normal" child. While recognizing the rule that the granting or denial of a petition for adoption rests in the discretion of the judge, the appellate court held that such discretion had been abused and accordingly reversed the judgment.

While it is clear the judge herein did not have the totally closed mind exhibited in *Richardson*, it is equally plain that his judgment was affected by serious misconceptions as to the importance of the involvement of parents in the purely physical aspects of their children's lives. We do not mean, of course, that the health or physical condition of the parents may not be taken into account in determining whose custody would best serve the child's interests. In relation to the issues at stake, however, this factor is ordinarily of minor importance; and whenever it is raised—whether in awarding custody originally or changing it later—it is essential that the court weigh the matter with an informed and open mind.

In particular, if a person has a physical handicap it is impermissible for the court simply to rely on that condition as prima facie evidence of the person's unfitness as a parent or of probable detriment to the child; rather, in all cases the court must view the handicapped person as an individual and the family as a whole. To achieve this, the court should inquire into the person's actual and potential physical capabilities, learn how he or she has adapted to the disability and manages its problems, consider how the other members of the household have adjusted thereto, and take into account the special contributions the person may make to the family despite—or even because of—the handicap. Weighing these and all other relevant factors together, the court should then carefully determine whether the parent's condition will in fact have a substantial and lasting adverse effect on the best interests of the child.

The record shows the contrary occurred in the case at bar. To begin with, the court's belief that there could be no "normal relationship between father and boys" unless William engaged in vigorous sporting activities with his sons is a further example of the conventional sex-stereotypical thinking that we condemned in another context. For some, the court's emphasis on the importance of a father's "playing baseball" or "going fishing" with his sons may evoke nostalgic memories of a Norman Rockwell cover on the old Saturday Evening Post. But it has at last been understood that a boy need not prove his masculinity on the playing fields of Eton, nor must a man compete with his son in athletics in order to be a good father: their relationship is no less "normal" if it is built on shared experiences in such fields of interest as science, music, arts and crafts, history or travel, or in pursuing such classic hobbies as stamp or coin collecting. In short, an afternoon that a father and son spend together at a museum or the zoo is surely no less enriching than an equivalent amount of time spent catching either balls or fish.

Even more damaging is the fact that the court's preconception herein, wholly apart from its outdated presumption of proper gender roles, also stereotypes William as a person deemed forever unable to be a good parent simply because he is physically handicapped. Like most stereotypes, this is both false and demeaning. On one level it is false because it assumes that William will never make any significant recovery from his disability. There was no evidence whatever to this effect. On the contrary, it did appear that the hearing was being held only one year after the accident, that William had not yet begun the process of rehabilitation in a home environment, and that he was still a young man in his twenties. In these circumstances the court could not presume that modern medicine, helped by time, patience, and determination, would be powerless to restore at least some of William's former capabilities for active life.

Even if William's prognosis were poor, however, the stereotype indulged in by the court is false for an additional reason: it mistakenly assumes that the parent's handicap inevitably handicaps the child. But children are more adaptable than the court gives them credit for; if one path to their enjoyment of physical activities is closed, they will soon find another. Indeed, having a handicapped parent often stimulates the growth of a child's imagination, independence, and self-reliance. Today's urban youngster, moreover, has many more opportunities for formal and informal instruction than his isolated rural predecessor. It is true that William may not be able to play tennis or swim, ride a bicycle or do gymnastics; but it does not follow that his children cannot learn and enjoy such skills, with the guidance not only of family and friends but also the professional instructors available through schools, church groups, playgrounds, camps, the Red Cross, the YMCA, the Boy Scouts, and numerous service organizations. As Dr. Share pointed out in his testimony, ample community resources now supplement the home in these circumstances.

* * *

We agree, and conclude that a physical handicap that affects a parent's ability to participate with his children in purely physical activities is not a changed circumstance of sufficient relevance and materiality to render it either "essential or expedient" for their welfare that they be taken from his custody. This conclusion would be obvious if the handicap were heart dysfunction, emphysema, arthritis, hernia, or slipped disc; it should be no less obvious when it is the natural consequence of an impaired nervous system. Accordingly, pursuant to the authorities cited above the order changing the custody of the minor children herein from William to Ellen must be set aside as an abuse of discretion.

Both the state and federal governments now pursue the commendable goal of total integration of handicapped persons into the mainstream of society: the Legislature declares that "It is the policy of this state to encourage and enable disabled persons to participate fully in the social and economic life of the state...." Thus far these efforts have focused primarily on such critical areas as employment, housing, education, transportation, and public access. No less important to this policy is the integration of the handicapped into the responsibilities and satisfactions of family life, cornerstone of our social system. Yet as more and more physically disabled persons marry and bear or adopt children—or, as in the case at bar, previously nonhandicapped parents become disabled through accident or illness—custody disputes similar to that now before us may well recur. In discharging their admittedly difficult duty in such proceedings, the trial courts must avoid impairing or defeating the foregoing public policy. With the assistance of the considerations discussed herein, we are confident of their ability to do so.

NOTES AND QUESTIONS

1. What are the duties of an adoption agency to inquire into genetic predisposition to disease in the biological parents' families? Should an adop-

tion agency be required to order genetic testing of the infant? Should prospective parents be able to ask that the infant be tested genetically—for example, for the genetic mutation for Huntington's disease? See Dorothy C. Wertz, et al., Genetic Testing for Children and Adolescents: Who Decides?, 272 JAMA 875 (1994) for the recommendation that children, including children given up for adoption, not be tested genetically for late-onset disorders. For a more extensive discussion of genetic testing of children, see Chapter 7.

2. The Trefethen article advocates "full disclosure" of medical information about a child who is available for adoption. Would this include information about a family history of breast cancer? What about criminality? The director of a sperm bank once asked one of the casebook authors whether he had a duty to inform women who used a particular donor's sperm that the donor had been arrested for murder. Lori B. Andrews & Nanette Elster, Adoption, Reproductive Technologies and Genetic Information, 8 Health Matrix: Journal of Law–Medicine 125 (1998).

3. Should the identification of a genetic disease have any bearing on whether a child should be considered adoptable? What if the disease has not yet manifested? What if the genetic test only indicates a higher than average predisposition to the disease? On remand, the Agency in the Valerie W. case supplied test results for Gregory showing no particular concerns and abandoned the idea of Vera and Juana adopting the children together. Instead, the Agency identified Juana as the prospective parent, with Vera providing significant support and back-up, allowing her to remain a part of the children's lives. The court agreed with this arrangement, and affirmed the termination of Greg W. and S.W.'s parental rights.

4. What is the standard for determining custody of a child when parents divorce?

5. When may a parent's disability, illness, or mental condition be taken into consideration when determining custody?

6. In a South Carolina case, a judge ordered a woman to be tested for Huntington's disease (at the instigation of her ex-husband) in order to terminate her parental rights. This precedent may foreshadow genetic battles in all custody cases, creating situations in which divorcing spouses each seek genetic testing of the other in order to find out which one is less likely to get cancer or heart disease and is thus likely to live longer. Such an evidentiary quest may put quantity of time with the child above quality, since the quality of a parental relationship is tougher to measure and prove than the presence or absence of a gene. With this approach, then, the child may not actually end up with the "better" parent. And the genetic predictions themselves may turn out to be wrong. Lori B. Andrews, Future Perfect: Confronting Decisions About Genetics 142–143 (2001).

7. In 1990, Congress enacted the Americans with Disabilities Act (ADA) to ensure persons with disabilities "equality of opportunity, full participation, independent living, and economic self-sufficiency." 42 U.S.C. § 12101(a)(8). To accomplish these goals, Title II of the ADA prohibits a public entity from excluding or denying participation in public services, programs, or activities on the basis of a person's disability. 42 U.S.C. § 12132(a). Some disabled parents have tried using the ADA to challenge the termination of their

parental rights, but nearly all have failed. Susan Stefan, Accommodating Families: Using the Americans with Disabilities Act to Keep Families Together, 2 J. Health L. & Pol'y 135 (2008).

8. In the Interest of B.K.F., 704 So.2d 314 (La. App. 1997), a Louisiana appellate court case, affirmed a lower court decision that a mother with schizophrenia could not raise a violation of the ADA as a defense against the State's petition for termination of parental rights. The mother, who was diagnosed with severe chronic undifferentiated schizophrenia, gave birth to the minor child B.K.F. while she was hospitalized for her mental illness. The child was taken into the custody of the state at birth and placed in foster care. It was intended that the child remain in foster care until such time as the child could be freed for adoption or a parent experienced a sufficient change in mental condition that reunification was possible. However, despite the mother's enrollment in rehabilitation and patenting classes, an evaluation revealed that she was unlikely to develop the skills necessary to care for her child and it was recommended that the best interests of the child would be served by not returning the child to the mother. The mother brought suit alleging, *inter alia*, that the state failed to make appropriate modifications in its policy, practice, or procedure to accommodate her disability and comply with the ADA. The court held, however, that "termination of parental rights proceedings are not 'services, programs, or activities' within the meaning of the ADA" and thus the ADA may not be used as a defense in such proceedings. The decision of the Louisiana appellate court is not unique in this regard. Other courts have reached similar conclusions. See Stone v. Daviess County Div. of Children & Family Services, 656 N.E.2d 824 (Ind. Ct. App. 1995); In re Torrance P., 522 N.W.2d 243 (Wisc. App. 1994); In re B.S., Juvenile, 693 A.2d 716 (Vt. 1997); In re Antony B., 735 A.2d 893 (Conn. App. 1999).

9. Various other cases have determined that custody of a child may be denied to a parent manifesting schizophrenia. See, e.g., D.W. v. State Department of Human Resources, 595 So.2d 502 (Ala. Civ. App.1992). The court in In re Juvenile 2006–833, 937 A.2d 297 (N.H. 2007), held that a mother who failed to take psychotropic medications she could not afford could have her parental rights terminated. Should custody be taken away from a parent prospectively if he or she has a gene mutation predisposing to schizophrenia?

CHAPTER 12

FORENSICS: GENETIC TESTING
FOR IDENTIFICATION

■ ■ ■

I. INTRODUCTION

Since 1985, law enforcement officials have increasingly used DNA testing in solving crimes. Genetic analyses have been used to help identify perpetrators by assessing the similarity of their DNA to that of semen, blood or other tissue from the crime scene. Since these comparisons provide a statistical probability that a given individual was present at the crime scene, courts face questions about whether an evolving series of DNA tests are admissible and what weight to give a DNA match. Law enforcement officials face questions about the circumstances under which they can compel suspects—or even the relatives of suspects—to provide blood, saliva, or other tissue for DNA testing.

In 1989, states began passing laws to require the collection of DNA samples from convicted violent offenders before their release from prison so their DNA could be compared to DNA collected from crime scenes. Law enforcement officials heralded the possibility of solving crimes with "the flick of a computer switch." All fifty states have passed laws to mandate the collection of DNA from offenders, but the collection of DNA in forensic banks raises constitutional, policy, and practical issues. Does the collection of DNA from convicted offenders violate the Fourth Amendment of the U.S. Constitution? Should DNA be banked, as it is in many states, from people convicted of lesser offenses, such as non-violent crimes, misdemeanors, juvenile offenses, or even from arrestees? Should DNA from all citizens be put in a DNA bank for law enforcement purposes?

As discussed in Chapter 13, Mental and Behavioral Genetics, DNA may also enter the criminal justice system at the behest of defendants who wish to claim that their genetic profile should exculpate them from conviction or mitigate their punishment. In the future, law enforcement officials may wish to use genetic information to attempt to predict the likelihood that someone might commit a crime (even though it is highly unlikely that such predictions will actually be valid).

The use of forensic DNA identification techniques goes beyond the criminal justice system, however. A military DNA bank has been established for future use to identify the remains of any soldiers killed in battle. In civil cases, including divorce, DNA testing has also been used for identification—for example, to prove adultery. In the future, DNA testing might be used to identify individuals as members of particular ethnic groups in order to provide social benefits.

II. ADMISSIBILITY OF DNA EVIDENCE IN CRIMINAL CASES

A. THE SCIENCE OF FORENSIC DNA TESTING

THE NATIONAL COMMISSION ON THE FUTURE OF DNA EVIDENCE, THE FUTURE OF FORENSIC DNA TESTING: PREDICTIONS OF THE RESEARCH AND DEVELOPMENT WORKING GROUP

13–20, 46–61 (U.S. Department of Justice, Washington, D.C., Nov. 2000).

The first genetic markers that were useful for human identification were the ABO blood groups discovered in the same year (1900) that Mendel's rules of inheritance were rediscovered. Nineteenth century scientists, investigating the causes of blood-transfusion reactions, mixed the bloods from different individuals in the laboratory. They soon discovered that when the bloods were incompatible, a clumping or precipitation of the red blood cells occurred. This allowed the scientists to identify the cell surface elements (called antigens) responsible for the reaction. They noted that human blood cells fell into four antigenic groups which Landsteiner (1900) designated A, B, AB, and O. It was quickly realized that the blood groups were inherited, but despite the seeming simplicity of the system, the genetic basis remained unclear. It was not until 1925 that the mode of inheritance was inferred from the population frequencies of the four groups * * *.

Different human populations were found to differ in the frequencies of the four types. For example, about 10 percent of Caucasian Americans are group B. If one of two blood samples was group A and the other group B, they must have come from different persons (in the absence of laboratory or other errors). On the other hand, if both were group B they could have come from the same person, but they could also have come from two different persons, each of whom happened to be group B. Over the years, several more independently inherited red blood cell systems were discovered. By 1960 there were some 17 systems, but not all were useful for identification. The most useful was the so-called HLA [human leukocyte antigen] system because it was highly polymorphic (i.e., with many alleles). Along with this battery of serological tests some laboratories included a few serum proteins and enzymes. Although it was quite probable that two blood samples from different persons would agree for one blood group or enzyme, it was less and less probable that two unrelated persons would agree for all loci as more tests were added.

The frequencies of a combination of such markers were typically one in a few hundred or less, although in some instances, when samples contained rare types, the probability of matching of samples could be much smaller. By the mid–1970s, analysis of evidence samples and calculations of random matches could be calculated. A combination of blood groups and serum proteins were sometimes used for identification in criminal investigations. Much more often, such probabilities were used in paternity testing and accepted as evidence of parentage, where civil criterion "preponderance of evidence," rather than the criminal criterion "beyond reasonable doubt," prevailed.

* * *

The nature of forensic identification changed abruptly in 1985. That year Alec Jeffreys and colleagues in England first demonstrated the use of DNA in a criminal investigation. He made use of DNA regions in which short segments are repeated a number of times [VNTRs—variable number of tandem repeats]. This number of repeats varies greatly from person to person. Jeffreys used such variable-length segments of DNA, first to exonerate one suspect in two rape homicides of young girls and later to show that another man had a DNA profile matching that of the sperm in the evidence samples from both girls. Soon after, some commercial laboratories made use of this "fingerprinting" procedure, and in 1988 the FBI implemented the techniques, after improving their robustness and sensitivity and collecting extensive data on the frequency of different repeat lengths in different populations.

* * *

After a first flush of immediate acceptance by the courts, the molecular methodology and the results of evidence analysis were challenged as unreliable. Although the majority of courts admitted the DNA evidence, a few highly publicized cases were overturned by higher courts, citing failure of sufficient DNA testing to meet the *Frye* or other standards for admissibility of scientific evidence as the reason.

* * *

During the decade 1985–1995, a revolutionary technical innovation became more and more widely used in molecular biology, so that by now it is almost universal. This is the polymerase chain reaction (PCR), a technique for amplifying a tiny quantity of DNA into almost any desired amount. It uses essentially the same principle as that by which DNA is normally copied in the cell, except that instead of a whole chromosome being copied only a short chosen segment of the DNA in a chromosome is amplified. This has made it possible to process the very tiny amounts of DNA often left behind as evidence of a crime and has greatly increased the sensitivity of the forensic systems available to the criminal justice system.

Thanks to PCR, minute amounts of DNA extracted from hairs, postage stamps, cigarette butts, coffee cups, and similar evidence sources can often be successfully analyzed.

* * *

STRs (short tandem repeats) are similar to VNTRs in that they are based on repeated sequences dispersed throughout the chromosomes. While methods of interpretation for STRs and VNTRs are similar, STRs have smaller repeat units (usually 3 to 5 base pairs) and fewer of them (usually 7 to 15 alleles per locus). The small size makes them amenable to PCR amplification so that much smaller quantities of DNA are needed for analysis.

* * *

The FBI has selected 13 STR loci to serve as a standard battery of core loci, and increasingly laboratories are developing the capability to process these loci. As laboratories throughout the Nation employ the same loci, comparisons and cooperation between laboratories are facilitated * * *. The FBI and others are actively involved in getting frequency data from a number of populations of different population groups and subgroups. These populations are being continuously subdivided. For example, there are data from Japanese, Chinese, Koreans, and Vietnamese. In the Western Hemisphere, there are data for Bahamians, Jamaicans, and Trinidadians. With the 13 core loci the most common profile has an estimated frequency less than 1 in 10 billion. Of the 10 STR loci that the British system now uses, 8 are included in the 13 core loci, so international comparisons are feasible.

* * *

Techniques for using mitochondrial DNA (mtDNA) have been available for some years, but application to problems of forensic identification began in 1990. Several laboratories now have the necessary equipment and techniques to use this system. Mitochondria are intracellular particles (organelles) outside the nucleus in the cytoplasm of the cell. They contain their own small DNA genomes; circular molecules of 16,569 base pairs and the variants are identified by sequence determination. Each cell contains hundreds to thousands of mitochondria. For this reason, a single hair shaft, old bones, or charred remains, which are generally unsuitable for chromosomal DNA, sometimes provide enough intact material for mtDNA analysis. Mitochondria are transmitted by the egg but not by the sperm, so mtDNA is uniquely suited for tracing ancestry through the female line. It was used recently to identify some of the bodies of the Russian royal family, the Romanovs. Limitations of mtDNA include its relatively low discriminatory power and the dependence for that power on the creation of large databases of mtDNA sequences.

EMERGING TECHNOLOGIES: YSTR, LOW
COPY NUMBERS AND SNPS

Standard STR DNA tests sometimes produce inconclusive results when the sample size is small or when there is a mixture of DNA, such as that of the rape victim and the rapist. New technologies are being developed to circumvent those problems. But, as each new technology is applied by forensic laboratories, the question of admissibility needs to be reconsidered.

As an alternative to the STR DNA test when there is an admixture of DNA, a method known as YSTR was developed which is specific to male DNA only. YSTR tests for short tandem repeats only on the Y chromosome. YSTR was held to be admissible under the *Frye* standard in Arizona v. Sanders, CR–2000 2900, December 16, 2003 and in Shabazz v. State, 592 SE2d 876 (Ga. Ct. App. 2004).

Low copy number (LCN) DNA tests were designed to deal with the problem of having just a small amount of DNA. However, because it multiplies the DNA in the sample by using more PCR cycles than traditional forensic DNA typing, there is more possibility of contamination. For example, the DNA of someone in the lab might be introduced into the sample. Consequently, the proponents of this technology recommend that the testing be done in a dedicated area; that the equipment be frequently treated with bleach and irradiated with UV light to diminish contamination; that staff wear disposable coats, gloves, and face masks; and that all results be run against a staff database. Peter Gill, Application of Low Copy Number DNA Profiling, 42 Croat. Med. J. 229–232 (2001). This technology was referred to in dicta in U.S. v. Kincade, 379 F.3d 813, 839 (9 Cir. 2004), which quoted Shaila K. Dewan, As Police Extend Use of DNA, a Smudge Could Trap a Thief, The New York Times, May 26, 2004 as follows, "Just as DNA permeates blood, semen, and saliva, it is recoverable from hair and epidermal cells—which even the most sophisticated criminals cannot help but leave behind. Techniques first developed in Britain have allowed scientists to generate DNA profiles from just 30–50 cells' worth of genetic material, and a new crime lab planned for New York City expects to generate profiles culled from as little as 6 cells' worth of genetic material collected at the scene of nearly every crime committed in the city—including all-too-common non-violent property offenses like home burglaries and auto thefts."

Another emerging forensic technology is based on SNPs. A single nucleotide polymorphism (SNP) represents a single base difference in the more than three billion bases of DNA in the human genome. SNPs are considered the most common form of genetic variation with each person carrying his or her own distinctive set of SNPs. SNP analysis purportedly can generate accurate matches using much shorter segments of DNA than other approaches. Although no public forensic DNA laboratory in the U.S.

routinely analyzes forensic evidence for SNPs, the technique has been used primarily for identification of human remains, as in the World Trade Center bombing. SNPs are not likely to replace STRs for most forensic applications, but SNPs may help solve special problems in forensic genetics. For instance, in November, 2003, the company Orchid Cellmark was awarded an FBI contract to develop a panel of SNP markers that can identify male DNA by measuring polymorphisms on the Y chromosome (found only in men) from degraded samples. This approach is expected to be particularly useful in constructing the male profile in samples that contain mixtures of DNA from both a man and a woman. November 2003, Forensic Focus Special edition, Orchid Cellmark Awarded FBI Contracts to Develop SNP Technology for Advanced Forensic, http://www.forensic focusmag.com/hotnews/3bh257343.html.

NOTES AND QUESTIONS

1. Short tandem repeats (STRs) are regions of DNA, usually shorter than 500 base pairs, that are comprised of adjacently repeated units two to seven base pairs long. A tandem repeat can be thought of as a stutter in the genome, e.g., ACCGACCGACCG. STRs are not full genes, and 12 of the 13 STRs used in forensics are in non-coding regions. The FBI relied upon STR analysis technology in creating the Combined DNA Index System (CODIS), which is a national database and searching mechanism that utilizes 13 STR loci designated by the FBI as "core loci."

The probability of a Caucasian American individual having a particular number of repeats at one STR locus ranges from approximately 3.6% to 19.5%, values much too large for effective forensic use. When data from all 13 core CODIS loci are used, however, the probability of a match is roughly one in 6×10^{14}, assuming that each STR locus is independent of the other. For an African American individual, the statistical likelihood of an accurate match is even greater: approximately one in 9×10^{14} assuming that each STR locus is independent of the other. National Institute of Justice, A Report from the National Commission on the Future of DNA Evidence, The Future of Forensic DNA Testing: Predictions of the Research and Development Working Group at 39 (U.S. Department of Justice, Washington, D.C., Nov. 2000), http://www. ncjrs.org/pdffiles1/nij/183697.pdf.

2. The STR technique, like other DNA forensic techniques, has been promoted based on the idea that the section of DNA analyzed is "junk DNA" from the non-coding regions of the genome and thus provides only identifying information and not information about the individual's health. However, as Chapter 2 made clear, the DNA in these regions turns out to have many important functions and may reveal health information about the individual.

Even if all the STR loci chosen for analysis are in non-coding regions, their analyses could provide health information. An STR variation could identify disease susceptibility when (1) the STR variation occurs in a regulatory region, e.g., promoter or intron splice site, and thereby alters gene activity; or (2) the STR variation occurs in an intron or outside a gene and is positioned close enough (typically within 200,000 base pairs) to a functional mutation that it is almost always inherited with the mutation. See Jennifer M. Kwon & Alison M. Goate, Genes and Mutations, 24 Alcohol Research & Health 167 (2000). See also, William E. Evans & Mary V. Relling, Pharmacogenetics: Translating Functional Genomics into Rational Therapeutics, 286 Science 487 (1999).

3. What privacy concerns are raised when forensic DNA testing also provides potential health information? Should care be taken to choose STR sites that are not likely to be in gene regulatory regions or near known disease mutations? Should laws be adopted to prevent third parties from gaining access to information and samples in forensic DNA banks? Should relatives of offenders have a right to prevent a criminal's DNA from being stored on the grounds that the DNA reveals health information about them as well?

B. THE LEGAL STANDARDS FOR ADMISSIBILITY

NATIONAL RESEARCH COUNCIL (NRC), THE EVALUATION OF FORENSIC DNA EVIDENCE

171–73 (1996).

GENERAL ACCEPTANCE AND SOUND METHODOLOGY

The technology used to examine VNTRs, STRs, or other loci must satisfy the standard required of scientific evidence. In the United States, two major standards exist for deciding whether scientific findings will be admitted into evidence: the "general-acceptance" test and the "sound-methodology" standard. In addition, some jurisdictions have adopted special statutes that provide for the admissibility of genetic testing in general or of DNA analyses in particular in criminal or civil cases. If a timely objection is raised, the judge must determine whether the applicable standard has been met.

The general-acceptance standard was first articulated in an influential 1923 federal case, Frye v. United States, 293 F. 1013 (D.C.Cir.1923). In jurisdictions that follow *Frye*, the proponent of the scientific evidence must establish that the underlying theory and methodology are generally accepted within the relevant portions of the scientific community. The biological and technological principles underlying the forensic methods for characterizing DNA variations have generated little controversy in court. Indeed, the 1992 NRC report proposed that courts "take judicial notice of [the] scientific underpinnings of DNA typing," and many courts have done so. Courtroom debate has revolved instead around the application of those principles to forensic samples and the procedures for declaring a match and interpreting its importance.

The sound-methodology standard is derived from phrases in the Federal Rules of Evidence. In Daubert v. Merrell Dow Pharmaceuticals [509 U.S. 579 (1993)], the Supreme Court held that these rules implicitly jettison general acceptance as an absolute prerequisite to the admissibility of scientific evidence. Instead of the *Frye* test, the Court prescribed a broader framework for deciding whether proposed testimony has sufficient scientific validity and reliability to be admitted as relevant "scientific knowledge" that would "assist the trier of fact." In that framework, the lack of general acceptance weighs against admissibility but is not invariably fatal. The Court discussed other factors that might be considered. Its nonexhaustive list includes the extent to which the theory and technology have been tested, the existence of a body of peer-reviewed studies, and the known error rates of the procedure.

Before *Daubert*, many state and federal courts had construed their rules of evidence as not including a rigid requirement of general acceptance. The 1992 NRC report described the "helpfulness standard" used in those jurisdictions as encompassing the following factors: "general acceptance of scientific principles," "qualifications of experts testifying about the new scientific principle, the use to which the new technique has been put, the technique's potential for error, the existence of specialized literature discussing the technique, and its novelty." Since *Daubert*, many state courts have suggested that their "helpfulness standard" was essentially identical with the approach articulated in *Daubert*; a few have characterized their rules as more permissive.

Labels like "general acceptance," "sound methodology," and "helpfulness" are just that—labels. Cases decided in each jurisdiction help to define the scientific community in which the degree of scientific acceptance is to be ascertained, the extent of disagreement that can be tolerated, the information that may be used to gauge the extent of consensus, and the specific factors other than general acceptance that bear on relevance and helpfulness. The degree of scientific consensus is important to the admissibility of scientific evidence in all jurisdictions, and pretrial hearings in hotly contested cases have lasted months and generated thousands of pages of testimony probing the opinions of experts on various aspects of DNA profiling. The courts have examined affidavits or testimony from scientists selected by the parties, specific papers in scientific periodicals, the writings of science journalists, the body of court opinions, and other scientific and legal literature, including the 1992 NRC report.

C. ASSESSING THE RELIABILITY OF DNA EVIDENCE

ERIC E. LANDER, DNA FINGERPRINTING: SCIENCE, LAW AND THE ULTIMATE IDENTIFICATION IN THE CODE OF CODES: SCIENTIFIC AND SOCIAL ISSUES IN THE HUMAN GENOME PROJECT

191–210 (Daniel J. Kevles & Leroy Hood, eds. 1993).

The rapidity with which the courts accepted DNA fingerprinting is understandable. In theory, the procedure is flawless: if enough sites of genetic variation are examined, it is certainly possible to determine whether two samples come from the same source.

In practice, however, DNA fingerprinting can be quite problematic. The difficulties become readily apparent from a comparison of DNA forensics with DNA medical diagnostics. DNA diagnostics can be conducted under optimal laboratory conditions: the samples are fresh, clean, and from a single individual. If uncertainty arises in the results, new samples can be taken and the test can be redone, which makes for a high standard of accuracy in the procedure. By contrast, DNA forensics compels the biologist to work with whatever samples happen to be found at the scene of a crime. Samples may have been exposed to numerous environmental insults: they may be degraded; they may be mixtures of samples from different individuals, as happens in a multiple rape. The forensic biologist often has only a microgram or less of sample DNA, enough to do perhaps only one test. If the test has ambiguous results, it often cannot be repeated because the sample will have been used up.

Moreover, DNA diagnostics usually asks only a simple question: which of two alternative * * * alleles has a parent passed on to his child? Because there are only two possible alternatives, there are natural consistency checks to guard against errors. By contrast, DNA forensics resembles analytical biochemistry. Given two samples about which we know nothing in advance, we wish to determine whether or not they are identical. We first need to determine if the band patterns match, a decision which requires us to make fine judgments about whether small differences between patterns are meaningful. If we decide that the patterns match at a few sites of variation, we must then assess the probability that the match might have occurred by chance. For this purpose, we must know the distribution of band patterns in the general population.

For these reasons, DNA forensics is considerably more challenging than DNA diagnostics. At the time that DNA fingerprinting was first introduced as evidence, however, the courts were not troubled by these potential problems—and neither were many other people, myself included. These issues have become obvious only in retrospect, as the result of experience.

* * *

Even if two samples show matching DNA patterns, it remains to determine the probability that the match might have occurred just by chance—that is, the probability expressed by the frequency of the pattern in the population. The most straightforward approach would be to compare the DNA pattern to a previously assembled data base containing the DNA patterns of a randomly selected population sample. If the DNA pattern in question matched no pattern in a data base of, say, 1,000 people, one would conclude that its frequency was probably less than 1 in 1,000. Such a conclusion would be completely defensible, provided that the sampling had been random. (In fact, the sampling schemes used by testing laboratories leave much to be desired in this regard: the FBI's original Caucasian data bases consist of samples from FBI agents, which hardly is a random sample with regard to ethnicity.)

DNA typing laboratories, however, claim much more extreme probabilities. They cite odds that range from 1 in 100,000, to 1 in 100 million, to 1 in 739 trillion in one case. How are such probabilities calculated? The explanation is simple: the laboratory assumes that each allele (that is, each band) in the DNA pattern is statistically independent and then multiplies the population frequencies of the alleles to produce the sometimes astronomical odds reported. Of course, the key is whether the assumption of statistical independence is correct.

The law has confronted the issue of statistical independence in the past. In a famous case called California v. Collins [438 P.2d 33 (Cal.1968)], an eyewitness reported seeing an interracial couple, the woman being a blonde, the man being black, leaving the scene of a crime in a yellow automobile. The police subsequently picked up such a couple. At the trial, a mathematician testified about the probability of finding a couple that matched this description. As part of his calculation, he multiplied (a) the frequency of blonde women in the population times (b) the frequency of black men times (c) the frequency of interracial couples. Using arithmetic of this sort, he reached the conclusion that the frequency of such couples was about 1 in 12,000,000; the jury convicted the defendants. The California Supreme Court overturned the conviction, because of this improper statistical testimony. Among several problems, the court noted that the three categories described in (a), (b), and (c) are certainly not statistically independent and so their frequencies cannot be multiplied.

In population genetics, the question of statistical independence comes down to whether the general population is randomly mixed or whether it contains genetically differentiated subgroups. If the latter is the case, then bands will not be statistically independent: if a band common among southern Italians is found at one locus, for example, it is more likely that the suspect has southern Italian heritage and thus it is more likely that a band common among southern Italians will be found at another locus.

* * *

The occurrence of false matches should come as no surprise: clinical laboratory errors occur in all areas at rates estimated at between 1 percent and 5 percent. Mistakes inevitably get made. Proficiency testing compels us to find our errors and confront their causes—with the result that procedures improve. It should also remind us that it makes no sense to report DNA fingerprinting results as accurate to one part in a hundred million, if the rate of laboratory errors is on the order of even 1 percent.

D. CONCERNS ABOUT DNA EVIDENCE

The Florida Supreme Court in Brim v. State, 695 So.2d 268, 271 (Fla. 1997) pointed out that "The fact that a match is found in the first step of the DNA testing process may be 'meaningless' without qualitative or quantitative estimates demonstrating the significance of the match." The DNA analysis assesses whether the accused's sample is similar to that from a crime scene. But a statistical analysis must be done to calculate the likelihood that such a match could occur by chance. The most common method of calculating these statistics is the multiplication or product rule. The product rule requires an expert to determine the frequency of certain genetic markers and then multiply those frequencies together.

Under the product rule, the probability of the joint occurrence of mutually independent events is equal to the product of the individual probabilities that each of the events will occur. If a person is rolling a die, there is a 1 in 6 chance that he or she will roll the number two. The chance that he or she will roll the number two twice in a row is 1/6 X 1/6—a 1 in 36 chance. But if the chance of a man having a beard is 1 in 6 and the chance of a man having a mustache is 1 in 6, these probabilities cannot be multiplied together to produce an estimate of 1 in 36, because the factors are not independent. (Many men with beards also have mustaches). So if a victim describes her assailant as a man with a beard and mustache and police arrest a man matching that description, it cannot be said that the probability that they have the wrong man is 1 in 36; the probability of a random match is higher.

Individual frequencies must be trustworthy for this rule to produce accurate results, but sometimes they are not because of the limited size of DNA databases. These limited databases, established for calculating population frequencies for broad racial categories, may not be representative of isolated subpopulations where intermarriage and inbreeding occur, subpopulations that are not in Hardy–Weinberg equilibrium.[1] The product rule also presents potential problems because it is based on an assumption that the genetic markers used for matching are independent (that is, not close enough to each other on chromosomes so that they are likely to be inherited together), but this is not always the case. See Paul C. Giannelli & Edward J. Imwinkelried, Scientific Evidence § 18 (3d ed. 1999). For instance, the admission of DNA evidence can be misleading in cases where the potential suspects are related and share common genetic markers.

One of the most common problems with DNA evidence has been termed the "prosecutor's fallacy," but often it becomes the jurors' fallacy as well. This occurs when DNA statistics are interpreted as being proof of the defendant's guilt simply because the DNA evidence matches the defendant's DNA, rather than proof that the defendant is one possible source of the evidence DNA. One author described this fallacy as one where the "question of the rareness of the evidence DNA profile" is considered identical to the "the probability that the defendant's matching DNA is the source of the evidence profile." Richard Lempert, Some Caveats Concerning DNA as Criminal Identification Evidence: With Thanks to the Reverend Bayes, 13 Cardozo L. Rev. 303, 306 (1991). This

1. According to the Hardy–Weinberg law, gene frequencies in a population will remain consistent over time assuming an infinitely large population with no migration, no mutation, no differential fertility or mortality, and random mating. For more explanation, see Stanford University, Stanford Encyclopedia of Philosophy, Population Genetics, http://plato.stanford.edu/entries/population-genetics/.

problem arises most often in cases where there is little evidence to link the defendant to the crime other than the DNA evidence. The "defendant's fallacy," on the other hand, occurs when jurors disregard other, non–DNA evidence and assume that any other person whose DNA is similar to that of the defendant is just as likely to have committed the crime. See Margaret A. Berger, Laboratory Error Seen Through the Lens of Science and Policy, 30 U.C. Davis L. Rev. 1081, 1106–08 (1997).

Notes and Questions

1. What are some of the distinctions between the *Frye* and *Daubert* standards for admissibility? Which seems more lenient?

2. Some form of forensic DNA testing is admissible in every state. As new DNA technologies are introduced, however, new *Frye* or *Daubert* analyses must be undertaken to determine whether it is appropriate to admit them. Sometimes the biotechnology companies have developed forensic DNA testing kits and marketed them to crime labs. This approach has led to difficulties in admissibility. For example, the Florida Supreme Court refused to admit evidence of a DNA match when the expert witness from the police lab, who had used a DNA testing kit, could not describe the underlying methodology. Murray v. State, 692 So.2d 157 (Fla. 1997). In a 2000 unpublished Vermont district court decision, State v. Pfenning, No. 57–4–96 GiCr (Apr. 6, 2000), http://scientific.org/distribution/archive/pfenning.pdf, the trial court refused to admit a new type of DNA forensic test that assessed six genetic loci. The test was marketed as a kit, and the manufacturer had refused to publish the genetic sequences used in the PCR technique, claiming they were trade secrets. This prevented others from assessing the reliability of the technique and led to a decision in a *Daubert*–style hearing not to admit the match evidence. The *Pfenning* court stated, "[T]he failure of the manufacturers of DNA testing systems to disclose the primer sequences they have created to permit amplification of DNA is problematic from the perspective of scientific knowledge and, consequently, validation. It is more than problematic, it is anti-scientific in that it inhibits the ability of scientists in the field (including defense experts) to test the manufacturers' claims * * *. The manufacturer's proprietary concerns * * * cannot trump Defendant's right to a fair trial, which includes the right to have only scientifically validated evidence admitted for the jury to consider in the State's case against him. Especially, with a new test, which has not been validated by long use in a variety of settings with a variety of sample types, it is unacceptable to deny independent scientists (including defense experts) access to primer sequences, which could allow the scientists to properly investigate the purported reliability and validity of the new technique." After courts in two other states made similar rulings, the manufacturer published the primer sequences.

3. Indigent defendants have a right to a court-appointed psychiatrist in criminal cases. In Ake v. Oklahoma, 470 U.S. 68 (1985), the Court held that when an indigent defendant makes a preliminary, threshold showing that his sanity at the time of the offense is likely to be a significant factor at trial, a state must provide the defendant access to a competent psychiatrist's assistance on this issue if the defendant cannot afford one. The court stressed the

importance of a defendant's "meaningful access to justice" and found that three factors are relevant in this type of inquiry: (1) the private interest that will be affected by the action of the state (e.g., the accuracy of the criminal proceeding); (2) the governmental interest that will be affected if the safeguard is to be provided; and (3) the probable value of the additional or substitute procedural safeguards sought, and the risk of an erroneous deprivation of the affected interest if those safeguards are not provided.

Should indigent defendants in criminal cases be entitled to a forensic DNA expert at the state's expense? For contrasting answers to that question, see Dubose v. State, 662 So.2d 1189, 1197 (Ala.1995) and Harrison v. State, 644 N.E.2d 1243, 1252–53 (Ind.1995). The *Ake* decision did not provide the lower courts with clear standards concerning the appointment of experts of all kinds to indigent defendants in criminal cases, and the law remains unsettled. For an in-depth discussion of this issue, see Paul C. Giannelli, Ake v. Oklahoma: The Right To Expert Assistance In A Post–Daubert, Post–DNA World, 89 Cornell L. Rev. 1305 (2004).

4. Why wasn't DNA evidence persuasive in the O.J. Simpson case? Blood drops at the crime scene were consistent with Simpson's DNA. Blood on a sock in his home matched the DNA of the victim, Nicole Brown Simpson's DNA. Yet the defense raised doubts about the interpretation and integrity of the DNA evidence by attacking how the evidence was handled at every turn, both at the crime scene and in the lab. For example, one of the blood samples found on a fence was not collected until two weeks after the murder, a lab technician admitted to spilling some of O.J. Simpson's blood shortly before conducting tests on other samples raising the possibility of contamination, and one officer revealed that he had carried a sample of O.J. Simpson's blood drawn at the police station around with him for three hours before delivering it to the lab for preservation and storage. Defense expert Barry Scheck also contended that the database used to establish the frequency estimates for certain alleles was not based on an adequate sample. William C. Thompson, Proving the Case: The Science of DNA: DNA Evidence in the O.J. Simpson Trial, 67 Colo. L. Rev. 827 (1996). See also, Gina Kolata, Simpson Trial Shows Need for Proper Use of Forensic Science, Experts Say, The New York Times, Oct. 11, 1995 at A 20. For an examination of the objections raised by the defense related to DNA evidence, see Defendant's Notice of Objections to Testimony Concerning DNA Evidence, California v. Orenthal James Simpson, Case No. BA097211, Los Angeles County Superior Court, March 13, 1995, http://www.scientific.org/distribution/archive/objection.doc.

5. Courts have grappled with the issues raised by Eric Lander regarding the difficulties of determining the probability of a random match when the accused individual is a member of a minority ethnic group and that group is not adequately represented in the genetic data base to which the sample from the crime scene is being compared. In United States v. Chischilly, 30 F.3d 1144 (9th Cir.1994), a Navajo man accused of murder argued that the FBI's database of Native American DNA was too small and contained too few Navajos to determine accurately the odds of a random match between the suspect's DNA and crime scene DNA. The defendant also raised questions about "substructuring"—the fact that there is less genetic variability among ethnically homogeneous, non-randomly mating populations and consequently

"the probability of a random match between two of its members is greater than the likelihood of such a match between two members of the population at large." The Ninth Circuit acknowledged that the defendant had raised legitimate concerns that may warrant review by the FBI and revision of its procedures. But the court held that these concerns went to the weight of the evidence, and not its admissibility.

6.   Other challenges to the weight of DNA evidence have focused on the probability of matches between the genetic profile of DNA evidence found at a crime scene and the genetic profiles stored in DNA databases, such as CODIS. The FBI estimates that a match between a crime scene sample and DNA in CODIS has the odds of occurring only one in 113 billion times. But a technician working in the Arizona Department of Public Safety Crime Laboratory, Kathryn Troyer, found 122 men in the Arizona database that matched at 9 loci, 20 at 10 loci, one match at 11 loci, and one match at 12 loci. Other laboratory workers claimed to have seen similar matches in their own crime labs. An analyst in the California Department of Justice, Steven Myers, explained Troyer's discovery as a mere "database effect." Typically, the DNA evidence found at a crime scene is sequenced to create a genetic profile of 13 loci and that specific profile is compared to the profiles stored in DNA databases. This is a different method from the one employed by Troyer, who compared all the profiles in the Arizona database against one another, looking for matches at any loci, not just the loci described by a particular profile. However, this analysis does not fully account for Troyer's results. According to Myers, only about 100 of the matches found by Troyer become statistically predictable when considering the "database effect." Jason Felch and Maura Dolan, The Verdict is Out on DNA Profiles, Los Angeles Times, July 20, 2008, http://articles.latimes.com/2008/jul/20/local/me-dna20.

7.   Scientists have developed a way to create blood or saliva samples containing anyone's DNA they choose. The process is simple—in fact, according to the author of a study in *Forensic Science International*, "any undergraduate in biology" can do it. First a small sample of a person's DNA is taken from a drinking cup or a hair follicle. Next, scientists use a process called "whole genome amplification" to make multiple copies of the persons DNA. This amplified DNA can be inserted into a fake saliva sample or a blood sample stripped of endogenous DNA. Someone with a basic background in biology can simply "engineer" a crime scene. Considering that "DNA is a lot easier to plant at a crime scene than fingerprints," do you think law enforcement officials place too much faith in DNA evidence? Andrew Pollack, DNA Evidence Can Be Fabricated, Scientists Show, The New York Times, Aug. 18, 2009 at D3.

8.   As part of the Dallas cold-case project, Sgt. Welsh tested 289 rape kits that were collected between 1983 and 1986 and identified matches in 23 of the cases. According to a recent law passed in Texas, both prosecutors and parole boards will now have access to view DNA evidence, like evidence found by Sgt. Welsh, which connects suspects to sexual assault cases where the statute of limitations has expired. The law will allow the DNA records to be attached to the suspect's criminal files and the information can then be used, among other things, to influence the terms of an inmate's parole. Troy Fox, administrator for the parole board stated that "this law could have an impact on an

inmate's term of parole * * *. The board considers all input for conditions it might want to impose on a parolee to protect society." Ann Zimmerman, Links to Sex Crimes to Follow Texas Suspects Law Will Let Prosecutors, Parole Boards See DNA Evidence Even When Statute of Limitations has Expired; Due Process Concerns, The Wall Street Journal, Aug. 31, 2009, A3.

Considering the "prosecutor's fallacy" concept, should DNA evidence that links an individual to a sexual assault case be attached to the individual's criminal record without any other evidence linking the individual to the crime? Does this violate an individual's due process rights?

9.   Hundreds of thousands of DNA analyses are conducted annually in the United States at more than 200 forensic laboratories, of which more than 175 are publicly funded and approximately 30 are privately funded. In 2005, Congress authorized the National Academy of Sciences ("NAS") to conduct a study on forensics science, including DNA analysis, in the Science, State, Justice, Commerce, and Related Agencies Appropriations Act of 2006. The NAS report notes that DNA analysis has been subjected to rigorous experimentation and validation prior to its use in forensic investigations, more so than any other forensic science discipline. The report ultimately concludes that DNA analysis is scientifically sound and has a high probative power for the following five reasons: "(1) there are biological explanations for individual-specific findings; (2) the 13 STR loci used to compare DNA samples were selected so that the chance of two different people matching on all of them would be extremely small; (3) the probabilities of false positives have been explored and quantified in some settings (even if only approximately); (4) the laboratory procedures are well specified and subject to validation and proficiency testing; and (5) there are clear and repeatable standards for analysis, interpretation, and reporting." National Research Council of the National Academies, Descriptions of Some Forensic Science Disciplines, Strengthening Forensic Science in the United States: A Path Forward, 130–131 (The National Academies Press: New York, 2009), http://books.nap.edu/catalog.php?record_id=12589.

The report further states that "DNA typing is now universally recognized as the standard against which many other forensic individualization techniques are judged." DNA has obtained this position because of its reliability and the fact that probabilities for false positives are quantifiable and often miniscule. However, the report does caution that even a very small, but nonzero, probability of false positives can affect the odds that a suspect is the source of a matching DNA profile. When errors occur, they usually involve one of three situations: where interpretational ambiguities occur, where samples were inappropriately processed or contaminated by the laboratory, or where only limited amount of DNA was available, which limits the amount of test information and increases the chance of misinterpretation. National Research Council of the National Academies, Descriptions of Some Forensic Science Disciplines, Strengthening Forensic Science in the United States: A Path Forward, 129–131 (The National Academies Press: New York, 2009), http://books.nap.edu/catalog.php?record_id=12589.

Although the NAS report confirmed the validity of DNA analysis in forensic testing, the report also indicated that the field of forensic science generally needs reform. "Problems [include] poor documentation, serious analytical and interpretative errors, the absence of quality assurance programs, inadequately trained personnel, erroneous reporting, the use of inaccurate and misleading statistics, and even 'drylabbing' (the falsification of laboratory results)." The NAS report recommends that serious study be undertaken to raise the standards of forensic science and also recommends that forensic labs be made independent of law enforcement agencies; knowledge of an ongoing investigation and the desired result can unduly influence scientific interpretation. National Research Council of the National Academies, Introduction, Strengthening Forensic Science in the United States: A Path Forward, 188, 193 (The National Academies Press: New York, 2009), http://books.nap.edu/catalog.php?record_id=12589. Do the reports of poor laboratory procedure undermine the probative value of DNA testing?

10.   Based on the claims of increased efficacy in solving crimes, one might expect that the percentage of crimes being solved or "cleared" would have increased as DNA databases expanded. However, while the crime rate has dropped over the past ten years, clearance rates have changed very little during that period. Moreover, the clearance rates for crimes typically associated with the availability of perpetrator DNA, homicide and forcible rape, were actually lower in 2007 than in 1995, meaning that law enforcement actually solved fewer of the reported crimes than it did when DNA databases were still in their infancy. FBI, Crime in the United States (1995) & (2007), http://www.fbi.gov/ucr/ucr.htm.

E.   DNA PROFILE WARRANTS

WISCONSIN v. DABNEY

663 N.W.2d 366 (Wis. Ct. App. 2003).

WEDEMEYER, P.J.

Bobby R. Dabney appeals from a judgment entered after a trial to the court where he was found guilty of kidnapping and two counts of first-degree sexual assault while using a dangerous weapon, contrary to Wis. Stat. §§ 940.31(1)(a), 940.225(1)(b) and 939.63 (2001–02). Dabney contends that the complaint and arrest warrant in this case, which initially only identified him by his DNA profile, were insufficient to confer personal jurisdiction. He further claims that the amended complaint, which identified him by name, was untimely and barred by the statute of limitations. Finally, he asserts that his due process rights were violated based on the six-year-plus delay between the criminal act and the prosecution in this case * * *.

* * *

II.   DISCUSSION

A.   DNA Complaint & Statute of Limitations.

Dabney contends that the original complaint and the arrest warrant, which were filed/issued three days before the expiration of the six-year statute of limitations, did not satisfy the "reasonable certainty" identification requirements of Wis. Stat. § 968.04(3)(a)4, thereby depriving the court of personal jurisdiction over him. He also argues that because the original complaint was insufficient, and the warrant was not timely issued, the six-year statute of limitations passed, and therefore bars this prosecution. We reject both arguments for the reasons that follow.

Whether a criminal prosecution is properly and timely commenced by a "John Doe" complaint and arrest warrant which identify the defendant solely by a DNA profile, is an issue of first impression in this state. The issue presented requires an interpretation of statutes and, thus, is a question of law for this court.

* * *

Although Dabney repeatedly argues that the "reasonable certainty" requirement applies to both the complaint and the arrest warrant, that is not the case. The "reasonable certainty" requirement is specific to the warrant only. The statutory requirements for a complaint require only that the complaint set forth "a written statement of the essential facts constituting the offense charged." Wis. Stat. § 968.01(2) * * *. The complaint must answer who is being charged and why. * * * Thus, we interpret Dabney's argument with respect to the complaint to suggest that the DNA profile fails to answer the question of who is being charged. Accordingly, in addressing this issue, we refer to both the complaint and the arrest warrant.

The question to be addressed is whether a complaint and an arrest warrant, which identify the defendant/suspect as "John Doe" with a specific DNA profile, satisfies the particularity and reasonable certainty requirements. Our supreme court considered a similar issue more than a century ago in a case where an unknown female was accused of larceny. See Scheer v. Keown, 29 Wis. 586, 588 (1872). In Scheer, the court held: "[T]he fact that her name was unknown should have been stated in the complaint and warrant, and the best description of the person prosecuted, which the nature of the case would allow, should have been given therein[.]" Thus, the particularity or reasonable certainty requirements do not absolutely require that a person's name appear in the complaint or warrant. When the name is unknown, the person may be identified with "the best description" available.

One treatise writer advises that a "John Doe" arrest warrant satisfies the particularity requirement if it describes the person's "occupation, his personal appearance, peculiarities, place or residence or other means of identification." 3 Wayne R. LaFave, Search and Seizure § 5.1(g) (3d ed. 1996 & Supp. 2003). The case law suggests that the complaint and warrant satisfy the sufficiency standard when the description clearly demonstrates that the "law enforcement authorities had probable cause to suspect a particular person of committing a crime." Powe v. City of Chicago, 664 F.2d 639, 646 (7th Cir. 1981).

Here, the complaint and arrest warrant identified the suspect as "John Doe" and set forth a specific DNA profile. We conclude that for purposes of identifying "a particular person" as the defendant, a DNA profile is arguably the most discrete, exclusive means of personal identification possible. "A genetic code describes a person with far greater precision than a physical description or a name." Meredith A. Bieber, Comment, Meeting the Statute or Beating It: Using "John Doe" Indictments Based on DNA to Meet the Statute of Limitations, 150 U. Pa. L. Rev. 1079, 1085 (2002). Thus, we agree with the State's arguments that the DNA profile satisfies the "reasonable certainty" requirements for an arrest warrant and answers the "who is charged" question for a complaint.

We are, however, persuaded by Dabney's suggestion that in addition to the DNA profile, the particular physical characteristics known to police would have further enhanced the completeness of the complaint and warrant. As Dabney points out, an individual would not necessarily recognize the DNA profile as his own. Thus, although the DNA profile satisfies the particularity requirements in identifying a suspect whose name is not known, it would be helpful, for notice purposes, to also include any known physical appearance characteristics. The lack of a more particular physical description in this case, however, does not defeat the State's argument.

Dabney also contends that because a DNA profile is not apparent to the naked eye, the warrant cannot be readily executed. This argument does not alter our conclusion that the particularity requirement was satisfied in this case. Clearly, a police officer with a DNA profile in hand could not walk up to an individual and arrest him/her on that basis. Rather, the officer would need to obtain a DNA sample from the individual to compare it with the one identified in the arrest warrant. This extra step, however, is not unique to a warrant based on DNA. No matter how well a warrant describes the individual, extrinsic information is commonly needed to execute it. If a name is given, information to link the name to the physical person must be acquired. Accordingly, we conclude that an arrest warrant based on a DNA profile can be readily and accurately executed.

Based on the foregoing, we conclude that the complaint and warrant in this case satisfy the statutory requirements; therefore, the documents were sufficient to identify Dabney and were sufficient to confer personal jurisdiction. Accordingly, the trial court did not err when it denied Dabney's motion to dismiss based on this argument.

* * *

Dabney's last claim is that his due process rights were violated for two reasons: (1) he was not given sufficient notice of the claim because the original complaint and warrant identified him only by his DNA profile; and (2) he was prejudiced by the pre-charging delay. We reject both arguments.

First, the fact that the original complaint and arrest warrant were issued as "John Doe" and contained only a DNA profile does not create any lack of "notice" issues. A defendant is not entitled to specific notice that the state is issuing a complaint and seeking an arrest warrant. "[A]n arrest warrant issues when it is signed by a judge with intent that it be executed and the warrant leaves the possession of the judge." State v. Mueller, 201 Wis. 2d 121, 129, 549 N.W.2d 455 (Ct. App. 1996). Thus, the warrant is issued without any involvement from the defendant and the defendant is not provided with any notice of the underlying charge until the warrant is executed. Here, the warrant was not executed until Dabney's name was substituted for "John Doe." Thus, whether or not Dabney knew his specific DNA profile is irrelevant.

Second, Dabney contends that the prosecutorial delay in filing the complaint violated his due process rights. He argues that the State intentionally delayed this case until it was able to obtain a positive DNA identification. He contends that, as a result, he has been prejudiced because "memories fade" and "witnesses become unavailable." We must reject this claim as well.

In order to demonstrate a due process violation on this basis, Dabney has to establish that he suffered: (1) actual prejudice as a result of the delay; and (2) that the delay arose as a result of an improper purpose, so as to afford the State a tactical advantage over him. State v. Wilson, 149 Wis. 2d 878, 903–05, 440 N.W.2d 534 (1989). Whether the pre-charging delay violated the due process clause is a constitutional question, which we review independent of the trial court. See generally State v. McMorris, 213 Wis. 2d 156, 165–66, 570 N.W.2d 384 (1997).

Dabney has failed to satisfy his burden. Although he alleges that "memories fade" and "witnesses become unavailable" as time passes, he does not set forth any specific facts to establish actual prejudice. Without any more specific factual allegations, he has failed to sufficiently present a claim of actual prejudice. See State v. Monarch, 230 Wis. 2d 542, 551, 602 N.W.2d 179 (Ct. App. 1999).

NOTES AND QUESTIONS

1. Other state courts have followed the *Dabney* court's logic. For example, a New York appellate court held that the use of a DNA profile in a criminal indictment did not violate a defendant's Sixth Amendment or state constitutional right to notice of the charges brought against him. The court reasoned that the charges read against the defendant at his arraignment provided him with sufficient notice. Therefore, the use of a DNA profile in the indicting document did not deprive the defendant of any constitutional rights. The court also noted that the use of DNA profiles for this purpose was increasingly popular due to the ability of DNA to accurately identify an individual and was therefore appropriate for use in an indicting document. People v. Martinez, 855 N.Y.S.2d 522 (N.Y.App.Div. 2008).

However, statutes of limitations and the policies behind them remain a stumbling block to the use of DNA profiles in John Doe warrants. As one commentator put it, statutes of limitations promote the security and stability of society; "the defendant will not be asked to defend against acts committed in the distant past, the innocent and unsure will be free from erroneous prosecution, the witnesses and victims will be provided the peace of mind that the ordeal has reached an end and is past, and the police are free to conclude investigation of the old case and redirect their attention to more recent affairs." Corey E. Delaney, Seeking John Doe: The Provision and Propriety of DNA–Based Warrants in the Wake of Wisconsin v. Dabney, 33 Hofstra L. Rev. 1091 (2005). What purposes does a statute of limitations serve? Are DNA warrants consistent with those purposes?

F.   OBTAINING DNA SAMPLES FOR A MATCH

LORI ANDREWS & DOROTHY NELKIN, BODY BAZAAR: THE MARKET FOR HUMAN TISSUE IN THE BIOTECHNOLOGY AGE

102–103 (2001).

Blair Shelton wept when the technician drew blood for a DNA test. The day before, police had come to Shelton's workplace, a T.J. Maxx, and quizzed the manager about him. They told his boss that a woman had been raped by a black male who stood between five foot seven and six foot two and was between twenty-five and thirty-five years old, implying that Shelton could be that man. Shelton, a thirty-seven-year-old African–American, owned his own home and held down two janitorial jobs, one at the T.J. Maxx and another at a local school. He lost the first job after the police questioned his boss about him.

Shelton was innocent, but the police would not take his word for it. Instead, they pressured him to submit a blood sample for testing by threatening to obtain a search warrant to extract the blood if he did not. Inexperienced in dealing with the police, Shelton was humiliated, intimidated, and reduced to tears when the sample was taken.

Shelton was just one of hundreds of African–Americans in Ann Arbor, Michigan, who were caught in this DNA dragnet operation. Based on the vague description of the rapist, Ann Arbor police stopped more than seven hundred men and took samples for DNA testing from 160 of them.

Shelton's DNA did not match the DNA from the rapist's samples, but that did not end the police intimidation of him. Over the next few weeks, police officers stopped him while he was waiting in line outside a theater, boarding a bus, buying bagels, and jogging around a baseball field. Each time he was required to show a receipt proving that his blood had already been tested. Once an officer held him at gunpoint until he could "prove" his genetic innocence. The receipt in effect became his "passport" to avoid further questioning. Once the rapist was found, Shelton sued the police to have his blood sample returned. In 1997 a court honored his request. Now, says Shelton, he keeps the two tubes in his refrigerator to "remind me how angry this whole thing makes me."

EDWARD IMWINKLERIED & D. H. KAYE, DNA TYPING: EMERGING OR NEGLECTED ISSUES

76 Wash. L. Rev. 413, 416–445 (2001).

Traditionally, DNA has been employed to link a suspect to a crime. Finding that a suspect's DNA matches the DNA left at a crime scene, for example, tends to incriminate the suspect. Inversely, when the DNA does not match, the suspect usually can be excluded as the source of the crime-scene DNA. If trace evidence is to be used in these ways, the police must secure samples of DNA from individuals who might have committed the crime under investigation. Officials can secure such samples in many ways. They can seek a court order to compel an individual to submit to sampling; they can turn to a preexisting collection of DNA samples; they can take a sample with the consent of the individual; or they can try to locate a sample that the suspect has abandoned.

As a matter of constitutional law, the principal constraint on such government action is the Search and Seizure Clause of the Fourth Amendment to the U.S. Constitution, which states:

> The right of the people to be secure in their persons, houses, papers, and effects, against unreasonable searches and seizures, shall not be violated, and no Warrants shall issue, but upon probable cause, supported by Oath or affirmation, and particularly describing the place to be searched, and the persons or things to be seized.

* * *

Because Schmerber [v. California, 384 U.S. 757 (1966)] established that the Fourth Amendment applies to removing material from a suspect's body, as a general rule, police must persuade a judge or magistrate that there is probable cause to believe that the desired DNA sample will produce evidence linking the suspect to the crime. With judicial authorization, police can use necessary force to extract the biological material. Furthermore, once the authorities legally have acquired a suspect's profile, they are permitted to compare it to profiles from unrelated, unsolved crime-scene stains. The current state of the law appears to allow evidence legitimately acquired for one purpose to be used for another purpose, at least if the additional use entails no further search or seizure of the person.

In some circumstances, however, either a warrant or probable cause might not be essential to obtain the sample in the first place. For instance, if a person is legitimately under arrest, the seizure of the person is justified, and routine, non-invasive DNA sampling of all arrestees solely for the purpose of creating a record of the true identity of the individual is probably constitutional * * *.

It also is likely that an order compelling a person to give a sample could be issued on something less than probable cause. In Davis v.

Mississippi [394 U.S. 721, 727 (1969)], the Supreme Court suggested in dictum such a procedure. A woman in Meridian, Mississippi, reported that "a Negro youth" broke into her home and raped her. Police, "without warrants, took at least 24 Negro youths," including Davis, "to police headquarters where they were questioned briefly, fingerprinted, and released without charge." After Davis's fingerprints were discovered to match those lifted from the windowsill, he was indicted, tried, and convicted. His objection to the admission of the fingerprint evidence was overruled, and the Mississippi Supreme Court affirmed the conviction on the theory that fingerprint evidence is so reliable that the Fourth Amendment exclusionary rule does not apply to this evidence. The U.S. Supreme Court reversed. The Court held that the Fourth Amendment requires the exclusion of evidence that is the fruit of an unreasonable search or seizure, regardless of how reliable that evidence may be. Reasoning that Davis was detained without a warrant and without probable cause, and that he was not merely fingerprinted but interrogated, the Court concluded that the resulting fingerprints were inadmissible. However, the Court's response to the state's argument that an arrest made solely for the purpose of obtaining fingerprints should be allowed without probable cause was less definitive. Although Justice Brennan, writing for the majority of the Court, emphasized that "detentions for the sole purpose of obtaining fingerprints are * * * subject to the constraints of the Fourth Amendment," he added that:

> It is arguable, however, that, because of the unique nature of the fingerprinting process, such detentions might, under narrowly defined circumstances, be found to comply with the Fourth Amendment even though there is no probable cause in the traditional sense * * *. Detention for fingerprinting may constitute a much less serious intrusion upon personal security than other types of police searches and detentions. Fingerprinting involves none of the probing into an individual's private life and thoughts that marks an interrogation or search. Nor can fingerprint detention be employed repeatedly to harass an individual, since the police need only one set of each person's prints. Furthermore, fingerprinting is an inherently more reliable and effective crime solving tool than eyewitness identifications or confessions * * *. Finally, because there is no danger of destruction of fingerprints, the limited detention need not come unexpectedly or at an inconvenient time.

The Court opened the door to the possibility that "the requirements of the Fourth Amendment could be met by narrowly circumscribed procedures for obtaining, during the course of a criminal investigation, the fingerprints of individuals for whom there is no probable cause to arrest." The Court virtually invited states to devise procedures to obtain evidence of identifying characteristics on the basis of something less than probable cause.

Many states seized on this invitation by adopting statutes or court rules permitting the police to obtain evidence of identifying physical characteristics after a showing of founded or reasonable suspicion. For instance, Arizona authorizes magistrates to issue "an order authorizing * * * temporary detention, for the purpose of obtaining evidence of identifying physical characteristics" on a showing of "reasonable cause for belief that a felony has been committed" and proof that the "physical characteristics * * * may contribute to the identification of the individual who committed such offense." As in this instance, the language of many of these statutes and court rules is broad enough to apply to DNA samples.

One might argue that these statutes or rules are too broad—that unlike the fingerprints in *Davis*, blood, urine, or hair samples should be treated differently because they have the potential to reveal information that is more significant than the pattern of whorls and ridges in a fingerprint. Some support for this distinction can be found in Skinner v. Railway Labor Executives' Ass'n [489 U.S. 602 (1989)], which involved drug testing of railway employees. The Court observed that "chemical analysis of urine, like that of blood, can reveal a host of private medical facts about an employee, including whether he or she is epileptic, pregnant, or diabetic." The same concern with "private medical facts" arises with any samples that can be subjected to DNA analysis. To this extent, it would be facile to say that DNA typing, like the fingerprinting in *Davis*, "involves none of the probing into an individual's private life and thoughts that marks an interrogation or search." Certain parts of one's genome—those that are related to otherwise nonobvious disease states or behavioral characteristics—are as much, if not more, a part of "an individual's private life" as are the hormones or other chemicals found in one's urine.

However, all the other factors listed in the *Davis* dictum apply to DNA sampling. Detention to obtain the sample cannot "be employed repeatedly to harass an individual, since the police need only one set of each person's [DNA types]." DNA analysis "is an inherently more reliable and effective crime-solving tool than eyewitness identifications or confessions." And, "the limited detention need not come unexpectedly or at an inconvenient time." Moreover, in describing these features of fingerprinting, the *Davis* Court recognized the possibility that the police might abuse even fingerprinting to harass or inconvenience a suspect. The suggestion of relaxing the probable cause requirement presupposes the police will conform to the court order and the judiciary will issue orders that avoid these problems. This premise applies as well to the informational privacy concern voiced in *Skinner*. Just as there is no need to detain an individual repeatedly or to detain a person in the middle of the night, there is no reason for the police to probe parts of the genome that conceivably could be used to indicate disease states, susceptibilities, or the like. Because the judicial order can limit the search to loci that are of strictly biometric interest, the analogy to *Davis* is apt. Detention for DNA typing, as much as detention for fingerprinting, "may constitute a much less serious intrusion upon personal security than other types of police searches and detentions." If a person can be compelled to submit to fingerprinting on reasonable suspicion rather than probable cause, he or she can be required to submit to DNA sampling on the same showing.

* * *

The police also might obtain a suspect's DNA sample surreptitiously, without detaining the person. Saliva deposited on a coffee cup at a restaurant, for example, can be collected and analyzed. Police unsuccessfully chasing a wounded felon might find sufficient blood has dripped onto the sidewalk for DNA profiling to be conducted. It could be argued that such activity is not a search (and hence requires neither probable cause nor a warrant) because the individual, having abandoned the material in a public place, retains no reasonable expectation of privacy in it. The Supreme Court used this reasoning in California v. Greenwood [486 U.S. 35 (1988)] in holding that the Fourth Amendment does not prohibit ''the warrantless search and seizure of garbage left for collection outside the curtilage of a home.'' The Court commented:

> It is common knowledge that plastic garbage bags left on or at the side of a public street are readily accessible to animals, children, scavengers, snoops, and other members of the public * * *. Moreover, respondents placed their refuse at the curb for the express purpose of conveying it to a third party, the trash collector, who might himself have sorted through respondents' trash or permitted others, such as the police, to do so.

> However, depositing DNA in the ordinary course of life when drinking, sneezing, or shedding hair, dandruff, or other cells differs from placing private papers in a container on the street to be collected as garbage. Depositing paper in the trash is generally a volitional act. Someone intent on preserving the secrecy of the papers can shred the papers or dispose of them in other ways that would defeat normal police surveillance. Leaving a trail of DNA, however, is not a conscious activity. The deposition of DNA in public places cannot be avoided unless one is a hermit or is fanatical in using extraordinary containment measures. In this setting, the inference of intent to abandon is markedly weaker.

> If the police collection of inadvertently deposited DNA cannot be justified solely on an abandonment theory, under Katz [v. United States, 389 U.S. 347 (1967), a case about the application of the Fourth Amendment to electronic eavesdropping on public phone booth calls], the question becomes whether society does or should recognize as reasonable the expectation that government agents will not follow one about to obtain and analyze DNA that almost inevitably is left in public places. A case can be constructed that such an expectation exists. The public is extremely concerned with preserving genetic privacy.

* * *

It seems clear that, in a public restaurant after a suspect departed, the police could pick up a coffee cup used by the suspect and, consistent with the Fourth Amendment, examine it for fingerprints. Courts may find it a small step to conclude that the warrantless collection of inadvertently abandoned DNA does not violate the Fourth Amendment.

Before taking this step, however, courts should consider the extent to which meaningful, personal information that would not be available to private citizens will fall into the hands of government agents interested in accessing this information. When society enters an era in which DNA analyzers are as accessible as home pregnancy-test kits, the argument for an expectation of privacy will be weak. But in a world still at the threshold of an age of molecular biology, what expectation is reasonable is less obvious. Privacy expectations should turn on the incentives and disincentives for the government to acquire DNA information that is truly sensitive as well as the risk that this information will be used to harm individuals.

* * *

IN THE MATTER OF A GRAND JURY INVESTIGATION
692 N.E.2d 56 (Mass.1998).

WILKINS, J.

A grand jury in Berkshire County is investigating the apparent rape of a twenty-one–year old woman who is profoundly retarded and autistic. The woman, who lives with her parents and brother, cannot talk and requires twenty-four hour supervision. In the fall of 1996, a physician determined that the woman was pregnant. The woman is incapable of identifying the man who caused her pregnancy. Police investigation led to the reasonable belief that either the woman's father or her brother caused her pregnancy. A State trooper sought to obtain blood samples from each for comparison testing, but, on advice of counsel, each declined to cooperate.

In February, 1997, the State trooper testified before the grand jury, presenting the information that we have just summarized. The district attorney then petitioned, on behalf of the grand jury, for a court order directing the father and the brother each to submit to the taking of a sample of blood by trained laboratory personnel under the direction of the State police. The father and the brother, represented by separate counsel, opposed the petition. They relied on the prohibition of unreasonable searches and seizures stated in both the Federal and State Constitutions but on appeal make no claim that the two provisions call for different results.

A judge in the Superior Court held a hearing on the petition and denied it. Relying on this court's opinion in Matter of Lavigne, 641 N.E.2d 1328 (Mass.1994), which concerned the right of the police to take a blood sample pursuant to a search warrant, the judge concluded that the Commonwealth must show that there is probable cause for believing that the person whose blood is sought committed the crime under investigation. Because, in his view, the Commonwealth failed to make such a showing, the judge declined to order the production of blood samples.

* * *

In Schmerber v. California, 384 U.S. 757 (1966), the Court balanced the State's interest in obtaining evidence against the defendant's rights. It held that a defendant's constitutional right not to be subjected to unreasonable searches and seizures was not violated when, in exigent circumstances and with probable cause to believe that the defendant had operated a motor vehicle while intoxicated, a doctor on direction of a police officer drew blood from the defendant shortly after a motor vehicle accident. "Such tests are a commonplace in these days of periodic physical examinations and experience with them teaches that the quantity of blood extracted is minimal, and that for most people the procedure involves virtually no risk, trauma, or pain." The Court emphasized that there was a clear indication that relevant evidence would be found because a blood test is an effective means of determining whether a person is intoxicated. The absence of an adequate alternative means of proof bears on the intensity of the State's interest in obtaining the evidence and is a factor to be considered in the balancing test stated in the *Schmerber* opinion. A more substantial bodily intrusion might require a different result, even if there were probable cause to believe that a defendant had committed a crime and the intrusion would produce relevant evidence, especially if the State's need for the evidence was not great. Although the *Schmerber* and Winston [v. Lee, 470 U.S. 753 (1985)] opinions indicate that drawing blood is not by itself unreasonable, they tell us little about the standard to be applied when a request comes from a grand jury.

* * *

* * * A standard that requires that a grand jury request must be reasonable in light of the facts seems appropriate. Given that a grand jury must find probable cause to indict, it would be peculiar to require them to demonstrate the same degree of probable cause to believe that a target of their investigation committed a crime before the grand jury could properly obtain evidence in aid of their investigation. ("A grand jury subpoena is thus much different from a subpoena issued in the context of a prospective criminal trial.... [T]he Government cannot be required to justify the issuance of a grand jury subpoena by presenting evidence sufficient to establish probable cause because the very purpose of requesting the information is to ascertain whether probable cause exists").

* * *

The grand jury uniquely "is a grand inquest, a body with powers of investigation and inquisition, the scope of whose inquiries is not to be limited narrowly by questions of propriety or forecasts of the probable result of the investigation, or by doubts whether any particular individual will be found properly subject to an accusation of crime.... [T]he identity of the offender, and the precise nature of the offense ... normally are developed at the conclusion of the grand jury's labors, not at the beginning." The Court has noted that "[t]he grand jury occupies a unique role in our criminal justice system. It is an investigatory body charged with the responsibility of determining whether or not a crime has been committed. . . . The function of the grand jury is to inquire into all information that might possibly bear on its investigation until it has identified an offense or has satisfied itself that none has occurred." A grand jury's investigative power is necessarily broad. It is, however, not unlimited.

A grand jury must have a reasonable basis for believing (have probable cause for believing, if you wish) that a blood sample will provide test results that will significantly aid (in this case perhaps indispensably aid) the grand jury in their investigation of circumstances in which there is good reason to believe a crime had been committed. In this case, an additional demonstration supports the issuance of orders for blood samples. There is reason to believe (it may even be more likely than not) that either the father or the brother caused the pregnancy. Proper testing certainly will exclude one, and could exclude both, from the grand jury's continuing interest. The test results, no matter what they are, will be a significant aid in the grand jury's inquiry. The reasonable expectation is that the test results will strongly point to, but not conclusively prove, the guilt of the man who caused the pregnancy.

The case is remanded to the single justice with instructions that an order shall be issued in the Superior Court directing the father and the brother each to submit to the taking of a blood sample by trained laboratory personnel under the supervision of the State police.

So ordered.

NOTES AND QUESTIONS

1. Was Blair Shelton's provision of a blood sample sufficiently coerced so as not to be considered "voluntary"? Under what circumstances should the police be able to request blood samples from individuals to match to a crime scene?

2. The Fourth Amendment protects individuals who have a reasonable expectation of privacy. Imwinkelried and Kaye state, "When society enters an era in which DNA analyzers are as accessible as home pregnancy-test kits, the argument for an expectation of privacy will be weak." How persuasive is their argument? Should the mere fact that technology makes certain invasions of privacy easier to accomplish override an individual's beliefs and social expectations that such information should be private? Just because a woman can readily learn whether she is pregnant or not through a home kit does not mean she expects that information to be publicly available.

In Kyllo v. United States, 533 U.S. 27 (2001), police used novel thermal imaging technology to scan an individual's home to obtain evidence that he probably was using high-intensity lamps that aided the indoor growth of marijuana. The trial court and the Ninth Circuit did not find the scanning to be a search in violation of the Fourth Amendment. The appellate court held that the defendant had shown no expectation of privacy because he had not attempted to conceal the heat emanating from his home. Plus, the imagery did not expose intimate details of his life.

The Supreme Court reversed, holding "Where, as here, the Government uses a device that is not in general public use, to explore details of the home that would previously have been unknowable without physical intrusion, the surveillance is a 'search' and is presumptively unreasonable without a warrant."

3. States are free to find that their state constitutions provide greater protection for privacy than the U.S. Constitution. In State v. Goss, 834 A.2d 316 (N.H. 2003), police executed a warrant to search the defendant's residence for marijuana and items used in marijuana cultivation. The warrant was based, in part, on a previous, warrantless search of the defendant's garbage, which had been left on the defendant's driveway in black plastic bags on the normal trash pick-up day. The defendant contended that he had an expectation of privacy in his garbage, and the search of his garbage did not fall within any of the recognized exceptions to the warrant requirement. The Supreme Court of New Hampshire agreed, saying, "Clues to people's most private traits and affairs can be found in their garbage. Almost every human activity ultimately manifests itself in waste products and any individual may understandably wish to maintain the confidentiality of his refuse." In reaching its decision, the court acknowledged that the U.S. Supreme Court had reached the opposite conclusion with regard to an expectation of privacy in garbage, but interpreted the New Hampshire Constitution as providing for greater protection than that found in the Federal Constitution.

4. Under what circumstances may law enforcement officials obtain genetic information (or even DNA samples) from physicians when their patients are suspected of committing a crime? The U.S. Department of Health and Human Services has promulgated health privacy regulations pursuant to the Health Insurance Portability Accountability Act of 1996 (HIPAA). A section of these regulations deal with the standards for disclosure for law enforcement purposes. See 45 C.F.R. § 164.512(f). Under the HIPAA privacy regulations, a health care provider or institution may disclose otherwise-protected health care information to law enforcement officials pursuant to a court order. Even if there is no court order, law enforcement officials may obtain certain protected health information (such as the type of injury, ABO blood type, and a description of distinguishing physical characteristics) for purposes of "identifying or locating a suspect, fugitive, material witness or missing person." However, without a court order, the police may *not* obtain "information related to the individual's DNA or DNA analysis, dental records, or typing, samples or analysis of body fluids or tissue."

5. Under what circumstances may law enforcement officials obtain genetic information from a suspect's blood-relative (such as a child) for use as a comparison to genetic evidence found at a crime scene? In Reno, Nevada, ten months after 19 year-old Brianna Denison was raped and murdered, police arrested a suspect based on an anonymous tip and DNA collected from the suspect's 4 year-old son. The mother of the child gave police permission to test the child's DNA to see if his father could be a potential match to the evidence

found at the scene. The DNA not only matched evidence from the rape and murder of Brianna Denison, but it also matched evidence from another sexual assault that occurred in 2007. See Mallory Simon, Tip, DNA Lead to Arrest in Student's Slaying, CNN.com, www.cnn.com/2008/CRIME/11/26/brianna. denison.arrest/index.html.

6.   John Paul Phillips had a fatal heart attack while on Death Row. Now police are asking that his body be exhumed and DNA testing undertaken to determine if he raped and murdered five additional women before his initial trial. Should the exhumation and testing be allowed? See Brett Nauman, Police Want Dead Man's DNA, Chicago Sun–Times, Oct. 5, 2001.

7.   Items abandoned in public lack Fourth Amendment protection against unreasonable search and seizure by law enforcement agents because the act of abandonment destroys any expectation of privacy that the owner might have previously possessed. But is DNA abandoned in the same way that garbage is left out on the street? The law surrounding this issue is currently in flux. For example, a New York court accepted that the DNA on a piece of gum that a suspect gave to police officers was abandoned. The suspect gave the gum to the officers while participating in a staged Pepsi taste-test that the police department had designed to acquire DNA evidence from the suspect. People v. LaGuerre, 815 N.Y.S.2d 211, 213 (N.Y. App. Div. 2006). But where the DNA was "abandoned" may make a difference. The North Carolina Court of Appeals prevented DNA from being used as evidence in a criminal trial because it had been collected from a cigarette butt found on the defendant's patio. The court concluded that the cigarette butt and the DNA on it were not abandoned because a reasonable expectation of privacy still attached to the cigarette butt, as it was seized on a private piece of property rather than in a public place. State v. Reed, 641 S.E.2d 320, 322–323 (N.C. Ct. App. 2007). See Laura A. Matejik, DNA Sampling: Privacy and Police Investigation in a Suspect Society, 61 Ark. L. Rev. 53 (2008) for a discussion of this issue.

8.   After Christa Worthington was murdered on Cape Cod, DNA samples from suspects were collected, but it took over a year for the state crime lab to analyze the results and identify her killer. Pam Belluck, Slow DNA Trail Leads to Suspect in Cape Cod Case, The New York Times, Apr. 16, 2005 at A1. Other women were outraged that her alleged killer had been allowed to remain free, perhaps to kill again during that time period. But such delays are common. In fact, a poll of U.S. law enforcement officials found a reluctance to collect DNA evidence, especially in cases involving non-violent offenses, because of a belief that due to cost, backlogs and storage problems, the evidence will never be sent to the lab and therefore never result in an arrest. See Nicholas P. Lovrich, Ph.D., et al., National Forensic DNA Study Report, Dec. 12, 2003, p. 21, at http://www.ncjrs.org/pdffiles1/nij/grants/203970.pdf.

9.   Some police departments have demonstrated a reluctance to submit rape kits for DNA testing. For example, as of February 2009, there were at least 12,669 untested rape kits in Los Angeles County. And of the 4,727 kits in the Los Angeles Sheriff's Department's storage facility, over 300 were beyond the ten-year statute of limitations and another 100 were within six months of that deadline. Sarah Tofte, Testing Justice: The Rape Kit Backlog in Los Angeles City and County, (Human Rights Watch: New York 2009).

Considering that rape is often a serial crime, this backlog allows for the possibility that thousands of assailants have gone unpunished or have committed additional sexual assaults. Solomon Moore, Progress is Minimal in Clearing DNA Cases, The New York Times, Oct. 24, 2008.

Despite being booked into evidence, the kits sit in evidence storage facilities because DNA testing and analysis has not been requested by a detective. One officer revealed that he did not request DNA testing in cases where the alleged perpetrator was known or where he thought the case was unfounded. Another officer did not request DNA testing unless he believed the kit would help to further the investigation. Sarah Tofte, Testing Justice: The Rape Kit Backlog in Los Angeles City and County, (Human Rights Watch: New York 2009). Are these valid exceptions to the policy of requiring every rape kit to be tested? Is this officer correct in believing that ''[m]ost rape cases are 'he said/she said,' and a rape kit isn't going to help you figure out who is telling the truth?''

Contrast Los Angeles with New York City, where a 16,000 DNA sample backlog from sexual assault and homicide cases in 1999 was eliminated by 2003 by sending every untested kit to a private crime lab. As of January, 2009, testing on the backlogged kits returned 2,000 cold hits, which resulted in 200 active investigations, arrests, or prosecutions. Amy Goodwin, Rape Kits in Cold Storage, Ms. Magazine, Winter 2009. Additionally, testing the kits exonerated a wrongfully convicted defendant, and the arrest rate for rape has increased from 40 percent to 70 percent. Prosecutions and convictions for rape have also increased. Sarah Tofte, Testing Justice: The Rape Kit Backlog in Los Angeles City and County, (Human Rights Watch: New York 2009). Do these figures demonstrate that testing rape kits is an important tool in stopping these crimes?

10.   Given the backlog in the processing of DNA evidence, should law enforcement agencies reopen cold cases that, because of older technologies, were not solvable in the past, but have a chance of being solved now? Should statutes of limitations be extended so that perpetrators of a crime can be brought to justice at some point in the future? Scott Turow fears ''that the growing capacity of today's forensics to reach farther and farther into the past seems likely to undermine the law's time-ingrained notions, embodied in statutes of limitations, about how long people should be liable to criminal prosecutions.'' Do you agree with this sentiment? Scott Turow, Still Guilty After All These Years, New York Times, April 8, 2007.

G.   POST–CONVICTION DNA TESTING

SETH AXELRAD & JULIANA RUSSO, SURVEY OF POST—CONVICTION DNA TESTING STATUTES

American Society of Law, Medicine, & Ethics, 2005.

Thirty-eight states and the federal government have passed statutes specifically providing for post-conviction DNA testing of biological evidence relating to a crime for which an offender has been convicted * * *.

* * *

- Who May Apply for Post–Conviction DNA Testing?

* * *

With respect to the severity of the offense, more than half of the state statutes limit eligible convicts to felons or a subset of felons. Kentucky and Nevada represent the extreme cases, limiting applicability to capital offenders. Less than half of the states, and the federal government, include those who have been convicted for any crime. The second criterion, [requiring that the individual be in] state custody, provides a means of restricting the potential postconviction remedy to those who need it to escape or reduce their imprisonment.

* * *

- What Evidence Can Be Tested? / What Criteria Must the Evidence Meet?

All of the state statutes place some restriction on the evidence that can be subjected to the requested DNA testing. The restrictions may be minimal, as in the case of Washington (requiring only that the evidence still exists); more common, however, are requirements that the evidence was secured in relation to the crime, was maintained or stored in a manner to ensure that the evidence has not degraded or been tampered with, and/or either was not previously tested, or was previously tested, but there exists good reason for retesting.

- Is the Prosecutor Involved in the Process?

The American criminal justice system is an adversarial system; accordingly, all of the post-conviction statutes except for North Carolina and Oregon explicitly provide for prosecutorial involvement. At the minimum is the requirement of notice to the prosecution of the motion for post-conviction DNA testing, and at the maximum is Washington's requirement for prosecutorial approval of the request. A typical statute will require notice to the prosecution and afford the prosecution an opportunity to respond to the motion.

* * *

- What Are the Review Criteria for the Petition?

This section lists the criteria that the decision-maker (usually the judge) will use in reviewing the defendant's motion for post-conviction DNA testing. Thus, this section identifies the barriers that the defendant must overcome in order to persuade a court to grant his or her post-conviction motion. In general, the courts require a showing that: the identity of the perpetrator (or accomplice) was an issue at trial; the evidence to be tested is relevant to the identity of the perpetrator; the evidentiary criteria have been met; and/or exculpatory DNA results, had they been introduced at trial, likely would have resulted in a different outcome at trial.

* * *

● Who Pays for the Costs of Testing?

This section identifies the allocation of the costs of DNA testing, if present in the statutory provision. The federal Justice for All Act of 2004 exemplifies a typical provision. The statute allocates the costs of testing to the applicant, except in cases where the applicant is indigent.

* * *

● What are the Consequences if the Results Do Not Favor the Petitioner?

* * * Some statutes, like Maryland, simply deny the petition for post-conviction relief upon unfavorable test results. Others penalize the petitioner in some manner, e.g., by requiring inclusion of the petitioner's DNA profile into the DNA database. The federal statute's punitive consequences arise as a result of its requirement that the petition for post-conviction DNA test contain an assertion of actual innocence under penalty of perjury; thus, upon the receipt of unfavorable test results, the petitioner can be held in contempt, or potentially prosecuted for making false assertions.

● What are the Consequences if the Results Do Favor the Petitioner?

In the event that the test results exclude the petitioner as the source of DNA evidence, the state and federal statutes specify the subsequent procedural steps a petitioner may take to challenge his conviction. The federal statute requires the petitioner to file a motion for a new trial, which the court shall grant upon a showing of compelling evidence that the new trial would result in an acquittal. The state statutes either similarly require a motion for a new trial, or provide the court more procedural flexibility upon reception of the favorable test results. North Carolina, for example, allows the court to enter any order "that serves the interests of justice," which may include an order setting a new trial or an order vacating and setting aside the petitioner's conviction.

* * *

● Will Compensation Be Awarded if the Petitioner is Exonerated?

Missouri, Montana, and Federal Government have statutes providing for restitution for wrongfully imprisoned persons exonerated through DNA testing. The Montana statute provides educational aid to exonerated petitioners, whereas the Missouri and Federal statutes provide direct financial restitution. [There are also other state laws, such as Mass. Gen. Laws Ann. Ch. 444 § 1, that provide compensation for certain exonerated individuals regardless of the nature of the evidence used to convict them.]

JUSTICE FOR ALL ACT

On October 30, 2004, President Bush, signed into law the "Justice for All Act of 2004" which provides for a number of improvements to the justice system. Specifically, as it relates to DNA, the Act enhances DNA collection and analysis efforts and provides for post-conviction DNA testing. Federal, State, and local forensic laboratories are slated for improvements and additional funding is earmarked for training, and assistance to ensure that this technology reaches its full potential to solve crimes.

More than 150 people have had their convictions overturned based on DNA testing. Most of these exonerations have involved faulty eyewitness testimony, coerced confessions or false testimony by prison inmates. The Innocence Protection Act of 2004, part of the Justice for All Act of 2004, grants prisoners convicted of a federal crime the right to petition a federal court for DNA testing for exoneration. 18 U.S.C. 3600 (a)(1) (2005). However, penalties are established if the testing actually inculpates the prisoner. 18 U.S.C. 3600 (f)(2) (2005). The Act also prohibits destruction of DNA evidence (except in limited circumstances) in a federal criminal case while the defendant remains incarcerated and increases the amount of compensation that may be awarded in cases of unjust imprisonment to $50,000 a year in non-capital cases and $100,000 a year in capital cases. 18 U.S.C. § 3600 (b)(2) (2005). See also Mark A. Rothstein, Genetic Justice, 352 New. Eng. J. Med. 2667–2668 (2005).

DISTRICT ATTORNEY'S OFFICE FOR THE THIRD JUDICIAL DISTRICT v. OSBORNE

129 S.Ct. 2308 (2009).

CHIEF JUSTICE ROBERTS delivered the opinion of the Court.

* * *

This lawsuit arose out of a violent crime committed 16 years ago, which has resulted in a long string of litigation in the state and federal courts. On the evening of March 22, 1993, two men driving through Anchorage, Alaska, solicited sex from a female prostitute, K. G. She agreed to perform fellatio on both men for $100 and got in their car. The three spent some time looking for a place to stop and ended up in a deserted area near Earthquake Park. When K. G. demanded payment in advance, the two men pulled out a gun and forced her to perform fellatio on the driver while the passenger penetrated her vaginally, using a blue condom she had brought. The passenger then ordered K. G. out of the car and told her to lie face-down in the snow. Fearing for her life, she refused, and the two men choked her and beat her with the gun. When K. G. tried to flee, the passenger beat her with a wooden axe handle and shot her in the head while she lay on the ground. They kicked some snow on top of her and left her for dead.

* * *

Six days later, two military police officers at Fort Richardson pulled over Dexter Jackson for flashing his headlights at another vehicle. In his car they discovered a gun (which matched the shell casing), as well as several items K. G. had been carrying the night of the attack. The car also matched the description K. G. had given to the police. Jackson admitted that he had been the driver during the rape and assault, and told the police that William Osborne had been his passenger. Other evidence also implicated Osborne. K. G. picked out his photograph (with some uncertainty) and at trial she identified Osborne as her attacker. Other witnesses testified that shortly before the crime, Osborne had called Jackson from an arcade, and then driven off with him. An axe handle similar to the one at the scene of the crime was found in Osborne's room on the military base where he lived.

The State also performed DQ Alpha testing on sperm found in the blue condom. DQ Alpha testing is a relatively inexact form of DNA testing that can clear some wrongly accused individuals, but generally cannot narrow the perpetrator down to less than 5% of the population. The semen found on the condom had a genotype that matched a blood sample taken from Osborne, but not ones from Jackson, K. G., or a third suspect named James Hunter. Osborne is black, and approximately 16% of black individuals have such a genotype. In other words, the testing ruled out Jackson and Hunter as possible sources of the semen, and also ruled out over 80% of other black individuals. The State also examined some pubic hairs found at the scene of the crime, which were not susceptible to DQ Alpha testing, but which state witnesses attested to be similar to Osborne's.

Osborne and Jackson were convicted by an Alaska jury of kidna[p]ping, assault, and sexual assault. They were acquitted of an additional count of sexual assault and of attempted murder. Finding it " 'nearly miraculous' " that K. G. had survived, the trial judge sentenced Osborne to 26 years in prison, with 5 suspended. His conviction and sentence were affirmed on appeal.

Osborne then sought postconviction relief in Alaska state court. He claimed that he had asked his attorney, Sidney Billingslea, to seek more discriminating restriction-fragment-length-polymorphism (RFLP) DNA testing during trial, and argued that she was constitutionally ineffective for not doing so. Billingslea testified that after investigation, she had concluded that further testing would do more harm than good. She planned to mount a defense of mistaken identity, and thought that the imprecision of the DQ Alpha test gave her " 'very good numbers in a mistaken identity, cross-racial identification case, where the victim was in the dark and had bad eyesight.' " [Osborne v. State, 110 P. 3d 986, 990 (Alaska App. 2005) (Osborne I)] Because she believed Osborne was guilty, " 'insisting on a more advanced ... DNA test would have served to prove that Osborne committed the alleged crimes.' " The Alaska Court of Appeals concluded that Billingslea's decision had been strategic and rejected Osborne's claim.

[The Alaska Court of Appeals subsequently rejected Osborne's claims of both a federal and state constitutional right to post-conviction DNA testing.]

* * *

Meanwhile, Osborne had also been active in federal court, suing state officials under 42 U.S.C. § 1983. He claimed that the Due Process Clause and other constitutional provisions gave him a constitutional right to access the DNA evidence for what is known as short-tandem-repeat (STR) testing (at his own expense). * * *

On cross-motions for summary judgment after remand, the District Court concluded that "there does exist, under the unique and specific facts presented, a very limited constitutional right to the testing sought." The court relied on several factors: that the testing Osborne sought had been unavailable at trial, that the testing could be accomplished at almost no cost to the State, and that the results were likely to be material. It therefore granted summary judgment in favor of Osborne.

The Court of Appeals affirmed, relying on the prosecutorial duty to disclose exculpatory evidence recognized in Pennsylvania v. Ritchie, 480 U.S. 39 (1987), and Brady v. Maryland, 373 U.S. 83 (1963). While acknowledging that our precedents "involved only the right to pre-trial disclosure," the court concluded that the Due Process Clause also "extends the government's duty to disclose (or the defendant's right of access) to post-conviction proceedings." [Osborne v. Dist. Attorney's Office, 521 F.3d 1118, 1128 (9th Cir. Alaska, 2006).] * * *

* * *

Modern DNA testing can provide powerful new evidence unlike anything known before. Since its first use in criminal investigations in the mid–1980s, there have been several major advances in DNA technology, culminating in STR technology. It is now often possible to determine whether a biological tissue matches a suspect with near certainty. While of course many criminal trials proceed without any forensic and scientific testing at all, there is no technology comparable to DNA testing for matching tissues when such evidence is at issue. DNA testing has exonerated wrongly convicted people, and has confirmed the convictions of many others.

At the same time, DNA testing alone does not always resolve a case. Where there is enough other incriminating evidence and an explanation for the DNA result, science alone cannot prove a prisoner innocent. The availability of technologies not available at trial cannot mean that every criminal conviction, or even every criminal conviction involving biological evidence, is suddenly in doubt. The dilemma is how to harness DNA's power to prove innocence without unnecessarily overthrowing the established system of criminal justice.

* * *

"No State shall . . . deprive any person of life, liberty, or property, without due process of law." U.S. Const., Amdt. 14, § 1. This *Clause* imposes procedural limitations on a State's power to take away protected entitlements. Osborne argues that access to the State's evidence is a "process" needed to vindicate his right to prove himself innocent and get out of jail. Process is not an end in itself, so a necessary premise of this argument is that he has an entitlement (what our precedents call a "liberty interest") to prove his innocence even after a fair trial has proved otherwise. We must first examine this asserted liberty interest to determine what process (if any) is due.

* * *

* * * Osborne seeks to defend the judgment on the basis of substantive due process ... He asks that we recognize a freestanding right to DNA evidence untethered from the liberty interests he hopes to vindicate with it. We reject the invitation and conclude, in the circumstances of this case, that there is no such substantive due process right. "As a general matter, the Court has always been reluctant to expand the concept of substantive due process because guideposts for responsible decisionmaking in this unchartered area are scarce and open-ended." Collins v. Harker Heights, 503 U.S. 115, 125 (1992). Osborne seeks access to state evidence so that he can apply new DNA-testing technology that might prove him innocent. There is no long history of such a right, and "[t]he mere novelty of such a claim is reason enough to doubt that 'substantive due process' sustains it." Reno v. Flores, 507 U.S. 292, 303 (1993).

And there are further reasons to doubt. The elected governments of the States are actively confronting the challenges DNA technology poses to our criminal justice systems and our traditional notions of finality, as well as the opportunities it affords. To suddenly constitutionalize this area would short-circuit what looks to be a prompt and considered legislative response. The first DNA testing statutes were passed in 1994 and 1997. In the past decade, 44 States and the Federal Government have followed suit, reflecting the increased availability of DNA testing. As noted, Alaska itself is considering such legislation. "By extending constitutional protection to an asserted right or liberty interest, we, to a great extent, place the matter outside the arena of public debate and legislative action. We must therefore exercise the utmost care whenever we are asked to break new ground in this field." [Washington v. Glucksberg], 521 U.S.[702], 720 (1997). "[J]udicial imposition of a categorical remedy ... might pretermit other responsible solutions being considered in Congress and state legislatures." Murray v. Giarratano, 492 U.S. 1, 14 (1989) (KENNEDY, J., concurring in judgment). If we extended substantive due process to this area, we would cast these statutes into constitutional doubt and be forced to take over the issue of DNA access ourselves. We are reluctant to enlist the Federal Judiciary in creating a new constitutional code of rules for handling DNA.

Establishing a freestanding right to access DNA evidence for testing would force us to act as policymakers, and our substantive-due-process rulemaking authority would not only have to cover the right of access but a myriad of other issues. We would soon have to decide if there is a constitutional obligation to preserve forensic evidence that might later be tested. If so, for how long? Would it be different for different types of evidence? Would the State also have some obligation to gather such evidence in the first place? How much, and when? No doubt there would be a miscellany of other minor directives.

In this case, the evidence has already been gathered and preserved, but if we extend substantive due process to this area, these questions would be before us in short order, and it is hard to imagine what tools federal courts would use to answer them. At the end of the day, there is no reason to suppose that their answers to these questions would be any better than those of state courts and legislatures, and good reason to suspect the opposite. * * *

* * *

The judgment of the Court of Appeals is reversed, and the case is remanded for further proceedings consistent with this opinion.

It is so ordered.

[JUSTICE ALITO'S concurring opinion is omitted.]

JUSTICE STEVENS, with whom JUSTICE GINSBURG and JUSTICE BREYER join, and with whom JUSTICE SOUTER joins as to Part I, dissenting.

The State of Alaska possesses physical evidence that, if tested, will conclusively establish whether respondent William Osborne committed rape and attempted murder. If he did, justice has been served by his conviction and sentence. If not, Osborne has needlessly spent decades behind bars while the true culprit has not been brought to justice. The DNA test Osborne seeks is a simple one, its cost modest, and its results uniquely precise. Yet for reasons the State has been unable or unwilling to articulate, it refuses to allow Osborne to test the evidence at his own expense and to thereby ascertain the truth once and for all.

* * *

The Fourteenth Amendment provides that "[n]o State shall ... deprive any person of life, liberty, or property, without due process of law." § 1. Our cases have frequently recognized that protected liberty interests may arise "from the Constitution itself, by reason of guarantees implicit in the word 'liberty,' ... or it may arise from an expectation or interest created by state laws or policies." Wilkinson v. Austin, 545 U.S. 209, 221(2005). Osborne contends that he possesses a right to access DNA evidence arising from both these sources.

* * *

* * * Osborne asserts a right to access the State's evidence that derives from the Due Process Clause itself. Whether framed as a "substantive liberty interest ... protected through a procedural due process right" to have evidence made available for testing, or as a substantive due process right to be free of arbitrary government action, see Harvey v. Horan, 285 F.3d 298, 315, 319 (CA4 2002) (LUTTIG, J., respecting denial of rehearing en banc), the result is the same: On the record now before us, Osborne has established his entitlement to test the State's evidence.

The liberty protected by the Due Process Clause is not a creation of the Bill of Rights. The "most elemental" of the liberties protected by the Due Process Clause is "the interest in being free from physical detention by one's own government." Hamdi v. Rumsfeld, 542 U.S. 507, 529 (2004) (plurality opinion).

[JUSTICE STEVENS notes that a prisoner retains some measure of constitutionally protected liberty interests while in prison, including the "fundamental liberty of freedom from physical restraint."]

Recognition of this right draws strength from the fact that 46 States and the Federal Government have passed statutes providing access to evidence for DNA testing, and 3 additional states (including Alaska) provide similar access through court-made rules alone, see Brief for State of California et al. as Amici Curiae 3–4, n. 1, and 2; ante, at 9. These legislative developments are consistent with recent trends in legal ethics recognizing that prosecutors are obliged to disclose all forms of exculpatory evidence that come into their possession following conviction. The fact that nearly all the States have now recognized some postconviction right to DNA evidence makes it more, not less, appropriate to recognize a limited federal right to such evidence in cases where litigants are unfairly barred from obtaining relief in state court.

* * *

Recent scientific advances in DNA analysis have made "it literally possible to confirm guilt or innocence beyond any question whatsoever, at least in some categories of cases." Harvey, 285 F.3d at 305 (Luttig, J.). As the Court recognizes today, the powerful new evidence that modern DNA testing can provide is "unlike anything known before." Ante, at 8. Discussing these important forensic developments in his oft-cited opinion in Harvey, Judge Luttig explained that although "no one would contend that fairness, in the constitutional sense, requires a post-conviction right of access or a right to disclosure anything approaching in scope that which is required pre-trial," in cases "where the government holds previously-produced forensic evidence, the testing of which concededly could prove beyond any doubt that the defendant did not commit the crime for which he was convicted, the very same principle of elemental fairness that dictates pre-trial production of all potentially exculpatory evidence dictates post-trial production of this infinitely narrower category of evidence." 285 F.3d at 317. It does so "out of recognition of the same systemic interests in fairness and ultimate truth." Ibid.

* * *

The majority denies that Osborne possesses a cognizable substantive due process right "under the circumstances of this case," and offers two meager reasons for its decision. First, citing a general reluctance to " 'expand the concept of substantive due process,' " ante, at 19 (quoting [Collins, 503 U.S. at 125]), the Court observes that there is no long history of postconviction access to DNA evidence. " 'The mere novelty of such a claim,' " the Court asserts, " 'is reason enough to doubt that "substantive due process" sustains it,' " ante, at 19 (quoting Reno v. Flores, 507 U.S. 292, 303 (1993)). The flaw is in the framing. Of course courts have not historically granted convicted persons access to physical evidence for STR and mtDNA testing. But, as discussed above, courts have recognized a residual substantive interest in both physical liberty and in freedom from arbitrary government action. It is Osborne's interest in those well-established liberties that justifies the Court of Appeals' decision to grant him access to the State's evidence for purposes of previously unavailable DNA testing.

The majority also asserts that this Court's recognition of a limited federal right of access to DNA evidence would be ill advised because it would "short circuit what looks to be a prompt and considered legislative response" by the States and Federal Government to the issue of access to DNA evidence. Such a decision, the majority warns, would embroil the Court in myriad policy questions best left to other branches of government. Ante, at 19–20. The majority's arguments in this respect bear close resemblance to the manner in which the Court once approached the now-venerable right to counsel for indigent defendants. Before our decision in Powell v. Alabama, 287 U.S. 45 (1932), state law alone governed the manner in which counsel was appointed for indigent defendants. "Efforts to impose a minimum federal standard for the right to counsel in state courts routinely met the same refrain: 'in the face of these widely varying state procedures,' this Court refused to impose the dictates of 'due process' onto the states and 'hold invalid all procedure not reaching that standard.' " Brief for Current and Former Prosecutors as Amici Curiae 28, n. 8 (quoting Bute v. Illinois, 333 U.S. 640, 668 (1948)). When at last this Court recognized the Sixth Amendment right to counsel for all indigent criminal defendants in Gideon v. Wainwright, 372 U.S. 335(1963) our decision did not impede the ability of States to tailor their appointment processes to local needs, nor did it unnecessarily interfere with their sovereignty. It did, however, ensure that criminal defendants were provided with the counsel to which they were constitutionally entitled. In the same way, a decision to recognize a limited right of postconviction access to DNA testing would not prevent the States from creating procedures by which litigants request and obtain such access; it would merely ensure that States do so in a manner that is nonarbitrary.

While it is true that recent advances in DNA technology have led to a nationwide reexamination of state and federal postconviction procedures authorizing the use of DNA testing, it is highly unlikely that affirming the judgment of the Court of Appeals would significantly affect the use of DNA testing in any of the States that have already developed statutes and procedures for dealing with DNA evidence or would require the few States that have not yet done so to postpone the enactment of appropriate legislation. Indeed, a holding by this Court that the policy judgments underlying that legislation rest on a sound constitutional foundation could only be constructive.

Osborne has demonstrated a constitutionally protected right to due process which the State of Alaska thus far has not vindicated and which this Court is both empowered and obliged to safeguard. On the record before us, there is no reason to deny access to the evidence and there are many reasons to provide it, not least of which is a fundamental concern in ensuring that justice has been done in this case. I would affirm the judgment of the Court of Appeals, and respectfully dissent from the Court's refusal to do so.

[JUSTICE SOUTER's dissenting opinion is omitted.]

NOTES AND QUESTIONS

1. Is a right to have DNA testing post-conviction analogous to the prosecutor's duty to disclose exculpatory evidence when it is not clear that the results of the DNA test will indeed exculpate the individual?

2. Should there be a duty to store evidentiary items that might have DNA on them? With the advent of DNA technologies, forensic officials who had been pack rats were able to convict people of decades-old crimes by applying the new techniques to stored evidence from the original crime scene evidence. Such evidence has also been retested through efforts like the Innocence Project, letting many innocent men go free. In fact, in 2009, volunteer lawyers in Virginia were trained on how to contact the 881 Virginia felons whose old cases included evidence ripe for potentially-exculpatory genetic testing.

With such technological miracles at hand, forensic specialists became reluctant to throw anything away. Beds, cars, clothes—who knew what new technologies would allow the CSI of the future to coax clues out of evidence?

The storage situation worsened in Colorado in 2008 when, after an innocent murder suspect was freed after nine years' imprisonment, a broad law was adopted requiring storage of every piece of evidence that might contain DNA. It required storage for the life of the defendant of "all reasonable and relevant evidence that may contain DNA." A recent amendment, Colorado Statutes Section 18–1–1104, made clear that an entire large item, such as a car, need not be stored if the DNA can be lifted off the item. The new law does not require retention "if DNA evidence is of such a size, bulk, or physical character as to render retention impracticable." What policies would you suggest for the storage of evidence?

III. DNA BANKS

A. CONSTITUTIONALITY OF FORENSIC DNA BANKS

JONES v. MURRAY
962 F.2d 302 (4th Cir.1992).

NIEMEYER, J.

Section 19.2–310.2 of the Virginia Code, effective July 1, 1990, requires convicted felons to submit blood samples for DNA analysis "to determine identification characteristics specific to the person" and provides for the creation of a data bank of the information for future law enforcement purposes. Six inmates have challenged the statute's constitutionality, contending that it authorizes the involuntary extraction of blood in violation of the Fourth Amendment prohibition against unreasonable searches and seizures.

* * *

II.

The principal argument advanced by the inmates is grounded on the contention that Virginia's blood testing program violates the inmates' Fourth Amendment rights against unreasonable searches and seizures by authorizing the search of their bodies in the absence of any individualized suspicion. They argue that the general purpose of enforcing the law by improving methods of identification is not sufficient to justify testing an entire class of people merely because the recidivism rate is higher for them. They note that several classifications of persons, for example, those affected by mental disease or environmental factors, who have never before been convicted of a crime, might statistically be equally likely to commit future crimes. They contend that the district court's ruling sustaining the Virginia program is "the first instance ... that a pure law enforcement search has ever been sustained in the absence of any individualized suspicion."

The Commonwealth of Virginia observes that if individualized suspicion must exist before any felon can be required to submit to a blood test, any meaningful DNA identification bank will be impossible. The very idea of establishing a data bank refutes the possibility of establishing individualized suspicion because the collection of the blood samples is designed to solve future cases for which no present suspicion can exist. It argues that the special needs of the government warrant application of the balancing test identified in Skinner v. Railway Labor Executives' Ass'n, 489 U.S. 602 [(1989)] and National Treasury Employees Union v. Von Raab, 489 U.S. 656 [(1989)]. When considering the minimal level of intrusion, the Commonwealth argues, demonstrably higher rates of recidivism among felons and the improved methods of identification provided by DNA analysis justify the search. They refer to studies, including one which concluded:

Of the 108,580 persons released from prisons in 11 states in 1983, representing more than half of all released State prisoners that year, an estimated 62.5% were arrested for a felony or serious misdemeanor within 3 years.... Before their release from prison, the prisoners had been arrested and charged with an average of more than 12 offenses each; nearly two-thirds had been arrested at least once in the past for a violent offense; and two-thirds had previously been in jail or prison.... An estimated 22.7% of all prisoners were rearrested for a violent offense within 3 years of their release.

* * *

It appears to be established, at least with respect to free persons, that the bodily intrusion resulting from taking a blood sample constitutes a search within the scope of the Fourth Amendment. And in the view of the inmates, all governmental searches conducted in the context of criminal law enforcement require individualized suspicion to satisfy the Fourth Amendment's requirement of reasonableness.

We have not been made aware of any case, however, establishing a per se Fourth Amendment requirement of probable cause, or even a lesser degree of individualized suspicion, when government officials conduct a limited search for the purpose of ascertaining and recording the identity of a person who is lawfully confined to prison. This is not surprising when we consider that probable cause had already supplied the basis for bringing the person within the criminal justice system. With the person's loss of liberty upon arrest comes the loss of at least some, if not all, rights to personal privacy otherwise protected by the Fourth Amendment. Thus, persons lawfully arrested on probable cause and detained lose a right of privacy from routine searches of the cavities of their bodies and their jail cells as do convicted felons. Even probationers lose the protection of the Fourth Amendment with respect to their right to privacy against searches of their homes pursuant to an established program to ensure rehabilitation and security.

Similarly, when a suspect is arrested upon probable cause, his identification becomes a matter of legitimate state interest and he can hardly claim privacy in it. We accept this proposition because the identification of suspects is relevant not only to solving the crime for which the suspect is arrested, but also for maintaining a permanent record to solve other past and future crimes. This becomes readily apparent when we consider the universal approbation of "booking" procedures that are followed for every suspect arrested for a felony, whether or not the proof of a particular suspect's crime will involve the use of fingerprint identification. Thus a tax evader is fingerprinted just the same as is a burglar. While we do not accept even this small level of intrusion for free persons without Fourth Amendment constraint, the same protections do not hold true for those lawfully confined to the custody of the state. As with fingerprinting, therefore, we find that the Fourth Amendment does not require an additional finding of individualized suspicion before blood can be taken from incarcerated felons for the purpose of identifying them.[2]

---

2. Because we consider the cases which involve the Fourth Amendment rights of prison inmates to comprise a separate category of cases to which the usual per se requirement of probable cause does not apply, there is no cause to address whether the so-called "special needs" exception, relied on by the district court, applies in this case. We do, however, find support for our holding in the fact that the Supreme Court has not categorically required individualized suspicion in the case of every search which advances a law enforcement objective. Only recently it concluded that a "slight" or "minimal" intrusion caused by the short stop of an automobile at a checkpoint, although directed at a class of people without individualized suspicion, may be justified as reasonable under the Fourth Amendment by a weightier interest advanced by the search. See Michigan Dep't Of State Police v. Sitz, 496 U.S. 444 (1990) (approving use of sobriety checkpoint to deter drunk driving).

In the absence of a requirement for individualized suspicion, assuming that the Fourth Amendment continues to apply to lawfully confined prisoners, we must nevertheless determine the reasonableness of any search. We recognize that the search effected by the taking of blood samples may be considered a greater intrusion than fingerprinting. Yet blood tests are commonplace, and the intrusion occasioned by them is "not significant." The procedure "involves virtually no risk, trauma, or pain." In *Skinner*, the Supreme Court upheld a program which required mandatory blood testing of an entire class of railway employees, albeit not for law enforcement purposes. In a similar vein, mandatory blood testing of all prisoners to detect the presence of the Human Immunodeficiency Virus, which causes Acquired Immune Deficiency Syndrome (AIDS), has been justified by the governmental interests in controlling AIDS in prison. These decisions instruct that blood testing can be reasonable under the Fourth Amendment, even with respect to free persons, where the slight intrusion is outweighed by the governmental interest advanced by the intrusion.

Against the minor intrusion, therefore, we weigh the government's interest in preserving a permanent identification record of convicted felons for resolving past and future crimes. It is a well recognized aspect of criminal conduct that the perpetrator will take unusual steps to conceal not only his conduct, but also his identity. Disguises used while committing a crime may be supplemented or replaced by changed names, and even changed physical features. Traditional methods of identification by photographs, historical records, and fingerprints often prove inadequate. The DNA, however, is claimed to be unique to each individual and cannot, within current scientific knowledge, be altered. The individuality of the DNA provides a dramatic new tool for the law enforcement effort to match suspects and criminal conduct. Even a suspect with altered physical features cannot escape the match that his DNA might make with a sample contained in a DNA bank, or left at the scene of a crime within samples of blood, skin, semen or hair follicles. The governmental justification for this form of identification, therefore, relies on no argument different in kind from that traditionally advanced for taking fingerprints and photographs, but with additional force because of the potentially greater precision of DNA sampling and matching methods.

Thus, in the case of convicted felons who are in custody of the Commonwealth, we find that the minor intrusion caused by the taking of a blood sample is outweighed by Virginia's interest, as stated in the statute, in determining inmates' "identification characteristics specific to the person" for improved law enforcement.

The inmates argue that the usefulness of DNA as an identification technique is largely limited to violent crimes, based upon the unlikelihood of recovering from the scene of a nonviolent crime a DNA sample from the perpetrator that is sufficient for comparison with the suspect's DNA. According to statistics presented by the inmates, there is only a remote possibility that a nonviolent offender will commit a future violent crime which will produce sufficient DNA for an identification match. These statistics indicate that 97% of the cases in which DNA evidence was used to link a defendant with a crime involved murder or rape, and further, less than 1% of all nonviolent offenders are later arrested on murder or rape charges. They contend therefore that the DNA program cannot be justified with respect to the testing of nonviolent felons.

These numbers persuasively demonstrate, given the DNA technology that is currently available, that Virginia's interest in DNA testing is significantly more compelling with regard to those felons convicted of violent crimes than those not. However, we note that the fact that fingerprints are not found at a particular crime scene does not negate the Commonwealth's interest in fingerprinting the criminal suspect when caught. There may be uses for DNA technology other than merely verifying a suspect's presence at the scene of a crime. As we have noted, a DNA print might be used to identify a criminal suspect who has attempted to alter or conceal his or her identity. Moreover, if DNA technology becomes more common (and particularly if it is established as a reliable and judicially accepted identification tool), then it is likely that law enforcement officials will become more aware of the technology and thus more likely to make use of the DNA clues that are left as a result of crimes other than murder or rape. The effectiveness of the Commonwealth's plan, in terms of percentage, need not be high where the objective is significant and the privacy intrusion limited.

It is not for us to weigh the advantages of one method of identification over another which is selected by the Commonwealth. While greater utility for use of DNA data can be supposed when the future crime is one of violence and those crimes can statistically be related more directly to inmates now incarcerated for crimes of violence, the utility of more exact identification in all cases still justifies the minor intrusion. We therefore agree with the district court's conclusion that § 19.2–310.2 does not violate the Fourth Amendment as applied by the Fourteenth Amendment to the Commonwealth of Virginia.

* * *

MURNAGHAN, J., concurring in part and dissenting in part:

To the extent that the majority opinion upholds the Virginia DNA testing procedure as applied to violent felons, and holds that the statute qualifies as an *ex post facto* law with respect to its effect on the mandatory release of prisoners convicted prior to its effective date, I concur in the decision. But I must respectfully dissent from the majority's determination of the constitutionality of the statute as applied to prisoners convicted of non-violent crimes. Prisoners do not lose an expectation of privacy with regard to blood testing, and the Commonwealth's articulated interest in the testing of non-violent felons does not counter-balance the privacy violation involved in the procedure.

I.

* * *

Prisoners most assuredly do give up specific aspects of their reasonable expectation of privacy because of practical concerns relating to living conditions, and because of the necessities involved in ensuring prison security. However, in the present case, appellants have not forfeited their expectation of privacy with respect to blood testing, and no practical penal concern justifies the departure involved in the DNA procedure. Accordingly, the Commonwealth's DNA testing procedure should be reviewed under the standard applied to a search of any individual when such a search is not based on individualized suspicion: the privacy interest of the prisoner in remaining free of bodily invasion should be balanced against the state interest in carrying out the search.

The majority cites the Supreme Court's opinion in Bell v. Wolfish, 441 U.S. 520 (1979), to support its sweeping conclusion about the extent of prisoners' loss of privacy rights. Although *Bell* allows for certain invasive search procedures, *Bell* does not suggest that probable cause detainees have abrogated the entire panoply of privacy protections. To the contrary, the *Bell* Court reaffirms the conclusion that privacy interests of detainees or prison inmates remain, and that these privacy interests must be balanced against the "significant and legitimate security interest of the [penal] institution."

The majority today implicitly holds that, whether violent or nonviolent, a prisoner loses a reasonable expectation of privacy which justifies the search in the present case. Citing Hudson v. Palmer, 468 U.S. 517 (1984), which held that a prisoner has no reasonable expectation of privacy in his prison cell, the majority indicates that prisoners lose the aspect of their right to privacy that protects them from routine searches. However, the majority goes a step further by applying the *Hudson* standard to the Commonwealth's DNA procedure and implicitly holding that the lack of a reasonable expectation of privacy in a prison cell extends to permit unjustified searches of bodily fluids of every felon, violent and non-violent alike.

A prisoner certainly cannot stake a claim to the kind of sanctity of dominion to a cell that a non-incarcerated individual can to a home. Moreover, the Supreme Court has indicated that there are situations in which even a private citizen's expectation of privacy diminishes, or disappears altogether. It is apparent, however, that the search involved in the present case, blood testing, violates a privacy interest that even a prisoner, living in close quarters under constant security surveillance, reasonably can expect to enjoy.

No precedential justification exists for the majority's holding that convicted felons, violent or non-violent, solely because of past criminal activity, lose the expectation that their bodily fluids will be free of unjustified search. As the Supreme Court stated in Skinner v. Railway

Labor Association, 489 U.S. 602 (1989), "it is obvious that this physical invasion [a blood test] penetrating beneath the skin, infringes an expectation of privacy that society is prepared to recognize as reasonable." Although *Skinner* involved the testing of free citizens, its determination that an individual has a reasonable expectation of privacy within one's own body applies equally to prisoners, unless the prisoner's privacy right is incompatible with the objectives of incarceration.

* * *

II.

The DNA testing of felons convicted of non-violent crimes is not justified, given the limited and non-compelling state interest in including them in the testing procedure. The only state interest offered by the Commonwealth for including non-violent felons is administrative ease. I cannot conclude that the government interest in administrative ease suffices to outweigh a prisoner's expectation of privacy in not having blood withdrawn from his body when that prisoner is not significantly more likely to commit a violent crime in the future than a member of the general population.

* * *

The record supports appellants' contention that there is an extremely tenuous link connecting persons convicted of non-violent felonies to the commission of future violent crime. It, therefore, contains nothing to substantiate a theory that DNA testing of non-violent felons would assist in solution of future crimes. United States Justice Department statistics provided in the record show that only 0.4% of non-violent felons are later arrested on rape charges, and only 0.8% are later arrested on murder charges. One might assume non-violent drug offenders would be more likely to commit violent crime subsequent to release than other non-violent felons; yet, only 0.4% of them are later arrested for rape, and 0.3% for murder.

The record does not provide similar percentage statistics for the general population. It can be readily inferred that the testing of all citizens, regardless of criminal record, would create a DNA data bank with a similar statistical likelihood of solving future crime as is provided by the testing of non-violent felons. Additionally, the testing of other discrete populations, e.g., racial minorities or residents of underprivileged areas, might produce significantly better statistics than 0.4%.[4]

Lacking a significant statistical likelihood to justify the inclusion of non-violent felons, the Commonwealth is forced to justify the inclusion of

---

4. An argument can be made that there is little likelihood that a state-sponsored program to create a DNA data bank of all racial minorities could survive an equal protection challenge, but it is clear that a similar program targeted at underprivileged citizens, having a disparate impact on these same minorities, would not be subject to equal protection analysis, given the non-"suspect" nature of wealth-based classifications. San Antonio Independent School Dist. v. Rodriguez, 411 U.S. 1 (1973).

these individuals based on its amorphous concern for administrative efficiency * * *. Therefore, the majority opinion, by implicitly approving the Commonwealth's stated justification, leads me to a deep, disturbing, and overriding concern that, without a proper and compelling justification, the Commonwealth may be successful in taking significant strides towards the establishment of a future police state, in which broad and vague concerns for administrative efficiency will serve to support substantial intrusions into the privacy of citizens.

KAEMMERLING v. LAPPIN

553 F.3d 669 (D.C. Cir. 2008).

SENTELLE, C.J.

Russell Kaemmerling, a federal prisoner, appeals from the district court's dismissal of his action seeking to enjoin application of the DNA Analysis Backlog Elimination Act of 2000 ("DNA Act" or "the Act"), *42 U.S.C. §§ 14135–14135e.* Kaemmerling alleged that the Act violated his rights under the Religious Freedom Restoration Act ("RFRA"), *42 U.S.C. §§ 2000bb–2000bb–4,* and the *First, Fourth,* and *Fifth Amendments of the United States Constitution.* * * * [W]e * * * affirm the dismissal of the case because his complaint fails to state a claim.

I

* * *

Kaemmerling was convicted of conspiring to commit wire fraud, a felony offense, and is currently incarcerated at the Federal Correctional Institution in Seagoville, Texas. Because he has committed a qualifying offense, the DNA Act requires the [Federal Bureau of Prisons (BOP)] to take a fluid or tissue sample from Kaemmerling for DNA analysis and inclusion in the CODIS. * * *

* * *

III

* * * Kaemmerling's complaint alleges violations of his rights under the RFRA and the *First, Fourth,* and *Fifth Amendments.* After thoroughly considering each of these challenges, we conclude that none of them state a claim upon which relief can be granted.

A

We begin with Kaemmerling's religious claim, which fails to allege a violation of the *Free Exercise Clause.* Kaemmerling contends that mandatory collection and analysis of his DNA under the DNA Act burdens the free exercise of his religious belief that "DNA sampling, collection and storage" "defile[s] God's temple." Even assuming this is true, it does not rise to the level of a constitutional violation. The right of free exercise protected by the *First Amendment* "does not relieve an individual of the obligation to comply with a valid and neutral law of general applicability on the ground that the law proscribes (or prescribes) conduct that his religion prescribes (or proscribes)." Kaemmerling does not suggest that the DNA Act is not, in theory or practice, a religion-neutral, generally applicable law, therefore he alleges no Free Exercise violation, even if the Act incidentally affects religiously motivated action.

B

But the *First Amendment* is not the only potential refuge for Kaemmerling's religious claim * * *. The RFRA prohibits the federal government from "substantially burden[ing]" a person's exercise of religion even if the burden results from a rule of general applicability unless the government can demonstrate that "application of the burden to the person—(1) is in furtherance of a compelling governmental interest; and (2) is the least restrictive means of furthering that compelling governmental interest." Congress instructs us that, in analyzing a claim under the RFRA, we must return to "the compelling interest test as set forth in *Sherbert v. Verner* and *Wisconsin v. Yoder*."

1

To apply this test, we first must determine if Kaemmerling alleges a substantial burden on his religious exercise. The RFRA defines "religious exercise" to include "any exercise of religion, whether or not compelled by, or central to, a system of religious belief." A litigant's claimed beliefs "must be sincere and the practice[] at issue must be of a religious nature." Because the burdened practice need not be compelled by the adherent's religion to merit statutory protection, we focus not on the centrality of the particular activity to the adherent's religion but rather on whether the adherent's sincere religious exercise is substantially burdened. A substantial burden exists when government action puts "substantial pressure on an adherent to modify his behavior and to violate his beliefs[.]" * * * An inconsequential or *de minimis* burden on religious practice does not rise to this level, nor does a burden on activity unimportant to the adherent's religious scheme.

In his complaint, Kaemmerling alleges that it is his sincere religious belief that DNA is "a foundational aspect . . . of God's creative work" and that "DNA sampling, collection and storage with no clear limitations of use, merely to satisfy the broadly overreaching efforts of secular authorities, politicians and their representatives" "defile[s] God's temple, as represented by one's mortal body, filled with the Holy Spirit." His complaint further alleges harms arising from government possession and storage of his DNA profile, including the potential that he could become an unwilling participant in future activities that violate his religious beliefs—including cloning experiments and stem-cell research—and use of his DNA profile by the anti-Christ, who according to Kaemmerling's religious beliefs will in the future rule the world and "make war against the saints," "forc[ing] everyone ... to receive a mark ... which is the ... number of his name."

* * * Kaemmerling makes abundantly clear that he does not challenge the collection of any particular DNA carrier—such as blood, saliva, skin, or hair—but rather that, regardless of the medium by which the government acquires access to his DNA, he objects to the government collecting his DNA information from any fluid or tissue sample they may recover. At oral argument, counsel emphasized that Kaemmerling objects to any collection of his DNA profile at all, even collecting DNA information from hair and skin that he naturally shed onto his clothes then turned over to prison officials for washing. * * * His objection to "DNA sampling and collection," then, must be a more specific objection to collection of the DNA information contained within any sample. It is not penetrating the body or collecting bodily material that Kaemmerling alleges violates his beliefs but rather collecting the "building block of life" specifically. Given these representations, we understand Kaemmerling's objection to "DNA sampling and collection" not to be an objection to the BOP collecting any bodily specimen that contains DNA material such as blood, saliva, skin, or hair, but rather an objection to the government extracting DNA information from the specimen.

* * * [W]e conclude that Kaemmerling does not allege facts sufficient to state a substantial burden on his religious exercise because he cannot identify any "exercise" which is the subject of the burden to which he objects. The extraction and storage of DNA information are entirely activities of the FBI, in which Kaemmerling plays no role and which occur after the BOP has taken his fluid or tissue sample (to which he does not object). The government's extraction, analysis, and storage of Kaemmerling's DNA information does not call for Kaemmerling to modify his religious behavior in any way[.] * * *

Kaemmerling alleges no religious observance that the DNA Act impedes, or acts in violation of his religious beliefs that it pressures him to perform. Religious exercise necessarily involves an action or practice * * *. Kaemmerling * * * alleges that the DNA Act's requirement that the federal government collect and store his DNA information requires the government to act in ways that violate his religious beliefs, but he suggests no way in which these governmental acts pressure him to modify his own behavior in any way that would violate his beliefs.

Nor does the criminal penalty for "fail[ure] to cooperate[]" in the collection of "a tissue, fluid, or other bodily sample ... on which a DNA analysis can be carried out[]" substantially burden Kaemmerling's exercise of religion. He objects only to the collection of the DNA information from his tissue or fluid sample, a process the criminal statute does not address, and he does not allege that his religion requires him not to cooperate with collection of a fluid or tissue sample. Moreover, he alleges that even "involuntary and/or forced collection" of his DNA would "violate[] [his] convictions." The criminal statute is therefore no inducement for Kaemmerling to cooperate and potentially violate his beliefs, because he alleges that collection of his DNA sample would violate his convictions whether or not he acquiesces in the process. Thus, Kaemmerling does not allege that he is put to a choice like the plaintiffs in *Yoder*, between criminal sanction and personally violating his own religious beliefs.

* * *

* * * Kaemmerling's objection to the DNA Act centers on the government's act of extracting and analyzing his DNA to collect its information and store an electronic DNA profile, without suggesting that the Act imposes any restriction on what Kaemmerling can believe or do. Like the parents in *Bowen* [*v. Roy*], Kaemmerling's opposition to government collection and storage of his DNA profile does not contend that any act of the government pressures him to change his behavior and violate his religion, but only seeks to require the government itself to conduct its affairs in conformance with his religion. Kaemmerling thus fails to allege a substantial burden on his religious exercise that would be cognizable under the RFRA.

To the extent that Kaemmerling challenges storage of his DNA profile or retention of the DNA sample itself based on fear of specific future misuses that would conflict with his religious beliefs, we emphasize that we must consider the statute as it exists and is applied today, complete with its protections against misuse, and we cannot pass on hypothetical future harms.

2

Even if Kaemmerling did allege a substantial burden on his exercise of religion, his complaint would still fail to state a claim for relief because the burden "is in furtherance of a compelling governmental interest" and "is the least restrictive means of furthering that ... interest," satisfying the RFRA exception.

The DNA Act serves the compelling governmental interest in accurately and expeditiously solving past and future crimes in order to protect the public and ensure conviction of the guilty and exoneration of the innocent.

Fundamental to the Act is the government's compelling interest in accurately identifying convicted offenders. DNA profiling furthers this interest in a way no other identifying feature can, because DNA is unique to each individual (excepting identical twins) and cannot, within current scientific knowledge, be altered or disguised.

Finally, courts also agree that the deterrent effect of compulsory DNA profiling under the Act serves "society's enormous interest in reducing recidivism."

Kaemmerling argues that the government has not shown—and cannot show, at this pre-evidentiary stage of the case—that the DNA Act serves a compelling interest as applied to him, "a first-time offender convicted of a non-violent crime that did not turn on DNA evidence." The RFRA demands that "the compelling interest test [be] satisfied through application of the challenged law 'to the person'—the particular claimant whose sincere exercise of religion is being substantially burdened." We must look beyond the "broadly formulated interests justifying the general applicability" of the statute to examine the interests the government seeks to promote as applied to Kaemmerling "and the impediment to those objectives" that would flow from granting him a specific exemption.

We first note that Congress specifically amended the DNA Act in 2004 to expand the qualifying federal offenses that subject an offender to DNA sampling to include "[a]ny felony." * * * This amendment is definitive evidence that nonviolent offenders were in fact the intended object of the compelling interests Congress sought to advance through the Act.

Indeed, the interests served by the DNA Act are compelling as to nonviolent first-time felons and violent recidivists alike. Kaemmerling's status as a nonviolent felon or first-time offender in no way undermines DNA profiling as an effective way to identify and "keep tabs on" him. * * * The identification purpose therefore serves interests aside from catching repeat offenders.

The government's compelling interest in accurately and expeditiously solving crime, by matching DNA evidence to an offender profile and by quickly excluding innocent offenders, also applies to felons previously convicted of nonviolent crimes and those who are first-time offenders. * * * Although it may be true that law enforcement officers currently use DNA evidence more often in solving violent crimes than nonviolent ones, the even stronger interest in collecting the DNA of violent offenders does not diminish the connection between taking and storing the DNA of nonviolent offenders and the government's crime-solving interest.

In addition, Kaemmerling's status as a first-time offender does not diminish the government's crime-solving interest as related to him. Even if Kaemmerling never re-offends, his DNA profile would still further this purpose because law enforcement uses the CODIS not only to identify a perpetrator but also to swiftly and efficiently eliminate countless potential suspects. Of course, all recidivists were once first-time offenders, so the government also has an interest in determining if Kaemmerling will be such a case, given that he has already demonstrated a willingness to commit a crime meriting imprisonment. * * *

Finally, because law enforcement officials can find usable DNA evidence related to both violent and nonviolent crimes, the Act's compelling interest in deterring recidivism applies undiminished to Kaemmerling, who has already displayed his need for a deterrent in his willingness, as mentioned before, to commit a felony meriting imprisonment. * * *

3

Having concluded that the government has a compelling interest in extracting and storing Kaemmerling's DNA information for identification, we have no trouble concluding that application of the DNA Act to Kaemmerling "is the least restrictive means of furthering that compelling governmental interest." A statute or regulation is the least restrictive means if "no alternative forms of regulation would [accomplish the compelling interest] without infringing [religious exercise] rights." While we acknowledge the government's argument that an intrusion like drawing blood might be considered an acceptably minimal invasion of privacy interests under the *Fourth Amendment*, it does not necessarily follow that it is the means least restrictive of religious exercise under the RFRA.

It is not the method of collecting the tissue or fluid sample for DNA analysis which Kaemmerling alleges burdens his religious exercise, so this is not a case like *United States v. Zimmerman* in which the religious adherent's beliefs prohibited him from giving blood, but the court considered whether other methods of obtaining a DNA sample would intrude less on his beliefs. Because Kaemmerling alleges that collecting his DNA information at all is what impedes his religious exercise, a less restrictive alternative would exist only if some means of identification other than DNA would accomplish the government's compelling purposes.

No less restrictive alternative exists. As Congress stated, DNA profiling is currently "the most reliable forensic technique for identifying criminals when biological material is left at a crime scene." Perhaps more importantly, it is the one identifying characteristic that criminals cannot change, disguise, or hide to avoid detection. * * *

* * *

C

Kaemmerling's complaint also alleges violations of his *Fifth Amendment* rights to equal protection and against self-incrimination and his *Fourth Amendment* right to be free from unreasonable searches and seizures. [The court held that collecting Kaemmerling's DNA did not violate his Fifth Amendment or Fourth Amendment rights.]

* * *

IV

For the foregoing reasons, we conclude that Kaemmerling's complaint fails to state a claim upon which relief can be granted and therefore should be dismissed. * * *

B. STATUTES GOVERNING FORENSIC DNA BANKS

N.Y. EXEC. LAW §§ 995

* * *

§ 995–c. State DNA identification index

* * *

3. Any designated offender subsequent to conviction and sentencing for a felony specified in subdivision seven of section nine hundred ninety-five of this article, shall be required to provide a sample appropriate for DNA testing to determine identification characteristics specific to such person and to be included in a state DNA identification index pursuant to this article.

* * *

5. The sample shall be collected, stored and forwarded to any forensic DNA laboratory which has been authorized by the commission to perform forensic DNA testing and analysis for inclusion in the state DNA identification index. Such laboratory shall promptly perform the requisite testing and analysis, and forward the resulting DNA record only to the state DNA identification index in accordance with the regulations of the division of criminal justice services. Such laboratory shall perform DNA analysis only for those markers having value for law enforcement identification purposes. For the purposes of this article, the term "marker" shall have the meaning generally ascribed to it by members of the scientific community experienced in the use of DNA technology.

6. DNA records contained in the state DNA identification index shall be released only for the following purposes:

(a) to a federal law enforcement agency, or to a state or local law enforcement agency or district attorney's office for law enforcement identification purposes upon submission of a DNA record in connection with the investigation of the commission of one or more crimes or to assist in the recovery or identification of specified human remains, including identification of missing persons, provided that there exists between the division and such agency a written agreement governing the use and dissemination of such DNA records in accordance with the provisions of this article;

(b) for criminal defense purposes, to a defendant or his or her representative, who shall also have access to samples and analyses performed in connection with the case in which such defendant is charged;

(c) after personally identifiable information has been removed by the division, to an entity authorized by the division for the purpose of creating or maintaining a population statistics database or for identification research and protocol development for forensic DNA analysis or quality control purposes.

7. Requests for DNA records must be in writing, or in a form prescribed by the division authorized by the requesting party, and, other than a request pursuant to paragraph (b) of subdivision six of this section, maintained on file at the state DNA identification index in accordance with rules and regulations promulgated by the commissioner of the division of criminal justice services.

8. The defendant, including the representative of a defendant, in a criminal action or proceeding shall have access to information in the state DNA identification index relating to the number of requests previously made for a comparison search and the name and identity of any requesting party.

9. Upon receipt of notification of a reversal of a conviction, or of the granting of a pardon pursuant to article two–A of this chapter, of an individual whose DNA record has been stored in the state DNA identification index in accordance with this article by the division of criminal justice services, the DNA record shall be expunged from the state DNA identification index, and the division shall, by rule or regulation, prescribe procedures to ensure that the record, and any samples, analyses, or other documents relating to such record, whether in the possession of the division, or any law enforcement or police agency, or any forensic DNA laboratory, including any duplicates or copies thereof, are returned to such individual, or to the attorney who represented him or her at the time such reversal or pardon, was granted. The commissioner shall also adopt by rule and regulation a procedure for the expungement in other appropriate circumstances of DNA records contained in the index.

* * *

§ 995–d. Confidentiality

1. All records, findings, reports, and results of DNA testing performed on any person shall be confidential and may not be disclosed or redisclosed without the consent of the subject of such DNA testing. Such records, findings, reports and results shall not be released to insurance companies, employers or potential employers, health providers, employment screening or personnel companies, agencies, or services, private investigation services, and may not be disclosed in response to a subpoena or other compulsory legal process or warrant, or upon request or order of any agency, authority, division, office, corporation, partnership, or any other private or public entity or person, except that nothing contained herein shall prohibit disclosure in response to a subpoena issued on behalf of the subject of such DNA record or on behalf of a party in a civil proceeding where the subject of such DNA record has put such record in issue.

2. Notwithstanding the provisions of subdivision one of this section, records, findings, reports, and results of DNA testing, other than a DNA record maintained in the state DNA identification index, may be disclosed in a criminal proceeding to the court, the prosecution, and the defense pursuant to a written request on a form prescribed by the commissioner of the division of criminal justice services. Notwithstanding the provisions of subdivision one of this section, a DNA record maintained in the state DNA identification index may be disclosed pursuant to section nine hundred ninety-five-c of this article.

* * *

§ 995–f. Penalties

Any person who (a) intentionally discloses a DNA record, or the results of a forensic DNA test or analysis, to an individual or agency other than one authorized to have access to such records pursuant to this article or (b) intentionally uses or receives DNA records, or the results of a forensic DNA test or analysis, for purposes other than those authorized pursuant to this article or (c) any person who knowingly tampers or attempts to tamper with any DNA sample or the collection container without lawful authority shall be guilty of a class E felony.

C. POLICY ISSUES IN FORENSIC DNA BANKS

MARK A. ROTHSTEIN & SANDRA CARNAHAN, LEGAL AND POLICY ISSUES IN EXPANDING THE SCOPE OF LAW ENFORCEMENT DNA DATA BANKS

67 Brooklyn L. Rev. 127 (2001).

The DNA data bank statutes have been challenged on several federal and state constitutional grounds. State constitutional arguments generally have tracked the federal arguments and neither have met with any success.

* * *

The most frequently raised argument, and the most substantial one, is that obtaining a DNA sample and using the genetic information derived from the sample constitutes an unreasonable search and seizure. The Fourth Amendment of the United States Constitution prohibits unreasonable searches and seizures, and applies to the states via the Fourteenth Amendment. Although nonconsensual searches conducted outside the judicial process are per se unreasonable, nothing in the Fourth Amendment expressly prohibits government searches without a warrant. The Fourth Amendment prohibits only searches that are unreasonable. The Supreme Court has interpreted the Fourth Amendment as establishing rules and presumptions that limit the government's ability to intrude upon matters of personal privacy.

* * *

Taking fingerprints or photographs upon arrest has not been held to violate the Fourth Amendment. Under the same reasoning, one could argue that taking DNA in a non-intrusive manner solely for identification purposes most likely would not violate the Fourth Amendment. Several courts bolster this point by focusing on the reduced expectation of privacy an offender has in his or her identity.

* * *

More recently, in Ferguson v. City of Charleston, [532 U.S. 67 (2001)] the Supreme Court applied the [City of Indianapolis v.] Edmond[, 531 U.S. 32 (2000)] "primary purpose test" to a case described by the lower court as a "special needs" case. In *Ferguson*, a state university hospital tested the urine of certain of its obstetrical patients suspected of drug use and notified police of positive drug screens. The hospital conducted the drug tests in accordance with a hospital policy developed in conjunction with law enforcement officials. Maternity patients arrested after testing positive for cocaine challenged the hospital's policy, claiming the drug tests were an unconstitutional search under the Fourth Amendment. The hospital policy provided for, among other things, a chain of custody for the urine sample so it could be used in later prosecutions, a range of possible criminal charges, and police notification and patient arrest after a positive test. The city argued that the hospital policy met the special needs exception to the Fourth Amendment's warrant requirement because the hospital had a need to facilitate the mother's drug treatment, and to protect the mother and unborn child—a need the hospital claimed was distinct from the normal needs of law enforcement.

The Supreme Court held that the hospital policy violated the Fourth Amendment. The Court noted the extensive involvement of police and prosecutors throughout the development of the policy and it held that, although the ultimate goal of the hospital policy may have been to get the women off drugs and into a substance abuse program for the benefit of both mother and baby, the policy was unconstitutional because "the immediate objective of the searches was to generate evidence for *law enforcement purposes....* " The Court said that "virtually any nonconsensual suspicionless search could be immunized under the special needs doctrine by defining the search solely in terms of its ultimate, rather than immediate, purpose." The Court distinguished its other special needs cases, which had legitimate civil objectives, and did not involve the extensive entanglement of law enforcement as did this case.

* * *

A broad, fingerprint-like identification exception would ignore the fundamental differences between DNA and fingerprints. A fingerprint reveals only unique patterns of loops and whorls. In contrast, a DNA sample is the information-containing blueprint of human life, revealing one's genetic predisposition to disease, physical and mental characteristics, and a host of other private facts not evident to the public. Unlike fingerprint analysis, DNA analysis does not necessarily end with a DNA identification profile. Typical law enforcement practice today is to retain the subject's DNA sample indefinitely on the chance that technological advancements might require re-testing of the samples. Indefinite sample retention increases the opportunity for misuse or abuse of the samples, and the intrusion on the privacy of individuals providing the identifiable samples. Moreover, many state statutes allow access to the samples for undefined law enforcement purposes and humanitarian identification purposes, or authorize the use of samples for assisting medical research or to support identification research and protocol development. No statutes provide for the informed consent of the DNA donors prior to conducting such research. Unlike the laboratory analysis of fingerprints, the Supreme Court has recognized that a laboratory analysis of blood and other bodily fluids constitutes a "second search" subject to the Fourth Amendment's reasonableness requirement. Thus, any reasonableness determination ought to include an analysis of the use that law enforcement authorities intend to make of the DNA sample.

SETH AXELRAD, USE OF FORENSIC DNA DATABASE INFORMATION FOR MEDICAL OR GENETIC RESEARCH

American Society of Law, Medicine, & Ethics, 2005.

The state legislatures in all 50 states established DNA databases in order to aid and enhance law enforcement. Alabama's statute declares, "[T]he creation and establishment of a statewide DNA database is the most reasonable and certain method or means to rapidly identify repeat or habitually dangerous criminals." Ala. Code § 36–18–20(g). The state statutes also recognize, however, that the criminals' DNA information can be used for other purposes, including for medical and genetic research.

Eight states—Indiana, Rhode Island, South Dakota, Texas, Utah, Vermont, Washington, and Wyoming—expressly prohibit the use of the DNA database to obtain information on human physical traits, predisposition to disease, or medical or genetic disorders. Alabama, on the other hand, explicitly authorizes the use of DNA information for medical research, and is the only state to do so. Ala. Code §§ 36–18–20 and 36–18–31.

Michigan authorizes use of anonymous database information for an "academic" or "research" purpose, although it is unclear from the statutory language whether the state legislature meant to include medical or genetic research as an authorized use of database information. Mich. Comp. Laws Ann. § 28.176. The remaining 40 state statutes are either silent on this issue (4), or they neither expressly authorize nor prohibit such research (36).

Thus, with regard to most state DNA database statutes, the issue of the use of database information for medical or genetic research is not directly addressed. An indirect answer to the question of research uses may be gleaned from those statutes which provide a list of "authorized uses." For example, Alaska limits use of the DNA database "only for (1) providing DNA or other blood grouping tests for identification analysis; (2) criminal investigations, prosecutions, and identification analysis; (3) statistical blind analysis; (4) improving the operation of the system; or (5) exoneration of the innocent." Alaska Stat. § 41.41.053(f). This exclusive list does not include medical or genetic research and, presumably, such research uses would violate the statute. Therefore, by examining the "authorized uses" provisions of the statutes, one may get a clearer picture of how most US states regulate research use of database information. Furthermore, where the authorized uses apparently exclude research use, the states also may deter the dissemination of DNA information to researchers by criminalizing the disclosure of database information to unauthorized persons. Thirty states currently criminalize such disclosures.

NOTES AND QUESTIONS

1. Illinois forensic DNA law states: "Any person who (a) intentionally discloses a DNA record, or the results of a forensic DNA test or analysis, to an individual or agency other than one authorized to have access to such records pursuant to this article or (b) intentionally uses or receives DNA records, or the results of a forensic DNA test or analysis, for purposes other than those authorized pursuant to this article or (c) any person who knowingly tampers or attempts to tamper with any DNA sample or the collection container without lawful authority shall be guilty of a class E felony." 730 Ill. Comp. Stat. 5/5–43 (f) (2005). Who may gain access to forensic DNA samples under the New York law and the Illinois law and for what purposes? Would researchers be able to get access to the New York or Illinois forensic DNA banks to undertake research on genetic markers for criminal behavior?

2. Should crime scene DNA be analyzed—and forensic DNA bank samples be analyzed—in order to attempt to ascertain the race of the perpetrator? "Recently, there has been increasing discussion and study of the possibility of using a DNA sample to determine characteristics of the person who left the sample. One possibility is to use the frequencies in the different databases to infer the population to which the person leaving the DNA belongs. If a crime-scene sample were more likely to have come from a Caucasian American than from an African American, this information would be useful in the search for the culprit. It would be similar to an eyewitness account, where the witness had only a fleeting glimpse that indicated the probable group of the culprit but provided no specific traits."

What about analyzing the DNA for specific physical characteristics? "Determining that a DNA sample was left by a person with red hair, dark skin pigment, straight hair, baldness, or color blindness may be practical soon, if not already." National Commission on the Future of DNA Evidence, The Future of Forensic DNA Testing: Predictions of the Research and Development Working Group 13–20, 46–61 (U.S. Department of Justice, Washington, D.C., Nov. 2000).

3. Discuss each of the following policies that have been recommended by Rothstein and Carnahan:

a) *DNA to be analyzed*—Only non-coding regions of DNA should be used for analysis, thereby ensuring that the only possible use of the DNA analysis is identification.

b) *Statistical and Reporting Issues*—All statistical methodologies used for determining a match between a crime scene or other sample and a DNA profile in the data bank should adhere to the latest scientific principles.

c) *Destruction of samples*—Law enforcement officials, including the FBI, favor retaining samples indefinitely for quality assurance and to re-type the samples in the event of changing technology. Twenty-nine state laws either authorize or require that agencies retain samples after analysis; only one state (Wisconsin) requires the destruction of samples, and no samples have actually been destroyed. The retention of samples, however, even under conditions of stringent security, raises concerns among the public that the samples could be re-analyzed for purposes other than identification. Therefore, samples should be destroyed immediately after analysis.

d) *Access to data bank*—Access to the data banks should be limited to law enforcement personnel, and data banks should not be used for any purpose other than identification, including research.

e) *Scope of data bank*—DNA data banks should be limited to DNA obtained from individuals convicted of violent sex offenses and other violent felonies.

What are the pros and cons of each recommendation? What are the pros and cons of retaining the printout of the DNA forensic tests instead of the samples themselves?

4. Why not create a database with everyone's DNA? Some people argue that creating a population-wide database would be more fair than the current database in which people of color are overrepresented. In contrast, Rothstein and Talbott argue that a nationwide DNA database requiring submission by everyone, criminals and non-criminals alike, could pose a serious threat to fundamental civil liberties. They argue that once everyone's genetic information is in law enforcement's possession, it will be difficult to prevent other more dangerous uses of the information by the government. They reiterate Justice Douglas's concern in Osborn v. United States that "[t]aken individually, each step may be of little consequence. But when viewed as a whole, there begins to emerge a society quite unlike any we have seen-a society in which government may intrude into the secret regions of man's life at will."

For Rothstein and Talbott, the social costs outweigh the possibility that increasing the scope of DNA banks will increase law enforcement's ability to capture criminals and prevent future crime. "Our concern is not that expanded DNA databases would transform our country into a 'nation of suspects.' Our concern is that we would become a nation with unfettered police powers." Mark A. Rothstein & Meghan K. Talbott, The Expanding Use of DNA in Law Enforcement: What Role for Privacy?, Journal of Law, 34 Medicine & Ethics 153–164 (2006).

5. If a suspect cannot be located, should police have the right to take DNA from the suspect's mother or sibling since the mitochondrial DNA from these individuals will be virtually identical to that of the suspect?

6. Newborns are screened for a variety of diseases, and hospitals may keep samples of newborn blood for years. In 1997, Australian police obtained a search warrant allowing them to seize children's newborn screening cards from the hospital after the mother refused to let her children undergo blood tests in an incest case. The test results helped lead to a successful conviction. At the time, there were no laws protecting the database.

Public concern that participation in the newborn screening public health program would decrease if the samples were used for forensic purposes led the

Western Australia Health Department to adopt a policy requiring the cards to be destroyed after two years. Other Australian states, including New South Wales and Victoria, have subsequently adopted policies that limit police access to newborn screening blood samples. The New South Wales policy limits access to samples suspected to come from a victim of a crime taken from a suspected crime scene. The police are required to make a reasonable effort to contact the next of kin or a parent to obtain consent except when doing so would be impracticable or would compromise an ongoing investigation. The Victoria policy requires specific court authority through a court order. Department of Human Services, Victoria, Australia Victorian Newborn Screening Review Committee Final Report for the Minister of Health–Supplementary Report of the Victorian Privacy Commissioner, (Aug. 2006). Should police have access to newborn blood for use in criminal investigations?

7. Courts have begun to assess the implications of the U.S. Supreme Court decisions in *Edmond* and *Ferguson* (described in the Rothstein and Carnahan excerpt) for assessments of the constitutionality of DNA banks. In the wake of those cases, the Ninth Circuit originally ruled that the federal law mandating DNA collection from federal parolees for a forensic bank was unconstitutional. That case, U.S. v. Kincade, 345 F.3d 1095 (9th Cir. 2003), held that blood draws for a forensic DNA bank were searches protected by the Fourth Amendment, that the parolees had a reasonable expectation of privacy with respect to their blood, and that the DNA bank did not meet a "special need" outside of law enforcement. However, in an *en banc* rehearing in the case, the Ninth Circuit upheld the constitutionality of the statute. Based on a "totality of the circumstances" test, the court held that parolees do have a diminished expectation of privacy, that DNA collection through blood sampling is minimally intrusive, and that an important social interest is furthered by the DNA collection. U.S. v. Kincade, 379 F.3d 813 (9th Cir. 2004)(en banc). Which decision do you find more persuasive? Is a holding that a DNA test is "minimally intrusive" in keeping with the way DNA tests are viewed in the clinical setting?

8. In Friedman v. Boucher, the Ninth Circuit found that law enforcement agents violated a clearly established right against unreasonable search and seizure when they forcibly swabbed the inside of the mouth of a detainee to obtain a DNA sample. 580 F.3d 847 (9th Cir. 2009). Friedman was an ex-convict who had pled guilty to sexual intercourse without consent in 1980 and had completed his sentence in 2001. In March 2003, Detective Boucher asked Friedman, who was then detained pending prosecution for unrelated charge, for a DNA sample to aid in the investigation of a cold case. Friedman refused and Boucher forcibly swabbed the inside of Friedman's mouth. The court found that "[t]he officer did not have a warrant or a court order authorizing the taking of the sample, nor was Freidman under any suspension of a crime which a DNA might be justified. The extraction occurred simply because the deputy district attorney wanted to put Friedman's DNA sample in a cold case data bank"

Boucher argued, among other things, that the search was "reasonable" because "pre-trial detainees have limited privacy rights that must yield to the desires of law enforcement to collect DNA samples for use in law enforcement databases." The court rejected this argument, finding that courts have traditionally limited administrative searches at detention facilities to those related to security concerns. Moreover, the court distinguished this search from previous cases that had upheld state laws requiring convicted felons that are currently under state supervision to submit DNA samples for use in a DNA bank. Friedman was not under state supervision and the detective's purpose of gathering human tissue for a law enforcement databank was in no way related to facility security. The court also concluded that "no reasonable detective or prosecutor could have thought that they could forcibly take a DNA sample from Friedman without violating his Fourth Amendment rights." Friedman v. Boucher, 580 F.3d 847 (9th Cir. 2009).

9.   The collection of DNA from convicted offenders has been justified as a way to solve future crimes committed by the offender after his or her release from prison. What justification might there be for collecting DNA from people who are on death row or who are serving a life sentence without the possibility of parole? In California, female death row inmates have brought a legal challenge to the requirements that they provide blood for the state forensic DNA bank. Their relatives have challenged it as well, asserting that any genetic predisposition to disease identified in the death row inmate's DNA might be used as a basis for discrimination in insurance or employment against law-abiding relatives.

10.   In December 2008, the European Court of Human Rights held that the collection of genetic information from innocent people in Britain violated international law. One-fifth of the genetic profiles in the DNA database in Britain are tied to individuals who have no criminal records. One criticism of the expansion of DNA databases stems from a fear of racial profiling and discrimination. The House of Commons reported that the genetic information of 42% of black males and 27% of the total population of black individuals in Britain are accounted for in a DNA database, while only 6% of white individuals are in the database. Are similar concerns appropriate in the U.S.? According to Hank Greely, 12% of the United States population is African–American, while 40% of the genetic profiles in the federal database belong to African–American individuals. Solomon Moore, F.B.I. and States Vastly Expanding Databases of DNA, The New York Times, April 19, 2009, at 1.

11.   Should genetic databases be established in which all people are tested at birth? Will genetic identification someday be as common as fingerprint identification and Social Security cards?

12.   The American Society of Law, Medicine and Ethics has undertaken a comprehensive project, funded by the National Human Genome Research Institute on "DNA Fingerprinting and Civil Liberties." The website for the project includes state-by-state analyses of the laws governing forensic DNA banks and post-conviction DNA testing. See "DNA Grant" at www.aslme.org.

13.   Originally, state and federal databases were limited to DNA samples from sexual offenders and a few other violent felons, such as murderers. However, as of 2008, every state collects DNA samples from convicted sex offenders, more than forty states from all felons, and at least thirty-eight from those convicted of certain misdemeanors. Dustin Hays, Genetics & Public Policy Center, DNA Forensics, and the Law, (August 2008), http://www.dnapolicy.org/images/issuebriefpdfs/DNA,%20Forensics,%20and%20the%20

Law%20Issue%20Brief.pdf. Several courts have held that collection of DNA from convicted, non-violent felons as a term of release from prison before parole, probation or supervised release does not violate those felons' Fourth Amendment rights. See e.g. Banks v. U.S., 490 F.3d 1178 (10th Cir. 2007); U.S. v. Weikert, 504 F.3d 1 (1st Cir. 2007).

This expansion has resulted in increased laboratory backlogs for DNA testing. For example, California's expansion of DNA testing from violent felons to all felons resulted in a ten-fold increase in demand and a quadrupling of its backlog. Tania Simoncelli, Dangerous Excursions: The Case Against Expanding Forensic DNA Databases to Innocent Persons, 34 J. L. Med. & Ethics 390 (2006).

Additionally, thirty-five states collect DNA from convicted juveniles. In the Matter of Appeal in Maricopa County Juvenile Action Numbers JV–512600 and JV–512797, 930 P.2d 496 (Ariz. App. 1996), an Arizona appellate court held that DNA collected from convicted juveniles was not subject to expungement and could be used beyond the age of majority, including in adult prosecutions, because such testing was not punitive.

In a striking departure from the approach of taking DNA from convicted felons, fifteen states collect DNA samples from individuals who have merely been arrested for certain offenses. Solomon Moore, F.B.I. and States Vastly Expanding Databases of DNA, The New York Times, April 19, 2009.

In 2006, the federal government authorized the collection of DNA samples from "individuals who are arrested, facing charges, or convicted ... under the authority of the United States." 42 U.S.C. § 14135(a)(1)(A). Regulations implementing the new provision went into effect in 2009. Prior to 2009, the federal government only collected DNA samples from individuals convicted of felonies, sexual offenses, or crimes of violence. Under the new rules, individuals arrested by federal agents who are fingerprinted must also have DNA collected from them. This rule applies to all federal arrestees— including persons arrested for criminal activities occurring in the context of demonstrations or protests. 73 Fed. Reg. 74932 (Dec. 10, 2008).

What are the pros and cons of allowing DNA collection on arrestees? Supporters of arrestee DNA collection claim that the policy will help law enforcement solve crimes more quickly and efficiently. Opponents claim that the expected 1.2 million DNA samples to be collected and processed at the federal level each year would significantly increase in the current workload and cost the country $45 million each year. Aside from the lack of resources and potential issues with quality control, the ability of all federal agencies to collect DNA evidence of arrestees raises constitutional issues. In light of the article written by Rothstein and Carnahan, does the collection of DNA by all federal agencies that have arresting powers infringe on an individual's constitutional rights?

Does the inclusion of individuals who have never been convicted of a crime in a criminal DNA database affect the notion of "innocent until proven guilty" in any way? Would the retention of an innocent individual's DNA by law enforcement violate Fourth Amendment privileges against unreasonable search and seizure? Under the new rules, the DNA database is to be expunged when the Attorney General or state receives a certified copy of a final court order establishing that each charge has been dismissed, resulted in an acquittal, or that no charge was filed within the applicable time period. 42 U.S.C. § 14132(d). How should law enforcement handle the DNA samples of individuals who have not been convicted of a crime?

14. The same rules that require federal agents to collect DNA samples from arrestees also apply to "non-United States persons who are detained under the authority of the United States," or illegal immigrants. What would the policy implications be if DNA samples were collected from a detained immigrant who has a legitimate claim to asylum or is granted legal resident status at a later date?

15. Should a convicted felon have a say about whether medical studies are undertaken on his or her DNA?

16. In 2008, the European Court of Human Rights found that The United Kingdom's policy of retaining DNA profiles, cellular tissues, and fingerprints from people charged with a crime but later acquitted violated Article 8 of the European Convention on Human Rights. Article 8 states, in relevant parts, "1. Everyone has the right to respect for his private and family life * * *. 2. There shall be no interference by a public a public authority with the exercise of this right except such as in accordance with the law and is necessary in a democratic society ... for the prevention of disorder or crime...." The Court found that:

> In addition to the highly personal nature of cellular samples, the Court notes that they contain much sensitive information about an individual, including information about his or her health. Moreover, samples contain a unique genetic code of great relevance to both the individual and his relatives. In this respect the Court concurs with [the lower court's decision that "there could be little, if anything more private to the individual than the knowledge of his genetic make-up."]

> Given the nature and amount of personal information contained in cellular samples, their retention *per se* must be regarded as interfering with the right to respect for private lives of the individuals concerned.

> * * *

> The Court observes ... that the [DNA] profiles contain substantial amounts of unique personal data. * * * In the Court's view, the DNA profiles' capacity to provide a means of identifying genetic relationships between individuals is in itself sufficient to conclude that there retention interferes with the right to the private life of the individuals concerned. The frequency of familial searchers, the safeguards attached thereto and the likelihood of detriment in a particular case are immaterial in this respect. * * *

The Court also found that "the possibility the DNA profiles create for inferences to be drawn as to ethnic origin makes their retention all the more sensitive and susceptible of affecting the right to private life." Additionally, in weighing the public interest of increasing the chances of capturing future offenders, the court concluded that

[T]he blanket and indiscriminate nature of the powers of retention of the fingerprints, cellular samples and DNA profiles of persons suspected but not convicted of offenses ... fails to strike a far balance between the competing public and private interests and that the respondent state has overstepped any acceptable margin of appreciation in this regard. Accordingly, the retention at issue constitutes a disproportionate interference with the applicants' right to respect for private life and cannot be regarded as necessary in a democratic society.

S. and Marper v. The United Kingdom, Nos. 30562/04 and 30566/04, 4 December 2008.

IV. DNA IDENTIFICATION OUTSIDE THE CRIMINAL SETTING

MAYFIELD v. DALTON

901 F.Supp. 300 (D. Haw. 1995), vacated as moot, 109 F.3d 1423 (9th Cir. 1997).

King, J.

* * *

Background

Beginning with Operation Desert Storm in 1991, the United States military has used DNA analysis to help with identification of soldiers' remains. Such analysis provides a means of identifying remains too badly damaged for identification through dental records or fingerprints. Identification is made by comparing DNA taken from the remains with a DNA sample previously taken from the decedent or his or her biological relatives.

Because of problems with obtaining reliable DNA samples during the Gulf War, the Department of Defense ("DOD") began a program to collect and store reference specimens of DNA from members of the active duty and reserve armed forces. That way, the reference samples would be available for use in identifying remains in future conflicts. The DOD DNA Registry, a program within the Armed Forces Institute of Pathology, was established pursuant to a December 16, 1991 memorandum of the deputy secretary of defense. Under this program, DNA specimens are collected from active duty and reserve military personnel upon their enlistment, reenlistment, or preparation for operational deployment. The military's goal is to obtain specimens from all active and reserve personnel by the year 2001.

The specimens consist of two small samples of dried blood stored on cards and a sample of epithelial cells taken from the inside of the subject's cheek using a cotton swab. One bloodstain card is sealed and stored in the service member's military health record, while the other bloodstain card and the swab sample are sent to the DOD DNA Repository. Once received by the repository, the bloodstain card is vacuum sealed, assigned a number and bar code, and stored in a refrigerated chamber. The swab sample is assigned an identical code and stored in alcohol. The specimens are to be stored in the repository for 75 years and then destroyed.

According to the military, except for a limited number of "quality assurance" tests in which the DNA is typed to ensure that the repository's storage and analytical mechanisms are working properly, DNA is not extracted from the samples unless and until there is a need for it to assist in the identification of human remains.

Also according to the military, access to the repository facility, computer system and the samples themselves is strictly limited. Specimens stored in the repository are not to be used for a purpose other than remains identification unless a request, routed through the civilian secretary of the appropriate military service, is approved by the assistant secretary of defense for health affairs. The Government notes that no such request from this program has ever been approved, though it is unclear how many, if any, such requests have been made.

Plaintiffs are members of the United States Marine Corps assigned to Company B, 1st Radio Battalion, Marine Forces Pacific. Scheduled to deploy in January 1995, the two were ordered to provide specimens for the DNA repository. Plaintiffs refused to do so, and each was charged with violation of an order from a superior commissioned officer. On May 23, 1995, the military judge in Plaintiffs' Court Martial dismissed the charges, holding that the regulations underlying the DNA Repository program were not punitive and thus no disciplinary action could be taken for refusal to provide the specimens. The Marine Corps has appealed the military judge's decision.

DISCUSSION

Plaintiffs' Constitutional Claims

Plaintiffs first allege that the collection, storage and use of DNA samples taken without their consent violates their "rights to freedom of expression, privacy, and due process under the First, Ninth, and Fifth Amendments to the United States Constitution, inter alia." In their moving papers and argument, however, Plaintiffs rely primarily on the Fourth Amendment to make their case for a constitutional violation.

The law is well-established that the Government's compulsory taking of blood and other bodily fluid or tissue samples constitutes a "seizure" subject to scrutiny under the Fourth Amendment. However, the Fourth Amendment prohibits only "unreasonable" seizures. The Court in Schmerber [v. California, 384 U.S. 757 (1966)] upheld a conviction for driving under the influence based in part on test results from a blood sample taken without the petitioner's consent. The court found the taking of the blood sample "reasonable" where there was probable cause that the petitioner was intoxicated and a delay to obtain a warrant might have resulted in a loss of evidence.

Plaintiffs herein suggest that *Schmerber* established a rule that the Government may not compel a subject to give a blood sample in the absence of a judicial warrant issued upon a showing of probable cause. The court made no such holding, however. What it did say was that it found nothing inherently unreasonable in the test chosen to measure the petitioner's blood alcohol level, noting that blood tests "are a commonplace in these days of periodic physical examination . . . and . . . for most people the procedure involves virtually no risk, trauma or pain."

In Skinner v. Railway Labor Executives Ass'n, 489 U.S. 602 (1989), the Supreme Court upheld a federally mandated drug and alcohol testing program for private railway workers. Citing *Schmerber*, the Court repeated its previous observation that the interference with privacy interests occasioned by a blood test is minimal. The Court weighed this minimal intrusion against the Government's compelling interest in testing railway employees whose jobs involved the safety of passengers and others and found the testing program to be reasonable. This was so even though the tests were conducted in the absence of probable cause or even any kind of individualized suspicion.

In National Treasury Employees Union v. Von Raab, 489 U.S. 656 (1989), the Court likewise upheld a U.S. Customs Service program requiring drug tests for employees entering positions involving drug interdiction or requiring the carrying of a firearm. The Court noted that certain public employees are necessarily subject to diminished expectations of privacy, and cited as an example members of the military and intelligence services, who "may not only be required to give what in other contexts might be viewed as extraordinary assurances of trustworthiness and probity, but also may expect intrusive inquiries into their physical fitness for those special positions."

The taking of blood samples and oral swabs for the purpose of remains identification presents, on its face, a far less intrusive infringement of Plaintiffs' Fourth Amendment privacy rights than the blood testing in either *Schmerber*, *Skinner* or *Von Raab*. The blood test at issue in *Schmerber* involved a seizure of evidence to be used in a possible criminal prosecution. In *Skinner* and *Von Raab*, blood, urine and breath tests were used to detect the illegal or illicit use of drugs or alcohol, the confirmation of which could be grounds for disciplinary action or criminal sanctions.

In the instant case, the blood and tissue samples at issue are not to be used as evidence against Plaintiffs, but only as a means of identifying their remains should they be killed in action with the Marine Corps. Although the military itself undoubtedly has a significant interest in being able to confirm which of its members have fallen in battle, and which ones may have been taken prisoner or are otherwise unaccounted for, it is the next of kin of service members who will derive the greatest benefit, and solace, from the speedy and definite identification of the remains of their loved ones.

Plaintiffs concede that the military's stated purpose for the DNA registry—remains identification—is a benign one. But they argue that the military could, at some point in the future, use the DNA samples for some less innocuous purpose, such as the diagnosis of hereditary diseases or disorders and the use or dissemination of such diagnoses to potential employers, insurers and others with a possible interest in such information. Plaintiffs have presented no evidence that the military has used or disclosed, or has any plans to use or disclose, information gleaned from the DNA samples for any purpose other than remains identification. A challenge to such hypothetical future use, or misuse, as the case may be, of the samples in the DNA repository does not present a justiciable case or controversy.

The court finds that the military has demonstrated a compelling interest in both its need to account internally for the fate of its service members and in ensuring the peace of mind of their next of kin and dependents in time of war. The court further finds that when measured against this interest, the minimal intrusion presented by the taking of blood samples and oral swabs for the military's DNA registry, though undoubtedly a "seizure," is not an unreasonable seizure and is thus not prohibited by the Constitution.

Breach of Contract

Plaintiffs also contend that the DNA sampling program constitutes a breach of their enlistment contracts with the Marine Corps. They note that the enlistment contracts they signed do not specifically warn recruits that blood and tissue samples will be taken for the DNA registry. Plaintiffs also argue that because they enlisted before the registry was begun, they cannot be deemed to have given their implied consent to the blood and tissue sampling.

In fact, the enlistment documents that Plaintiffs concede they signed make amply clear that military enlistees may be subjected to a plethora of laws, regulations, and requirements that would not normally apply to civilian employees of the Government.

* * *

The enlistment documents promise no limits on the military's ability to take blood or tissue samples or perform other medical tests on enlistees, whether for purposes of assessing physical fitness, detecting the use of illegal drugs, or otherwise. Indeed, Plaintiffs were undoubtedly subjected to such tests in connection with their enlistment. The sampling performed in connection with the DNA registry is not so qualitatively different so as to require a separate, more specific form of consent than that required for other testing.

The court finds that the military's taking of blood samples and oral swabs for purposes of obtaining DNA samples for the DOD DNA Registry is not a violation of any enlistment contract between Plaintiffs and the military.

Regulations Governing Research on Human Subjects

Plaintiffs also rely on 32 C.F.R. Part 219, Protection of Human Subjects, which governs human research conducted, supported or regulated by the military or civilian branches of the federal government. They contend that the military has failed to comply with all of the requirements of the part, which is apparently intended to protect human research subjects and thus prevent a recurrence of past abuses, such as those connected with Government experiments involving exposure to radiation from nuclear blasts or the unwitting ingestion by service personnel of mind altering drugs.

The regulations in question define research as "a systematic investigation, including research development, testing and evaluation, designed to develop or contribute to generalizable knowledge." 32 C.F.R. § 219.102(d). Defendants argue, and the court agrees, that the DOD DNA Registry does not meet the regulatory definition of "research." The DNA samples in question are maintained for a particularized purpose, i.e., the identification of the remains of the samples' donors. According to the military, the only other purpose for which the samples are removed from their repository is for tests to ensure the integrity of the storage process. The registry does not have as its purpose the development of generalizable knowledge about DNA, the traits of service personnel, or anything else.

Moreover, and perhaps more importantly, there is no evidence that Plaintiffs or their fellow service members are being subjected to any kind of experimentation or research. Once a blood sample and oral swab are taken and stored, the individual service member's relationship with the registry becomes dormant. The sample is not retrieved and scrutinized unless and until the service member is believed to have died in action. Even then, the military's inquiry is limited to determining whether the DNA in the sample matches that in the remains believed to be those of the service member. The service members whose DNA samples are kept in the registry are no more human guinea pigs than are the millions of service members whose dental records were kept on hand by the military to provide for remains identification in past wars.

The court finds that the DOD DNA Registry and related blood and tissue sampling does not violate 32 C.F.R. Part 219.

* * *

CONCLUSION

For the foregoing reasons, Plaintiffs' Motion for Summary Judgment and Plaintiffs' Motion to Certify Class were DENIED and Defendants' Cross Motion for Summary Judgment was GRANTED.

NOTES AND QUESTIONS

1. Since the *Mayfield* case, other servicemen have refused to provide DNA to the Department of Defense (DOD) DNA bank. In April 1996, Sergeant

Warren Sinclair, an Air Force medical equipment repairman, refused to submit blood and tissue samples for genetic testing. Sinclair, an African–American, was convinced that DNA samples would be used to support racist claims. He said, "Would we ask Jews to give their genes to Germans? No * * *. Until the issue of racism is resolved, Afro–Americans should maintain possession of their genetic material." He was convicted by court-martial on May 10, 1996, and sentenced to fourteen days of hard labor and a two-grade reduction in rank.

Donald P. Power, a first class petty officer and navy nuclear technician on the USS Arkansas, refused to give a DNA specimen because it violated his religious principles as a member of a Native American lodge. Power lost a stripe and his nuclear classification as well as 40 percent of his income. He was reassigned to a shore unit during discharge proceedings. Subsequently he applied for a waiver on grounds of religious freedom. Eighteen months later, a religious waiver was accepted, his rank was restored, and his nuclear classification was reinstated. But few members of the armed services will be able to make use of the narrow religious exemption; moral objections alone are not enough to avoid military rules. See Lori Andrews & Dorothy Nelkin, Body Bazaar: The Market for Human Tissue in the Biotechnology Age 113–114 (2001).

2.   Should the Department of Defense (DOD) be allowed to use the DNA in its bank for any purposes other than identification of remains? Under what circumstances, if any, should law enforcement officials be able to gain access to the DOD DNA bank to see if a soldier's DNA matches DNA found at a crime scene? Under what circumstances, if any, should genetic researchers be able to gain access to samples in the DOD DNA bank? If identification is the only permissible use of the DOD DNA bank, should members of the military be able to direct that the DNA be held privately by the soldier's relatives rather than in the government DNA bank?

3.   An amendment to Nanette Sexton's prenuptial agreement allowed her to collect millions in a divorce if her husband committed adultery. To prove that he had been unfaithful, Sexton authorized DNA testing from her husband's bedsheets, which identified his DNA and that of a woman other than Sexton. The judge upheld a mediator's order that the DNA test was admissible. Mary McLachlin, Divorce Twist: Wife Says DNA Test Proves His Tryst, Palm Beach Post, Dec. 26, 2000, at 1A.

4.   In the 1999–2000 session, the following bill, "An Act Related to DNA Testing and Native Americans" was introduced in the Vermont legislature: "The commissioner shall by rule establish standards and procedures for DNA–HLA testing to determine the identity of an individual as a Native American, at the request and the expense of the individual. The results of such testing shall be conclusive proof of the Native American ancestry of the individual." If such a bill does pass, what use might Native Americans make of DNA testing? Can you envision situations in which such testing might be used to disadvantage Native Americans?

CHAPTER 13

MENTAL AND BEHAVIORAL GENETICS

■ ■ ■

I. INTRODUCTION

Anyone who has a canine companion knows about behavioral genetics. In the last few thousand years, through selective breeding hundreds of breeds of dogs have been bred from wolves. Besides their wide range of sizes, shapes, and colors, dogs have been bred for their temperament, including herding, hunting, retrieving, and contented sleeping on the couch next to their human companions.

Experts agree that the temperament and behavior of other animals, including humans, also is affected by genetics. But, this is practically where the agreement ends. There is widespread disagreement about the range of behaviors influenced by genetics. Many experts consider mental illness, intelligence, addictive behavior, and sexual orientation to be influenced by genes. Others add to the list a genetic predisposition to rage, happiness, impulsivity, shyness, daydreaming, or suicide. Still others assert that contentment, spatial abilities, nurturing behavior, perfect pitch, and a sweet tooth are influenced by genes. One study claims to demonstrate that one's attitude toward reading books, abortion, playing organized sports, roller coaster rides, and the death penalty are influenced by genes, but not one's attitudes toward gender roles, easy access to birth control, being assertive, and playing bingo.

As important as the types of behaviors influenced by genes is their degree of heritability. Are genes responsible for 5% of intelligence or 50%? One of the most common ways of attempting to estimate the degree of heritability is the use of twin studies, a research method developed by Francis Galton in the 19th century. By comparing the behavioral traits of monozygotic (MZ) twins with dizygotic (DZ) twins and twins reared apart and reared together, association between heredity and environment ("nature and nurture" in Galton's words) can be estimated. Some twin studies have been criticized on methodological grounds, such as the similarities of twins raised apart are not necessarily attributable to genetic influences when the environments are similar. Nevertheless, some of the similarities of twins reared apart are astounding.

In one celebrated example, MZ (identical) twins Jim Lewis and Jim Springer were adopted into different families in Western Ohio, about 100 miles apart. They were reunited after 39 years when they were part of a twin study conducted at the University of Minnesota. The investigators discovered several coincidences: each had been given the same name by their adoptive families, each had an adoptive brother named Larry and a dog named Toy. Other coincidences were more striking: each married and divorced a woman named Linda and remarried a woman named Betty; they named their first sons James Allan and James Alan. In school, both liked math and disliked spelling; both enjoyed carpentry and mechanical drawing; both became deputy sheriffs in different Ohio towns; both drove similar blue Chevrolets; both vacationed on the same beach in Florida; both had nearly identical patterns of chain smoking and drinking; both had a white bench around a tree in their backyard; both made miniature furniture in their wood shop; both had vasectomies; both followed stock car racing and hated baseball. The similarities went on and on. See Lawrence Wright, Twins and What They Tell Us About Who We Are 43–47 (1997). What, if anything, was gene-mediated? What similarities would they have with other men of the same age in the same part of the country of the same socio-economic background? In what ways were they different?

Behavioral genetics is a very complicated field, fraught with scientific and statistical obstacles to correlations that can be verified and replicated. Three of the leading problems are (1) defining the endpoint (e.g., accurately diagnosing mental illnesses or variations in personality traits); (2) accounting for the multiple genetic and environmental factors influencing behavior; and (3) excluding possible confounding factors. In fact, the difficulty in proving associations and the frequency with which research findings have been retracted have led to at least one area of inquiry, the genetics of schizophrenia, to be referred to as "the graveyard of molecular geneticists."

This chapter will explore the social and legal significance of behavioral genetics. In particular, it will consider the effect of behavioral genetics on criminal law and tort law. New discoveries in behavioral genetics challenge some of the basic assumptions of religion, philosophy, and the law involving free will and moral culpability. The law's response to behavioral genetic research will shape our law and society for years to come.

II. HISTORY OF MENTAL AND BEHAVIORAL GENETICS

MARK A. ROTHSTEIN, BEHAVIORAL GENETIC DETERMINISM: ITS EFFECTS ON CULTURE AND LAW IN BEHAVIORAL GENETICS: THE CLASH OF CULTURE AND BIOLOGY

89–96 (Ronald A. Carson & Mark A. Rothstein eds., 1999).

* * *

The popularity of genetic determinism, like other beliefs about science, has been cyclical. The golden age of genetic determinism began in the second half of the nineteenth century. As Sir Francis Galton, the father of eugenics, phrased it, the debate centers on whether "nature or nurture" is more important to human development. In mid-nineteenth-century England there was little doubt that inherited explanations of behavior were gaining popularity. Lewontin et al. observe the influence of this theory in Charles Dickens' popular novel *Oliver Twist*, which was published serially between 1837 and 1839. When ten-year-old Oliver first meets Jack Dawkins, the "artful dodger," on his way to London, Oliver is described as having a genteel nature and speaking with perfect grammar, in stark contrast to the streetwise Dawkins. Oliver's mode of expression is inexplicable, inasmuch as he had lived virtually all of his life in a parish workhouse, with no mother and no education. What explains this phenomenon? Oliver's father was from a well-off and socially prominent family; his mother was the daughter of a naval officer. According to Lewontin et al., "Oliver's life is a constant affirmation of the power of nature over nurture."

At the turn of the century, Alfred Binet, director of the psychology laboratory at the Sorbonne, abandoned his work in the field of craniometry (using brain size and structure to measure intelligence) to develop a test that could directly measure inherited, native intelligence. The purpose of his first test, developed in 1905, was to identify Parisian children needing special education. In the second version of his test, published in 1908, he assigned an age level to each task in the test to establish a mental age for each child. In 1912, a year after Binet's death, German psychologist Wilhelm Stern divided mental age by chronological age to establish an intelligence quotient, and the IQ, the supposed expression of innate intelligence, was born. Stanford professor Lewis Terman created a paper-and-pencil version of the basic test, the Stanford–Binet Intelligence test.

In 1914, seventy-six years after *Oliver Twist*, George Bernard Shaw's *Pygmalion* was first performed. Shaw was a follower of Galton, and according to Shaw's vision, culture was not immutably fixed by biology, but nearly so. Only after six months of arduous work and the talent of phoneticist Professor Higgins could an ignorant flower girl overcome the deprivation of her station in life and appear to be a duchess. Liza Doolittle, of course, was a white English-woman. Were she nonwhite or from central or eastern Europe, the task surely would have been impossible. At this time, pauperism and shiftlessness—not to mention intelligence—were widely believed to be overwhelmingly or exclusively genetic.

English translations and American revisions of the basic intelligence test, primarily the Army Alpha Test, were used on a mass scale during World War I as a way to screen troops. The findings of the test were "startling." The test was given only in English, and immigrants from southern and eastern Europe scored much lower than either native-born Americans or immigrants from northern Europe. * * * [T]hese test results helped to sway Congress in 1924 to reduce immigration from southern and eastern Europe.

It is small wonder that genetic determinism is linked with eugenics. If genes determine the human condition (physical, psychological, behavioral, and social), then improving the gene pool will improve the human condition. The efforts at improvement take on two forms—negative eugenics, preventing the reproduction of the genetically "unfit"—and positive eugenics—encouraging the mating of those with "favored" genetic endowments.

* * *

In 1990, seventy-six years after Shaw's *Pygmalion*, the popular American film *Pretty Woman* was released. The premise, though hardly original, was simple. Even a lowly streetwalker in Los Angeles could become a member of high society literally overnight so long as she had good looks, a rich benefactor, and designer clothes. (Cinderella required supernatural intervention to accomplish a comparable, though morally pure, transformation.) In popular culture, the pendulum had swung completely from *Oliver Twist*.

The Human Genome Project officially began in 1990. It heralded a period in which claims for a genetic basis for homosexuality, aggression, impulsive behavior, nurturing, and numerous other behaviors was asserted. This has contributed to a resurgence of behavioral genetic determinism that is based on the misapprehension and misapplication of scientific discoveries and that threatens to have grievous social consequences.

* * *

Flawed scientific theories can be refuted by more rigorous science. A more perplexing social problem involves the permissible societal response to legitimate discoveries in behavioral genetics. Undoubtedly, there is *some* correlation between certain genes and behavioral traits. The only serious scientific dispute concerns the overall degree of correlation and the applicability of genetic factors in a range of specific behavioral traits. What, then, are the likely psychological, social, political, and legal consequences of such correlations?

As an example, take the case of alcoholism. Several past and ongoing studies have explored whether there is a genetic component to alcoholism. Assume there is such a component in some cases of alcoholism. Does that mean that, as a society, we will be more or less tolerant of alcoholics, more or less inclined to mandate genetic testing for such an allele or alleles, or more or less likely to embrace the disease model of alcoholism? On the one hand, it could be argued that the genetic component vitiates the moral taint from individuals with alcoholism. On the other hand, the genetic, heritable nature of the disorder may increase the stigma associated with alcoholism; it may increase the pressure for genetic screening for the mutation; it may contribute to individuals feeling a sense of resignation and a reluctance to enter treatment; and it may lead to disdain for individuals who, despite knowledge that they have the mutation, proceed to drink nonetheless. Research to find an association between genes and alcoholism is being conducted at the Ernest Gallo Clinic and Research Center at the University of California–San Francisco. If a genetic link to alcoholism were to be established, some of the social pressure against alcoholic beverages and their purveyors might be deflected onto "faulty" genes.

Similar issues are raised with regard to a possible genetic link to homosexuality. If we find a "gay gene," will it mean greater or lesser tolerance? My suspicion is that it will not change the way most people view homosexuals. For individuals who are tolerant of homosexuals, it will reaffirm that the behavior is physiologically based and does not represent moral depravity. On the other hand, for individuals who are intolerant of homosexuality, it will confirm their view that such individuals are "abnormal." It also could lead to proposals that those affected by the "disorder" should undergo treatment to be "cured" and that measures should be taken to prevent the birth of other individuals so afflicted.

III. SCIENTIFIC ISSUES

STEVEN E. HYMAN, USING GENETICS TO UNDERSTAND HUMAN BEHAVIOR: PROMISES AND RISKS IN WRESTLING WITH BEHAVIORAL GENETICS: SCIENCE, ETHICS, AND PUBLIC CONVERSATION

113–116 (Erik Parens, Audrey R. Chapman, & Nancy Press eds. 2006).

For both ethical and practical reasons, human genetics is an observational, not an experimental, science. Thus, the practice of human genetics differs markedly from study of other organisms in which breeding and environmental factors can be rigidly controlled, mutagenesis can be performed, and, in some cases, genes can be directly inserted or deleted. Before the advent of molecular genetics, human behavioral genetics was limited largely to analyses that attempted to quantify genetic versus nongenetic influences on behavioral phenotypes and to determine the modes of inheritance in cases in which genes proved relevant. Quantitative (or classical) genetic studies of behavior depended on observational designs in which genetic and environmental influences might be teased apart or in which patterns of segregation of genes might be inferred. These designs included multigenerational family studies, twin studies, and adoption studies. Multigenerational family designs permit the analysis of modes of inheritance across generations. Based on their relative convenience and analytic power, many behavioral genetic studies investigated phenotype concordance in twins, comparing identical twins versus fraternal twins raised together. That is, they investigated how similar identical twins raised together were with respect to some trait (e.g., height or schizophrenia or "IQ") and compared those observations with observations regarding how similar fraternal twins raised together were with respect to the same trait. On the assumption that identical twins are raised in the same environment and that fraternal twins are too, and given the fact that identical twins share 100 percent of their DNA and fraternal twins on average only 50 percent of theirs, researchers make inferences about the magnitude of the role of genes in the emergence of a particular trait. To be sure, the methodology of twin studies has the weakness that the 100 percent shared-DNA condition (identical twins) cannot truly be balanced by a 100 percent shared-environment condition in humans. Indeed, creating truly identical conditions even for lab rats has proved to be very difficult.

Studies of individuals who had been adopted away from their biological families early in life better distinguished the influences of heredity and environment, and studies of twins separated early in life provided an even more powerful design. But adoption studies are difficult to perform, since they depend on societies making both records and people available for examination and interview. Moreover, the selection of adoptive families by social service agencies and the phenomenon of gene-environment covariation (whereby the individual helps select or create his or her own experiential environment) have moved some observers to question the validity of the investigators' assumption that the environments of the adoptees are really so different.

Measures frequently used in thinking about disease phenotypes and other traits that can be derived from both twin and family studies are recurrence risk ratios (λ), which quantify the likelihood of sharing a phenotype with another person as a function of relatedness and therefore as a function of percentage of DNA shared. As I will discuss at greater length later, recurrence risk ratios, like heritability estimates can serve as a rough and ready measure to prioritize disease phenotypes for molecular investigation based on the notion that the greater the contribution of genes to a phenotype, the higher the likelihood of identifying the genetic loci that contribute risk. Both heritabilities and recurrence risk ratios are measures of the *aggregate* genetic contribution to a phenotype no matter how complex the genetic contribution; thus, a high recurrence risk ratio is not a guarantee of success in identifying *actual loci* contributing to a phenotype.

Extensive family and twin studies and a smaller number of adoption studies have led to the conclusion that genes contribute significantly to risk of autism, schizophrenia, bipolar disorder, major depression, anxiety disorders, alcoholism, and other disorders of brain and behavior. Recurrence risk ratios derived from many studies are consistent with a major role for genes in risk of mental illness. With the development of modern genomic and other molecular tools, we can now begin to address the extraordinary challenge of how genetic differences influence biochemical and cellular networks that affect the emergence of complex traits; thus, the traditional quantitative genetic analyses are no longer a goal in themselves, but a tool.

The goal of behavioral genetics in the twenty-first century is to identify the precise genetic variants that contribute to behavioral phenotypes. These discoveries, in turn, become tools of inquiry for neuroscience and for the neurobiology of disease. To provide just one kind of example of how gene identification provides tools for neuroscience, genes found to be associated with Alzheimer disease, Parkinson disease, or Rett syndrome in humans have been inserted into mice or used to replace the endogenous mouse gene, thus producing animal models for research and treatment development. Clearly, mouse models will never provide perfect replicas of human cognitive and behavioral disorders such as schizophrenia, but they can prove very useful as partial models. For example, a knock-in-mouse (i.e., a mouse in which the endrogenous gene was replaced by a gene of the investigator's choosing) made to express a human Rett disease mutation in the causative MEPC2 gene shows abnormalities in social behavior. This experiment was possible because Rett is a Mendelian (single-gene) disorder; what might not have been predicted is that human social deficits could be even partially modeled in a mouse. Overall there is growing evidence that useful, if imperfect mouse models can be constructed by inserting genes that confer disease risk in humans.

In sum, the importance of quantitative or classical genetic analyses of behavior now lies in helping to define phenotypes, suggesting paths of gene–environment interaction, and setting priorities for molecular analyses. The scientific future for behavioral genetics lies in providing tools to understand the brain in health and disease, and to point the way toward new therapies for brain disorders.

ROBERT PLOMIN, JOHN C. DEFRIES, IAN W. CRAIG, & PETER MCGUFFIN, BEHAVIORAL GENETICS IN BEHAVIORAL GENETICS IN THE POSTGENOMIC ERA

10–14 (Plomin et al. eds. 2003).

QUANTITATIVE GENETICS: BEYOND HERITABILITY

Most of what is known today about the genetics of behavior comes from quantitative genetic research. During the past three decades, the behavioral sciences have emerged from an era of strict environmental explanations for differences in behavior to a more balanced view that recognizes the importance of nature (genetics) as well as nurture (environmental). This shift occurred first for behavioral disorders, including rare disorders such as autism (.001 incidence), more common disorders such as schizophrenia (.01), and very common disorders, such as reading disability (.05). More recently, it has become increasingly accepted that genetic variation contributes importantly to differences among individuals in the normal range of variability as well as for abnormal behavior. The most well-studied domains of behavior are cognitive abilities and disabilities, psychopharmacology, personality, and psychopathology.

Although twin and adoption studies of individual differences in previously neglected behavioral domains such as learning might yield important new insights into their etiology, asking only whether and how much genetic factors influence such domains would not fully capitalize on the strengths of quantitative genetic analysis. New quantitative genetic techniques make it possible to go beyond these rudimentary questions to investigate how genes and environment affect developmental change and continuity; *comorbidity* and *heterogeneity*, the links between disorders and normal variation; and interactions and correlations between genetic and environmental influences. Using these techniques, quantitative genetic research can lead to better diagnoses based in part on etiology rather than solely on symptomatology. They also can chart the course for molecular genetic studies by identifying the most heritable components and constellations of disorders as they develop and as genetic vulnerabilities correlate and interact with the environment. In this sense, quantitative genetics will be even more important in a post genomic era. The future of behavioral genetic research lies in identifying specific genes responsible for heritability, which will make it possible to address these same questions with much greater precision.

* * *

BEHAVIORAL GENOMICS

Despite the slower–than–expected progress to date in finding genes associated with behavior, the substantial heritability of behavioral dimensions and disorders means that DNA polymorphisms exist that affect behavior. We are confident that some of the genes responsible for this heritability will be found. Although attention is now focused on finding specific genes associated with complex traits, the greatest impact for behavioral science will come after genes have been identified. Few behavioral scientists are likely to join the hunt for genes because it is difficult and expensive, but once genes are found, it is relatively easy and inexpensive to use them. DNA can be obtained painlessly and inexpensively from cheek swabs—blood is not necessary. Cheek swabs yield enough DNA to genotype thousands of genes, and the cost of genotyping is surprisingly inexpensive.

It is crucial that the behavioral sciences be prepared to use DNA in research and eventually in clinics. What has happened in the area of dementia in the elderly population will be played out in many other areas of the behavioral sciences. The only known risk factor for late-onset Alzheimer's dementia (LOAD) is a gene, apolipoprotein E, involved in cholesterol transport. A form of the gene called allele 4 quadruples the risk for LOAD but is neither necessary nor sufficient to produce the disorder; hence, it is a QTL. Although the association between allele 4 and LOAD was reported less than a decade ago, it has already become a *de rigueur* in research on dementia to genotype subjects for apolipoprotein E in order to ascertain whether the results differ from individuals with and without this genetic risk factor. Genotyping apolipoprotein E will become routine clinically if this genetic risk factor is found to predict differential response to interventions or preventative treatments.

In terms of clinical work, DNA might eventually contribute to gene-based diagnoses and treatment programs. The most exciting potential for DNA research is to use DNA as an early warning system that facilitates the development of primary interventions that prevent or ameliorate disorders before they occur. These interventions for behavioral disorders, and even for single-gene disorders, are likely to be behavioral rather than biological, involving environmental rather than genetic engineering. For example, PKU, a metabolic disorder that results postnatally in severe mental retardation, is caused by a single gene on chromosome 12. This form of mental retardation has been largely prevented, not by high-tech solutions such as correcting the mutant DNA or by eugenic programs or by drugs, but rather by a change in diet that prevents the mutant DNA from having its damaging effects. Because this environmental intervention is so cost-effective, newborns have been screened for decades for PKU to identify those with the disorder so that their diet can be changed. The example of PKU serves as an antidote to the mistaken notion that genetics implies therapeutic nihilism, even for a single-gene disorder. This point is even more relevant to complex disorders that are influenced by many genes and by many environmental factors as well. With behavior-based interventions, psychotherapists eventually will be in the business of preventing the consequences of gene expression.

The search for genes involved in behavior has led to a number of ethical concerns. For example, there are fears that the results will be used to justify social inequality, to select individuals for education or employment, or to enable parents to pick and choose among their fetuses. These concerns are largely based on misunderstandings about how genes affect complex traits, but it is important that behavioral scientists knowledge-able about DNA continue to be involved in this debate. Students in the behavioral sciences must be taught about genetics to prepare them for this postgenomic future.

* * *

NOTES AND QUESTIONS

1. Chapter 3 discussed the eugenics movement in the late-nineteenth and early-twentieth centuries. Although one of the ways of improving the "genetic stock" of the population was to decrease or eliminate individuals with physical disabilities, eugenics was even more concerned with eliminating people who were considered to be stupid and evil. Accordingly, eugenic measures were soon applied beyond individuals with disabilities to individuals and then entire groups of people who were allegedly intellectually and morally inferior. Often the two, intellect and morality, were tied together, as in Buck v. Bell, 274 U.S. 200 (1927), where the eugenic sterilization was precipitated by Carrie Buck's having a child out of wedlock. Thus, eugenics was closely linked with behavioral genetics.

2. The controversy surrounding behavioral genetics has not been lessened by the contemporary rejection of eugenics. As long as certain behaviors are assigned values by society, studying those behaviors to find biological links will raise highly contentious issues, from whether the research should be attempted at all, to the methodology, to the findings, to the implications of the findings. The possibility of group stigmatization from associations with behavioral traits such as violence, addictive behavior, and low intelligence makes behavioral genetics a lightning rod for genetic research.

3. One of the main concerns surrounding behavioral genetics is that weak associations between genetic traits and behaviors will be incorrectly viewed in deterministic terms. According to biologist Steven Rose: "It is my argument that such naive neurogenetic determinism is based on a faulty reductive sequence whose steps include: reification, arbitrary agglomeration, improper quantification, belief in statistical 'normality', spurious localization, misplaced causality, and dichotomous partitioning between genetic and environmental causes." Steven Rose, The Rise of Neurogenetic Determinism, 373 Nature 380 (1995). For similar criticism, see Jonathan Michael Kaplan, The Limits and Lies of Human Genetic Research (2000); Richard C. Lewontin, Steven Rose & Leon J. Kamin, Not in Our Genes: Biology, Ideology, and Human Nature (1984). See also Kenneth S. Kendler, "A Gene for . . . ": The Nature of Gene Action in Psychiatric Disorders, 162 Am. J. Psychiatry 1243 (2005).

IV. CRIMINAL LAW

A. OVERVIEW

TROY DUSTER, BEHAVIORAL GENETICS AND EXPLANATIONS OF THE LINK BETWEEN CRIME, VIOLENCE, AND RACE IN WRESTLING WITH BEHAVIORAL GENETICS: SCIENCE, ETHICS, AND PUBLIC CONVERSATION

154–156 (Erik Parens, Audrey R. Chapman, & Nancy Press eds. 2006).

While there is no single or simple answer to the question of why certain behaviors are subjected to a genetic explanation and others are not, there is a major avenue that is undertheorized, unexplored, and less appreciated for the rich potential for getting at the answer(s). Again, an impressive array of different kinds of data strongly suggests that the answer lies in what the Germans call the Zeitgeist, roughly translated as "the spirit of the times." If this begs the question of why "in these times," then that is precisely the point of entry for an explanation of what it is about "these times" that makes for the selection of particular behaviors as genetically explorable and explainable. Behavioral genetics has long been interested in "the genetics of criminality." At the same time the prospect of discerning a relationship between genes and violent behavior has been very contentious.

Critics have raised a variety of issues. One concern is whether violent behavior is a well-defined classification amenable to scientific analysis. Crime, by definition an act or the commission of activity that is forbidden, is socially constructed; that is, the very categorization of an act as criminal depends on social standards of behavior, the identity of the actor, and the environment in which it takes place. Criminal behavior can be a one-time phenomenon (impulsive homicide after discovery of adultery), or it can be a profession (the cat burglar—the professional thief, or the "hit-man" specialist for organized crime). The theoretical warrant for examining the impulsive homicide as having a completely different etiology than the professional thief is well developed. In the case of the latter, the empirical literature on both the professions and professional thievery is predictive of the manners and patterns of routinized behavior. That is in sharp contrast to the literature and conceptual framework with which one approaches an understanding of most homicides, where even if impulsivity sometimes gives way to planning, patterns of jealousy, shame, and rage predominate. Crime can be an occasional diversion from one's ordinary life, such as depicted in Cameron's classic study of shoplifting, or it can be a compulsive-neurotic habituation (sexual abuse of the young by adults); alternatively, crime can be a rational, calculated decision (stealing a loaf of bread to feed one's family), or a routine occupational imperative, as was the case with the price-fixing scandal among the largest electrical companies in the United States. Crime can be a bureaucratic response to turf invasion, such as with organized crime during Prohibition, or a violation of existing social stratifying practices, such as the crime of teaching a slave to read—or assisting a slave to run away.

In short, what is criminal is as variable, and as variably explained, as any wide range of human behaviors that are legal. To place in the same taxonomic system the theft of bread, exposing oneself in public, cat burglary, and euthanasia, as a single, examinable phenotype is to engage in a breathtaking mystification of the classification of crime. The theoretical warrant in each of these instances is both well articulated and highly differentiated in the best empirical work in criminology. As noted above, Cameron's research on shoplifting remains the standard and the classic— distinguishing and documenting how and why this form of crime is primarily performed by "amateurs." In so doing, Cameron explained why shoplifting has the lowest rate of recidivism when the perpetrator, almost always (over 90%) the "amateur," is confronted. At the other end of the continuum is the pickpocket, almost always a professional who works with groups of other professionals—where the rate of recidivism is, by contrast, extraordinarily high. The pickpocket regards arrest as an occupational hazard, and has strategies for minimizing its effect on his (usually) behavior. The arbitrary features of the social fabrication of the criminal law comes to us more clearly by looking back to a much earlier time. In late eighteenth-century England, for example, stealing linens from a linen factory was a crime punishable by death. With the hindsight of two centuries, we now see this more clearly as a narrow, politically and economically motivated specification of a "serious crime." But that is because we have a few centuries' hindsight. Today, we place in the same criminal category someone who leaves lethal nerve gas on a subway station (anonymous killings) and someone who shoots in the back a doctor working in an abortion clinic. Fifty years from now, if some researcher went through the police records to show whether adoptees had a similar "inclination to commit crime" as did those in then biological families, someone might point out the quite reasonable objection that the system of classification was constructed in such a way as to make any claims about a genetic basis for these crimes highly problematic. The search for a genetic explanation for such a demonstrably variegated "phenotype" (criminal) requires a theoretical warrant that has never been delivered. The closest that one can come is in the abstract notion of an "antisocial personality," but even for this abstracted version, the obstacles to linking phenotypes and genotypes are huge. That is, given this demonstrably high empirical variability (sometimes arbitrary, sometimes systemic reach of the criminal justice system) in what constitutes a crime, and even more demonstrably high empirical variability in what constitutes "antisocial behavior" across social time and space, how is it possible to search for a genotype? The answer, and the conclusion provide strong reasons for deep concern.

It is therefore not possible to study criminal behavior without taking the circumstances in which the behavior takes place into account. The very classification of criminals or criminal behavior as a biological category may also affect the way people understand a particular kind of behavior. The sheer knowledge of such categories can have a looping effect. That is, it may affect people's attitudes and behavior in a way that feeds back on the classification scheme itself.

MARK A. ROTHSTEIN, APPLICATIONS OF BEHAVIOURAL GENETICS: OUTPACING THE SCIENCE?

6 Nature Reviews Genetics 793, 795–796 (2005).

* * *

SPECIFIC APPLICATIONS

Criminal Law. Genetic explanations of anti-social behaviour represent an important area of research and one of the earliest applications of behavioural genetics. Behavioural genetics could potentially be used in several ways—from the earliest stages of a criminal investigation through to almost every aspect of the criminal justice system.

DNA forensic techniques are used by law-enforcement agencies around the world. In the absence of a match between the evidence from a crime scene and the profiles stored in forensic DNA databases, DNA forensic profiling can be used for several purposes—to identify the gender of and make predictions about the race or ethnicity, health status, age, or physical characteristics of the sample source. Behavioural genetic forensic profiling might be increasingly used in law enforcement to predict the perpetrator's behavioural traits and psychiatric conditions, such as learning disabilities and personality traits.

Once a suspect is arrested and charged with a crime, behavioural genetic information could be presented at a bail hearing. Prosecutors might urge that bail should not be granted or should be set at a high amount because of the defendant's genetic predisposition to impulsivity (for example, risk of flight) or aggression (for example, risk of committing further crimes).

At trial, evidence of behavioural genetic variations within the normal range is unlikely to establish an independent basis for acquittal. More extreme deviations might be part of the scientific evidence used to support an insanity defence. Behavioural genetic evidence might also be used to claim that the defendant lacked the mental capacity to form the intent necessary to commit the crime. For example, on this basis a defendant charged with premeditated murder might be convicted of a lesser offence, such as manslaughter.

In many states in the United States it is common for convicted defendants to introduce evidence that relatives across many generations have engaged in violent criminal activities, that the defendant has inexplicably engaged in antisocial activities from a young age, or that the individual has been diagnosed with a neurogenetic disorder. This is then used to assert that defendants who commit crimes caused at least in part by a genetic predisposition or compulsion are not as morally culpable and do not deserve the harshest sentences. It is difficult to determine whether such arguments have had an effect on the sentences imposed, but the willingness of some courts to consider such evidence leaves open the possibility that behavioural genetics could be afforded greater weight in the future.

Behavioural genetic information could also be introduced in parole hearings. Ironically, the positions of the government and the inmate with respect to the behavioural genetic evidence are likely to be the opposite of their arguments at the trial. At a parole hearing, the government might attempt to use genetic predisposition as a basis for denying parole; the inmate might use the absence of genetic predisposition as a basis for release under the theory that he or she is less likely to commit another crime in the future.

Finally, many states in the United States have enacted 'sexual predator laws', which permit the indefinite confinement of individuals who have been convicted of multiple sex crimes against children and who are considered likely to commit further crimes if released. In theory, behavioural genetic evidence might be used to predict the likelihood of the individual committing future sex crimes.

B. CULPABILITY

LORI B. ANDREWS, PREDICTING AND PUNISHING ANTISOCIAL ACTS: HOW THE CRIMINAL JUSTICE SYSTEM MIGHT USE BEHAVIORAL GENETICS IN BEHAVIORAL GENETICS: THE CLASH OF CULTURE AND BIOLOGY

120–122 (Ronald A. Carson & Mark A. Rothstein eds. 1999).

Criminal law is viewed as a "choosing system" in that people are seen as having a choice about whether to engage in criminal behavior. People are seen as culpable when they *choose* to violate the law. This involves both a voluntary wrongful act (*actus rea*) and the mental state to know that the act was wrongful (*mens rea*). In situations in which the individual was not acting under free will, however, the law provides a variety of mechanisms to avoid traditional criminal penalties.

Evidence of one's genotype might be used to exculpate an individual or to mitigate punishment. A person may claim that his genes provoked involuntary actions that caused the inappropriate act (such as involuntarily physically harming someone during a seizure). Or he may argue that his genotype influenced his mental processes so as to prevent him from realizing his act was wrongful and controlling himself. Or he might argue that it is unjust to punish him because his actions are compelled by an illness rather than a "chosen" behavior.

With respect to the voluntary act requirement for criminal conviction, genetic defenses would be unlikely to be accepted if there was evidence that the individual could have ascertained his or her genetic status and done something about it. For example, a driver who unexpectedly blacks out and causes a fatal accident would not be criminally liable; however, a driver who knows he is prone to blackouts could be found guilty of manslaughter if he has a fatal traffic accident during a blackout. This is in keeping with the traditional legal approach, which holds that "the powerful influences exercised by one's hereditary make-up by his developmental and environmental background are not ignored, but the law takes the position 'that most men, in most of the relations of life, can act purposefully and can inhibit antisocial, illegal tendencies.' "

There is more potential to prove that a particular genotype influenced a defendant's mental status. If a person's genetic status causes him or her to be insane, the individual can be found not guilty by reason of insanity. There are a variety of legal tests for insanity, with twenty states applying a strict rule requiring proof that the defendant did not know the nature or the quality of the act he was committing, or if he did know it, that he did not know he was doing wrong. In twenty-seven states and the District of Columbia, a more liberal approach is taken, requiring the defendant to prove that he lacked substantial capacity to appreciate the criminality of his or her conduct or to control that conduct to the requirements of law.

At the federal level, the insanity test was changed significantly after John Hinckley was acquitted on the grounds that he could not conform his conduct to the requirements of the law. Now, under federal law, individuals can be found not guilty by reason of insanity only if they are unable to appreciate the nature and quality or wrongfulness of their acts. Merely not being able to conform their conduct is not enough.

Also in response to the Hinckley situation, the majority of states amended their criminal laws to create a verdict of guilty but mentally ill to avoid (except in rare instances) acquitting someone who had committed an antisocial act. This newer "guilty but mentally ill" verdict recognizes culpability but allows mitigation of the sentence in terms of its length or the type of facility in which the offender is institutionalized.

In traditional criminal law, several justifications are put forth for punishing people who have committed antisocial acts. People are institutionalized to deter them from committing future antisocial acts, to rehabilitate them, to deter others from committing antisocial acts, to incapacitate them, and to exact retribution (an institutionalized vengeance). If a genetic deterministic view is taken, the first two justifications may be eliminated on the ground that there would be nothing that could be done to change the individual. However, institutionalizing the offender might serve other purposes by deterring others from committing crimes (or from attempting to "game" the system by purporting to have a genetic defense), by preventing the offender (through incarceration) from having the opportunity to commit another crime, and by satisfying society's need for revenge.

Lawyer Maureen Coffey advocates that, "In light of increasing knowledge and understanding, traditional yet outdated notions of freedom and responsibility should be modified to square with a scientific view of human conduct." She argues that people with genetic susceptibilities for antisocial behavior are "innately different from the 'normal' person," but that their lessened free will should not make such individuals immune from punishment. Rather, punishment should be based, not on a subjective, moral culpability justification, but on "the legitimate objectives of social control and public welfare." Even though she acknowledges that "punishing an individual for crimes for which he is not responsible in the traditional sense seems to be morally offensive," she feels it can be outweighed by the greater social good.

Coffey's argument will probably be attractive to policymakers, who seem to have given up on a rehabilitative model of prison in favor of a punitive one. Thus, even in instances in which it is proven that the defendant acted in conformity with a genetic predisposition, people who argue that their genes caused them to commit an antisocial act may ultimately be incarcerated to prevent them from committing other acts, to deter others, or to satisfy society's need for vengeance.

MILLARD v. MARYLAND

261 A.2d 227 (Md. Ct. Spec. App. 1970).

MURPHY, J.

Charged with the offense of robbery with a deadly weapon, appellant filed a written plea that he was insane at the time of the commission of the crime under Maryland Code, Article 59, Section 9(a), which provides:

> "A defendant is not responsible for criminal conduct and shall be found insane at the time of the commission of the alleged crime if, at the time of such conduct as a result of mental disease or defect, he lacks substantial capacity either to appreciate the criminality of his conduct or to conform his conduct to the requirements of law. As used in this section, the terms 'mental disease or defect' do not include an abnormality manifested only by repeated criminal or otherwise antisocial conduct."

The basis for appellant's insanity plea, as later unfolded at the trial, was that he had an extra Y chromosome in the brain and other cells of his body which constituted, within the meaning of Section 9(a), a mental defect resulting in his lacking substantial capacity either to appreciate the criminality of his conduct or to conform his conduct to the requirements of law.

At the trial before a jury in the Circuit Court for Prince George's County, the State established the corpus delicti, adduced proof of appellant's criminal agency, and then rested its case. Thereafter, under the prescribed Maryland procedure, it became incumbent upon the appellant in undertaking to establish his insanity defense to first adduce sufficient competent proof in support thereof, out of the presence of the jury, from which the trial judge could properly find, as a preliminary matter of law, that the presumption of sanity had been rebutted and a doubt raised in the minds of reasonable men as to his sanity. To this end, and in conformity with the approved procedure, appellant adduced evidence through the testimony of a Lieutenant at the Prince George's County jail showing that while in confinement appellant was agitated, nervous, upset, and became so violent on occasions that he had to be handcuffed and shackled in leg irons; that appellant cut himself five or six times on his arm between the elbow and the wrist, resulting in severe bleeding, although no arteries were severed; that these cuts "ran the gamut from scratches to very severe cuts requiring quite a number of sutures"; and that as a result of his condition, appellant was sent to three different hospitals for treatment and evaluation.

Dr. Cecil Jacobson, the appellant's only medical witness, testified that he was an Assistant Professor in the Department of Obstetrics and Gynecology and Chief of the Reproduction Genetics Unit of the George Washington University School of Medicine; that he had obtained a degree in genetics from the University of Utah in 1960 and was "a research teacher teaching the full-time faculty" at the University; that he had published 42 articles in the field of genetics, had conducted extensive research in the field, supervised a number of genetics laboratories, and was a consultant in genetics to the Federal Government. He stated that in 1964 he also obtained a medical degree and was licensed to practice medicine in Maryland, Virginia and the District of Columbia; that he had interned for one year in 1964–1965 but did not serve a residency in medicine but "went directly into the academic program [at George Washington University] because he had an active teaching responsibility as a medical student." He testified that while he received formal training in psychiatry as a medical student, and had received clinical experience in the psychiatric wards during his medical internship, he was not a psychiatrist, had received no post-graduate training in psychiatry, was neither Board eligible nor Board certified, and had "no competence" in the field of psychiatry beyond that possessed by "the conventional physician." * * *

Dr. Jacobson testified that on December 16, 1968, appellant was examined and his body cells found to contain an extra Y chromosome (XYY); that the presence of this extra chromosome constituted a "basic defect in the genetic complement of the cell" affecting not only the way the cells grow in the body, but also the physical growth of the body itself; that the presence of the extra Y chromosome caused "marked physical and mental problems" affecting the manner in which persons possessing the extra Y chromosome "will react to certain stimulus; certain physiological problems; certain behavioral characteristics." Dr. Jacobson then told of approximately 40 published reports indicating that persons possessed of an extra Y chromosome tended to be very tall, with limbs disproportionate to their body; that such persons had marked antisocial, aggressive and schizoid reactions and were in continual conflict with the law.

Dr. Jacobson stated that he had never previously testified in court. Asked whether he was familiar with the Maryland test of insanity, as defined in Section 9(a), he said that he had never read it, but believed it contained two parts—"One, whether there was a basic defect involved, and, secondly, whether or not the person is competent for his act." Section 9(a) was then read to Dr. Jacobson, and he was then asked whether appellant was insane. Dr. Jacobson responded with a professorial narrative of appellant's genetic make-up, after which he concluded that "if the definition of insanity has a mental defect, the answer is yes, he has a mental defect based upon his abnormal [chromosome] test." Asked whether the "defect" was such as to cause appellant to lack "substantial capacity either to appreciate the criminality of his conduct or to conform his conduct to the requirements of law," Dr. Jacobson answered:

> "I cannot say that because I have not examined him as a psychiatrist. I have no competence in that area."

Appellant's counsel then told the court that he intended to show through "case histories" that individuals having the extra Y chromosome have extremely aggressive personalities, "to the extent that most of them end up in jail for one reason or another because of their aggressive reactions." Dr. Jacobson was then asked to examine appellant's arms to determine whether the cuts thereon were "suicidal or merely attention cuts." Dr. Jacobson did so briefly and stated that based on his experience as a medical doctor, he believed the cuts constituted an actual attempt at suicide; that based on this fact, and his brief questioning of appellant during a five-minute court recess, he felt appellant's "reactions" were not normal; that appellant had a fear of "forceful activity with an attempt at extension of this regression and a lack of adequately controlling this;" that although he was "greatly restricted" by not knowing the "developmental history" of appellant, he believed, based upon the testimony of the jail lieutenant concerning appellant's conduct while in confinement, including the suicide attempts, coupled with appellant's genetic defect, that "this does not fall within the realm of sanity, as I understand it." Dr. Jacobson then testified that the extra Y chromosome in appellant's genetic make-up affected his behavioral patterns, as reported in other cases of persons similarly possessed of the extra Y chromosome. He conceded that persons having the extra Y chromosome may differ among themselves depending upon "what other physical effects are found in the body of the XYY," environment also being a factor accounting for differences between XYY individuals.

Under further questioning by the trial judge, the prosecutor, and defense counsel, Dr. Jacobson stated that appellant's genetic defect—which he characterized as a mental defect—influenced "his competence or ability to recognize the area of his crime;" that appellant had a "propensity" toward crime because of his genetic abnormality; that based upon the medical literature, the appellants' conduct and behavioral patterns, and his genetic defect, he was insane and not even competent to stand trial. The doctor defined insanity in terms of the "ability to comprehend reality" or the "inability to judge one's action as far as consequence." Dr. Jacobson next testified that he had "insufficient evidence" upon which to base a conclusion whether appellant appreciated the consequences of his action, but that because he had attempted to commit suicide, such an act constituted "an inability to comprehend the consequences of his act, the act of suicide, being death;" and that appellant's actions were "not consistent with sanity."

* * *

At the conclusion of Dr. Sauer's testimony, the trial judge ruled that he was not persuaded that reasonable minds could differ as to appellant's sanity; that the appellant's defect was physical and not mental; and that Dr. Jacobson's testimony did not, with reasonable medical certainty, overcome the presumption that appellant was sane. The trial judge thus declined to submit the issue of appellant's sanity to the jury. The jury subsequently found appellant guilty of robbery with a deadly weapon and he was sentenced to eighteen years under the jurisdiction of the Department of Correction.

We see no merit in appellant's contention on appeal that the trial judge erred in ruling that there had not been presented evidence of insanity under Article 59, Section 9(a) sufficient to overcome the presumption of sanity. Dr. Jacobson's testimony, if believed, clearly established that appellant possessed an extra Y chromosome (XYY) and that he was therefore genetically abnormal. It also tended to show in a general way that appellant's possession of the extra Y chromosome caused him to be antisocial, aggressive, in continual conflict with the law, and to have a "propensity" toward the commission of crime. But, * * * the test of responsibility for criminal conduct under Section 9(a) is predicated upon "mental disease or defect," the existence of which is "first and foremost a medical problem;" and that an opinion as to the ultimate fact whether an accused is insane under Section 9(a) should be reached "by a medical diagnosis," based on "reasonable medical certainty." The mere fact then that appellant had a genetic abnormality which Dr. Jacobson characterized as "a mental defect" would not, of itself, suffice to show that, under Section 9(a), he lacked, because of such defect, "substantial capacity either to appreciate the criminality of his conduct or to conform his conduct to the requirements of law." And to simply state that persons having the extra Y chromosome are prone to aggressiveness, are antisocial, and continually run afoul of the criminal laws, is hardly sufficient to rebut the presumption of sanity and show the requisite lack of "substantial capacity" under Section 9(a). Moreover, we think it entirely plain from the record that in testifying that appellant had a "mental defect," Dr. Jacobson did so only in a most general sense, without full appreciation for the meaning of the term as used in Section 9(a), and particularly without an understanding that such term expressly excludes "an abnormality manifested only by repeated criminal or otherwise antisocial conduct." But even if it were accepted that appellant had a "mental defect" within the contemplation of Section 9(a), Dr. Jacobson, by his own testimony, indicated an inability to meaningfully relate the effect of such defect to the "substantial capacity" requirements of the subsection. Not only did Dr. Jacobson candidly admit that he had "no competence" in the field of psychiatry, but he demonstrated that fact by showing that he had not theretofore familiarized himself with the substance of Section 9(a); indeed, his conception of the test of criminal responsibility in Maryland was shallow at best, at least until the test was read to him during his testimony. While Dr. Jacobson did ultimately testify in conclusory fashion that he thought appellant insane and even incompetent to stand trial, his testimony in this connection was obviously predicated on a definition of "insanity" different than that prescribed under Section 9(a)—a definition so general as to encompass as insane a person who would attempt suicide.

* * *

That Dr. Jacobson was a well qualified geneticist was clear beyond question. Equally clear is the fact that he was not a practicing physician, and his experience in mental illness was related essentially to his practice in the field of genetics. He conceded a lack of competence in the field of psychiatry, admitted having no prior familiarity with the provisions of Section 9(a), had not subjected appellant to any psychiatric examination, and defined "insanity" in terms different than those prescribed by the applicable law * * *. [T]o constitute proof of insanity sufficient to raise a doubt in the minds of reasonable men, competent medical evidence must be adduced to the positive effect that the accused, as a result of mental disease or defect, lacked substantial capacity either to appreciate the criminality of his conduct or to conform his conduct to the requirements of law; and evidence of some undefined mental disorder or instability is insufficient proof to overcome the presumption of sanity. On the record before us, we think Dr. Jacobson's opinion as to appellant's sanity under Section 9(a) was not competent in that it was not based on reasonable medical certainty, and that the trial judge, had he so concluded, would not have been in error.

NOTES AND QUESTIONS

1. Based on the Andrews excerpt, what would a criminal defendant have to prove to make out a genetic defense to a crime? How, if at all, would it differ from an insanity defense? For a further discussion of these issues, see Jeffrey R. Botkin et al. eds., Genetics and Criminality: The Potential Misuse of Scientific Information in Court (1999).

2. In 1965, a chromosomal study of 197 mentally subnormal males with dangerous, violent, or criminal tendencies in an institution in Scotland found that seven of the men had a karyotype of XYY. This was a surprisingly high percentage of 3.5%. In addition, the average height of the seven men was 6 feet, 1 inch, whereas the average height for the rest of the men was 5 feet, 7 inches. It was not long before an XYY genetic defense was asserted in several criminal cases, based on the assumption that men with an extra Y chromosome were genetically programmed to commit violent acts for which they should not be responsible. The courts generally rejected the defense. See, e.g.,

People v. Tanner, 91 Cal.Rptr. 656 (Cal. Ct. App. 1970); People v. Yukl, 372 N.Y.S.2d 313 (N.Y.Sup.1975); State v. Roberts, 544 P.2d 754 (Wash.App. 1976). Subsequent research indicated that men with an XYY karyotype tend to have lower intellectual functioning or even to be mildly retarded. Cognitive impairment, irrespective of genetic makeup, correlates with being institutionalized for crime.

3.   The court in *Millard* adopted the majority view in rejecting the XYY defense. The expert witness for the defense, whose testimony was discredited by the court, became infamous several years later. In 1992, Dr. Cecil B. Jacobson was convicted of 52 felony counts for mail fraud, wire fraud, travel fraud, and perjury. Between 1976 and 1986, Dr. Jacobson, while owning and operating the Reproductive Genetics Center, Ltd., a fertility clinic, fraudulently injected his own sperm into patients instead of the promised sperm of the patient's husband or an anonymous donor during artificial insemination procedures at the clinic. As many as 75 children were born from these insemination procedures. Dr. Jacobson was sentenced to five years in prison, ordered to pay a $75,000 fine, and required to refund the $39,205 that patients had paid for his services. In addition to the federal criminal action, Dr. Jacobson was named in at least six civil suits brought by the parents of the children Jacobson allegedly fathered. The suits alleged various counts of fraud, battery, negligence, outrage, negligent infliction of emotional distress, medical malpractice, and child support.

4.   Glenda Sue Caldwell was tried for the murder of her son and the aggravated assault of her daughter. She was found guilty but mentally ill and sentenced to life imprisonment. Her defense at trial was that she was insane, brought on by the fear of contracting Huntington disease and the stress of her separation from her husband. The psychiatrist who testified for the defense said that she was under stress and exhibited a borderline personality disorder, but she was not psychotic. Caldwell v. State, 354 S.E.2d 124 (Ga. 1987). After spending nine years in prison, Caldwell was granted a new trial and subsequently acquitted. By the time of the retrial, her Huntington disease symptoms had become more pronounced, which may have convinced the judge that she was not responsible for the shootings. Blaming Illness, Woman Cleared of Killing Son, The Record, Sept. 29, 1994. What effect, if any, should her later development of symptoms of Huntington disease have on her guilt or innocence? As predictive testing improves for various late-onset neurological disorders and dementias, what principles should the courts apply in determining the admissibility and effects of this evidence?

5.   For a further discussion, see Nita A. Farahany & James E. Coleman, Jr., Genetics and Responsibility: To Know the Criminal from the Crime, 69 L. & Contemp. Probs. 115 (2006); Karen H. Rothenberg & Alice Wang, The Scarlet Gene: Behavioral Genetics, Criminal Law, and Racial and Ethnic Stigma, 69 L. & Contemp. Probs. 343 (2006).

C. SENTENCING

HILL v. OZMINT

339 F.3d 187 (4th Cir. 2003).

King, Circuit Judge:

In October of 1995, David Hill was sentenced to death for the murder of Major Spencer Guerry, the Deputy Police Chief for the City of Georgetown, South Carolina. After the South Carolina courts denied relief on both direct appeal and collateral review, Hill sought habeas corpus relief in the District of South Carolina. The district court denied relief, and it declined to issue a certificate of appealability ("COA").

* * *

V. The IAC [Ineffective Assistance of Counsel] claim

In his IAC claim, Hill maintains that his defense lawyers were ineffective in calling Dr. Edward Burt to testify during the trial's sentencing phase. At sentencing, Hill's lawyers sought to show that Hill suffered from a genetically-based serotonin deficiency, which resulted in aggressive impulses. After his arrest and incarceration, Hill had been prescribed medication that they believed had successfully curbed these impulses. Thus, according to Hill's lawyers, the death penalty was not warranted because Hill's aggressive behavior was genetic (i.e., beyond his control) and treatable. To this end, Hill's lawyers presented the testimony of Dr. Emil Coccaro, who explained the role of serotonin in brain chemistry, as well as how genetics affects serotonin levels. Next, the defense called Dr. Bernard Albiniak, a forensic psychologist, who had performed a series of spinal taps on Hill to monitor his serotonin levels. Dr. Albiniak opined that Hill suffered from a chronic serotonin deficiency.

Finally, the defense called Hill's psychiatrist, Dr. Edward Burt. Dr. Burt was expected to testify that he has prescribed Prozac to treat Hill's serotonin deficiency, and that Hill had responded favorably to the medication. Dr. Burt's testimony sought to establish that Hill's serotonin deficiency caused his aggressive behavior, and that a long history of violence and suicide in his family indicated that his aggressive impulses resulted from a genetic condition. Dr. Burt, however, apparently suffered a breakdown while on the witness stand. Thus, while testifying during the trial's sentencing phase, Dr. Burt had difficulty responding to questions, particularly on cross-examination.

Hill contended * * * that his defense lawyers should have known that Dr. Burt was incapable of testifying effectively. According to Hill, his lawyers also knew that, approximately eight months before trial, Dr. Burt had been arrested for public intoxication. Hill maintained that, in light of his lawyers' knowledge of Dr. Burt's problems, the decision to call him as a witness fell below an objective standard of reasonableness. Further, the decision to present Dr. Burt's evidence, Hill maintained, prejudiced his defense because it undermined the compelling evidence of Drs. Coccaro and Albiniak.

The state court summarily rejected Hill's IAC claim. It concluded that, although Dr. Burt "was not as effective as [Hill] would have liked," Hill's lawyers were not constitutionally ineffective in calling him as a witness because they had properly investigated him and prepared him for trial. The district court also denied relief on the IAC claim, concluding that the state court's rulings were neither "contrary to" nor an "unreasonable application of" clearly established federal law. Hill now challenges the district court's ruling. Although we have issued a COA on this claim, we decline to award Hill any relief.

NOTES AND QUESTIONS

1. Suppose Dr. Burt had been able to present his testimony as scheduled. Should it be used to mitigate the sentence of the defendant?

2. Do you think that introducing genetic evidence at the sentencing stage is going to help or hurt the defendant? Although genetic propensity may explain the predisposition of the plaintiff (ostensibly militating toward a less harsh sentence), the determinist view of genes argued by the defendant may cause the court to think that a maximum sentence is necessary to keep the defendant off the streets as long as possible.

3. In Mobley v. State, 455 S.E.2d 61 (Ga.), cert. denied, 516 U.S. 942 (1995), Stephen Mobley was convicted of murdering a Domino's Pizza store manager. Mobley's attorneys attempted to use his "genetic makeup" as a mitigating factor in sentencing. Based on his family history of violence, the defense requested expert and financial assistance to conduct a genetic analysis to determine whether Mobley had a genetic mutation associated with monoamine oxidase A (MAOA) deficiency, which some studies have linked with a predisposition to aggression and violence. The trial court denied the request based on an insufficient scientific evidence of correlation between MAOA deficiency and aggression. The Georgia Supreme Court affirmed. Mobley subsequently filed a habeas corpus petition in which he alleged ineffective assistance of counsel for attempting to present such an unorthodox mitigation defense, using genetic evidence. A trial judge vacated his sentence, but the Georgia Supreme Court reversed and held that Mobley's counsel had made a "reasonable strategic decision." Turpin v. Mobley, 502 S.E.2d 458 (Ga. 1998). The Eleventh Circuit agreed with the Georgia Supreme Court. Mobley v. Head, 267 F.3d 1312 (11th Cir. 2001), cert. denied, 536 U.S. 968 (2002). For a further discussion, see generally Nita A. Farahany & James E. Coleman, Jr., Genetics and Responsibility: To Know the Criminal from the Crime, 69 Law & Contemp. Probs. 115 (2006); Dianne E. Hoffmann & Karen H. Rothenberg, Judging Genes: Implications of the Second Generation of Genetic Tests in the Courtroom, 66 Md. L. Rev. 858 (2007).

4. Richard M. Ewanisyzk was an attorney who abused alcohol and misappropriated client funds. His disbarment was affirmed by the courts. In re Ewaniszyk, 788 P.2d 690 (Cal.1990). John David Baker was an attorney

who abused alcohol and misappropriated client funds. The state bar and the courts considered it to be a mitigating factor that Baker conceded that he "had a genetic predisposition to addiction." He was suspended rather than disbarred. Baker v. State Bar of California, 781 P.2d 1344 (Cal.1989). To what degree, if any, should the genetic basis of the addictive behavior (assuming it could be established) affect the appropriate discipline in these cases or sentencing in criminal cases?

5. Similar issues could arise at all stages of the criminal justice system, from bail to parole. As to bail, in United States v. Salerno, 481 U.S. 739 (1987), the Supreme Court upheld the use of predictions of future criminal conduct as a factor in deciding whether to grant bail and the proper amount. As to parole, a wide range of considerations may be used by parole boards, and the boards are given a wide range of discretion, subject to considerations of due process. See Greenholtz v. Inmates of Nebraska Penal & Correctional Complex, 442 U.S. 1 (1979).

6. In general, a more lax evidentiary standard is used in bail, sentencing, and parole matters than is applied at trial. What standard should be applied to the introduction of proffered behavioral genetic evidence?

7. In Roper v. Simmons, 543 U.S. 551 (2005), the Supreme Court held that it was unconstitutional to execute individuals who were under 18 years old at the time they committed their crime. The decision was based largely on "evolving national and international standards of decency" and the consensus that children lack the emotional and mental maturity necessary for the most culpable criminal intent. Amicus briefs submitted on behalf of the defendant emphasized, among other things, that teenagers have "an underdeveloped sense of responsibility." Studies using modern neuroscience imaging techniques were offered to show that the brain does not mature until the age of 20–25 and therefore teenagers do not have fully developed frontal lobes capable of impulse control. Based on this line of reasoning, how should the Supreme Court rule in a future case in which the defendant argues that it is cruel and unusual punishment to execute an adult who does not suffer from mental retardation, but whose impulse control has been compromised by a genetic mutation?

D. COMMITMENT PROCEEDINGS

KANSAS v. CRANE

534 U.S. 407 (2002).

JUSTICE BREYER delivered the opinion of the Court.

This case concerns the constitutional requirements substantively limiting the civil commitment of a dangerous sexual offender—a matter that this Court considered in Kansas v. Hendricks, 521 U.S. 346 (1997). The State of Kansas argues that the Kansas Supreme Court has interpreted our decision in *Hendricks* in an overly restrictive manner. We agree and vacate the Kansas court's judgment.

I

In *Hendricks,* this Court upheld the Kansas Sexually Violent Predator Act, Kan. Stat. Ann. § 59–29a01 *et seq.* (1994), against constitutional challenge. In doing so, the Court characterized the confinement at issue as civil, not criminal, confinement. And it held that the statutory criterion for confinement embodied in the statute's words "mental abnormality or personality disorder" satisfied "substantive due process requirements."

In reaching its conclusion, the Court's opinion pointed out that "States have in certain narrow circumstances provided for the forcible civil detainment of people who are unable to control their behavior and who thereby pose a danger to the public health and safety." It said that "[w]e have consistently upheld such involuntary commitment statutes" when (1) "the confinement takes place pursuant to proper procedures and evidentiary standards," (2) there is a finding of "dangerousness either to one's self or to others," and (3) proof of dangerousness is "coupled . . . with the proof of some additional factor, such as a 'mental illness' or 'mental abnormality.'" It noted that the Kansas "Act unambiguously requires a finding of dangerousness either to one's self or to others," and then "links that finding to the existence of a 'mental abnormality' or 'personality disorder' that makes it difficult, if not impossible, for the person to control his dangerous behavior." And the Court ultimately determined that the statute's "requirement of a 'mental abnormality' or 'personality disorder' is consistent with the requirements of . . . other statutes that we have upheld in that it narrows the class of persons eligible for confinement to those who are unable to control their dangerousness."

The Court went on to respond to Hendricks' claim that earlier cases had required a finding, not of "mental abnormality" or "personality disorder," but of "mental illness." In doing so, the Court pointed out that we "have traditionally left to legislators the task of defining [such] terms." It then held that, to "the extent that the civil commitment statutes we have considered set forth criteria relating to an individual's inability to control his dangerousness, the Kansas Act sets forth comparable criteria." It added that Hendricks' own condition "doubtless satisfies those criteria," for (1) he suffers from pedophilia, (2) "the psychiatric profession itself classifies" that condition "as a serious mental disorder," and (3) Hendricks conceded that he cannot " 'control the urge' " to molest children. And it concluded that this "admitted lack of volitional control, coupled with a prediction of future dangerousness, adequately distinguishes Hendricks from other dangerous persons who are perhaps more properly dealt with exclusively through criminal proceedings."

II

In the present case the State of Kansas asks us to review the Kansas Supreme Court's application of *Hendricks.* The State here seeks the civil commitment of Michael Crane, a previously convicted sexual offender who, according to a least one of the State's psychiatric witnesses, suffers from both exhibitionism and antisocial personality disorder. After a jury trial, the Kansas District Court ordered Crane's civil commitment. But the Kansas Supreme Court reversed. In that court's view, the Federal Constitution as interpreted in *Hendricks* insists upon "a finding that the defendant cannot control his dangerous behavior"—even if (as provided by Kansas law) problems or "emotional capacity" and not "volitional capacity" prove the "source of bad behavior" warranting commitment. And the trial court had made no such finding.

Kansas now argues that the Kansas Supreme Court wrongly read *Hendricks* as requiring the State *always* to prove that a dangerous individual is *completely* unable to control his behavior. That reading, says Kansas, if far too rigid.

III

We agree with Kansas insofar as it argues that *Hendricks* set forth no requirement of *total* or *complete* lack of control. *Hendricks* referred to the Kansas Act as requiring a "mental abnormality" or "personality disorder" that makes if *"difficult,* if not impossible, for the [dangerous] person to control his dangerous behavior." The word "difficult" indicates that the lack of control to which this Court referred was not absolute. Indeed, as different *amici* on opposite sides of this case agree, an absolutist approach is unworkable. Insistence upon absolute lack of control would risk barring civil commitment of highly dangerous persons suffering severe mental abnormalities.

We do not agree with the State, however, insofar as it seeks to claim that the Constitution permits commitment of the type of dangerous sexual offender considered in *Hendricks* without *any* lack-of-control determination. *Hendricks* underscored the constitutional importance of distinguishing a dangerous sexual offender subject to civil commitment "from other dangerous persons who are perhaps more properly dealt with exclusively through criminal proceedings." That distinction is necessary lest "civil commitment" become a "mechanism for retribution or general deterrence"—functions properly those of criminal law, not civil commitment. The presence of what the "psychiatric profession itself classifie[d] ... as a serious mental disorder" there consisted of a special and serious lack of ability to control behavior.

In recognizing that fact, we did not give to the phrase "lack of control" a particularly narrow or technical meaning. And we recognize that in cases where lack of control is at issue, "inability to control behavior" will not be demonstrable with mathematical precision. It is enough to say that there must be proof of serious difficulty in controlling behavior. And this, when viewed in light of such features of the case as the nature of the psychiatric diagnosis, and the severity of the mental abnormality itself, must be sufficient to distinguish the dangerous sexual offender whose serious mental illness, abnormality, or disorder subjects him to civil commitment from the dangerous but typical recidivist convicted in an ordinary criminal case.

We recognize that *Hendricks* as so read provides a less precise constitutional standard than would those more definite rules for which the parties have argued. But the Constitution's safeguards of human liberty in the area of mental illness and the law are not always best enforced through precise bright-line rules. For one thing, the States retain considerable leeway in defining the mental abnormalities and personality disorders that make an individual eligible for commitment. For another, the science of psychiatry, which informs but does not control ultimate legal determinations, is an ever-advancing science, whose distinctions do not seek precisely to mirror those of the law. Consequently, we have sought to provide constitutional guidance in this area by proceeding deliberately and contextually, elaborating generally stated constitutional standards and objectives as specific circumstances require. *Hendricks* embodied that approach.

* * *

For these reasons, the judgment of the Kansas Supreme Court is vacated, and the case remanded for further proceedings not inconsistent with this opinion.

It is so ordered.

JUSTICE SCALIA, with whom JUSTICE THOMAS joins, dissenting.

Today the Court holds that the Kansas Sexually Violent Predator Act (SVPA) cannot, consistent with so-called substantive due process, be applied as written. It does so even though, less than five years ago, we upheld the very same petitioner (the State of Kansas) from the judgment of the very same court. Not only is the new law that the Court announces today wrong, but the Court's manner of promulgating it—snatching back from the State of Kansas a victory so recently awarded—cheapens the currency of our judgments. I would reverse, rather than vacate, the judgment of the Kansas Supreme Court.

NOTES AND QUESTIONS

1. After remand of his case, doctors determined that Mr. Crane was no longer a threat, and he was released in January 2002. On October 14, 2003, Crane was found guilty of forcible rape, kidnapping, third-degree assault, and three counts of forcible sodomy that stemmed from the raping of a woman in an apartment complex parking lot in Kansas City, Missouri. He was sentenced to life in prison.

2. About one-third of the states have laws similar to the Kansas law upheld in *Hendricks*, and new bills are introduced every year. See Ariz. Rev. Stat. Ann. § 36–3701; Cal. Welf. & Inst. Code § 6600; D.C. Code Ann. § 22–3808; Fla. Stat. Ann. § 394.910; 725 Ill. Comp. Stat. Ann. § 207/40; Iowa Code Ann. § 229A.1; Kan. Stat. Ann. § 253B.02; Minn. Stat. Ann. § 632.480; Mo. Rev. Stat. § 632.480; N.J. Stat. Ann. § 30:4–82.4; N.Y. Correctional Law § 402; N.D. Cent. Code § 25–03.3–13; S.C. Code Ann. § 44–48–20; Tex.

Health & Safety Code Ann. § 841.081; Va. Code Ann. § 37.1–70.9; Wash. Rev. Code Ann. § 71.09.010; Wis. Stat. Ann. § 980.06.

3. If you were a member of a state legislature, would you support such legislation? Why or why not?

4. In Robinson v. California, 370 U.S. 660 (1962) (narcotic addiction) and Powell v. Texas, 392 U.S. 514 (1968) (alcohol addiction), the Supreme Court held that individuals may be convicted for unlawful acts, but it is unconstitutional to punish an individual for having the status of an addict. If an individual were found to have a genetic mutation linked to a predisposition to violence, would incarcerating the individual before he or she committed a crime be cruel and unusual punishment? Would it matter what degree of correlation there was between the mutation and the likelihood of committing the violent act? Would *Robinson* and *Powell* prohibit compelled treatment of an individual to prevent the commission of acts of violence, or to prevent the commission of additional acts of violence for an individual who already has been convicted?

V. EDUCATION

Assessing cognitive ability is the largest potential application of mental and behavioral genetics in educational settings. There are numerous scientific, technical, and moral concerns about whether to attempt to distinguish among individuals based on the genetics of cognitive ability. These concerns are heightened when dealing with children, who are often vulnerable to familial and peer-based stigmatization, self-fulfilling prophecies, and confusion about the deterministic effects of genetic predispositions. Nevertheless, it is likely that the use (or misuse) of genetics in educational settings will become increasingly important legal and social issues.

Potentially, there are two main types of genetic tests with relevance in educational settings. First, children might be tested for fragile X syndrome, autism, and various learning and behavioral disorders or predispositions. Second, children and young adults could be tested for the genetic component of cognitive ability, including "gifted" status and relative strengths and abilities in certain fields, such as musical ability and numeracy. Of course, the scientific research does not currently support such widespread uses, and ethical and legal considerations might even limit the use of scientifically valid testing.

MARK A. ROTHSTEIN, GENETICS AND THE WORK FORCE OF THE NEXT HUNDRED YEARS

2000 Colum. Bus. L. Rev. 371, 377–379 (2000).

The "channeling" or "tracking" of children based on their genetic endowment would be consistent with educational methods used in varying degrees for most of the twentieth century, which relied on IQ tests and standardized tests such as the SAT. It would also be consistent with elitist and even racist notions of worthiness of education and social advance-ment, which date back at least to the nineteenth century. For example, Herbert Spencer, the father of social Darwinism, opposed free public education in nineteenth century England on hereditarian grounds. In his view, parents who could not afford to pay for the education of their children, necessarily must lack the intellect, determination, and good character to succeed in life. Because he believed that these traits were heritable, it followed that the offspring of such individuals would possess similar defective traits and therefore public education would be a waste of public money.

* * *

The tracking of school children based on IQ has been criticized on a variety of grounds, including that it is inaccurate, unsound educationally and socially, discriminatory on the basis of race and ethnicity, stigmatiz-ing, and a self-fulfilling prophecy. Perhaps the most important criticism, as we contemplate even more extensive tracking based on genetic predis-position, is that it is undemocratic. "The practice of sorting children into ability groups and providing them with a differentiated educational experi-ence is inherently undemocratic and is contrary to the spirit of equality that is so important to Americans." Interestingly, the critics almost always focus on the asserted unfairness in the educational process rather than the larger effects on society of having an individual's future opportu-nities for the good life so severely limited at a young age and creating a *de facto* caste system.

GARY E. MARCHANT & JASON S. ROBERT, GENETIC TESTING FOR AUTISM PREDISPOSITION: ETHICAL, LEGAL AND SOCIAL CHALLENGES

9 Hous. J. Health L. & Pol'y 203, 221–222 (2009).

* * *

Accurate and timely diagnosis is critical for addressing autism in clinical settings. Establishing a diagnosis and understanding the underly-ing etiology may aid in predicting the prognosis, determining accurate recurrence risk, starting appropriate treatment and health maintenance planning, and offering family members considerable emotional relief. Children exhibiting symptoms or characteristics of autism might be genet-ically tested for autism predisposition genes to assist in diagnosing autism early in its development. The threshold question for this application is: how will the identification of a genetic marker in a child assist in the diagnosis or treatment of that child's condition? For example, will there be different treatment options based on the results of genetic testing? If not, will there be any other benefits for the child from identifying a genetic contributing cause? Will there be any benefits to the parents in terms of planning for future children? What are the risks that such testing might entail (e.g., in terms of parent-child relations, child's own self-image, and insurability)? How well characterized and validated must the genetic test be before it can be used for such purposes?

It is also important to understand how individuals perceive the genetic risk of their child developing autism given that genetic testing for complex diseases such as autism provides only the probability of developing the disease. It is unlikely that there will be a bright line between disease and non-disease status in people exhibiting autism traits, so how will genetic markers contribute to delineation of disease status from non-disease status? It has been shown that, regarding results from genetic testing, individuals often interpret probabilities as either presence or absence of the disease. The fact that mutations or polymorphisms are reported as either present or not present (despite the fact that the risk of developing the disease is probabilistic) may further exacerbate the problem. Knowledge that a young child and possibly other family members carry a genetic predisposition to autism may create a whole series of stigmas and negative perceptions related to being "at risk." There is some evidence associated with other genetically influenced diseases that the existence of a genetic explanation for a child's disease can provide emotional relief for the parents. However, a parent who is found to have contributed the genetic marker to an autistic child may have feelings of guilt and responsibility. Siblings of an individual with autism who are found to carry the same genetic marker but who did not develop autism may have misgivings and anxieties about becoming a parent and passing on such a trait to their children.

EMILY CHANG, IN CHINA, DNA TESTS ON KIDS ID GENETIC GIFTS, CAREERS

CNN.com (August 3, 2009),
http://edition.cnn.com/2009/WORLD/asiapcf/08/03/china.dna.children.ability/index.html

CHONGQING, China (CNN)—At the Chongqing Children's Palace, experts are hoping to revolutionize child-rearing with the help of science. About 30 children aged 3 to 12 years old and their parents are participating in a new program that uses DNA testing to identify genetic gifts and predict the future.

For about $880, Chinese parents can sign their kids up for the test and five days of camp.

When Director Zhao Mingyou first heard about the technology earlier this year, he instantly knew it could be a success in China.

"Nowadays, competition in the world is about who has the most talent," said Zhao. "We can give Chinese children an effective, scientific plan at an early age."

The test is conducted by the Shanghai Biochip Corporation. Scientists claim a simple saliva swab collects as many as 10,000 cells that enable them to isolate eleven different genes. By taking a closer look at the genetic codes, they say they can extract information about a child's IQ, emotional control, focus, memory, athletic ability and more.

"For basketball, we can test for height and other factors," said Dr. Huang Xinhua, a leading scientist on the project. "We also test listening ability so that can tell us if (the child) might be talented at music."

DNA testing has been used more widely to determine susceptibility to genetic disease. The test can identify mutations in the genetic code that lead to certain disorders, allow patients to assess risk levels and decide whether they want preventative treatment.

* * *

But according to Chinese scientists, this is the first time the test is being offered to children in China to help discover their natural talents.

For about $880, Chinese parents can sign their kids up for the test and five days of summer camp in Chongqing, where the children will be evaluated in various settings from sports to art. The scientific results, combined with observations by experts throughout the week, will be used to make recommendations to parents about what their child should pursue.

Dr. Huang said the testing can even help project careers down the road.

Examining one child's results, he told CNN: "This child is very thoughtful and focused, so I suggest she go into management."

Clinical psychologist Dr. Rob Blinn said the DNA test can be accurate but only "within a sort of limited field" and that results will not be "dramatic."

"You're not going to be able to predict that someone's going to be like the next Einstein. It's more like this person may have an IQ that's maybe 5 or 10 points greater than this other person because of the absence or presence of these particular genes," he said.

Still, parents are convinced it will help their child. It is no secret that China's one-child policy often produces anxious and ambitious parents with high expectations for their only child.

"China is different from Western countries," said Yang Yangqing, the lab's technical director. "There is only one child in our families so more and more parents focus on their children's education and they want to give them the best education."

Along with parents, the Chinese government is also interested in giving talented children an early start on their careers. Children as young as two are regularly hand-picked by the government to represent China on the international stage.

Future gymnasts, musicians, and basketball players are sent to rigorous training camps and specialized sports schools, and sometimes paid a government salary.

* * *

"It's better to develop her talents earlier rather than later," Chen Zhongyan said of her four-year-old daughter, who is attending the genetics camp. "Now we can find when she is young, and raise her based on what her natural gifts are."

Her daughter, Lai Hongni, has already shown a strong aptitude for dancing, while four-year-old twin boys Luo Lianzhao and Dong Liangtong appear to be good at drawing.

"This way we can really understand our kids," said the twins' father, Mr. Dong, referring to the program.

In the end, are these parents giving their kids a head start or taking a shortcut? Critics of the program said such analysis has frightening implications.

"Kids, especially at younger ages, they need to have fun, they need to enjoy themselves, they need to find meaning in life," Dr. Blinn said. "They need to have rich deep emotional interchange with their families and parents."

"Whether it's really good for a two- or three-year-old to be sent off to a camp to be genetically tested, you know, and put in this track so early in life, I have some real doubts about whether that's in the child's best interest," Blinn added. "It seems to be more in the parents' best interest."

LAURA F. ROTHSTEIN, GENETIC INFORMATION IN SCHOOLS IN GENETIC SECRETS: PROTECTING PRIVACY AND CONFIDENTIALITY IN THE GENETIC ERA

317–320 (Mark A. Rothstein ed. 1997).

Although little genetic information is being systematically collected or used in educational settings, this could change at any time. Well meaning but unthinking school officials could adopt programs of genetic screening or genetic classification of students. School officials also could acquiesce in commercial pressures by facilitating the collection of genetic information about students. The possibility of using genetic information in schools, obtained or maintained for any reason, raises a variety of important ethical, legal, and social issues that are poorly addressed by current policy.

WHY SCHOOLS WOULD ACQUIRE, HAVE, OR USE GENETIC INFORMATION

Educational purposes. A school could acquire, have, or use genetic information for four main reasons. If a school has genetic information about a condition such as dyslexia or fragile X syndrome, it may be able to provide appropriate educational programming for a particular child. If the school personnel believe that the basis for a child's weak academic performance is genetic, then the school may be able to intervene more appropriately in programming the child's education. Arguably, if problems are identified before a child begins school, difficulties can be anticipated and planned for. Diagnosing dyslexia through nongenetic means usually occurs only once a child is about eight years old. If diagnosis were to occur at a much earlier age through genetic testing, it is believed that interventions would be much more effective. Early speech and language therapy and physical therapy may be positive interventions for children with fragile X syndrome.

The second purpose for using genetic information is that where conditions relate to potential behavioral and disciplinary problems, the school can provide more appropriate behavior management or observe a particular child more closely in anticipation of problems. In most cases, behavior will also affect educational development because it will affect the child's ability to focus and understand. Children with fragile X syndrome have been shown to have positive behavior changes when treated with folic acid. Benefits also have been shown to derive from taking methylphenidate (Ritalin), dextroamphetamine (Dexedrine), and pemoline (Cylert). Identifying fragile X syndrome as the basis for certain behaviors also may ensure that appropriate behavior management techniques (e.g., "time outs") are used.

The third educational purpose relates to conditions that involve health impairments. The benefit of knowing such information is that the school can provide appropriate related services, such as diagnosis and physical therapy, for children whose health or physical ability has been adversely affected. If public health agencies were to provide population-wide information about the incidence of certain types of health impairment in a state based on genetic screening at birth, schools would be better able to budget and plan for related services in anticipation of the entry of these children into public schools.

The fourth reason relates to accountability. Schools must measure abilities and performance to meet the mandates of school excellence expectations as well as to obtain funds under special education laws. Having a genetic marker for certain conditions may in theory assist in better measuring students' eligibility for special education and for determining which students should and should not be held to certain performance expectations.

Noneducational purposes. Schools may in turn be able to provide genetic information to other social service agencies for public health services and planning. If public health officials were convinced that genetic screening of children promoted public health, then schools would be the ideal setting in which to conduct such screening. In almost every state schools already screen children for various public health purposes, including conducting screenings for tuberculosis and scoliosis, as well as dental, vision, and hearing tests.

Public health screening agencies could plan for appropriate interventions in response to the information they obtained through screening. It could be argued that schools are the logical screening and intervention point for many public health issues because (with the exception of children in home schooling) they are the one institution in which everyone is mandated by law to participate. Though not educational in nature, such programs as comprehensive vaccination efforts benefit society as a whole.

By screening all individuals of school age for certain conditions, public service providers could plan for future needs and requirements. For example, if children were screened for certain cancers, the medical community could plan for the required services. If there were comprehensive screening for various late-onset genetic disorders, such as Alzheimer's disease, society at large could make preparations for the number of individuals expected to develop the disorders. Not only could society at large make general preparations, but in some cases, individuals with the genetic marker could begin planning for services.

Schools might also facilitate genetic testing and screening by others for monetary reasons. It is not hard to imagine commercial enterprises providing financial and other incentives to schools to allow them to gain access to children or the names of children with certain genetic traits. In a case involving the Genentech Corporation, schools facilitated the acquisition of information about children who were unusually short for their age. The school board approved the school nurse's provision of information about children's heights, which Genetech then used in marketing its human growth hormone.

There are risks associated with commercial interests joining forces with the schools. Even assuming that the schools' motives are entirely benign, in most cases the administrators who grant permission to carry out such evaluations probably do not appreciate the consequences. One need only think of how television sets and commercial programming have found their way into many schools to realize that financially strapped schools are not averse to exploring opportunities for economic support. This in turn brings to mind the *Jurassic Park* problem: when commercial interests use science, they are unlikely to think through the moral and ethical implications of what they are doing.

DOE v. KNOX COUNTY BOARD OF EDUCATION

918 F.Supp. 181 (E.D. Ky. 1996).

COFFMAN, J.

This matter is before the Court upon the defendants' motion to dismiss.

BACKGROUND

The plaintiff, Jane Doe, files this action pursuant to 42 U.S.C. § 1983. She claims that the defendants violated her civil rights, in that they violated the Family Educational Rights and Privacy Act of 1974 ("FERPA"), 20 U.S.C. § 1232(g); the right to academic privacy guaranteed by the Equal Protection Clause of the Fourteenth Amendment to the United States Constitution; and the Kentucky Family Education Rights and Privacy Act ("KFERPA"), K.R.S. 160.700, et seq. The plaintiff also asserts two tort claims: intentional infliction of emotional distress and invasion of privacy. The defendants' memorandum in support of their motion to dismiss addresses the plaintiff's federal and state FERPA claims and, indirectly, the tort claims. Their memorandum does not address the plaintiff's equal protection claim.

The plaintiff is a thirteen-year-old hermaphrodite. In 1994, a dispute arose between the plaintiff's mother, Mary Doe, and defendant Knox County Board of Education ("Board"). Mary was not satisfied with her daughter's educational plan and requested a due process hearing on the issue. A hearing officer held the hearing on August 18, 19 and 20, 1994. During the hearing, the hearing officer entered a protective order prohibiting the disclosure of the plaintiff's confidential records. The plaintiff alleges that the defendants discussed the plaintiff's educational placement, medical condition and disability with a newspaper reporter. The defendants allege that, in accordance with applicable law, the members of the Board discussed the reasons for emergency purchases made on behalf of the plaintiff and that discussions with the reporter were in that context. In any event, the following appeared in the *Mountain Advocate*:

> As an alternative to the residential placement, the emotional behavior disorder (EBD) unit was established at Lay Elementary at the beginning of the 1994–95 school year for the fifth through eighth grade.

> A written explanation in the board of education agenda from recent meeting stated that the EBD unit was created because of a 12–year-old female with severe emotional and behavioral problems, resulting primarily from a medical condition, hermaphroditism.

> Hermaphroditism is a person born having both male and female reproductive organs.

The plaintiff is suing the superintendent of the Knox County School District and several members of the Board in their individual and official capacities. The plaintiff is also suing the Board.

THE ELEVENTH AMENDMENT AND SOVEREIGN IMMUNITY

* * *

Therefore, sovereign immunity bars the plaintiff's state tort claims against the Board and against the superintendent and the members of the Board in their official capacities. Likewise, sovereign immunity bars the plaintiff's claim for damages against the Board and against the superintendent and the Board members in their official capacities for the defendant's alleged violation of KFERPA. Claims for injunctive or declaratory relief against those entities, however, may proceed.

FERPA

The plaintiff claims that the defendants violated her civil rights when they violated FERPA. The defendants argue that, even if they did violate FERPA, they are not liable to the plaintiffs because FERPA does not provide a private cause of action. The plaintiff does not dispute this but argues that a FERPA violation may be the basis for a claim under 42 U.S.C. § 1983. The defendants point out that all jurisdictions have not agreed on whether a plaintiff may recover under § 1983 for a violation of FERPA. However, the Sixth Circuit has addressed the issue. In an unpublished decision, the Sixth Circuit stated, "The district court correctly noted that FERPA itself does not give rise to a private cause of action, but does create an interest that may be vindicated in a § 1983 action." This holding is in accord with decisions in several other federal courts. The plaintiff's FERPA–based § 1983 claim may thus proceed.

Consequently, the Court must determine the applicability of FERPA to the plaintiff's claim. The plaintiff alleges that the defendants violated FERPA by releasing specific identifiable information without the consent or knowledge of the plaintiff. 20 U.S.C. § 1232(g)(b)(1) provides as follows:

> No funds shall be made available under any applicable program to any educational agency or institution which has a policy or practice of permitting the release of education records (or personally identifiable information contained therein other than directory information ...) of students without the written consent of their parents to any individual, agency, or organization, other than to the following....

The statute proceeds to list the exceptions, none of which includes newspapers or newspaper reporters.

Thus, the question becomes whether the information disclosed in the due process hearing and reported by the *Mountain Advocate* was personally identifiable. The defendants argue that the information was not identifiable and that one who did not already know this student would not have learned the identity of the student based on the information in the newspaper article. The defendants may be correct but that is an issue of fact that the jury must decide at trial.

KFERPA

The plaintiff's claim pursuant to KFERPA against the superintendent and Board members in their individual capacities for full relief and against the Board and the superintendent and Board members in their official capacities for declaratory and injunctive relief remains. K.R.S. 160.720(2) provides, "Educational institutions shall not permit the release or disclosure of records, reports, or identifiable information on students to third parties ... without parental or eligible student consent...." The statute proceeds to list several exceptions, none of which includes newspapers or newspaper reporters.

The defendants argue that the information was not identifiable. As discussed above, this is a question of fact for a jury to decide at trial. The defendants also argue that K.R.S. 160.990 provides the exclusive remedies available under this statute. The Court disagrees. K.R.S. 160.990 is not part of KFERPA, and its provisions apply to statutes that are not part of KFERPA. Accordingly, the defendants' motion to dismiss fails with regard to the individual-capacity KFERPA claims and any KFERPA claims for injunctive or declaratory relief against the Board or the Board members and the superintendent in their official capacities.

QUALIFIED IMMUNITY

The Board members and superintendent argue that they are entitled to qualified immunity with regard to the claims against them in their individual capacities. Government officials performing discretionary functions generally are immune from personal liability for civil damages so long as their conduct does not violate clearly established statutory or constitutional rights of which a reasonable person would have known. When analyzing whether a right is clearly established, a district court must carefully define the right at issue.

The issue in the present case is whether the plaintiff's right to avoid disclosure of the information printed in the *Mountain Advocate* was clearly established by federal statute or by the constitution. FERPA clearly establishes a right of freedom from a board of education's disclosure of personally identifiable information contained in education records. The defendants do not dispute that the information was contained in education records. Therefore, the question becomes whether the disclosed information was personally identifiable. The defendants argue that it was not. However, for purposes of a motion to dismiss, the Court must view the plaintiff's factual allegations in a light most favorable to the plaintiff. Viewed in this way, the information reported in the *Mountain Advocate* was personally identifiable. This is especially true within the context of a motion to dismiss, when the parties have had insufficient opportunity to develop the facts. Subsequent discovery will shed greater light on this issue, and the defendants may raise their qualified immunity argument in a motion for summary judgment or at trial if appropriate. The defendants have not raised directly the argument that the Board's members reasonably thought the disclosure complied with FERPA. However, the Court notes that if the information was identifiable, disclosing it to the press was not reasonable. For purposes of the motion to dismiss, the Court will not hold, at this stage, that the Board members had qualified immunity for purposes of the § 1983 claim that the Board members violated FERPA.

Because the parties have not addressed thoroughly the § 1983 claim that the Board members violated the plaintiff's Constitutional right to academic privacy, the Court will not rule on the Board members' qualified immunity argument as it applies to that claim.

CONCLUSION

Accordingly, the Court ORDERS that

1) The defendants' motion to dismiss is GRANTED with respect to the plaintiff's state tort claims against the Board and the superintendent and Board members in their official capacities and the plaintiff's claim for damages under KFERPA against the Board and the superintendent and Board members in their official capacities.

2) The defendants' motion to dismiss is DENIED on all other grounds and for all other claims.

NOTES AND QUESTIONS

1. Which of the educational motivations of schools mentioned in the Rothstein excerpt do you think will be the most likely source of pressure to use genetic information in schools? What genetic disorders or traits do you think will be most relevant to schools?

2. For a discussion of a likely application of genetics in educational settings, see Robert Plomin & John C. DeFries, The Genetics of Cognitive Abilities and Disabilities, Scientific Am., May 1998, at 62–69.

3. In the *Doe* case, one of the defenses raised was that the name of the plaintiff never appeared in the newspaper article. How difficult do you think it would be for the readers of the *Mountain Advocate* to identify Jane Doe?

4. There are currently no laws that directly address the issue of genetic information in schools. The Family Educational Rights and Privacy Act (FERPA), which safeguards the privacy of school records, applies only to recipients of federal financial assistance and provides for limited remedies. 20 U.S.C. § 1232g. In addition, it is not clear whether genetic information would be considered a "school record" subject to the Act. State school record laws are probably a better vehicle for protecting genetic privacy and confidentiality. These laws could be enacted or amended to limit the access of school personnel to genetic information in a student's record, grant parents a right to view and correct educational records, require that medical and other genetic information be stored in files separate from other educational records, and set time schedules and procedures for the destruction of the files.

VI. TORT LAW

CARLSEN v. WACKENHUT CORP.

868 P.2d 882 (Wash. Ct. App. 1994), review denied, 881 P.2d 255 (Wash. 1994).

ALEXANDER, J.

Ronda Carlsen appeals an order of the Pierce County Superior Court granting summary judgment to the Wackenhut Corporation, dismissing Carlsen's claims against Wackenhut for Wackenhut's alleged negligence in hiring and supervising an employee. We reverse.

On May 10, 1989, two 16-year-old girls, Ronda Carlsen and her friend, Heather, attended a rock concert at the Tacoma Dome with some acquaintances. The concert featured a group of musicians known as "Bon Jovi". During the course of the concert, Carlsen and Heather became separated from their companions. Consequently, they sought assistance from someone in authority to "help us find our friends". Toward that end, they approached a man who they believed was a "security guard".

The man, William Futi, indicated his willingness to help the two girls. After speaking with them for a short time, he asked them if they wanted to get closer to the stage and perhaps even meet the band members. The two girls were eager to meet the entertainers, so they accompanied Futi toward the stage of the Tacoma Dome. Their route required them to go under the bleachers. Carlsen indicated that "neither Heather or I wanted to go under the bleachers with him but since we were together and he was a security guard, we felt reasonably comfortable in proceeding." Part way to the stage, Futi mentioned that he could only take them one at a time. After Futi took Heather to the stage and returned, he told Carlsen that they would have to travel a different way back. As Futi led Carlsen under a set of bleachers, he threw her down and attempted to rape her. Carlsen screamed but she was not heard over the noise of the concert. Futi was eventually frightened away when the music ended and the lights came on.

Futi was charged in Pierce County Superior Court with second degree attempted rape. He later pleaded guilty to an amended charge of indecent liberties.

Carlsen brought suit against the Wackenhut Corporation, the company that had employed Futi at the Tacoma Dome. She claimed that Wackenhut had been negligent in its hiring of Futi in that it knew or should have known that Futi, who had a prior conviction for robbery, was unfit for employment with Wackenhut. She also claimed that Wackenhut was negligent in its supervision of Futi and that it was liable for Futi's actions under the theory of respondeat superior.

* * *

Although Futi's job was not high paying, the circumstances of his employment put him in a position of responsibility. A jury might well conclude that it was reasonable for concert patrons to look upon Futi as one authorized to perform security functions, and that, therefore, Wackenhut should have more extensively examined Futi's background before hiring him. The need for such a determination by a jury seems especially compelling in light of the limited information and inconsistencies in Futi's applications for employment. This additional investigation might well have disclosed Futi's prior juvenile record.

Wackenhut argues, finally, that even if it had performed a check of Futi's criminal record, nothing in that record indicated a propensity for sexual violence. Carlsen responds that robbery (only one of Futi's four convictions) involves the use of force or a threat of force which is indicative of a propensity toward violence. We agree with Carlsen that robbery is a crime of violence. Upon discovery of a prior robbery conviction, a prospective employer would be on notice that the prospective employee has a propensity for violent behavior. In short, we conclude that, although Wackenhut did not have actual knowledge that Futi was potentially dangerous, a trier of fact could find that the corporation breached its duty of ordinary care by not doing more to determine whether Futi was fit to work in the job he performed for Wackenhut.

NOTES AND QUESTIONS

1. Tort liability is based on the employer's failure to determine the potential employee's dangerousness or propensity to engage in violent conduct. These actions are usually termed negligent hiring, negligent retention, or negligent supervision. See Mark A. Rothstein et al., Employment Law § 1.12 (4th ed. 2009).

2. Can you think of other contexts in which third parties would be interested in learning about an individual's propensity to engage in violent conduct as a way of avoiding tort liability? Consider the following hypothetical.

> Suppose a young camper at summer camp unexpectedly and deliberately hit another camper in the head with a baseball bat, causing serious injury. Because the statutory liability of parents for the intentional torts of their children is quite limited, and because a child is unlikely to have adequate assets to satisfy a judgment, a negligence action might be brought against the camp. Assuming the boys were adequately supervised, the injured child's lawyer might assert that had the camp required behavioral genetic testing of all campers, it would have learned that the aggressor child was predisposed to violent behavior. It then could have refused to admit the child, thereby preventing the injury. If the injured child is able to obtain a judgment, or even a settlement, then the risk-averse behavior for every other summer camp, boarding school, college dormitory, and other entities might be to require a review of behavioral genetic test results. Pressure to do so also could come from parents.

Mark A. Rothstein, Behavioral Genetic Determinism: Its Effects on Culture and Law, Behavioral Genetics in The Clash of Culture and Biology 107 (Ronald A. Carson & Mark A. Rothstein eds. 1999).

3. Are there any negative consequences from screening individuals to make predictions about their genetic predisposition to violence? What are the most likely sources of legal protection against unreasonable conduct on the part of employers and other third parties?

4. If there were "some" scientific basis for doing so, would you oppose the Navy's use of genetic testing for predisposition to claustrophobia before assigning sailors to serve on submarines? Would you oppose an auto insurance company's use of genetic testing for predisposition to risk taking behavior in basing insurance rates? If you oppose these uses, do you oppose *any* use of behavioral genetics or only certain kinds? Why?

CHAPTER 14

PRIVACY, CONFIDENTIALITY, AND DISCRIMINATION

■ ■ ■

I. INTRODUCTION

For experts and lay people alike, privacy is the defining issue in determining whether advances in genetics can be integrated into medical practice and other aspects of daily life without unacceptable social consequences. Virtually everyone is in favor of genetic privacy in the abstract, but agreement among individuals and interest groups on this issue rarely extends beyond the abstract.

On closer examination, it is extraordinarily difficult to: (1) reach consensus on the definition of privacy and the related concepts of confidentiality, security, and anonymity; (2) distinguish genetic privacy from more general notions of medical privacy; (3) differentiate among the tangible and intangible benefits and harms associated with the presence or absence of privacy, including the complex concept of genetic discrimination; (4) balance the interests in genetic privacy and confidentiality against other valid social interests, such as research, clinical care, public health, law enforcement, and cost; and (5) devise thoughtful, practical, and effective legislative and regulatory measures to protect genetic privacy.

This chapter challenges you to think critically about genetic privacy and confidentiality. There are few cases in the chapter because cases based on alleged invasions of privacy tend to be context-specific and therefore they are included in, for example, succeeding chapters on insurance and employment. Nevertheless, the readings and statutory materials are crucial because they explore the conceptual foundations on which all genetic privacy and confidentiality law, ethics, and policy are based.

SISSELA BOK, SECRETS: ON THE ETHICS OF CONCEALMENT AND REVELATION

20 (1983).

Control over secrecy provides a safety valve for individuals in the midst of communal life—some influence over transactions between the world of personal experience and the world shared with others. With no control over such exchanges, human beings would be unable to exercise choice about their lives. To restrain some secrets and to allow others freer play; to keep some hidden and to let others be known; to offer knowledge to some but not to all comers; to give and receive confidences and to guess at far more: these efforts at control permeate all human contact.

Those who lose all control over these relations cannot flourish in either the personal or the shared world, nor retain their sanity. If experience in the shared world becomes too overwhelming, the sense of identity suffers. Psychosis has been described as the breaking down of the delineation between the self and the outside world: the person going mad "flows out onto the world as through a broken dam." Conversely, experience limited to the inside world stunts the individual: at best it may lead to the aching self-exploration evoked by Nietzsche: "I am solitude become man.—That no word ever reached me forced me to reach myself."

In seeking some control over secrecy and openness, and the power it makes possible, human beings attempt to guard and to promote not only their autonomy but ultimately their sanity and survival itself. The claims in defense of this control, however, are not always articulated. Some take them to be so self-evident as to need no articulation; others subsume them under more general arguments about liberty or privacy. But it is important for the purposes of considering the ethics of secrecy to set forth these claims. Otherwise it will not be possible to ask, in particular cases, to what extent they should apply and what restraints they might require. Nor will it be possible to study the extrapolations made from them in support of collective practices of secrecy.

NOTES AND QUESTIONS

1. There are many descriptions of the importance of privacy. Here is another one.

> Why we as Americans so cherish our privacy is not easy to explain. Privacy covers many things. It protects the solitude necessary for creative thought. It allows us the independence that is part of raising a family. It protects our right to be secure in our own homes and possessions, assured that the government cannot come barging in. Privacy also encompasses our right to self-determination and to define who we are. Although we live in a world of noisy self-confession, privacy allows us to keep certain facts to ourselves if we so choose. The right to privacy, it seems, is what makes us civilized.

Ellen Alderman & Caroline Kennedy, The Right to Privacy xiii (1995). How do you compare their view of privacy with Sissela Bok's?

2. Is the right to privacy valued more or less today than in earlier times? Do we have more or less privacy today? What threats to privacy do you see in daily life? What, if anything, does the growth in social networking websites indicate about public attitudes about privacy? Compared with other fields, such as consumer credit, educational records, and vital statistics, do we have more or less medical privacy?

II. GENETIC PRIVACY AND CONFIDENTIALITY

A. ANALYTICAL FRAMEWORK

ANITA L. ALLEN, GENETIC PRIVACY: EMERGING CONCEPTS AND VALUES IN GENETIC SECRETS: PROTECTING PRIVACY AND CONFIDENTIALITY IN THE GENETIC ERA

31, 33–34 (Mark A. Rothstein ed. 1997).

THE FOUR DIMENSIONS OF GENETIC PRIVACY

The word *privacy* has a wide range of meanings. It is used ambiguously in law and morals to describe and prescribe, denote and connote, praise and blame. "Genetic privacy" is no less rich with ambiguity than "privacy." Although the expression "genetic privacy" is a product of recent developments in science, it does not stand for a wholly new concept. "Genetic privacy" signifies applications of the familiar concept of privacy to genetic-related phenomena.

When used to label issues that arise in contemporary bioethics and public policy, "privacy" generally refers to one of four categories of concern. They are: (1) informational privacy concerns about access to personal information; (2) physical privacy concerns about access to persons and personal spaces; (3) decisional privacy concerns about governmental and other third-party interference with personal choices; and (4) proprietary privacy concerns about the appropriation and ownership of interests in human personality. "Genetic privacy" typically refers to one of these same four general categories.

"Genetic privacy" often denotes informational privacy, including the confidentiality, anonymity, or secrecy of the data that result from genetic testing and screening. Substantial limits on third-party access to confidential, anonymous, or secret genetic information are requirements of respect for informational privacy. However, family members may possess moral rights to undisclosed genetic data that patients and the professionals who serve them legitimately withhold from other third parties.

George Annas had informational privacy in mind when he warned that "control of and access to the information contained in an individual's genome gives others potential power over the personal life of the individual by providing a basis not only for counseling, but also for stigmatizing and discrimination." Likewise, Alan Westin was thinking of informational privacy when he defined "genetic privacy" by reference to what he called the "core concept of privacy"—namely, "the claim of an individual to determine what information about himself or herself should be known by others." Westin's definition captures well much of the informational dimension of genetic privacy and its connection to ideals of self-determination. Although it is adequate for purposes of a discussion of informational privacy, Westin's definition leaves important physical, decisional, and proprietary dimensions of genetic privacy in the shadows.

The genetic privacy concerns heard today range far beyond informational privacy to concerns about physical, decisional, and proprietary privacy. Briefly, issues of physical privacy underlie concerns about genetic testing, screening, or treatment without voluntary and informed consent. In the absence of consent, these practices constitute unwanted physical contact, compromising interests in bodily integrity and security. Decisional privacy concerns are heard in calls for autonomous decision making by individuals, couples, or families who use genetic services. A degree of choice with regard to genetic counseling, testing, and abortion are requirements of respect for decisional privacy. The fourth category of privacy concern, proprietary privacy, encompasses issues relating to the appropriation of individuals' possessory and economic interests in their genes and other putative bodily repositories of personality.

* * *

The human genome contains many mysteries that await scientific discovery. The air of mystery that shrouds gene science often shrouds discourse about genetic privacy, too. Yet genetic privacy is only an expansive concept, not an unfathomable one.

DAVID ORENTLICHER, GENETIC PRIVACY IN THE PATIENT–PHYSICIAN RELATIONSHIP IN GENETIC SECRETS: PROTECTING PRIVACY AND CONFIDENTIALITY IN THE GENETIC ERA

77, 78–81 (Mark A. Rothstein ed. 1997).

Privacy permits patients to retain control over the amount of intimate information they divulge about themselves and to whom they divulge it. Society demonstrates its respect for people when it gives them control over important aspects of their lives, including decisions about career, marriage, reproduction, and medical treatment. Control over personal information is of fundamental importance to individuals. It assures people that they can avoid the shame of having embarrassing intimate information disclosed publicly. It also assures individuals that they can pursue deeply held beliefs that are politically unpopular or engage in behavior that is unconventional without risk of opprobrium or retaliation. Privacy in personal information allows people the freedom of self-exploration as they shape their identity without the risk that, at some later date, they will be penalized for experiments with behavior or life-styles that they later rejected. Informational privacy is not only about shielding facts that might be viewed negatively by others, it is also about shielding facts that are generally viewed positively by others. For many people, for example, charity is noblest when given anonymously. Most fundamentally, informational privacy is valuable regardless of whether the information it shields is viewed positively or negatively by others. Informational privacy allows people to pursue their education, careers, friendships, romances, and medical care without the oversight, interference, or other unwelcome involvement of others. By controlling personal information, individuals can control the extent to which other people can participate in their lives.

* * *

Concerns about privacy in medical information are particularly present with genetic information. Genetic makeup is at the heart of personality. Genetics not only has a profound influence on such physical characteristics as height, weight, skin color, and eye color, but it almost certainly affects less tangible traits, such as shyness, altruism, sociableness, artistry, and intellectual skills. Indeed, a chief argument against the cloning of embryos has been the concern that the creation of genetically identical sibling embryos deprives those individuals who develop from the embryos of their unique identity. Individuals may not want to know whether they are at risk for a genetic disease, like Huntington disease, for which nothing can be done by way of prevention or treatment in advance. Such persons may conclude that they will be better off psychologically not knowing, and they may therefore decline medical testing to discover genetic information about themselves.

Disclosure of genetic information to others is also of particular concern. One's genetic makeup may one day provide a detailed blueprint of the person, thereby enabling others to alter their relationship with the person on account of that genetic information. Employers may decide to fire or not hire persons with undesirable traits, and landlords may refuse to rent housing to them. Disclosures of genetic information also may lead to self-fulfilling categorizations or stigmatizations. People who are expected to develop certain traits will be perceived as having those traits and will be encouraged by others to develop those traits. For example, children for whom adults have low expectations and who are therefore not challenged educationally or otherwise will not do as well as if adults had high expectations for them. Moreover, because genetic information can indicate tendencies for medical problems years or even decades in the future, disclosure of genetic risks for disease can elicit the stigmatization and discrimination that ordinarily result from actual illness far before the development of any illness or even in cases when a person at elevated risk for disease would not actually develop the disease.

* * *

Privacy is especially important with genetic information also because an individual's genetic makeup reveals information not only about the individual but also about family members. If a person carries the gene mutation for Huntington disease, it follows that one of the person's parents also carries the mutation that each of the person's children has a 50% chance of carrying the mutation, and that each of the person's siblings also has a 50% chance of carrying the mutation. Violations of a patient's privacy with respect to genetic information may also mean that the privacy of many other persons has been violated.

NOTES AND QUESTIONS

1.   Genetic privacy has both a tangible and an intangible aspect. As David Orentlicher notes, people are concerned about protecting their genetic privacy, regardless of whether there are any tangible, adverse consequences. Yet people are also concerned about how third parties may use "private" genetic information to the detriment of the individual. Which aspect of genetic privacy, tangible or intangible, is most important to people? See Mary R. Anderlik & Mark A. Rothstein, Privacy and Confidentiality of Genetic Information: What Rules for the New Science?, 2 Ann. Rev. Genomics & Human Genetics 401 (2001).

2.   As research shifts to gene function, it will become increasingly important to review the medical records of individuals to correlate genotype and phenotype. This "second stage genomics," going from identifying the location to learning the function of genes, raises additional privacy issues. See John A. Robertson, Privacy Issues in Second Stage Genomics, 40 Jurimetrics J. 59 (1999).

3.   Privacy is not the same as confidentiality. Confidentiality means that information disclosed in the course of a confidential relationship (e.g., physician-patient) will not be redisclosed outside of the relationship without the consent of the individual who supplied the information. It has been a core value of the medical profession ever since the time of the Hippocratic Oath, which provides, in pertinent part: "And whatsoever I shall see or hear in the course of my profession, as well as outside my profession in my intercourse with men, if it be what should not be published abroad, I will never divulge, holding such things to be holy secrets." The principle of confidentiality is also widely endorsed by the modern ethical codes of the medical profession. See Mark A. Rothstein, Privacy and Confidentiality, Medical Ethics: Analysis of the Issues Raised by the Codes, Opinions and Statements ch. 6 (Baruch A. Brody et al. eds. 2001).

4.   The confidentiality of genetic information was addressed by the Institute of Medicine's Committee on Assessing Genetic Risks:

> Confidentiality as a principle implies that some body of information is sensitive, and hence, access to it must be controlled and limited to parties authorized to have such access. The information provided within the relationship is given in confidence, with the expectation that it will not be disclosed to others or will be disclosed to others only within limits. The state or condition of nondisclosure or limited disclosure may be protected by moral, social, or legal principles and rules, which can be expressed in terms of rights or obligations.

Committee on Assessing Genetic Risks, Institute of Medicine, Assessing Genetic Risks: Implications for Health and Social Policy 205 (Lori B. Andrews et al. eds. 1994). See also Eugene Pergament, A Clinical Geneticist Perspective of the Patient–Physician Relationship in Genetic Secrets: Protecting Privacy and Confidentiality in the Genetic Era 92 (Mark A. Rothstein ed. 1997): Madison Powers, Genetic Information, Ethics, Privacy and Confidentiality: Overview, in 1 Encyclopedia of Ethical, Legal, and Policy Issues in Biotechnology 405 (Thomas H. Murray & Maxwell J. Mehlman eds. 2000).

5. The relationship between genetic privacy and discrimination is explored in Section V of this Chapter.

LORI B. ANDREWS, FUTURE PERFECT: CONFRONTING DECISIONS ABOUT GENETICS

140–141 (2001).

The problems of improper disclosure and misuse of genetic information are aggravated by the poor protections given to medical information in general. Secretary of Health and Human Services Donna Shalala says, "Every day, our private health information is being shared with fewer federal safeguards than our video store records."

Patient information is frequently disclosed. Dr. Mark Siegler describes a pulmonary patient who became concerned about the confidentiality of his medical record when he learned that the respiratory therapist had access to it. When the patient threatened to leave the hospital if confidentiality could not be guaranteed, Siegler inquired about the number of health care professionals and hospital personnel who had access to the patient's chart. When he revealed to the patient that seventy-five people had access to the chart in furtherance of his care, the patient stated, "I always believed that medical confidentiality was part of a doctor's code of ethics. Perhaps you should tell me just what you people mean by 'confidentiality'!"

In addition to the revelation of information to enhance patient care, the types of disclosures that a health care provider might be tempted to make range from pure gossip unrelated to the patient's well-being to disclosures to outside third parties that are thought to be in the best interest of the patient, another individual, or society. The individuals seeking disclosure from physicians might include law enforcement officials, public health authorities, relatives of the patient, employers, insurance companies, schools, and lawyers.

It is shocking how little protection exists for private medical information. In some states, laws protect only doctor-patient confidentiality and do not apply to other health care providers. Medical information collected in the workplace rather than the doctor's office is not protected in some states, so genetic screening and monitoring of employees is not covered. Even genetic information collected in a traditional health care setting may be unprotected, depending on *who* collects it. Some existing medical confidentiality statutes protect only medical information in the hands of *doctors* and will not cover genetic information in the hands of Ph.D. geneticists or genetic counselors.

Moreover, even states in which genetic information cannot be released without the individual's permission do not offer sufficient protection. As long as insurers and employers can continue to ask people to "consent" to the release of their genetic information, people will be discriminated against based on their genotype, no matter what the state's law is on medical confidentiality.

NOTE

It is difficult to separate the social issues surrounding genetic privacy or even medical privacy from the larger issue of privacy in general. As a society, we are constantly faced with the issue of determining how much privacy we have, how much privacy we want, and how much privacy we are willing to pay for. These issues are played out almost daily in the context of computer privacy, consumer privacy, educational privacy, governmental privacy, as well as medical privacy.

B. COSTS AND BENEFITS

ALEXANDER DOROZYNSKI, PRIVACY RULES BLINDSIDE FRENCH GLAUCOMA EFFORT

252 Science 369 (1991).

Paris—A team of researchers sifting through 5 centuries of French village records for patterns of mental illness has instead turned up an astonishing pattern of blindness caused by hereditary juvenile glaucoma—a pattern that goes all the way back to a single couple living in a village in Brittany in the l5th century. The researchers have since traced no fewer than 30,000 living Frenchmen and Frenchwomen who are descended from that couple, and they have found that more than half of all reported French cases of juvenile glaucoma have occurred in people in that direct lineage.

The researchers, from the Institut National d'Etudes Demographique (INED), were elated—treated early with drugs or surgery, this form of glaucoma can be arrested; blindness occurs only in untreated sufferers. So INED's data could be invaluable in pinpointing families at risk and ensuring that they get early treatment. But then came a revelation: French privacy law, designed to protect at almost any cost the privacy of the French citizenry, would prevent any such use of the information.

"I know the names of the people, often young ones, who risk becoming blind tomorrow, but I cannot alert them," says Andre Chaventre, director of INED's Department of Anthropology and Genetic Demography, who led the team that traced the genealogy of the disease. And Chaventre isn't the only one who's incensed. Claude Evin, minister of Social Affairs and Solidarity, recently announced the results of the INED study at a medical ethics conference and has since done his best to get the privacy rules changed.

The identification of potential bearers of the putative glaucoma gene is the fortuitous result of a study Chaventre started 3 years ago with psychiatrist Edouard Zarifian of the Caen University Hospital. They were trying to trace the genetic pattern of manic depression and soon realized that there was a strong, but so far unexplained, statistical link between this disease and a common variety of congenital juvenile glaucoma known as open-angle glaucoma. The disease is insidious: The patient, often a child, does not become conscious of the disease until vision is affected, but by that time a large proportion of optic fibers are irreversibly damaged.

Chaventre came across a 1979 medical thesis reporting a high incidence of juvenile glaucoma in the Nord–Pas-de-Calais region, near the English Channel, and quickly recognized it had a familial pattern. Chaventre contacted ophthalmologists in Lille and Paris and established a protocol to trace the genealogy of manic depression, glaucoma, and diabetes, which is known to be associated with glaucoma. The study was extended to relatives of glaucoma patients, who were given an ophthalmologic examination, glaucoma tests, and, whenever possible, psychiatric evaluation.

INED researchers assembled bits and pieces of a genealogic tree, using town and village records, often kept in several copies by the traditionally punctilious French administration. Posted on a wall, the tree was several tens of meters long. Computer analysis unequivocally pointed to a single couple, who died in 1495 in a small hamlet near the village of Wierre–Effroy in the departement of Pas-de-Calais, as the original source of the disease. (An 11th-century chapel in Wierre–Effroy, dedicated to Sainte Godeleine, contains a cistern filled with water that was believed to cure blindness; even today, pilgrims gather there every year in July to pray for the healing of the blind. "This," says Chaventre, "is not a coincidence.").

From this 15th-century couple, the gene spread rapidly throughout the region and the country. "This can go very fast," says Chaventre. "We have found records of affected parents who had as many as 18 children." The data are now coded and stored on a computer in the INED building in Paris. And if the Commission Nationale d'Informatique et des Libertes (CNIL) gets its way, that's where they will stay.

In 1988 Chaventre consulted CNIL, which was created in 1978 to protect individuals from potential abuses of computerized data, about a plan to inform physicians of the names of at-risk individuals living in their area. Physicians would then be able to keep a close watch on specific patients and, when necessary, recommend an examination in ophthalmology departments of designated hospitals. The CNIL cut the ground out from under the plan, however, by ruling that it would be fine for INED to tell physicians to keep an eye out for juvenile glaucoma among their patients, but it couldn't mention the names of any individuals. INED, it said, can alert physicians only to the symptoms and hereditary nature of the disease.

Chaventre objects that alerting physicians without telling them which patients are at risk would be ineffective, and that a national screening campaign would overwhelm specialized centers. "Giving physicians the names of individuals registered in their neighborhood, who are on the INED list would be far more efficient," he says. But Vulliet Tavernier, an official at CNIL, counters that distributing a list of individuals obtained by a genealogic study would constitute an authoritarian public health measure that would infringe on individual liberty and privacy. CNIL is concerned that circulating the names of potential carriers of genes predisposing to diseases might lead to discrimination in hiring or insurance.

CNIL bases its legal case on a 1978 law that states that individuals about whom information is collected must know how the information will be used. The law specifically notes that "even in the domain of medical research, such information can, in certain cases, cause prejudice to a patient because it informs him he is affected by a severe disease." Although a proposal was floated in 1989 to change this legislation to permit some types of data to be released to protect public health, it was rejected because "they did not provide for a satisfactory equilibrium between the interests of public health, the respect of fundamental liberties, and the rights of men, notably the right to respect privacy," CNIL president Jacques Fauvet wrote at the time.

NOTE

A similar problem, although not dealing with genetics, has recently been reported in the United Kingdom. Under the 1998 Data Protection Act, personal data collected for one reason may not be used for another reason without the informed consent of the individual. Reportedly, physicians who had supplied government-sponsored researchers with individual patient data refused to continue doing so when they were informed that they were subject to prosecution. Concerns also are said to be arising about the impact of data protection laws in Japan, South Africa, and Canada. David Adam, Data Protection Law Threatens to Derail UK Epidemiology Studies, 411 Nature 509 (2001).

MARK A. ROTHSTEIN, MEDICAL PRIVACY—AN OXYMORON?

Newsday, March 15, 1999, at A25.

To Americans, medical privacy is like motherhood and apple pie. We all are in favor of it. Yet most people don't realize how little medical privacy we have or that new efforts to protect medical privacy would not be free—either in financial or social costs.

In some other countries, the public is willing to pay a high price for medical privacy. For example, in 1991, French researchers studying mental illness were surprised to discover a pattern of blindness caused by hereditary juvenile glaucoma. More than half of all cases of juvenile glaucoma in France were traced to descendants of a single couple living in the 15th century.

Even though the disease, open-angle glaucoma, can be cured if treated promptly, and even though the researchers knew the names of those at risk of becoming blind, French privacy laws prevented the researchers from notifying them.

In the United States, we have yet to determine the level of medical privacy we want and the costs we are willing to pay to achieve it. Today's two greatest challenges to medical privacy are computerization and managed care. At many hospitals, all patient medical records can be accessed by anyone with entry into the hospital computer system, from billing clerks to food-service workers. Various abuses have been reported, such as hospital personnel snooping in the files of celebrities or other hospital employees.

Hospitals could increase privacy by permitting access to medical records only by health care providers seeing the records of their own patients, encrypting sensitive information, requiring passwords for access to the system and using audit trails that record each entry into the records. These measures would protect privacy, but they would increase the cost of health care and might make access more time-consuming and burdensome for those with legitimate needs to see the records.

Most patients don't realize that, when they have a blood test or tissue biopsy, their biological specimens are often retained for quality control or research purposes. If the hospital or researchers were required to get each former patient to provide new consent to experiment on the sample, it would be an impediment to medical research. On the other hand, many of these samples still contain the names of the patients, and the patients probably never consented to having the sample used for purposes unrelated to treatment. Computer networks can coordinate patient medical records stored in several different sources. "Smartcards"—credit card-sized memory cards—can store an individual's entire medical record on a single, portable card. Software is inexpensive. Already used in Europe, the cards would be invaluable for treatment of individuals in accidents or medical emergencies, for people who don't speak English well or those who have mental disabilities. In the absence of strict privacy protection, however, third parties might demand to view the cards as a condition of employment, insurance or some other transaction. If one's card is lost, the finder might be able to learn the most intimate details of the individual's treatment for mental illness or substance abuse, HIV or reproductive status, the results of genetic tests or other sensitive information.

Large managed-care organizations can use computerized medical records to assess whether individuals have received all necessary preventive health services, as well as the periodic check-ups necessary to monitor their specific medical conditions. By analyzing data from medical records, researchers could determine what procedures and medications were most effective in treating certain conditions. Computers also could help auditors from the government and other payers to uncover fraud or abuse in billing. The unresolved question, however, is when is it appropriate to use individual medical records for purposes other than treatment?

Patients frequently overestimate the extent to which their medical records are private. In fact, in most jurisdictions video rental records and consumer credit reports have more legal protection than medical records. Despite abstract support for medical privacy, we tolerate a system with little privacy and are seemingly indifferent to the specific measures needed to protect medical privacy. It also remains unclear whether we consider medical privacy worth the additional costs to public health, medical research and law enforcement.

In my view, medical privacy is essential to human dignity. It is worth protecting, and it may be possible to minimize the costs of doing so. Our national debate needs to focus more clearly on the costs and benefits of medical privacy. We also need to move expeditiously to implement policies and laws that reflect our shared values before new technology eliminates what little medical privacy we have.

NOTES AND QUESTIONS

1.   Recent studies reveal significant public concerns about genetic privacy, and the belief that genetics is different from other conditions. One study involved 100 individuals from each of the following six disease groups at a major medical center: cystic fibrosis, sickle cell disease, diabetes, HIV infection, breast cancer, and colon cancer. When asked whether special privacy protections should be in place for certain medical conditions, the results produced the following table.

Abortion history	68.6%
Mental health history	60.1
HIV/AIDS	54.0
Genetic test results	46.5
Drug/Alcohol history	44.4
Sexually transmitted disease	44.0
Breast cancer	29.0
Colon cancer	23.5
Family history of cancer	20.4
Sickle cell disease	19.8
Cystic fibrosis	17.7
Huntington disease	15.5
Diabetes	12.0
Cholesterol level	10.7
Heart disease	10.3

Laura Plantinga et al., Disclosure, Confidentiality, and Families: Experiences and Attitudes of Those with Genetic versus Nongenetic Medical Conditions, 119 Am J. Med. Genetics, Part C, 51 (2003).

2. Another study sought to explore the concerns of at-risk relatives of colon cancer patients about genetic discrimination and their awareness of legislative protections. About half the respondents rated their concern about genetic discrimination as high. A significant majority (79%) learned about genetic discrimination from one of the following media sources: television, magazines, newspapers, or radio. Fewer than 5% said they had heard of laws dealing with genetic discrimination. Kira A. Apse et al., Perceptions of Genetic Discrimination Among At–Risk Relatives of Colorectal Cancer Patients, 6 Genetics in Med. 510 (2004).

3. What, if anything, do these studies suggest about the need to protect genetic privacy, the preferred legislative or other method of protecting it, or the public and professional education needed about these issues? See generally Sheri Alpert, Privacy Issues in Clinical Genomic Medicine, or Marcus Welby, M.D., Meets the $1000 Genome, 17 Cambridge Q. Healthcare Ethics 373 (2008).

4. In the French glaucoma study reported in *Science*, the families also were at risk for manic depression. Would the concerns and analysis be different if that was the disorder being publicized?

C. ELECTRONIC HEALTH RECORDS AND NETWORKS

AMY L. MCGUIRE ET AL., CONFIDENTIALITY, PRIVACY, AND SECURITY OF GENETIC AND GENOMIC TEST INFORMATION IN ELECTRONIC HEALTH RECORDS: POINTS TO CONSIDER

10 Genetics in Med. 495, 495, 499 (2009).

The clinical use of genetic/genomic information is becoming an increasingly important aspect of modern health care delivery. At the same time, the increasing role of health information technology platforms in organizing health information has led to the need to review the confidentiality, privacy, and security of electronic information. Electronic health records (EHRs) provide a useful way to manage complex medical information; as such, EHRs will become established in the future as the means to manage the large and complex datasets that accompany genetic/genomic tests and interpretations. The inclusion of genetic/genomic information in EHRs should inform the determination of disease risk, appropriate drug dosing to avoid adverse events, and the selection of effective treatment. However, electronic health information is portable and mobile; the ease with which information can be disseminated through EHRs raises concern about the potential for unauthorized access to and use of this information. A major policy question, then, is whether special protections should be created for genetic/genomic information that is stored in the EHR.

* * *

The inclusion of genetic/genomic information in the EHR will greatly impact personalized health care by informing disease risk determination, appropriate drug dosing, and the selection of effective treatment or preventive action. To realize the full potential of personalized medicine, however, policies must be implemented to protect the confidentiality, privacy, and security of genetic/genomic test information appropriately with regard to access and use. Genetic/genomic information features a series of attributes that must be carefully considered in the aggregate with regard to policy development. Genetic/genomic data should be afforded the same provisions as other sensitive health information with regard to potential restricted access in the EHR. Protection against potential discrimination based on genetic/genomic information must be ensured, and proper disclosures must also be made for the use of such data for research purposes. Attention to the issues raised by these discussions will help policy developers and health care professionals ensure that confidentiality, privacy, and security are appropriately maintained for genetic/genomic information contained in the EHR.

NOTES AND QUESTIONS

1. The American Recovery and Reinvestment Act of 2009 (ARRA), Pub. L. 111–5, 123 Stat. 115 (2009), includes the Health Information Technology for Economic and Clinical Health Act (HITECH ACT), which commits the nation to shifting from paper to electronic health records (EHRs) in an attempt to make the practice of medicine safer, more effective, and more efficient. The ARRA provides substantial grants to develop new technologies and assist in their adoption and implementation. Similar efforts to shift from paper records are ongoing in much of the developed world.

2. There are three essential attributes of EHRs and the networks designed to connect them. First, they are interoperable, meaning that they may be accessed and used from remote locations and utilize a standard system for transmitting and receiving information. Second, they are comprehensive, meaning that they compile information from all of an individual's health care encounters with various physicians, hospitals, pharmacies, laboratories, etc. Third, they are longitudinal, meaning that they contain an individual's records over an extended period of time. These three attributes enhance coordination of care, help avoid duplication of services, prevent errors, improve effectiveness of care, and facilitate outcomes and other research. They also challenge privacy, confidentiality, and security by providing easier access to a wider range of health information—sometimes when health care providers have no need to know the information. See generally Sharona Hoffman & Andy Podgurski, In Sickness, Health, and Cyberspace: Protecting the Security of Electronic Private Health Information, 48 B.C.L. Rev. 331 (2007): Mark A. Rothstein, Health Privacy in the Electronic Age, 28 J. Legal Med. 487 (2007); Nicolas P. Terry & Leslie P. Francis, Ensuring the Privacy and Confidentiality of Electronic Health Records, 2007 U. Ill. L. Rev. 681 (2007).

3. As described in Chapter 9, personalized medicine using genetic and genomic data requires information-rich health records. This increased quanti-

ty and different type of health information raises the issue of whether individuals should have greater rights to control the uses and disclosures of genetic information than other health information. "Genetic exceptionalism" describes treating genetics differently from other health conditions or information. It is further explored in Section III of this chapter.

4. Current limitations of privacy protections in EHRs are also discussed in Chapter 16, in the context of employment discrimination.

D. COMPELLED DISCLOSURES

MARK A. ROTHSTEIN & MEGHAN K. TALBOTT, COMPELLED DISCLOSURE OF HEALTH INFORMATION: PROTECTING AGAINST THE GREATEST POTENTIAL THREAT TO PRIVACY

295 JAMA 2882–2883 (2006).

* * *

In the United States, laws to protect health information privacy and confidentiality are largely designed to protect against the unauthorized access to, use of, and disclosure of personal health information. A variety of state and federal laws attempt to make health information secure from snoops, hackers, and rogue health care employees. Some laws specify the form in which health records may be stored or transmitted; other laws attempt to punish unauthorized access through civil or criminal sanctions. Although these laws are valuable, they fail to address the compelled, authorized disclosure of personal health information.

As a condition of applying for employment, various types of insurance, and certain benefit programs such as Social Security Disability Insurance or workers' compensation, millions of Americans each year sign authorizations for the release of vast amounts of personal health information maintained in the files at their physicians' offices, hospitals, and other health care settings. There can be no effective protection of health privacy and confidentiality unless compelled, authorized disclosures of health information are regulated. Yet, legally and practically, this will be difficult to accomplish.

Few current laws place any restrictions on the scope or level of detail of information that third-parties may require individuals to release pursuant to an authorization. Even if there were legal restrictions, it would be practically impossible in most instances for the custodians of health records to limit the disclosure. Typical paper-based health records, such as most hospital and physician office records, are often a montage of disparate reports and clinical encounters involving wide-ranging conditions over a prolonged period of time. The records may intermingle routine clinical data with sensitive information, such as mental health, genetic test results, sexually transmitted diseases, human immunodeficiency virus (HIV) antibody status, sexual history, history of abortions and other reproductive matters, domestic violence, and drug and alcohol abuse. The disclosure of such sensitive health information to entities without a treatment relationship, without a need to know, and for non-medical purposes may lead to embarrassment and stigma. The mere possibility of such a disclosure also may lead individuals to forgo some potentially beneficial medical tests and procedures or even medical care altogether.

* * *

Disclosure of sensitive health information may result in the inability to obtain insurance or employment. In addition, individuals may experience embarrassment, humiliation, shame, anxiety, and depression if their health secrets are revealed. That is why many individuals withhold some sensitive health information from their loved ones, closest friends, and even their physicians. Yet, these individuals may not be able to withhold sensitive health information from other unknown third parties if they want to be considered for employment, other essential life activities, or insurance.

NOTES AND QUESTIONS

1. The total number of compelled authorizations for disclosure of health records is unknown. The following table contains the only published estimates.

Annual Compelled Authorizations in the United States

Type of Authorization	Estimate
Employment entrance examinations	10,203,000
Individual health insurance applications	550,000
Individual life insurance applications	6,800,000
Individual long-term care insurance applications	200,000
Individual disability insurance applications	200,000
Disability insurance claims (individual and group)	1,500,000
Automobile insurance claims	1,360,000
Social Security Disability Insurance applications	1,700,000
Workers' compensation claims	1,560,000
Veterans' disability claims	632,000
Personal injury lawsuits	300,000
Total	25,005,000

Adapted from Mark A. Rothstein & Meghan K. Talbott, Compelled Authorizations for Disclosure of Health Records: Magnitude and Implications, 7 Am. J. Bioethics No. 3, at 38, 40 (2007).

2. The privacy problem does not stem from the fact that health information is frequently disclosed to various third-parties with a legitimate need to access the information. It is based on the fact that there is no feasible method of restricting the amount of information disclosed and therefore it is commonplace for custodians of health records to respond to any request for health records by sending the entire record. As the use of comprehensive, longitudi-

nal electronic health records expands, the quantity of information disclosed to third parties, such as employers and insurers, will increase dramatically. Without a way to limit the disclosures there could be serious public health consequences; for example, individuals might be reluctant to seek care for sexually transmitted diseases, mental illness, domestic violence, or other stigmatizing conditions if the information will be disclosed in perpetuity. Would these same concerns affect the willingness of some individuals to undergo genetic testing?

III. GENETIC EXCEPTIONALISM

GEORGE J. ANNAS, GENETIC PRIVACY: THERE OUGHT TO BE A LAW

4 Tex. Rev. L. & Politics 9, 9–13 (1999).

If you don't believe in privacy, you probably don't believe in genetic privacy. I believe in privacy, including the constitutional right of privacy. But my interest is not to persuade you to believe in privacy, but rather to expose the major issues involved in genetic privacy. What makes genetic information different from other sensitive medical information? Are we getting carried away? Are we just treating DNA-based information differently because it is new?

We protect certain sensitive medical information by statute: mental health information, information about alcoholism, drug treatment, and abortion. There is a lot of information we take very seriously and treat very, very privately. The question is whether we should treat genetic information like other especially sensitive medical information, or whether new rules are needed. They would not be constitutional rules—I would certainly agree with Judge Bork on that issue. If we want to protect genetic information, the protection must be statutory. I want to begin by talking about why we might see genetic information as special.

Historically, we have thought of privacy in this country in at least four different ways. There is private *information*— information that we do not want revealed about ourselves. There are private *relationships:* husband-wife, priest-penitent and lawyer-client. The law also recognizes private *decisions:* whether or not to use contraception, or whether or not to have an abortion. Finally, there are private *places* where we have an expectation of privacy: the bedroom or the phone booth, for example.

Genetic information actually transects three of these four, and that is one argument for why such information is more powerfully private than other types of information. It is information about us, very private information about our likely future health. Moreover, this information is not just about us. It could also be seen relationally, because it tells us information about our parents, our siblings, and our children. If you happen to be a genetic twin—an unusual circumstance—then your genes tell exactly the same story about your twin as they tell about you. It is also information that is very important for private decision-making: who to marry, whether or not to have a child, whether or not to undergo prenatal testing, and the future health of your child. Given that, I think it is worth looking at each of the types of privacy in a bit more detail to see if we can say that there is something unique about genetic information.

First, let us examine the nature of privacy and why genetic information is private. The first thing that must be understood is that *all* your genetic information is contained in the nucleus of each of your cells. All that a geneticist needs is one cell from you to read your genetic code. It could be a blood cell—most genetic testing is done with blood cells. It could also be hair cells or even saliva. Once someone has a drop of your blood, or, perhaps, hair or saliva, they have your DNA from which your genetic code can be extracted.

Therefore, we have to think of one drop of blood as a medical record. It is in code, it is a code that has not been broken yet, and it will require sophisticated codebreakers to break it. But the fact remains that it is a complete record of your DNA. You do not have to agree with many boosters of the Genome Project who think it is the Book of Life, that your DNA is going to tell the story of your life. I would not get that carried away, but it does contain an enormous amount of information about you and your probable medical future.

* * *

A second way to think about that drop of blood is to understand it as information, not just about you, but about your family as well. We may not care what people know about our DNA or the probability that we will get cancer, a stroke, or whatever in the future. But most of us would probably care more about what someone else knows about our children. *Your* DNA may reveal information about your children. Of course, your spouse will be protected, but your DNA will reveal information about your children, your parents, and your siblings. There may be considerable differences in the family as to who is willing to share that information with whom. For example, in large pedigree studies conducted around the country and around the world to identify families that have a greater than usual expected incidence of certain diseases, like the Huntington's Disease Group in Venezuela, there have been many cases where family members are not interested in knowing whether they carry a specific gene, whether they have transmitted it to their children, or what their genetic fate is likely to be. I think that should also be their choice.

Third, not only is genetic information powerful in the sense of telling us things about ourselves we may or may not want to know, but genetic information also has historically been subject to tremendous abuse and misuse in society. It is not the geneticists' fault necessarily, but we do not have to think hard to recognize how genetics have been abused in this century. The Nazis infamously misused genetic information in incredibly discriminatory, invidious, and ultimately genocidal ways.

* * *

But we have a tendency to see genetic information as somehow more accurate, more pure, more correct than other information. This tendency leads us to make decisions, or maybe think about making decisions, based on more than just predispositions to disease. Rather, the decisions now are who should be employed or maybe even who should be watched. Judge Bork suggested that perhaps there is a genetic tendency to rage or to crime, and we might want to watch these people more carefully. I do not think we are going to lock up people with genetic predispositions yet, but can we doubt that there will be many people who want to watch them more carefully? Will the government want to screen our children's genes and watch our children or us more carefully based on their genes?

These reasons are enough, for me at least, to say that genetic information is uniquely private and should be protected by law. Much of the discussion in this country is directed at two problems with respect to genetic information: employment discrimination and insurance discrimination, usually health care insurance discrimination. But this discussion assumes that the information has already been *collected, analyzed,* and *stored* somewhere. I believe that if you are really interested in genetic privacy, you have to protect people before the information has been collected by giving people a choice to participate or not. To make privacy protection more meaningful, the law should make it clear that each of us *owns* our DNA.

DOUGLAS H. GINSBURG, GENETICS AND PRIVACY

4 Tex. Rev. L. & Politics 17, 22–23 (1999).

I believe it was Dr. Annas who coined the term "future diary" to describe the information in our genes. The metaphor derives its power from the jealousy with which people guard the secrets in their written diaries and therefore implicitly supports genetic exceptionalism. Upon analysis, however, the metaphor breaks down. First, our future diaries are much less diverse than our written ones: "while a child is 99.95 percent the same as its genetic mother at the level of the DNA molecule, it is also 99.90 percent the same as any randomly chosen person on the planet earth." Second, unlike the past thoughts and actions contained in our written diaries, the secrets that our future diaries are supposed to hold, like our family histories, speak only to probabilities. Indeed, the inability to distinguish between genetic and non-genetic diseases practically, conceptually, or morally led a task force of the joint NIH–Department of Energy Working Group on the Ethical, Legal, and Social Implications of the Human Genome Project to abandon the notion of genetic exceptionalism, albeit reluctantly. As Thomas H. Murray, a member of that task force, ultimately concluded:

> [T]here is a vicious circularity in insisting that genetic information is different and must be given special treatment. The more we repeat that genetic information is fundamentally unlike other kinds of medical information, the more support we implicitly provide for genetic

determinism, for the notion that genetics exerts special power over our lives.

The sober, unexciting realization that genetic information is but the latest iteration of our evolving medical knowledge yields one final suggestion: areas in which changes in degree are endemic are not well suited to statutory solutions. Courts, following in the common law tradition, can address the issues that genetic information raises as the extension of an existing phenomenon. Recognizing that genetic information is not qualitatively different from other types of medical information allows courts to draw upon past experience and to adapt that experience to meet new challenges. Engrafting a unique statutory solution for genetic information onto this common law landscape will simply create two divergent legal regimes for what is essentially a single problem.

Our fascination with the building blocks of human beings runs deep— from Mary Shelley's *Frankenstein* to Aldous Huxley's *Brave New World,* and now to the prospect of human cloning. Not surprisingly, genetic exceptionalism is a psychologically compelling position. Yet the questions that genetic information raises are not sufficiently different from those raised before—either qualitatively or as a matter of degree—to justify the creation of unique legal solutions—solutions likely to serve only to press the popular debate ever more toward the reductionist forms of genetic exceptionalism.

THOMAS H. MURRAY, GENETIC EXCEPTIONALISM AND "FUTURE DIARIES": IS GENETIC INFORMATION DIFFERENT FROM OTHER MEDICAL INFORMATION? IN GENETIC SECRETS: PROTECTING PRIVACY AND CONFIDENTIALITY IN THE GENETIC ERA

60, 71 (Mark A. Rothstein ed. 1997).

The paths I have explored lead to one destination. Genetic information is special because we are inclined to treat it as mysterious, as having exceptional potency or significance, not because it differs in some fundamental way from all other sorts of information about us. Portions of that mystery and power come from the opaqueness of genetic information, the possibility that others will know things about the individual that he or she does not know, and how genetic information connects individuals to immediate family and more distant kin. The more genetic information is treated as special, the more special treatment will be necessary. Yet none of these factors is unique to genetic information.

I propose that genetic exceptionalism—the plea to treat genetic information as different from other health-related information—is an overly dramatic view of the significance of genetic information in our lives. It is a reflection of genetic determinism and genetic reductionism at least as much as the product of genuinely distinctive features of genetic information. There is a disturbing corollary to this thesis: there is a vicious circularity in insisting that genetic information is different and must be given special treatment. The more we repeat that genetic information is fundamentally unlike other kinds of medical information, the more support we implicitly provide for genetic determinism, for the notion that genetics exerts special power over our lives.

NOTE

George Annas is perhaps the leading academic voice in support of genetic-specific privacy and anti-discrimination legislation. Also supporting this position are Colin S. Diver & Jane Maslow Cohen, Genophobia: What Is Wrong with Genetic Discrimination?, 149 U. Pa. L. Rev. 1439 (2001) and Ronald M. Green & Mathew Thomas, DNA: Five Distinguishing Features for Policy Analysis, 11 Harv. J. L. & Tech. 571 (1998). Among the allegedly unique aspects of genetic information are (1) DNA's informational nature; (2) its longevity; (3) its use as an identifier; (4) the familial risks indicated by the information; and (5) the effects on communities. So far, genetic exceptionalism has been heavily criticized in the literature, but the approach has been adopted by legislatures, see Section B infra, where the laws have generally addressed genetics separately from other health issues. See generally Lawrence O. Gostin & James G. Hodge, Jr., Genetic Privacy and the Law: An End to Genetics Exceptionalism, 40 Jurimetrics J. 21 (1999); Deborah Hellman, What Makes Genetic Discrimination Exceptional?, 29 Am. J.L. & Med. 77 (2003); Trudo Lemmens, Selective Justice, Genetic Discrimination, and Insurance: Should We Single Out Genes in Our Laws?, 45 McGill L. J. 347 (2000).

MARK A. ROTHSTEIN, GENETIC EXCEPTIONALISM AND LEGISLATIVE PRAGMATISM

35 Hastings Center Report no. 4, at 27–33 (2005).

THE ALTERNATIVE TO GENETIC EXCEPTIONALISM

I have argued that genetic-specific laws have limited value in preventing or redressing harms caused by the uses and disclosures of genetic information. Genetic-specific laws also reinforce the stigma of genetic disorders (by treating them differently from nongenetic conditions) and ignore the underlying social problems that genetic privacy and discrimination exemplify. The fundamental issue raised by genetic discrimination in health insurance is the fairness of our system for allocating access to health care; the fundamental issue raised by genetic discrimination in employment is how to balance the rights of employers and employees in controlling access to employee health information and in deciding what role, if any, current or predictive health status should play in employment opportunities.

General legal standards are more effective in dealing with these problems than genetic-specific laws. As mentioned, genetic discrimination is not a concern for health care finance systems that are not based on individual medical underwriting. For example, genetic discrimination is irrelevant in government-sponsored programs, such as Medicare and Medicaid, and group-based health insurance. But individual underwriting in any insurance product is synonymous with "discrimination" (that is to say, with differentiation) since eligibility and rates are determined by risk classification. Thus, it will be virtually impossible to devise any effective measures to prevent genetic discrimination in a system based on discrimination.

* * *

WHEN IS HALF A LOAF BETTER THAN NOTHING?

Legislative champions for genetic-specific laws are easy to find, and they include sympathetic and persuasive advocates. Opponents are few, especially if the proposed legislation is narrow in scope. Only a small number of elected officials realize that genetic-specific laws are largely ineffective and may be counterproductive. To most lawmakers, it seems obvious that if there is a problem with genetic discrimination, then the solution is to enact legislation making genetic discrimination illegal.

More savvy lawmakers still may be reluctant to propose generic, rather than merely genetic, legislation, since generic legislation is extraordinarily difficult to enact. Support for logical, effective, and sweeping legislation is hard to find. The underlying issues—such as the right of access to health care, the relative rights of employers and employees to decide about health hazards in the workplace, and the principles to apply in medical underwriting for life and disability insurance—are extremely contentious. To date, efforts to address these issues have often been unsuccessful.

Because of the difficulty in enacting sweeping reforms, the policy question is whether it is a good idea to enact a genetic-specific law when there is insufficient support for broader legislation. In legislative circles it is often said that the perfect is the enemy of the good. In other words, many people would argue that it is better to have limited or even flawed protection against discrimination than no protection at all. On the other hand, enacting and then touting feel-good legislation with little or no substantive protection may mislead members of the public to rely on the law to their detriment. It may also encourage people to believe in genetic exceptionalism, thereby making it a self-fulfilling prophesy, and it may erroneously convince legislators that they have resolved the underlying issues, thereby delaying enactment of meaningful legislation.

In my view, four conditions need to be met before it is appropriate to support a genetic-specific law as a fallback position to more sweeping legislation. First, there must be some value to the law, both in the sense that there is a demonstrated need for legislative action and that the proposed legislation will help to resolve one or more aspects of the problem. Second, the law must be drafted carefully to avoid unintended consequences, such as interfering with clinical care or medical research, or unreasonably interfering with the economic interests of third parties such as insurers or employers. Third, enacting the law must not serve to delay the enactment of legislation better designed to promote public policies, such as not coercing individuals into genetic testing and not dissuading at-risk individuals from being tested for fear of the social consequences. And fourth, both legislators and the public must realize that the law is not ideal but merely the best that can be achieved at the moment.

* * *

It is difficult to assess whether enacting a weak or ineffective law delays the enactment of more meaningful legislation. On the one hand, the initial enactment may be viewed as "a foot in the door" or the first step to stronger legislation. Since 1995, every state to enact a law establishing a DNA forensic database for use in law enforcement has amended its law to add more categories of offenders who are required to provide DNA samples. This expansion reflects the continuing efforts of the law enforcement community and its legislative advocates to promote forensic DNA banks.

On the other hand, "legislative-fatigue" is sometimes used to describe the notion that having enacted *something,* legislators are ready to move on to the next issue and have no interest in reconsidering a problem they thought was resolved. For example, few amendments have been made to the privacy and antidiscrimination laws enacted in the last decade, especially to extend the privacy protections for individuals. Whether genetic legislation will be a precursor to stronger legislation or give way to legislative fatigue will depend on whether powerful legislative champions are satisfied with the initial version of the law.

My fourth condition is that legislators and the public realize that a genetic-specific law is not ideal. Unfortunately, in the press conferences and self-congratulation that usually follow enactment of legislation affording protection against genetic discrimination there is rarely any mention of the limitations of the new laws. Many people, including legislators, probably assume that the problem has been solved. Legislative sponsors and supporters would then view it as a sign of weakness or ineptitude to admit that the bill they advocated is flawed or ineffectual. If media descriptions of the new laws are based on press releases and interviews with advocates of the legislation, then the gaps in protection are unlikely to be noted.

NO SHORTCUTS

* * *

Genetic exceptionalism undercuts this essential reconsideration of the role of predictive health information in society. It allows elected officials to avoid difficult issues by enacting genetic-specific laws that seem to respond to a perceived new crisis, but in fact offer little or no protection and may even be counterproductive. It is not surprising that elected officials would want to avoid fundamental and controversial issues and focus instead on nominally protecting the public against the highly publicized evils of invidious genetic discrimination. For the time being, at least, it seems that the public is genetically predisposed to let them.

IV. LEGAL PROTECTIONS FOR MEDICAL AND GENETIC PRIVACY

A. CONSTITUTIONAL LAW

WHALEN v. ROE

429 U.S. 589 (1977).

MR. JUSTICE STEVENS delivered the opinion of the Court.

The constitutional question presented is whether the State of New York may record, in a centralized computer file, the names and addresses of all persons who have obtained, pursuant to a doctor's prescription, certain drugs for which there is both a lawful and an unlawful market.

The District Court enjoined enforcement of the portions of the New York State Controlled Substances Act of 1972 which require such recording on the ground that they violate appellees' constitutionally protected rights of privacy. We noted probable jurisdiction of the appeal by the Commissioner of Health, and now reverse.

Many drugs have both legitimate and illegitimate uses. In response to a concern that such drugs were being diverted into unlawful channels, in 1970 the New York Legislature created a special commission to evaluate the State's drug-control laws. The commission found the existing laws deficient in several respects. There was no effective way to prevent the use of stolen or revised prescriptions, to prevent unscrupulous pharmacists from repeatedly refilling prescriptions, to prevent users from obtaining prescriptions from more than one doctor, or to prevent doctors from over-prescribing, either by authorizing an excessive amount in one prescription or by giving one patient multiple prescriptions. In drafting new legislation to correct such defects, the commission consulted with enforcement officials in California and Illinois where central reporting systems were being used effectively.

The new New York statute classified potentially harmful drugs in five schedules. Drugs, such as heroin, which are highly abused and have no recognized medical use, are in Schedule I; they cannot be prescribed. Schedules II through V include drugs which have a progressively lower potential for abuse but also have a recognized medical use. Our concern is limited to Schedule II, which includes the most dangerous of the legitimate drugs.

With an exception for emergencies, the Act requires that all prescriptions for Schedule II drugs be prepared by the physician in triplicate on an official form. The completed form identifies the prescribing physician; the dispensing pharmacy; the drug and dosage; and the name, address, and age of the patient. One copy of the form is retained by the physician, the second by the pharmacist, and the third is forwarded to the New York State Department of Health in Albany. A prescription made on an official form may not exceed a 30-day supply, and may not be refilled.

The District Court found that about 100,000 Schedule II prescription forms are delivered to a receiving room at the Department of Health in Albany each month. They are sorted, coded, and logged and then taken to another room where the data on the forms is recorded on magnetic tapes for processing by a computer. Thereafter, the forms are returned to the receiving room to be retained in a vault for a five-year period and then destroyed as required by the statute. The receiving room is surrounded by a locked wire fence and protected by an alarm system. The computer tapes containing the prescription data are kept in a locked cabinet. When the tapes are used, the computer is run "off-line," which means that no terminal outside of the computer room can read or record any information. Public disclosure of the identity of patients is expressly prohibited by the statute and by a Department of Health regulation. Willful violation of these prohibitions is a crime punishable by up to one year in prison and a $2,000 fine. At the time of trial there were 17 Department of Health employees with access to the files; in addition, there were 24 investigators with authority to investigate cases of overdispensing which might be identified by the computer. Twenty months after the effective date of the Act, the computerized data had only been used in two investigations involving alleged overuse by specific patients.

A few days before the Act became effective, this litigation was commenced by a group of patients regularly receiving prescriptions for Schedule II drugs, by doctors who prescribe such drugs, and by two associations of physicians. After various preliminary proceedings, a three-judge District Court conducted a one-day trial. Appellees offered evidence tending to prove that persons in need of treatment with Schedule II drugs will from time to time decline such treatment because of their fear that the misuse of the computerized data will cause them to be stigmatized as "drug addicts."

* * *

Appellees contend that the statute invades a constitutionally protected "zone of privacy." The cases sometimes characterized as protecting "privacy" have in fact involved at least two different kinds of interests. One is the individual interest in avoiding disclosure of personal matters, and another is the interest in independence in making certain kinds of important decisions. Appellees argue that both of these interests are impaired by this statute. The mere existence in readily available form of the information about patients' use of Schedule II drugs creates a genuine concern that the information will become publicly known and that it will adversely affect their reputations. This concern makes some patients reluctant to use, and some doctors reluctant to prescribe, such drugs even when their use is medically indicated. It follows, they argue, that the making of decisions about matters vital to the care of their health is inevitably affected by the statute. Thus, the statute threatens to impair both their interest in the nondisclosure of private information and also their interest in making important decisions independently.

We are persuaded, however, that the New York program does not, on its face, pose a sufficiently grievous threat to either interest to establish a constitutional violation.

Public disclosure of patient information can come about in three ways. Health Department employees may violate the statute by failing, either deliberately or negligently, to maintain proper security. A patient or a doctor may be accused of a violation and the stored data may be offered in evidence in a judicial proceeding. Or, thirdly, a doctor, a pharmacist, or the patient may voluntarily reveal information on a prescription form.

The third possibility existed under the prior law and is entirely unrelated to the existence of the computerized data bank. Neither of the other two possibilities provides a proper ground for attacking the statute as invalid on its face. There is no support in the record, or in the experience of the two States that New York has emulated, for an assumption that the security provisions of the statute will be administered improperly. And the remote possibility that judicial supervision of the evidentiary use of particular items of stored information will provide inadequate protection against unwarranted disclosures is surely not a sufficient reason for invalidating the entire patient-identification program.

Even without public disclosure, it is, of course, true that private information must be disclosed to the authorized employees of the New York Department of Health. Such disclosures, however, are not significantly different from those that were required under the prior law. Nor are they meaningfully distinguishable from a host of other unpleasant invasions of privacy that are associated with many facets of health care. Unquestionably, some individuals' concern for their own privacy may lead them to avoid or to postpone needed medical attention. Nevertheless, disclosures of private medical information to doctors, to hospital personnel, to insurance companies, and to public health agencies are often an essential part of modern medical practice even when the disclosure may reflect unfavorably on the character of the patient. Requiring such disclosures to representatives of the State having responsibility for the health of the community, does not automatically amount to an impermissible invasion of privacy.

Appellees also argue, however, that even if unwarranted disclosures do not actually occur, the knowledge that the information is readily available in a computerized file creates a genuine concern that causes some persons to decline needed medication. The record supports the conclusion that some use of Schedule II drugs has been discouraged by that concern; it also is clear, however, that about 100,000 prescriptions for such drugs were being filled each month prior to the entry of the District Court's injunction. Clearly, therefore, the statute did not deprive the public of access to the drugs.

* * *

A final word about issues we have not decided. We are not unaware of the threat to privacy implicit in the accumulation of vast amounts of personal information in computerized data banks or other massive government files. The collection of taxes, the distribution of welfare and social security benefits, the supervision of public health, the direction of our Armed Forces, and the enforcement of the criminal laws all require the orderly preservation of great quantities of information, much of which is personal in character and potentially embarrassing or harmful if disclosed. The right to collect and use such data for public purposes is typically accompanied by a concomitant statutory or regulatory duty to avoid unwarranted disclosures. Recognizing that in some circumstances that duty arguably has its roots in the Constitution, nevertheless New York's statutory scheme, and its implementing administrative procedures, evidence a proper concern with, and protection of, the individual's interest in privacy. We therefore need not, and do not, decide any question which might be presented by the unwarranted disclosure of accumulated private data—whether intentional or unintentional—or by a system that did not contain comparable security provisions. We simply hold that this record does not establish an invasion of any right or liberty protected by the Fourteenth Amendment.

Reversed.

MR. JUSTICE BRENNAN, concurring.

I write only to express my understanding of the opinion of the Court, which I join.

The New York statute under attack requires doctors to disclose to the State information about prescriptions for certain drugs with a high potential for abuse, and provides for the storage of that information in a central computer file. The Court recognizes that an individual's "interest in avoiding disclosure of personal matters" is an aspect of the right of privacy, but holds that in this case, any such interest has not been seriously enough invaded by the State to require a showing that its program was indispensable to the State's effort to control drug abuse.

The information disclosed by the physician under this program is made available only to a small number of public health officials with a legitimate interest in the information. As the record makes clear, New York has long required doctors to make this information available to its officials on request, and that practice is not challenged here. Such limited reporting requirements in the medical field are familiar, and are not generally regarded as an invasion of privacy. Broad dissemination by state officials of such information, however, would clearly implicate constitutionally protected privacy rights, and would presumably be justified only by compelling state interests.

What is more troubling about this scheme, however, is the central computer storage of the data thus collected. Obviously, as the State argues, collection and storage of data by the State that is in itself legitimate is not rendered unconstitutional simply because new technology makes the State's operations more efficient. However, as the example of the Fourth Amendment shows, the Constitution puts limits not only on the type of information the State may gather, but also on the means it may use to gather it. The central storage and easy accessibility of computerized data vastly increase the potential for abuse of that information, and I am not prepared to say that future developments will not demonstrate the necessity of some curb on such technology.

In this case, as the Court's opinion makes clear, the State's carefully designed program includes numerous safeguards intended to forestall the danger of indiscriminate disclosure. Given this serious and, so far as the record shows, successful effort to prevent abuse and limit access to the personal information at issue, I cannot say that the statute's provisions for computer storage, on their face, amount to a deprivation of constitutionally protected privacy interests, any more than the more traditional reporting provisions.

In the absence of such a deprivation, the State was not required to prove that the challenged statute is absolutely necessary to its attempt to control drug abuse. Of course, a statute that did effect such a deprivation would only be consistent with the Constitution if it were necessary to promote a compelling state interest.

MR. JUSTICE STEWART, concurring.

In Katz v. United States, 389 U.S. 347, the Court made clear that although the Constitution affords protection against certain kinds of government intrusions into personal and private matters, there is no "general constitutional 'right to privacy.' ... [T]he protection of a person's *general* right to privacy—his right to be let alone by other people—is, like the protection of his property and of his very life, left largely to the law of the individual States."

MR. JUSTICE BRENNAN's concurring opinion states that "[b]road dissemination by state officials of [the information collected by New York State] ... would clearly implicate constitutionally protected privacy rights...." The only possible support in his opinion for this statement is its earlier reference to two footnotes in the Court's opinion. The footnotes, however, cite to only two Court opinions, and those two cases do not support the proposition advanced by MR. JUSTICE BRENNAN.

NOTES AND QUESTIONS

1. *Whalen* remains the leading case on the constitutional dimension of medical privacy. Yet, it is a very narrow decision that is subject to different interpretations, and even the concurring justices disagreed as to the scope of the holding. See generally Lawrence O. Gostin, Health Information Privacy, 80 Cornell L. Rev. 451 (1995); Seth F. Kreimer, Sunlight, Secrets, and Scarlet Letters: The Tension Between Privacy and Disclosure in Constitutional Law, 140 U. Pa. L. Rev. 1 (1991).

2. Individuals attempting to assert claims for invasion of medical privacy have not always fared well in the courts. For example, in Doe v. Southeast-

ern Pennsylvania Transp. Authority (SEPTA), 72 F.3d 1133 (3d Cir.1995), cert. denied, 519 U.S. 808 (1996), the plaintiff was an employee who was the manager of his company's employee assistance program. Before he had a prescription filled under the company's drug plan he asked his supervisor, the head of the medical department, whether the company was able to identify what prescriptions individual employees had filled. When he was assured that the company did not get such information, the employee had his prescription for AZT, an antiviral drug used to treat AIDS, refilled under the company plan. When the pharmacy chain submitted its mandatory utilization report, which included a list of the names of all employees and the medications they were taking, the employer's medical department, including this particular employee's supervisors, learned that he was HIV-positive, a fact that they then indiscriminately shared. In an action for invasion of privacy, the jury awarded the plaintiff $125,000, but the Third Circuit Court of Appeals reversed. The court held that the employer's "important interests" in the prescription information outweighed the "minimal intrusion" into the plaintiff's privacy. For a discussion of possible tort actions for invasion of genetic privacy, see June Mary Z. Makdisi, Genetic Privacy: New Intrusion a New Tort?, 34 Creighton L. Rev. 965 (2001).

3. In what settings and in what ways do you think constitutional privacy issues could be raised with regard to genetics?

4. There are numerous exceptions to the general principle that an individual's medical records may not be disclosed. The most common exception is consent, but this is not so simple. For example, some of the questions raised by consent include: who may consent when the patient is a child; can consent be made a condition of employment or insurance (discussed in Chapters 15 and 16); do the same rules on consent apply to all medical records, including psychiatric summaries and genetic test results; and can consent be revoked? Other exceptions include law enforcement, domestic violence reporting, communicable disease reporting, public health, research, and health care fraud investigations. How strong is the justification for each of these conditions to be an exception to the rule of consent?

B. LEGISLATION

In 1995, Professors George J. Annas, Leonard H. Glantz, and Patricia A. Roche drafted a proposed Genetic Privacy Act. The proposal, excerpted below, sets forth detailed procedures for obtaining consent to genetic testing and limits the disclosure of the results of the genetic tests. Some of the principles set out in the proposal were included in bills filed in Congress and some state legislatures. In general, the approach they advocated was not enacted because the procedures they endorsed were seen as onerous and unnecessary, too time-consuming and expensive, and perhaps would interfere with patient care and research. As you read the proposal, consider whether you think these criticisms are warranted.

GEORGE J. ANNAS, LEONARD H. GLANTZ & PATRICIA A. ROCHE, THE GENETIC PRIVACY ACT AND COMMENTARY

vii-ix (1995).

Under the Act, each person who collects a DNA sample (e.g., blood, saliva, hair or other tissue) for the purpose of performing genetic analysis is required to:

- provide specific information verbally prior to collection of the DNA sample;

- provide a notice of rights and assurances prior to the collection of the DNA sample;

- obtain written authorization which contains required information;

- restrict access to DNA samples to persons authorized by the sample source;

- abide by a sample source's instructions regarding the maintenance and destruction of DNA samples.

Special rules regarding the collection of DNA samples for genetic analysis are set forth for minors, incompetent persons, pregnant women, and embryos. DNA samples may be collected and analyzed for identification for law enforcement purposes if authorized by state law, and for identifying dead bodies, without complying with the authorization provisions of the Act. Research on individually identifiable DNA samples is prohibited unless the sample source has authorized such research use, and research on nonidentifiable samples is permitted if this has not been prohibited by the sample source. Pedigree research and research involving DNA from minors are also governed by specific provisions of the Act.

Individuals are prohibited from analyzing DNA samples unless they have verified that written authorization for the analysis has been given by the sample source or the sample source's representative. The sample source has the right to:

- determine who may collect and analyze DNA;

- determine the purposes for which a DNA sample can be analyzed;

- know what information can reasonably be expected to be derived from the genetic analysis;

- order the destruction of DNA samples;

- delegate authority to another individual to order the destruction of the DNA sample after death;

- refuse to permit the use of the DNA sample for research or commercial activities; and

- inspect and obtain copies of records containing information derived from genetic analysis of the DNA sample.

A written summary of these principles and other requirements under the Act must be supplied to the sample source by the person who collects the DNA sample. The Act requires that the person who holds private genetic information in the ordinary course of business keep such information confidential and prohibits the disclosure of private genetic information unless the sample source has authorized the disclosure in writing or the disclosure is limited to access by specified researchers for compiling data.

NOTE

Besides the philosophical and political problems of genetic exceptionalism, the Genetic Privacy Act (GPA) and similar proposed and enacted legislation are plagued by a very practical problem, which relates to the volume of genetic information increasingly generated in health care. Even if the extensive procedural requirements, such as written notice and written informed consent, were feasible in a prior era of occasional genetic testing for rare disorders, they will be infeasible in an era when pharmacogenomic testing precedes prescribing drugs for common conditions and when genotyping is used to more closely identify subtypes of malignancies and strains of infectious diseases. Thus, irrespective of whether genetic information ought to be regarded as exceptional for legal purposes, in fact, generating genetic information will be routine as a matter of modern clinical care.

Another controversial aspect of the GPA is giving the individual a property interest in his or her DNA. Section 104 provides: "An individually identifiable DNA sample is the property of the sample source." This principle has been challenged on the grounds that it unnecessarily infringes upon clinical care and research and it confuses property interests with privacy interests. For a detailed discussion of this point, see Sonia M. Suter, Disentangling Privacy from Property: Toward a Deeper Understanding of Genetic Privacy, 72 Geo. Wash. L. Rev. 737 (2004). The issue is further discussed in Chapter 5.

MICHIGAN COMMISSION ON GENETIC PRIVACY AND PROGRESS FINAL REPORT AND RECOMMENDATION

47 (1999).

1. The commission recommends that genetic information be protected just as all medical information is protected. The commission does not recommend special protection for genetic information since the commission feels that it is critically important to protect all medical information and it would not be useful to create a separate set of laws for genetic information. The commission believes it is important to consider both use of and access to information. The commission believes that research uses are important and access can be controlled in a way that keeps confidentiality intact. Exceptions to confidentiality should exist for criminal investigations, court proceedings, paternity disputes, decedent identification,

convicted criminals and newborn screening. After the federal government enacts privacy legislation the state can conduct an analysis to determine the need for any state legislation.

NOTES AND QUESTIONS

1.   Notwithstanding the recommendation of the Commission "that genetic information be protected just as all medical information is protected," Michigan has still enacted genetic-specific legislation prohibiting genetic discrimination in employment and health insurance rather than attempting to prohibit genetic discrimination in the same way as it prohibits other forms of medical discrimination. See Mich. Comp. Laws Ann. § 37.1201 (West 2000) (genetic discrimination in employment); § 333.17020 (West 2000) (informed consent for a genetic test); § 500.3407b (West 2000) (genetic discrimination in health insurance).

2.   As of 2010, laws in 16 states require informed consent for a third party to perform or require a genetic test or obtain genetic information. Many of these laws apply only to physicians. Eighteen states require informed consent to disclose genetic information. Some states define genetic information as personal property. Why do you think this is so? For a further discussion of who owns genetic information, see Chapter 5. Four states mandate individual access to personal genetic information, and 16 states establish civil or criminal penalties for violations of the genetic privacy law. The National Conference of State Legislatures maintains an updated website of these laws, www.ncsl.org/programs/health/genetics/charts.htm.

3.   Refer back to Anita Allen's excerpt at the beginning of the chapter. Which aspects of genetic privacy do these state genetic privacy laws advance?

NEW MEXICO GENETIC INFORMATION PRIVACY ACT
(ENACTED 1998).

N.M. Stat. Ann.

§§ 24–21–2 Definitions.

As used in the Genetic Information Privacy Act [24–21–1 to 24–21–7 NMSA 1978]:

§§ 24–21–3 Genetic analysis prohibited without informed consent; exceptions.

A.   Except as provided in Subsection C of this section, no person shall obtain genetic information or samples for genetic analysis from a person without first obtaining informed and written consent from the person or the person's authorized representative.

B.   Except as provided in Subsection C of this section, genetic analysis of a person or collection, retention, transmission or use of genetic information without the informed and written consent of the person or the person's authorized representative is prohibited.

C. A person's DNA, genetic information or the results of genetic analysis my be obtained, retained, transmitted or used without the person's written and informed consent pursuant to federal or state law or regulations only:

(1) to identify a person in the course of a criminal investigation by a law enforcement agency;

(2) if the person has been convicted of a felony, for purposes of maintaining a DNA database for law enforcement purposes;

(3) to identify deceased persons;

(4) to establish parental identity;

(5) to screen newborns;

(6) if the DNA, genetic information or results of genetic analysis are not identified with the person or person's family members;

(7) by a court for determination of damage awards pursuant to the Genetic Information Privacy Act [24–21–1 to 24–21–7 NMSA 1978];

(8) by medical repositories or registries;

(9) for the purpose of medical or scientific research and education, including retention of gene products, genetic information or genetic analysis if the identity of the person or person's family members is not disclosed; or

(10) for the purpose of emergency medical treatment consistent with applicable law.

D. Actions of an insurer and third parties dealing with an insurer in the ordinary course of conducting and administering the business of life, disability income or long-term care insurance are exempt from the provisions of this section if the use of genetic analysis or genetic information for underwriting purposes is based on sound actuarial principles or related to actual or reasonably anticipated experience. However, before or at the time of collecting genetic information for use in conducting and administering the business of life, disability income or long-term care insurance, the insurer shall notify in writing an applicant for insurance or the insured that the information may be used, transmitted or retained solely for the purpose of conducting and administering the business of life, disability income or long-term care insurance, the insurer shall notify in writing an applicant for insurance or the insured that the information may be used, transmitted or retained solely for the purpose of conducting and administering the business of life, disability income or long-term care insurance.

E. Nothing in Paragraph (5), (6), (8), (9) or (10) of Subsection C of Section 3 [24–21–3 NMSA 1978] of the Genetic Information Privacy Act authorizes obtaining, retaining, transmitting or using a person's DNA, genetic information or the results of genetic analysis if the person, his authorized representative or guardian, or the parent or guardian of a minor child, objects on the basis of religious tenets or practices.

* * *

§§ 24–21–5 Rights of retention.

A. Unless otherwise authorized by Subsection C of Section 3 [24–21–3 NMSA 1978] of the Genetic Information Privacy Act, no person shall retain a person's genetic information, gene products or samples for genetic analysis without first obtaining informed and written consent from the person or the person's authorized representative. This subsection does not affect the status of original medical records of patients, and the rules of confidentiality and accessibility applicable to the records continue in force.

B. A person's genetic information or samples for genetic analysis shall be destroyed promptly upon the specific request by that person or that person's authorized representative unless:

(1) retention is necessary for the purposes of a criminal or death investigation or a criminal or juvenile proceeding;

(2) retention is authorized by order of a court of competent jurisdiction;

(3) retention is authorized under a research protocol approved by an institution review board pursuant to federal law or a medical registry or repository authorized by state or federal law; or

(4) the genetic information or samples for genetic analysis have been obtained pursuant to Subsection C of Section 3 of the Genetic Information Privacy Act.

C. Actions of an insurer and third parties dealing with an insurer in the ordinary course of conducting and administering the business of life, disability income or long-term care insurance are exempt from the provisions of this section. However, before or at the time of collecting genetic information for use in conducting and administering the business of life, disability income or long-term care insurance, the insurer shall notify in writing an applicant for insurance or the insured that the information may be used, transmitted or retained solely for the purpose of conducting and administering the business of life, disability income or long-term care insurance.

D. Nothing in Paragraph (3) or (4) of Subsection B of Section 5 [24–21–5 NMSA 1978] of the Genetic Information Privacy Act authorizes retention of a person's authorized representative or guardian, or the parent or guardian of a minor child, objects on the basis of religious tenets or practices.

NOTES AND QUESTIONS

1. As of 2010, 31 states had enacted genetic privacy laws similar to the New Mexico law in at least some respects, although they may be limited to certain entities, such as employers or insurers. These laws typically contain

one or more of the following provisions: (1) personal access to genetic information is required; (2) informed consent is required to perform a genetic test or obtain, retain, or disclose genetic information; (3) define as personal property genetic information or DNA samples; and (4) provide penalties for violations. State genetic privacy laws are collected and updated by the National Conference of State Legislatures on its website at www.ncsl.org/programs/health/genetics/charts.htm.

2. What are the benefits of enacting a law such as New Mexico's? Are there costs?

HEALTH INSURANCE PORTABILITY AND ACCOUNTABILITY ACT (HIPAA)

The Health Insurance Portability and Accountability Act (HIPAA), 42 U.S.C. §§ 300gg–300gg–2, enacted in 1996, contains a provision that required Congress to enact privacy legislation by August 21, 1999. If Congress failed to enact legislation by the deadline, the law directed the Secretary of Health and Human Services to promulgate regulations for the privacy of medical information. Following unsuccessful attempts to pass federal legislation, proposed regulations were issued in November 1999. After considering over 52,000 comments, the final regulations were issued on December 2000, and had a compliance date of April 2003. The regulations appear at 45 C.F.R. Parts 160 and 164. The key substantive provisions of HIPAA related to genetics and group health insurance are discussed in Chapter 15. The following excerpt describes in very basic terms the complicated and detailed HIPAA Privacy Rule.

OFFICE FOR CIVIL RIGHTS, DEPARTMENT OF HEALTH AND HUMAN SERVICES, SUMMARY OF THE HIPAA PRIVACY RULE

www.hhs.gov/ocr/privacy/hipaa/understanding/summary/privacysummary.pdf

WHO IS COVERED BY THE PRIVACY RULE

The Privacy Rule, as well as all the Administrative Simplification rules, apply to health plans, health care clearinghouses, and to any health care provider who transmits health information in electronic form in connection with transactions for which the Secretary of HHS has adopted standards under HIPAA (the "covered entities").

Health Plans.

Individual and group plans that provide or pay the cost of medical care are covered entities. Health plans include health, dental, vision, and prescription drug insurers, health maintenance organizations ("HMOs"), Medicare, Medicare + Choice and Medicare supplement insurers, and long-term care insurers (excluding nursing home fixed-indemnity policies). Health plans also include employer-sponsored group health plans, government and church-sponsored health plans, and multi-employer health plans.

Health Care Providers.

Every health care provider, regardless of size, who electronically transmits health information in connection with certain transactions, is a covered entity. These transactions include claims, benefit eligibility inquiries, referral authorization requests, or other transactions for which HHS has established standards under the HIPAA Transaction Rule.

Health Care Clearinghouses.

Health care clearinghouses are entities that process nonstandard information they receive from another entity into a standard (i.e., standard format or data content), or vice versa. In most instances, health care clearinghouses will receive individually identifiable health information only when they are providing these processing services to a health plan or health care provider as a business associate.

What Information is Protected

Protected Health Information.

The Privacy Rule protects all *"individually identifiable health information"* held or transmitted by a covered entity or its business associate, in any form or media, whether electronic, paper, or oral. The Privacy Rule calls this information *"protected health information (PHI)."*

General Principle for Uses and Disclosures

Basic Principle.

A major purpose of the Privacy Rule is to define and limit the circumstances in which an individual's protected health information may be used or disclosed by covered entities. A covered entity may not use or disclose protected health information, except either: (1) as the Privacy Rule permits or (2) as the individual who is the subject of the information (or the individual's personal representative) authorizes in writing.

Required Disclosures.

A covered entity must disclose protected health information in only two situations: (a) to individuals (or their personal representatives) specifically when they request access to, or an accounting of disclosures of, their protected health information; and (b) to HHS when it is undertaking a compliance investigation or review or enforcement action.

Permitted Uses and Disclosures

Permitted uses and disclosures.

A covered entity is permitted, but not required, to use and disclose protected health information, without an individual's authorization, for the following purposes or situations: (1) To the Individual (unless required for access or accounting of disclosures); (2) Treatment, Payment, and

Health Care Operations; (3) Opportunity to Agree or Object; (4) Incident to an otherwise permitted use and disclosure; (5) Public Interest and Benefit Activities; and (6) Limited Data Set for the purposes of research, public health or health care operations. Covered entities may rely on professional ethics and best judgments in deciding which of these permissive uses and disclosures to make.

AUTHORIZED USES AND DISCLOSURES

Authorization.

A covered entity must obtain the individual's written authorization for any use or disclosure of protected health information that is not for treatment, payment, or health care operations or otherwise permitted or required by the Privacy Rule. A covered entity may not condition treatment, payment, enrollment, or benefits eligibility on an individual granting an authorization, except in limited circumstances.

An authorization must be written in specific terms. It may allow use and disclosure of protected health information by the covered entity seeking the authorization, or by a third party. Examples of disclosures that would require an individual's authorization include disclosures to a life insurer for coverage purposes, disclosure to an employer of the results of a pre-employment physical or lab test, or disclosures to a pharmaceutical firm for their own marketing purposes.

All authorizations must be in plain language, and contain specific information regarding the information to be disclosed or used, the person(s) disclosing and receiving the information, expiration, right to revoke in writing, and other data.

LIMITING USES AND DISCLOSURES TO THE MINIMUM NECESSARY

Minimum Necessary.

A central aspect of the Privacy Rule is the principle of "minimum necessary" use and disclosure. A covered entity must make reasonable efforts to use, disclose, and request only the minimum amount of protected health information needed to accomplish the intended purpose of the use, disclosure or request. A covered entity must develop and implement policies and procedures to reasonably limit uses and disclosures to the minimum necessary. When the minimum necessary standard applies to a use or disclosure, a covered entity may not use, disclose, or request the entire medical record for a particular purpose, unless it can specifically justify the whole record as the amount reasonably needed for the purpose.

The minimum necessary requirement is not imposed in any of the following circumstances: (a) disclosure to or a request by a health care provider for treatment; (b) disclosure to an individual who is the subject of the information, or the individual's personal representative; (c) use or disclosure made pursuant to an authorization; (d) disclosure to HHS for complaint investigation, compliance review or enforcement; (e) use or disclosure that is required by law; or (f) use or disclosure required for compliance with the HIPAA Transaction Rule or other HIPAA Administrative Simplification Rules.

STATE LAW

Preemption.

In general, State laws that are contrary to the Privacy Rule are preempted by the federal requirements, which means that the federal requirements will apply. "Contrary" means that it would be impossible for a covered entity to comply with both State and federal requirements, or that the provision of State law is an obstacle to accomplishing the full purposes and objectives of the Administrative Simplification provisions of HIPAA. The Privacy Rule provides exceptions to the general rule of federal preemption for contrary State laws that (1) relate to the privacy of individually identifiable health information and provide greater privacy protections or privacy rights with respect to such information, (2) provide for the reporting of disease or injury, child abuse, birth, or death, or for public health surveillance, investigation, or intervention, or (3) require certain health plan reporting, such as for management or financial audits.

ENFORCEMENT AND PENALTIES FOR NONCOMPLIANCE

Compliance.

Consistent with the principles for achieving compliance provided in the Rule, HHS will seek the cooperation of covered entities and may provide technical assistance to help them comply voluntarily with the Rule. The Rule provides processes for persons to file complaints with HHS, describes the responsibilities of covered entities to provide records and compliance reports and to cooperate with, and permit access to information for, investigation and compliance reviews.

CIVIL MONEY PENALTIES.

HHS may impose civil money penalties on a covered entity of $100 per failure to comply with a Privacy Rule requirement. That penalty may not exceed $25,000 per year for multiple violations of the identical Privacy Rule requirement in a calendar year. HHS may not impose a civil money penalty under specific circumstances, such as when a violation is due to reasonable cause and did not involve willful neglect and the covered entity corrected the violation within 30 days of when it knew or should have known of the violation.

CRIMINAL PENALTIES.

A person who knowingly obtains or discloses individually identifiable health information in violation of HIPAA faces a fine of $50,000 and up to one-year imprisonment. The criminal penalties increase to $100,000 and up to five years imprisonment if the wrongful conduct involves false pretenses, and to $250,000 and ten years imprisonment if the wrongful conduct involves the intent to sell, transfer, or use individually identifiable health information for commercial advantage, personal gain, or malicious harm. Criminal sanctions will be enforced by the Department of Justice.

NOTE

Title XIII of the American Recovery and Reinvestment Act of 2009, P.L. No. 111–5, 111th Cong., 1st Sess. (2009), contains the Health Information Technology for Clinical Health Act (HITECH Act). Among the amendments to the HIPAA Privacy Rule contained in the Act are the following: (1) business associates of covered entities are subject to regulation and enforcement activities of the Department of Health and Human Services (HHS); (2) covered entities are required to notify the public in the event of a serious breach of security; (3) enforcement of the Privacy Rule by HHS is to increase; (4) additional restrictions are to be placed on the use of protected health information in marketing; and (5) public and professional educational programs of HHS are to be expanded.

C. COMMON LAW

MARK A. ROTHSTEIN, GENETIC STALKING AND VOYEURISM: A NEW CHALLENGE TO PRIVACY

57 Kan. L. Rev. 539, 546–548 (2009).

* * *

In 1890, two young law partners from Boston, Samuel D. Warren and Louis D. Brandeis, published a seminal article on the right to privacy at common law. According to most historians, the impetus for the article was Warren's great concern about the allegedly intrusive social reporting of the Boston press, but it is not clear what, if any, specific stories aroused his ire. Brandeis collaborated with Warren to write their seminal and legendary law review article, *The Right to Privacy*. Although it was inspired by perceived abuses by the press, Warren and Brandeis argued more broadly in favor of a comprehensive common law right of individuals to be free of unwanted and unreasonable intrusions of their "inviolate personality."

Warren and Brandeis expanded on Judge Thomas M. Cooley's notion of privacy as the right "to be let alone." They proposed a general legal principle of protecting "the privacy of private life" and urged creating a cause of action to redress "the more flagrant breaches of decency and propriety . . ." They concluded their article by observing the irony between the different standards used by the law in dealing with public and private interferences with peaceful habitation: "The common law has always recognized a man's house as his castle, impregnable, often, even to its own officers engaged in the execution of its commands. Shall the courts thus close the front entrance to constituted authority, and open wide the back door to idle or prurient curiosity?"

Despite its well-deserved acclaim in the academic literature, the Warren and Brandeis article did not immediately translate into a concrete common law doctrine that could be invoked to redress private wrongs. Beginning in the 1930s, courts in several states began to recognize a right of privacy, but the contours of the right were not well defined. The task of developing a cohesive doctrine fell to William L. Prosser who, in a famous law review article in 1960, proposed that the common law right to privacy was actionable in tort in four discrete situations: (1) intrusion upon the plaintiff's seclusion or solitude, or into his private affairs; (2) public disclosure of embarrassing private facts about the plaintiff; (3) publicity which places the plaintiff in a false light in the public eye; and (4) appropriation, for the defendant's advantage, of the plaintiff's name or likeness.

Some scholars have argued that, in carving out limited categories of protected interests, Prosser engaged in reductionism and oversimplification of the human dignity embodied in the right to privacy. Nevertheless, the *Restatement (Second) of Torts* adopted Prosser's classifications, and the limited, categorical approach to common law torts for invasion of privacy steadily gained widespread acceptance in the United States.

NOTES AND QUESTIONS

1. Of the four common law torts for invasion of privacy, public disclosure of private facts is the one most likely to be alleged in the context of genetics. According to the *Restatement (Second) of Torts* § 652D, there are four essential elements to the tort: (1) disclosure to the public or a large number of persons; (2) of a fact that is private in nature; (3) which would be highly offensive to a reasonable person; and (4) is not of a legitimate concern to the public. This theory has been used when other types of health information was unreasonably disclosed without consent. See, e.g., Urbaniak v. Newton, 277 Cal.Rptr. 354 (Cal. Civ. App. 1991) (disclosure of HIV status); Levias v. United Airlines, 500 N.E.2d 370 (Ohio App. 1985) (disclosure of reproductive health).

2. The other invasion of privacy tort of likely significance to genetics is appropriation of name or likeness, where an individual's genetic information or biological specimen has been used for private gain without consent. This tort, and the related tort of conversion, is explored in Chapter 5.

3. How valuable do you think common law actions are for invasion of genetic privacy? What should the relationship be between statutory and common law remedies?

V. DEALING WITH GENETIC DIFFERENCES

The first part of this chapter explored how the ability to maintain some aspects of one's person, including genetic information, free from access by or disclosure to others advances an individual's highly valued interest in privacy. This aspect of the ability to protect one's genetic privacy may be considered as a way of avoiding the intangible harm associated with a loss of privacy. Another, sometimes overshadowing concern, is the ability to avoid the adverse treatment that might flow from a third party's access to one's genetic information, and this may be considered a tangible harm. It is often equated with genetic discrimination.

MARK A. ROTHSTEIN, LEGAL CONCEPTIONS OF EQUALITY IN THE GENOMIC AGE

25 Law & Inequality 429, 455–460 (2007).

* * *

The genetic nondiscrimination and genetic privacy laws implicitly attempt to advance the vision of a "genome-blind" society. It is questionable whether genome-blind public policy is needed to assuage public concerns about eugenics or whether such a strategy ever could be successful. It is even more doubtful whether such an approach ought to be pursued.

The civil rights model of "sameness" and the fiction that all "difference is irrelevant" are inappropriate legal models for genetic diversity. Moreover, ignoring difference is not the only way to protect privacy and prevent invidious discrimination based on genetic variation.

* * *

Purging genetic information from all aspects of public and private life will become an increasingly untenable and counter-productive policy. As I have argued elsewhere, it is seemingly easier for legislators to enact laws prohibiting access to genetic information or outlawing genetic discrimination than it is to address the more fundamental and contentious underlying issues. For example, genetic discrimination in health insurance is really about access to health care, distributive justice, and health care finance, all of which most policy makers would prefer to avoid tackling. At the same time, separate legislative treatment of genetic information is certain to increase the level of stigmatization of individuals at risk for genetic disorders. Furthermore, protecting privacy and preventing discrimination are only two of the many public policies to be achieved with regard to obtaining, using, and disclosing genetic information.

In the pre-genomic age, legal conceptions of equality were based on the political ideal of equality of rights, the social goal of equality of opportunity, and the biological fiction of population homogeneity. In the genomic age, the political foundations and social aspirations remain the same, but the likelihood of achieving them will be enhanced by recognizing the biological reality of individual variation and, in appropriate situations, taking variation into account in formulating or revising various legal doctrines. Recognizing genotypic and phenotypic diversity of individuals is perfectly consistent with respecting and valuing every individual. It is also consistent with improving individual and population health, protecting health privacy, ensuring equal access to health care and other social goods, and guaranteeing civil rights.

NOTES AND QUESTIONS

1.   The Rothstein article argues that the nation's legislative policy on antidiscrimination, as exemplified by Title VII of the Civil Rights Act of 1964 (prohibiting employment discrimination based on race, color, religion, sex, and national origin), is based on the "sameness" model. That model assumes that all people are essentially the same and therefore they ought to be treated the same in all respects. By contrast, under the "difference" model, the law recognizes that people differ in important ways and therefore the law ought to take these differences into account. The Americans with Disabilities Act, with its reasonable accommodation requirement, is presented as an example of the difference model. Is this conceptualization of discrimination instructive in thinking about genetic discrimination?

2.   How would a legal approach recognizing genetic differences differ from a "genome blind" approach?

3.   How difficult is it to obtain an individual's DNA sample without consent and to have it analyzed? Should such activity be prohibited? Is it feasible to do so? Consider the following article.

MARK A. ROTHSTEIN, GENETIC STALKING AND VOYEURISM: A NEW CHALLENGE TO PRIVACY

57 Kan. L. Rev. 539, 539–543, 576–578 (2009).

A new website has just been launched with the URL of celebritygenetics.com ("Celebrity Genetics").[1] Designed to appeal to the public's seemingly insatiable appetite for information about celebrities, Celebrity Genetics sells genetic information about hundreds of entertainers, politicians, athletes, and other public figures. For a fee ranging from twenty dollars to several hundred dollars, individuals and commercial publishers (such as blogs or tabloids) can purchase genetic information about selected celebrities, such as relatedness to other celebrities (e.g., paternity); ancestral place of origin; cognitive ability; behavioral genetic profile (e.g., genetic contribution to sexual orientation, propensity to addiction, and degree of risk-seeking behavior); and predisposition to various illnesses.

The analysis of celebrity DNA samples is merely the latest application of new genetic technologies to test individuals without consent and for purposes other than health care. In the late 1980s, law enforcement officials began matching DNA left at crime scenes with samples donated to police by suspects, often in "DNA dragnets," to identify serial murderers and rapists. Soon thereafter, law enforcement officers began obtaining

---

1.   The author owns the domain name, www.celebritygenetics.com, to prevent its use by others for commercial purposes. Of course, numerous similar names are available. Even if no commercial website is ever created, the genetic privacy issues, including the possibility of nonconsensual testing on a smaller, noncommercial scale, are important to consider.

DNA samples from suspects without consent and, in some cases, surreptitiously or by ruse from licked envelopes and stamps, soft drink cans, cigarette butts, chewing gum, and other objects.

At about the same time, fathers with child support obligations who were suspicious of their child's paternity were urged by billboard advertising and other mass marketing techniques to have DNA testing of themselves and their children (without the knowledge or consent of the child's mother) to confirm or rebut paternity. At first, the "doubtful dads" brought their children to genetic testing laboratories for the sample collection. Soon, on-line entrepreneurs began advertising paternity testing services using home-collection kits involving cheek swabs, which captured buccal cells in saliva.

It was not long before an "anything goes" atmosphere permeated the internet world of DNA-based parentage testing, and the trend has continued unabated. For a fee, virtually any source of DNA that can be tested will be tested. For example, one web-based laboratory offers a list of items it will test and the cost for each, including the following: chewed chewing gum ($240—Wrigley Juicy Fruit© is claimed to work best); cigarette butts ($240—six should be sent); hard candy ($300—well-sucked lollipops are preferred); used condoms ($300); semen stains on clothing ($300); used tampons or feminine pads ($240); sweaty hats or ball caps ($300); "hocked loogies" ($300—best if uninfected); plucked hair ($240—three to ten strands); Q-tips with ear wax ($300—up to three swabs); snotty Kleenex ($300—best if full of mucus) and fecal matter ($360—must be frozen immediately).

Celebrity Genetics thus entered an already sleazy world of covert genetic analysis to offer yet another unsavory DNA testing service. Unlike testing for personal use, however, Celebrity Genetics assumes that the test results will generate more widespread and commercial interest. Celebrity Genetics' business depends on maintaining interest in the genetic information of celebrities and replenishing the supply of DNA for analysis, and the company uses an ingenious method to do both. Celebrity Genetics' website has a section called "DNA Wanted." Hundreds of celebrities are listed, each with a price or bounty for the first collector who submits a sample of the celebrity's DNA. As a result, Celebrity Genetics has created an army of thousands of amateur "gene-*arazzi*" from all over the world who hope to (and in some cases, do) make money and achieve fleeting notoriety by obtaining and selling the DNA of listed celebrities. The Celebrity Genetics website does not specify the method of sample collection; it merely lists some suitable items for DNA testing, such as used chewing gum and cigarette butts.

In attempting to verify that the DNA sample submitted is that of the celebrity claimed, the collector uses a cell phone or camera to obtain a digital image of the celebrity using a particular object (for example, a napkin in a restaurant). Then the collector places the object in a special mailing envelope sold by Celebrity Genetics to the DNA sleuths. Once received, the DNA is analyzed and the results are offered for sale on the Celebrity Genetics website. In their frenzy to obtain samples, DNA collectors in Hollywood, Cannes, Monte Carlo, Washington, Beijing, and other places have scavenged through the trash cans of political candidates, movie stars, judicial nominees, and Olympic athletes; pilfered napkins and utensils from chic restaurants; bribed bartenders and chambermaids for used glasses, towels, and linens; stolen dirty clothes from laundries and dry cleaners; and vandalized barber and beauty shops. Privacy advocates and various celebrities are concerned about the intrusions and disruptions in obtaining the DNA, and in publication of the test results.

Are Celebrity Genetics and its inevitable "copy-cat" websites merely the harmless, twenty-first century versions of gossip columns and tabloid photographs from an earlier era? Or, does this phenomenon represent an insidious infringement on the rights of individuals to be let alone and to prevent their intimate personal health information from being involuntarily generated, publicized, and exploited?

* * *

In the futuristic film *Gattaca*, the female lead, played by Uma Thurman, surreptitiously obtains a hair of her romantic interest, the film's protagonist, played by Ethan Hawke. She takes the hair to a laboratory that appears to specialize in the stealth genetic assessment of prospective mates. For a seemingly nominal fee, and in a matter of seconds, the laboratory presents her with the results of a full genome sequence analysis and an overall assessment of "9.3" which, she is told, makes the sample source "quite a catch." This aspect of the futuristic world portrayed in *Gattaca* is not science fiction; it is here today. The only differences are that today's genetic testing is not available "while you wait," only genome-wide association analyses rather than full sequence data are commercially available today, and the genetic testing of the future presumably would be more accurate than what is commercially touted today.

Genetic stalking and voyeurism involving celebrities serve to draw attention to the issue, but the underlying privacy concerns of surreptitous genetic testing are anything but frivolous and have population-wide applicability. Genetic information is among the most sensitive health and personal information about an individual. Without legislation prohibiting nonconsensual DNA analysis, human dignity and public civility will be irretrievably lost. Society will have succeeded in reaching a level of "zero" privacy and it will not be easy or desirable to "get over it."

* * *

Today, in the health care setting, a genetic test intended to benefit the patient may be ordered only by a licensed physician with informed consent from the patient, the testing must be performed by a certified clinical laboratory, and the confidentiality of the results must be maintained in accordance with the HIPAA Privacy Rule. Should strangers be permitted to acquire an individual's DNA sample on an inanimate object surreptitiously without any consent, arrange for an unregulated laboratory to perform genetic testing on the sample, and widely publish the results when the motivation is curiosity, commercial exploitation, or some other trivial, voyeuristic, or nefarious purpose?

NOTES AND QUESTIONS

1. Do any of the legal remedies mentioned in the previous part of this chapter offer adequate protection against nonconsensual genetic testing and the exploitation of the results? If not, what would you recommend?

2. Reports of plans to engage in the "genetic stalking" of England's Prince Harry was a prime motivation for the enactment of Section 45 of the United Kingdom's Human Tissue Act of 2004, which makes it unlawful for any individual, without proper consent, to possess any "bodily material" with the intent to have DNA testing performed. There are exceptions for medical treatment, law enforcement, research, and other uses. Violators are subject to fine and imprisonment.

3. During the 2008 Presidential election campaign, someone placed for sale on eBay part of the uneaten breakfast and utensils used by Barack Obama, advertising that the buyer could perform genetic testing on the sample. Peter Aldhous & Michael Reilly, Who Is Testing Your DNA?, New Scientist, April 24, 2009, at 8, 11. Should this be prohibited by U.S. law? Only a few states make it unlawful to perform nonconsensual genetic testing. On the other hand, Presidential candidates typically release their medical histories. Should they also release their genetic profiles? See Teneille R. Brown, Double Helix, Double Standards: Private Matters and Public People, 11 J. Health Care L. & Pol'y 295 (2008); Robert C. Green & George J. Annas, The Genetic Profile of Presidential Candidates, 359 New Eng. J. Med. 2192 (2009).

4. Genetic information often is a powerful predictor of an individual's likely future health. Because there are frequently many other individuals and entities with an interest in learning the likelihood of any particular individual's future health, genetic privacy involves weighing the relative interests of the individual with those of the third parties. Insurance (Chapter 15) and Employment (Chapter 16) are examples explored in the following chapters, as is the use of genetic information in education, discussed in Chapter 13. Notes 5–7 discuss other less explored, but nonetheless important, possible uses of genetic information.

5. Mortgage lenders make substantial investments in real estate based on the presumed ability of the borrower to make payments over a prolonged period of time—frequently up to 30 years. Although the mortgage companies have collateral in the form of the real estate itself, repossession and resale are a last resort for lenders. Along with the loan application and credit report, there is currently no law that would prevent a mortgage company from requiring a genetic test to predict the future health of the borrower. Some possible legal theories under which the practice could be challenged involve Title III of the Americans with Disabilities Act, the Fair Housing Act, and state and federal consumer credit and banking laws. The applicability of any of these laws is unclear.

6. As baby boomers age, retirement communities are likely to experience a boom as well. Many retirement communities like to project the image of vigorous and active lifestyles, with golf, tennis, swimming, and other activities featured prominently in promotional materials. Residents sitting in the lobby in wheel chairs or with attendants caring for the basic needs of residents with dementia would not be good for business. Would it be lawful for a retirement community (either rental or sale properties) to require pre-approval genetic testing to determine the genetic risks of Alzheimer's disease, Parkinson's disease, or other debilitating conditions? Some of the legal theories challenging such practices would be similar to those mentioned in the prior note. What are the ethical and policy arguments that could be made for each side of the issue?

7. There are various possible government uses of genetic tests and genetic information. These include tests by government security agencies (e.g., concerns abut genetic predisposition to mental instability); state motor vehicle licensing agencies (e.g., concerns about genetic predisposition to neurological impairments); and government benefits agencies (e.g., using genetic information to determine eligibility). Among the possible uses of genetic information by the military are to predict susceptibility to certain harmful environments, to assess the likelihood of developing post-traumatic stress disorder, to determine fitness for duty, and to establish the source of disability. See Susannah Baruch & Kathy Hudson, Civilian and Military Genetics: Nondiscrimination Policy in a Post–GINA World, 83 Am. J. Human Genetics 435 (2008).

CHAPTER 15

INSURANCE

■ ■ ■

I. INTRODUCTION

Insurance is a system for pooling resources against contingent risks. In the United States, the insurance market is a private, largely for-profit enterprise, and there are thousands of companies selling insurance. Many of the insurance products, such as homeowners insurance, auto insurance, fire and flood insurance, property and casualty insurance, and professional liability insurance attempt to protect against the harms caused by natural occurrences or human errors. Other product lines, including medical expense insurance (health insurance), life insurance, disability insurance, and long-term care insurance, attempt to provide expenses or replacement income in the event of unpredictable illness or death.

Risk classification lies at the heart of insurance. To use life insurance as an example, it is impossible to predict how long any particular individual will live. But, it is possible to predict how long the average member of a clearly defined group will live. Thus, if we know the individual's age, current health status, occupation, lifestyle (e.g. smoking, drinking), and other relevant factors, it is possible to predict the average life expectancy of a group of individuals with the same relevant characteristics. Underwriting is the process of assigning individuals to actuarially relevant groups for purposes of predicting risk and thus deciding the appropriate terms and rates for insurance coverage.

Predictive genetic assessments of individuals have a curious relationship with insurance. If insurance is based on coverage against unknown risks, to the extent that any individual's future illness or death becomes predictable, then insurance would be either (1) unnecessary (where there is little chance of serious illness or death within a given period of time) or (2) unavailable or unaffordable (where there is a virtual certainty of serious illness or death in a given period of time).

Genetic prognostications involving asymptomatic individuals have not yet reached the point where it is possible to make accurate estimates of future illness and death. This is true for monogenic disorders with high penetrance rates, and predictions are even more venturesome for complex

832

disorders and disorders with lower rates of penetrance. Nevertheless, because risk classification is concerned with group experience rather than individual experience, it is clear that genetic information may well be relevant in risk classification.

The interests of consumers and insurers may be summarized in the following way. First, consumers are concerned that genetic information may be used inaccurately, such as during the early 1970s when some unaffected carriers of sickle cell trait were denied access to insurance despite a lack of scientific evidence of increased risk of morbidity or mortality. Second, they are concerned about the invasion of their privacy in insurance companies requiring that they undergo genetic tests they would prefer not to take or companies obtaining, retaining, and disclosing their genetic information. Third, consumers assert that even actuarially accurate insurance decisions may result in great unfairness in denying them access to essential services such as health care and long-term care.

On the other hand, insurers are extremely worried about adverse selection. This is the tendency of those who need insurance the most to purchase it and in the greatest amounts. Insurers argue that as more genetic tests are run in the clinical setting, greater numbers of individuals learn of their genetic risks. Those who learn that they are at greater risk of illness are more likely to seek insurance. Insurers assert that unless they have access to the same information as the individuals, then it is impossible to assign policy holders to the appropriate risk pool for purposes of underwriting. The result is that low-risk individuals are subsidizing the policies of high-risk individuals who have knowledge of their genetic risks, resulting in unfairness among policy holders as well as threatening the economic viability of the insurance companies.

Because of conflicts between the consumer and insurer positions, the use of genetic information in insurance is one of the most contentious social issues arising from the genetics revolution. Among the many questions raised are the following: First, when is the science sufficiently developed that it is appropriate to use genetic information in risk classification? Second, even if actuarially justified, are there social reasons why genetic information should not be used? Answering this question demands an inquiry into the social function of the particular insurance product; the harms associated with obtaining, storing, and using the information; and the existence of alternatives to a genetic-based risk classification scheme. Third, how should the insurance industry be regulated to accomplish social policy?

In this chapter we will consider the use of genetic information in four main contexts: health, life, disability, and long-term care insurance. Although this area has been a fertile ground for scholarship and legislative activity at all levels, there have been few cases thus far. As you consider these materials, try to determine the underlying social policies at issue and whether each proposal or enactment operates to further those policies.

II. HEALTH INSURANCE

A. BACKGROUND

MARK A. ROTHSTEIN & YANN JOLY, GENETIC INFORMATION AND INSURANCE UNDERWRITING: CONTEMPORARY ISSUES AND APPROACHES IN THE GLOBAL ECONOMY IN HANDBOOK OF GENETICS AND SOCIETY: MAPPING THE NEW GENOMIC ERA

128–129 (Paul Atkinson, Peter Glasner, & Margaret Lock eds. 2009).

HEALTH INSURANCE

Countries around the world differ in their health finance systems, including the degree to which they finance health care by optional private sector health insurance (also known as medical expense insurance). Of developed countries, the United States is the most pronounced example of a health care system that assigns a prominent role to private health finance, although the importance of private health insurance continues to grow in several publicly financed and 'mixed' health systems. Thus, analyzing the possible use of genetic information in health insurance is relevant to many countries besides the United States.

Health insurance is generally sold as either a group or an individual policy. In the United States, most individuals with private health insurance obtain their coverage through an employer-sponsored group plan. Underwriting for group health insurance is overwhelmingly group based. Thus, if pricing is experience rated (based on past claims experience, as opposed to 'community rating', in which all policy holders pay the same rate regardless of health status), the experience of the group is considered. In 1996, the United States Congress enacted the Health Insurance Portability and Accountability Act. Among other things, this law makes it unlawful for employer-sponsored group health plans (involving both commercial health insurance and employer self-insured plans) to charge individuals different rates or vary coverage based on health status, including genetic predisposition.

With regard to individual health insurance policies, a substantial majority of the states in the United States have enacted laws prohibiting health insurance companies from requiring a genetic test as a condition of applying for insurance or basing coverage or pricing decisions on the results of a genetic test. There is a substantial and legitimate concern that fear of genetic discrimination, especially in health insurance and employment, causes individuals to decline genetic testing in the clinical and research settings. Although survey research and reports from genetic counsellors confirm these fears to some extent, there is no evidence that the enactment of state genetic nondiscrimination laws has either changed public perceptions or affected health insurance purchasing behavior.

NOTE

According to the U.S. Census Bureau, in 2008, 66.7% of the U.S. population had private health insurance. Of that total, 58.5% was employment-based group coverage and 8.9% was individual coverage or "direct purchase." During 2008, 29.0% of the population had government health coverage under Medicare (14.3%), Medicaid (14.1%), or military and veterans insurance plans (3.8%). That left 15.4% of the population, 46.3 million people without any health insurance coverage. Note that multiple coverage and rounding errors account for the differential sums. U.S. Census Bureau, Income, Poverty, and Health Insurance Coverage in the United States: 2008 (Sept. 2009), at 20–23.

Government-sponsored health benefits are not medically underwritten. If an individual satisfies the statutory criteria for coverage, such as age or income level, then the individual's health status is not relevant. Similarly, pursuant to the Health Insurance Portability and Accountability Act (HIPAA), employer-sponsored group health plans may not discriminate in eligibility, coverage, or rates based on health status, including "genetic information." Thus, it might appear at first glance that, even before the 2008 enactment of the Genetic Information Nondiscrimination Act (GINA), only those individuals with individual health insurance policies would be concerned about the possibility of discrimination based on genetic information. Such a view would be incorrect, however. Individuals often change the basis of their coverage. For example, an employee currently covered by an employer-sponsored health plan might lose his or her job or decide to become self-employed. Because individual health insurance is often the default option for coverage, and because all of society has an interest in the health status of its members, the possibility of health based, including genetic based, discrimination is a widespread concern.

NANCY E. KASS, THE IMPLICATIONS OF GENETIC TESTING FOR HEALTH AND LIFE INSURANCE IN GENETIC SECRETS: PROTECTING PRIVACY AND CONFIDENTIALITY IN THE GENETIC ERA

299, 300–302 (Mark A. Rothstein ed. 1997).

In the individual health insurance market, applicants are screened individually for their medical history and health risks. Typically, this process begins with a simple written questionnaire that the applicant completes. A statement or medical record is requested from the applicant's physician for approximately 20% of applicants, usually because of a particular response on a health history questionnaire or because of the applicant's age or other factors. A physical examination is required of only 4% of applicants for individual health insurance. Approximately 75% of individual insurance applicants are approved for coverage. Another 15–20% are approved as "substandard," meaning that either they are charged higher premiums or their coverage will exclude payments for a preexisting condition. Applicants are denied insurance altogether if their chance of disease exceeds three times the risk for others of their age and sex. Approximately 8% of applicants are denied coverage.

* * *

It is fundamental to the contemporary insurance market to assess risk. According to one industry spokesperson, "The insurance industry is built upon a basic insurance principle: the ability to appropriately and accurately evaluate risks and, in turn, price the product." The industry wants to be able to predict who is likely to develop a serious disease and whose disease is expected to be prolonged or expensive. Indeed, each of the 50 states and the District of Columbia have legislation known as Unfair Trade Practices acts. These acts prohibit unfair discrimination "between individuals of the same class and of essentially the same hazard in the amount of premium, policy fees, or rates charged for any policy or contract of [life or] health insurance." Unfair Trade Practices acts have been interpreted not only as providing protection against differential treatment for individuals of the same risk but also, more germane to the issue of genetic testing, as justification for rendering differential treatment to individuals of *different* risk. It is the philosophy of the insurance industry that an insurance company "has the responsibility to treat all its policyholders fairly by establishing premiums at a level consistent with the risk represented by each individual policyholder."

The United States does not require individuals to have health insurance, nor does it require employers to provide their employees with health insurance. The insurance industry argues, therefore, that only or predominately persons who believe they have special reason to need insurance will want to buy it. The industry is concerned about adverse selection, whereby an applicant has information about his or her health unavailable to the insurer and this information might lead the applicant to buy insurance or to buy a greater amount of insurance than he or she would without such knowledge. Insurance companies argue that if they were required to accept all applicants, without being able to screen for preexisting conditions or risk factors (in order, they argue, to "level the playing field"), rates for individual insurance would rise and healthier individuals would choose to stop buying insurance. This concept is difficult to test empirically.

B. STATE LAWS

After the Human Genome Project officially began in 1990, the use of genetic information in health insurance was the first issue to receive widespread public attention. In 1993, a special task force of the National Institutes of Health–Department of Energy (NIH–DOE) Working Group on Ethical, Legal, and Social Implications of Human Genome Research issued a report on genetics and health insurance. Among its recommendations was the following. "The U.S. health care system should ensure universal access to and participation by all in a program of basic health services that encompasses a continuum of services appropriate for the healthy to the seriously ill.'' In the absence of sweeping health system reform, state legislatures took the lead in enacting laws prohibiting genetic discrimination in health insurance.

KAN. STAT. ANN. § 40–2259
(ENACTED 1997).

40–2259. Genetic screening or testing; prohibiting the use of; exceptions. (a) As used in this section, "genetic screening or testing" means a laboratory test of a person's genes or chromosomes for abnormalities, defects or deficiencies, including carrier status, that are linked to physical or mental disorders or impairments, or that indicate a susceptibility to illness, disease or other disorders, whether physical or mental, which test is a direct test for abnormalities, defects or deficiencies, and not an indirect manifestation of genetic disorders.

(b) An insurance company, health maintenance organization, non-profit medical and hospital, dental, optometric or pharmacy corporations, or a group subject to K.S.A. 12–2616 et seq., and amendments thereto, shall not:

(1) Require or request directly or indirectly any individual or a member of the individual's family to obtain a genetic test;

(2) require or request directly or indirectly any individual to reveal whether the individual or a member of the individual's family has obtained a genetic test or the results of the test, if obtained by the individual or a member of the individual's family;

(3) condition the provision of insurance coverage or health care benefits on whether an individual or a member of the individual's family has obtained a genetic test or the results of the test, if obtained by the individual or a member of the individual's family; or

(4) consider in the determination of rates or any other aspect of insurance coverage or health care benefits provided to an individual whether an individual or a member of the individual's family has obtained a genetic test or the results of the test, if obtained by the individual or a member of the individual's family.

(c) Subsection (b) does not apply to an insurer writing life insurance, disability income insurance or long-term care insurance coverage.

(d) An insurer writing life insurance, disability income insurance or long-term care insurance coverage that obtains information under paragraphs (1) or (2) of subsection (b), shall not:

(1) Use the information contrary to paragraphs (3) or (4) of subsection (b) in writing a type of insurance coverage other than life for the individual or a member of the individual's family; or

(2) provide for rates or any other aspect of coverage that is not reasonably related to the risk involved.

NOTES AND QUESTIONS

1. As of 2010, laws similar to the one in Kansas had been enacted in virtually all of the states. The updated listing of state laws on the issue is maintained by the National Conference of State Legislatures at www.ncsl.org/programs/health/genetics/charts.htm.

2. Would the Kansas law prohibit discrimination in health insurance based on an individual's family history of genetic disease? Should insurers be prohibited from considering such information? Does the Kansas law prohibit an individual from voluntarily submitting favorable genetic information to an insurer to get a lower rate?

3. Because of the preemptive effect of the Employee Retirement Income Security Act (ERISA), 29 U.S.C. §§ 1001–1461, state laws do not apply to employer-sponsored group health plans. Therefore, the laws generally apply only to individual health insurance policies and small, non-employer group plans. Some state laws apply to one but not the other. For example, Hawaii's law, Haw. Rev. Stat. §§ 4331–10a–118, 432–1–607, 432d–26, applies only to individual policies; Arizona's law, Ariz. Rev. Stat. §§ 20–448, 448.02, applies only to small group policies.

4. The exclusion in the Kansas law of life, disability, and long-term care insurance is typical of most of the state laws. These other forms of insurance are discussed later in this chapter.

MARK A. HALL, LEGAL RULES AND INDUSTRY NORMS: THE IMPACT OF LAWS RESTRICTING HEALTH INSURERS' USE OF GENETIC INFORMATION

40 Jurimetrics 93, 94–99, 122 (1999).

Researchers and advocacy groups have reported cases of employers and health, life, and disability insurers using this new-found genetic information to deny coverage, raise rates, or limit the extent of coverage. Fear of genetic discrimination of this sort was shown to factor strongly into patients' and family members' decisions and concerns about undergoing genetic testing.

These laws are thus intended to achieve two kinds of social benefit: (1) to prevent unfair use of genetic information, however accurate that use might be as a source of underwriting information; and (2) to encourage more genetic testing for purposes of research, prevention, treatment, and family planning. This article reports on an extensive empirical study designed to assess what impact these laws have had, and why. This article focuses on only the first purpose of the legislation—preventing genetic discrimination. Other publications will explore the second purpose.

Several distinctive features of these laws must be considered in assessing their purpose and intended effects. First, they mostly target only comprehensive (or "major medical") health insurance, not life, disability, or long-term care insurance, and not employment discrimination. A few states address these other arenas, but the great majority so far have addressed only ordinary health insurance. This limitation results from two factors: health insurers put up less resistance to this legislation than do life insurers, and most people care more about maintaining health insurance than about other types of insurance.

The second crucial feature of these statutes is that they typically cover only certain types of genetic information: *presymptomatic* information derived from genetic *tests*. Most states still allow insurers to consider family history of disease, although an increasing number appear to prohibit this as well; however, almost every state allows health insurers to underwrite based on observed clinical signs and symptoms of medical conditions, regardless of their genetic status. The reasons are partly pragmatic, and partly central to the law's purpose. Since health insurers have always used symptoms of existing disease in medical underwriting, it would be infeasible and unjustified to distinguish between diseases with and without significant genetic components. One would either have to prohibit all medical underwriting, which cannot be done as long as the purchase of health insurance is voluntary, or to target only specific sources of information. Information from genetic tests is the sensible point of concern because that is where the fear of insurance discrimination has the greatest discernible impact.

* * *

For purposes of this study, genetic discrimination is defined as the denial, limitation, or increased price of health insurance based on the results of presymptomatic genetic information. In other words, genetic discrimination, as defined by these laws, means insurers using genetic information as part of medical underwriting to predict future health problems for people who currently do not have the genetic disease in question. A majority of states prohibit only information from genetic *tests*, but a substantial and growing minority also prohibit the use of family history information. However, almost no state defines genetic discrimination to include observed signs and symptoms of genetic disease, or medical tests other than genetic tests. Genetic discrimination could be defined more broadly, but then it would be impossible to distinguish it from other, non-genetic sources of information commonly used in medical underwriting. Presymptomatic genetic information is different because it results in branding someone as a high health risk who presently has no disease. However, we do not use "discrimination" necessarily as a pejorative term, but rather in the more neutral sense of differentiation. Thus, genetic discrimination includes insurers' use of genetic information regardless of whether that use might be considered fair or actuarially justified.

It appears from several independent sources that genetic discrimination by health insurers is very low or nonexistent, both before these laws were enacted and afterwards, and in states with and without these laws. Thus, these laws have had no discernible impact on actual genetic discrimination by health insurers. Although it is difficult to prove a negative assertion like this conclusively, strong confirmation exists if thorough examination of many reliable sources of information all point to the same conclusion. That is the case here. However, these laws have had an impact: they have discouraged health insurers from even considering the possibility of using genetic information.

* * *

These examples and explanations apply to much of what we have observed about genetic discrimination laws. In this instance, there has not been a change in industry behavior, but the law has helped to preserve the status quo. The insurance industry struggles with competing norms of actuarial fairness and social fairness. Actuarial fairness says that insurers not only may, but should, use the best available information about risk to determine each person's risk status. Social fairness says that certain types of risk classification unfairly penalize people for factors they cannot control or for which they should not be held responsible. Usually in these debates the industry is univocal in defending the norm of actuarial fairness; this occurred, for instance, with AIDS testing. But, in this instance, as with racial discrimination, laws prohibiting health insurers from using genetic information have helped move the industry norm toward social fairness. Having done so, these laws operate more effectively and with broader sweep than if they had to be actively enforced against a reluctant industry looking for ways to circumvent them.

Rather than criticizing these laws for responding to a problem that does not exist, one can maintain that the law has a legitimate function in simply expressing the social judgment that it is wrong to use genetic information in health underwriting. Even though insurers and agents do not have widespread and accurate knowledge of these laws, these laws have fortified their impression of social disapproval by creating a general climate of legal condemnation. Health insurers avoid the use of genetic information not so much because of the specific threat of law but because the law reinforces the instinct that doing otherwise would be socially wrong. To this extent, they have been effective. However, the expressive effect of the law can also have unintended negative consequences. It may be that, rather than calming fears about genetic discrimination and therefore encouraging more people to undergo beneficial genetic testing, these laws have heightened fears without substantial justification by calling undue attention to a problem that, in large measure, does not exist.

Whether these laws, on balance, are a success depends also on an appreciation of their potential harms. Although the harms are not great, that is because genetic information simply is not much used by health insurers, for either adverse or favorable purposes. But, once adverse uses become possible, so too do favorable ones. At that point, the potential for inhibiting favorable use by those who wish to clear up a suspect family or medical history becomes real, and this potential seems to be roughly as great as the potential for these laws to protect against adverse use. The difficult judgment social policy makers must make is whether this trade-off is socially desirable.

NOTES AND QUESTIONS

1. Hall's article is the first effort to study asserted discrimination in health insurance in a methodologically rigorous manner. Prior attempts to document anecdotal reports of discrimination relied on self reports. See, e.g., Paul R. Billings et al., Discrimination as a Consequence of Genetic Testing, 50 Am. J. Human Genetics 476 (1992); E. Virginia Lapham et al., Genetic Discrimination: Perspectives of Consumers, 274 Science 621 (1996). The problem with the case reports is that they often do not distinguish between asymptomatic and symptomatic individuals, and it is also difficult to verify self-reports of discrimination. Nevertheless, self-report studies are still widely cited in the media and elsewhere as evidence of health insurance discrimination. For a critical discussion of the popular literature on genetic discrimination, see Philip R. Reilly, Genetic Discrimination, in Genetic Testing and the Use of Information (Clarisa Long, ed. 1999).

2. Another common assumption is that individuals decline to undergo genetic testing because they are afraid of discrimination by health insurance companies. Hall and his colleague Stephen S. Rich attempted to study whether the enactment of state laws prohibiting genetic discrimination in health insurance had any effect on the willingness of at-risk individuals to undergo genetic testing. The study involved detailed interviews with genetic counselors and medical geneticists in selected states with and without antidiscrimination legislation. Hall and Rich found that the enactment of state laws had little effect on the willingness of individuals to undergo genetic testing:

> Although genetic counselors report that their patients have great concern about insurance discrimination, many counselors think that this concern does not rank so high as the psychological impact of learning one's genetic fate, or they believe this concern is important only when the need for the information is low. Thus, discrimination concerns are often overshadowed by other barriers to testing, or by the pressing need for the information.

> Where discrimination fears actually deter testing, there is little reason to believe that the legal protections so far have offered much reassurance or have altered any testing decisions. These laws provide little reassurance because counselors do not perceive them as significantly reducing the actual risk of discrimination, or counselors do not yet have sufficient confidence in these laws. These protections have not received nearly so much publicity as has the potential risk of discrimination, so patients' primary source of information about these laws is from genetic counselors. Although counselors mention these laws, they continue to place more stress on alerting patients to the potential risks than on reassuring them of the legal protections.

Mark A. Hall & Stephen S. Rich, Genetic Privacy Laws and Patients' Fear of Discrimination by Health Insurers: The View from Genetic Counselors, 28 J. L. Med. & Ethics 245, 254 (2000).

3. If there is little genetic discrimination in health insurance today, to what do you attribute it? Antidiscrimination laws? The fact that most health insurance is group based? The desire of agents and companies to sell policies? The fact that there are few genetic tests performed in the clinical setting now? The fact that adverse selection is less of a risk in health insurance? Other factors?

4. Assuming that fears of health insurance discrimination are not well founded, which of the following arguments do you support: (1) there is no need to enact legislation and it is bad policy to pass laws to assuage the irrational fears of consumers; or (2) the risk of discrimination may increase in the future, the laws have a valuable psychological effect, and if there is no discrimination going on then the laws are not interfering with the commercial practices of insurance companies.

5. What is the risk of harm to individuals? Is it the same harm these laws seek to address? Is it that (1) health insurers are requiring individuals to undergo genetic testing as a condition of health insurance coverage; (2) using the results of predictive genetic tests to deny coverage to currently health individuals; or (3) having the legal ability to refuse to renew individual health insurance policies or increase rates substantially after an individual becomes ill? Consider how this issue affects the development of federal laws, discussed in the next section.

C. FEDERAL LAWS

HEALTH INSURANCE PORTABILITY AND ACCOUNTABILITY ACT

42 U.S.C. §§ 300gg–300gg–2.

(ALSO CODIFIED IN PART AT 26 U.S.C. § 9801, AND IN FULL AT 29 U.S.C. §§ 1181–1191c.)

PART A—GROUP MARKET REFORMS

Subpart 1—Portability, Access, and Renewability Requirements

§ 300gg. Increased portability through limitation on preexisting condition exclusions

(a) Limitation on preexisting condition exclusion period; crediting for periods of previous coverage

Subject to subsection (d) of this section, a group health plan, and a health insurance issuer offering group health insurance coverage, may, with respect to a participant or beneficiary, impose a preexisting condition exclusion only if—

(1) such exclusion relates to a condition (whether physical or mental), regardless of the cause of the condition, for which medical advice, diagnosis, care, or treatment was recommended or received within the 6–month period ending on the enrollment date;

(2) such exclusion extends for a period of not more than 12 months (or 18 months in the case of a late enrollee) after the enrollment date; and

(3) the period of any such preexisting condition exclusion is reduced by the aggregate of the periods of creditable coverage (if any, as defined in subsection (c)(1) of this section) applicable to the participant or beneficiary as of the enrollment date.

(b) Definitions

For purposes of this part—

(1) Preexisting condition exclusion

(A) In general

The term "preexisting condition exclusion" means, with respect to coverage, a limitation or exclusion of benefits relating to a condition based on the fact that the condition was present before the date of enrollment for such coverage, whether or not any medical advice, diagnosis, care, or treatment was recommended or received before such date.

(B) Treatment of genetic information

Genetic information shall not be treated as a condition described in subsection (a)(1) of this section in the absence of a diagnosis of the condition related–to such information.

* * *

§ 300gg–1.

(a) In eligibility to enroll

(1) In general

Subject to paragraph (2), a group health plan, and a health insurance issuer offering group health insurance coverage in connection with a group health plan, may not establish rules for eligibility (including continued eligibility) of any individual to enroll under the terms of the plan based on any of the following health status-related factors in relation to the individual or a dependent of the individual:

(A) Health status.

(B) Medical condition (including both physical and mental illnesses).

(C) Claims experience.

(D) Receipt of health care.

(E) Medical history.

(F) Genetic information.

(G) Evidence of insurability (including conditions arising out of acts of domestic violence).

(H) Disability.

(2) No application to benefits or exclusions

To the extent consistent with section 701, paragraph (1) shall not be construed—

(A) to require a group health plan, or group health insurance coverage, to provide particular benefits other than those provided under the terms of such plan or coverage, or

(B) to prevent such a plan or coverage from establishing limitations or restrictions on the amount, level, extent, or nature of the benefits or coverage for similarly situated individuals enrolled in the plan or coverage.

(3) Construction

For purposes of paragraph (1), rules for eligibility to enroll under a plan include rules defining any applicable waiting periods for such enrollment.

NOTES

1. HIPAA was enacted in 1996, and the language applicable to genetic information was included late in the legislative process. HIPAA applies to employer-sponsored group health plans, the main avenue by which individuals obtain health care coverage in the private sector. According to HIPAA, genetic information may not be considered to be a preexisting condition and may not be used as a basis for denying coverage or setting rates.

2. HIPAA does not require that any employer offer health benefits, it does not set a defined minimum benefits package, it does not limit the amount of money that employers charge employees to participate in the plan, and it does not prohibit an employer from dropping coverage altogether. HIPAA also does not apply to individual health insurance policies or non-employer group plans.

GENETIC INFORMATION NONDISCRIMINATION ACT (GINA)
P.L. 110–233 (2008).

* * *

SEC. 2. FINDINGS.
Congress makes the following findings:

* * *

(5) Federal law addressing genetic discrimination in health insurance and employment is incomplete in both the scope and depth of its protections. Moreover, while many States have enacted some type of genetic non-discrimination law, these laws vary widely with respect to their approach, application, and level of protection. Congress has collected substantial evidence that the American public and the medical community find the existing patchwork of State and Federal laws to be confusing and inadequate to protect them from discrimination. Therefore, Federal legislation establishing a national and uniform basic standard is necessary to fully protect the public from discrimination and allay their concerns about the potential for discrimination, thereby allowing individuals to take advantage of genetic testing, technologies, research, and new therapies.

TITLE I—GENETIC NONDISCRIMINATION IN HEALTH INSURANCE

SEC. 101. AMENDMENTS TO EMPLOYEE RETIREMENT INCOME SECURITY ACT OF 1974.

(a) NO DISCRIMINATION IN GROUP PREMIUMS BASED ON GENETIC INFORMATION.—Section 702(b) of the Employee Retirement Income Security Act of 1974 (29 U.S.C. 1182(b)) is amended—

* * *

(3) NO GROUP-BASED DISCRIMINATION ON BASIS OF GENETIC INFORMATION.—

(A) IN GENERAL.—For purposes of this section, a group health plan, and a health insurance issuer offering group health insurance coverage in connection with a group health plan, may not adjust premium or contribution amounts for the group covered under such plan on the basis of genetic information.

* * *

SEC. 102. AMENDMENTS TO THE PUBLIC HEALTH SERVICE ACT.

* * *

(b) AMENDMENT RELATING TO THE INDIVIDUAL MARKET.—

(1) IN GENERAL.—The first subpart 3 of part B of title XXVII of the Public Health Service Act (42 U.S.C. 300gg–51 et seq.) (relating to other requirements) is amended—

SEC. 2753. PROHIBITION OF HEALTH DISCRIMINATION ON THE BASIS OF GENETIC INFORMATION.

(a) PROHIBITION ON GENETIC INFORMATION AS A CONDITION OF ELIGIBILITY .—

(1) IN GENERAL.—A health insurance issuer offering health insurance coverage in the individual market may not establish rules for the eligibility (including continued eligibility) of any individual to enroll in individual health insurance coverage based on genetic information.

(2) RULE OF CONSTRUCTION.—Nothing in paragraph (1) or in paragraphs (1) and (2) of subsection (e) shall be construed to preclude a health insurance issuer from establishing rules for eligibility for an individual to enroll in individual health insurance coverage based on the manifestation of a disease or disorder in that individual, or in a family member of such individual where such family member is covered under the policy that covers such individual.

(b) PROHIBITION ON GENETIC INFORMATION IN SETTING PREMIUM RATES.—

(1) IN GENERAL.—A health insurance issuer offering health insurance coverage in the individual market shall not adjust premium or contri-

bution amounts for an individual on the basis of genetic information concerning the individual or a family member of the individual.

(2) RULE OF CONSTRUCTION.—Nothing in paragraph (1) or in paragraphs (1) and (2) of subsection (e) shall be construed to preclude a health insurance issuer from adjusting premium or contribution amounts for an individual on the basis of a manifestation of a disease or disorder in that individual, or in a family member of such individual where such family member is covered under the policy that covers such individual. In such case, the manifestation of a disease or disorder in one individual cannot also be used as genetic information about other individuals covered under the policy issued to such individual and to further increase premiums or contribution amounts.

(c) PROHIBITION ON GENETIC INFORMATION AS PREEXISTING CONDITION.—

(1) IN GENERAL.—A health insurance issuer offering health insurance coverage in the individual market may not, on the basis of genetic information, impose any preexisting condition exclusion (as defined in section 2701(b)(1)(A)) with respect to such coverage.

(2) RULE OF CONSTRUCTION.—Nothing in paragraph (1) or in paragraphs (1) and (2) of subsection (e) shall be construed to preclude a health insurance issuer from imposing any preexisting condition exclusion for an individual with respect to health insurance coverage on the basis of a manifestation of a disease or disorder in that individual.

(d) GENETIC TESTING.—

(1) LIMITATION ON REQUESTING OR REQUIRING GENETIC TESTING.—A health insurance issuer offering health insurance coverage in the individual market shall not request or require an individual or a family member of such individual to undergo a genetic test.

(2) RULE OF CONSTRUCTION.—Paragraph (1) shall not be construed to limit the authority of a health care professional who is providing health care services to an individual to request that such individual undergo a genetic test.

MARK A. ROTHSTEIN, GINA'S BEAUTY IS ONLY SKIN DEEP

22 Gene Watch No. 2, at 9–10 (April–May 2009).

* * *

GINA's prohibition on genetic discrimination in health insurance is largely a mirage. The Health Insurance Portability and Accountability Act (HIPAA) contains a little-known provision prohibiting employer-sponsored group health plans from denying individuals coverage, charging them higher rates, or varying their coverage based on "genetic information." Significantly, HIPAA prohibits discrimination by group health plans on the basis of any health information. Because HIPAA prohibits genetic discrimination for the largest source of private health coverage (group plans), GINA's main value is to cover people with individual health insurance policies in the few states that did not previously enact a state genetic nondiscrimination law.

Unfortunately, the protections afforded individuals under either state laws prohibiting genetic discrimination in health insurance or GINA are not particularly robust or valuable. (Because state laws and GINA are similar in substance, for simplicity, I'll merely refer to GINA.) The problem is that GINA only applies to asymptomatic individuals. There are few incentives for health insurers to discriminate against asymptomatic individuals and few laws to prohibit them from discriminating against symptomatic individuals.

An example will bring this problem more clearly into focus. Under GINA, it is unlawful for an individual health insurance company to refuse to offer coverage, charge higher rates, or exclude certain conditions on the basis of genetic information, including the results of a genetic test. For example, it would be unlawful to deny coverage to a woman with a positive test for one of the breast cancer mutations. Now, suppose some months or years later, the woman develops breast cancer. GINA simply does not apply. The insurance company's permissible response would depend on state insurance law. In virtually every state, the health insurance company could lawfully react to the changed health status of the individual by refusing to renew the policy (at its typically annual renewal date), increase the rates to reflect the increased risk (and the rates might be double or triple), or renew the policy but exclude coverage for breast cancer.

GINA does have some limited value in this scenario. Because of GINA, an at-risk woman is no worse off in terms of insurability due to having a genetic test, and there might be psychological or medical benefits from being tested, depending on the results. Yet, the overall picture in terms of health policy remains bleak. So long as individual health insurance is medically underwritten at the initial application and for renewals, individuals who are ill or more likely to become ill are extremely vulnerable. Many advocates and policy makers have concentrated on the issue of genetic discrimination in health insurance, but the issue is much broader and cannot be resolved by such a narrow focus. To state the obvious: Under any system of universal access to health care, the issue of genetic discrimination in health insurance disappears.

NOTES AND QUESTIONS

1. The express purpose of GINA is to allay fears of individuals that if they undergo genetic testing they will be subject to discrimination. GINA does not apply to life, disability, long-term care or other forms of insurance, and its health insurance provisions only apply to individuals who are asymptomatic. Do you think these limitations undermine the stated intent of GINA?

2. The essential problem of GINA is captured with the following example from Russell Korobkin & Rahul Rajkumar, The Genetic Information

Nondiscrimination Act—A Half–Step Toward Risk Sharing, 359 New Eng. J. Med. 335, 335 (2008).

> Consider three Americans—one with an increased genetic risk for colon cancer, one with a family history of colon cancer, and one with colonoscopic finding of several large adenomatous polyps. Under the Genetic Information Nondiscrimination Act (GINA), which was recently signed into law by President George W. Bush, health insurance companies may not refuse to cover and may not raise premiums for the first two people, whose genetic information or family history puts them at higher risk for colon cancer. Insurers could, however, refuse to sell the third person an individual policy or quadruple his or her premiums.

3. The precursor bill of GINA was introduced in 1995, and it took 13 years before legislation was finally enacted. In the final vote, only one member of the House of Representatives and no member of the Senate voted against GINA. How can you explain this?

4. GINA can be fairly characterized as limited in scope and an example of genetic exceptionalism. Given these facts, if you were in Congress, would you have supported this bill? Reconsider the following article from Chapter 14, Mark A. Rothstein, Genetic Exceptionalism and Legislative Pragmatism.

5. Title II of GINA, dealing with genetic discrimination in employment, is discussed in Chapter 16.

D. COVERAGE DECISIONS

KATSKEE v. BLUE CROSS/BLUE SHIELD

515 N.W.2d 645 (Neb. 1994).

WHITE, JUSTICE.

In January 1990, upon the recommendation of her gynecologist, Dr. Larry E. Roffman, appellant consulted with Dr. Henry T. Lynch regarding her family's history of breast and ovarian cancer, and particularly her health in relation to such a history. After examining appellant and investigating her family's medical history, Dr. Lynch diagnosed her as suffering from a genetic condition known as breast-ovarian carcinoma syndrome. Dr. Lynch then recommended that appellant have a total abdominal hysterectomy and bilateral salpingo-oophorectomy, which involves the removal of the uterus, the ovaries, and the fallopian tubes. Dr. Roffman concurred in Dr. Lynch's diagnosis and agreed that the recommended surgery was the most medically appropriate treatment available.

After considering the diagnosis and recommended treatment, appellant decided to have the surgery. In preparation for the surgery, appellant filed a claim with Blue Cross/Blue Shield. Both Drs. Lynch and Roffman wrote to Blue Cross/Blue Shield and explained the diagnosis and their basis for recommending the surgery. Initially, Blue Cross/Blue Shield sent a letter to appellant and indicated that it might pay for the surgery. Two weeks before the surgery, Dr. Roger Mason, the chief medical officer for Blue Cross/Blue Shield, wrote to appellant and stated that Blue Cross/Blue

Shield would not cover the cost of the surgery. Nonetheless, appellant had the surgery in November 1990.

Appellant filed this action for breach of contract, seeking to recover $6,022.57 in costs associated with the surgery. Blue Cross/Blue Shield filed a motion for summary judgment. The district court granted the motion. It found that there was no genuine issue of material fact and that the policy did not cover appellant's surgery. Specifically, the court stated that (1) appellant did not suffer from cancer, and although her high-risk condition warranted the surgery, it was not covered by the policy; (2) appellant did not have a bodily illness or disease which was covered by the policy; and (3) under the terms of the policy, Blue Cross/Blue Shield reserved the right to determine what is medically necessary.

* * *

Blue Cross/Blue Shield contends that appellant's costs are not covered by the insurance policy. The policy provides coverage for services which are medically necessary. Blue Cross/Blue Shield denied coverage because it concluded that appellant's condition does not constitute an illness, and thus the treatment she received was not medically necessary. Blue Cross/ Blue Shield has not raised any other basis for its denial, and we therefore will limit our consideration to whether appellant's condition constituted an illness within the meaning of the policy.

The policy broadly defines "illness" as a "bodily disorder or disease." The policy does not provide definitions for either bodily disorder or disease.

An insurance policy is to be construed as any other contract to give effect to the parties' intentions at the time the contract was made. When the terms of the contract are clear, a court may not resort to rules of construction, and the terms are to be accorded their plain and ordinary meaning as the ordinary or reasonable person would understand them. In such a case, a court shall seek to ascertain the intention of the parties from the plain language of the policy.

Whether a policy is ambiguous is a matter of law for the court to determine. If a court finds that the policy is ambiguous, then the court may employ rules of construction and look beyond the language of the policy to ascertain the intention of the parties. A general principle of construction, which we have applied to ambiguous insurance policies, holds that an ambiguous policy will be construed in favor of the insured. However, we will not read an ambiguity into policy language which is plain and unambiguous in order to construe it against the insurer.

* * *

We find that the language used in the policy at issue in the present case is not reasonably susceptible of differing interpretations and thus not ambiguous. The plain and ordinary meaning of the terms "bodily disorder" and "disease," as they are used in the policy to define illness, encompasses any abnormal condition of the body or its components of such a degree that in its natural progression would be expected to be problematic; a deviation from the healthy or normal state affecting the functions or tissues of the body; an inherent defect of the body; or a morbid physical or mental state which deviates from or interrupts the normal structure or function of any part, organ, or system of the body and which is manifested by a characteristic set of symptoms and signs.

The issue then becomes whether appellant's condition—breast-ovarian carcinoma syndrome—constitutes an illness.

Blue Cross/Blue Shield argues that appellant did not suffer from an illness because she did not have cancer. Blue Cross/Blue Shield characterizes appellant's condition only as a "predisposition to an illness (cancer)" and fails to address whether the condition itself constitutes an illness. This failure is traceable to Dr. Mason's denial of appellant's claim. Despite acknowledging his inexperience and lack of knowledge about this specialized area of cancer research, Dr. Mason denied appellant's claim without consulting any medical literature or research regarding breast-ovarian carcinoma syndrome. Moreover, Dr. Mason made the decision without submitting appellant's claim for consideration to a claim review committee. The only basis for the denial was the claim filed by appellant, the letters sent by Drs. Lynch and Roffman, and the insurance policy. Despite his lack of information regarding the nature and severity of appellant's condition, Dr. Mason felt qualified to decide that appellant did not suffer from an illness.

Appellant's condition was diagnosed as breast-ovarian carcinoma syndrome. To adequately determine whether the syndrome constitutes an illness, we must first understand the nature of the syndrome.

The record on summary judgment includes the depositions of Drs. Lynch, Roffman, and Mason. In his deposition, Dr. Lynch provided a thorough discussion of this syndrome. In light of Dr. Lynch's extensive research and clinical experience in this particular area of medicine, we consider his discussion extremely helpful in our understanding of the syndrome.

According to Dr. Lynch, some forms of cancer occur on a hereditary basis. Breast and ovarian cancer are such forms of cancer which may occur on a hereditary basis. It is our understanding that the hereditary occurrence of this form of cancer is related to the genetic makeup of the woman. In this regard, the genetic deviation has conferred changes which are manifest in the individual's body and at some time become capable of being diagnosed.

At the time that he gave his deposition, Dr. Lynch explained that the state of medical research was such that detecting and diagnosing the syndrome was achieved by tracing the occurrences of hereditary cancer throughout the patient's family. Dr. Lynch stated that at the time of appellant's diagnosis, no conclusive physical test existed which would demonstrate the presence of the condition. However, Dr. Lynch stated that this area of research is progressing toward the development of a more determinative method of identifying and tracing a particular gene throughout a particular family, thus providing a physical method of diagnosing the condition.

Women diagnosed with the syndrome have at least a 50–percent chance of developing breast and/or ovarian cancer, whereas unaffected women have only a 1.4–percent risk of developing breast or ovarian cancer. [*sic*] In addition to the genetic deviation, the family history, and the significant risks associated with this condition, the diagnosis also may encompass symptoms of anxiety and stress, which some women experience because of their knowledge of the substantial likelihood of developing cancer.

The procedures for detecting the onset of ovarian cancer are ineffective. Generally, by the time ovarian cancer is capable of being detected, it has already developed to a very advanced stage, making treatment relatively unsuccessful. Drs. Lynch and Roffman agreed that the standard of care for treating women with breast carcinoma syndrome ordinarily involves surveillance methods. However, for women at an inordinately high risk for ovarian cancer, such as appellant, the standard of care may require radical surgery which involves the removal of the uterus, ovaries, and fallopian tubes.

Dr. Lynch explained that the surgery is labeled "prophylactic" and that the surgery is prophylactic as to the prevention of the onset of cancer. Dr. Lynch also stated that appellant's condition itself is the result of a genetic deviation from the normal, healthy state and that the recommended surgery treats that condition by eliminating or significantly reducing the presence of the condition and its likely development.

Blue Cross/Blue Shield has not proffered any evidence disputing the premise that the origin of this condition is in the genetic makeup of the individual and that in its natural development it is likely to produce devastating results. Although handicapped by his limited knowledge of the syndrome, Dr. Mason did not dispute the nature of the syndrome as explained by Dr. Lynch and supported by Dr. Roffman, nor did Dr. Mason dispute the fact that the surgery falls within the standard of care for many women afflicted with this syndrome.

In light of the plain and ordinary meaning of the terms "illness," "bodily disorder," and "disease," we find that appellant's condition constitutes an illness within the meaning of the policy. Appellant's condition is a deviation from what is considered a normal, healthy physical state or structure. The abnormality or deviation from a normal state arises, in part, from the genetic makeup of the woman. The existence of this unhealthy state results in the woman's being at substantial risk of developing cancer. The recommended surgery is intended to correct that morbid state by reducing or eliminating that risk.

Although appellant's condition was not detectable by physical evidence or a physical examination, it does not necessarily follow that appellant does not suffer from an illness. The record establishes that a woman who suffers from breast-ovarian carcinoma syndrome does have a physical state which significantly deviates from the physical state of a normal, healthy woman. Specifically, appellant suffered from a different or abnormal genetic constitution which, when combined with a particular family history of hereditary cancer, significantly increases the risk of a devastating outcome.

* * *

In the present case, the medical evidence regarding the nature of breast-ovarian carcinoma syndrome persuades us that appellant suffered from a bodily disorder or disease and, thus, suffered from an illness as defined by the insurance policy. Blue Cross/Blue Shield, therefore, is not entitled to judgment as a matter of law. Moreover, we find that appellant's condition did constitute an illness within the meaning of the policy. We reverse the decision of the district court and remand the cause for further proceedings.

NOTES AND QUESTIONS

1. A study published in 2001 demonstrates that prophylactic bilateral total mastectomy for women who have a BRCA1 or BRCA2 mutation substantially reduces the risk of breast cancer. Hanne Meijers–Heijboer et al., Breast Cancer After Prophylactic Bilateral Mastectomy in Women with a BRCA1 or BRCA2 Mutation, 345 New. Eng. J. Med. 159 (2001). The decision whether to undergo such radical surgery is a difficult one, and it is not clear how many women will want to do so. It is virtually certain, however, that this study will increase the demand for prophylactic surgery. Will health insurers and health care plans have to pay for it? See generally Alexandra K. Glasier, Genetic Predispositions, Prophylactic Treatments and Private Health Insurance: Nothing Is Better Than a Good Pair of Genes, 23 Am. J.L. & Med. 45 (1997); Mark A. Rothstein & Sharona Hoffman, Genetic Testing, Genetic Medicine, and Managed Care, 34 Wake Forest L. Rev. 849 (1999).

2. A woman discovered a lump in her breast, and a biopsy indicated stromal fibrosis and confirmed that the lump was noncancerous. After her consulting specialist included in her treatment options a prophylactic mastectomy, the woman elected the surgery. Her insurer's medical director denied coverage, stating that "breast removal is not an appropriate or recommended treatment for fibrocystic disease, for 'cancer phobia,' or for a patient with a family history which is positive for hereditary breast cancer." The woman sued to compel the health plan to pay. What result? See Anderson v. HMO Nebraska, Inc., 1993 WL 61839 (Neb. Ct. App. 1993)(health plan abused its discretion in refusing the surgery), rev'd on other grounds, 505 N.W.2d 700 (Neb. 1993).

3. Physicians also need to be careful to provide patients with informed consent and a range of treatment options. In Brown v. Dibbell, 595 N.W.2d 358 (Wis. 1999), a malpractice action was brought against a physician in which the plaintiff successfully argued that her physician failed to provide her

with treatment options or adequately discuss the risks and benefits prior to her electing to undergo a prophylactic mastectomy. See Mary R. Anderlik & Elaine A. Lisko, Medicolegal and Ethical Issues in Genetic Cancer Syndromes, 18 Seminars in Surgical Oncology 339 (2000).

4. During the early 1990s a series of cases were brought challenging the denial of medical benefits under ERISA–qualified health plans for high-dose chemotherapy with autologous bone marrow transplants to treat advanced cases of breast cancer. The procedure costs in excess of $150,000, and most plans denied coverage on the ground that it was "experimental." Most of the cases upheld the denial of benefits. See, e.g., Harris v. Mutual of Omaha Companies, 992 F.2d 706 (7th Cir. 1993); Holder v. Prudential Insurance Co. of Am., 951 F.2d 89 (5th Cir. 1992). Some courts, however, held that the procedure was not experimental and ordered the plans to pay for the procedure. See, e.g., Kekis v. Blue Cross and Blue Shield of Utica-Watertown, Inc., 815 F.Supp. 571 (N.D.N.Y. 1993); Wilson v. Group Hospitalization & Medical Services, Inc., 791 F.Supp. 309 (D.D.C. 1992). Subsequently, scientific studies have shown that the procedure does not improve the survival of women with metastatic breast cancer. See Edward A. Stadtmauer et al., Conventional–Dose Chemotherapy Compared with High–Dose Chemotherapy Plus Autologous Hematopoietic Stem–Cell Transplantation for Metastatic Breast Cancer, 342 New Eng. J. Med. 1069 (2000). Do courts have the expertise to decide cases involving the coverage of various medical procedures?

III. LIFE INSURANCE

MARK A. ROTHSTEIN & YANN JOLY, GENETIC INFORMATION AND INSURANCE UNDERWRITING: CONTEMPORARY ISSUES AND APPROACHES IN THE GLOBAL ECONOMY IN HANDBOOK OF GENETICS AND SOCIETY: MAPPING THE NEW GENOMIC ERA

130–132 (Paul Atkinson, Peter Glasner, & Margaret Lock eds. 2009).

LIFE INSURANCE

Unlike health insurance, which varies based on the health care finance system of each country, life insurance is more uniform internationally in its product line and social function. Also, unlike health insurance, most life insurance is individually underwritten, thereby increasing the concern that genetic predictions of mortality risk could be used in deciding an individual's insurability. In the United States, as evidenced by public opinion surveys and the degree of legislative attention, the use of genetic information in life insurance is of less concern than its use in health insurance. Nevertheless, the possible effect of genetics on life insurance is of substantial concern in the United States, Canada, Western Europe, and throughout the developed world. For example, according to one survey, all of the UK genetic centers reported that they had patients who refused to be tested for genetic susceptibility to breast cancer because of a fear of being unable to obtain insurance.

At the present time, genetic information is not widely used by life insurers. Also, the advent of more widespread genetic testing has not changed the percentage of policy applicants offered coverage. In the United States, 88% of applicants are offered coverage at preferred or standard rates, 6% are offered coverage at higher rates, and 6% are declined. Notwithstanding the current lack of use of genetic information, the situation could change. As the focus of genetic testing shifts from rare, monogenic disorders to more common, chronic, complex disorders (e.g., asthma, diabetes, epilepsy, hypertension), the amount of genetic information in the health records of individuals will expand. This information will be disclosed to insurers via individual authorizations in the process of medical underwriting. Furthermore, individual concerns about possible genetic discrimination already operate to discourage some at-risk individuals from undergoing genetic testing.

* * *

It is too soon to tell the effects of genetic information on consumer behavior. A source of great frustration for policy analysts and policy makers is the virtual absence of peer-reviewed research. One of the only empirical studies in the United States suggests that women who learn of their increased risk of breast cancer do not attempt to purchase additional life insurance. It is also too soon to tell the effect of legislative or voluntary industry practices on commercial activity. For example, it has been asserted that no British insurers "have endured financial hardship in the 3–5 years of the moratorium [on using genetic tests for life insurance for mortgage cover below £500,000]". It is often noted that life insurance in the United Kingdom is necessary to obtain a residential mortgage; therefore it is asserted to be a different product, presumably more immune from pressures of adverse selection. Nevertheless, it is the effect on insurers, not the reason for seeking coverage, that determines whether underwriting practices are undermined by individuals' knowledge of their mortality risks.

The ethical and policy issues depend on the social function or "moral mission" of life insurance. If life insurance is considered a purely commercial transaction or a type of investment for estate building purposes, then a strong case can be made that limitations should not be placed on any type of medical underwriting so long as it is actuarially sound and the confidentiality of personal health information is scrupulously maintained. On the other hand, if providing a death benefit to survivors or ensuring the availability of a residential mortgage is deemed an essential public policy, then the government would be justified in regulating the process and criteria for obtaining life insurance coverage.

J. ALEXANDER LOWDEN, GENETIC RISKS AND MORTALITY RATES, IN GENETICS AND LIFE INSURANCE: MEDICAL UNDERWRITING AND SOCIAL POLICY

95–98 (Mark A. Rothstein ed. 2004).

WHY WOULD LIFE INSURERS CONSIDER GENETIC TESTING?

Before offering coverage to an applicant, life insurers attempt to identify factors that may shorten the person's usual life expectancy at a given age. If identifiable risks exist, the underwriter uses actuarial and medical information to calculate life expectancy and determine an appropriate premium. Genetic tests may offer a means to identify future health risks and potentially could improve those calculations. At the present time most genetic tests for predisposition to disease lack valid actuarial information. The likelihood of developing a disease when a mutation in a particular gene is identified is often uncertain. More important, the risk may be greatly altered in the future as we learn how to use genetic knowledge to lower it.

There are many different types of life insurance products and their particular features play different roles in determining the price of each one. Whereas most of the cost of insurance can be determined from experience, actuarial tables, and corporate business practices, expected survival varies with the state of health of the applicant and consideration of future health risks. Because life expectancy is defined as the age at which half the insureds will have died, it is a moving target that increases with the age of the individual at the time of application. To estimate an individual's life expectancy, underwriters consider medical history, current health status, laboratory test results, family history, and lifestyle.

Risk is increased in applicants who have not experienced a clinical event, such as myocardial infarction, but who have evidence of risk in their medical status. Obesity and untreated hypertension trigger an added premium because they are associated with early mortality. Some laboratory tests may also indicate increased risk. Elevated cholesterol, indication of hepatitis C infection, or early evidence of diabetes can be uncovered in people who are otherwise in apparent good health but who, on the basis of a laboratory test showing such a disorder, can be expected to have a shortened life expectancy. Their insurance premiums must reflect the added risk.

The primary goal of medical underwriting is therefore to anticipate the impact of health history and current health status, including laboratory tests, on survival. Unanticipated events do occur. That is one of the reasons for purchasing insurance, but underwriters try to determine what is likely to happen to an applicant and price a policy accordingly. Genetic testing brings a somewhat different aspect to this picture. It potentially provides information about risks that are not anticipated and that may be unrelated to medical or family history.

Causes of death vary with age. Accidental death or trauma is a major factor in younger people, heart disease in middle and later life, and cancer in older people. Almost all mortality, however, has a genetic basis (table 5.1). Our knowledge about how mutations are linked to disease has escalated in a logarithmic fashion in the past few years. The HGP will provide many new insights into mechanisms of disease and will continue to identify genes associated with early mortality.

TABLE 5.1

Genetic basis	Number of deaths/100,000 lives
Chromosomal	380
Single gene defects	2,000
Somatic mutations	24,000
Multifactorial disease	64,600

Some genetic tests could possibly bring changes to underwriting decisions. In a person with no family history and no medical history, a series of tests might be able to predict an increased risk of unanticipated disease. Will, or should, insurers have the right to this information? How will they use it if they do acquire it? To approach the answers to these questions, let us consider knowledge of some common genetic diseases that may lead to early mortality in adults. People with many of these disorders can be underwritten and, for the most part, offered insurance at affordable rates. The secret to what might appear speculative underwriting practice is in knowing the risk and doing something to mitigate possible loss.

Making lifestyle changes or therapeutic decisions may not alter one's genetic risk today, but we live in a world in which scientific discoveries occur at an ever-increasing rate. If an individual has a fatal genetic mutation today, will developments lead to new methods of management or treatment in the next ten years? Will the mutation have been expressed before new therapy is available? The HGP was not devised to bring new genetic tests to market, but to use genetic information to improve health. In time, people who have genetic tests and know they have certain health risks will be better off than their untested peers for, with knowledge, will come the ability to prevent mutant gene expression. Thus, predicting future scientific developments as well as health risks based on new information makes medical underwriting extremely difficult.

CATHLEEN D. ZICK ET AL., GENETIC TESTING, ADVERSE SELECTION, AND THE DEMAND FOR LIFE INSURANCE

93 Am. J. Med. Genetics 29, 29–32, 35–38 (2000).

Both sides of the insurance and genetic testing debate have made assertions without extensive supporting data. In this paper, we capitalize on survey information from two groups of women to assess insurers' claims regarding consumer behavior. Specifically, we examine whether or not consumers exploit the information asymmetry created when genetic test results are kept private. The first group in our study is comprised of women in a large kindred whose members are at risk of carrying a specific mutation of the BRCA1 gene that dramatically increases their lifetime risk of developing breast and ovarian cancer. These women have been tested for this mutation and they know their genetic test results. Their insurance companies do not have this information unless these women choose to reveal their test results to them. We separate the tested women into two sub-samples: those who tested positive for the mutation (carriers) and those who tested negative (non-carriers). The second group of women in the study is a sample of the general public who have not undergone testing for the BRCA1 gene mutation. The demand for life insurance among the tested and non-tested groups of women is estimated. Comparisons across the tested and non-tested women allow us to assess the potential behavioral implications of asymmetric information in the life insurance market attributable to a genetic test for a BRCA1 gene mutation.

* * *

In general, several conditions must be met for adverse selection to occur: (1) there must be heterogeneity of risk among consumers; (2) insurers must not be able to detect (appropriately price) this risk; (3) consumers must have access to information that allows them to predict their personal risk better than insurers; and (4) consumers must seek and obtain additional insurance coverage based on this information. These conditions, in combination, imply that high-risk consumers (i.e., asymptomatic individuals who test positive for a gene mutation associated with a serious illness) will have greater demand for life insurance than low-risk consumers (i.e., those who test negative for a gene mutation associated with a serious illness) and in the analysis that follows, we test this proposition.

* * *

Standard economic models of life insurance markets presume that consumers know more about their own risks than do insurers. Life insurers respond to this information asymmetry by categorizing insurance applicants into risk pools based on observable characteristics that are highly correlated with actual mortality risk. Thus, when completing life insurance applications, consumers must typically provide information on such attributes as age, occupation, marital status, personal and family health histories, and personal smoking history. Consumers classified in the higher risk groups are then charged higher prices for a given level of coverage than are consumers in lower risk groups. The premium difference reflects the higher risk of mortality that members of these former groups face. In this context, life insurance company representatives argue that consumer knowledge of genetic predisposition to potentially life-threatening diseases must be shared with insurance companies so that policies may be appropriately underwritten.

In the context of our study, a rather straightforward test for evidence of adverse selection is to compare the demand for life insurance among otherwise comparable respondents who test positive, respondents who test negative, and respondents who are not tested for the BRCA1 gene mutation. We estimate five different models that examine how knowledge of genetic test results influences life insurance demand where demand is measured by: (1) the likelihood of having life insurance; (2) the number of life insurance policies purchased; (3) the amount of life insurance carried in the respondent's primary policy; (4) the total amount of life insurance carried; and (5) a combination of the likelihood of having insurance and the amount of insurance carried among those who choose to purchase a policy.

Typically, life insurance purchases are thought to be a function of: (1) household income; (2) age; (3) the presence or absence of minor children in the home; (4) marital status; (5) education; and (6) employment status.

We include three key regressors in our model to test for the presence of adverse selection. They are family history of breast or ovarian cancer, genetic test status, and involvement in the early BRCA1 research. A family history of breast or ovarian cancer raises the risk of mortality and thereby the demand for life insurance. But the relationship between family history and the demand for life insurance may be tempered if the premiums charged to such high risk individuals are adjusted upward by insurers (that in turn would decrease the quantity purchased). If the insurance company does not use family history in its underwriting procedures, then the potential for adverse selection will continue to exist and we would predict that the coefficient associated with family breast/ovarian cancer history would be positive and statistically significant with respect to the demand for life insurance.

Testing positive for the BRCA1 gene mutation also increases mortality risk. But, in our sample, a tested respondent knows the result whereas the insurance company does not. As a consequence, there is the potential for consumers to exploit this information asymmetry and purchase additional life insurance at rates that are below what would be actuarially justified. If we find a positive statistically significant coefficient associated with testing positive relative to the untested group, this would be supportive of the adverse selection hypothesis. If we find that individuals who test negative have lower insurance coverage than the untested group, this would further support the adverse selection hypothesis.

* * *

The variables that test for the presence of adverse selection in this final specification again show little support for the contention that consumers are exploiting their information asymmetry. The test status dummy variables are always statistically insignificant. Moreover, the coefficients associated with participating in the early BRCA1 research are *negative* and statistically significant in both equations. This is opposite of what would be expected if these consumers who participated in the early

BRCA1 research were capitalizing on their informational advantage. Finally, we find moderate evidence of interactions between price and family cancer history (P < 0.10) suggesting that those with one or more first-degree relatives who have had cancer may be less sensitive to price increases than are those individuals who have no first degree relatives who have had cancer.

Our discussion must be prefaced with a cautionary note. The analyses done here make use of a somewhat homogeneous sample. All of the study participants are white women and most identify themselves as being active members of the Church of Jesus Christ of Latter Day Saints. The impact of asymmetric information on the demand for life insurance may vary by gender, ethnicity, and personal life style (as proxied by religious affiliation).

We also focused on the testing for one gene mutation that is associated with two potentially fatal illnesses, breast and ovarian cancer. Learning the results of a test for a gene mutation that is associated with a non-life-threatening disease (e.g., the sickle cell trait) versus a gene mutation that leads to the contraction of a disease that is always fatal (E.g., Huntington disease) may have a different behavioral impact than the gene mutation studied here.

* * *

Our research shows that the women who test positive for the BRCA1 gene mutation do not capitalize on their informational advantage by purchasing more life insurance than those women who have not undergone genetic testing. Thus, life insurers' claims that consumers will use information about their genetic test results to engage in adverse selection is not supported here.

Why are women who carry the potentially life threatening BRCA1 gene mutation not exploiting their informational advantage in the market for life insurance? One possible answer is that positive genetic test results may simply serve to confirm something that these women *and* their insurers have known all along based on their family histories. If learning that they have tested positive simply confirms the suspicions of many of these women, it may have little behavioral impact on their life insurance purchasing behavior. Consistent with this argument is the research finding that women who test positive for the BRCA1 mutation experience little short-run change in psychological distress between the pre-and post-test interviews because for many it only serves to affirm what they already suspected.

Alternatively, the reason we observe little evidence of adverse selection may be because our follow-up period of one-year is too short. Women who have learned that they carry the BRCA1 mutation may be preoccupied with more immediate concerns such as what they can do to reduce their risk of breast or ovarian cancer. Indeed, we find that 87% of the women in K2082 [the kindred] who test positive are contemplating undergoing surgery to remove their ovaries (17% for breasts) to reduce their cancer risk one year after testing. Behavioral changes regarding life insurance may be delayed while these women work through the more immediate and very serious health care choices that they face.

* * *

Policymakers should be cautious as they move forward with the legislative debate on genetic testing and life insurance underwriting practices. They should view with some skepticism the contention that the denial of access to genetic test results (and hence the denial of their use in underwriting) will threaten the insurance industry's economic viability in the immediate future. We find no evidence to support this position. Indeed, our findings suggest that if insurers continue to use family cancer history in their underwriting process, they have little need to worry about the impact that genetic tests for cancer-related gene mutations will have on consumer demand for life insurance.

NOTES AND QUESTIONS

1. Zick's article reports on the first empirical study of the effect of genetic testing on life insurance purchasing behavior. Although the limitations of the study are noted, it certainly raises the question of the degree to which adverse selection can be expected to actually take place.

2. Is there a difference between requiring that insurance companies have access to the results of genetic tests already performed and allowing insurers to require genetic testing as a condition of coverage? Should different rules apply for different coverage amounts? Should individuals be allowed to use their "good results" on genetic tests to obtain life insurance at lower rates?

3. Would it be lawful for a life insurance company to tell an applicant that because she has tested positive for a BRCA1 mutation that she is not eligible for life insurance unless she has a prophylactic mastectomy?

4. Lowden suggests that genetic tests are no different from other medical tests for underwriting purposes. Should the insurance company have to demonstrate the actuarial significance of any medical criteria used? In theory, state unfair trade practices laws already have such a requirement, but, in practice, insurers are given great deference by state insurance commissioners and the courts. Should insurers be required to prove that adverse selection will occur if they are denied access to predictive health information or predictive genetic test results?

VERMONT. STAT. ANN. TIT. 18, CH. 217
(ENACTED 1997).

§ 9331. Definitions

For purposes of this chapter:

* * *

(2) "DNA" means deoxyribonucleic acid and "RNA" means ribonucleic acid.

* * *

(6) "Genetic information" means the results of "genetic testing" contained in any report, interpretation, evaluation, or other record thereof.

(A) "Genetic testing" means a test, examination or analysis that is diagnostic or predictive of a particular heritable disease or disorder and is of:

(i) a human chromosome or gene;

(ii) human DNA or RNA; or

(iii) a human genetically encoded protein.

(B) The test for human genetically encoded protein referred to in subdivision (A)(iii) of this subdivision shall be generally accepted in the scientific and medical communities as being specifically determinative for the presence or absence of a mutation, alteration, or deletion of a gene or chromosome.

(C) For the purposes of sections 9332 and 9333 of this title, as they apply to insurers, section 9334 of this title, and section 4727 of Title 8, and notwithstanding any language in this section to the contrary, "genetic testing" does not include:

(i) a test, examination or analysis which reports on an individual's current condition unless such a test, examination or analysis is designed or intended to be specifically determinative for the presence or absence of a mutation, alteration, or deletion of a gene or chromosome; or

(ii) a test, examination or analysis of a human chromosome or gene, of human DNA or RNA, or of a human genetically encoded protein that is diagnostic or predictive of a particular heritable disease or disorder, if, in accordance with generally accepted standards in the medical community, the potential presence or absence of a mutation, alteration or deletion of a gene or chromosome has already manifested itself by causing a disease, disorder or medical condition or by symptoms highly predictive of the disease, disorder or medical condition.

(8) "Insurance" means a policy of insurance regulated under Title 8, offered or issued in this state, including health, life, disability and long-term care insurance policies, hospital and medical service corporation service contracts, and health maintenance organization benefit plans.

* * *

§ 9334. Genetic testing as a condition of insurance coverage

(a) No policy of insurance offered for delivery or issued in this state shall be underwritten or conditioned on the basis of:

(1) any requirement or agreement of the individual to undergo genetic testing; or

(2) the results of genetic testing of a member of the individual's family.

(b) A violation of this section shall be considered an unfair method of competition or unfair or deceptive act or practice in the business of insurance in violation of section 4724 of Title 8.

(c) In addition to other remedies available under the law, a person who violates this section shall be subject to the enforcement provisions available under Title 8.

§ 9335. Remedies

(a) Any person who intentionally violates section 9333 or subsection 9334(a) of this chapter shall be imprisoned not more than one year or fined not more than $10,000.00, or both.

(b) Any person aggrieved by a violation of this chapter may bring an action for civil damages, including punitive damages, equitable relief, including restraint of prohibited acts, restitution of wages or other benefits and reinstatement, costs, and reasonable attorney's fees and other appropriate relief.

NOTES AND QUESTIONS

1. Although most states have enacted legislation addressing genetic discrimination in health insurance, only a handful of states have enacted legislation dealing with other forms of insurance.

2. What effects, if any, do you think the Vermont law will have on the availability of insurance in the state, the willingness of individuals to undergo genetic testing in the state, or the price structure of insurance in the state?

3. Do you think that criminal sanctions are appropriate for violations?

CHABNER v. UNITED OF OMAHA LIFE INSURANCE CO.

225 F.3d 1042 (9th Cir. 2000).

HUG, J.

* * *

Howard Chabner suffers from a progressive condition called facioscapulohumeral muscular dystrophy (FSH MD), a rare form of muscular dystrophy. The condition has confined Chabner to a wheelchair since 1991 and has caused "marked wasting" of his extremities. Chabner takes medication to help control the condition, and his doctor administers annual electrocardiograms to detect any cardiomyopathy that may arise.

On May 3, 1993, Chabner, who was 35 years old at the time, applied to United for whole life insurance. United forwarded Chabner's application to an underwriter who had experience in underwriting insurance policies for applicants with muscular dystrophy, but not with FSH MD. United possessed no internally developed actuarial data for people with FSH MD, and so its underwriter turned to external sources to estimate Chabner's mortality risk. The underwriter, who was not a doctor, arranged to have Chabner examined by a paramedic, reviewed Chabner's medical records, and consulted two underwriting source materials: the Cologne Life Reinsurance Company's "Life Underwriting Manual" ("Cologne manual"); and "Medical Selection of Life Risks" by R.D.C. Brackenridge and W. John Elder ("Brackenridge manual"). After reviewing these materials, the underwriter authorized a policy with a "Table 6" rating, which corresponded to a mortality rate of 150 percent above standard.

United offered Chabner a $100,000 whole life policy at a cost of $1,076 per year. Of the $1,076 annual premium, $305.44 was applied to the cost of insurance, and the remainder was invested in the policy's cash accumulation and surrender values. By contrast, even though the annual premium for a standard whole life policy (without an increased mortality rating) would have been the same $1,076, only $155.44 of that annual premium would have been applied to the cost of insurance, which would result in an additional $150 being invested in the policy's cash accumulation and surrender values each year.

Chabner accepted the policy, but inquired about the reason for his nonstandard premium. United's Vice President and Senior Medical Director of Underwriting sent Chabner a letter attempting to explain the nonstandard rating. In the letter, United acknowledged that FSH MD "has only a small effect on mortality" and stated that it reduced life expectancy by four years for a non-smoking man of his age. Unsatisfied, Chabner wrote United on two more occasions to inquire why his premium was 96.5% greater than standard if his condition had only a small effect on mortality. United did not respond, and Chabner filed this action.

Chabner filed his original complaint in California Superior Court on January 3, 1995, alleging violations of California's Insurance Code, its Business and Professions Code, its Unruh Civil Rights Act, and common law fraud. After United removed the case to federal court based on diversity jurisdiction, Chabner amended his complaint to add a claim under the ADA. Chabner sought class certification and moved for summary judgment on all but his fraud claim. The district court denied class certification, but granted Chabner's motion for summary judgment. The district court held that the ADA applies to insurance underwriting, that California law provides Chabner with a private cause of action for the alleged violation of the state insurance code, and that United's actions in this case violated the ADA, the California Insurance Code and the Business and Professions Code, and the Unruh Civil Rights Act.

* * *

I. THE ADA

Chabner alleges that the nonstandard premium that United charged him for his insurance policy violated the ADA. Recently, however, we held that although Title III of the ADA requires an insurance office to be physically accessible to the disabled, it does not address the terms of the policies the insurance companies sell. See Weyer v. Twentieth Century Fox Film Corp., 198 F.3d 1104, 1115 (9th Cir.2000). We therefore hold that United did not violate the ADA by offering Chabner a nonstandard policy.

Title III of the ADA provides: "No individual shall be discriminated against on the basis of disability in the full and equal enjoyment of the goods, services, facilities, privileges, advantages, or accommodations of any place of public accommodation by any person who owns, leases (or leases to), or operates a place of public accommodation." 42 U.S.C. § 12181 (a). The ADA also includes a "safe harbor" provision, which says that "[the ADA] shall not be construed to prohibit or restrict . . . an insurer . . . from underwriting risks, classifying risks, or administering such risks that are based on or not inconsistent with State law. . . . " 42 U.S.C. § 12201(c).

Weyer, which was handed down after the district court's order was issued, concerned the question of whether an insurance company that administers an employer-provided disability plan was a "place of public accommodation" under Title III of the Americans with Disabilities Act. We found that the term "place of public accommodation" required a connection between the good or service complained of and an actual physical place. As we explained: "[c]ertainly, an insurance office is a place where the public generally has access. But this case is not about such matters as ramps and elevators so that disabled people can get to the office. The dispute in this case, over terms of a contract that the insurer markets through an employer, is not what Congress addressed in the public accommodations provisions." In adopting this approach, we followed the Third and Sixth Circuits, each of which agreed that an insurance company that administered an employer-provided disability plan was not a "place of public accommodation" under the ADA because the employees received their benefits through employment, and not through a public accommodation. See Parker v. Metropolitan Life Ins. Co., 121 F.3d 1006, 1010–12 (6th Cir.1997) (en banc); Ford v. Schering–Plough Corp., 145 F.3d 601, 612–13 (3d Cir.1998). Taking these cases at face value, we are led to conclude that a similar distinction between "access" and "content" applies to this case. Here, we reiterate our observation, set forth in Weyer, that "an insurance office must be physically accessible to the disabled but need not provide insurance that treats the disabled equally with the non-disabled." Therefore, we do not uphold the district court's decision based upon the ADA.

II. CALIFORNIA LAW

A. Business and Professions Code section 17200 and Insurance Code section 10144

In his complaint Chabner alleged violations of California Insurance Code section 10144, and California Business and Professions Code section 17200. Insurance Code Section 10144 provides, in relevant part: "No insurer issuing [life insurance] shall refuse to insure, or refuse to continue to insure . . . or charge a different rate for the same coverage solely because of a physical or mental impairment, except where the refusal . . . or rate differential is based on sound actuarial principles or is related to actual and reasonably anticipated experience. . . ." Cal. Ins. Code § 10144. This statutory provision would have prohibited United from charging Chabner a nonstandard premium due to his FSH MD, unless the premium was based on sound actuarial principles or was related to actual and reasonably anticipated experience. However, it is unclear whether this insurance code section provides Chabner with a private cause of action. The parties did not address this issue in their briefs, and therefore we do not address it.

Chabner, however, also claimed violations of California Business and Professions Code section 17200. Section 17200 is part of the Unfair Competition Law, Cal. Bus. & Prof. Code §§ 17200–18209, and provides, in relevant part, that "unfair competition shall mean and include any unlawful, unfair or fraudulent business act or practice." Cal. Bus. & Prof. Code § 17200. Private causes of action for violations of Business and Professions Code section 17200 are authorized by Business and Professions Code section 17204. The district court held that Insurance Code section 10144 may be used to define the contours of a private cause of action under Business and Professions Code section 17200. We agree.

* * *

As applied to this case, the district court was correct in holding that Chabner could maintain a cause of action under section 17200 for United's alleged violation of section 10144. Setting the premium for a life insurance policy can quite "properly be called a business practice." Also, United's alleged misconduct (charging Chabner a discriminatory premium that is neither actuarially sound nor based on reasonably anticipated experience) would run afoul of section 10144, if proven. Accordingly, the prerequisites for "borrowing" a violation of section 10144 and treating it as a violation of section 17200 exist in this case.

* * *

B.   *The Unruh Civil Rights Act*

Chabner also claims that United's actions violated California's Unruh Civil Rights Act. The Unruh Civil Rights Act provides, in relevant part, that "[a]ll persons within the jurisdiction of this state are free and equal, and no matter what their . . . disability are entitled to the full and equal accommodations, advantages, facilities, privileges, or services in all business establishments of every kind whatsoever." Cal. Civ. Code § 51. The Act also provides that a violation of the ADA is also a violation of the Unruh Act. Cal. Civ. Code § 51. The district court held that because

United had violated the ADA, it also violated the Unruh Act. In light of our decision in Weyer v. Twentieth Century Fox Film Corp., 198 F.3d 1104 (9th Cir.2000), as discussed above, the district court's decision cannot be upheld on this basis.

We may, however, "affirm the district court on a ground not selected by the district judge so long as the record fairly supports such an alternative disposition." Chabner, and the State of California as amicus curiae, argue that United's actions violated the Unruh Act, regardless of whether they also violated the ADA. We agree that Chabner's allegations support an Unruh Civil Rights Act claim independently of the alleged ADA violation.

The Unruh Civil Rights Act works to ensure that all persons receive the full accommodations of any business within California, regardless of the person's disabilities. Cal. Civ. Code § 51. The insurance business is subject to the Unruh Civil Rights Act. Cal. Ins. Code § 1861.03 (a). Unruh prevents more than discrimination in access to a business or its services; it also prevents discrimination in the form of pricing differentials. However, disparities in treatment and pricing that are reasonable do not violate the Unruh Act. The critical question, therefore, is whether the nonstandard premium United charged Chabner was "reasonable."

To determine whether the nonstandard premium was reasonable, we are again informed by Insurance Code section 10144. Section 10144 prevents an insurer from charging "a different rate for the same coverage solely because of a physical or mental impairment," unless the "rate differential is based on sound actuarial principles or is related to actual and reasonably anticipated experience." Cal. Ins. Code § 10144. If Chabner's nonstandard premium was based on "sound actuarial principles" or "actual and reasonably anticipated experience," then it would certainly be reasonable for purposes of the Unruh Act because it would have been specifically allowed by statute. By contrast, if the premium was not based on one of the section 10144 prongs, then there would be no reasonable justification for it, and in that case we may consider the nonstandard premium to be arbitrary and a violation of the Unruh Act. Therefore, we hold that if United violated Insurance Code section 10144, it also violated the Unruh Act, but if section 10144 authorized United's actions, then Chabner's Unruh Act claim necessarily fails as well.

* * *

D. *Summary Judgment*

* * *

The parties argue at length about the proper definitions of "sound actuarial principles" or "actual and reasonably anticipated experience." For example, they dispute whether an insurance company must base its rating decisions on "hard data" that is specific to each person, or whether it may take into account more generalized estimates of mortality when it lacks specific data. We need not resolve the debate about exactly what can justify a mortality decision as actuarially sound or related to actual and reasonably anticipated experience, for in this case there is no question that United's mortality rating was arbitrarily high.

The mortality rating United assigned to Chabner was not actuarially sound. United assigned Chabner a "Table 6" rating, which corresponds with a 150% mortality rating. The 150% mortality rating, in turn, reflects an estimate that Chabner's life expectancy is nine to eleven years less than that of a standard male non-smoker. United points to the Brackenridge manual, which recommended a mortality rating of 75%—150%, and the Cologne manual, which recommended a mortality rating of 300%, to argue that the 150% mortality rating was justified. However, United's own admissions subvert its reliance on these manuals. In his letter to Chabner, Dr. Robert Quinn, the Vice President and Senior Medical Director of Underwriting at United, admitted that FSH MD "has only a small effect on mortality." Moreover, Dr. Quinn estimated Chabner's life expectancy to be only four years less than standard. Even assuming that the estimate of a four year decrease in life expectancy is correct, it does not justify a rating that estimates a nine to eleven year decrease. Accordingly, by United's own admission, the 150% mortality rating (i.e., the estimate of a nine to eleven year decrease in life expectancy) was not actuarially sound.

Nor does the second prong of section 10144, which allows rate differentials if they are based on actual and reasonably anticipated experience, provide refuge for the 150% mortality rating. United's underwriter handling Chabner's application had experience with muscular dystrophy, but not with Chabner's rare fascioscapulohumeral muscular dystrophy. She thus had no "actual experience" with underwriting applicants with FSH MD. Moreover, she was not a doctor, she did not have a doctor examine Chabner, and she did not have a doctor review Chabner's medical records. Thus, the underwriter's basis for "reasonably anticipated experience" in evaluating an applicant with FSH MD was virtually nonexistent, especially considering that Dr. Quinn, who was a medical doctor and who was familiar with FSH MD, subsequently admitted that FSH MD has little effect on mortality. Therefore, viewing the evidence in the light most favorable to United, we hold that no reasonable jury could find that the 150% mortality rating was either based on sound actuarial principles or related to actual and reasonably anticipated experience. Section 10144 did not justify the discriminatory premium, and summary judgment on Chabner's Business and Professions Code section 17200 claim, and on his Unruh Civil Rights Act claim, was therefore proper.

* * *

Conclusion

For the foregoing reasons, the district court's grant of summary judgment for Appellee Chabner, and its judgment ordering Appellant United to modify the insurance policy, are AFFIRMED.

1.   The Ninth Circuit's holding that Title III of the ADA does not permit individuals to challenge the substantive provisions of insurance contracts is in accord with the weight of authority. See, e.g., Pallozzi v. Allstate Life Insurance Co., 198 F.3d 28 (2d Cir.1999). See generally Maxwell J. Mehlman et al., When Do Health Care Decisions Discriminate Against Persons with Disabilities?, 22 J. Health Pol., Pol'y & L. 1385 (1997).

2.   State unfair trade practice laws or other regulation of insurance practices exist in every state, although the remedies and the interpretation of the statutory provisions differ widely. Who should have the burden of proof with regard to underwriting decision making? What degree of deference, if any, should be given to the insurance company?

3.   The most commonly raised issue regarding genetics and life insurance is that actuarial fairness does not necessarily equate with moral fairness when allocating essential goods. *Chabner* raises a second concern, that the medical underwriting will not be based on sound actuarial principles. Which of the two issues is the more vexing problem? Why?

MARK A. ROTHSTEIN, POLICY RECOMMENDATIONS, GENETICS AND LIFE INSURANCE: MEDICAL UNDERWRITING AND SOCIAL POLICY

252–261 (Mark A. Rothstein ed. 2004).

1.   Establish a moratorium on requiring genetic testing and use of genetic information.

A moratorium could be imposed legislatively or voluntarily by individual insurers. There is no agreement on the length of time for the moratorium, although five years is frequently mentioned. Moratoria already have been adopted in some countries, including France, Germany, and the United Kingdom.

The theory behind a moratorium is that scientific and policy issues will be clarified in the next few years and appropriate policies can then be determined. From a scientific standpoint, this is wishful thinking. Although the relationship between some genotypes and mortality risks may be better established, the basic scientific issue—use of genetic information when its actuarial significance is not definitely established—will remain. As scientists accumulate better data on some associations, other associations will be suspected and investigated. Thus, the uncertainty simply will be shifted to a different group of genetic variations. With regard to policy, the question of the degree to which life insurance underwriting and pricing should be regulated to promote social considerations will remain the same.

* * *

2. Prohibit genetic testing and using genetic information.

At first glance, prohibiting insurers from requiring genetic testing and using genetic information would appear to be the most effective way to "avoid the creation of an uninsurable underclass of individuals." By prohibiting use of genetic information, however, family health histories and other traditional measures of risk assessment also would be prohibited. As a result, major changes would be required in the way life insurance is underwritten and priced.

3. Prohibit insurers from requiring genetic testing, but permit use of genetic information.

Under this option individuals would not be compelled to undergo insurer-ordered genetic testing as a condition of applying for life insurance. Insurers, however, could use the results of genetic tests already performed and in a person's medical record. This compromise option raises problems for both insurance companies and consumers. For insurers, individuals who were tested in research studies, anonymously, or off the record would be able to apply for life insurance without any way for underwriters to know of the results of the test. This is a recipe for adverse selection. Individuals, however, would not do well under this approach either. They would be deterred from having genetic testing in the health care setting, where it would be most beneficial, because the results would be placed in their medical record. Moreover, even without such test results, persons at increased risk because of family health history would still be subject to higher rates or denial of coverage.

Advocates of prohibiting life insurers from requiring genetic testing also must deal with another fundamental issue. If companies are permitted to require some medical tests (e.g., cholesterol, HIV, hepatitis B and C), on what basis should genetic tests be treated differently? Assuming the tests are predictive, is there something inherent in the fact that they are genetic suggest they should not be used?

* * *

4. Establish a maximum amount of coverage that can be obtained without genetic testing or genetic information.

Establishment of maximum levels of coverage without genetic test results of other genetic information (sometimes referred to as a "safe harbor" or a "monetary threshold" approach) is popular in Western Europe, and some attempts have been made to introduce similar legislation in the United States. In Europe, however, life insurance has a different social role, because it is essential to have life insurance to obtain a mortgage. It is a different product with a different public interest at stake.

In European countries that adopted this approach, about $100,000 is the lowest level of life insurance coverage available without genetic testing or consideration of genetic information. With the average policy in the United States in 2000 of $134,800, a substantial percentage of the market would be included under a comparable proviso. In practice, establishing

maximum levels of coverage without genetic information would be difficult. First, it would be necessary to define "genetic." Does the prohibition
apply only to genetic testing or does it also apply to genetic information?
As discussed previously, either definition raises serious problems. Second,
it would be necessary to have some way of determining whether people
had policies from more than one insurance company so that those at risk
could not obtain a series of policies below the maximum. Third, some
market adjustments in pricing would be necessary. For example, if companies could not consider information in underwriting policies of $100,000 or
less, the rates for a $110,000 policy for a low-risk person (using genetic
information) would likely be lower than for a $100,000 policy in the all-
applicant (not using genetic information) pool. This would encourage
individuals to undergo genetic testing and then apply for the higher
amount if they tested negative and the lower amount if they tested
positive. This would increase the price disparity between the genetically
underwritten and nonunderwritten pools in a spiraling fashion. Thus,
additional regulation or subsidies would be necessary to adjust the pricing
structure.

5.   Prohibit insurance companies from offering preferred rates based
on the results of genetic tests or genetic information.

One scenario in which life insurance companies may be compelled by
market forces to require genetic testing or use of genetic information is
the following. Company A begins to offer a "good gene" discount of 25%
on its life insurance to individuals who voluntarily take ten selected
genetic tests and are found not to have any deleterious mutations. Low-
risk individuals will flock to company A for the discount. Company B,
having lost some of its low-risk insureds, will then be forced either to raise
rates for remaining policy holders and new applicants or also use genetic
tests. This could quickly put pressure on other companies to do the same
and, eventually, the rest of the industry would become segmented by
whether genetic information was used.

Although it is not clear that the science would currently justify such
an adjustment in the pricing structure merely based on the absence of ten
deleterious mutations, the possibility of at least some companies attempting this approach cannot be dismissed. To prevent this from occurring,
legislation could be enacted to prohibit life insurance companies from
using the results of genetic tests or genetic information to sell policies at
preferred rates (below standard). This is now expressly permitted under
Indiana law, whereas Oregon prohibits the use of favorable genetic information to induce the sale of insurance.

* * *

6.   Permit individuals to use results of genetic tests to obtain coverage at regular rates.

An insurance company that is not permitted to use results of genetic
tests would be forced to charge higher premiums to an individual who had

a familial risk of a serious illness, but who had undergone genetic testing and learned that he or she did not inherit the lethal mutation. To prevent this from occurring, it has been suggested (and actually enacted in some states) that people should be allowed to use the results of genetic tests if they are favorable.

To prevent the assessment spiral from occurring, as well as coercing individuals into genetic testing, the individual should be permitted to obtain coverage at the regular rate he or she would be offered if genetic information were not considered. Thus, genetic information could not be the basis for a preferred rate, but a preferred rate could be offered to someone with a negative genetic test who would otherwise qualify for a preferred rate for other reasons, such as non-smoking and health lifestyle.

* * *

7. Prohibit use of predictive testing or predictive information in group life insurance.

About one-third of all life insurance policies are purchased by employers or associations or as credit insurance under group policies. In theory, the group is underwritten, but individuals in the group are not. Nevertheless, there is some degree of medical underwriting in group life insurance, depending on the size and nature of the group.

Legislatures should prohibit use of predictive medical information in group health insurance as part of the federal Health Insurance Portability and Accountability Act of 1996. Such a measure might increase the price of group life insurance slightly, but only to the extent that underwriting takes place in group policies.

* * *

8. Establish high-risk life insurance pools.

Previous options attempted to make adjustments to the current system of medical underwriting to prevent insurers from considering an individual's genetically increased risk of illness. If the ultimate goal of legislation dealing with genetic (or predictive) information is to provide an opportunity for high-risk individuals to purchase life insurance at affordable rates, it is better to confront the issue directly. The most likely way of ensuring access to life insurance is to create high-risk pools. These are already established in various other insurance product lines, including health, auto, and workers' compensation insurance. In the United States, if public policy supports taxpayer subsidization of flood insurance for beachfront vacation homes, some subsidies should be possible for life insurance for high-risk individuals.

NOTES AND QUESTIONS

1. Which, if any, of the proposals do you favor? Why? Are there any proposals that would be worse than the status quo? Which proposals do you think are the most and least politically viable?

2. In addition to these "substantive" proposals, Rothstein proposes the following procedural reforms: (1) regulate the use of predictive medical tests; (2) regulate testing laboratories; (3) regulate medical decision makers; (4) require informed consent for all medical examinations and tests; (5) require life insurers to disclose the medical basis of an adverse underwriting decision; and (7) prohibit use of medical information across insurance product lines or to underwrite family members. Which, if any, of these proposals do you think would be valuable?

IV. DISABILITY INSURANCE

Disability insurance policies pay a percentage of the wages of the insured individual (often about 70% to reflect after-tax income) in the event of short-term or long-term disability. Disability is tied to the ability to work in one's chosen profession and, not surprisingly, most disability policies are issued through employer-sponsored groups. Risk selection and pricing is done on a group basis, and the percentage of income replacement offered and premiums charged are influenced by the nature of the employment and the claims experience of the employer. Some employment-based group policies offer individuals a "buy up" option whereby they can purchase additional coverage. These supplements may be individually underwritten or they may be offered on a group-rate basis, where the pricing structure takes into account the likelihood for adverse selection.

Individual policies represent about 12 percent of all policies sold. Because of the cost, these policies are mostly bought by self-employed individuals and professionals such as lawyers and physicians. As with other individual policies (e.g. life, health), there is individual underwriting.

There are three main government disability insurance programs. Workers' compensation provides income replacement for workers who are injured or become ill from workplace exposures. Except for a few categories of workers, such as federal employees, employee eligibility, benefit levels, and administration are determined by the states. Social Security Disability Insurance (SSDI) provides disability payments to workers (and survivors of disabled workers) who qualify for Social Security but who become permanently and totally disabled before reaching retirement age. Supplemental Security Income (SSI) provides disability payments linked to financial need.

Disability insurance policies are regulated at the state level, but the policies adopted by the states on issues such as the use of predictive genetic information in underwriting may have an effect on both state and federal disability insurance programs.

Unlike other forms of insurance, little legislative attention has thus far been paid to disability insurance. The following states limit insurers' use of genetic information in disability insurance in some way: Arizona, California, Kansas, Maine, Massachusetts, Montana, New Jersey, Vermont, and Wisconsin.

SUSAN M. WOLF & JEFFREY P. KAHN, GENETIC TESTING AND THE FUTURE OF DISABILITY INSURANCE: ETHICS, LAW, AND POLICY

35 J.L. Med. & Ethics (Supp. 2) 6, 11, 13 (2007).

Genetics may play a larger role in private disability insurance than private health insurance or life insurance. State and federal statutes place some limits on health insurers' use of such information, and very few limits on disability insurers. Further, in the realm of private individual life insurance, individual underwriting is less stringent than in disability insurance, as life insurers cover a single event—death. Because an individual may be disabled early in life precluding decades of income, disability insurers are exposed for longer periods of time than life insurers and for potentially much larger amounts of money. This exposure creates an incentive for disability insurers to use predictive medical information including genetic information, since genetics may help predict whether a disability precluding work will manifest at all, when, how, and for what duration.

To underwrite individual disability insurance, the insurer must carefully review the medical history of the applicant. On the basis of that information, the insurer may issue the coverage as applied for, charge additional premiums for the coverage, exclude specific conditions from coverage, change the benefit or elimination periods, or refuse to issue the coverage. As noted above, disability insurers providing individual policies generally rely less than group insurers on pre-existing conditions exclusions. The insurer is thus motivated to perform careful health research on an applicant. The insurer is also motivated by the requirement in most states that the policy include an incontestability clause. The incontestability clause provides that after two years, the insurer cannot deny benefits or cancel a policy if it discovers error in the information supplied by the applicant, so long as the insured did not intentionally defraud the insurer. Once this period has expired, the insurer thus loses the option to deny or cancel a contract due to pre-existing conditions that it failed to uncover. Incontestability clauses add to the insurer's incentives to discover as much as possible about an applicant's medical history—including genetic susceptibility to future disability—at the time of application, or at least within two years of it.

* * *

Given the importance of disability insurance, ideally legislators and regulators would impose the same restrictions on disability insurers as they do on health insurers. Norman Daniels analyzes the implications of setting up a disability insurance social safety net by eliminating medical underwriting (including consideration of genetics) while requiring that everyone have a minimum amount of disability insurance. Daniels does not go so far as to advocate this, but he recognizes it as an option to preserve equality of opportunity in the face of disability disrupting employment and income. For many individuals, this goal might be met through group insurance and public disability programs. When an individual can obtain the minimum amount of disability insurance needed through these other mechanisms, then individuals with a higher level of income can buy additional private individual insurance for additional income protection. Yet there will be some individuals without access to group insurance and unable to qualify for public programs who need access to a minimum safety net of individual disability insurance.

NOTES AND QUESTIONS

1. As with health insurance, public and private interests clearly intersect in the area of disability insurance. Disability income replacement is an important part of the Social Security system (SSDI), and private disability insurance provides supplemental protection for many workers. How might Social Security be affected by changes in the way that private disability insurance is regulated with regard to the use of genetic information?

2. Based on the legislative treatment of health insurance vs. life insurance, at the moment, U.S. public policy seems to regard health insurance more as an entitlement or right to which all individuals have a claim, whereas life insurance is considered more of a commercial transaction to which actuarial principles should apply. Assuming this analysis is correct, how should disability insurance be regarded, and how might this consideration affect public policy for disability insurance?

V. LONG–TERM CARE INSURANCE

MARK A. ROTHSTEIN, PREDICTIVE GENETIC TESTING FOR ALZHEIMER'S DISEASE IN LONG–TERM CARE INSURANCE

35 Ga. L. Rev. 707, 714–731 (2001).

The number of individuals purchasing long-term care insurance doubled from 1995 to 2000. The total number of long-term care insurance policies sold increased from approximately three million in 1992 to 5.8 million in 1998. The number of policies purchased in 1997 and the first half of 1998 alone increased by more than 880,000. The long-term care insurance market has grown an average of 21% each year from 1987 to 1997. The average household income for people who purchase long-term care insurance is $35,000 a year. Insurance policies sold include individual, group association, employer-sponsored, and riders to life insurance policies that accelerate the death benefit for long-term care.

The majority of long-term care insurers sell policies in the individual market. Eleven sellers have been identified as having sold 80% of the 5.8 million long-term care insurance policies. These policies covered nursing home care, care at an assisted living facility, home health care, and hospice care. Additionally, all of them provided coverage for Alzheimer's disease. In 1999, approximately one-fourth of long-term care insurance carriers sold policies in either the employer-sponsored or life insurance market. The employer-sponsored market has seen a 40% average annual growth rate since 1997, to about 800,000 policies cumulatively, and more than two thousand employers offered long-term care insurance to employees. The employer-sponsored and life insurance markets represented 20% of all long-term care policies sold as of 1997, up from less than 3% in 1988.

* * *

Long-term care insurance is expensive; paying for the costs of long-term care out-of-pocket can be a catastrophic financial experience for individuals and their families. As long-term care for the elderly increases in expense and a larger portion of the population closes in on their twilight years, the number of insurance policies should be expected to grow. Nevertheless, private insurance is likely to have only a limited role in financing long-term care unless at least the following three things occur: First, long-term care insurance must become a more widely available employee benefit offered through "cafeteria plans" by employers and purchased by employees with pre-tax dollars. Second, because younger, working employees are unlikely to purchase a benefit that they probably will not need, if at all, until after they retire and are no longer paying the premiums needed to keep the policy in force, some "paid up" forms of long-term care insurance will be necessary.

* * *

On average, Alzheimer's disease patients live eight to ten years after they are diagnosed. Consequently, each additional patient with Alzheimer's disease represents a significant increase in the likely expenditures for long-term care. Insurance companies can easily identify symptomatic individuals, but identifying those asymptomatic individuals who are likely to get Alzheimer's disease is much more difficult. Any tests used today by insurers would be poor predictors of future cognitive impairment in asymptomatic and younger applicants. If new tests, including genetic tests, were developed that were better predictors of future dementia (or if they were believed to be better predictors), long-term care insurance companies would have a considerable economic interest in using them. If predictive testing were available, then insurers could learn of the individual's risk status, which may cause adverse selection. Testing by insurers would thus be merely "defensive" in nature.

* * *

In trying to discern the appropriate public policy for the use of predictive genetic information in long-term care insurance, it is valuable to contrast the public policy for health insurance with that for life insurance. For health insurance, restrictions on access due to genetic-based predictions of future health status are unacceptable. There are not clear indications of the specific reasons for this public policy. It may well be a combination of at least the following reasons: (1) the importance of private health insurance to well-being in a nation that does not provide for universal access to health care; (2) the lack of alternatives to health insurance as a way of spreading risk and, in the era of managed care, obtaining health services at negotiated rates; (3) the speculative nature of many types of predictive genetic information; (4) the asserted moral blamelessness of individuals with genetic predisposition to illness; and (5) successful lobbying by groups with an interest in genetic-specific health protections—genetic disease advocacy groups, public health officials, and pharmaceutical and biotechnology companies concerned that individuals will not take their genetic tests if they fear discrimination.

For life insurance, at least in the United States, restrictions on access or cost based on predictions of future health status currently are generally acceptable. The reasons for this policy are likely to include at least the following: (1) life insurance serves a valuable role in promoting peace of mind and in providing financial security for one's heirs, but it is not a necessity for the person who is insured; (2) there are various investment alternatives to some forms of life insurance; (3) medical underwriting based on predictions of mortality risk are commonly performed for various health and lifestyle measures, including smoking and drinking habits, diet, occupation, recreational activities, and various presymptomatic health measures ranging from weight to cholesterol levels; (4) unlike health insurance, where the benefits are largely defined, life insurance can be purchased in extremely large amounts, thereby increasing the incentives for adverse selection; and (5) life insurance has not yet been the subject of intense lobbying activity.

If the preceding arguments generally capture the current public sentiments with regard to health and life insurance, to determine the appropriate policy for long-term care insurance one must merely resolve the following question: As a policy matter, is long-term care insurance more like health insurance or life insurance? Arguing in favor of long-term care insurance being closer to health insurance is the fact that long-term care is a type of health care which is merely provided in a different setting, and even though there are different pricing levels among long-term care facilities, commercial policies are generally sold with certain defined benefits. Arguing in favor of long-term care insurance being closer to life insurance is the fact that there are alternatives to long-term care policies and the premium structure is based on mortality risk, much the way that life insurance (and disability insurance) is.

* * *

As with the use of genetic information in numerous other contexts, the issue of using genetic information in long-term care insurance cannot be resolved in isolation. If public policy prohibits long-term care insurers from requiring genetic testing or using the results of a genetic test, what about using predictive genetic information based on family history? If the use of *any* predictive genetic information should be prohibited, what about non-genetic health information predictive of dementia, such as a history of head trauma, smoking, or drinking? What about other non-health factors predictive of dementia, such as socio-economic status? What about underwriting based on medical and nonmedical factors predictive of other disabling conditions?

Ultimately, the question becomes who should have access to long-term care, or, at least, who should have access to long-term care insurance? The most logical, and defensible line of demarcation for risk classification may not be genetic versus nongenetic factors. It may be whether the applicant is asymptomatic or symptomatic, with only age as an underwriting factor for individuals who are asymptomatic and all actuarially relevant criteria permitted in underwriting symptomatic individuals.

CATHLEEN D. ZICK ET AL., GENETIC TESTING FOR ALZHEIMER'S DISEASE AND ITS IMPACT ON INSURANCE PURCHASING BEHAVIOR

24 Health Affairs 483, 484–488 (2005).

STUDY DATA AND METHODS

Study Design.

The Risk Evaluation and Education for Alzheimer's Disease (REVEAL) Study is a recently completed randomized controlled trial (RCT) evaluating the impact of a genetic education and counseling program for adult children of Alzheimer's patients. As the largest study of its kind, it provides a rare opportunity to gain initial insights into the relationship between genetic testing for Alzheimer's disease and insurance purchasing behavior.

Participants in the REVEAL Study were either self-referred or systematically ascertained through their family's membership in existing Alzheimer's research registries in Boston, Cleveland, or New York City. Recruitment began in August 2000, and the last of the follow-up respondents surveys was completed in October 2003. A total of 162 participants were randomized into the clinical trial. All study participants were at higher-than-average risk for developing Alzheimer's because they have at least one parent affected by the disease.

In the control arm of the REVEAL Study, participants were informed of their risk of developing Alzheimer's based on sex and family history alone, with lifetime risk estimates ranging from 18 to 29 percent. Meanwhile, intervention-group participants learned their APOE genotype and were informed of their risk on the basis of sex, family history, and genotype, with lifetime risk estimates ranging from 13 to 57 percent.

Of the 162 people in the study, 148 were included in the analyses that follow. The remaining fourteen were excluded because they had missing data on one or more of the covariates. Among the 148 subjects, 46 were in the arm of the study where there was no APOE disclosure, 54 learned that they were a4 negative, and the remaining 48 learned that they were a4 positive (that is, had one or two a4 alleles).

Participants characteristics.

Participants' sociodemographic information illustrates that the RE- VEAL sample, like all research volunteer samples, is not a representative sample of the population. People in this study were more likely to be white, female, and well educated than members of the general population. Participants were also typically older than the general population, since participants had to be an adult child of a diagnosed Alzheimer's patient. Before intervention, it was ascertained that 97 percent of the sample had health insurance, 78 percent had life insurance, and 19.8 had long-term care insurance. These high rates of insurance coverage likely reflect the age, education, and ethnic composition of the sample.

* * *

Adverse selection.

First, there was little evidence of adverse selection in the health, life, and disability insurance markets despite the fact that the sample consisted of highly motivated people (that is, all had a family history of Alzheimer's disease and were highly educated) who were participating in a closed research trial where confidentiality of genetic information was guaranteed. This finding might be expected, however, given the ages of the participants, the relatively short period of follow-up (one year), people's typical insurance buying patterns, and the unique attributes of various insurance products.

Long-term care insurance.

Second, the one insurance domain where we found suggestive evidence of adverse selection is long-term care. Almost 17 percent of those who tested positive subsequently changed their long-term care insurance coverage in the year after APOE disclosure, compared with approximately 2 percent of those who tested negative and 4 percent of those who did not receive APOE disclosure. The overall percentage with long-term care insurance rose from 19.8 percent at baseline to 27 percent just one year later. Roughly three quarters of this increase is attributable to study participants' having learned that they had tested positive for the a4 allele. Controlling for other insurance-related covariates, we found that participants who tested positive were 5.76 times more likely to change their long-term care insurance coverage during the subsequent year than were those who did not receive APOE disclosure (although this finding is not reinforced by the sensitivity analyses).

Potential for adverse selection.

Policymakers who are attempting to balance consumers' concerns regarding potential genetic discrimination against insurers' concerns that the withholding of genetic test results would make insurance markets unprofitable should proceed with caution. Our findings imply that the potential for adverse selection may vary considerably by insurance market, thus making it difficult to design a public policy that works well in all instances.

It may be that the natural history of Alzheimer's disease combines with APOE testing and the characteristics of the mostly private long-term care insurance market to create the "perfect storm" with regard to adverse selection. That is, (1) Alzheimer's is a condition that has a high probability of requiring formal, long-term care services; (2) APOE testing gives significant, albeit incomplete, predictive information for the at-risk population; and (3) long-term care insurance is generally a private insurance market where an information asymmetry can have serious consequences. Taken in combination, these conditions create a situation where adverse selection may occur and where its consequences for insurers and consumers may be significant. This premise is consistent with the fact that we observe a positive relationship between testing positive and changing one's long-term care insurance coverage even in our relatively small sample.

NOTES AND QUESTIONS

1.   Taken together, what do the Rothstein and Zick articles indicate about the nature and consequences of genetic information for long-term care insurance?

2.   If you favor laws prohibiting long-term care insurers from using genetic information in underwriting, would you do so through genetic-specific or more general laws? If the latter, how would you structure such a law?

3.   Genetic information may have an effect on a variety of other insurance products. Medical malpractice (for negligence in diagnosis or treatment) and products liability (for pharmacogenomic medications) quickly come to mind. But there are other less obvious implications as well. For example, would it be permissible for an auto insurance company to test applicants to determine whether they were genetically predisposed to be risk takers? See Chapter 13 on Behavioral Genetics. In a claim filed under a homeowners or premises liability policy, can an insurer require genetic testing of an injured plaintiff to assess causation or determine life expectancy? See Chapter 17.

CHAPTER 16

EMPLOYMENT DISCRIMINATION

■ ■ ■

I. INTRODUCTION

Along with genetic discrimination in insurance, the topic of Chapter 15, genetic discrimination in employment is a topic of enormous concern to individuals and policy makers. Employment is not only a source of income but also the source of health insurance for the majority of Americans. Therefore, it is extremely important to resolve whether employers may get access to individual genetic information and, if so, what they may lawfully do with it. At the same time, it is necessary to consider the employers' interests in efficiency, employee health, and the health and safety of the public.

Employers have a keen interest in the health of their employees. A healthy work force is more stable, more productive, safer, and less costly in various ways than one composed of workers who are ill or likely to become ill in the future. Accordingly, medical screening of workers, the use of medical criteria in selecting and maintaining a work force, makes sense from a business standpoint and, if appropriately performed, from a health and policy standpoint as well. Medical screening of workers is not new; the only recent changes have been in the specific financial incentives for having healthier employees and the science used to make such determinations.

Medical screening became common in the United States at the beginning of the twentieth century. With industrialization, and the emergence of large manufacturing and other centralized employment facilities, employers attempted to ensure that their employees were free of tuberculosis and other communicable diseases. They also wanted to determine whether applicants and employees had the necessary vision, hearing, strength, stamina, dexterity, and other physical (and later mental) attributes necessary to perform the job safely and efficiently. Thus, "factory surgeons" were hired to screen out individuals who were deemed to be unacceptable. The nascent state of occupational medicine and the vulnerability of employer-paid physicians to making decisions for non-medical reasons, such as screening out union sympathizers for "medical reasons," sometimes compromised the integrity of the medical screening process during the first half of the twentieth century.

After World War II, there were new incentives to use more extensive medical screening. Besides workers' compensation and unemployment compensation liability for injuries and illnesses and employee turnover, employers began assuming a portion of employee (and later dependent) health insurance costs and, for some employers, disability insurance. In 1970, the Occupational Safety and Health Act subjected employers to civil penalties for safety and health violations, including those associated with occupational diseases or employee-caused accidents. The prospect of substantial tort liability for physical injuries and property damage sustained by the public resulting from employee-based mishaps further encouraged employers to select employees carefully based on medical criteria.

While pressures to increase medical screening were growing, civil rights legislation was enacted to limit employer prerogatives in employee selection. Title VII of the Civil Rights Act of 1964, as amended, and the Age Discrimination in Employment Act of 1967 (ADEA) prohibited discrimination based on race, color, religion, sex, pregnancy, national origin, or age. These laws had the effect of prohibiting employers from using stereotypical assumptions of individuals' abilities, thereby requiring an individualized determination of physical ability. In 1990, Congress enacted the Americans with Disabilities Act (ADA), which differed from Title VII and the ADEA in at least two important ways. First, Congress realized that it had to go beyond merely prohibiting discrimination based on disability; it was also necessary to address the previously unregulated process of selecting employees based on medical criteria. Thus, the ADA limits the timing and permissible scope of medical inquiries so that individuals with disabilities will not be excluded from consideration because of their disabilities before they have a chance to demonstrate their abilities. Second, the ADA requires that employers provide "reasonable accommodation" to enable individuals with disabilities to perform their jobs.

In 2008, Congress enacted the Genetic Information Nondiscrimination Act (GINA), Title II of which prohibits discrimination in employment on the basis of genetic information. Following the general framework of state laws enacted in the 1990s, GINA's main purpose is to reassure individuals that they can undergo genetic testing or genetic consultations without adverse consequences to their employment.

This chapter considers the broader context of genetic information and discrimination in the workplace. It explores what it means to "discriminate," whether genetic-specific or more general laws would be more effective in preventing discrimination, and the specifics of GINA and other legislation applicable to genetics in employment.

A. WHAT IS GENETIC DISCRIMINATION?

MATT RIDLEY, NATURE VIA NURTURE

260–262 (2003).

MORAL 4: MERITOCRACY

As the last candidate left the room, the chairman of the committee cleared his throat.

"Well, esteemed colleagues, we must choose one of those three people for the job of financial controller of the company: which is it to be?"

"Easy," said the red-haired woman. "The first one."

"Why?"

"Because she is a qualified woman and this company needs more women."

"Nonsense," said the portly man. "The best candidate was the second one. He has the best education. You can't beat Harvard's business school. Besides I knew his father at college. And he goes to church."

"Pah," scoffed the young woman with the thick glasses, "When I asked him what seven times eight is, he said 54! And he kept missing the point of my questions. What use is a good education if you haven't got a brain? I think the last candidate was by far the best. He was smooth, articulate, open, and quick. He didn't go to college, true, but he's got a natural grasp of numbers. Besides, he's got a real personality and the chemistry's right."

"Maybe," said the chairman. "But he's black."

Question: Who in this scene is guilty of genetic discrimination? The chairman, the red-haired woman, the portly man, or the woman with the glasses? Answer: All except the portly man. Only he is prepared to discriminate on the grounds of nurture. He is a true blank-slater, believing firmly that all human beings are born equal and stamped with their character by their upbringing. He is prepared to put his faith in the church, Harvard, and his college friend to create the right character whatever the raw material. The chairman's racism is based on the genetics of skin color. The red-haired woman's adherence to affirmative action for women is discrimination against people with Y chromosomes. The young woman in the glasses prefers to ignore qualifications and look for intrinsic talent and personality. Her discrimination is more subtle, but it certainly is genetic, at least in part: personality is strongly inherited, and her dismissal of the candidate from Harvard is based on the fact that his "nurture genes" have failed to take advantage of his education. She does not believe he is redeemable. I suggest that she is just as much of a genetic determinist as the chairman and the red-haired woman—and of course I hope her candidate got the job.

Every job interview is about genetic discrimination. Even if the interviews correctly ignore race, sex, disability, and physical appearance and discriminate on the grounds of ability alone, they are still discriminating, and unless they are prepared to decide on the basis of qualifications and background alone—in which case, why hold an interview?—then they are looking for some intrinsic, rather than acquired talent. The more they are prepared to make allowances for a deprived background, the more they are genetic determinists. Besides the other point of the interview is to take into consideration personality, and remember the lesson of twin studies: personality is even more strongly heritable in this society than intelligence.

MARK A. ROTHSTEIN & MARY R. ANDERLIK, WHAT IS GENETIC DISCRIMINATION AND WHEN AND HOW CAN IT BE PREVENTED?

3 Genetics in Med. 354, 354–355 (2001).

The two most common uses of the term discrimination differ dramatically in the degree of disapproval they connote. On the one hand, the term discrimination may be used to indicate a type of distinction that invariably is or should be socially unacceptable. We refer to this as the civil rights definition. For example, the Council for Responsible Genetics position paper on genetic discrimination does not define the term discrimination, but the negative connotation is clear from its use. Discrimination is linked to evaluating people based on "questionable stereotypes" rather than their individual merits and abilities, invading people's privacy, the morally and publicly unacceptable stratification of the community into "haves" and "have-nots," and the punishment of people for characteristics over which they have no control in violation of cherished beliefs in justice and equality. The proper response to discrimination is legal prohibition.

On the other hand, the term discrimination may be used as an all-purpose descriptor for the practice of making distinctions. Further, some individuals and entities link social unacceptability with irrationality, that is, they believe that only irrational distinctions should be socially unacceptable. We refer to this as the actuarial definition. For example, in the insurance industry, the term discrimination is considered neutral and simply refers to classification for purposes of underwriting. On the industry view, discrimination only becomes problematic where there is no sound actuarial basis for the manner in which risks are classified, or individuals with equivalent risks are treated differently. Often, in the business context, "irrational" means that the distinction cannot be defended in economic terms or, in the case of insurance, by reference to sound actuarial principles.

For both definitions, the term genetic discrimination also conveys that adverse treatment is based solely on the genotype of asymptomatic individuals. Differential treatment on the basis of phenotype is frequently rational and accepted as a social necessity, such as where an employer bases a hiring decision on a job-related need for visual acuity. Cases of adverse treatment based on the phenotypic expression of a genetic characteristic fit well within the analytical framework of laws dealing with disability-based or health status-based discrimination generally. The most important of these laws is the Americans with Disabilities Act. To the contrary, cases of adverse treatment of phenotypically "normal" individuals fit poorly within the disability discrimination framework. A large majority of the public considers discrimination against these individuals as unfair because current opportunities are being denied to seemingly unaffected individuals merely because a genetic test or assessment indicates an increased risk of future incapacity.

We define discrimination as drawing a distinction among individuals or groups plus an element of either irrationality or social unacceptability or both. Our definition draws upon elements of both the civil rights and actuarial definitions. When discrimination is defined in this way, the term clearly has a negative connotation, but it does not necessarily equate with a legal proscription of the classification. The appropriate legal and policy response to social unacceptability—a widely shared sense within a polity that some activity or state of affairs is "wrong"—will depend on the circumstances. In addition to or in lieu of legal prohibitions backed by criminal, civil, or administrative penalties are withdrawals of public funding, public condemnation, professional standards, and direct citizen action against the offending parties, for example, in the form of an economic boycott. Our definition recognizes that some forms of irrational discrimination are accepted, or at least tolerated, by society and some forms of discrimination are socially unacceptable despite the fact that they are rational.

Table 1 illustrates the application of our definition of discrimination by indicating how a sample of selection criteria for employment would be arrayed along dimensions of social acceptability and rationality. Note that standards for judging social acceptability will vary according to the context. While employers are generally not prohibited from basing hiring decisions on Zodiac signs, even though this is clearly irrational, an insurer would have to offer some actuarial basis for the distinction in order to meet the requirements of state insurance laws. One justification for differences in the law of employment and insurance is that, in our society, there is no history of systematic mistreatment of Virgos relative to Capricorns in employment, and the costs of policing idiosyncratic factors in isolated hiring decisions would be very high. On the other hand, risk classification in insurance involves assigning individuals to risk pools and hence insurance practices have the potential to *create* systematic mistreatment. Insurance underwriting policies also are more amenable to regulation than hiring decisions.

Table 1. Categories of Discrimination in Employment

	Rational	Irrational
Acceptable	• Choosing based on relative skill or other job-related criteria • Choosing based on medical assessment of ability to perform the job	• Choosing based on Zodiac sign • Choosing based on a coin toss
Unacceptable	• Excluding persons with cancer based on concerns about health care costs • Excluding pregnant women because they may shortly go on maternity leave	• Excluding based on religion (in a secular enterprise) • Excluding based on national origin

NOTES AND QUESTIONS

1. "Genetic discrimination" has long been an essential and accepted component of employee selection practices. For example, genes are a factor in height, vision, cognitive ability, and numerous other attributes of interest to employers. Thus, in a sense, it is "genetic discrimination" for a professional basketball team to select players based on their height. It is also "genetic discrimination" for an employer to refuse to hire an individual whose intellectual deficits preclude understanding key assignments or whose expressed genetic disorder precludes him or her from working. These forms of discrimination are generally considered legally and ethically permissible. Thus, "genetic discrimination" of a legally and ethically problematic nature, and as the term is commonly used, really means discrimination based on an unexpressed genotype. It is discrimination against presymptomatic or at-risk individuals.

2. Based on this definition, where would you place genetic discrimination on the preceding table?

3. Can you make an argument for including genetic discrimination in any of the other "boxes"?

4.   What is the nature of the harm suffered by a victim of genetic discrimination? How does it compare with the harm suffered by the victims of other forms of discrimination in employment?

RICHARD A. EPSTEIN, THE LEGAL REGULATION OF GENETIC DISCRIMINATION: OLD RESPONSES TO NEW TECHNOLOGY
74 B.U. L. Rev. 1, 12–13 (1994).

* * *

At this point it is critical to note that the plea for privacy is often a plea for the right to misrepresent one's self to the rest of the world. In and of itself that may not be a bad thing. We are certainly not obligated to disclose all of our embarrassing past to persons in ordinary social conversations; and it is certainly acceptable to use long sleeves to cover an ugly scar. White lies are part of the glue that makes human interaction possible without shame and loss of face. Strictly speaking, people may be deceived, but they are rarely hurt, and they may even be relieved to be spared an awkward encounter. However, when a major change in personal or financial status is contemplated by another party, the white lies that make human interaction possible turn into frauds of a somewhat deeper dye. In order to see why this is the case, recall that the traditional tort of misrepresentation stressed the usual five fingers: a false statement, known to be false, material to the listener, and relied on, to the listener's detriment. There is little question, whether we deal with marriage or with business, that concealment of relevant genetic information satisfies each element. The only question, therefore, is whether one can *justify* what is a prima facie wrong.

I am hard pressed to see what that justification might be. No doubt the individual who engages in this type of deception has much to gain. But equally there can be no doubt that this gain exists in all garden variety cases of fraud as well. To show the advantage of the fraud to the party who commits it is hardly to excuse or to justify it, for the same can be said of all cases of successful wrongs. On the other side of the transaction, there is a pronounced loss from not knowing the information when key decisions have to be made. For example, a woman may choose the wrong husband; an employer may pass up a good employee with a strong medical record and a clear upward path in favor of a worker who will, in the end, be the source of enormous personal and financial costs. To show that the condition is one for which the speaker is not responsible hardly justifies concealment at all: Lying about one's age or about the place of one's birth is often fraud even though these facts are immutable—just ask the Immigration and Naturalization Service.

False statements about or deliberate concealment of genetic information is as much a fraud as false statements about or concealment of any other issue. The only possible justification for concealment, therefore, would be that it is unfair for the person with the pending disorder to deal alone with the suffering and financial loss. Yet, that loss is not sustained because of the wrong of another. Could the victim of a natural catastrophe keep it secret, and single out one other person to bear some substantial fraction of the loss? If not, then why give that same privilege to the victim of a genetic defect? Today, it is easy to find strong support for socializing losses. But why should a person laboring under a genetic defect be entitled to pick the person or group that has to pay the subsidy?

In sum, genetic discrimination raises problems no different from those associated with any other sort of misfortune, and calls for no different response. The greater knowledge that comes from testing increases the informational asymmetries that are always the bane of insurance markets. When testing is possible, dangers from strategic behavior are only enhanced. Accordingly, the case for insisting on standard insurance norms is greater than it was before. Full disclosure of material information in response to direct questions is an indispensable part of that system. If we have reason to suspect that a system of disclosure could prove unreliable, we should allow the employer or insurer to test in order to obtain the knowledge already available to the employee. The person who wants privacy need not apply for the position or the insurance coverage. But he should not be able to have it both ways, and at someone else's expense.

NOTES AND QUESTIONS

1. Do you agree that the desire for privacy should be equated with misrepresentation?

2. Epstein assumes that the individual has already undergone genetic testing and is withholding the results. Does an individual have an obligation to undergo genetic testing or to submit to genetic testing so that third parties can more accurately calculate the risk of future illness?

3. What scientific, economic, and social assumptions underlie Epstein's theory?

4. For a similar view, see Colin S. Diver & Jane Maslow Cohen, Genophobia: What is Wrong with Genetic Discrimination?, 149 U. Pa. L. Rev. 1439 (2001) (advocating ''genetic transparency'' in which all parties have access to genetic information).

B. THE WHY AND HOW OF EMPLOYER ACCESS TO GENETIC INFORMATION

Employers have a considerable interest in the current and future health of their employees. The nature of the business and the work force will determine the specific interests, but in general, a healthy work force will be more productive; have less absenteeism and turnover; have fewer workers' compensation, disability insurance, and unemployment compensation claims; have fewer Family and Medical Leave Act requests for personal leave; require fewer accommodations under the Americans with Disabilities Act; and cause fewer OSHA violations.

The most important economic reason to have a healthy work force is to control health insurance costs. In the United States, about 85% of individuals who have privately financed health care coverage obtain their health benefits through their employer. The cost of health care coverage is the largest single non-salary compensation expense and, despite a moderating of increases in the 1990s attributable to managed care, the costs have begun increasing at a faster rate. In any given year, 5% of claimants represent 50% of expenditures, and therefore if the high-cost users could be excluded, dramatic savings (or cost-shifting to other, largely public payers) would be realized.

Employers attempting to limit their health insurance costs by selecting employees based on their health status may run afoul of the Americans with Disabilities Act as well as the Health Insurance Portability and Accountability Act of 1996 (HIPAA), 42 U.S.C. § 300gg et seq. HIPAA applies to employer-based group health plans (self-insured plans) and commercially issued group health insurance. HIPAA curtails the use of exclusions for preexisting conditions. Employers and insurers may apply a maximum, one-time 12-month exclusion to illnesses that were diagnosed or treated within the six months prior to enrollment, but individuals must be given credit for time they were covered under another plan. Therefore, an individual with at least one year's continuous coverage who changes jobs is eligible immediately for all benefits. No exclusions at all may be applied for pregnancy, newborns, or adopted children. Genetic information may not be treated as a preexisting condition in the absence of a diagnosis. For a further discussion of HIPAA, see Chapter 15

Note on Employer Access to Employee Health Information

Employers *lawfully* obtain medical information about employees in numerous ways. The following are 10 of the most common ways.

1. *Application forms.* Under the Americans with Disabilities Act (ADA), it is unlawful for an employer to make any medical inquiries of an applicant for employment until after there has been a conditional offer of employment. Therefore, it would be unlawful for an employer to require that the individual provide medical information on an application form. It is lawful, however, for an application form to ask an individual about previous jobs held and the reason why the individual left each prior job. The answer to one of these questions might be: "took time off work for cancer treatment."

2. *Interviews.* It is unlawful for an employer to ask about health matters at the interview before a conditional offer of employment. But nothing would prevent an employer from asking, for example, why the individual is interested in working for a particular employer. The answer to such a question could be: "Your health benefits are excellent, and there is a good chance I will need a liver transplant in a few years."

3. *References.* References sometimes disclose information about individuals that the individual would prefer not to have divulged to a potential

employer. For example, a reference, trying to be helpful might say: "He has not let the fact that he tested positive for the Huntington disease mutation affect his positive outlook on life."

4. *Post-offer medical exams.* Under the ADA, after a conditional offer of employment, the employer can require that the individual submit to a preplacement medical examination. These examinations may be unlimited in scope, regardless of the nature of the job or the individual's health history.

5. *Releases of medical records.* Under the ADA, after a conditional offer of employment, an employer may require that an individual sign a blanket release authorizing disclosure to the employer of all of the individual's medical records. Under GINA, it is unlawful for an employer to request, require, or purchase genetic information about an employee or family member of an employee, but genetic information is generally interspersed with non-genetic information in medical records. Because there is no easy or low-cost method of separating this information in paper or electronic health records, the custodians of health records often send the entire files in response to a more limited request.

6. *FMLA requests.* Under the Family and Medical Leave Act (FMLA), an employer of 50 or more employees is required to provide up to 12 weeks of unpaid leave for, among other things, the worker's own serious health condition that prevents him or her from working. The employer may require medical certification of the employee's need for leave, notwithstanding the ADA, which otherwise prohibits employers from requiring current employees to undergo non-job-related medical examinations. GINA, which prohibits employers from requesting genetic information from their employees, contains an exception for information related to an FMLA certification.

7. *Periodic medical exams.* Employers often require that employees periodically undergo medical examinations. For jobs with certain work-place exposures, periodic examinations are required under the Occupational Safety and Health Act. Under the ADA, medical examinations of current employees must be job-related or voluntary.

8. *Workers' compensation claims.* Employees sustaining work-related injuries and illnesses are eligible for workers' compensation. By submitting a claim, however, the employee places his or her medical condition at issue. The employer is therefore entitled to an independent medical examination of the claimant as well as access to the employee's medical records.

9. *Health insurance claims.* Employers often have widespread access to claims information submitted under an employer-sponsored health benefits plan. With a self-insured, self-administered plan, the physicians' bills and fee explanations are sent directly to the employer for payment. Even when a third-party administrator is used, employers often have access to the information. Employers also gain access to the health claims of the employee's dependents.

10. *Voluntary disclosure.* One of the most frequently used forms of disclosure of health information in the workplace occurs when employees voluntarily disclose their illnesses to co-workers and supervisors.

NOTES AND QUESTIONS

1. Individuals *fear* workplace genetic discrimination and they *report* they have been subject to adverse treatment. See, e.g., E. Virginia Lapham et al., Genetic Discrimination: Perspectives of Consumers, 274 Science 621 (1996). Yet, there have been very few cases brought under the Americans with Disabilities Act or other laws. Why?

2. To what extent do you think the lack of cases reflects the fact that genetic testing is an emerging technology and therefore few individuals' medical records contain the results of DNA based tests? Is it because individuals do not want to identify themselves as having a genetic predisposition? Is it because individuals often do not know the reason they are refused employment? Is it because discrimination based on future health risk is most likely to occur at the preplacement stage and applicants do not have such a financial or emotional interest in a job such that they are likely to sue? Other reasons?

3. The public health concern underlying genetic discrimination in the workplace is that at-risk individuals who want to be tested for prevention or other health-related reasons will not do so if they are afraid they will be subject to discrimination, including in employment. Is allaying an irrational public fear an adequate reason for enacting antidiscrimination legislation, such as GINA?

4. To what extent do you believe antidiscrimination legislation is encouraged by researchers and commercial interests concerned about the willingness of the public to undergo genetic testing in the absence of legislative assurances of nondiscrimination?

II. GENETIC DISCRIMINATION UNDER THE AMERICANS WITH DISABILITIES ACT (ADA)

A. COVERAGE

The Americans with Disabilities Act of 1990 (ADA), 42 U.S.C. §§ 12101–12213, was the first comprehensive federal law to prohibit discrimination in employment against the estimated 43 million Americans with physical or mental disabilities. The ADA's five titles deal with employment (Title I), public services (Title II), public accommodations operated by private entities (Title III), telecommunications (Title IV), and miscellaneous issues (Title V). The ADA draws heavily upon Title VII of the Civil Rights Act of 1964, 42 U.S.C. § 2000e, and the Rehabilitation Act of 1973, 29 U.S.C. §§ 701–796i.

The ADA applies to employers with 15 or more employees. It also applies to state and local government employers and the United States

Congress. Federal employees are not covered by the ADA, but they are covered by comparable provisions of section 501 of the Rehabilitation Act.

Section 102(a) of the ADA contains the general prohibition on employment discrimination. "No covered entity shall discriminate against a qualified individual with a disability because of the disability of such individual in regard to job application procedures, the hiring, advancement, or discharge of employees, employee compensation, job training, and other terms, conditions, and privileges of employment." There can be no liability if the employer did not know that the individual had a disability at the time it took the adverse action and therefore direct or circumstantial proof of employer motive is often determinative.

Besides the ADA, nearly every state has its own civil rights law prohibiting discrimination in employment on the basis of disability or handicap. Section 501(b) of the ADA provides that the ADA does not preempt any state or local law "that provides greater or equal protection for the rights of individuals with disabilities than are afforded by this [Act]." There are three main ways in which state laws are important to complement the protections of the ADA. First, the state law may apply to a wider class of employers. Twenty-five states and the District of Columbia have laws that apply to employers with fewer than 15 employees. Second, the state law may apply to a wider range of impairments than the ADA, such as individuals who are obese, who have substance abuse problems, or whose disabilities are not severe enough to meet the ADA definition. Third, the state law may more closely regulate certain medical or hiring procedures in employment. For example, in California and Minnesota preplacement medical examinations must be limited to assessing job-related health conditions. Medical examinations are discussed in Section IIB of this Chapter.

EEOC COMPLIANCE MANUAL VOL. 2

EEOC Order 915.002, Section 902 (1995).

This part of the definition of "disability" applies to individuals who are subjected to discrimination on the basis of genetic information relating to illness, disease, or other disorders. Covered entities that discriminate against individuals on the basis of such genetic information are regarding the individuals as having impairments that substantially limit a major life activity. Those individuals, therefore, are covered by the third part of the definition of "disability."

Example—CP's genetic profile reveals an increased susceptibility to colon cancer. CP is currently asymptomatic and may never in fact develop colon cancer. After making CP a conditional offer of employment, R learns about CP's increased susceptibility to colon cancer. R then withdraws the job offer because of concerns about matters such as CP's productivity, insurance costs, and attendance. R is treating CP as having an impairment that substantially limits a major life activity. Accordingly, CP is covered by the third part of the definition of "disability."

NOTES AND QUESTIONS

1. The abbreviation "CP," used in the example, stands for "charging party," the individual who is alleging the unlawful conduct. "R" stands for respondent, in this case the employer. An "unofficial" interpretation in 1991 by EEOC said that genetic discrimination was not covered under the ADA. The EEOC's 1995 interpretation is not binding on the courts.

2. The ADA's definition of the term "disability" is as follows:

(2) DISABILITY—The term "disability" means, with respect to an individual—

> (A) a physical or mental impairment that substantially limits one or more of the major life activities of such individual;
>
> (B) a record of such an impairment; or
>
> (C) being regarded as having such an impairment.

Section 3(2), 42 U.S.C. § 12102(2).

3. Why do you think that, according to the EEOC, individuals subjected to genetic discrimination would be covered under the "third prong" of the definition of disability (regarded as having an impairment) rather than under the "first prong" of the definition as having an impairment?

4. The ADA Amendments Act of 2008, P.L. 110–325, 110th Cong., 2d Sess. (2008), was signed into law on September 25, 2008. It was specifically enacted to overturn Supreme Court decisions narrowly interpreting the definition of an individual with a disability. The essence of the new amendments is captured by the following rule of construction: "The definition of a disability in this Act shall be construed in favor of broad coverage of individuals under this Act, to the maximum extent permitted by the terms of this Act." ADA Amendments Act § 3(4). Among the Supreme Court decisions overturned were Sutton v. United Air Lines, Inc., 527 U.S. 471 (1999), and its companion cases. In Sutton, twin sisters with correctable vision problems were denied an opportunity to become airline pilots because their uncorrected vision did not meet the airline's medical standards. In the ADA action, however, the airline argued that they were not covered by the ADA because in their "mitigated" state they did not have a substantially limiting impairment. The Supreme Court, rejecting the EEOC's interpretation that impairments should be considered in their unmitigated state, held that the lower court was required to consider the effect of eyeglasses on their condition. The Court relied on the congressional finding that the ADA provided coverage to 43 million Americans with disabilities to conclude that the ADA was only intended to apply to individuals with substantially limiting impairments. Most observers had concluded that the EEOC's 1995 interpretation on the coverage of genetic predisposition under the ADA did not survive Sutton. Although Congress rejected Sutton, the ADA Amendments Act did not address the issue of genetic discrimination or discrimination based on the risk of future impairment. Perhaps Congress did not believe this was necessary in light of GINA, which was signed into law on May 21, 2008.

B. MEDICAL EXAMINATIONS

AMERICANS WITH DISABILITIES ACT

42 U.S.C. §§ 12101–12213.

SECTION 102. (§ 12112) DISCRIMINATION

(a) GENERAL RULE.—No covered entity shall discriminate against a qualified individual with a disability because of the disability of such individual in regard to job application procedures, the hiring, advancement, or discharge of employees, employee compensation, job training, and other terms, conditions, and privileges of employment.

* * *

(d) MEDICAL EXAMINATIONS AND INQUIRIES.—

(1) IN GENERAL.—The prohibition against discrimination as referred to in subsection (a) shall include medical examinations and inquiries.

(2) PREEMPLOYMENT—

(A) PROHIBITED EXAMINATION OR INQUIRY.—Except as provided in paragraph (3), a covered entity shall not conduct a medical examination or make inquiries of a job applicant as to whether such applicant is an individual with a disability or as to the nature or severity of such disability.

(B) ACCEPTABLE INQUIRY.—A covered entity may make preemployment inquiries into the ability of an applicant to perform job-related functions.

(3) EMPLOYMENT ENTRANCE EXAMINATION.—A covered entity may require a medical examination after an offer of employment has been made to a job applicant and prior to the commencement of the employment duties of such applicant, and may condition an offer of employment on the results of such examination, if—

(A) all entering employees are subjected to such an examination regardless of disability;

(B) information obtained regarding the medical condition or history of the applicant is collected and maintained on separate forms and in separate medical files and is treated as a confidential medical record, except that—

(i) supervisors and managers may be informed regarding necessary restrictions on the work or duties of the employee and necessary accommodations;

(ii) first aid and safety personnel may be informed, when appropriate, if the disability might require emergency treatment; and

(iii) government officials investigating compliance with this Act shall be provided relevant information on request; and

(C) the results of such examination are used only in accordance with this title.

(4) EXAMINATION AND INQUIRY.—

(A) PROHIBITED EXAMINATIONS AND INQUIRIES.—A covered entity shall not require a medical examination and shall not make inquiries of an employee as to whether such employee is an individual with a disability or as to the nature or severity of the disability, unless such examination or inquiry is shown to be job-related and consistent with business necessity.

(B) ACCEPTABLE EXAMINATIONS AND INQUIRIES.—A covered entity may conduct voluntary medical examinations, including voluntary medical histories, which are part of an employee health program available to employees at that work site. A covered entity may make inquiries into the ability of an employee to perform job-related functions.

(C) REQUIREMENT.—Information obtained under subparagraph (B) regarding the medical condition or history of any employee are subject to the requirements of subparagraphs (B) and (C) of paragraph (3).

NOTES AND QUESTIONS

1. Section 102(d) of the ADA has three different sets of rules for employee medical examinations and inquiries, depending on the stage of employment at which the examination or inquiry is conducted. Can you summarize the three different sets of rules? Are these privacy protection rules or antidiscrimination rules?

2. Even though post-offer medical examinations need not be job-related, an employer may not withdraw a conditional offer of employment based on a medical examination unless the withdrawal is based on the individual's inability to perform the essential functions of the job, § 102 (b)(6), 42 U.S.C. § 12112 (b)(6). Thus, it was held to be unlawful for a city to perform nonconsensual HIV testing at the post-offer stage and then withdraw conditional offers from those who tested positive. Doe v. City of Chicago, 883 F.Supp. 1126 (N.D.Ill.1994).

3. For a discussion of the legislative history of this section, see Chai Feldblum, Medical Examinations and Inquiries Under the Americans with Disabilities Act: A View From the Inside, 64 Temp. L. Rev. 521 (1991); Sharona Hoffman, Preplacement Examinations and Job–Relatedness: How to Enhance Privacy and Diminish Discrimination in the Workplace, 49 U. Kan. L. Rev. 517 (2001). For a discussion of the ADA and genetics, see Mark A. Rothstein, Genetic Discrimination in Employment and the Americans with Disabilities Act, 29 Hous. L. Rev. 23 (1992).

OTHER LAWS APPLICABLE TO GENETIC DISCRIMINATION IN EMPLOYMENT

Title VII of the Civil Rights Act of 1964 prohibits discrimination in employment on the basis of race, color, religion, sex, and national origin. 42 U.S.C. § 2000e–2(a)(1). Because genetic disorders often appear in higher frequencies in distinct population groups, discrimination against individuals with certain disorders or traits (e.g., sickle cell) might be alleged as disparate impact discrimination under Title VII. This was the theory used in Norman–Bloodsaw v. Lawrence Berkeley Laboratory, 135 F.3d 1260 (9th Cir. 1998). Without their knowledge or consent, blood and urine samples of certain employees obtained during their preplacement medical examinations were tested for pregnancy, syphilis, and sickle cell trait. Seven current and former employees sued under the U.S. and California Constitutions, Title VII, and the ADA. The Ninth Circuit, in reversing the district court's dismissal of all claims, held that the facts raised a valid constitutional claim. "One can think of few subject areas more personal and more likely to implicate privacy interests than that of one's health and genetic make-up." 135 F.3d at 1269. The court also held that a cognizable Title VII claim for sex discrimination was alleged by the pregnancy testing and a race discrimination claim because the sickle cell testing was limited to black employees. The dismissal of the ADA claims was affirmed, however, because, under the ADA, preplacement medical examinations can be of unlimited scope and need not be job-related.

The Employee Retirement Income Security Act (ERISA) makes it unlawful to discriminate against a participant or beneficiary "for the purpose of interfering with the attainment of any right to which such participant may become entitled under the plan * * *." 29 U.S.C. § 1140. However, ERISA applies only to current employees and therefore is inapplicable to a refusal to hire based on perceived future health insurance costs. The ADA and state genetic nondiscrimination laws would be the best recourse for discrimination before hiring.

III. GENETIC NONDISCRIMINATION LAWS

A. STATE LAWS

State laws prohibiting genetic discrimination in employment date back to the 1970s. At that time, widespread and ill-advised carrier testing for sickle cell trait caused confusion, resulting in discrimination against unaffected carriers. Florida, Louisiana, and North Carolina enacted laws prohibiting discrimination based on sickle cell trait. The first comprehensive genetic nondiscrimination law was enacted in Wisconsin in 1991. In the years since then, over half the states have enacted laws prohibiting genetic discrimination in employment, and new measures are introduced in more states every year.

The laws fall into two general categories. First, the laws in all but two of the states to enact genetic nondiscrimination legislation prohibit employers from requiring genetic testing as a condition of employment and prohibit discrimination based on genetic information. The definition of genetic information includes family health history in some states; in others it is limited to the results of a DNA-based genetic test. The laws do not prohibit employers from requiring that individuals sign a blanket release of their medical records after there has been a conditional offer of employment. The second category of laws, represented by only California and Minnesota, adopt a more generic approach, and prohibit employers from obtaining any non-job-related medical information at any time. Presumably, this also prohibits employers from requiring broad releases of medical information, which could include genetic information and family health history information from which genetic risks may be inferred.

B. FEDERAL LAWS

GENETIC INFORMATION NONDISCRIMINATION ACT OF 2008 (GINA)

P.L. 110–233, 122 Stat. 881 (2008).

The Genetic Information Nondiscrimination Act of 2008 (GINA), was signed into law by President Bush on May 21, 2008, after a 13–year struggle in Congress. Previously, in 2000, President Clinton issued Executive Order 13145, which prohibited genetic discrimination in federal government employment. The executive order was designed to pave the way for legislation covering the private sector, but GINA was considered unnecessary or intrusive by some members of Congress until various objections were resolved.

Title II of GINA prohibits discrimination in employment. Specifically, it prohibits employers from requesting, requiring, or purchasing genetic information about employees or applicants. Genetic information is defined as information about the individual's genetic tests, the genetic tests of family members, or the manifestation of a disease or disorder in a family member. It does not apply to manifested diseases or disorders of the individual. Thus, as with Title I, applicable to health insurance (discussed in Chapter 15), Title II of GINA applies only to individuals who are asymptomatic.

Employers are prohibited from engaging in various unlawful employment practices, including refusing to hire, discharging, or discriminating in terms or conditions of employment, based on genetic information. There are several exceptions to the ban on acquiring genetic information, including inadvertent acquisition (e.g., disclosures by the employee), employer requests for health information in accordance with the Family and Medical Leave Act (FMLA), and optional genetic monitoring for the effects occupational exposures.

For private sector employers, GINA has the same coverage and remedies as Title VII, except that disparate impact claims may not be brought. Title II took effect on November 21, 2009, 18 months after GINA was signed law. The Equal Employment Opportunity Commission (EEOC) has responsibility for issuing regulations and enforcement of GINA.

GENETIC INFORMATION NONDISCRIMINATION ACT OF 2008 (GINA)

P.L. 110–233, 122 Stat 881 (2008).

* * *

TITLE II—PROHIBITING EMPLOYMENT DISCRIMINATION ON THE BASIS OF GENETIC INFORMATION

§ 201. DEFINITIONS

* * *

(4) GENETIC INFORMATION—

  (A) IN GENERAL—The term 'genetic information' means, with respect to any individual, information about—

   (i) such individual's genetic tests,

   (ii) the genetic tests of family members of such individual, and

   (iii) the manifestation of a disease or disorder in family members of such individual.

  (B) INCLUSION OF GENETIC SERVICES AND PARTICIPATION IN GENETIC RESEARCH—Such term includes, with respect to any individual, any request for, or receipt of, genetic services, or participation in clinical research which includes genetic services, by such individual or any family member of such individual.

  (C) EXCLUSIONS—The term 'genetic information' shall not include information about the sex or age of any individual.

(5) GENETIC MONITORING—The term 'genetic monitoring' means the periodic examination of employees to evaluate acquired modifications to their genetic material, such as chromosomal damage or evidence of increased occurrence of mutations, that may have developed in the course of employment due to exposure to toxic substances in the workplace, in order to identify, evaluate, and respond to the effects of or control adverse environmental exposures in the workplace.

(6) GENETIC SERVICES—The term 'genetic services' means—

  (A) a genetic test;

  (B) genetic counseling (including obtaining, interpreting, or assessing genetic information); or

  (C) genetic education.

(7) GENETIC TEST—

(A) IN GENERAL—The term 'genetic test' means an analysis of human DNA, RNA, chromosomes, proteins, or metabolites, that detects genotypes, mutations, or chromosomal changes.

(B) EXCEPTIONS—The term 'genetic test' does not mean an analysis of proteins or metabolites that does not detect genotypes, mutations, or chromosomal changes.

§ 202. EMPLOYER PRACTICES.

(a) Discrimination Based on Genetic Information—It shall be an unlawful employment practice for an employer—

(1) to fail or refuse to hire, or to discharge, any employee, or otherwise to discriminate against any employee with respect to the compensation, terms, conditions, or privileges of employment of the employee, because of genetic information with respect to the employee; or

(2) to limit, segregate, or classify the employees of the employer in any way that would deprive or tend to deprive any employee of employment opportunities or otherwise adversely affect the status of the employee as an employee, because of genetic information with respect to the employee.

(b) Acquisition of Genetic Information—It shall be an unlawful employment practice for an employer to request, require, or purchase genetic information with respect to an employee or a family member of the employee except—

(1) where an employer inadvertently requests or requires family medical history of the employee or family member of the employee;

(2) where—

(A) health or genetic services are offered by the employer, including such services offered as part of a wellness program;

(B) the employee provides prior, knowing, voluntary, and written authorization;

(C) only the employee (or family member if the family member is receiving genetic services) and the licensed health care professional or board certified genetic counselor involved in providing such services receive individually identifiable information concerning the results of such services; and

(D) any individually identifiable genetic information provided under subparagraph (C) in connection with the services provided under subparagraph (A) is only available for purposes of such services and shall not be disclosed to the employer except in aggregate terms that do not disclose the identity of specific employees;

(3) where an employer requests or requires family medical history from the employee to comply with the certification provisions of section 103 of the Family and Medical Leave Act of 1993 (29 U.S.C. 2613) or such requirements under State family and medical leave laws;

(4) where an employer purchases documents that are commercially and publicly available (including newspapers, magazines, periodicals, and books, but not including medical databases or court records) that include family medical history;

(5) where the information involved is to be used for genetic monitoring of the biological effects of toxic substances in the workplace, but only if—

(A) the employer provides written notice of the genetic monitoring to the employee;

(B)(i) the employee provides prior, knowing, voluntary, and written authorization; or

(ii) the genetic monitoring is required by Federal or State law;

(C) the employee is informed of individual monitoring results;

(D) the monitoring is in compliance with—

(i) any Federal genetic monitoring regulations, including any such regulations that may be promulgated by the Secretary of Labor pursuant to the Occupational Safety and Health Act of 1970 (29 U.S.C. 651 et seq.), the Federal Mine Safety and Health Act of 1977 (30 U.S.C. 801 et seq.), or the Atomic Energy Act of 1954 (42 U.S.C. 2011 et seq.); or

(ii) State genetic monitoring regulations, in the case of a State that is implementing genetic monitoring regulations under the authority of the Occupational Safety and Health Act of 1970 (29 U.S.C. 651 et seq.); and

(E) the employer, excluding any licensed health care professional or board certified genetic counselor that is involved in the genetic monitoring program, receives the results of the monitoring only in aggregate terms that do not disclose the identity of specific employees; or

(6) where the employer conducts DNA analysis for law enforcement purposes as a forensic laboratory or for purposes of human remains identification, and requests or requires genetic information of such employer's employees, but only to the extent that such genetic information is used for analysis of DNA identification markers for quality control to detect sample contamination.

(c) Preservation of Protections-In the case of information to which any of paragraphs (1) through (6) of subsection (b) applies, such information may not be used in violation of paragraph (1) or (2) of subsection (a) or treated or disclosed in a manner that violates section 206.

* * *

§ 206. CONFIDENTIALITY OF GENETIC INFORMATION.

(a) Treatment of Information as Part of Confidential Medical Record—If an employer, employment agency, labor organization, or joint labor-management committee possesses genetic information about an employee or member, such information shall be maintained on separate forms and in separate medical files and be treated as a confidential medical record of the employee or member. An employer, employment agency, labor organization, or joint labor-management committee shall be considered to be in compliance with the maintenance of information requirements of this subsection with respect to genetic information subject to this subsection that is maintained with and treated as a confidential medical record under section 102(d)(3)(B) of the Americans With Disabilities Act (42 U.S.C. 12112(d)(3)(B)).

(b) Limitation on Disclosure—An employer, employment agency, labor organization, or joint labor-management committee shall not disclose genetic information concerning an employee or member except—

(1) to the employee or member of a labor organization (or family member if the family member is receiving the genetic services) at the written request of the employee or member of such organization;

(2) to an occupational or other health researcher if the research is conducted in compliance with the regulations and protections provided for under part 46 of title 45, Code of Federal Regulations;

(3) in response to an order of a court, except that—

(A) the employer, employment agency, labor organization, or joint labor-management committee may disclose only the genetic information expressly authorized by such order; and

(B) if the court order was secured without the knowledge of the employee or member to whom the information refers, the employer, employment agency, labor organization, or joint labor-management committee shall inform the employee or member of the court order and any genetic information that was disclosed pursuant to such order;

(4) to government officials who are investigating compliance with this title if the information is relevant to the investigation;

(5) to the extent that such disclosure is made in connection with the employee's compliance with the certification provisions of section 103 of the Family and Medical Leave Act of 1993 (29 U.S.C. 2613) or such requirements under State family and medical leave laws; or

(6) to a Federal, State, or local public health agency only with regard to information that is described in section 201(4)(A)(iii) and that concerns a contagious disease that presents an imminent hazard of death or life-threatening illness, and that the employee whose family member or family members is or are the subject of a disclosure under this paragraph is notified of such disclosure.

(c) Relationship to HIPAA Regulations—With respect to the regulations promulgated by the Secretary of Health and Human Services under part C of title XI of the Social Security Act (42 U.S.C. 1320d et seq.) and section 264 of the Health Insurance Portability and Accountability Act of 1996 (42 U.S.C. 1320d–2 note), this title does not prohibit a covered entity under such regulations from any use or disclosure of health information that is authorized for the covered entity under such regulations. The previous sentence does not affect the authority of such Secretary to modify such regulations.

§ 207. REMEDIES AND ENFORCEMENT.

(a) Employees Covered by Title VII of the Civil Rights Act of 1964—

(1) IN GENERAL—The powers, procedures, and remedies provided in sections 705, 706, 707, 709, 710, and 711 of the Civil Rights Act of 1964 (42 U.S.C. 2000e–4 et seq.) to the Commission, the Attorney General, or any person, alleging a violation of title VII of that Act (42 U.S.C. 2000e et seq.) shall be the powers, procedures, and remedies this title provides to the Commission, the Attorney General, or any person, respectively, alleging an unlawful employment practice in violation of this title against an employee described in section 201(2)(A)(i), except as provided in paragraphs (2) and (3).

(2) COSTS AND FEES—The powers, remedies, and procedures provided in subsections (b) and (c) of section 722 of the Revised Statutes of the United States (42 U.S.C. 1988), shall be powers, remedies, and procedures this title provides to the Commission, the Attorney General, or any person, alleging such a practice.

(3) DAMAGES—The powers, remedies, and procedures provided in section 1977A of the Revised Statutes of the United States (42 U.S.C. 1981a), including the limitations contained in subsection (b)(3) of such section 1977A, shall be powers, remedies, and procedures this title provides to the Commission, the Attorney General, or any person, alleging such a practice (not an employ-

ment practice specifically excluded from coverage under section 1977A(a)(1) of the Revised Statutes of the United States).

* * *

(f) Prohibition Against Retaliation—No person shall discriminate against any individual because such individual has opposed any act or practice made unlawful by this title or because such individual made a charge, testified, assisted, or participated in any manner in an investigation, proceeding, or hearing under this title. The remedies and procedures otherwise provided for under this section shall be available to aggrieved individuals with respect to violations of this subsection.

(g) Definition—In this section, the term 'Commission' means the Equal Employment Opportunity Commission.

§ 208. DISPARATE IMPACT.

(a) General Rule—Notwithstanding any other provision of this Act, 'disparate impact', as that term is used in section 703(k) of the Civil Rights Act of 1964 (42 U.S.C. 2000e–2(k)), on the basis of genetic information does not establish a cause of action under this Act.

* * *

§ 209. CONSTRUCTION.

(a) In General—Nothing in this title shall be construed to—

(1) limit the rights or protections of an individual under any other Federal or State statute that provides equal or greater protection to an individual than the rights or protections provided for under this title, including the protections of an individual under the Americans with Disabilities Act of 1990 (42 U.S.C. 12101 et seq.) (including coverage afforded to individuals under section 102 of such Act (42 U.S.C. 12112)), or under the Rehabilitation Act of 1973 (29 U.S.C. 701 et seq.);

* * *

(4) limit or expand the protections, rights, or obligations of employees or employers under applicable workers' compensation laws;

(5) limit the authority of a Federal department or agency to conduct or sponsor occupational or other health research that is conducted in compliance with the regulations contained in part 46 of title 45, Code of Federal Regulations (or any corresponding or similar regulation or rule);

(6) limit the statutory or regulatory authority of the Occupational Safety and Health Administration or the Mine Safety and Health Administration to promulgate or enforce workplace safety and health laws and regulations; or

* * *

(1) with respect to such an individual or family member of an individual who is a pregnant woman, include genetic information of any fetus carried by such pregnant woman; and

(2) with respect to an individual or family member utilizing an assisted reproductive technology, include genetic information of any embryo legally held by the individual or family member.

(c) Relation to Authorities Under Title I—With respect to a group health plan, or a health insurance issuer offering group health insurance coverage in connection with a group health plan, this title does not prohibit any activity of such plan or issuer that is authorized for the plan or issuer under any provision of law referred to in clauses (i) through (iv) of subsection (a)(2)(B).

§ 210. MEDICAL INFORMATION THAT IS NOT GENETIC INFORMATION.

An employer, employment agency, labor organization, or joint labor-management committee shall not be considered to be in violation of this title based on the use, acquisition, or disclosure of medical information that is not genetic information about a manifested disease, disorder, or pathological condition of an employee or member, including a manifested disease, disorder, or pathological condition that has or may have a genetic basis.

§ 211. REGULATIONS.

Not later than 1 year after the date of enactment of this title, the Commission shall issue final regulations to carry out this title.

* * *

§ 213. EFFECTIVE DATE.

This title takes effect on the date that is 18 months after the date of enactment of this Act.

MARK A. ROTHSTEIN, GINA, THE ADA, AND GENETIC DISCRIMINATION IN EMPLOYMENT

35 J.L. Med. & Ethics 837, 838–839 (2008).

* * *

GINA

Both the health insurance and employment provisions of GINA expressly limit their protections to asymptomatic individuals who have been subjected to adverse treatment based on genetic information. GINA defines "genetic information" as information about an individual's genetic tests, the genetic tests of family members, and the manifestation of a disease or disorder in family members. Of critical importance, GINA provides that it is not unlawful to use, acquire, or disclose medical information "about a manifested disease, disorder, or pathological condition of an employee ... , including a manifested disease, disorder, or pathological condition that has or may have a genetic basis."

Unfortunately, GINA does not define "a manifested disease, disorder, or pathological condition." GINA instead defines a "genetic test" as "an analysis of human DNA, RNA, chromosomes, proteins, or metabolites, that detects genotypes, mutations, or chromosomal changes." The definition does *not* include "(1) an analysis of proteins or metabolites that does not detect genotypes, mutations, or chromosomal changes; or (2) an analysis of proteins or metabolites that is directly related to a manifested disease, disorder, or pathological condition that could reasonably be detected by a health care professional with appropriate training and expertise in the field of medicine involved." These definitions do not provide much guidance as to the types of tests considered genetic, let alone when a disease, disorder, or pathological condition is "manifested."

READING THE ADA AND GINA TOGETHER

As illustrated in Figure 1, the coverage of the ADA and GINA are mirror images at the extremes. In the context of genetic discrimination in employment, asymptomatic individuals are unlikely to be covered by the ADA, but they are expressly covered by GINA. Conversely, severely affected individuals are covered by the ADA, but they are expressly not covered by GINA. The greatest uncertainty is in the middle. Under the ADA, an individual with a mild, temporary, or presymptomatic condition does not come within the statutory definition of an individual with a disability. Similarly, under GINA, an individual with a genetically based, biologically determinable difference beyond genotypic variation but short of phenotypic variation is unlikely to be protected.

FIGURE 1

COVERAGE OF GINA AND THE ADA

	ASYMPTOMATIC	BIOMARKERS, ENDOPHENOTYPES, MILD SYMPTOMS	MANIFESTATION OF DIESEASE
GINA	Yes*	?	No
ADA	No	No	Yes†

* Prohibits discrimination based on genetic information, which includes an individual's genetic tests, the genetic tests of the individual's family members, and family history.
† Prohibits discrimination based on an impairment that constitutes a substantial limitation of a major life activity.

The problems in interpreting GINA stem from the fact that the law is based on a scientifically dubious dichotomy between genetic and non-genetic information, tests, and disorders. It has been generally acknowledged by scientists for decades that virtually all human disease has both genetic and environmental components. New developments in proteomics, transcriptomics, metabonomics, epigenetics, and other fields have blurred the line between asymptomatic and symptomatic. The various biological processes by which a gene becomes expressed are still being elucidated.

Increasingly sensitive biomarkers and sophisticated analyses of endophenotypes add further complexity to disease mechanisms. Regardless of the policy issues implicated by different definitions under GINA, the distinctions drawn in the statute are scientifically untenable today and are likely to be increasingly problematic.

CONCLUSION

The employment discrimination provisions of GINA take effect November 21, 2009, and the EEOC is charged with issuing regulations implementing GINA by May 21, 2009 [29 CFR §§ 1635.1–1635.12]. One of the most important tasks for the EEOC is to devise practical, understandable, and scientifically compelling rules for determining what degree of biological response or symptoms constitutes manifestation of a disease, thereby precluding an individual from coverage by GINA. Under any conceivable definition of "manifestation," however, an individual will be too affected to be covered under GINA long before having a substantial limitation of a major life activity necessary to be covered under the ADA.

LAWS v. PACT, INC.

2000 WL 777926 (N.D. Ill. 2000).

GETTLEMAN, J.

Plaintiff Patricia Laws has brought a two count amended complaint against her former employer, Pact, Inc., alleging violations of § 504 of the Rehabilitation Act, 29 U.S.C. § 794 (Count I), and the Americans With Disabilities Act ("ADA"),42 U.S.C. § 12101 et seq. and 42 U.S.C. § 1981 (Count II). Defendant has moved for summary judgment on both counts. For the reasons set forth below, defendant's motion is granted.

Defendant is a non-profit agency that assists developmentally disabled clients and their families in locating residential, vocational, recreational and day program options, and links clients with funding sources. Plaintiff was employed by defendant in a variety of positions from September 1990 until her termination in May 1997. Plaintiff's last position with defendant was as an Individual Service Coordinator ("ISC") in the Case Coordination Unit ("CCU").

In August 1996 plaintiff's mother died, leaving plaintiff as executor of the estate and sole guardian of her disabled sister. Around that time, plaintiff was suffering from depression and began to experience some symptoms of what she later learned to be Huntington's Disease, which is an "inherited progressive degenerative disease of cognition, emotion, and movement." It "affects men and women equally and is transmitted by a single autosomal dominant gene on the short arm of chromosome 4." The disease is usually diagnosed in the late 30s to early 40s but may begin as early as age 4 in the juvenile form or as late as 85 years in the late-onset form. The onset of the disease is often heralded by insidious changes in behavior and personality, including depression, irritability and anxiety.

On February 21, 1997, plaintiff asked for a one month leave of absence to deal with her family affairs. The request did not mention either her depression or any other medical condition, nor did it indicate in any way an inability to handle her work load. That request was denied based on staffing problems, but defendant suggested an alternative of five days leave.

One week later, February 28, 1997, plaintiff submitted another request, this time seeking at least 2 1/2 weeks leave, based on recommendations of her therapist and psychiatrist who were treating her for depression. That request was granted. On March 4, 1997, plaintiff informed defendant that "under no circumstances am I able to continue to perform in my present position as Individual Service Coordinator at this time." Plaintiff therefore requested a disability leave without pay, from March 8, 1997, through April 11, or 15, 1997. Submitted with her March 4, 1997, letter was a letter from her primary care physician, requesting that plaintiff be put on disability leave for 25 to 30 days, based on her depression. Again, nothing in either of plaintiff's memos or the doctor's letter mentioned Huntington's Disease.

Around the same time, plaintiff apparently informed Karen Delhotal, whom plaintiff calls her immediate supervisor, that she had been diagnosed with Huntington's Disease. Plaintiff had not yet actually been formally diagnosed with Huntington's, but was undergoing testing. Plaintiff asked Delhotal not to reveal the diagnosis to anyone, but plaintiff has presented evidence that Delhotal told a co-worker that plaintiff had Huntington's. There is no evidence, however, that Delhotal told either Steve Boisse, Associate Director, or Dr. Joseph Straka, the Executive Director, the ultimate decision makers on personnel matters.

Plaintiff was told that her position might be filled while she was on leave, due to staffing problems. The position was filled shortly after her leave began. On April 2, 1997, Boisse wrote to plaintiff informing her that her position had been filled and that there were no positions currently available, but that she would be given preference should any position for which she was qualified open. On May 5, 1997, the date plaintiff was finally medically cleared to return to work, there were no such positions available. Boisse informed plaintiff of that in a letter dated May 5, 1997, in which he terminated her employment and informed her that pursuant to company policy she would be given preference for any opening in a similar position.

Defendant had an employee policy in effect which provided that "every attempt will be made to reinstate those employees who have been granted an authorized leave of absence in the same, similar, or vacant position for which they are qualified." Pursuant to that policy, on June 2, 1997, Boisse spoke with plaintiff and offered her a position similar to her previous position. According to plaintiff, the position offered was in the Bogard Department, for which she was qualified but would need additional training. According to defendant, the offer was for an ISC position, although it is unclear whether that position was in the Bogard Unit. Plaintiff considered the offer for two days then rejected it because of a slightly lower salary and because the Bogard Unit had an aging, dying population which plaintiff and her doctor decided would be difficult for her to handle.

Defendant has moved for summary judgment on a number of grounds: 1) plaintiff is not now, and was not disabled at the time of her termination; 2) the claims are time barred; and 3) the actions are not discriminatory.

Defendant first argues that plaintiff can not establish that she was disabled. To establish a claim of discriminatory treatment under the ADA or the Rehabilitation Act, plaintiff must demonstrate that she suffers from a disability as defined in those statutes. Disability is defined as: a) a physical or mental impairment that substantially limits one or more of the major life activities of an individual; b) a record of such impairment; or c) being regarded as having such an impairment. EEOC regulations define major life activities to include "functions such as caring for oneself, performing manual tasks, walking, seeing, hearing, speaking, breathing, learning and working." Substantially limited means that the person is either "unable to perform in a major life activity or is significantly restricted as to the condition, manner or duration under which the individual can perform a major life activity as opposed to the average person in the overall population."

In the instant case, it is undisputed that at the time of the actions in question, plaintiff was not yet substantially limited in her ability to care for herself, perform manual tasks, walk, see, speak, breath, learn, or work. Although she may have begun to exhibit early signs of Huntington's Disease, her own testimony established that it had only minor effects on her activities. Plaintiff argues that once she told Delhotal that she had been diagnosed with Huntington's, defendant perceived her as disabled, but she has no evidence to support that theory. Although Delhotal may have known that plaintiff had the disease, knowing that plaintiff was ill and perceiving her as disabled are different matters. To perceive plaintiff as disabled, Delhotal (who arguably was not plaintiff's supervisor) must have perceived plaintiff as substantially limited in a major life activity, and there is no evidence to support that theory.

Plaintiff also argues, however, that Huntington's Disease substantially limits reproduction, which *Bragdon v. Abbott*, 524 U.S. 624 (1998), holds is a major life activity. A person with Huntington's Disease has a 50% risk of passing the disease on to a child, a risk certainly substantial enough to control a decision. Plaintiff testified that she elected not to have a child based on this risk. Plaintiff had not yet been diagnosed with Huntington's when she made her decision, however, leaving open the question as to whether the *Bragdon* holding is applicable. The court need not reach the complicated issue of whether plaintiff's decision not to reproduce because she might have had Huntington's Disease constitutes a disability, because even if plaintiff was disabled, her claim of disability discrimination fails. Plaintiff's claim is for discriminatory treatment based on her disability. Therefore, she must establish that her disability impacted on defendant's decisions. She has not done so.

Plaintiff's theory of the case is that once learning of her disease, defendant began to scheme to terminate her. Thus, plaintiff argues that there was no need to immediately replace her, and that her replacement was hired simply to assure that there would be no position for her to return to once being medically cleared for work. This argument is negated by plaintiff's own original request for leave, however, in which she acknowledged that "I realize that this is not the best time for the Case Coordinator Department, in terms of staff availability and caseload. . . . " According to plaintiff, once defendant learned of her illness, it wanted her out to reduce its health insurance costs. Her only evidence to support this theory is that once plaintiff's replacement transferred to a new position, Boisse recommended that plaintiff's former position be eliminated. Straka's memorandum to Boisse accepting the recommendation listed a number of factors, including keeping down rising health insurance costs.

The problem with plaintiff's theory is that it is undisputed that plaintiff was offered a position that was substantially similar to the one she vacated. Had plaintiff accepted the position, defendant's health insurance costs would not have been reduced, destroying her theory. She argues that defendant (Boisse and Straka) knew that she could not take the position, but has no evidence to support that claim. Indeed, plaintiff took several days to determine that she did not want the position. Even under a reasonable accommodation theory, plaintiff does not have the right to pick and choose her position among reasonable accommodations. Plaintiff elected not to take the position offered by defendant. There is no evidence that Boisse and Straka based their decisions to offer her that particular position based on her condition. Indeed, there is no evidence to suggest that Boisse or Straka even knew of her condition. Absent such knowledge, plaintiff could not have been terminated "because of" her disability as required by the ADA. Accordingly, because there is no evidence of a causal connection between plaintiff's alleged disability and defendant's decisions, and because plaintiff turned down a position that constituted a reasonable accommodation, defendant's motion for summary judgment is granted.

NOTES AND QUESTIONS

1. In deciding whether the plaintiff was covered under the ADA, the court observed that, at the time the case was brought, the plaintiff was not yet substantially limited in a major life activity, although she had begun to exhibit symptoms of Huntington's disease. Therefore, she was not covered under the ADA. Note, that if the plaintiff had brought suit after she was suffering from more severe symptoms, then she would probably be held to be unqualified for her job.

2. The plaintiff tried, unsuccessfully, to rely on *Bragdon* by claiming that her Huntington's disease adversely affected her reproductive plans. For a

further discussion of this theory, see Brian R. Gin, Note, Genetic Discrimination: Huntington's Disease and the Americans with Disabilities Act, 97 Colum. L. Rev. 1406 (1997). See also Laura F. Rothstein, Genetic Discrimination: Why Bragdon Does Not Ensure Protection, 3 J. Health Care L. & Pol'y 330 (2000).

3. *Laws* was brought under the ADA, but a similar plaintiff still would not be able to prevail today under GINA because the plaintiff's Huntington's disease already was "manifested," even though it was not yet a substantially limiting condition. Do you think individuals in the position of Patricia Laws should be protected by antidiscrimination law? If so, how would you structure such a law? Would you use a genetic-specific law or a more generic one?

4. In 2009, the University of Akron adopted a policy that the school reserves the right to require any prospective faculty, staff or contractor to submit a "DNA sample for the purpose of a federal criminal background check." Why would the university adopt such a policy? Would imposing such a condition of employment violate GINA? Would it violate federal or state DNA forensic statutes to use law enforcement data banks, such as CODIS, to perform background checks of employees? See Chapter 11. After considerable adverse publicity, the university appears to have abandoned the policy. See Declan McCullagh, University Backs Away From New–Hire DNA Testing (Nov. 6, 2009), www.cbsnews.com/sections/taking_liberties/main504383.shtml?contributor=45134.

Professor David Kaye, while noting the ridiculousness of the Akron policy, raises the legitimate question of whether an employer *ever* is justified in requiring a DNA sample of employees. For example, New York City requires police officers who handle crime-scene materials to provide DNA samples. "A laboratory that does forensic DNA typing, for instance, might wish to build a database of its employee's profiles so that it, the police, prosecutors, and judges and juries can be assured that the DNA profiles reported out by the laboratory are free of any effects of contamination from the employees' DNA." Should such DNA collection be excluded from the prohibitions of GINA? If so, how broad should the exclusion be? Section 202(b)(6) of GINA contains an exception to the ban on acquisition of genetic information for employees working in forensic laboratories. See David H. Kaye, Foolishness in Akron Raises a Serious Question about GINA (Oct. 31, 2009), www.personal.psu.edu/dhk3/blogs/DoubleHelixLaw/2009/10/foolishness-in-Akron-raises-a-serious-question-about-GINA.html.

CHAPTER 17

ENVIRONMENTAL AND OCCUPATIONAL REGULATION AND PERSONAL INJURY CASES

■ ■ ■

I. INTRODUCTION

Prior chapters have explored the relationship between genetic and environmental factors in human health and development in the context of clinical genetics (Chapters 6–8), pharmacogenomics (Chapter 9), and behavioral genetics (Chapter 13). Another interaction between genetics and the environment with important legal applications involves laws that protect the air, water, earth, wildlife, and food supply from pollutants. Similar issues are raised by laws that attempt to ensure that workers have safe and healthful workplaces. The overarching question is the degree to which human genetic variation should be considered in setting exposure limits and in prescribing other measures to prevent harm. One concern is that an overemphasis on genetic factors will shift the blame from polluters to the "faulty genes" of certain individuals. The regulatory consequences of adopting such an approach could include changing the focus from lowering exposures merely to warning at-risk individuals or, in the workplace setting, excluding them from employment. At the same time, it may simply not be technologically or economically feasible to lower all exposures to levels where the most vulnerable individuals can be exposed without any adverse health effects. It is difficult to decide what ethical and legal principles should be applied in these circumstances, especially when the scientific evidence is incomplete or inconclusive.

Regulatory agencies have begun considering genetic studies, and to a lesser extent epigenetic studies, in assessing the human health risks from environmental and occupational exposures. This chapter will consider the legal significance of developments in toxicogenomics and related avenues of scientific inquiry. In addition to discussing the applicable statutes, the chapter will also consider the admissibility and significance of genetic information proffered by either plaintiffs or defendants in personal injury litigation to prove or disprove exposure, causation, and damages. These legal actions could be based on negligence, strict liability, products liability, or other theories.

II. REGULATION

A. ENVIRONMENTAL

NATIONAL RESEARCH COUNCIL, APPLICATIONS OF TOXICOGENOMIC TECHNOLOGIES TO PREDICTIVE TOXICOLOGY AND RISK ASSESSMENT

186–189 (2007).

Toxicogenomic data have numerous potential applications in environmental, pharmaceutical, and occupational health regulation. Regulatory agencies such as the Environmental Protection Agency (EPA) and the [Food and Drug Administration (FDA)] have already produced guidance documents on the incorporation of genomic information into their regulatory programs. Some examples of potential regulatory applications of toxicogenomics and their implications are discussed below.

DEFINING NEW ADVERSE EFFECTS

Many regulatory requirements are based on a finding of "adverse effect." For example, national ambient air-quality standards set under the Clean Air Act are set at a level that protects against adverse effects in susceptible populations. Some subclinical effects (for example, changes in erythrocyte protoporphyrin concentration in blood) have been found to be adverse effects under this statutory provision and have required more stringent standards to prevent such effects from occurring in exposed populations. Furthermore, many EPA regulations for noncarcinogenic substances are based on the reference concentrations (RfC) or reference dose (RfD). Some gene expression or other changes measured with toxicogenomic technologies may constitute new adverse effects under these programs and thus lower RfDs and RfCs, resulting in more stringent regulations. Manufacturers of pesticides and toxic chemicals are required to notify the EPA of new scientific findings about adverse effects associated with their products. In pharmaceutical regulation, the detection of a biomarker that suggests an adverse effect may likewise trigger additional regulatory scrutiny or restrictions.

Therefore, a critical issue in the regulatory application of toxicogenomics will be determining whether and when a change constitutes an adverse effect. Many changes in gene expression, protein levels, and metabolite profiles will be adaptive responses to a stimulus that are not representative or predictive of a toxic response. Other toxicogenomic changes may be strongly indicative of a toxic response. Therefore, it will be important to distinguish true biomarkers of toxicity from reversible or adaptive responses and to do so in a way that is transparent, predictable, and consistent for the affected entities. At least initially, phenotypic anchoring of toxicogenomics changes to well-established toxicologic end points will likely be necessary to identify toxicologically significant markers.

REGULATORY DECISIONS BASED ON SCREENING ASSAYS

The availability of relatively inexpensive and quick toxicogenomics assays that can be used for hazard characterization of otherwise untested materials offers a number of potential regulatory opportunities. Full toxicologic characterization of the approximately 80,000 chemicals in commerce using a battery of traditional toxicology tests (for example, chronic rodent bioassay) is not economically or technologically feasible in the foreseeable future. Screening with a toxicogenomic assay, such as gene expression analysis that classifies agents based on transcript profiles, might be useful to quickly screen chemicals for prioritizing substances for further investigation and possible regulation. Another possibility is to require the manufacturer of a new chemical substance, or an existing substance that will be used in a new application, to include the results of a standardized toxicogenomics assay as part of a premanufacturing notice required under Section 5 of the Toxic Substances Control Act.

PROTECTION OF GENETICALLY SUSCEPTIBLE INDIVIDUALS

Many regulatory programs specifically require protection of susceptible individuals. For example, the Clean Air Act requires that national ambient air-quality standards be set at a level that protects the most susceptible subgroups within the population. Under this program, the EPA focuses its standard-setting activities on susceptible subgroups such as children with asthma. Recent studies indicate a significant genetic role in susceptibility to air pollution, which may lead to air-quality standards being based on the risks to genetically susceptible individuals. Regulations under other environmental statutes, such as pesticide regulations under the Food Quality Protection Act and drinking water standards under the Safe Drinking Water Act, may likewise focus on genetically susceptible individuals in the future, as might occupational exposure standards promulgated by the Occupational Safety and Health Administration. Likewise, pharmaceutical approvals may require considering and protecting individuals with genetic susceptibilities to a particular drug.

The identification of genetic susceptibilities to chemicals, consumer products, pharmaceuticals, and other materials raises a number of regulatory issues. One issue is the question of the feasibility of protecting genetically susceptible individuals. On the one hand, protecting the most susceptible individual in society may be extremely costly, and perhaps even infeasible without major, formidable changes in our industrial society. On the other hand, the concept of government regulators leaving the health of some individuals unprotected, who through no fault of their own are born with a susceptibility to a particular product or chemical, also seems politically and ethically infeasible. As more information on individual genetic susceptibility becomes available, regulators and society generally will confront difficult challenges in deciding whether and how to protect the most genetically vulnerable citizens in our midst.

GARY E. MARCHANT, TOXICOGENOMICS AND ENVIRONMENTAL REGULATION, IN GENOMICS AND ENVIRONMENTAL REGULATION: SCIENCE, ETHICS, AND LAW

11–14 (Richard R. Sharp, Gary E. Marchant, & Jamie A. Grodsky eds. 2008).

Major uncertainties and data gaps limit the utility and credibility of risk assessment for informing regulatory decisions. These uncertainties include extrapolating results from animals to humans and from high-dose to more typical low-dose human exposures, understanding the mechanism of action of a toxicant and its implications for risk assessment, determining the shape of the dose-response curve, and estimating the exposure levels for actual human populations. Gene expression data have the potential to help address many of these unknowns.

Toxicogenomic data can improve risk assessment in several ways. First, gene expression data, by providing a characteristic "fingerprint" of different toxicological mechanisms, can be used to characterize the mechanism or mode of action of a toxicant. Regulatory agencies such as the U.S. Environmental Protection Agency (EPA) have recently focused on mode of action as a key factor in risk assessment, because this information is critical for addressing the issues raised above and for deciding whether an agent is likely to exhibit a threshold below which there is no significant toxicity. As noted in EPA's 2002 Interim Policy on Genomics, toxicogenomics will "likely provide a better understanding of the mechanism or mode of action of a stressor and thus assist in predictive toxicology, in the screening of stressors, and in the design of monitoring activities and exposure studies."

Second, gene expression will be useful in extrapolating results obtained in animal and epidemiology studies that typically involve higher dose levels than those more relevant for the general human population. Until now, low-dose effects have generally been refractory to empirical analysis, and risk assessors have had to rely on models to extrapolate results from high to low dose levels. A finding that gene expression changes characteristic of the carcinogenic response of a particular agent at high doses are also observed in low-dose groups, even though those low-dose animals may not develop tumors, may indicate that low-dose exposures present a carcinogenic risk in large populations. Alternatively, the absence of any characteristic gene expression response in low-dose animals may suggest that the carcinogenetic response occurs only at high doses.

Third, gene expression patterns may help to assess the relevance of animal studies for humans. Most toxicology data comes from animal studies, which are often but not always relevant to humans. By providing a quick and inexpensive test of whether a chemical is causing a similar response in rodents and humans, gene expression assays can help prevent false positives for chemicals that cause toxicity in rodents but not in humans and false negatives for chemicals that cause toxicity in humans but not rodents.

Fourth, gene expression data may also be beneficial for exposure assessment. Many types of environmental exposures lack adequate exposure data, which severely limits the ability to accurately determine the relationship between dose and response that underlies risk-assessment estimates. By characterizing gene expression patterns in exposed persons, microarrays have the potential to provide more precise quantitative estimates of exposure to specific toxic substances in contemporaneous and prospective human studies.

Fifth, gene expression profiling may be particularly useful for evaluating the toxicity of chemical mixtures, which is difficult to do with traditional chemical-by-chemical toxicological methods. DNA microarrays permit the simultaneous monitoring of all gene expression changes within a cell in a single experiment, thus they are "particularly suitable to evaluate any kind of combinational effect resulting from combined exposure to toxicants."

These potential applications of gene expression data may help reduce many of the most important uncertainties in risk assessment, although by no means eliminating such uncertainties altogether. The effect may be to give risk regulation greater credibility and certainty, which will allow environmental regulation to more directly target the most serious risks to human health and the environment.

HIGH-THROUGHPUT TOXICITY SCREENING OF CHEMICALS

The majority of chemicals in commercial use in the United States have not been comprehensively tested for human toxicity and carcinogenicity potential. EPA and the chemical industry have begun to address this data gap for chemical risk assessment with the high-production volume (HPV) chemical testing initiative. However, given that there are now some 80,000 chemicals in commerce, it is not feasible to conduct full toxicological testing for all or even most of these chemicals using existing methods. As the then-director of the National Institute of Environmental Health Sciences testified to Congress in 2002, many commercial products require additional testing, but "we can never satisfy this testing requirement using traditional technologies."

Gene expression assays have the potential to provide rapid, inexpensive, and high-throughput screening of chemicals for a wide range of genotoxic and nongenotoxic responses. Microarrays can be used to interrogate the gene expression of cells either in tissue culture or in living laboratory animals that have been treated with putative toxic agents. The resulting gene expression profiles can be used to classify those chemicals in specific toxicological categories to characterize likely risks. In addition to their relatively low cost and rapid results, microarrays offer possible advantages as a screening assay. Microassays can monitor changes in the expression of all genes within a cell, potentially permitting simultaneous evaluation of all toxicological endpoints in a single assay, something that is not possible with traditional toxicological technologies. In addition, microassays allow a more sensitive assay of potential toxicity, because they test for the initial molecular events in a toxic response. This is more sensitive than other assay methods that tend to monitor clinical effects that do not occur until much later in the disease process.

Initially, gene expression assays will need to be conducted in association with traditional toxicity testing until a sufficiently robust and validated data set has been accumulated to reliably correlate specific gene expression profiles with particular toxicological mechanisms and endpoints. Used in conjunction with traditional toxicology tests, gene expression data have the potential to improve the sensitivity and interoperability of the standard tests. After an adequate relational database has been established, gene expression assays might replace some or all of the current toxicological screening and testing assays or at least select the specific assays indicated by the observed gene expression pattern.

NOTES AND QUESTIONS

1.   Toxicogenomics is defined as the application of genomic technologies to study the adverse effects of environmental and pharmaceutical chemicals on human health and the environment. National Research Council, Applications of Toxicogenomic Technologies to Predictive Toxicology and Risk Assessment 12 (2007).

2.   There are thousands of commonly used industrial and consumer chemicals that could have toxicogenomic-mediated adverse effects on human health. A possible strategy to protect individuals is to issue warnings, perhaps because of regulatory requirements or the desire to limit tort liability. Imagine the shelves of the neighborhood grocery or hardware store, with numerous products containing genotype-specific warnings about exposures and harms. How helpful do you think this information would be? Might there be harms from such warnings?

3.   One likely effect of toxicogenomics is to increase the amount of individual genomic information. Refer back to chapter 14. What risks to privacy, stigma, and discrimination are raised by this additional information? How, if at all, would you protect against the adverse uses and effects?

MARK A. ROTHSTEIN, YU CAI, & GARY E. MARCHANT, ETHICAL IMPLICATIONS OF EPIGENETICS RESEARCH

10 Nature Revs. Genetics 224 (2009).

* * *

First we consider environmental justice. Epigenetic effects have been associated with exposure to various toxic chemicals, airborne pollutants, pesticides and other harmful substances. Many of these exposures are linked with poverty, discriminatory land use, and substandard living and working conditions. At the same time, many individuals with these harmful exposures are considered medically vulnerable because of pre-existing health conditions that are frequently complicated by poor clinical management. Both the exposure to environmental hazards and the social, nutritional, medical and psychological stresses of low-income communities can separately and, perhaps even more importantly, cumulatively cause epigenetic changes that place exposed populations at increased risk. Epigenetics therefore provides a new window for understanding and possibly addressing the co-morbidities associated with disparate environmental exposures.

The second issue regards the intergenerational effects and equity of epigenetics research. A key implication of epigenetics research is that many environmental and hazardous exposures will affect not only the exposed individuals, but possibly their progeny and subsequent generations. This insight will create new challenges for environmental and health regulation, as well as for intergenerational equity. Intergenerational equity refers to the obligations of each generation to serve as a custodian or steward of the planet and its inhabitants for future generations. Thus, it could be asserted that each generation has an obligation to its decendants not to damage the genomes and epigenomes of future generations, such as through exposure to environmental hazards. It remains to be seen whether or how the possible transgenerational damage caused by environmentally induced epigenetic changes will affect environmental regulatory policies.

* * *

Some of the ethical concerns discussed above are similar to those already raised by genetics, but the role of environmental exposures in producing epigenetic effects adds new concerns. The use of epigenetics in environmental risk assessment will probably be among the first applications of the new research. Once epigenetic testing of individuals becomes available, concerns are likely to arise about possible privacy violations and epigenetic discrimination. The prospect of such non-genetic discrimination casts doubt on the wisdom and efficacy of current genetic-specific laws, and it suggests that broader laws are needed to prohibit adverse treatment on the basis of health status or biological markers.

Epigenetic research raises other profound issues, including individual and societal responsibilities to prevent hazardous exposures, monitor health status and provide treatment. Epigenetics also serves to highlight the effects of inequality in living and working conditions and adds a multigenerational dimension to environmentally caused adverse health effects.

NOTES AND QUESTIONS

1. As discussed in Chapter 2, epigenetics literally means "above the genetics." It refers to modifications of the genome that do not involve a change in the DNA sequence. The recent understanding of epigenetic processes stands in contrast to the traditional assumption that genetic variation was exclusively the result of changes in DNA sequence. Epigenetic changes or "marks" result from a wide range of environmental exposures, including diet, toxic substances, and environmental stressors. Epigenetic changes tend to occur at much higher rates than mutations in DNA sequences from similar exposures. Susceptibility is not only a function of dose, but also of the stage of development when exposure takes place, such as prenatal and neonatal exposure. Whereas genetic mutations tend to be irreversible, epigenetic changes can be reversed. How, if at all, should these factors influence legal regulation of substances causing epigenetic changes?

2. A distinctive feature of epigenetics, especially changes resulting from the process of methylation, is that the effects may persist in future generations despite the lack of DNA sequence modification. Thus, parental exposures (e.g., to diesel exhaust fumes) may be expressed not only in the exposed generation in the form of respiratory disease, but in future generations as well. The issue of intergenerational equity raised in the article excerpt has been applied in the context of various environmental hazards, such as nuclear waste disposal, climate change, and extinction of species of plants and animals. Do you think the present generation is the steward of the genomes and epigenomes of future generations? If so, how can such an abstract concern be implemented in laws?

3. There are many unresolved scientific questions surrounding epigenetics that will have significant effects on social policy. For example: How many substances and environmental conditions cause epigenetic effects, at what exposure levels, and at what time during human development? Are there predispositions that make certain individuals more susceptible to epigenetic changes? When will tests be commonly available to measure epigenetic effects? When will therapies be available to reverse epigenetic effects? Is it possible to regulate in the absence of answers to these questions?

4. For further discussion, see Mark A. Rothstein, Yu Cai, & Gary E. Marchant, The Ghost in Our Genes: Legal and Ethical Implications of Epigenetics, 19 Health Matrix 1 (2009).

B. OCCUPATIONAL

MARK A. ROTHSTEIN, OCCUPATIONAL HEALTH AND DISCRIMINATION ISSUES RAISED BY TOXICOGENOMICS IN THE WORKPLACE IN GENOMICS AND ENVIRONMENTAL REGULATION: SCIENCE, ETHICS, AND LAW

184–188 (Richard R. Sharp, Gary E. Marchant, & Jamie A. Grodsky eds. 2008).

The Occupational Safety and Health Act of 1970 is the primary federal law regulating worker safety and health. The OSH Act covers employment in every state and territory—an estimated six million workplaces and ninety million employees. Unlike many labor and unemployment laws, there is no minimum number of employees or dollar volume of business needed for coverage. The OSH Act applies to all employers engaged in a business affecting interstate commerce—an easy standard to satisfy.

Among other requirements, each covered employer must comply with two provisions of the statute. First, section 5(a)(1) requires each covered employer to keep its workplace free from recognized hazards that are causing or likely to cause death or serious physical harm to its employees. Second, section 5(a)(2) requires each covered employer to comply with occupational safety and health standards promulgated by the Occupational Safety and Health Administration (OSHA) of the U.S. Department of Labor. The failure to comply with these requirements may result in the assessment of a range of civil penalties depending on the nature and gravity of the violation as well as on other factors.

STANDARD SETTING

Section 6 of the statute provides for the promulgation of standards in three ways. First, under section 6(a) the secretary of labor was authorized from 1971 to 1973 to adopt as OSHA standards, without rulemaking procedures, two types of existing standards—national consensus standards (developed by private organizations) and established federal standards (promulgated under other federal laws). This provision was designed to ensure the existence of OSHA standards soon after the effective date of the OSH Act in 1971, by adopting standards with which industry already was familiar. Second, under section 6(b), the secretary may modify, revoke, or issue new standards by complying with detailed rule-making procedures. This is the most important standards promulgation provision for new health standards. Third, under section 6(c), the secretary may issue emergency temporary standards in extraordinary circumstances, which may remain in effect for up to six months. Because standards promulgated under this provision have been difficult to sustain on judicial review, it has been rarely used.

Occupational safety and health standards generally have not been developed with an explicit concern for individual variability in response to toxic substances. Although such standards are designed to provide the maximum protection possible, OSHA has recognized that it may not be possible to protect workers with heightened sensitivity. For example, the preamble to the coke oven emissions standard provides: "Because of the variability of individual response to carcinogens and other factors, the concept of a 'threshold level' may have little applicability on the basis of existing knowledge. Some individuals may be more susceptible than others. Thus, while a 'threshold' exposure level, below which exposure does not cause cancer, may conceivably exist for an individual, susceptible individuals in the working population may have cancer induced by doses so low as to be effectively zero." New toxicogenomic studies will identify an increasing number of substances for which a particular genotype confers greater risk of illness based on occupational exposures. OSHA will need to decide if, or to what extent, individual variability should be incorporated into the agency's standards promulgation strategy.

As an initial matter, it is necessary to consider OSHA's statutory authority to promulgate health standards and the judicial construction of the exercise of that authority. Section 6(b)(5) of the OSH Act, which deals with the promulgation of standards for toxic substances and harmful physical agents, provides in part: "The Secretary of Labor shall set the standard which most adequately assures, to the extent feasible.... that no employee will suffer material impairment of health." This seemingly absolute language might be read as requiring OSHA to set standards at a level where even the most sensitive employee could work without ill effects. However, in *Industrial Union Department, AFL–CIO v. American Petroleum Institute* (1980)—also known as the *Benzene* decision—the Supreme Court rejected the notion that the OSH Act requires regulation at the level of zero risk.

The *Benzene* decision involved an industry challenge to OSHA rule-making that lowered the permissible exposure limit for benzene from 10 parts per million to 1 part per million. In striking down the benzene standard, the Fifth Circuit held that, based on section 3(5) of the OSH Act, the secretary was required to prove that the benefits of the standard bear a reasonable relationship to the costs. The Supreme Court affirmed, but on different grounds. According to the plurality opinion, the secretary must initially demonstrate the need for a new standard by establishing that exposure at current levels poses a "significant risk" of harm. Because the secretary failed to make this finding, the benzene standard was struck down. The Court also cautioned that the duty imposed on employers by the statute was not absolute. "The statute was not designed to require employers to provide absolutely risk-free workplaces whenever it is technologically feasible to do so ... [but] was intended to require the elimination, as far as feasible, of significant risks of harm."

Although the Supreme Court never explicitly stated whether the OSH Act requires employers to set exposure levels that would protect the most sensitive workers, *Benzene* implicitly holds that it does not. OSHA standards for toxic substances could be set to avoid requiring absolute levels of protection in two main ways: they could be limited to control measures that are economically and technologically feasible, or they could establish permissible exposure levels that would not protect the most sensitive workers. Although these appear to be distinct concepts, as a scientific and practical matter, they are closely related. Figure 11.1 plots a hypothetical linear dose-response curve.

As the dose increases (along the horizontal axis), the percentage of affected workers increases (along the vertical axis), and as the percentage of workers increases, even less sensitive individuals will exhibit the biological response. The lowest feasible level for reducing exposure is indicated by f. The intersection of f with the dose-response line, point 0, results in setting the susceptibility cutoff at s. Consequently, a standard lowering exposures only to the *Benzene* requirement of feasibility will necessarily result in a lack of protection for some of the most susceptible workers.

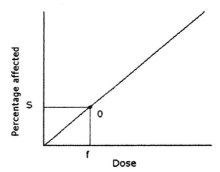

Figure 11.1. The Intersection of feasibility
and susceptibility in dose-response analysis

NOTES AND QUESTIONS

1. The *Benzene* case implicitly acknowledges it is impossible to protect the most sensitive workers from adverse health effects caused by occupational exposures. If Congress or the Supreme Court were to make this principle more explicit, what would it say? What would be the likely public reaction?

2. The *Benzene* case fills 118 pages of the U.S. Reports—an indication of the complexity of the issues and the divisions within the Court. Toxicogenomics is likely to make the scientific issues even more complicated. Is judicial review of regulatory action now beyond the technical competence of the judiciary? Are there alternatives?

3. In American Textile Mfrs. Institute, Inc. v. Donovan, 452 U.S. 490 (1981), the Supreme Court rejected the industry argument that the OSH Act requires the use of cost-benefit analysis. Relying on the plain meaning of the word "feasible" in § 6(b)(5) as "capable of being done," the Court held that imposing a cost-benefit requirement would be inconsistent with the mandate of Congress.

MARK A. ROTHSTEIN, GENETICS AND THE WORK FORCE OF THE NEXT HUNDRED YEARS

2000 Colum. Bus. L. Rev. 371, 393–95 (2000).

Autonomy and paternalism conflict in the area of genetic predisposition to occupational disease. Should workers be screened for polymorphic markers of varied sensitivity to toxic chemicals and other hazards in some workplaces? One view is that workers should not be screened; instead, the employer should be required to make the workplace safe and healthful for all workers. The problem is that reducing exposures to levels where even the most sensitive individual can work safely is neither technologically nor economically feasible because of the wide variability among individuals and because the difficulty and cost of reducing exposure levels increases exponentially as exposures are reduced to very low levels. The opposite view is that employers should be free to use genetic screening as a way of protecting the health of employees and their own financial interests. This approach, however, shifts the economic burden of working with dangerous substances from the employer to the worker, removes an important incentive to clean up workplaces for the benefit of even "low-risk" workers, and runs counter to the notion of autonomy embraced in *Johnson Controls* [In International Union, UAW v. Johnson Controls, Inc., 499 U.S. 187 (1991), the Supreme Court held that the employer's rule prohibiting assignment of any fertile women to work with exposure to lead (which may cause in utero birth defects to the fetus of a pregnant woman employee) was sex discrimination because women have the right to decide which risks to their reproductive health are acceptable] as well as the ADA [Americans with Disabilities Act].

A middle position is that a worker who is currently capable of performing the job should have the option of learning whether he or she is at increased risk of occupational disease based on genetic factors. This information should not be available to the employer, but should be used by the employee in deciding whether to accept or continue in the position. A threshold issue is whether a scientific test has sufficient analytical and clinical utility to be used as a screening device for individuals, as opposed to a research tool for population studies. Another issue is what criteria should be used in evaluating whether there is scientific justification for the individual to avoid a job with a certain exposure. Finally, other logistical questions include how individuals get referred for genetic testing, who pays for the testing, and who has access to test results.

In my view, where employers know or should know that research has identified genetic markers of increased risk based on exposure to substances in their workplace, they have a duty to inform applicants and employees. The applicants and employees then should have the option of undergoing genetic testing at the employer's expense, administered by a physician of the applicant's or employee's choosing, with the results available only to the individual. If the test is positive, the physician or a genetic counselor should discuss the risks of employment with the individual. The choice of whether to accept or continue in the job would rest with the individual. Only where employment of an individual would create a direct, immediate, and severe risk of harm to self, others, or property would the employer be justified in performing its own testing and excluding the individual from employment. These situations are likely to be rare.

NOTES AND QUESTIONS

1.   Section 202(b)(5) of GINA, provides that it is not unlawful for an employer to offer employees voluntary genetic monitoring to determine whether prior occupational exposures have caused genetic changes. GINA does not permit employers to offer new employees and those initially being assigned to work where there are certain exposures voluntary genetic screening to assess whether they are at increased risk from occupational exposures. Would you favor extending the exception to pre-exposure genetic screening?

2.   One of the first applications of toxicogenomic testing in the workplace involves occupational exposure to beryllium, a lightweight metal widely used in aircraft components, nuclear weapons, and a variety of industrial products. Exposure to beryllium can result in chronic beryllium disease (CBD), a serious respiratory condition. Individuals with a particular genetic marker, HLA–DPB1–Glu69, have been shown to be at an increased risk of CBD. At least two employers have used voluntary genetic screening for new workers, who could elect to undergo testing at no cost by an independent laboratory, with individual results not reported to the employer. Such efforts at genetic screening have raised a variety of scientific, ethical, and legal issues, many of them stemming from the low positive predictive value of the test. For a further discussion, see Ken Silver & Richard R. Sharp, Ethical Considerations in Testing Workers for the–Glu69 Marker of Genetic Susceptibility to Chronic Beryllium Disease, 48 J. Occup. & Envtl. Med. 434 (2006).

GENETIC TESTING FOR SUSCEPTIBILITY
TO CARPAL TUNNEL SYNDROME

Burlington Northern Santa Fe Railroad (BNSF) is the nation's second largest railroad company. The railroad operates 33,500 route miles of track covering 28 states and two Canadian provinces. In March 2000, BNSF began a pilot program that included genetic testing for employees who claimed work-related carpal tunnel disease. Rail industry safety rules and negotiated union contracts allow BNSF to require employees to undergo medical examinations to evaluate work-related injury claims. Since the initiation of the new policy, approximately 125 of its 40,000 active employees filed claims for carpal tunnel-related injuries. Of those 125, genetic testing was performed on 23 employees. None of the employees was told that the blood sample they were giving was being sent to a research laboratory for genetic analysis.

BNSF's practice of requiring genetic tests came to the attention of the Equal Employment Opportunity Commission (EEOC) when Janice Avary, a registered nurse and wife of a BNSF employee, began looking into the reason why BNSF was requiring her husband to submit seven vials of blood after he filed a claim for a carpal tunnel injury. Avary was concerned that her husband was asked to furnish such a large amount of blood and that he was not instructed to fast to ensure accurate results, as is typical when blood tests are taken. Two days before the scheduled exam, Avary called the company to ask for an explanation and to get a list of the lab tests that her husband would undergo. When the company's medical liaison mentioned possible genetic tests, Avary became alarmed. She called the railroad's headquarters to inform them that they could not subject her husband to a genetic test without his permission (under Iowa state law). According to Avary, BNSF told her that if her husband refused the exam, he could face an investigation for insubordination.

As a result of this experience, Gary Avary filed a complaint with the EEOC. Soon after, five more workers told the EEOC that they had given blood during the medical exams but were unaware of its ultimate use. While the union and the EEOC were investigating the claims against BNSF, Gary Avary received a disciplinary letter from BNSF as a result of his failure to comply with the examination. In response to this letter and to BNSF's practice of requiring genetic testing, on February 9, 2001, EEOC filed its first court action challenging genetic testing. EEOC v. Burlington Northern Santa Fe R.R. Co., No. C01–4013 (N.D. Iowa, filed Feb. 9, 2001). In its petition, the EEOC asked for a preliminary injunction against BNSF requiring the company to end genetic testing of employees who have filed claims for work-related injuries based on carpal tunnel syndrome. The EEOC alleged that the employees were unaware that they were submitting to a genetic test and further, that they were not asked to consent to such a test. The EEOC asked the court to order the railroad to end its nationwide policy of requiring employees who have submitted claims of work-related carpal tunnel syndrome to provide blood samples which are then used for a genetic DNA test for a chromosome 17 deletion associated with hereditary pressure palsy neuropathy, a rare condition which may predict some forms of carpal tunnel syndrome. For a discussion of the scientific basis of the genetic testing, see Paul A. Schulte & Geoffrey Lomax, Assessment of the Scientific Basis for Genetic Testing of Railroad Workers with Carpal Tunnel Syndrome, 45 J. Occup. & Envt'l Med. 592 (2003).

The EEOC also sought to halt any disciplinary action or termination of an employee who has refused to submit a blood sample. The EEOC claimed that the genetic testing violated the Americans with Disabilities Act (ADA) because it is not job-related or consistent with business necessity. Section 102 (d)(4) of the ADA provides that any medical examinations or inquiries of current employees must be either voluntary or job-related and consistent with business necessity, meaning that they measure the ability to perform the job safely and efficiently. EEOC's position was that the unproven test was not job-related. On February 12, 2001, BNSF announced that it would suspend its practice of requiring genetic testing, and a settlement agreement was approved by the court on April 18, 2001.

The *Burlington Northern* case generated a substantial amount of publicity. It was widely reported as the first action brought by the EEOC alleging genetic discrimination. Part of the publicity may be attributable to the fact that the case arose within days of the joint publication in *Nature* and *Science* of the completed draft sequence of the human genome. Thus, it provided the counterpoint for the scientific marvel—the possibility that genetics could result in discrimination. Yet, it is arguable that the case has little to do with genetics. What ADA and common law legal theories could be asserted by the EEOC and individual plaintiffs? How strong a case is this? What is the central ethical issue surrounding this incident?

III. LITIGATION

A. INJURY

BRYSON v. PILLSBURY CO.

573 N.W.2d 718 (Minn.Ct.App.1998).

KALITOWSKI, J.

Appellant Nora Bryson challenges the district court's grant of summary judgment in favor of respondents Pillsbury Company, et al., arguing the district court erred because: (1) Bryson submitted evidence that raised a genuine issue of material fact as to whether she suffered a present injury; and (2) Bryson presented sufficient evidence to establish her claim for damages based on her alleged increased risk of developing cancer.

FACTS

Appellant Nora Bryson boarded her horse at the farm of an individual who, like Bryson, was an employee of respondent Pillsbury's subsidiary, Green Giant (company). On July 23, 1990, Bryson discovered that her horse had fallen into a pit filled with water from a storm. The pit, which was 20 feet by 20 feet with a 17–foot depth, had allegedly been used by the company to dispose of waste. Bryson entered the pit in an attempt to rescue the horse and, while in the pit, observed what she believed to be Captan–treated seeds floating in the water. Captan is a chemical treatment for seed that protects it from insects in the soil until germination.

Bryson and others succeeded in getting the horse out of the water. Later that day, Bryson broke out in a rash that covered her body. She presented evidence that she has subsequently developed additional rashes. Bryson, through her expert from the University of Minnesota, presented evidence that she suffered extensive chromosome breakage as a result of exposure to Captan and that, because of the chromosome breakage, she has an increased risk of developing cancer. The company made a motion for summary judgment arguing: (1) Bryson assumed the risk of harm by not leaving the pit when she saw the Captan–treated seeds; and (2) Bryson's alleged damages were too speculative. The district court denied the company's summary judgment motion on assumption of risk, but granted summary judgment in favor of the company stating that Bryson suffered no present injury and concluding that her claimed damages for future harm were too speculative as a matter of law.

ISSUES

1. Did Bryson present sufficient evidence to support her claim of a present injury?

2. Did Bryson present sufficient evidence to support her claim for damages based on her alleged increased risk of developing cancer?

ANALYSIS

* * *

Bryson contends the district court erred in granting summary judgment, claiming she presented sufficient evidence to raise a genuine fact issue as to whether her chromosome damage constituted a present injury. The company asserts that because Bryson's claimed chromosome damage is asymptomatic, it does not constitute a legally compensable present injury. In a memorandum supporting its order for summary judgment, the district court, without reference to Bryson's allegations regarding present damages, stated: "In this matter there are no present injuries * * *." We conclude the district court erred by granting summary judgment where there is a genuine issue of disputed material fact regarding whether there was a present injury.

In Werlein v. United States, 746 F.Supp. 887, 901 (D.Minn.1990), vacated in part on other grounds, 793 F.Supp. 898 (D.Minn.1992), the United States District Court addressed a case in which the plaintiffs claimed that exposure to contaminated air and drinking water resulted in chromosome damage. The defendants argued that the plaintiffs did not suffer a present injury. In denying the defendants' summary judgment motion, the court in Werlein stated that it could not

> rule as a matter of law that plaintiffs' alleged injuries are not "real" simply because they are subcellular. The effect of volatile organic compounds on the human body is a subtle, complex matter. It is for the trier of fact, aided by expert testimony, to determine whether plaintiffs have suffered present harm.

The asymptomatic, subcellular damages claimed in Werlein are similar to the injury claimed by Bryson. Here Bryson's expert witness presented evidence that Bryson's exposure to Captan resulted in chromosome breakage, and that such breakage is a "real and present physical and biologic injury." This testimony was disputed by the company, whose expert testified that an elevated number of chromosome aberrations are not considered an "injury" per se because they do not in and of themselves result in any physical impairment.

Following the reasoning of *Werlein,* we conclude the trier of fact should resolve this fact dispute.

Further, like the plaintiffs in *Werlein,* Bryson claims emotional distress damages and medical monitoring expenses because of her alleged chromosome damage. The court in *Werlein* determined that the existence and extent of these alleged damages also presented fact questions for the jury. Again, following *Werlein,* we conclude that because there are genuine fact issues concerning the existence of Bryson's present injuries and damages, summary judgment on this claim is inappropriate.

Bryson next argues that because she has offered expert evidence that she has a present injury, she need only present evidence that is "fair comment" on the medical implications of chromosome breakage to establish future damages resulting from her increased risk of cancer. Alternatively, Bryson argues that she has presented sufficient evidence to a reasonable medical certainty that entitles her to compensation for future damages as a result of her increased risk of cancer. The district court concluded that because Bryson can neither prove that her increased risk of future harm is more likely than not to occur, nor quantify her increased risk of developing cancer, her claimed damages for increased risk of future harm are too speculative as a matter of law. We agree.

A plaintiff must prove every element of a claim by a preponderance of the evidence. For Bryson to establish her claim for future damages, she must show: (1) that the future harm is more likely than not to occur; and (2) that her future damages are not too speculative. Bryson failed to present evidence on both issues.

We disagree with Bryson's contention that she need only present evidence that is "fair comment" on the medical implications of chromosome breakage. The term "fair comment" has been used to characterize expert medical testimony for purposes of determining the admissibility of evidence, not to provide the standard for proving future injury. Here, Bryson's expert admitted that Bryson's increased risk of cancer could not be measured or quantified. Thus, the evidence presented by Bryson does not, as a matter of law, permit a factfinder to determine that Bryson is more likely than not to develop cancer.

Further, this court [has] affirmed the principle that plaintiffs may not recover damages that are too speculative. The determination of whether damages are too speculative or remote "should usually be left to the judgment of the trial court." Because Bryson has presented no evidence to quantify her risk of developing cancer, we conclude the district court properly granted summary judgment in favor of the company on Bryson's claim for future damages.

DECISION

The district court properly granted summary judgment in favor of the company on Bryson's claim for damages based on an alleged increased risk of future harm because: (1) Bryson has not presented evidence that it is more likely than not that she will develop cancer; and (2) Bryson's claimed damages for the increased risk of cancer are too speculative as a matter of law. We conclude, however, Bryson has presented sufficient evidence to establish a genuine issue of material fact concerning the existence of a present injury and damages as a result of the alleged injury. We, therefore, reverse and remand this claim for further proceedings.

Affirmed in part, reversed in part, and remanded; motion to strike denied.

SHORT, J. (concurring in part, dissenting in part).

I concur insofar as the majority concludes the trial court properly granted summary judgment in favor of Pillsbury Company on Bryson's "risk of cancer" claim. I respectfully dissent on the narrow remand concerning Bryson's "chromosome breakage" claim because there is no evidence supporting an award of damages for present physical injury. Mere allegations of emotional distress and possible medical monitoring expenses are insufficient to create a fact issue on whether Bryson now suffers from a present physical injury.

Even if an asymptomatic chromosome condition constitutes evidence of a present physical injury, Bryson also failed to offer any evidence that her alleged damages are capable of proof to a reasonable certainty. Under these circumstances, Bryson has no compensable injury and Pillsbury Company is entitled to judgment as a matter of law. I would affirm the trial court's grant of summary judgment.

NOTES AND QUESTIONS

1. How can biomarkers of a genetic, unexpressed or preclinical "injury" help to prove causation and to establish a compensable harm?

The power of biomarkers to validate latent risk claims is demonstrated by the following hypothetical. A young woman is exposed to vinyl chloride emitted by a nearby factory. A blood test reveals the presence of DNA adducts in her lymphocytes that are consistent with a significant recent exposure to vinyl chloride. Two years later, the woman has a son with a mutation that inactivates ("knocks out") one of his two copies of the $p53$ tumor suppressor gene. The mutation has the "genetic fingerprint" that is characteristic of vinyl chloride. Genetic testing of the mother reveals that most of her cells contain no such mutation, although a few of her cells have similar mutations. Moreover, other sequence variations in the mother's $p53$ genes confirm that the son's defective copy of the gene came from the mother, thus indicating that the mutation must have arisen in the mother's germ cells. With only one functioning copy of the $p53$ gene, the son is at a permanent, significantly increased risk of cancer. A mutation to the remaining functional copy of the *p53* gene, arising either spontaneously or from some other exposure later in life, would almost certainly result in cancer. By providing objective and specific evidence of an increased risk and the probable cause of such risk, the genetic biomarker strengthens the case for such a plaintiff to recover damages for his permanent and irreversible risk.

Gary E. Marchant, Genetic Susceptibility and Biomarkers in Toxic Injury Litigation, 41 Jurimetrics 67, 87 (2000). See also Jamie A. Grodsky, Genomics and Toxic Torts: Dismantling the Risk–Injury Divide, 59 Stan. L. Rev. 1671 (2007); Gary E. Marchant, Genetic Data in Toxic Tort Litigation, 14 J.L. & Pol'y 7 (2006).

2. Is subclinical damage compensable, either by itself or because it signifies increased risk? In general, the courts have not been receptive to such claims based on products liability, see In re Rezulin Products Liability Litigation, 361 F. Supp.2d 268 (S.D.N.Y. 2005), or emotional distress, see Parker v. Wellman, 230 Fed. Appx. 878 (11th Cir. 2007). A physical injury or disabling sign or symptom is required.

3. The measure of the damages for increased risk of future harms will, undoubtedly, be smaller than the damages for any harms that actually occur. Why not simply wait to see whether the injury manifests itself and then sue? What effect would statutes of limitation have in calculating whether to sue immediately after the injury or wait until the damage appears clinically? See Christopher H. Schroeder, Corrective Justice and Liability for Increasing Risks, 37 UCLA L. Rev. 439 (1990).

4. Two other issues are also relevant: (1) the availability of damages for the psychological harm of worrying whether certain illnesses will become manifest, see James F. D'Entremont, Fear Factor: The Future of Cancerphobia and Fear of Future Disease Claims in the Toxicogenomic Age, 52 Loy. L. Rev. 807 (2006); and (2) the damages associated with increased medical monitoring to detect the early symptoms of disease at a time when treatment will be most effective, see James M. Garner et al., Medical Monitoring: The Evolution of a Cause of Action, 30 Envt'l L. Rep. 10,024 (2000).

B. CAUSATION

WINTZ v. NORTHROP CORP.

110 F.3d 508 (7th Cir.1997).

COFFEY, J.

Plaintiffs-appellants Van Wintz and Jill Wintz, both individually and on behalf of their daughter Jessica (the "Wintzes"), appeal the district court's order granting the jointly-filed motion for summary judgment of defendants-appellees Northrop Corporation ("Northrop") and Eastman Kodak Company ("Kodak"). The Wintzes sought damages for injuries allegedly suffered by Jessica as a result of her *in utero* exposure to the chemical bromide, allegedly contained in photographic developing material manufactured by Kodak and used by Jill Wintz in the course of her employment with Northrop. The questions presented are whether the district court erred in excluding the proffered testimony of a toxicologist hired by the Wintzes, and whether, absent that testimony, the Wintzes failed to establish a genuine issue of fact as to whether exposure to bromide caused injury to Jessica. We affirm.

I. BACKGROUND

Prior to and during her pregnancy with Jessica, Jill Wintz was employed by Northrop as an Industrial Engineer Associate in Northrop's Defense Systems Division. Her employment with Northrop began in May 1979, and continued through March 1982. From March 1980 through October 1980, while she was pregnant, Jill's duties involved the mixing of certain chemicals manufactured by Kodak to develop photographic film used in the manufacturing process of the "black box" for jet fighter aircraft. One of these chemicals, Kodalith Developer B, contained bromide. The chemicals came in powdered form in paper-type bags, and Jill poured them from the bag into a container for mixing with water. During this process, the powder from the bags would create a dust in the air, and Jill alleges that she inhaled this dust while mixing the chemicals. According to Jill's affidavit, she was "never given or advised to use any type of protective breathing mask or other protective equipment during mixing or use of the chemical powders." Jill Wintz worked in this capacity for Northrop from March 1980 until she took a maternity leave of absence on October 31, 1980, approximately five weeks before giving birth to Jessica, and she mixed the chemicals on a daily basis during this period.

Jessica was born at Lutheran General Hospital in Park Ridge, Illinois on December 6, 1980, and shortly thereafter she began displaying a number of atypical symptoms for newborns. Most noticeably, according to the deposition of Dr. Henry Mangurten, a neonatologist who treated Jessica at that time, she displayed hypotonia (low muscle tone), poor sucking reflexes, and weak or infrequent cry, as well as abnormal facial features. When she was but four days old, the baby was placed in a neonatal intensive care unit and came under Dr. Mangurten's care. In an effort to determine the cause of these abnormal behavioral symptoms, Dr. Mangurten ordered a variety of tests but they came back inconclusive, at which time the specialist saw fit to interview and gain additional background information from Jill Wintz. Upon learning that Jill worked in an environment in which bromide was present, Dr. Mangurten, based on his previous experience in which he had treated a baby with elevated bromide levels and who had displayed symptoms similar to Jessica's, ordered a bromide test on the baby. A urine sample was obtained when she was 11 days old and prior to learning the results of this test, Jessica's condition showed signs of improvement and she was released from the neonatal intensive care unit when she was but 13 days old. Shortly thereafter, the test revealed elevated levels of bromide in Jessica's system. The doctor, at this time, ordered another urine sample taken when Jessica was 20 days old and this test again revealed the presence of bromide in her system but at a decreased level. This time, Dr. Mangurten also ordered a bromide test on her mother, Jill, which also revealed elevated bromide levels in her system as well.

Dr. Mangurten stated that Jessica's condition had improved somewhat, though not entirely, at the time she was released from the neonatal intensive care unit. According to Dr. Mangurten, Jessica's condition was tracked for roughly four years after she left Lutheran General pursuant to a follow-up program the hospital maintains for infants who have spent time in the neonatal intensive care unit. In an affidavit, Dr. Barbara Burton, Director for the Center of Medical and Reproductive Genetics at Michael Reese Hospital in Chicago, who reviewed Jessica's complete medical records, stated that Jessica has continued to display abnormal symptoms through the present, including strabismus (deviation of the eye), myopia, frequent upper respiratory infections, enamel defects in her teeth, and delayed development in mental and physical milestones. Dr. Burton, who is an expert in genetics and genetic disorders, opined in her affidavit that Jessica's symptoms are all "classical" symptoms of a person afflicted with a genetic disorder known as Prader–Willi Syndrome ("PWS").[1]

In the course of her follow-up care after being discharged, it was learned (and is not disputed by the Wintzes) that Jessica was in fact born with PWS. PWS is caused by a deletion of genetic material from the father's chromosomes. It is a purely genetic disorder which occurs prior to conception, and it cannot be caused by environmental exposure. As the Wintzes have acknowledged, all of the abnormal symptoms Jessica has experienced throughout her life are very similar, if not identical, to those experienced by children with PWS. During his deposition, Dr. Mangurten agreed with the statement that Jessica's developmental problems have "almost certainly" been caused by PWS.

In addition to Dr. Mangurten, the Wintzes listed Gilbert Elenbogen ("Elenbogen"), a toxicologist, as an expert witness. The Wintzes asserted that Elenbogen would testify that exposure to bromide caused Jessica's abnormalities. Elenbogen opined in an affidavit that Jill Wintz's exposure to bromide while mixing the photographic chemicals caused Jessica to be exposed to bromide, and that this exposure, as stated in Elenbogen's affidavit, "caused the child's symptoms at birth and her permanent developmental damage and problems." Elenbogen did acknowledge that Jessica had PWS, and that her symptoms which he attributed to her prenatal exposure to bromide were identical to those caused by PWS. No other expert testified for the Wintzes on the issue of causation.

Kodak and Northrop filed a combined motion for summary judgment after deposing Elenbogen and Mangurten. They argued that Elenbogen's testimony was inadmissible under rule 702 of the Federal Rules of

---

1. Prader–Willi Syndrome is defined as "a congenital disorder characterized by rounded face, almond-shaped eyes, strabismus, low forehead, hypogonadism, hypotomia, insatiable appetite, early hypotonia, failure to thrive, and mental retardation." *Dorland's Illustrated Medical Dictionary* 1638 (28th ed. 1994).

Evidence as interpreted by the Supreme Court in Daubert v. Merrell Dow Pharmaceuticals, 509 U.S. 579 (1993). They argued that the toxicologist Elenbogen was not a licensed physician and surgeon and lacked sufficient experience with bromide or with PWS, and was thus not qualified to render an opinion as an expert as to the cause of Jessica's injuries. Northrop and Kodak further argued that, because Elenbogen's opinion that bromide caused Jessica's injuries was inadmissible due to his lack of qualifications, and because Dr. Mangurten agreed in his deposition testimony that PWS was the cause of Jessica's developmental problems, the Wintzes failed to establish a genuine issue of material fact as to whether bromide exposure was a proximate cause of any of Jessica's abnormalities. In a memorandum opinion dated December 21, 1995, the district judge agreed with Kodak and Northrop. The district court entered a summary judgment order in favor of Kodak and Northrop on December 21, and the Wintzes appealed.

* * *

In the present case, Dr. Mangurten's deposition established in clear and unequivocal language that, in his opinion, PWS caused Jessica's long-term developmental problems. It also established that he could not offer an opinion with any reasonable degree of medical certainty that Jessica's short-term problems at birth were caused by bromide, notwithstanding the observation that her symptoms decreased at the same time the bromide levels decreased. Whatever support the Wintzes hope to find in [Champion v. Knasiak, 323 N.E.2d 62 (Ill.App.Ct. 1974)], we do not agree that it can be read to suggest that they did not have the obligation to come forward with affirmative evidence to support their causation argument. Thus, the trial court did not err in concluding that Dr. Mangurten's testimony was insufficient to create a genuine issue of fact as to whether bromide caused any of Jessica's long-term or short-term symptoms.

The district court's decision excluding the proffered testimony of the Wintzes' toxicologist was not manifestly erroneous, and the evidence, when considered in its totality, fell short of raising a genuine issue of material fact as to the cause of Jessica's short-term or long-term symptoms. WE AFFIRM the grant of summary judgment in favor of Kodak and Northrop.

NOTES AND QUESTIONS

1. As indicated in *Bryson* and *Wintz,* genetic information may be helpful to the plaintiff or the defendant.

2. Genetic testing has been used by plaintiffs' lawyers to prove that a plaintiff's condition was *not* the result of a genetic disorder, thereby rebutting a defendant's claim to the contrary. See Lori B. Andrews, Future Perfect 143 (2001).

3. The issue of causation has been one of the great conundrums of tort law. Toxic injuries and toxicogenomics add a layer of complexity to the issue

of causation in fact. For example, scientists may demonstrate convincingly that if 1,000 people are exposed to substance A at B levels for C amount of time per day, over D number of years there will be E cases of cancer, which greatly exceeds the F number of cases for a similar group of unexposed people. Are these facts enough to establish that any particular individual's exposure to substance A caused his or her cancer? If not, what additional evidence is necessary? Genetic biomarkers may help to prove that the exposure actually caused a particular individual's cancer. If the science has not developed appropriate measures for the substance and disease at issue, what level of statistically increased risk should be required to prove causation in fact for legal purposes? See Daniel A. Farber, Toxic Causation, 71 Minn. L. Rev. 1219 (1987); Sander Greenland & James M. Robins, Epidemiology, Justice, and the Probability of Causation, 40 Jurimetrics J. 321 (2000).

C. DAMAGES

MARK A. ROTHSTEIN, PREVENTING THE DISCOVERY OF PLAINTIFF GENETIC PROFILES BY DEFENDANTS SEEKING TO LIMIT DAMAGES IN PERSONAL INJURY LITIGATION

71 Ind. L.J. 877, 878–891 (1996).

Imagine the following situation: Dr. Jane Smith is a thirty-five year-old neurosurgeon who entered private practice three years ago upon completion of her training. She has an annual income of $200,000. One day, while crossing the street from the doctors' parking lot to the hospital, she is run over by a Zippy Express delivery truck, whose unlicensed, intoxicated driver was speeding to a delivery and failed to stop for a red light. As a result of the accident, Dr. Smith has become quadriplegic and will be unable to perform surgery again.

In a negligence action against Zippy Express, a key component of Dr. Smith's economic damages is her lost income. Assuming she would have been able to work for thirty more years, with an income of $200,000 per year, this would amount to six million in current dollars, exclusive of projected earnings increases, merely for lost income.

Suppose, however, that Dr. Smith is in the unaffected, presymptomatic stage of Huntington's disease, amyotrophic lateral sclerosis, or some other late-onset genetic disorder. Further suppose that experts will testify that, in all likelihood, irrespective of the accident, she would not have been able to practice medicine beyond age forty-five and that her life expectancy is fifty years. Applying traditional damages principles, this information would reduce her recovery for economic injury by at least four million dollars.

Zippy Express and its insurers therefore would have a great economic incentive to discover information about Dr. Smith's genetic profile and to introduce this information at trial. Should the defendants be able to discover this information by obtaining access to Dr. Smith's medical records? Should they be able to obtain a court order directing Dr. Smith to submit to genetic testing? Should it matter whether genetic testing previously had been performed on Dr. Smith or whether there was something in her family or medical history to suspect a genetic disorder? Should it matter whether Dr. Smith was suspected of having a genetic risk of a monogenic disorder, such as Huntington's disease, or a multifactorial disorder, such as cancer? What effect, if any, should be given to the penetrance, variable expressivity, and treatability of the disorder? Should it matter if Dr. Smith objects to genetic testing?

* * *

II.   DAMAGES FOR LOST FUTURE EARNINGS

In personal injury litigation, special damages for quantifiable losses are based on the increased expenses and lost income caused by the injury. The latter component, lost future earnings, is a function of income level and work life expectancy. A claim for lost future earnings or lost earning capacity is "an estimate of lost present ability to work in appropriate occupations, now and in the future." By contrast, a claim for lost earnings refers to the loss of income from the time of injury until the date of the trial. Ordinarily, damages for lost future earnings are only relevant after the plaintiff proves that he or she has suffered a permanent injury. Thereafter, the evidence focuses on two issues: (1) the plaintiff's expected rate of earnings, and (2) the plaintiff's expected number of lost years of earning capacity.

* * *

The first part, rate of earnings, is relatively easy to compute. It is based on the plaintiff's abilities, training, experience, and preinjury earnings. Prospects for wage increases and loss of fringe benefits also are considered. Loss of future earnings is not all-or-nothing; thus, reduction of future earnings as well as inability to generate any earnings at all are recoverable.

The second part, determining life expectancy, is already more difficult, and it is likely to become increasingly complicated in the new era of genetics and predictive medicine. Currently, life expectancy is based initially on standard mortality tables. These tables, however, are merely the starting point for making a determination of life expectancy or work expectancy.

* * *

The courts have permitted a wide range of information to be introduced by either party in attempting to ascertain the plaintiff's life expectancy and work expectancy with more precision than mortality tables. These additional factors include the plaintiff's work history, as well as past and current health, constitution, and habits. In a minority of jurisdictions, mortality tables proffered by the plaintiff are deemed inadmissible if the plaintiff had a preexisting condition, the theory being that mortality tables are based on the lives of "healthy people."

* * *

There are two types of evidence that could indicate that the plaintiff has a shorter life expectancy than the standard mortality tables. The first type of evidence involves previously diagnosed diseases. If the plaintiff already had been diagnosed with cancer, heart disease, or some other life-threatening illness at the time of the injury, this evidence would be admissible to show a reduced life expectancy. The second type of evidence involves factors that predict the likelihood of disease which would cause premature mortality. The courts have admitted a wide range of evidence of behavioral factors in attempting to prove that the plaintiff had a diminished life expectancy at the time of the injury. These factors include the plaintiff's use of drugs, alcohol, or cigarettes.

If evidence of cigarette smoking is admissible to show that the plaintiff's life expectancy is lessened because of the possibility of lung cancer, emphysema, or heart disease, then evidence that the plaintiff was genetically predisposed to such a disorder also would seem to be admissible. From the defendant's standpoint, the only issue is how to obtain access to such genetic information. The main ways include discovery of existing medical records, questioning the plaintiff at deposition, compelling a medical examination of the plaintiff, and questioning the plaintiff's physicians by interrogatories or depositions.

Although virtually all of the cases involve the defendant's attempt to introduce evidence of the plaintiff's shorter life expectancy, it is also possible for the plaintiff to introduce evidence of longevity.

* * *

With genetic prediction becoming increasingly sophisticated, it may be possible to estimate increased longevity. Nevertheless, for the foreseeable future, it is likely that decreased life expectancy will be the primary focus in personal injury litigation.

* * *

III.   DISCOVERY OF MEDICAL RECORDS

The easiest way for a personal injury defendant to learn a plaintiff's prior medical history is to discover the plaintiff's medical records. Requests for the medical records of personal injury plaintiffs are considered routine and are rarely challenged.

Courts considering the issue of discovering a plaintiff's medical records have applied the general principle that discovery requests are liberally granted. In general, parties may discover any nonprivileged matter relevant to a claim or defense of any party to a lawsuit. If evidence of a plaintiff's preinjury health status is admissible on the issue of damages, then medical records indicating health status are presumptively discoverable. Thus, courts routinely order the discovery of medical records, including records relevant to the issue of damages for lost future earnings. Even sensitive information, such as psychiatric records, have been ordered disclosed.

* * *

IV. COMPELLED MEDICAL EXAMINATIONS

The most intrusive form of medical discovery is the compelled medical examination. Rule 35 of the Federal Rules of Civil Procedure provides that a mental or physical examination may be ordered by the court in an action in which the mental or physical condition of a party is "in controversy," upon a showing of "good cause." The rules of civil procedure of every state, except Mississippi, contain similar provisions.

In Schlagenhauf v. Holder, [379 U.S. 104 (1964)] the Supreme Court considered the meaning of the terms "in controversy" and "good cause."

* * *

Schlagenhauf has been interpreted by both federal and state courts to mean that any time a plaintiff seeks to recover for physical injuries, his or her physical condition is "in controversy." Although this may establish the discoverability of a plaintiff's medical records pursuant to Rule 26, it does not necessarily establish the existence of good cause for a medical examination. An important question is whether information in the plaintiff's medical records can establish good cause for a medical examination. This is crucial to the issue of genetics, because information in the plaintiff's medical record may cause the defendant to suspect an underlying genetic condition, and then seek to have a court-ordered medical examination that includes genetic testing.

* * *

Even when the "in controversy" and "good cause" requirements of Rule 35 are satisfied, the court has discretion in deciding whether to compel an examination. In general, the cases in which courts order a physical or mental examination fall into three categories.

First, the information must not be available elsewhere. The movant must show that other discovery procedures, such as the production of medical records, have been exhausted. Second, it must be established that useful information is likely to be gained from the examination. For example, repetitive examinations will not be permitted unless special circumstances justify an additional examination. Third, the examination must not create health risks to the examinee. Although most of the cases involving health risks are concerned with physical risks, there is some support for the view that the feelings, reputation, and psychological impact on the examinee also should be considered. For example, in Doe v. Roe, [139 Misc.2d 209, 526 N.Y.S.2d 718 (N.Y. Sup. Ct. 1988)] maternal grandparents attempted to gain custody of their grandchild from the allegedly unfit father. They sought an order requiring the child's father to have an HIV test. In rejecting the motion, the court noted that "the psychological impact of learning that one is [HIV-positive] has been compared to receiving a death sentence."

The potential psychological and social harm to the examinee is merely one factor to consider in the context of genetics. Public policy concerns about confidentiality and conservation of resources, discussed in the next section, also need to be weighed against the need for the information revealed by the testing. These issues are likely to arise in motions to compel genetic testing under Rule 35. The few cases that have been decided under this rule, however, have not developed the issues sufficiently to provide needed guidance to courts dealing with a genetics case of first impression.

NOTES AND QUESTIONS

1.   The argument has been made that advocating limitations on defendants' ability to obtain genetic information in medical records or require genetic testing of plaintiffs amounts to genetic exceptionalism (discussed in Chapter 14). Do you agree?

2.   Should the same rules apply to discovery of genetic information for proof of harm and causation as applied to estimations of life expectancy?

3.   If you think that limits should be placed on the compelled disclosure of genetic information to defendants for proof of damages, should the limitation be judge-made through application of procedural rules or pursuant to legislative enactment?

4.   For a further discussion of these issues, see Diane E. Hoffmann & Karen H. Rothenberg, Judging Genes: Implications of the Second Generation of Genetic Tests in the Courtroom, 66 Md. L. Rev. 858 (2007); Anthony S. Niedwiecki, Science Fact or Science Fiction? The Implications of Court–Ordered Genetic Testing Under Rule 35, 34 U.S.F.L. Rev. 295 (2000).

INDEX

References are to Pages

†